JEWISH-AMERICAN HISTORY AND CULTURE:
AN ENCYCLOPEDIA

Garland Reference Library of the Social Sciences
(Vol. 429)

Jewish-American History and Culture:
AN ENCYCLOPEDIA

Edited by

Jack Fischel and Sanford Pinsker

GARLAND PUBLISHING, INC.
New York and London
1992

Library of Congress Cataloging-in-Publication Data

Jewish-American history and culture : an encyclopedia / edited by Jack Fischel and Sanford Pinsker.
      p. cm. — (Garland reference library of the social sciences ; vol. 429)
      Includes index.
      ISBN 0-8240-6622-7 (alk. paper)
1. Jews—United States—Encyclopedias. 2. United States—Civilization—Jewish influ-ences—Encyclopedias. I. Fischel, Jack. II. Pinsker, Sanford. III. Series: Garland reference library of social science ; v. 429.
E184.J5J48 1991
973'.04924'003—dc20
                                             91-14188
                                              CIP

Printed on acid-free, 250-year-life paper
Manufactured in the United States of America

The entry "Civil Rights" by Murray Friedman is reprinted by permission of the U.S. Commission on Civil Rights, from the Fall 1985 edition of *New Perspectives*.

The entry "Fiction" is adapted from Daniel Walden, "The American Yiddish Writer: From Cahan to Singer," *Ethnic Literature Since 1776: The Many Voices of America Part 2*, edited by Wolodymyr T. Zyla and Wendell M. Aycock (Lubbock: Texas Tech University Press, 1978). Used by permission of Texas Tech University Press.

The entry "Theater" is adapted from Sarah Blacher Cohen, *From Hester Street to Hollywood* (Bloomington: Indiana University Press, 1983). Used by permission of Indiana University Press.

To Dr. David Zubatsky, Director of Library Services, Millersville University, a person of great intellect and extraordinary common sense.

Contents

Preface

If it is true that collaborative efforts can turn former friends into bitter enemies, it is also true that collaborative efforts can turn good friends into better ones. *Jewish-American History and Culture: An Encyclopedia* was both an ambitious project, one that cried out for collaboration, and a stern testing of the skills we had developed as co-editors of the *Holocaust Studies Annual*. That the volumes managed to make their way from an idea to a reality is, in some measure, proof that disagreements can resolve themselves in dialogue and that controversies can end in accommodation. We are stronger colleagues now than we were when this project began some three-and-a-half years ago.

A natural division of academic labor helped our cause: as a professor of history, Jack Fischel had both the expertise and the necessary contacts to take on those areas of the encyclopedia dealing with "history"; as a professor of English, Sanford Pinsker agreed to man the table called "culture." Neither of us was especially surprised when there was overlap, disagreements about the overlap, or worse, when certain topics fell through the cracks of our collective expertise. During the many hours that we debated about which categories were essential, which expendable, and, of course, which personalities should, or should not, be included, each of us added a few nuggets to the store of what we know, but, perhaps even more important, each of us ended up with a clearer idea of what we do not know.

Our distinguished Board of Advisers was especially helpful in shaping our discussions and the results. Some helped us refine the original proposal; others suggested categories, organizations, events,

and personalities that had not crossed our minds, or had not been there in the first place. Gradually, an outline of the encyclopedia began to take shape. About one thing we had been clear from the beginning: our encyclopedia would include comprehensive essays—on subjects ranging from "Academe" to "Zionism"—and shorter entries focusing on specific personalities or events.

At this point, our focus shifted from what essays and entries ought to be written to the more practical question of who should write them. Not surprisingly, we hoped to enlist the best people possible, but a mare's nest of complications lay inside that overly simple solution. Again, our advisers proved invaluable, occasionally in their willingness to write a key essay themselves, but most of the time in their generous suggestions about fellow scholars who were doing work in areas that our encyclopedia should cover.

We soon discovered several truisms of academic life—namely, that the "best" people are also the busiest, the most heavily committed; that those who have written the definitive book on a subject are the ones most likely to write a first-rate essay on the topic; and, on occasion, that it is sometimes easier to extract a scholar's promise than a scholarly article.

The making of an encyclopedia—*any* encyclopedia—is likely to be a study in frustration, whether it comes from the sheer headaches of bookkeeping or so many disparate authors crowded into the same kitchen. Too many cooks (or more correctly, *chefs*) have spoiled even the best-laid plans for an encyclopedic stew.

We wanted to stress, wherever possible, the Jewish connection or content of an entrant's contribution. Sometimes, as with people such as Isaac Meyer Wise or Isaac Bashevis Singer, the Jewishness of their identities is self-evident; at other times—as with certain scientists, politicians, and a wide range of entertainers—definition becomes much more complicated. We have, therefore, adopted a generous stance, one we feel is not out of harmony with the broadest possible definition of what is meant by the term Jewish-American.

An encyclopedia such as ours cannot avoid celebrating Jewish life in America, nor should it. Jewish-American life has been extraordinarily rich on *both* sides of this awkward, hyphenated term. But "celebration," however warranted, must also coexist with the sober judgments of scholarship, analysis, and critical detachment. Thus, *Jewish-American History and Culture: An Encyclopedia* is much more than a litany of success stories: its essays and entries represent the efforts of scholars from an extremely diverse field of disciplines—history, literature, film studies, political science, religious studies, Yiddish studies, biology, women's studies—to survey the distinctive experience of Jews in America. This diversity suggests that Jewish-American life is, indeed, a rich tapestry and that these volumes not only will fill a reference need for students at all levels, but also will be of interest to those who enjoy browsing among the artifacts, institutions, and intriguing personalities who have added so much to the life of Americans in general and to Jewish Americans in particular.

Jack Fischel
Sanford Pinsker

Acknowledgments

The publication of *Jewish-American History and Culture: An Encyclopedia* would not have been possible without the assistance of many people. The following made significant contributions to the organization of the encyclopedia: Sheri Schramm, Margaret Eichler, Michael Harmatz, and "Cookie" Faust. Tracey Showalter created our indispensable filing system, and Patricia Levin was invaluable in the initial meetings that helped set the project's focus. Seymour J. Colen's vast knowledge of the field of Jewish social services helped us to locate contributors. Michael Birkner, Gettysburg College, and Reynold Koppel, Millersville University, made helpful suggestions, and Deans Linda Clark and Christopher Dahl, Millersville University, are thanked for their on-going support of the project.

Kennie Lyman and Shirley Cobert, Garland Publishing, Inc., are thanked for their patience, guidance, and helpful suggestions. Janet Dotterer, a Millersville University graduate assistant and European history major in the Millersville Master's program, was invaluable in dealing with the routine detail work that is necessary in a work of this kind.

Our wives, Julie and Ann, are thanked for putting up with the endless meetings, late-hour phone calls, and, in general, living with the project for close to four years.

We would like to thank the administration of both Millersville University and Franklin and Marshall for their financial aid for making resources available that ultimately made these volumes possible.

Finally, we are indebted to Susan Liss for proofreading the manuscript and to Irit Gal for her help as a translator.

Introduction

Jewish-American History and Culture: An Encyclopedia is a one-volume reference work that seeks to survey the Jewish experience in the United States. Because we have defined our task broadly, readers will find a wide spectrum of information—about historical events and figures, about literature and the arts, about popular entertainment, about the range of Jewish religious life and communal organizations, about the contributions Jewish Americans have made to our nation's public life, and a great many other miscellaneous topics. The result is a panoramic view, one designed to supplement, rather than to replace, more specialized encyclopedias. In this sense, our work is selective rather than comprehensive, and as such, it is the first encyclopedia that takes the whole of Jewish-American life as its purview.

At the heart of the *Encyclopedia* is a series of essays that reflect the best that has been thought and said on a particular topic—e.g., Jews in Colonial America, Jews on the Left, Communal Organizations. Contributors were chosen from among established experts in various fields; more important, they were given an opportunity to express themselves with a freedom not usually associated with the dry, impersonal style of reference works. The results are essays as lively as they are informative. And because we have made every effort to make them as current as possible, a reader will find the essays extremely useful as informed, reliable introductions to a variety of topics. Moreover, the essays include a short bibliography that can be the basis for further, more advanced study.

If the essays provide an "overview," the *Encyclopedia*'s shorter entries provide a snapshot of an especially noteworthy personality or event. Admittedly, the choice of entries is subjective; nonetheless, we have tried to imagine what our readers would expect to find in perusing the volume and have tried to weigh these expectations against an honest effort to balance the coverage assigned to past and present, Judaism's various religious branches, culture and politics, the genders, and other similar categories. We apologize in advance if a reader's expectation about a specific entry is unfulfilled, but we refer that reader to the index, where we are confident that the disappointment will be rectified in one of the surveying essays. Moreover, the *Encyclopedia* provides a user-friendly system of cross-referencing, so that readers who encounter the name "Saul Bellow" in the essay on Literature are directed to the entry more narrowly focused on Bellow's work and his contribution to Jewish-American letters.

The shaping idea behind the *Encyclopedia* is that the Jewish-American presence has made significant contributions to American history and culture. It is for this reason that we have emphasized the more serious aspects of history and culture rather than the trivial ones. To provide an undue coverage of the more mundane aspects of Jewish life—e.g., cultural stereotypes, food preferences—would be to dilute this important truth. Thus, we do not include an entry on the "bagel," nor is there an essay on "Jewish Foods" that mentions it. No doubt some readers will wonder about the omission, but we felt that there was little profit, and a possible danger, in confusing the trivial with the decidedly more important.

By contrast, we have tried to survey the more substantial institutions of Jewish-American life. For example, we have tried to represent the major religious denominations with scrupulous balance and to devote as much space as possible to examples of Jewish communal/service organizations and to Jewish communities. Naturally, we could not include every city, town, and hamlet where Jewish Americans have erected synagogues and community centers, day schools, and chapters of B'nai B'rith. But we have tried to show, by selecting examples within the usual geographic divisions of North, South, East, West, and Midwest, something of the representative Jewish-American landscape.

At the same time, however, we have also included essays that survey important Jewish contributions to secular American life. Therefore, the reader will find essays on such diverse topics as the Left, popular music, rock and roll, labor, and civil rights. Balancing religious contributions with secular ones is not an easy task, but we remain committed to the *Encyclopedia*'s goal of surveying the broad panorama of Jewish-American life rather than to assessing it from a specific theological or ideological perspective.

With popular entertainers and widely popular public figures, we selected entries that struck us as culturally important, as likely to remain important for the foreseeable future, and wherever possible, as reflecting, in one way or another, their "Jewishness." Admittedly, such choices are not easily defended. That we have included entries on such disparate figures as the Lubavitcher Rebbe or Woody Allen requires no special explanation; that we have also included entries on such publicly nonidentifying Jews as Judah P. Benjamin and Hyman Rickover is more problematic. But we felt that there were moments when principles of selection must bow to inclination and instinct. Finally, we refer those readers interested in more specialized coverage to the bibliographies that follow each essay.

The story of the Jewish impact on America, and of the American impact on "Jewishness," can perhaps best be thought of as a rich, multifaceted tapestry. Among its threads there are surely justifiable cause for pride, as well as occasion for continuing disagreement and debate. That is part of the story; perhaps it *is* the story. Aspects of the saga have been told before, but never in a comprehensive one-volume reference work, and never quite in the systematic "Abram, Morris Berthold" to "Zionism" way that is presented here.

List of Contributors

Howard Adelman
Smith College

Zalman Alpert
Yeshiva University

Mark D. Angel
Rabbi, Congregation Shearith Israel

Bruce Armon
Franklin & Marshall College

Jerald S. Auerbach
Wellesley College

Evelyn Avery
Towson State University

Zachary M. Baker
YIVO Institute for Jewish Research

Mark K. Bauman
Atlanta Metropolitan College, Atlanta, GA

Alan L. Berger
Syracuse University

Graenum Berger
Jewish Communal Planner and Educator

Marc A. Bernheim
Miami University of Ohio

Mashey M. Bernstein
University of Michigan

Maxine Berkman Bernstein
Writer

Michael Birkner
Gettysburg College

Wolf Blitzer
Military Affairs Correspondent for the Cable News Network

Timothy Boxer
Columnist, author

Robin Brabham
University of North Carolina at Charlotte

Joseph Brandes
William Paterson College of New Jersey

S. Daniel Breslauer
University of Kansas

Robert Bresler
Pennsylvania State University–Harrisburg

Stephen F. Brumberg
City University of New York

Stephen R. Centola
Millersville University

Elaine Shizgal Cohen
McGill University

Sarah Blacher Cohen
SUNY at Albany

Abraham Cooper
Simon Weisenthal Center

David G. Dalin
University of Hartford

David Desser
University of Illinois, Urbana-Champaign

Haisa R. Diner
University of Maryland, College Park

Leonard Dinnerstein
University of Arizona

Michael N. Dobkowsky
Hobart, Williams & Smith

Elliot N. Dorff
University of Judaism, Los Angeles

Janet L. Dotterer
Millersville University

Lawrence J. Epstein
Suffolk Community College

Patricia Brett Erens
Rosary College

Eli Evans
President, Charles H. Revson Foundation

Ira N. Feit
Franklin & Marshall College

Donald Feldstein
Council of Jewish Federation

Ellen S. Fine
City University of New York

I.M. Finegood
American Vets of Israel

Jack Fischel
Millersville University

Joshua Fischel
Pennsylvania State University

Stanley Fogel
St. Jerome's College

Murray Friedman
Former Vice Chairman of U.S. Commission on Civil Rights; American Jewish Committee

Saul Friedman
Youngstown State University

Lawrence H. Fuchs
Brandeis University

Richard K. Gerlitzki
Millersville University

Neil Gillman
Jewish Theological Seminary

Abraham Gittelson
Central Agency for Jewish Education, Florida

Linda Glazer
Hadassah

Allen Glicksman
Polisher Research Institute of the Philadelphia Geriatric Center

Eric A. Goldman
Founder and President of Ergo Media

Katherine Green
Millersville University

Lawrence Grossman
American Jewish Committee

Jeffrey S. Gurock
Yeshiva University

Irving Halperin
San Francisco State University

Miriam Joyce Haron
Spertus College of Judaica, Chicago

Kathryn Hellerstein
University of Pennsylvania

Gertrude Hirschler
author, editor and translator

Dwight D. Hoover
Ball State University

Judith Brin Ingber
University of Minnesota

Robert A. Jacobs
Leo Baeck Institute

Jenna Weissman Joselit
Annenberg Research Institute, Philadelphia

Jacob Kabakoff
Professor Emeritus, Lehman College of the City University of New York

Benjamin Kahn
The American University, Washington, D.C.

Abram Kanof
Professor Emeritus, State of New York Medical School; Past President, American Jewish Historical Society

Kenneth Kanter
Rabbi, Mezpah Congregation, Chattanooga, TN

W. Kirschenbaum
Workmen's Circle, New York

Norman Kleeblatt
Jewish Museum

Harvey Klehr
Emory University

Dennis B. Klein
Anti-Defamation League of B'nai B'rith, International Center for Holocaust Studies

Hannah Kliger
University of Massachusetts at Amherst

Reynold Koppel
Millersville University

Seymour Lainoff
Professor Emeritus, Yeshiva University

Stephen Lehmann
University of Pennsylvania

Elinor Lerner
Stockton State College

Dianne Levenberg
Kutztown University

Nora Levin
Gratz College (deceased)

Patricia Levin
University of Pennsylvania

Joseph A. Levine
Former Faculty Member, Jewish Theological Seminary, Constors Institute

Rhoda G. Lewin
Academic Council, American Jewish Historical Society

Franklin H. Littell
Temple University

John Livingston
University of Denver

Archie K. Loss
Penn State-Erie

Steven M. Lowenstein
University of Judaism, Los Angeles

Bonnie Lyons
University of Texas at San Antonio

Donald McEvoy
National Conference of Christians & Jews

Alan Mandel
American University

Marvin S. Margolis
Millersville University

Will Maslow
American Jewish Congress

Deborah Dash Moore
Vassar College

Pamela S. Nadell
American University

Judah Nadich
Rabbi Emeritus, Park Avenue Synagogue, New York City

Edna Nahshon
Jewish Theological Seminary of America

Henry Neiger
92nd Street YMHA, New York

Amnon Netzer
Hebrew University of Jerusalem

Jacob Neusner
Florida State University

Edgar Leon Newman
University of New Mexico

William A. Orbach
University of Louisville

David Oshinsky
Rutgers University

Sherry Ostroff
School District of Lancaster, PA

Bruce Pandolfini
New York Chess Club

Abraham J. Peck
Hebrew Union College–Jewish Institute of Religion

Elizabeth Petuchowski
University of Cincinnati

Matthew Pinsker
Brasenose College, Oxford

Sanford Pinsker
Franklin & Marshall College

Marcia W. Posner
Jewish Book Council

Yakov M. Rabin
Universite de Montreal

Leslie Y. Rabkin
Seattle Psychological Assessment & Referral Center

Michael Riff
Leo Baeck Institute

Leonard Rogoff
Writer

David M. Rosen
Brandeis University

Philip Rosen
Gratz College

Gilbert S. Rosenthal
Rabbi, Jewish Theological Seminary.

Michael Roth
Franklin & Marshall College

Earl Rovit
City College of New York

Brian D. Rozen
Duquesne University, Pittsburgh, PA

Sayeeda Yasmin Saikia
University of Wisconsin

Henry Sapoznik
YIVO Institute for Jewish Research

Eva Sartori
University of Nebraska

Michael Schiraldi
Millersville University

Louis Schmier
Valdosta State College

Shuly Rubin Schwartz
Academic Consultant for Florence Melton Mini School

Charles Selengut
County College of Morris (NJ)

Gerald Serotta
Hillel Rabbi and Jewish Chaplain, George Washington University, Washington, D.C.

Howard Shaker
Writer

Jeffrey Shandler
Critic

Baila R. Shargel
Jewish Theological Seminary of America

Mark Shechner
SUNY at Buffalo

Beatrice Shustko
Educational Alliance

William Simons
SUNY at Oneonta

Brett Singer
Pennsylvania State University

Robert Singerman
University of Florida Libraries

June Sochen
Northeastern Illinois University

Gerald Sorin
SUNY at New Paltz

Henry W. Spiegal
Emeritus Professor of Economics, The Catholic University of America

Jacob J. Staub
Reconstructionist Rabbinical College

Ilan Stavans
City University of New York

David Stern
University of Pennsylvania

Gerald Stern
University of Iowa

Lance J. Sussman
SUNY at Binghamton

Richard Taskin
North Adams State College

S.D. Temkin
SUNY at Albany

David A. Teutsch
Reconstructionist Rabbinical College

Melvin I. Urofsky
Virginia Commonwealth University

Kenneth von Gunden
Pennsylvania State University, State College

Max Vorspan
University of Judaism

Alan Wald
University of Michigan

Daniel Walden
Pennsylvania State University

Albert Waldinger
Defense Language Institute, Presidio of Monterey, CA, and Hartnell College, Salinas, CA

Bernard Wax
American Jewish Historical Society

Chaim I. Waxman
Rutgers University

Miriam Weiner
co-editor of The Encyclopedia of Jewish Genealogy

Harold Wechsler
Northwestern University

Stephen J. Whitfield
Brandeis University

Phillip Wiener
Journal of the History of Ideas, *Executive Editor, Emeritus*

Michael Witmer
Temple University

Earl Yaillen
Association of Jewish Family and Children's Agency

Irwin Yellowitz
City University of New York

David Zubatsky
Millersville University

List of Entries

RELIGION AND RELIGIOUS THEORY

SCIENCE

SOCIAL SCIENCES

Jewish-American History and Culture:
An Encyclopedia

A

Abram, Morris Berthold (b. 1918). A strong advocate for individual rights and freedoms, Morris B. Abram is a retired partner of a prominent New York law firm (Paul, Weiss, Rifkind, Wharton and Garrison), a former president of Brandeis University (1968–1970), and a sometime lecturer at Oxford University (1981, 1983). He has held political appointments on various national commissions, often as chairperson, has represented the United States at the United Nations, and has presided over several major organizations.

Abram was born in the small Georgia town of Fitzgerald. His father, Sam, a Romanian immigrant, scratched out a living running a series of small stores. His mother, Irene Cohen, was a strong, ambitious woman from a German Jewish background. Educated at the local public schools, Abram excelled in his studies and in debating. Although he had minimal Jewish exposure in his Reform home, he took it upon himself to describe Judaism to the largely Gentile Fitzgerald community. He was influenced by Isadore Gelders, a Jewish socialist newspaper editor for whom he worked, but his sense of Jewishness was more a result of the happenstance of birth and the identity forced upon him by non-Jews. He experienced social and professional anti-Semitism, which he associated to some extent with southern provincialism.

His horizons broadened as he attended the University of Georgia (B.A., 1938), the University of Chicago Law School (J.D., 1940), and served in the U.S. Air Force Intelligence (1941–

1945). While a Rhodes Scholar at Oxford University, he served as a member of the American prosecution staff (1946) of the Nuremberg Trials. This experience solidified his position as a Zionist and advocate of Jewish rights.

He returned to Atlanta to practice law in 1948 and in the years that followed handled several controversial cases, including a 14-year battle against the county unit system. This was finally won before the U.S. Supreme Court (*Sanders v. Gray*, 1963) with the phrase "one man, one vote." Though unsuccessful in running for Congress in 1954, he was appointed chair of the Atlanta Citizens Crime Committee (1958–1961). He had already served on other community committees, for example, as assistant to the director for the Committee for the Marshall Plan (1948) and as counsel and public board member of the Regional Wage Stabilization Board for the South (1951).

Abram's chief involvement in politics has been through appointed positions and assisting in the election campaigns of others, although he did consider running for the Senate from New York. As John F. Kennedy's Georgia campaign manager in 1960, he recommended Kennedy's intervention when Martin Luther King, Jr., was jailed in Atlanta. He also negotiated King's release. Nationally, he served as first general counsel of the Peace Corps (1961), and he sat on the UN Subcommittee on Prevention of Discrimination and Protection of Minorities (1962–1964), working with his close friend Adlai Stevenson. While the U.S. representative to the UN Commission on Human Rights (1965–1968), he helped draft an international treaty outlawing racial discrimination and condemning religious bigotry. As a result of his position regarding Soviet Jewry and immigration restrictions, Russian representatives launched personal attacks on him. In 1965, Arthur Goldberg appointed Abram senior adviser to the U.S. mission to the United Nations. This appointment lasted three years.

As a member of the executive committee of the Lawyers Committee for Civil Rights Under Law, he took the first case fought by the group, *Aelony v. Pace*, which defended voter registration advocates in Americus, Georgia, who had been jailed for sedition. The courts found the law under which the individuals had been prosecuted to be unconstitutional. Abram was also a member of the National Advisory Council on Economic Opportunity (1967–1968). In 1968, Lyndon Johnson sent him to Vietnam on a fact-finding mission. He gradually came to the conclusion that the war was unwinnable, thus breaking with the President.

During the Carter administration, he urged the President to pursue a policy of human rights in foreign affairs, but he became frustrated at the naive administration of the policy. In 1980, Abram supported the presidential campaign of Ronald Reagan.

As chair of the New York Moreland Act Commission (1975–1976), his investigation of nursing home care criticized the management and supervision of the homes, placing ultimate responsibility on former Governor Nelson Rockefeller. After a successful struggle against cancer, he became an advocate of patients' rights and chaired the President's Commission for the Study of Ethical Problems in Medicine and Biomedical and Behavioral Research (1979–1983).

Abram felt stifled in the South, and in 1962 when his four children from his first marriage to Jane Maguire experienced anti-Semitism, he decided to move to New York. He nurtured his continued intellectual stimulation through participation in the Field Foundation (president, 1965–1981), a liberal philanthropy, and in the Twentieth Century Fund (board member, 1958–), a liberal think tank.

His views have been sought as a southerner who also advocated individual rights for blacks. In the late 1940s, he coauthored a pamphlet, "How to Stop Violence in Your Community," advocating five laws to limit activities of the Ku Klux Klan. Two of these, which prohibited the public wearing of masks and the burning of crosses without the permission of the property owner, were adopted in 5 states and 55 cities. He also served on the board of Morehouse College (1959–1985) and chaired the United Negro College Fund (1970–1979). Yet as the civil rights movement began to advocate a "Third World perspective," preferential treatment, and special programs defined by race, Abram became disillusioned. These changes had gradually become apparent when he co-chaired the planning session of the White House Conference on Civil Rights (1965) and when he presided over Brandeis University. At Brandeis (1968–1970) Abram had difficulty with its former president, Abram Sachar, and with what he perceived as petty academic politics. Always the rationalist, he wanted to keep the university out of politics and supported what he considered an elitist approach to education through a sound grounding in theory based on a rigorous classical core curriculum. He opposed a separate black studies program, and he viewed the violence of student demonstrators at the university as destructive to the free exchange of ideas. When he left Brandeis in 1970, his departure seems to have been mutually agreeable. He emerged from this and other experiences as an outspoken opponent of the "quota system," and his appointment as co-chair (1983–1986) of the U.S. Civil Rights Commission was opposed by many civil rights advocates. Abram's position for color-blind justice and equal opportunity was consistent: it was the movement that had changed.

As a struggling young lawyer, Abram had involved himself as a part-time employee of the Atlanta chapter of the American Jewish Committee. He rose to become the youngest president of the national body (1963–1967). In the late 1960s, he and a group of other leaders, including Francis Cardinal Spellman, interceded with Pope Paul VI to obtain a positive statement denouncing anti-Semitism. As chair of the National Conference on Soviet Jewry, he traveled to the Soviet Union in 1987 to encourage the lifting of immigration barriers and the opening of opportunities within that country for the practice of Judaism. In 1986, he became chair of the Conference of Presidents of Major American Jewish Organizations. He serves on the board of the Weizman Institute of Science (1966–) and was chair of the board of the Benjamin N. Cardozo Law School of Yeshiva University (1976–1979). President George Bush appointed Abram Chief U.S. delegate to the Paris Conference on Human Rights and Ambassador to European headquarters of the United Nations in Geneva.

Abram has received honorary degrees from several universities, is a fellow of the American Academy of Arts and Sciences (1969-), and is the author of many popular and scholarly articles. His insightful autobiography, *The Day is Short* (1982), is based upon his extensive oral memoirs conducted by Eli Evans for the Weiner Oral History Collection of the American Jewish Committee.

In many ways, Morris Abram illustrates the classical marginal-man type. He was born Jewish, but not raised as a practicing Jew. He was a liberal in the conservative South, then a southerner in the North. A brilliant and successful attorney and leader of major commissions and organizations, he has chartered his own course as an independent thinker in behalf of individual rights and democratic participation for all.

MARK K. BAUMAN

BIBLIOGRAPHY

Abram, Morris. *The Day Is Short: An Autobiography.* New York: Harcourt Brace Jovanovich, 1982.

Academe. The Jewish encounter with American higher education is an important barometer of the Jewish position in American society. The denominational bent of the nine colonial American colleges limited Jewish contact to an occasional student matriculation. Judah Monis was the first man of Jewish origin on an American college faculty. However, his conversion to Christianity preceded his appointment. Isaac Nordheimer, also of Jewish origin, taught at the University of the City of New York for several years during the 1830s. Some accounts imply that he converted to Christianity before his death. The situation remained unchanged until the late nineteenth century, when some nascent universities, anxious to abandon their pietistic ethos in favor of broader missions of research and community service, viewed a Jewish faculty and student presence as evidence of their catholicity. Academic receptivity led American Jews to view the nation's colleges and universities not as hostile, Gentile-dominated institutions but as possible vehicles for educational, cultural, and social acceptance and advancement. The change was reflected in the steady flow of students appearing in a larger number of institutions. Indeed, by 1910, City College in New York City was a predominantly Jewish institution. Similarly, a small but significant number of Jewish faculty showed up on college and university rosters around the country, reflecting the loosening of denominational ties and the perception that Jewish faculty might well contribute to a broadened educational mission. Finally, Jewish philanthropists perceived institutional receptivity and hospitality and increasingly supported institutional initiatives.

In the early twentieth century, the rise of anti-Semitism on the campus reflected the general social anti-Semitism that accompanied the large East European Jewish migrations. Academic appointments became difficult to obtain, especially in the humanities. The social life of Jewish college students became increasingly segregated, the rapid increase in Jewish fraternities being one indicator. And, after World War I, the imposition of admissions restrictions at institutions hitherto viewed as open to all of merit and character left a scar on American Jewry that has not yet completely healed. The American university shifted from an emphasis on research, theoretical and practical, to a concern with collegiate life and to social criteria for leadership. In the latter realm, Jews were often considered "undesirable."

During the 1920s and 1930s, Jews attended American colleges, although not always the ones they regarded as most desirable; graduate school acceptances proved more difficult to obtain, particularly those at medical and engineering schools. After World War II, while some restrictions on student admissions and faculty appointments persisted, most Jews seeking access to higher education found opportunities and increasingly at the schools of their choice. The growth of public higher education, the lessening of anti-Semitic attitudes after the war, a renewed emphasis on scholarship, passage of antidiscrimination legislation, and increased competition for competent faculty in the 1950s and early 1960s overcame most remaining prejudices. Student access to fraternities and sororities was still a gray area, but the diminished influence of Greek societies in the 1960s made this issue less pressing than in earlier decades. By the 1980s, Columbia and Princeton had their first Jewish presidents; Yale would have joined their company had not Henry Rosovsky declined the honor. Higher education became a "shorthand" for the Jewish encounter with American society. The education it provided offered a route into the middle and upper-middle classes. The socialization it provided offered an introduction to their social mores. The recognition it provided offered tangible evidence of social and economic success.

Here, we will address three topics: *faculty*, *students*—their admission and participation in collegiate activities—and *Jewish learning* in colleges and universities.

FACULTY. In the nineteenth century, the college or university-based American Jewish academic barely had an intellectual or social role to play. Today, Jews comprise over 10 percent of the American professoriat (they comprise about 2 percent of the American population). At certain "elite" institutions the proportion of Jewish academics approaches 40 percent and more. Both early exclusion and more recent inclusion have posed dilemmas.

Most colleges in the nineteenth century stressed the inculcation of Christian discipline and piety rather than mastery of specific subject matters. Many, including public colleges such as the University of Michigan, applied informal or explicit religious tests to prospective faculty. Colleges found it relatively easy to impose a particular religious orientation among faculty, whereas religious homogeneity in the student body required foregoing of essential tuition dollars.

Antebellum colleges hired some Jewish faculty: English mathematician Joseph Sylvester taught at the University of Virginia beginning in 1841 and later at Johns Hopkins, for example, because his Jewishness prohibited his appointment to an English university. Only in the late nineteenth century, when American colleges and nascent universities relinquished their explicitly Christian orientation in favor of research and subject mastery, did the Jewish academic emerge as a distinct professional type.

Doubtless, in the late nineteenth century, colleagues, administrators, and trustees all identified Jewish faculty as Jews first and professor of literature, for example, next. Sometimes this worked to a candidate's benefit, especially in situations where a university courted new constituencies able to finance desired growth. Yet even when Jewish identification had prejudicial connotations, conditions were better in late nineteenth-century America than in England or Germany. In England, the religious prohibitions that thwarted Sylvester continued to block appointments of Jewish faculty until the late nineteenth century. In Germany at that time a Jew's chances for any academic appointment were slight, and senior status was next to impossible. In the United States, while each appointment had to reckon with the Jewish origins and/or beliefs of the candidate,

exclusion was far from outright. There were Jewish faculty members in the American universities, often near large Jewish population centers and often under the aegis of philo-Semitic presidents.

Indeed, several college presidents of this period evinced quite strong pro-Jewish sympathies: Daniel Coit Gilman, the first president of Johns Hopkins University, founded in 1876, had attended Jewish services as a child and maintained a strong interest in Judaism during his adult life. William Rainey Harper's interest in the teaching of the Hebrew language and in the defense of the Bible from the extremist European "higher critics" led him to cultivate acquaintances with Jews having similar interests during his presidency of the University of Chicago (1892–1906). Charles W. Eliot, who presided over Harvard's transformation (1869–1909), from a college into a major university, was not disingenuous when he told the Menorah student society in 1906 that "some of my best friends are of Jewish descent." And, given the increasing wealth and status of the German Jewish community in late nineteenth-century America, presidential and Jewish communal interests proved complementary.

The story of Temple Sinai's financial contribution to the University of Chicago quickly became part of both institutions' organizational sagas. The Jewish community's reward for a key contribution to the university's financial canvass was a seat on the trustees and the appointment of the Sinai rabbi Emil G. Hirsch to the faculty. Other Jewish appointments followed, including physicist Albert Michaelson and economist Isaac A. Hourwich. Hourwich, who sympathized with the populists and later with a number of left-wing causes, was dismissed by President Harper after two years of service. He subsequently worked as a government statistician and an official of the International Ladies Garment Workers Union.

Under President Seth Low (1889–1901), Columbia University accepted many endowments and contributions from New York's Jewish community. A former mayor of Brooklyn, New York, when it was still an independent city, Low emphasized Columbia's public role, including the provision of impartial access to all positions and facilities. While Columbia's prejudiced trustees did not invite a Jew to membership for another third of a century, Low appointed or reappointed several Jewish faculty, including Romance language professor Adolph Cohn, Semitics and rabbinics professor Richard Gottheil, economist E. R. A. Seligman, and literature professor Joel

Spingarn. Writing of Columbia in the early twentieth century, Alvin Johnson implied that some of those appointments required presidential intervention. He was not sanguine about the academic future for Columbia's Jewish graduate students:

> There was much private discussion among students and faculty of the position of Jews. A favorite dogma was that the Jew is a middleman, with great acquisitive capacity, but not a pioneer, with originality and inventiveness. I used to point out that E. R. A. Seligman, who joined the faculty when Columbia was just a young gentleman's finishing school, where a course in economics could be given but could not be credited toward a degree, had managed to build up one of the greatest departments of economics in America. I made much of the fact that Felix Adler was the only important original ethical teacher in America after the decease of William James, and that [Franz] Boas had placed American anthropology on an extremely new footing. But no man profits by arguing with balky mules or professors with fixed ideas. (Alvin Johnson, memoir in Louis Finkelstein, ed., *American Spiritual Autobiographies: Fifteen Self-Portraits* [New York: Harper, 1948], 46.)

The *Jewish Encyclopedia* (1901–1905) contained an entry for most of the major American universities, each listing the Jewish representation on the faculty. Most institutions listed from three to seven names; the University of California appointed one of the first Jewish women, economist Jessica Blanche Peixotto. From reading these lists, one may conclude that appointments could be obtained by assimilated second-generation German Jews, especially those coming from prominent families. A significant number (about 16) taught in Semitics departments: the rest were spread over a large number of disciplines. Jews had the most difficulty obtaining appointments in fields that interpreted past and present Western, Christian culture, that is, history, religion, English literature, and art. Franz Boas's leadership in anthropology assured continued Jewish representation in that field, and Jews secured appointment to prominent posts in other "newer" disciplines. This pattern persisted through the 1960s when Jews, by then well represented in the social sciences and professions, still were underrepresented in the humanities.

Jewish women also remained underrepresented. Several Jewish women served on the faculty of Hunter College in New York City, including Elizabeth Vera Loeb, Anna Jacobson, Dora Askwith, and Adele Bildersee (who then moved to Brooklyn College). The *Universal Jewish Encyclopedia*, published in the early 1940s, included several other female Jewish faculty, such as Florence Bamberger of Johns Hopkins, Bessie Bloom Wessel of Connecticut College, Theresa Wolfson of Brooklyn College, and Elizabeth Brandeis of the University of Wisconsin, among others. It commented, "On the whole, however, few Jewish women served in women's colleges." Louis Feuer's list of 52 Jewish faculty in *American Jewish History* includes no females.

As the East European Jewish migrations increased in numbers and visibility and as more East European students appeared in the graduate and undergraduate classrooms of elite institutions in the early twentieth century, academic anti-Semitism flourished. Although the growth of American colleges and universities after World War I might have predicted an influx of Jewish faculty, the occasional Jewish student who obtained admission to graduate school seldom went on to a significant academic career. While Jewish representation on European university faculties slightly increased early in the century, their population in American institutions declined.

Dan A. Oren's account in *Joining the Club* (1986) illuminates the shift from mild to outright anti-Semitism occurring at Yale after World War I. In contrast to universities where graduate education reigned supreme, Yale's greatest honor consisted of an appointment to the undergraduate faculty. No Jew obtained a tenured position on this faculty before World War II. A few Jews had graduate and professional school appointments, such as physiological chemist Lafayette B. Mendel, appointed first to the Sheffield Scientific School and then in 1896 to the graduate school. Universally acknowledged as an extraordinary talent (he discovered vitamin B), Mendel, Oren states, was, "like the idealized product of the *Haskalah*, the Jewish Enlightenment, . . . a Jew at home and an ordinary man on the street." He regularly attended Sabbath services at Congregation Mishkan Israel and received the respect of both the academic and Jewish community. At Yale and elsewhere, a meritocratic urge occasionally overcame a deepening hostility toward Jews.

However, such instances required increasingly greater merit and often decreasing visibility of Jewishness. And, as Jewish college students simultaneously learned, all too often all the academic and social merit just did not help them overcome campus anti-Semitism.

To deal with this almost inevitable prejudice, a Jew required exceptional talent and considerable luck. Sociologist Lewis Feuer phrased the issue in terms of necessary and sufficient conditions for appointment. Strong sponsorship and an excellent thesis often did not prove sufficient. The necessary conditions included the strong backing of a sponsor "who would testify to the authorities that this man, though a Jew or an immigrant or from the working class, was not insisting on his Jewishness, was devoid of 'pushing' traits, was courteous, and quiet in disposition." Much discouragement occurred—even in fields such as chemistry where the possibility of nonacademic appointments existed.

Confronted with admissions and placement dilemmas, sympathetic Gentile faculty advisers found it easier to counsel individual Jewish students than to confront the prejudices of their colleagues. They usually offered verbal and written support for their Jewish students' attempts at placement. But at a time when, as one critic noted, "racial prejudice is so thoroughly ingrained that no one takes much notice of it except in particularly flagrant cases," efforts confined to support of individual candidates were doomed.

So long as the predominant faculty attitude remained anti-Semitic, outside exhortations would produce little change, especially in an era where antidiscriminatory legislation was rare or nonexistent. In one of the few instances of faculty action in this area, a 1939 Harvard faculty committee, with a membership including Arthur M. Schlesinger, Sr., and Felix Frankfurter, candidly summarized the typical interwar situation:

> In the United States anti-Semitic feeling has operated within the universities themselves, in the form of a prejudice which is difficult to prove and never officially proclaimed. Though the prejudice has not, as in totalitarian countries, caused the wholesale dismissal of professors, it has made it difficult for Jews otherwise eligible to obtain initial appointment and, there is reason to believe, has retarded their advancement to higher rank when appointed.

The committee deemed anti-Semitism a betrayal of Harvard's and the nation's best traditions (fair play and equal opportunity), costly to Harvard's efforts to recruit the best intellects and to attain scholarly diversity, and, last, a deprival of the opportunity for "America's oldest university . . . to set a high standard for its sister institutions in this and other countries" (Special Committee appointed by the President of Harvard University, *Report of Some Problems of Personnel in the Faculty of Arts and Sciences* [Cambridge: Harvard University, 1939], 150–153).

The Harvard report took issue with commonly invoked rationales for discrimination, such as the intolerance of the undergraduate. "The extent of this undergraduate attitude can easily be exaggerated," argued the committee. "In a number of departments Jewish tutors have met with conspicuous success." Other defenders of discrimination expressed fears of being "overrun" by a minority group, or they invoked "democracy" (here defined as majority rule, even at the expense of minority right) and "diversity" (defined as restrictions on the growth of any "distinctive" group liable to "overwhelm" overall composition). And, in an ultimate irony that some discriminators must have understood, their absence from college faculties would lead to yet more criticism of Jews themselves. One critic noted, "The situation is very serious because Jews are gradually being eliminated from the educational field and will ultimately be charged with making no contribution to it" ("Community Organization in the United States," *American Jewish Yearbook* 39 (1937–1938): 62).

In the hands of those hostile to Jews, words lost their meaning, a fact of life understood by some Jews who had gained a foothold in academe. Sidney Hook recounted that he advised Lionel Trilling to make a scene and accuse his chair of anti-Semitism when faced with the prospect of nonreappointment to Columbia's English Department faculty. He assumed that the Columbia faculty, located in a city where everyone had Jewish friends and acquaintances, ultimately did not have the courage of its prejudices. Trilling, Hook continued, followed his advice and eventually was reappointed (Sidney Hook, "Anti-Semitism in the Academy: Some Pages of the Past," *Midstream* 25 [January 1979]).

Factors reversing the pervasive discrimination of the interwar years included the general liberalization of attitudes that occurred during and after World War II, the appointment of significant numbers of refugee scholars, many of whom were Jewish, to university faculties, and changing demographic and economic conditions.

American colleges played a significant role in the war effort, and Jews capitalized on opportunities when stationed at colleges where opportunities would have previously been restricted. At Yale, Isidore Dyen's knowledge of Malayan languages and Bernard Bloch's of Japanese led first to wartime appointments and then to lengthy academic careers. And at Yale, as elsewhere, once the war mandated intellectual considerations over social ones in faculty appointments, there was no turning back.

Knowledge of the results of European anti-Semitism further silenced objections to Jewish appointments. And once Jews appeared in a college or university hierarchy, their views on subsequent appointment and promotion decisions had to be considered. Finally, the rapid growth in undergraduate enrollments, due first to the G.I. Bill and then to the rising birth rate and the increase in women attending college, created a severe faculty shortage. In the early 1960s, sociologist E. Digby Baltzel wrote that colleges and universities could afford to discriminate only at the peril of their existence; there were just not enough good faculty to go around.

The intellectual migration of the 1930s and early 1940s is a story in itself. Laura Fermi compiled a list of over 1900 European refugees who settled in the United States between 1930 and 1941 and held academic appointments or made significant intellectual contributions to their fields. Not all such refugees were Jewish, nor were they all located in academe. But a significant proportion were both, and even in the humanities, where Jews still experienced the greatest discrimination, refugee Jews brought such impeccable credentials that their presence could only be considered an asset.

The refugee Jewish contribution to a reorientation of American scholarship during these years is well known. Jews contributed to nearly every physical and biological science, and they revitalized American sociology and psychology. Sociologist Lewis Coser described the refugees as "salutary disturbers of America's intellectual peace," although the intellectual jousting which must have taken place in some fields is not yet fully documented. We know even less about the effect of such refugee appointments on the subsequent appointment of native-born Jews or those arriving during earlier periods of migration.

Coser and Hook imply that the former facilitated the latter, although it should be recalled that many refugees worked in fields, such as physics, already open to American Jews.

The intellectual and social tension in many newly integrated departments may explain a key problem faced by Jewish academics during a period of inclusion: the conflict between academic norms and the expectations of the Jewish community. Indeed, by the late 1960s, articles began to appear in Jewish and academic publications with such titles as "How Jewish are Jewish Academicians?" and "The Socialization of Jews Into the Academic Subculture." Most articles assumed that Jewish professors were well into the process of socialization into secular, intellectual subcultures with the result that a widening gap existed between their outlooks and those of their fellow Jews. Indeed, to some membership in the academic guild resembled religious membership in that both required specialized knowledge, intensive commitment, formal ethical codes, and distinctive modes of communication.

Statements about secularization, while not without considerable truth, must be placed in context. First, perhaps in no other decade in the twentieth century did American academics appear as autonomous as they did during the 1960s. With a growing flow of federal and foundation grants, with increased public prominence, with a strong demand for their services as undergraduate and graduate enrollments rose, faculty members found themselves subject to relatively few constraints. Soon, the end of expansion and the leveling off and decline of grants lessened the autonomy of all professors, not only Jewish ones. Thus, some of the "priorization" of academic over Jewish agendas reflected the general ability of American professors to set their own terms for public service participation.

Second, anti-Semitic attitudes were still extant, although declining, during the 1960s. In response, Jewish academics continued to behave with some circumspection. Since many Jewish academics had often obtained their academic positions precisely because they were assimilated, drastic behavioral changes over a short time span would be unlikely.

Third, as sociologists began to collect data concerning the beliefs and practices of Jewish academics, a more complex picture emerged. Jews, by any measure, displayed greater academic achievements than their Gentile colleagues. The percentage of Jews in the American academic profession had greatly increased from its nadir in the 1920s through the 1960s, when Jews comprised 12 percent overall of American college faculty and over 20 percent in elite institutions. They were more likely to publish a greater number of books and articles, attain higher rank, and command higher salaries than their Gentile colleagues. At the same time, the association between scholarly attainments and irreligion was "surprisingly weak." That is, the evidence that scholarship came at the cost of religious observance was not compelling. One could participate in the "universalistic culture" and still observe some mitzvoth.

Fourth, patterns of Jewish observance and communal participation remained relatively stable after the 1950s. Studies show that "the proportion of younger Jewish academics who regard themselves as not having any religious identification, who do not attend services, or are hostile to religion does not differ greatly from the older." While these results suggest that any desired change in Jewish identification will come only as a result of considerable effort, they also suggest that the worst fears of the critics will not be realized.

Fifth, other studies carefully distinguish between the personal identity and observance of Jewish academics, on the one hand, and communal participation, on the other. A low level of group participation, researchers found, did not imply low levels of observance. Many contemporary Jewish academics have modified Lafayette Mendel's mode of conduct: "a Jew at home, and a professor on the street."

In short, Jewish academics are probably not the "disaster area" of the Jewish community. Within a generation, they overcame an academic anti-Semitism that diminished their numbers and penalized strong Jewish identification. Today, they reflect general American Jewish patterns of identification (especially among professionals) more than they differ from them; they neither lead nor follow the organized Jewish community. Their presence in American colleges and universities has proved salutary in many respects, not the least of which is the decided Jewish influence on a number of the academic disciplines.

Thorstein Veblen once attributed much of the intellectual achievement associated with Jews to their marginality; their position on the social periphery offered Jews the opportunity for insight denied to those wholly immersed in the dominant culture. Jews, today, are less marginal, yet continued creativity and productivity can be thoroughly documented. Perhaps some of these qualities may not result from social marginality but from Judaic insight, which even assimilated academics have somewhere in their genes.

JEWISH STUDENTS. Those acquainted with traditional Jewish thought understood its ambivalence about the worth of secular higher education and did not anticipate the influx of Jewish students into American colleges and universities during the first decades of the twentieth century. Indeed, Jewish reluctance to expose their young to Protestant-sponsored institutions explains much of their neglect of the nineteenth-century college. On the other side, those imbued with the prejudices of that century believed that Jewish "acquisitiveness" preempted interest in the discipline and culture of liberal education.

Yet, increasing numbers of Jews ignored Orthodox prohibitions. Many Jews believed that their participation in the secular schools would help reduce anti-Semitism. At bottom, secular education attracted Jewish students and their parents as it became clear that economic advancement required education obtainable through the schools and universities. As institutions of higher learning opened or incorporated extant professional schools, they raised these schools' entrance requirements to include a bachelor's degree. Thus attendance at an undergraduate institution became virtually inescapable for those seeking the economic and social advancement attainable via a professional degree. Conversely, increased economic security among Jews made feasible a longer period of postsecondary education.

In the United States, the Jewish student population exhibited rapid growth, high visibility, and strong geographic, institutional, and disciplinary concentrations. No sooner had initial expectations of Jewish indifference or hostility to higher education been proved incorrect than Jewish students found themselves blamed for their own success. Initial concern was moderate: from its start in the late nineteenth century through World War I, the influx had been gradual, involving, for the most part, assimilated Sephardic- and German-Jewish students, who raised fewer questions for authorities. Some expected that informal discrimination, sometimes tacitly sanctioned, practiced by students (especially fraternities and sororites) might discourage Jewish enrollments. Further, the general movement toward liberalized access to American colleges that occurred between 1890 and 1910 discouraged any proclivity toward restriction. Last, the philo-Semitic presidents who hired the first significant numbers of Jewish faculty would not have countenanced admissions discrimination.

Such factors continued to influence admissions policies after World War I; however, the balance soon shifted. With a college education now imperative to social advancement, officials faced with increased applications from Jewish students questioned the effects of competition for large enrollments and of previously effected admissions liberalizations. Finally, apathetic or anti-Semitic presidents succeeded sympathetic ones. Fear of the foreigner and racial categorization had become commonplace by the 1920s, and Jews had attained enough upward mobility to translate an abstract "threat" into a present reality. Many Gentiles concluded that if not dealt with promptly, the Jewish presence might reduce higher education's attractiveness to the traditional Gentile constituency.

Discrimination in college admissions and the enactment of immigration restrictions occurred simultaneously. Admissions restrictions most frequently occurred at or near major Jewish population centers. Two restrictive devices were developed: selective admissions and quotas.

Devised and elaborated at Columbia University after World War I, *selective admissions* postulated that the individual characteristics of *some* Jewish students created a "problem" and that mechanisms existed to distinguish between "desirable" and "undesirable" students. Applications eliciting social characteristics, "psychological" (intelligence or aptitude) tests, photographs, character references, and personal interviews were near simultaneous innovations designed to facilitate such distinctions. Viewing "desirability" as an individual property, Columbia authorities concluded that, given adequate information about each applicant and a large enough applicant pool, one could compose a freshman class containing an academic and social mix acceptable to all concerned. This usually meant the exclusion of East European Jews.

Harvard president Abbott Lawrence Lowell (1910–1933) viewed the presence of Jews as a group as problematic apart from any member's personal characteristics. All interests, therefore, would be best satisfied by placing a *quota* (a strict limitation) on the number of Jewish students—even if all who applied appeared individually desirable.

Advocates of selective admissions viewed the expanded dossier on each student as a way of evaluating social desirability while retaining the focus of admissions decisions on the individual student. The result was a Jewish enrollment of desired level. The cost for these institutions was a laboriousness and subjectivity in admissions procedures. The gains consisted of an "acceptable" student body, according to the administration's narrow definition. Selective admissions deflected much criticism precisely because it singled out no single status as "key." Quota establishment, to the contrary, remained indefensible (a university was not, after all, a social club or summer resort). Consequently, it was a covert, though common, practice.

While private institutions had nearly free reign to change their admissions policies, the U.S. Constitution's Fourteenth Amendment confined public colleges concerned about a Jewish presence and lacking an indigenous Jewish population to restricting out-of-state matriculations. The existence of restricted housing at state schools with dormitory shortages also proved effective. Even if legally prohibited from the invidious use of selective admissions, college officials retained broad discretion over admissions. External agencies, such as the courts, exhibited little enthusiasm for substituting their own judgment for that of an admissions committee—the latter alone had the expertise to evaluate each applicant's credentials and to decide whether he or she best corresponded to that of the institution's ideal client. After World War II, colleges confronted with litigation and regulatory legislation (such as the 1948 Fair Education Practices Act in New York State) still managed to save the selective admissions process (and its subjective and discretionary methods), while having to cease all discrimination on the grounds of race, creed, color, or national origin. Several eastern states passed antidiscrimination legislation, and Title VI of the 1964 Civil Rights Act, though primarily aimed at equal treatment for blacks and Hispanics, also assured equal treatment for Jews. Today, few charge selective institutions with anti-Jewish discrimination, although it is not clear precisely when discriminatory practices ended at a number of institutions.

On the campus social level, Jewish students received little help from college officials when confronted with student ostracism. However, they occasionally obtained the support of Jewish philanthropists to "neutralize" their fellow students' anti-Semitism. Jacob Schiff, the financier, anonymously endowed the student center at Barnard College as a countermove to the self-selecting student culture. Centrally located, its facilities would be open to all. At the same time, Schiff urged authorities at American colleges to abolish fraternities and sororities that discriminated against Jewish students. To such requests, most administrators responded that changes in interpersonal relationships could come about only through education, that administrative coercion would probably only result in greater anti-Semitism. (However, sociological courses specifically designed to reduce student prejudice were woefully unsuccessful.) Even after World War II, most colleges only reluctantly pressured fraternities and sororities to abolish discriminatory charter provisions or to disaffiliate from national orders mandating discriminatory policies.

Jewish students responded to social exclusion either with renewed emphasis on their academic work (thereby earning the reputation of "grinds") or by the establishment of predominantly Jewish academic and social organizations. At Harvard College in 1906, a group of Jewish undergraduates organized the first Menorah Society, which had as its purpose "the promotion in American colleges and universities of the study of Jewish history, culture and problems, and the advancement of Jewish ideals." Far more resembling typical nineteenth-century collegiate literary societies than fraternities, Menorah societies flourished on a number of college campuses before and after World War I. Deliberately eschewing a primarily social purpose, Menorah quickly found itself caught between Jewish student organizations whose objectives differed from its academic goals, such as the Student Zionist Organization, and a quickening demand for Jewish fraternities and sororities.

The first Jewish fraternity in the United States was founded in New York City in 1898. Established under the watchful eye of Columbia University Semitics professor Richard J. H. Gottheil, the Zeta Beta Tau fraternity originally professed ideals more ambitious than friendship and brotherhood. It aimed, wrote an early member, "to inspire the students with a sense of Jewish national pride and patriotism" (Zeta Beta Tau, *The First Twenty Years* [New York: Zeta Beta Tau, 1924], 15). Although the fraternity movement's early Zionist orientation gradually diminished, it attempted to retain the intellectual and service ideals on which it was founded. Indeed, some

feared that the distinctive missions of Menorah and ZBT might confirm and even enhance Jewish stereotypes. But, by the 1920s, Jewish fraternities and sororities became virtually indistinguishable from their Gentile counterparts and Menorah societies began to atrophy.

Some Jewish students eschewed all organizations that might have offered them membership. "White Jews" aspired to full inclusion in Gentile culture, sometimes succeeding—more often learning that their Jewishness per se was an inescapable status. Other students aspired neither to inclusion in the Gentile nor Jewish student cultures. In traveling a difficult road, some relied on their Jewishness for strength, others redoubled their academic efforts, while others sublimated their frustrations into some creative endeavor. Some perhaps never fully recovered from the status attached to them by their Gentile counterparts.

Post-World War II Jewish students moved into the student mainstream, abetted in the 1960s by the decline of fraternities and sororities as mainstays of student culture. Some identifiably Jewish organizations, such as Menorah, declined, while others, such as Hillel, grew. Some Jewish students, however, thought they detected an undertone of anti-Semitism in comments made about student demonstrations of the late 1960s and early 1970s, which, sociologists noted, included a disproportionate number of Jewish participants. In the 1980s, a more blatant anti-Semitism emerged in the form of "JAP-bashing," aimed against Jewish women. Academically, Jewish students opted for a broader spectrum of institutions as overt and covert discrimination declined and as public higher education increased in size to absorb the baby boom. They opted for majors leading to a larger number of occupations, as discrimination declined in professions dominated by firms (e.g., engineering) rather than individual practice (e.g., medicine). In this climate, assimilation (and, less openly, a fear of intermarriage) replaced inclusion as the main problem perceived by the concerned Jewish community.

On the basis of more than half a century of data on college students, it is possible to comment on the "threat of assimilation." While religious identification of all students declines during the years they attend college, Jewish *identity* declines less than Catholic or Protestant identity. In *Four Critical Years: Effects of College on Beliefs, Attitudes, and Knowledge* (1977), Alexander Astin suggests that the place of college attendance affects identity. For example, matriculation in northeastern colleges appears to reinforce Jewish student identification. On the other hand, what is considered Jewish "behavior" exhibits a greater decline. Jewish students also exhibit greater-than-average increases in liberalism. Astin also found that they are less likely to marry while in college and more likely to attend graduate and professional school. They are more inclined to activism and less attracted to student government.

JEWISH STUDIES. During the nineteenth century, the founders of *Wissenschaft des Judentums* (the scientific study of Judaism) dreamed of seeing this study incorporated into the curriculum of German universities, a move that would have heralded the acceptability of Jews and Judaism in German society and culture. But German officials rejected all petitions and the study of Judaism remained in communal institutions. In contrast, numerous institutions in the United States added Jewish studies to their curriculum beginning in the late nineteenth century. By the late 1960s, about one-third of all liberal arts colleges offered one or more courses in some branch of Jewish learning, and enrollments reached 50,000. Today, more Americans study the field in collegiate than communal institutions.

Although biblical Hebrew was part of the colonial American college curriculum, it was confessional, not scientific. With the decline of Protestant (particularly Puritan) Hebraism from the middle of the eighteenth through the nineteenth centuries, the study of Hebrew also declined. In 1755, Harvard relegated the subject to elective status, leading to a significant drop in enrollment. In the nineteenth century, Columbia claimed to offer Hebrew but actually dropped the subject for decades. Biblical criticism briefly flourished at Harvard and Andover in the nineteenth century, but its influence waned after mid-century. California, Johns Hopkins, and Cornell appointed scholars to Semitics (the philological study of the language family that included Hebrew) posts in the 1870s, but none of these appointments lasted a decade. With Paul Haupt's appointment to the Johns Hopkins faculty in 1884, Semitic scholarship found a lasting home. Once established, Semitics allowed Judaica to emerge as a significant subfield. Columbia soon appointed Richard J. H. Gottheil to a Semitics chair, and the University of Pennsylvania appointed Morris Jastrow to such a post. In 1897, William Rosenau published a paper identifying 15 colleges and universities offering Semitics. Of these, the University of Chicago,

Columbia, Johns Hopkins, and the University of Pennsylvania offered instruction in specifically Jewish materials (rabbinic and medieval Jewish texts). These were all large, well-off, and research-oriented institutions. Harvard and the University of California, which began their scientific Judaica programs shortly after the Rosenau survey, shared these characteristics.

The field's intellectual agenda was shaped by the state of the art in Semitics research, the place of the Jew in American society and on the campus, and the nature of the college or university that housed it. William F. Albright, the Biblical archaeologist, characterized the nineteenth century as "the heroic age of philology." The excitement generated by philology in America can be demonstrated by Gottheil's comment that he had become "a full-fledged philological worm, who at best can creep from one root to another and nibble a little here and there." Gottheil's play on the word "root" suggested both flora and etymology. Though trained in rabbinics and occupying a chair of rabbinics and philology, Gottheil expended most of his professional efforts on the latter field. He did so partly because the area of language per se was exciting and because this work was most likely to produce recognition from his professional colleagues. And he did so partly in self-protection. Gottheil and other practitioners knew their position was tenuous. By 1898, Gottheil reduced his offerings in Judaica to two half-year courses in rabbinics. By 1906, he reported that he was devoting himself more and more to Arabic. Gottheil exhibited a socially grounded ambivalent stance toward Jewish scholarship, fairly typical of his contemporaries. He wished to be seen as a disengaged scientist, not an apologist. This required shifting the focus of research to other areas of Semitics or concentrating on technical problems of language. Either would save him from religious forces hostile to the critical examination, analysis, and interpretation of texts. While Gottheil asserted the centrality of history as well as philology for a scholarly agenda, this remained a prescription for others, rather than a description of his own work. George Foote Moore, a Gentile, became the first important American university-based scholar to engage in interpretive analyses of Jewish historical and religious materials. For a Jew, humanistic scholarship might prove too dangerous.

A generation later, Harvard's Harry Wolfson faced the problem of legitimizing his subject in the humanities curriculum. "Medieval philosophy is the only branch of Jewish literature . . . which binds us to the rest of the literary world," he wrote. While Jewish Semitics professors acknowledged the significance in Jewish intellectual and spiritual life, the Talmud and its commentaries (the core of yeshiva studies) were too uniquely Jewish for a university course. Jewish learning had to make sense to university colleagues, lest practitioners be perceived as rabbis. Traditional rabbinics would not become part of the university Judaica curriculum for another forty years.

Although Wolfson's emphasis on philosophy extended the scope of Judaica within universities, its high culture subject matter and approach kept the field restricted to research universities attracting an elite student body. Further growth required access to mass institutions and a curriculum appropriate to such institutions. In 1933, Abraham Katsh, a graduate student at New York University, proposed the introduction of *modern* Herbrew into an adult education unit; soon after, a program of Jewish studies began in the School of Education. At NYU, the program emphasized the modern period, and Hebrew was viewed as a living language—that of the Jewish settlers in Palestine. The program grew in the adult and the undergraduate professional divisions—not the graduate school. In the research institutions, by contrast, the field was centered on the graduate level and was located in the arts and sciences faculty. The NYU model was adopted by Brooklyn College in 1938, Hunter College in 1940, and City College of New York and Temple University in 1948.

During the 1950s and 1960s, the field developed further. Scholars conducted more and more sophisticated social-scientific inquiries into Jewish life. With the growing body of reading materials, and the availability of interested scholars, it became possible to introduce undergraduate courses focused on the lives of ordinary Jews. The textual and intellectual-historic orientation of classical *Wissenschaft* shared the field with social history, sociology, and related disciplines. Concurrently, departments of religion at private colleges became less confessional and apologetic and allowed for the study of Judaism with religious studies. The 1963 Supreme Court decision in the *Schempp* case (allowing study *about* religion in public educational institutions) permitted a significant expansion of the study of Judaism in public college religion departments. While early scholars were obsessed with problems of language and texts, their intellectual successors became less concerned with data for data's sake and more concerned with the meaning of data.

The field's growth pattern from the 1920s through the 1970s reflects the growing acceptability of Jews and Judaism in America, the field's transformation as described above, and the changing size and character of American higher education institutions. American colleges experienced substantial enrollment growth during the twentieth century. This allowed many institutions to go beyond a restricted curriculum. Increased size allowed for appointment of professors in a greater number of specialties. Although the field shifted from a primarily graduate to a primarily undergraduate orientation, it is still mainly found in larger institutions with graduate programs in areas of high Jewish population density and enrolling large numbers of Jewish students.

By any measure, the field's growth outstripped that of higher education in general. During the 1920s and 1930s (a period of anti-Semitism on many campuses), growth was very slow, but from the 1940s through the mid-1950s, growth accelerated rapidly. From the late 1950s through the mid-1960s, the rate of growth significantly declined. From the latter 1960s through the 1970s, the growth rate again accelerated sharply. The pattern of endogenous growth displayed by the field from the 1920s through the 1960s suggests that the field grew without much impact from events outside the academic world. The Holocaust and creation of Israel may have influenced the content of courses, but not their number. The field spread from campus to campus with new undergraduate programs emerging in response to the availability of faculty. At the same time, new faculty were trained in response to demands created by the growth of undergraduate programs. This pattern remained stable for 40 years. However, in the late 1960s, the boundary between American higher education and the rest of American society became more permeable; concurrently America experienced an ethnic revival. This propelled the field's upward rate of growth rapidly.

Jewish learning, and more generally, the Jewish presence in American higher education, is secure for now. Jewish students and faculty may still be occasional victims of anti-Semitism (in the mid-1980s, fraternity-instigated anti-Semitic attacks seemed on the rise) and Jewish learning might be the victim of budgetary cutbacks. On the other hand, institutions with lengthy histories of anti-Semitism, such as Columbia and Princeton, now have Jewish presidents. Jewish learning appears in the catalogues of institutions hitherto unrepresented, and endowments for chairs continue to be awarded. The future of the Jew and of Jewish learning in American higher education depends on the continued belief among Jews that American colleges and universities are benign, indeed supportive, institutions and on the willingness of the Jewish community to be involved in the financial and political support of American higher education in general, and Jewish learning in particular. It also depends upon continued tolerance and encouragement by external agencies. *See also* Economics, Hillel, Historiography, Jewish Studies.

HAROLD S. WECHSLER

BIBLIOGRAPHY

Baltzel, E. Digby. *The Protestant Establishment.* New York: Random House, 1964.

Band, Arnold J. "Jewish Studies in American Liberal Arts Colleges and Universities." *American Jewish Yearbook* (1966):3–30.

Coser, Lewis. *Refugee Scholars in America: Their Impact and Their Experiences.* New Haven: Yale University Press, 1984.

Fermi, Laura. *Illustrious Immigrants: The Intellectual Migration from Europe, 1930–1941.* Chicago: University of Chicago Press, 1968.

Feuer, Lewis S. "The Stages in the Social History of Jewish Professors in American Colleges and Universities." *American Jewish History* 71 (June 1982).

Fleming, Donald, and Bailyn, Bernard, eds. *The Intellectual Migration: Europe and America 1930–1960.* Cambridge: Harvard University Press, 1969.

Higham, John. *Send These to Me.* New York: Atheneum, 1975.

——. *Strangers in the Land.* New Brunswick, N.J.: Rutgers University Press, 1955.

Jick, Leon, ed. *The Teaching of Judaica in American Universities: The Proceedings of a Colloquium.* New York: Ktav, 1970.

Lipset, Seymour M., and Ladd, E. C. "Jewish Academics in the United States: Their Achievements, Culture and Politics." *American Jewish Yearbook* (1971): 89–128.

Neusner, Jacob. *The Academic Study of Judaism.* 2 vols. New York: Ktav, 1975, 1977.

Oren, Dan. *Joining the Club: A History of Jews and Yale.* New Haven: Yale University Press, 1986.

Ritterband, Paul, and Wechsler, Harold. "Jewish Learning in American Universities." *Encyclopedia Judaica Yearbook* (1977–1978): 71–75.

——. "Jewish Learning in American Universities: The Literature of a Field." *Modern Judaism* 3 (October 1983): 253–289.

Synnott, Marcia. *The Half-Opened Door: Discrimination and Admissions at Harvard, Yale, and Princeton, 1900–1970.* Westport, Conn.: Greenwood Press, 1979.

Wechsler, Harold S. *The Qualified Student: A History of Selective College Admission in America.* New York: Wiley-Interscience, 1977.

——. "The Rationale for Restriction: Ethnicity and College Admission in America 1910–1980." *American Quarterly* 36 (Winter 1984): 643–667.

Actors and Actresses. *See* COMICS AND COMEDY; FILM STARS; RADIO; TELEVISION; THEATER; THEATER, YIDDISH; VAUDEVILLE.

Adler, Cyrus (1863–1940). Born in Arkansas and raised in Philadelphia, Cyrus Adler received his B.A. from the University of Pennsylvania and his Ph.D. from Johns Hopkins University in 1887. The first person to receive a doctorate in Semitics from an American university, Adler taught Semitics at Johns Hopkins and was, for many years, curator of Semitics and subsequently librarian and assistant secretary of the Smithsonian Institution in Washington, D.C.

For close to 50 years, between the 1890s and his death in 1940, Adler played a unique role in American Jewish public life. One of the most gifted and farsighted Jewish public servants and communal leaders of his generation, Adler was instrumental in the creation and development of an extraordinary number of Jewish institutions and communal enterprises. He was one of the founders of the Jewish Publication Society (1888), on whose various committees he would serve as chairman throughout his life. Adler was also a founder of the American Jewish Historical Society (1892) and its president for more than 20 years. Together with Louis Marshall, Jacob Schiff, Oscar Strauss, and other Jewish leaders, Adler played a pivotal role in organizing the American Jewish Committee (1906) and served as its president from 1929 until his death.

In 1908, Adler left the Smithsonian to become president of the Dropsie College for Hebrew and Cognate Learning in Philadelphia. During his 32 years as president, Adler shaped the institution into one of the preeminent institutions of higher Jewish learning in America. When Solomon Schechter died in 1915, Adler succeeded him to the presidency of the Jewish Theological Seminary, with which he had been closely associated since its founding in 1886, while remaining president of Dropsie as well. Serving as president of the Seminary for 25 years, Adler was a leading figure in the founding of the United Synagogue of America, whose presidency he also held, and was widely recognized as one of the preeminent leaders of Conservative Judaism in America. An editor of the *American Jewish Year Book*, Adler was also the sole editor for many years of the *Jewish Quarterly Review*, the only English-language journal then devoted to Jewish scholarship. Although a committed non-Zionist, Adler (during the 1920s) worked closely with Chaim Weizmann and Louis Marshall in the creation and development of the expanded Jewish Agency for Palestine. Adler was in the forefront in forging the rapprochement between the Zionist and non-Zionist leadership of the Jewish Agency and must be credited with being one of its most influential architects and farsighted leaders. During the last years of his life, Adler was instrumental in helping to rescue, resettle, and secure academic positions for Jewish refugee scholars from Nazi Germany.

A friend and confidant of presidents, U.S. senators, philanthropists, rabbis, and Jewish scholars, Adler was involved in and influenced virtually every aspect of Jewish life in America and abroad from the 1890s through the 1930s. His success as one of the preeminent Jewish public servants of his era lay in his unique ability to bridge worlds that early in the twentieth century had little common ground. A religiously observant Jew, knowledgeable in the field of Jewish scholarship, Adler was also well known and respected in the world of American government and scholarship. A tireless communal leader and creative and constructive administrator, Adler was uniquely able to interpret the needs of traditional-minded Jews to the men of wealth and influence in American Jewry.

DAVID G. DALIN

BIBLIOGRAPHY

Adler, Cyrus. *I Have Considered the Days*. Philadelphia: Jewish Publication Society, 1941.

Dalin, David G. "Cyrus Adler, Non-Zionism and the Zionist Movement: A Study in Contradictions." *Association for Jewish Studies Review* (Spring 1985).

——. "Cyrus Adler and the Rescue of Jewish Refugee Scholars." *American Jewish History* (March 1989).

Neuman, Abraham A. *Cyrus Adler: A Biographical Sketch*. New York: American Jewish Committee, 1942.

Robinson, Ira, ed. *Selected Letters of Cyrus Adler*. 2 vols. Philadelphia: Jewish Publication Society, 1985.

Agenda. *See* NEW JEWISH AGENDA.

Agriculture. Traditional Jewish concerns with farming can be traced back to biblical times, when farmers in Judaea and Israel planted a variety of crops. The pattern continued even after dispersion from the Holy Land, from ancient to medieval periods, wherever they were permitted to till the soil. In modern times, thousands of Jewish families subsisted as farmers in Eastern Europe, despite increasingly oppressive government policies, particularly in Russia.

Religious practices and Talmudic law, including the cycle of holidays, continued replete with agrarian references. And with the crumbling of ghetto walls, many Jews turned to farming as a means of normalizing their place in the larger society. Some saw it as a proper response to accusations that they preferred mercantile endeavors to the more "honest" toils of husbandry.

In nineteenth-century America, many hardworking immigrant peddlers dreamed of a time when they could cease their wanderings and earn the respect of their neighbors on some rural frontier. In an age of Jeffersonian-Jacksonian shibboleths, farm life was idealized also among Jews, even when industrial change had already begun.

Thus, the quixotic Jewish playwright-politician Mordecai Manuel Noah proclaimed the establishment of Ararat (1825) as a haven for his oppressed brethren. There, in northern New York (near Buffalo), they could "till the soil, reap the harvest . . . raise flocks," enjoying a new-found freedom. A decade after this effort failed, some German-Jewish immigrants (members of New York City's Anshe Chesed congregation) formed the Sholem farm colony near Ellenville, New York; it folded in the depression of the 1840s. Group settlement versus individual farming would always present tantalizing dilemmas for Jewish agriculturists, even into the twentieth century.

In the wake of more racist European bigotry and Russian pogroms of the 1880s, issues of haven and resettlement became ever more urgent. A self-help movement was formed by young

Russian Jewish intellectuals and idealists convinced that group settlement on farm lands in America was the answer. Calling themselves Am Olam (eternal or world people), they adopted the slogan, "Work on the land [for] the spiritual and physical revival of our people."

As they made their way out of Europe, the Am Olam groups carried a flag with the twin design of a plow and the Ten Commandments bearing the psalmist's message of regeneration: "Arise from the dust, throw off the contempt of the nations, for thy time has come!" They could even count on aid from their more affluent Western brethren—through "establishment" organizations such as the Franco-Jewish Alliance Israélite, the American Hebrew Emigrant Aid Society, the Baron de Hirsch Fund (incorporated in New York), and (by 1900) the Jewish Agricultural Society.

Out of such joint efforts and disparate dreams emerged many Jewish immigrant communities throughout the rural United States. One of these was located in Catahoula Parish, Louisiana, some 400 miles north of New Orleans, boldly incorporated on November 16, 1881, as the "First Agricultural Colony of Russian Israelites in America." Yet, of the 42 original settlers, none had farming experience. Their hard labor would be wasted when floods washed away crops of cotton and corn. Their families succumbed to malaria and a sense of isolation. Consequently, the project was abandoned; some headed for urban jobs, while others joined Jewish farm ventures elsewhere.

More groups of the Am Olam helped found colonies in far-off places—such as Beersheba, near Cimarron, Kansas; Palestine, near Bad Axe, Michigan; even New Odessa in Oregon; Clarion, Utah; Bethlehem-Yehudah, South Dakota; Cotopaxi, Colorado; and Happyville, South Carolina. American Jewish leaders offered practical aid as well as moral support. For example, Isaac M. Wise, the renowned Reform rabbi of Cincinnati, worked with the Beersheba colony (Kansas).

In his influential journal, *The American Israelite*, Wise pleaded, "Let us make as many Jewish free farmers as can be made." His son, Leo, endured the hardships of homesteading along with the colonists. Similarly, Michael Heilprin, a distinguished American Jewish scholar-journalist, became a zealous advocate of "Jewish agricultural colonization" and cofounder of the Montefiore Agricultural Aid Society (Philadelphia).

But the paths of agrarianism were fraught with hazards. Poor soil and lack of water, as in Utah, meant that Jewish farmers sowing wheat and alfalfa were constantly preoccupied with repairing inadequate irrigation channels. Elsewhere, lack of wood and other materials, distance from transportation and markets, burdensome mortgages, prairie fires, and inexperienced leadership represented some of the common denominators of impending collapse. Ideological and ethnic/religious priorities were divisive factors diminishing the cooperation required among the settlers themselves, as also with their American benefactors. Disputes over cooperative/collective farming as opposed to individual enterprise, as well as Orthodox observance, sometimes caused communal disintegration.

However, in New Jersey the Jewish farmers achieved longevity. Among the earliest and certainly the longest-lasting Jewish agrarian communities were those in rural southern New Jersey, in Salem, Cumberland, and Cape May counties. First was Alliance, started in the spring of 1882, so named in honor of the Alliance Israélite, but dubbed "Jewtown" by townspeople in neighboring Vineland. The nearly 400 East European Jewish pioneer settlers (including over 100 children) recalled being "dumped off" at the nearest Jersey Central Railroad stop. The original tract, purchased from Vineland developers, was thickly overgrown with scrub oak and pine woods. It was an area of sandy soils affected by the Delaware Bay, described even by some geographers as one of the "most desolate areas" in the East.

The immigrants were undaunted. They cleared land for family farms of 12 to 15 acres and built small frame homes. At first, near the west bank of the Maurice River, large temporary buildings provided shelter, with families assigned small rooms like cabins on a steamship. These were dubbed the "barracks" by some; for others, it was Castle Garden (the New York City entry center for immigrants) all over again.

The early years were marked by the hardships of pioneering. Farm implements and household necessities were delayed in transit; there was a lack of draft animals; drinking water was scarce and cooking stoves few; only the infamous mosquitoes abounded. It was hard to get to a doctor in town for lack of horse and wagon, so some mothers would try to heal an open wound with home remedies such as a poultice made of sour black bread (a precursor, of sorts, to penicillin).

Before the first crops came in, and later to supplement meager incomes, the immigrants provided cheap labor throughout the area. Entire families, including mothers and children, trudged for miles to find jobs picking cranberries, strawberries, and blackberries. Children used worn-out stockings on their hands and arms for protection from the thorns, for a family working quickly could earn $3 to $4 a day. Some slaved as pickers as far away as New Egypt; others cut corn at Palatine or Deerfield; still others made bricks in the Vineland factory or produced glass in Millville.

The area press worried over the new "installments of persecuted Russians" (or Russian Hebrews). At times, there were comments on the hundreds of "Jews residing in Alliance returning to their homes across the Maurice River, flush with money from the cranberry bogs." Natives poked fun at older immigrants trying to learn farming, some who did not even know if potatoes grew above or below ground. And the most stubborn tree stumps in Alliance were not cleared until World War I, when the Du Pont Company tested its dynamite on them.

Even native farmers were discouraged by low farm prices and lower wages and the inability to compete with western bonanza farms. The newcomers, however, suffered in addition both a lack of experience and the immigrant's sense of alienation. The process of becoming American was especially difficult for the old, whose traditional values were challenged.

Despite all these difficulties, more Jewish communities emerged in rural south Jersey—Carmel, Rosenhayn, Norma, even Zion, Hebron, and Mizpah. And when Woodbine was founded in Cape May County (1891) and later incorporated as a township, it seemed a fulfillment of ethnic aspirations. Thus, New York's Educational Alliance claimed proudly that agrarian Woodbine was "the first self-governed Jewish community since the fall of Jerusalem." More impressed by its prize-winning poultry shows, local farmers would prefer the mundane title of "Chickenville."

Progress came in the wake of hardships. Immigrant farmers in Alliance/Norma produced Irish potatoes successfully, along with tomatoes, lima beans, and other truck crops. But the corn, fruit, and sweet potatoes (the famous "Vineland sweet") grown in their "New Jerusalem" drew special praise.

Even the parochial *Vineland Journal* admitted (1887) that "the quality of local berries as raised by the Jews has been largely improved on, and some fruit is now grown there as fine as in Vine-

land proper." The previously cool *Elmer Times* admitted, too, that the immigrants had made progress within a few years. "Those who suppose the Jews are a worthless set [should] pay their villages a visit," advised the *Elmer Times*. "What a few years ago was a worthless tract of land has been transformed by the hand of these men and their wives into farms in a good state of cultivation."

Do-gooders from Philadelphia, only 35 miles away, brought back news of the immigrants' industriousness, cleanliness, and such American virtues as voting and paying off mortgages. They felt it important to note that the large bathhouses were "frequented by most of the colonists daily," not to mention summertime swims in the Maurice River.

If such friendly observers represented the more established American Jewish community (of Sephardic or German origin), they were also sympathetic to their rural cousins' practical needs. For example, the Alliance farmers cultivated grapes, drawing the Philadelphia *Exponent's* praise for their "large quantities of excellent wines." A marketing cooperative was formed to aid these vintners and to promote the local juice as well as kosher wines for Passover. Such varied products of Jewish farms were proudly exhibited in New York's Educational Alliance, even if New York was much more distant (about 115 miles) than Philadelphia.

Alliance/Norma proved, through countless family experiences, that Jews could be honest-to-goodness "dirt-farmers." In nearby Rosenhayn also, Jewish farmers were paying off their mortgages with proceeds from strawberries, lima beans, spring chickens, and eggs; their strawberries alone reached record annual shipments of 86,000 crates by the turn of the century. A model agricultural enterprise, Allivine Farm, was funded in Alliance by Philadelphia's philanthropic Fels family (Joseph, Maurice, and Samuel), introducing scientific techniques to all of the area's growers. It was operated by the Russian Jewish agronomists Raymond and Jacob G. Lipman.

The Allivine project was supplemented with a canning factory (also built by the Fels brothers) to offer good prices for all local staples as well as production jobs to supplement seasonal incomes. At the same time, the farm provided low-cost fertilizer, a model for the care of crops and livestock, as well as varied extension services. Such activities would be curtailed only in the unstable economic conditions following World War I and the expansion nearby of Seabrook Farms Co. with its mass production methods.

At the other end of the agrarian spectrum in New Jersey was Woodbine, planned as a balanced community of both farms and factories so that immigrants could supplement their income in the hard times confronting American farmers. Developed during the depression of the 1890s, this concept preceded the Subsistence Homesteads of the 1930s New Deal by more than a generation. Woodbine included, at the outset (1891), a large three-story shirt factory in addition to the first 50 homesteads built on 30-acre farm plots. Woodbine's manager, Hirsch Loeb Sabsovich, devoted a lifetime to agricultural research, teaching, and administration.

A growing recognition that farmers required education in the latest scientific techniques led to the establishment of Woodbine's Baron de Hirsch Agricultural School (1894). A generation of young Jews of immigrant families (as many as 250 students at a time) acquired a background in the sciences and mechanical arts as well as applied experience in the school's model dairy farm, orchards, nurseries, gardens, and laboratories. More of an emphasis on "applied skills" was offered by the National Farm School in Doylestown, Pennsylvania, founded by Rabbi Joseph Krauskopf to educate Jewish immigrant boys for farming (1897). Only the exigencies of the entry of the United States into World War I ultimately forced the closing of the pioneer Baron de Hirsch school (1917). Its graduates included Jacob G. Lipman, later dean of Rutgers' Agricultural College; Joseph A. Rosen, who developed the "Rosen rye," a prize-winning grain for infertile soils; as well as other noted agronomists and farm managers.

Ultimately, the chronic depression of American agriculture in the rising industrial era, as well as a general desire for education, led young men away from the family farm. To attend high school, some had to move to Vineland; thence, even college beckoned and then the world of letters and professions.

One such son of Alliance farmers was Gilbert Seldes, who became a noted author and literary critic—as did the journalist Gershon Agronsky and his son Martin Agronsky. But Arthur Goldhaft, a son of immigrant farmers in south Jersey who graduated from the University of Pennsylvania, came back to Vineland, developing vital poultry vaccines in his Vineland Poultry Laboratories. Even by the early 1900s, poultry and egg production offered a practical means to supplement depressed farm incomes, and Jewish farmers began their pioneering role in the cooperative movement. Some decades later, Arthur Goldhaft and his son, Tevis Goldhaft, would help provide scientific know-how to poultry farmers in Israel.

The onset of the twentieth century was another occasion for soul-searching within the Jewish community. Thus, a moral challenge was presented in a graduation address (1904) at the Baron de Hirsch Agricultural School by Rabbi Solomon Schechter, new president of the Jewish Theological Seminary. He was of East European birth like most of Woodbine's people. He knew the rural community's achievements and of the school's graduates; they and others like them "proved" that Jews could be productive farmers. But more important, he asked, "Will the farmer succeed as a Jew?" Would the farmers be able to retain essential religious-cultural values when confronted with assimilation?

In fact, these were issues related to the perennial tensions between group identity and Americanization in the "melting-pot" era. For most, there was no question of retaining religious institutions, even if differences developed over form. Thus, prayer services were held in Alliance from the outset, and a major event was the founding of its first synagogue—a distinctive two-story building of stone foundation, brick, and clapboard. Here, in their *Eben Ha' Ezer* (Rock of Deliverance, completed 1888) were celebrated most weddings; it was also the place for recreation and dramatics, for politics and social clubs, and housed a library as well. Its comprehensive activities formed a classic example of the community-center concept in American Jewish life, even before New York's Educational Alliance.

A striving for community as well as self-help continued to mark Jewish agrarianism in the twentieth century. Changing circumstances required social innovation and response. Amidst urbanization and technological revolution, it was necessary for those already on the land to support themselves and even to assist in the absorption of additional settlers by adapting to unstable economic conditions. For example, poultry farming grew more popular. Group settlement gave way to individual homesteads, from Chesterfield, Conneticut, to Petaluma, California. Farmers supplemented their income, as in New York's Catskill Mountains, by attracting vacationers to country room and board.

In the interwar years, new clusters of Jewish

farming flourished, as, for example, in Ocean County, New Jersey, about 50 miles northeast of the old pioneering Vineland colonies, especially in Farmingdale and Toms River. These communities had been first guided there by the Jewish Agricultural Society in the brief depression that followed World War I. By the mid-1920s, about 60 families organized the Toms River Community of Jewish Farmers. Though many received loans from the Jewish Agricultural Society, the farmers remained independent operators who risked their own savings and united mainly for such specific objectives as cooperative purchasing. At the same time, as a Jewish community of farmers, they were bound to the historic worldwide agrarianism of their people—in Palestine, Argentina, Canada, and even the Soviet Union.

The Toms River Community of Jewish Farmers prospered, with a peak membership of 360 families, including refugees of the 1930s and of World War II. Even during the Great Depression, their sense of responsibility for brethren abroad was never lost, whether in the form of aid for the Palestine *Yishuv*, collections for the Joint Distribution Committee, or protests against anti-Jewish boycotts in Poland. The National Labor Committee and the Poale Zion (Labor Zionists) were as active in Toms River as in the old Vineland communities where Arthur Goldhaft headed the local drives of the United Palestine Appeal. And the Norma Athletic Hall resounded with benefit dances on behalf of incoming German refugees.

As one of the Alliance pioneers explained, it was only natural that they help the immigrants of the 1930s. After all, had not the newcomers of the 1880s received aid from *their* German Jewish brethren in America? Likewise, the East European survivors of the Holocaust—the "displaced persons" of the 1950s—could look for help in setting up poultry farms, reinvigorating such old communities as Vineland or establishing new ones.

In the long run, the social engineering represented by Jewish agrarianism could not be measured by magnitude alone. At its peak in the 1920s the Jewish farm population in the United States was less than 100,000. Numerous settlers eventually dispersed to towns and cities, as American agriculture generally diminished. Nonetheless, there remains this heritage of Jewish idealism, of self-help and philanthropy, individualism and cooperation.

Joseph Brandes

BIBLIOGRAPHY

Brandes, Joseph. *Immigrants to Freedom: Jewish Communities in Rural New Jersey Since 1882*. Philadelphia: University of Pennsylvania Press, 1971.

Davidson, Gabriel. *Our Jewish Farmers and the Story of the Jewish Agricultural Society*. New York: Fischer, 1943.

Dobin, Abraham. *Fertile Fields: Recollections and Reflections of a Busy Life*. New York: Barnes, 1975.

Dubrovsky, Gertrude. *The Land Was Theirs: Jewish Farmers in the Garden State*. Tuscaloosa, Ala.: University of Alabama Press, 1991.

Goldberg, Robert A. *Back to the Soil: The Jewish Farmers of Clarion, Utah, and Their World*. Salt Lake City: University of Utah Press, 1986.

Herscher, Uri D. *Jewish Agricultural Utopias in America, 1880–1910*. Detroit: Wayne State University Press, 1981.

Norman, Theodore. *An Outstretched Arm: A History of the Jewish Colonization Association*. London: Routledge & Paul, 1985.

Agudath Israel Of America. Agudath Israel is a world movement to preserve Jewish Orthodoxy. It was founded to present a viable alternative to Reform Judaism, Zionism, Bundism, and assimilation. A broad range of activites in religious, economic and political affairs as well as in social welfare have been developed to help strengthen Torah-true Judaism. As established, the Agudath Israel was fundamentally anti-Zionist because it did not agree with the idea of a secular Jewish society in the Holy Land. After the Holocaust its opinion changed on the establishment of Israel; the leaders then saw Israel as a conduit for uniting the people under the Torah—politically, economically, and religiously.

The movement was founded in May 1912 in Kattowitz, Upper Silesia, by German, Hungarian, Polish, and Lithuanian Orthodox rabbis in opposition to the Tenth Zionist Congress that recognized secular Jewish culture as coexisting with the religious. In 1922, the world organization attempted to establish an American branch without success. A youth section, though, the Zeirei Agudath Israel, was set up. Finally, in 1939, Agudath Israel of America was founded. Rabbi Aaron Kotler (1892–1962), a member of the supreme rabbinical council of the world organization, the Mo'etset Gedolei ha-Torah, who arrived in the United States in 1941, had a great influence on the American branch. He was committed to the establishment of institutions for exclusively Orthodox interests. Agudath Israel also drew considerable support from Adath Jeshurun (Breuer), a well-organized community in Washington Heights, New York City, which supported the traditions of German Austritt-Orthodoxie (seccessionist Orthodoxy) as well as from certain Hasidic rebbes. It was active in the rescue efforts of Jews in Europe during and after World War II, and Rabbi Kotler established the Va'ad Hazzalah (Rescue Committee) of the Agudat ha-Rabbanim to aid war refugees. At the meeting of the Central World Council in 1947, three centers of the movement were established: Jerusalem, New York, and London.

Agudath Israel of America has had a number of impressive accomplishments but has been unable to duplicate the successes and dominance enjoyed by the parent organization in pre-war Europe. This can be attributed to its late arrival in America and the growing right-wing sectarianism of the yeshiva world. The leaders of the Agudah, such as Rabbi Kotler, were also heads of the yeshivot and trained the younger generation to value only traditional Jewish learning. This led to a devaluation of and a disinterest in political and social activities in the Jewish community. The youth organization is vital and important but deliberately avoids controversial topics of communal concern within the Orthodox community, and its local activities pertain only to religious study and *musar* (moral exhortation). Through the National Commission on Youth, more than 15,000 young people are led by 1000 volunteer leaders in separate divisions (Pirchei Agudath Israel for young boys, Bnos Agudath Israel for girls, and Zeirei Agudath Israel for adolescent boys) in 200 local chapters throughout the nation that meet weekly to engage in essentially religious and Torah-study activities.

There is dissension within the Agudah on whether it should work with those outside the right-wing Orthodox community. Despite this, a significant outreach program run by the Agudah, the Jewish Education Program (JEP), has been established. In this program Jewish public school children are taken to nearby synagogues and yeshivot by yeshiva students to receive religious instruction. The JEP has also established Orthodox summer camps for these children as well as providing Orthodox homes for those who are boarding yeshiva students on the Sabbath and holidays.

The Agudath Israel has four central institutions: (1) the Mo'etset Gedolei ha-Torah (Council of Torah Sages), whose members are chosen on the basis of preeminence in talmudic learning; (2) Kenesiyyah ha-Gedolah (the Great Assembly), the highest political authority in the association; (3) the Central World Council, which is elected by the Great Assembly; and (4) the World Executive Committee. At the head of Agudath Israel stands the Mo'etset Gedolei ha-Torah, formerly headed by Rabbi Kotler (1954–1962) and by Rabbi Moses Feinstein (from 1962 until his death in 1986). Since 1986, the council has been comprised of Rabbis Mordechai Gifter, Avraham Pam, Israel Spira, and Elya Svei and has functioned without a titular leader. The Mo'etset is officially responsible for formulating all positions taken by the Agudah concerning important religious and political decisions. Critics claim that the Mo'etset is simply a front for the professional and lay leadership since the rabbinic sages are too removed from practical affairs to make meaningful decisions. In reality, the truth probably is somewhere in between. The Mo'etset today appears to be moving in a more activist direction. It has begun to consider the Agudah's responsibilities toward Russian and Iranian immigrants and has applied Torah ethics to the business and professional world.

Agudath Israel of America at the end of the 1980s emerged as a prime advocate of religious rights of Jews. It organized a Commission of Legislation and Civic Action to protect the rights of Orthodox Jews by presenting the interests of the yeshivot to governmental and legislative bodies. Protected have been Jewish ritual slaughtering (the guarantee that all items sold as kosher are not misrepresented), the rights of the Sabbath observer in public and private employ, and the religious needs of Orthodox Jews when hospitalized. It has worked for the recognition of Jewish higher education and established a program called Project COPE (Career Opportunities and Preparation for Employment) that prepares Orthodox men and women who have not attended college for such fields as computer programming, bookkeeping, and electronics.

In 1978, the Agudath Israel set up the Orthodox Jewish Archives to document a history of the world movement. The archives include material about Orthodox Jewry nationally and internationally, as well as a major section on the rescue of Jews during the Holocaust. Its establishment underscores the "coming of age" of the organization. Unfortunately, a fire in 1988 destroyed much of the collection.

Agudah's influence will remain limited if it maintains the present policy of opposition to participation of other Orthodox bodies in organizations that include non-Orthodox elements, such as the Synagogue Council of America. *See also* Orthodoxy.

MICHAEL N. DOBKOWSKI
JANET L. DOTTERER

BIBLIOGRAPHY

Archives of Agudath Israel of America, New York City.

Dobkowski, Michael N., ed. *Jewish American Voluntary Organizations.* Westport, Conn.: Greenwood Press, 1986.

Encyclopedai Judaica. Jerusalem: Macmillan, 1971.

Jewish Observer and *Dos Yiddishe Vort,* journals.

Liebman, Charles. "Orthodoxy in American Jewish Life." *American Jewish Year Book* (1965).

AIPAC. *See* AMERICAN ISRAEL PUBLIC AFFAIRS COMMITTEE.

Allen, Woody (b. 1935). American film director, screenwriter, playwright, actor, and author, Woody Allen was born Allen Stewart Konigsberg in Brooklyn, New York. He attended Midwood High School and then New York University and City College of New York but did not attain a degree. Although he has worked in a variety of media, Allen is unquestionably best known for his films, which include *Sleeper* (1973), *Love and Death* (1975), *Annie Hall* (1977), *Manhattan* (1978), *Zelig* (1981), *Hannah and Her Sisters* (1986), and *Crimes and Misdemeanors* (1989).

Allen began his career in show business as a gag writer, submitting jokes to newspaper and television personalities. He wrote for such television shows as "The Tonight Show" and "Your Show of Shows" starring Sid Caesar, where he worked with other comic writers who have become well known, e.g., Mel Brooks, Neil Simon, Larry Gelbart, and Carl Reiner. At the urging of his agents, he became a stand-up comic in the early 1960s and created the persona of the little loser, the schlemiel, who is in awe of women and unable to succeed with them. Nightclub and television appearances led to his early work in film. His work for Sid Caesar and his nightclub act clearly influenced his first screenplays. *What's New, Pussycat?* (1965, in which Allen plays a

supporting role) continues Allen's image as insecure and sex-obsessed, while *Casino Royale* (1967) is a parody of James Bond-style spy films. In between these assignments he redubbed a Japanese spy thriller to create the comic *What's Up, Tiger Lily?* (1966).

He made his directorial debut with *Take the Money and Run* (1969), a parody of the documentary form, which features Allen as an incompetent outlaw. Filmic parody and the schlemiel persona again dominate this film, which also incorporates a handful of ethnic gags. In this, his first film as writer-director-star, Allen begins to focus on his Jewish background, and as will often be the case in his later films, the images are disturbing. Twice in the film he uses the image of a rabbi for humor. In the first instance, as a prisoner he is given an experimental drug whose side effects, the audience is told, turn him into a rabbi—visually, an Hasidic rabbi. Later, in a TV-game show parody, an elderly rabbi is featured on a segment of "What's My Perversion?" Much of the rest of the ethnic humor is subtle—the image of Allen's character beaten up by neighborhood bullies looks forward to the more explicitly anti-Semitic nature of such beatings claimed for the character of Zelig in the film of that name.

The specifically Jewish dimensions to his work in the period leading up to *Annie Hall* are few and sometimes covert. *Sleeper,* for instance, features Allen as an alien in a futuristic dystopia, which encapsulates the Jewish experience of living as an outsider in a dominant culture. A memorable "dinner table" scene features non-Jewish characters unintentionally and humorously mangling Yiddish words and phrases. Many of the characters in the various sketches of *Everything You Always Wanted to Know About Sex* (*but were afraid to ask)* (1972) are recognizably Jewish (characters portrayed, for instance, by Gene Wilder or Lou Jacobi), but little is made of this. However, his short-story contributions to the *New Yorker,* to which he began submitting in 1966, are often more explicitly Jewish and overtly intellectual. The best of these stories show Allen working in a stream of Jewish humor whose essential strategy is to link the sacred and the mundane.

Annie Hall marked a turning point in his career, both as his establishment as a filmmaker of international stature and as a chronicler of the American Jewish experience. The film is a virtual compendium of Jewish-American issues. Allen's autobiographical Alvy Singer and his relationship to midwestern *Annie Hall* reproduces a central motif of Jewish-American literature and cinema: the Jewish male and the shiksa. Interactions between Alvy and Annie's family point out the ambivalent attitude toward WASP society and the phenomenon of Jewish self-hatred. Through a complex narrative structure, Allen cuts a swath through Jewish-American culture and history, pointing up Jewish involvement in political causes, the Jewish educational achievement in America, and Jewish involvement in show business. Allen's character, who is unable to feel happy about his life and searches for some kind of ultimate meaning, is a virtual Jewish archetype.

His willingness to confront his own feelings and situation led to the making of *Stardust Memories* (1980), a thinly disguised self-analysis in which Allen agonizes over his role as a comic filmmaker, and *Zelig* (1983), a technically stunning story of a fictionalized celebrity of the 1920s who was a "chameleon man." The latter film is another expression of Jewish fear and paranoia and reveals the desperate desire to fit in, to achieve total assimilation with mainstream society. Like many of his short stories, *Zelig* has a particular Jewish appeal and can be seen as a kind of "in joke" of American Jewish intellectual life as he brings to bear on this fictional story a number of real-life "witnesses," like Irving Howe, Susan Sontag, Bruno Bettelheim, and Saul Bellow, all of whom, of course, are Jewish.

However, Allen has continually been accused of anti-Semitism, or at least self-hatred, for his almost always comic use of recognizably Jewish figures and for his portrayals of Judaism, which, though rare, are consistently negative. In *Hannah and Her Sisters* (1986), Allen's own character, a Jewish TV writer-producer stricken with metaphysical paralysis, tries Catholicism and other religions before finding solace in movies and romance. Put-downs of Yom Kippur, the most holy day in Judaism, recur in *Annie Hall* and *Radio Days* (1987). It is questionable, moreover, if the cinematic visions of his Jewish childhood as seen in *Take the Money and Run, Love and Death, Annie Hall, Stardust Memories,* and *Radio Days* are really affectionate. Nevertheless, his films may be taken as paradigms of the Jewish experience in America as Allen's semiautobiographical characters move up the economic ladder as his film career progresses and attain more than a degree of confidence, competence, success, and status. *See also* Comics and Comedy.

DAVID DESSER

BIBLIOGRAPHY

Brode, Douglas. *Woody Allen: His Films and Career.* Charleston, N.C.: Citadel Press, 1985.

Lax, Eric. *On Being Funny: Woody Allen and Comedy.* New York: Charterhouse, 1975.

———. *Woody Allen: A Biography.* New York: Knopf, 1991.

Pogel, Nancy. *Woody Allen.* Boston: Twayne, 1987.

Alter, Robert (b. 1935). The literary critic Robert Alter was born in New York City. After receiving his B.A. from Columbia University in 1957 and his M.A. and Ph.D. from Harvard University in 1958 and 1962, Alter began what seemed to be a conventional, albeit successful, career as a secular literary scholar/critic. His first books—*Rogue's Progress* (1965) and *Fielding and the Nature of the Novel* (1968)—were well regarded. But they were exactly what one might expect from a bright young man out to establish credentials in the University of California's English Department at Berkeley.

With the publication of *After the Tradition* (1969)—a series of essays on Jewish writing, many of which had first appeared in *Commentary* magazine—it became clear that Alter brought an uncommon measure of intelligence and Jewish learning to his literary criticism. *Defenses of the Imagination: Jewish Writers* and *Modern Historical Crisis* (1978) solidified his reputation as an essayist equally at home with a wide range of Jewish writing whether it was produced in the United States, in Israel, or in Europe.

Alter's books on the Bible as literature—for example, *The Art of Biblical Narrative* (1983), *The Art of Biblical Poetry* (1983), and *The Literary Guide to the Bible* (1987) (co-edited with Frank Kermode)—are even more noteworthy. As a professor of comparative literature at UC–Berkeley, Alter had gained a considerable reputation as a Hebraist and as one of the few American literary critics who read the fictions of S. Y. Agnon, Amos Oz, Yehuda Amichai, or A. B. Yehoshua in the original. His 1975 anthology, *Modern Hebrew Literature*, was an important contribution to the Jewish literary scene, for it helped to popularize the writers included, in particular, and modern Hebrew literature in general. His books on the Bible, however, had a much wider impact, influencing the way in which literary scholars taught the literature of the Bible at all levels—from introductory humanities courses to upperclass and graduate seminars.

Alter has added chairing the Jewish Studies program at Berkeley to his academic duties in the comparative literature department, and the result—rather like his books on Jewish writing, on the Bible, and on modern Hebrew literature—has been to provide a program with wide appeal and one that makes significant contributions to scholarship. Indeed, it would be hard to think of a Jewish-American literary critic who has managed to be so successful at both. *See also* Critics, Literary.

SANFORD PINSKER

American Council for Judaism (ACJ).

The Reform rabbis of the Central Conference of American Rabbis (CCAR) in 1942 founded the American Council for Judaism (ACJ) in protest of a resolution of the CCAR supporting the establishment of a Jewish army in Palestine. The ACJ functioned as a Jewish lobbying group against the creation of a Jewish state, putting the organization in direct conflict with the Zionists. After the creation of Israel it survived as a group outside the Jewish consensus. At its height, the ACJ claimed membership of 20,000. Members consider themselves as American in nationality and Jewish in religion. ACJ considers Israel as the homeland of all those who live there: Moslem, Christian, and Jewish citizens. This ideological stance reflects that of Reform Judaism's nineteenth-century founders, and for this view the ACJ and its members have been accused of being pro-Arab.

One of the founders and leading spokesman of the ACJ, Rabbi Elmer Berger, was director and executive vice-president until 1968. Berger emphasized his stand in the following books: *Emancipation: The Rediscovered Ideal* (1945), *The Jewish Dilemma* (1946), *Who Knows Better Must Say So!* (1955), and *Judaism of Jewish Nationalism* (1957). In *The Jewish Dilemma* he names two men especially who supported the emancipation of Jews versus the creation of a Jewish state: Lessing J. Rosewald, first president of ACJ, and Rabbi Isaac M. Wise, founder of a religious revival of the 1880s to integrate Jews in America (the Reform Judaism Movement).

In 1964, the ACJ testified before Congress in opposition of the United States Government giving direct support to Israel. That same year Berger wrote a letter to the editor of the *Christian Century* stating: "The State of Israel and the World Zionist Organization officially claim that Israel is the 'sovereign state' of 'the Jewish People.' It is also a matter of record that Israeli officials and their American Zionist Associates have persistently ignored the distinction between 'Jew' and 'Israeli.'"

Berger and the ACJ feared the status of Jews in the world would be compromised by the establishment of a Jewish state, and even after the creation of Israel the ACJ continued to press for the assimilation of Jews into American society.

Berger best supported his stance of the ACJ and its fears in a speech in Texas before the Dallas Council of World Affairs, on November 4, 1965:

> [T]he State of Israel and the Zionist movement claim, in fact and in law, that the nationality constituency of the State of Israel included all Jews, regardless of their legal citizenship and nationality. If unchallenged, these claims may become established, through custom, in international law, and as such, discriminate among Americans on the basis of religious faith.

He went on to say:

> [C]ontemporary Zionist-Israeli insistence that the State of Israel's nationality constituency is still "the Jewish people" accounts for those of us today who, as American nationals of Jewish faith, are unequivocally anti-Zionist. We reject and repudiate this political-national "Jewish people" concept with its system of nationality rights and obligations pertaining to the State of Israel.

Berger contended that anti-Zionism among Jews had existed since 1897 when the World Zionist Organization claimed to speak for "the Jewish people." In his speech he gave three fundamental facts for this historic position in the United States:

> 1. Judaism is a religion. The sphere of its moral and ethical influence in history has been universal—not tribal or nationalistic. . . .
> 2. In the democratic tradition, Jews are . . . those individual citizens who voluntarily identify themselves with the spiritual fellowship of this universal faith.
> 3. It is a perversion of any manifestation of contemporary Judaism to assign its devotees, because they are Jews,

any element of secular nationality related to any national sovereignty.

Berger saw the differences between the ACJ and the Zionists as a dilemma for all Jews who must choose between Israel as a homeland and Judaism as a religion and not a nationality.

Much of this changed after the Six-Day War in 1967. During the war Berger assisted in writing a speech for the Syrian ambassador to the United Nations to present to the Security Council. Many ACJ members felt that he had gone too far, and Berger was ousted from the organization in 1968. After this the Reform congregations, organized under the ACJ's influence, distanced themselves from ACJ, and though the members never became pro-Zionist, many became pro-Israel.

The American Council for Judaism continues into the 1990s under the leadership of its Executive Director, Allan C. Brownfeld, who succeeded Rabbi Elmer Berger in 1968. The position of the organization toward Israel has not changed and is perhaps best exemplified in Brownfeld's words: "To the extent that the State of Israel and its organizational supporters in the U.S. promote the idea that American Jews are 'exiles' in their own country, they are interfering in the internal affairs of the U.S. and of American Jews."

JANET L. DOTTERER

BIBLIOGRAPHY

Berger, Elmer. *The Jewish Dilemma*. New York: Devin-Adair, 1946.

——. *Memoirs of an Anti-Zionist Jew*. Beirut: Institute for Palestine Studies, 1978.

——. "The United States and the Middle East." *Vital Speeches* 32 (January 1, 1956): 184–190.

Cohen, Naomi W. *American Jews and the Zionist Idea*. New York: Ktav, 1975.

Dawidowcz, Lucy S. *On Equal Terms: Jews in America, 1881–1981*. New York: Holt, Rinehart and Winston, 1982.

Dobkowski, Michael N., ed. *Jewish American Voluntary Organizations*. Westport, Conn.: Greenwood Press, 1986.

Kolsky, Thomas A. *Jews Against Zionism, the American Council for Judaism, 1942–1948*. Philadelphia: Temple University Press, 1990.

Waxman, Chaim I. *America's Jews in Transition*. Philadelphia: Temple University Press, 1983.

"What Pope Paul's Visit Was Not." *Christian Century* 81 (April 22, 1964): 524.

American Israel Public Affairs Committee (AIPAC). AIPAC is the leading pro-Israel lobbying organization in the United States and is one of the leading forces behind the shaping of United States policy in the Middle East. Its goal is to secure public and government assistance on behalf of Israel to insure the future of an independent Jewish state. AIPAC is not an Israeli lobby, but an American one. All its funding comes from individual Americans. It has been able to draw on the sympathy of the various administrations, Congress, and the American public for the Israeli cause and has become one of the most effective lobbying groups in Washington.

In 1949, after the establishment of the State of Israel, the American Zionist Council (AZC) was created by I. L. Kenen, a registered foreign agent for Israel, to provide a unified Zionist public relations program. It was composed of 14 leading Zionist groups and headed by Louis Lipsky, the aging Zionist leader. The AZC floundered from 1949 to 1953 trying to find a raison d'être for itself. It lobbied in Washington for increased military and economic support for Israel and opposed all groups organized to challenge the Zionist Movement, especially the American Council for Judaism. It issued literature and tried to coordinate Zionist activities in the United States. Because Israel assumed responsibility for speaking to the American government, AZC's functions were undermined. Furthermore, at the end of 1953, the tensions between the Eisenhower administration and Israel's supporters were so acute that there were rumors that the administration would investigate the American Zionist Council. Therefore, an independent lobbying committee was founded under the name American Zionist Committee for Public Affairs. In 1959, it assumed the name American Israel Public Affairs Committee (AIPAC). Rabbi Irving Miller replaced Lipsky as head of the council, and soon afterward the council decided to discontinue all of its distinctly political activities. After 1954, all pro-Israel lobbying was coordinated through the single office of AIPAC.

AIPAC submits policy statements to the President, State Department, and Congress as well as circulates the *Near East Report*, a Washington weekly on American policy in the Middle East, to government officials. It arranges policy conferences to alert members of Congress and key administration officials of issues important to Israel. The 28th Annual Policy Conference, held in May 1987, for example, was attended by 1500 delegates. AIPAC's largest conference ever focused on United States-Israel strategic and economic cooperation and current issues on the legislative agenda: arms sales to Israel's enemies, foreign aid, and the Israeli economy.

AIPAC encourages legislators to travel to Israel with their constituents to see firsthand the strategic and economic realities that Israel faces. It works with hundreds of Jewish student groups on college campuses to help sensitize Jewish students to their political responsibilities concerning Israel. In 1979, AIPAC established the Political Leadership Development Program (PLDP) to respond to the anti-Israel campaign on campuses and published *Myths and Facts*, a record of the Arab-Israeli conflict. According to Thomas A. Dine, executive director since 1980, AIPAC operates on the grass-roots level, which includes U.S. college campuses.

From 1959 to 1987, AIPAC grew from 9000 contributing households to 55,000 and from an annual budget of $1.4 million to $6 million. As of 1987, the membership consisted of roughly 90 to 95 percent American Jews and the remaining 5 to 10 percent were evangelical Christians sympathetic to Israel.

The committee's ability to mobilize votes in the House and Senate has given it stature with the executive branch. AIPAC has been successful in its lobbying efforts because (1) its message is simple, coherent, and motivated by a single-minded devotion to a cause; (2) it never endorses or gives money to candidates, but through contributions of its members is perceived to influence many campaign contributions; (3) it already has the sympathy of many in Congress who wish to help Israel; and (4) it is able to supply timely and reliable information to members of Congress. *See also* United States-Israeli Relations, Zionism.

MICHAEL N. DOBKOWSKI
JANET L. DOTTERER

BIBLIOGRAPHY

AIPAC's annual legislative reports, *Near East Report*, and *AIPAC on Campus*, a newsletter.

"The American Zionist Emergency Council: An Analysis of a Pressure Group." *American Jewish Historical Quarterly* 60 (September 1970): 82–105.

Cohen, Naomi W. *American Jews and the Zionist Idea.* New York: Ktav, 1975.

Halperin, Samuel. *The Political World of American Zionism.* Detroit: Wayne State University Press, 1961.

Pear, Robert with Berke, Richard L. "Pro-Israel Group Exerts Quiet Might as It Rallies Supporters in Congress." *New York Times*, July 7, 1987, A8.

Shipler, David K. "On Middle East Policy, A Major Influence." *New York Times*, July 6, 1987, A1, 4.

Urofsky, Melvin. *American Zionism from Herzl to the Holocaust.* New York: Anchor Press/Doubleday, 1975.

———. *We Are One.* New York: Anchor Press/Doubleday, 1978.

American Jewish Archives. Authorized in 1947 by Nelson Glueck, president of the Hebrew Union College, the American Jewish Archives was founded in Cincinnati in the aftermath of World War II at a time when the enormous tragedy of the European Holocaust was becoming known to a still unbelieving American Jewish community. It was created at a time when the Jews of America, now the largest and best-educated Jewish community in history, faced the awesome responsibility of preserving the continuity of Jewish life and learning.

Glueck appointed Jacob Rader Marcus director. Marcus in the very first year outlined the archive's raison d'être, one that remains valid and that still pertains: "We propose to collect the records of this great Jewish center . . . We seek to understand how [American Jews] lived, how they worked, how they established their own cultural religious community, how they interacted with this novel environment, creating a new Jewish life and at the same time helping to give birth to a new American world."

To a large degree, the creation of the archives may be said to have reflected American Jewry's revived sense of its own distinctive ethnicity, as Stanley Chyet has described it. This was a major turning point in the evolution of an American Jewish identity away from the apologetics that had symbolized the earlier writing of American Jewish history toward "a dispassionate, scholarly productivity" that marked the awareness and acceptance of a distinctly pluralistic American society.

In 1990, the American Jewish Archives contained over 8 million pages of documentation. It published a semiannual historical journal and had three separate publication series.

The Archives has developed a philosophy of sharing its historical treasures not only with scholars but with the American public. Its aim is not only to teach about the role of Jews in the history of the American republic, but also to encourage the study of the historical interaction of Jews with the many other religio-ethnic groups in our society.

ABRAHAM J. PECK

BIBLIOGRAPHY

American Jewish Archives. *Preserving a Heritage.* Cincinnati: American Jewish Archives, 1987.

Clasper, James W., and Dellenbach, M. Carolyn. *Guide to the Holdings of the American Jewish Archives.* Cincinnati: American Jewish Archives, 1979.

Proffitt, Kevin. "The American Jewish Archives: Documenting and Preserving the American Jewish Experience." *Ethnic Forum: Journal of Ethnic Studies and Ethnic Bibliography* 5 (1985): 20–29.

White, Paul F. *Index to the American Jewish Archives.* Vols. I–XXIV. Cincinnati: American Jewish Archives, 1979.

American Jewish Committee. The history of the American Jewish Committee (AJC), the oldest American Jewish defense organization, sheds considerable light on the evolution of Jewish life in twentieth-century America. The impetus that brought the organization into being in 1906 was the desire of a group of prominent Jews to do something about the persecution of their coreligionists abroad. As the pioneer Jewish communal agency, it has had a profound impact on American Jewish attitudes toward, and strategies to deal with, the political, economic, social, and religious problems facing American Jews. Over the years the committee, reflecting American Jewry's integration into American society, gradually expanded its scope, exercising its influence on issues of public policy that were, and are, of interest to Americans in general, not only Jews. The committee has come to function effectively in an environment very different from the one in which it was founded.

Outraged by a series of bloody pogroms in Russia, 34 wealthy and prestigious American Jews of German origin met in 1906 to organize the American Jewish Committee. Among them were Jacob Schiff, Louis Marshall, Oscar Straus, and Cyrus Adler. The first AJC president was Judge Mayer Sulzberger. The new agency's declared purpose was to use its influence against the deprivation of Jewish rights anywhere in the world. Deliberately designed not to be a mass democratic organization, the AJC at first limited its membership to Jews who came from the same social background as the founders.

The organization's opposition to czarist Russia's anti-Jewish policies led it to press for abrogation of a long-standing commercial treaty between the United States and Russia, a goal that was achieved in 1913. The AJC quickly became involved in the struggle over immigration restriction. Despite serious misgivings about the character and habits of their East European coreligionists who sought to enter the United States in the early twentieth century, AJC leaders fought against literacy tests and other measures aimed at keeping them out of the country. With the onset of World War I, the AJC played a key role in organizing relief supplies for Jews stranded in the European war zone. After the war, the AJC sent delegates to the Versailles peace conference and helped secure guarantees of minority rights for Jews in the newly created states of Eastern Europe.

Fighting anti-Jewish discrimination in the United States became the AJC's major priority in the 1920s. It sought to discredit the anti-Semitic *Protocols of the Elders of Zion*, and it was Louis Marshall, AJC president, who engineered Henry Ford's public apology for printing material from it in his newspaper. Subsequently, AJC surveyed American public opinion about Jews, publicized the links between American anti-Semites and German Nazis, and launched an educational campaign to show that anti-Semitism threatened not only Jews, but democratic society as a whole.

The committee's attitude toward Zionism was deeply ambivalent. AJC willingly backed the right to settle in Palestine for those Jews who wished to do so. Yet it feared any assertion of Jewish nationalism that could possibly undermine the legitimacy of Jewish citizenship elsewhere in the world. While officially non-Zionist, the AJC welcomed the Balfour Declaration of 1917 that supported a Jewish homeland in Palestine and joined with Zionists in the 1920s to create an expanded Jewish Agency for the purpose of building up the economy of Jewish Palestine. Although the committee criticized the British for curtailing Jewish immigration into Palestine in the 1930s, it opposed calls for the creation of an independent Jewish state there until after World War II. Hailing the establishment of the State of Israel in 1948, the AJC consistently maintained that the political allegiance of American Jews was solely to the United States and that American Jewry was under no moral obligation to transplant itself to Israel. Jacob Blaustein, AJC president, elicited an agreement to that effect from Israeli Prime Minister David Ben-Gurion in 1950. The AJC was the first American Jewish organization to open a permanent office in Israel.

A major turning point in AJC's history was a 1944 decision to open membership and establish chapters around the country. Given the passing from the scene of the eminent prewar Jewish "elite" and the acculturation of the Eastern European immigrants, the committee had to expand and democratize in order to survive.

After World War II, under the professional leadership of executive vice-presidents John Slawson and Bertram H. Gold, AJC became heavily involved in intergroup-relations work. Active in the movement for civil rights, the agency developed programming in Jewish-Christian relations and in interethnic understanding. Its legal staff crafted numerous *amicus* briefs on First Amendment questions, concentrating especially on preserving the separation between church and state. The AJC distinguished itself in the field of research with its sponsorship of social scientific studies of prejudice and anti-Semitism. Concerned about the possible internal erosion of American Jewish life, the committee initiated programs to enhance the Jewish knowledge and Jewish identity of its members.

Today, the American Jewish Committee, headquartered in New York City, has 50,000 members in 32 chapters across the United States, in addition to a Washington office that deals directly with government officials and representatives of foreign nations. It also continues to maintain its Israel office. The agency works through four program departments: international affairs, interreligious affairs, national affairs, and Jewish communal affairs. Two of its publications, *Commentary* magazine and the *American Jewish Year Book*, have achieved international renown.

The fading of the distinction between German and East European Jews and the founding of a plethora of other Jewish organizations have blurred what used to be the special character of the American Jewish Committee. Yet even today it remains unique in its broad agenda not confined to Israel or anti-Semitism; in its ideologically diverse membership encompassing liberals and conservatives, Democrats and Republicans; and in its emphasis on coalition building with other religious and racial and ethnic groups to achieve its goals.

In February 1990, the AJC board of governors tackled long-standing budgetary problems by cutting back on programs. Concluding that AJC's focus had become unclear because it had branched off into too many areas, the board decided to concentrate on combating anti-Semitism, safeguarding Israel, supporting human rights, promoting intergroup relations, enriching American Jewish life, and influencing American policy in the areas of civil rights, immigration, and church-state relations.

Later that year, the AJC named as its executive vice-president David A. Harns, a 43-year-old staff member and expert on international affairs.

LAWRENCE GROSSMAN

BIBLIOGRAPHY

Adler, Cyrus. *I Have Considered the Days*. Philadelphia: Jewish Publication Society, 1945.

Cohen, Naomi W. *Not Free to Desist: The American Jewish Committee, 1906-1966*. Philadelphia: Jewish Publication Society, 1972.

Feingold, Henry L. "The Continued Vitality of the American Jewish Committee at 80." *American Jewish Year Book* 81 (1981): 341-361.

American Jewish Conference. On August 29, 1943, the American Jewish Conference was convened for the purpose of unifying American Jewish organizations behind the Biltmore Program. The inspiration for the conference came from Henry Monsky, president of B'nai B'rith, who invited 34 Jewish organizations to come to Pittsburgh in January 1943 for the purpose of forging a consensus in regard to the postwar status of Jews and the future of a Jewish Palestine.

Thirty-two organizations accepted, and only the then anti-Zionist American Jewish Committee and the non-Zionist Jewish Labor Committee declined the invitation. Delegates to the forthcoming assembly were to be chosen as a result of a nationwide election both among cooperating national Jewish organizations and popularly elected delegates. In this election, which was held in the 48 mainland states plus the District of Columbia, 500 delegates were selected to represent 65 organizations. The new president of the American Jewish Committee, Judge Joseph Proskauer, accepted the second invitation sent to the committee to participate on the condition that the organization change its name from the American Jewish Assembly to the American Jewish Conference in order to avoid the idea of a specific Jewish political identity.

The elections resulted in the conference being dominated by organizations belonging to the Zionist Organization of America or its affiliates. With its majority, the Zionists were able to control the first conference session, held at the Waldorf-Astoria Hotel in New York City on August 29, 1943. The delegates passed resolutions that called for the fullfillment of the Balfour Declaration and the reconstitution of a Jewish commonwealth in Palestine. The delegates also called for the abrogation of the British White Paper of 1939. With the passage of these resolutions, the American Jewish Committee withdrew its participation from the conference.

The conference continued to function until 1949. It attempted to unify American-Jewish organizations behind the rescue of what was left of European Jewry, proposing plans for the postwar reconstruction of Jewish life, including aid to displaced persons, and continued its efforts to build a Jewish homeland in Palestine.

The creation of the State of Israel in 1948 made the conference's primary function extraneous. In addition, the fragile unity that had made the organization functional began to unravel as old ideological and personal rivalries once again surfaced. In 1949, the conference ceased to function. *See also* Zionism.

LINDA GLAZER

BIBLIOGRAPHY

Dobkowski, Michael. *Jewish Voluntary Organizations.* Westport, Conn.: Greenwood Press, 1986. Pp. 39–44.

Kohansi, Alexander S., ed. *The American Jewish Conference: Its Organization and Proceedings of the First Session.* New York: American Jewish Conference, 1944.

Urofsky, Melvin. *We Are One.* New York: Anchor Press/Doubleday, 1978.

American Jewish Congress. After years of agitation for a democratically elected central body of American Jews with authority to make decisions on all questions affecting American Jewry, the American Jewish Congress was founded in 1918. The main movers for the creation of such a body were the leaders of American Zionism: Rabbi Stephen S. Wise, Justice Louis D. Brandeis, and Federal Judge Julian W. Mack. The Zionist Movement had reached the conclusion that the work to reconstruct a Jewish homeland left no time or energy to alleviate the needs and woes of Diaspora Jews and therefore another allied Jewish movement was necessary. Recently arrived Russian Jewish immigrants, the so-called "downtown" Jews, whose numbers had multiplied in the first part of the century and who were no longer content to let the "uptown" German-Jewish leadership determine their future, enthusiastically embraced these new ideas.

The nationwide elections for delegates to the first American Jewish Congress took place on June 10, 1917, and some 350,000 ballots were cast. After some delay, the newly elected delegates plus representatives of 30 national organizations convened in Philadelphia on December 15, 1918. The first business of the congress was to adopt a program to be submitted to the peace conference meeting in Versailles. The American Jewish Congress program demanded that clauses be inserted in the treaties with the defeated powers that would protect the rights of Jews and other minorities in those countries. The delegation that was sent to Versailles achieved its mission, and the so-called minority clauses were inserted in the peace treaties.

In 1920, AJCongress delegates meeting in Philadelphia for the second time dissolved the Congress, pursuant to prior agreement. A few minutes later, however, the delegates reconvened and made plans to establish a permanent American Jewish Congress. This was done in 1922 without the participation of the American Jewish Committee or the National Workmen's Committee.

During that stage in the lifespan of AJCongress, the organization was a federated body of organizations. Its leader was Rabbi Stephen S. Wise, then the best-known Jew in America. The congress struggled along during the 1920s without funds, accomplishing little.

When Hitler rose to power, the leadership of the Congress began to mobilize. Rabbi Wise, over the opposition of more conservative elements in American Jewry, organized a nationwide boycott of German goods and began the worldwide struggle against Nazism, which led in 1936 to the organization of the World Jewish Congress with Wise and Nahum Goldmann as its leaders.

Meanwhile the affiliation of the various national Jewish organizations in the congress weakened, and in 1940 Wise opened the membership to individuals. Soon the congress was distinguished from other American Jewish organizations by its liberal point of view and its emphasis upon the fight against widespread discrimination against Jews. Wise created a Commission Against Economic Discrimination and a Commission on Law and Legislation to carry out these campaigns. In 1945, Wise's son-in-law, Shad Polier, and his daughter, Justine Wise Polier, took the lead in restructuring the organization. New staff members were engaged, among them David W. Petegorsky, Alexander Pekelis, and Will Maslow, and a new commission entitled the Commission on Law and Social Action (CLSA) was created, displacing the older bodies.

CLSA insisted on ignoring anti-Jewish prejudice and concentrating instead on combatting discrimination in the courts by litigation and in the state houses by legislation. Its slogan was "Full equality in a free society."

CLSA soon made a name for itself by its fight against the quota system in medical schools, which resulted in 1948 in a New York law against the quota system in medicine. It also began to fight for the separation of church and state, in which Leo Pfeffer on the CLSA staff distinguished himself. Another distinguishing feature of CLSA was its insistence that it should fight for the rights of all minorities, particularly blacks, and CLSA formed a close alliance with the National Association for the Advancement of Colored People. Within a decade, CLSA's philosophy was copied by the American Jewish Committee and the Anti-Defamation League of B'nai B'rith.

The preeminence of AJCongress in the area of civil rights was recognized in 1963 when the organizers of the March on Washington chose Rabbi Joachim Prinz, then president of AJCongress, to march alongside the Reverend Martin Luther King, Jr., and represent American Jewry.

Shortly thereafter the rise of "Black Power" and black separatism diminished the role of AJCongress in the civil rights struggle. When blacks succeeded in persuading the Nixon administration to establish a system of so-called affirmative action based on preferences for blacks and women, the participation of AJCongress in civil rights agitation diminished still further. Nevertheless, it persisted in its continuous struggle for equal rights for all.

In the sixties, AJCongress broadened its concerns, setting up a Commission on Urban Affairs and, in the eighties, a Commission on Women's Equality. During those years, AJCongress led the successful struggle against the effort to abolish the Electoral College, which many felt would seriously weaken the political power of American

Jews and American blacks. It also set up an anti-boycott unit to organize a national struggle against the Arab boycott of Israel.

Throughout the seventy years of its existence, AJCongress sought to strengthen the relationship of American Jews to Israel and its people. It organized a travel program that has enabled 250,000 American Jews to visit Israel. It established a yearly Dialogue in Israel between American Jewish intellectuals and their counterparts in the Jewish state and in countless ways sought to protect the Jewish state. *See also* Zionism.

WILL MASLOW

BIBLIOGRAPHY
Curtis, Michael, ed. *Antisemitism in the Contemporary World.* Boulder, Colo.: Westview Press, 1986.

Dobkowski, Michael, ed. *Jewish American Voluntary Organizations.* Westport, Conn.: Greenwood Press, 1986.

Frommer, Morris. "The American Jewish Congress: A History, 1914–1950." Ph.D. dissertation, Ohio State University, 1978.

Urofsky, Melvin. *American Zionism from Herzl to the Holocaust.* Garden City, N.Y.: Doubleday, 1975.

American Jewish Historical Society.

Founded in 1892 in conjunction with the anniversary of Columbus's landing in the Western Hemisphere, the American Jewish Historical Society, located in Waltham, Massachusetts, is the oldest immigrant historical association continuously in existence in the United States. The society is one of the chief repositories of documents and other primary material related to Jewish life in North America. Its headquarters houses over 80,000 volumes in its library as well as over 6 million manuscripts, 250 paintings and artifacts, and over 500 American Yiddish theater and film posters.

The origins of the society cannot be separated from the question of Jewish fate in America at the end of the nineteenth century, widely regarded as an era in which racial bigotry spread. The massive wave of Jewish immigrants at this time not only aroused nativist fears, but also transformed the character of Jewish life. Even their co-religionists wondered about the capacity of the refugees from persecution and from economic privation in Eastern and Central Europe to Americanize themselves. The strangeness of these new immigrants seemed to threaten patriotic assumptions as well as the security of Anglo-Saxon hegemony. To counteract these reactions, Jews proclaimed rather anxiously the value of Jewish contributions to the American polity and economy. Such "challenges" to the established Jewish-American way of life helped stimulate interest in Jewish historical organization. Another force in founding such an organization was the prestige of "scientific history" stemming from German higher learning.

The mixture of motives can be discerned in the pride that Oscar S. Straus, merchant and philanthropist, felt upon learning that Columbus's crews included several baptized Jews. "If it were historically shown that our race had a direct part in the discovery of America," Straus wrote in 1891, ". . . this would be an answer for all time to come to any anti-Semitic tendencies in this country which doubtless will come to the surface sooner or later by reason of the large Russian immigration to our country." Historical research would not be conducted for the sake of satisfying curiosity alone; rather it would directly enhance the defense of Jewish communal interests and rights. One historian who attended the founding meeting at the Jewish Theological Seminary in New York was convinced that historical investigations would "eliminate whatever prejudice lingers against the Jews."

Straus served as first president of the society (1892–1898) and was succeeded by another of its pivotal organizers, Cyrus Adler (1899–1921), of Johns Hopkins University. Since the third president, Abraham Rosenbach, served from 1922 until 1948, such continuity meant that for the first half-century of the life of the society, only three men served at its helm. Until the second half-century, mostly well-to-do Americanized Jews of German background, living on the East Coast, directed the fortunes of the society.

Membership rolls have always been small. As of 1990, its membership hovered around 3400, or approximately 0.06 percent of the Jewish population in the United States. The society was based in New York until 1968, when it was relocated on the campus of Brandeis University and was housed in a building provided by a bequest from the late Lee M. Friedman, an attorney and historian who had succeeded Rosenbach as president of the society.

The results of research into the American Jewish past and the interpretation of its meaning have been primarily disseminated through a scholarly journal, initially called the *Publications of the American Jewish Historical Society*, later the *American Jewish Historical Quarterly*, and today *American Jewish History*. For the first 50 years, the subjects of over half the articles in the journal were confined to colonial and early American Jewry up to about 1815, an emphasis that avoided controversial topics (like Zionism, radicalism, or anti-Semitism) and underscored the claims of Jews to full citizenship.

In recent decades efforts to rid the society and its quarterly of filiopietism have been largely successful, and the policy to sponsor research that would cast only the most favorable and patriotic light upon the Jewish community has been suppressed. As the American Jewish community became more secure—and increasingly distant from its own immigrant origins—the humble, elusive but honorable aim of locating the facts of that community's development became more important than showing that development only sympathetically or heroically. Academic historians who were professionally trained have largely replaced amateurs, however gifted their abilities, and antiquarians, however necessary their labors. The society has been especially interested in encouraging communal histories, as well as the histories of organizations and congregations. Its catalogued manuscript collection also has a strong concentration of materials dealing with individuals or families.

The society is run by a lay board whose members have generally felt bound to contribute to the fulfillment of its purposes. There is a professional staff as well as an advisory council of academicians.

American Jewish History publishes about four articles, plus book reviews, every quarter and lists relevant articles and books published elsewhere. Other publications by the society include a newsletter and special volumes, such as the *Guides to America-Holy Land Studies*. For the five-hundredth anniversary of Columbus's landing and the centenary of the society, a five-volume history of the American Jewish community has been commissioned under the general editorship of Henry L. Feingold. A national conference is held annually, and scholarly sessions on American Jewish history have been held as joint meetings with the American Historical Association.

Except for the American Jewish Archives in Cincinnati, no other institution has taken as its mandate the collection, preservation, and dissemination of information on the heritage of Jews in North America. The society is therefore an important entry point into the experience of the most powerful, affluent, and successful community in the long history of the Diaspora.

STEPHEN J. WHITFIELD

BIBLIOGRAPHY

Appel, John J. *Immigrant Historical Societies in the United States, 1880-1950.* Salem, N.H.: Ayer, 1980.

Kaganoff, Nathan M. "AJHS at 90: Reflections on the History of the Oldest Ethnic Historical Society in America." *American Jewish History* 71 (June 1982): 466-485.

***American Jewish Joint Distribution Committee* (AJJDC** or **JDC)**. Usually referred to as "the Joint," the committee was formed at the beginning of World War I. The civilian populations caught by the war in Europe were suffering greatly. European Jews suffered even more, caught between the problems brought on by the war and the usual anti-Semitism. In addition to the problems faced by the Jews in Europe, a blockade by the Ottoman Empire was causing severe hardship to the people of Palestine.

To aid these people, avoid duplicating needed services, coordinate fund raising, and show the world a united front in dealing with the various foreign governments, a single, united agency was necessary. In 1914, the American Jewish Joint Distribution Committee was founded with Felix Warburg as its first chairperson. It was the first organization that was able to unite the Jews of the United States regardless of their religious, social, or cultural background. Through the Joint, American Jewry began to establish itself in international Jewish affairs.

The goal of the Joint Distribution Committee was to organize and subsidize rescue, relief, and rehabilitation programs. It worked throughout World War I and continued to assist Jews to reestablish themselves at the conclusion of the war. It distributed food, clothing, and medicine; extended small loans; founded schools; and taught new trades. Many Zionists criticized the Joint for overemphasizing aid to European and Russian Jews while not devoting enough energy and funds to Palestine. The work done by the Joint was, nonetheless, exemplary. Herbert Hoover, who headed the major American postwar relief projects in Europe, stated in 1923, "There is no brighter chapter in the whole history of philanthropy than that which could be written of the work of the American Jews in the last nine years."

The work done by the Joint during and after World War II was even greater. Under the direction of Joseph Schwartz, the Joint gave money to any group working to save the lives of Jewish people and was involved in every important refugee operation. False passports were obtained; placement was found for all the people on the infamous ship *St. Louis*; when France was conquered, Jewish children were smuggled into Switzerland; through Spain and Portugal, ships were chartered or berths were purchased on regular passenger ships for Jews; sustenance was provided to the Polish ghettos; Jews from Russia who were forcibly relocated to a bleak area near the border of Iran were assisted; Jews stranded in Shanghai were supported; through Sweden, food, medical supplies, and clothing were smuggled into concentration camps. The Joint even established indirect negotiations with the Nazis to attempt to ransom the Jews of Europe.

From 1945 to 1952, the Joint spent over $342 million to help victims of the war through emigration and relief programs. Its programs assisted thousands of Jews in DP camps. The Joint also participated in Operation Magic Carpet, the secret air lift of Yemenite Jews to Israel.

As the worldwide immigration crisis eased, the Joint gave up this part of its operation. It continues to provide health, education, and assistance programs for hundreds of thousands of needy Jews in countries all over the world. At the end of 1980, the Joint again assisted Jews leaving the Soviet Union and participated in training programs for them as well as resettlement in Israel.

LINDA GLAZER

BIBLIOGRAPHY

Bauer, Yehuda. *My Brother's Keeper: A History of the American Jewish Joint Distribution Committee.* Philadelphia: Jewish Publication Society, 1974.

Feldstein, Stanley. *The Land That I Show You.* New York: Anchor Press/Doubleday, 1978.

Karp, Abraham J. *Haven and Home.* New York: Schocken, 1985.

Klaperman, Gilbert and Libby. *The Story of the Jewish People.* Vol. 4. New York: Behrman House, 1961.

Sanders, Ronald. *Shores of Refuge.* New York: Holt, 1988.

American Revolution. At the beginning of the American struggle for independence, there were approximately 2500 Jews in the colonies.

Most of them sided with the Revolution; only a small minority remained loyal to Great Britain. When hostilities began, Jews were actively involved in all aspects of the struggle for independence. They served in the military, contributed to the financing of the Revolution, and provided necessary supplies for the waging of war.

Jewish merchants were among those who adopted the non-Importation Resolution in 1765, and when warfare erupted, the majority of colonial Jewry joined the revolutionary cause. In South Carolina, "Jews Company," consisting primarily of Jewish soldiers, distinguished itself at the Battle of Beaufort; Francis Salvador of South Carolina was killed in battle; David Emanuel, later a state governor, fought the British with his fellow Georgians. Colonel David Salisbury Franks of Philadelphia was included in Jefferson's planned delegation to the peace conference. Isaac Franks, a relative of David Franks, joined the rebel army after the Battle of Lexington and served under Washington in the Battle of Long Island. Among other Jews who figured prominently in the Revolutionary Army were Lieutenant Colonel Solomon Bush of Pennsylvania; Major Benjamin Nones, who arrived from France in 1777 to assist the American cause; the three Pinto brothers, Solomon, William, and Abraham of Connecticut; Captain Jacob Cohen of Virginia, who commanded a cavalry company; Captains Jacob De Leon and Jacob De Lamotta, who fought with General DeKalb at Camden, New Jersey; and Dr. Phillip Moses Russel, who served as a surgeon and was praised by Washington for his faithful attention to the sick and wounded. Russel was with the army at Valley Forge during the winter of 1777–1778.

Jewish participation in the revolutionary cause was also important in finance. Haym Salomon is perhaps the best known of the financiers of the American Revolution. The Polish-born Salomon raised great sums of money for the revolutionary cause and was ultimately appointed by Robert Morris as broker of the Office of Finance. He also served as the paymaster for the French troops in America and negotiated many loans for the cause with France and Holland without taking a commission.

Aaron Lopez, reputedly the wealthiest Jew in the colonies, lost most of his fortune in behalf of the Revolution when the British confiscated his fleet of merchant ships. Bernard and Michael Gratz helped to finance the Northwest expedition of George Rogers Clark, and Israel Moses donated a large sum of his personal fortune to buy food for the Revolutionary Army.

Jews particularly distinguished themselves in supplying the army with commodities necessary to fight the war. One of the difficulties the colonists faced in fighting the British was lack of supplies. The economy in 1776 was basically agrarian. What little industry and manufacturing existed was in its infant stage of development and limited to the coast, where the British blockade was in effect. The imperatives of war required clothing, shoes, rifles, and blankets, all in short supply. The American Jews who were engaged in commerce attempted to meet this demand, and their success was a major factor in the outcome of the war.

One method used to acquire supplies was to send armed merchant ships out to prey on enemy commerce. Jews as pirates? Jewish merchants who participated in such forays did not consider themselves as such. Mordecai Sheftall and Jonas Phillips, for example, saw themselves as blockade runners. Jonas Phillips of Philadelphia wrote his "shopping list" in Yiddish with the hope that if caught, the British would let his ship and "list" go because they could not read it. One such list was intercepted, and, unfortunately for Phillips, the British concluded that the list was a code and impounded both the list and his ship.

The American Quartermaster Department had to depend on men like Jonas Phillips for supplies because its own techniques of procurement were often inadequate and primitive. Thus a working relationship between the Quartermaster Department and civilian purveyors arose in order to obtain the badly needed supplies. Jewish merchants played an important role in meeting the needs of the Department, for example, Hayman Levy of Philadelphia, Barnard and Michael Gratz also of Philadelphia, and Michael Gratz's father-in-law, Joseph Simon of Lancaster, Pennsylvania.

Joseph Simon's interest in the American cause went back to 1774 when he had donated funds for the relief of Boston as that city felt the effects of the British blockade. After the Battle of Lexington and Concord, Simon, together with his partner, Andrew Levy, supplied powder and lead for the Patriot cause. In 1777, Simon donated the money to open a messenger service between Lancaster and Washington's army.

Simon, along with another partner, William Henry, manufactured rifles in Lancaster. Ultimately, their rifles were used by American commissioners to pacify the Indians on the Ohio frontier, thus relieving the Revolutionary Army from having to fight a war on two fronts—the Indians in the backcountry and the English in the East.

Men like Jonas Phillips and Joseph Simon managed to supply the necessary war material even in the darkest days of the war. Keeping commodities flowing was, perhaps, the real Jewish contribution to the war effort.

A small but influential number of Jews did remain loyal to Great Britain. The motivation for their decision to oppose the War for Independence was not unlike those of their non-Jewish counterparts. Tory Jewish families such as the Newport Harts and some members of the Philadelphia Franks took pride in being part of the British empire. Others felt that they would lose valuable economic privileges and contacts should independence be won. Still others remained Tories because they felt that Great Britain would triumph, and they wanted to be on the winning side.

The American Revolution also impacted socially and politically on colonial Jews. It led to wartime Jewish immigration, which, in turn, changed the population distribution of Jews in the emerging new nation. The war also divided families. The Gomez, Franks, Polock, and Hart families were among those who divided their allegiances between Whigs and Tories.

Most significantly, Jews viewed the War of Independence as an opportunity to improve their social and political status. Having shed blood for their country, Jews now felt that they had earned for themselves the right to demand full equality in all spheres of American life, especially with regard to the removal of religious barriers for political office and general acceptance by the overall society. As Jonathan Sarna has pointed out, in post-Revolutionary America Jews displayed their patriotism conspicuously and diligently copied prevailing Protestant standards of behavior. Nevertheless, it would not be until the twentieth century that American Judaism would evolve from a barely tolerated religion to one of the three great American faiths. *See also* Colonial America; Military, The.

JACK FISCHEL

BIBLIOGRAPHY

Marcus, Jacob. *The Colonial American Jew.* Vol. III. Detroit: Wayne State University Press, 1970.

Rezneck, Samuel. *Unrecognized Patriots: Jews in the American Revolution.* Westport, Conn.: Greenwood Press, 1975.

Sarna, Jonathan D. "The Impact of the American Revolution on American Jews." In *The American Jewish Experience,* edited by Jonathan D. Sarna. Pp. 21–28. New York: Holmes & Meier, 1986.

Wolf, Simon. *The American Jew as Patriot, Soldier and Citizen.* Boston: Gregg Press, 1972.

Annenberg, Walter (b. 1908). Philadelphia publisher and philanthropist, Walter Annenberg was born in Milwaukee, the only son and the sixth of nine children born to Moses Louis and Sadie Cecilia (Friedman) Annenberg. He received his early education at Milwaukee University School. In 1920, the Annenberg family moved to Great Neck, Long Island, New York. Annenberg enrolled in the Wharton School of Finance at the University of Pennsylvania in 1927 but remained there for only one year. Thereupon he joined his father's business, Triangle Publications, as an assistant in the bookkeeping office and progressed up the executive ladder of the firm, becoming its head when his father died in 1942.

Annenberg made brilliant additions to his father's publishing legacy. Among the first was *Seventeen*, a popular monthly magazine for teenage girls, which was founded in 1944. In its first issue the magazine sold 400,000 copies. In 1945, Annenberg acquired WFIL-AM and FM, one of Philadelphia's leading radio stations, and made it a television outlet two years later. Since then Triangle Publications has acquired radio and television stations throughout the United States. Annenberg's television interests have led him into one of his most successful ventures, the publication of *TV Guide*, which he established in 1953. In 1957, Annenberg acquired the *Philadelphia Daily News*. As head of Triangle Publications, Annenberg has gained a reputation as a conservative editorialist and a pro-Republican, with stress on "law and order" issues. He is known to be pro-Israel in politics and contributed $1 million to the Israeli emergency fund after the outbreak of the Six-Day War in June 1967.

In 1969, he was appointed ambassador to Great Britain, during the administration of President Richard M. Nixon, a position he held until 1974. While serving as ambassador, he donated to various worthy British causes, such as the Royal Opera House and Convent Garden, commissioned a statue of former British Prime Minister Harold Macmillan, and facilitated a touring exhibition of part of his extensive art collection, lending 32 French Impressionist and Postimpressionist paintings from his own collection to London's Tate Gallery.

Known as one of Philadelphia's most open-handed philanthropists, Annenberg serves as president of the M. L. Annenberg Foundation, a charitable organization established in memory of his father. He is also president of the Annenberg Fund, Inc., and of Philadelphia Inquirer Charities, Inc. Annenberg is also a major sponsor of the Philadelphia Art Museum and Philadelphia Orchestra. He is the founder and president of the Annenberg School of Communications, at the University of Pennsylvania, donor of the Walter Annenberg Library and the Master House of the Peddie School in Hightstown, New Jersey, and a founder and member of the Board of Overseers of the Albert Einstein College of Medicine in New York City. He has donated $50 million to the United Negro College Fund and $15 million to Operation Exodus.

Among the many honors Annenberg has received are the gold medals of the Freedoms Foundation, the Pennsylvania Meritorious Service Medal, and the Humanitarian Award of the Federation of Jewish Agencies. He holds honorary degrees from Temple University, Pennsylvania Military College, LaSalle College, Albert Einstein College of Medicine, Dropsie College, and the University of Pennsylvania. He has been decorated by the governments of Italy and Finland and is an officer of the French Legion of Honor. From 1950 to 1966, he was a commander of the U.S. Naval Reserve.

From his first marriage to Veronica Dunledman (divorced), Annenberg has one daughter, Wallis. In 1951, he married Leonore Cahn. Annenberg maintains his Jewish identity, although he is not a practicing Jew. In his office he keeps a plaque with the quotation from Winston Churchill, "Look not for reward from others but hope that you have done your best."

SAYEEDA YASMIN SAIKIA
JANET L. DOTTERER

BIBLIOGRAPHY

Cooney, John. *The Annenbergs: The Salvaging of a Tainted Dynasty*. New York: Simon & Schuster, 1982.

Foonzi, Gaeton. *Annenberg: A Biography of Power*. New York: Weybright and Talley, 1970.

Anti-Defamation League. *See* B'NAI B'RITH INTERNATIONAL.

Anti-Semitism. A significant percentage of Americans, perhaps as many as 20 to 25 percent, still harbor anti-Semitic stereotypes. Gary Tobin in his book *Jewish Perceptions of Anti-Semitism* (1988) has demonstrated that Jews on the whole feel that anti-Semitism is still a problem. They point to the greater visibility of neo-Nazi political tendencies in Western Europe, Canada, and the United States and the growth of Holocaust revisionism. In 1985, for example, Canada witnessed the much publicized trials of Ernst Zundel in Ontario and Jim Keegstra in Alberta, both dealing with the denial of the Holocaust. They are disturbed when organizations such as the White Aryan Resistance, the Aryan Nations, the Order, and the revitalized Ku Klux Klan promulgate anti-Semitic and racist rhetoric and literature and indicate their intention to do acts of violence against blacks and Jews. They are concerned when bigoted groups of youth known as "Skinheads" are growing across the country, possibly numbering as many as 3500 in 35 cities, and are being supported by older racist groups. These groups have been blamed for crimes ranging from intimidation and arson to murder. Jews are made anxious by the increased violence directed against them, including such heinous crimes as the bombing of synagogues, the desecration of cemeteries, and the assassination by Aryan extremists of Denver radio personality Alan Berg in 1984. Finally, they are made uneasy by the blurring of the distinctions between genuine criticism of specific Israeli policies and vitriolic anti-Zionist diatribes that go well beyond legitimate political criticism or discourse and that use Israel as a surrogate for traditional anti-Semitic beliefs and attitudes; the rise of a fundamental Christianity that claims that God does not hear the prayers of Jews; the apparent increase of black anti-Semitism; and the anti-Semitic slurs of a candidate for the United States presidency. To be sure, a difference exists between Europe and America, but has America been different enough? This question is central ever since a once-civilized country exploded in this century in an unprecedented orgy of anti-Semitism and genocide. It is a question that permits no easy answers.

Given this reality, the relative neglect of anti-Semitism by students of American history contrasts interestingly with the intense fascination it has held for scholars of European history. Historians of American Jewry have tended to view anti-Semitism as an exception, a quirk of fate, an abnormal situation caused by temporary social and economic factors.

Notwithstanding the tendency of many to see anti-Semitism behind every furtive glance and frustrated desire, clearly not every negative statement or sentiment regarding Jews is anti-Semitic. To some extent, Jewish immigrants to America experienced hostility simply for being impoverished, unacculturated foreigners. American pride in this country as a haven for the oppressed and the liberal traditions of tolerance, individuality, and equal opportunity helped create the ambivalent attitudes that Americans have had concerning Jews, often combining feelings of hostility with feelings of friendship and acceptance. Moreover, mitigating circumstances contributed toward tolerance within the historical tradition of American Christianity. John Higham, the historian, has argued, for example, that a certain strain of sentiment among American Protestants admired Jews and Judaism. Puritan orthodoxy held that the Jews were God's chosen people, miraculously saved and sustained as proof of God's greatness, a view that lent itself to sympathy and positive identification with the Jews.

Because of these factors, scholars of the American experience did not really look at the issue of anti-Semitism until after the Holocaust. Prominent social scientists and psychologists, in the wake of that tragedy, attempted to analyze and understand the social, economic, religious, and psychological factors that predispose some individuals and societies to reactions of extreme hostility and hatred directed toward racial and religious groups. The writing of Theodor Adorno, Bruno Bettelheim, Morris Janowitz, Seymour Martin Lipset, Alan Davies, Gordon Allport, Charles Stember, Rodney Stark, and Harold Quinley are indicative of the vast social science research that has been done in this area.

In particular, Glock and Stark, in *Christian Beliefs and Anti-Semitism* (1966), propounded a correlation between professing anti-Semitic beliefs and levels of Christian affiliation. Gary Marx's *Protest and Prejudice* (1969) found blacks no more anti-Semitic than whites; to the extent that black anti-Semitism exists, it results largely from unfavorable social and economic contact between Jew and black.

The Tenacity of Prejudice (1969), a survey analysis by Selznick and Steinberg, isolates the independent variables that contribute to anti-Semitism. The researchers developed an "Index of Anti-Semitic Belief," which they submitted to 2000 respondents. Analyzing the results, they found that education, more than age, generation, geographical location, and religious beliefs, was the most important independent variable in determining the extent of anti-Semitic bias. They went on to predict the gradual disappearance of anti-Semitism with the spread of education.

Anti-Semitism in the United States: A Study of Prejudice in the 1980s (1982), by Gregory Martire and Ruth Clark, is very much in the same tradition. Also using survey analysis, the authors attempt to provide "the first comprehensive trend study of anti-Semitism in the United States, and . . . to examine the factors that are associated with American anti-Semitism in the 1980s." Drawing on the Selznick and Steinberg study, plus a 1977 study on attitudes toward Israel by Yankelovich, Skelly, and White, Inc., Martire and Clark conducted 50 in-depth interviews with Jews and non-Jews from across the nation and compiled a quantitative survey based on 1215 personal interviews representing all adult groups in the contiguous United States.

The authors conclude that, although a minority, "Individuals holding anti-Semitic beliefs clearly represent a significant social problem in the United States." One in four whites (23 percent) can be characterized as prejudiced. Though anti-Semitic beliefs continue to present a serious problem, the authors found a decline since 1964 in the prevalence of many traditional anti-Semitic stereotypes, such as negative images relating to shrewdness, dishonesty, assertiveness, or willingness to use shady business practices. The decline resulted not from changes in the attitudes of individuals, but rather from generational change—the coming of age of those who were children in the mid-1960s, who as young people tended to be relatively unprejudiced and who showed an increased tolerance of diversity.

Martire and Clark did not find any particular correlation between political conservatism, energy crisis concerns, dual loyalty fears, or religious fundamentalism and anti-Semitism. Instead, their study indicates that anti-Semitism is associated most strongly with three demographic characteristics: age, education, and race. "The level of anti-Semitism is higher among adults who are older, less educated, or black," thus pointing to the generational variable as the most important determinant. This finding has a number of significant implications for the authors. "It suggests that an individual's attitude toward Jews is probably relatively enduring. . . . It also suggests that the decline in anti-Semitism should continue as the better-educated and more tolerant young adults continue through the life cycle."

The only exception to this hopeful prognosis is the black community. The authors found that race is the other demographic factor most closely associated with anti-Semitism. About 23 percent of whites can be characterized as prejudiced compared to 37 percent of blacks. Black anti-Semitism appears to stem primarily from the tensions caused by the middleman minority, or retailer-consumer, relationship that characterizes the economic interactions of the two groups.

Notwithstanding that these studies have made an important contribution to the growing body of social science literature on the subject of anti-Semitism, some weaknesses in the approach need highlighting. Since such studies lack a historical orientation and because, as Lucy Dawidowicz pointed out in her book *The Jewish Presence* (1977) of "its single focus on opinion," the survey analysis method is "not properly geared to study the etiology of anti-Semitism. Useful for periodic pulse-taking, it nevertheless serves ultimately to limit our understanding of anti-Semitism, which is a phenomenon marked by a high degree of multiformity and contradictoriness." Furthermore, these works of social research do not explain the earlier and specifically American manifestations of anti-Semitism.

Beginning in the late 1960s, American scholars apparently became more sensitive to the issue of American anti-Semitism and the role of ideology. Critical of the grading-over process of consensus historiography, they initiated a revisionist critique of the problem. Several factors account for this development. American historians of the time engaged generally in a critical rethinking of assumptions long taken for granted concerning the political, economic, and social realities of our past. American Jewish scholars, just beginning to come into their own in academia, were drawn toward aspects of the American Jewish experience previously unexamined. The pluralistic attitudes characteristic of the 1960s' culture brought Jews and Jewish scholars out of the closet, so to speak, and made it easier for them to discuss publicly issues of Jewish concern. The growing interest in the Holocaust, spurred on by the 1961-1962 Eichmann trial, the 1967 Arab-Israeli war and predictions of a second Holocaust, and the emergence of Elie Wiesel as folk hero and witness to atrocity generated interest in the problem of anti-Semitism.

In addition, Israel's creation in 1948 had posed theological problems for many Christians. These people believed that Judaism ceased as a creative and legitimate force with the rise of Christianity and that the destruction of the Temple in 70 C.E. had marked the death of Judaism and the Jewish people as viable, living entities. The perception that Jews were "a fossilized relic of Syriac society," as British historian Arnold Toynbee put it, apparently made it difficult for many Christians to support the modern state created by this "anachronistic" people. Yet these negative factors, one can surmise, facilitated a positive response in some areas and a renewed interest in Jewish-Christian relations in America and the desire to look closely and critically at the problem of American anti-Semitism.

Nineteenth-century American society probably was unaware of the European historical background that had built anti-Semitism into its societal structure. Except for a few knowledgeable individuals, America hardly knew of the medieval ecclesiastical statutes limiting the types of economic activity available to Jews. Consequently, while the origins of the structurally created anti-Semitism in European and American society had been forgotten, the symbolic expressions of these origins remained embedded in the literature and sensibilities of Western society in the form of pejorative stereotypes.

What is the relationship of these images to the tendency to discriminate against Jews? Do all negative images lead inevitably to discrimination? Are some more dangerous than others? What elements in society benefit from discrimination? What impact have these negative images had on Jewish self-perception and self-esteem? Has their existence fostered the rush towards assimilation?

Among the relatively few books and articles that examine American anti-Semitism from a historical perspective, one finds only tentative answers to these questions. The best-known works—the studies by Oscar Handlin, John Higham, Arnold Rose, Leonard Dinnerstein (*The Leo Frank Case*), Corey McWilliams, and Richard Hofstadter—argue that anti-Semitism is the consequence of objective socioeconomic factors and tensions operative in society that affect marginal groups. Sander Diamond (1974) and Leo Ribuffo (1980) have extended this analysis of social conflict to include those individuals who have created or joined radical right and Christian right organizations.

Before we can generalize about their findings, we need to know why certain individuals are attracted to extremist movements. As William Schneider has pointed out, Joseph McCarthy, George Wallace, and more recent right-wing ideologues such as Jerry Falwell and Pat Robertson have not been associated openly with anti-Semitic sentiments: "These right-wing figures . . . conscientiously avoided the exploitation of anti-Semitism among their followers. Indeed, some candidates of the New Right have made explicit overtures to Jews, arguing that Jews should consider their self-interest and not merely their ideology."

Similarly, it is not enough to say, for example, that all fundamentalists are anti-Semitic. As Ribuffo has argued, there is "no necessary connection between conservative theology and far right activism . . . nevertheless, the convention associating fundamentalism with bigotry and reaction, created during the 1920s, was widely disseminated. . . . Following World War II, this convention, combined with surfacing suspicion of 'simple folk,' would decisively influence interpretations of the far right." In their 1982 study of anti-Semitism in America, Martire and Clark have concluded, in fact,

> that the relationship between Christian orthodoxy and anti-Semitism is due almost entirely to three demographic factors: education, race, and age. . . . After controlling for education, race, and age, we find that the partial correlation between religiousness and anti-Semitism virtually disappears, indicating that the apparent relationship is actually due to the fact that individuals who are traditional in their religious outlook are more likely to be older, less educated, and black—all factors that are associated with higher levels of anti-Semitic belief.

Finally, anti-Semitic ideology and anti-Semitic attitudes are insufficient in themselves to explain America's anti-Jewish tendencies. Most contemporary analyses of American anti-Semitism show, disturbingly, that in the late-nineteenth and early twentieth centuries, anti-Semitism was separated from analysis of capitalist development, thereby locating the American-Jewish problem in a structural vacuum independent from other economic or social tendencies.

Yet, the fact remains that anti-Semitism erupted even in reformist and libertarian sectors of American society. The democratic impulse was not and may not be always resolute enough to overcome the psychological and social momentum of anti-Semitic stereotyping. True, America never visited mass physical oppression upon its Jews. But there are more subtle types of oppression—economic, social, and cultural—that are also damaging and painful. For example, during the Civil War General Ulysses S. Grant issued General Order No. 11 on December 17, 1862, that called for the expulsion of all Jews "as a class" from his army department. In addition, Jews faced the serious problem of social discrimination. Such famous resort areas as Saratoga, Nahant, Newport, Long Branch, Lakewood, soon became battlegrounds—even New York City. Signs like "No Jews or Dogs Admitted Here" were common in many of America's finest resorts. Advertisements in the *New York Times* and the New York *Tribune* often used euphemisms like "restricted clientele," "discriminating families only," and "Christian patronage." Rather than accept this, some prominent Jews, like Nathan Straus, retaliated by buying several of the leading hotels that excluded Jews.

Discrimination at summer resorts, private schools, and clubs increased during the years before World War I. The Century Club in New York rejected the distinguished scientist Jacques Loeb because he was a Jew. Most Masonic lodges excluded Jews. Some of the most prestigious preparatory schools, such as Exeter, Hotchkiss, and Andover, had small Jewish quotas. After 1900, few Jews were elected to the Princeton clubs or to the fraternities at Yale, Columbia, and Harvard. The literary and gymnastic societies at Columbia kept Jews out entirely. As a result, Jewish students gradually formed their own fraternities, the first appearing at Columbia in 1898. The anti-Semitic feelings also infected college faculties. It was common knowledge that few Jews could gain entry or advancement in American academic circles.

Social discrimination reached a climax in the quota systems adopted by colleges and medical schools in the years after World War I. Many colleges set limits on Jewish enrollment. Some established alumni committees to screen applicants. Others, under the pretext of seeking regional balance, gave preference to students outside the East, thereby limiting the number of Jews, who were heavily concentrated there. The most common method of exclusion came with the introduction of character and psychological examinations.

Before the 1920s, scholastic performance was the most important criteria used in admissions policies. Now admissions committees devised tests to rank students on such characteristics as "public spirit," "fair play," "interest in fellows," and "leadership," traits not usually associated with Jews in the popular mind. Here we see that negative imagery can have social consequences. According to the prevailing opinion, "public spirit" and "interest in fellows" were Christian virtues; Jews were excessively clannish and cared only for their group. "Leadership," again, was seen as a Protestant virtue; Jews exhibiting it would be regarded as aggressive and pushy. By 1919, New York University instituted stringent restrictions and introduced psychological testing. Chancellor Elmor Brown justified this policy, citing the "separateness" of the Jewish student body. Columbia University cut the number of Jews in the incoming classes from 40 to 20 percent. At Harvard, where elite Protestant students and faculty feared the university's becoming a "new Jerusalem," President A. Lawrence Lowell in 1922 recommended a quota system, openly adopting what other institutions were doing covertly. "There is a rapidly growing anti-Semitic feeling in this country," he wrote in June of that year, "caused by . . . a strong race feeling on the part of the Jews." Smaller colleges, perhaps more rigid than some large, urban ones, used more subjective criteria, such as requiring a photograph of the candidate and enforcing a geographic distribution. This was even a greater problem in medical schools, where formidable barriers spread throughout the country, severely limiting Jewish enrollments and causing undue hardship. So what began quite explicitly at Columbia, New York University, and Harvard, namely the adoption of a Jewish quota, reflected what was going on behind the scenes, between 1920 and the mid-1940s, at most eastern private liberal arts colleges and elite universities, in the major state universities in the South and MidWest and nationally in many medical, dental, and law schools. As Marcia Graham Synnott has argued, the reasons for these limitations was "to perpetuate the economic and social position of middle- and upper-middle-class, white, native-born Protestants." This policy also had social and economic implications since "few manufacturing companies, corporate law firms, private hospitals, or such government bureaucracies as the State Department welcomed Jews."

The 1920s also saw the proliferation of the "restrictive covenants" in housing where owners pledged not to sell their homes and property to Jews and other undesirable groups. Economic discrimination also grew. In banking, insurance, and public utilities firms, Jews could not find positions. Employment agencies also found that Jews were unacceptable to most employers. The Alliance Employment Bureau in New York City, for example, wrote to Cyrus Sulzberger, president of the United Hebrew Charities, in 1928: "We are finding great difficulty in placing our Jewish boys and girls, an increasing number of employers absolutely refusing to take them." The Katharine Gibbs School for secretarial training informed a Jewish applicant in 1928 that its policy was "not to accept students of Jewish nationality." Insurance companies, such as Connecticut Mutual Life Insurance Co., the Shawnee Fire Insurance Co., and the New Jersey Fire Insurance Co., urged their agents not to insure Jewish clients because they are "an extraordinary hazardous class."

The most significant ideological attack against Jews also occurred during the 1920s and 1930s. It focused not on religious issues or Jewish social climbing but on race and political subversion. A resurgent Ku Klux Klan activated the other myths about Jews as Christ killers and race polluters. More significantly, the country witnessed the resurrection of the international stereotype of the Jew as half banker and half Bolshevik, conspiring to seize control of the nation. This belief, having been foreshadowed during the Civil War, emerged in the 1890s during the Populist ferment and crystallized in the early 1920s around auto magnate Henry Ford. In May 1922, Ford's newspaper, the Dearborn *Independent*, launched an anti-Semitic propaganda campaign without precedent in American history. It lasted for about seven years. In time, the newspaper "exposed" Jewish control of everything from the League of Nations to American politics, from baseball and jazz to agriculture and movies. If any pattern of ideas activated discrimination, it was the conspiratorial ferment to which the Populists, Henry Ford, and the KKK contributed.

With the approach of World War II, these issues were further clouded by events in Europe. As Hitler proved to be virulently anti-Semitic, American Jews began to argue for intervention in the affairs of Europe, a stand resented by isolationists committed to keeping America out of the impending conflagration. On September 11, 1941, American aviation hero Charles Lindbergh warned that the Jews and President Roosevelt were conspiring to bring the nation into a war against Germany and that such a war would prove catastrophic for America.

This sentiment fed into a form of Catholic anti-Semitism best represented by Father Charles Coughlin, who spoke for the beliefs of small-town America. Beginning in 1936, in his journal, *Social Justice*, and on his widely aired radio broadcasts (with 20 to 30 million listeners), he began to argue that European fascism was a legitimate response to the more pernicious threat of communism that was largely inspired by Jews. His diatribes continued until 1942, when he was finally taken off the air. However, Fritz Kuhn's German-American Bund, Gerald L. K. Smith, Dudley Pelley, and other pro-Nazi and anti-Semitic groups and individuals kept the issue alive. In fact, over 100 anti-Semitic organizations were formed in the United States in the 1930s, including the Silver Shirts, the Friends of Democracy and the National Union for Social Justice, to name just three.

The situation became more acute when European Jews began to seek refuge in this country. The growing isolationism and xenophobia of the 1930s, as well as public opinion polls of the period, have shown how stereotyping reinforced insensitivity and misunderstanding and contributed to governmental inertia in the face of an unprecedented human tragedy. The critical decade of the 1930s witnessed the rise of Nazism in Europe as well as a high degree of acceptance and approval of anti-Semitism in America. Although sympathetic to the plight of the refugees, many Americans remained unalterably opposed to admitting them.

Consequently, only approximately 127,000 refugees, or on the average a little over 18,000 a year, came to the United States between 1933 and 1940. Without congressional action, 183,112 could have entered the United States from Germany and Austria. Obstruction and red tape, largely caused by insensitivity to their plight, kept out at least 60,000 deserving others.

When you add up all the individual cases of American anti-Semitism before World War II, they may not seem very significant. But when viewed differently, the callous lack of concern for Nazi refugees and refusal to admit them that led to certain death for countless thousands, the reality becomes painfully disturbing.

As indicated previously, however, matters began to improve dramatically after 1945. Whether as a result of guilt feelings and sympathy for Jews because of the Holocaust, or the greater effectiveness of American Jewish organizations committed to fighting anti-Semitism, or the diminished appeal of ideologies of all sorts in postwar America, the fact is that the intensity and effect of anti-Semitism in the United States declined significantly in the late 1940s into the 1950s. Universities and colleges began to loosen their quota restrictions. Medical, dental, and law schools showed dramatic increases in the numbers of Jewish students. Public opinion polls in the early 1950s began reflecting the more positive attitudes that non-Jews had concerning Jews. Major public opinion surveys published in 1964, 1966, 1981, and 1982 indicated that the trend was continuing. Institutional discrimination against Jews in housing and employment was sharply reduced. Jews began to enjoy greater political success. Jews were elected to the Congress, the Senate, and other high political offices in numbers far disproportionate to the size of the Jewish population. In the 101st Congress sworn in on January 3, 1989, there were 31 Jewish members of the House of Representatives and 8 Jewish Senators, one of whom is believed to be the first Orthodox Jew elected to the chamber. By the 1980s, some would feel that anti-Semitism in the United States, once a serious problem, was a thing of the past.

While there is no question that Americans today are much more accepting of Jews and far less intolerant than they were in the pre-World War II period, there still are some significant areas of concern. There is one notable exception to the apparent decline of anti-Semitic attitudes, and it appears in the black community with which Jews have been historically linked in their collective struggles for civil rights and equal opportunities. Recent public opinion surveys reveal that on almost every indicator blacks, particularly young blacks, hold more negative views of Jews than whites. This is troubling for two reasons. First, contrary to what is happening among whites, black anti-Semitism is inversely related to age and education (the strongest anti-Semitism is expressed by the most educated and by younger blacks). Second, although anti-Semitism is not now generally politically acceptable in America, the one exception to this is in the black community. The more politically conscious and active blacks appear to be more negative than the majority of blacks. When such very public personalities as Jesse Jackson used terms like "hymies" to refer to Jews during his 1984 campaign for the Democratic presidential nomination and when he, and other black leaders, did not repudiate Louis Farrakhan who introduced anti-Semitic rhetoric into national politics, and gave a muted response to Congressman Gus Savage's remarks, about Jews, then there is cause for concern.

What this indicates is that the historic alliance between Jews and blacks, forged during the long civil rights struggle, seems to be drawing to a close. The sources for these tensions go back several decades. As early as the 1960s, many black activists began to feel that Jews in the civil rights movement were patronizing in their attitudes and were reluctant to give up leadership roles to blacks. Meanwhile there were developments in American society that brought new conflicts between blacks and Jews. The population of blacks in America's Northeast cities, where Jews lived in disproportionate numbers, continued to increase, and this caused social friction between adjacent black and Jewish communities. Jews, like other whites, tended now to link the problem of crime to the "problem" of blacks. Resentment and fear intensified, and they surfaced with acute force during such controversies as the New York City teachers' strike of 1968. That strike developed over the issue of school decentralization. The catalyst was a decision made by the Ocean Hill-Brownsville board in April 1968 to dismiss 19 teachers considered in opposition to the experimental project in decentralization. Almost all were Jews. When Superintendent of Schools Bernard Donovan called for the reinstatement of the teachers, local parents, most of whom were black, prevented the teachers from entering the schools. In September, approximately 95 percent of the teachers went on strike. The lines were now drawn between a white, largely Jewish school system and the United Federation of Teachers facing a largely black student and parent body. This situation unleashed a plethora of racist and anti-Semitic expressions that appeared in print and on the radio, like the anti-Semitic poem, written by a 15-year-old schoolgirl read on WBAI-FM on December 26, 1968. "Hey, Jew Boy, with that yarmulka on your head/You pale-faced Jew boy—I wish you were dead." Remarks like these and the tensions they unleashed led many Jews to fear that black anti-Semitism was a serious concern. Furthermore, recalling a history of quota systems and anti-Semitic hiring practices in the United States, many felt that the merit system was the Jews' one protection and this was threatened by differences between the two communities on social issues such as decentralization, affirmative action, quotas, busing, political rights, and economic competition. Differences over Israel ex-

acerbated the problem. Many blacks identify with liberation struggles around the globe and have aligned themselves with the Arab and PLO struggles against Israel. This is legitimate when it is based on reasoned, careful analyses of the situation. Unfortunately, it often blends into an anti-Zionism verging on anti-Semitism when Israel is unfairly described as a kind of conspiratorial state with demonic qualities characterized by its alleged arrogance and its colonialist, imperialist, and racist tendencies.

In the overall community, new stereotypes have emerged and younger non-Jews are more likely than older non-Jews to hold them. Education and generation appears not to have brought the hoped-for end to anti-Semitism. Stereotypic Jewish American Princess jokes, for example, and "JAP-baiting" generally may not always be intended as anti-Semitism but may reveal latent prejudice. Ultimately, it is the relationship between attitude and behavior that is important here, and it may not be much consolation that only 20 to 25 percent of Americans have anti-Semitic attitudes in light of the apparent increase of anti-Semitic incidents in recent years. Audits of anti-Semitic incidents produced by the Anti-Defamation League since 1979 show an average of over 600 reported occurrences a year. The number has grown from about 400 in 1980 to almost 1000 in 1981 and then down to 638 in 1985 and 906 in 1986 and up to 1018 in 1987. The upward trend continued in 1988–1989 with harassments up 41 percent and vandalism 19 percent, reaching a total of nearly 1300 incidents. These include arsons, cemetery desecrations, anti-Semitic graffiti, threats, and harassments. Some of the more serious vandalism incidents were perpetuated by members of neo-Nazi youth gangs called "Skinheads" in several cities, including Chicago, San Diego, Los Angeles, and Miami. While vandalism involving hate groups had accounted for no more than 1 or 2 incidents over the past several years, the number jumped to about 20 in 1987. There has also been an increase of anti-Semitic incidents on college campuses in 1988 into 1989: drawing of swastikas at Yale University, the State University of New York at Binghamton, and Memphis State University; an attack against a Yeshiva University student in Manhattan by a gang of youths shouting anti-Semitic epithets as they beat, robbed, and stabbed the 19 year old; and a depiction of Dartmouth College's Jewish president, James Freedman, by a conservative college newspaper,

Dartmouth Review, as another Hitler. When evaluated in the context of the growth of such other extremist groups as the Ku Klux Klan, the Liberty Lobby, the Aryan Nations, the Posse Comitatus, Willis Carto's Liberty Lobby, Lyndon LaRouche's organization, and a number of pseudoreligious groups such as the Sword and the Christian Patriot's Defense League, we may be witnessing the beginning of a trend. The guilt feelings felt by many non-Jews concerning the Holocaust may be disappearing.

This is consistent with a growing amnesia about the Holocaust that has taken various forms. As indicated, neo-Nazi tendencies have erupted in Western Europe, Canada, and the United States. Books in the United States, Britain, and France, as well as other countries, have denied or minimized the reality of the Holocaust. The publication of Arthur Butz's *The Hoax of the Twentieth Century* in 1976, the launching of the Institute for Historical Review in the late 1970s and its sophisticated journal, the *Journal of Historical Review* in 1980, were designed to earn scholarly and academic acceptance for revisionism. Robert Faurisson's *Mémoire en Défense: contre eux qui m'accusent de falsifier l'histoire La question des chambres à gaz* (1980), with an introduction by Noam Chomsky, gave this thrust even more legitimacy.

This amnesia has shown itself in other ways as well, such as public apathy concerning unpunished war criminals and the controversial invitation by Chancellor Helmutt Kohl to President Ronald Reagan to visit the German military cemetery at Bitburg, where members of the Waffen SS lay buried.

So there are some dark clouds that punctuate the brighter horizon. Conditions for Jews in America have certainly improved since World War II and anti-Semitism has subsided generally, although it has not disappeared completely. To answer the question posed at the beginning of this essay: yes, America is different than Europe, but it is not different enough. To be sure, Jews are more fully accepted in American society than ever before, but there still are areas of inequality, there still is ideologically based anti-Semitism and stereotyping, and there are the new troubling specters of a Holocaust revisionism and an ideologically motivated anti-Zionism that wishes to strip Jews of their particularity, their history, and their right to self-determination in a world that has too often demonstrated its tragic indifference.

MICHAEL N. DOBKOWSKI

BIBLIOGRAPHY

Dawidowicz, Lucy. *The Jewish Presence.* New York: Holt, Rinehart and Winston, 1977.

Diamond, Sander. *The Nazi Movement in the United States: 1924–1971.* Ithaca, N.Y.: Cornell University Press, 1974.

Dinnerstein, Leonard. *Uneasy at Home.* New York: Columbia University Press, 1987.

Dobkowski, N. Michael. *The Tarnished Dream: The Basis of American Anti-Semitism.* Westport, Conn.: Greenwood Press, 1979.

Gerber, David, ed. *Anti-Semitism in United States History.* Urbana: University of Illinois Press, 1986.

Glock, Charles Y., and Stark, Rodney. *Christian Beliefs and Anti-Semitism.* New York: Harper & Row, 1966.

Kaufman, Jonathan. *Broken Alliance.* New York: Scribner, 1988.

Martire, Gregory, and Clark, Ruth. *Anti-Semitism in the United States.* New York: Praeger, 1982.

Marx, Gary. *Protest and Prejudice.* New York: Harper & Row, 1969.

Quinley, Harold E., and Glick, Charles Y. *Anti-Semitism in America.* New Brunswick, N.J.: Transaction, 1983.

Ribuffo, Leo. *The Old Christian Right.* Philadelphia: Temple University Press, 1983.

Selznick, Gertrude J., and Steinberg, Stephen. *The Tenacity of Prejudice.* New York: Harper & Row, 1969.

Synnott, Marcia Graham. "Anti-Semitism and American Universities: Did Quotas Follow the Jews." In *Anti-Semitism in United States History*, edited by David Gerber. Urbana: University of Illinois Press, 1986.

Tobin, Gary A. *Jewish Perceptions of Anti-Semitism.* New York: Plenum Press, 1988.

Weisbord, Robert, and Stein, Arthur. *Bitter-Sweet Encounter.* New York: Schocken, 1972.

Archives. See AMERICAN JEWISH ARCHIVES; LIBRARIES AND ARCHIVES IN THE UNITED STATES AND CANADA, JEWISH.

Arendt, Hannah (1906–1975). Political theoretician and philosopher, Hannah Arendt is known for her nonconformist opinions and dialectical approach, which have aroused both admiration and opposition. Her originality is attributable partly to her humanistic understanding of her fields and partly to her courage in voicing independent views. She is best known for her critical writing on Jewish affairs and the study of totalitarianism.

Arendt grew up in Konigsberg, East Prussia, home of both her parents, who were liberal Jews. A sickly child, she compensated for absences from school through independent reading. While still in high school, she audited Greek and Latin lectures at the University of Berlin, where the Roman Catholic theologian Romano Guardini aroused her interest in theology. She earned her Ph.D. in 1928 after studying at the Universities of Marburg, Freiburg, and Heidelberg. She studied theology, German literature, and philosophy under Martin Heidegger, philosopher and exponent of existentialism; Rudolf K. Bultmann, leading twentieth-century New Testament scholar and follower of existentialist philosophy; Edmund Husserl, philosopher and founder of phenomonology (description and analysis of consciousness); and Karl Jaspers, philosopher and existentialist. Philosophy and her grounding in Western classics shaped her political theories.

Whereas religion played no part in Arendt's life, her Jewish identification was influenced by Kurt Blumenfeld (1884–1963), a leading German Zionist spokesman. Blumenfeld, presenting Zionism in German ideological terms, convinced Arendt of the futility of assimilation. Henceforth, Judaism meant solutions to the "Jewish Problem" for Arendt. Her unsystematic *Rahel Varnhagen*, begun in 1929, finished in 1938, but not published until 1958 (London; Munich, 1959; New York, 1974) deals with assimilation as it affected the life of a late-eighteenth-century German literary Romantic figure. Seminal ideas recur in the much more independent "The Jew as Pariah" (1944).

While doing research on Varnhagen in the Prussian State Library, Berlin, in 1933, Arendt entered practical Jewish politics by illegally collecting archival anti-Semitic material to substantiate the Zionist position at the upcoming Zionist Congress. After the Reichstag (Parliament) fire in Berlin, February 27, 1933, she harbored opponents of the National Socialist regime. She was apprehended by the police as she left the archives, was questioned, and was held for eight days. Without documents, Arendt and her mother fled Germany, first to Prague, then to Geneva and Paris.

From autumn of 1933 until the Vichy takeover, Arendt worked in France for the settlement of Jewish children in Palestine and for Youth Aliyah. At the same time, she took Hebrew lessons from Polish immigrant Chanan Klenbort. In the spring of 1935, accompanying a group of Youth Aliyah trainees to Palestine, she met German immigrants of Kurt Blumenfeld's circle.

Arendt met her second husband, Heinrich Blucher, later a professor of philosophy, in the spring of 1936 in Paris. Married in January 1940, they applied for U.S. immigration papers in October of that same year. France fell to the Germans before they were able to leave. Arendt was interned in Gurs, while Blucher was held elsewhere in France. Both managed to get to Marseilles, where they eluded the police, and from where with Arendt's mother traveled to Portugal and then to the United States, where they arrived in May 1941.

Arendt aptly described commonly experienced difficulties of Jewish escapees in "We Refugees" (*Menorah Journal* 1943). In New York she worked for the Conference on Jewish Relations (later Jewish Social Studies) from 1944 to 1946 and for Jewish Cultural Reconstruction, Inc. (1949–1952), locating and cataloguing European Jewish cultural objects. She was an editor for Schocken Books from 1946 to 1948. After leaving Schocken, she wrote the essays that made up *The Origins of Totalitarianism* (1951 and later editions), establishing herself as a scholar. She was awarded grants from the Walgreen, Guggenheim, and Rockefeller foundations to write her award-winning *The Human Condition* (1958). After adjunct and temporary academic appointments (e.g., 1945–1947 European history, Graduate Division, Brooklyn College; a semester at Berkeley, spring 1955), she became a professor at Princeton (1959).

Arendt modified her earlier Zionist views ("Zionism Reconsidered," 1945) because she thought the nation state to be obsolete. During World War II she pleaded for a worldwide Jewish army, hoping it would focus resistance to Hitler. Withdrawing from the Committee for a Jewish Army when she learned of its Revisionist sponsorship, she worked for an independent pro-Jewish army group and formulated its ideology in *Aufbau*. She opposed plans for a binational Arab-Jewish State (the Ihud [Unity] party) advocated by chancellor and first president of the Hebrew University of Jerusalem, Rabbi Judah Magnes. But, after the establishment of the State of Israel, she supported Magnes in his advocacy of peace between Jews and Arabs.

Arendt covered the 1961 Eichmann trial in Jerusalem for the *New Yorker* because she had been unable to attend the Nuremberg trials of the major war criminals in 1946. Her *New Yorker* articles appeared as *Eichmann in Jerusalem* (1963, revised 1965; Munich 1964). This volume did not provoke the desired thoughtful response that she sought. Instead, for years she was subjected to the acrimony of her co-religionists and others due to her emphasis on the supposed cooperation of Jewish community leaders with the Nazis to exterminate the Jews during World War II. Old friends who did not forgive her included Gershom Scholem, who saw in her book a lack of "love of the Jewish people." As a philosopher, she maintained that Eichmann, the incarnation of evil, looked so ordinary and deduced that evil looked deceptively ordinary. As a moralist, she warned that evil goes unrecognized. The book contained factual errors, and created heated debate over her concept of "the banality of evil." Written with strained objectivity, it differed altogether from other books about the Holocaust and still remains a subject of controversy in Holocaust historiography. Arendt produced innumerable notable essays, including "Organized Guilt" (1945) and "Concentration Camps" (1948). Currently, her work is undergoing reassessment.

ELIZABETH PETUCHOWSKI
JANET L. DOTTERER

BIBLIOGRAPHY

Barnouw, Dagmar. *Visible Spaces. Hannah Arendt and the German-Jewish Experience.* Baltimore: Johns Hopkins University Press, 1990.

Kateb, George. *Hannah Arendt, Politics, Conscience, Evil.* Totowa, N.J.: Rowman & Allanheld, 1983.

Young-Bruehl, E. *Hannah Arendt: For Love of the World.* New Haven: Yale University Press, 1982.

Armed Forces. *See* MILITARY, THE.

Artists. The emergence of Jewish painters and sculptors as mainstream participants in the American art scene is a phenomenon that evolved rather slowly. In general, it followed Western European patterns of Jewish participation in the arts. These relate to long-standing prohibitions against Jewish membership in guilds, which were swept away with the emancipation of Jews in the early nineteenth century. Because of these long-lived professional constraints that dated from the Middle Ages and the Renaissance—a time when most art was associated with Christian religious functions

and subject matter—Jewish individuals (at least those with no intention of converting to Christianity) had naturally veered away from occupations in the plastic arts. While the civil liberties resulting from this emancipation presented new professional possibilities for Jews, Jewish occupational patterns often changed more slowly than legal rights permitted.

America never imposed such vocational restrictions. Nevertheless, the majority of Jews were generally content to continue in the mercantile and trading professions and minor artisanal jobs common to its European forbears.

During the seventeenth and eighteenth centuries few Jews are recorded as practitioners of painting and sculpture in the United States. Myer Myers (1723–1795), a New York silversmith, would have to rank as the first important Jewish artist in America, even though he was essentially a craftsman. One of the more gifted silversmiths of the colonial period, Myers's work encompassed Jewish ritual objects as well as the domestic wares for the colonial and early federal bourgeoisie.

While no Jewish painter or sculptor emerged during this period, Jews were nevertheless important commissioners of portraits—the stock-in-trade of eighteenth- and early-nineteenth-century American painting. Most of the major Christian portraitists painted the likenesses of sitters from the tiny Jewish population of the period. This list of painters includes such notables as Gilbert Stuart, Rembrandt Peale, Charles Willson Peale, Thomas Sully, and John Wesley Jarvis; the list of sitters, such prominent families as Levy, Seixas, Mendes, Phillips, Gratz, Etting, Hays, Franks, and Mordecai.

Although the nineteenth century produced a small number of Jewish painters and sculptors, not one is recognized as a significant figure in American art. For many of these individuals, portraiture, still popular but far less important after the invention of photography in 1838, served as their largest source of income and their most important creative outlet. In addition to these likenesses, the artists often produced a few subjects from the Hebrew Bible as well as the occasional portrait of a major political figure. The latter, usually neither commissioned work nor painting from life, served as statements of the artist's political beliefs as well as a vehicle of patriotic association.

A natural sociological outgrowth of the activity of this new, if small, group of Jewish artists is the considerable patronage from within the

American Jewish community. The modest register of Jewish creativity in the plastic arts left a paucity of Jewish import on American art history. In the latter nineteenth century there exists no *corpus* of important Jewish portraits by Jewish artists compared to the significant group of Jewish portraits by the more artistically significant non-Jewish talents previously mentioned. This phenomenon is due in large measure to the rather minor stature of late-nineteenth-century Jewish artists and sculptors.

The two most notable Jewish painters and sculptors of the nineteenth century were Solomon Nunes Carvalho (1815–1897) and Moses Jacob Ezekial (1844–1917), both Jews of Sephardic descent. Their careers have recently been reconsidered in exhibitions that feature their work, first, in the social context of American Jewish history and, second, within the larger framework of American art. Nevertheless, their impact on the latter remains minor. Carvalho, a painter and inventor, was also the first Jewish photographer. His broad interests led him to accompany the controversial political and military leader John Charles Frémont on an expedition to the West as visual documentarian. He painted portraits of numerous coreligionists, such as the important leader Rabbi Isaac Lesser, as well as the Indian chief of the Utah Tribe and a posthumous portrait of Abraham Lincoln.

Moses Jacob Ezekial, who studied sculpture in Berlin, worked in an academic classical manner that seemed dated even during his own lifetime. His *retardataire* style was due to his preference for the hard, linear Italian-based style whose popularity had already waned as a result of the preeminence of French *Beaux-Arts* tradition. Even though he lived past World War I, in both his style and his subject matter he must be considered a nineteenth-century artist. He spent most of his life as an American expatriate artist in Rome, following the example of an elite group of American painters and sculptors. The mainstay of his work were portraits of Victorian heroes, religious themes, and funerary monuments. A man of his time, Ezekial was influenced by the post-Civil War era's interest in the myriad commissions of public monuments, many of which were a direct reaction to the issue of slavery and the traumatic impact of the war. Ezekial did receive some notable commissions, including one from the original Corcoran Gallery, the Edgar Allan Poe monument for Syman Park in Baltimore (1916), and his Confederate monument for Arlington Cemetery (1912). His best known commission from the Jewish community came from B'nai B'rith for a monument for Philadelphia's Fairmount Park, titled *Religious Liberty*. This project marked the celebration of the centennial of American independence. This work, and the large number of his busts of Jews, demonstrate the Jewish patron's predilection for using Jewish artists.

Other Jewish artists that are recorded in nineteenth-century American art are essentially minor figures. Even more than in the previous two examples, neither their careers nor their work figure substantively in the history of American art. Joshua Cantor (1767–1826) and his brother John Cantor (1782–1823), both Danish in origin, served as directors of the Charleston Academy of Fine Arts. Theodore Moise (1808–1885) was another Charleston portraitist who later moved to New Orleans. Jacob Hart Lazarus (1822–1891), a New York artist, is another of the group of portraitists dependent on Jewish commissions for a large portion of his work. Theodore Sidney Moise (1806–1883) is perhaps better known for his role in the Confederate Army than for his artistic output, and Henry Mosler (1841–1920) illustrated various Civil War battles for *Harper's Weekly*.

The two major schools of Realism and Romanticism that emerged in American painting after the Civil War all but excluded Jewish participation. No Jewish artists number among those involved in the historically important Hudson River School, the Native Realism of Homer and Eakins or the school of American Impressionism, except if one tangentially includes the early work of Louis Eilshemius.

Other artists of the later nineteenth century include Max Weyl, a landscapist of German origin, Herman N. Hyneman (1849–1907), Frank Moss (1837–1924), and Max Rosenthal (1833–1918). The most prominent, and indeed most imaginative, of these nineteenth-century Jews was Robert F. Blum (1857–1903), whose work shows a distinct personal style based on the renewed classicism in English art as exemplified by that country's artist Albert Moore. As opposed to the earlier examples, Blum must be considered a full-fledged figure within the history of American art.

The twentieth century was indeed the era when Jews, breaking with the traditional Jewish professions, became painters and sculptors in ever increasing numbers and with an impact on the art world heretofore unimaginable. As the century progressed a large number established important reputations in the history of twentieth-century American art, a considerable number achieving international renown.

There are several reasons for this phenomenon. First, the massive immigrations of Eastern European Jews between 1880 and 1920 created a greater Jewish population from which artists might emerge. It was in large measure these Eastern European immigrants who made the reputation of the Jews in the annals of American art. The significant American Jewish artists reflect a mixture of recent immigrants and first-generation Americans. Some of the former received part of their early training in their native lands in Eastern and Central Europe. In these countries, art academies had recently opened their doors to Jews in the late nineteenth century. Second, the shift away from the academic traditions in art, which often focused on religious, mythological, and historical subjects, made it easier for Jews to relate to a new, increasingly secular, and sometimes totally abstract, subject matter for art. The themes of paintings and sculpture became secondary to formal innovations in such rapidly successive movements as Realism, Post-Impressionism, Fauvism, Cubism, Dada, and Surrealism. Essentially, the phenomenon of this rapid succession of styles freed the Jews from associations that had been foreign to their cultural consciousness. They could now concentrate on art for art's sake, only occasionally exploring issues connected to Jewish identity and experience. It has been argued that the secular nature of Modernism—be it in medicine, politics, literature, music, or art—fostered a great influx of Jews into these fields. Consequently, Jews were often in the vanguard of the formation and codification of radical departures from traditional modes of thought (e.g., Freud, Marx, Levi-Strauss). However, fewer such individual examples exist within the history of art.

Because of the large influx of Jews into twentieth-century art, it would be impossible to cover all or even a substantial percentage of Jewish artists in twentieth-century America. Nevertheless, one can begin to comprehend their impact through a few examples from the art movement of successive decades.

The establishment of the art school at The Educational Alliance, the leading Jewish settlement house in New York City, certainly assisted young immigrant and first-generation Jews in acquiring rudimentary training. Furthermore, the mere example of an art school as a part of this agency's program gave an *imprimatur* of respectability to this profession. Beginning in the late 1890s, art classes were held at this agency, but they were suspended in 1905. The art school was reestablished in 1917 and gave a sizable number of notable American artists—mostly of Jewish origin—its first encounter with painting and sculpture.

Abraham Walkowitz (1878-1965) and Jacob Epstein (1880-1959) were among the Jewish artists to emerge in the first decade of this century and among those who studied at the Educational Alliance. While Epstein emigrated to England in 1905 and his later oeuvre is considered part of the British School, his early work, as well as that of Walkowitz, encompasses many visions of the people on New York's Lower East Side. Other artists—including Saul Baizerman, Leonard Baskin, Peter Blume, Jo Davidson, Philip Evergood, Mark Rothko, Adolph Gottlieb, Louise Nevelson, Barnett Newman, Isaac and Moses Soyer—either studied or taught at the Education Alliance school. Louis Lozowick, the noted precisionist painter and printmaker, gave lectures on art history there. Lozowick later promoted Jewish artists through his articles in the *Menorah Journal* in the 1920s and 1930s. In an era of nationalistic chauvinism, ethnicity and style were frequently considered to be connected, and Lozowick responded to these ideas in his writings and lectures on Jewish art. For Lozowick, Jewish art depended not on the piety of the artist or the specificity of his subject matter, but rather on the religion of his birth and his desire to affiliate culturally, however tangentially, with Judaism.

Of course, success within the framework of American art hinged on training and associations more mainstream than the rather modest and somewhat insular Educational Alliance. Therefore, many Jews, following the example of other painters and sculptors in New York, trained at the Art Students League and the National Academy of Design. (For the purposes of this discourse, the author will use the city of New York, America's greatest Jewish population, as the primary example although artists in other American cities followed similar career paths.) In fact, Leon Kroll, one of the earliest Jewish members elected to the prestigious National Academy, was considered by some younger Jewish artists to have served as an important precedent for the future possibilities open to them.

Jews participated in considerable numbers in

major early-twentieth-century exhibitions, such as the seminal Armory Show of 1913, the Forum Exhibition at the Anderson Gallery in 1916, and later in exhibitions at the then recently founded Museum of Modern Art. Samuel Halpert, Bernard Karfiol, Leon Kroll, Morton Schamberg, Abraham Walkowitz, and William Zorach were among those who exhibited at the Armory Show, the exhibition that was instrumental for its introduction of modernist trends and avant-garde European artists to the still rather provincial American audiences. Five of the 32 artists whose work was shown in the Museum of Modern Art's "Painting and Sculpture by Living Americans Exhibition (1930–1931)" were Jewish, and 12 Jewish artists were represented in the museum's exhibition American Painting and Sculpture, 1862–1932. Many of these artists were considered representative leaders in twentieth-century American art and included Max Weber, Leon Kroll, Peter Blume, William Zorach, Samuel Halpert, Stefan Hirsch, Bernard Karfiol, Abraham Walkowitz, Jo Davidson, Maurice Sterne, and Jacob Epstein.

This new influx of Jews and other ethnic and national minorities onto the art scene in America was sometimes problematic for conservative patrons and critics who wished to keep American art isolated from European aesthetic influence and free of the taint of minority Americans. References to these issues were apparent in the attack on modern art by the noted art critic Royal Cortissoz, who, in 1923, cautioned against the "invasion of American art by aliens"—or what he called "Ellis Island Art." Other critics, like Walter Dyer, were more outwardly positive in their response to the beneficial effects of immigrants on American art. Nevertheless, as opposed to the reception of other minorities into the art world (blacks, Hispanic Americans, and women), the acceptance of the Jew was a fairly rapid phenomenon.

The response to such critical attacks and the mainstream art scene top heavy with its hierarchy of the socially and economically more privileged individuals prompted numbers of Jewish (and non-Jewish) artists to band together to form art groups. These had the general effect of affording cultural identification from within, and their attendant exhibitions provided possible outlets for the sale of works in a contemporary art market that was sluggish at best in the early years of the twentieth century.

An early example of such a Jewish-aligned group was the People's Art Guild established by John Weichsel and active between 1915 and 1918. Perhaps this organization, and its exhibition program, was formed in partial response to the profound effect of the 1913 Armory Show. The guild, as well as Weichsel's own strong Marxist ideology, was a doctrine that was shared by many recent immigrants from Eastern Europe and their children. Moreover, it also reflects the ethos of the Progressive Era then in America. This left-wing orientation for recent immigrants and their children is considered to have had its origins within the Jewish participation in the political restructuring of Eastern Europe during the early years of the twentieth century.

Essentially, the People's Art Guild sought to exhibit art for, and to market directly to, the working classes, whose opportunity to see or own art was severely limited by the elitist museum and gallery structure of that era. The association organized a large exhibition at the headquarters of the Yiddish newspaper the *Jewish Daily Forward* in 1917. Exhibiting were such Jewish artists as Abraham Walkowitz, Joseph Foshko, Jennings Tofel, Samuel Halpert, Bernard Gussow, Leon Kroll, Theresa Bernstein, William Meyerowitz, and Jo Davidson. Established and highly important non-Jewish artists were also represented, including the Synchromist Stanton Macdonald-Wright, the Ashcan artists Robert Henri, John Sloan, and George Bellows, the latter Regionalist Thomas Hart Benton, as well as the Modernists John Marin and Marsden Hartley. The People's Art Guild published its brochures in Yiddish and English and held its meetings at special dinners on Friday evenings, in a sense substituting mainstream culture for Jewish ritual in its aesthetic sanctification of the Sabbath eve, a hallowed time in Jewish religious life. Its program showed little interest in specific Jewish iconography in general or religion in particular. The Guild had begun as a coalition of Jewish artists seeking recognition mainly among their coreligionists. In all, the guild demonstrated the mounting complexities of defining the role of Jewish culture in American art. The organization, as reflective of the progressive era, came to an end with the end of World War I.

The war, which forced Americans into an international arena, had a great effect on attitudes toward immigrants and eventually resulted in the restrictions to immigration in 1924. This new isolationism encouraged new Jewish arts organizations associated with these new attitudes. As such, some Jews had a tendency to focus in on themselves and their own specific culture in the expansion into artistic realm of two literary societies in the 1920s—*Di Junge* (established in 1907) and the Jewish Art Center. *Di Junge* was chiefly an organization of Yiddish poets and writers whose mandate led its members to shift from the Jewish subjects generally associated with that language and to make Modernism and its attendant nonheroic, nontraditional subjects (i.e., the subjects of modern life) the focus of their work.

A number of artists became associated with the Jewish Art Center, for example, Max Weber, Benjamin Kopman, Jennings Tofel, Abraham Harriton, Ben Benn, Chaim Gross, Abraham Walkowitz, and Louis Lozowick. The center was founded by Tofel and Kopman. For the most part, the members' art subscribed to the Modernist stylistic idiom and subject, yet, as predicated by Lozowick's previously mentioned definition of Jewish art, the cultural identification was frequently associated with the birth religion of these artists, which, after all, had a major impact on shaping their lives and thought. The center also served as an exhibition vehicle, and it was there, for example, that the Social Realist Raphael Soyer exhibited for the first time.

The 1930s and the Depression created the impetus for the formation of a new movement in American art in response to the social and financial hardships of the era. This movement, known as Social Realism, sought to invest art with the power to change society largely by depicting with great pathos the startling verities of America's troubled plight. An amazing number of Jews were prominent in this movement, which seemed to capture for a great many immigrant and first-generation Jews an idealist purpose for the creation of art, a use of their new-found profession to better the human condition. These Jews now had the potential to show through their art the depth of America's social and political dilemma. These artists, in large part left-wing, responded to the times with a visual assault on poverty, unemployment, racism, etc., incorporating some of the basic Modernist tenets in their style but using a more conservative naturalism as a means to their didactic ends. One must count in this group once again the Soyer brothers (Raphael, Isaac, and Moses), who showed the humble workers, the unemployed—in essence, the general deprivation and alienation, the mood of the period. The work of such artists as Philip Evergood, Peter Blume, Aaron Goodelman, Jack Levine, and Ben Shahn

cried out against every form of injustice, including the plight of the black man in America (whose situation was frequently exploited as a metaphor for that of the recent history of Jews in Europe), Nazism, and eventually the brutality of World War II.

A number of painters and sculptors, however, continued to practice an art during the Depression and war years that was concerned with simply formal issues. Included in this group are Elie Nadelman, William Zorach, Chaim Gross, and Jo Davidson and the geometric abstractionists, such as Gertrude Greene and Ilya Bolotowsky. Despite the nature of individual style or ethnic background, artists banded together ideologically to fight society's ills and the threat of fascism with the formation in 1934 of the Artist's Union and in 1936 the establishment of the Artist's Congress Against War and Fascism. A Jewish version of the latter was inevitable and YKUF (or Yiddisher Kultur Farband), an anti-Nazi, antifascist popular-front organization, was formed in 1938.

As much as Jews formed a large percentage of Social Realist artists, other Jews were absolutely seminal to turning American art toward less political, less naturalistic forms, and the eventual ascendancy of abstraction as the most important direction for American art at mid-century. In reaction to the dominant mode of Social Realism, nine Jewish men formed the first version of a group called The Ten, also known as the Whitney Dissenters. Why the original group was entirely Jewish and what that configuration might mean is yet unexplained, but this circle began to turn the tide of American art from realism toward painterly abstraction. The original members included Mark Rothko, Adolf Gottlieb, Joseph Solman, and Ben-Zion. Among these artists, the latter was the only one heavily involved in Jewish subject matter. This advocacy of abstraction would lead such members as Rothko and Gottlieb toward the formation of the new movement of Abstract Expressionism, which was embraced as the major international art movement during the 1950s in the United States and Europe. Here, Jews were among the leading participants and highly important in the dissemination of the movement's ideology of universalism. One would certainly not recognize the impact of the crusade of Abstract Expressionism without such names as Barnett Newman, Mark Rothko, Adolph Gottlieb, and Phillip Guston, four of the perhaps dozen or so major painters within that movement. Abstract

Expressionist sculpture, while less appreciated at present than its painting counterpart, also counted many Jews as sculptors, for example, Ibram Lassaw, Herbert Ferber, and Seymour Lipton.

It is with the Abstract Expressionists that Jews really assumed a pivotal role in an art that now exerted international force. Some sense of the impact of the movement is evident in its being dubbed "the triumph of American painting," which is ironic considering most of its participants, whether Jewish or not, were either foreign-born or children of immigrants. As it absorbed the European culture of the vast number of highly educated emigrés who found themselves in New York both during and after World War II, that city now became the center of the art world. Parented by European Surrealism and influenced by the impact of Freudian and Jungian movements, Abstract Expressionist painting became personal and highly charged emotionally, totally nonobjective, and its implicit subject matter tended toward the universal. Frequently, biblical themes jockeyed with mythological subjects as conceptual representations of major human psychological issues, seeking to absorb the richness and diversity of Western thought and history in a purposefully open-ended, antinarrative work. Not only were such a large number of Abstract Expressionist painters Jewish, but the critics who interpreted and popularized this "epitome" of American art were as well. Harold Rosenberg and Clement Greenberg had immense impact on American taste in their exegesis of its ideology and aestheticism through their extensive critical writings.

While abstraction was considered until recently by many art historians to be the major force from the late 1940s through the early 1960s, it is considered by some to have overshadowed (sometimes for political ends) the realist tendencies that ran concurrently to abstraction. A number of Jews, such as Ben Shahn, Jack Levine, and Leonard Baskin, continued their varied realistic approaches in works that frequently encompassed Jewish subject matter. Levine's mystic rabbis, Shahn's calligraphic notations on biblical liturgy, and Baskin's interpolation of biblical figures take part in the sizable group of Realist postwar painters who are just beginning to receive greater attention, as the hard-line linear approach to the stylistic succession imposed by traditional art history begins to recede. The Jewish subjects of these Realists were extremely popular with the now enlarged groups of bourgeois Jewish Americans who could use these images to identify themselves culturally as Jews and economically as successful Americans, even when they were not particularly connoisseurs or collectors.

The 1960s, 1970s, and 1980s saw an even greater increase in the participation of Jewish artists in an American art scene that increasingly dominates the international art world, including the new media of performance and video. The post painterly abstraction of Helen Frankenthaler and Morris Louis, who came to the fore of the art scene in the 1950s, the Pop artists like Jim Dine, Larry Rivers, Alex Katz, and George Segal who gained prominence in the early 1960s, the Minimalism and Process artists Eva Hesse, Sol Lewitt, Joel Shapiro, and Mark di Suvero later that decade—all continued the international reputation for American Jewish artists. In a society that is increasingly secular and in an artistic community that is fairly stable and relatively free of prejudice against Jews, one finds with these artists infrequent reference to Jewish subject matter.

The return to imagery of the 1980s, however, witnessed a new preoccupation with specific Jewish imagery that relates themes of personal identity and group marginality, seminal issues of that decade. Additionally, the Holocaust, the most shattering and profound event of the twentieth century, has become so central an intellectual issue in this decade that it could not help but be embraced by artists, especially Jewish ones. The list of Jewish artists during the 1980s is an exhaustive one and includes the movements of Neo-Expressionism popular in the first half of that decade with, for example, the two seminal American exponents—Julian Schnabel and David Salle —who introduced this European-born movement to a new art world now defined as post-modern. Political art and neo-pop, with their searing commentary on consumerism and feminism and other socially oriented issues included such eminent artists as Barbara Kruger, Sherrie Levine, Ida Appelbroog, Haim Steinbach, Meyer Vaisman, and R. M. Fisher. They were vital players in an exuberant and volatile art scene that continued its international scope.

NORMAN L. KLEEBLATT

BIBLIOGRAPHY

Goodman, Susan T. *Jewish Themes: Contemporary American Artists.* New York: Jewish Museum, 1982.

———. *Jewish Themes: Contemporary American Artists II.* New York: Jewish Museum, 1985.

Gutmann, Joseph. "Jewish Participation in the Visual Art of Eighteenth and Nineteenth-Century America." *American Jewish Archives* 15 (April 1963): 21–57.

Kampf, Avram, *Chagall to Kitaj: Jewish Experience in 20th Century Art.* London: Lund Humphries in association with Barbican Art Gallery, 1990.

Kleeblatt, Norman L., and Chevlowe, Susan. *Painting a Place in America: Jewish Artists in New York, 1900–1945.* New York: Jewish Museum in cooperation with Indiana University Press, 1991.

London, Hannah R. *Portraits of Jews.* Rutland, Vt.: Tuttle, 1969.

McCabe, Cynthia Jaffee. *The Golden Door: Artist-Immigrants of America, 1876–1976.* Exhibition catalogue. Washington, D.C.: Smithsonian Institution Press, 1976.

———. *Myer Myers; American Silversmith.* Exhibition catalogue. New York: Jewish Museum, 1965.

Roth, Cecil. "Jewish Art and Artists before Emancipation." *Jewish Art*, edited by Cecil Roth. pp. 175–190. Boston: New York Graphic Society, 1971.

Schwarz, Karl. *Jewish Artists of the 19th and 20th Centuries.* Freeport, N.Y.: Books for Libraries Press, for the Philosophical Library, 1949, repr. 1970.

Werner, Alfred. "Ghetto Graduates." *The American Art Journal* 5 (November 1973): 71–82.

———. "Jewish Art of the Age of Emancipation." *Jewish Art*, edited by Cecil Roth. pp. 191–206. Boston: New York Graphic Society, 1971.

Asimov, Isaac (b. 1920). The writer and scientist Isaac Asimov was born in a shtetl in Petrovichi, Russia, 16 kilometers outside of the Jewish Pale in White Russia.

In 1923, the Asimov family immigrated to the United States and settled in the East New York Section of Brooklyn, where they opened a candy store. The young boy's encounter with science fiction magazines on the store's shelves greatly influenced his deep love for the science and writing that he pursued later in life.

Asimov's religious training, while growing up in Brooklyn, was very inconsequential. Despite the fact that his father was trained in the Orthodox tradition, he was not religious. Thus, Asimov became a freethinker and refers to himself as "a kind of second-generation atheist." At the age of 10, Asimov entered Boy's High School in Brooklyn, from which he graduated at the age of 15. He then enrolled at Columbia University, where he received his B.S. in 1939, a M.S. in 1941, and his Ph.D. in biochemistry in 1948.

Currently, Asimov is a professor of biochemistry at the University of Boston, where he has been teaching since 1979.

Isaac Asimov's professional writing career began with a short story published in 1938. Since then he has published over 250 books on a wide variety of subjects, including books on history (*The Land of Canaan*, 1971), science (*Asimov Guide to Science*, 1972); (*History of Physics*, 1984), the Bible (*Asimov's Guide to the Bible*, 1971), as well as writing science fiction, for which he is best known (*I, Robot*, 1950; *The Robots of Dawn*, 1983; *Foundation Trilogy*, 1951–1953).

Asimov has been very influential in the realm of science fiction. Much of his writing deals with robotics, which has influenced many scientists in the field of artificial intelligence. Further, Asimov is credited with establishing the "Three Laws of Robotics," which codify robot behavior. These laws have influenced the field of science fiction.

Asimov's voluminous writing has brought him many awards. *Foundation Trilogy* earned the "Best All-time Stories Series" by the Hugo Science Fiction Achievement Award (1966). *The Gods Themselves* (1972) won Hugo and Nebula awards. In 1984, the author won the *Humanist* Magazine of the Year Award. His most recent book is *Neptune, the Icy Planet* (1990).

JOSHUA FISCHEL

BIBLIOGRAPHY
Asimov, Isaac. *In Joy Still Felt: The Autobiography of Isaac Asimov 1954–1978.* New York: Doubleday, 1980.

———. *In Memory Yet Green: The Autobiography of Isaac Asimov 1920–1954.* New York: Doubleday, 1979.

Erlanger, Ellen. *Isaac Asimov: Scientist and Story Teller.* Minneapolis: Lerner, 1986. Juvenile biography.

Gable, Neil. *Asimov Analyzed.* Baltimore: Mirage, 1972.

Assimilation. There are few terms in the vocabulary of ethnicity and ethnic groups, and especially that of Jews, that evoke as many emotions and debates as that of *assimilation*. It stands to reason that any self-conscious ethnic group that strives to survive either as a minority group within a dominant society and culture or even as an ethnic group within a pluralist society and culture will undertake efforts to resist the tendency for members of that group to lose their identity and identification with the ethnic group. Assimilation is popularly conceived of as a unidimensional process within which the members of the ethnic and/or religious group totally blend in with the larger society and culture and cease to consider themselves as part of the ethnic group, but research indicates that the process is much more complex.

With regard to the American Jewish community, the major concern regarding assimilation hinges on its future vis-à-vis the question of intermarriage. But the issue of intermarriage is complex because it involves a variety of subsets of questions, many of which are ideologically laden. The one empirical matter upon which there is consensus is that the rate of intermarriage has risen sharply during the past quarter of a century. Until the early 1960s, American Jews were characterized as an overwhelmingly endogamous group, that is, the overwhelming majority of Jews married Jews. Since then, while precise data are, for a variety of reasons, difficult to obtain, the available evidence suggests that, nationally, approximately 30 percent of all Jews marry non-Jews. However, this figure is deceptive because it obscures wide regional variations. For example, the intermarriage rate is lower in the Greater New York City area than it is in Los Angeles, and it is highest in Denver, where it reaches well over 50 percent. Even with this in mind, what the increase in the intermarriage rate means, both quantitatively and qualitatively, is the crux of the disagreement.

There are two basically different types of intermarriage, namely, mixed marriage and conversionary marriage, which apparently have very different consequences. In the former, the non-Jewish spouse remains non-Jewish, whereas in the latter, the original non-Jewish spouse converts to Judaism. The available evidence strongly suggests that the levels of Jewish ritual practice are substantially higher in conversionary Jewish households than in mixed-marriage households. However, we do not have the longitudinal studies that are necessary to determine the future Jewish identification of the children of even conversionary intermarried couples. Nor do we have the in-depth qualitative studies that are necessary to determine the impact of having both Jewish and non-Jewish relatives, such as grandparents, uncles, aunts, and first cousins, upon children of even conversionary intermarried couples. We do not know how having non-Jewish close relatives affects these children's own sense of Jewish identity, nor do we know whether, in the future, they will continue to identify as Jews. After all, the fact

that half of the family of a child of an intermarried couple is not Jewish gives that child an option that is unavailable to the child of an endogamous couple. The child of the intermarried couple, therefore, has a much greater degree of freedom to choose not to identify as a Jew. To what extent such children will exercise that option remains to be seen.

From a strictly demographic perspective, the impact of intermarriage is largely dependent upon the proportion of conversionary marriages among all intermarriages. This is so because all of the available data indicate that it is extremely rare for American Jews to overtly leave the Jewish group. Apostasy, in which case the Jew converts to another religion, appears to be minimal, and even cases of defection from the Jewish population without joining another religion appear statistically insignificant. However, as the Israeli demographers Uziel Schmelz and Sergio DellaPergola point out, the data may be biased because they inherently omit those ex-Jewish men and, probably even more commonly, women who live in non-Jewish neighborhoods, behave in non-Jewish ways, or in other ways manage to evade the researchers conducting population studies for Jewish communal organizations.

Assuming that, in any case, the rate of defection from the Jewish population is low, intermarriage need not spell decline if there is a high rate of conversion to Judaism. If a large proportion of the formerly non-Jewish spouses convert to Judaism, not only is there no inevitable demographic loss; there may well be a gain. The optimists, such as Calvin Goldscheider, convey the general impression that the rate of conversion to Judaism in intermarriages has increased and that now perhaps even more than 50 percent of intermarried couples raise their children as Jews. Charles Silberman argues even more strongly that intermarriage does not pose a threat to Jewish continuity in America. He strongly argues that if even only half of the children of intermarriages are raised as Jews, there will be no net reduction in the size of the Jewish population, no matter how high the intermarriage rate is, and he, too, argues that the evidence indicates an increasing tendency for intermarried couples to raise their children as Jews.

With respect to Goldscheider's assertion of an increasing level of conversion, however, a number of studies paint a rather different picture. Their data indicate that not only is the conversion rate not increasing; it is decreasing. For example, in Greater Los Angeles, the second largest Jewish population center, not only in the United States but in the world, Neil Sandberg found that mixed marriages outnumber conversionary marriages among all Jewish intermarriages by three-to-one. The rate of mixed marriage increases by generation, from 11.6 percent among first generation American Jews to 43.5 percent among those in the fourth generation. Both types of intermarriage are related to religious affiliation, with the rates varying from 8.3 percent for the Orthodox, 20 percent for the Conservative, 37.7 percent for Reform, to a high of 66.7 percent of the unaffiliated of the fourth generation. In addition, Sandberg found a higher rate of intermarriage in remarriages. Given the rising divorce and remarriage rates of America's Jews, it is likely that the intermarriage rates will rise even higher.

Sandberg's is not the only study to find such patterns. Bruce Phillips' studies of Jewish communities on the West Coast (1984) also found that the proportion of mixed marriages among all intermarriages is rising rather than declining, as Goldscheider suggests. In Denver, for example, the percentage of intermarried households rises from 53 percent among those ages 30–39 to 72 percent among those ages 18–29, and the percentage of conversionary households among the intermarried households decreases from 25 percent among those ages 30–39 to 9 percent among those ages 18–29. Similar patterns were also found in Phoenix, with the percentage of intermarried households increasing from 43 percent to 72 percent and the percentage of conversionary households among intermarried households decreasing from 40 percent to 17 percent between the 30–39 and 18–29 age cohorts.

Nor are such patterns limited to the West Coast. Although the percentages are definitely smaller, similar patterns manifest themselves in Philadelphia (1984) as well. The percentage of intermarried households there increases from 27 percent among those ages 30–39 to 38 percent among those ages 18–29, and the percentage of conversionary households among intermarried households decreases from 16 percent among those 30–39 to 12 percent among those 18–29. If patterns such as these are characteristic of the national American Jewish trends, there is a sound basis for questioning the optimism of what has been termed "the new Jewish sociology."

On the other hand, as the optimists point out, intermarriage is not an isolated variable. The extent to which intermarriage is indicative of the decline of the community is also related to the response of the community to intermarriage. Until recently, it was accepted as axiomatic that Jews who intermarry have rejected the Jewish community and their intermarriage is their final step in leaving that community. The new Jewish sociology argues that this is most frequently not the case. Conditions have changed, they argue, and many, if not most, of those who intermarry do so for reasons unrelated to their feelings about being Jewish or the Jewish community. They marry for love or other reasons, and, at the time of their marriage, they do not consider their Jewishness to be a problem. It is only later, usually when they have children, that the Jewish issue arises. When it does arise, they frequently find that the Jewish community is unwilling to accept them. Their subsequent alienation from the Jewish community, so the argument goes, was not of their own doing. For example, on the basis of his analysis of studies of the Boston Jewish community, Goldscheider (1985) argues that he did not find any ideological basis for intermarriage that favors out-marriages among Jews. Nor did he find any evidence that intermarriage reflects values that emphasize assimilation. The young Jews in his studies—those in their late teens and early twenties—do not see a significant connection between intermarriage and total assimilation, he claims. If alienation from the Jewish community does occur, it is a consequence of the Jewish community's unwillingness to accept them.

Both the reality of the sharp rise in intermarriage and this new perspective on the social psychology of intermarriage have sparked major policy changes within the organized American Jewish community. It is, today, extremely rare to find the traditional Jewish rites of mourning being practiced by the families of those who intermarry. The only organized communal refusal to accept intermarriage is that of the relatively small Syrian Jewish community, which has a firm policy prohibiting any conversion, no matter how sincere the particular individual involved might be, so that no member of that community even thinks that his or her intermarriage might ever be accepted. Aside from this rare exception, no similar explicit organized communal action exists. All of the religious branches of American Judaism have, to one degree or another, adopted a stance that David Singer has characterized as "living with intermarriage."

Reform Judaism has taken the most explicit

and dramatic steps to deal with intermarriage. It first adopted as policy a proposal to embark on a major outreach campaign to encourage the conversion of the non-Jewish spouses among intermarried couples. While no such *de jure* formal policy has been adopted by either Conservative or Orthodox Judaism, several Conservative and Modern Orthodox rabbis have recently written articles urging that traditional Judaism change its stance from one that discourages toward one that encourages conversion. Increasingly, however, it is *de facto* policy of most Conservative and Orthodox rabbis to encourage conversion among mixed-marriage couples.

The second major step of Reform Judaism in this regard was the adoption of a new criterion, at least in terms of the last 2000 years, of determining Jewish status. Whereas traditional Judaism has historically defined a Jew as one born of a Jewish mother or one who converted to Judaism, Reform Judaism's policy of patrilineal descent now recognizes as a Jew the child of either a Jewish mother or a Jewish father, providing the child wishes to so be recognized. The objective of this new policy is to keep the children of intermarrieds within the community.

Although there has been substantial criticism of this policy of patrilineal descent from both the Conservative and Orthodox rabbinic bodies, in addition to some dissent from within the Central Conference of American Rabbis (Reform) itself, there has been no major joint effort to rescind it, and the whole issue has largely vanished from the organizational agendas of those rabbinic organizations. Ironically, the only place where it is still a priority issue for some is in Israel, where it is part of the broader struggle over the "Who is a Jew?" issue.

Although, as suggested earlier, intermarriage is the major issue of contention between those who perceive assimilation and those who perceive transformation, it is not the only issue. The transformationists point to the fact that the vast majority of respondents in survey after survey report some degree of participation in both religious and communal Jewish activities. If identificational assimilation were taking place, they argue, the data ought to show much larger numbers of totally unaffiliated and unidentified among the respondents. That they do not, the transformationists argue, is clear evidence the assimilationists are wrong. They may be wrong because they are blinded by their own ideologies—for example,

Israeli Zionists and Orthodox rabbis have an ideological vested interest in defining any behavior that deviates from that which their ideologies define as proper as assimilation. Even if they have no vested interest in depicting assimilation, they may be simply misled by communal leaders who use their own high standards of communal involvement as the standard and are, thus, unrealistic in their expectations of the involvement levels of the masses. This is especially true with respect to those who derive their predictions of the future based upon the present involvement levels of the youth and young adults of today. What such forecasters frequently overlook is the fact that young adults have a much lower rate of communal participation than others and that rate changes significantly once the young adults become parents. Rather, the transformationists argue, there are many signs of not only enduring but increasing Jewish vitality in American society. These signs may be different than the previous ones—the expression of Jewishness through religious forms is on the decline—but there are many alternative modes of Jewish expression. Greater involvement with Israel, through reading, organizations, and visiting there, is perhaps the clearest manifestation of this phenomenon, aver the transformationists.

Others, however, are unconvinced by these arguments. Social scientists with such varied backgrounds and perspectives on other issues as Herbert Gans, Nathan Glazer, and Charles Liebman are virtually agreed in their skepticism with respect to the ability of America's Jews to withstand the forces of assimilation. Glazer is the most ambivalent, in that he sees merit in the arguments of both the transformationists and the assimilationists. Gans, viewing the whole question within the context of the sociology of ethnicity, sees contemporary American Jewish ethnicity as but "symbolic ethnicity," an ethnicity that is "worn very lightly" and thus, implicitly, probably will not endure for more than several generations.

Perhaps the strongest critic of the transformationist perspective is Charles Liebman. He is unpersuaded by the argument that new forms of identification have replaced the religious ones because he does not believe that Jewish life can be measured independent of Judaism. In fact, Steven Cohen's own data, (1985) as well as those from Paul Ritterband's study of the Jews of New York City, (1985) indicate that there is a direct correlation between ritual observance and support for

Israel as well as with involvement in other forms of Jewish expression.

In addition, Liebman puts little faith in survey research as a means for assessing the vitality of American Jewish life because of a variety of problems associated with the representativity of and the interpreting of data derived from questionnaires.

Although there are a variety of signs of Jewish revival in American society, they do not necessarily apply to the majority of American Jews. Thus, while a minority is experiencing invigorated Jewish life, the trend for the majority is in the opposite direction. Jews may not be disappearing biologically but, Liebman avers, the quality of Jewish life is obviously eroding, and the sociologists of American Jewry ought to formulate their projections more precisely to make this clear.

There has been one empirical study designed to test the validity of the two contrasting perspectives. As part of a survey of Jews in New York City, Steven Cohen (1988) included categories of questions designed to measure the changes over time in various dimensions of Jewishness and Jewish involvement. Those findings do not resolve, however, the debate between the perspectives conclusively. There are portions of the findings that lend credence to the assimilationist perspective, other portions that lean in the direction of the transformationist perspective, and large portions that suggest that both of those perspectives may be extremes. Rather, a more moderate pattern that is neither clearly assimilationist nor clearly transformationist may be the reality. In any case, the whole issue is far from resolved and only serves to highlight the difficulties of prediction in the social sciences. *See also* Conversion, Intermarriage.

CHAIM I. WAXMAN

BIBLIOGRAPHY

Cohen, Steven M. *American Assimilation or Jewish Revival?* Bloomington: Indiana University Press, 1988.

——, and Liebman, Charles S. "The Quality of American Jewish Life—Two Views." In *Facing the Future: Essays on Contemporary Jewish Life*, edited by Steven Bayme. Hoboken, N.J.: Ktav, 1989.

——, and Ritterband, Paul. *Intermarriage: Rates, Background and Consequences for Jewish Identification*. Queens, N.Y.: Department of Sociology, Queens College, 1985.

Glazer, Nathan. "New Perspectives in American Jewish Sociology." In *Facing the Future: Essays in Contemporary Jewish Life*, edited by Steven Bayme. Hoboken, N.J.: Ktav, 1989.

Goldscheider, Calvin. *Jewish Continuity and Change: Emerging Patterns in America*. Bloomington: Indiana University Press, 1986.

——, and Zuckerman, Alan S. *The Transformation of the Jews*. Chicago: University of Chicago Press, 1984.

Gordon, Milton M. *Assimilation in American Life*. New York: Oxford University Press, 1964.

Liebman, Charles S. *Deceptive Images: Toward a Redefinition of American Judaism*. New Brunswick, N.J.: Transaction Books, 1989.

Silberman, Charles E. *A Certain People: American Jews and Their Lives Today*. New York: Summit Books, 1985.

Baeck Institute. *See* LEO BAECK INSTITUTE.

Baron, Salo Wittmayer (1895–1989). Among the foremost Jewish historians of the twentieth century, Salo W. Baron came to the United States in 1926. He was born in Tarnow, Austria, studied rabbinics in Krakow, and, with the outbreak of World War I, moved to Vienna with his family. Baron studied at the university there, earning doctorates in philosophy (1917), political science (1922), and law (1923). He also received rabbinical ordination from the Jewish Theological Seminary in Vienna (1920). He married Jeannette Meisel (1934), an important collaborator in his research. Baron was the first member of an American history faculty to teach Jewish studies, at Columbia University, from 1930 to 1963, when he became professor emeritus. Throughout his career he was a prolific writer on Jewish history and culture.

Inspired by the historian Heinrich Graetz, Baron decided early in his life to devote himself to Jewish history. He believed this necessitated broad-based knowledge, which he obtained through his rabbinical ordination and doctoral studies. Baron taught history at the Jewish Teachers College (Juedisches Paedagogium) in Vienna (1919–1926) and then went to New York (1926) to teach at the Jewish Institute of Religion. He left in 1930 to fill the chair of Jewish History, Literature, and Institutions established by the Miller Foundation at Columbia University. Baron also served as director of Columbia's Center of Israel and Jewish Studies (1950–1968), taught at the Graduate School for Jewish Social Work in New York (1928–1938), Rutgers University (1936–1969), and the Jewish Theological Seminary of America (1954–1971).

Active in many scholarly and communal endeavors, Baron served as president of the American Academy for Jewish Research for intermittent periods (1940–1943, 1958–1963, 1967, 1973–1979) and was named honorary president in 1980. He also headed the American Jewish Historical Society (1953–1955) and the Conference on Jewish Social Studies (1941–1954, 1963–1967, serving as honorary president for 1955–1962 and again from 1968 until his death). For the latter, Baron was an editor of *Jewish Social Studies*, from its inception (1939), and was a consulting editor of the *Encyclopaedia Judaica* (1971). In addition, he was founder and president (1947–1980) of Jewish Cultural Reconstruction, a corporation dedicated to the recovery and distribution of Jewish religious and cultural treasures seized by the Nazis. After 1952, he also served as a Corresponding Member of the UNESCO-sponsored International Commission for a Scientific and Cultural History of Mankind. Baron was president of the academic council of Hebrew University (1940–1950) and a trustee of Tel Aviv University (1967–1989) and Haifa University (1970–1989). At the Eichmann Trial (1961), Baron was the historical witness.

During his long tenure at Columbia, Baron influenced numerous students, many of whom currently fill Judaic studies chairs at universities throughout the United States and Israel, and the plethora of such positions owes much to his example. Baron was the recipient of several honorary degrees, and countless dissertations and other scholarly works have been dedicated to him. *Essays on Jewish Life and Thought*, edited by Joseph Blau et al. (1959) was presented to him by his students in honor of his sixtieth birthday; the *Salo Wittmayer Baron Jubilee Volume* was published on the occasion of his eightieth birthday (1974). The Salo Wittmayer Baron professorship in Jewish History, Culture, and Society was named in his honor at Columbia University (1979). The first appointee was Yosef Hayim Yerushalmi, one of Baron's last students.

Baron published over 500 articles and books on both general and specialized topics in Jewish history, the most ambitious being his multivolume *A Social and Religious History of the Jews* (3 vols., 1937; 2nd ed., vols. 1–18, in progress, 15 of which had been published as of 1989). The breadth of his interests and expertise can be seen in the wide range of topics in his works. His first major study, *Judenfrage auf dem Wiener Kongress* (1920), dealt with the Jewish question at the Congress of Vienna. Among his subsequent books are *The Jewish Community: Its History and Structure to the American Revolution*) 3 vols., 1942, 1972), *Modern Nationalism and Religion* (1947), with Joseph Blau, *The Jews in the United States, 1790–1840: A Documentary History* (3 vols., 1963), *History and Jewish Historians* (1964), *The Russian Jew Under the Tsars and the Soviets* (1964, rev. ed. 1976), *Steeled by Adversity: Essays and Addresses on American Jewish Life* (1971), and *Ancient and Medieval Jewish History: Essays* (1972). Baron's magnum opus, *A Social and Religious History of the Jews*, covers the period from the beginnings of the Jewish people to the Jews in the Ottoman Empire in the late Middle Ages.

More than any other historian, Baron succeeded in placing Jewish history within the context of world history. Central to his outlook was the conviction that the Jewish experience through the ages has not happened in isolation. Also crucial to his conception of history is the interplay between Judaism as an idea and the reality of living Jewish communities struggling with their milieu. In his view, the Jews have been the bearers of a messianic religion of universal import. But whereas other peoples are created in space, on their lands, Jewry lives in time, as a people exemplifying universal moral ideas. Because of this

view, Baron's studies stressed communal life, the setting within which these Jewish ideas are imbedded, rather than focusing on individuals or literature as was common in previous research.

Finally, Baron's writings were motivated in part by the desire to combat "the lachrymose theory of Jewish history" (a term he coined early in his career), the view that Jewish history is predominantly a chronicle of suffering. Baron did not neglect the long periods of Jewish suffering; his more optimistic outlook, however, called attention to the ages of quiet and even cooperation between Jews and Gentiles.

Baron will always be remembered as an instrumental figure in the tremendous growth of Jewish scholarship in America in the twentieth century. His institutional and communal involvements helped strengthen the field, while his works, with their copious notes, provided scholars with indispensable tools of research. Above all, his example motivated countless students to make careers in scholarship and pioneer new areas of research. Baron permanently altered scholars' perceptions of the Jewish past, inspiring them to study it in all its fullness.

SHULY RUBIN SCHWARTZ

BIBLIOGRAPHY

Baron, Jeannette Meisel. "A Bibliography of the Printed Writings of Salo Wittmayer Baron." In *Salo Wittmayer Baron Jubilee Volume on the Occasion of his Eightieth Birthday* 3 vols. Edited by Saul Lieberman. Jerusalem: Academy for Jewish Research, New York: Columbia University Press, 1974. Pp. 1–37.

Directory of American Scholars. New York: Bowker, 1974.

Gilson, Estelle. "A Portrait of Salo W. Baron." *Jewish Digest* 28 (March/April 1983): 55–63.

Katz, Steven T. "Modern Jewish Historians." *Shefa Quarterly* 1 (April 1978): 63–79.

Nutkiewicz, Michael. "Jewish Historians and the Historical Sublime." *The Reconstructionist* 50 (April/May 1985): 30, 34.

Baruch, Bernard M. (1870–1965). Businessman, statesman Bernard Baruch, in 50 years of public service, took stands, even if unpopular at the time, for what he believed to be for the good of all people. Known for his organizational abilities during World War I, Baruch, also a self-made millionaire, was highly respected during his life, serving as adviser to seven presidents. In addition,

Baruch, an exceptional orator, possessed fine persuasive speaking abilities.

Born in Camden, South Carolina, Baruch was the second of four sons of German Jewish immigrant parents. His father, Dr. Simon Baruch, served as a physician in the Confederate Army and was a prisoner of war for a short time. At the age of 11, Baruch and his family moved to New York City.

At age 14, he entered the College of the City of New York to study science and foreign languages. Shortly after graduating, Baruch secured a position in the stock firm of A. A. Housman & Co., earning $5 a week. While working at Housman, Baruch became interested in playing the stock market. He did so well in speculating that he not only made a fortune for himself, he soon owned one-third of the Housman firm.

The year 1912 was a turning point in Baruch's life; he became interested in politics. He met with Woodrow Wilson at the Plaza Hotel in New York City and gave financial support to his campaign, which resulted in Baruch being appointed to the Advisory Commission, or the Council, of National Defense in 1916, later to be known as the War Industries Board, of which he served as chairman. During the Wilsonian period, Baruch turned down an appointment as secretary of the treasury. Baruch was always so engrossed in facts that President Wilson referred to him as "Dr. Facts."

After World War I, Baruch served on the Supreme Economic Council of the Versailles Peace Conference. Through the 1920s he continued to stress the "preparedness for any emergency that might arise." As a result, many considered him to be an alarmist. Because of mobilization skills and the abilities that he gained during World War I at the War Industries Board, President Franklin Roosevelt called upon Baruch for advice and assistance during World War II.

After World War II, Baruch was active in forming United States policy on atomic control. In a speech on June 14, 1946, to the United Nations Atomic Energy Commission, he stated, "We are here to make a choice between the quick and the dead. That is our business. . . . We must elect World Peace or World Destruction." As U.S. representative on that commission, Baruch set forth a plan calling for the United States to destroy its atomic bombs and to share its scientific knowledge with other nations on the condition that (1) an international authority be created to monitor the peaceful use of atomic energy; (2) the authority would have the power of inspection, control, and license of all atomic activities; (3) any country violating the agreement would meet with "immediate, swift, and sure punishment." Although the United States had the monopoly on atomic bombs, the Soviet Union rejected the Baruch Plan in 1948, resulting in the end of the commission. Shortly after, in 1949, the Soviet Union successfully tested its own atomic bomb.

In 1947 the *New York Herald Tribune* listed Baruch as one of the 100 most important men in the world. Another journalist stated of Baruch, "There has been no man in our history held in such esteem." Baruch devoted his life not only to business, but also to public life and the betterment of all mankind. Baruch considered himself an assimilated Jew and was not active in any Jewish organizations. He was criticized by the Orthodox community for not being religious enough, by the political liberals for being too conservative, and by the Zionists for his lack of public support for their programs.

Baruch used his intelligence to predict and prevent problems in the future. As an adviser to presidents, both Republican and Democrat, spanning four decades, he helped shape U.S. policy at home and abroad. In return for his service in public office, he never accepted any payment.

MICHAEL SCHIRALDI

BIBLIOGRAPHY

Baruch, Bernard M. *Baruch, the Public Years.* New York: Holt, Rinehart and Winston, 1960.

Coit, Margaret L. *Mr. Baruch.* Boston: Houghton Mifflin, 1957.

Field, Carter. *Bernard Baruch, Park Bench Statesman.* New York: Wittlesey House McGraw-Hill, 1944.

Rosenbloom, Morris V. *Peace Through Strength: Bernard Baruch and a Blueprint for Security.* Washington, D.C.: American Surveys in association with (New York) Farrar, Straus and Young, 1953.

Belkin, Samuel (1911–1976). American rabbi, scholar, and educator, Samuel Belkin was born in Poland. He received a traditional rabbinical education, culminating in his ordination as a rabbi (1928). He came to the United States in 1929 and enrolled at Brown University, where he received a doctorate in classics (1935). After serving on the faculty of the Rabbinical College of New Haven, he joined the faculty of Yeshiva College in New York City, teaching classics and Greek at the college and Talmud at the Rabbi Isaac Elchanan Theological Seminary. He held several administrative positions at Yeshiva College, and on the death of Bernard Revel, he was elected president of the college (1943). Belkin served as president until 1975, when he assumed the title of chancellor. As president, he greatly expanded the scope and nature of Yeshiva. A prolific author, Belkin wrote numerous articles and books, among them *The Alexandrian Halachah in Apologetic Literature* (1939) and *Philo and the Oral Law* (1940).

As president of Yeshiva, Belkin was chiefly responsible for expanding it from its core college and rabbinical seminary into a well-known university with a number of graduate schools.

Among his major accomplishments were the establishment of the Albert Einstein College of Medicine (1955), which was the first medical school under Jewish auspices in the United States. Belkin was also instrumental in the establishment of the Wurzweiler School of Social Work as a graduate component of Yeshiva University (1957). This school stressed the tradition of cultural pluralization in the United States and emphasized ethnic identity as a factor in the social system of the United States. Belkin also laid the groundwork for the Benjamin Cardozo School of Law (1976) although the school was actually established when he was no longer president. Belkin was a firm believer in the positive role of women in Orthodox Jewish life, and as such, he established Stern College, the undergraduate women's school of Yeshiva University. Like Yeshiva College, it offered a dual program of secular and Judaic studies to college-age women. This institution was the first of its kind in the Jewish world.

As a scholar, Belkin was chiefly interested in the culture and scholarship of the Hellenistic Jews of Alexandria and Philo, one of the leading scholars of this culture. He posited that the Alexandrian community was influenced by normative rabbinic Judaism, as were Philo's writings and teachings. Yet Belkin saw, as one of the reasons for the decline of this community, its lax attitude toward classical Judaic knowledge and texts. In Belkin's view, only through intensive study of the primary Jewish sources, the Bible and Talmud (in its original language—Hebrew) could the Jewish nation insure its continuity. He saw the Jewish community in Spain in the Middle Ages as an example of a community that both studied secular and Jewish studies and retained its Jewish identity. This, Belkin held, was due to its positive attitude toward the study of Jewish texts. This

duality was the goal Belkin set for Yeshiva University, to produce rabbinic leaders and lay leaders who would be modern well-educated men and women as well as committed to the study of Jewish texts.

As a leader of the so-called modern sector of Orthodoxy, Belkin not only was a proponent of the ideology of a synthesis between the secular world and the Jewish religious world, but also advocated Orthodox cooperation with non-Orthodox religious groups, as well as advocating a positive approach toward Zionism and the State of Israel.

By developing Yeshiva University into a large and well-known educational institution, Belkin placed modern Orthodox Judaism as a major force in the Jewish religious scene in the United States.

Zalman Alpert

BIBLIOGRAPHY

Gurock, Jeffrey S. *The Men and Women of Yeshiva: Higher Education, Orthodoxy and American Judaism.* New York: Columbia University Press, 1988.

Klaperman, Gilbert. *The Story of Yeshiva University, the First Jewish University in America.* New York: Macmillan, 1969.

Bellow, Saul (b. 1915). Foremost among his generation in achieving major literary success, Saul Bellow has been the recipient of multiple honors and awards, including the Nobel Prize for Literature (1976), National Book Awards (1954, 1965, 1971), and the Pulitzer Prize for Fiction (1976). Born in Lachine, Quebec, he was brought up in Montreal and Chicago, was educated at Northwestern University and the University of Wisconsin, and has maintained flexible connections with academe for most of his career. One measure of his accomplishment has been his success at integrating an exemplary career as an internationally acclaimed novelist, respected academic (professor of social thought, University of Chicago, 1962–), and recognized spokesman for the Jewish-American intellectual community.

Further, his has been a career that has remained scrupulously independent of partisan intellectual or political positions. As a novelist, Bellow has been an engaged social critic (as in his masterly analysis of anti-Semitism in *The Victim*, 1947, or his scathing portraits of urban disorder in *Mr. Sammler's Planet*, 1970, and *The Dean's December*, 1982). Both within and outside his fiction (*To Jerusalem and Back*, 1976), he has commented widely and incisively on the broad range of social issues that have roiled contemporary history since 1950. But he has followed no camp and been subservient to no policy save that of his own artistic and philosophical vision. Creating a body of work remarkable for its prolificity and steady excellence, Bellow has worked within the highest Jewish-American traditions of humanism while always remaining his own man.

Scarcely to be predicted from his first two novels (*Dangling Man*, 1944; *The Victim*, 1947), Bellow's breakthrough out of a relatively restricted Jewish readership came with his first National Book Award winner, *The Adventures of Augie March* (1953). In this novel—surprisingly more broadly scoped and freely cast than the earlier books—the continent-sprawling adventures of his picaresque title character (sometimes dubbed a Jewish Huck Finn) gained a wide mainstream audience and, for the first time, established a Jewish-American perspective and twist of pragmatic idealism at the very center of American letters. *Augie March*, along with Bernard Malamud's *The Magic Barrel* and J. D. Salinger's *Catcher in the Rye*, marked the real acceptance of Jewish writers in American fiction. From then on, it was recognized that although Bellow was intensely interested in Jewish concerns, he could be appreciated outside of the Jewish-American community as an unhyphenated American novelist. It is fair to suggest that those Jewish-American writers who have since emerged with varying degrees of popularity (Philip Roth, Stanley Elkin, Cynthia Ozick) would hardly have attained their own considerable successes in the American marketplace without Bellow's prior groundbreaking example.

With the publications of *Seize the Day* (1956) and *Herzog* (1964), the fictional world that has come to seem characteristically Bellovian fell into place. (*Henderson the Rain King*, 1959, a spirited excursion into a mythical Africa, is Bellow's one significant exception.) This world is relentlessly urban—sometimes comfortable Chicago, sometimes the more frenzied purlieus of New York, sometimes quick snapshot visits to Paris, Warsaw, Jerusalem, Budapest. The main character is a male Jewish professional who is in the very vocal process of suffering multiple beleaguerments. He tends to be having problems with women (a marriage breaking up, a new liaison in incipient formation); he tends to be having problems with money, these usually related to alimony, taxes,

and lawsuits; and he tends to be in a scratchy state of irritation with the social scene and what he believes to be its meretricious and insipid values. But beneath the scrim of his day-to-day worries, he is beset by a deeper and more difficult problem: Is it possible to live "a good life" and to be "a good man" in the second half of the American twentieth century?

The Bellow hero struggles constantly to reconcile his conventional Jewish upbringing and his recollections of an intense immigrant family life with the very different situation of being an uprooted intellectual in the increasingly hectic world of plastic products and synthetic relationships. More specifically, he struggles to balance the optimism of eighteenth-century rationalism and the deterministic pessimisms of nineteenth-century romanticism against his irrepressible faith in a God and a moral ethic that he cannot rationally justify. In *Herzog* and the novels that follow (*Humboldt's Gift*, 1975; *More Die of Heartbreak*, 1987), this theme and the many variations that it generates can be seen as the supporting armature of Bellow's work: Can modern Western man live the life of a moral integer in a world given over to binary computation?

Bellow's comic genius is intransigently at the service of a profoundly serious ethical enterprise. Beneath the wisecracking, the self-deprecating mockery, the blatant satire, and the thick layers of narrative irony through which Bellow projects and riddles his realistic milieus and his frequently extravagant characterizations, the dominant question of his fictions is ultimately a moral one. Starting from the fact that the Holocaust has indelibly redefined the limitations and possibilities of the human condition, he consistently aims in his work at exploring the extent and degree to which traditional morality—Mosaic morality—continues to exert viable claims on human behavior.

In dealing with this problem, Bellow has oscillated in his tone from savage to wry, from exuberant to bleakly depressive. He has created a richly textured chronicle of American Jewry improvising new lives in a new land—grappling, adapting, discarding major supporting elements of their past even as they strive to retain a grip on traditional Jewishness. No writer has presented a fuller or cannier portrait of the American Jewish experience in the twentieth century. No writer has explored more keenly the incomparable value of the intelligence as well as its virtual impotence in resisting the blind demands of the senses. And no writer has demonstrated more tellingly the grim and gaudy vacancies that have replaced the once nurturing soil in which the religious spirit could take root. In spite of this, however, Bellow continues to insist, unapologetically and without qualification, on some primal and prior obligation of the soul, which, in fact, both the rational mind and the greedy senses deny. It is this fundamental testament of faith, perhaps, that is the fruit of Bellow's comedies and the clearest index of his adherence to his heritage. *See also* Fiction, Theater.

EARL ROVIT

BIBLIOGRAPHY

Bradbury, Malcolm. *Saul Bellow.* London: Methuen, 1982.

Clayton, John J. *Saul Bellow: In Defense of Man.* Bloomington: Indiana University Press, 1968.

Cohen, Sarah Blacher. *Saul Bellow's Enigmatic Laughter.* Urbana: University of Illinois Press, 1974.

Fuchs, Daniel. *Saul Bellow: Vision and Revision.* Durham, N.C.: Duke University Press, 1984.

Miller, Ruth. *Saul Bellow: A Biography of the Imagination.* New York: St. Martin's Press, 1991.

Opdahl, Keith. *The Novels of Saul Bellow.* University Park: Pennsylvania State University, 1967.

Rovit, Earl, ed. *Saul Bellow: A Collection of Critical Essays.* Englewood Cliffs, N.J.: Prentice-Hall, 1975.

Benevolent Societies. *See* COMMUNAL ORGANIZATIONS, LANDSMANSHAFTEN.

Benjamin, Judah P. (1811–1884). Perhaps more than any other Jewish American, Judah P. Benjamin achieved the greatest power in American history, certainly in the nineteenth century. Known as a brilliant legal mind and orator, he was elected to the United States Senate from Louisiana (1852); was offered a seat on the Supreme Court 60 years before Louis Brandeis (1853); as well as offered the ambassadorship to Spain (1858). After the outbreak of the Civil War, he became known as "the brains of the Confederacy" and was appointed by President Jefferson Davis successively as attorney general (1861), secretary of war (1861–1862), and secretary of state to the Confederacy (1862–1865). After the war, Benjamin fled to England where he rose to prominence, first, as a barrister in the English bar and, later, as Queen's Counsel, qualified to practice in the House of Lords.

Judah Benjamin was born on the island of St. Croix in the British West Indies to Sephardic Jewish parents who had left London in pursuit of greater opportunities in the new world. His family moved to the United States in 1813, when he was a child, and settled in 1821 in Charleston, S.C., at that time one of the largest Jewish communities in America. They were poor aristocrats (from his mother's forebearers) and opened a small fruit shop near the docks. His father was well versed in Jewish law and was one of the 12 founders in 1824 of Beth Elohim in Charleston, the first Reform congregation in America. Indeed, young Benjamin was probably one of the first boys confirmed within the new congregation (the records were lost in a fire, but he was 13 years old at the time).

At the age of 14, Benjamin became one of the earliest Jews to attend Yale University, where, despite spectacular academic success as a law student, he suffered both as a Jew and a Southerner. He never graduated and was forced to leave after his second year under circumstances that have remained clouded to this day.

With $5 in his pocket, Benjamin went to apprentice as a lawyer in the bustling, open city of New Orleans, a place of enormous economic activity and growth in the 1830s and 1840s, a city where one's religion mattered less than one's willingness to work hard.

He enhanced his reputation by co-writing a book on Louisiana law, and in 1833, at the age of 21, he entered into a strategic marriage with Natalie St. Martin, the 16-year-old heiress of one of the Catholic Creole ruling families. As a talented attorney, Benjamin had a spectacular rise and attracted the attention of the political boss of New Orleans, John Sidell. By the early 1840s, he had made enough money to buy a large sugar plantation called Bellechase (the purchase included 140 slaves), but not long after he moved there, his wife left for Paris, which was to remain her home for the rest of her life, taking their only child with her. In 1850, he sold the plantation and for 10 years before the Civil War was one of the few major southern political figures who did not own slaves.

In 1852, with Sidell's backing, he was elected to the United States Senate. Early in 1853, after his election to the Senate, outgoing President Millard Fillmore offered him a seat on the Supreme Court; Benjamin rejected the offer, preferring life in the Senate, with the freedom to represent clients before the Court (as many Senators did).

When Louisiana, along with the other southern states, seceded from the Union, Benjamin decided to cast his lot with the new Confederacy, delivering a farewell address on the floor of the Senate on New Year's Eve, 1860, which many historians consider one of the greatest speeches in American history. The newly elected Confederate president, Jefferson Davis, out of respect for Benjamin's reputation as a lawyer and U.S. senator, appointed him first as attorney general and later as secretary of war and secretary of state. Working in the new Confederate capital of Richmond, Benjamin commonly worked 12- and 14-hour days at Davis's side, advising on all matters, writing speeches, and even occasionally acting for Davis when he was incapacitated by one of his frequent illnesses or away from Richmond on trips to battlefields.

His lack of military background and his loyalty to Davis ensured that Benjamin as secretary of war would not be independent of President Davis. He became a useful scapegoat for disgruntled generals and the anti-Semitic target for a bitterly critical press. As secretary of state, he was more appropriately experienced, since he spoke several languages and had traveled extensively as a lawyer before the war. He labored long and hard to lure Britain and France into the struggle on the side of the Confederacy.

As the military situation worsened, Benjamin became convinced that the only chance for a victory for the South was foreign intervention. As early as 1863, he began to organize behind the scenes an effort to convince President Davis to issue a Confederate Emancipation Proclamation, offering the slaves freedom in exchange for service in the Confederate army. It was a controversial step, supported eventually by General Robert E. Lee, and one that Benjamin believed would result in European entry into the war. However, by the time the idea surfaced publicly for debate, it was too late, and soon after, the Confederate Cabinet was in flight from Richmond.

After a series of adventure-story escapes, Benjamin made his way to England, where at the age of 55, as an almost destitute political refugee, he enrolled as a law student and set about fashioning a new career. After a few years, he wrote a book known as *Benjamin on Sales* (1868), which is still considered a classic treatise on international commercial law. He met Disraeli, Gladstone, and Tennyson and won a place as a barrister and finally as Queen's Counsel, arguing major cases in wig and robes before the House of Lords.

Unlikely and unfounded allegations from America followed him—that he had stolen part of the Confederate gold, that he and Jefferson Davis somehow were part of the plot to assassinate Lincoln. For the most part, however, he led a quiet life without notoriety or public speeches and followed a lifelong pattern of burning all of his personal papers, as if he wanted to remain totally apart from his Civil War history. His last years were calm and very successful; he made a fortune practicing law and died (in 1884) in a grand mansion he had built for himself in Paris.

His life, a British newspaper commented in 1884, "is not likely to be repeated [with] all the fascinations of a brilliantly narrated romance." It had been tumultuous and adventuresome. In the final years before the Civil War, Benjamin was widely admired nationally in both the Jewish and non-Jewish communities for his prestige as a southern leader and his eloquence as an orator. His election as the first acknowledged Jew in the U.S. Senate was a watershed for American Jews. Because of the war, he became the first Jewish political figure to be projected into the national consciousness. Jews in the South were especially proud of his achievement because he validated their legitimacy as Southerners. A pivotal figure in American Jewish history, Benjamin broke down the barriers of prejudice to achieve high office. After him, it was more acceptable for Jews to be elected to office and aspire to service in the councils of national power.

ELI N. EVANS

BIBLIOGRAPHY

Butler, Pierce. *Judah P. Benjamin.* New York: Chelsea House, 1907, rept. 1980.

Evans, Eli N. *Judah P. Benjamin: The Jewish Confederate.* New York: Free Press, 1988.

——. *The Provincials: A Personal History of Jews in the South.* New York: Atheneum, 1973.

Korn, Bertram. *American Jewry and the Civil War.* New York: World, 1970.

——. *The Early Jews of New Orleans.* Philadelphia: Jewish Publication Society, 1969.

Meade, Robert Douthat. *Judah P. Benjamin, Confederate Statesman.* Salem, N.H.: Ayer, 1943, rept. 1975.

Berg, Gertrude (1899–1966). Actress, author, and producer, Gertrude Berg was primarily responsible for the popular radio and television program, "The Goldbergs," which was unique in presenting an emphatically Jewish, if sentimentalized, family to the American mass audience. Among radio series only "Amos 'n' Andy" exceeded it in popularity and longevity, and so indelibly associated with the show was its creator and star that Mrs. Berg herself usually signed autographs as the fictitious Molly Goldberg.

She was born Gertrude Edelstein in the Harlem section of New York City. Her father was in the restaurant and hotel business. After graduation from high school, she wanted to become a playwright, an idea that had begun with skits for the guests of her father's resort hotel in the Catskill Mountains. While enrolled in extension courses in drama at Columbia University, she married an engineering student, Lewis Berg, in 1918; they had two children.

In 1929, she drew upon her observations and memories of her parents and immigrant grandparents to invent a family named the Goldbergs. The series was intended to be a saga of upward mobility, from the East Bronx to Park Avenue. Jake, the father, was incessantly seeking new business opportunities; the nice if a bit undisciplined children were Sammie and Rosalie; Uncle David was a direct link to the Old World. But the center of the household was Molly: her English may have been broken, but her secure sense of humanity guaranteed that her home was not. Gertrude Berg recalled that, when she first submitted her script to NBC, she made it illegible so that she would have to read it aloud, thus auditioning for the main role at the same time. "The Rise of the Goldbergs" was inaugurated, at first only locally in New York, on November 20, 1929.

Its impact was so powerful that by 1931 NBC was broadcasting "The Goldbergs" over the national network five evenings a week, from 7:30 p.m. till 7:45. When she began the program, Mrs. Berg received a salary of $75 per week, out of which she was expected to pay her cast. Later, she enjoyed peak earnings of 100 times that amount, a trajectory a bit more spectacular than that of the Goldbergs themselves, who remained trapped in the Great Depression.

The program exuded an air of lower-class authenticity, and its language contributed to a sense of everyday working people. Mrs. Berg had grown up in a home in which Yiddish was rarely spoken, so ethnic expressiveness percolated through the scripts not so much in vocabulary as in syntax and intonations. More than 200 characters were drawn from relatives and friends whom Mrs. Berg had known. Plot devices were rarely imaginative or even necessary; often nothing much seemed to be happening on East Tremont Avenue except demonstrations of Molly Goldberg's domestic skills. The heart of "The Gold-bergs" remained its creator and protagonist. Mrs. Berg made Molly the operational definition of the Jewish mother: warm, nurturing, supremely competent, but with a special flair for nagging her husband and children. In dispensing wisdom as well as blintzes, in soothing tensions that her own manipulations often provoked, Molly was an early stereotype that the mass media have refined as well as satirized in subsequent decades.

In her own career, Gertrude Berg revealed hints of a hunger to transcend such material, but her identification with "The Goldbergs" was too complete to permit escape. The series temporarily went off the air in 1935, enabling her to write and produce a radio series set in the Catskills called "The House of Glass." Though moderately successful, it was soon dropped, and "The Goldbergs" returned in 1936, this time on CBS. The series enjoyed an uninterrupted run until 1945 and then reappeared for the 1949–1950 season. By then Mrs. Berg had written over 5000 scripts. She also wrote a Broadway play in which she starred, *Me and Molly* (1948).

For no genre or medium seemed impenetrable to "The Goldbergs." Mrs. Berg co-wrote the screenplay for Paramount Pictures' *Molly* (1951), in which she starred. From 1949 until 1951, an estimated 13 million television viewers also tuned in to CBS's "The Goldbergs." Then Philip Loeb, the actor who played Molly's husband on the television show, was subjected to right-wing political pressures. At first Mrs. Berg's resistance to replace him was effective, and he remained as Jake. But General Foods dropped its sponsorship of the program. When NBC picked up "The Goldbergs" in 1952, Loeb was not in the cast, and three years later he committed suicide. By then the series was off the air, despite Mrs. Berg's efforts to avoid controversy.

Though she won a Tony award on Broadway for her portrayal of a Brooklyn widow in *A Majority of One* (1959), Gertrude Berg could not elude identification with a fictional Jewish mother who greeted her tenement neighbor with "Yoo-hoo, Mrs. Bloom!" on a program bathed in good cheer and informal humor. She died in New York City. *See also* Television.

STEPHEN J. WHITFIELD

BIBLIOGRAPHY

Berg, Gertrude. *Molly and Me*. Mattituck, N.Y.: American Ltd, 1961.

Freedman, Morris. "The Real Molly Goldberg." *Commentary* 21 (April 1956): 359–364.

Bernstein, Leonard (1918–1990). As a conductor, composer, pianist, lecturer, author, music educator, and spokesman for the arts—especially music—Leonard Bernstein enjoyed worldwide esteem and international popularity.

The son of Russian Jewish immigrants, Bernstein was born in Lawrence, Massachusetts. Upon his graduation from Harvard University (1939), he continued his studies at the Curtis Institute of Music and the Berkshire Music Center in Massachusetts ("Tanglewood"). His teachers included Fritz Reiner, Walter Piston, Randall Thompson, and Serge Koussevitzky. Bernstein was appointed assistant conductor of the New York Philharmonic Orchestra under Artur Rodzinski (1943) and was catapulted into fame when he substituted on short notice for the ailing Bruno Walter in November of that year. He was named music director of the New York Philharmonic in 1958, and upon his retirement from that position was named Conductor Laureate (1969). In addition to his worldwide conducting appearances and numerous recordings, which included an association with the Israel Philharmonic Orchestra dating from 1947, Bernstein composed music for operas, theater works (notably *West Side Story*, 1957), ballets (*The Dybbuk*, 1974), songs, and pieces for orchestra, chorus, and smaller ensembles. He hosted the "Young People's Concerts" television presentations for 15 years (1958–1973), thus demystifying the world of serious concert music for millions of children and adults alike. Bernstein was a Norton Lecturer of Poetry at Harvard University (1973), wrote five books, and taught at Brandeis University and at Tanglewood. His personal magnetism—mixing ebullience with an almost rabbinic sense of moral (and at times political) fervor—kept him in demand as a public speaker.

Bernstein remained active as a guest conductor throughout the world until the end of his life, although he did officially retire shortly before his death on October 14, 1990. He recorded several works in his later years, mostly with the Vienna Philharmonic, and produced new musical compositions, among them *A Quiet Place* (1983). His many honors include the receipt of a John F. Kennedy Center for the Performing Arts Honor for Outstanding Contribution to the Performing Arts in the United States (1980), election to the American Academy and Institute of Arts and Letters (1981), and scores of honorary degrees.

Throughout his career, Bernstein amalgamated his Jewish heritage into his compositional language. His Symphony no. 1 (*Jeremiah*, 1942), utilizes Ashkenazic liturgical chant and scriptural cantillation as primary thematic material, as well as a solo in Hebrew of verses from the Book of Lamentations; the Symphony no. 3 (*Kaddish*, 1963) features this Jewish doxology in the original Aramaic; the *Chichester Psalms* (1965), composed for orchestra, soloists, and chorus, uses various Psalm texts in the original Hebrew. By birth and training Bernstein was heir to a whole tradition of Eastern European Jewish musical culture, which made itself felt in the passion and drama of his performances (Beethoven, Schumann, Tchaikovsky, Shostakovich), as well as in his close identification with the music of Gustav Mahler. His own description of Mahler (*Findings*, p. 255) has defined Bernstein himself as well: a man of the modern age, caught painfully yet profitably between composing and conducting, between concert music and opera, between sophistication and naivete, between belief and doubt, and—as demonstrated in *Mass* (1971)—between his Jewish origins and his attempts to come to terms with Christianity.

BRIAN D. ROZEN

BIBLIOGRAPHY

Bernstein, Leonard. *Findings*. New York: Simon & Schuster, 1982.

———. *The Infinite Variety of Music*. New York: Simon & Schuster, 1966.

———. *The Joy of Music*. New York: Simon & Schuster, 1959.

———. *The Unanswered Question*. Cambridge: Harvard University Press, 1976.

———. *Young People's Concerts*. New York: Simon & Schuster, 1970.

Freedland, Michael. *Leonard Bernstein*. London: Harrap, 1987.

Gottlieb, Jack, ed. *Leonard Bernstein: A Complete Catalog of His Works*. New York: Jalni, 1988.

Gradenwitz, Peter. *Leonard Bernstein: The Infinite Variety of a Musician*. Leemington Spa, U.K.: Berg, 1987.

Peyser, Joan. *Bernstein: A Biography*. New York: Beech Tree Books, 1987.

———. "Leonard Bernstein." Edited by H. W. Hitchcock and S. Saide. *The New Grove Dictionary of American Music*. Vol. 1, pp. 195–200. New York: Grove Press, 1984.

Bettelheim, Bruno (1903–1990). Psychologist Bruno Bettelheim, descended from an Hungarian Jewish family, was born in Vienna. The events of his life thereafter were to influence his understanding of meaning and identity for the most seriously disturbed child as well as for adults pressured by the stresses of a modern society. He himself underwent psychoanalysis for help with personal problems and was drawn to the profession. He obtained his doctorate in psychology in 1938 and studied psychoanalysis with Sigmund Freud in Austria. A year later he was sent to the concentration camps of Dachau and Buchenwald. It was there that Bettelheim used his training in observation and human behavior to study how the camp guards broke the identity of their prisoners. But not everyone could be broken, and it was his observation of this difference in human reaction and behavior that propelled a distinguished internationally acclaimed and controversial career for the next 52 years. His writings, particularly, "Individual and Mass Behavior in Extreme Situations" (1943), *Love Is Not Enough* (1950), and *The Uses of Enchantment* (1976), embodied these experiences and portrayed their diverse applications.

Bettelheim was released from the concentration camps in 1939 due to the efforts of Gov. Herbert Lehman of New York and Eleanor Roosevelt. He emigrated to the United States, where he briefly taught at Rockford College (Ill.), next becoming a distinguished professor of psychology and psychiatry at the University of Chicago, where he headed the Sonia Shankman Orthogenic School from 1944 to 1972. In 1943, Bettelheim wrote "Individual and Mass Behavior in Extreme Situations," which analyzed the ability of those under the reign of Nazi terror to adapt to unusual stress. Bettelheim observed that those Jews and other concentration camp prisoners who survived the pressures of social systems retained a personal autonomy and integrity and had a highly developed belief system and sense of morality. At the same time he criticized the Jews in Europe for not doing enough to resist the Nazis, an unpopular position in the Jewish community. These themes were further articulated over the years in *The Informed Heart* (1960) and *Surviving and Other Essays* (1976).

In his work with seriously disturbed and autistic children, Bettelheim reversed the dehumanizing methods of the concentration camp guards that he had witnessed during his year of imprisonment. His Orthogenic School was based on the concept of providing a 24-hour "therapeutic mileu" that fostered caring, individual attention, and constant availability of therapists in an effort to reestablish the identity and self-esteem of the children. Unlike prisons, which are locked from within to keep the prisoners imprisoned, the school was locked to the outside to keep the children safe from the outside. A series of four books detailed the philosophy behind the school and the treatment techniques used: *Love Is Not Enough* (1950), *Truant From Life* (1955), *The Empty Fortress* (1967), *A Home for the Heart* (1974). These books, and related articles, were impassioned, insightful, and compelling. Bettelheim claimed an 85 percent cure rate and implicated "schizophrenogenic" mothers in the problems of their seriously disturbed children. Critics believed that the rates of success were exaggerated, and the pronouncement of blame unacceptable. In 1987, Bettelheim wrote *A Good Enough Parent*, which somewhat reversed this position by fostering the notion that children are innately good and that parents are "good enough."

In his never ending quest to understand and help children, Bettelheim visited Israeli kibbutzim for seven weeks and analyzed the personalities of the children resulting from this communal system of care and education. In 1969, *The Children of the Dream* was published detailing those experiences. But it was the landmark book *The Uses of Enchantment* (1976), which explored children's use of fairy tales to cope with their problems and fears in life, that earned him the National Book Critics Circle Award (1976) and the National Book Award (1977). Bettelheim viewed the fairy tale as therapeutic in that children could read about and believe in triumph over an individual's trials and tribulations.

While he never overcame the nightmares that plagued him about his experiences in the concentration camps, he used these experiences to help others cope with, understand, and survive life. At the age of 86, diminished by a stroke and the death of his wife of 43 years, Bettelheim put an end to his own life on March 13, 1990. Fifty-two years earlier, to the day, the Nazis marched into Austria and changed his life forever. Through his work and writings he, in turn, changed the lives of countless others.

KATHERINE GREEN

BIBLIOGRAPHY
Bettelheim, Bruno. *The Empty Fortress*. New York: Free Press, 1972.

———. *A Good Enough Parent*. New York: Random House, 1987.

———. *A Home for the Heart*. Chicago: University of Chicago Press, 1985.

———. "Individual and Mass Behavior in Extreme Situations." *Journal of Abnormal and Social Psychology* 38 (1943): 417–552.

———. *The Informed Heart*. New York: Free Press, 1960.

———. *Love is not Enough*. New York: Free Press, 1950.

———. *Surviving and Other Essays*. New York: Random House, 1980.

———. *Truants from Life*. New York: Free Press, 1955.

Biltmore Conference. The Biltmore Conference was an extraordinary Zionist meeting held at the Biltmore Hotel in New York between May 6 and May 11, 1942, to discuss and reformulate the aims of the movement. The eight-point Biltmore Program that was adopted reflected the new militancy of Zionism. It urged that Palestine be established as a Jewish commonwealth and that the Jewish Agency replace the British Mandatory Administrative Authority as the body responsible for the development of the country.

In August 1939, with the world conflict rapidly approaching, the Twenty-first World Zionist Congress, meeting in Geneva, recognized that its headquarters in Jerusalem might be cut off from the rest of the movement. Accordingly, the Congress decided to establish an Emergency Committee for Zionist Affairs in New York, which, if necessary, could be called upon to assume the full functions of Zionist leadership. It was also set up to incorporate the Zionist Organization of America (ZOA), Hadassah, Mizrachi, and Poale Zion into one organization for the purpose of spreading the Zionist message to the American public, since the role of the American government was obviously going to be central after the war.

The Emergency Committee's ambitious program was slow in developing. Not infrequently the committee had to resolve an internecine Zionist feud occasioned by the claims of one group, usually the ZOA, at the expense of the others. Much of the committee's time was also spent protesting the British White Paper of 1939 and opposing the Revisionists. The catastrophe that was occurring in Europe and the threat to the Yishuv posed by German forces in Egypt finally overcame the caution of American Zionists to speak out against the German tyranny and dissi-

pated much of the divisiveness that had weakened American Zionism. To secure a common platform on which they could all stand, the Emergency Committee called a special meeting at the Biltmore Hotel in New York in early May 1942. The 586 American delegates, as well as 67 foreign leaders, represented every faction in the movement. They heard the aged Rabbi Stephen S. Wise call for a Jewish commonwealth in Palestine. They sat in silence as the distraught Chaim Weizmann told them of the horrors European Jews were suffering. He admitted that England had not kept its word on Palestine, yet he implored the delegates to support Britain in its war against Nazi Germany. In the momentum of the conference, leadership passed from the cautious old guard to a new and more militant group led by David Ben-Gurion, chairman of the Jewish Agency Executive, and the fiery Rabbi Abba Hillel Silver from Cleveland. For them, there was only one solution to the Jewish problem—and that was a Jewish state in Palestine. They called for a full-scale effort to achieve this end.

The declaration adopted unanimously by the Biltmore Conference clearly indicated the new maximalist mood of American Zionism. "The Conference demands that the gates of Palestine be opened; that the Jewish Agency be vested with control of immigration into Palestine . . . ; and that Palestine be established as a Jewish Commonwealth. . . ."

The Biltmore Conference marked a clear turning point in American Zionism. Before Biltmore, American Zionists saw Palestine as a refuge, as a cultural center; after Biltmore, they fought for a Jewish state.

MICHAEL N. DOBKOWSKI

BIBLIOGRAPHY

Cohen, Naomi. *American Jews and the Zionist Idea*. New York: Ktav, 1975.

Halperin, Samuel. *The Political World of American Zionism*. Detroit: Wayne State University, 1961.

Urofsky, Melvin. *American Zionism from Herzl to the Holocaust*. New York: Anchor Press/Doubleday, 1975.

Black-Jewish Relations. Few issues in American Jewish culture and history have engendered as heated a discussion and as sparse an objective and analytic literature as black-Jewish relations. Both Jews and blacks have reacted intensely to each other, both positively and negatively, and have invested a great degree of energy in the "special relationship" between the two groups.

It is much easier to analyze the nature of the relationship of Jews and blacks on a leadership level and in terms of political issues. It is, however, not clear if the opinions expressed by the leadership, either black or Jewish, at any given time expressed the true sentiments of the masses of both groups. It is much more difficult to ascertain the nature of mass Jewish or mass black opinion.

Until the early twentieth century, only minimal contact occurred between Jews and blacks, partly because so few Jews lived in the South where the bulk of the black population resided. There is some recorded Jewish proslavery sentiment, particularly in southern communities. The leader of the Reform Movement, Isaac Mayer Wise, expressed support for the confederate cause during the Civil War. A number of Jews owned slaves, and a handful profitted from the plantation system as cotton brokers. Judah P. Benjamin, of Louisiana, held three posts in the Confederate cabinet. On the other hand a smattering of Jews, such as Mauritz Pinner from Missouri and August Bondi from Kansas, were associated with the antislavery cause and rabbis delivered antislavery sermons, comparing the plight of American blacks with the slavery of the Jews in Egypt.

By the early twentieth century, the nature of Jewish–black relations changed. In the North a number of important and highly visible Jews participated in the beginnings of the civil rights movement. The Jewish participation was particularly intense in the National Association for the Advancement of Colored People (NAACP), launched in 1909, where Jews served in the highest offices of the organization, provided a huge share of its funding, and participated in the association's legal, political, and public educational efforts. Such individuals as Joel and Arthur Spingarn, Louis Marshall, Jacob Schiff, Herbert Lehman, Herbert Seligman, and Jacob Billikopf involved themselves in the NAACP's civil rights efforts. Similarly, in the field of philanthropy for social services in black communities, Jews played a prominent role both by funding projects and supporting the efforts of institutions like the National Urban League, founded in 1911. Julius Rosenwald, for example, donated millions of dollars for black education at every level, black recreational facilities, and black medical care. Jews were also involved in the intellectual battle against

racism. The scholarly endeavors of a group of Jewish anthropologists, particularly Franz Boas, Alexander Goldenweiser, and Melville Herskovitz destroyed the scientific basis of antiblack sentiment in white America.

The Jewish involvement with civil rights and the improvement of race relations in America was not limited to the upper- and upper-middle-class Jews with money to donate to civil rights or philanthropic efforts. The Jewish trade unions, especially the International Ladies Garment Workers Union and the Amalgamated Clothing Workers Union, made strident efforts to organize black workers in their trade and participated in other attempts to unionize blacks. The Yiddish press, read by recent immigrants from Eastern Europe, covered American race relations closely and expressed a high degree of empathy and sympathy with the plight of black Americans.

Most of the Jews involved noted the parallels between blacks and Jews: the similarities between the poverty and civil disabilities endured by blacks and the degraded conditions of Jews in Europe. Indeed, many of the demands of the civil rights movement were crucial to Jews as well. Jews were still the frequent victims of economic discrimination, educational quotas, and prejudicial treatment in housing.

Generally, however, the Jewish involvement with blacks existed primarily at a leadership level and did not involve constant, everyday relations at a face-to-face level. Jewish merchants owned many of the small retail businesses in southern towns and their encounter with blacks was primarily a merchant-customer relationship, although black servants were employed by wealthy Jewish families. By the early decades of the twentieth century, as black migration to the North began, Jews once again operated stores that serviced the developing black neighborhoods in the large cities. The masses of Jews and blacks, however, did not live in the same neighborhoods, attend the same schools, or interact freely as peers. In general, though, Jews put up little resistance to black movement into their neighborhoods, in part because they were in the process of abandoning those sections anyhow for better, more middle-class housing.

Blacks for their part expressed ambivalent feelings about Jews. On the one hand, black leaders such as Booker T. Washington, who had close ties to philanthropists like Julius Rosenwald, exhorted blacks to emulate Jews, and to put their resources into education, to support each other, and to develop positive habits of thrift and frugality. Black political leaders and the black press noted with gratitude the high level of Jewish involvement with the civil rights struggle and commented on how unusual Jews were among white Americans for rendering that service.

On the other hand, anti-Semitism seems to have always existed among blacks in varying degrees. Black anti-Semitism may have had its roots in black Christian fundamentalism, which assigned to Jews blame for the crucifixion of Jesus. It may also have grown out of a black perception that Jews, relative newcomers to America, were experiencing rapid mobility and economic success by means of their black customers, while they, blacks, remained mired in poverty. Some black intellectuals and activists, much as W. E. B. DuBois, resented Jewish involvement in the civil rights movement, and while DuBois recognized that the movement was dependent upon Jewish assistance, he believed that Jews behaved in a patronizing manner toward blacks.

Like much classic anti-Semitism, even black statements of admiration for Jews contained within them elements of hostility, attributing to Jews power and wealth far beyond that which objective conditions merited. Blacks tended to overstate the degree of Jewish political influence and financial resources.

While it is possible to see the preconditions for black–Jewish conflict earlier in the twentieth century, it was not until the mid-1960s that the public began to discuss openly tensions and animosities between the two groups. Until then press coverage, for example, emphasized the alliance between the two groups and the similarity of their political agendas. Since 1965, however, many highly publicized, emotionally charged events have sparked intense public discussions about a seeming breakdown in that alliance. In 1968, New York City's public school teachers went on strike over the issue of community control, and for the first time the issues of Jewish racism and black anti-Semitism became the focus of community debate. In 1979, Andrew Young, the United States ambassador to the United Nations, met with a representative of the Palestine Liberation Organization, and when he was subsequently fired by President Carter, blacks charged that Young was the victim of Jewish racism. In the 1980s black Muslim leader Louis Farrakhan denounced Judaism as a "gutter religion," while presidential aspirant Jesse Jackson referred to New York as "hymietown."

Jews and blacks have differed politically over a number of issues. Jews have generally opposed racial quotas in hiring and university admissions, while blacks have seen these as critical programs for their economic advancement. Some black leaders, such as Jackson, have expressed strong support for the Palestinian cause and have, in varying degrees, condemned Israel. To a large percentage of American Jews, on the other hand, no issue is as emotional as Israel, and any threat to its security and support is responded to immediately and sharply.

While a good deal of the public discussion since the late 1960s has emphasized conflict and bitter feelings between the two groups, Jews and blacks continue at least on a political level to work together and share some issues. Jews, for example, in mayoralty elections in the 1980s in Chicago, New York, Philadelphia, and for governor of California voted in greater number for black candidates than any other group of white voters, and Jewish–black dialogue groups in many communities in the 1970s and 1980s laid the basis for common action on local issues of mutual concern. Black and Jewish congressional representatives tend to vote similarly and cooperate with each other.

Black–Jewish relations remain an ongoing concern of both communities, and scholars have tended to read back into the history of that relationship their contemporary views of the current conflict. *See also* Civil Rights.

HASIA R. DINER

BIBLIOGRAPHY

Diner, Hasia R. *In the Almost Promised Land: American Jews and Blacks, 1915–1935.* Westport, Conn.: Greenwood Press, 1977.

Dinnerstein, Leonard. "Black Antisemitism." In *Uneasy at Home: Antisemitism and the American Jewish Experience.* New York: Columbia University Press, 1987.

Black Jews In America. Over the years, the subject of black Jews in the United States has been treated, often misportrayed, in newspapers, magazines, radio, television, and books, all of which purported to tell the real, albeit partial, story of their origins and practices. Most dealt with black Jews as "exotic" phenomena at best. Few of the individuals or groups described were representative of those who are authentically black Jews.

Despite the headlines, rhetoric, and statistics offered, black Jews have never been numerous. There has been no widespread impulsion on the part of blacks to become Jews, nor has there been interest by the organized Jewish community to bring them into the Jewish fold. Not a scintilla of evidence exists to indicate that blacks will become Jews in any significant numbers in the future.

Affirmative attitudes of numerous blacks toward the Hebrew Bible and toward Zionism, witnessed in the late nineteenth and early twentieth centuries, and toward the State of Israel after it was established, have not increased in recent decades and, indeed, may have waned. These early spiritual and nationalistic influences on black Americans were never extensive, and today they do not motivate blacks to affiliate with Jewish organizations. Black African countries broke with Israel after the 1973 Yom Kippur War—relations that had been fostered by Israel and that had provided excellent services to these budding African nations. In recent years, a few have restored their ties. Black youth in America also cut former close relationships with Jewish individuals and organizations during the late 1960s. This rupture has not been repaired, despite the attempts of Jewish communal relations groups to renew and foster such contacts.

While scholars, white and black, in search of black origins have written imaginatively about their roots in ancient Israel, or their stemming from the Falashas (Ethiopian Jews), or the so-called ubiquitous spread of Jewish religious and nationalistic influences and practices on the African continent over thousands of years, these writings are inventive rather than historical. Cultural parallelism (comparable religious and communal customs) should not be confused with an umbilical association with historical Judaism or with Jews.

While an association with Ethiopian Jews, and its legendary origins, going back to Moses or the union of King Solomon and the Queen of Sheba, might provide the mythology for an ancient linkage with Judaism and royalty, such efforts to develop genuine connections by American and Caribbean blacks are fantasies and spurious.

In the colonial period and after the United States was formally established at the end of the eighteenth century, while some Jews were slave holders, there is no evidence that any of their "chattel" were converted to Judaism. What is more, according to Jewish law, any slaves would have had to be freed after six years, thus conferring no benefits for the slave owner. Some Jews did emancipate their slaves in their wills. Furthermore, it would not have been in a black's interest to convert to Judaism because Jews themselves suffered from civic disabilities and prejudice during the early period in American history. In many states, particularly in the South, both relationships and marriages between whites and blacks were forbidden by law and custom until recent decades.

Accounts were printed occasionally in the nineteenth century of individual blacks who were described as Jews. A few were allowed to attend congregational services. It was written that some had been converted, but no names of the rabbinical authorities were provided. It was only in the early part of the twentieth century that there were reports in the press of the existence of black Jews as actual congregations in the northeastern and north central parts of the United States. At times they were recognized as Jews by individual white Jews. In the main they attended small synagogues or temples founded and led by blacks, whose leaders called themselves "rabbis." Under the charismatic direction of Wentworth Arthur Matthew of New York, these black Jews were organized into a council of rabbis and synagogues. He trained and "ordained" them as "rabbis." This union no longer exists. Among these groups were those that retained Christian elements and symbols.

Some blacks turned to Judaism after their disillusionment with Christianity following the demise of the Marcus Garvey "Back to Africa" movement in the 1920s. Garvey heralded the Jew as a model to emulate, for the Jew was pridefully "interested first in himself as a Jew," quickly became economically self-sufficient, and wanted to reestablish his own homeland in Palestine. Garvey claimed that compensation was due the blacks for centuries of slavery, persecution and discrimination. His followers (he died in 1940) asserted that this should be done by the United States Government, just as the Jews were given reparations by Germany in compensation for all that they had lost under the Hitler-Nazi tyranny.

Despite black anti-Semitism, which emerged with the socialization of slaves in the American culture, and which had its roots in the teachings of white Protestant fundamentalism and anti-Jewish expressions in American folklore, black Judaism had its largest growth during the 1930s, when black anti-Semitism attacked Jews with the charges of "Christ Killers" and "economic exploiters."

Blacks entered Judaism by deliberate choice as they sought a new or alleged older Jewish identity. Others became Jews through theological conviction, communal association, conversion, and marriage. Some were also Jews automatically because the mother (black or white) was Jewish, whether through marriage or an illicit relationship. Individuals, if not initially rebuffed, affiliated with a white Jewish congregation, Orthodox, Conservative, or Reform. They were conspicuous, but some became fully accepted as congregants.

There are several synagogues that have only black congregants; for example, in Chicago and New York City synagogues follow an Orthodox ritual tradition in text and costume. Some have distinctive dress, jewelry, and musical and liturgical forms for their services. Some observe kashrut (or practice vegetarianism), the Sabbath, and Jewish holidays and have a Torah. The spiritual leaders and the congregants are robed in prayer shawls and wear kippahs.

Many of the congregants have converted to Judaism. In a few instances, a black group that banded together in a synagogue of its own design and with its own religious leadership, after instruction, was converted en masse to Judaism.

With a few exceptions, black synagogues and their leaders have not attained legitimacy from the formal religious or secular Jewish community, or such embracing organizations as national denominational groups, local rabbinical councils, or from rabbis whose halakic authority is unquestioned. A few black groups have made applications, only to have their candidacy ignored. Most have never requested such affiliation.

Only one black leader, Rabbi Avraham R. Coleman, has ever received official rabbinic ordination. Others have never applied, because they did not have the aboriginal Jewish credentials by birth or conversion, or because they did not have the academic status by study or graduation from an approved religious seminary, or because they have never met the test of a qualified rabbi or Bet Din. While nearly all heads of black congregations use the title "Rabbi," they acknowledge that they use it in the more limited, albeit original, sense of "teacher."

There are not enough benefits to be derived by being Jewish today to warrant any mass movement by black people to adopt Judaism, even if the most vigorous and hospitable recruiting tactics were undertaken by white Jewish synagogues. Most white Jews have been reluctant to accept converts, white or black. Converts who enter the Jewish fold, usually come voluntarily, often induced by one or the other partner in a marriage. While unions and conversions between whites have flourished in recent decades, this has not occurred frequently between blacks and whites, even when one is Jewish. Efforts to obtain records on black conversions to Judaism have been futile.

A group of American blacks calling themselves Black Hebrews or Israelites found their way clandestinely into Israel in 1969.

While not claiming to be Jews, they decided to settle there permanently in their own enclave. Their numbers grew by births and illegal immigration to several thousands. There has been endless controversy about their presence, their illegal status, their lifestyle. The black Israelites refuse to convert to Judaism as a condition for living there and will not leave. Since they have torn up their American passports, they are stateless. Some have been expelled for criminal acts. Initially Israel was persuaded by American Jewish community relations organizations not to do anything that would arouse interracial animosities for Jews in the United States or court further antagonism from African and Third World nations. Their status in Israel remains in limbo.

There has been no authoritative census on the number of black Jews in the United States. Figures cited are without foundation. Several books, which have not yet been published, will seemingly indicate that there are many more black Jewish congregations and individuals than cited herein because the authors apparently do not accept the restrictive Halakah test of who is a Jew and include anyone or group that simply professes to be Jewish.

Despite these assertions, it is questionable whether there are more than 5000 black Jews in America, about half through birth from a Jewish mother, white or black, and the remainder by occasional conversions.

In the 1960s for a short time there existed an organization Hatzaad Harishon (First Step) in New York City. It was created by blacks and a few white Jews to foster a closer identity with the white Jewish community and to obtain entry, at least for authentic black Jewish children, into Jewish schools, summer camps and to Israel. It never received the backing of most black congregations. The organization stimulated a number of formal conversions and affiliations with predominantly white or mixed congregations. It terminated when efforts were made by its black Jewish leaders to welcome only bona fide black Jews into its ranks.

In the future, acceptance and integration within the larger white Jewish community will continue to be difficult for black Jews. Those blacks who elect to convert should be welcomed with total hospitality into the House of Israel. All authentic black Jewish synagogues should be recognized. Others, however, should not be treated as a dissident Jewish sect.

GRAENUM BERGER

BIBLIOGRAPHY

Berger, Graenum. *Black Jews in America: A Documentary with Commentary.* New York: Federation of Jewish Philanthropies, 1978.
———. *Graneum.* Hoboken, N.J.: Ktav, 1987.
Bratz, Howard. *The Black Jews of Harlem: Negro Nationalism and the Dilemmas of Negro Leadership.* New York: Free Press, 1964.

Bloom, Harold (b. 1930). One of the most prolific and influential of American literary critics, Harold Bloom was born in New York City on July 11, 1930. He had been a steady, even distinguished, worker in the vineyard of the Romantic period, but with the publication of *The Anxiety of Influence* (1973), he became one of criticism's dominant voices. Prior to that provocative study, critics generally agreed that the literary tradition worked as a gathering up of the best each age had thought and said—an addition without loss. Bloom argued for quite a different view, one in which each successive generation of poets reacted violently against their predecessors in what often took on the dimensions of an Oedipal struggle. Subsequent books such as *A Map of Misreading* (1975) both refined and extended this general view.

But as important as Bloom's contributions to our understanding of literary history—and especially of how to estimate "influence"—have been, he is equally important for books such as *Kabbalah and Criticism* (1975) and *The Breaking of the Vessels* (1982) that simultaneously applied the scholarship of Gershom Scholem (*Major Trends in Jewish Mysticism*) to literary texts and introduced these largely unfamiliar terms to a wider American audience. That Jews in recent decades have figured prominently in Ivy League English departments (Bloom, for example, teaches at Yale) is no longer considered extraordinary; however,

that a Harold Bloom can write about "Kabbalah and literature" would have been unthinkable before he did it. Nor did Bloom stop there. His writings on the Hebrew Bible, Hebrew poetry, and Jewish history have been every bit as controversial, and as influential, as have his commentaries on Romantic poets such as Shelley or Blake.

In an age where university professors are only rarely iconoclastic, Bloom is the sort of character around whom apocrypha swirl. He is said to have read English before he spoke it, and stories of his extraordinary memory (he can, for example, cite whole books of *Paradise Lost* by heart) are legendary. In an age of the computer, he writes his books longhand (occasionally at the dinner table) and eschews any copyediting whatsoever because neither Ralph Waldo Emerson nor Thomas Carlyle were so edited. Nonetheless, his own books and articles keep churning out, along with literally hundreds of books that he has edited for such series as *The Chelsea House Library of Literary Criticism*, *Modern Critical Interpretations*, and *Modern Critical Views*. For a man who launched his career by shaking the very underpinnings of what the Anglo-American tradition had defined as "tradition," Bloom has become something of a scholarly tradition himself, although one so rich, so complicated, and so altogether extraordinary that it is hard to imagine him as either "anxious" or as threatened by those who might seek to unseat him.

SANFORD PINSKER

BIBLIOGRAPHY

Fite, David. *Harold Bloom: The Rhetoric of Romantic Vision.* Amherst: University of Massachusetts Press, 1985.
Handelman, Susan A. "The Critic as Kabbalist: Harold Bloom and the Heretic Hermeneutic." In *The Slayers of Moses.* Albany: State University of New York Press, 1982.

B'nai B'rith International. Twelve German Jews of New York City founded in 1843 B'nai B'rith (Sons of the Covenant) as a fraternal order for the then American Jewish population of 15,000. In its early years its goals and activities centered around social service projects: orphanages, hospitals, homes for the aged, help for victims of the great Chicago fire, adjustment of new immigrants to the New World.

By the twentieth century, in response to new needs and challenges, B'nai B'rith expanded its concerns. Then, in 1913, a time of anti-Semitic excesses, exemplified by the murder trial in Georgia of Leo Frank, the Anti-Defamation League of B'nai B'rith (ADL) was founded. Its purpose was to confront the defamation of Jews and fight discrimination against all citizens. In the 1920s, ADL joined other groups in fighting the Ku Klux Klan and took the lead in publicizing the Klan's danger to Americans. In the 1930s and 1940s, ADL's focus shifted to confront fascism in America and its links to Nazi front groups. After World War II, ADL turned to the issue of discrimination in American life. It was active in the support of the Civil Rights Act of 1964 and subsequent civil rights legislation. ADL was also in the forefront of Jewish organizations protesting the march of American Nazis in Skokie, Illinois, the winter of 1975-1976.

In the 1980s and 1990s, ADL continued to be involved in issues of concern to American Jewry, such as the plight of Jews in the Soviet Union, the American commitment to Israel, black–Jewish relations, and the ongoing fight against anti-Semitism.

Needs also emerged that went beyond defense of Jewish rights into concerns for Jewish youth, upon whose Jewish identity survival depended. So, in 1923 at the University of Illinois, the first Hillel Foundation came into being, eventually expanding to 400 campuses in 31 countries.

Two years later the B'nai B'rith Youth Organization for teenagers was created to serve, like Hillel, their social, cultural, community service, religious, and counseling needs. B'nai B'rith program also includes a Career and Counseling Service.

B'nai B'rith is administered by democratically elected officers and a board of governors with representatives of districts coming from 41 countries. The organization has often been defined as a conglomerate. As the membership grew to half a million men, women, and youth, its departments (called "Commissions") have proliferated. Each commission is headed by its own staff and governing body. The commissions include Continuing Jewish Education, which sponsors Institutes of Jewish Learning, a lecture bureau, and a publication program. The Community Volunteer Services Commission is the vehicle for B'nai B'rith's concern for the veteran, the poor, the elderly. Its Senior Citizens Housing Program, continually expanding, has received substantial support from the United States Government.

Other major departments included the Israel Commission, which organizes tours and volunteer programs in Israel, among them the highly successful ARI (Active Retirees in Israel) program and which has promoted the sale of Israel bonds and trees.

The International Council is the instrument for coordinating B'nai B'rith activities and interests in the 41 countries where B'nai B'rith serves. Through its United Nations office it protects world Jewish interests.

B'nai B'rith Women, founded in 1897, is a parallel branch for developing programs for women and support of the youth program. A highlight of its ongoing program is the B'nai B'rith Women Children's Home in Jerusalem. In 1990, at its biennial convention, B'nai B'rith admitted women to full membership. At the same time the B'nai B'rith Women became a part of B'nai B'rith through a formal affiliation, with its own agenda and with female members only.

B'nai B'rith international headquarters is at 1640 Rhode Island Avenue, N.W., in Washington, D.C. In its building also is the B'nai B'rith Klutznick Museum. The organization publishes the *B'nai B'rith Monthly* magazine, *The Insider* for the lay leadership, and *Tachlis*, the newsletter for the staff. In addition, it periodically issues studies on current Jewish issues.

The twelve Jews who founded B'nai B'rith could never have foreseen that within a century it would become an international organization, the largest anywhere in the Jewish world. *See also* Hillel.

BENJAMIN M. KAHN

BIBLIOGRAPHY
Belth, Nathan. *Not the Work of a Day.* New York: Anti-Defamation League, 1965.
Bisgyer, Maurien. *Challenge and Encounter.* New York: Crown, 1967.
Dobkowski, Michael, ed. *Jewish American Voluntary Organizations.* Westport, Conn.: Greenwood Press, 1986.
Grusd, Edward E. *B'nai B'rith: The Story of a Covenant.* New York: Appleton, 1966.
Klutznick, Philip. *No Easy Answers.* New York: Farrar, Straus and Cudahy, 1961.
Moore, Deborah Dash. *B'nai B'rith and the Challenge of Ethnic Leadership.* Albany: State University of New York Press, 1982.

Borscht Belt. As soon as the immigrant Jews could leave the crush of the tenements in which they lived, they fled—if only for a week or two in the summer. And the place where many of the more fortunate happily went was known simply as "the mountains," or to be more precise, the Catskills in southeastern New York State. As one longtime Jewish resident put it, "You keep going until you get to where there's two stones to every dirt. Then you're there."

Jewish-Americans had been *there* from as early as 1890. Indeed, by 1893 the Rand-McNally *Guide to the Hudson River and Catskill Mountains* observed that Tannersville "is a great resort of our Israelite brethren, who love to gather where they can be together." There is little doubt that the "brethren" were German Jews and still less doubt that there was little enthusiasm—and indeed, often much undisguised hostility—for the East European Jews who began flooding into the area during the late 1890s.

But there was no stopping those yearning to breathe reasonably priced mountain air, and in a few decades the movement from *kokhaleyns* (where guests did their own cooking or shared communal cooking facilities) and unadorned boardinghouses to clusters of hotels catering to a Jewish-American clientele from all over the United States was complete. From the late 1920s until the early 1960s (the peak period of Borscht Belt popularity) many of the Catskill hotels that had become symbols of luxurious vacation living—Grossinger's, Kutcher's, Brown's, the Nevele, and the Concord, to name only a few—competed with each other in terms of size, entertainment, lavish architecture and facilities (which included nightclubs, theaters, swimming pools, tennis courts, riding paths, boating, ice skating, later ski runs—whatever the demanding guest would want for his or her pleasure was available), and, of course, limitless quantities of good food. From Rip Van Winkle onward, the Catskill Mountains had inspired legends, and the stories that grew up around those who built "Jewish" hotels were no exception. When Arthur Winarick (who made his fortune with an invention called Jeris Tonic, a hair restorative) set out to make his Concord Hotel the most spectacular watering hole in the area, he asked his Scottish landscaper, "How big a golf course has Grossinger's got?" "Eighteen holes," the landscaper replied. Winarick commanded, "Then build me a fifty-hole golf course."

The term "Borscht Belt" was originated by the entertainers who played the Catskill circuit, going from one hotel to another in the region. They named the circuit after the popular Eastern European beet soup that was a staple of the area's menus. For them the term symbolized the overabundance of food served at the hotels where they performed. The name caught on, and the area became widely known as the Borscht Belt.

Although the Borscht Belt is an easy target of satire—especially by those who cut their show business teeth in its auditoriums and lounges and by its poolsides—the fact of the matter is that it provided a valuable training ground for a wide variety of Jewish-American entertainers, including Joey Adams, Milton Berle, Danny Kaye, Red Buttons, Eddy Fisher, Jan Pierce, Jerry Lewis, and Mel Brooks. *See also* Comics, Vaudeville.

SANFORD PINSKER

BIBLIOGRAPHY

Adams, Joey, with Henry Tobias. *The Borscht Belt.* New York: Bobbs-Merrill, 1966.

Frommer, Harry and Myrna Frommer-Katz. *It Happened in the Catskills.* New York: Harcourt Brace Jovanovich, 1991.

Kanter, Stefan. *A Summer World.* New York: Farrar, Straus and Giroux, 1989.

Pomerantz, Joel. *Jennie and the Story of Grossinger's.* New York: Grosset & Dunlap, 1968.

Taub, Harold J. *Waldorf-in-the-Catskills.* New York: Sterling, 1952.

Boston. With a metropolitan area of over 2 million people, Boston boasts a Jewish population of 230,000, many of whom are recent arrivals, migrating to the area for education and jobs. Recent newcomers include sizable numbers of Russians and Israelis.

It was not until 1842 that a Jewish community began in one of the nation's oldest cities, founded in 1630. This, despite the fact that the first known Jew in the United States, Solomon Franco, arrived in 1649. Ohabei Shalom, the initial Jewish congregation in Boston, held its first services in 1842, but it was not until the influx of East European Jews in the 1880s and 1890s that there were substantial numbers, resulting in social clubs, literary programs, settlement houses, self-help societies, and landsmanschaften. Even Jewish baseball teams were formed in the 1880s. By 1900, there were 400 Jewish institutions, including the Federated Jewish Charities founded in 1895, the first Jewish federation in the United States and the forerunner of Boston's current Combined Jewish Philanthropies.

Jewish cultural institutions had been founded

much earlier by the initial German immigrants and had included the Hebrew Literary Society (1846) and the Mendelsohn Verein (1855). It was during the Civil War that the leading charitable institutions began with the founding of the United Hebrew Benevolent Association in 1864. There followed the Progress Cultural Club (1864), the Hebrew Educational Society (1868), and the Young Men's Hebrew Association (1875).

Members of the initial Jewish community resided in the South End, while the newcomers in the latter part of the century moved to the North End and West End and later to Roxbury, Dorchester, and Mattapan. Subsequent migrations took them to the suburbs of Brookline and Newton and, particularly after World War II, to the suburbs west and south of the city, such as Framingham and Randolph. Responsive to this geographic and demographic trend, two major Jewish community centers serving thousands of families were built in the 1980s in Newton and Stoughton.

The immigrants arriving in the 1890s and after the turn of the century came at a fortunate time and place for economic opportunities that meshed with the skills and training Jews traditionally followed. New England had reigned as the center of the nation's textile industry, and European Jews had already been involved in the garment industry. They went to work in factories or sweatshops or did piecework at home. Others became peddlers and shopkeepers, and some, like William Filene, succeeded in becoming major department store owners. Since World War II, Boston's economy has grown in such areas as law, education, medicine, and computer high technology enterprises, fields in which many Jews were educated and trained and where they have provided leadership.

Boston also proved to be a center of Yiddish culture and at one time supported seven Yiddish-language papers of its own, numerous Yiddish stage productions, and even a Yiddish theater. By mid-century, this interest in and the need for Yiddish language and culture diminished considerably as Jews adopted and adapted to American language and customs.

Education of all varieties proved to be a passion for the newcomers with religious school begun at the same time as the founding of the first congregation. Labor unions, Zionist organizations, and Yiddish culture groups also opened schools, while Boston was among the first cities to support IVRIA, schools where Hebrew was the language of instruction. Hebrew Teachers College (now Hebrew College) and the Bureau of Jewish Education were among the first in the nation. The famed Menorah Society was founded at Harvard College and proved to be a precursor of the Hillel Foundations. Brandeis University, the nation's first secular Jewish institution of higher learning, was founded in 1948 in Waltham, a suburb of Boston. Over the years Boston has attracted more Jewish college students than any other city in the nation so that student life has played a major role in Boston's Jewish culture. The Jewish college student movement of the late 1960s and 1970s found its start in Boston, where such publications as *Genesis, Response*, and *Moment Magazine* had their start.

Despite the growth and success of the community during the period prior to World War II and even after, anti-Semitism was a major concern, with attacks upon the community by Father Feeney locally and Father Coughlin nationally. The Jewish Community Council (now the Jewish Community Relations Council) was founded in 1944 to represent the community in its dealings with intergroup and intragroup conflicts.

Boston has nurtured such twentieth-century Jewish luminaries as Louis D. Brandeis, Horace M. Kallen, Felix Frankfurter, and Abram L. Sachar, as well as numbers of Nobel Prize winners in various catagories, including Elie Wiesel, who teaches at Boston University.

Boston's Jewish community under the leadership of Jacob DeHaas, Brandeis, and Elihu D. Stone served as one of the centers of American Zionism with Stone successfully lobbying for the 1922 Lodge-Fish Congressional Resolution calling for the establishment of a Jewish state. In 1948, David K. Niles and Dewey D. Stone played significant roles in advising President Harry S. Truman to recognize the newly established State of Israel.

The community has been home to leaders of Judaic studies and diverse religious leaders, such as Professors Isadore Twersky and Harry A. Wolfson and Rabbis Roland B. Gittlesohn, Levi I. Horowitz, and Joseph B. Soloveitchik.

According to a 1985 demographic survey, out of the total population of 230,000 Jews in the Greater Boston area, approximately 27,000 households contribute to the campaign of the Combined Jewish Philanthropies. It is estimated that in Greater Boston there is an intermarriage rate of 29 percent, while only 41 percent of the

Jewish population have a synagogue affiliation. Despite these figures, 75 percent of the households have had or will have such an affiliation, and it is anticipated that 83 percent of the Jewish children in the area will obtain some Jewish education prior to adulthood.

BERNARD WAX

BIBLIOGRAPHY

American Jewish Historical Society. *On Common Ground: The Boston Jewish Experience, 1649–1980.* Philadelphia: American Jewish Historical Society, 1981.

Solomon, Barbara. *Ancestors and Immigrants: A Changing New England Tradition.* New York: Wiley, 1956.

Wieder, Arnold A. *The Early Jewish Community of Boston's North End.* Waltham, Mass.: Brandeis University, 1962.

Brandeis, Louis Dembitz (1856–1941). One of the greatest legal minds in American history, Louis Brandeis served on the United States Supreme Court from 1916 until 1939. He was born in Louisville, Kentucky. His parents, Adolphe and Frederika Brandeis, immigrated from Prague because the new government resulting from the Revolution of 1848 imposed greater restrictions on Jews and their future prospects seemed uncertain. The events surrounding the Brandeis family experience in Europe would infuse their son with a spirit of "political democracy" and "national liberation." In addition, an uncle, Attorney Lewis Dembitz, would be most influential in shaping Brandeis's chosen profession and liberality that would become the hallmark of his life's work.

As a child, Brandeis's intellectual brilliance was apparent. He graduated from high school at the age of 14 with the highest honors, and during a three-year stay in Europe he attended school in Dresden, Germany. Before the age of 21, Brandeis graduated first in his class from Harvard Law School in 1878, earning the best academic record in the school's history.

Brandeis began his law practice in Boston with a fellow Harvard graduate, Samuel Warren. He also taught law at Harvard, and when offered a full-time professorship, he rejected the position to pursue his first love, trial law. With a successful growing law practice, Brandeis accidentally entered the realm of advocacy of the public interest

when a friend protested the misuse of public money for private interest.

Brandeis's practice as a public-cause attorney brought him cases concerning the privacy rights of individuals, municipal corruption, labor relations, and abuses in state-run facilities for the indigent. Additionally, he tackled monopolistic industry and large corporations, such as Equitable Life Insurance in 1906, and the plight of women performing hard labor, representing the plaintiff in *Muller v. Oregon* in 1908. He often took up the causes for those he considered defenseless at reduced fees and frequently for no fee. As a result of his activities, Brandeis was dubbed the "people's attorney" and "troublemaker"; his position made him an enemy of the rich. What was truly revolutionary about his legal career was his incorporation of economic and sociological facts into legal issues.

In 1916, President Woodrow Wilson appointed Brandeis to the Supreme Court. His confirmation was a difficult one, partly because of his religion. Once approved, he served on the Court with distinction until 1939.

Brandeis's Jewish identity was late in arriving. It was not until the age of 54, when he was called to negotiate a settlement in a strike among the garment workers in New York's Jewish East Side, that Brandeis developed a kinship with fellow Jews. At first he distanced himself from the Zionist Movement so as not to jeopardize his Supreme Court nomination, but the transition from people's advocate to Zionist fighter for Jewish rights seemed a natural one. Again he was coming to the aid of the defenseless.

At the close of World War I, Brandeis was instrumental in sending Zionist representatives to the peace conference in Paris to discuss Jewish hopes for a homeland in Palestine. Brandeis also petitioned the British government to improve conditions for Jews in Palestine: removal of anti-Semitic British soldiers, reconsideration of Jewish immigration restrictions, cessation of unfair practices that favored Arabs and caused disharmony with their Jewish neighbors. The violence of Arab against Jew in 1929 and 1936 proved the urgency of his appeal. Hitler's rise in Germany and the increase of anti-Jewish programs enhanced Brandeis's Zionist energies. The danger for Jews in Germany made it imperative for Jews to be able to immigrate to Palestine. Brandeis's position and prestige allowed him to speak to influential world leaders, including the British prime minister and President Franklin Roosevelt, to convince them of this need.

Shortly before his eighty-fifth birthday, Brandeis suffered a fatal heart attack; never regaining consciousness, he died on October 5, 1941. Lawyer, teacher, public advocate, and Supreme Court justice would have been enough to fulfill the ambitions of most, but not for Justice Brandeis. He strove to defend the defenseless, to be their champion, and this tireless effort is what sets Louis Brandeis apart. *See also* Law and Lawyers, Zionism.

SHERRY OSTROFF
HOWARD SHAKER

BIBLIOGRAPHY

Gal, Allon. *Brandeis of Boston.* Cambridge: Harvard University Press, 1980.

Mason, Alpheus Thomas. *Brandeis: A Free Man's Life.* New York: Viking, 1946.

Paper, Lewis J. *Brandeis.* Englewood Cliffs, N.J.: Prentice-Hall, 1983.

Rabinowitz, Cezekiel. *Justice Louis D. Brandeis: The Zionist Chapter of His Life.* New York: Philosophical Library, 1968.

Urofsky, Melvin I. *Louis D. Brandeis and the Progressive Tradition.* Boston: Little, Brown, 1981.

Brandeis University. Named after U.S. Supreme Court Justice Louis Dembitz Brandeis, Brandeis University was founded in 1948 by a group of visionary communal leaders as the first Jewish-sponsored nonsectarian university in North America. It is an accredited, private, coeducational institution of higher learning and research located on a 230-acre campus 10 miles west of Boston in Waltham, Massachusetts. From an initial beginning of 107 matriculants and 14 faculty, the school's enrollment has increased dramatically to include 2900 undergraduates and 800 graduate students. For the 1989–1990 academic year there were 365 full-time faculty members.

The undergraduate College of Arts and Sciences encompasses the Schools of Humanities, Creative Arts, Science, and Social Science. As a liberal arts college, Brandeis affirms the importance of a broad and critical education and offers more than 30 fields of concentration as well as special interdisciplinary research and bachelor-master's programs.

Undergraduate education is enhanced by Brandeis's position as one of only 100 recognized research institutions in the nation. A member of the Association of American Universities and accredited by the New England Association of Schools and Colleges, Brandeis provides access to highly advanced research, making its senior scholars and researchers available to freshmen as well as to graduate students.

The Graduate School of Arts and Sciences, established in 1953, offers master's and doctoral degrees in the arts and humanities, the social sciences, mathematics, and science, American civilization, contemporary Jewish studies, Near Eastern and Judaic studies, and theater arts. The Florence Heller Graduate School for Advanced Studies in Social Welfare (1959) is an internationally known professional school conducting a multidisciplinary, policy-oriented research program on a wide range of health and welfare issues. It confers a master's degree in Management of Human Services and a doctoral degree in Social Policy Analysis. Postgraduate training in medical science is undertaken through the Rosenstiel Basic Medical Sciences Research Center; graduate study in international business is provided by the Lemburg Program in International Economics and Finance; and the Gordon Public Policy Center—designed to serve as a locus of shared research among experts in economics, political science, history, and law—is the nation's first interdisciplinary multiuniversity program for the study of public policy.

Reflecting Brandeis's Jewish heritage, the School of Near Eastern and Judaic Studies offers the largest, most comprehensive program in the field in any university outside Israel. It has an intensive teaching and research program in all the main areas of Judaic studies, the Ancient Near East, and the Modern Near East. The Maurice and Marilyn Cohen Center for Modern Jewish Studies is devoted to the study of contemporary Jewish life, such as Jewish identity, family, political behavior, and anti-Semitism. The Tauber Institute for the Study of European Jewry seeks to study the history and culture of European Jewry in the modern period—especially the causes, nature, and consequences of the European Jewish catastrophe—and seeks to explore them within the context of modern European diplomatic, intellectual, political, and social history. In addition to these programs, the Benjamin S. Hornstein Program for Jewish Communal Services prepares students for professional careers in Jewish communities and Jewish education.

International in scope, the student community draws its members from every state and 55 foreign countries. The Wien International Scholarship Program, designed to further international understanding through education, provides exceptionally gifted foreign students with an opportunity to study in the United States and enriches the intellectual and cultural life of the Brandeis campus.

In addition to distinguished academic programs, Brandeis maintains an active year-round schedule of concerts, theater performances, and art exhibits centered around the Slosberg Music Hall, the Spingold Theater, and the Rose Art Museum.

The Brandeis University libraries, consisting of the Bertha and Jacob Goldfarb Library, Leonard L. Farber Library, Rapaporte Treasure Hall, and the Gerstenzang Science Library have combined collections of 850,000 volumes, 735,000 microforms, 300,000 U.S. documents, 7,500 publications, and 62 newspapers. The rapid development of the library was the result of the continuous efforts and support of the Brandeis University National Women's Committee, whose role has evolved to include a diverse range of local and national activities and fund raising.

In May 1991 Brandeis University selected Samuel O. Thier to be its sixth president.

DAVID M. ROSEN

BIBLIOGRAPHY

Goldstein, Israel. *Brandeis University: Chapter of its Founding.* New York: Bloch, 1951.

Bruce, Lenny (1926–1966). Nightclub comedian and social satirist, Lenny Bruce was born Leonard Alfred Schneider in Mineola, Long Island (N.Y.), the son of Mickey and Sadie Schneider. After his parents' divorce in 1933, Bruce first lived with relatives and then with his father. He grew up in rural Bellmore, Long Island. The 16-year-old Bruce enlisted in the Navy in 1942 and served on the cruiser *Brooklyn*. Following his discharge in 1946, he studied acting in Hollywood on the G.I. Bill. In 1951, Bruce married Honey Harlow (Harriet Lloyd), a stripper. Bruce's only child, a daughter named Kitty, was born in 1955, and in 1957 he and Honey were divorced. After three arrests for obscenity and one for possession of drugs, Bruce's career was all but over by the end of 1963. Bruce died of a drug overdose on August 3, 1966.

In 1947, Bruce made his first appearance as a comic and impressionist at a Brooklyn nightclub and successfully appeared on the "Major Bowes Hour" and "Arthur Godfrey's Talent Scouts." While Bruce was working in strip clubs, he wrote and appeared in his first film, *Dance Hall Racket* (1954). The film also starred Bruce's wife Honey and his mother, now an entertainer named Sally Marr. Bruce co-wrote the children's film *The Rocket Man* (1954) and also made *Dream Follies*, which has since disappeared. A successful run at Ann's 440 in San Francisco in 1958 led to Bruce's critical and popular "discovery," and he signed a recording contract with Fantasy Records. A favorite of the "Beatniks" and labeled a "sick comic" by some social commentators, Bruce made TV appearances in 1959 on "The Steve Allen Show" and on New York City's public TV station Channel Thirteen's "The World of Lenny Bruce." Bruce was profiled in the *New York Times Magazine* in an article by Gilbert Millstein called "Man, It's Like Satire" (May 3, 1959). Bruce knew he had arrived when columnist Walter Winchell dubbed him "America's No. 1 Vomic!"

At San Francisco's hungry i nightclub Bruce taped his breakthrough album, *The Sick Humor of Lenny Bruce*. His other albums include *Live at the Curran Theater*, *The Best of Lenny Bruce*, *Interviews of Our Time*, *The Real Lenny Bruce*, *Thank You Mask(ed) Man*, and *Togetherness*. Bruce wrote two books, *Stamp Help Out!* (1964) and *How to Talk Dirty and Influence People: An Autobiography* (1965), and John Cohen edited *The Essential Lenny Bruce* (1967). John Magnuson based an animated short, *Thank You Mask Man*, on Bruce's famous routine, and Magnuson and Bruce released a concert film, *Lenny Bruce*, in 1965.

Works about Bruce include *Lenny* (1974), a Bob Fosse film adapted from Julian Barry's play, and *Ladies and Gentlemen—LENNY BRUCE!!*, by Albert Goldman (1974). In October 1963, *Playboy* published the first of six installments of Bruce's autobiography, *How to Talk Dirty and Influence People*.

Bruce's first obscenity arrest occurred in San Francisco in 1961, but he was found not guilty. He was arrested again for obscenity in Chicago in 1962, but his conviction was reversed by the Illinois Supreme Court. After a 1963 narcotics' conviction, Bruce received a suspended sentence and probation. Although the Supreme Court refused to review Bruce's 1964 New York City conviction on obscenity charges, he would probably have been exonerated but for his refusal to file a proper appeal.

Inspired by the funny men he observed in Jewish neighborhoods—nonprofessional comics whose angry in-group situational humor used the language of the Jewish lower classes to skewer the foibles and insanity of everyday life—Bruce incorporated their Jewish "spritz" into his act and made it his own. Familiar with jazz and jazzmen, Bruce became a master of hip sensibility: able to take a rap on music or sex, movies or religion and able to wring improvisations on it until he came up with a "bit" that soared and dove, that made audiences laugh while it made them think. Although he appeared on television and in films and made comedy records, Bruce's forte was the nightclub with its intimate "let-me-tell-you-a-story" atmosphere. Still, Bruce rejected being labeled merely a comedian, hoping instead to gain recognition as a filmmaker, philosopher, and social satirist.

At the end of his life, he had a saying: "I'm not a comedian, I'm Lenny Bruce." Labeled a "sick" and "dirty" comic, Bruce was, in reality, a romantic whose middle-class values were formed by his Jewish culture and his eager consumption of thousands of Hollywood films. Unfortunately, his casual (almost *innocent*) use of four-letter words and sexual references only served to obscure his brilliant attacks on prejudice, hypocrisy, and narrow-mindedness. Bruce was a point man for the 1960s upheaval in social and political values, and he paid a stiff price for his innovative comedy. Bruce's contributions to humor, alternately downplayed and magnified, remain substantial. Bruce's ultimately successful legal battles over obscenity helped make possible the careers of comedians with a similar approach to comedy—including Richard Pryor, George Carlin, Redd Foxx, Richard Belzer, Sam Kinison and Eddie Murphy.

KENNETH VON GUNDEN

BIBLIOGRAPHY

Barry, Julian. *Lenny: A Play Based on the Life and Words of Lenny Bruce.* New York: Grove Press, 1971.

Goldman, Albert. *Ladies and Gentlemen: LENNY BRUCE!!.* New York: Random House, 1974.

Millstein, Gilbert. "Man, It's Like Satire." *New York Times Magazine*, May 3, 1959, 28–30.

C

Cahan, Abraham (1860–1951). Born in Podberezy, Russia, the only son of Shachne and Sarah Goldarbeiter Cahan, Cahan at the age of 5 moved with his family to Vilna, where he studied the Torah and Talmud in several traditional Jewish heders (schools) and then, after learning Russian, attended the new Vilna Teachers Institute, a Russian-government school for Jewish teachers. After graduating in 1881, he began teaching in Velizh, near Vitebsk. At the same time he became deeply immersed in radical, underground anticzarist activities. Forced to flee the region, he joined a group of immigrants bound for America. He arrived in Philadelphia on June 5, 1882, and the next day went to New York, resolved to evolve a new Jewish identity.

After a brief stint in a cigar factory, Cahan began tutoring his Lower East Side countrymen in primitive English. On the completion of a course in English at the Chrystie Street School, he published his first article in English in the *New York World* and soon became the first immigrant employed to teach English at the YMHA's evening school. On July 7, 1882, he delivered a public political speech in Russian; not long afterward he gave the first political speech in Yiddish in the United States. In 1886, he married Anna Bronstein, of Kiev, a gymnasium graduate, an educated and cultured woman to whom he was married for some 60 years. In 1890, Cahan became the editor of the weekly *Arbeiter Zeitung*, the paper of the United Hebrew Trades. Among the pseudonyms he used for columns were Socius, David Bernstein, the Hester Street Reporter, and the Proletarian Preacher. In this last guise he used Russian fables, mixed with Talmudic parables and Marxist lessons, to spread his message.

In 1892, Cahan published in the *Arbeiter Zeitung* his first short story in Yiddish, "Mottke Arbel and His Romance," a rather crudely written story of an immigrant peddler. Translated into English and revised, "A Providential Match" was published in 1895. It was seen by William Dean Howells, the dean of American letters. In large part due to Howells's efforts, *Yekl: A Tale of the New York Ghetto* came out in 1896. Howells, in a front-page review in the *New York World*, praised Cahan as "a new star of realism" and the equal of and in the same class as Stephen Crane and Hamlin Garland. *The Imported Bridegroom and Other Stories* (1898) and *The White Terror and the Red* (1905) were published amidst a flurry of a dozen realistic stories that appeared in *Cosmopolitan*. *Yekl*, a novella that evolved out of Cahan's experiences, observations, and attitudes, specifically deals with the effects, positive and negative, of Americanization. In addition, it reflects the tensions that developed in the immigrant American experience. In Jake Podgorny's words (he was Yekl in Russia), "During the three years since he had set foot on the soil, where a 'shister' (shoemaker) becomes a mister and a mister a shister, he had lived so much more than three years . . . that his Russian past appeared to him a dream and his wife and child, together with his former self, fellow characters in a charming tale, which he was neither willing to banish from his memory nor able to reconcile with the actualities of his American present."

Jake, an operative in a cloak shop, speaking a Boston Yiddish and a fragmented, often grotesque English, was very defensive when his social habits were questioned. "Once I live in America," he declared, "I want to know that I live in America. *Dot'sh a'kin a man I am*! One must not be a *greenhorn*. Here a Jew is as good as a Gentile." He shaved his upper lip, cut his hair, and dressed like an American. He worked, always accompanied by the staccatos of the machines. In Povodye he'd been Yekl or Yekele, but here he was proudly Jake, "American." Three years ago he'd left his family in Povodye (his father's smithy couldn't support two families), his wife, and half-year-old son; he'd exchanged his broken Russian for a broken English, his bellows for a sewing machine, his religious habits for American ones. Subsequently he'd moved to New York, the center of the cloak-making industry. Soon he was Jake, and soon he worked on Saturdays, if it was necessary, or he played on the Sabbath. Yekl Podkovnik became Jake Podgorny.

Every month Jake mechanically sent his wife Gitl a remittance of ten rubles, and every month he asked the price of a steerage voyage from Hamburg to New York. But he also quickly let his mind drift to more important matters, such as working, dancing, and women. He conjured up Gitl's sweet, rustic face, as he thought of the loose morals of the women he knew (intimately); once, in an emotional state, he borrowed his landlady's prayer book and for the first time in three years recited the bed prayer. A few weeks later Jake, looking like an American, freshly shaven and smartly dressed in his best clothes and ball shoes, anxiously waited at one of the desks at the Immigration Bureau of Ellis Island for Gitl and Yossel. Impatient and anxious, his heart sank at the sight of his wife's appearance. Jake, now in a state of unspeakable misery, "was anxious to flee from his wretched self into oblivion." An Americanized East European Jew, he saw Gitl as an immigrant, Mamie as an American. Torn between thought of his cozy home (shared with Bernstein, a lodger), and his yearning for Mamie, his blonde shopmate, he ran headlong toward Chrystie Street; perhaps, he thought, Mamie would aid him. Amid thoughts of his dead father and his child, he protested his love for her, promised that he would divorce Gitl. After satisfying herself of his sincerity, Mamie extended her open bank book with its balance of $340 to him. The plan was quickly made, and carried out. While Gitl thought of a happy future with Bernstein, their lodger, Jake

felt a gnawing feeling that he was not a conqueror but a victim; he was soon to give up his recently acquired freedom and liberty. Each time the Third Avenue cable car came to a halt, taking Jake and Mamie and two witnesses to the mayor's office to get married, the distance between his past as husband, father, and lord of the house and his present grew larger. His future loomed dark and impenetrable. "Each time the car came to a halt he wished the pause could be prolonged indefinitely; and when it resumed its progress, the violent lurch it gave was accompanied by a corresponding sensation in his heart."

At the suggestion of the editor, Cahan wrote a two-part series in 1913 for *McClure's* magazine titled "The Autobiography of an American Jew," then expanded it to a four-part series. Four years later his masterpiece, *The Rise of David Levinsky*, the story of an immigrant who became a very successful garment manufacturer, marked the climax of his career as a novelist. Widely acclaimed as the best immigrant novel ever written, it was a mythic novel of the immigrant Jewish experience; at the same time it was a parody of and satire on the American dream of Success.

The Rise of David Levinsky was a first-person narration of an immigrant-become-successful garment manufacturer who looks back on his life and rise to success with a mixture of self-satisfaction and regret. Starting with his past in a small Russian town, where his mother is killed by gentile hoodlums, Cahan continues David's life through his arrival in New York in the 1880s and his experiences thereafter. David's early dream of going to the City College of New York is shattered by his overwhelming dream of making it, American style. Using the excuse of an accident in his shop as the precipitating factor, his employer fires Levinsky. His meteoric rise dates from that event. Vivid scenes of New York's Lower East Side's teeming streets and tenements—the pushcarts, the insides of shops and factories, kitchens and apartments—abound in the book. Cahan also details the takeover from the German Jews by the East European Jews of the ready-made clothing industry, the restaurants, the trains, the real estate speculators, and the Catskills when it became the Borscht Belt.

What is more memorable are the changes wrought upon David Levinsky by the success he enjoys, his inability to forget his tradition and its values, and the resultant inner tension and conflict. Levinsky wound up a "lonely millionaire," a man without a wife though wanting one, a man who admits that sometimes success can be a tragedy. As Levinsky put it, reflecting his uneasy perch at the top of the corporate ladder, "his past and his present do not comport well." He lived a life of luxury, but he was not happy—nor could he be happy. The ironies and subtleties of his position are clear. David Levinsky's drive made him a wealthy man, but he was still searching for that elusive wholeness of soul and character that should have been his but never would. The cost of success was in what he lost as a *mensch*.

Cahan, an immigrant genius who began as a political radical but became a pragmatic American socialist, paralleled his career as a novelist and short story writer with a long, distinguished career as a newspaperman and editor. After an internship on small Yiddish papers, Cahan worked as a reporter for Lincoln Steffens on the *New York Commercial Advertiser* (1897–1901) and served as editor of the *Jewish Daily Forward* (1903–1946), where he transformed a socialist daily into a mass circulation pacesetter for the Yiddish press. His dynamic leadership, his inventiveness—he pioneered unusual columns, including the *Bintel Brief* (Bundle of Letters), an early version of the Dear Abby "Letters to the Editor" column—his use of everyday Yiddish instead of literary Yiddish made the *Forward* a powerful voice in journalism, a national institution, and made him an influential voice in American society, especially in liberal and progressive circles.

Abraham Cahan was a successful and enterprising Americanizer and interpreter of the Jewish immigrant experience. His memoirs, in five volumes, titled *Bleter fun mein Leben* (Leaves From My Life), published 1926–1931, spanned the decades from the 1860s in Russia to the beginning of World War I. After the war he remained active, serving as a member of the American press delegation to Versailles in 1919, visiting Palestine in the 1920s, and helping President Franklin Roosevelt and reporting the Lindbergh kidnapping trial in the 1930s. He succumbed to the demands of age in 1946 when he suffered a stroke, at which time he gave up the editor's chair at the *Forward*.

Cahan was a uniquely gifted journalist-writer-friend of the ghetto, as Ernest Poole called him, whose ability to mediate between the various traditions, belief systems, sensitivities, and languages of the Lower East Side places him at the very center of American Jewish culture and Jewish writing. As Moses Rischin put it, Cahan was the single most influential personality in the total cultural life of well over 2 million Jewish immigrants and their families during his life. His life and works were the bridge across the chasm between past and future that will enable us to understand the world that has made us all. *See also* Jewish Daily Forward; Literature, Yiddish.

DANIEL WALDEN

BIBLIOGRAPHY

Chametzky, Jules. *From the Ghetto: The Fiction of Abraham Cahan*. Amherst: University of Massachusetts Press, 1977.

Howe, Irving. *World of Our Fathers*. New York: Harcourt Brace Jovanovich, 1976.

Rischin, Moses. *The Promised City*. Cambridge: Harvard University Press, 1962.

Sanders, Ronald. *The Downtown Jews*. New York: Harper & Row, 1969.

Stein, Leon; Conan, Abraham P.; and Davison, Lynn, trans. *The Education of Abraham Cahan*. Philadelphia: Jewish Publication Society, 1969.

Call It Sleep (1934). Henry Roth's *Call It Sleep* is an intricate novel remarkable for its artful plot, deft characterization, evocative detail, convincing dialect, linguistic virtuosity, firm symbolic structure, and complex interweaving of symbols and motifs. It is often acclaimed as the best American Jewish novel and one of the great novels of this century.

Call It Sleep is a profound psychological study of David Schearl, who is at once a sensitive child and a mystic in search of divine illumination. Redemption, the underlying theme of the novel, is developed through an intricate pattern of symbols. Although the novel is superficially constructed in an episodic manner, certain symbols, specifically cellar, picture, coal, and rail, provide a firm unifying structure, as well as the names of the four books of the novel. In the first book, David associates the cellar with filth, bodily corruption, shameful sexuality, guilt, and death. The picture represents the past, including his mother Genya's previous sexual relationship with a non-Jew in Poland and his father Albert's highly charged relationship with his own father. While the symbol of the cellar involves uniformly negative emotional connotations and the picture's meanings are ambiguous, the symbol of the coal combines conflicting or opposing meanings. Because it is black and dirty, coal has inevitable connections with uncleanliness for David. He confuses this ordinary coal with the coal or burning ember that purified Isaiah and is unable to reconcile the blackness of coal he knows with purity. In the brilliant last section of the novel, David, who believes that God's purifying coal is in the car tracks, rushes madly through the streets and plunges a milk ladle into the tracks. Knocked unconscious, he experiences a vision that enables him to transcend the horrors of the cellar, the oppression of the picture, and the conflict of the coal.

Call It Sleep can be fruitfully studied using a variety of approaches. It is an unsurpassed novel about childhood, a grittily accurate urban novel, a subtle psychological novel, an accomplished modernist or Joycean novel, and an evocative immigrant novel.

While it is a great novel in any terms, *Call It Sleep* is also a profoundly Jewish novel in its language, allusions, and narrative materials. As an illustration of immigrant Jewish life in the early years of this century, it is fascinating for its historical and sociological insights into that crucial period of American Jewish life.

On a linguistic level, there is a delicate interplay of Yiddish (symbolically the mother tongue and rendered as pure English), Hebrew (transliterated and considered God's tongue), and English (the language of the streets spoken falteringly by the parental generation and maimed by the children). Judaism is central to the characters' speech and thoughts, their allusions and comparisons. Casual references to Jacob and Esau, Moses and the burning bush, Solomon, and Adam and Eve are found throughout the novel, defining the characters' background and cultural identity. Isaiah and Moses are vivid and known; Odysseus and Helen of Troy are outside their sphere.

Call It Sleep is Jewish in more than its language, allusions, and narrative material; the basic materials that Roth manipulates to define and describe David's quest develop thematically and imagistically out of two major Jewish sources: the significance and associations of the Isaiah story and the Passover celebration. In Roth's articulation of his central theme, David Schearl's mystical quest, the novel manipulates Jewish materials as the texture of the narrative.

Although it was generally well received when it first appeared in 1934, the novel was not well known until it was republished in 1960 by Cooper Square Publishers and then as a paperback by Avon in 1964. Greeted by extraordinary reviews when it reappeared, the novel has become a great popular and critical success.

After publishing *Call It Sleep* Roth began a second novel, which Maxwell Perkins predicted would be great, but Roth destroyed it and began but never completed a third. A few short stories and memoirs have appeared since then. Roth dropped out of literary life by 1940 and worked over the years as a teacher, precision tool grinder, attendant in a state hospital, tutor, and water fowl farmer in Maine. Roth and his wife left their Maine farm permanently in 1968 after 19 years. Except for periods of travel, they have lived since then in Albuquerque, New Mexico. *Shifting Landscapes*, a collection of Roth's shorter work before and after *Call It Sleep*, was published by the Jewish Publication Society in 1987. In 1990, he was working on a long memoir and a sequel to *Call It Sleep*.

An extraordinary work of art and the single most accomplished American Jewish novel, *Call It Sleep* has made Henry Roth a major literary figure in spite of the fact that he is, thus far anyhow, a one-novel writer. *See also* Roth, Henry.

BONNIE LYONS

BIBLIOGRAPHY

Lyons, Bonnie. *Henry Roth: The Man and His Work*. New York: Cooper Square, 1977.
Studies in American Jewish Literature 5 (Spring 1979). Special Henry Roth Issue.

Cantor, Eddie (1892–1964). One of the preeminent Jewish entertainers of his era, without underscoring his own ethnic origins or identity, Eddie Cantor distinguished himself as a comedian in a variety of genres—vaudeville, Broadway, movies, radio, television. He was born into an impoverished Russian immigrant family named Iskowitz on the Lower East Side of New York. Cantor, who never finished elementary school, managed to transcend economic hardship through a natural and irrepressible capacity for performance. His career was astonishingly successful, whether by breaking precedent by starring in *Ziegfield's Follies* or by topping "Amos 'n' Andy" in the radio ratings. Incorporating wholesome anecdotes about his wife (née Ida Tobias) and their five daughters in his routines also enhanced Cantor's popularity, as did his unstinting devotion to various charities and causes, from the March of Dimes to Zionism.

He made his vaudeville debut in 1907 as a member of a song-and-dance team; the following year his professional career began on the Bowery.

Soon Cantor was famous as a blackface comedian, putting on eyeglasses as a special touch. His mimicry of ethnic accents also won him considerable applause. His long association with the famous Broadway impresario Florenz Ziegfield began when he was hired for the musical *Midnight Frolic* (1917) and the *Follies* (1917–1919). When the Schubert brothers cast Cantor in *Midnight Rounders* (1920), his name on the marquee appeared for the first time above the name of the show. He also wrote most of the material for Ziegfield's *Kid Boots*, which ran for three years (1923–1926). For the same producer's *Whoopee* (1928–1930), Cantor earned a weekly salary of $5000, making him probably the highest-salaried comedian in history up to that time.

When most of that wealth evaporated at the onset of the Great Depression, Cantor quickly wrote a popular joke book, *Caught Short!* (1929) and then began earning nearly half a million dollars a year in Hollywood. He starred in a series of Samuel Goldwyn musical comedies throughout the decade, but it was his radio show that earned him his widest audience and popularity. By 1933, his show headed the comedy roster of NBC's "red" network; unexcelled vigor and unabashed sentimentality guaranteed Cantor's success on radio for two decades. Just as the decline of vaudeville compelled him to make a smooth transition to radio, television posed a challenge that could not be resisted. In this medium he appeared in several comedy and variety shows in the 1950s, including "The Eddie Cantor Comedy Theatre" (1955). Cantor's last film was biographical, *The Eddie Cantor Story* (1953), starring Keefe Brasselle. The Warner Brothers movie was released a year after a heart attack forced him into semi-retirement. He died in Hollywood in 1964.

Pop-eyed wonder had been Cantor's trademark on stage and in the visual media, along with his dancing and the relentless energy that animated every movement and gesture. Cantor's popularity can be attributed to his dignified yet boyish charm and to his irresistible human warmth. Like other comedians of his generation who exerted so powerful an impact on the American mass audience, Cantor concealed explicit indications of his Jewish origin. But he once refused to open a show of *Ziegfield's Follies* because it was Yom Kippur, and he did not pretend to be anyone other than a Jew offstage. Cantor was not a satirist, and he was neither profound nor original. George Jessel, who was probably his best friend, nevertheless called him "the most resourceful comic figure that there ever was in America." *See also* Vaudeville.

STEPHEN J. WHITFIELD

BIBLIOGRAPHY

Cantor, Eddie. *As I Remember Them.* New York: Duell, Sloan & Pierce, 1963.

———. *My Life Is in Your Hands.* New York: Harper, 1928.

———. *Take My Life.* New York: Doubleday, 1957.

Cantorial Music. *See* MUSIC, CANTORIAL.

Cardozo, Benjamin Nathan (1870–1939). Supreme Court justice, author, and reluctant Zionist, Benjamin Nathan Cardozo was born in New York City, the youngest child of Albert Cardozo, who was forced to resign his seat on the New York Supreme Court due to allegations of misusing his office in the Boss Tweed scandal. The American branch of the Cardozo family had settled in North America prior to the Revolutionary War; several family members gained notoriety by signing the repeal of the Stamp Act. Through the years Cardozos have been rabbis and presidents of Jewish congregations.

At the age of 15, with both parents deceased, Benjamin Cardozo entered Columbia University. He distinguished himself by serving as vice-president of his class and participating in public debates. He earned his bachelor's degree in 1889 and his master's from Columbia in 1890. Although Cardozo passed the bar examination in 1891, he never received his law degree due to a dispute with the university.

With his brother Albert, Cardozo began his law practice with the goal of clearing his father's name. He achieved recognition on the basis of his own merit, regardless of his father's tarnished legacy. Cardozo attained immediate success as an attorney because of his ability to put complex issues into clear language. His legal aptitude was acclaimed by many, and he was often called "a walking encyclopedia" of law and a "lawyer's lawyer." He devoted much of his time and practice to small claims that did not bring in large fees; he would charge less for those clients who could not afford the usual fees.

In 1913, Cardozo successfully ran for a judgeship on the New York Supreme Court. Two months later he was appointed to New York's highest court, the Court of Appeals, eventually becoming the chief justice. He served for 20 years. His decisions usually involved integrating legal issues with the social and economic needs of the people. An example was the case of *MacPherson v. Buick Motor Co.* in 1916. The case involved implied warranty, and Cardozo's decision, adopted throughout the United States, stated that a person who purchased faulty merchandise has a right to expect compensation from the manufacturer even though the retailer actually owned the product immediately before the purchase.

In 1920, Cardozo was invited to lecture at Yale Law School. He delivered a series of lectures on how a judge reaches a decision. Cardozo's most famous work, *The Nature of the Judicial Process* (1921), was an outgrowth of this series.

In 1932 President Herbert Hoover nominated Cardozo to fill the vacancy on the United States Supreme Court on Justice Oliver Wendell Holmes's resignation. There were objections to his nomination on two grounds. First, many were not anxious to have a "bleeding-heart" liberal whose first priority was individual rights rather than the concerns of big corporations. Second, Cardozo was a Jew. With Brandeis already on the bench, many felt one Jew was enough. Through the support of Idaho Senator William Borah and Justice Harlan Stone, who threatened resignation, Cardozo was nominated and seated at the age of 62.

Although Cardozo was born into an Orthodox Jewish family, he did not share his family's religious fervor; however, he did maintain membership in a New York Sephardic congregation and opposed any change to traditional worship. Zionism did not interest Cardozo until he was moved to action with Hitler's rise in Germany and the resultant danger for European Jews. Cardozo realigned his support for Zionism when he realized a homeland for Jewish refugees was essential for their survival.

Cardozo earned many accolades and praise throughout his career. Franklin Roosevelt wrote of him, "I know of no jurist more learned in law, more liberal in its interpretation, more insistent on simple justice, keeping step with the progress of civilization and bettering the lot of the average citizen who make up mankind." Cardozo combined his keen intellect with his foremost concern—the rights and protection of ordinary citizens versus monopolies and big banks. He attributed his attitude to the lessons to be learned from 20 centuries of Jewish oppression. This, he claimed, was the basis for his compassionate decisions on social welfare issues.

After serving for six years in the Supreme Court, Cardozo died from heart disease and a stroke in Port Chester, New York. *See also* Law and Lawyers.

SHERRY OSTROFF
HOWARD SHAKER

BIBLIOGRAPHY

Levy, Beryl H. *Cardozo and Frontiers of Legal Thinking, With Selected Opinions.* Cleveland: Press of Case Western Reserve University, 1969.

Morris, Clarence, ed. *The Great Legal Philosophers: Selected Readings of Jurisprudence.* Philadelphia: University of Pennsylvania Press, 1959.

Paper, Lewis J. *Brandeis.* Englewood Cliffs, N.J.: Prentice-Hall, 1983.

Posner, Richard. *Cardozo: A Study in Reputation.* Chicago: University of Chicago Press, 1990.

Celler, Emanuel (1888–1981). Elected as a Democrat in 1922, "Mannie" Celler represented Brooklyn, New York, in the United States House of Representatives for half of a century until his retirement in 1973. For many years, he was chairman of the House Judiciary Committee and, after 1965, senior member of the House. A prominent progressive, Celler supported the New Deal and opposed the House Committee on Un-American Activities, but he truly built his reputation during a long career of battling immigration restrictions and monopolies.

Celler was born in Brooklyn and spent his entire life as a Brooklyn resident. He graduated from Brooklyn Boy's High School and then Columbia College. His parents died while he was in Columbia, but an uncle helped finance his education. Celler also earned money as a wine salesman, a job he kept even after he graduated from Columbia Law School and became a lawyer. Prior to World War I, he married Stella Baar, his high school girlfriend. While he worked for the government during the war, he began considering a political career. Running for Congress in 1922, Celler spoke about "the evils of prohibition and the virtues of the league of Nations" and won by a slim majority in a previously Republican district.

"All my life, in one way or another," Celler wrote in his autobiography, *You Never Leave Brooklyn* (1953), "I had been involved and associated with the immigrant and with the facets of immigration and naturalization." His fierce opposition to the Johnson Immigration Act (1924), which established national origin quotas, brought the young congressman his first acclaim. During the thirties, Celler consistently supported President Roosevelt's domestic policies.

After World War II, Celler became quite powerful in Washington. He first became chairman of the Judiciary Committee in 1949. Celler, a Zionist since the age of 25, pushed for the creation of the State of Israel. He opposed McCarthyism bitterly, voting against the Mundt-Nixon Communist Registration Bill (1948) and the Internal Security Act (1950). His major legislative success was the Celler-Kefauver Anti-Merger Act (1950), a significant addition to antitrust policies. He also authored the Civil Rights Acts of 1957 and 1960.

Celler once summed up his public philosophy in a sentence borrowed from Adlai Stevenson: "There is nothing more important than the people." In a long career, Celler demonstrated his determination to help the people who often could not help themselves: immigrants, workers, and minorities. His political courage carried him through 50 of the most turbulent years in American politics. Celler began his remarkable journey with campaigns for the League of Nations and ended it just before the scandals of Watergate. Thoughout that time, he remained tirelessly devoted to the people of Brooklyn in New York's Tenth Congressional District.

MATTHEW PINSKER

BIBLIOGRAPHY

Celler, Emanuel. *You Never Leave Brooklyn.* New York: Day, 1953.

Chess. Chess has held a place in Jewish culture since the Middle Ages, and many of the game's greatest players have been of Jewish descent. Why Jews have had an affinity for chess is unclear. Some experts say that the habit of mind engendered by Talmudic dialectic is similar to chess analysis. Grandmasters Akiba Rubinstein (1882–1961) and Aron Nimzovich (1886–1935), for example, emerged from schools of Talmudic training. There is no doubt that the game's intellectual qualities mesh well with the traditional Jewish love of learning.

Since the late nineteenth century, American Jews have been vital to the growth and popularity of chess worldwide. Wilhelm Steinitz (1836–1900), the first world champion, was an Austrian Jew who resided in America in his later years. It was in New York, St. Louis, and New Orleans that Steinitz played the first official world championship match in 1886 against Johannes Zukertort (1842–1888), a Polish Jew. Steinitz won by a score of 10-5 with five draws. Steinitz developed the theory of positional chess—the basis for the modern game—where a player tries to accumulate small, lasting advantages, and he popularized these ideas in his writings and public appearances.

Steinitz lost the title in 1894 to Emanual Lasker (1868–1941), a German Jewish mathematician, by a score of 10-5 with four draws. Lasker's toppling of the great Steinitz astounded the chess world. American chess fans, many of whom were recent Jewish immigrants, had a new hero. Lasker would finish his career with the highest winning percentage of any world champion, holding the title for an unprecedented 27 years. His victory at the age of 56 in the great New York 1924 tournament, ahead of his younger rivals Jose Raoul Capablanca (1888–1942) and Alexander Alekhine (1892–1946), is one of the high marks of chess history. Undoubtedly, American hegemony in international chess during the 1930s, when the United States won four consecutive Olympiads (Prague 1931, Folkestone 1933, Warsaw 1935, and Stockholm 1937), can be traced to the groundwork laid by Steinitz and Lasker.

In 1920, Samuel Reshevsky (b. 1911), a Polish Jew, immigrated with his parents to the United States. The 9-year-old "Sammy" gave memorable blindfold exhibitions throughout America—exploits no chess prodigy has ever surpassed. Reshevsky went on to capture six U.S. championship tournaments (1936, 1938, 1940, 1942, 1946, and 1969) and at his height was ranked in the world's top three players. If Reshevsky had not taken a five-year hiatus from serious competition during his adolescence to pursue religious studies, it is likely he would have won the world championship.

The first native-born American Jew to distinguish himself in international chess was Isaac Kashdan (1905–1985). During the late 1920s and early 1930s he was America's best player, though he was never able to capture the U.S. title. In 1928 at the Hague Olympiad, he spearheaded the U.S. team to second place behind Germany. Kashdan won the first-board prize with a score of 13-2. For many years he was the chess editor of the *Los Angeles Times*, but perhaps his most outstanding achievement was the founding of *Chess*

Review in 1933 with Al Horowitz (1907–1973) and Fred Reinfeld (1910–1964).

Reshevsky's true rival in the 1930s and 1940s was Reuben Fine (b. 1914). Although Fine never won the U.S. championship, his achievements internationally outstripped Reshevsky's. In 1937, Fine was the second for world champion Max Euwe (1901–1981) in his title defense against Alekhine. Then, in 1938, he was co-winner, along with Estonia's Paul Keres (1916–1975), of the AVRO (an acronym for a Dutch radio station) tournament, thought by many to be the strongest tournament of all time. It consisted of the world's top eight players in head-to-head matchups. (In the same tournament, Reshevsky finished fourth-sixth, tied with Alekhine and Euwe.) The world's top speed-chess player in the late 1930s and early 1940s, Fine opted not to compete in the 1948 Hague–Moscow world championship tournament, retiring from competition for a career as a Freudian psychoanalyst.

Other American Jews who competed successfully in the pre-Fischer years were Arnold Denker (b. 1914), 1944 U.S. champion; Herman Steiner (1905–1955), 1948 U.S. champion; Arthur Bisguier (b. 1929), 1954 U.S. champion; and Larry Evans (b. 1932), winner of four U.S. championships (1951, 1961–1962, 1968, and 1980).

During this period, important literary contributions were made by Horowitz, publisher of *Chess Review* (1933–1969), chess editor of the *New York Times* (1963–1973), and the author of more than 20 books; Irving Chernev (1900–1981), a brilliant writer and coauthor, with Kenneth Harkness (1898–1972), of the best-seller *Invitation to Chess*; and Reinfeld, the most prolific writer in the history of the game, with more than 200 titles to his credit.

The highest rated chess player of all time, with a final ELO rating of 2780, is Robert James Fischer (b. 1943). The son of a Jewish-American mother and a West-German father, "Bobby" was born in Chicago, Illinois, and moved to Brooklyn, New York, with his family in 1949. He was taught how to play chess that same year by his 11-year-old sister, though, according to Fischer, he did not "get good" until he was 12.

Once Fischer got going, there was no stopping him. In 1956, he won the U.S. junior championship. Later that year, in the Rosenwald Tournament, he played the "game of the century" against Donald Byrne (1930–1972), brother of Robert Byrne (b. 1928), long-time chess editor

of the *New York Times*. Experts consider this game the greatest ever played by a prodigy. At 14, Fischer became the youngest player ever to win the U.S. championship. Indeed, he has won it all eight times that he has competed (1957–1958, 1958–1959, 1959–1960, 1960–1961, 1962–1963, 1963–1964, 1965, and 1966). In 1958, at 15, he became the youngest grand master ever, finishing fifth in the Portoroz Interzonal Tournament. At Bled, Yugoslavia, 1961, Fischer went undefeated, finishing second to world champion Mikhail Tal (b. 1936) and beating him in their individual encounter. Fischer won the 1962 Stockholm Interzonal Tournament without losing a single game (13 wins, 9 draws), and in the 1963–1964 U.S. championship, Fischer triumphed over the entire field 11–0, the first and only time a U.S. champion has won all his games.

Fischer's greatest achievements, however, occurred in the early 1970s. In 1970, he crushed former world champion Tigran Petrosian (1929–1984)—two wins, two draws, and no losses—in the USSR-vs-the-Rest-of-the-World Match. He then won the Palma de Mallorca Interzonal, with fifteen wins, seven draws, and one loss. Fischer's victory made him one of the eight official challengers for the world championship held by Russia's Boris Spassky (b. 1937).

To meet Spassky, Fischer had to defeat three of the world's top grand masters in head-to-head matches. First up was Russia's Mark Taimanov (b. 1926), who Fischer overwhelmed 6–0, the first shutout of a grand master in modern times. Next was Denmark's Bent Larsen (b. 1935), and once again Fischer annihilated his opponent, 6–0. That left only former champion Petrosian, and, as in their previous 1970 showdown, Fischer won easily, with five wins, three draws, and one loss, winning the last four games straight.

Fischer and Spassky began their historic world championship match in Reykjavik, Iceland, on July 11, 1972. Remarkably, Fischer blundered away the first game and failed to show up for the second, forfeiting it and giving Spassky a two-game edge. But then Fischer won the third, fifth, sixth, eighth, and tenth games (the fourth, seventh, and ninth were drawn), building a lead that Spassky found insurmountable. When Spassky resigned the twenty-first game on September 1, Fischer had become the first American to win the world chess championship and the only non-Russian to hold the title since 1937.

Fischer opted not to defend his title in 1975, having withdrawn from public life after his 1972 victory, and thus Anatoly Karpov (b. 1951) of the Soviet Union was awarded Fischer's title without having defeated Fischer across the board. (In 1985, Karpov lost his title to compatriot Garry Kasparov [b. 1963], a Jew from Baku.)

In Fischer's absence, American Jews are still making important contributions to championship chess. In the vanguard are Lev Alburt (b. 1948), 1985 and 1986 U.S. champion; Joel Benjamin (b. 1964), 1987 U.S. champion; Michael Wilder (b. 1962), 1988 U.S. champion; Michael Rohde (b. 1959), 1989 national open champion; and Max Dlugy (b. 1966), 1985 world junior champion. The United States, once again, is becoming a world power in chess, and, as always, American Jews are leading the way.

BRUCE PANDOLFINI

BIBLIOGRAPHY

Gaige, Jeremy. *Chess Personalia: A Biobibliography.* Jefferson, N.C.: McFarland, 1987.

Hooper, David, and Whyld, Ken. *The Oxford Companion to Chess.* New York: Oxford University Press, 1984.

Pandolfini, Bruce. *The Best of Chess Life and Review.* Vols. 1 and 2. New York: Simon & Schuster, 1988.

Ribalow, Harold, and Ribalow, Meir. *The Great Jewish Chess Champions.* New York: Hipprocene, 1987.

Spanier, David. *Total Chess.* New York: Dutton, 1984.

Whyld, Ken. *Chess: The Records.* New York: Oxford University Press, 1986.

Chicago. The Jewish population of metropolitan Chicago in the late 1980s was approximately 248,000. This population, which included almost 6000 Russian immigrants who arrived between 1971 and 1981, had been relatively stable in the previous 30 years, declining less than 10 percent. Among the Jewish communities in the United States Chicago ranked fifth.

The community supported 21 Conservative synagogues affiliated with the United Synagogues of America, 32 Reform temples affiliated with the Union of Hebrew Congregations, and 25 Orthodox synagogues affiliated with the Chicago Rabbinical Council. The community also supported the nondenominational Spertus College of Judaica, the Spertus Museum of Judaica, and modern Orthodox Hebrew Theological College.

Jews were among the earliest settlers in the city of Chicago, which was chartered in 1837. They came to the United States from the small towns of Bavaria and from other German states. A small group of German Jews living in New York in 1841 formed an association to set up a colony in a western state, and they purchased a farm near Schamberg, Illinois. But these were urban people, and most left the farm for Chicago, where they found that several Jewish shopkeepers had preceded them. The small community in 1845 purchased an acre of land from the city for a cemetery. Then at a meeting on October 3, 1846, in the dry goods store of Rosenfeld and Rosenberg at 155 Lake Street, 15 men organized Chicago's first congregation—an Orthodox congregation—Kehilat Anshe Maarav, KAM. The congregation, in 1851, built a small frame synagogue on Clark Street, south of Adams Street. Two years later those members of KAM who were natives of German Poland left the congregation to form their own synagogue, B'nai Shalom.

Reform Judaism arrived in Chicago in the person of German-born teacher Bernhard Felsenthal (1822–1908), who in June 1858 brought together a group of Chicago men interested in organizing a Jewish Reform Society. As a result, these men left KAM to establish Chicago's first Reform temple, Congregation Sinai, which Felsenthal served as rabbi. He left in 1864 to take the pulpit of Chicago's newly established second Reform temple, Temple Zion.

When the Civil War began, Chicago favored the Union. Chicago Jews, numbering 1500 in a total population of 10,260, generously contributed men and money to the cause. One of the companies of the Eighty-second Regiment of Illinois volunteers was formed by Jews. Within three days in August 1862, the Chicago community recruited 100 men and raised $10,000 to provide a bonus for each soldier. The *Chicago Tribune* praised the Jewish community, saying its patriotic efforts could not be surpassed.

After the Civil War, the city grew rapidly, but development came to an abrupt halt as a result of the Great Chicago Fire of October 1871 that began on the eve of Simchat Torah and devastated the entire city. When the building's roof collapsed, thirteen patients in the Jewish hospital, which had been built by the United Hebrew Relief Association in 1868, died in their beds. The fire also destroyed five synagogues and four B'nai B'rith lodges. Jews took an active role in relief and in the rebuilding of the city. The efforts of banker Henry Greenebaum (1833–1914), who had been the first Jew to serve on the city council (1856), so impressed the editors of the *Chicago Tribune* that the newspaper put forward his name as a possible mayoral candidate.

By 1880, the growing city had a population of 500,000, including 10,000 Jews. Then pogroms in Russia triggered the mass exodus of Eastern European Jews from the Russian empire, and thousands of Jewish refugees made their way to Chicago. Displacing earlier arrived Irish, German, and Bohemian immigrants, these Yiddish-speaking Orthodox Jews settled west of the Chicago River and south of Harrison Street in what became one of the poorest, most congested areas of the city. The Eastern Europeans established their own small congregations, religious schools, relief societies, *landsmanschaften*, and, in 1906, the Marks Nathan Home, their own orphanage. That same year the Fifth Illinois District elected a Bohemian Jewish immigrant, Democrat Adolph J. Sabath (1866–1952), to Congress. A champion of liberal causes and a devoted Zionist, Sabath remained in Congress until his death.

During the period of Eastern European immigration, the pulpit of Sinai Congregation was occupied by the outstanding radical reform rabbi of the era, Emil G. Hirsch (1851–1923). With some degree of guidance from Hirsch, Jewish women played an important role in looking after the welfare of the immigrants. One of the pioneer organizations in this field was the National Council of Jewish Women founded by Hannah Greenebaum Solomon (1858–1942) at the Chicago World's Fair of 1893. The previous year three prosperous south-side women had established Chicago's first Jewish orphanage, the Chicago Home for Jewish Orphans. In addition, Congregation Sinai set up the Ladies' Industrial School for Girls, which in October 1890 became the Chicago Jewish Training School.

Julius Rosenwald (1862–1932), president of Sears and Roebuck, was another prominent Chicagoan who looked after the welfare of the Eastern Europeans. Among his many important contributions was support for the Associated Jewish Charities of Chicago, for which in 1907 he served as president. Rosenwald was also active in the affairs of the Chicago Hebrew Institute, after 1922 known as the Jewish Peoples Institute. The JPI became a national model for future Jewish community centers.

Zionism came to Chicago with the Eastern European immigrants. The Chicago Zion Society was formed in 1895, and two years later a small group of Chicago Jews organized a fraternal society called the Knights of Zion. When in November 1917 the British government published the Balfour Declaration, a mass meeting attended by the governor of Illinois was held at the Chicago Hebrew Institute. According to the Jewish communal newspaper the *Sentinel*, the crowd responded to an appeal for funds by throwing $15,000 in small bills on to the stage. In the period between World War I and World War II under the leadership of Judge Julian Mack (1866–1943), Judge Harry Fisher (1882–1952), and Rabbi Solomon Goldman (1893–1953), Chicago Jewry continued to be active in the movement to establish a Jewish state in Palestine.

After World War I, the Jewish community came together to support the American Jewish Joint Distribution Committee's national campaign to raise $14 million for European Jewry. Jacob M. Loeb (1875–1944) created the slogan "Suppose you were starving!" Chicago exceeded its million-dollar quota by $850,000. Chicago's concern for European Jewry continued, and during the 1930s the community responded to the plight of refugees fleeing Hitler. A special effort was made on behalf of refugee scholars. The Federation of Jewish Charities worked out a plan whereby the University of Chicago hired refugee scholars and the Federation paid their salaries.

After World War II, Chicago's Jewish population numbered 268,969. Large numbers of Jews began to leave the city for the northern suburbs, including the village of Skokie, where approximately 7000 Holocaust survivors settled. The unity of the city and suburbs was underlined when in 1975–1976 a small group of American Nazis attempted to march through Skokie and met well-organized resistance.

MIRIAM HARON

BIBLIOGRAPHY

Berkow, Ira. *Maxwell Street: Survival in a Bazaar.* Garden City, N.Y.: Doubleday, 1977.

Cutler, Irving. "The Jews of Chicago: From Shetetl to Suburb." In *Ethnic Chicago*, edited by Peter D'Alroy Jones and Melvin Holli. Grand Rapids, Mich.: Eerdmans, rev. ed. 1983.

Kramer, Sydelle, and Masur, Jenny, ed. *Jewish Grandmothers.* Boston: Beacon Press, 1976.

Mazur, Edward. "Jewish Chicago: From Diversity to Community." In *Ethnic Chicago.* Edited by Peter D'Alroy Jones and Melvin Holli. Grand Rapids, Mich.: Eerdmans, rev. ed. 1983.

Wirth, Louis. *The Ghetto.* Chicago: University of Chicago Press, 1956.

Children's Literature. *See* JEWISH CHILDREN'S LITERATURE.

Civil Rights. Widespread prejudice and intolerance toward Jews and blacks existed in the United States at the turn of the century. Americans believed that blacks and newly arrived immigrants were mentally and physically inferior and were responsible for rising rates of poverty and crime. Distinguished newspapers and magazines popularized vulgar caricatures, and school texts accepted and passed these on as a matter of course. Even leading social scientists, many of them active in social reform movements, contributed to an ethos of racial exclusivity. Beginning in the late nineteenth century and reaching a climax in the 1920s, harsh and restrictive immigration laws cut back sharply on East and South European immigrants and Asian immigrants and favored fair-haired and lighter-skinned peoples from Northern Europe.

Between 1890 and 1910, the disenfranchisement of blacks in the South that began following the Civil War was completed. Laws requiring segregation in education and other areas of life were enacted in other parts of the country as well as in the South. In 1896, the Supreme Court held in *Plessy v. Ferguson* that as long as facilities provided to blacks were equal to those of whites—which they rarely were—separate racial facilities were constitutionally permissible. The system was reinforced by a reign of terror. In 1907, Governor Vardaman of Mississippi warned, "If necessary, every Negro in the state will be lynched: it will be done to maintain white supremacy." Black soldiers returning from World War I, expecting to enjoy the fruits of winning the "battle to preserve democracy," were greeted instead with the "red summer" of 1919. There were more than 20 bloody race riots in every part of the country that summer; more than 70 blacks were lynched: 11 black men, some of them soldiers in uniform, were burned alive. The National Association for the Advancement of Colored People (NAACP) reported that between 1889 and 1918 some 3224 men and women had been lynched, and no one knows how many had disappeared without a trace.

The situation in which Jews found themselves was also difficult. Having grown up in a small Jewish community in Fitzgerald, Georgia, Morris B. Abram recalls in his autobiography being unnerved by the lynching in 1915 of a young Jewish manufacturer, Leo Frank, falsely convicted of murdering a young girl. A revived Ku Klux Klan targeted Jews, Roman Catholics, and blacks as foreign and evil forces. In the 1920s, Henry Ford's *Dearborn Independent* spewed forth a steady stream of anti-Semitism. While Ford appealed crudely to the passions of small-town and rural Protestantism, more sophisticated forms of prejudice and discrimination were used in society's most elevated circles: major universities, such as Columbia and New York University, limited the enrollment of Jewish students by quotas. Only a sharp reaction by Jews and others to the public announcement that Harvard planned to follow suit caused Harvard to abandon its plan. (Instead, informal quotas were used.)

It was in this social and psychological setting that Jewish defense agencies were organized. The American Jewish Committee was founded in 1906 in the wake of the Kishinev pogrom in Russia, mainly by a group of wealthy German Jews. Those unhappy with the "uptown" character of the American Jewish Committee organized the American Jewish Congress in 1918 with a constituency drawn primarily from East European Jews. The Anti-Defamation League (ADL) was formed by B'nai B'rith during the murder trial of Leo Frank in 1913.

The *Frank* case sent a wave of fear surging through the Jewish community. Faced with outright anti-Semitic violence, Jews became more involved with the broader movement for civil rights in America. Philanthropists such as Julius Rosenwald, Herbert Lehman, and Samuel and Mary Fels were major contributors to the NAACP, the Urban League, and other black organizations. Earlier, Rosenwald emerged as the leading force in the creation of educational facilities for blacks in the South.

Not long after the formation of the NAACP in 1909, a Jew was named chairman of the board—Joel Spingarn of New York. For most of the period between 1911 and 1934, he and social worker Mary White Ovington shared the NAACP board chairmanship. During this time, Spingarn, working with W. E. B. DuBois, the black social scientist, was the major NAACP policy strategist and activist, making eloquent public appeals for the cause of black equality. In 1914, Spingarn established the Spingarn Award given annually by the NAACP to the black American who has "made the highest achievement during the preceding year or years, in any honorable field of endeavor." Following Spingarn's death in

1939, DuBois dedicated his autobiography to him.

But the seeds of later conflicts were sown by this early white and Jewish involvement in black civil rights efforts. When the black nationalist Marcus Garvey visited DuBois at the NAACP's headquarters, he was "dumbfounded" that "but for Mr. Dill, DuBois, and the office boy" he could not tell whether he was in "a white office or that of the National Association for the Advancement of Colored People."

In the 1920s, Louis Marshall (a board member of the NAACP who, as head of the American Jewish Committee, had carried the *Frank* case to the Supreme Court) argued a number of the early NAACP cases before the Supreme Court. His attack on restrictive covenants was not successful in 1926, but in 1948 the Court adopted his view that restrictive covenants were not legally enforceable. In 1927, Marshall wrote a brief for the NAACP whose arguments were later followed by the Court when it outlawed the exclusion of blacks from voting in the Texas white primary.

Years later, Jack Greenberg served as the assistant counsel of the NAACP's Legal Defense and Education Fund under Thurgood Marshall and then became its head in 1961, running the organization through the 1970s.

Jews with access to centers of power helped, also, in the development of black leadership. When Howard University President Mordecai Johnson decided to set up a law school, he turned to the first Jewish justice on the Supreme Court, Louis D. Brandeis, for advice. Brandeis urged him to get a full-time and "real faculty out there or you're always going to have a fifth-rate law school." Johnson recruited Charles Houston, a student and lifelong protégé of Felix Frankfurter. Under Houston and later Thurgood Marshall, a brilliant group of black attorneys was trained at Howard University and fed into the NAACP and its Legal Defense Fund. This group would soon take over the assault on segregation in all areas of American life.

Welcome as it was, the role of Jews was, at times, patronizing. Brandeis told Johnson that he could always tell when he was reading a brief prepared by a black attorney because of its poor preparation. Hasia Diner has argued that an altruistic desire to help blacks was not the only thing motivating wealthy and assimilated Jews involved in early campaigns for civil rights. German Jews were reluctant to fight anti-Semitism openly,

Diner suggests, for fear of being seen as too "pushy" or "demanding." So they expressed their frustration through association with a number of progressive causes, including the cause of black equality. If blacks gained greater acceptance, the position of Jews would also be improved. There is probably some truth to these assertions; self-interest of one kind or another undoubtedly played a part.

However, a new revisionism has emerged among a number of black historians that assigns a degree of almost malevolent design to the German Jews' efforts. David Levering Lewis, for example, refers to the "caginess" of elite Jews and argues that court victories that Jews helped to bring about deflected blacks from grappling with more important economic and political needs. This view notwithstanding, blacks and Jews agreed that certain legal barriers had to be removed before economic and political gains could even be attempted, let alone achieved. Without doubt, what was truly at stake in those years, for both groups, was fulfillment of an American ideal: equality of opportunity. Upper-class Jews continued to suffer from restrictions, and because of this they empathized with the plight of blacks. Their philosophy, growing in part out of Reform Judaism's emphasis on social justice, was that no minority was safe until the rights of all minorities were protected. Moreover, Jews at all levels of the social scale identified with blacks and threw themselves wholeheartedly into the fight for their rights. The organ of immigrant Jews, the socialist *Jewish Daily Forward*, compared the East St. Louis riot of 1917 to the Kishinev pogrom of 1903: "Kishinev and St. Louis, the same soil, the same people." Jewish labor unions were among the first to accept blacks as members when other unions would not.

Perhaps the most significant role played by Jews in attacking the racist thinking of the times was through the fledgling field of social science, which was devising new theories of environmental causation and new notions of equality. Two of the leading votaries of this new science in the United States were W. E. B. DuBois and Franz Boas—a black and a Jew.

DuBois's 1899 book, *The Philadelphia Negro*, was the first major sociological study of blacks in the United States. With extraordinary richness of detail it delineated the social circumstances that contributed to poverty, crime, and other problems among the black underclass in that city. DuBois, however, was barred from any important place in academic circles because of his color.

Boas, who had experienced anti-Semitism in Germany before coming to the United States in 1896, taught for four decades at Columbia. In *The Mind of Primitive Man* (1911) he attacked the "common sense" of the day that held inferior treatment of blacks to be justified because of innate inferiority. The traits of the Negro, Boas argued, were explained by his historical experience, especially his former slave status. The Negro was torn from his native soil and old standards of life and thrust into slavery, family disorganization, and severe economic struggle against great odds—all these facts provided sufficient explanation for his inferior position in society without resort to hereditary or genetic theories.

Boas trained a group of American sociologists and anthropologists that included Alexander Goldenweiser, Ruth Benedict, A. L. Krober, Margaret Mead, Melville Herskovits, Edward Sapir, and Robert H. Lowie, all of whom became prominent figures in the broader American culture. In their zeal to assault conventional notions of racial and genetic differences, and thereby overcome prejudice and discrimination, these scholars inadvertently laid the groundwork for later difficulties. By developing important concepts of cultural evolution and societal conditioning, they seemed to be suggesting, in the words of one, that blacks were "only white men with black skins, nothing more, nothing less"—strip away extraneous barriers that limited their opportunities and they would be like anyone else. This, it has become clear more recently, ignored the long-term effects of discrimination and disadvantage. Often alienated from their own ethnic or religious backgrounds, these thinkers paid little attention to the positive aspects of group identity and seemed to be urging blacks and other ethnic outsiders to disappear into the melting pot. Thus when the civil rights revolution took a turn years later toward black nationalism and black power, it seemed as if the cultural pride of blacks was going one way and this sociological and "Jewish" emphasis on cultural assimilation and integration was going another.

In the 1940s, the older generation of upper-class German Jewish leaders was passing from the scene to be replaced by full-time professionals who broadened the outlook of the Jewish defense—or, as they now came to be called, community relations—organizations. Unlike their more conservative predecessors, these lawyers, social workers, and social psychologists were generally from poor East European backgrounds and were

men of the political Left. In a 1945 essay entitled "Full Equality in a Free Society," Alexander Pekelis of the American Jewish Congress declared "American Jews will find more reasons for taking an affirmative attitude toward being Jews as members of an organized movement, if they are part and parcel of a great American and human force working for a better world . . . whether or not the individual issues touch directly upon so-called Jewish interest." Working for a society in which economic disadvantage and intolerance would have no place became for Jews "an almost religio-cultural obsession."

During World War II, the American Jewish Committee under John Slawson undertook a major examination of the roots of prejudice. Utilizing a group of refugee German Jewish scholars of the "Frankfurt School," Slawson commissioned the famous Studies in Prejudice series, the lead volume of which was *The Authoritarian Personality* (1950). These studies focused on the personality of the bigot rather than the victim and suggested that prejudice arose out of early child-rearing practices of rigid conformity. Published at the height of the McCarthy phenomenon, the works had an enormous impact. They spawned several hundred allied studies in subsequent years whose ideas soon found their way into the mainstream of American life.

The ADL in the meantime launched massive educational efforts confronting racial and religious intolerance with films, filmstrips, car cards, and radio (later television) announcements that reached virtually every nook and cranny in the land. "What difference does it make what his race or religion is," said the caption of a typical car card showing a little black boy standing on a baseball field in tears, surrounded by white children. "He can pitch can't he?"

Critical of such "brotherhood sloganeering," which they thought was ineffective, the more populist American Jewish Congress set up a Commission on Community Interrelations (CCI) in 1944 under the refugee social psychologist Kurt Lewin. Lewin and his associates were among the first to develop a comprehensive rationale for legislative efforts on behalf of civil rights. The following year the American Jewish Congress established a Commission on Law and Social Action under Pekelis. Discrimination, Pekelis argued, had its roots in "private governments"—concentrations of power in the hands of executives of giant corporations, university trustees, real estate boards, and professional associations.

The Jewish agencies with their experienced staffs—the American Jewish Congress had more civil rights attorneys at this point than the Justice Department—launched major campaigns across the country to break those concentrations of power. They demanded fair educational opportunities, fair employment, and, later, fair housing practices. Legislation on these issues was drafted in their national or regional offices or by local Jewish community relations councils. Public campaigns were organized in cooperation with church, labor, civic, and black groups to secure its enactment. In the South, Morris Abram and Alexander F. Miller, ADL's Atlanta director, coauthored a widely distributed pamphlet, "How to Stop Violence in Your Community." Some 5 states and 55 cities soon adopted two of the most important laws discussed in the pamphlet, those prohibiting the wearing of masks and the burning of crosses without permission, moves that stripped the Klan of anonymity and consequently much of its power.

By the early 1960s, there were 20 states and 40 cities with some kind of fair employment law covering 60 percent of the total population and about 50 percent of the country's minorities. Spurred by a 1958 New York City initiative, 17 states and cities had, by 1963, enacted laws banning discrimination in the rental or sale of housing. Even as prejudice and discrimination began to ease for Jews, their funds, institutional manpower, and influence continued to press forward the civil rights agenda, to the dismay of supporters of the status quo.

Howard Law School by this time was graduating a skilled group of black attorneys to lead the civil rights fight, for which Jews and Jewish groups marshaled social-scientific support. In 1950, the year *The Authoritarian Personality* was published, the American Jewish Committee hired black psychologist Kenneth B. Clark to prepare a paper on the impact of segregation on children for presentation at the White House Conference on Children. Based in part on the Studies in Prejudice series, the paper showed the psychological damage that segregation caused black children. Following the conference, Clark was invited by NAACP attorneys to collaborate with them on expert testimony in three of the four cases they were preparing to argue before the Supreme Court. In its historic *Brown* decision of 1954, the Supreme Court ruled that racial segregation in public schools had a deleterious effect on the "hearts and minds" of black children. The Court

based its decision, in part, on "modern authority," referring in its famous footnote 11 to the original Clark manuscript prepared for the American Jewish Committee, as well as two CCI (American Jewish Congress) investigations.

Blacks were now charting new strategies and leading civil rights battles. Starting with the Montgomery bus boycott in 1955 led by Martin Luther King and then through sit-ins, freedom rides, and other direct action techniques, they, along with sympathetic whites, began to challenge official systems of subordination by putting their bodies on the line. It is sometimes said that as blacks took over their fight, Jews resented this and began to withdraw from it. Jews joined enthusiastically and in disproportionate numbers in these often physically dangerous confrontations. In the summer of 1961, they made up two-thirds of the white Freedom Riders who traveled into the South to desegregate interstate transportation. In 1964, they comprised from a third to a half of the Mississippi "Freedom Summer" volunteers led by the Student Nonviolent Coordinating Committee (SNCC). It was in Mississippi that two Jewish youths, Andrew Goodman and Michael Schwerner, were martyred along with a black, James Chaney.

These protest tactics had their basis in the earlier labor and socialist movements in which Jews were so conspicuously involved. Two products of this movement were A. Philip Randolph and Bayard Rustin. Randolph forced the Roosevelt administration to issue an executive order in 1941 creating the first Fair Employment Practices Commission and later suggested the famous 1963 March on Washington, which Rustin organized.

Recent research makes clear that an Afro-American–Jewish radical community survived occasional internal conflicts during the 1930s, 1940s, and 1950s to become "a seedbed for civil rights activism during the 1960s." It was in this milieu, one scholar reports, that "blacks gained awareness of protest and propaganda techniques and a faith that these techniques, despite the fact that they were used by small numbers of radicals, might someday change American society." Several of the leaders of the new phase of the civil rights revolution that came forward in the 1960s were graduates of this Afro-American–Jewish radical culture. It was through Morris Milgram of the Workers Defense League, and through the Young Peoples Socialist League, that James Farmer began as a labor organizer in the South. Farmer helped invigorate a dormant Congress on

Racial Equality (CORE) and led it through its most tumultuous year. Stokely Carmichael, head of SNCC, had been strongly influenced by Jews he met at the Bronx High School of Science in New York, where he associated with various Socialist and Communist youth groups. Carmichael's first demonstration—ironically, in light of his later views—was on behalf of Israel.

The conflicts that began to take place increasingly between blacks and Jews were not caused by the Jews being displaced in the crusade for civil rights. Neither were they caused by any failure on the part of Jews to show enthusiasm for the growing black identity movement, for that matter. Rather, there was a transformation of the civil rights revolution into a race revolution. This brought forward a new group of black leaders, men like Malcolm X., Carmichael, Eldridge Cleaver, and H. Rap Brown, who wanted to withdraw from alliances with whites in order to build black identity and black power. These men associated themselves with left-wing revolutionary movements around the world and turned away from the liberal-reformist strategies of Martin Luther King and others, strategies by which ethnic outsiders have traditionally sought and gained full entry into American life. The embattled state of Israel became, for the new breed, an outpost of "Western imperialism" in the Middle East. This thrust was often accompanied by provocative, anti-Semitic statements, which rankled at a time when Israel was the cause of renewed *Jewish* pride and identity. Finally, the desire of black leaders to use racial preferences as a means of making up for past injustices worried Jews. Attempts by Jewish agencies to challenge quotas in the courts exacerbated the situation further. Jews by this time were turning inward, particularly following the Six Day War in 1967 and the Yom Kippur War in 1973. They reacted strongly to confrontations like the teachers' strike in New York City in 1968 and the effort to put in low-cost housing in a predominantly Jewish area of Queens a few years later. Tensions have arisen in the 1980s, most notably following appearances around the country by black nationalist leader Louis Farrakhan, who expressed anti-Jewish sentiments along with appeals for black empowerment. These appearances put local black leaders on the spot. The bid by Jesse Jackson, who was critical of Israel's position in the Middle East, to capture the Democratic Party's presidential nomination in 1984 and 1988 has also exacerbated relations. In addition, some black leaders have expressed concern about Israel's trade relations with South Africa and its policies on the West Bank.

A considerable amount of good will continues to exist, nevertheless, in both communities. It is reflected in the strong bonds between Jewish and black politicos on Capitol Hill in Washington. The former have been in the vanguard of legislative attacks on apartheid in South Africa, while the latter have given consistent backing for economic and military aid to Israel. Whatever the future may hold, the fact remains that Jews, Jewish groups, and blacks, working together with other allies, have created in the twentieth century what political scientist John P. Roche has called "a new ideology of civil liberty" that stands as a major expansion of the democratic idea. *See also* Black–Jewish Relations.

MURRAY FRIEDMAN

BIBLIOGRAPHY

Benson, Lenora E. *The Negroes and the Jews.* 1971.

Diner, Hasia. *In the Almost Promised Land: American Jews and Blacks, 1915–1935.* Westport, Conn.: Greenwood Press, 1977.

Kaufman, Jonathan. *Broken Alliance.* New York: New American Library, 1989.

Civil War. At the onset of the Civil War in 1861, the population of the Jewish communities in the North and South numbered about 150,000, a fraction of a percent of the general community, with most residing in the North. For each, the war was a struggle to establish principles of justice and equality, for both communities suffered from expressions of ignorance, prejudice, and intolerance exacerbated by the conditions of war. It is in this era that the concept of an America comprised of Catholics, Protestants, and Jews first took hold. In part, this came about as a result of the efforts of Rabbi Arnold Fischel of New York, who urged that Jewish clergy be appointed to the Corps of Chaplains in the Union forces. A congressional act of July 22, 1861, provided that only regularly ordained Christian ministers could serve as chaplains. It took over a year for authorities to recognize the need for a Jewish chaplain, but on September 19, 1862, Jacob Frankel became the first American rabbi to serve as an army chaplain. Surprisingly, no such religious restrictions had applied in the Confederacy.

The other major incident that concerned the Jewish community was covered by General

Order No. 11 issued by General Ulysses S. Grant on December 17, 1862, which called for the expulsion of all Jews "as a class" from his army department. The order blatantly reflected the prejudices of not only Grant but also that of high officials in both the Union Army and the United States Government. Cesar Kaskel of Paducah, Kentucky, immediately traveled to Washington to ask President Abraham Lincoln, whom many Jews admired and revered, to intercede, while others vigorously lobbied against Grant's action. As a result, on January 4, 1863, the order was revoked by Henry W. Halleck, the General-in-Chief of the Army. It should be noted, however, that following this episode Grant's relationship with the Jewish community was exemplary, and he became an intimate friend of many individual Jews.

Of the approximately 10,000 Jews who served in the armies, 7000 were in the Union forces, while 3000 were in the Confederate forces; over 500 lost their lives. All these numbers reflected a Jewish presence far beyond their proportion in the general population. Despite their activities on behalf of their respective communities, Jews were subjected to anti-Semitic diatribes. The tragedies and difficulties of war caused many, especially in the Confederacy, to resort to such outbursts. Southern Jews were particularly vulnerable because of the prominence of Judah P. Benjamin, who held numerous high offices in a losing cause and served as a personal adviser and confidant of Confederate President Jefferson Davis.

During the Civil War period, the majority of Jews in the North became aligned with the Republican Party, an alliance maintained until just before the New Deal of the 1930s. The prospects of unrestricted immigration, increased industrialization and urbanization, a transcontinental railroad, liberalized and expanding banking as well as seemingly unlimited economic opportunities, formed the basis of this political loyalty as well as the basis for both future business enterprises and fortunes. *See also* Military, The.

BERNARD WAX

BIBLIOGRAPHY

Evans, Eli N. *Judah P. Benjamin: The Jewish Confederate.* New York: Free Press, 1988.

Korn, Bertram W. *American Jewry and the Civil War.* Philadelphia: Jewish Publication Society, 1951.

Publication of the American Jewish Historical Society, No. 4 (June 1961).

Cohen, Arthur A. (1928–1986). Novelist, theologian, cultural critic, and publisher, Arthur A. Cohen, who was born in New York City and educated at the University of Chicago and the Jewish Theological Seminary, was one of the most distinctive figures in recent American Jewish intellectual life. Cohen's first books—*The Natural and the Supernatural Jew* (1962) and *The Myth of the Judaeo-Christian Tradition* (1970)—earned him an early reputation as a highly original Jewish thinker. From the early seventies onward, Cohen turned increasingly to writing fiction. In five novels, including *In the Days of Simon Stern* (1973) and *An Admirable Woman* (1983), he explored further the questions that had dominated his earlier writing—the shape of belief and of imagination in the modern world, the situation of the Jewish artist and intellectual, and, in particular, the relationship between religion and literature.

In both his theology and fiction, Cohen offered a vision of Jewish belief that was existential in tone yet also deeply sensitive to the realities of history, particularly to the modern historical experience of the Jewish people in the Nazi death camps and in the aftermath of World War II. Cohen's religious thinking was influenced by Martin Buber and Franz Rosenzweig. Distinguishing between the "natural" Jew who lives in history and the "supernatural" Jew who exists in the timeless realm of covenantal belief, Cohen was extremely sensitive to the paradoxes of Jewish existence in the context of modern Christian culture. Though personally involved in dialogue with Christian theologians (and deeply influential among them), Cohen polemicized in one famous essay against "the myth of the Judaeo-Christian tradition" (1979). Yet he also emphasized the shared problematics, the common ultimacy, that Jewish and Christian theology alike faced in the aftermath of "the Tremendum," as Cohen called the crisis of belief created by the Holocaust for both Judaism and Christianity.

The sense of situational paradox that informs his theological writing—the fact, as Cohen once remarked, that one cannot think about God without also considering the mind that is thinking about God—can help to explain why Cohen turned from theology to writing fiction. *In the Days of Simon Stern* (1973), his most representative novel, Cohen narrates the life of Simon Stern, a millionaire businessman in New York City who, in the aftermath of the Holocaust, attempts to save the survivors of the death camps and ensure the renewal of Judaism by building for them what is in effect a new "Temple." By the book's end, however, this sanctuary undergoes destruction just as the two previous temples in Jewish history.

More than simply an attempt to recast the messianic theme in Judaism in contemporary terms, *Simon Stern* is actually an incredibly ambitious elaboration in narrative of a concept that is essentially theological, the idea of the "failed," as opposed to false, messiah. This is a concept that Cohen would later extend in his post-Holocaust theology to the notion of a God who is imperfect but not impossible, less than omnipotent yet not utterly powerless or dead. In the novel the idea is elevated to story; or more precisely, the fictional life of Simon Stern turns, in the course of the narrative, from novel to hagiography to theological myth, acquiring a compelling force that exceeds its success judged solely within the terms of the novel or the theological treatise. If one wished to specify the book's true genre, it would probably be necessary to invent a new name for it, something on the order of the theological epic. For what Cohen was primarily attempting was to use narrative to recover for theology its epic grandeur, a monumentality of form comparable to its subject matter.

In his last published novel, *An Admirable Woman* (1983), Cohen found the fictional persona closest perhaps to his own voice—in the character of a German Jewish emigré intellectual who was reminiscent of Hannah Arendt and other scholar writers who came to America from Europe during and after the war. That Cohen should have found his voice in such a persona was not accidental. In many ways, his own literary career was more typical of the European intellectual than of the American. For one thing, Cohen eschewed the academic establishment: he did not hold advanced degrees or a university appointment, making his living instead as a publisher (of Noonday Press and Meridian Books, two houses he founded) and as a dealer in rare art documents. A genuine man of letters, Cohen was an acknowledged authority on the history of modern typography and design; he wrote frequently on art history and general culture and edited several influential anthologies.

Rosenzweig once wrote that theology must be smuggled into life; Cohen smuggled theology into literature. Although often elusive and difficult, the remarkable character of Cohen's writing lies in his desire to invent a literary discourse for the singular matters—Jewish and imaginative—

that obsessed him, a language that would at once be sufficiently expressive, articulate, and grand to meet the requirements of the difficult, often obscure subjects he wrote about. The passionate, idiosyncratic writing that resulted was like nothing else in contemporary American Jewish literature.

DAVID STERN

BIBLIOGRAPHY
Theology
Cohen, Arthur A., and Kaplan, Mordechai M. *If Not Now, When?* Wycote, PA: Reconstructionist Press, 1973.
——. *Martin Buber.* New York: Hilary House, 1957.
——. *The Myth of the Judaeo-Christian Tradition.* New York: Harper & Row, 1970.
——. *The Natural and the Supernatural Jew.* New York: Behrman House, rev. ed. 1979.
——. *The Tremendum.* New York: Crossroad, 1988.

Fiction
Cohen, Arthur A. *Acts of Theft.* Chicago: University of Chicago Press, 1980.
——. *An Admirable Woman.* Boston: Godine, 1983.
——. *Artists and Enemies: Three Novellae.* Boston: Godine, 1987.
——. *The Carpenter Years.* New York: New American Library, 1967.
——. *A Hero in His Time.* New York: Random House, 1976.
——. *In the Days of Simon Stern.* Chicago: University of Chicago Press, 1987.

Art and Literary Criticism
Cohen, Arthur A. *Herbert Bayer.* Cambridge, Mass.: MIT Press, 1984.
——. *Osip Emilevich Mandelstam: An Essay in Antiphon.* New York: Ardis, 1974.
——. *Sonia Delaunay.* New York: Abrams, 1988.

Readers and Anthologies
Cohen, Arthur A. *Arguments and Doctrines: A Reader of Jewish Thinking in the Aftermath of the Holocaust.* New York: Harper & Row, 1970.
——, and Mendes-Flohr, Paul. *Contemporary Jewish Religious Thought.* New York: Scribner, 1986.
——. *The Jew: Essays from Der Jude.* University: University of Alabama Press, 1980.

Cohen, Morris Raphael (1880–1947).

Morris Raphael Cohen was a thinker, a philosopher, and perhaps most important of all, an influential teacher. He was born in Minsk, Russia, emigrating to the United States in 1892. For most of his life Cohen lived in New York City in the predominantly Jewish neighborhoods of Manhattan and the Bronx.

When he was 20 years old, Cohen graduated from the College of the City of New York (CCNY); two years later he became an instructor there in mathematics and then advanced to the philosophy department. He received his Ph.D. degree in philosophy from Harvard University, where he had been an able student with, though not a disciple of, William James.

At Harvard, Cohen roomed with Felix Frankfurter, a law student destined to become an Associate Justice of the U.S. Supreme Court. As a token of his roommate's friendship, Cohen named his first-born son Felix. He later became a law student and, still later, the author of *Law and Ethics.*

Cohen became a legendary teacher at CCNY, famous not only for his unswerving commitment to the Socratic method, but also for the sharp interchanges that this method of endless questions and answers took in his classrooms. Though critical of the radical empiricism of William James, Cohen admired the democratic and friendly attitude of James to students who were seeking to orient themselves morally, religiously, and economically. Cohen made it a point to recommend that his own students read James's lectures on *The Will to Believe* (1897) and *The Varieties of Religious Experience* (1902).

Cohen resisted any orthodoxies that he felt might restrict the Socratic search for truth. At CCNY, this often meant that he had sharp differences of opinion with the revolutionary Marxists in his class; at the University of Chicago (where Cohen was a visiting professor from 1938 to 1942), it meant that he challenged both the positivist, antimetaphysical restrictions and the equally dogmatic Thomistic strictures on liberal thought.

When a student once demanded to know why he persisted in answering his questions with yet another question, Cohen replied: "Why not?" Simple cruelty was not his motive, despite the fact that Cohen could be a sharp, abrasive teacher. Rather, he was combative with, and for, a purpose—to further the search for truth and to teach young minds what it meant to think with rigor and precision. Cohen succeeded admirably on both counts.

PHILIP WIENER

BIBLIOGRAPHY

Cohen, Morris Raphael. *American Thought: A Critical Sketch.* Glencoe, Ill.: Free Press, 1954.
——. *A Dreamer's Journey.* Boston: Beacon Press, 1949.
——. *The Faith of a Liberal.* Freeport, N.Y.: Books for Libraries Press, 1945.
——. *Law and the Social Order.* Hamden, Conn.: Archon Books, 1939.
——. *A Preface to Logic.* New York: Holt, 1944.
Howe, Irving. *World of Our Fathers.* New York: Harcourt Brace Jovanovich, 1976.

College and University Education. See ACADEME.

Colonial American Jewry. In 1654, 23 Jewish refugees landed in Dutch New Amsterdam. They had fled from Brazil, which had been reconquered from the Dutch by the Portuguese. To Governor Peter Stuyvesant, this group of insolvent Jews who had disembarked from the ship *St. Charles* was an undesirable element. He wrote to his employers, the West India Company of Amsterdam, asking that "the Jewish nation" be banned from the community, but the company did not agree, and he was forced to accept the newcomers. The suffering of the Jews in the war with Portugal, as well as the large shareholdings in the company by Amsterdam Jews, probably accounted for this action.

In 1739, in the thirteenth year of the reign of George II, Parliament passed an act exempting certain religious minorities, including Jews, residing in the American colonies from such religious requirements that had previously prevented them from becoming naturalized citizens. Jews were no longer required to receive the Sacrament of the Lord's Supper, and they were permitted to omit the words "upon the true faith of a Christian" when subscribing to any of the required oaths.

It is one of the curious anomalies of history that while Jews residing in the British colonies in America after 1740 could become naturalized subjects of the Crown, Jews living in England could not. In 1753, Parliament attempted to rectify this by passing an act specifically applicable to Jews. It became popularly known as the Jew Bill of 1753 and provoked considerable opposition. Despite its passage, hostility toward the act did not abate. On the contrary, it grew until in the following year sufficient opposition could be mustered in Parliament to repeal the act. Encouraged by its repeal, an attempt was made to repeal the earlier statute of 1740, but this effort failed.

In the colonies, occasionally, a Jew did experience difficulty in being naturalized. For example, in 1761, Aaron Lopez and Isaac Elizar, two Jews residing in Newport, R. I., petitioned the legislature of the colony to be naturalized under the act of 1740. The Upper House did not concur with the Assembly, which had approved the petition, on the grounds that the terms of the act specified that the matter was to be referred to the courts.

Undismayed, the petitioners hastened to submit their request to the Superior Court of Judicature in the County of Newport. The court, acting contrary to the act of 1740, denied the petition and in so doing stated "the principal Views with which this Colony was settled & by a Law made and passed in the year 1663 no Person who does not profess the Christian Religion can be admitted free of this Colony. This Court therefore unanimously dismiss the said Petition as absolutely inconsistent with the first principles upon which the Colony was founded & a Law of the same now in full Force."

Aaron Lopez then moved to Swansey, across the border in Massachusetts, and after residing there two months petitioned the Superior Court of Judicature in the county of Bristol to be naturalized. After presenting the court proof of compliance with the act of 1740 and subscribing to the necessary oaths, three in all, Lopez was declared naturalized. The year was 1762. Isaac Elizar, who also left Rhode Island, was naturalized in New York in 1763.

Between 1755 and 1770, about 184 Jews were naturalized in the British colonies in the Americas, 150 of whom resided in Jamaica, 24 in New York, 8 in Pennsylvania, 1 in Maryland, and 1 in South Carolina.

From a community of 23 in 1654, the Jewish population in the thirteen colonies grew to be an estimated 1500 to 2500 by 1776. The cities of greatest Jewish settlement were New York, Newport, Philadelphia, Charleston, and Savannah.

The Jew in early America was almost invariably a businessman, usually one of modest circumstances. At times he was a craftsman. He normally resided in an urban community. Many of these entrepreneurs engaged in trade took economic risks. Some sought their fortune in whaling, slave trading, or the fur and military supply businesses. Such entrepreneurial risks were matched by frequent participation in lotteries as well as by land speculation and the establishment of banking and insurance companies.

The small Jewish community soon realized the opportunities for political freedom afforded by living in the new nation. The American Revolution had made it possible for its members to achieve complete political equality and thus not be looked upon as outsiders. A Jew became not only an economic, cultural, and possibly a social peer of his fellow Americans, but also a political one. He read and spoke English, did not have earlocks, nor did he wear special clothing. He could reside in a neighborhood that was not a ghetto but, in some cases, one in which he had access to a kosher butcher shop, a Jewish school, a ritual bathhouse, and, of course, a synagogue and a cemetery.

At the end of the Revolution, socially, Jews were part of the middle class and mingled with their gentile counterparts. There were some artisans and workingmen, but almost none were impoverished. Those that were were aided by fellow Jews. Whatever differences that existed within the Jewish community, they were not frozen: there was ample opportunity for upward mobility. Even newcomers advanced considerably soon after becoming adapted to their new environment.

The ties that bound the early Jewish colonists together were thus social, ethnic, economic, and political rather than exclusively religious. The synagogue served not only as a house of worship, but also as a symbol of the Jewish community to the outside world and provided its members with an identity.

Following are pertinent historical facts about the six oldest Jewish communities in the United States as represented by their synagogues:

CONGREGATION SHEARITH ISRAEL, New York City. (More popularly known as The Spanish-Portuguese Synagogue of New York. It is the first and oldest continuous Jewish community in North America.)

    1654—Twenty-three Jews from Recife, Brazil, arrive in New Amsterdam.
ca. 1686—First public services held.
ca. 1695—First synagogue established.
    1706—Constitution adopted.
    1728—Adopted the name Congregation Shearith Israel (Remnant of Israel).

1730—Dedication of the new synagogue building on Mill Street (the first to be built as such on the North American mainland; the building is no longer standing).

CONGREGATION YESHUAT ISRAEL, Newport, R. I. (The Touro Synagogue).

1678—Jewish burial ground purchased.

1754—The Congregation called Nephuse Israel (Scattered Ones of Israel).

1759—Title to the land for a new synagogue building acquired by Jacob Rodrigues Rivera, Israel Hart, and Moses Lopez.

1763—New synagogue building consecrated. (The oldest extant synagogue building in the United States, on August 31, 1947, it was formally designated a national historic shrine.)

1764—Congregation name changed to Yeshuat Israel (Salvation of Israel).

Many of the Jews of Newport fled with the British occupation in 1776, a blow from which the Jewish community never recovered. By the time the war ended, Newport was on the decline, and by 1822, there were no Jews left in Newport. The community was revitalized ca. 1880 with the arrival of Jews from Eastern Europe.

1883—Touro Synagogue reopened and reconsecrated.

CONGREGATION MIKVEH ISRAEL, Philadelphia.

1738—A burial plot purchased by Nathan Levy on Spruce Street, which was enlarged two years later for a family cemetery. By the 1760s, through additional purchases, it became a communal cemetery and remained in use until the second half of the nineteenth century.

1771—A permanent congregation established. (It is not certain when the name Mikveh Israel was first adopted; it was definitely in use by 1782.)

1782—Consecration of the first synagogue building to be erected. (Haym Salomon, the Philadelphia financier of the American Revolution, was given a prominent role in the dedication ceremonies.)

CONGREGATION BETH ELOHIM, Charleston, S. C.

1749—Congregation founded.

1756—Rules of the congregation adopted.

1775—Land purchased for building a synagogue. (About the same time, Jacob Tobias granted the congregation a 7-year lease, gratis, of two rooms over the westernmost part of his new house for a temporary synagogue.)

1792—First synagogue constructed. It was destroyed in the great fire of 1834.

1840—The present synagogue built, which is the second oldest extant synagogue building in the United States and the oldest in continuous use.

CONGREGATION MICKVE ISRAEL, Savannah, Ga.

1733—In July, 41 Jews landed. The congregation established during the first year of Jewish settlement; however, services discontinued after 1740, when a large segment of the community left for the more flourishing town of Charleston.

1735—The name Mickve Israel (Hope of Israel) adopted.

1771—The number of Jews in Savannah estimated to be 49.

1774—Mordecai Sheftall invited the Jews to worship in his home and reestablish a synagogue.

1790—Incorporated as a body politic with the name Parnass and Adjunta of Mickve Israel at Savannah.

1820—First synagogue building erected and dedicated; destroyed by fire in 1827.

CONGREGATION BETH SHALOME, Richmond, Va.

1782—Four names of Jewish persons appeared in the city's census.

1791—29 heads of family mentioned in the membership of the congregation.

1822—Dedication of the first synagogue building of Beth Shalome.

1891—Congregation Beth Shalome merged with Beth Ahabah, a Reform congregation.

In 1789 George Washington was inaugurated as the first President of the United States. In June 1790, Shearith Israel, in New York, sent a letter to the other five established congregations in the new nation proposing that a united letter of congratulations be drafted and sent to Washington.

The congregations were asked to submit a draft of what each thought ought to be said in this the first attempt to speak on behalf of all the Jews of the nation. But a united voice it was not to be. Because of the time that had elapsed between the inauguration and the New Yorker's letter, the congregation in Savannah, "without any previous notice," had already sent its own congragulatory message.

Moses Seixas, answering for Congregation Yeshuat Israel of Newport, felt it would be improper for them, "so small in number," to address the President before the legislature as other large bodies in Rhode Island did; he did castigate Shearith Israel and other congregations who could with propriety have sent congratulations sooner for having delayed so long.

Savannah's letter had gone off over a year before. The draft of the joint address seemed to be making no progress in New York. Consequently, on August 17, 1790, when Washington made an official visit to Newport, the congregation there presented its own communication. In November, Charleston rather impatiently asked what had happened to the draft that it had submitted to Shearith Israel. Then Philadelphia, not having heard any further news, told Isaac Moses that it had prepared an address and was going to present it to the President on the occasion of the move of the capital from New York to Philadelphia. That at least crystallized the affair. The *parnass* of Shearith Israel sent Josephson drafts he had received from Charleston and Richmond and agreed that Philadelphia should go ahead with its plans.

On December 13, Manuel Josephson took the "Address of the Hebrew Congregations in the cities of Philadelphia, New York, Charleston, and Richmond" to President Washington. He "had the honour to present the same to him in person, and was favoured with his answer." He assured the officials of the New York congregation that he had "made it a point to inform the President verbally, the reasons for your Congregation's seeming remissness in not having paid their respects before; and he appeared perfectly satisfied." The letter had been largely prepared by Josephson, who signed it on behalf of all the congregations, and, with apologies for having been "prevented by various circumstances" from adding their congratulations before.

Washington, who had already replied to Newport—stating that the government gives "to bigotry no sanction, to persecution no assistance"—and to Savannah, now acknowledged the congratulations of the remaining four congregations. *See also* American Revolution; Military, The.

BERNARD WAX

BIBLIOGRAPHY
Marcus, Jacob. *The Colonial American Jew*. 3 vols. Detroit: Wayne State University Press, 1970.

Comics and Comedy. In the United States, the roll call of Jewish comics who have made their mark on stage and screen or in nightclubs, vaudeville, radio, and television spans the alphabet from A to Y, from Allen to Youngman, and if we read every booking contract from Grossinger's resort in New York's Catskills to New York's Second Avenue, we would be certain to find a Z—maybe a dozen Zs—among the hundreds of Jewish comedians who came and went in vaudeville or on the famous Borscht circuit in the Catskills. American comedy has sometimes appeared to be a Jewish invention, and according to a survey reported in *Time* magazine, while Jews constitute some 3 percent of the American population, they make up about 80 percent of professional comedians (*Time*, October 2, 1978:76).

So dominant have Jews been in comic theater that in the period between roughly 1920, when they joined the mainstream of American entertainment, until the present, Jews revolutionized American comedy. The earthiness of their wit, the boldness of their idioms, and the tautness of their one-liners, the extravagance of their routines, and the brio and agility of their deliveries constituted a new comic style—comic modernism—that replaced the droll and folksy humor associated with the likes of Mark Twain and Will Rogers and, in more recent times, Garrison Keillor of "A Prairie Home Companion." "Indeed it is difficult," observe William Novak and Moshe Waldocks in *The Big Book of Jewish Humor*, "to imagine what would remain of American humor in the twentieth century without its Jewish component." Joey Adams, Woody Allen (Alan Stewart Konigsberg), Morey Amsterdam, Belle Barth, Jack Benny (Benjamin Kubelsky), and Mary Livingstone (Sadie Marks), Milton Berle (Milton Berlinger), Shelly Berman, Joey Bishop, David Brenner, Fanny Brice, Mel Brooks (Melvin Kaminsky), Lenny Bruce (Leonard Schneider), Myron Cohen, Rodney Dangerfield (Jacob Cohen), Shecky Green, Buddy Hackett (Leonard Hacker), Goldie Hawn, George Jessel, Danny Kaye (David Daniel Kaminsky), Alan King, Robert Klein, David Letterman, Jack E. Leonard (Leonard Lebitsky), Sam Levenson, Joe E. Lewis (Joe Klewan), Jerry Lewis (Joseph Levitch), the Marx Brothers, Jackie Mason (Yacov Moshe Maza), Bette Midler, Nichols and May (Michael Peschkowsky and Elaine Berlin), Don Rickles, the Ritz Brothers, Joan Rivers, Mort Sahl, Smith and Dale (Joe Sultzer and Charlie Marks), Sophie Tucker, Weber and Fields (Morris Weber and Moses Schanfield), Ed Wynn, and Henny Youngman—all are names extracted from a list so long that an encyclopedia entry could be composed of names alone. So persistent indeed is the comic strain in Jewish life that even practitioners of "higher" arts display a strong comic impulse, and among American Jewish novelists who have paid their respects to comedy are Saul Bellow, Philip Roth, Bernard Malamud, Joseph Heller, Wallace Markfield, Stanley Elkin, and Bruce Jay Friedman. Moreover, many prominent Jewish comedians are or were lapsed concert musicians, including Amsterdam, Benny, Victor Borge, Harpo Marx, and Youngman. Woody Allen is still a concert clarinetist.

This fact—the Jewish presence in American comedy—demands explaining, and there is no shortage of explanations. Those most commonly cited are variants on the "laughter through tears" thesis, that humor arose among the Ashkenazic Jews of Eastern Europe and Russia during times of poverty and persecution as a way of maintaining community morale in the face of oppression. Hillel Halkin, a translator of Sholem Aleichem, praises the "therapeutic force" of Aleichem's humor, which left the Jews of his time "feeling immeasurably better about themselves and their fate as Jews" (Sholem Aleichem, *Tevye the Dairyman and The Railroad Stories*, trans. Hillel Halkin [New York: Schocken, 1987], xvi). The therapeutic explanation has much to recommend it, for it does seem that humor and comedy flourish among the downtrodden, who cultivate laughter

as a balm for their wounds. The rich traditions of comedy in Ireland and black America appear to give independent confirmation of the thesis that laughter is a universal human device for coping with pain.

While this thesis says something about the social functions of Jewish humor and comedy, it says nothing about their unique forms—the trenchant social observation, the nervous patter, the mayhem—or about how it was that Jews should flourish as comics in the United States, where the tears of the past were stanched by opportunities on a scale unparalleled in the history of Galut. It also leaves us unenlightened about how one ethnic group's comedy of tears gained such eager applause from the tearless and the Gentile. Though Jewish comedy underscored the uniqueness of Jewish culture and history, it also served to ease assimilation by bringing Jewish voices into the center of American life and demonstrating that, for all their differences, Jews could express the suffering, and also the resiliency, of people everywhere. From Allen to Youngman, Jewish voices have spoken a universal language.

It is one of the paradoxes of this comedy that the universal language of the Jewish comics has been English, and an English, moreover, steeped in the tumult, the grief, and the homely realism of Yiddish. Jewish humor and comedy—and the two should be distinguished—arrived in the New World intact, embodied in a tradition of storytelling, a treasury of anecdotes, and an astringent wit that needed only the opportunity and the media of dissemination to become staples of American entertainment. It would not be amiss to say that, despite the dire circumstances of Jewish history or the unremitting sobriety of the Jewish holy books, the propensity for humor has been a defining feature of Ashkenazic Jewish culture. Not only did laughter in the face of woe mark the life of that culture, but humor, no less than piety, was a cornerstone of its identity.

The sources of this comic spirit are little understood, however, as they are buried in the unrecorded folk life of Ashkenazic Jewry. Humor had little place in the Jewish holy books and played virtually no role in rabbinic Judaism, and as for the theater, it was disdained by the rabbis of the Middle Ages as the "seat of the scornful." The one significant point of contact between rabbinic Judaism and the Yiddish comic spirit was in the festival of Purim. Purim, which celebrates the rescue of the Persian Jews from Haman, lieutenant of King Ahasuerus, by Queen Esther and Mordecai was traditionally celebrated by the Ashkenazim as a festival of license in which common restraints were abandoned and conventional pieties mocked. Drunkenness was encouraged, masquerading and cross-dressing between men and women promoted, and mockery of Torah and Talmud practiced.

The heart of the Purim festivity was the Purim *shpil*, the recitation by a "Purim rabbi" of a ludicrous "Purim Torah," which parodied some familiar liturgical text and ridiculed the subtleties of Midrash. The Purim *shpil* was sometimes accompanied by a comic play performed by clowns and fools, and there was even, according to Nahmah Sandrow, historian of the Yiddish theater, a typology of such clowns: "the *lets, nar, marshelik, badkhen,* and *payets*" (*Vagabond Stars: A World History of Yiddish Theater* [New York: Harper & Row, 1977]). *Lets* and *nar* were simple clowns who did slapstick and pratfalls, while the *marshelik* was a master of ceremonies who specialized in Talmudic wordplay and disputation. The *badkhen*, also a master of wordplay, traditionally performed at weddings, where he recited long rhymed sermons. The *payets* was the narrator and stage director of the Purim play.

While such festivities are now out of fashion in most Jewish communities, their spirit remains alive in secular forms: as comic types, the fool (Ed Wynn, Rodney Dangerfield, Gene Wilder), the master of ceremonies (Jack Benny, Alan King, Sid Caesar, Milton Berle), the trickster (Marx Brothers, Ritz Brothers, Mel Brooks) adapted ancient social roles to new times and new media.

It is significant that the Jewish comic spirit should intersect the religious in that ceremony in which Jews were licensed to feign irreverence and act out impieties that are elsewhere proscribed. This normalization of the comic spirit under the umbrella of the Purim festivity suggests a way in which the religious life accommodated the comic and turned its anarchic tendencies to the service of religion itself, binding the restless Yiddish folk humor by giving it the limited sanction of a festival all its own. For except in the oral tradition of joke and storytelling, the Jewish comic impulse had no other public outlet until the rise of Yiddish theater in the nineteenth century, which developed out of the same secularist stirrings that produced the Jewish socialist movement and the Yiddish literary renaissance.

If the Purim *shpil* and the Yiddish theater are the proximate ancestors of modern Jewish

comedy, then comedy inherited something of the rebelliousness of those institutions, inherited, indeed, the tension between rabbinic Judaism and cultural Yiddishism that reached a pitch in the nineteenth century, when Yiddish asserted itself as a language of art and culture. Jewish humor is continuous with the folk life of the Ashkenazic Jews, touching with affection all things, sacred and secular, that constituted that life, but Jewish comedy dispenses with that affection; it is mutinous and discordant. The humorist acts as a mirror, reflecting back to the community that which it already possesses, its particular slant on life. The comedian, however, is a figure apart, in the community perhaps but not of it. At his most extreme he is a shaman who takes upon his shoulders the sins of the community and purges them through his sufferings. Lenny Bruce was an instance of this. If we think of Jewish humor as it crystallized in the writing of Sholom Aleichem and would be carried to the stage by the likes of Myron Cohen or Sam Levenson and if by comedy we mean the low farce and mad antics of the Marx Brothers, Sid Caesar, or Mel Brooks, or the insult comedy of Don Rickles, Jack E. Leonard, and Joan Rivers, then it is plain that we are dealing with different forms of the comic spirit and very different refractions of Jewish life. The humorists are sentimental, *gemutlich*, and warm; the comics agitated, theatrical, and frequently cold.

Jewish humor has its life in the community and is at one with it. Sholem Aleichem was the very embodiment of the Jewish people about and for whom he wrote. Comedy, on the other hand, takes its departure from the community, exploiting its dreams and nightmares, its values, its habits of mind and speech, in a spirit of something less than reverence. While humor aims at binding communities together, comedy tends toward the separation of the comic. Consider these typical examples of Jewish humor. Two impoverished *melamedim* are heard in conversation. "If I were Rothschild, I would be richer than Rothschild." "How could that be?" "I would do a little teaching on the side." Another: "The rabbis once asked themselves what God does with His day. How, after the world has been created, does the Almighty spend at least part of the time? Answer: studying the Torah." Compare those with Groucho Marx's monologue from *Animal Crackers*:

One night I shot an elephant in my pajamas. How he got in my pajamas I don't know. Then we tried to remove the tusks, but they were embedded in so firmly that we couldn't budge them. Of course, in Alabama, the Tuskaloosa. But that's entirely irrelevant to what I was talking about. We took some pictures of the native girls—but they weren't developed. But we're going back again in a couple of weeks.

What have these two varieties of humor in common? On the face of it, nothing at all. Where the one reflects upon the life of the Old World Jews—the longings of the impoverished for riches and their affection for a personal, anthropomorphic God—the other employs a Jewish character trait, verbal agility, to achieve a theatrical coup. The humor of one lies in real juxtapositions: the *shtetl* Jew and Rothschild, while the comedy of the other lies in purely verbal juxtapositions: in Alabama the Tuskaloosa.

Then again, these forms of the comic are connected through the social base that gave rise to both—Ashkenazic Jewish life itself—and they are contrasting examples, of the comedy of content and that of manner. The one is a window onto diaspora life; the other is a little epiphany of Jewish manner. A fuller example may clarify what is meant by a comedy of manner, which is not the same thing as a comedy of "manners," not at least when performed by a stand-up monologist. It is rather a comedy of manner*isms* in which an entire national character is compressed into a repertoire of gestures. Jackie Mason does a routine about his visit to a psychiatrist that goes like this:

> There was a time when I didn't know who I was. I went to a psychiatrist; he took a look at me and he said, "This is not you."
>
> I said, "This is not me then who is it?"
>
> He said, "I don't know either."
>
> I said, "What do I need you for?"
>
> He said, "To find out. Together we're going to look for the real you."
>
> If I don't know who I am, how do I know who to look for, and even if I find me, how will I know if it's me; and if I want to look for me, why do I need him? I can look myself. I can take my friends; we know where I was; and besides, what if I find the real me and I find that he's worse than me. Why do I need him? I don't make enough for myself,

why do I need a partner? Ten years ago I'd have been happy to look for anybody. Now I'm doing good; why should I look for him? If he needs help, let him look for me.

> He said, "The search for the real you will have to continue. That will be one hundred dollars."
>
> I said to myself, "If this is not the real me, why should I give him the hundred dollars. I'll look for the real me, let *him* give him the hundred dollars. What if I find the real me and he doesn't think its worth a hundred dollars? For all I know, the real me might be going to a different psychiatrist altogether. He might even be a psychiatrist himself." I said, "Wouldn't it be funny if you were the real me and you owe me a hundred dollars?" I said, "I'll tell you what. I'll charge you fifty dollars, we'll call it even."

This is a wonderful routine in which the manner is the sole comic device, not the content. (This being the case, the whole repertoire of gestures, facial expressions, movements, and tonal nuances—the extensions of mannerism into body language—that are the comedian's stocks-in-trade are lost in the transcription.) It is not the psychiatric situation reduced to absurdity that provides the comedy but the convoluted reasoning, the ingenuity of the pilpul. Here is the method of Purim Torah applied to a psychiatric situation, armed with something that sounds like logic to serve nonlogical and egotistical ends: stubbornness, parsimony, and self-esteem. And that should tell us what Mason is to his audiences, who know him for an ordained rabbi who has forsaken the pulpit for the stage and traded in his congregation for an audience. He is the Purim rabbi himself, the comedian in whom the remnants of a culture founded on law and observance come out topsy-turvy but in whose delivery it remains pure and unadulterated.

Besides being a gifted comedian, then, Mason is also a study in Judaism and comedy, a crossover figure who brings to his comedy not only a wealth of Halakic learning but a manner that is so saturated in the past that every shrug, every pause, every crook of the finger, turn of the hand, and lift of the arm is a syllogism rooted in diaspora life, as ritualized and choreographed, as balletic indeed, as a Balinese dance or a Japanese Noh drama. Only the ballet here is verbal, a riotous pas de deux with an imaginary analyst, who is reeling at the end just as surely as Mason's audience.

We can also see in Mason's routine the tendency of pilpul comedy to gravitate toward the absurd and surreal, to create its own Boschean land of fantasmagoric ideas and images. But Mason, finally, is a comedian of measure and restraint; whatever his instincts may be, and surely they are wilder than his performances, he is a professional who is sensitive to the limits of what a middle-class audience will accept and does not push the logic of his method as far as it will go. Philip Roth, by contrast, who lacks Mason's training in pilpul but has an instinct for the outrageous and the impious, occasionally experiments with driving his monologues toward the terra incognita of the surreal, as if to expose the core of the absurd that is embedded deeply in the comic. In a fantastical and funny Roth story entitled "On the Air," Milton Lippman, a talent scout, writes to Albert Einstein to ask if Einstein would agree to star on a radio program that Lippman hopes to negotiate with the networks, "The Jewish Answer Man." It will demonstrate to the world that "the Greatest Genius of all Time is a Jew." When his first approach to Einstein goes unanswered, Lippman bravely writes again:

Dear Mr. Einstein:
I can understand how busy you must be thinking, and appreciate that you did not answer my letter suggesting that I try to get you on a radio program that would make "The Answer Man" look like the joke it is. Will you reconsider, if the silence means no? I realize that one of the reasons you don't wear a tie or even bother to comb your hair is because you are as busy as you are, thinking new things. Well, don't think that you would have to change your ways once you become a radio personality. Your hair is a great gimmick, and I wouldn't change it for a second. It's a great trademark. Without disrespect, it sticks in your mind the way Harpo Marx's does. Which is excellent. (Now I wonder if you even have the time to know who The Marx Brothers are? They are four zany Jewish brothers, and you happen to look a little like one of them. You might get a kick out of catching one of their movies. Probably they

don't even show movies in Princeton, but maybe you could get somebody to drive you out of town. You can get the entire plot in about a minute, but the resemblance between you and Harpo and his hair and yours might reassure you that you are a fine personality in terms of show business just as you are.)

This is a brilliant routine, taking Albert Einstein for a quiz show star and his Harpoesque coiffure for a commercial logo. So outrageous are its premises that this comedy leaps across into absurdity, and, indeed, it takes on increasingly surreal dimensions as the story of Lippman's pilgrimage to Princeton unfolds. Consider the very incongruity of the proposition! Milton Lippman to join forces with Albert Einstein, the man who revolutionized our understanding of space and time to be managed and marketed by this *landsman*, this marginal hustler and jobber whose voice keens with the desperate wisdom that comes of 2000 years working bum territories: Egypt, Spain, the Pale of Settlement, New Jersey.

Again, Lippman to Einstein:

Perhaps I should have told you that my fee is ten percent. But truly and honestly I am not in this business for money. I want to help people. I have taken colored off the streets, shoeshine kit and all, and turned them into headline tap dancers at roadhouses and nightclubs overnight. And my satisfaction comes not from the money, which in all honesty is not so much, but in seeing those boys getting dressed up in dinner jackets and learning to face an audience of people out for a nice time. Dignity far more than money is my business.

Both examples, Mason and Roth, fall under the heading of Jewish comedy: performative, theatrical, dependent for their effect on the verbal resourcefulness and corrosive imagination of the comedian himself. They are also hooked right into Jewish history: the people of the book were also the people of the deal; the people of the Freudian couch also the people of the purse. What Mason and Roth do is draw out with great skill the comic ramifications of this encounter of learning and business, of psychoanalysis and stinginess, in the same culture.

Few comics are pure practitioners of either humor or comedy, which are ideal categories, unevenly blended in most of their work. Jackie Mason's comedy is performative and virtuostic but also warm. So is Roth's, despite the air of rancor that sometimes hangs about it. At the start of the last decade of the twentieth century Woody Allen is the prime example of the comic-cum-humorist who embodies qualities that Judaism has traditionally held dear—modesty, wit, verbal agility—but turns those qualities into a performance in which modesty becomes a boast and verbal agility is continuous with verbal aggression. The ambiguity of his later films—*Zelig, Broadway Danny Rose, The Purple Rose of Cairo, Radio Days, Hannah an Her Sisters, Another Woman*—is the ambiguity of a comedian in search of humor who desires to merge with a community and nourish it from within but can find none to merge with. The bouyancy and invention of his comedy is darkened by the pathos of his ambition to transcend it and cut deeper into the human condition. Compare him, for example, with Mel Brooks, who is less culturally ambitious and is happy to live from punch line to punch line.

Comedy, then, is to humor as theater is to community; it stands in dialectical and uneasy relation to the culture from which its has emerged. That tells us something about the broad appeal of Jewish comedy in America, where its anarchism spoke to the anarchic instincts of a nation of immigrants let loose from the chains of Old World servitude. A classic image of this in American film was the Marx Brothers' use of Margaret Dumont as a constant foil in the films *The Coconuts, Animal Crackers, Duck Soup, A Night at the Opera* and *A Day at the Races*. Proper, quintessentially Anglo-Saxon, and the very caricature of a *lady*, she was the perfect straight-woman for the Marx Brothers' comedy of immigrant *ressentiment*, and what Irishman, what Italian, what Pole, what black could resist a comedy in which Yankee propriety was vexed time and time again by immigrant cunning?

No word on Jewish comedy is complete without some remarks on the place of Yiddish in its formation. Jewish comedy is Yiddish comedy; its entire repertoire of mannerisms originates in the Yiddish language, whose earthiness and realism, pungency and concision made it the perfect vehicle for comic deflation. Some of those qualities that fitted Yiddish for comedy reflect its subordination, as a homely *jargon*, to the *loshen ha-kodesh* of the Jews: Hebrew.

The Ashkenazim of Eastern Europe dwelled in two sharply divided worlds. One was the world of labor and trade, money, politics, love, marriage, family, trouble, death. Its domain was the six days from Saturday night through Friday, and its language was Yiddish. The other was the world of the Sabbath, of prayer and study, Torah and Talmud, faith and prophecy. Exalted and transcendent, its language was Hebrew. In daily life the languages tended to fuse, as Yiddish penetrated the language of prayer and Hebrew formed a sacred canopy over common speech, but for all that, Ashkenazic life was one of vast contradictions, to which the two languages gave emphasis. The Yiddish scholar Max Weinreich once referred to this as the "internal bilingualism" of Ashkenazic Jewry. The literature of the Yiddish renaissance reflects these contrasts vividly: it was a literature in which quotations from sacred texts mingled with colloquialisms and the exalted was intersected by the popular.

It was this juxtaposition of higher and lower worlds within the mental economy of the Jewish people that established the terms for a comedy of deflation, whose basic trope was a sudden thrusting downward from the exalted to the workaday. From Sholem Aleichem to Woody Allen, this comedy of internal juxtaposition has been fundamental. In Aleichem's *The Adventures of Mena-hem-Mendl*, for example, the ritual openings of all the letters between the wandering Menahem-Mendl and his long-suffering wife, Sheineh-Sheindl are Hebrew/Yiddish melanges, in which the exalted sentiments of the Hebrew salutation are brought low by plain truths uttered in Yiddish.

> To my dear, esteemed, renowned, and honored husband, the wise and learned Menahem-Mendl, may his light shine forever.
>
> In the first place, I want to let you know that we are all, praise the Lord, perfectly well, and may we hear the same from you, please God, and never anything worse.
>
> In the second place, I am writing to say, my dearest husband, my darling, my sweet one—may an epidemic sweep all enemies away! You villain, you monster, you scoundrel, you know very well that your wife is on her deathbed after the reparation which that wonderful doctor made on me—I wish it on all your Yehupetz ladies! The result is I can hardly drag my feet. And all the trouble

I'm having with your children, with their teeth, their tonsils, their diphtherias, and all the other plagues on my enemies' heads!

Even in translation the comedy of the elevated and formal (and false) being sabotaged by the plain and vernacular (and honest) comes across unambiguously. Bilingualism translates, however roughly, into English, which has its own traditions of vaporous rhetoric and plain speech to draw upon. Woody Allen's humor too is an almost ritual yoking of the exalted and the worldly, which sometimes produces explosive punch lines. In "God," a one-act play on the death of God, a modern rendition of a Greek tragedy goes haywire and gets away from both cast and playwright, until Zeus is lowered from on high to put things in order and is accidentally strangled by the machinery. "God is dead," announces an actor. "Is he covered by anything?" responds a physician who has rushed up from the audience.

The comic doubletake is a standard technique of Jewish humor. Here are some routines by one Jules Farber, the comedian hero of Wallace Markfield's novel, *You Could Live If They'd Let You*, a book in praise of stand-up comedy and the desperation for which it stands.

> And they shall beat their swords into plowshares—and then, then first they'll give it to you with those plowshares.
>
> By the waters of Babylon I sat down and I wept that I have not bought a little property.
>
> If your brother should weaken and fall, don't move him until you first have at least two witnesses.
>
> "Then spake Rabbi Israel: And the sages do say that we shall weaken their vitals, yea, with fish sticks and red hots shall we pierce their bowels. For hath he not promised us, blessed be His Name of Names, that He will send us an angel, and the angel will put them in confusion and alarm, for He shall cause their shelves to be empty of Campbell's Soups, and we shall fall upon them, yea, we shall smite them with the slats from our venetian blinds. . . ."

Or this, which strikes this writer as one of the cleverest of Woody Allen's short routines:

> And it came to pass that a man who sold shirts was smitten by hard times.

Neither did any of his merchandise move nor did he prosper. And he prayed and said, "Lord, why hast thou left me to suffer thus? All mine enemies sell their goods except I. And it's the height of the season. My shirts are good shirts. Take a look at this rayon. I got button-downs, flare collars, nothing sells. Yet I have kept thy commandments. Why can I not earn a living when mine younger brother cleans up in children's ready-to-wear?"

And the Lord heard the man and said, "About thy shirts. . . ."

"Yes, Lord," the man said, falling to his knees.

"Put an alligator over the pocket."

"Pardon me, Lord?"

"Just do what I'm telling you. You won't be sorry."

And the man sewed on to all his shirts a small alligator symbol and lo and behold, suddenly his merchandise moved like gangbusters, and there was much rejoicing while amongst his enemies there was wailing and gnashing of teeth.

The fun here is of just the sort that has been discussed: a sudden thrusting downward from the exalted to the workaday, from the tragic to the trivial, from the Hebrew to the Yiddish, from the biblical cadence to the commercial slogan. It is the Lord who comes up with the alligator. But the indispensable element in each, without which these jokes would be scarcely more than routine exercises in ironic juxtaposition, is the cultural flavoring. Something of the humiliations and fears of Jewish life itself has been captured in these juxtapositions: the Jewish fear of violence, the sense of shame that underlies the show of pride, the fetish of insurance for a people who were vulnerable for 2000 years, the failing line of goods, the fear of a lawsuit in a world of shysters, the skepticism of a people who know from experience that even plowshares can be beaten into swords.

Finally, we might note that the taste for parody, which has been a staple of Jewish comedy, also profits from this genius for deflation, and there is no better representative of that than S.J. Perelman, who built a career on doing parodic send-ups of other writers, great and small. His "Waiting for Santy," a depression era parody of

Clifford Odets's play "Waiting for Lefty," was a stunning x-ray of "Proletarian" rhetoric; the revolt in Santa's workshop, led by revolutionary Marxist elves, was not the least among the causes of the Proletarian literary movement's quick demise.

It is this ready availability, then, of formal devices that are also ancient properties of the Jewish mind in exile, rather than the specific details of Jewish history, that gave rise to these special brands of humor and comedy. And it is this slant on life—earthy, blunt, rebellious—that promises a continued vitality for Jewish comedy even as the culture that gave birth to it is being transformed—in America, in Israel, in Russia—into something quite different from what it had been. *See also* Films, Radio, Television, Vaudeville.

MARK SHECHNER

BIBLIOGRAPHY

Ausubel, Nathan. *A Treasury of Jewish Humor*. New York: Doubleday, 1951.

Cohen, Sarah Blacher, ed. *From Hester Street to Hollywood: The Jewish-American Stage and Screen*. Bloomington: Indiana University Press, 1986.

———. *Jewish Wry: Essays on Jewish Humor*. Bloomington: Indiana University Press, 1987.

Novak, William, and Waldoks, Moshe, eds. *The Big Book of Jewish Humor*. New York: Harper & Row, 1981.

Smith, Ronald Lande. *The Stars of Stand-up Comedy: A Biographical Encyclopedia*. New York: Garland, 1986.

Weinreich, Max: "Internal Bilingualism in Ashkenaz." *Voices from the Yiddish: Essays, Memoirs, Diaries*, edited by Irving Howe and Eliezer Greenberg. Ann Arbor: University of Michigan Press, 1972.

Whitfield, Stephen. "Laughter in the Dark: Notes on American-Jewish Humor." *Midstream* (February 1978): 48–58.

Communal Organizations. From their beginnings as small self-help groups in the seventeenth century, Jewish communal organizations in the United States burgeoned by the 1980s to 204 comprehensive community federations supporting a variety of human services. In addition, 364 other national Jewish organizations are listed in the *American Jewish Yearbook* under the rubric of religious, educational, cultural, community relations, overseas aid, social welfare, social, mutual benefit, Zionist, and pro-Israel. These include professional associations as well as womens', youth, and student organizations. In turn, these national organizations have thousands of branches or local affiliates. There are also synagogues, Jewish community centers, and family agencies scattered throughout the fifty states. Initially, the Jewish communal enterprise spent a few hundred dollars to take care of the poor, homeless, and sick amongst the 23 Jews who landed in New Amsterdam in 1654. More than 300 years later, it now raises hundreds of millions of dollars annually to provide for the estimated U.S. Jewish population of 6 million through social agencies and synagogues with gross budgets in the billions. It also has assumed obligations overseas for Jews in Israel and other lands exceeding $750,000,000 annually.

A definitive "map" of the Jewish communal structure in America has been attempted several times but has never quite captured the complex realities of the situation. Attempts have been made by the American Jewish Congress in the 1980s, Jonathan Woocher in 1983, and Jerome Chanes and Daniel Elazar in 1989. Most would agree that U.S. Jewish organizations fall into four general categories—(1) *the religious organizations*, congregational, rabbinical and scholarly, nationally and locally; (2) *the philanthropic social service network*, generally referred to as the "communal" system, which includes support of Jewish education and community relations; (3) *special interest groups*, political, Zionist, and Israel-oriented; and (4) *face-to-face associational groups*, at one time primarily the landsmanschaftens, then the great membership organizations such as B'nai B'rith and Hadassah. Today the local synagogue has become the primary associational group for American Jews who wish to affiliate.

HISTORICAL OVERVIEW. When the first Jews were allowed to stay in New Amsterdam (New York) on condition that "the poor among them shall be supported by their own nation," they did not become a "burden" to the greater community then or in the succeeding centuries. In large part this was due to the time-honored Jewish religious communal traditions of humanitarian obligations to the less fortunate, albeit abetted by the settlers' extraordinary capacity for rapid economic advancement. Despite continued discrimination, which denied the Jews of New Amsterdam their own synagogue, the right to hold public office, the right to stand guard in the militia against any common enemy, or the right to become craftsmen or enter retail trade, somehow, ingeniously, they thrived, were taxed, and courageously protested all prohibitions until these were ultimately rescinded.

Self-help was not only imposed, but assumed, for in the colonial period and for some time thereafter there were few central governmental instrumentalities for assisting the poor, whether unemployed, ill, widowed, or orphaned. The instruments that did exist were either very localized or creations of special affinity groups. So the Jewish settler, like his Gentile neighbors, had to provide for coreligionists who fell victim to ill fortune through loss of a job, or any shift in the unregulated economy, or when a ship foundered at sea, ruining a merchant's investment, or when a penniless Jew turned up at the harbor from abroad.

As the number of Jews grew in the New World before and immediately after the American Revolution, social problems arose that required remedy. All communities provided modest accommodations for religious worship and a cemetery to bury the dead. The presence of a synagogue with or without a rabbi, the need to maintain or reaffirm one's identity as distinguished from other self-conscious groups, the general disregard of the needy by the majority culture, and the expectation that they should help their own cemented the small Jewish band and encouraged support for its modest charitable endeavors. To the middle of the nineteenth century, private charity in the larger general community played a relatively insignificant role. No Jewish poor class developed. All were encouraged by their fellow Jews to become self-sufficient. In 1801, Charleston, South Carolina, established the first Hebrew Orphan Society and developed a formal benevolent society. Women in congregations sewed clothing for the poor. When a Jewish Revolutionary War veteran could not sustain himself with a meager government pension, New York City Jews started a welfare society. Philadelphia soon followed suit. Generally, all social services emanated from the leadership of a synagogue. A rabbi writing in 1848 reported, "In all our congregations, where necessity demands it, there are ample provisions made for the support of the poor, and we endeavour to prevent, if possible, any Israelite from being sent to the poorhouse, or sink into crime for want of the means of subsistence." Charity was neither generous nor extensive until the advent of considerable Jewish immigration and the impact of the industrial revolution later in the nineteenth century. And the development of communal social services organi-

zations, apart from the synagogue, were often "spinoffs" of the synagogues. The Spanish-Portuguese Synagogue in New York, for instance, spun off Mount Sinai Hospital in the 1840s.

However, by the eve of the Civil War (in 1861), Jews had begun to create a host of Jewish organizations, lodges and charities and were testing reform (and Reform) in their traditional religious practices. Jewish education was not widespread. Some Jews even assisted non-Jewish philanthropies. On his death the wealthy Judah Touro (1775–1854) left bequests in unprecedented sums for that time to local, national, and even a Palestinian Jewish institution.

Many Jewish merchants prospered during the Civil War as the demand grew for uniforms, military supplies, food, and transportation. When prejudice was manifested against Jewish entrepreneurs in the border states, B'nai B'rith (founded in 1843) and the New York Board of Delegates of American Israelites (organized in 1856) vigorously remonstrated against these injustices. They mounted protests against the dismissal of Mordecai Manuel Noah as consul to Tunis, against the anti-Semitic outrage in Damascus, against the prohibition of Jews to travel to Switzerland, and against the kidnapping and baptism of Edgardo Mortara in Italy.

An observer in 1872 noted that Jews "generally united in objects of benevolence . . . they are very solicitous for the welfare of their needy brethren. They will never suffer the destitute to be an incubus on society. Rarely is any of their faith an inmate of the almshouse, and more rare is any arrested as a vagrant or an outlaw." With the influx of large numbers of immigrants and the spontaneous creation of many more organizations, he went on to state that "the directors . . . endeavour to correct the evil by fusion of all charities, under the guidance of a board of managers. These are men that have the capacity to discriminate, and the leisure to examine into each case."

As late as 1885, after the first mass influx of East European Jewish immigrants to the United States, the largest single group of applicants at the United Hebrew Charities in New York (formed in 1874 by a merger of six societies) was of non-East European stock. Shortly after that time, however, the vast majority were of Russian and East European origin.

Jewish relief agencies and settlement houses established toward the end of the century adopted the guiding philosophy, social thought, and patrician practices of the non-Jewish agencies of that time. Scientific philanthropy insisted on a thorough investigation of the needy applicant, emphasized economic and vocational rehabilitation, and espoused the professionalization of welfare services. The sociological view of poverty accented environmental forces and prevention.

Nineteenth-century American cities were "disorderly, disease ridden, and dangerous places to live in." Efforts to reform the condition were challenged by social scientists such as William Graham Sumner, who wondered whether "voluntary charity is mischievous" and "whether legislation which forces one man to aid another is right and wise."

It was into this somewhat inhospitable physical and human environment that the newer Jewish immigrant was expected to make a superhuman adjustment; and to his everlasting credit, he ultimately did. To the credit of the Sephardic and Ashkenazic Jews who had come earlier, they accepted responsibility for aiding and Americanizing the new Eastern European immigrant, in spite of finding him distasteful.

When the efforts of all local organizations proved to be inadequate, wider local relief committees were created. Finally, a national conference for relief was called to initiate radically new approaches.

THE RISE OF NATIONAL JEWISH ORGANIZATIONS. As early as 1876, the United Hebrew Relief Association of St. Louis suggested the need for a National Association of Jewish Charities, paralleling the nonsectarian National Conference of Charities and Correction (1873). Another quarter of a century elapsed before the National Conference of Jewish Charities was finally established in 1899. This was the forerunner of the Conference of Jewish Communal Services, which now covers both the United States and Canada. This national organization was founded only four years after the creation of the first federations of Jewish philanthropies in Boston and Cincinnati in 1895. National organizations could result only after there had been demonstrations of greater unity, efficiency, and vision on a local plane. In 1900, there were only three local federations. In 1989, there were 204.

While the Jew at the end of the nineteenth century was fleeing Europe for his life (largely from the brutalities of the Russian regime), for freedom, and for new opportunities, America needed cheap labor to expand westward, to build its sprouting cities, its railroads, its factories, harness its rivers, till the soil, and mine its minerals. The time was mutually beneficial for both. Recruiters from the United States for workers abounded in Europe. Steamboat steerage tickets were not expensive. Emma Lazarus exhorted democratic America to welcome the "tired, your poor, your huddled masses, yearning to breathe free."

The 230,000 Jews in the United States in 1880 absorbed 3 million immigrants in the next 50 years. The sheer numbers placed unprecedented burdens on the predominantly German Jewish population of the United States, and its institutions, which were never designed to serve such a vast clientele. The financial panics of 1893 and 1907 temporarily dried up sources of self-help funds. Unemployment during these intervals complicated the relief problems. Attempts were made to resettle newcomers in the Midwest and Southwest and on farms outside of New York. Efforts were made to retrain them out of their former concentrations in the needle trades, peddling, and unprofitable small businesses into farmers and skilled mechanics. The Baron de Hirsch Fund, the Jewish Agricultural Society, the Industrial Removal Office, the Hebrew Sheltering and Immigrant Aid Society (HIAS), the National Desertion Bureau, the National Council of Jewish Women and hospitals for consumptives were some of the national instrumentalities developed to cope with these multitudinous problems.

The first major national organization attempting to represent Jewish interests was the American Jewish Committee, founded in 1906. Comprised of the Jewish elite, it took on the traditional Jewish role of *shtadlon*, or intercessor, with the general authorities. It advocated a U.S. response to Russian pogroms and more open immigration and was instrumental in spawning the New York Kehillah and the American Jewish Joint Distribution Committee.

Uptown New York Jews organized a Kehillah (an experiment in self-government) in 1908 in an effort to curb the growing crime, desertion, and prostitution rate among the Jewish residents. It endeavored to coordinate all Jewish welfare programs, improve Jewish education, train modern professional personnel, and collect accurate data. The necessary unity for a successful Kehillah never emerged, and the Kehillah died.

Quarrels developed between employer and worker, which bordered on fratricidal war, as employees with conflicting political ideologies struck against low wages and inhuman and hazardous working conditions. These were partially resolved with the emergence of communal statesmen, including astute attorneys, labor union representatives, and civic-minded rabbis.

The immigrant, even if he was poor, did not come empty-handed. Ambitious, he was soon off relief, went from one job to a better one, and from a windowless, toiletless, railroad flat to a better residence and different neighborhood. Most Jews came with their families. To some degree they shared the social problems of all poor immigrant groups. But they had a thirst for learning. They nourished new synagogues, although many abandoned religion altogether. Charles Liebman has pointed out in the *American Jewish Yearbook* (1967) that most Russian Jews came knowing only Orthodoxy but tended to be neither scholarly nor deeply religious. Orthodox Judaism was weak and shrinking until after World War II when new immigrants came to an infrastructure developed by a few pioneers. Their dress became modish. Originally, they spoke Yiddish, but they soon learned English. They went to night school and to night college. They supported the theater, music, newspapers—all in Yiddish. They formed their own labor unions, credit unions, landsmanschaften, and charitable societies. They demanded a voice in the citywide and national Jewish organizations. They rejected injustice, exploitation, and human degradation. They voted as they pleased and elected socialists to the state and federal legislative bodies.

The Jewish labor movement uniquely developed a wide range of welfare programs that included banks, health institutions, leisure facilities, and social insurance.

Immigrant Orthodox Jews took the initiative toward meeting the crisis facing Eastern European Jewry during World War I. The American Jewish Committee and the Jewish socialists created separate instrumentalities. The trio was eventually merged into the American Jewish Joint Distribution Committee (JDC), which still exists to help Jews in distress outside the United States.

American Jewry had come of age philanthropically by the end of World War I, obligated and able to take care of most of its own domestic problems through local federations along with overseas organizations for relief and for the development of Palestine. While this last was popular with the Eastern European masses, many organizations and much of Reform Judaism actively opposed Zionism.

SOCIAL WELFARE. In the main, Jews turned to the Jewish organizations for assistance, but many utilized non-Jewish and public charitable services, often located in areas in which the Jews replaced the former settler. Some of the wealthier, often totally assimilated, were invited to serve as trustees of Christian institutions which had become nonsectarian.

While Jews have contributed immeasurably to the development of philanthropy in the United States, one cannot overlook the fact that the social gospel impelled individual Christians to establish their own network of social services (often in Jewish neighborhoods) and even propel the government into assuming responsibility for those that could not be accommodated under voluntary auspices. Care for the sick, the insane, the criminals, the blind, the orphaned, and the aged were largely initiated by Christian institutions. Many social work pioneers were the daughters of ministers.

That Jewish philanthropy should not only emulate general philanthropy, but actually seek to become nonsectarian, should not be surprising. This was an early issue among the leaders of Jewish philanthropy. While it ran counter to fostering Jewish cultural and religious activities in Jewish institutions, it gained a sufficient foothold in both lay and professional thinking, so that the debate continued into the 1960s.

The comradeship of *landsleit* and the need for family benefits in case of disability or death produced in New York alone by 1917 over 1000 groups, benevolent associations, and fraternal orders. Originally part of the congregations, they steadily developed into separate entities. They stimulated the chartering of the Hebrew Free Loan Society (1892). Beth Israel Hospital (1890) was organized in New York to make kosher food available for Orthodox patients and to provide employment for physicians of East European origin.

The landsmanschaften banded together for nostalgia and comfort under the names of the communities from which they originated and developed self-help instruments for their mutual assistance. These included charitable support, cemeteries, medical assistance, and loan societies. It is estimated that while the first was established as early as 1855, they came into their full efflorescence after the massive migrations. At their height they numbered 3000 in New York alone with a constituency of 500,000 members. They become more political, occasionally joined together in federations, and when World War I broke out, they undertook large-scale relief programs for their kinsmen in Europe, finally joining the JDC. Since World War II, they have gone into decline or disappeared, as their children became integrated within the overall Jewish organizations and American life. There was no parallel for such a large scale development among other immigrant populations.

Offshoots of these organizations were the Free Loan Societies, which the immigrants brought from Europe. By 1927, there were 500 in the United States. In the early 1900s, few banks offered low-interest personal loans and small-business entrepreneurs also needed capital to launch their ventures. Credit cooperatives (Akisiyes) were also developed among the Jews as a device for self-sufficient management of their savings and financing of their personal needs.

In the 1920s, the immigrant Jew, stabilized geographically and economically, began to challenge the former German Jewish hegemony over all of Jewish civil life and began to rise to leadership in the old and many of the new communal and welfare agencies.

Despite the depression of the early 1920s and the prejudices against Jewish admissions to the Ivy League universities and the anti-Semitic campaigns, Jews managed to prosper, assimilate, and build conspicuous religious, cultural, and welfare monuments throughout the land. The Graduate School of Jewish Social Work was established to professionalize the personnel for the Jewish social agencies. The school expired in 1939, when the Jewish community failed to support it, in part due to the rather widely held view that Jewish-trained social workers were not essential on the American Jewish scene. In the post-World War II period, efforts were made to revive the institution, but they failed.

In the 1930s, private, voluntary, social welfare was radically altered. The Great Depression of that decade brought mass unemployment, affecting tens of thousands of Jewish workers and small businessmen. It was not uncommon for the long-time patrons of many Jewish communal services to lose their fortunes and their leadership roles. Independent Jewish institutions and even those affiliated with federations were sometimes unable to raise the funds necessary for the maintenance of programs, and campaigns for overseas assistance raised insignificant sums.

To the rescue came a reluctant government. Direct relief was finally assumed by the munici-

palities, then by the state, and eventually by the federal government, and such relief was for all time given up as a principal responsibility of Jewish agencies for their coreligionists. Social security and unemployment insurance would follow to distribute by check and computer permanent, catastrophic, and long-term relief for the exceptional, the aged, and children, further removing primary obligation from the Jewish community. The residual question of the adequacy of public support and its direct contribution toward the expanding "relief" population has ever since been argued in the civic arena by the public, the politician, and the professional. Government encouragement and protection was also afforded unions.

Many of the agencies in the health and welfare fields were only able to maintain their programs and to some extent expand their services through the substantial assistance provided by the government, which assigned manpower and finally cash. As an unexpected dividend, many Jews were recruited for the field of Jewish communal service who otherwise might never have chosen such a career.

JEWISH EDUCATION. There was a steady rise in the Jewish school census during the first 20 years of the twentieth century due to immigration and childbirth. Schools, however, suffered during the 1930s, for families were unable to pay tuition and communal support dwindled. Some schools closed. This blow came at a period when advances were being made in Jewish education, witnessing the early development of the Jewish day school, improvements in the Sunday school, the establishment of Jewish secondary education, the initiation of summer resident camps with both a Hebraic and Yiddish accent, the development of teacher-training seminaries, the rise of the Conservative Movement's congregational schools and the establishment of bureaus of Jewish education.

REFUGEE AID. Anti-Semitism in the 1930s was blatant. It was fanned by such as Father Charles E. Coughlin, the German-American Bund, and the American Firsters, which gave round-the-clock work to the American Jewish Congress, the American Jewish Committee, the Anti-Defamation League, and the Jewish War Veterans.

To aid the incoming refugees from Germany and other European countries, the National Coordinating Committee for Aid to Refugees and Emigrants was established (1934), which eventually merged with HIAS (1950). Following World War II, the New York Association for New Americans (NYANA) was organized. The American Jewish Joint Distribution Committee again provided relief and rescue from Soviet Russia, Europe, South America, North Africa, Ethiopia, Iran, and eventually for Palestine and then Israel. The resettlement of Jewish immigrants became one of the basic parts of the Jewish communal system, done primarily by NYANA in New York and by Jewish Family Agencies around the country.

Despite the greater need for a permanent haven for Jews, the Zionist Movement was actually weakened during the first part of the 1930s, only to take on a major thrust during World War II, when all other avenues for a safer haven were severely limited.

EMERGENCE OF COMMUNITY COUNCILS. The 1930s saw the formation of the Council of Jewish Federations and Welfare Funds (1932) (now the Council of Jewish Federations), an outgrowth of early forms of national Jewish communal cooperation. Its program was to provide better coordination of local Jewish communal services, improve the character of fund raising, reduce conflict and overlapping of local and national agencies, achieve a more rational distribution of funds collected between domestic and overseas demands, assemble more and accurate data on demography, and stimulate programs for more efficient operation. It has often made the local federations the central address for most Jewish communal services in the United States and Canada.

In many cities Jewish community councils emerged to defend Jewish rights at home and abroad. The typical Jewish federation today is a merger of a Jewish welfare fund that supported Jewish local social services and a council or united appeal that raises funds for social needs abroad and in Israel. The last such merger was in 1986 between New York's United Jewish Appeal and its Federation of Jewish Philanthropies.

The National Community Relations Advisory Council (1944) was eventually formed, which curiously did not insert the word "Jewish" before "Community" until 1968. NJCRAC was set up to coordinate community relations efforts, but it never superseded the three major community relations organizations that continue to dominate this field. NJCRAC has nurtured local community relations efforts and has achieved some coordination of functions.

The end of World War II, the calamitous revelations of the Holocaust in Europe, the refugee camps, all gave impetus to the creation of the State of Israel and called for unity, leadership, manpower, and enormous financial assistance. American Jewry was not found wanting. After the establishment of Israel, anti-Zionism died as a major force in the Jewish community.

American Jewry, originally concentrated in the cities, began a wholesale exodus to the suburbs, where it had to build anew a vast network of institutions. Simultaneously, it had to reconstruct many of the outmoded facilities in the "inner city." Hospital centers of immense proportions, homes for the aged, child care institutions, rehabilitation centers, community centers, camps, day camps, synagogues, day schools, office buildings to house the local federations and national services were erected with a lavish hand. Funds for capital construction eventually ran into the billions. To support both domestic and international programs, including Israel, the central campaigns soared from $28.4 million in 1939 to 205 million in 1949 (creation of the State of Israel), $317.7 million in 1967 (Six-Day War), sums that have been exceeded in subsequent years. If there is a gross national Jewish communal product in the United States, it would approximate $3 billion, including user's fees, memberships, tuition, contributions (with a generous government tax deductibility), United Way support and income from endowment funds and legacies. If the Jewish GNP was to include the budgets of all Jewish agencies, including third-party payments and government grants, it could be as high as $5 billion. Israel has benefitted from these major fundraising campaigns via the United Jewish Appeal Israel Bond drives and the efforts of scores of organizations interested in some special aspect of Israel: Hadassah, universities, hospitals, religious groups, community centers, homes for youth, etc.

The Jewish Welfare Board (1917) is the major Jewish service agency for more than 200 Jewish community centers and YM-YWHAS and camps, whose constituency numbers over 1 million in the United States and Canada. JWB is also a United States Government-accredited agency for providing services and programs to Jewish military personnel and their families and hospitalized Jewish veterans. Each of the local agency networks, family agencies, vocational, educational, and the like has a similar, if smaller, national service organization. In May 1990, the organization changed its name to the Jewish

Community Center Association of North America. It retained, however, JWB in its work with the men and women in the armed forces.

Immediately after World War II, there was vaunted Jewish prosperity, widespread acceptance of Jews in the social and economic structure, a reduction of anti-Semitism, vast governmental assistance to Jewish charitable enterprises, boundless sums raised for capital and operational programs, with an unprecedented outpouring of aid for overseas relief and Israel.

The 1960s and especially 1967 witnessed a 180-degree turn in the thrust of the entire Jewish communal enterprise. Up to the 1960s, Jewish communal agencies had been interested in Jewish education or culture, in serving Jews, whatever their needs, in providing specific services, the thrust of the enterprise was in helping Jews to succeed in America—to fight anti-Semitism and discrimination—to help Jews to overcome barriers to employment in certain industries—to be accepted at the best colleges and faculties, etc. In the mid-sixties all of this changed. Jews had by and large "made it" in all of the above areas. In addition, Jews were a dominating force in the American literary and intellectual establishment. At the same time the American Welfare State took another great leap forward, the first since the 1930s with the advent of Medicare and Medicaid. This removed from the voluntary private charitable sector one of its major functions—support for the aged—and turned it over to the public sector. The 1960s also saw the beginning breakdown of the liberal-labor-Jewish-black coalition that had marched together on almost all issues, at least since World War II. Finally, the Six-Day War awakened in the consciousness of hundreds of thousands of American Jews a realization that had always been below the surface—that the survival of the State of Israel was a matter of basic import to the mass of American Jews. From that point forward, the thrust of the American Jewish communal enterprise was on maintenance and the enhancement of Jewish life in America: to help Jews remain Jews in freedom rather than to help them become good Americans.

The change has occurred in spurts and discrete steps, but it has been overwhelming and continuous since the late 1960s. It has changed the focus of the federation from an organization primarily involved in efficient fund raising and allocations to an organization concerned with building community as an end in itself. The federations have become community-building organizations that have as major functions fund raising and allocations and social planning; however, the building of community has become more and more essential. One can see this in the massive changes in allocations toward Jewish education, culture, community relations, and college campus services and the decline of allocations to Jewish hospitals. Further, if community building is the goal, then service is no longer charitable in the older sense, that is, directed at poor and needy Jews. Services are for the *entire* Jewish community of *all* economic classes. It is one thing to insure that any Jewish parent who wants a Jewish education for his or her child can receive one. It is another thing to advocate that Jewish parents provide Jewish education for their children.

The new emphasis has brought new issues to the fore. The birth rate was declining. Divorce rates increased. Intermarriage had become widespread and more acceptable. Jewish family life structure was changed.

SHIFT IN EMPHASIS OF THE COMMUNITY ORGANIZATIONS. Jewish organizations had to take stock and adopt a course that would stem and even reverse the seeming inevitable trends. As new problems arose or new needs had to be satisfied, the American Jewish community was fertile in creating new instrumentalities to deal with these issues. The Jewish Restitution Successor Organization (1947) and the Conference on Jewish Material Claims Against Germany (1951) processed claims, received and assisted in the recovery of Jewish heirless or unclaimed property, utilizing such assets to provide for the relief, rehabilitation, and resettlement of surviving victims of Nazi persecution, all arising from agreements with the German Federal Republic for the indemnification of Jewish victims and survivors. A network of organizations concerned with Soviet Jewry arose to work on their behalf, to further exodus from the USSR to Israel and elsewhere. Organizations to develop programs and provide resources to further understand the Holocaust and its impact on civilization were established and will result in the last decade of this century in the creation of major memorial buildings in New York, Washington, and Los Angeles. The creation of the State of Israel led to the formation of the Conference of Presidents of Major American Jewish Organizations (1955) to coordinate the activities of 37 major groups as they relate to American-Israeli affairs and problems affecting Jews in other lands. The American Israel Public Affairs Committee (1954) was registered to lobby on behalf of legislation affecting Israel and prevent a tilt toward the Arab states. It represents Americans who believe support for a secure Israel is in the U.S. public interest and works for stronger United States–Israel ties. Special organizations like the American Association for Ethiopian Jews (1974) are another example that however well organized, the Jewish communal system is not monolithic.

While Jewish domestic concerns could not be and were not ignored, it was Israel that assumed the center of the world Jewish stage, consuming the energies even of the presidents of the United States. First, the 1967 Six-Day War with its unexpected massive victory for Israel, then the reaction of Arabs through worldwide terrorism and the use of their oil, which brought about scarcities, unprecedented higher costs, and eventually contributed to exceptional inflation, disrupting the world and the American economy. It culminated in the American government initiative, which led to the Camp David Treaty in 1979 between Egypt and Israel. By 1990, Jewish communal organizations were divided in regard to the issue of "Land for Peace," as that controversy continued to fester in Israel.

In the postwar period, the American Jewish community rebuilt Jewish communities in Europe. Until German reparations were made available, the total burden rested on Jewry, American and worldwide. Israel's needs obviously competed with the distribution of the American philanthropic dollar. This problem has not yet been resolved, and there is now a careful review of expenditures made on the Israeli scene. The unprecedented exodus of Jews from Soviet Russia in 1990–1991 and the war in Kuwait and Iraq in 1991 has once again turned the American-Jewish community's attention to Isreal.

Threats to the Jewish communities in Iran and in South Africa, for those still remaining in the Arab-Moslem world and Ethiopia, as well as the major effort to press for massive immigration of Soviet Jewry, have occupied the attention of large sections of American Jewry.

WOMEN'S ORGANIZATIONS. Jewish women played a secondary role in Jewish community organizational life until the end of the nineteenth century. Initially, they were largely active in sewing circles and sisterhoods of temples, which were concerned with charitable activities and sometimes literary expression. Occasionally they were organizers of religious schools and child care orphanages where, as volunteers, they were teachers or social workers. In most instances, men administered and dominated both charities and religious institutions.

This began to change with the creation of the National Council of Jewish Women (1893), perhaps the first major national Jewish women's organization. It played a decisive role in activities associated with new immigrants and their absorption into American society. This was followed by its establishment of settlement houses and summer camps. Currently, it operates programs in education and social and legislative action and promotes education and research in Israel.

B'nai B'rith Women became an independent organization in 1897 with a program comparable to the men's group. In 1990, it formally became a part of B'nai B'rith International. Hadassah, led by Henrietta Szold, was initiated in 1912, and while best known for its medical services and Youth Aliyah programs in Israel, it is also concerned with the Zionist youth movement in America and in Jewish educational programs. In recent years it has aided distressed countries around the world.

Initially, most women were volunteers. Later some became professionals in medical care and social welfare. Lillian Wald is perhaps the earliest example of a Jewish woman involved in improving the plight of the poor through the Henry Street Settlement House in New York and the Visiting Nurse Service.

Following World War II, a number of other Jewish women's organizations sprang up—Zionist, religious, and welfare—that sponsored programs of their own in this country and in Israel.

In recent years, it has become not uncommon for women to become presidents of synagogues, mostly Reform, local Jewish federations, and national Jewish organizations like the Council of Jewish Federations and the National Jewish Community Relations Advisory Committee. Today there are few Jewish organizations not open to female leadership. Some women have become rabbis and cantors in the Reform and Conservative movements. The exceptions are the traditional religious organizations, where men still dominate the volunteer and professional scene. Professional Jewish communal service also still lags, and there has not been a woman chief executive in a major federation.

YOUTH ORGANIZATIONS. Youth groups were usually appendages of adult organizations, due to efforts by the adult community to pass on its ideological viewpoints and maintain closer ties between the generations. Young Judea, B'nai B'rith Youth, and a variety of Zionist organizations developed as a consequence. Summer camps and tours of Israel were also initiated. Later each of the dominant religious organizations introduced youth units and camps, and sponsored trips to Israel.

In 1923, the first of the B'nai B'rith Hillel campus groups was established to provide Jewish programs for Jewish youth attending the universities in ever greater numbers. There are now nearly 400 units. The recent growth of Jewish studies as units or departments of the university provides study opportunities for Jews as well as non-Jews. Rabbis and lay Jewish educators thus offer beyond instruction a distinctive leadership for Jewish students away from home.

Among the independent Jewish youth organizations were Jewish fraternities and sororities, which began to develop around the turn of the century, usually as a consequence of discrimination and exclusion of Jews from these collegiate societies. In recent years, their numbers have declined. Many had to become integrated. They are no longer exclusively Jewish. Yet at one time they played an important role in maintaining a Jewish presence and identity on the campus.

DENOMINATIONAL GROUPS. The homogeneity that existed in American Jewish life until after the Civil War, whether Sephardic or Ashkenazic (German), began to disintegrate with the rapid adjustment of immigrant groups that came from Eastern Europe beginning in the 1880s. The diversified groups began to develop their own indigenous rabbinical leaders, first Reform Judaism through the Hebrew Union College (1875). The Jewish Theological Seminary (Conservative) and Yeshivah University (Orthodox) established their own institutions in 1886 in part to counter the Reform trend as well as to provide native professional leadership for its own constituencies, constantly fed by the inflow of migrants. Other institutions of rabbinical training were created during the twentieth century among the diverse Orthodox sects, Reform, and later the Reconstructionists. Traditional groups, such as the Hassidim, also developed independent seminaries.

Each denomination formed a network of supplementary national organizations for education, for lay people (men and women), for youth, for Israel, obviously competing with each other. While Conservative and Reform Judaism at the end of the twentieth century have the largest following, Orthodox Judaism is steadily catching up with recent immigrants, with families having many more children, and with its more intensive day-school program. These religious affiliations have slowed down the process of total integration into the larger American community.

In the last decade of the twentieth century, the Jewish community will be faced with major problems that will affect its census and its substantial influence, despite its limited population of less than 3 percent.

The aged will increase due to continued better economic circumstances, better diets, and better medical care. Intermarriage has become a serious problem. Unless the non-Jewish spouse converts to Judaism (in which case their children are almost always educated Jewishly), this may produce the largest erosion in the Jewish population. While in the main urban dwellers, the Jewish residency is more dispersed, shifting to the south and the western part of the country. Mobility tends to depress affiliation rates. The Jewish divorce rate grows, while still about 50 percent of the Protestant rate. However, Jews are more likely to remarry than others. Marriage is later, and Jewish singles constitute an ever growing problem although marriage is still considered the desirable pattern of adult life.

Though there are many Jews who fall into the poverty or marginal economic categories, Jews will be proportionately higher wage earners, with most Jewish women entering the working force creating double incomes. The financial position of most Jewish families will improve or at least hold its own. Jews still continue to field business and professions, which are now open to them in every branch of American economic and institutional life from universities to major business corporations.

Most Jewish organizations will be supported by federations, government subsidies, third parties, endowment funds, foundations, and legacies.

At the moment there is disunity in both Israel and on the American Jewish scene. Yet, when either is threatened, instrumentalities for cooperation will arise as much out of defense as for the developing conservative trends in the overall Jewish population.

While federations are only the largest or most powerful of the Jewish communal institutions, a number of their attributes are characteristic of the Jewish communal enterprise more generally. The characteristics of the Jewish voluntary structure have been analyzed by Daniel Elazar and Jonathan Woocher, among others.

The characteristics include:

1. *Voluntarism.* Unlike a state system or certain Jewish autonomous communities in prior times in Europe, participation is totally voluntary. Therefore, it can never be taken for granted.

2. *Consensus.* Jewish establishment organizations tend to be conservative. They may change gradually and incrementally and in a measured way. They work very hard to maintain as broad an umbrella as possible, keeping as many forces and interests in the community under that umbrella. The organization is a democratizing force in that it is very easy for some interest or group to be heard. Decisions are by consensus. The final outcome of a consensus process is usually that some bow toward any particular interest group that has made itself heard, and accommodations are made for the overall goal. Smaller Jewish organizations can be more fast moving. The tension between such organizations and the large established ones maintains some sort of balance so that change does occur.

3. *Localism.* The Jewish federation system and the agency system are fiercely autonomous and local. In a time of need for better technology in communications, in a time of a great deal of mobility and dispersion in the Jewish population, this localism may be becoming increasingly dysfunctional and be a factor in the loss of Jewish affiliation and association. The federation system is beginning to adjust to this, for example, in adopting collective responsibility for the financing of resettlement of Soviet refugees.

It is also noteworthy that while American Jews are divided on certain policy issues particularly vis-à-vis Israel, they tend to be united on the very same issues on which Israeli Jews are united, such as the centrality of Jerusalem to Israel, and divided on the very same issues on which Israelis are divided, such as the degree of willingness to trade land for peace.

Barring a recurrence of American anti-Semitism or the merging of world forces against Israel, both of which are always possibilities, Jews, despite their modest number, will be able to maintain positions of strength and influence, seeking alliances with hospitable non-Jewish groups, who may be in equal jeopardy, largely in the free world, pressuring governments to defend Jews by law and defend Israel in the name of human rights and democracy.

GRAENUM BERGER
DONALD FELDSTEIN

BIBLIOGRAPHY

Berger, Graenum, ed. *The Turbulent Decades: Jewish Community Service in America, 1956–1978.* 2 vols. New York: Conference of Jewish Communal Services, 1981.

Dobkowski, Michael N., ed. *Jewish American Voluntary Organizations.* Westport, Conn.: Greenwood Press, 1986.

Elazar, Daniel J. *Community and Polity: The Organizational Dynamics of American Jewry.* Philadelphia: Jewish Publication Society, 1976.

———. *People and Polity.* Detroit: Wayne State University Press, 1989.

Conference of Presidents of Major American Jewish Organizations.

To avoid the duplication of effort and confusion that often results from the plethora of organizations that have similar agendas, officials of major Jewish organizations began meetings in 1954 in order to coordinate policy with regard to American-Israeli relations.

In 1955, Nahum Goldmann, president of the World Jewish Congress, convened a meeting of leaders of the major Jewish organizations in Washington, D.C. The result of this gathering was the creation of the Conference of Presidents of Major American Jewish Organizations (COMAJO). Initially, the organization was formed to provide a single American Jewish public voice regarding Israel. In fact, it did become, for many years, the most important quasi-official spokesperson for American Jewry on matters pertaining to Israel.

This leadership role, in regard to Israel, was eclipsed in the 1970s by the growth of the American-Israel Political Action Committee (AIPAC) as the principal American Jewish lobby for Israel.

In 1963, COMAJO added to its agenda issues that affected the entire international Jewish community. By 1984, the conference included 38 major Jewish organizations, both religious and secular, and could boast of representing a majority of Jewish community organizations. Today,

COMAJO's activities include educating public opinion on a myriad of Jewish issues, such as the plight of Societ Jewry, the precarious status of Iranian, Ethiopian, and Syrian Jews, the controversy over the statute of limitations for Nazi war criminals, and its ongoing concern for Israel's security.

Past chairmen of the COMAJO were Dr. Nahum Goldmann (1955–1959), Philip M. Klutznick (1959–1960), Label A. Katz (1960–1961), Rabbi Irving Miller (1961–1963), Lewis H. Weinstein (1963–1965), Rabbi Joachim Prinz (1965–1967), Rabbi Herschel Shachter (1967–1969), Dr. William A. Wexler (1969–1972), Jacob Stein (1972–1974), Rabbi Israel Miller (1974–1975), Rabbi Alexander M. Schindler (1976–1978), Theodore R. Mann (1978–1980), Howard M. Squadron (1980–1982), Julius Berman (1982–1984), Kenneth J. Bialkin (1984–1986), Morris B. Abram (1986–1989), Seymour D. Reich (1989–1990), and Shoshana Cardin (1991–).

JACK FISCHEL

Conservative Judaism. The largest of the four major religious classifications of Jews in the Americas with institutions in Europe and Israel as well, Conservative Judaism is a form of Judaism that openly seeks to embrace and balance tradition and modernity. Although specifically Conservative institutions arose only in the nineteenth century in response to emancipation, Conservative Judaism traces its roots back to the rabbis of the Talmud and sees itself as the continuation of talmudic Judaism in the modern world.

HISTORY. Enlightenment ideology, which defined people as individuals rather than as members of a group, freed Jews from the second-class status that they had suffered for centuries. In the late eighteenth and nineteenth centuries, Jews in central and western Europe and in the United States, where Enlightenment ideology was adopted, could participate much more fully in the educational, cultural, economic, and political life of their countries. Jews understandably welcomed this new-found freedom, but Jewish leaders worried about the massive assimilation and intermarriage that emancipation produced. In response they formed the Conservative, Reform, and neo-Orthodox movements, all three motivated primarily by the need to combat assimilation and only secondarily by differences with each other as to how best to do that.

The Conservative response, called originally Positive-Historical Judaism, applauded the emancipation and the Westernization of Jews, and it recognized that these new conditions required changes in Jewish modes of thought and behavior. It affirmed, however, the value and, indeed, the divine imperative of maintaining traditional Judaism in the modern world, and it asserted that any necessary changes could and should be made within Jewish law. That differentiated it sharply from Reform Judaism, which claimed that all post-biblical law was created by people who intended it to have authority only during their time period and that the biblical prophets had established that only the moral laws of the Torah should be binding.

In contrast to neo-Orthodoxy, however, Conservative spokesmen maintained that, while Jewish law continues to be binding, its content should evolve to meet modern circumstances, just as it had always done. This claim of evolution in Jewish law and culture was rooted in the new, historical method by which Conservative adherents studied the tradition. In addition to learning and examining classical Jewish texts internally, probing all of the Jewish commentaries written over the centuries to see how the tradition understood itself, this method required the student to gain information external to the Jews to understand how the tradition looked from the outside. Jews had never applied objective ("positive") historical techniques to the study of Judaism, and when they began doing so in the nineteenth century, they discovered that Judaism had indeed changed over time in response to new conditions. Leaders of "positive-historical Judaism" maintained that this traditional process should be continued.

The ideological progenitors of Conservative Judaism were the scholars of the Science of Judaism (*Wissenschaft des Judentums*) in the mid-nineteenth century, particularly Zecharias Frankel and the rabbinical seminary he established and directed in Breslau. Frankel broke with his Reform scholarly compatriot, Abraham Geiger, in insisting on the importance of Hebrew in Jewish prayer, one of the factors that continues to differentiate Conservative Judaism from Reform. While some of the scholars of the European Science of Judaism were among the leaders during the early years of the Conservative Movement in the United States, the American movement developed in response to American realities, independent of what was happening in Europe.

Only 12 of the 200 synagogues in America in 1880 identified themselves as other than Reform. After the "Trefah Banquet" in celebration of the first graduating class of Hebrew Union College in 1883 and the Reform Movement's Pittsburgh Platform of 1885, these traditionalists found that they differed too much with the Reformers to be part of the same group. They established the Jewish Theological Seminary of America in New York City in December 1886 to advocate a form of Judaism that, as Professor of Talmud Alexander Kohut put it at the time, "acknowledges the necessity of observing the Law as well as studying it." In founding the Seminary, the traditionalists organized themselves around a school, and that academic grounding and leadership have characterized the Conservative Movement ever since.

Solomon Schechter was brought from Cambridge University to reorganize and direct the Seminary in 1902. Despite many attempts, he was unable to convince some segments of the many Eastern European immigrants arriving in those years to join with him in forming one movement of American traditional Judaism. When the Orthodox broke off, he established the United Synagogue of America in 1913 as an organization of synagogues affiliated with the Seminary and its modern, but yet traditional, approach. The Rabbinical Assembly, originally consisting exclusively of the Seminary's alumni, was established shortly thereafter, and it is those three organizations—the Jewish Theological Seminary, the United Synagogue, and the Rabbinical Assembly—that still form the nucleus of the Conservative Movement in North America.

The Conservative Movement grew by leaps and bounds in the mid-twentieth century. As the children of the Eastern European immigrants became adults, they sought a form of Judaism that expressed their American identity and style and yet retained much of the traditional Judaism of their youth. This sociological phenomenon made Conservative Judaism by far the largest movement in American Judaism from the 1930s through the 1960s. In the 1970s and the 1980s, as the third generation of the Eastern European immigrants reached adulthood, they found ever more opportunities to blend into the American society, producing soaring increases in assimilation and intermarriage. In this environment, most Jews do not affiliate with any religious movement, and so Conservative Judaism, along with the other movements, has had to define its ideology and program much more clearly in an effort to attract the new generation.

INSTITUTIONS. Over the years, the Conservative Movement has established a number of organizations to accomplish its mission. The Seminary, together with its affiliated campuses at the University of Judaism in Los Angeles and Neve Schechter in Jerusalem, has, in addition to its academic activities of teaching and publishing, sponsored the six Ramah camps in North America and the Ramah programs in Israel, the Jewish Museum and the Institute for Religious and Social Studies in New York, and the Eternal Light and Commitment radio and television series. In addition to the Rabbinical Assembly, other Conservative professional organizations include the Cantors Assembly, the Jewish Educators Assembly, the Jewish Youth Directors Association, and the National Association of Synagogue Administrators, the latter four of which are officially arms of the United Synagogue of America. Among its many activities, the United Synagogue also sponsors a large youth department, an education department, and a book publication service. The Federation of Jewish Men's Clubs and Women's League for Conservative Judaism carry on their own religious, educational, and social programs as well as aiding in the sponsorship and direction of many programs of other Conservative affiliates.

While North America has been the primary locus of Conservative Judaism, important arms of the movement now exist in Latin America, Europe, and Israel. Rabbi Marshall Meyer, a Seminary graduate, established the Seminario Rabbinico Latin Americano in Buenos Aires in 1963, the only rabbinical seminary in Latin America. Staffed by local people and many visiting Israeli and Seminary scholars, the Seminario has educated many native Latin American rabbis and teachers in addition to its programs in adult education; it has published Jewish educational and liturgical materials in Hebrew, Spanish, and Portuguese; and it has established Ramah camps in Argentina, Chile, and Colombia. Its graduates are now the rabbis in almost all South and Central American synagogues that have a rabbi, and the Seminario also provides the only institutional supervision of kashrut available in Latin America.

The Conservative Movement has not been as successful in Europe, where there are only a handful of synagogues affiliated with its World Council of Synagogues. In Israel, the Conservative Movement, called *Yahadut M'soratit* (Traditional Judaism), has been handicapped until 1987 by the structure of the Jewish Agency and the Israeli government, both of which channeled all funds for religious activities to the Israeli Orthodox establishment. Beginning in 1987, however, the Jewish Agency for the first time gave money directly to the Foundation for Conservative Judaism in Israel, and the likelihood is that that will expand. Even without such funding, the Conservative Movement to date has established over 40 synagogues, a network of Ramah day camps and youth groups, and, in 1983, a rabbinical program for Israelis.

CONSERVATIVE IDEOLOGY: JEWISH LAW. At the heart of Conservative ideology is a commitment to Jewish law (Halakhah). That commitment is justified in various ways by Conservative writers, as we shall describe below, but all Conservative ideologues assert that observing Jewish law is central to what it means to be a Jew. They simultaneously affirm that the content of Jewish law developed over time in response to historical conditions and that, using the same legal techniques, it must do so today.

Rationale for the Law's Authority. All Conservative thinkers accept the results of modern biblical scholarship, according to which the Torah is composed of several documents from different time periods. That removes the intellectual innocence of centuries of rabbinic scholars—although such people as Abraham ibn Ezra and Azariah de Rossi came remarkably close to these results. The documentary thesis also precludes, however, the tradition's straightforward rationale for the authority of Jewish law, i.e., that God said that we should obey in the record we have of His words. Too much is now known about the text of the Torah to maintain that it is the literal transcription of God's words at Sinai. Some of it is based on cultural traditions antedating Sinai, and much of it derives from various periods thereafter. All of it, however, was committed to writing and edited in the form that has been in our hands centuries after Sinai. That puts the text's claim to divine authority one step removed: it is, at best, what human beings remembered generations later of what God said at Sinai.

Despite this textual problem, some within the Conservative Movement (e.g., Abraham Joshua Heschel, David Novak) maintain that Jewish law is authoritative because God commanded it in words at Sinai. Our text may not be a verbatim transcription, but it is the closest we have. Moreover—and this point will be important in the other approaches too—the Jewish people have sanctified this text and its rabbinic interpretations by basing their lives (and sometimes their martyred deaths) on it. Consequently, one should obey Jewish law because Jews through the centuries have understood it as God's word—in other words, for a combination of divine and human reasons.

Others within the Conservative Movement raise questions not only about the text of the Torah, but also about the process of revelation. Some (e.g., Ben Zion Bokser, Robert Gordis) maintain that human beings wrote the documents out of which the Torah is composed, but they were divinely inspired. God, in other words, did not speak words at Sinai but rather inspired Moses to articulate His message in Moses's own words.

Others (e.g., Louis Jacobs, Seymour Siegel) claim that God did not reveal propositions at all but rather opened Himself to an encounter with human beings, who then articulated their experience and its implications with as much fidelity as possible. God thus commands that we obey Jewish law, but not through words or inspiration; rather, the experiences of the Jewish people with God lead them to understand God's will, and that understanding is articulated in laws. One can feel the influence of Franz Rosenzweig in these existentialist approaches—and indeed Jacobs and Siegel refer directly to Rosenzweig—but one must note that, in contrast to the use of Rosenzweig by Reform theologians, Jacobs and Siegel stress the communal and nomian nature of the encounter with God.

Still others (e.g., Jacob Agus, David Lieber, Elliot Dorff) take a more objectivist view of the encounter with God, basing the authority of the law on the products of reason (rationalists) and experience (empiricists) we all share rather than on personal encounters with God. Jewish law, then, is the will of God as understood by the Jewish people in their reaching for God.

What characterizes all of these philosophies is an insistence on the binding character of the law based upon both divine and human elements. Moreover, the human factor is largely understood in communal terms; that is, it is the Jewish people, through the method described below, who determine the meaning and application of a given text, not individuals.

How the Law Is Determined. Because of its strong historical grounding, the Conservative Movement makes its legal decisions in the two ways in which that was done historically. Specifically, when a community is sufficiently organized to have a central, governing body, then that body makes the decisions. Even when that is the case (and certainly when it is not), the local rabbi (*mara d'atra*) makes many of the decisions.

Thus when a person has a question in Jewish law, he or she first asks the rabbi. In the vast majority of cases, the rabbi answers, and that is the end of the matter. If the rabbi wants advice about how to answer, however, he or she can address the question to the Committee on Jewish Law and Standards (the "Law Committee"), a committee consisting of 25 rabbis, 15 appointed by the Rabbinical Assembly, 5 by the Jewish Theological Seminary of America, and 5 by the United Synagogue of America. Until 1985, when there was disagreement, the committee issued majority and minority opinions, where a "minority" consisted of at least 3 members, and individual rabbis were then free to follow any of the opinions issued. In 1985 the constitution of the Rabbinical Assembly was revised to provide that the agreement of 6 members is required to constitute an official position of the Law Committee.

In addition, according to the 1985 revision, if a proposal is presented for vote as a standard of the movement, and if four-fifths of the members present at a meeting of the Law Committee vote for it, followed by four-fifths of the committee members polled by mail and a majority of those present at the next convention of the Rabbinical Assembly, then the proposal becomes a standard of the movement, binding upon all Conservative rabbis and synagogues on pain of expulsion. The first standard to be adopted under the new rules defines a Jew solely through matrilineal descent or conversion in accordance with Jewish law.

Almost all of the decisions of the Committee on Jewish Law and Standards, however, including those that attain unanimous approval, are not standards; they are decisions of the committee that the individual rabbi must then decide how to implement. Moreover, some regions of the Rabbinical Assembly have adopted policies within their own region, and Conservative rabbis in Israel have constituted a group to answer questions specifically related to Israel. The Conservative method for determining matters of Jewish law thus provides ample room for diversity among the many Conservative rabbis and synagogues. The coherence of the movement is preserved in the most extreme cases through officially adopted standards, but it rests much more upon the shared perspectives and values of the members of the movement.

Some Conservative Decisions. The operating principle of Conservative legal activity is that traditional Jewish law is to be upheld and applied unless there is strong reason to do otherwise. The burden of proof is always on the person who wishes to change Jewish law, not on the one who wants to maintain it. Thus, by and large, decisions of Conservative rabbis and of the Committee on Jewish Law and Standards have simply invoked the law. Of course, that process often calls for judgments to be made since there may be varying opinions in the traditional sources on a given issue or several possible ways to construe a new case. Is food and hydration given intravenously, for example, to be understood as medication such that it can be removed from a patient under certain circumstances, or is it the equivalent of food and water ingested through the mouth so that a patient may never be deprived of it? But the vast majority of Conservative legal decisions have simply been applications of the received law.

A few, however, have taken the law in new directions, particularly in areas of the law concerning women. The marriage contract (*ketubbah*) used by Conservative rabbis since the 1940s includes a clause that records the husband's agreement to follow Jewish law in issuing a writ of divorce to his wife in the event that there is a civil divorce. That clause, upheld in 1983 by the highest court in New York, then led to new legislation in that state requiring both parties to a divorce to remove all impediments for the other to remarry. These measures help to alleviate the woman's inability in Jewish law to institute a writ of divorce.

While the clause in the marriage contract is all but universally accepted within the movement, other measures changing the status of women have not been. The Committee on Jewish Law and Standards permitted women to be called to the Torah for an *aliyah* in 1954, and in 1973 it permitted women to be counted for a prayer quorum (*minyan*). After a protracted process of consideration, involving representatives of all segments of the movement, women were admitted to the Rabbinical School of the Jewish Theological Seminary of America as of October, 1983. The first woman to be ordained by the Seminary was Amy Eilberg in May 1985. Women were also admitted to membership in the Rabbinical Assembly as of June 1984 and subsequently to the Seminary's Cantorial School. These changes are not embraced by all constituents of the Conservative Movement; indeed, some oppose such changes bitterly. It was, in fact, the decision to ordain women that led to the founding of the Union of Traditional Conservative Judaism to oppose that and other such changes. Conservative synagogues vary widely in these matters, ranging from those that do not permit women to assume any leadership role in the liturgy to those that are totally egalitarian. Synagogue governance, however, including the office of president, in all but a handful of Conservative synagogues is open to women.

Aside from the decisions concerning women, probably the best-known Conservative responsum is that permitting driving to synagogue services on the Sabbath if one would not otherwise attend. First promulgated in 1950, it was restricted in 1960 to driving to one's own synagogue. Two other practices within the Conservative Movement often differentiate traditional, Conservative Jews from Orthodox Jews—specifically, many Conservative Jews use electricity on the Sabbath for purposes not forbidden in themselves (e.g., for lights but not for clothes washers) and many will eat dairy foods in a nonkosher restaurant. Not all Conservative Jews accept these leniencies, but a significant number do.

Since these ground-breaking decisions are the ones that have gained a degree of notoriety, it is important to reiterate that they are not the norm. The Conservative Movement sees itself as a movement grounded in, and guided by, Jewish law, and its decisions are most often simply an application of the tradition to modern circumstances.

The Gap Between the Rabbinate and the Laity. In all of the American religious movements there is a gap between the Jewish practices of the rabbinate and those of the laity, but that has been most pronounced and disturbing in the Conservative Movement. This is especially evident in ritual areas, such as observance of the Sabbath and the dietary laws.

To combat this, Conservative synagogues and organizations have undertaken major efforts in recent years to teach constituents what to do and why. United Synagogue Youth has instituted a Shabbat Enhancement Program, which has provided concrete suggestions to teenagers as to how to enhance their observance of Shabbat, even if their parents and/or friends do not observe it. One of its first activities, for example, was to make sure that members knew how to arrange to take college aptitude examinations on a day other than Saturday. The Federation of Jewish Men's Clubs initiated a Hebrew literacy program in the

1970s that has already taught over 100,000 people how to read the Hebrew of the prayer book. In cooperation with the University of Judaism, the Federation of Jewish Men's Clubs has also published a book giving instructions to families of many different configurations (singles, couples without children, etc.) as to how to observe the Friday night Shabbat rituals, together with many practical suggestions and personal comments by laypeople to make it more meaningful, and another, similar book on the Passover Seder has also appeared. Many synagogues have instituted family education programs to teach young families how to observe the Sabbath and festivals, and synagogues have also instituted special services for learners to teach adults how to pray. Adult bar and bat mitzvah programs are also quite common now, in which a first or second bar or bat mitzvah serves as a rubric for enticing adults to learn how to pray and lead the services. And then, of course, the increasing numbers of Conservative children who attend day schools and/or one of the Ramah camps means that more and more of them are attaining a familiarity with Jewish prayer, dietary laws, and Sabbath and festival observance. One should also remember that Conservative Jews have played a pivotal role in communal activities that carry out some of the moral aspects of Jewish law, such as feeding the hungry and caring for the sick.

While these and other similar efforts have not removed the gap in practice between the real and the desirable, they do indicate a new seriousness within the Conservative Movement in its commitment to Jewish law.

CONSERVATIVE IDEOLOGY: JEWISH BELIEF. Conservative ideology has been defined more by its commitments to historical study of the tradition and to Jewish law as both binding and developing than it has to a particular version of other Jewish beliefs. Conservative thinkers, in fact, have varied widely in their theologies. Some have been rather eclectic in their thought (e.g., Simon Greenberg, Louis Jacobs), while others have concentrated on one specific approach, including forms of naturalism (e.g., Mordecai Kaplan) and humanism (e.g., Eugene Kohn), panentheism (Jacob Kohn), predicate theology (Harold Schulweis), rationalism (Jacob Agus, Ben Zion Bokser, Robert Gordis), Hegelianism (Milton Steinberg), organic thinking in the mode of Whitehead (e.g., Max Kadushin), existentialism of both an atheistic (Richard Rubenstein) and theistic (Herschel Matt, Seymour Siegel, Arnold J. Wolf) sort, and phenomenology (Abraham J. Heschel). Conservative leaders have gloried in this diversity since it marks an intellectually and spiritually open and dynamic movement.

Nevertheless, over the years there has been some discomfort with the lack of an overall statement of belief for the movement. This feeling has become especially keen in the 1980s, when sociological realities have meant that Conservative synagogues and organizations must actively recruit constituents rather than simply expect that many people would join. Recruitment requires a reasonably sharp and convincing statement of belief. That, together with the internal need to have a statement of what unites the Conservative Movement within all its diversity, led to the establishment of a Commission on Conservative Philosophy. Chaired by Robert Gordis, the commission was originally constituted in October 1985 by the Seminary and the Rabbinical Assembly and had seven representatives of each. Subsequently, four representatives of the United Synagogue of America and one each of the Women's League for Conservative Judaism, the Federation of Jewish Men's Clubs, the Educators Assembly, and the Cantors Assembly were added, together with a corresponding member of the Israel Region of the Rabbinical Assembly, so that its ultimate statement could indeed reflect the entire movement. At the March 1988 Rabbinical Assembly Convention the commission presented its 40-page *Emet Ve'Emunah*, Conservative Judaism's first Statement of Principles. Neil Gillman, a member of the commission and professor of Jewish philosophy at the Jewish Theological Seminary, in a preliminary assessment stated: "First, it's important to remember that the document itself has no official standing. . . . It would be effective to the extent that it would enable Conservative Jews to understand who they are and what they stand for. If it fails to do this, it will be filed away and become one more footnote in the Movement's century-long attempt to clarify its ideology." As of the fall of 1990, the "verdict" on its adoption was as yet not in. It was still being studied and debated by the movement's rabbis, scholars, and laity.

The work of the commission has demonstrated beyond any doubt that, despite the many different theological approaches taken by Conservative writers, there are many commonalities that make the Conservative Movement cohesive and identifiable. Part of the reason why Conservative leaders were satisfied to remain without a statement of their ideology for so long is undoubtedly that they felt this all along.

One of these commonalities is the vision of Judaism as an evolving, religious civilization. That idea, first formulated in full by Mordecai M. Kaplan in his 1934 book, *Judaism as a Civilization*, means, on the one hand, that Jewish identity is not simply a matter of the Jewish religion, but rather it encompasses all of the elements that make up the Jewish civilization—an attachment to the land of Israel, Hebrew, Jewish dance, art, music, literature, foods, clothing, and so forth. On the other hand, the nucleus of that civilization is the Jewish religion, and so a person whose Jewish identity is based on one or more elements of the Jewish civilization but not its religion has latched onto peripheral elements in Jewish identity and neglected its core. Furthermore, all elements of the Jewish civilization, including its religious beliefs and law, have evolved over time and continue to develop.

In line with this understanding of being Jewish, the Conservative Movement is primarily a religious movement in that it is centered on religious practice (prayer, Shabbat, the festivals, the dietary laws, Jewish moral obligations, etc.) and the study of religious texts, all based on some central religious beliefs. The Conservative Movement, however, has also devoted considerable energies to transmitting and developing other parts of the Jewish civilization. Thus its educational programs in both schools and informal settings teach Israeli literature, songs, and dances, and its youth programs have sponsored educational trips to Israel for the summer or school year and to sights of Jewish significance in Eastern Europe. Moreover, learning both classical and modern Hebrew continues to be a central curricular objective for both children and adults. Some have even said, with some merit, that what characterizes the Conservative Movement most is its emphasis on Jewish peoplehood (*K'lal Yisrael*, which Schechter translated, "catholic Israel"), together with its cultural products.

While the Conservative Movement has adopted this idea of Kaplan's, it has largely rejected his naturalist theology together with its understanding of Jewish rituals as simply folk customs. Most Conservative thinkers affirm a personal, theistic God and ascribe divinity to Jewish law in some way. Conservative liturgical publications reflect this ongoing theism. They also continue to apply the word "chosen" to the People Israel, in contrast to Kaplan's principles. As a result, followers of Kaplan on these issues ultimately formed an independent Reconstructionist Movement rather than remaining the Conservative Movement's "left wing."

Conservative thinkers vary widely in their conceptions of God, but they all affirm the religious and philosophical necessity to speak in theological language. A purely secular view of the world is understood to be inadequate to account for human experience and to respond to it. Conservative writers also maintain many other classical Jewish beliefs: for example, the sanctity of the human being, including the human body as well as the human mind, emotions, will, and soul; human free will and its attendant moral and legal responsibility; the importance of the family, the community, and education; the centrality of Israel for Jews accompanied by an affirmation of the legitimacy and significance of strong Diaspora Jewish communities; the mission of the People Israel to be "a light unto the nations" and to fix the world, leading hopefully one day, with God's help, to a messianic existence for all humanity.

PROBLEMS AND PROSPECTS. The sociological realities of the 1980s, with the other movements becoming more militant and most Jews not affiliating with any religious movement, have made Conservative Judaism in recent years more assertive—communally, legally, and theologically.

On a communal basis, Conservative leaders are now insisting on the leadership positions in Jewish communal agencies and the Jewish communal funding for Conservative institutions and projects commensurate with Conservative numbers. That was not the case previously, in part because the strength of the movement made it unnecessary and in part because of a reticence to cause controversy within the Jewish community. The Conservative community now has more financial needs, however, as it attempts, in an environment of declining rates of affiliation and rising numbers of new day schools, to maintain synagogues, train new personnel, and create new materials and programs.

Similarly, in Israel, Conservative leaders are no longer willing to let the Orthodox establishment have all of the funds earmarked for synagogues and religious schools. Consequently, in 1987, after a vigorous campaign, Mercaz, the Conservative Zionist organization, gained the

third largest number of seats of any delegation on the board of the Jewish Agency, which allocates the funds raised among American Jews to Israeli institutions. Moreover, in that year for the first time grants were made by the Jewish Agency directly to Conservative Movement projects in Israel, thereby bypassing the Orthodox stranglehold on monies allocated by the Israeli government. Steps are also being taken to revise the legal disabilities of Conservative rabbis in Israel.

These steps mark an important, new understanding of the Conservative commitment to *K'lal Yisrael.* The good of the Jewish community in general is still a primary goal of the Conservative Movement, but it aims to achieve that goal in new ways and with new tactics. The "good of the community" no longer means "the community minus the Conservative Movement," nor does it mean "the communal vision of everyone except those of the Conservative Movement." For good or for ill, the Conservative Movement is politically coming of age.

Some of this new assertiveness grows out of the sense that Conservative Judaism has a distinctive, and correct, approach to being Jewish in the modern age and that it has been too meek in promoting it. Its Committee on Jewish Law and Standards no longer is intimidated by the Orthodox or the Reform in making what it considers to be appropriate decisions in Jewish law that are both traditional and modern. Its rulings on the role of women in Judaism are probably the most well known, but the topics it has touched range the whole gamut of moral, ritual, and communal issues, including matters of birth and burial, medical ethics and copyright, the Sabbath and dietary laws. A mark of this new confidence is the plan to organize and publish the committee's decisions on an ongoing basis so that rabbis can consult them readily and use them in classes and discussions with their congregants. Conservative Jewish law is coming out in the open.

And this is true because of a new assertiveness and openness in theology. With the major exception of Mordecai M. Kaplan, Conservative thinkers rarely published works regarding matters of belief until the 1950s, in part, probably, because they feared that spelling out the theological implications of the historical approach to Jewish law and tradition would undermine the whole system. Since then, however, writers affiliated with the Conservative Movement have published a spate of creative theology, including books by Jacob Agus, Ben Zion Bokser, Robert Gordis, Simon

Greenberg, Abraham Joshua Heschel, Louis Jacobs, Jacob Kohn, Harold Kushner, David Novak, Richard Rubenstein, Harold Schulweis, and Milton Steinberg, in addition to many articles by them and others. All of this comes of a renewed sense that Conservative ideology is not only historically authentic but philosophically true, and Conservative ideologues need to explore and explain the reasons why.

Is all of this enough to sustain Conservative Judaism in the future? Nobody knows. But an atmosphere of open inquiry combined with commitment to Jewish law and community have become the distinguishing marks of Conservative Judaism as it continues to develop a modern, traditional form of Judaism. *See also* Reconstructionism, Soloman Schecter.

Elliot N. Dorff

BIBLIOGRAPHY

Davis, Moshe. *The Emergence of Conservative Judaism.* Philadelphia: Jewish Publication Society, 1963.

Dorff, Elliot N. *Conservative Judaism: Our Ancestors to our Descendants.* New York: United Synagogue of America, 1977.

Emet Ve-Emunah: Statement of Principles of Conservative Judaism. New York: The Jewish Theological Seminary of America, The Rabbinical Assembly, The United Synagogue of America, 1988.

Gillman, Neil. "Toward a Theology for Conservative Judaism." *Conservative Judaism* 37 (1984–1985): 4–22.

Gordis, Robert. *Understanding Conservative Judaism.* New York: Rabbinical Assembly, 1978.

Judaism 26 (Summer 1977). The entire issue devoted to articles on Conservative Judaism.

Klein, Isaac. *A Guide to Jewish Religious Practice.* New York: Jewish Theological Seminary, 1979.

Siegel, Seymour, ed. *Conservative Judaism and Jewish Law.* Hoboken, N.J.: Ktav, 1985.

Sklare, Marshall. *Conservative Judaism: An American Religious Movement.* Lanham, Md.: University Press of America, 1985.

Conversion to Judaism. Although conversion to Judaism in America has always existed, it is only in the last several decades that the numbers of converts have been large. While Jewish attitudes toward converts have changed from indifference to more widespread acceptance, conversions have also become part of a significant interreligious disagreement within Judaism.

There have been converts to Judaism in America from colonial times to the present. In colonial America, a large number of converts were black slaves. Some of their descendants maintained their new faith and formed various black Jewish congregations.

After the failed German revolution in 1848, many Jews and Christians sought political refuge in the United States. These refugees were religious liberals; so, despite differences of faith, their common political, national, and linguistic bonds resulted in intermarriages. A large number of the children of such marriages sought to convert to Judaism as adults. Various Jewish periodicals, especially *The Occident* (1843–1869) and *The American Israelite* (founded 1854), frequently carried stories about individuals who had converted.

The most well-known of these early converts was Warder Cresson (1798–1860). In 1844, Cresson was appointed as the first American consul to Jerusalem. Despite a later cancellation of the appointment, Cresson traveled to Jerusalem. Caught up in the revival of Jewish nationalism, and sympathizing with the downtrodden Jews, Cresson decided to convert to Judaism in 1848. Anxious to settle the affairs of his life in the United States, Cresson returned to Philadelphia. His wife and son, shocked at his religious conclusions, had a court declare him insane. In a sensational trial in 1851, a jury found Cresson sane. Cresson returned to Jerusalem, married a Sephardic Jewish woman and worked for Jewish causes.

The greatest changes in conversion occurred in the twentieth century.

The first modern Jewish group to seek converts was the United Israel World Union, established in 1944 by journalist David Horowitz. Union converts established congregations in West Olive, Michigan, and West Union-Wilbur, West Virginia. The union received little rabbinic or Jewish organizational support, in part because Horowitz included among his beliefs the notion that the ten lost tribes of Israel actually exist in the world and that a union must take place between Jews and members of these tribes. One of the union's aims is convincing some non-Jews that they are descendants of these lost tribes.

Other organizations devoted to conversion were also founded. The Jewish Information Society, headquartered in Chicago, was founded by Ben Maccabee in 1959. He received considerable support from some important rabbis, but most Jews greeted the society's efforts with indifference. Financial support dwindled, and the society went out of existence after 13 years. In 1960,

Rabbi Moshe M. Maggal founded the National Jewish Information Service to seek converts. In 1973, Rabbi Allen S. Maller founded the National Jewish Hospitality Committee (an outgrowth of Jews United to Welcome Gentiles). The committee is not a proselytizing organization, but it does aid converts, prospective converts, and others.

The cumulative effect of all these organizations was very limited, in large part because American Jews were not yet ready to welcome converts and an insufficient number of rabbis were convinced of the need to welcome converts.

By the late 1970s, though, much had changed. Most importantly, the intermarriage rate had soared, a fact that caused alarm in the Jewish community but also brought about an unexpected development. Between 20 and 30 percent of those marriage partners not born Jewish were converting to Judaism. In 1954, it was estimated that 3000 people a year were converting to Judaism. By the late 1970s, the annual number topped 10,000. Most estimates were that by the mid-1980s there were 150,000 converts and that by the year 2000, another 150,000 people would convert. Conversion began to be seen as a demographic defense against the loss of numbers brought about by intermarriage.

There were other reasons for a changing Jewish attitude. Jews had never felt more secure in America. They felt freer to place their religious "product" up for sale in the marketplace of ideas. Jews were more supportive of converts as well because American Jewry's fundamental character is voluntary. In a sense, all American Jews choose to remain Jews. Gentiles who choose to convert validate the choice of those born Jewish to remain Jewish. Finally, support for converts has increased because of the enormous contributions made by the converts themselves to Jewish life.

Sensing the change in attitude, Rabbi Alexander Schindler, president of the Union of American Hebrew Congregations (UAHC), a Reform group, delivered an address in December 1978. He proposed that Jews should try to convert "unchurched" non-Jews to Judaism, especially non-Jewish partners in an intermarriage. The outreach program was designed to be unobtrusive, taking its form in the establishment of information centers, educational courses, and publications. By 1983, the UAHC had joined with the Central Conference of American Rabbis to establish a UAHC/CCAR Commission on Outreach as a permanent body to oversee the Reform Movement's conversion program. The emphasis in the program has come to center on welcoming and integrating converts rather than actively seeking them.

Other religious groups in America established comparable programs. In 1979, the Reconstructionists developed formal Guidelines on Conversion, including an outreach program. Their program, though, was aimed directly at those who had already converted in order to help them integrate into the community.

The Conservative Movement, eschewing the original mission idea inherent in Schindler's approach, nevertheless saw the value of preventing intermarriages by encouraging an intermarried non-Jew to convert and making Judaism available (as opposed to proselytizing) to those who are interested. In 1985, the movement's Rabbinical Assembly approved a statement viewing the increase in conversions as a "positive" aspect of Jewish life, both as a reaction to intermarriage and as a personal religious quest. In 1987, the movement held its first Conference on Intermarriage and Conversion and was planning a common syllabus to use in teaching potential converts and other related efforts.

All of these movements began using the term "Jews by Choice" instead of "converts," a term at least some objected to despite its familiarity. In addition to common language use, the three movements faced a common critic: the Orthodox Movement.

The Orthodox, in principle, accept converts who agree to abide by Jewish religious law. However, the Orthodox Movement does not recognize conversions by non-Orthodox rabbis, believing both that such rabbis are unqualified to serve as religious witnesses and that the formal conversion requirements and practices of those rabbis do not conform to traditional Jewish Law. There are, therefore, thousands of non-Orthodox converts not recognized as Jews by the Orthodox. Such a situation carries within it the potential danger of a formal split between the Orthodox and non-Orthodox.

As the number of converts increases, there are continuing efforts to integrate these converts and find a way to allow for recognition of the converts by all religious segments of Judaism, in order to maintain the unity of the Jewish people. *See also* Assimilation, Intermarriage.

LAWRENCE J. EPSTEIN

BIBLIOGRAPHY

Bamberger, Bernard J. *Proselytism in the Talmudic Period.* New York: Ktav, 1968.

Kaellis, Eugene. *Toward a Jewish America.* Lewiston, N.Y.: Mellen Press, 1987.

Kukoff, Lydia. *Choosing Judaism.* New York: UAHC Press, 1981.

Rosenbloom, Joseph R. *Conversion to Judaism: From the Biblical Period to the Present.* New York: Behrman House, 1978.

Wigoder, Deborah. *Hope is My House.* Englewood Cliffs, N.J.: Prentice-Hall, 1966.

Copland, Aaron (1900-1990). Composer Aaron Copland, a man of many talents and musical styles, was most famous for his ballet pieces *Billy the Kid* (1938), *Rodeo* (1942), and *Appalachian Spring* (1944) and his concert pieces *El Salón México* (1937), *Fanfare for the Common Man* (1942), and *Lincoln Portrait* (1942).

Copland was born in Brooklyn, the youngest of five children of Harris and Sarah Copland. His maternal grandfather, Aaron Mittenthal, for whom he is named, came to America in 1868 from Russia. Copland's father, born in Lithuania, immigrated to America in 1877. He owned a successful dry-goods store in Brooklyn—Copland's Department Store—until 1922, when he retired.

Aaron Copland left Brooklyn in the early 1920s to study music in France, where he studied at the Palace of Fontainebleau under Nadia Boulanger. He returned to America in 1924. Soon after, he and Roger Sessions founded Copland-Sessions Concerts. Throughout the late 1920s and early 1930s, their concert series introduced New York audiences to the works of the more important composers.

Copland's compositions have varied throughout the years. In the 1920s he incorporated jazz into his work, for example, in such pieces as *Music for the Theater* (1925) and the *Piano Concerto* (1927). This was followed by the period in which he strove for greater simplicity in his music. This period coincided with his support of liberal and left-wing causes during the 1930s and 1940s. The best example from this period is *El Salón México.* During this period he also incorporated American folk tunes and cowboy tunes into his works. The best known of these works are *Rodeo* and *Billy the Kid.* Perhaps his best adaptation of Americana into his music was in *Appalachian Spring* (1944), where he used the open-fifth harmonies of country fiddlers and featured the Shaker hymn "Simple Gifts" for his elaborate finale. He received the Pulitzer Prize for Composition for the suite from *Appalachian Spring.* During this period of his work he also wrote the movie scores for *Our Town* and *Of Mice and Men.*

In the 1950s, he adopted the 12-tone system. The most famous of these pieces is *Inscape.* After composing four more pieces using the 12-tone system, Copland virtually retired from composing in 1970. He continued to direct and lecture into the mid-1980s, but the poor reception of his later pieces was a great disappointment to him.

One of Copland's best-known pieces was written at the request of Eugene Goossens, conductor of the Cincinnati Symphony Orchestra. He asked Copland to write a fanfare to open a concert that would make a "stirring and significant contribution to the war effort." In response to this request Copland wrote *Fanfare for the Common Man* in 1942. It was played in March 1943 and dedicated to the "average" man having to pay his income taxes. Eventually, Copland used the fanfare as a finale to his Third Symphony. *Fanfare for the Common Man* has since been used on many auspicious occasions, including the groundbreaking ceremony for the Lincoln Center and for the presidential inauguration of Richard Nixon. There have also been a number of different arrangements of the piece used by such musicians as Woody Herman, the pop group Emerson, Lake, and Palmer, and the rock group the Rolling Stones.

During his splendid career Copland also published several books. Among them were *What to Listen for in Music* (1939), *Our New Music* (1941), which was revised and published in 1968 as *The New Music 1900-1960,* and *Music and Imagination.* In 1984, he published his autobiography *Copland: 1900 Through 1942,* which was followed in 1989 by the second and final volume *Copland Since 1943.*

Copland received many honors and awards. Among them was the honor of being the director of the First Festival of Contemporary Music at Yaddo, held in Saratoga Springs, New York in 1932. He was also president of the American Composers Alliance (1937-1945), member of the executive board of directors of the League of Composers, and member of the faculty at the Berkshire Music Center at Tanglewood, Lennox, Massachusetts, for 25 years. He received the Presidential Medal of Freedom in 1964, the Henry Howland Memorial Prize from Yale University in 1970, the Gold Baton from the American Symphony Orchestra League in 1978, and the Kennedy Center Award in 1979.

Copland was preeminent among the composers of the twentieth century and will long be remembered for his use of folk songs and incorporation of Americana into his music.

JANET L. DOTTERER

BIBLIOGRAPHY

"Aaron Copland, U.S. Composer, Dies at 90." Obituary. *New York Times*, December 3, 1990, Al, D11.

Berger, Arthur. *Aaron Copland*. Westport, Conn.: Greenwood Press, 1953.

Butterworth, Neil. *The Music of Aaron Copland*. New York: Universe, 1986.

Copland, Aaron, and Perlis, Vivian. *Copland: 1900 Through 1942*. New York: St. Martin's Press, 1984.

———. *Copland: Since 1943*. New York: St. Martin's Press, 1989.

Skowronski, Joann. *Aaron Copland: A Bio-Bibliography*. Westport, Conn.: Greenwood Press, 1985.

Council of Jewish Federations. The stated purpose of the Council of Jewish Federations (CJF) is to aid local agencies in "fund raising, community organization, health and welfare planning, personnel recruitment, and public relations." Originally known as the Council of Jewish Federation Welfare Fund, the council was formed in 1932 to establish a coordinated communal fund-raising organization and to provide a forum for professionals from many organizations to discuss common problems and possible solutions.

Beginning in the late 1800s, Jewish community organizations in the United States began to join together to form local federations. The first federations were formed in Boston and Cincinnati. By the end of World War I, there were 42 federations. It soon became obvious that those local federations would benefit from a national umbrella organization, and the Council of Jewish Federations was established. The real strength of the council developed during the Depression, when a massive relief effort was needed to prevent the various agencies from being overwhelmed. By speaking with one voice, the council was able to appeal to the federal government for assistance. The formation of the Council of Jewish Federations reflected a Jewish community that was beginning to develop a sense of national identity.

CJF helped many communities with a Jewish population establish local federations. Within a few years after the council's formation, there were 200 federations across the United States. The communities that have a federation use it for the basic organizational functions of financing, budgeting, planning and coordination, and leadership development for Jewish interests. The federation is a voluntary citizen's movement. Local federations retain their independence but rely on the Council of Jewish Federations to represent them at the national and international level.

Federations are committed to support Israel. In 1950, the Council of Jewish Federations took part in a conference to set the framework for aid to Israel. A four-part program was organized: (1) contributions; (2) bonds, to be used as loans for development by the Israeli government; (3) intergovernmental loans; and (4) private investment for businesses.

CJF also helps Jewish communities during emergencies. When Hurricane Agnes devastated Wilkes Barre, Pennsylvania, and when floods devastated Johnstown, Pennsylvania, and Jackson, Michigan, CJF sent monetary assistance and provided counseling.

The council is the only Jewish institution that has been able to develop a program of service to the entire Jewish community. Its campaign supports many causes: the United Jewish Appeal is the largest beneficiary. In 1959, CJF established the National Foundation for Jewish Culture and the National Council of Jewish Cultural Agencies. These organizations were given the responsibility to help develop Jewish scholarly research, publications, archives, and other cultural resources. Universities were encouraged to establish Judaic studies curricula. The foundation also assists Ph.D. candidates in Judaic studies.

The strength of the council has been felt frequently, especially when it has been able to bring unity on divisive issues. In 1939, two organizations were conducting separate, vigorous fund-raising campaigns. The Joint Distribution Committee was raising money for worldwide rescue and relief; the United Palestine Appeal was raising money for settlements and absorption in Palestine. Through the Council of Jewish Federations, local federations pushed for some means of cooperation. The local federations were issued allocation guidelines. The two competing organizations merged campaigns and created the United Jewish Appeal (UJA). The council has exerted the pressure necessary to keep UJA united. More recently, the council proved how effective it was during the Israelis' General Assembly 1988 debate over "who is a Jew." The council was instrumental in explaining the feelings of American Jewry to the Israelis.

Julian Freeman, former president of CJF, summarized the Council's work in his address to the 1951 CJF General Assembly: "There was a vacuum in Jewish life which had to be filled—the need for communities to counsel together on their needs and responsibilities, to learn from each other, so that they could face more intelligently and more successfully, the local problems which pressed upon them—and act jointly on the national responsibilities which all share. That was the vision on which the Council was established. And the movement has grown because it has worked." *See also* Communal Organizations.

LINDA GLAZER

BIBLIOGRAPHY

"Council of Jewish Federations, 50 Years of Building a Jewish Community, 1932–1982." New York: Council of Jewish Federations.

Karp, Abraham J. *Haven and Home.* New York: Schocken, 1985.

Meller, Charles. "An Introduction to the Jewish Federation." New York: Council of Jewish Federations, 1985.

"Semi-Centennial Minutes, 1982." New York: Council of Jewish Federations, 1982.

Yoffe, James. *The American Jews.* New York: Random House Paperback Library Edition, 1969.

Criminals. Throughout their long residence in North America, a residence that dates back to the mid-seventeenth century, Jews had a reputation for being among the more law-abiding and peaceful of the nation's citizenry. "If we enter a penitentiary or prison of any description," remarked one nineteenth-century journalist, "the marked face of the Israelite is rarely to be seen within its walls."

As the nineteenth century gave way to the twentieth, however, Jews increasingly appeared as members-in-full of the underworld, especially in such metropolitan areas as New York City. Manhattan's Lower East Side, home to the single largest concentration of Eastern European Jewish immigrants in the New World, was now viewed as a "distinct center of crime," and its residents "the worst element in the entire make-up of New York life." By 1908, none other than Theodore Bingham, New York's high-ranking police com-

missioner, could publicly proclaim that Jews constituted more than half of his city's underworld, a statement that rocked New York Jewry to its very core, shocking them with his revelations. Armed with a battery of seemingly incontestable statistics, the official declared that "it is not astonishing that with a million Hebrews, mostly Russian, in the city . . . perhaps half of the criminals should be of that race."

Though a concerned Jewish citizenry took vigorous exception to Bingham's remarks, challenging the accuracy and statistical rigor of his assertions, few were inclined to dispute Bingham's basic point: the existence of a sizable Jewish criminal class. No informed Jewish leader dared question that during the years of mass immigration the Lower East Side had become, in fact, a "real police problem," as another, perhaps more restrained, police commissioner had observed several years earlier. In an area of only one square mile, authorities estimated there to be approximately 200 brothels, 336 gang "hangouts," and over 200 pool hall cum betting establishments; dance halls, a common rendezvous of pimps and procurers, were found every two-and-one-half blocks, while gambling parlors blanketed the neighborhood. With its fair share of prostitutes, pickpockets, extortionists and gangs, the East Side, noted the *American Hebrew* soberly, "is spoken of as one vast habitat of the underworld."

Vice and crime were not only widespread on the Lower East Side, they were also highly visible. With no segregated crime areas, vice, lamented Abe Shoenfeld (a keen student of the underworld and chief investigator for the Kehillah's Bureau of Social Morals, a "Jewish police station"), was everywhere and respectable residents "rubbed shoulders" with the criminal element. In the cramped quarters of the Lower East Side, it was hard not to. That brothels were scattered throughout the area was a matter of common knowledge. "If a woman called out to you as you walked down Allen Street," recalled former resident Judge Jonah J. Goldstein, "you knew she wasn't calling you to a *minyan*." Seedy restaurants and saloons were contiguous to public schools, and Jewish gang members loitering on the street was not an uncommon sight.

Frequenting the area's cafes, saloons, and disorderly houses, the pre-World War I Jewish criminal element made the Lower East Side and other Jewish neighborhoods like it their home. If deviant in their choice of occupation, the members of the Jewish underworld were in other respects tied to the larger Jewish community. Comfortable with their own kind, such well-known Jewish criminals as Big Jack Zelig, a master pickpocket turned gunman, and Mother Rosie Hertz, a wealthy madam, lived alongside their more law-abiding coreligionists. At the zenith of his career, Zelig lived on Broome Street, in the heart of the Lower East Side, while Rosie chose to pitch her tent among the affluent Jews of Brooklyn's Borough Park neighborhood. Like the other Jewish inhabitants of the Empire City, the members of the Jewish underworld often spoke Yiddish among themselves, giving rise to a host of slang criminal phrases of Yiddish origin such as *simcha* for a pimp and *shomis* for a detective. They not only spoke Yiddish but enjoyed eating at the Grand Street Cafeteria, attended weddings and bar mitzvahs at Arlington Hall, a popular local catering facility, and even attended synagogue on occasion. "It makes no difference whatever I do," one prostitute related. "On Yom Kippur and Rosh Hashannah, I go to *schul*."

Interestingly enough, the Jewish underworld element prior to World War I evinced a distinctive economic profile: even their illicit form of upward mobility was rooted in the Jewish ethnic economy. The most common crimes—burglary and theft, dealing in stolen goods, labor racketeering, arson and horse-poisoning, a form of extortion—were bound up with the specific economic contours of the Jewish Lower East Side, and their victims were largely Jewish; prostitution and the white slave trade similarly engaged Jewish prostitutes, procurers, and customers. Although focusing overwhelmingly on property-related offenses, Jewish criminals, to be sure, did commit assault, engage in rape, abandon their wives, and periodically murder. "The Jews of this city as a class," noted a contemporary in 1916, "are possessed of all the vices of the people with whom they live." And yet, violent crimes accounted for a disproportionately small percentage of offenses for which Jews were arrested or even convicted. "The Jewish population is not apt, unless under great pressure, to resort to force or to commit crimes of violence," observed one official. Much the same could be said of its more deviant members. Like their respectable counterparts, even the Jewish criminal element tended to stay clear of violent crimes and to concentrate most directly on those relating to property. "The Christians commit crimes with their hands, while the Jews," declared sociologist Arthur Ruppin, "use their reason."

As World War I drew to a close, New York Jews began to make great strides economically and socially and to move into middle-class neighborhoods. Leaving behind the gray cramped tenements of the city's densest Jewish quarters, they had left behind as well its social dislocation, poverty, and criminal pathologies. Although the advent of Prohibition offered untold possibilities to a number of imaginative and resourceful Jewish underworld figures, such as bootlegger Waxy Gordon, and instances of labor racketeering became especially pronounced in the garment trades, criminal activity among New York's Jews during the interwar years actually declined. During this period, fewer and fewer turned to crime as a vehicle of upward mobility; so marked was this trend that one court official observed in 1931 that "there has been a drop in delinquency and criminality among the Jews almost beyond belief. The number of Jewish prisoners," he added, "is sinking to practically a negligible quantity."

Ironically enough, though, it was during the interwar years that Jewish criminals enjoyed their great celebrity and in one celebrated instance, their greatest notoriety. Arnold Rothstein, reputed "czar of the underworld" and man-about-town, was perhaps the best-known Jewish underworld figure of the 1920s. With a flair for business and business organization, Rothstein (the model for F. Scott Fitzgerald's fictional character Meyer Wolfsheim) reportedly transformed criminal activity from a haphazard, poorly organized enterprise into "big business," rationalizing the enterprise and financing its illegal business ventures. And yet, with the exception of his involvement in labor racketeering (he furnished strong-arm gangs during labor disputes), Rothstein derived little of his income from the Jewish ethnic economy nor for that matter was he tied culturally to a Jewish environment: he remained a Jewish criminal by virtue of his origins and little else. Much the same can be said of Murder, Inc., an ethnically mixed Brownsville (a Brooklyn neighborhood) gang of bookmakers, money-lenders, racketeers, and, toward the latter part of its career, professional murderers whose unsavory deeds were widely chronicled during the late thirties and early forties by the metropolitan press. Little bound that gang to an avowedly Jewish context, nor, for that matter, did their activities represent the advance guard of a future, gun-toting generation of Jewish n'er-do-wells. Two anomalies, both Rothstein and Murder, Inc., each in its own way, signified the "last hurrah" of the American Jewish criminal experience.

Despite the intense glare of publicity that surrounded Rothstein and Murder, Inc., or even the legendary postwar exploits of Meyer Lansky, the general public refrained from branding the Jewish community as a whole as a criminal underclass. "There are Jews in America who still recall with a shudder, the [Bingham] incident," observed the *American Hebrew* almost 25 years later. In the face of the diminishing numbers of Jewish criminals, "we can now say," concluded the influential weekly, "that the scar left by Bingham is now ENTIRELY HEALED." *See also* New York City.

JENNA WEISSMAN JOSELIT

BIBLIOGRAPHY

Bingham, Theodore A. "Foreign Criminals in New York." *North American Review* 187 (September 1908).

Goren, Arthur. *New York Jews and the Quest for Community: The Kehillah Experiment, 1908–1922.* New York: Columbia University Press, 1970.

Joselit, Jenna Weissman. *Our Gang: Jewish Crime and the New York Jewish Community, 1900–1940.* Bloomington: Indiana University Press, 1983.

McAdoo, William. *Guarding a Great City.* New York: Harper, 1906.

Ornitz, Samuel. *Haunch, Paunch and Jowl.* Garden City, N.Y.: Doubleday, 1923.

Critics, Literary. Jewish-American literary scholars have become prominent only since the 1940s. The most sustained and influential contributions to contemporary criticism are probably those of Lionel Trilling (1905-1975), Philip Rahv (1908-1973), Alfred Kazin (b. 1915), Leslie Fiedler (b. 1917), and Irving Howe (b. 1920). All are associated with the tradition of the "New York intellectuals," sharing a common genesis in the Jewish-American encounter in the 1930s between Marxist political radicalism and the European avant-garde literature of T. S. Eliot and James Joyce that we now call "Modernism."

Prior to World War II, Jewish-American literary scholars were rarely represented in universities and academic journals. In the postwar era, there were few Jews among the leading practitioners of the two dominant critical movements—the New Criticism, sanctifying the autonomy of the work of art, and the Chicago School, emphasizing the Aristotelian elements of action, plot, and character. In subsequent years, prominent Jewish-American critics, such as Harry Levin,

Daniel Aaron, Stanley Fish, and Harold Bloom, were identifiable as Jews more by their names than by subject or methodology, although Bloom borrowed from the Jewish tradition for some of his interpretations of Western literature in *Kabbalah and Criticism* (1975).

However, between the early 1930s and the early 1950s, a largely Jewish school of "New York intellectuals" gradually coalesced. Based in New York City and associated with publications such as *Partisan Review*, *Commentary*, and *Dissent*, this lively group of men and women has written prolifically and often polemically about the social implications of the arts for nearly five decades. In addition to Trilling, Rahv, Kazin, Fiedler, and Howe, other Jewish-American literary critics frequently linked to the tradition are Lionel Abel, Stephen Marcus, William Phillips, Norman Podhoretz, Isaac Rosenfeld, Delmore Schwartz, Susan Sontag, and Diana Trilling.

The intellectual achievement of this group constitutes an important chapter in the cultural history of upwardly mobile second-generation American Jews. Mostly from immigrant families, they began their careers as rebellious "outsiders" but ended as part of the very establishment they once abhorred. In varying degrees, their political and literary views accommodated the changes in their status over the decades, although some cultural historians argue that such transformations were justified by international and domestic new political developments.

Cultural historians also differ in their assessments of the relative weight of the diverse elements coming together to forge these individuals, along with an interlocking network of associates and disciples, into an identifiable "group." Most agree, however, that the pioneering work of these critics was part of a common effort to reconcile tensions in three areas.

First, the founders of the tradition of the New York intellectuals were inspired by Karl Marx's vision of a rational and humane society but frustrated by the development of the totalitarian system that they called "Stalinism" in the Soviet Union. Second, they applied European Modernist categories and standards to literature of the United States. Third, they struggled to affirm a secular Jewish identity while rejecting particularism.

Thus, despite variants and eccentricities, at the outset of their careers these men and women tended to counterpose authentic communism to its Soviet aberration, cultural vanguardism to academic convention, and internationalist universalism to a particular ethnic identity. At the close of the period, they tended in varying degrees and with a few exceptions to support the United States (euphemistically renamed "The West") against Stalinist expansionism; cling to classical Modernism as the last hope of sanity against the Beats, the counterculture of the 1960s, and post-Modernism; and sentimentalize their Jewish upbringings when their internationalism waned.

Philip Rahv, comparatively the least productive of the group, was in many ways its architect and guiding spirit through his brilliant editing of the journal *Partisan Review*. A Russian immigrant who educated himself while working at odd jobs, Rahv was born Ivan Greenberg but changed his name to Rahv—the Hebrew word for rabbi—when he joined the Communist Party in 1933. In 1934 he cofounded *Partisan Review* as an organ of the Communist Party's writers' organization, the John Reed Clubs.

The journal's initial effort was to promulgate a Marxist literary criticism eschewing the political coding of literary forms and the judgment of art according to the politics of the artist. By 1937, after the Communist Party had abandoned its "proletarian literature" orientation for the liberal populism of the Peoples Front, Rahv had assembled a core group of writers, many of whom would later be known as the New York intellectuals. What these individuals had in common was a commitment to relaunching the journal independent of and in opposition to the Communist Party from the Left. The new *Partisan Review* brought a dissident revolutionary communism, partly influenced by the ideas of the exiled Bolshevik Leon Trotsky, into a tensive relation with literary Modernism.

For his entire career, Rahv aspired to become the ideological leader of dissident literary intelligentsia. Throughout the later Great Depression years, World War II, the postwar era, the McCarthyite witch-hunt, and the revival of radicalism in the 1960s, he maneuvered the journal through political and cultural debates with a skill that turned the pages of *Partisan Review* into one of the most widely discussed documents of the intellectual life of our times.

The first essays of Rahv garnering influence beyond the literary Left appeared in the late 1930s, in certain respects demarcating the terrain of his future career. "Proletarian Literature: A Political Autopsy" (1939, *Southern Review*) was an ambiguous dismissal of the literary movement to which he had devoted the formative part of his career. The effort in the early 1930s to foment a renaissance of "proletarian literature"—that is, literature explicitly about class struggle and, where possible, penned by authentic workers—is excoriated as the political creature of the Communist Party. Whether such a project had an independent viability remains unexplained. A characteristic lacuna in the essay is Rahv's virulent denunciation of Stalinism as a perversion of Marxism, without a forthright explanation of the politicocultural program of the purer Marxism-Leninism to which he apparently adhered at that moment.

"Paleface and Redskin" (*Kenyon Review*, 1939) and "The Cult of Experience in American Writing" (*Partisan Review*, 1940) offer a perspective on American literary culture, possibly formulated in opposition to what he saw as the literary nationalism of the Popular Front. Rahv was considerably impressed with Henry James's observations about the limitations of American culture in contrast to that of Europe; he was also influenced by Van Wyck Brooks's view of the existence of a cultural bifurcation between refined and vulgar authors (Rahv substituted "Paleface" and "Redskin" for Brooks's "Highbrow" and "Lowbrow") during the nineteenth and twentieth centuries. In a strategy that would also be employed by Trilling and Howe, Rahv set out to give a fresh interpretation of such protomodernist views reconceptualized with Marxist notions of the historical matrix of culture.

For Rahv, a successful work of art is refined yet boldly confronts reality; thought and being are bound together in the fictional word. His exemplars are the European novels of Leo Tolstoy, Fyodor Dostoyevsky, Gustav Flaubert, Marcel Proust, James Joyce, Thomas Mann, D. H. Lawrence, and Franz Kafka. On the theoretical plane, Rahv likens artistic practice to the Marxist model of a material substructure giving birth to a superstructure of multiple forms of consciousness; these, in turn, act and react upon the material base.

From this perspective, Rahv proposes a skeletal frame in which nineteenth-century America—due to an alleged lack of European historical depth, the isolation of the intelligentsia from seats of power, and the repressive legacy of Puritanism—was dominated by Paleface writers of the Hawthorne tradition, cerebral and isolated from experience. After industrial and urban forces were unleashed toward the end of the century, the United States moved from an economy of accumulation to one of consumerism. This assisted the dominance of Redskin writers in the Walt Whitman tradition, hostile to complex ideas and responding to reality as if it were an undifferentiated whole.

Rahv held that the Redskins maintained the upper hand into the late 1930s, but he believed that international factors would soon transform intellectual life. Nevertheless, such historical determinism, while overwhelming on a grand scale, did not at all preclude unique and heroic individual efforts at recreating the European blend, exemplified most clearly in the late novels of James.

Rahv, who never attended college, was appointed a professor at Brandeis University in 1957. Unable to sustain a book-length work, his oeuvre survives in a series of collections of his essays and reviews, often with duplications, such as *Image and Idea* (1949), *The Myth and the Powerhouse* (1965), *Literature and the Sixth Sense* (1969), and the posthumous *Essays on Literature and Politics, 1932–1972* (1978).

The typical essay by Rahv is initiated by a dialectically provocative first sentence affirming a complex but plausible thesis with the air of great certainty. Often the thesis is hard to sustain, breaking down rather easily in light of attempts at broader application. Yet the results are frequently scintillating, as in Rahv's tracing of female archetypes in Hawthorne ("The Dark Lady of Salem," *Partisan Review* [September–October 1941]) and James ("The Heiress of All the Ages," *Partisan Review* [May–June 1943]).

Although there is little development in scope or methodology, key moments in his literary itinerary include his defense of Kafka as a repository of rationalism, chapters from a projected book on Dostoyevsky, a righteous assault on the mystifications of myth and symbol criticism, and a series of animadversions on renegade ex-Marxist intellectuals when Rahv returned to left-wing political thought in the 1960s. A high Modernist to the end, in 1969 Rahv broke with William Phillips, his longtime co-editor of *Partisan Review*, on the grounds that *Partisan Review* had capitulated to the 1960s counterculture. In 1971, he founded *Modern Occasions*, which lasted only six issues.

Lionel Trilling is widely recognized as one of the most influential American intellectuals of the post-World War II decades. He began his career in the 1920s as a frequent contributor to the *Menorah Journal*, a nonreligious magazine of Jewish culture, and in the 1930s contributed to left-wing journals such as the *Nation, Modern Monthly,*

and *Partisan Review*. The publication of *The Liberal Imagination* (1950) secured him a broader reputation as a cultural critic of unusual range, subtlety, and perspicacity. Trilling denied allegiance to any particular theory of criticism, but his many books—including *Matthew Arnold* (1939), *The Opposing Self* (1955), *Beyond Culture* (1965), and *Sincerity and Authenticity* (1972)—reveal a special preoccupation with psychoanalysis, contemporary politics, mass culture and high culture, rebellion and conformity, and manners and morals.

Even though Trilling commented on Jewish matters only a few times after he had become a famous professor of literature at Columbia University, his attitude toward his Jewish upbringing and the Jewish community is the subject of some debate. Those critical of Trilling for a lack of sufficient identification with Judaism frequently cite his February 1944 statement in the *Contemporary Jewish Record* that "I do not think of myself as a 'Jewish writer.' . . . I know of writers who have used their Jewish experience as the subject of excellent work; I know of no writer in English who has added a micromillimetre to his stature by 'realizing his Jewishness'."

A more balanced expression of Trilling's point of view appeared in his memoir of *Commentary* critic Robert Warshow. Trilling wrote in the introduction to Warshow's posthumous collection, *The Immediate Experience* (1962), that Warshow's life resembled his own in that Warshow "acknowledged, and with pleasure, the effect that a Jewish rearing had had upon his temperament and mind, and he was aware of, and perhaps surprised by, his sense of connection with Jews everywhere—and [yet he] found that the impulses of his intellectual life were anything but Jewish, and that the chief objects of his thought and feeling were anything but Jewish."

This is confirmed by the fact that little, if any, of Trilling's professional and literary activities after the 1920s correlate to Jewish culture—except, indirectly, through his lifelong interest in Marx and Freud, whose Jewish aspects he hardly considered. Instead, his body of critical writing takes its theme from Matthew Arnold's view of literature as a criticism of life, and his numerous essays agonize over the dilemma of the self seeking freedom in a culture that both nurtures and inhibits that desire for freedom.

For example, while he shared Rahv's perspective on the inadequacies of American culture, he placed a greater emphasis and responsibility on the struggle of human consciousness to respond to the ambiguities of "reality" and "experience." Although it is difficult to determine who influenced whom in the forging of such similar perspectives, there is no doubt that a considerable amount of cross-fertilization took place among the founders and later adherents of the tradition of New York intellectuals.

After repudiating his allegiance to radical movements in the 1930s, Trilling affirmed what he believed to be a liberal spirit in intellectual life while also insisting that liberal ideas had a tendency to degrade themselves when entering the sphere of politics because they gave themselves too easily to simplistic solutions and utopias. As an antidote, Trilling sought to foster Keats's concept of "negative capability," which he defined as being the outlook of a person who can live with perpetual contradictions and uncertainties.

Moreover, there was a persistent political theme in his writing: an assault on the mentality of fellow travelers of communism, which can be seen in his famous collection of essays, *The Liberal Imagination*, as well as in his novel, *The Middle of the Journey* (1946). His one novel, along with a half-dozen stories, constitutes his achievement in fiction, although his original goal had been to be a novelist, not a critic.

Alfred Kazin, a critic noted for his ability to analyze literature in conjunction with the lives of the authors and the prevailing social climate of the times, was born in 1915 into a poor Jewish immigrant family in New York. A student at the City College of New York who commuted home at night to Brownsville, he received a Bachelor of Social Science degree in 1935 and an M.A. in English from Columbia University in 1937. He subsequently worked as a tutor while aspiring to be a writer in New York City.

During the Great Depression he was an armchair left-wing socialist, attracted to Marxist intellectuals but not to Marxism as a doctrine. Over the next 40 years he evolved to left liberalism, abandoning socialism entirely by the 1980s. Nevertheless, he distanced himself considerably when an important wing of the New York intellectuals around Norman Podhoretz's *Commentary* and the art critic Hilton Kramer's *New Criterion* embraced neoconservatism during the late 1970s.

On Native Grounds: an Interpretation of Modern Prose Literature (1942), established Kazin as a major force in the study of United States literature. The book inaugurates the enduring theme of his life's work: the estrangement of American writers from the very ground on which they live—and that is full of fascination for them. Among the frustrating and painful consequences of that dilemma is a tendency to turn inward, repeating oneself and failing to reach maturity. For example, in the case of literary Modernism, Kazin suggests that American writers used Modernism as an instrument without fully assimilating its substance.

Although Kazin omits consideration of poetry and drama, *On Native Grounds* in many ways summarizes the most impressive intellectual qualities of the 1930s. The book is rich in its social texture, firm in its humane point of view, and for its time relatively nonelitist in scope and valorizations. Methodologically, however, *On Native Grounds* was imbalanced in the degree to which it hammered away at the weaknesses of other critics—especially those closest to him in preoccupation, if not talent, such as Granville Hicks—while being vague about the alternatives proposed. Still, the literary establishment was astonished by the sheer learning exhibited by the 27-year-old Kazin as the chapters marched steadily from Howells to Steinbeck, covering perhaps 50 twentieth-century American writers of three generations in considerable detail.

Numerous subsequent works—*The Inmost Leaf* (1955), *Contemporaries* (1962), and *Bright Book of Life* (1973)—established Kazin's reputation as a reviewer and essayist able to communicate quickly and aptly the unique styles of a range of writers. On the other hand, Kazin gives relatively little emphasis to formal analysis, even less to the unconscious intent of the author, and almost none to abstract theory.

An American Procession: The Major American Writers from 1830–1930, The Crucial Century (1984) failed to match his first book in vigor and erudition but nevertheless sustained his reputation as a powerful voice in the tradition of humane critics who aspire to enrich intellectually their readers. Once more Kazin exhibits a talent for immersing himself in writers' works and lives to recapitulate in concise form their ideas and emotions.

An enterprise paralleling his literary scholarship has been his autobiographical trilogy, *A Walker in the City* (1951), *Starting Out in the Thirties* (1965), and *New York Jew* (1978), which begins more forcefully than it ends. The first volume sensuously evokes the immigrant Jewish community in which Kazin was reared, dramatizing the dialectical interplay of the cultural conflict between the insular Brownsville of Brooklyn and the lure of Manhattan that so profoundly shaped his childhood.

Starting Out in the Thirties, which extends from his inauguration as a book reviewer in 1934 to his viewing of films of concentration camp victims in 1945, describes his involvement with the intellectual life of the 1930s. The book is most effective in its accounts of meetings and descriptions of performances, but it is vague about the ideological issues of the day, leaving the reader with an unclear conception of Kazin's "socialism."

New York Jew, which covers 1942 until the 1970s, is far more expansive and ambitious than the preceding volumes but consequently weaker in the integration of narration and portraits. Nevertheless, with wit, lyricism, and insight it effectively communicates a lively sense of the changing times in which Kazin and the other New York intellectuals evolved and came to influence.

Throughout his career, Kazin has been closer to indigenous cultural traditions and less fixated on the Modernist tradition than other New York intellectuals; such qualities, along with a reluctance to put literary criticism at the service of political struggle, have facilitated his distinctive voice and achievement. Yet it is symptomatic of the narrowness of the group that, as late as the mid-1980s, Kazin, one of its less Eurocentric members, could publish a book so bound to traditional canons as *An American Procession*. Purporting to interpret the "major writers" who created a voice for our culture, Kazin inexplicably omits all nonwhites, including the great figures of the Harlem Renaissance, and all females save Emily Dickinson. By and large, Kazin is at one with Rahv and Trilling in a reluctance to champion unconventional writers and theories after the 1930s.

Such steadfast literary traditionalism contrasts markedly with the curious career of Leslie Fiedler. Fiedler has spent little time in New York City, but he shares many common formative experiences with a second generation of those in the tradition of the New York intellectuals.

Born in 1917 in Newark, New Jersey, he switched from the Communist to the Trotskyist movement during his final year at New York University. Following graduate studies at the University of Wisconsin, he took a teaching job at Montana State University, his home base until he moved to the State University of New York at Buffalo in 1964. After a few months in Montana, he drifted away from left-wing organizations for nonideological reasons. During World War II, he learned Japanese, serving as an interrogator of war prisoners.

A June 1948 essay in *Partisan Review*—"Come Back to the Raft Ag'in, Huck Honey!"—brought Fiedler considerable notoriety. The iconoclastic essay charged that classic American writing was actually a "boys' literature," masking a homoerotic fantasy of love between white and dark-skinned men in response to the guilt complex of the European invaders of the continent. The central burden of his scholarship was thus established as the exposure of the hidden intentions at the core of literature. From the outset, critics of Fiedler have been uncertain as to whether he uses literature as an excuse for wild speculations about the psyches of the authors or whether such speculations ultimately return us to an enriched understanding of our national culture.

Two collections of essays, *An End to Innocence* (1955) and *No! In Thunder* (1960), confirmed Fiedler's ability to provoke his audience. Reviewers were once more polarized as to whether he was a creative genius or a charlatan huckstering sensational theses. In *Leslie Fiedler* (1985), an admiring Mark Winchell found he could only label Fiedler's method "creative eclectism."

In 1960 *Love and Death in the American Novel* elevated his early psychoanalytical themes about the disabling role of guilt and sexual immaturity in the American consciousness to a grand scale, with the result that the book won a place among the most influential texts in United States literary studies. Fiedler explores the psychodynamic drives underlying our national myths in startling and original ways; his special attention to issues of race, gender, ethnicity, and marginality anticipate the scholarship of generations to come.

Fiedler's argument about American literature was extended in *Waiting for the End* (1964) and *The Return of the Vanishing American* (1968). In 1982, *What Was Literature?* not only defended the original thesis, but reworked it impressively with examples from mass culture. In the meantime, Fiedler continued to issue an extraordinary group of writings that ranged from polemics against formalism to meditations on black-Jewish relations to the defense of literary criticism on ethical grounds. *The Stranger in Shakespeare* (1972) explored the treatment of women, Jews, Moors, and native peoples, while *Freaks: Myths and Images of the Secret Self* (1978) was a landmark of popular culture treating human oddities.

Fiedler's 1959 monograph, "The Jew in the American Novel," is credited with reorienting the understanding of Jewish-American literature. Not only did he deflate the earlier tradition based on Ludwig Lewisohn and Ben Hecht, asserting a lineage that included Abraham Cahan, Daniel Fuchs, Henry Roth, and Nathanael West, he also extended his inquiry into the role of "middlebrow" and science-fiction writers. In a collection of essays on Jewish themes, *To the Gentiles* (1971), Fiedler argued that the self imagined by the Jewish writer in a non-Jewish culture tended to be that of a "dream-merchant."

Originally a poet who fell by accident into literary criticism, Fiedler is also a prolific fiction writer. Many of these stories and novels treat themes of Jewish identity, although just as frequently the themes are sexuality, academe, and Bohemia. Admired for his honesty, he is also criticized for overanalyzing his characters. His novels include *The Second Stone* (1963), which narrates the love triangle of a rabbi in Rome; *Back to China* (1965), depicting a Jewish philosophy professor who sterilizes himself in atonement for the dropping of the atomic bomb on Japan; and *The Messengers Will Come No More* (1975), a science-fiction novel of twenty-fifth-century Palestine. Collections of stories are *Pull Down Vanity* (1962), *The Last Jew in America* (1966), and *Nude Croquet* (1969). *Being Busted*, a partial autobiography, dealing largely with his 1968 arrest for allowing marijuana to be smoked in his home, appeared in 1970.

At the start of World War II, Fiedler considered himself an independent Trotskyist, but by the 1950s, he was writing essays that allegedly challenged both Left and Right in regard to the Alger Hiss case, the execution of Julius and Ethel Rosenberg, and the anti-Communist witch-hunt of Senator Joseph McCarthy. Within a short time Fiedler underwent another sharp change in his thinking, finding himself increasingly drawn to the Vernon Parrington tradition of indigenous American populism. In the 1960s, he embraced a self-styled anarchist libertarianism and became an enthusiastic proponent of the counterculture, a turn heralded by an essay, "The New Mutants" (*Partisan Review* [Fall 1965]). Fiedler is among the few in the New York intellectuals' tradition to become antielitist; what is troubling, however, is that the "outsider" trends embraced by Fiedler were usually those on the ascendancy.

Irving Howe was born Irving Horenstein in the East Bronx in 1920, the son of immigrants who ran a small grocery store that went out of business during the Great Depression. A socialist activist even before he entered City College of New York, Howe remained a member of a sequence of Trotskyist organizations until the fall of 1952, resigning at the time he began an associate professorship at Brandeis University.

From 1936 to 1940, he attended City College of New York, followed by a brief period of graduate work at Brooklyn College. After his release from three years of military service, a good part of which he spent reading in Alaska, he initiated a literary career, expanding from left-wing publications such as Max Shachtman's *New International* and Dwight Macdonald's *Politics*, to Elliot Cohen's *Commentary* and Philip Rahv and William Phillips' *Partisan Review*. In 1954, he founded his own radical socialist journal, *Dissent*.

His first book was *The U.A.W. and Walter Reuther* (1949), written in collaboration with B. J. Widick, a chief steward of the United Auto Workers and comrade of the Trotskyist movement. Written in swift, incisive prose, the book is a sympathetic account of the interrelationship of Reuther and the union, combined with observations about the appropriate goals of the labor movement.

This was followed by two impressive critical studies, *Sherwood Anderson* (1951) and *William Faulkner* (1952). Both are part of Howe's effort to view novelists from a modern perspective, a project he continued in *Thomas Hardy* (1967). All three books treat the work of their subjects as part of a "regional literature," enabling Howe to emphasize social issues and context. Thus Howe established himself as a socially oriented, although not "sociological," critic who usually subordinated form and symbolism to the story itself.

Howe is a prolific reviewer and writer of essays. His major literary collections include *A World More Attractive* (1963), *Steady Work* (1966), *Decline of the New* (1970), *The Critical Point* (1973), and *Celebrations and Attacks* (1979). For the most part, Howe writes in crisp, felicitous prose, revealing a skill at literary description and a quick grasp of the relevant issue. In his writings on contemporary subjects, he frequently emphasizes the existence of a cultural crisis in the United States, attributed to the loss of firm moral values in our age. A noteworthy legacy of his political experiences is a capacity for formidable polemics. Howe's pungency of style, fluency, and individual tone allow him to be scholarly without being pedantic, but his "lead-pipe" sarcasm occasionally backfires, appearing cruel and unfair.

Politics and the Novel (1957) is essentially a study of the intrusion of political themes and passions into the literary imagination. Howe's view is that great writers affirm the autonomy of the imagination while acknowledging the imperious presence of the social world. Surveying nineteenth- and twentieth-century European and Euro-American writers from Stendhal to Orwell, he concludes that their quality declines as the novel becomes increasingly dominated by politics.

The American Communist Party: A Critical History (1958), written in collaboration with sociologist Lewis Coser and political activist Julius Jacobson, was an unsympathetic but witty and analytical treatment of the major left-wing organization in the United States. By this time Howe had moved decisively from the revolutionary socialist politics of his Trotskyist years into a firm social democratic posture that would leave him ill prepared to cope with the New Left soon to emerge. During the 1960s and early 1970s, in fact, Howe was regarded as a major antagonist of the student radicals, feminists, and black nationalists, with the odd twist that he claimed to be arguing from a socialist perspective.

A 1978 study of *Leon Trotsky* exhibited surprising sympathy for his former Bolshevik mentor, but Howe's intellectual autobiography, *A Margin of Hope* (1982), and a subsequent political testament, *Socialism and America* (1985), confirm that his one-time Marxism has evaporated as completely as his youthful Leninism. In fact, both suggest that his notion of "socialism" has become nearly indistinguishable from the welfare state of Franklin D. Roosevelt's New Deal. A subsequent book-length work, *The American Newness: Culture and Politics in the Age of Emerson* (1987), holding that Emerson was the chief spokesperson for the democratization of United States culture, argues in a manner that further distances him from traditional notions of socialism.

Howe achieved national acclaim for his bestselling *World of Our Fathers* (1976), a massive social and cultural history of the immigration of Eastern European Jews and the life they made in New York City. An impressive example of local history, the book looks back affectionately, but not piously, on the decline of a once vigorous community. A continuous theme is the role of socialism and the labor movement on the lower East Side; among the most impressive sections is the chapter on Jewish-American novelists that applies his conception of "regional literature" to

argue that a subculture finds its authentic voice as it approaches disintegration.

Howe's work was sharply criticized from a number of perspectives. He was accused of a politically biased treatment of Communist-connected unions and publications, a failure to examine seriously religious and Zionist elements of the Jewish community, a reluctance to explore fully the impact of the Holocaust, an absence of a comparative dimension with other immigrant groups, an underemphasis of the hostility with which Jewish immigrants were met and the degree to which they consequently were forced into their characteristic cultural patterns, a downplaying of Jewish gangs and prostitutes, and an exaggeration of the degree to which Yiddishkeit is irretrievably moribund.

Nevertheless, the book stands without parallel as a comprehensive history of the American phase of secular Judaism, presented in a rich web of analysis full of effective anecdotes and quotation. The book especially benefits from its fluent, readable style that aptly communicates the ambivalences felt by the community in the face of pressures to assimilate.

Howe has additionally contributed to the preservation of Yiddish literature by editing and introducing, in collaboration with Eleazer Greenberg, *A Treasury of Yiddish Stories* (1954), *A Treasury of Yiddish Poetry* (1969), and *Voices from the Yiddish: Essays, Memoirs, Diaries* (1972). In 1966, he published *Selected Short Stories of Isaac Bashevis Singer*.

Howe's response to Judaism in *The World of Our Fathers* is fairly typical of those New York intellectuals who are of Jewish descent; for them, Jewish identity has functioned primarily as a mark of alienation, facilitating their attraction to Modernism, Marxism, and nineteenth- and twentieth-century European thought. All but a few are decidedly in the secular tradition, demonstrating little interest in religion or Zionism.

As a school of literary criticism, the New York intellectuals express not so much a distinctive methodology as a hybrid sensibility closely connected to its moment of birth in the 1930s. At that time, the founders sought to appropriate Modernism for the Left. Critics associated with the tradition of the New York intellectuals focus on the relation of literature to society, hold in common an opposition to Stalinist politics (originally on socialist premises), wrestle with a sense of the inadequacy of American culture in comparison to that of Europe, express an ambivalence toward the realism and naturalism of the 1930s, exhibit hostility to academe (modulated as they joined its ranks), and display—with the exception of the later work of Fiedler—condescension toward mass and popular culture.

With the death of central figures such as Rahv and Trilling, the end of Modernism as a vanguard sensibility, and the conservative mood of the 1980s, the tradition of the New York intellectuals has become increasingly diffuse. Nevertheless, the continuing vitality of the work of Kazin, Fiedler, and Howe suggests that its impact on literary criticism, while diminished, is hardly terminated. Moreover, it is unlikely that any other school of critics of Jewish-American descent will ever leave so vivid and substantial a mark on our culture.

ALAN WALD

BIBLIOGRAPHY

Barrett, William. *The Truants: Adventures Among the Intellectuals*. Garden City, N.Y.: Anchor Press/Doubleday, 1982.

Bloom, Alexander. *Prodigal Sons: The New York Intellectuals and Their World*. New York: Oxford University Press, 1986.

Longstaff, S. A. "The New York Family." *Queen's Quarterly* 83 (Winter 1976): 108–129.

O'Neill, William L. *A Better World—The Great Schism: Stalinism and the American Intellectuals*. New York: Simon & Schuster, 1982.

Pells, Richard. *The Liberal Mind in a Conservative Age: American Intellectuals in the 1940s and 1950s*. New York: Harper & Row, 1985.

Rosenberg, Bernard, and Goldstein, Ernest, eds. *Creators and Disturbers: Reminiscences by Jewish Intellectuals in New York*. New York: Columbia University Press, 1982.

Rosenfeld, Alvin H. "Alfred Kazin and the Conditions of Criticism Today." *Midstream* 19 (November 1973): 68–73.

Shechner, Mark. *After the Revolution: Studies in the Contemporary Jewish Imagination*. Bloomington: Indiana University Press, 1987.

Winchell, Mark R. *Leslie Fiedler*. Boston: Twayne, 1985.

Cults. Studies of American cults report a disproportionate percentage of Jewish members. Although Jews comprise 2.5 percent of the population of the United States, about 18 percent of all Hare Krishna cult members, between 8 percent and 10 percent of Rev. Moon's Unification Church and

10 percent of Scientologists come from Jewish background. Other popular American cults, particularly those based upon Eastern mysticism, also show high rates of Jewish membership. The high rates of Jewish defection to cults coupled with rising rates of intermarriage and the still recent memory of Jewish losses in the Holocaust have made cults an important concern for the Jewish community.

What is a cult? Some scholars claim all established religions begin as cults, and the cult stage is but the first stage in the development of a religious tradition (Stark and Bainbridge, 1985). Most scholars, however, contrast cults with conventional religion in the following ways: (a) cults require complete obedience to the cult leader, (b) cults demand a total commitment of time and money to the cult, (c) cults separate the cult member from his family and friends, and (d) cults restrict social contact to members of the cult (Rudin and Rudin, 1980). Some cults, such as the infamous People's Temple in Guyana, where a mass suicide of almost 1000 people took place in 1978, and Bhagwan Shree Rajneesh's Rajneesh Param commune in Antelope, Oregon, which disbanded in 1986, were totalistic cults requiring complete obedience and separation from the rest of society. Other cult groups, such as certain "New Age" movements who believe the human mind has untapped powers for human betterment or some charismatic Christian groups, are less extreme in their demands for obedience and permit greater contact with outsiders.

There are no entirely reliable figures on the number of cult groups or cult members. Scholars estimate that there are between 1500 and 2000 cultlike groups active in the United States. Most are small groups limited to a few hundred members. Among the largest groups, with membership totaling in the thousands, are the Unification Church, the International Society for Krishna Consciousness (Hare Krishnas), the Church of Scientology, and The Way International.

What all cult groups have in common is a rejection of religious pluralism and an emphasis on obedience to the charismatic cult leader. Cult members are taught that the cult is privy to an ultimate truth that is available only to cult members. The cult teaches that it alone has the answers to the ambiguities and problems of modern life. Decisions about work, marriage and family, health care, or residence are only taken after consultation with cult authorities. The separation between public and private life—an integral aspect of modern life—is absent in cult communities. In the cult, all activities and elements in a person's life are directed to the realization of the aims of the cult: spreading the group's doctrine, recruiting new members, and obtaining financial support so that the movement will prosper. Frequently, members of cults are told they may violate social rules—at times, legal procedures—to get people to join or support their groups.

Life in a cult is intense, with regular prayer or meditation sessions, all-night study sessions, and secret rituals with group leaders. Cults usually have a set pattern of religious rituals and prohibitions that are to be observed by all members. For example, the Hare Krishna community, a fundamentalist offshoot of Orthodox Hinduism, which attracts a significant number of Jewish converts, is strictly vegetarian. All food eaten in Hare Krishna communities is first offered in an elaborate ritual to the deities (physical representations of the gods in the Hare Krishna Pantheon) who occupy a central place in the Krishna temples. Devotees are required to chant the Hare Krishna mantra for a period of no less than 2 hours daily (and this activity is strictly monitored by local temple administrators), and they must also attend temple services at daybreak (usually at 4:30 a.m. in the American temples) and be present at the evening meeting at sundown. Celibacy is the highest religious status; marriage is permitted but highly regulated, with rigid guidelines for social and sexual relations. Participants in temple activities are also required to avoid Western clothes and don the dhoti for men and the sari for women. All temple activities are also strictly segregated by gender: women and girls pray or chant in a separate room or in a separate section of the temple.

The Unification Church, in contrast, has less elaborate ritual requirements, but its members also pray and meditate daily, concentrating on the figure of Reverend Moon, asking for his guidance, and praying for the success of his messianic mission. In the Unification Church, religious activity means working directly or providing financial support for the program of the church. The special goal of the Unification Church is a one-world society under the leadership of Reverend Moon; any activity that the church authorities recommend to help to bring about this world transformation is defined as religious activity. The authority of the church leader is to be unquestioned because it is through his guidance that messianic transformation will be achieved.

Research studies report that the typical Jewish cult joiner is a college student between 18 and 28 years old from a well-to-do and well-educated family that identified itself as Jewish and, in most cases, affiliated with a synagogue or temple and attended services on High Holidays and during family celebrations. One study reports that over 90 percent of Jewish cult members celebrated the Passover seder and Hanukkah with their family during childhood and adolescence. Approximately 45 percent come from families affiliated with Reform congregations, 33 percent with the Conservative Movement, 3 percent were members of Orthodox congregations, and 17 percent are unaffiliated (Selengut, 1988).

In spite of high levels of synagogue membership, studies show that the religion practiced in the families of cult joiners was essentially an ethnic or cultural religion with an emphasis on child-oriented and social activities. It was largely an ethnic religiosity with little attempt to stress the religious significance of rituals, the importance of biblical texts, the clear definition of the sacred and the profane. The rituals were performed with little consideration of the Jewish understanding of the Almighty's role in history.

The Jewish converts to cults do not so much reject the Jewish religion as make a break with family and Jewish secularism. The movements they join speak openly and unabashedly about God or Divine Presence and about God's relationship with the faithful. They stress God's directives to humankind, God's demands for ethical and ritual observance, and the need for personal discipline and obedience to religious authority. Above all, the cults provide powerful messianic visions that are to be realized only if the faithful, and others who can be converted, come together in devotion to these cult ideals. Many of the Jewish cultists are attracted to this intense religiosity, which they did not experience in their Jewish milieu.

Some young Jews are also attracted by the professed (though by no means realized) universalism of cult movements. The new cults encourage the converts to shed their Jewish identity. They need no longer be Jewish but can through cult membership become part of a universal faith open to all humankind—Catholics, Protestants, Jews, and others. Since every new convert, whether Jew or Gentile, surrenders a former religious or ethnic identity, membership in a minority group is also discarded. For young Jews who were uncomfortable with their marginal Jewish identity, this is a serious incentive for joining a new religious movement.

Some commentators have suggested that cults seek to gain converts through mind control and systematic attempts at "brainwashing" whereby the prospective cult member loses his ability to think clearly and rationally and make individual decisions. While many cults do engage in aggressive recruitment and proselytizing, often misleading the prospective recruit about the true nature of life in a cult, most scholars reject the idea of mind control and brainwashing. Instead, current scholarly thinking focuses upon the breakdown of strong family ties and the consequent search for a warm and caring community among large numbers of young adults. Cults, many experts believe, now fulfill many of the functions formerly satisfied by the extended family and community. Psychologists, rabbis, and social workers, therefore, encourage parents who have a child in a cult to maintain contact and continue a loving relationship with the child.

Whatever the precise reason for the rise of cult membership, Jewish scholars are in agreement that more attention be given to Jewish learning and spiritual values in Jewish life. Cults appeal primarily to individuals who have had little religious education or experience, despite formal affiliation with a Jewish congregation. Experts suggest that increasing Jewish educational opportunity, providing expanded opportunities for religious experiences, and developing greater personal and communal ties in synagogue life are some ways to encourage greater Jewish religious involvement and curtail conversion to cults.

CHARLES SELENGUT

BIBLIOGRAPHY

Bromley, David G., and Shupe, Anson D. *Strange Gods: The Great American Cult Scare.* Boston: Beacon Press, 1981.

Rudin, A. James, and Rudin, Marcia R. *Prisoner Paradise: The New Religious Cults.* Philadelphia: Fortress Press, 1980.

Selengut, Charles. "American Jewish Converts to New Religious Movements." *Jewish Journal of Sociology* 30, No. 2 (December 1988): 95.

Stark, Rodney, and Bainbridge, William Sims. *The Future of Religion: Secularization, Revival and Cult Formation.* Berkeley: University of California Press, 1985.

Dance. In the United States Jewish dance has become less and less a part of community life, although Israeli folk dance has its place in providing identity and group expression. However, Jewish dancers and choreographers, some working within the coummunity, others members of dance companies, have created new theater dances around Jewish themes. Together, they have found an audience and made a name for themselves—and for Jewish dance tradition—in American ballet, modern dance, dance of social conscience, and the newest postmodern and eclectic performance-oriented dance.

From ancient times, Jewish identity was synonymous with dance. After the Exodus and the parting of the Red Sea, Miriam danced in victory. When the Ark was brought to Jerusalem, David danced. Through the centuries, Jews of all ages, with no formal dance training, have danced with the Torah scrolls on Simchat Torah, danced at Purim, danced in celebration of births and B'nai Mitzvot, and at weddings, it is written in the Talmud, Jews are commanded to dance before the bride and groom to insure their happiness.

Dance created a festive atmosphere at holidays and celebrations, gave the community a participatory activity, and embodied the essential Jewish expression of joy and the sanctity of life.

The Sephardic Jews who were the first to arrive in the New World seem not to have made the same impact on American Jewish dance culture as the later arrivals, even though Sephardim may have continued to dance in the prescribed ritual ways; this for many Americans of Sephardic descent is an improvised dance form, often to Ladino tunes passed down for generations.

The Ashkenazic Jews who were the next to arrive, coming from Germany and Western Europe in the main in the 1840s, quickly discarded ways of celebration that were considered "old country" and danced in the fashion of the day. The Richmond, Virginia, *Enquirer* reported that on February 7, 1849, at a fund-raising ball for the Hebrew and English Institute, "every portion of the room sparkled with flashes from the eyes of Gentile and Hebrew beauties; the gay quadrille and graceful waltz kept time to the fine music of the Armory Band." Many of the Ashkenazim embraced the Reform Movement, which stripped Judaism of much of its ethnicity; wedding celebrations, for example, became simplified and Americanized, with the traditional mitzvah dances eliminated.

Two of the earliest dance impresarios in America, however, were Imre (1845–1919) and Bolossy Kiralfy (1848–1932), Hungarian Jews who arrived in 1869. They produced indoor and outdoor ballet spectacles involving hundreds of performers, including *The Fall of Babylon* and *The Destruction of Jerusalem*, which were extremely popular at an amusement park Bolossy founded on the Palisades in New Jersey overlooking the Hudson River. Imre Kiralfy staged an extravaganza called *America!* for the 1893 World's Fair in Chicago.

It was the massive Jewish immigration from Eastern Europe, 1881–1924, however, that made Jewish dance part of the artistic life of urban

America. The young newcomers who flocked to settlement houses and community centers found programs and classes in Jewish dance, as well as in English and citizenship. Many East European Jews in the United States continued to dance at traditional celebration times, especially the Hasidim among them, for whom the Baal Shem Tov had decreed that the highest form of prayer is that which not only moves the soul, but also sets all the limbs in motion.

One of the earliest professional expressions of Jewish dance in the United States was in vaudeville. A tradition of Yiddish vaudeville had existed in Europe, where actors sang and danced in the *shantan* (from the French *cafe-chantant*, meaning "nightclub"). Fanny Brice, born Fannie Borach (1891–1951), starred in the Ziegfeld Follies; among her best-known routines are characterizations of girls from the Lower East Side who wanted to be dancers. Others who followed in this genre include comedian Danny Kaye, born David Daniel Kominsky (1913–1987), who toured as a dancer with A. B. Marcus reviews and danced in most of his film and Broadway appearances, and more recently Joel Grey, born Josel Katz (b. 1932), who achieved stardom as the master of ceremonies in *Cabaret*. Grey began his career as a child traveling with his father, Mickey Katz, a Yiddish comic with the Borscht-Capades.

The East European immigrants, most of whom had never seen a professional stage production in the Old Country, also popularized the Yiddish theater. They came to see tableau, music, song, and dance that evoked memories of Old Country ways, as well as for serious theatre. And although they were not aware of it at the time, it was the Yiddish theater and its satellite, the Borscht Belt, that opened the way for Jewish dance and dancers to move into the larger community. It also set the example of what Jewish dance seemed to connote in its characterizations, humor, and narrative as time went on.

When the Russian-Jewish Habima Theatre production of *The Dybbuk* opened in New York in 1926, its *Beggars' Dance* and its magnificent use of stylized mitzvah wedding dance created a furor in the American dance world. *The Dybbuk* was probably the single most inspirational work for Jewish choreographers from that time on. In 1933, Maurice Schwartz's Yiddish Art Theatre created a similar excitement with *Yoshe Kalb*, based on Israel Joshua Singer's novel about a Hasidic village, with the traditional dances reinterpreted by choreographer Lillian Shapiro

Rausch (1908–1988). She was in Martha Graham's first company, directed her own group, and also had other Yiddish theater choreographic successes.

Meanwhile, at the Neighborhood Playhouse in New York City, Irene and Alice Lewisohn had begun giving dance lessons and directing theatrical productions in 1915. Jewish ritual and tradition supplied materials for productions like *Jephthah's Daughter* and for ensemble works featuring notable modern dancers such as Benjamin Zemach, who came to New York with the Habima Theatre and decided to stay in the United States. The Playhouse was second only to the Denishawn Company in training and offering performance opportunities to aspiring young American dancers, but the atmosphere at the Playhouse was notably different, for Ted Shawn and Ruth St. Denis reportedly limited Jewish students to 10 percent of their company.

Irene Lewisohn directed the Neighborhood Playhouse Festival Dancers, assisted by Blanche Talmud. Other teachers included Sophie Bernsohn Finkle, who had starred in Max Reinhardt's *The Eternal Road*, with choreography by Zemach, and Senia Gluck-Sandor, who went on to the Metropolitan Opera Ballet, then joined Adolf Bolm's company and helped direct the WPA Federal Dance Project in the 1930s. Talmud also trained Lily Mehlman (b. 1903), Helen (Becker) Tamiris (1902–1966) Sophie Maslow, and Anna Sokolow (b. 1910). All performed with the Martha Graham Company and the New Dance League; later, for the New Dance Group, Maslow choreographed *Dust Bowl Ballads* (1941), *Folksay* (1942), her important *The Village I Knew* (1949)—reminiscent of shtetl life—*Ladino Suite* (1969), and a dance inspired by *The Dybbuk* called *Neither Rest Nor Harbor* (1968). From 1955 to 1962, she choreographed pageants and dances for Israel bond rallies at Madison Square Garden in New York City and in 1962 staged New York City Opera productions of *The Dybbuk* and *The Golem*.

Other Neighborhood Playhouse alumni were Miriam Blecher (1909–1979), Edith Segal (b. 1902), Anna Sokolow (b. 1910), and Helen Tamiris (1905–1966). All were social protesters and dynamic artists, often choreographing together in a group way. A later New Dance Group piece Blecher created focused on dances of protest against fascism, *Van deLubbe's Head*.

The reputations of many of the important dance figures who were not themselves Jewish (among them Martha Graham, Doris Humphrey, Hanya Holm, Alwin Nikolais, Merce Cunningham, and George Balanchine) were enhanced by Jewish company members.

Sokolow danced with Graham (1930–1938), but Sokolow's own choreographic works were produced independently. Her first work, *Anti-War Cycle* (1933), foreshadowed the intense social responsibility of much of her later work. Her dances on Jewish themes include Theatre Guild's production with Louis Horst of *Noah* (1935); *Exile* (1939); *Kaddish* (1945)—often pictured in dance books with Sokolow's dancers bound in tefilin-like black strips; *The Bride* (1946); *Song of the Semite* (1944); *Visitors of Ruth and Naomi, March of the Semite Women, The Dybbuk* (1951); her important *Dreams*, an indictment of the Nazi camps (1961); *Rooms*, about loneliness in urban America, *Song of Songs, Ellis Island* (1976); *The Holy Place* (1977); *Songs Remembered* (1978); *Homage to Gertrud Kraus*, pioneer of modern dance in Israel (1977); and *Queen Esther* (1980). Sokolow went to Israel in 1953 at the request of Jerome Robbins to work with the Inbal Dance Theater, the Yemenite modern dance company, on modern technique and stagecraft. In 1962, she started her own Israeli company, the Lyric Theatre, which survived through 1964. She teaches at Juilliard in New York City, directs the Players Project, a dance troupe presenting her works in concert, and continues to make periodic work trips to Israel. She was honored in 1986 with a gala "A Tribute to Anna Sokolow" at the National Foundation for Jewish Culture's first International Festival on Jewish Dance in New York City, and again in 1990 on her eightieth birthday at the Rubin Academy in Jerusalem (where she teaches in the summer) and the 92nd Street YMHA in New York City.

Another New Yorker, Robert Cohan (b. 1925), was also a noted Graham Company dancer. He was a member of the company from 1946 through 1957 and again from 1962 until 1969, during which period he served briefly in 1966 as Graham's co-director. Since 1967, Cohan has been director of the London School of Contemporary Dance and associated with the London Contemporary Dance Theatre, for which he has choreographed. In 1980, he served as artistic adviser to the Batsheva Dance Company in Tel Aviv and choreographed for them as well.

Helen (Becker) Tamiris, with her social conscience created dances of poignancy (*Negro Spirituals*). She was chief choreographer for the WPA Federal Dance Theater during the 1930s. She also formed the Dance Repertory Theatre with Martha Graham, Doris Humphrey, and Charles Weidman, which was her effort to create a cooperative venture in the factionalized world of modern dance. She did the choreography for several Broadway musicals, including *Annie Get Your Gun* (1946).

Benjamin Zemach (b. 1901), trained in Stanislavsky dramatic technique as well as dance, remained in New York from 1928 to 1932 after defecting from the Habima Theater, creating *Ruth* and *Farewell to the Queen Sabbath*. In 1932, he left for Hollywood to teach and choreograph dance. There he created *Jacob's Dream, The Menorah, "Three Palestinian Folk Songs,"* and *Psalms*. In 1933, his *Fragments of Israel* became the first ballet with Jewish content to be presented at the Hollywood Bowl. In 1936, he returned to New York to choreograph Max Reinhardt's Broadway production of *The Eternal Road* and stayed until 1947, when he returned to California to join the University of Judaism Theater and Dance Department, assisted by dancer Miriam Rochlin. His students included Alan Arkin, Herschel Bernardi, and Lee J. Cobb. In 1971, he moved to Israel.

One of the finest dancers to perform with Zemach was Hadassah (b. 1910). Born in Jerusalem, Hadassah Spira was descended from generations of Hasidic rabbis. She fled with her family to Istanbul during the Ottoman regime. There, she saw Dervishes dance. Later, she was introduced to Indian dance and became very accomplished in the styles of India. In 1938, she moved to New York and married artist Milton Epstein, who designed costumes and sets for her solo concerts. Her signature dance, *Shuvi Nafshi* (Return, Oh My Soul, based on Psalm 116), was danced to music by Cantor Liebele Waldman. Other works, such as *Israeli Suite, The Cantor, The Wanderer*, and *Water*, dealt with Jewish tradition and spirituality. Hadassah presented dance concerts in Israel in the 1940s and 1950s and also appeared at the American dance center Jacob's Pillow (Massachusetts) and throughout America and India. For many years she headed the Ethnic Dance Department of the New Dance Group.

The 92nd Street YMHA in New York played a leading role in development of American modern dance and Jewish dance in America. Hadassah and Zemach both danced there. William Kolodney began the Dance Department in 1935, sponsoring programs that produced countless choreographers, performers, and dance teachers.

In the 1950s the 92nd Street Y's Jewish Dance Division was created by Fred Berk (1911–1980). Francis Aleinkoff (b. 1920) and her AVIV Company were also based at the 92nd Street YMHA. Born Fritz Berger in Vienna, Berk came to the United States in 1941, leaving behind a career as an Expressionist modern dancer started with Gertrud Kraus in Vienna. In the United States, he was reunited with Katya Delakova and Claudia Vall Kauffman, who had also performed with Kraus's company. Berk and Delakova first taught dance at the Jewish Theological Seminary in New York. They then opened their own school and launched a company, the Jewish Dance Guild, to perform dances with Jewish themes. They also were the first to make dance tours to American colleges, sponsored by the Hillel Foundation and the National Jewish Welfare Board. Hillel and JWB continue to support dance in their programming.

In the early 1950s, he created the Camp Blue Star Folk Dance Camp, which still continues. In addition, he founded several different dance companies at the Y, including the Hebraica and the Merry-Go-Rounders, which he cofounded in 1953, creating his signature piece, *Holiday in Israel*, for them.

Fred Berk also directed Israeli Folk Dance Festivals in New York from 1952 until his death, working with hundreds of Jewish youth from Zionist and religious movements. He created the Israeli Folk Dance Department of the American Zionist Youth Foundation, which, in addition to the festival, sponsored summer folk dance tours to Israel and published materials edited by Berk, including *Hora* magazine. Ruth Goodman continues his work, directing the Jewish Dance Division at the Y, the Israeli Independence Festivals, and the Israeli Dance Institute. Berk also performed in Israel and lived there briefly in the late 1970s while he worked with the Histadrut Israeli folk dance committee. He presented Israeli folk dance workshops throughout the United States and produced records and manuals on Israeli folk dance and books on Jewish dance, first in collaboration with Delakova and then independently.

During their brief marriage, Katya Delakova and Berk performed duet concerts featuring their own choreography, as well as choreographing for their Jewish Dance Guild. Among their renowned dances are *Hora, Halutzim, Golem, The Deathless Voice*, and *Nameless Heroes*. Delakova is artistic director of the Echobow Company, producing large-scale works like *Visions and Prophe-cies* and *The Tower of Babel*, set to music by Moshe Budmor.

Another Gertrud Kraus dancer who escaped to the United States before World War II was Jan Veen (1903–1967), born Hans Wiener, who joined the faculty of the New England Conservatory of Music. *Hora Staccato* (1948) is a noted example of his choreography.

Felix Fibich and his wife, dancer Judith Berg, both originally Polish, performed in Russia during the 1940s. She was known for her choreography and performance in the pre-war Polish film version of *The Dybbuk*. Later the couple taught dance in European displaced persons camps. Arriving in New York in the 1950s, they continued their work, focusing on choreography for Yiddish schools, camps, film, Broadway, and the Jewish Theological Seminary's television series, "Lamp Unto My Feet." Their credits include a revival of *Rebecca, the Rabbi's Daughter* on Broadway, *Sing, Israel, Sing* for the film version of *The Chosen*, and a dance film of Yiddish folk tales, *Higher and Higher*, featuring their own Fibich Dance Ensemble.

During the 1940s and 1950s, many others also performed, taught, and created records and books with Jewish dance themes. Nathan Visonsky organized his own Jewish Ballet Company in Chicago and published *Jewish Folk Dances*. Corinne Chochem directed her own dance group, Rikkud Ami, and taught at the Jewish Theological Seminary, Cornell University, and the University of California. She published two books, *Palestine Dances* and *Jewish Holiday Dances*, and was the first in the United States to record Jewish and Palestinian dances, using arrangements by such composers as Leonard Bernstein and Darius Milhaud.

Dvora Lapson, director of the Dance Department of the Board of Jewish Education, New York City, conducted teacher-training seminars, gave lectures, wrote erudite articles, particularly on her experience performing her solos in Poland, and created dance curriculum for use in religious day schools throughout the New York area. Lapson's noted student was Joyce Mollov, who also founded her own Jewish Dance Ensemble in New York and organized the Jewish Dance Educators Network of CAJE (Conference on Alternative Jewish Education) in 1986.

Another Jewish dance educator who has also had performing groups is Harriet Berg, who has worked at the Detroit Jewish Community Center. Carole and Paul Kantor have been at the

Jewish Community Center in Cleveland. Jo Anne Tucker founded and directs Avodah Dance Ensemble. Tucker and Susan Freeman wrote *Torah in Motion*, which is based on their work.

Pauline Koner (b. 1912), noted soloist with Doris Humphrey and Jose Limon, made a solo tour to Alexandria and Tel Aviv in 1932 as one of the first modern dancers to tour there. She choreographed *Yael* to Palestinian folk songs (1931), *Hasidic Song and Dance* (1931) and *Yemenite Song* (1933) to music by Bracha Tsvira, and "Voice in the Wilderness" (1948).

Jewish dancers also joined other dance companies. Bethsabee de Rothschild, for many years Graham's main patron, had founded the Batsheva Company when she moved to Israel in 1962. Some of Batsheva's American dancers included Rina Gluck, who did her first choreography at the 92nd Street Y, Laurie Freedman, and Pamela Sharni. Batsheva also hired American Jewish choreographers, including Jerome Robbins, Anna Sokolow, Lar Lubovitch, Ze'eva Cohen, Pearl Lang, Matthew Diamond, and Daniel Ezralow. Ezralow is also known for his work with Jonathan Woken in the Philobolus Company with Paul Taylor and most recently with his own company, ISO, along with Morleigh Steinberg. Irving Burton, longtime performer and co-creator of "Paper Bag Players," performed his dance "Zey . . . (They)" and recited the Yiddish Mani Leyb poem in New York City in 1990 and 1991. The Merce Cunningham Company had several Jewish dancers too, including Judith Dunn and Remy Charlip, both of whom left to choreograph. Unfortunately, Charlip's extensive creative work is not associated with Jewish themes; the same can be said for Murray Louis, who has been associated with Alwin Nikolais and has had his own company since the mid-1950s, which merged with Nikolais in the late 1980s. Arnie Zane (1948–1988) collaborated with African-American Bill T. Jones, choreographing dances of social comment until his death. Phyllis Lamhut, David Dorfman, Laura Dean, Liz Keen, David Gordon and his Pick Up Dance Company, Bella Lewitzky, and others too numerous to mention do not deal with their Judiasm in their dance art.

Anna Halprin (b. 1920) is more oriented to universal Jewish themes and values in her work; her earliest memories of dance focus on watching her Orthodox grandfather praying. Trained in the modern dance techniques of the 1950s, she traveled in Israel and created *Daughter of the Voice*, *The Story of Hannah*, and *The Prophetess*. Halprin formed her own company, the San Francisco Dancers Workshop, creating dances on such themes as atonement, interracial performance projects, and what she calls "contemporary ritual dances" like *Kadosh* (1970), *Ritual and Celebration* and her work for world peace, *Circle the Earth*. She has worked with hundreds of performers over intense periods of time and has a very large following.

Meredith Monk (b. 1942) is a noted postmodern performance artist who choreographs, composes, and dances her reflections on Jewish issues, inspired by tales of her grandparents' life in Europe and by Jewish cantorial tradition. Her first Expressionist modern dance was with Fred Berk, and she also studied at the Graham studio and with Bessie Schönberg at Sarah Lawrence College. Her full evening work *Quarry* (1976) is a condemnation of the Nazis and war. Her *Ellis Island* was televised as a film portrait of immigrants entering America. In 1989 she was at work on a full-length feature film about European ghetto life in the Middle Ages. Monk has performed all over Europe, Israel, and the United States with her ensemble, and her company—The House—and has received numerous awards, including two Guggenheim grants, an "Obie," and a "Bessie" (a prestigious New York dance award) for Sustained Creative Achievement.

Other dance artists today include Lanny Harrison (*Return of the Good Doctor*, 1980), Ellen Kogan and Judith Brin Ingber (solo modern dance performers who work with themes from Jewish and dance history), Fanchon Shur (a student of Nathan Vishonsky) and her noteworthy ceremonial ritual performance work (*Tallit: Prayer Shawl*, 1971), and Jane Kosminsky. Kosminsky performed with Paul Taylor and Bruce Becker and in the late 1980s directed the modern dance program at the 92nd Street Y. Lisa Green founded a company called the Jewish German Dance Theatre, started in 1985, as a collaborative ensemble based in Philadelphia. It works mainly on themes about the Holocaust. This group, composed of Gentile and Jewish American and German dancers, has appeared in the United States and Germany.

Israelis working in modern dance in the United States include Domi Reiter-Soffer; Hadassah Badoch; Ze'eva Cohen, also a featured dancer in Anna Sokolow's company and independent soloist, choreographer and teacher at Princeton University; Ohad Naharin, who formed his own company in the United States before returning to Israel; Zvi Gatheiner; Igal Pery, who directs a school and company in New York City; Margalit Oved, known for her teaching of Yemenite Jewish dance in the UCLA dance department and also for her company; and Ya'acov Sharir, who teaches at the University of Texas as well as directing and choreographing for his own Houston company.

In the world of classical ballet, many dancers of note have been Jews, but their religious background has been more a fact than an influence. Louis Herve Chalif (1876–1948) came to the United States in 1907 and opened the first of many schools. Noted choreographer David Lichine (1910–1972) was associated with the Ballet Russe de Monte Carlo and moved to the United States in the 1940s. His best-known work is *Graduation Ball* (1940), always in repertoire in America and Europe. Jewish dancers with the American Ballet Theatre have included Anne (Wolfson) Wilson, Nora Kaye, Miriam Weiskopf, Betty Bruce (Eisner), and Leda Anchutina. Ruthanna Boris was one of George Balanchine's first pupils in the United States. She became a ballerina with the Ballet Russe, guest artist with the New York City Ballet, and a popular teacher and choreographer (*Cakewalk*, 1951). Balanchine was brought to the United States and supported in all his seminal endeavors in creating dances and the New York City Ballet by Lincoln Kirstein (b. 1907), who thereby had a tremendous effect on American dance. Other Jewish dancers with Balanchine included Annabelle Lyon (who also danced with Ballet Caravan and American Ballet Theatre, creating key roles in Antony Tudor and Agnes DeMille ballets), Melissa Hayden (now a renowned teacher at the North Carolina School for the Arts), and Jillana (Zimmerman).

The Jewish ballet dancer who has made the most important contributions to the American ballet and musical theater is Jerome Robbins, born Rabinowitz (b. 1918). Robbins joined the American Ballet Theatre in 1940 and became an outstanding interpreter of comic and dramatic characters. His first choreographic work, *Fancy Free* (1944), was expanded into a hit Broadway musical, *On the Town*. On a 1951 visit to Israel, he staged his ballet *Interplay* (1945), "discovered" the new Israeli dance company, Inbal, and introduced them to Sol Hurok, who became their international agent, and to Anna Sokolow, who became their technique teacher. His other Broadway choreography includes *The King and I*, *West Side Story* (1957), *Gypsy* and the East European Jewish theme *Fiddler on the Roof* (1964). He also created a ballet for the New York City Ballet

based on *The Dybbuk*, called *The Dybbuk Variations* (1974), set to music by Leonard Bernstein, who was also his collaborator on *West Side Story*.

American Ballet Theatre has also had several other Jewish performers and choreographers of note, among them Michael Kidd (b. 1917), born Milton Gurenwald. Kidd is best known for his work on Broadway, having won four "Tony" awards for his choreography for the musicals *Guys and Dolls*, *Can-Can*, *Finian's Rainbow*, and *The Rothschilds*. Herbert Ross (b. 1926) collaborated with Leonard Bernstein on *Serenade for Seven Dancers*, established the Ballet of the Two Worlds with his ballerina wife, Nora Kaye, in 1960, and toured Europe with his ballets, including his own version of *The Dybbuk*. He is also a film director, whose works include *The Turning Point*, *Nijinsky*, and *Dancers*.

Nora Kaye (1920–1987), born Nora Koreff, was considered America's greatest dramatic ballerina, starring in Antony Tudor's psychological ballets as the repressed spinster Hagar in *Pillar of Fire* (1942) and in Agnes deMille's *Fall River Legend* (1948) and Jerome Robbins's *The Cage* (1951). She also starred in a ballet version of *The Dybbuk* choreographed by her husband, Herbert Ross. She was associate director of Ballet Theater from 1977 to 1983 and served as co-producer on seven of Ross's movies.

Eliot Feld (b. 1943) performed first in Robbins's *West Side Story*, and then became an American Ballet Theatre dancer in 1963. His first ballet, *Harbinger*, was created for ABT in 1967 and met with enormous critical acclaim, followed by the riveting *At Midnight*. In 1969, he created his own company, the Eliot Feld Ballet Company, and has choreographed over 50 works for them. While Feld never set out to make a statement about his Jewishness, two of his ballets, both choreographed in 1974, have specifically Jewish themes. *Tzaddik*, with music by Aaron Copland, was dedicated to Feld's grandmother and introduced by the epigram, "A Jew without learning is incomplete." *Sephardic Song* explores aspects of the Sephardic tradition and was described by dance critic Clive Barnes as "a poem scribbled in the soul of his forgotten memory." Bruce Marks is a noteworthy former principal of the Ballet Theater and now director of the Boston Ballet, as are Annabelle Lyon and Muriel Bentley.

The youngest member of the Ballet Russe was a Jewish dancer, Rochelle Zide-Booth (b. 1938). She became a soloist in 1957, has been ballet mistress of the Joffrey Ballet, artistic director of the Netherlands Dance Theater, an associate professor of dance at Adelphi University, and a choreographer, doing *Glory Songs* for the Kibbutz Dance Company in Israel.

In sum, Jews in dance have reflected the multifaceted ways in which America's Jews have responded to and reinterpreted their Judaism. Some have identified fully with their Jewishness, consistently working with Jewish thematic material or Jewish stories. Some are nostalgic, others have a caustic response, some try to create new art inspired by Judaism, some reflect little, if any, of their Judaism in their performance and choreography.

Meanwhile, however, Jews of all ages and training continue to express themselves in dance. A community of Sephardim in Los Angeles, originally from Rhodes, improvises dances called *A La Turka* to generations-old Ladino music. The estimated 75,000 Hasidic Jews living in Brooklyn, each in their different "courts," adhere to the ancient tradition of separate dances for men and women, each with different dance characteristics. Lubavitcher Hasidic men, for example, dance a *Kozatske* medley at weddings that combines a Russian Cossack step with mime and acrobatics; the women's dances incorporate the *mayim* step from Israeli folk dance.

Israeli folk dance repertoire has also come to the United States as a new expression of American Jewish identity, replacing the *sherele* and other *mitzvah tanzs* at many weddings, holidays, and celebrations. Beginning in the 1940s, folk dancing spread via Jewish summer camps, the Zionist and Habonim movements with teachers such as Shulamit Kivel, at YMHAs and Jewish community centers, youth programs in day schools and after-school Hebrew classes, and Sunday schools and youth groups, particularly in Conservative synagogues. With the establishment of the State of Israel, some of the yearning expressed in early modern dance left the theater stage. Later, Israelis came to the United States to teach and direct Israeli folk troupes, and many settled here. Danny Uziel and Moshe Eskayo in New York, Danni Dassa and Shlomo Bachar on the West Coast, Ya'acov Eden in the Midwest, and David Edrey in New York have all been influential.

In America, as it has through the ages, Jewish dance continues to provide many Jews with feelings of participatory identification at weddings and other celebrations. In addition, Jewish dance and Jewish themes have become a part of American theater and film tradition, enjoyed broad public acceptance in performance, and produced a growing list of leaders in every field of dance performance, theory, and education. *See also* Yiddish Theater.

JUDITH BRIN INGBER

BIBLIOGRAPHY

Ingber, Judith Brin. *Victory Dances, The Life of Fred Berk*. Minneapolis: Emmet, 1985.

Prevots, Naima. *Dancing in the Sun, Hollywood Choreographers 1915–1937*. Ann Arbor, Mich.: UMI Research Press, 1987.

Day Schools. See JEWISH EDUCATION.

Diseases Common to Jewish Communities. See GENETIC DISORDERS.

Dropsie University. Moses Aaron Dropsie, founder of Dropsie College in Philadelphia in 1907, was inspired by a single goal: "the establishment of a non-sectarian, non-theological postgraduate institution of higher learning" where academic freedom protects scholarship and learning is valued. Students studied Hebrew, biblical and rabbinic literature, the Middle East, Jewish education, and communications. One of its most important goals was to train scholars for research, and, to that end, the Abraham I. Katsh Center for Manuscript Research was established to acquire, preserve, and encourage the use of primary sources.

On June 6, 1909, a charter was granted to the institution under the name of Dropsie College for Hebrew and Cognate Learning. It was the first postgraduate center for Jewish studies in America. The school had only three presidents: Cyrus Adler, Abraham Neuman, and Abraham Katsh. It was the only graduate institution in America completely dedicated to Hebrew, Bible, and Middle Eastern studies. It also published the *Jewish Quarterly Review*, an English-language publication of scholarly articles and reviews on Jewish issues.

Dropsie College (changed to Dropsie University on September 1, 1969) never fully realized its dream. Financial problems plagued the university throughout most of its history and finally closed its doors as Dropsie in 1986. In 1987, it reopened as the Annenberg Research Institute after receiving a grant from publisher Walter Annenberg. The resources of Dropsie continue to be available for use by students and the general public and the *Jewish Quarterly Review* is still published, but degrees are no longer issued.

LINDA GLAZER

BIBLIOGRAPHY

Katsh, Abraham. *The Mission of the Dropsie University.* Philadelphia: Dropsie University, 1976.

Rubenstein, Frank J. *The Dropsie University: The Early Years, 1908–1919.* Philadelphia: Dropsie University, 1977.

E

Economics.

JACOB NUÑEZ CARDOZO: ECONOMIC THEORIST OF THE ANTEBELLUM SOUTH.

The first Jew to contribute to economic theory in America was not a product of academic life but a child of the antebellum culture of the South, which provided a fertile ground for economic studies at a number of places. This pioneer was Jacob Newton (a.k.a. Nuñez) Cardozo (1786-1873), a native of Savannah, Georgia, who spent most of his active life as a resident of Charleston, South Carolina. In this center of culture and learning, the self-taught man became a prominent journalist. Cardozo (whose uncle was the great grandfather of Justice Benjamin Nathan Cardozo), like David Ricardo, was born into a Sephardic family. He lived the life of an Orthodox Jew, while his brother became a leader in the contemporary Reform movement. Similar to Ricardo, Cardozo possessed great gifts of analytical thinking and achieved a high level of abstraction in economic theory.

Specialists in American economic thought remember Cardozo as the author of *Notes on Political Economy*, which was published in Charleston in 1826. This book provided an early attempt at a systematic critique of Ricardian economics and developed ideas that were to return later in the writings of a number of American economists. The classical system, as it emerged in the writings of Malthus and Ricardo, had undertones that were profoundly pessimistic and that earned economics the name of the "dismal science." Cardozo argued that these pessimistic features—with their threat of overpopulation, diminishing returns, declining profits, increasing land rents, stable wages at the subsistence level, and a stationary state rather than unlimited progress beckoning in the future—did not seem to fit into the American environment, with its scarce population, plentiful resources, and wide-open spaces. Cardozo also discovered that Ricardo's theory of rent failed to take into account the "increased facility of production," that is, technological progress, that would result in expansion of agriculture and manufacturing. He believed that economic development would not principally benefit the landowners, as Ricardo had concluded, but benefit everyone. His theory stated that as wage goods would become available more cheaply, both wages and profits would rise under a policy of free trade. Cardozo strongly endorsed Ricardo's economic theory, but he adapted it to the regional preferences prevailing in the America of the time. More adequately than the theories of the classics, Cardozo's views reflect the future economic progress of the United States.

DANIEL DE LEON, INTERPRETER OF MARX.

Economic development was not without cost, and industrialization and urbanization brought social problems and conflicts. Beginning in the 1870s and for a 50-year period, the history of the United States was replete with labor troubles, riots, violent strikes, and severe repression. Radical movements arose that provided outlets for the aspirations of the discontented. A number of labor unions and several socialist parties appealed for followers. Often their internecine struggles occupied them as much as the struggle against the capitalists. Karl Marx, who had moved the First International to America, gained supporters. The man whom many consider to be the outstanding interpreter of Marx in the United States was Daniel De Leon (1852–1914). He led the Socialist Labor Party for many years, fighting capitalists and the rival Socialist Party. In the emerging American labor movement, De Leon favored a highly politicized type of industrial union and opposed the business or reform unionism of the American Federation of Labor. He was also among the founders of the Industrial Workers of the World. As a theorist, he attempted to fill some of the gaps in Marx's ideas, and he developed his own ideas about the changing nature of society. Instead of the commonly found regional organization of society, De Leon proposed an organization by trades or industries. He also developed the notion of industrial councils, which was similar to Lenin's soviets. Leninism has other affinities with De Leonism. Lenin himself admired De Leon and suggested that a work of his be translated into Russian. This attempt was unsuccessful. De Leon, however, was not a professional economist but a radical agitator, one who participated in many of the radical movements of his time.

De Leon was born in Curaçao in the West Indies. Like Cardozo, he was a Sephardic Jew, but unlike Cardozo, De Leon eventually denied his Jewish origin. After coming to the United States, he earned a law degree at Columbia University. He had such an impressive record there that he was invited to lecture on Latin American diplomacy, which he did for a few years until his political activities interfered. Like a number of socialists, he started out as a follower of Henry George but gradually shifted his allegiance in the direction of more pronounced radicalism.

With the growth of a democratic trade union movement and the social-service state in the United States, socialist parties and the radical labor movement have weakened, leaving only a dim memory of De Leon.

ISLANDS IN A WASPISH SEA. After Harvard set up a separate professorship of economics in 1871, an increasing number of institutions followed suit, and economics became an established discipline in the college curriculum. Professorships grew into departments, and the number of academic economists rose accordingly. When the American Economic Association was founded in 1885, it had less than 200 members. In 1911, there were over 2,000, and in 1984 20,000.

During the first 35 years of its existence, the American Economic Association had three Jews among its presidents, Edwin R. A. Seligman (1902–1903), Frank W. Taussig (1904–1905), and Jacob H. Hollander (1921–1922). During this period, and even during the following two decades, academic economics was largely a "Wasp" affair, and the three exceptions mentioned (who were affiliated with Columbia, Harvard, and Johns Hopkins, respectively) had very few counterparts elsewhere because of widespread discrimination.

Seligman (1861–1939) and Taussig (1859–1940) both were children of immigrants, who had arrived in the United States around 1840—Seligman's father, Joseph, from Germany, and Taussig's from Bohemia. Their fathers had become founders of flourishing business establishments: banking in Seligman's case, and manufacture in Taussig's case. After extensive European travel and training at Columbia and Harvard, Seligman and Taussig became distinguished members of their respective economics faculties. Their European travel had exposed them to the influence of the German historical school of economics. These schools were hostile to abstract economic theory and generally favored government intervention in the economy. Although Seligman, Taussig, and the many other American economists of the time were not enormously influenced by these German ideas, these ideas may have prevented their dogmatic attachment to laissez faire.

Edwin Robert Anderson Seligman specialized in the field of public finance. He contributed publications about progressive taxation, the shifting and incidence of taxes, and related theoretical matters of great practical importance. In his other writings, he produced a critical account of the economic interpretation of history, documenting an interest in the work of Karl Marx, which he shared with his colleague F. G. Simkhovitch (1874–1959) and later with M. M. Bober (b. 1891). In the history of economic thought Seligman explored the lesser-known byways and brought a number of forgotten figures of the past to the attention of his contemporaries. He possessed a substantial library of economic works and used these books to bring past economic thought before new readers. The crowning achievement of his career was his shared editorship, with Alvin Johnson, of the *Encyclopaedia of the Social Sciences*, a 15-volume set that was prepared between 1927 and 1933 and published between 1930 and 1935. The aging Seligman lent his name and prestige to this enterprise, which reached completion shortly before his death, and it served generations of readers as an authoritative source of information. It is interesting to note that the editor of a similarly authoritative work, R. H. Inglis Palgrave, was also of Jewish origin. This smaller scale 3-volume set, called *Dictionary of Political Economy*, was first published in England between 1894 and 1899.

Both Seligman and Taussig were internationally recognized scholars, and in the early years of the twentieth century, Taussig was among the most influential American teachers of economics. Taussig made foreign trade his specialty and became the leading authority in this field. His principal work was the systematic restatement of the theory of international trade, in which he complemented what the classicists and their successors had accomplished in outline form. His attachment to the real-cost doctrine of the classics at a time when new interpretations came to the fore attests to his conservative temper.

Taussig also wrote a history of the United States tariff and explored the tariff question in other writings. His empirical disposition is illustrated by his tariff history, his study of the social origins of American business leaders, and his interest in the mechanism of adjustment of international payments. To general economics, Taussig contributed an analysis of the wages-fund doctrine, a theory that John Stuart Mill had abandoned and Taussig attempted to revive.

Taussig edited the *Quarterly Journal of Economics* during its first 40 years. He opened the journal to writers of diverse methodological and theoretical preferences, some of which he did not agree with. He also ushered in the new trend of public service that was to become increasingly more effective in later years. During World War I, he supported price control, and held the important post of chairman of the U.S. Tariff Commission.

Jacob Viner (1892–1970), Taussig's pupil and friend, started his teaching career at the University of Chicago around 1920, becoming as respected an authority in the international economics field as Taussig had been. Viner, a native of the Montreal ghetto, was also an outstanding student of the history of economics and of intellectual history in general. He made significant contributions to general economic theory and developed the theory of cost that has become the standard version used in textbooks. In other works, he anticipated what later became known as the theories of monopolistic competition, and the kinked demand curve, an approach to oligopolisitic pricing. Viner educated generations of economists in his course on economic theory, first at Chicago and later at Princeton. As co-editor of the *Journal of Political Economy*, he helped to establish a rival of the *Quarterly Journal of Economics*.

A few Russian immigrant contemporaries of Viner made names for themselves in other departments across the United States. At Wisconsin, Selig Perlman (1888–1959) became a favorite pupil of John R. Commons and continued his mentor's study of labor economics. The gist of Perlman's theory of the labor movement was that the American workman was job-conscious rather than class-conscious. At Michigan, Isaiah Leo Sharfman (1886–1969) served as chairman of the Economics Department from 1927 to 1954 and wrote a monumental study of transport regulation. Joseph Dorfman (b. 1904), a professor at Columbia, wrote a monumental study on the history of American economic thought. Both Viner and Sharfman served as presidents of the American Economic Association, the former in 1939 and the latter in 1945. Viner's appointment in 1939 was the first time that this distinction had been given to a Jew since Hollander had been so honored in 1921.

GOVERNMENT SERVICE. During the 1930s, many Jewish economists were drawn into the expanding field of labor economics. A few Jewish economists had an academic interest in Marx, but the upsurge of radicalism during the Great Depression did not create any prominent Jewish economists proclaiming attachment to the doctrines of Marx. Instead, as the Roosevelt administration began a number of new programs to fight unemployment and the depression, many Jewish economists filled the ranks of the government services. Here opportunities for the employment of Jews became available earlier than in the academic world, where discrimination persisted for a longer period. During World War II, a number of wartime agencies had positions to fill and the trend of the 1930s continued. Jews attracted to labor economics left their mark in this and related fields in government service. Some influenced the course of legislation, and a few even moved into policy-making positions. Jews assisted in establishing social security, labor legislation, and an international financial organization that rendered useful services during the postwar decades.

Many Jews rose to prominence in the economic sector of the government. Isador Lubin (1896–1978) served as U.S. Commissioner of Labor Statistics from 1933 to 1946. Wilbur J. Cohen (1913–1987) worked for social security from 1934 to 1956, rose to under secretary of the Department of Health, Education, and Welfare in 1965 (the year Medicare was enacted) and became secretary of the department for 1968 and 1969. Leon H. Keyserling (1908–1987) was an assistant to Senator Robert F. Wagner when the Wagner, or National Labor Relations, Act was passed in 1935. He later became vice-chairman and eventually chairman of President Truman's Council of Economic Advisers (1946–1953). Samuel Berger (1911–1980), a scholar trained in labor economics, became the foreign services' first labor attaché in 1941 through 1944, and later rose to the rank of ambassador. In the Department of State, Herbert Feis (1893–1972) was economic adviser from 1931 to 1937, serving as a one-man forerunner of what later became a large staff. Robert R. Nathan (b. 1908) pioneered in the preparation of national-income estimates for the federal government; later he held important posts in wartime planning and again pioneered in the new field of economic consulting that developed after World War II.

Jewish economists also held important positions in the Department of Agriculture. Mordecai Ezekiel (1899–1974), a theorist who had developed the cobweb theorem of price fluctuations, was economic adviser to the secretary of agriculture from 1933 to 1944. In the same department, Louis Bean (b. 1896) investigated agricultural price instability and served as economic adviser to the Agricultural Adjustment Administration from 1933 to 1939. In the Treasury Department, which was headed by Secretary Henry Morgenthau, Jr., a Jew, Harry D. White (1892–1948), a pupil of Taussig's, was assistant secretary (1945–1946), when he negotiated with the renowned English economist John Maynard Keynes the Bretton-Woods Agreements that established the World Bank and the International Monetary Fund.

A number of Jews were prominent in government finance. Emanuel A. Goldenweiser (1883–1953), who became president of the American Economic Association in 1946, served on the Federal Reserve Board. So did Arthur Marget (1899–1962), a great scholar, who relinquished

an academic career at the University of Minnesota for a position in Washington. Arthur F. Burns (1904–1987), after a distinguished career at Rutgers and Columbia universities and service as director of research at the National Bureau of Economic Research, became chairman of the President's Council of Economic Advisers (1953–1956), chairman of the Board of Governors of the Federal Reserve System (1970–1978) and eventually ambassador to the Federal Republic of Germany (1981–1985). Alan Greenspan (b. 1926), chairman of the Council of Economic Advisers under President Ford, became chairman of the Federal Reserve Board in August 1987.

CONTRIBUTION OF THE EUROPEAN IMMIGRANTS IN THE 1930s and 1940s.

The migration of Jewish intellectuals from Europe during the 1930s and 1940s included a fair number of economists. Some were mature scholars, others in life's mid-passage, and still others were young students. The early arrivals faced a situation in which employment opportunities, because of the Great Depression and prejudice, were meager. Even during these years of retrenchment and prejudice, the newcomers could avail themselves of opportunities for teaching positions in economics that were relatively more plentiful than they would have been in their country. This disparity reflected differences in the college curricula. On the continent, economics, as a rule, was not part of a student's general education. Instead, economics courses were the preserve of future professional economists and a mandatory requirement for law students. The newcomers faced a different situation in the United States, where introductory economics courses were mandatory for many students as part of their general education requirement. Nevertheless, it was not easy to find places for so many newcomers. Some congregated at the New School for Social Research in New York, which Alvin Johnson attempted to turn into a "university in exile." A few found employment at elite institutions. The majority had to compete for jobs in small and middling colleges. Sometimes black or Catholic institutions offered a much desired refuge. However, a number of institutions barred the newcomers, fearing they might be communists. Those immigrants who did find academic employment brought color, liveliness, and cosmopolitanism into an environment that was often drab and parochial.

Numerically, the largest and earliest contingent of the new arrivals came from Germany.

There (but not in Austria) economics was still under the spell of the historical school, whose rejection of economic theory was shared in the United States by only a handful of followers of institutional economics. Many newcomers had to become acclimatized to the different approach in the new teaching experience, but what may have impressed them as a handicap also equipped them with a wider perspective.

The Nestor of the German contingent was Franz Oppenheimer (1864–1943), a distinguished social reformer, who had taught in Berlin and Frankfurt and had once been the teacher of Ludwig Erhard, later West German chancellor. At the New School Adolph Lowe (b. 1898) taught for many years and attempted to develop a rival approach to conventional equilibrium economics. Some of his students themselves became well-known economists, such as the American-born Robert Heilbroner (b. 1919). Among the original members of the New School faculty were also Gerhard Colm (1897–1968), who specialized in public finance and eventually held a leading position in the Bureau of the Budget in Washington; Emil Lederer (1882–1939), the principal economic expert of the Social-Democratic Party in Germany, who did not live long enough in the United States to continue his studies of technological unemployment; and others. Among newcomers from Germany working elsewhere was Fritz Redlich (1892–1978), who placed the study of entrepreneurial and financial history on a new basis, but only found satisfactory employment in 1952.

Of the German contingent, only one was elected president of the American Economic Association. This was Jacob Marschak (1898–1977), a Russian native educated in Germany, who died while president-elect.

The newcomers with the widest appeal came from the Austrian contingent, led by Ludwig von Mises (1881–1973), a brilliant doctrinaire. Mises, born in Lemberg but educated in Vienna, was an advocate of laissez faire and an opponent of public policy. When Mises came to America around 1940, he was already well known, but his extreme views accompanied with his powerful personality made it difficult for him to find a position. Mises's fame continued to grow after his death. He became the subject of a cult movement that was organized and financed by conservative businessmen. Fritz Machlup (1902–1983) deserves mention because of his contributions to general economic theory and international economics. He also served as president of the American Association of University Professors (1962–1964) and of the International Economic Association (1971–1974). William Fellner (1905–1983), a Hungarian, had a distinguished academic career at Berkeley and Yale and published a study of oligopoly. Both Machlup and Fellner served as presidents of the American Economic Association, the former in 1966, the latter in 1969. The only newcomer who attained both the presidency of the American Economic Association (in 1976), and the Nobel Prize in Economic Science was an Italian immigrant, Franco Modigliani (b. 1918), who was trained both in Italy and at the New School.

THE POSTWAR SCENE: THE INCLUSION OF THE EXCLUDED. During the postwar decades, the huge increase in college enrollment, together with other factors, greatly increased the demand for economists. The other factors included the growing employment of economists by business firms and the increasing need for economic consultants. The concomitant increase in the supply of economists coincided with what Joseph Alsop has designated as "the inclusion of the excluded," that is, the opening up of opportunities for people of different races, nationalities, and religions and for the one-half of the population that is made up of women. All these trends greatly increased employment opportunities for Jewish economists. Milton Friedman and Paul A. Samuelson are only two amongst a long list of those who rose to the opportunities. In general, it suffices to state that since the mid-fifties about one-half of the presidents of the American Economic Association have come from Jewish extraction. Approximately the same proportion prevails among the American winners of the Nobel Prize in Economic Science since it was instituted in 1969.

THE QUALITY OF THE JEWISH CONTRIBUTION TO AMERICAN ECONOMIC THOUGHT. A few Jewish contributions to American economics are unique. Joseph Dorfman's *The Economic Mind in American Civilization*, published in five volumes from 1946 to 1959, presents a history of economic thought in the United States. I. L. Sharfman's *The Interstate Commerce Commission*, likewise published in five volumes, from 1931 to 1937, also provides an important contribution to economics in America. Outstanding as these contributions are, they are devoted to topics that are not of worldwide interest, nor would they establish a new "paradigm" in economic thought.

The Jewish contributions to American economics are a mirror image of the contribution of other Americans. True, Jewish economists were drawn to labor economics in the 1930s, but this was a passing phase that ended with the lapse of interest in this field, which was later reborn under the name of manpower economics. In the postwar years, they were drawn to development economics and the mathematization of economics, but so was the great majority of the profession. The profession itself, no longer Waspish and including not only Jews but also newcomers from other minorities and foreign countries, would be attracted to the mathematization of economics for reasons similar to those that years ago, under the multinational Austrian empire of the Hapsburgs, had made abstract configurations such as pure economics, the pure theory of law, and the like so suitable and attractive. In the multiethnic American domain, quantifications and highly abstract generalizations presented in mathematical language have a similar appeal because they can be used as instruments of homogenizing or integrating ethnic, linguistic, historical, or other differences into a melting pot. Turning economics into a pseudonatural science with a mathematical approach did not only appeal to Jews, but to many other economists as well.

Jewish-American Nobelists did make significant contributions to economics even if they, like non-Jews, did not establish any new paradigms. Paul A. Samuelson (b. 1915) discovered a mathematical reformulation of the various parts of economic theory. Simon Kuznets (1901–1985) specialized in empirical measurement. Milton Friedman (b. 1912) is a libertarian and has pronounced views on monetary policy. Herbert Simon (b. 1916) has broken new paths in organization and decision theory. Lawrence Klein (b. 1920) works on econometric models and forecasting. Franco Modigliani (b. 1918) has explored the role of anticipations. Kenneth Arrow (b. 1921) developed the paradox of voting and made other contributions to economic theory. Robert M. Solow (b. 1924) explored the factors of long-term growth.

By studying current alignments in economic thought, it is apparent that these different approaches are equally well represented by Jews and non-Jews. In mainstream economics there are monetarists, on the one hand, and various branches of Keynesianism on the other. The monetarists are led by Milton Friedman, but he has many followers that are not Jewish. Again, among the Keynesians there are Jews and non-Jews. Among the peripheral movements there are the radicals, the new Austrians, and the supply-side economists. As for the radicals, in the immediate postwar period Paul Baran (1910–1964), a Russian-born Jew, was the only academician at Stanford University who openly professed Marxist economics. As the number of radical economists increased during the 1960s, more non-Jews became prominent among them. The leader of the new Austrians is Friedrich von Hayek, a non-Jew, but they have followers of all persuasions and denominations. The same is true of supply-side economics. It may be said that there are no distinctive qualities of Jewish contributions to American economic thought. However, it is also true that Jews have contributed disproportionately to their numbers in the overall population to the growth of economics in the United States.

HENRY W. SPIEGEL

BIBLIOGRAPHY

Blaug, Mark, ed. *Who is Who in Economics: A Biographical Dictionary of Major Economists, 1700–1986.* 2nd ed. Cambridge, Mass.: MIT Press, 1986.

Cardozo, Jacob Nuñez. *Notes on Political Economy (1826).* With an Introduction by Joseph S. Dorfman. New York: Kelly, 1960.

Craver, Earlene. "The Emigration of the Austrian Economists." *History of Political Economy* 18 (Spring 1986): 1–32.

Dorfman, Joseph. *The Economic Mind in American Civilization.* 5 vols. 1946–1959. New York: Kelly, 1966.

Leiman, Melvin M. *Jacob N. Cardozo: Economic Thought in the Antebellum South.* New York: Columbia University Press, 1966.

Seligman, Ben B. *Main Currents of Modern Economics: Economic Thought Since 1870.* Glencoe, Ill.: Free Press, 1962.

Seretan, L. Glen. *Daniel De Leon: The Odyssey of an American Marxist.* Cambridge: Harvard University Press, 1979.

Spiegel, Henry W., and Samuels, Warren J., eds. *Contemporary Economists in Perspective.* 2 vols. Greenwich, Conn.: JAI Press, 1984.

Education. See ACADEME, JEWISH EDUCATION, JEWISH STUDIES.

Educational Alliance. A committee of German-Jewish philanthropists created the Educational Alliance in the 1880s to reach out to recent East European Jewish immigrants. A majority of these immigrants came to the United States between 1881 and 1890 and settled on the Lower East Side of New York in crowded tenements. They were poverty-stricken, knew little English, and were forced to work in the local garment-making shops ("sweat shops") for 14 hours a day. Upon seeing the poor conditions these coreligionists were forced to live in, the more affluent, well-established "uptown" German Jews felt duty-bound to help.

Among the founders of the Educational Alliance were Isidor Straus, Judge Samuel Greenbaum, Myer S. Isaacs, Jacob Schiff, and Isaac Seligman. These men met and planned a fund-raising fair to build a large educational building on the Lower East Side as an outreach to the recent immigrants. In this building merged the Hebrew Free School Association, the Aguilar Free Library Society, and the Young Men's Hebrew Association. The building was completed in 1891 and in 1893 was named the Educational Alliance.

The Educational Alliance was created to "Americanize" the recent immigrants and help them assimilate into the American culture. According to the legal agreement of May 4, 1893, "the scope of the work shall be of an Americanizing, educational, social and humanizing character." This program, supported by funds from the Baron de Hirsch Fund, prepared the immigrants' young children for entry into the public schools.

Day and evening classes were also provided for adults, with instruction in the English language and civics and all necessary preparations to become a naturalized American citizen. Lectures were given and motion pictures were shown on American history and the structure and function of the American government as well. The Educational Alliance served as a bridge between urban New York and the world of the immigrant—the Torah and the ghetto—by having the classes taught in Yiddish.

From the beginning, the Educational Alliance served as a major educational, cultural, intellectual, and service center for the residents of the Lower East Side. The Alliance Aguilar Free Circulating Library was provided at the building since there was no public library in the city. On average, the adult reading room and library served 500 to 1000 people each day.

The Educational Alliance took over the work of the Hebrew Free Schools Association and continued the education of Jewish religion and history for children ages 3 to 5. There were also children's services and Bible and story hours on Saturday. For young people a wide range of classes was offered: art; Greek; Roman and American history; American, English, German, and French literature; botany; biology and physiology; chemistry; electricity and physics; piano, violin, and mandolin lessons; English composition; stenography; typewriting; bookkeeping; telegraphy; manual training; and preparation for Regents and Civil Service exams.

For adults, a People's Synagogue was established, which offered special free services for the Holy Days. From 1898 to the middle 1920s, the world-renowned Russian-Jewish preacher, Zevi Hirsh Masliansky, lectured on Friday evenings in Yiddish at the People's Synagogue.

In 1898, David Thompson, a Scottish-born historian of education, conducted a series of four lectures at the Alliance. These lectures were followed by daily lectures that were the foundation of the Breadwinners' College based at the Alliance. One of Thompson's "disciples," Morris Raphael Cohen, also gave a series of lectures. After Thompson's death in 1900, Cohen and other "disciples" began the David Thompson Society, which continued the Breadwinners' College until 1917.

In 1901, the Educational Alliance opened a boy's camp in Cold Spring-on-the-Hudson. This was followed some years later by a camp for girls in Oceanic, New Jersey, and a summer vacation home for mothers and young children.

Special bureaus were set up to meet the problems and needs of the neighborhood. The Legal Aid Bureau was established with Yiddish-speaking lawyers and clerks to help the immigrants communicate with their employers and landlords and to protect them from swindlers. The Desertion Bureau was established to help locate husbands and fathers who had deserted their families and to obtain help from the United Hebrew Charities to prevent starvation and eviction for the abandoned families.

In 1915, an alumni association was formed to insure a continuity of interest in the Educational Alliance and the ideals for which it stands and to renew old friendships. The association has established a hall of fame to honor those who have rendered conspicuous service to the Alliance or who have become famous in their professions, including, to name only some, Monty Banks, Leonard Baskin, Peter Blume, Irving Caesar, Eddie Cantor, Morris Raphael Cohen, Israel Cummings, Jo Davidson, Sir Jacob Epstein, Philip Evergood, John Garfield, Judge Abraham J. Gellinoff, George Gershwin, Ruby Goldstein, Adolph Gottlieb, Chaim Gross, Elinor Guggenheimer, Jacob Holman, Nat Holman, George Jessel, Alan King, Louis J. Lefkowitz, Judge Arthur Markewich, Judge Allen Murray Meyers, Zero Mostel, Arthur Murray, Louise Nevelson, Jan Peerce, Judge Saul Price, Judge Simon H. Rifkind, Billie Schiffres Rosen, Judge Leon Sandler, Brig. Gen. David Sarnoff, Ben Shahn, Charles H. Silver, Isaac Soyer, Moses Soyer, Michael Howard, and Arthur Tracy.

Until 1917, the Educational Alliance was supported by the fund-raising efforts of the founding trustees, board members, and women's auxiliary. Endowments and bequests provided another source of income. In 1917, the Educational Alliance became a charter member agency of the Federation of Jewish Philanthropic Societies of New York and received annual budgetary allowances that supported its major budget. In 1990, the Educational Alliance had an annual operating budget of over $4.2 million. Approximately 20 percent of its income comes from the Federation of Jewish Philanthropies of New York and the Greater New York Fund/United Way; approximately 55 percent from federal, state, and city grants; 18 percent from membership and tuition fees; and the balance from other sources—contributions from trustees, alumni, bequests, and grants from foundations for special programs.

In recent times the Educational Alliance has altered its services to match the changes occurring on the Lower East Side. Since World War II, the neighborhood has changed dramatically. Today Jews make up only 30 percent of the population in the neighborhood. The remainder is Hispanic, Asian, Afro-American, Italian, Ukrainian, and Polish.

Over the years, in line with the needs of the people it serves, the "melting-pot" philosophy of Americanization has evolved into the "cultural-pluralism" approach. The purpose of the Educational Alliance is manifold and focuses on serving all inhabitants of the neighborhood with special commitment to the Jewish community. The organization is concerned that people be able to accept their own cultural heritage as well as to accept others who are different. Thus many special programs are geared to the needs of different groups. The Alliance maintains an active community outreach program, and it endeavors to build bridges among ethnic groups to work toward a more united cooperating community among its inhabitants.

The Educational Alliance offers a diverse and multifaceted program to its more than 10,000 members of all ethnic, economic, and social backgrounds. This program reaches all age groups. Services for children include day care, head start, schools for the emotionally disturbed and economically disadvantaged children (ages 5 to 9), nursery school, and kindergarten; an after-school religious school for school-age children, "Kol Tov" program for Jewish Orthodox-oriented boys and girls, and "B'nos Agudath" also for Jewish Orthodox-oriented children (ages 5 to 14); and programs for teens such as recreational outings, project CONTACT to reach the drug-addicted teens and runaways, and a Young Adult Alcoholism Service Program (YAASP).

Services to adults and older adults also cover a wide range. Included is the Educational Alliance Art School, which was founded in 1917 by Abbe Ostrowsky. Among the gifted students who have attended are Saul Baizerman, Elias Grossman, Dina Melicof, Eli Nadelman, Louis Ribak, Iver Rose, Mark Rothko, and Abraham Walkowitz. There is also a Photography Institute, Alliance of Figurative Artists, a sports-fitness program, and special services to older adults, including a crime prevention program.

This is only a partial listing of the outreach program the Educational Alliance offers. In the 1990s, as when it was founded in the 1880s, the Educational Alliance strives to provide programs specifically designed for its neighborhood residents and its members. *See also* New York City.

BEATRICE SHUSTKO
JANET L. DOTTERER

BIBLIOGRAPHY

Bellow, Adam, and Keens, Bill. *The Educational Alliance: A Centennial Celebration.* In press.

Gorelick, Sherry. *City College and the Jewish Poor: Education in New York, 1880–1924.* New Brunswick, N.J.: Rutgers University Press, 1981.

Howe, Irving. *World of Our Fathers.* New York: Harcourt Brace Jovanovich, 1976.

Rischin, Moses. *The Promised City: New York's Jews, 1870–1914.* Cambridge: Harvard University Press, 1962.

Sanders, Ronald. *The Downtown Jews: Portraits of an*

Immigrant Generation. New York: Harper & Row, 1969.

Waxman, Chaim I. *America's Jews in Transition*. Philadelphia: Temple University Press, 1983.

Einstein, Albert (1879–1955). German-American physicist, formulator of the Special and General Theories of Relativity, and winner of the Nobel Prize for Physics (1921) for his work on the photoelectric effect and other contributions to theoretical physics, Albert Einstein is considered one of the most important physicists of modern times.

Born in Ulm, Germany (1879) and educated in Germany and Switzerland, Einstein developed many of his early theoretical concepts while working as a patent examiner in Bern (1901–1909). During this period, he announced the Special Theory of Relativity (1905), which revolutionized the logical foundations with which physicists think about the world. Discarding classical Newtonian conceptions of absolute space and time, Einstein showed that we exist in a four-dimensional space-time continuum in which distances can shrink or expand, time can slow down or speed up, and the mass of a body can increase or decrease as the velocity of our four-dimensional coordinate measuring system changes relative to the event being measured. Although at slow relative velocities Einstein's equations are approximated by the classical Newtonian formulation, his relativistic mechanics not only can be verified experimentally at high relative velocities but also *must* be used for correct atomic and cosmological calculations. Also during this period, Einstein formulated the theory of Brownian movement, the irregular dance of tiny particles such as bacteria or dust suspended in a liquid or gas. This was one of the earliest actual demonstrations that atoms and molecules actually exist, that a physical event has no alternative interpretation other than the atomic model.

Recognition of his work led to his appointment to professorships in Zurich, Prague, and Berlin, the latter including the directorship of the prestigious Kaiser Wilhelm Institute of Physics (1913). In 1916, Einstein made two new major contributions to physics. His General Theory of Relativity deals with systems accelerating rather than moving at constant velocity relative to one another as in the Special Theory. The General Theory incorporates gravitation into the relativity concept by explaining it geometrically: gravitational attraction is caused by the bending of the four-dimensional space-time continuum by material bodies. Einstein's explanation of the photoelectric effect, the emission of electrons when certain metals are struck by light, was one of the earliest proposals of the quantization of light, the concept that light may be considered as composed of particles or "photons." This work on the photoelectric effect was emphasized when Einstein was awarded the Nobel Prize for Physics (1921) and the Theory of Relativity was not explicitly mentioned in the award.

For the rest of his research career, Einstein attempted to create a unified field theory of physics, one in which the forces of electromagnetism and gravitation emerge from geometrical considerations of the space-time continuum. At the same time, he fought a lonely battle against the widely accepted new field of quantum mechanics; this opposition was ironic since his work on the photoelectric effect had led to the quantization of the concept of light. Nevertheless, the essential theoretical foundation of quantum mechanics is based on the fundamental simultaneous indeterminacy of the position and velocity (or momentum) of the electron and other particles. Einstein, on the other hand, expressed his conviction this way: "I cannot believe that God plays dice with the universe."

Einstein, who from his childhood on had difficulties with aspects of German education, science, and politics, watched with dismay as the situation in Germany deteriorated in the 1920s and early 1930s. Finally, he accepted a position at the Institute for Theoretical Physics in Princeton, New Jersey (1933–1945). Stripped of his property and German citizenship by the Nazis (1934), Einstein subsequently became an American citizen (1940). After his retirement, Einstein continued as an Associate at the Institute until his death in Princeton in the spring of 1955.

Concerned about the possibility of development by the Nazis of an atomic bomb, in part made possible by the mass-energy equivalence implicit in his theory of relativity, Einstein represented a group of leading scientists when he wrote (1939) to President Roosevelt urging an atomic bomb development program by the United States. Despite his key role in the decision to implement such a program, Einstein remained a lifelong devoted and articulate pacifist.

Although ambivalent in his identification with traditional Judaism, Einstein was an ardent Zionist. He was offered, but declined, the first presidency of the State of Israel. Representing the Jewish philosopher-scientist in his highest development, Einstein summed up his view of the universe in this way: "God is subtle, but he is not malicious."

IRA N. FEIT

BIBLIOGRAPHY

Bernstein, Jeremy E. *Einstein*. New York: Viking Press, 1973.

Clark, Ronald W. *Einstein, The Life and Times*. New York: World, 1971.

Einstein, Albert. *Out of My Later Years*. New York: Philosophical Library, 1950.

———. *The World as I See It*. New York: Philosophical Library, 1934.

Frank, Philipp. *Einstein, His Life and Times*. New York: Knopf, 1953.

Hoffmann, Banesh, and Dukas, Helen. *Albert Einstein, Creator and Rebel*. New York: Viking Press, 1973.

———. *Albert Einstein, The Human Side: New Glimpses from his Archives*. Princeton, N.J.: Princeton University Press, 1979.

Holton, Gerald, and Elkana, Yehuda, eds. *Albert Einstein, Historical and Cultural Perspectives: The Centennial Symposium in Jerusalem*. Princeton, N.J.: Princeton University Press, 1982.

Pais, Abraham. *Subtle is the Lord: The Science and Life of Albert Einstein*. New York: Oxford University Press, 1982.

Stachel, John, et al. *The Collected Papers of Albert Einstein: The Early Years, 1879–1902*. Vol. 1. Princeton, N.J.: Princeton University Press, 1987.

Eisenstein, Ira (b. 1906). A leader of the Reconstructionist Movement throughout his adult life, Ira Eisenstein was the first president of the Reconstructionist Rabbinical College. The most important confidant, disciple, and collaborator of Mordecai Kaplan, Eisenstein served as editor of the *Reconstructionist* magazine from 1959 to 1981. He co-edited the Reconstructionist prayer books for the Sabbath (1945), High Holidays (1948), and the pilgrimage festivals (1958), and the Reconstructionist Haggadah (1941), as well as being the author of several books and dozens of articles.

Born and raised in New York City, he received his B.A. in 1927 and Ph.D. in 1941, both from Columbia University. He was ordained by the Jewish Theological Seminary in 1931 and received an honorary D.D. in 1958. He served as the assistant rabbi of the Society for the Advance-

ment of Judaism (SAJ) from 1931 to 1945 and as rabbi until 1954. With Mordecai M. Kaplan as senior rabbi, the SAJ was the fountainhead of Reconstructionist thought and activity.

After the publication of Kaplan's *Judaism as a Civilization* in 1934, Eisenstein played a crucial role in spreading Kaplan's key ideas through his books *Creative Judaism* (1936), *What We Mean By Religion* (1938), and *Judaism Under Freedom* (1958). He was active in the launching of the *Reconstructionist* magazine (1935), the Jewish Reconstructionist Foundation (1940), and the Reconstructionist Press.

An ardent Zionist, Eisenstein spent a substantial amount of time in Israel and devoted considerable thought and energy to fostering a strong relationship between American and Israeli Jews. While he did consider becoming a permanent resident of Israel, he saw his essential mission as helping to create a vital Jewish life in the United States.

From 1954 to 1959, Eisenstein served as senior rabbi of congregation Anshe Emet in Chicago. He returned to New York in 1959 to assume the editorship of the *Reconstructionist* and head the Jewish Reconstructionist Foundation, determined to build the Reconstructionist Movement as a separate entity. Though he had served as president of the Conservative Rabbinical Assembly (1952–1954), he saw a pressing need to create a progressive, non-Halakhah movement based upon Reconstructionist ideals.

The movement in that period suffered from financial and organizational problems. Its volunteer leadership was pessimistic, and Kaplan was ambivalent about the future direction of the Reconstructionist enterprise. At that key juncture, Eisenstein played a pivotal role in altering the movement's fortunes.

His efforts culminated in the 1968 founding in Philadelphia of the Reconstructionist Rabbinical College, which he served as president until 1981. After his retirement, he wrote *Reconstructing Judaism: An Autobiography*, published in 1986.

Eisenstein's wife is Judith Kaplan Eisenstein, the daughter of Mordecai M. Kaplan and a noted musicologist. Together they wrote five widely popular cantatas.

Eisenstein was a leader in the building of Reconstructionism into an enduring fourth branch of American Judaism. Its growth and continued evolution in recent years, as well as the success of the rabbis trained at the Reconstructionist Rabbinical College, are tributes to Eisenstein's vision, energy, and unswerving commitment to his mission. *See also* Reconstructionism.

DAVID A. TEUTSCH

BIBLIOGRAPHY

Eisenstein, Ira. *Reconstructing Judaism: An Autobiography.* New York: Reconstructionist Press, 1986.

Elderly, The. "Old age" has been an important subject in Jewish life from earliest times. The Bible takes two conflicting approaches to aging. The first approach views old age as a reward for observance of commandments, especially the commandment to honor father and mother (Exodus 20:12). The second approach views aging as a time of physical and cognitive decline. The twelfth chapter of Ecclesiastes is a description of the ravages of old age.

This dual tradition continues in the Talmud and is codified in several ways. The elderly are entitled to special respect. One who has achieved a certain age is assumed to have gained wisdom as well. However, the Talmud does not endorse gerontocracy, that is, rule by the elderly. The Talmud continues to place learning above age as a criteria for leadership. The writers of the Talmud also assumed that physical and cognitive decline are part of old age, and for this reason set a mandatory retirement age of 70 for members of the Sanhedrin.

Although there was disagreement about the meaning of aging, there was never any disagreement on the importance of caring for the old. The Bible describes a wicked society as one where the aged are not cared for (Isaiah 3:5). In general, the Talmud views care of the elderly as the responsibility of the family. However, when the family was unable to help because of poverty or other reasons, the responsibility for care fell on the community.

The one exception to the rule that families must care for their own elderly is a decision of Maimonides that if caring for an older parent becomes too much of a strain for a family, the parent can be sent to be cared for by another person. The strain referred to seems to be the type of psychological strain that often accompanies caring for a demented relative.

The tradition of family care for the aged began to break down in the seventeenth century. The reasons for this breakdown were the large number of aging parents with no one to care for them because of the murder of their adult children by the Cossacks and the beginning of vast population movements across Europe, which for the first time left some older Jews living far from their children. For these reasons the first Jewish old-age homes were established.

THE JEWISH ELDERLY IN AMERICA: AN HISTORICAL VIEW. The earliest recognition of an aging Jewish population in the United States comes from colonial times when some sermons delivered in synagogue seem to castigate congregants for not helping more with the elderly. In early America, as in Europe, it was thought that the family must care for the elderly, and communal support was limited to the elderly who were poor and without family.

While there are no precise statistics on the Jewish family, it is fair to say that the number of family members living in the same dwelling was larger in the nineteenth century and early twentieth centuries than it is today. There were also more households with three generations living under one roof. However, one must also remember that the "older generation" was much younger than today because childbearing began at earlier ages and life expectancy was shorter. In addition, many immigrant families suffered from desertion by the father; thus even though there may have been three generations in the household, a nuclear family was not always at the core.

Institutionally, the American Jewish community has been searching for an appropriate way to deal with the elderly population who needed communal help almost since Jews began to arrive in the seventeenth century. Before the middle of the nineteenth century, the major institutional response came from the synagogues. The synagogues dispensed charitable funds for the poor and others in need. Some elderly were given a regular "old-age" pension by local synagogues. This occurred as early as 1760 in congregation Shearith Israel in New York. Some Jews participated in non-Jewish charities both as donors and as recipients, but as soon as each community was able, charitable services, including those to the elderly, were handled through the synagogue.

The first home for the Jewish elderly in the United States, established in New York in 1848 by B'nai B'rith, was set up along the lines of homes for the Jewish aged in Germany. This home, like the next one established in 1855 in St. Louis, was designed for poor elderly German Jews without families.

Immigrants also strove to care for their parents left in Europe, either by sending them money or arranging for them to immigrate to the United States.

The arrival of Jews from Eastern Europe had a significant effect on the provision of services for the Jewish elderly. Before 1900, 9 homes for the Jewish elderly with Eastern European backgrounds were established, 8 between 1900 and 1909, and 14 from 1910 to 1919. Many of these homes were in the same communities as those already supported by the German Jews in order to meet the special needs of the East European Jews; that is, they served kosher food and the staff spoke Yiddish. Few if any of these homes were under "religious" auspices such as the institutional structures of the Reform or Orthodox movements. Most were supported by the community at large, a model learned in Europe.

In their own old age, these Eastern European immigrants often had a hard time adjusting. Cut off from their past and alienated from American culture, which they never fully embraced, they were denied the cultural and social supports that are often needed in old age. Their children often had no grandparents and therefore no model learned from their parents on how to treat the elderly. Nevertheless, the majority of the elderly were never abused or abandoned, even though such tales always made exciting reading in the Jewish press and literature.

The event that most transformed care of the Jewish elderly, along with the nation's elderly as a whole, was the establishment of the Social Security system, followed 30 years later by the institution of Medicare. While Social Security and Medicare never covered all the needs of the elderly (and were never intended as such), they did provide a great deal of help that had previously been provided by local Jewish social service agencies. While these agencies continued to provide a variety of services and programs, many of these were now paid for by the government.

CONTEMPORARY ISSUES. The elderly, those individuals 65 years of age or older, constitute approximately 18 percent of the American Jewish population. This is an increase from 12 percent in 1971. It is estimated that by the year 2000 the elderly will make up 20 percent of the American Jewish population. In the overall American population approximately 10 percent were elderly in 1971, and by the year 2000 approximately 12 percent of the American population will be 65 or older. Thus, not only is the proportion of elderly in the American Jewish population higher than the proportion of elderly in the American population as a whole, the Jewish community is also aging at a faster rate.

There are more women than men in the elderly American Jewish population. The 1971 National Jewish Population Survey reported a breakdown of 44 percent male and 56 percent female in the elderly population. Jewish males have greater longevity than non-Jewish males. One effect of the greater longevity of Jewish males is that there are more married couples among the Jewish than the non-Jewish elderly.

One-third of the Jewish elderly are over the age of 74, and 10 percent are 85 years or older. These "old old" (75+) are more likely to be immigrants, in poorer health, and in worse financial circumstance than the "young old," those 65 to 74 years of age. As people live longer, we can expect a larger proportion of the elderly to live past the age of 85, until age 100 or beyond.

The current generation of "young old" are a generation of transition. A large proportion of them are first-generation Americans, making them a bridge between their immigrant parents and their acculturated American children. They are also less likely than the "old old" to participate in Jewish ritual observance or dietary laws.

It is clear that there is great disparity in the wealth of older Jews. This is in part due to the differences in work experience between the "old old" and the "young old." The single greatest impact on the social status of the Jewish elderly is the expansion in the number of Jews who complete college degrees. Among the "young old," 61 percent have at least some college experience, and this proportion will increase as new cohorts enter old age.

Of the noninstitutionalized Jewish elderly, about a third live alone. Some elderly live near their adult children, but seldom do they live near their grandchildren. Only 7 percent of American Jewish households contain three generations.

The current generation of Jewish elderly are disproportionately urban residents and apartment dwellers, much more so than the general American elderly population. More older Jews live in the suburbs, and fewer live in the poorest sections of urban areas than in 1970. Almost 25 percent of American Jewish households are headed by an elderly person.

The Jewish elderly are more mobile than the general older population, just as the American Jewish community is more mobile than the population as a whole. Most of the movement involves widows who move near their adult children. Of the elderly who move because of retirement, 60 percent move to Florida. Aside from communities such as Sarasota, Florida, and Palm Springs, California, which are retirement communities, some smaller Jewish communities, such as Scranton, Pennsylvania, and Dayton, Ohio, have a high proportion of elderly inhabitants because the younger cohorts have left these cities for better opportunities elsewhere. Many Jewish organizations are now finding that a significant portion of their membership is 65 years of age or older.

There are special populations among the Jewish elderly, including Holocaust survivors and Soviet Jews. Some Holocaust survivors bring special emotional problems into old age. In addition, they have a stronger aversion than most of the elderly population to placement in nursing homes because of their fear of returning to an institutional environment. Soviet Jewish elderly often have a difficult time adjusting to life in the United States. The poor health and lack of resources that many Soviet Jews suffer from also make caring for them a special challenge for Jewish communal agencies. Eventually, the American Jewish community will face dealing with other aging subpopulations, such as Israelis who immigrated to the United States.

The Jewish elderly are in effect in a double minority status as both Jews and elderly. They also suffer from other social changes, such as the rising rate of divorce. Divorce often places the older parents (usually of the wife) in the position of providing both financial and social support. In large part because of the divorce rate, more money flows from aging parents to their adult children than the other way around.

Older Jews come into contact with community institutions more often than the non-Jewish elderly both as providers and receivers of service. The Jewish elderly use more formal services for the aged than the non-Jewish elderly and are more frequent participants in social activities, especially volunteering.

The choices made by older Jews regarding housing are also often different from the choices made by the non-Jewish elderly. The Jewish elderly have been hesitant to move to life-care communities where a large down payment and regular monthly fees guarantee services for the rest of one's life. While some have interpreted this hesitancy as a desire to leave as much as possible to the children, it seems that a better explanation is

the desire of many Jewish elderly to retain some control over their own lives. The "big buy in" means giving up a large sum of money, sometimes the entire life savings, and never seeing the money again. A higher proportion of Jewish elderly are in nursing homes than non-Jewish elderly.

The desire for control is one facet of the psychological status of the Jewish elderly. The immigrants brought with them into old age their traditions, manners of expression, and world view. East European Jews are fond of expressing their aches and pains, and these expressions can make it difficult to distinguish between depression and a style of expression. More recent generations of American Jews, born and acculturated in the United States, continue to be as expressive as their parents. However, over time, this may change.

While most of the problems that face the Jewish elderly are the same that face most older people—declining health, limited financial resources—there are some that seem to affect the Jewish elderly more often.

For many of the American-born children of the Jewish elderly, there is a constant struggle between proper behavior in terms of American values, which means success that often can only be achieved by a high degree of geographic mobility, and proper behavior in terms of how Jewish values are understood, taking care of aging parents that requires living in close proximity. This tension affects both the adult children, who never feel that they are doing enough for their parents, and the aging parents, who are torn between admiration for their children's success and a desire for their children to live in close proximity so that the children can care for them when they become ill. Such tensions are expressed in many different ways but most often in relationships between adult children and their parents that can become a source of guilt.

On an institutional level, two issues have emerged in the recent past that reflect a conflict between Jewish and modern norms. The first issue is the struggle between traditional Jewish norms about decision making for the critically ill, the definition of death, and similar issues versus the demands and rules of health care institutions such as hospitals and nursing homes. A second issue revolves around the problem of taking nonsectarian funds (United Way, governmental) for sectarian institutions. How "Jewish" can such institutions be and still be entitled to funds designed to provide services regardless of religious background? While neither of the problems are unique to agencies serving the Jewish elderly, they do appear most often in the context of agencies serving the old.

On a societal level, some groups espouse a philosophy of spending less on the elderly and more on children. This approach is directly antithetical to the position of traditional Judiaism, which requires support of all in need. Some Jewish agencies are beginning to respond to the challenge presented by such organizations.

THE FUTURE. It is clear that the Jewish elderly form a unique and special segment of both the American Jewish community and the elderly population of the United States. How this population will change in Jewish terms over time depends almost entirely on how the people entering old age were socialized as children. For those who were raised in strong Jewish homes, Jewishness will be a source of comfort and strength in old age. For those who were alienated from their Jewish heritage as children, Jewishness will play little role and be of little comfort in later years. *See also* Communal Organizations.

ALLEN GLICKSMAN

BIBLIOGRAPHY

Dulin, Rachel. *A Crown of Glory: A Biblical View of Aging.* New York: Paulist Press, 1988.

Glicksman, Allen. *The New Jewish Elderly: A Literature Review.* New York: American Jewish Committee, 1991.

Myerhoff, Barbara. *Number Our Days.* New York: Simon & Schuster, 1980.

Ellis Island. The United States government in 1892 opened an immigrant reception center in New York Harbor at Ellis Island. By the time it closed in 1954, some 12 million immigrants—including a majority of the 2 million Jews who fled Russia, Austria-Hungary, and Romania between 1881 and 1924—had passed through its portals. On September 10, 1990, after six years of restoration, the restored immigrant center reopened as the National Museum of Immigration.

Prior to 1890, the states handled immigrant reception. After 1855, immigrants to New York landed at Castle Garden in Lower Manhattan, but it became evident in the 1880s that Castle Garden could not handle the increased traffic of the great migration. Shortly after federal authorities took over immigration affairs in 1890, they opened Ellis Island.

For Jewish immigrants it was but the last stop in a long journey, the majority of whom had traveled furtively across the Russian frontier and on to the seaports of Hamburg, Bremen, Antwerp, Rotterdam, or Liverpool. From there they sailed amid the crowds and filth of steamship steerage to Ellis Island.

As they piled into its massive Great Hall, they lined up for the dreaded medical examinations. Those who exhibited symptoms of one of the "loathsome and contagious diseases" for which America sent back would-be immigrants—including the "Jewish disease," tuberculosis—found a letter chalked on their coats. Those who passed would then be interrogated by multilingual inspectors about their character, politics, criminal activities, finances, relatives, and work plans. The last question often confused the immigrants, for to have a job already violated federal law prohibiting the importation of contract labor.

Most immigrants passed through in a day. Those detained for further examination or to appear before a Board of Inquiry could spend weeks there. After 1900, Jewish detainees found a kosher kitchen, a feature of the new station built to replace the wooden one completely destroyed—along with all immigration records back to 1855—by fire in 1897.

One's view of Ellis Island depended upon where one stood. Many, meeting harsh and frightening treatment, named it the "isle of tears." Others, however, understood its inspectors' overwhelming tasks and the need for haste because these officials saw in a single year, 1907, for example, more than 1 million people. Jewish immigrants found their difficulties smoothed somewhat by sensitive Jewish immigrant inspectors, among them Philip Cowen, and agents, like Alexander Harkavy, of the Hebrew Sheltering and Immigrant Aid Society (HIAS).

PAMELA S. NADELL

BIBLIOGRAPHY

Corsi, Edward. *In the Shadow of Liberty.* Hamden, Conn.: Arno Press, 1969.

Howe, Irving. *World of Our Fathers.* New York: Harcourt Brace Jovanovich, 1976.

Pitkin, Thomas M. *Keepers of the Gate: A History of Ellis Island.* New York: New York University Press, 1975.

Epstein, Abraham (1892–1942). Abraham Epstein has been credited as the person who was most influential in the passage of the Social Security Act in 1936.

Epstein, a Russian Jew, emigrated to New York City at the age of 18 in 1910. His parents were Leon and Bessie Levovits Epstein. Early in life he identified with the economically disadvantaged. He became passionately committed to social insurance, and in the 1920s he served, for almost nine years, as a research director for the Pennsylvania Commission for Old Age Pension. After leaving that post, he founded the American Association for Old Age Security (AAOAS) in 1927. The organization's first major act was to prepare a bill for introduction to Congress calling for federal grants-in-aid to states adopting old-age insurance laws, with Epstein as the chief draftsman. The bill never made it out of committee.

Epstein was an expert in the social security field and a powerful writer on the subject. In 1928, he published *The Care of the Aged*, which enlarged on his *Facing Old Age*, a study of old-age dependency and old-age pensions, first published in 1922.

Epstein, along with Isaac Rubinow, became embroiled in the social security debate of the Roosevelt administration. There were two proposals before Congress, the Wisconsin Plan and the Ohio Plan. Their differences included the control of funds (public vs. private), employer and employee contributions, and amount of compensation and length of time employees would be compensated. Epstein preferred the Ohio Plan.

In November 1934, a National Conference on Economic Security met in Washington. Conspicuously missing from the committee were unemployment insurance experts Epstein and Rubinow, as well as Paul Douglas and Eveline Burns, all known for their advocacy of a national system as opposed to a state or private system. As this conference met, Epstein and Rubinow met with Barbara Armstrong, a law professor at the University of California, and drafted an "Outline of Old Age Security Program" that established two ways of paying benefits. Either benefit payments would be a percentage of prior individual earnings or benefit payments would be made on a flat rate for everyone, regardless of previous earnings. The latter was rejected as un-American because it standardized incomes and contributions of the higher paid would be shifted to benefit the less well paid.

A compromise was suggested, fusing pay-as-you-go with government deficit financing. Epstein eventually rejected the idea because the proposal appeared to be a "compromise" of contradictions. He rejected "contributory payment" and believed that the employee contribution should be held to a minimum. The government rejected Epstein's advice and continued the pay-as-you-go, joining it with a partial reserve and future partial funding annually from general revenues. Epstein also opposed the reserve fund for social security because it shifted the burden of providing for aging workers to the younger wage earners. Epstein is quoted as stating, "Our programs actually relieve the wealthy from their traditional obligation under the ancient poor laws."

Finally, Epstein warned that the real losers of the Social Security Act would be the blacks because the bill excluded the occupations where blacks were most heavily concentrated and contained no specific prohibitions against discrimination in any of the areas the bill did cover. He warned in 1934 that the way the bill was set up would lead to long-range problems. He even predicted that in the 1980s social security would be in serious financial trouble with the way it was set up.

Epstein was a leading advocate of unemployment and old-age insurance in the 1930s. He was knowledgeable in the field, but because of his abrasive personality and argumentativeness his word was not heeded in the 1930s and few of his ideas were actually implemented in the Social Security Act. In spite of this, it was Epstein who kept the idea of social insurance alive in America in the 1920s and 1930s.

JANET L. DOTTERER

BIBLIOGRAPHY

Davis, Kenneth S. *FDR: The New Deal Years, 1933–1937. A History.* New York: Random House, 1979.

Schlesinger, Arthur M., Jr. *The Age of Roosevelt: The Coming of the New Deal.* Boston: Houghton Mifflin, 1958.

Weiss, Nancy J. *Farewell to the Party of Lincoln: Black Politics in the Age of FDR.* Princeton, N.J.: Princeton University Press, 1983.

Ethiopian Jews, American Response to.

Ethiopian Jews made the front page of the *New York Times* and other major newspapers around the world in 1985 when it was disclosed that 8000 refugees in Sudan had been transported secretly to Israel, the land of their prayers and dreams for centuries. Until then, even the presence of an equal number in Israel had been rarely revealed. Previous efforts by organizations such as the American Association for Ethiopian Jews to aid them in their efforts to reach Israel for more than a decade (although there were groups interested in their welfare for the better part of the twentieth century) had met with relatively little success.

Who were these black Jews? With a past shrouded in mystery, with many conflicting and imaginative conceptions of their origin, they may be the longest continuous Jewish group in the millenial Jewish experience. Theories as to their beginnings include perhaps the offspring of relationships with Moses, whose two wives were Ethiopian; or descendants of the union of King Solomon and the Queen of Sheba; offsprings of the Ten Lost Tribes, most notably that of Dan; Jews who left Egypt, trekked up the Nile to Ethiopia; Jews who sailed across the Red Sea from Yemen and South Arabia, some or all intermingling with the natives through settlement, intermarriage, and conversion. Some contend that they became Jews only in the fourteenth century, although the Judaization of Ethiopia since biblical times would dispute such a belated notion. The Bible has numerous references to contacts of ancient Israel with Ethiopia (Cush). Isaiah included them in the "remnants of Israel" scattered over the Near East, the Mediterranean and Red Sea regions as far back as 750 B.E. Ancient Israelites reached the land in the northeast section of Africa through military incursions, trade, and diplomatic relations.

In the ninth century, Eldad-Hadani traveled to North Africa from what is believed to be Ethiopia to chronicle a thriving Jewish community. From the eleventh to the seventeenth centuries, a Jewish kingdom reigned in a large part of Ethiopia, dominating it with its military prowess, thriving on agriculture and skills in construction. It took the Ethiopian kings over 600 years to conquer this stiff-necked Jewish tribe, after which they were reduced by death and forced conversion, with the remainder assigned to serfdom. Those who did not convert to Christianity could not inherit the land and became "Falasai," landless. Thus the name "Falasha" was foisted on them as a pejorative term. By government policy they became pariahs. At the same time, those who rose to leadership of the Jewish villages determined that their followers would remain Jews despite ubiquitous prejudice and persecution. Their census before final defeat has been variously estimated at 500,000 to 1 million.

With the extirpation of most of their religious and lay leaders, along with their sacred shrines, literature, and symbols, some opted for monasticism as a way of life, isolated from their foes. This movement attracted some high-ranking Christians as converts into their Jewish ranks.

They were thus forced to turn to crafts and iron work together with tenant farming to survive. Their numbers since the seventeenth century contracted steadily as the result of poverty, disease, and conversion to other faiths, Christian and Moslem. By the middle of the nineteenth century, their count had diminished to less than 150,000.

James Bruce, in his "Travels to Discover the Source of the Nile" in the latter part of the eighteenth century, noted the distinctive differences between Jews and others living in that country, portraying the "Falashas" in a more favorable life style due primarily to their religious practices.

Christian missionaries from Europe, and particularly from England, descended upon them, seeking conversions to Protestant sects. A book by a meshumad (convert) in 1862 attracted the interest of European Jews to the extent that they dispatched Joseph Halevy, an eminent French scholar of that region and its languages, to Ethiopia. When he returned and published that they were indeed Jews, most of the European Jewish world ignored his revelations. The one response that was forthcoming was from Jews in Philadelphia, who sent money to help these poverty-stricken Jews. Despite these efforts, the Ethiopian Jews continued in their poverty, prey to missionaries, suffering daily discrimination and further decline in their numbers.

A student of Halevy, Jacques Faitlovitch, took up their cause in the beginning of the twentieth century. For 50 years he tried to overcome the indifference of world Jewry through Pro-Falasha committees to save this remnant by educating some of their young and brightest in Europe and Palestine. He hoped they would return and teach modern Judaism to a people struggling to survive in a hostile land, one of the poorest in the world, and where the benefits of education and medical care were amongst the lowest on the globe. In response to Faitlovitch's appeal, a rabbi at Hebrew Union College in Cincinnati wrote a lengthy letter in 1910 questioning the authenticity of the Jews and suggested that aid be supplied directly to Ethiopia rather than educate or resettle the Ethiopian Jews in the Jewish world.

Shortly after Faitlovitch's article on "The

Falashas" appeared in the *American Jewish Year Book* in 1920, the American Pro-Falasha Committee was organized, and under the leadership of the American Jewish Joint Distribution Committee, a fund was set up to assist in developing a medical and educational program for Ethiopian Jews. A number of national American Jewish organizations contributed to this fund. With the Depression in the 1930s and the urgent needs of European Jewry under the German Nazi regime, this fund petered out.

While it was always their fervent prayer to reach Jerusalem, the center of Israel, and sporadic efforts had been attempted over the centuries to settle in the Promised Land, there was no interest by the Jewish world before the State of Israel was established, nor in the decades after its creation, to encourage the movement of Ethiopian Jews in that direction.

In 1955 and 1956, the Israelis brought 27 Ethiopian Jewish youth to Israel to study. At that very time, they were denied the right to emigrate, and embassy blocks were put in their way of even coming as tourists. The excuse given was that there was doubt as to their authentic Jewishness, despite a number of decrees that had been rendered by prominent rabbis from Palestine, Egypt, and Europe since the sixteenth century that they were indeed Jews. The other excuse was that the emperor would not allow them to leave the country.

In the 1960s, the British Falasha Welfare Association, aided and abetted by the interests of some Americans and the Torah Department of the Jewish Agency, provided modest funds to maintain their primitive schools and medical clinics. At best, these important services reached only a small portion of the Ethiopian Jewish population scattered over more than 400 villages. It was only with the creation of the American Association for Ethiopian Jews that an earnest effort was made to involve American Jewry.

The American Association for Ethiopian Jews (AAEJ) was organized in 1974 and became an advocate for the outright migration of Ethiopian Jews, now reduced to 42,000, in an effort to save them as a distinctive Jewish group as well as to spare their lives from continued privations.

After some prodding, the two chief rabbis, Ovadia Joseph in 1973 and Shlomo Goren in 1975, reaffirmed their Jewishness, following which the Israeli government declared that they were eligible to enter under the Law of Return. Finally, 121 were assisted by the Menachem

Begin Israeli government to enter clandestinely in 1977. By then Ethiopia had undergone a revolution and was in the midst of a civil war with Eritrean secessionists and other guerilla groups. The country then became a satellite of Soviet Russia with Cuban troops brought in to carry out a communist style of political life.

From 1976 to 1981, World Ort conducted a modest nonsectarian education, medical, and agricultural program in several villages where some of the Ethiopian Jews lived. It did not promote aliyah to Israel, nor did it provide relief for the impoverished natives. Since 1985, the American Jewish Joint Distribution Committee has also sponsored a nonsectarian program, building a medical clinic in one village, where few Jews reside. It did not undertake migration nor a relief program for Ethiopian Jews, who suffered along with the other inhabitants during the severe drought and famine that overtook the country in 1984–1985 and recurred in 1987–1988.

The organized American community resisted all efforts to help until 1984, when with the aid of the national government, a major, but clandestine, rescue was undertaken by Israel. When it was discovered that Ethiopian Jews, like their Christian and Moslem counterparts, were escaping from Ethiopia into Sudan to avoid the harsh policies of the government, the internecine war, and the famine, and there was no effort to help them escape by either Israel or the rest of world Jewry, the American Association for Ethiopian Jews undertook two rescue missions from Sudan to demonstrate that it was possible to bring them to Israel. This was followed by sustained pressure and exposure of the issue on the Jewish and general public. Israel then undertook secret rescue missions, which over a period of five years brought 7000 Ethiopian Jews to Israel. Little information was provided about their arrival or their absorption, and no fund-raising efforts were made on their behalf, although the adjustment process was costly.

In 1984, when the Ethiopian Jews learned that their only hope of escaping the horrendous conditions under which they were forced to live, plus being threatened by arrest and torture for being Jews and Zionists and for covertly attempting to flee, 12,000 left their villages, trekked for weeks until they reached Sudan, thousands dying of hunger, disease, and banditry en route. The AAEJ undertook a campaign in the press, assisted in the development of a movie, national TV exposure, organized the Senate and House of Representatives of the United States Government to pressure Israel and provide funds for a massive rescue effort. This push occurred simultaneously with the revelations of the drought and famine in Ethiopia that affected millions of people and was portrayed gruesomely on television each day. Following this, the Israeli and the American governments undertook a covert massive rescue, which resulted in saving another 8000 Jews.

By the end of 1985, there were 17,000 Ethiopian Jews in Israel. The American Jewish community raised upward of $60 million to integrate them into Israel's economy. Following this "Operation Moses," a number of groups sprang up around the United States that in one way or another helped in their further rescue and resettlement. In addition, major Jewish organizations supported special projects—medical, educational, and vocational—seeking support from American Jewish contributors.

With a population of 22,000 Ethiopian Jews in Israel in 1990, there is every possibility for their survival as a community. There are still problems with the chief rabbinic leaders, who insist on the Ethiopian Jews undergoing some rites that they assert are an effort to make them accept a form of conversion before marriage. Various schisms have sprung up amongst the Ethiopians to oppose such strictures as well as to demonstrate for the rescue of the remaining approximate 17,000 of their kinsmen still left in Ethiopia, whose lot is worsening.

The newly arrived immigrants in Israel have shown a capacity for rapid adjustment. Many are already thriving in the school programs, training for vocations, entering universities. They now receive constant press coverage. In 1984–1985, the United Jewish Appeal undertook a huge and successful campaign to aid in their integration within Israel. They have proven to be rapid learners, good workers, and able soldiers. It is predicted that despite all the difficulties they experienced in their native land and on the way to Israel that they will make good and permanent citizens in the State of Israel.

In the late 1980s articles appeared frequently in the American general and Jewish press about the condition of the Ethiopian Jews, as their lot grew more foreboding with the civil war and economic collapse in their native country. In 1990, most of the Jews left in Ethiopia were fleeing to Addis Ababba, the capital, seeking relief and awaiting papers, so that they might leave and be reunited with their families already in Israel. In 1991, Israel, the Jewish Agency, the JDC, and the AAEJ brought nearly all of the remaining Ethiopian Jews to Addis Ababba. They were all flown to Israel by the end of the year. In 1990, there were about 50 Ethiopian Jews in the United States and another 75 in Canada.

GRAENUM BERGER
JANET L. DOTTERER

BIBLIOGRAPHY

Ashkenazi, Michael, and Alex Weingrad. *Ethiopian Jewish Immigrants in Beersheba*. Highland Park, Ill.: American Association for Ethiopian Jews, 1984.

Baron, Salo W. *A Social and Religious History of the Jews*, Columbia Un. and JPS, Vol. 18, 1983. Pp. 363–389 and 585–600.

Berger, Graenum. *Graenum*. Hoboken, N.J.: Ktav, 1987.

———. "Why Doesn't Jewish World Save the Falasha?" *Jewish Post and Opinion* (Indianapolis), September 23 and 30, 1977.

Faitlovitch, Jacques. "The Falasha." *American Jewish Year Book*. Philadelphia: Jewish Publication Society, 1920, pp. 80–100.

Kessler, David. *The Falashas*. London: Allen & Unwin, 1982.

Leslau, Wolf. *Falasha Anthology*, New Haven: Yale University Press, 1951.

Messing, Simon D. *The Story of the Falashas*. Brooklyn, N.Y.: Balshon, 1982.

Quirin, James. *The Beta-Israel (Falasha) in Ethiopian History*. Ann Arbor: University of Michigan, 1977.

Rapoport, Louis. *The Lost Jews*. New York: Stein & Day, 1980.

———. *Redemption Song*. New York: Harcourt Brace Jovanovich, 1986.

Farming. *See* AGRICULTURE.

Feminist Movement. Jewish women have had a long and crucial involvement with American feminism. The connection between American Jewish women, Jewish organizations, and the feminist movement has taken several forms: participation of individual Jews in feminist organizations and with feminist causes, connections between Jewish women's groups and the feminist movement, support for feminist issues by the Jewish community. From at least the mid-1800s, with the involvement of Ernestine Rose in the abolition and suffrage movements, to the resurgence of the women's movement in the 1970s, Jewish women have been prominent in the feminist movement and have been active in all areas of women's concern, such as suffrage, labor organizing, legislative and social reform, politics, pacifism, reproductive rights, and artistic expression. Most American Jewish women worked on feminist issues in predominantly Gentile women's groups, although some maintained associations with Jewish organizations (both secular and religious) and some worked extensively with a Jewish constituency such as women garment workers.

Probably the first noted American Jewish feminist, Ernestine Rose (1810–1892) was a prominent suffragist and abolitionist. An ally of Elizabeth Cady Stanton and Susan B. Anthony for over 20 years, she was a founder of the National Woman Suffrage Association, and worked for social and legal rights for women. The daughter of a Polish rabbi, Rose was known for her brilliant oratory.

From the start of the twentieth century, many Jewish women were involved in activities related to women's issues. Although some were better known for activities not exclusively "feminist" (such as labor organizing and social welfare movements), these activities were part of their commitment to feminism and were usually conducted under the auspices of feminist organizations. Among these were Lillian Wald, Maud Nathan, Rose Schneiderman, Emma Goldman, and Rose Pastor Stokes, women whose activities encompassed the main concerns of feminists up to World War II.

Social reformer Lillian Wald (1867–1940) was a founder of the settlement house movement. Working from her New York City settlement, Henry Street House, she was active in suffrage, child welfare legislation, pacifism, and school reform. Maud Nathan (1862–1946), from a prominent New York family, was a founder of the National Consumers' League, which strove to better working conditions for women, support unionization, and educate the public about women's working conditions. She was one of the few leading Jewish feminists who remained religiously affiliated and active in Jewish organizations. With associations spanning both Jewish and Gentile groups, Nathan was active in both the suffrage movement and the National Council of Jewish Women.

Rose Schneiderman (1882–1972) dedicated her life to improving the lives of working women.

Starting as a garment worker, she became a national organizer for the International Ladies Garment Workers Union (1915–1916) and president of the Women's Trade Union League (1926–1950), an organization to aid in unionization of women and improved working conditions for them. Schneiderman was also active in suffrage, socialism, and the women's peace movement.

Emma Goldman (1869–1940), a prominent anarchist, writer, and organizer, was an advocate of sexual freedom for women, birth control, and women's unions. Like Schneiderman and Goldman, Rose Pastor Stokes (1879–1933) came from a poor immigrant family. Starting as a cigar maker, she became a writer, union activist, and socialist politician. Stokes worked for suffrage, women's unions, and birth control, and she became one of the founders of the American Communist Party.

Not only were individual Jewish women active feminists, several organizations of Jewish women supported feminist causes, working in active coalitions with other women's groups. For example, the National Council of Jewish Women, whose activities, like those of other Jewish women's community organizations, were mainly concerned with civic, cultural, and religious issues in the Jewish community, joined the Women's Joint Congressional Committee (WJCC), an umbrella group formed in 1920 to lobby for congressional legislation dealing with women's issues. Among the issues that WJCC worked for were child labor laws, vocational training, antilynching legislation, peace, and internationalism.

There was also extensive Jewish community support for women's issues, and Jewish women were eager to use feminist services and take advantage of feminist gains. Jews as a group were a major base of support for woman suffrage. Jewish women were leaders and community workers in the suffrage movement; Jewish male community leaders, such as Rabbi Stephen Wise, supported suffrage, and Jewish men voted for it in state referenda. On the local level, Jewish women, of all classes, were among the most dedicated, hardworking suffragists. Another indication of Jewish community support for women's concerns was the participation of Jewish women in the birth control movement and the eagerness of Jewish women to use the services of birth control clinics. In response to demand, one of the first birth control clinics in the United States was opened by Margaret Sanger in 1916 in a Jewish neighborhood of Brownsville, New York.

The involvement of Jewish women in organizing women workers and the large numbers of Jewish women who joined unions and struggled for better working conditions for women have been well documented. Jewish women were particularly influential in the garment trades and the textile industry, where tens of thousands of Jewish women participated in strikes, fighting for unions and improved working conditions. While some, such as Schneiderman and Bessie Abramowitz Hillman (1889–1970), rose to moderate levels of influence and position in the union structure, most found their leadership positions in affiliated women's organizations, such as the Women's Trade Union League or the National Consumers' League. These early Jewish women labor activists left their mark on the labor movement, in addition, through their introduction of innovative union-sponsored social programs, such as labor studies schools for women workers.

From the 1920s through the 1940s, Jewish feminists, along with other activists, turned to policy making. They held legislative and informational positions in government and national organizations in addition to participating in mass organizational work. For example, Rose Schneiderman was appointed by President Roosevelt to the Labor Advisory Board of the National Recovery Act (1933–1935) and was secretary of the New York State Department of Labor (1937–1943). Dorothy Jacobs Bellanca (1894–1940), organizer for the Amalgamated Clothing Workers of America, served on various national and state committees concerned with labor and child welfare. Anna Rosenberg (1902–1983) served as President Truman's assistant secretary of defense.

While most Jewish secular organizations and communities supported the basic programs and strategies of feminism, until the 1970s there was not a Jewish feminism as such. Until the revival of the feminist movement in the late 1960s the feminism of American Jewish women had been expressed in secular, rather than religious, terms, and the women usually worked on women's issues in organizations that were not contained within the Jewish community.

Jewish women's activities in feminist organizations have been hampered over the years by anti-Semitism and controversies concerning international politics and Israel. In the 1930s and 1940s disagreements over the creation of Israel made it difficult for Jewish women to participate in some international feminist organizations. For example, the International Alliance of Women, with headquarters in London and largely British leadership and with Jewish and Middle Eastern membership in leadership positions, experienced serious internal dissension in political disagreements over the establishment of Israel. Since the 1970s, policy disagreements over Israel and the Middle East have continued to surface, especially in international settings, such as the United Nations conferences on women.

Only since the 1970s have Jewish women sought to develop a distinctly Jewish feminism. Much of their work concentrates on modifying and rewriting Jewish ritual, religious practices and writings/theology to eliminate sexism, to reflect equality between the genders, and to introduce women's values and perspectives. They attempt to modify rituals of Jewish life, both secular and religious, to incorporate women and feminist ideals. Results include a variety of publications, from revised feminist Haggadahs to feminist magazines (*Lilith*) which was first published in 1976, and the formation of religiously oriented Jewish feminist organizations. Feminists have extended their demands to reforms of organized religious practices, such as more equality in religious services (e.g., seating, what constitutes a "quorum") and more participation in formal religious organizations with women being accepted as representatives of the faith. There has been an increase of women in religious study, religious training, public participation in religious rituals, and practicing as rabbis. By 1972, Hebrew Union College, the seminary of the Reform Movement, had ordained the first woman rabbi, Sally Priesand. In 1974 the Reconstructionist Movement ordained its first woman rabbi, and the Conservative Movement did so in 1985.

Also women have been demanding a greater presence and power, as women, in traditional Jewish organizations. For example, although progress has been slow, women have worked for greater access to leadership positions in the Council of Jewish Federations and its member organizations. By the end of the 1980s, more than 150 women were presidents of Reform and Conservative congregations. However, within B'nai B'rith a rift evolved in the 1980s as to the equal status of women in the parent B'nai B'rith International organization. In 1990, women were formally admitted as full members of the International.

In this period, as in the past, a remarkable number of feminist theorists and leaders in mainstream feminist organizations have been Jewish women. Two of the most recognized are Betty Friedan (b. 1921), author of *The Feminine Mystique* (1963), the book often cited as being the forerunner of the feminist revival, and Gloria Steinem (b. 1934), cofounder of *Ms.* magazine. In politics, Bella Abzug (b. 1920) was nationally identified with feminist organizations and programs.

Since the 1960s, Jewish feminism has become important in academic, cultural, and political arenas. Feminists were very active in the civil rights movement. Jewish women teachers and researchers have been creating courses on Jewish women, Jewish feminism, and Jewish theology. The 1970s and 1980s saw a large output in writings, including scholarship, reflective essays, and fiction by Jewish feminists, dealing with a wide range of topics from rewriting and reinterpreting the Halakah to exploring family relationships. Among the many essayists, poets, and fiction writers where feminist concerns appear clearly in their work are Irena Klepfisz, Grace Paley, and Adrienne Rich. Jewish feminist scholars have been publishing large numbers of studies on the social, economic, and political history of American Jewish women, as well as theoretical/philosophical works on religion. This creative work by scholars and artists has served to develop a whole new, large body of work and theory and has created the intellectual and academic subdiscipline of Jewish women's studies. *See also* Women.

ELINOR LERNER

BIBLIOGRAPHY

Baum, Charlotte; Hyman, Paula; and Michel, Sonya. *The Jewish Woman in America.* New York: Dial Press, 1976.

Heschel, Susannah, ed. *On Being a Jewish Feminist.* New York: Schocken, 1983.

Koltun, Elizabeth, ed. *The Jewish Woman: New Perspectives.* New York: Schocken, 1976.

Marcus, Jacob. *The American Jewish Woman: A Documentary History.* Hoboken, N.J.: Ktav, 1981.

Mazow, Julia, ed. *The Woman Who Lost Her Names: Selected Writings by American Jewish Women.* New York: Harper Religious Books, 1980.

Fiction. In the early modern era there began to develop in Eastern European Judaism a tension between *chesed* (piety) and the Haskalah (the Enlightenment). *Chesed*, one of the 613 commandments, is something like loving-kindness or what Christians call grace. In early Yiddish literature, in the works of Mendele, Peretz, and Sholom

Aleichem, there is an attempt to deal with or circumvent the tension. The aggudic content (tales, folklore, acts, etc.) of Jewish writing became central as these writers tried to open the eyes of their readers to their condition and to the outside world. What they did was to turn away from the Halakhah (hard core code of Jewish law) as they turned toward the ethical, as they emphasized the story, as they evoked socioeconomic and moral lessons.

Strangely, it was a Jewish manqué, Baruch Spinoza, who best exemplified this tension, when he argued that laws, or mitzvoth, were a bogus notion; he was saying that God was not a law-giver but a "Deus sive Natura," a God of Nature. The laws have to do with nature, he argued, not the arbitrary, man-defined mitzvoth. To be enlightened, then, was to realize that the nature of God is incompatible with commandment or piety. Law equaled the laws of nature, not the rabbinic tradition, or the talmudic tradition.

From Mendele into the present, from I. B. Singer's *The Slave* and *The Family Moskat* through Chaim Grade's *The Yeshiva*, from Abraham Cahan and Henry Roth to Saul Bellow, Bernard Malamud, and Philip Roth and to Cynthia Ozick and Chaim Potok, whether raised in an Orthodox or Reform or secular environment, it is the divided person who predominates as protagonist. The axis around which almost all turn is the *musar* (the ethical) rather than the ritual or traditional. Even Martin Buber, the leading scholar on Hasidism, in a letter to Franz Rosenzweig, wrote: "It is beneath the dignity of God to be a lawgiver," to have a covenantal relationship on the basis of mitzvoth. As you can see, what developed was an equation of polar opposites: piety, on the one side, related to tradition and Orthodoxy; on the other, the *mitnagdim* (the resisters), the enlightened ones, those who believe that the ethical core in a developing Jewish civilization was most important.

For some writers in the twentieth century, the locus of the conflict was in the erotic excesses, the frenzy of the characters. The significance of eros in the twentieth century, whether you use Freudian theory or not, is apparent. Eros is the point at which the conflict is embodied; it is the mental-spiritual embodiment of the conflict. In turn, the Hebraic and American versions are called marriage, adultery, and seduction; making decisions whether to marry and to whom, whether to commit adultery or seduce are part of the conflict. Relatedly, whether to honor the tra-

ditions of the past or to adapt to the present are also part of the conflict. In short, it is in the context of the pressures to be American, to acculturate, even assimilate, that Jews by and large live. It is in this frame of reference that American Jewish literature reflects the experiences and the tensions that develop between the atavistic pull of the past—of tradition, ritual, mitzvoth—and the seemingly stronger pull of the present and future—of getting ahead, adaptation, compromise—mixed with the wish to be ethical and be loved, all in the modern context of alienation, disorder, and chaos.

The first Jews who came to America in 1654 were descendants of those who had been expelled from Spain and Portugal in the 1490s. At the time of the American Revolution, these Sephardic Jews, who numbered less than 2500, had made extraordinary contributions to their new homeland. By the eve of the Civil War they had gained a large measure of economic rights, and political and religious acculturation followed. In turn, acculturation led to widespread intermarriage and conversion, on the one hand, and the establishment of Reform Judaism, on the other. As Rabbi Gustavus Poznanski, Charleston's German-educated leader of the Sephardic congregation, put it, "America is our Zion, and Washington is our Jerusalem."

Beginning in the 1830s, thousands of German Jews arrived in the United States. There were now about 50,000 Jews in America, mostly on the East Coast. Since they came from a country where the Enlightenment had spread its doctrine of rationalism, these Jews embraced and extended Reform Judaism. With the organization of the Central Conference of American Rabbis in 1889, however, the religious issue was joined. The Russo-Polish Jews, who began arriving in the 1880s, came from the Orthodox tradition, and though they subsequently diluted their religion, they were not yet ready to abandon it. Another issue soon emerged. The German Jews, many of whom began as itinerant peddlers, succeeded magnificently in everything material. Unfortunately, though much biography, history, and sociology attests to the German and Sephardic Jews' accession to wealth, little more than the plays of Manuel Noah (e.g., *The Fortress of Sorrento*, 1808) and poetry of Penina Moise (e.g., *Fancy's Sketchbook*, 1833), Adah Isaacs Menken, and Emma Lazarus (a Sephardic Jew) reflects their spiritual-creative life. Commenting on what had happened to her people, Lazarus regretted that "the light of the perpetual lamp is spent/That an undying radiance was to shed." With the news of the assassination of Czar Alexander II in 1881 and the subsequent massacres of Jews in Russia, she extended her heart to the "huddled masses yearning to breathe free." Between 1881 and 1914, more than 2 million Jews from Russia-Poland arrived in America. It was the "promised land" to Mary Antin (*The Promised Land*, 1912), fresh from Polotzk. It was also the land of opportunity where Abraham Cahan's David Levinsky was told, "It isn't Russia. . . . Judaism has not much of a chance here. . . . A man must make a living here," (*The Rise of David Levinsky*, 1917).

Coming from Russia-Poland, most from shtetls, the Jews of the New Immigration and their descendants have dominated American Jewish life numerically, economically, and culturally almost since they arrived. But they have lived with a paradox: At the same time that they wanted more than anything else to be American, they wanted to remain Jews. Like one of America's foremost scholars, W. E. B. DuBois, who experienced the "double vision" and "Two-ness" of being both American and black, they were troubled by the efforts to integrate themselves into the society while retaining and passing on an ethnic identity: as Jews, as American Jews, and—since World War II—increasingly as Americans who are Jews. The attempts to define what it meant to be a Jew in the Old Country, what it meant to be a Jew here, and how a Jew was acculturated (and perhaps assimilated in an ever-changing culture) while still holding to an ethnic identity, are grist for the writers who have described the unique experience of being Jewish. That set of experiences, these problems, this people, are the source and reason for the American Jewish writers and their works.

The new immigrants, numbering perhaps 500,000 by 1900 and close to 3 million in 1914, came to the New World with little or no money and few skills. Arriving too late to duplicate or even carry on the experience of the German Jews, they were received with hostility by most Christians and viewed with contempt by the German Jews. Speaking a despised language, Yiddish, they were called coarse peasants and were seen as a threat to the comfortable assimilation and economic stability of their predecessors. The threat proved to be real; as we know from historians Moses Rischin and Ronald Sanders and from Abraham Cahan's classic, *The Rise of David Levinsky* (1917), the Russian Jews succeeded the

German Jews as entrepreneurs, owners, and workers in the clothing industry in New York City. As Russian Jews became more visible, anti-Semitism surfaced and grew. Fortunately, the plans to cut off immigration did not become effective until well after World War I. By that time, 3.5 million Jews had landed. Ironically, though it is often forgotten, Catholic immigrants from Russia, Poland, Italy, and Greece were far more numerous and visible.

Most Jews who arrived here between 1881 and 1914 were nominally Orthodox. Those willing to venture to the New World were those least committed to the practice of their religion. Beaten down by several hundred years of persecution and ghettoization, the Jews of Eastern Europe came alive only in the eighteenth century under the twin spurs of Hasidism and the Jewish Enlightenment. Hasidism taught them to find God everywhere and in everything; to pray with joy and enthusiasm was more important than rote, ritual, and exegesis. These latter elements, along with a new emphasis on scholarship, would come later. From the Enlightenment, Jews learned how to enter European civilization; literature from outside the Jewish community (like Dostoyevsky, Tolstoy, and Marx), science, and the impact of urbanism combined to dissolve the medieval isolation of the ghettos. As a synthesis developed, it became clear that the ideas of the Enlightenment had been diluted even as they penetrated the ghetto, while the orthodoxy of extreme piety and ritual crumbled even as the essence of the Jewish heritage held on. That there would be two Zions in their lifetime, one in the United States and the other in Israel, was not foreseen. That Yiddish culture, Eastern European culture, would endure, though the Yiddish language would diminish, was also not seen. Driven by pogroms at home and lured by the American Dream, they chanced the journey to what was literally a New World.

For most Jews in America the question of observing the Sabbath and the dietary laws was often related to their feelings about becoming American and climbing out of the ghetto. Those who insisted on adhering to Orthodox practice were in the minority. Those who erected a facade or who chose to pursue American ways and a new identity were in the majority. It was a shock, for instance, to discover that success meant learning the way things were done, doing them better than anyone else, and becoming (and even looking) American as soon as possible. Shaving off beards and sideburns (*payess*) and married women not wearing wigs (*shaytls*) were serious religious matters. The wearing of American clothes paled by comparison. Looking to material values was even more traumatic, even for freethinkers. In the Old Country, one achieved prestige (*yiches*) by learning and Torah study, and one's duty on Friday night and Saturday was simply to welcome the Sabbath. In America, as Cahan's David Levinsky and Samuel Ornitz's Meyer Hirsch (*Haunch, Paunch, and Jowl*, 1923) learned, one achieved prestige and social acceptance at greater cost. That many Jews worked for themselves or for other Jews so as not to be forced to work on the Sabbath is a fact; that many decided to be Jews outside their homes, regardless of the cost (though they could not see the future cost), is also a fact. Their children and their children's children have departed even further from the old ways. In a society dominated by acquisitiveness and technology, people chose whatever roots and pillars were available, hoping to temper the mix with humanism whenever possible.

By the 1920s, America's Jews, now American Jews, with one foot in the Old country and one in the New, were struggling with problems no longer tied to the ghetto. As Jews, their adherence to traditional values and ethics was honored. As American Jews, shown in Samuel Ornitz's anonymously published novel *Haunch, Paunch and Jowl* (1923), the compulsion to succeed and to wield power, no matter how corruptly, surfaced for the first time. Though it was an isolated case, surrounded by pathos and humor, it went beyond David Levinsky's acceptable entrepreneurship in its earthiness—so much in the Yiddish tradition—and grotesqueness. Myron Brinig's Singermann family saw some of the same forces and emotions. In a country in which an allegedly "lost generation" flourished, emulation was common. As the drama of the generations was played out, Jews as Jews and as American Jews rebelled against their parents, struggled for their own identities, succeeded and failed, cried and laughed, as did others. Jews were in the forefront in creative areas. The success of George and Ira Gershwin, Irving Berlin, Eddie Cantor, and Al Jolson in the world of entertainment matched the success of Albert Einstein, Marc Chagall, and Ben Shahn and many others in science and in the creative arts.

In the 1930s, in the grip of the Great Depression, Jews moved into prominence in movies, in the theater, and in literature. Luther and Stella Adler, John Garfield, and the playwright Clifford Odets made their marks in legitimate theater; Paul Muni, Edward G. Robinson, Irving Thalberg, and many producers in Hollywood enriched the screen. In literature, whether through proletarian novels or novels with social impact, writers fought the system that bound and fought their families as well. Nathanael West, Tillie Lerner, Albert Halper, Daniel Fuchs, Michael Gold, Henry Roth, Nelson Algren, Meyer Levin, and Edward Dahlberg were some of those in whose works social and economic and generational and religious problems appeared. Writing about intellectuals and workers, hoboes and farmers, they concentrated on the attempts of people to identify with the poor and the oppressed. Some glorified the new energy of the Soviet Union or the Communist Party at home, as alternatives to what appeared a sick society. Michael Gold's *Jews Without Money* (1934), a novel from an ideologue, surprisingly kept to its last pages a plea for Communist brotherhood. Most, characteristically, reflected the external pressures of a depression-ridden society in which Jews struggled to be Americanized and survive. Many also joined in the decade's widely supported protests, spearheaded by President Roosevelt's New Deal for some and the Communists' program for others. Exchanging religious attachments for secularism, they sought new answers, perhaps new messiahs, in the social order. As Mike Gold wrote, "We had no Santa Claus, but we had a Messiah." No wonder he promised his mother, ideologically, "I must remain faithful to the poor because I cannot be faithless to you."

Caught up in the conflict of generations, young Jewish writers sometimes moved beyond acculturation. Nathanael West, escaping from Nathan Weinstein, was refused admission to a gentile fraternity at Brown University and expanded his rebellion; turning his anger inward, he attacked Jews in his novels. Ben Hecht, on the first page of *A Jew in Love* (1931), described "Jew faces in which race leers and burns like some biologic disease." Within a few years, however, he had become an ardent Zionist—spurred by Hitler's horrors, the inability of the West to act, and the efforts of Jews to escape to Palestine and elsewhere, Hecht strongly criticized those (including Rabbi Stephen Wise) who did not act as quickly as he. As other examples of questionable taste or Jewish anti-Semitism, Ornitz, Halper, and Dahlberg were named. Even Ludwig Lewisohn was criticized by fellow Jews, though he early became a Zionist and a Judeophile. That their motives were good, they argued, ranging from a belief in assimilation to a belief in class over religion, meant little. To a people recently arrived from Eastern European persecution, sensitive to overt anti-Semitism in America, excuses or rationales were hard to accept.

It was almost unique that Henry Roth's *Call it Sleep* (1934) shifted focus in so many ways. Unlike any other novel of the era, this superb psychological work, seen through the eyes of a child, summed up the truths and the traumas of the immigrants' experience. Confronted by a father who was maddened by ghosts of the past and present poverty and despair, little David Schearl's existence balanced precariously between the traditional values of his mother and the heder (religious school) and those of the outside world. The most Freudian of the interwar novels, involved with Oedipal conflict, God, and phallic imagery, it is, said Leslie Fiedler, "the best single book by a Jew about Jewishness written by an American, certainly through the thirties and perhaps ever." Whether *Call it Sleep* is a proletarian novel, which is doubtful, is unimportant. What comes across is the inner psychic pain of the second generation and its social and familial revolts. In Ludwig Lewisohn's view, the literary reflections of the historical and generational circumstances were part of an ongoing dialectical process that would eventuate in a return to Judaism, characteristically liberal not only in the religious field but in politics and love and sex as well. Although Lewisohn was a prophet for the thirties through the fifties, it appears that the continuing process has wreaked havoc with his words in the post World War II era.

Even before 1930, American Jewish novelists used the themes of sex and love. They are persistent needs in the works of Bruno Lessing, Anzia Yezierska, and James Oppenheim. Cahan's David Levinsky, a kind of Jewish Horatio Alger, continually tried to find love. That he ended with loneliness, a millionaire, only highlighted the paradox: His success was a measure of his estrangement from the community of old. "There are cases when success is a tragedy," David knew. He never forgot the Jewish greenhorn who arrived here penniless and without friends. He never forgot what might have been if he had gone to the City College of New York. Similarly, the Jew as Don Juan conflicted with the traditions of the Old Country, as Ludwig Lewisohn, Myron Brinig, and Meyer Levin found out. The hold of ghetto mores, the fear of what "they" would say, were

barriers. Until the 1960s, American Jewish writers did not easily use these themes. In any case, the image of the Jew was more meaningful than it had been. An inarticulate sense of inherited identity, later to be articulated, reflected a growing interest. Secular and cultural Judaism generational problems, intermarriage, all vied with traditional forms. Apparently there were millions of Americans who wondered about the God of their fathers, the American Dream, man's manipulation of man, and the necessary persistence of the natural and compulsory Jewish communities of earlier days.

American Jewish writers have had to fashion their product out of the life they knew, and they worked usually in an uncaring or hostile framework. For too long, as in the case of black literature, stereotypes persisted, drawn mainly by the host culture but aided and abetted by the minority. Even as Sambo and Amos and Andy perpetuated the black stereotype, so Potash and Perlmutter, Cohen on the telephone, the Goldbergs, Mickey Katz, and chocolate matzos continued the travesty of Jews by Jews. Overcoming these images was one aspect of the writers' problem. Learning the language and the symbols was another. Most important, the writers had to deal with a Jewish image brought into existence by gentiles and Jews and then create what had never existed before—an American Jewish literature.

America's major writers from the early nineteenth century on have been preoccupied with man's condition and his attempts to find meaning in it. Observing the tendency to overintellectualize and pervert the humanistic spirit of the Founding Fathers, Hawthorne, Melville, Whitman, and Twain stressed the importance of following the dictates of the heart, of the spiritual as against the material values of society. They were conscious of the disparity between what Americans said they believed in and what they did. Sensitive to this gap, to the fraudulent, self-righteous, commercial aspects of American culture that overshadowed the ethical-human, they used their insights to hold mirrors up to us all.

In the twentieth century, this socioliterary examination and analysis continued in the works of Dreiser, James, Hemingway, Dos Passos, Faulkner, Fitzgerald, and Wolfe, to name a few. In this tradition, the American Jewish writers came of age. They are American writers, of course, but they are also American Jewish writers because they were born Jewish, and, regardless of the intensity of their religious or cultural commitment, they have written about some essential aspect of the Jewish experience in America. Unlike the Lost Generation writers—Gentiles who seldom wrote about urban or ethnic conditions—the Jewish writers had to wait until they had become American Jews and the Jewish community was defined enough to support their work. In the cultural vacuum that existed in the early 1940s, American Jewish writers responded as no other group to the country's urgent cultural need. The biblical past, the rise of Hitler, the Holocaust, the new State of Israel, and the need of Americans to again believe in humanity helped. As Saul Bellow put it, affirming his belief in the humanity of the patriarch Abraham, he knew his debt (*Mr. Sammler's Planet*, 1970)—it had to do with the presence and continuation of life.

For the American Jewish writers, from the cities, towns, and shtetls of Russia-Poland, arriving at a time of national reform and psychic crisis, of primary importance were the problems of adjustment to the new culture and reconciliation of their Old Country culture with that of the New World. Scrambling for a dollar, everyone working, they endured so that their children might become Americans. "Who has ever seen such optimism?" asked Harry Golden. For the American Jewish writer, under the pressures of the Americanizing process, new problems were added. With disdain for his parents' ways, dress, and accent, he often opted for the New at the expense of the Old. Traditions, values, religion—all were subordinated to the need to emulate the American or the Jews who were no longer greenhorns. The joys and the tragedies of the generational experience were not unique, of course, but the works of those writers, from Cahan on in the first generation and from Ornitz through Henry Roth in the next, show that the context, the insights, and the style of the generational experience are novel, a breakthrough. For the first time, Jews who bridged the two cultures in a host country wrote of the ongoing bridging experience. Their literary talents explored the sociological dimensions of a minority. And as the up-from-the-ghetto literature gave way to fiction as a living form, as Jewish self-consciousness benefited from the national and international processes, so the American Jewish writer wrote of himself, his people, anti-Semitism, the war, middlebrow America, and the attempt to understand himself and the society he inhabited. That some of the works fall short of excellence may be true; that they are therefore irrelevant to the main lines of development of American fiction is absurd. The fact of their quest for identity, the effort to create a literature in a non-WASP context, the excellent and near excellent quality of the work seem significant because they created a new genre in literature and demonstrated that the American Jew was beginning to feel at home. Because of the writing of the Jewish Thirties, fertile, talented minds, conversant with the subject, created the images of the American Jew; the gross, distorted portraits of the past, as a result, have been dissolved in the subtler and more artful, and thus truer, images of the American Jewish moderns.

When Abraham Cahan's *The Rise of David Levinsky* appeared, it was seen by some, incorrectly, as an anti-Semitic book. "Had the book been published anonymously," observed one critic, "we might have taken it for cruel caricature of a hated race by some anti-Semite." In the succeeding decades, anti-Semitism has been denounced readily, whenever it appeared—if at times questionably. Recently most of the animus in American Jewish literature has been directed at Philip Roth, though novels like Budd Schulberg's *What Makes Sammy Run?* (1941) and Herman Wouk's *Marjorie Morningstar* (1955) have come in for their share of denunciation.

The question of what constitutes anti-Semitism (or more correctly anti-Judaism) is a ticklish one. When Roth's *Goodbye, Columbus* (1959) was published, with "The Conversion of the Jews," "Defender of the Faith," and "Epstein" included, the issue was again raised. *Portnoy's Complaint* (1969) and *The Breast* (1972) have exacerbated the problem. To the charges that he was an anti-Semite and a pornographer, Roth answered that he was a writer who was a Jew. "How are you connected to me as another man is not?" is one of the questions he started with. The question really, he believed, was who was going to address men and women like men and women—and who would address them like children. Castigating the oratory of self-congratulation and self-pity too often heard from the pulpits, he argued that many Jews found the stories the novelists told more provocative and pertinent than the sermons of the rabbis. Maybe so, but as Irving Howe says, Roth, since *Portnoy's Complaint*, has not really been involved in the Jewish tradition. He is "one of the first American Jewish writers who finds that it yields him no sustenance, no norms or values, from which to launch his attacks on middle-class complaisance." And yet he continues introspectively.

When a Gentile commits an anti-Judaic act, the deed is usually clear and can be recognized and dealt with. Organizations like B'nai B'rith's Anti-Defamation League, backed by law, stand ready to discuss, persuade, or act. When a Jew is accused, the facts are harder to come by. The forces can be exceedingly subtle, pro and con. For example, when a Jew describes another Jew in gross terms and the description does not proceed out of love or honest concern, there is little room for argument. To describe a Jew as a lecher or a parvenu or a corrupt businessman in the 1960s or 1970s, even if he is good to his mother, is another thing. Thus, Philip Roth says that in his "Epstein" he was interested in the condition of a man who was a lecher and who was Jewish, in that order. It is understandable that the older generation, still so close to the pogroms in Russia-Poland, the Holocaust, and overt anti-Semitism, both in Europe and the United States, would be hostile to a writer washing dirty linen in public. But since World War II, in the United States, the situation has changed; public opinion and law are antagonistic—officially—to anti-Judaism, and the tendency to cut the ties that bind, to forgive and forget, is strong. Many of America's Jews have succeeded materially. Their children, fortunate to have middle-class parents, are Americans who are Jewish. Their dress, their likes and dislikes, their speech, their music, their foods, are urban- and exurban-oriented, with no memories of Europe's death camps and little active acquaintance with anti-Judaism at home.

A generation brought up on the Jewish experiences of Allen Ginsberg, Abbie Hoffman, Bob Dylan, and Don Rickles is not likely to look to Dachau or the heder for its reference points. Yet, uncertain as they are of their precise Jewish identity, for many there is no struggle with being identified as Jewish. Influenced by the Kennedys, Martin Luther King, the Vietnamese War, rock 'n' roll, and the Youth Cult, they are also possessed by the desire to understand the human condition, themselves, and the country they live in. Rejecting that part of America where the bland lead the bland, they seek roots and truth. In the same way, the contemporary American Jewish writers were influenced by the same forces, as well as those of the Depression, the Spanish Civil War, Hitler and World War II, Franklin D. Roosevelt, the Korean War, and McCarthyism. In their common quest, compelled by an indefinable feel of one's heritage, it is the writers who have asked the questions about other Jews—because that is whom they know, and love, and hate and because they care deeply and want to find out what it means to be a Jew or an American Jew or an American who is a Jew.

Jews in the United States have responded in many ways to the pressures of the New World. Some from the beginning and into the present desired to be and were quickly or eventually assimilated. Some attempted to find a middle way by which they could become Americans and still retain their sense of being Jews. Some were so alienated or estranged as to drop out and pass into the great other—the Gentile world. Still others were doubly alienated, no longer at home either in the Jewish or non-Jewish context. And some did not care one way or the other. Arthur Koestler, for example, after World War II, bade goodbye to Judaism, opting for total assimilation. Meyer Levin, accepting biculturalism, wrote, "Godless though I profess myself, I have responded with more than warmth to the mystical elements of Hasidism. As a writer, I have considered that I accept the material as folklore. But in my soul I know that I take more than this from these legends." Albert Halper spoke of Yiddish as a "bastardized language," while Edward Dahlberg, a Jew who was in a Catholic, and then a Jewish, orphan asylum, sought a faith he could not find. And Ben Hecht vacillated from self-hating and nearly anti-Semitic prose to some essays and stories in the 1940s calling on Jews to defend Jewish rights. For Saul Bellow, who has had no struggle in identifying himself as Jewish, there has been unconcern for the definition of what that means. As for Herbert Gold, who has traveled far, he has returned to his Jewishness, as he describes his pilgrimage in *My Last Two Thousand Years* (1972).

These opinions and these insights have been used by American Jewish writers since World War II. Though some critics would call the authors collectors of pathological characters, anti-Semitic, or simply nonwriters because their concerns are not in accord with a set of predefined goals, it is clear that they are writers first, who are Jews. Some will ask that a writer be held to a specific commitment (individually defined) to a specific religious framework in which the writing goes on. In the writer's view, the duty of a writer is clear: a story that is on the right side of God but is not well written will neither make an impression nor live. Similarly, a tale that is sexy, if it is not honest and well crafted, will not persist. Searching for truth takes many forms. One form it will take only perilously will be that of the didactic story or essay; however, the search must take the form that the characters and their situations determine. If Jews in America are religious or not, or are rooted in the values of the past or not, so be it. If they are engaged in a generational conflict, so be it. And if they are Americans who are Jews, who are trying to find their way in a world that has meaning and structure somewhat different from that of the past, or that seems to lack meaning, or that needs new interpretations of the past—as is the way of the Talmud—so be it. The writer's province is insight and honesty, not religious or political activism, and the degree to which he succeeds as a writer, as an American Jewish writer, is the most important criterion.

Since the early 1940s, millions of Americans have read the works of Bellow, Mailer, Salinger, Malamud, Miller, Friedman, Roth, Wouk, Heller, Ozick, Rosen, Schwartz, Trilling, Potok, Singer, and Wiesel. Because I. B. Singer usually writes in Yiddish and Elie Wiesel in French, and their concerns are for Jews outside of America, they can not be considered as American Jewish writers. Similarly, though Mailer, Salinger, Trilling, and Heller are Jewish, because they deal only peripherally with Jews they will not be considered American Jewish writers, though one could contend that they write as they do because they are Jewish. Bellow, Malamud, Roth, and the others, however, are American Jewish writers because their novels and stories, whose literary and cultural reference points are Jewish, reflect their essential concerns. In spite of their individual differences, they usually deal with Jews in the American experience.

From World War I through World War II, American literature was dominated by such concepts as alienation and the wasteland. In spite of the fact that estrangement produced some masterpieces, its time passed. When the older generation passed on, there seemed to be few replacements. At this point in time, in Bellow's opinion, the writer had to exercise his own intelligence, to think, and not merely of his own narrow interests and needs. For Bellow, who had no fight about being a Jew—"I simply must deal with the facts of my life, a basic set of primitive facts," he said in 1964—the Jewish people's experience was a universal metaphor. Inasmuch as the modern writer specializes in what are called grotesque facts, and cannot compete with the news itself, as both Bellow and Roth pointed out, he or she must go beyond reality. The writer must turn away from

current events, but without losing focus. For what seems lacking, concluded Bellow, was a firm sense of the common world, a coherent community, a genuine purpose in life. Man had to strive for a life of significant pattern.

With the same goals in mind, Malamud sought moral salvation and self-realization. Whether he is writing about Morris Bober and his assistant, or Fidelman, or a Levin who would like to be a "freeman" in a world that is not easy for Jews, the theme of meaningful suffering is present. Bober (*The Assistant*), for example, knew painfully that he had been a failure in the eyes of the world. But, as became clear in the end, he was a good man in the biblical sense of the word. As one of the Hasidic rabbis said, "I would rather be devout than clever, but rather than both devout and clever, I should like to be good." Achieving the essential Jew, therefore, by his own actions is what was sought. But that goal, shared by Philip Roth, is at least distantly related to what Bellow refers to as consummation of a heart's need.

That there are similarities in the works of some American Jewish writers can be demonstrated. The differences are more striking. Roth, for instance, has written most often about extreme behavior in ordinary situations. From the beginning, he was concerned with men and women whose moorings had been cut, who had been swept away from their native shores and out to sea, sometimes on a tide of their own righteousness or resentment. Take "The Conversion of the Jews," a story of a little Jewish boy who could no longer stomach his rabbi's evasions and rote answers, a child who could no longer act like a little rabbi. Take Alexander Portnoy, a productive member of society on the job, whose problems, rightly or wrongly understood, lead him to live beyond his psychological and moral means. In short, we learn from Roth, the fantastic situation must be accepted as reality at the same time as the reality of the fantastic and horrible. Or, to go back to an earlier explanation, the world of fiction, wrote Roth, "frees us of circumscriptions that society places upon feeling . . . and allows both writer and reader to respond to experience in ways not always available in day-to-day conduct."

Through writing and reading, people pass on their collective experience. From Yiddish literature the Old Country can be remembered; even some of that whole wonderful body of literature, in English translation, can bring back the hard, dirty, primitive life of the shtetls. It will also bring back the warmth and earthiness of life in a Jewish family in a Jewish community in a world that no longer exists. So it is with the sensitively written recollections of Harry Golden and Alfred Kazin and the creative memories of the American Jewish writers from Abraham Cahan into the present. Thus, Bellow, as he recreates the joys and sadnesses of growing up in Montreal and Chicago, or describes an Augie March or a Herzog, also demonstrates an ambivalent faith in man's ability to realize himself in an ambiguous world. The resonance of "two-ness" is always present. For Malamud, redemptive suffering is what comes through, from a New York city past; for Roth, who grew up outside of Elizabeth, New Jersey, insanity or estrangement are not what he sees as the good life, yet an examination of what appears insane in a framework of normality is compelling. For others, the flight from impotence into machismo, in Bruce Jay Friedman, and the significance of the existential, in Edward Lewis Wallant, are important. And no wonder. If one recalls the shtetl (in spite of the romanticized "Fiddler on the Roof") or the Holocaust, as in Wallant's *The Pawnbroker* (1961), then pain is an everyday experience that coexists with love and comfort. What Jew over 40 years of age can ever forget the death camps in Germany and Poland? How many can forget how their grandparents hid in the forests from the Cossacks or townspeople or fled Russia to avoid the draft, persecution, humiliation, and often forced conversion? But, the question must be asked, what has all this to do with the 1970s? The 1980s? The 1990s?

To young Americans who are Jews, the memories and suffering of the past are subordinated to the middle-class comforts and security of post-World War II America, as they should be. Like Descartes, they ask: "I am certain that I am, but what am I?" The case of Franz Kafka, an acculturated Jew, might be a help. Conscious of being an outsider, he somehow felt his way into Jewishness. "The Metamorphosis" was "no dream," he wrote. What was at stake, according to young Jewish Americans, was that many struggles were going on, the outcomes of which were dreadfully important to them. They had to find a way to bring peace to the contending forces; to find some harmonic middle way between the material-hedonistic and the ethical-moral was necessary. No longer capable of determining their destinies, though taught individualism as a supreme virtue, they alternately pursued the chimera of achievement and escape from the frustration of despair. It was clear to them that the love of suffering, of what they saw as the dead past, was a waste of time. It was not clear that playing the doomsday theme, or playing at crises, alienation, apocalypse, and desperation, with tools like mind expanders and religious cults, were also suffering. They did not see that individualism cut two ways. A triumph, on the one hand, for justice and self-realization, it was also a bearer of possible trouble with its dream of unlimited leisure and liberty. Why can't I do anything I want? they asked. Why can't I have everything I want? The answer is not in the power of money to buy. The answer is in the nature of being Jewish, in the time-honored, ages-long meaning. Perhaps as Bellow's Dr. Sammler put it, the best is "to have some order within oneself. Better than what many call love. Perhaps it *is* love." That is, to be a Jew because of anti-Semitism is not enough. Similarly, to be a Jew because of the bravery of the State of Israel cannot be convincing. And to be a Jew because your parents say so is also a transparent excuse. But the experience *of being Jewish*, of living the warmness of community, with or without ritual, of having roots, as in Henry Roth, Bellow, Malamud, Ozick, Gold, and Potok, of being a part of an organic, progressive community that has existed proudly and contributed mightily for thousands of years—this might be enough. *See also* Jewish Children's Literature; Literature, Yiddish; Poetry; Poetry, Yiddish.

DANIEL WALDEN

BIBLIOGRAPHY

Eisenberg, Azriel, ed. *The Golden Land*. New York: Yoseloff, 1965.

Gittleman, Sol. *From Shtetl to Suburbia*. Boston: Beacon Press, 1978.

Guttmann, Allen. *The Jewish Writer in America*. New York: Oxford University Press, 1971.

Liptzin, Sol. *The Jew in American Literature*. New York: Bloch, 1966.

Malin, Irving, ed. *Breakthrough: A Treasury of Contemporary American Jewish Literature*. New York: McGraw Hill, 1964.

Shechner, Mark. *After the Revolution*. Bloomington: University of Indiana Press, 1987.

Walden, Daniel, ed. *Twentieth Century American Jewish Fiction Writers*. Detroit, Mich.: Gale, 1984.

Fiedler, Leslie (b. 1917). Prolific writer and talker—as he describes himself in "Who Was Leslie Fiedler?" (*What Was Literature: Class Culture and Mass Society* [1982])—Leslie Fiedler, in extended works and in aperçus, has written irreverently, wittily, and learnedly fiction, poetry, and criticism as well as compiled anthologies. Because of its range, Fiedler's work eludes classifications. He treated, idiosyncratically, the American myth in *Love and Death in the American Novel* (1960), *Waiting for the End* (1964), and *The Return of the Vanishing American* (1968). He has explored the Jew's place as artist, symbol, and stereotype in *To the Gentiles* (1973). Other works of literary and cultural criticism include *Freaks: Myths and Images of the Secret Self* (1978) and *The Stranger in Shakespeare* (1972) and collections of essays such as *An End to Innocence* (1955) and *Cross the Border, Close the Gap* (1977). He has published novels, among them *Back to China* (1965) and *The Last Jew in America* (1966), as well as a science fiction novel, *The Messengers Will Come No More* (1974).

Fiedler was born in Newark, New Jersey. He received a B.A. from New York University and an M.A. and Ph.D. from the University of Wisconsin. He also studied at the Japanese Language School (University of Colorado) and served as a Japanese interpreter with the United States Navy from 1944 through 1945. Currently Distinguished Professor at the State University of New York at Buffalo, he was for many years the Samuel L. Clemens Professor there.

Visceral, argumentative, iconoclastic, Fiedler has battled the professionalizing of literary criticism, the canonization of "high" culture, and the sterility of university literacy. To that end, he has written about and produced science fiction, pop culture as well as the classics, and treated sympathetically marginal texts, people, and activities. The university's power to name and act as the custodian of culture is one of his major targets; to subvert it, he champions many dissident approaches: the redefinition of criticism by minorities; an erotics as well as a thematics of literature; espousal of pornographic and popular as well as what we would call elitist fiction. With a mythopoeic approach, Fiedler links disparate texts, revealing the congruity of their social vision. He manages to be insightful about bad literature, and he writes incisively about critical theory in a way that is free of jargon. The ambiguity he articulates regarding freaks (in *Freaks*) defines his nondogmatic approach to texts of all kinds: "the normality of Freaks, the freakishness of the normal, the precariousness and absurdity of being, however we define it, fully human."

In a passionate yet scholarly way Fiedler explores the situation of Jews as writers and as characters in literature; the Jew as outsider; his/her integration into American society: these are topics, similar to those that are the focus in *Love and Death in the American Novel*, that Fiedler examines. He also traces the genealogy of the Jewish-American writer, finding ironically that the first such writer, whose pseudonym was Sidney Luska, was really Henry Harland, a Protestant American. *See also* Critics, Literary.

STANLEY FOGEL

BIBLIOGRAPHY

Fiedler, Leslie. *The Collected Essays of Leslie Fiedler.* New York: Stein and Day, 1971.
Winchel, Mark Royden. *Leslie Fiedler.* Boston: Twayne, 1985.

Film. The history of Jewish representation on the American screen is a history of gradual assimilation, resulting temporarily in a virtual disappearance and followed by a resurgence of activity that is still in full bloom. Jewish images proliferated during the silent cinema, revealing stories of European hardships and the tribulations of American immigrant life, all redeemed by opportunities in the Land of Promise. These stories were contrasted by a large number of comedies featuring ethnically stereotyped Jewish performers.

During the 1930s and until the end of World War II, there was a gradual decline in the number of Jewish characters, coupled with a tendency to depict only highly whitewashed Jews, usually played by non-Jewish actors and actresses. Despite the oppression of Jews in Europe and the rise of anti-Semitism at home, Jewish Hollywood producers, perhaps nervous about calling attention to themselves, skirted such subjects. Following the cease fire in Europe, several films did confront the issues of anti-Semitism, but such controversial tendencies were soon brought to a halt by the hearings of the House Un-American Committee in which many Jewish liberals were blacklisted or jailed.

During the 1950s, Jewish characters once again appeared in motion pictures. Films preached religious tolerance, and Jewish themes were universally edifying. However, beginning in the mid-1960s, ethnicity returned to the screen, affecting all groups and providing a great deal of space for Jewish performers and Jewish concerns.

The decades of the 1970s and 1980s saw a

plethora of films depicting Jewish life and reflecting a Jewish sensibility. As in the past, Jews have made a large contribution to the development of comedy, although currently they are more likely to speak as Jews rather than as nonspecified characters.

Throughout the history of American motion pictures, Jews have dominated film production, serving as producers, writers, composers, and businessmen. In recent years they have also become directors and performers in growing numbers.

The first studios were run by non-Jews, such men as Thomas A. Edison and D. W. Griffith. Yet even before the turn of the century, Sigmund "Pop" Lubin had begun producing films. Other early Jewish entrepreneurs were Gilbert Max Anderson, better known as Broncho Billy, who was a partner in Essanay Studios; Carl Laemmle, founder of Universal Pictures; William Fox, founder of Fox Film Corporation; Adolph Zukor, who along with Jesse L. Lasky formed what later became Paramount Pictures; and Samuel Goldwyn, who worked independently.

The first documented appearance of a Jewish character on the movie screen was drawn from the scandal surrounding the Dreyfus Affair in France. Presented as fact, these reconstructed newsreels and pseudonewsreels were produced in France by Lumiere in 1897, by Pathe in 1899, and by Melies in 1899.

In the United States the first images were also documentaries. In 1903, Thomas Edison released two one-minute films called *Arabian Jewish Dance* and *A Jewish Dance at Jerusalem* featuring Hasidic men doing a hora.

Following these actualities, short comedies and dramas appeared in profusion. Typical of the earliest films was *Cohen's Fire Sale* (1907), which featured a large-nosed, gesticulating merchant who makes profits on naive customers. Produced by the Edison company, it reflected the accepted anti-Semitism of the day.

More sympathetic were films such as *The Romance of a Jewess* (1908), directed by D. W. Griffith, which dramatizes the tragic consequences for young Ruth of going against her father's wishes by marrying the man of her choice.

In the main, the films that follow fall into three general categories. *Ghetto films*, the first, depict immigrant life on New York's Lower East Side and establish several character types who persist through the decades—namely, the patriarchal father with Orthodox commitments; the

prodigal son, who chooses a different path, usually toward assimilation; and the Rose of the ghetto, the innocent virginal typical of the Victorian era, ever on the verge of being violated. These characters turn up in such films as: *Child of the Ghetto* (1910), *The Ghetto Seamstress* (1910), *Solomon's Son* (1912), *The Jew's Christmas* (1913), and *A Passover Miracle* (1914).

The second dramatic genre are the *pogrom films* that drew inspiration from events in czarist Russia. Here Jewish oppression was graphically portrayed, with rescues provided by the intervention of Christian lovers. Often these works ended as the family set off for the Promised Land. Over a dozen of these films were made. Titles include *In the Czar's Name* (1910), *Russia, the Land of Oppression* (1910), *The Sorrows of Israel* (1913), *Escape From Siberia* (1914), and *Vengeance of the Oppressed* (1916).

Two dramas deserve special mention: *A Passover Miracle* and *The Jew's Christmas*. The first feature chronicles a prodigal son's philandering and eventual return to the fold. Produced and distributed with the aid of the Bureau of Education of the Jewish Community of New York, the film is an early effort to depict Jewish life and ritual in the hopes of furthering religious tolerance.

The second work, produced by Lois Weber and Phillip Smalley, non-Jews, also aimed at interfaith understanding, but through different means. Here intermarriage is not only condoned, but the patriarchal rabbi ends up celebrating Christmas, as emotion triumphs over religious difference. It is this scenario that becomes the dominant message in the years to come.

The third genre of note are the *comedies*. Here character types include scheming merchants as in *Levitsky's Insurance Policy* (1908) or *Foxy Izzy* (1911) or Jewish weaklings as in *The Yiddisher Cowboy* (1909 and 1911) and *How Mosha Came Back* (1914), who use their brains to overcome their physical limitations.

In addition to these three categories, Jews appeared in the various adaptations of classic literature, such as *The Merchant of Venice* (1908, 1912, 1914) and *Oliver Twist* (1909, 1910, 1912, 1916), serving to perpetuate anti-Semitic stereotypes.

During the twenties, there was a plethora of films with Jewish subjects. Most were outgrowths of the primitive period, especially stories from the New York ghetto. Many character types persisted—the patriarchal father, the prodigal son, and the Rose of the ghetto. Added to these is a new figure, the long-suffering mother. The struggle for dominance within the immigrant family and the conflict between traditionalism and assimilation continue to be the central concerns. However, during the twenties the balance of power clearly shifts to the younger generation. Sons reject their fathers. Families are reconstituted, but seldom do sons "go back home again."

An important feature of this period is the emphasis placed on "making it." Many films deal with sudden financial success and the movement out of the ghetto, reflecting the upward mobility of many Jews during this period. Closely tied to satisfying this great American dream is the ready acceptance of assimilationist ideas. As in the earlier period, this usually manifests itself in a marriage contract between Jew and Gentile, a narrative element that constitutes a happy ending to a large number of works. "The melting-pot" mentality also emerges through the portrayal of relationships with the Gentile community at large. Frequently non-Jews appear as business partners as well as romantic lovers in films with such wonderful titles as *Kosher Kitty Kelly* (1926) and *Clancy's Kosher Wedding* (1927). As in the earlier films, the Irish appear over and over again.

During the twenties, comedies blossom from one- and two-reelers to feature works. Like the melodramas, many center on ghetto life. Jewish merchants continue to conduct business, but the scheming merchant disappears. The comedies tend to be structured around several leading Jewish performers, each of whom developed a unique film persona. The most popular was George Sidney. Beginning with *Busy Izzy* in 1915, he played throughout the silent era the small, rotund immigrant, struggling to stay on top of the situation. These appearances culminated in the 1926 film, *The Cohens and Kellys*, a blockbuster that spawned six sequels. In addition, Alexander Carr and Sammy Cohen found their niches, creating comic characters such as Morris Perlmutter and Sammy Nosenbloom.

Representative of the twenties are several prominent motion pictures. Inaugurating the decade is *Humoresque* (1920), a prestige production released by Paramount, based on a work by Fannie Hurst. The story follows the life of Leon Kantor, who, spurred on by the encouragement and sacrifice of his mother, rises to great fame as a violinist. As one critic pointed out, "The spectator is not looking at the Jewish family life from the outside in but from the inside out." In large measure, *Humoresque* set the pattern for the films to follow, including *The Good Provider* (1922), *Hungry Hearts* (1922), and *Salome of the Tenements* (1925).

Also influenced by *Humoresque* is the decade's most celebrated feature, *The Jazz Singer* (1927). Remembered in history as the first talking film, *The Jazz Singer* featured Al Jolson as Jack Robin, a prodigal son, intent upon following a Broadway career rather than becoming a fifth-generation cantor as his father wishes. Supported by a loving mother, Jack not only reaches his ambition, but also captures the heart of the lovely Mary, the *shiksa*. The film's popularity made this term known to millions of non-Jewish Americans.

In between these two melodramas were several other ghetto films, most importantly *His People* (1925), *We Americans* (1928), and *The Younger Generation* (1929). Both *His People*, directed by Edward Sloman, and *The Younger Generation*, directed by Frank Capra, feature immigrant families and peddler fathers. Starring eminent actors such as Rudolph Schildkraut and Jean Hersholdt, the films depict sons who achieve the American dream as lawyers, boxers, and successful businessmen. Although these works begin to question the price for such upward mobility, in the main they affirm the goal. *We Americans* goes a step further, depicting intermarriage among different national groups and different religions as the natural result of good-hearted men.

The comedies echoed many of the same themes as the dramas. Two series typify the era—the three Potash/Perlmutter comedies (1923–1926), featuring two erasible Jewish partners and the mishaps of the Cohens and Kellys (1926–1929).

The decade ended with perhaps the most affirmative plea for intermarriage, *Abie's Irish Rose*, released in 1928 with talking sequences. Clearly, Levy and Murphy, the fathers, represent the "old way" as well as the "Old World," while their children, Abie and Rosemary, have solved the problems of religious difference through marital bliss and the birth of a baby. As with the dramas, this resolution becomes more dominant as we approach the thirties.

It is during the 1920s that the Jewish Hollywood moguls whose names have become household words solidify their power, although most of these men entered the business during the teens. Studio and corporate heads included Harry Cohn, Louis B. Mayer, the Warner brothers (Harry,

Albert, Jack, and Sam), Irving Thalberg, B. P. Schulberg, and Nicholas and Joseph Schenck.

In the two years following Warner Brothers' *The Jazz Singer*, Hollywood frantically set about converting to sound. As the studios began importing New York talent, many Jews landed in Hollywood. Among the Jewish performers who made their way west were Jack Benny, Ben Blue, Fanny Brice, George Burns, Harry Green, Ted Lewis, the Marx Brothers, Sophie Tucker, and Ed Wynn. In addition, directors and writers shifted from theater to film, including men such as George Cukor, Reuben Mamoulian, Sidney Buchman, Norman Krasna, Charles Lederer, Joseph Mankiewicz, S. J. Perelman, Robert Riskin, Morrie Ryskind, and Ben Hecht.

In film, the Hollywood mogul soon replaces the Jewish businessman as an object of jest and a character of self-parody. He turns up in *Once in a Lifetime* (1932), wherein the producer Julius Saxe demands a scenario of Genesis in 300 words, and in *The Cohens and Kellys in Hollywood* (1932).

Upward mobility continues to occupy the minds of screenwriters; however, in the films of the 1930s, there is an increasing ambivalence or, at least, a sombering realization that every gain has its concomitant loss. Sometimes this theme is treated nostalgically, as in *Symphony of Six Million* (1932), when Felix Klauber decides to give up his fancy Park Avenue medical practice and return to the ghetto; sometimes comically, as in *The Heart of New York* (1932), where the Mendels do the same thing in an effort to once again be with their old friends; and sometimes dramatically, as when George Simon, the protagonist of Elmer Rice's *Counsellor-at-Law* (1933), must reexamine the values that made him one of New York's top criminal attorneys.

By the mid-thirties even assimilated Jews were of little interest to studio producers. The degree to which Hollywood eliminated a Jewish presence can be assessed by comparing *The House of Rothschild* (1934) with *The Life of Emile Zola* (1937). The former deals with the famous banking family and forthrightly depicts historic anti-Semitism rampant in the Germany of their day (and by analogy the 1930s as well). In this film, starring George Arliss who had twice depicted Benjamin Disraeli on the screen, there is no question of Rothschild's identity.

In contrast, *The Life of Emile Zola* treats the infamous Dreyfus Affair, yet oddly, throughout the entire film the fact that Dreyfus was a Jew is never mentioned. Instead, he is portrayed as just an innocent French officer unfairly accused.

Despite Hitler's election as Supreme Chancellor of the Third Reich in 1933, growing militarization, civilian restrictions, and legislated discrimination against Jews, Hollywood remained totally silent on the subject throughout the thirties. The producers reflected the neutralist philosophy emanating from Washington. MGM's *Three Comrades* (1938) and Warner Brothers' *Confessions of a Nazi Spy* (1939) merely intimated at the true horror.

Only one voice dealt directly with the plight of Jews. Charlie Chaplin, a non-Jew who had worked independently since the 1920s, broke ranks by producing *The Great Dictator* (1940), a film that depicted contemporary conditions in his mythical Tomania. Despite its comic demeanor, the film ends with a passionate plea for hope and triumph over evil.

With the onset of World War II, Hollywood set about dealing with fascism, although it was less explicit about Jewish persecution. Several titles reached the screen at the beginning of the 1940s: *Escape*, *The Mortal Storm*, and *So Ends Our Night*. It is not until the Japanese bomb Pearl Harbor in December 1941, however, that Hollywood goes to war in full force. Increasingly, the victims are identified as Jews rather than non-Aryans—ironically a Nazi classification. Titles include *The Pied Piper* (1942), *None Shall Escape* (1944), and *Address Unknown* (1944).

The war also saw the rise of the combat film, which depicted a fighting unit of ethnically and geographically diverse soldiers. Among the films with Jewish characters who were fighting to keep the world safe for democracy were *Air Force* (1943), *Bataan* (1943), *Guadalcanal Diary* (1943), and *Action in the North Atlantic* (1943). Most typically the Jews' function was to provide the comic relief.

More serious depictions of Jewish participation in World War II can be found in *The Purple Heart* (1944) and *Pride of the Marines* (1945). Consistently, all the characters evidence intelligence, bravery, and patriotism.

Following the war and the full knowledge of the Nazi atrocities, it was natural to ask, "How could this happen?" "Could it happen here?" The response to these questions were two works, both released in 1947—RKO's *Crossfire* and 20th Century-Fox's *Gentleman's Agreement*.

Crossfire treats anti-Semitism as the cause for a seemingly unmotivated murder in a typical

1940s *film noir. Gentleman's Agreement* presents journalist Gregory Peck posing as a Jew to get first-hand experience of what it feels like to suffer discrimination. Both films received critical and popular acclaim and, despite initial concern on the part of the Jewish agencies, both works proved through testing to be effective tools in combating prejudice. Although advanced for its day, the message of *Gentleman's Agreement* (we are all alike except for what we call ourselves) leaves something to be desired.

Another response to the war was the creation of the Motion Picture Project in 1947, an organization funded by the major U.S. Jewish agencies which sought to encourage Jewish themes in Hollywood films and to create positive images. Headed by a former schoolteacher, John Stone, the project accomplished its task quietly and effectively, working with producers and screenwriters behind the scenes. It accomplished its task so successfully that it was disbanded in 1967.

The postwar period also produced an unexpected backlash against Jews, most particularly in Hollywood. Spurred on by anti-Communist fears, conservative individuals were able to act out their prejudices through the workings of the House Un-American Activities Committee. Of the original Hollywood ten who faced investigation and charges, seven were Jewish. Also, anti-Semitism emerges from the official records, as evidenced by comments such as Representative John Rankin's description of Walter Winchell as "a little slime-mongering kike."

In many ways the films of the 1950s that deal with Jewish characters and themes can be seen as a direct result of the Motion Picture Project. In no decade are the screen Jews so intelligent, patriotic, and unqualifiably likable. At no other time is religious tolerance and good will so consistently echoed.

Beginning in 1951 with the "bio-pic," *The Magnificent Yankee*, in which Louis Brandeis, a paragon of wisdom and virtue, fights to become the first Jewish Supreme Court justice, until 1960 when a sensitive, young Jewish cadet, wounded by social discrimination, commits suicide in the screen adaptation of *Dark at the Top of the Stairs*, the films all preach the same message—Jews are deserving of full acceptance; anti-Semitism is no longer acceptable; anti-Semitism is un-American. As if to prove the point, most of the Jewish roles were taken by non-Jewish actors, thus playing down differences, but also confusing the issue.

In between these two works, several important films came to the screen. In 1952, Dory Schary adapted *Ivanhoe*, with Elizabeth Taylor in the role of Rebecca. Her father, Isaac of York, a moneylender, is not only distinguished in his white beard, but proves his loyalty by ransoming Richard the Lion-Hearted. In 1953, the first remake of *The Jazz Singer* appeared with Danny Thomas in the lead role. The once Orthodox family have now become assimilated Reform Jews. In *Good Morning, Miss Dove* (1955), Jennifer Jones uses the presence of a Polish immigrant to teach her class a lesson in religious tolerance, first by studying Palestine and second by visiting a Jewish home.

Three Brave Men (1957) deals with the Abraham Chasanow case, in which a government employee is accused of Communist activities. Not only do the charges prove false, but the film's main characters are clearly the exemplary all-American family. Other positive images appear in *Home Before Dark* (1958), which portrays a Jewish college professor, and *The Last Angry Man* (1959), in which Paul Muni plays a kindly doctor who puts the welfare of his patients before material ambition. Two war films depict anti-Semitism in the United States Army—*The Naked and the Dead* (1958) and *The Young Lions* (1958), with much sympathy going out to Montgomery Clift in the role of Noah Ackerman.

Only *Marjorie Morningstar* (1958), *Me and the Colonel* (1958), and *The Diary of Anne Frank* (1959) deal with other themes. *Marjorie Morningstar*, which was filmed on the strength of its popularity as a novel, is one of the first films since the 1920s to focus on Jewish domestic life and looks forward to the ethnic interest of the 1960s, especially in its self-critical approach to contemporary Jewish values. Both *Me and the Colonel* (starring Danny Kaye) and *The Diary of Anne Frank* were based on successful Broadway plays, and both treat the plight of Jews during the war. As initial steps into a difficult terrain, they are to be applauded. In comparison with the more directly engaged material that is to follow, these efforts seem light indeed. Also of note, the major roles of Marjorie Morningstar and Anne Frank, following precedent, went to non-Jewish actresses—Natalie Wood and Milly Perkins.

Lastly, *The Juggler* (1953), starring Kirk Douglas, becomes the first U.S. production shot entirely in Israel, and it sets the tone for a positive image of the land. This film is later eclipsed by the epic *Exodus* (1960), which not only creates heroic men and women, but also fixes Israel in the American imagination for years to come.

With the arrival of the 1960s, the scene is set for major changes. Not since the silent era have so many Jewish characters appeared, especially in major roles. And once again, Jewish actors and actresses are cast for these parts, although there are some glaring exceptions.

During this decade, there also emerges a growing recognition of the Jew as an identifiable individual who has experienced a unique fate. This is mirrored on screen by several Jewish characters of great suffering, dignity, or courage–Sol Nazerman in *The Pawnbroker* (1965), Col. Mickey Marcus in *Cast a Giant Shadow* (1966), and Yakov Bok in *The Fixer* (1968).

The reawakening of ethnic identity was being felt by almost all national, racial, and religious groups. For the most part, Jews had followed a path of acculturation, assimilating in their public life while keeping Jewish customs in the privacy of their homes and synagogues. By the 1960s, new attitudes were being voiced by many minorities.

Beginning in 1968, a series of comedies set a new direction and established Jewish humor as a major trend for the next two decades. Most prominent are *Bye, Bye Braverman* (1968), *The Producers* (1968), *Funny Girl* (1968), *Take the Money and Run* (1969), and *Goodbye, Columbus* (1969). Together they highlight the urban experience, the continued drive to succeed, and the outsider's perspective.

The comedies also introduced to film audiences a group of young Jewish actors and actresses who openly acknowledged their heritage by the parts they chose to play, by their personal publicity, and by the sound of their names. Unlike the Jewish performers in Old Hollywood (Edward G. Robinson, Sylvia Sydney, John Garfield, Tony Curtis, and Jerry Lewis, among others not previously mentioned), the new performers were able to assume star roles without having to sacrifice their religious or ethnic identities. Barbra Streisand clearly led the way in *Funny Girl*. Other members of this group include Dustin Hoffman, Richard Benjamin, Richard Dreyfuss, Elliott Gould, Jeannie Berlin, and, of course, the director-actors Mel Brooks and Woody Allen.

Although comedy dominates the decade in terms of Jewish film, the Holocaust is approached in two works with forceful impact. First, *Judg-ment at Nuremburg* (1961) soberly approaches the range of Nazi injustices. Although Jews as a group are perplexingly not mentioned, documentary footage of the camps is shown as part of the trial. In 1965, *The Pawnbroker*, independently produced and distributed by Ely Landau, stars Rod Steiger in the role of a German survivor. The film is the first American fictional work to treat the camp experience with such harrowing reality.

Closely related, *The Fixer*, starring Alan Bates, depicts Jewish victimization under the czarist regime, and by implication called attention to current Soviet discrimination.

The decade closes with one of the most celebrated films about Jewish life ever to reach the screen—*Fiddler on the Roof* (1969). Based on Sholem Aleichem's story of Tevya and his five daughters, the film exposed millions around the world to the warmth of Jewish family life and the traditions associated with life in the Russian *shtetl*.

Overwhelmingly the Jewish films of the seventies concentrated on speaking the unspoken. For such purposes, comedy represented an ideal medium, and it is not surprising that a majority of the films in this decade are comedies, seriocomedies, or comic romances.

As in the twenties, the Jewish family once again emerges as central. However, although the same character types appear—father, mother, son, and daughter—many shifts have occurred. Whereas the father-son conflict dominated earlier ghetto films, the contemporary works focus on the mother-son relationship. In many cases, the father is totally absent.

In his place appears the mother, totally metamorphosized. In the ghetto films, although her position is insignificant, she is the adored long-suffering mother. Beginning in the post-war period, she slowly evolves into the suffocating mother, an object of fear and scorn. By the 1970s, the central conflict is no longer the need to break with traditional Judaism and assimilate, but rather the son's efforts to sever the emotional umbilical cord and to establish his manhood and autonomy.

Two films that portray the suffocating mother are *Where's Poppa* (1970) and *Portnoy's Complaint* (1972). As the memorable Mama Hocheiser, Ruth Gordon in the former was obscene and senile and intent upon making her son's life as miserable as possible. Likewise, Lee Grant as Sophie Portnoy appeared dominating and self-serving, holding her son emotionally captive.

Quite expectedly, these women produced neurotic sons, the heroes of the above-mentioned works, as did mothers in *Move* (1970), *The Steagle* (1971), *Play It Again Sam* (1972), *Annie Hall* (1977), and *Manhattan* (1979). These sons were fearful, indecisive, and insecure men, craving boundless sex and affection, most frequently from *shiksas* as unlike their mothers as possible. Despite their infantile tendencies, these characters were frequently sympathetically presented, a result of their Jewish male authorship.

Jewish womanhood came off little better during this period. The Jewish heroines of *Such Good Friends* (1971), *Made For Each Other* (1971), *The Heartbreak Kid* (1972), and *Sheila Levine Is Dead and Living in New York* (1975) are equally insecure and dependent as their brothers, a marked contrast to the Jewish-American princess of the previous generation. Only those films with a strong female input—such as *The Way We Were* (1973), starring Barbra Streisand; *Hester Street* (1975), written and directed by Joan Micklin Silver; and *Girlfriends* (1978) written and directed by Claudia Weill—avoid the stereotypes. These works also make other contributions, e.g., *The Way We Were* implies intermarriage does not always work; *Hester Street* focuses on Orthodox Jewish life, a topic untreated since the late 1920s; and *Girlfriends* depicts an autonomous Jewish woman who is not looking for a husband.

The seventies also introduce many new types: the Jewish gambler (*The Gambler*, 1974), the Jewish madam (*For Pete's Sake*, 1974), blacklisted artists (*The Front*, 1976), the Jewish gumshoe (*The Big Fix*, 1976), the Jewish lesbian (*A Different Story*, 1978), a Yiddish cowboy (*The Frisco Kid*, 1979), a Jewish union organizer (*Norma Rae*, 1979), a Jewish murderess (*The Last Embrace*, 1979), and an elderly Jew pushed to violence (*Boardwalk*, 1979).

The Frisco Kid deserves special mention. Despite its high comedy, the film is one of the few Hollywood works to treat Jewish values as a serious topic. Briefly stated, the film shows the confrontation between Talmudic piety and American pragmatism (as the two influenced each other) as Jew met Gentile in the New Land.

The Holocaust and Israel continue to provide material for scenarios; however, the tendency is to create thrillers from this material rather than thought-provoking works. Only *The Man in the Glass Booth* (1975), based on a stage play, stands apart. The other titles include *The Odessa File* (1974), *Marathon Man* (1976), and *The Boys From Brazil* (1978), plus *The Jerusalem File* (1975), *Rosebud* (1975), *The Next Man* (1976), and *Black Sunday* (1977).

In the main the eighties and the onset of the nineties are a continuation of themes and characters from the 1970s, with a preponderance of comedies and a barrage of minor characters, some familiar like doctors, lawyers, businessmen, moguls, and performers; others more novel like werewolves, basketball coaches, and cops.

The major comedies focus once again on domestic life, some with a nostalgic look toward the past; others with a derisive look at the present. Films include *My Favorite Year* (1982), *Down and Out in Beverly Hills* (1986), *Brighton Beach Memoirs* (1987), and *Radio Days* (1987).

Jewish women finally come to the fore with great strength, in the main a result of Jewish women's participation in production. Beginning with *Private Benjamin* (1980), co-produced and starring Goldie Hawn as the Jewish American princess who finally grows into an autonomous woman, Jewish women are admirably depicted in *Tell Me a Riddle* (1980), *Baby, It's You* (1983), *Hannah K* (1983), *Yentl* (1983), *St. Elmo's Fire* (1985), *Sweet Lorraine* (1987), and *Dirty Dancing* (1987). Among the Jewish women active in film as directors, screenwriters, and producers are Barbra Streisand, Susan Seidelman, Claudia Weill, Lee Grant, Joan Micklin Silver, Gail Parent, and Sherry Lansing.

Several of the works of the eighties feature exclusively Jewish worlds, even Orthodox worlds—e.g., *Tell Me a Riddle*, *The Chosen* (1981), *Yentl*, *Brighton Beach Memoirs*, *Sweet Lorraine*, *Dirty Dancing*, *Crossing Delancey* (1988), *Enemies: A Love Story* (1989), *The Plot Against Harry* (1989). Here the Gentiles are the outsiders, the marginal group.

In fact, the differences between "us" and "them" continue to fascinate filmmakers who deal with Jewish subject matter. Whereas during the 1940s, films seemed to go to great lengths to prove we were all alike under the skin, contemporary works stress the opposite. Woody Allen, long obsessed with this issue, deals with it again in *Hannah and Her Sisters* (1986), in *Radio Days* (1987), and in *Crimes and Misdemeanors* (1989). Likewise, it seems at the heart of such diverse works as *The King of Comedy* (1983), *Desperately Seeking Susan* (1985), *Dirty Dancing*, and *Broadcast News* (1987), or even in *Sophie's Choice* (1982), where the traditional roles of victim and victimizer are reversed.

It is hard to predict what new avenues will open in terms of Jewish images and themes. The drive toward acceptance and assimilation for American Jews has been nearly complete, and this is reflected in contemporary cinema. Jewishness has fairly well pervaded all character types. A Jew can now be anything in an American film. Better yet, recent Jewish characters can be major narrative heroes and heroines without losing their specificity, without having to be just like everyone else, and without deteriorating into ethnic stereotypes. Perhaps best represented by the roles of Barbra Streisand, Jewish characters are now persons in their own right.

Likewise, a wide variety of Jewish themes have been treated visually. Still, being Jewish in American cinema is primarily an ethnic rather than a religious distinction, and, in the main, American Jewish preferences lean toward social identification. It is not surprising, therefore, that comedies outnumber dramas or that practically no works deal with the spiritual side of Judaism. For the present, the future looks to be a continuation of the trends already noted for the last two decades, and although this does not augur major innovations, it does evince a healthy reflection of Jewish life in America. *See also* Movie Moguls, Films, Yiddish.

PATRICIA BRETT ERENS

BIBLIOGRAPHY

Cripps, Thomas. "The Movie Jew as an Image of Assimilation, 1903–1927." *Journal of Popular Film* 4(1975): 190–207.

Doneson, Judith E. *The Holocaust in American Film.* Philadelphia: Jewish Publication Society, 1987.

Erens, Patricia. *The Jew in American Cinema.* Bloomington: Indiana University Press, 1984.

French, Philip. *The Movie Moguls: An Informal History of the Hollywood Tycoons.* Chicago: Regnery, 1971.

Friedman, Lester D. *Hollywood's Image of the Jew.* New York: Ungar, 1982.

Gabler, Neal. *An Empire of Their Own: How the Jews Invented Hollywood.* New York: Crown, 1988.

Suber, Howard. "Politics and Popular Culture: Hollywood at Bay, 1933–1953." *American Jewish History* LXVII (June 1979): 517–533.

Weinberg, David. "The 'Socially Acceptable' Immigrant Minority Group: The Image of the Jew in American Popular Film." *North Dakota Quarterly* (Autumn 1972): 60–68.

Zierold, Norman. *The Moguls.* New York: Coward-McCann, 1969.

Film, Yiddish. As an effort to retain identity and heritage in the face of the "melting-pot myth," Yiddish cinema transcended territorial, political, and aesthetic boundaries in celebrating the richness of Jewish life. It was a cultural expression that began before World War I as a tool for combatting czarist anti-Semitism and as a vehicle for presenting Yiddish theater to the masses. Later with the arrival of sound, Yiddish movies became a mechanism for entertaining non-English-speaking Jewish immigrants. At its zenith, between 1936 and 1940, Yiddish cinema provided an effective vehicle for strengthening Jewish identity. To be sure, Yiddish pictures were made to entertain, not to indoctrinate, but their stories and themes continually reinforced a belief in Jewish peoplehood and survival.

In 1911, the age of Yiddish cinema began simultaneously in Poland, Russia, and the United States. In Warsaw, A. Y. Kaminsky arranged to have plays, produced by his Yiddish theater troupe, filmed directly from the stage. The film prints were then sent to be seen by Jewish communities all across the Austro-Hungarian empire. Most of Kaminsky's films starred his actress wife Esther Rokhl Kaminska (known as the mother of Yiddish theater) with daughter Ida (much later of *The Shop on Main Street* and *The Angel Levin* fame) appearing in some. At the same time in Moscow, Alexander Arkatov successfully adapted an original story about Jewish life in Russia for the screen. Arkatov used nonactors for his films. Kaminsky continued his theater film recordings until 1914 when the war made film stock rare and distribution impossible, while Arkatov's last film, an adaptation of a Sholem Aleichem story, was completed in 1917, on the eve of the Russian Revolution.

In the United States, the first Yiddish pictures were made by Sidney Goldin. To protest harsh anti-Semitism in czarist Russia, Goldin identified a new film genre. After World War I, Goldin made films in Austria, using noted artists from the Yiddish stage, such as Maurice Schwartz and Molly Picon.

The 1920s brought us fine Yiddish films produced in Poland and the Soviet Union. In Poland, with Yiddish theater again thriving, artists from the Warsaw Yiddish Art Theater helped create fine pictures. Artists like Zygmund Turkow, Jonas Turkow, and Henryk Szaro took Yiddish cinema outdoors to deal with difficult issues of the day. In the Soviet Union, where cultural development was encouraged by the

Communist Party, Yiddish movie-making was seen as an integral part of Soviet cinema production. Several films, directed, written, and featuring the most talented of Soviet artists, including Alexander Granovsky, Isaac Babel, Solomon Mikhoels, Benjamin Zuskin, Grigori Roshal, and G. Gricher-Cherikover, were produced during the period. By the end of the decade, though, with changing Soviet ideology, almost all Yiddish film production in Russia ceased. A sound motion picture, Peretz Markish's *The Return of Nathan Becker*, was made in 1932.

Despite a dominance of Jews in the film industry of the 1920s, American producers were not interested in making pictures aimed at any one ethnic group, especially their own. Still, Jewish subject films with Jewish characters were made, often stories of Jews who sought intermarriage and assimilation. Upon achieving "the American dream," their Jewishness was almost always left behind.

These films, with their "melting-pot ideology," seemed to appeal to the broad American audience. Yet for many Jews these films proved objectionable, especially when intermarriage of Jew and Gentile was suggested. As use of sound in film became the norm by 1927–1928, the problem became even more acute. American-born Jews had little difficulty with English-language Jewish subject pictures; they were integrated into American society. English was their language and for many, intermarriage was a fact of life. For immigrant Jews, Yiddish was still their *mame-loshn*, English a language only acquired. A tradition was maintained that encouraged education, upward mobility, and acceptance into society while still remaining a Jew and seeing that one's children would also maintain their Jewishness. Yiddish was not just a spoken language; it was a way of life. Hollywood's film product was just not acceptable.

In response to Hollywood's portrayal of Jews and as a means of providing the 10 million Yiddish-speaking audience with talking pictures they could understand, a Yiddish film industry began to evolve in the 1930s. At first, pictures were cheaply made, churned out in someone's kitchen or off the theater stage. By the mid-1930s, independent producers realized that better, well-crafted pictures could bring in greater box-office returns. Some of the greats of Yiddish theater participated in the films, actors like Boris Thomashevsky, Ludwig Satz, and Celia Adler. Most of the films dealt nostalgically with Jewish

life in Eastern Europe, which many Yiddish-speaking Jews still considered "home." There, in the shtetl, Jewish values and culture seemed more clearly defined. In the West, assimilation and acculturation had changed the mores of Jewish existence; the shtetl represented a pure Jewish spirit, lost in Americanization.

In 1935, Joseph Green, a Polish-born American, went back to Warsaw to revolutionize the Yiddish film industry. Bringing Molly Picon, now a household name on the Yiddish stage, to Poland and coupling her with actors from the Warsaw theater, he made the Yiddish musical, *Yidl Mitn Fidl* (Yidl with a Fiddle), the story of a girl who masquerades as a boy in order to join a troupe of klezmorim (traveling musicians). The film did exceptionally well in Poland. When Green brought the picture to New York City the following year, the lines stretched for blocks.

Green had proven that quality Yiddish pictures could be made and could be profitable. *Yidl Mitn Fidl* ushered in a "Golden Age of Yiddish cinema," a period of five years, 1936–1940, when productions of the highest level were made. Green returned to Poland in 1937 and 1938, with Europe in chaos, to produce and direct three more Yiddish pictures. Many issues were tackled in his films, all revolving around family and holiday celebration.

Sidney Goldin, "grandfather" of the Yiddish cinema, wanted to bring the Golden Age to America. Pointing to the success of Joseph Green's *Yidl Mitn Fidl*, he was able to raise sufficient funds for a large-budget film, at least by Yiddish film standards. He engaged Moyshe Oysher, one of the great voices in Yiddish theater, to star in what was actually an adaptation of the singer's story. Unfortunately, in September 1937, Goldin died in the middle of the production of *Dem Khazns Zundl* (The Cantor's Son). Like Moses, who saw the promised land only from a distance, Goldin did not live to witness the presentation of quality, well-produced Yiddish pictures in America.

In Poland, 11 pictures (including Green's films), were produced during the Golden Age. The films, all of which exist today, provide a living testament to a vanished world. Performances by Avrom Marevsky, Dzigan and Schumacher, and Dina Halpern add vitality to movies written by some of the finest Yiddish writers of the twentieth century. Some of the films, such as *The Dybbuk* and *Yidl Mitn Fidl*, won international recognition and attracted large non-Jewish audiences. Yiddish cinema in Poland was a phenomenon. As Nazi activity in Europe increased, so did creative Yiddish cinema, as if an expression of resistance.

In America, Edgar G. Ulmer brought his European and Hollywood training to New York and helped usher in the Golden Age. With his technical know-how and the support of such Yiddish theater directors as Jacob Ben-Ami, he successfully adapted theater classics for the screen, his first film being Peretz Hirschbein's *Green Fields*. Others, like the noted Yiddish actor Maurice Schwartz and producers Roman Rebush and Abraham Leff, followed his lead. Ten classics were made between 1937 and 1940, including *Tevye, Mirele Efros*, and *The Light Ahead*; four were directed by Ulmer. There were also numerous low-budget films produced during this period.

With the outbreak of World War II, Yiddish film production worldwide ground to a halt. One last "elaborate" production, *Der Vilner Balabesl* (The Vilna Petit-Bourgeois) was begun in America in 1940. The picture would bring the Golden Age of Yiddish cinema to a close. Independent producers Ira Greene and Ludwig Landy lavished the Yiddish screen with opulence. They wanted faithful reproduction quality and emulated a Hollywood picture with expensive costumes and a wide variety of elegant sets unprecedented in Yiddish movies. It was to be the last "high-budget" Yiddish picture.

With the end of World War II came the last effort to bring Yiddish cinema back to life. Several films were made in Poland, West Germany, and the United States. Yet in 1950, the same year that the Yiddish Art Theater closed in New York, Yiddish film production ceased. In Europe, there no longer was a Yiddish-speaking audience. In America, Jews were beginning to view themselves differently—how they lived, where they lived, what professions they chose, and how they entertained themselves. Having largely recovered from the trauma of the Holocaust, American Jews, both native and foreign-born, were finding it easy and comfortable to be just as "American" as their Gentile neighbors. A Yiddish picture, with its language and plot tied to an Eastern Europe of a bygone era, was of little interest. The Holocaust had shattered the illusion of comfort and peace in the "Old Country." American Jews, more than ever, wanted American culture.

In the 1980s, efforts have been made to restore and rehabilitate Yiddish pictures, and interest in such films has grown tremendously, drawing a new audience. As world Jewry has begun to rediscover its Jewish heritage, more and more young Jews are drawn to the Yiddish film form. Cinema historians and enthusiasts have turned their attention to this creation of an ethnic minority as one of the more interesting examples of the independent cinema. Yiddish films were made in the 1980s and have been shown on television across Europe; Yiddish film festivals took place in France, Italy, and West Germany at the close of the 1980s. Several Yiddish films are now available on videocassette.

At one point there seemed little future for the Yiddish cinema. Yiddish pictures were made for a Yiddish-speaking audience, and as that audience dwindled in size, it would become less possible or practical to produce Yiddish pictures. Yet, since 1980, Yiddish pictures were produced in Belgium, Israel, Poland, and the United States; others are in the process of development. A revival, at least a reappraisal, seems very much to be in the making.

ERIC A. GOLDMAN

BIBLIOGRAPHY

Goldman, Eric A. *Visions, Images and Dreams*. Teaneck, NJ: Ergo Media, 1989.
Kafanova, Ludmila. "Remembering Solomon Mikhoels." *New Leader* 61 (March 13, 1978): 16–17.

Film Stars. Show business in America often seems to be a Jewish invention. *Variety*, for example, is called the Bible of Hollywood. The film industry was created in large part by Jewish immigrants shortly after the turn of the century. Thus, Carl Laemmle came from Germany and founded Universal Studios. Louis B. Mayer, a native of Russia, and Samuel Goldwyn (born Shmuel Gelbfisz), a glove salesman from Poland, organized Metro-Goldwyn-Mayer (MGM). Adolph Zukor, a furrier from Hungary, was responsible for Paramount Pictures. William Fox, whose parents also came from Hungary, and who started out in the cloth business, formed the Fox Film Corp. Benjamin Warner, born in Russia, became a peddler in Youngstown, Ohio, where he raised four sons—Harry, Sam, Albert, and Jack—who went on to build Warner Bros. Studio.

These Jewish heads of studios had migrated to the West Coast because the anti-Semitic social barriers in the East prevented them from making inroads in big business and high society. In Hollywood they fashioned a WASP society from which they had fled in their own image. To that end, these movie moguls changed their names, altered their manner of dress, had non-Jewish wives, camouflaged any Jewish traits or abandoned altogether all outward connections with their heritage, took up mistresses as well as golf, and lorded over a baronial empire of the silver screen. To maintain their hegemony, the film magnates pressured their clients, Jew and gentile alike, to change their foreign-sounding names and ethnic manners into a WASP mold.

Julius Garfinkle, a product of the Lower East Side, had already changed his name to Jules Garfield when he signed a contract with Warner Bros. in the 1930s. That was not good enough. Jack Warner wanted to change it to James Fielding. The actor resisted, so he became John Garfield, star of *Pride of the Marines*, *Gentleman's Agreement*, and many other films.

Other Jewish stars who changed their names included Edward G. Robinson (Emanuel Goldberg), Paul Muni (Muni Weisenfreund), Paulette Goddard (Marion Levy), Melvyn Douglas (Melvyn Hesselberg), Lee J. Cobb (Leo Jacobi). Of course, this trend to de-emphasize one's religious and ethnic background took root early in vaudeville, nightclubs, Broadway, and television with such names as Joey Bishop (Joseph Gottlieb), Bea Arthur (Bernice Frankel), Tony Randall (Leonard Rosenberg), Shelley Winters (Shirley Schrift), Tony Curtis (Bernie Schwartz), Kirk Douglas (Issur Danielovitch), Elliott Gould (Elliott Goldstein), Jack Carter (Jack Chakrin), Red Buttons (Aaron Chwatt), Joel Grey (Joel David Katz), Freddie Roman (Fred Kirschenbaum), Joan Rivers (Joan Molinsky), Monty Hall (Monty Halparin), Robert Merrill (Merrill Miller).

In contemporary times it is no longer *de rigueur* to change one's ethnic name or deny one's roots to succeed in show business. Such Jews as Barbra Streisand, Tovah Feldshuh, Dustin Hoffman, Richard Dreyfuss, David Steinberg, Jeff Goldblum, and Steve Guttenberg have become screen stars with family names intact. Gentiles, too, such as Robert De Niro, Danny Aiello, Arnold Schwarzenegger and Danny De Vito, for example, see no need to drop their surnames for WASP-sounding appellations.

Whereas in the heyday of the studio system (1920–1950), producers and stars assimilated to such an extent that they were reluctant to expose their Jewish family background, today the atmosphere has changed radically. Due either to the tragedy of the Holocaust or the triumph of the state of Israel, Hollywood Jews have begun to express an interest and a pride in their roots. Indeed, a majority of the screen stars and related industry colleagues such as producers, directors, agents, writers, are lending their names and prestige to various cultural, religious, and charitable causes.

Ron Leibman and his wife Jessica Walters went to Israel to make a fund-raising film for the United Jewish Appeal. Barbra Streisand and Dustin Hoffman helped the UJA honor Time-Warner co-chairman Steven Ross. Ron Silver and Robert Klein helped sell Israel Bonds. Elliott Gould and Melissa Gilbert participated in a telethon for Chabad House of Los Angeles. George Burns raised money for Hebrew University. The list of Hollywood performers coming out for Israel and in support of Jewish organizations is endless.

Many of the stars have actually begun to rediscover their heritage. Some have begun to observe religious rituals and commandments.

TIM BOXER

BIBLIOGRAPHY

Boxer, Tim. *The Jewish Celebrity Hall of Fame.* New York: Shapolsky, 1987.

Chetkin, Len. *Guess Who's Jewish?* 1985. Norfolk, Va.: Donning, 1985.

Friedman, Lester D. *The Jewish Image in American Film.* Secaucus, N.J.: Citadel, 1987.

Gabler, Neal. *An Empire of Their Own: How the Jews Invented Hollywood.* New York: Crown, 1988.

Finance. Even before the discovery of America, Jews participated in European financial activity. The church's prohibition against Christians practicing usury probably drove Jews into financial activity. European kings and queens often used "the court Jew" as a financial middleman through whom money passed in a long journey from the pockets of peasants into the royal exchequer's vaults. Moorish rulers did not restrict Jews to narrow moneylender or tax collector roles. In their lands among a list of popular Sephardic (Jewish) occupations, "bullion merchant" ranked twelfth while "physician" lead the list followed by "public official" and "clerk of the treasury."

Jews provided important financial services to the Spanish royalty before 1492. In one report, they were "in key positions as ministers, royal counselors, farmers of state revenue, financiers of military enterprises and as major domos of the estates of the Crown and of the higher nobility." A prominent Jewish banker, Don Isaac Abravanel, was one of the first to offer Christopher Columbus financial backing. When Columbus needed still more money and Isabella almost abandoned the project for lack of funds, Abravanel turned to other Jewish bankers, including Luis de Santangel, Gabriel Sanchez, and Abraham Senior.

Because of their supposed "talent" at international and wholesale trade, in seventeenth-century Holland the Dutch thought that Jews should be channeled into these activities for the good of the country. Dutch Jewish contributions to international finance helped balance Holland's economic position in relation to her competitors, England, Portugal, and Spain. The Dutch claimed that retailing "distracted" Jews from their more important international business. They felt the same focus of Jewish attention was necessary in America's New Amsterdam.

Jews were well known in trading and commerce in early America and helped to establish the institutions of a capitalist economy there. They participated in setting up the New York Board of Stockholders, which preceded the New York Stock Exchange. Almost from America's beginning, there existed a few Jewish private bankers and factors. Stephen Birmingham writes that "Mendes Seixas Nathan was a banker who was one of the little group who gathered one day under a buttonwood tree in lower Manhattan to draw up the constitution of the New York Stock Exchange."

Robert Morris, the Philadelphia financier who founded the Bank of North America, employed Haym Salomon (1740-1785), who was a Polish-born Jewish American of Sephardic descent. Morris, whose personal credit at one point during the Revolution was better than the government's, assigned Salomon to negotiate war loans. Salomon sold the infant government's bonds in various markets. He sold them so well that soon people called him "the most successful of the war brokers." Though he charged only a modest 0.25 percent for his services, his account at the Bank of North America grew until it was nearly as large as Robert Morris's.

Salomon was proud of his position as the Revolution's leading bond broker. Other Jewish brokers—Isaac Franks, Benjamin Nones, and Lion Moses—also bought and sold government notes. But Salomon did the biggest volume of business. In 1782, he asked Morris for permission to advertise himself as "Broker to the Office of Finance."

There is no proof that Salomon lent "vast sums" to the government, personally paid soldiers' salaries, and "paid for the Revolution." He did, however, extend personal loans to many prominent individuals and members of the Continental Congress without charging them interest. In particular, he aided Thomas Jefferson, James Madison, and James Monroe at different times when they were short of ready cash. He also sold hundreds of thousands of dollars' worth of American bonds. The bonds found their way to the bourses of Paris, London, and Frankfort and helped to establish the standing of America's credit in European bond markets.

After the Revolution and following the Jeffersonian ideal, the United States became a nation of small farmers and business people. By 1830, the typical Jewish American of the time was an immigrant from Germany who chose a business career as a peddler, trader, or middle person.

As America intensified its industrialization after the Civil War, the Gentile elite founded vast empires in steel, oil, railroads, shipping, coal, and chemicals. Gentiles tended to hire other white Anglo-Saxon Protestants for management posts. As a consequence, most Jews did not make a career in these fields. Instead, they first chose retailing and only later financial activity. In the process, a German-born Jewish elite became successful beyond the wildest dreams they may have had when they were in German ghettos. They became merchant princes.

Finance matured in America between 1860 and 1890 with the coming of a golden age for investment banking. Along with the increasing industrialization of America came an increasing need for financial investment. German Jewish investment bankers participated in the golden age. The founders of many of these firms were originally peddlers. Thus the Seligmans of J. & W. Seligman & Co., the Lehman brothers, Abraham Kuhn and Solomon Loeb, Philip Heidelbach of Heidelbach, Ickelheimer, and Marcus Goldman of Goldman, Sachs all progressed from peddling to banking via cotton brokerage or clothing stores and then to dealing in commercial paper. Most of these banking houses climbed the ladder to become full financial institutions without any outside financial or political help. Jewish-owned banks in Germany did establish a few of them, however.

The eight Seligman brothers of J. & W. Seligman & Co. began as peddlers and clothing dealers before they entered banking. They first built a peddling business into a chain of small stores. Then they opened an importing business in New York. After the discovery of gold in California in 1849, the Seligmans sent two brothers to San Francisco to establish a branch of the business there. Soon the New York Seligman's most profitable import became gold from California. When they did not trade the gold on the New York market, they sent it on to Europe to purchase new supplies for their stores.

The Seligmans still dealt in dry goods, etc., but as buyers and sellers of bullion they found themselves, almost before they knew what had happened to them, in the banking business. To become a banker in those days was as simple a matter as saying, "I am a banker." Gradually, they began to sell the federal government's obligations in the early years of the Civil War. Finally, in 1864, they opened a bank, and by 1870, they advertised that they were a "fiscal agent of the United States State Department." In the 1870s, they became importantly involved in government finance. They were an influential banking house before J. P. Morgan and Kuhn, Loeb came to dominate the business.

Goldman, Sachs & Co. began in 1869 when Marcus Goldman left peddling to become a dealer in commercial paper; that is, he bought the promissory notes of small businessmen and resold them to banks both in the United States and abroad. In 1882, Goldman formed a partnership with his son-in-law, Samuel Sachs, and the present firm emerged in 1885, primarily as a commercial-paper house. The firm started in the underwriting business in the early 1900s by specializing in the underwriting of retail store securities, which the leading houses then thought an undignified business. By 1917, when it had already taken over the financing needs of Sears, Roebuck, May Department Stores, F. W. Woolworth, and others, Goldman, Sachs was the leading underwriter of retail store securities.

Several of the Jewish houses had their forebears in Frankfort or Hamburg, Germany. For example, Philip Speyer & Co., which opened a branch in the United States in 1837, went back to at least the middle of the fourteenth century. James Speyer became the senior partner of the firm in 1899. While he achieved great prestige, he was a loner. He had no interest in the continued existence of the firm. Since he trained no successor, the house dissolved upon his retirement.

Some German Jewish houses did grow and prosper with the help of talent and capital imported from the long-established banking houses of Frankfort and Hamburg. The leading example was Kuhn, Loeb & Co., which benefited immensely through the inclusion of members of the Schiff and Warburg families. Jacob H. Schiff, who came to the United States in 1865 and shortly became a senior partner in the firm, married one Loeb daughter while Paul Warburg married another.

Abraham Kuhn and Solomon Loeb were originally peddlers who operated general stores in Indianapolis and Cincinnati before entering the banking business. In 1867, they opened private banking offices in the downtown financial district of New York City. Their house eventually became second in fame and prestige to J. P. Morgan. But it did not begin to ascend to its pedestal until Jacob Schiff and the Warburgs, all from families associated with old-line Jewish banking houses in Germany, entered the business. Schiff entered in the early 1870s and the Warburgs later.

Jacob H. Schiff (1847–1920), born in Frankfort, emigrated to the United States at an early age and worked his way up in Horatio Alger fashion to become a powerful financier. Among his many financial negotiations was his participation in the reorganization of the Union Pacific Railroad. Schiff viewed capitalism as an ideology that rewarded people with profit for doing things well—the Puritan ethic at work. He hated czarist Russia because of its anti-Semitic policies. He floated a $200 million bond issue for Japan to help that country defeat Russia in their 1905 war.

August Belmont (1816–1890) started in the United States in 1837 as an agent of the Rothschilds. He was born in Germany, but once in the United States, he disassociated himself from anything Jewish. He soon went his own way and gained the wide respect of the financial community even though he came to spend more and more of his time at the races and in "high" society.

Of all the financial institutions in the decades after 1890, the leading investment banking houses were unparalleled in terms of power and influence. The most prominent of these houses was the Gentile firm of J. P. Morgan & Co. Only one other firm, Kuhn, Loeb & Co., possessed comparable prestige and authority. A step lower in the hierarchy were such less well-known but highly respected and influential houses as Speyer & Co., J. & R. Seligman, August Belmont & Co. As an economist would say, the business of investment banking was a highly concentrated oligopoly.

Firm entry was difficult because of the large amount of financial capital required. The very nature of the business, which demanded reputation and the "right business connections" as essential assets, also blocked entry.

South-Carolina-born Bernard Baruch (1870–1965) profited from his investments in railroads and other industries at the turn of the century. He became a millionaire financier without starting his own investment bank. In World War I, he was appointed chairman of the War Industries Board and coordinated the entire industrial establishment of the country.

During the war, German influence declined in the United States. The same decline in influence affected the German Jewish investment banks. The German Jews could not eliminate their sympathies for Germany entirely and Kuhn, Loeb's Schiff refused to help finance the Russian war effort against Germany. As a result, other American banks expanded while the German Jewish banks contracted.

In 1914, three popular Russian Jewish banks on the Lower East Side, run by the brothers M. and L. Yarmulowsky, Adolf Mandel, and Max Kobre, collapsed. The founders had established the banks casually and made big promises to their depositors. The owners had little banking expertise and nonrigorous loan policies. In August of that year, responding to rumors that the banks were in an unsound financial condition, the New York State banking superintendent closed all three. There was an immediate panic in the Lower East Side. The investigation that followed confirmed the banking commission's worst fears. The Yarmulowskys' bank, for example, was insolvent since it owed $1,703,000 and had assets of only $654,000. Similarly, the Mandel bank owned $1,250,000 less than what it owed. The hard-earned savings of thousands of immigrants were lost in the bank closings.

Joseph S. Marcus formed the Bank of the United States in 1913 with an initial capital of $100,000. It grew slowly until Marcus's death in late 1928, when it had a capital of $6 million and six branches in New York City. Despite the grandiose name, the bank was throughout the period a small local bank, serving a predominantly Jewish clientele in Manhattan. The scenario changed when the founder's son, Bernard K. Marcus, succeeded to the presidency of the bank upon his father's death. Bernard embarked on a vigorous program of expansion and fraud that ended with the bank's failure in late 1930.

The collapse of the Bank of the United States, with over $200 million of deposits (then the largest American bank ever to fail) in mid-December was of particular significance, for many people at home and abroad mistakenly assumed that the bank was an official institution. The failure or refusal of local clearing house banks and the Federal Reserve System to save the institution caused much additional alarm.

Like New York City, Philadelphia also experienced bank failures. Competing banks refused to grant financial assistance to a Philadelphia bank that was primarily Jewish owned at a crucial point in 1930, and it folded. As in New York City, several Philadelphia banks that were in trouble and were not owned by Jews did receive assistance, and some survived.

Were the failures of the banks in New York City and Philadelphia the result of anti-Semitism? American monetary and financial historians disagree on the issue. Milton Friedman, who investigated the period in detail, claims there was anti-Semitism. Other historians who have studied the period doubt the anti-Semitism charge.

During the Depression years, United States economic activity declined and therefore its financial activity declined also. Jewish businesses declined the same as everyone else's. After the failure of many banks in the early 1930s, the U.S. Congress passed many new banking laws that made banks safer, e.g., federal deposit insurance. The new laws also made entry into banking more difficult. Adolph Hitler came to power in Nazi Germany in the period, and he frequently and publicly spoke of the harmful effects of powerful Jewish bankers and financiers. The irony was that at that time Jewish ownership of financial institutions in Germany, the United States, or anywhere else was usually insignificant.

While the Depression was traumatic for everyone, not least for America's Jews, there was one bright spot. Several young and talented Jews who might ordinarily have become scientists instead chose to study economics. They did so partly out of a sense of social conscience because they wanted to help improve the economic system of the United States after the Depression debacle. They brought a new rigor to economic analysis for which they later were awarded Nobel laureates in economics. Among such university economists were Paul A. Samuelson (b. 1915) and Robert M. Solow (b. 1924) at MIT, Milton Friedman (b. 1912) at the University of Chicago, and Kenneth J. Arrow (b. 1921) at Harvard and Stanford universities.

An economist of Jewish heritage, Arthur F. Burns (1895–1981), served as chair of the Federal Reserve Board for the first eight years in the 1970s. The Federal Reserve Board is the decision-making body for the Federal Reserve System, which is the central bank of the United States. Because the Federal Reserve controls the lifeblood of the economy, the nation's money supply, it is one of the economically most powerful governmental institutions in America.

Burns was born in Austria and came to the United States in 1910. He earned a Ph.D. in 1934 from Columbia University and stayed there as a professor. At the same time he served as a researcher for the National Bureau for Economic Research (NBER), one of several think tanks financed by the corporate community. The NBER focuses almost exclusively on economic policies. From 1945 to 1953, he served as the NBER's research director, and, in 1957, he became its president. Through the NBER programs and publications and his speeches to business groups as an NBER executive, he became well enough known in the corporate community to be invited to be a member of the board of a top-level insurance company, the Mutual Life of New York.

Alan Greenspan (b. 1926) is also of Jewish background, although different in philosophy from most Jews in that he admires the superindividualism of Ayn Rand. He was never an investment banker or a corporate lawyer. Yet in 1977 he joined the boards of Morgan Guaranty Trust, Mobil, and General Foods, three of the larger corporate entities in the world.

Greenspan followed another path to become eventually chair of the Federal Reserve, that of expert adviser. An economist and business consultant, he founded his own consulting and forecasting firm, Townsend-Greenspan & Co. He was the firm's president from 1954 to 1974 before taking his first full-time job with the government in July 1975 as chairman of President Nixon's (and then President Ford's) Council of Economic Advisers. Presently, he serves as chair of the Federal Reserve Board in Washington.

Milton Friedman (b. 1912) is a leading monetary economist and academic whose economic and monetary ideas strongly influenced United States economic policy. Together with Anna J. Schwartz, he wrote a book that describes in detail the monetary history of the United States for the years 1867 to 1960. He also argues that "classical" capitalistic ideas have more in common with traditional Judaic principles than do socialistic ideas.

According to Werner Sombart's 1913 book, *The Jews and Modern Capitalism,* "Jews transformed economic life in Europe . . . by creating credit instruments." Prior to 1945, it was not obvious what new financial instruments American Jews created. After 1945, however, young, self-made Jewish entrepreneurs in America began to rise to wealth and prominence on Wall Street. Featured on the front pages of major United States newspapers and magazines as traders, deal makers, investment bankers, high-risk venturers, and corporate raiders, the men have achieved success through vision, daring, and driving ambition. Some central players are Felix Rohatyn, Sanford I. Weill, John Gutfreund, Ivan Boesky, Carl Icahn, Lew Glucksman, Saul Steinberg, Ace Greenberg, and Mike Milken, among others. These men represent profound transformations in American business and corporate culture and spectacular realizations of the American dream. They also helped introduce new language on Wall Street: terms such as "greenmail," "LBOs," "junk bonds," "white knights," and "poison pills."

Three of the leaders and their firms are Felix Rohatyn (b. 1928) of Lazard Freres, Sanford I. Weill (b. 1933) of Shearson, and John Gutfreund (b. 1929) of Salomon Brothers. The three arose from ordinary circumstances without immediate access to the Wall Street establishment or major corporations. They benefited from the new economic and social opportunities available to Jews after World War II. In the course of four decades, they outdistanced the previous generations of WASP and German Jewish gentlemen bankers.

Jews found career choices limited in the world of finance and in corporate America before 1945. They were held back by deep-rooted prejudices against them, Only in 1963 did Morgan Stanley hire its first Jew. At the end of World War II, many Jews lacked the credentials and contacts required to reach the highest levels of corporate management.

In the United States and on Wall Street after 1945, performance, instead of old money and connections, closed a deal or made a sale. Young Jewish newcomers who were outsiders had nothing to lose in taking risks. They were quick to adapt to the market-responsive climate and eager to take advantage of new resources and strategies open to them to make their fortunes. Having no other way to enter, they would go where the opportunities were.

They began with small up-and-coming Jewish firms in the fields of brokerage, deal making, and trading. In these firms and fields, they did not have to contend with the closed bureaucracies of large corporations or the tradition-bound ways of old-line bankers, German Jewish or otherwise.

Sanford I. Weill (b. 1933) amassed a brokerage empire and eventually became president of American Express. Then he became chairman, chief executive officer, and president of Primerica, like American Express a large diversified financial services company. He is recognized as one of the most powerful Jewish businessmen in the United States.

John Gutfreund (b. 1929) helped transform a small scrappy bond trading house into one of the more important securities firms in the Western world, before runaway expenses in 1986 led to questions about its continuing leadership. As chairman and chief executive officer of Salomon Inc, he personified the consummate Wall Street player and boss, whose strength in trading and deal making spanned the globe.

Felix Rohatyn (b. 1928), a master merger, reshaped American business for much of the past three decades by arranging corporate combinations. As the man who helped save New York City during its mid-seventies fiscal crisis, he gained a national reputation.

There are many other Jewish names in contemporary American finance. They include Ira Harris of Salomon and later Lazard Freres, Stephen Friedman of Goldman, Sachs, and Bruce Wasserstein. Wasserstein, formerly of the financial firm First Boston, formed his own merger firm with Joe Perella. Jerome Kohlberg and his partner Henry Kravis of Kohlberg Kravis Roberts became stars of the continuing merger mania that struck in the late seventies. Henry Kravis made many leveraged buyouts (LBOs) of the era, including one involving $25 billion for RJR Nabisco. That LBO, the largest ever, took LBOs past the financial pages and onto the editorial and front pages of the press.

Peter Cohen (b. 1946), Sandy Weill's protégé, engineered two landmark deals of his own after he succeeded Weill as chief executive of Shearson. In 1990, he resigned as Chief Executive Officer of American Express. Within a half-dozen years, Carl Icahn (b. 1936) rose from obscurity to become one of the most feared corporate raiders in the country. He became chairman of TWA, the largest shareholder in Texaco and USX (formerly U.S. Steel), and a billionaire. Saul P. Steinberg (b. 1939), using as his base a staid insurance company, fought pitched battles with the corporate

establishment. He survived political and personal scandal.

A controversial figure who earned over a billion dollars in a few years, young Michael Milken (b. 1946) of Drexel Burnham Lambert, took part of Wall Street West. Operating from Los Angeles, his financial activities led financiers and heads of corporations to beat a path to his door. His wealth rose from the marketing of once obscure securities commonly known as "junk bonds." The securities quickly became used as a major source of financing for hostile takeovers. Some called Milken the most formidable American financier since J. P. Morgan.

The very personality traits and business conditions that enabled so many other Wall Street Jews to succeed through risk taking became transmuted in a few individuals who pushed beyond the boundaries of securities law. In May 1986, Dennis Levine, a deal maker at Drexel Burnham Lambert, pleaded guilty to charges of "insider trading" (profiting from the use of material confidential information), which led investigators to uncover one of the most publicized and still unfolding scandals in Wall Street History. At the time, the two men implicated were among the important players in corporate takeovers: arbitrageur Ivan Boesky and deal maker Martin Siegel. A number of other Jews were caught among the more than twenty men named in the story of the insider trading cases. More than two years after the scandal began, Michael Milken, the biggest target of them all, was indicted as a result of his connection with Boesky. In April 1990, he pleaded guilty to six felony charges and was sentenced to jail.

Perhaps one of the richest Jewish families in the United States is the Pritzker family of Chicago, collectively worth between $700 million and $1 billion. The founding father, Nicholas J. Pritzker (1871–1957), came from Kiev at age 9 in 1880, in the first wave of Russian immigrants. The basis of the family fortune is Chicago real estate, which Pritzker began acquiring in the early 1900s when the city was still young and raw.

In conclusion, American Jews have played an active role in American financial activity throughout the country's history. As the American economy progressed from 1654 to 1990, Jews participated and assisted as America's financial system also became necessarily more sophisticated. Whether Sephardic or Ashkenazic, German or Russian, America's Jews have contributed their share to the development of the nation's many financial instruments and institutions. The instruments and institutions are necessary in order that a highly industrialized country like the United States may maintain its standard of living.

MARVIN S. MARGOLIS

BIBLIOGRAPHY

Auletta, Ken. *Greed and Glory on Wall Street*. New York: Random House, 1986.

Birmingham, Stephen. *The Grandees: America's Sephardic Elite*. New York: Harper & Row, 1971.

——. *"Our Crowd": The Great Jewish Families of New York*. New York: Harper & Row, 1967.

——. *"The Rest of Us": The Rise of America's Eastern European Jews*. Boston: Little, Brown, 1984.

Bruck, Connie. *The Predator's Ball: The Inside Story of Drexel Burnham and the Rise of the Junk Bond Raiders*. New York: Penguin, 1989.

Chernow, Ron. *The House of Morgan: An American Banking Dynasty and the Rise of Modern Finance*. New York: Atlantic Monthly Press, 1990.

Dimont, Max I. *The Jews in America: The Roots, History, and Destiny of American Jews*. New York: Simon & Schuster, 1978.

Ehrlich, Judith R., and Rehfeld, Barry J. *The New Crowd: The Changing of the Jewish Guard on Wall Street*. Boston: Little, Brown, 1989.

Krefetz, Gerald. *Jews and Money: The Myths and the Reality*. New York: Ticknor & Fields, 1982.

Krooss, Herman E., and Blyn, Martin R. *A History of Financial Intermediaries*. New York: Random House, 1971.

——. and Gilbert, Charles. *American Business History*. Englewood Cliffs, N.J.: Prentice-Hall, 1972.

Zweigenhaft, Richard L., and Domhoff, G. William. *Jews in the Protestant Establishment*. New York: Praeger, 1982.

Finkelstein, Louis (b. 1895). Conservative rabbi, scholar, educator, communal leader, Louis Finkelstein was born in Cincinnati. He graduated from the College of the City of New York (1915), received his Ph.D. from Columbia University (1918), and was ordained at the Jewish Theological Seminary of America (1919). He served as rabbi of Congregation Kehillath Israel in New York City (1919–1930), but from 1920 on, his career centered about the Seminary where he taught Talmud and theology, later becoming the Solomon Schechter Professor of Theology. He assumed a series of administrative positions culminating in his appointment as president

(1940) and chancellor (1951). He became chancellor emeritus in 1972.

In his time, Finkelstein was one of the most influential personalities in American Jewish life. He played a decisive role in shaping the education of generations of Conservative rabbis, and under his leadership, the Jewish Theological Seminary achieved international renown as a preeminent center for the scholarly study of Judaism, its graduates assuming academic positions in universities throughout the world. As chancellor, Finkelstein also functioned as the head of American Jewry's Conservative Movement. While espousing a more traditionalist stance to Jewish practice, he also encouraged an open, historical, and scientific approach to Jewish scholarship.

Finkelstein's concerns extended far beyond parochial interests. The Seminary's Institute for Religious and Social Studies and Conference on Science, Philosophy and Religion, which he launched in 1938 and 1940, respectively, were pioneering efforts to open lines of communication among the leadership of the Jewish, Roman Catholic, Protestant, and other religious communities and among academicians in the sciences and the humanities. He also created the Seminary's innovative and prize-winning "Eternal Light" radio and television programs, using these media to disseminate the Jewish perspective on common social and interpersonal concerns to the public at large. In *The Jews: Their History, Culture and Religion* (2 vols., 1949, 1960), which he edited, he invited the outstanding Judaica scholars of the day to summarize the findings of their respective fields, thus opening the best of Jewish scholarship to the English-speaking world.

Finkelstein pursued a wide-ranging scholarly career of his own, largely in late biblical and early rabbinic Judaism. Among other volumes, his *The Pharisees: The Sociological Background of Their Faith* (2 vols., 1938, rev. ed., 1963) advanced the then radical thesis that Pharasaic ideology and practice were influenced by economic and sociological factors. His *Akibah: Scholar, Saint and Martyr* (1939) is an imaginative attempt to construct a spiritual biography of a major Talmudic master out of references scattered throughout rabbinic literature.

In a more technical vein, he published critical editions of the *Sifre* (1939, reprinted, 1969) and the *Sifra* (vols. II and III, 1983; vols. I, 1989, and IV, 1990), rabbinic commentaries on Deuteronomy and Leviticus, respectively, as well as over 100 scholarly articles on the formation of the classical Jewish liturgy and issues in Talmudic literature. *A Bibliography of the Writings of Louis Finkelstein* was published by the Seminary in 1977.

In recognition of his position as spokesman for American Jewry, Finkelstein was appointed by President Roosevelt to serve as presidential adviser on America's efforts to rebuild Europe after World War II and, by President John F. Kennedy, as a member of the American delegation to the coronation of Pope Paul VI. *See also* Conservative Judaism.

NEIL GILLMAN

BIBLIOGRAPHY

Parzen, Herbert. *Architects of Conservative Judaism.* New York: Jonathan David, 1964.

Sklare, Marshall. *Conservative Judaism: An American Religious Movement.* New York: Schocken, 1972.

Waxman, Mordecai. *Tradition and Change: The Development of Conservative Judaism.* Philadelphia: Maurice Jacobs, 1958.

Florida. By the early 1990s, Florida, which had less than 3000 Jews a century previous, contained the third largest Jewish population of all the states, over 600,000 residents.

While it is still open to conjecture whether or not there were Marranos with the explorers Ponce de León or Hernando de Soto in the sixteenth century, the first record of Jewish settlement in the state was that of three merchants who came to Pensacola in 1763, fleeing the Spanish rule in New Orleans. In 1821, Moses Elias Levy, a Morroccan Jew who had become wealthy through his timber dealings in the Caribbean region, secured over 50,000 acres of land near Jacksonville. Levy sought to establish a New Jerusalem for Jewish settlers from Europe, but his plans came to naught. His son, David Levy Yulee, became active in Florida territorial politics, and in 1845, he was selected as the state's first U.S. Senator, becoming the first Jew in the Senate. Levy County and the city of Yulee, are named after the family, while Fort Myers, a city on the Gulf coast, was named after Abraham C. Meyers, a quartermaster in the army during the Seminole Indian Wars of 1836–1838 and 1841–1842.

By the 1880s there were Jewish communities in Pensacola, Jacksonville, Tampa, Gainesville, Deland, Palm Beach, and Ocala. Congregations had been formed in Pensacola in 1874, in Jacksonville in 1882, in Key West in 1887, and in Tampa in 1892. By the 1880s, Jewish mayors had been elected in Jacksonville (Morris Dzialynsky) and in Tampa (Herman Glogowsky).

While Key West was a major Jewish community in this period, it was the extension of the railroad to Miami in 1896 that was crucial to the development of the "Magic City" and to its becoming the Jewish center of the state. Among the first Jewish pioneers was the merchant Isidore Cohen, who became a leader in civic and communal affairs. The first congregation, Bnai Zion, later renamed Beth David, was formed in 1913. By the early twenties, Reform and Orthodox synagogues had been organized both in Miami and Miami Beach, which was originally developed in the early 1900s as a place to grow coconuts and mangoes—and as a "restricted haven." By 1943 Miami Beach had its first Jewish mayor. By 1970, the population was 80 percent Jewish.

The major impetus to settlement in Florida followed World War II when Miami served as training grounds for U.S. servicemen. There they, their families, and service employees came to appreciate the state's climate and its facilities. Coupled with the advances in air travel, increasing mobility and the lure of continuing warm weather, the Jewish population increased from less than 50,000 statewide in 1939 to 125,000 in 1960, over 250,000 in 1970, and close to 600,000 by the late 1980s. While in-migration was composed overwhelmingly of those from the northern states, there were, especially in southeast Florida, recognizable groups of Cuban, Russian, and South and Central American Jews.

By the 1980s, Jews were active in civic and political life on all levels: as local councilmen and mayors, as state representatives and senators, as judges, and as U.S. representatives and senators (Richard Stone, 1974). Culturally and religiously, there were close to 200 synagogues throughout the state, 21 day schools, 5 Judaic studies programs in major universities, 10 Jewish federations, and branches of almost every national Jewish organization. Hillel Foundations were found in almost all of Florida's public and private universities. Jews were especially prominent in the hotel business, light industry, trade, tourism, entertainment, commerce, and the scientific community at the space center at Cape Canaveral.

ABRAHAM GITTELSON

BIBLIOGRAPHY

American Jewish Yearbook, 1990. Philadelphia: Jewish Publication Society, 1991.

Adler, Joseph Gary. "Moses Elias Levy and Attempts to Colonize Florida." In *Jews of the South*, edited by Samuel Proctor and Louis Schmier. Macon, Ga.: Mercer University Press, 1984.

Green, Henry. *Mosaic: Jewish Life in Florida*. Central Agency for Jewish Education, Jewish Community Center of Greater Fort Lauderdale. Coral Gables: Jewish Studies Program, University of Miami, 1986.

Sheskin, Ira, ed. "Florida Jewish Demography." Vol. 4, No. 1. December 1990. Geography Department, University of Miami.

Tebeau, Charlton W. *Synagogue in the Central City: Temple Israel of Greater Miami, 1922–1972*. Coral Gables, Fla.: University of Miami Press, 1972.

Fortas, Abe (1910–1982). Abe Fortas was born in Tennessee. His immigrant parents provided an Orthodox Jewish home for their youngest child in the poorest Jewish neighborhood in Memphis. Fortas completed high school in three years, graduating at the age of 15 with the highest honors. Insufficient funds would have denied him a college education except for the generosity of a local rabbi, Hardwig Perez, who set up a $10,000 scholarship to aid a poor Jewish boy to attend Southwestern University. It did not concern the rabbi that Southwestern was a Presbyterian college, and Fortas was the first to receive the award.

Fortas matriculated at Southwestern in 1926, one of six Jews in a student body of 500. The academic program included mandatory religious instruction at daily chapel service which he refused to participate in and for this reason Fortas found social acceptance difficult. At 19, however, Fortas graduated earning highest honors in English and economics.

He entered Yale in 1930 as the youngest member in the law school. He was the editor-in-chief of the *Yale Law Journal*. The faculty was so impressed with Fortas that they awarded him a $500 scholarship for graduate work so he could join the staff as a professor of law.

Fortas taught at Yale from 1933 to 1937, but during summer recesses, with the encouragement and influence of his professor and mentor, William O. Douglas, he worked at a variety of New Deal posts in Washington, D.C.: Agricultural Adjustment Administration, Securities and Exchange Commission, and the Public Works Administration. His work was admired by Interior Secretary Harold Ickes, who suggested to President Roosevelt that Fortas be named undersecretary of the Interior. Roosevelt had reservations about appointing another Jew to a powerful position, but Ickes convinced Roosevelt that Fortas did not possess what he thought were irritating Jewish characteristics and his ability was needed. Fortas worked full time for the government until 1946.

He then entered private practice with the firm of Arnold, Fortas and Porter in Washington, where he represented big business as well as poor criminals for free. He defended political dissenter Owen Lattimore, who was accused by Senator Joseph McCarthy of being a Russian spy, on a pro bono basis. The case cost the firm $30,000. In 1948, attorney Fortas met Lyndon Baines Johnson, who was having difficulty keeping his name on the Texas ballot for Senate due to irregularities. Fortas came to Johnson's legal rescue and saved his political life. The two became friends, and Johnson did not forget his friends.

When President, Johnson wanted Fortas on the Supreme Court although there was no vacancy. Johnson pressured Justice Arthur Goldberg to vacate his seat by offering him the ambassador's post to the United Nations as a possible stepping stone to the vice-presidency. Goldberg accepted the post, and Fortas was nominated and immediately confirmed by the Senate in 1965. The Supreme Court vacancy filled by Fortas was generally viewed as the "Jewish seat" and was previously held by Brandeis, Cardozo, Frankfurter, and Goldberg.

During his four years on the Supreme Court, Fortas supported liberal decisions regarding censorship, racial discrimination, rights for political dissenters, and separation of church and state, but he quickly realized the Supreme Court was not for him. He preferred the quick pace of his law practice and the exciting social life that Washington offered. As a justice, Fortas found that people avoided his company and were afraid to be open and candid because of his position. This sterile environment led Fortas to Louis Wolfson and the Wolfson Family Foundation, a philanthropic organization. Fortas offered Wolfson his consultant services for $20,000 a year, which would be in addition to his $39,000 salary as a justice. Problems were inherent in this decision. It seemed unethical for a justice to accept payment from an outside interest; it could jeopardize his objectivity. More importantly, Wolfson's unsound financial practices were being scrutinized by the Securities Exchange Commission. When Chief Justice Earl Warren announced his retirement, the Senate refused to confirm Fortas as chief justice because of his association with Wolfson and his continued close relationship with Johnson as political adviser while serving as a justice. Fortas resigned from the Court on May 15, 1969.

Fortas returned to private law practice until his death. As a lawyer, his career was brilliant, but Fortas could not carry that success to the Supreme Court. It was there he lacked the understanding of the strict ethical code that all justices must adhere to for successful membership in the Supreme Court. *See also* Law and Lawyers.

SHERRY OSTROFF

BIBLIOGRAPHY
Kalman, Laura. *Abe Fortas: A Biography*. New Haven, Conn.: Yale University Press, 1990.
Murphy, Bruce Allen. *Fortas: The Rise and Ruin of a Supreme Court Justice*. New York: Morrow, 1988.

Forward, The. *See* JEWISH DAILY FORWARD.

Frank *Case, The.* Leo Frank, born in Texas in 1884 and reared in New York City, was accused and convicted of murdering a 13-year-old girl in his pencil factory in Atlanta in 1913. The murder occurred on April 26, 1913—Confederate Memorial Day—and the trial took place in July and August. The girl's body had been brutally assaulted, and the state's main witness, a black janitor in the factory, so convincingly told a preposterous tale as to how it occurred that the jurors found the defendant guilty. Moreover, newspaper accounts and statements from the police and the prosecuting attorneys in the weeks before the trial began convinced the public that Frank had indeed been the culprit.

Subsequent analyses showed conclusively that Frank could not possibly have been guilty of the crime, but his defense attorneys—reputedly the best in the South at that time—made many blunders. Thus, as every tribunal to which the case was brought on appeal, and that included the Georgia and the United States Supreme Courts, refused to sanction a new trial, the public became increasingly sure of his guilt.

Frank was also badly served by national publicity. His friends in Atlanta were convinced that he had been victimized by anti-Semitism—and there is no denying that it had been a factor in his arrest and conviction—and they sought aid from coreligionists in the North. Northern Jews provided financial and legal assistance for appeals and stimulated newspaper and public awareness of Frank's plight. In Georgia, however, the national attention was seen as Jewish interference, and a state campaign emerged, led by former Populist Tom Watson, arguing that there must be the same law for the rich as well as for the poor. Watson's original forays on the subject were applauded by readers of his journals, who praised him more for his attacks on Jews than they did for his pleas on equality of individuals before the law. Picking up on what his correspondents desired, Watson became increasingly vicious in his anti-Semitic condemnations.

By the time that the United States Supreme Court turned down Frank's last appeal, in May 1915, Watson's columns had made significant impressions in Georgia. The state governor, John M. Slaton, who received the plea for commutation, had to deal with both the case and the anti-Semitic hysteria that Watson had helped to foment. Slaton evaluated the evidence, concluded that Frank was innocent, but only commuted the sentence to life imprisonment because that was all that Frank's attorneys had requested.

On the prison farm where the governor sent Frank, another convict slit his throat. As he was recovering from the wound, a band of men stormed the prison, removed Frank, and drove him back to Marietta, Georgia, the hometown of the murdered girl, and lynched him.

In the 1980s, an elderly gentleman, Alonzo Mann, who had been a 13-year-old office boy in the pencil factory in 1913, came forth to say that he had seen the janitor carrying the girl's body on the day of the murder but had refrained from telling the authorities about it because the janitor had threatened to kill him if he revealed what he had seen. Mann's evidence led to a reexamination of the case by the Georgia Board of Pardons, which recommended a posthumous pardon for Frank in 1985.

LEONARD DINNERSTEIN

BIBLIOGRAPHY
Dinnerstein, Leonard. *The Leo Frank Case*. New York: Columbia University Press, 1968.

Frankfurter, Felix (1882–1965). Supreme Court Justice and educator Felix Frankfurter was born in Vienna, Austria, to a family with a strong religious background and a 300-year rabbinical history. The anti-Semitic climate of Vienna propelled the Frankfurter family to immigrate to the United States in 1894, where they settled in New York City.

Problems with language and prejudice did not deter Frankfurter from success in his educational pursuits. He graduated third in his class from City College of New York in 1902. In 1906, he graduated from Harvard Law School with highest honors.

After a few months in private practice, Frankfurter joined the office of the U.S. Attorney Henry Stimson in the Southern District of New York. The primary concern for Stimson and Assistant U.S. Attorney Frankfurter was a trust-busting campaign ordered by President Theodore Roosevelt. Frankfurter aided Stimson in this capacity from 1906 to 1910 and was involved in legal action against the New York Central Railroad and American Sugar Refining Company. When Stimson returned to Washington, Frankfurter followed, taking on the position of law officer in the Bureau of Insular Affairs; he served in this capacity until 1914. The personal satisfaction he gained by his work for the public interest influenced Frankfurter to remain in the government's employ or to teach law. He never returned to private practice.

In 1914, Frankfurter was invited to teach at Harvard Law School. Louis Brandeis, convinced that Frankfurter would be a gifted teacher, offered a monetary contribution to Harvard so Frankfurter could be paid more than the average salary for law professors.

While at Harvard, where he remained until 1939, Frankfurter became involved in many current issues of the day. During World War I he was chairman of the War Labor Policies Board and at the end of the war attended the Paris Peace Conference at the request of Justice Brandeis and others. His mission was to present the Zionist cause to the peacemakers, including President Wilson, James Balfour, and Prince Feisel, the representative for the Arab people.

In 1927, Frankfurter gained national fame when questioning the fairness of the Sacco-Vanzetti trial and the subsequent robbery-murder conviction and death sentence in Massachusetts. Frankfurter claimed the conviction of Nicola Sacco and Bartolemeo Vanzetti was prejudiced due to their immigrant background and the heightened fear caused by the Red Scare of the 1920s. Frankfurter published his views on the case even though his liberalism on this issue risked his position at Harvard. Frankfurter also became

involved in the Scopes trial. He was a founder of the American Civil Liberties Union (ACLU) and served as legal adviser to the National Association for the Advancement of Colored People. In addition, he wrote books on constitutional and administrative law, including *The Commerce Clause Under Marshall, Taney and Waite* (1937).

Frankfurter joined President Roosevelt's New Deal "brain trust," and on January 5, 1939, President Roosevelt nominated him to the Supreme Court. Twelve days later he was appointed to the seat left vacant by the death of Justice Benjamin Cardozo. Objections to his nomination included his association with the ACLU, his defense of Sacco and Vanzetti, and his Jewish background.

While on the Supreme Court, Frankfurter made numerous decisions regarding minority issues; for example, *West Virginia Board of Education v. Barnette*, concerning the refusal of Jehovah Witnesses to salute the flag, and *McCollum v. Board of Education*, which called for release-time religious instruction within the public school. Frankfurter remarked that many of his judicial decisions affecting minorities were influenced by his Jewish heritage. "One who belongs to the most vilified and persecuted minority in history is not likely to be insensible to the freedoms guaranteed by our Constitution." Frankfurter's Jewish heritage and his frustrating experience with intolerance when expounding the Zionist cause was again visible in the landmark case of group libel, *Beauharnais v. Illinois*. This involved the publication of a pamphlet with degrading information about the black race. Frankfurter wrote the opinion of the Court and declared that protection for minority groups was essential.

Frankfurter was raised in an observant Jewish family, but he found himself unable to join in religious worship in good conscience. He claimed that the prayers and synagogue service were no longer meaningful for him, and after his college years he never attended service again. Frankfurter described himself as a "reverent agnostic." Although he divorced himself from the religious side of his heritage, he remained faithful in representing the Jewish cause. He consistently pursued Zionism in the wake of World War I and the tragic events unfolding with the rise of Adolf Hitler. He tried to make Americans aware of Nazi atrocities in the hope that this knowledge would prompt the American government to act against Germany.

After a series of strokes, Frankfurter retired

from the Supreme Court in 1962. A year later he was awarded the Presidential Medal of Freedom with Special Distinction.

Many authorities consider Frankfurter as one of the finest Supreme Court justices in American judicial history, because of his relentless pursuit of equal protection under the law for all minorities. *See also* Law and Lawyers.

SHERRY OSTROFF
HOWARD SHAKER

BIBLIOGRAPHY

Burt, Robert. *Two Jewish Justices: Outcasts in the Promised Land.* Berkeley: University of California Press, 1988.

Frankfurter, Felix. *Felix Frankfurter Reminisces.* New York: Reynal, 1960.

Simon, James F. *The Antagonists: Hugo Black, Felix Frankfurter and Civil Liberties in Modern America.* New York: Simon & Schuster, 1989.

Friedlaender, Israel (1876–1920).

Judaic scholar, communal figure, and Zionist leader, Israel Friedlaender was born into a middle-class family and raised in Praga-Warsaw in a traditional, yet enlightened home. Early on, he displayed prodigious command of the classical Jewish texts and mastery of German language and literature. Pursuing modern scholarship in Berlin, he enrolled in both the Hildesheimer Rabbinical Seminar, where he studied Bible with David Hoffmann, and the University of Berlin, where he studied Semitics and philosophy with Julius Wellhausen, Franz Julius Delitzsch, and Wilhelm Windelband. He transferred to Strasbourg to take his doctorate in medieval Islamic studies with Theodor Noeldeke and to initiate new scholarly projects, which he would complete in the United States, for, despite Noeldeke's encouragement, he realized that as a Jew he was unlikely to secure a permanent academic post in Europe. In 1903, at age 27, he became professor of biblical literature and exegesis at the Jewish Theological Seminary, newly reorganized under Solomon Schechter.

As a Bible scholar, Friedlaender cherished traditional Jewish exegesis even as he utilized the newer tools of archaeology and contemporary philology to place ancient Israel in its Near Eastern matrix. He also presented the Bible as the primary textbook of modern spiritual Zionism. His scholarly expertise lay, however, in the field of medieval Semitic philology and history. His dissertation on Maimonides's *Guide to the Per-*

plexed was followed by several important studies of Jewish and Moslem heterodoxy and messianic movements. His *Khadirlegende* was a pioneering study in the field of comparative religion.

Renowned as a distinguished scholar and an inspiring teacher, Friedlaender was also a communal activist, a founder and trustee of many organizations, including the Menorah Society, Young Judea, Young Israel, the Achavah Club, and the New York Kehillah and its constituent body, the Bureau of Jewish Education. For these and other groups he served as spokesman and guide, not only setting forth reasons for their establishment, but also nurturing them through difficult formative years. To pursue his overarching objective of Jewish renewal in America, Friedlaender wrote many essays that appeared in the Jewish and general press and lectured before lay audiences in New York and many other cities. His well-honed English translations and summaries of the ideas of Ahad Ha'am and Simon Dubnow brought these important figures to the attention of the American Jewish public. With great eloquence he presented the ideas of Historical (Conservative) Judaism to lay and rabbinic audiences.

A prominent leader of the early American Zionist Movement (the Federation of American Zionists and the World War I Provisional Executive Committee for General Zionist Affairs), Friedlaender also produced works defending Zionist principles. For this he was rewarded with an appointment to the American Red Cross wartime commission to Palestine in 1918. On the eve of his departure he was inexplicably compelled to resign. In compensation, he was sent on an American Jewish Joint Distribution Committee rescue mission to the Ukraine. There, on July 5, 1920, Friedlaender was murdered, acquiring through a martyr's death the universal recognition that had eluded him in life.

BAILA R. SHARGEL

BIBLIOGRAPHY

Die Chadirlegende und der Alexanderroman: Eine Sagengeschichtliche und Literarhistorische Untersuchung. Leipzig and Berlin: Teubner, 1913.

Cohen, Boaz. *Israel Friedlaender: A Bibliography of His Works with an Appreciation.* New York: Moinester, 1936.

Dubnow, Simon. *History of the Jews in Russia and Poland, from the Earliest Times Until the Present Day.* 3 vols. Philadelphia: Jewish Publication Society, 1916, 1918, 1920.

Friedlaender, Lillian. "A Chassid's Service to American

Judaism: The Work of Israel Friedlaender."
Menorah Journal 6 (December 1920): 337–344.

Magnes, Judah. "Friedlaender the Student: The Work of
Israel Friedlaender." *Menorah Journal* 6 (December
1920): 351–354.

Marx, Alexander. *Essays in Jewish Biography*. Philadelphia: Jewish Publication Society, 1947.

———. "Friedlaender the Scholar: The Work of Israel
Friedlaender." *Menorah Journal* 6 (December 1920):
344–350.

Past and Present: A Collection of Jewish Essays. 1st ed.
Cincinnati: Ark Publishing, 1919.

Past and Present: A Collection of Jewish Essays. 2nd ed.
New York: Burning Bush Press, 1961. (Some dele-
tions from 1st ed.)

Shargel, Baila R. *Practical Dreamer, Israel Friedlaender
and the Shaping of American Judaism*. New York:
Jewish Theological Seminary, 1985.

Friedman, Milton. (b. 1912). A leading American economist, Milton Friedman was born in New
York City. He received his undergraduate education at Rutgers University and did graduate work
at Chicago and Columbia universities. Prior to
1946, he held several positions either in research
or short-term teaching. In that year he joined the
University of Chicago, where he remained until
his retirement as professor emeritus in 1983. He
then went to the Hoover Institution on the campus of Stanford University. While a member of
the economics department at Chicago, known for
its conservative leanings, Friedman became the
recognized and influential leader of the Chicago
School, which supported conservative or old-time
liberal thought, and a leader of such thought in
general. He was elected president of the American
Economic Association in 1967 and received the
Nobel Prize in Economic Science in 1976. In
1981 he was appointed to President Reagan's
Economic Advisory Board.

Monetarism and attachment to laissez faire
are the key words for the interpretation of Friedman's economic thought. John M. Keynes had
considered income and expenditure the relevant
variables in the economy without neglecting that
"money matters." Friedman rejected Keynes's
approach and instead made monetary variables
the central element in the economy. He proposed
to revive the old-established quantity theory of
money, which Jean Bodin had formulated in the
sixteenth century but which had been discredited
and pushed into the background by more recent
developments in economic theory. The quantity

theory, in its crudest form, relates changes in the
quantity of money to changes in the price level; as
the quantity of money changes, so does the price
level. In Friedman's form of monetarism, changes
in the quantity of money are not to be left to the
whims of monetary authorities but are to occur
automatically in accord with certain rules or formulas. This leads directly to Friedman's laissez-
faire views, which makes him suspicious of and
hostile to public policies that interfere with the
operation of ostensibly free markets. Practical policy proposals that Friedman endorsed include a
voucher system that parents could use for the payment of tuition to a school of their choice, a negative income tax that would guarantee everybody a
minimum income, floating exchange rates, and the
replacement of the draft by a voluntary army.

Among Friedman's contributions to general
economics are studies in economic method and a
refined version of the consumption function. He
also wrote the authoritative monetary history of
the United States and in his younger years did
distinguished empirical work. His views on
money and laissez faire, however, are highly controversial. He popularized them in widely read
columns of news weeklies.

HENRY W. SPIEGEL

BIBLIOGRAPHY

Friedman, Milton. *Capitalism and Freedom*. Chicago:
University of Chicago Press, 1962.

———. *Essays in Positive Economics*. Chicago: University of Chicago Press, 1953.

———. *A Program for Monetary Stability*. New York:
Fordham University Press, 1959.

———. *A Theory of the Consumption Function*. Princeton, N.J.: Princeton University Press, 1957.

———. *There's No Such Thing as a Free Lunch*. 1st ed.
LaSalle, Ill.: Open Court, 1974.

———, and Friedman, Rose. *Free to Choose: A Personal
Statement*. New York: Harcourt Brace Jovanovich,
1980.

———, and Kuznets, Simon. *Income from Independent
Professional Practice*. New York: National Bureau of
Economic Research, 1945.

———, and Schwartz, Anna J. *A Monetary History of the
United States 1867–1960*. Princeton, N.J.: Princeton University Press, 1963.

Gordon, Robert J., ed. *Milton Friedman's Monetary
Framework: A Debate with His Critics*. Chicago:
University of Chicago Press, 1974.

Spiegel, Henry W., and Samuels, Warren J., eds.
Contemporary Economists in Perspective. 2 vols.
Greenwich, Conn.: JAI Press, 1984.

G

Galveston Plan. The mass migration of Jews from Russia at the turn of twentieth century, as a result of the czar's anti-Semitic policy, contributed to overcrowding in the Jewish ghettos of the major eastern seaboard cities. Many of New York City's prominent "uptown" German Jews were concerned about growing negative stereotyping of Jews as a result of the congestion and the rising crime statistics among the newly arrived Russian Jews. This soon led to the establishment of the short-lived Kehillah Experiment. There were also concerns about proposals in Congress to limit immigration by imposing a head tax, requiring a certificate of character from the country of origin, and administering a literary test.

Jacob Schiff, a wealthy New York banker, who had led the fight against legislative attempts to limit immigration, went to London to meet with Israel Zangwill, a Polish Zionist who had settled in England. Zangwill proposed that Schiff buy up large tracts of land in the South and West of the United States to create a Jewish National homeland. Schiff, an anti-Zionist, adamantly refused to accept Zangwill's proposal.

There was, however, an alternate strategy that became known as the "Galveston Plan." The idea was to divert Jewish immigrants from the eastern seaboard and use Galveston, Texas, as a port of entry. If San Francisco or San Diego were used as an entry port, the same situation would arise that existed in New York. Galveston was selected because it had little to offer as a permanent home; it did however have a rabbi.

Rabbi Henry Cohen was a schoolmate of Israel Zangwill and a "circuit-riding rabbi" to about 12,000 Jews in Texas. The plan was proposed to Rabbi Cohen, and he agreed to support it wholeheartedly.

Morris Waldman, sent by the Industrial Removal Office, an offshoot of the Jewish Agricultural Society, arrived in Galveston to establish the headquarters of the Jewish Immigrants Information Bureau (JIIB), which was totally funded by Jacob Schiff. Waldman's primary objective was to locate employers in the Southwest and Midwest who would hire newly arrived immigrants. He met with Rabbi Cohen and set up a headquarters office.

In Europe, Israel Zangwill began to funnel Jewish immigrants from Eastern Europe to the North German Lloyd Line steamers he had chartered for Galveston. The first steamer arrived in Galveston in July 1907 carrying 60 Russian Jewish families. Rabbi Cohen and the mayor of Galveston met them as they disembarked. They were given a hot meal and a bath, then presented with train tickets, and JIIB certificates that identified them as "an object of charity." This entitled the immigrants to reduced train fare rates. The immigrants were then sent on their way to inland communities where jobs were waiting for them.

The Galveston Plan attempted to ease the congestion of the eastern ghettos and extend the total area of Jewish settlement. The plan also promised respectable jobs and a wholesome atmosphere in which to live. There was also a provision to subsidize farmlands for Jewish farmers in an effort to redirect immigrants from the needle trades in the cities.

The plan did not live up to expectations and was only nominally successful. The great majority of the Russian Jewish immigrants still came into the United States at Ellis Island and continued to crowd the Eastern seaboard ghettos.

RICHARD K. GERLITZKI

BIBLIOGRAPHY

Manners, Ande. *Poor Cousins*. New York: Coward, McCann & Geoghegan, 1972.

Margolis, Max L., and Marx, Alexander. *A History of the Jewish People*. Philadelphia: Jewish Publication Society, 1947.

Roth, Cecil. *A History of the Jews*. Rev. ed. New York: Schocken, 1970.

Urofsky, Melvin. *American Zionism From Herzl to the Holocaust*. New York: Anchor Press, 1975.

Genealogy. Beginning with the earliest Jewish traditions, interest in genealogy has continued throughout history. Today, in Jewish communities throughout the world, tracing family roots has become a popular as well as a scholarly pursuit.

The listing of "family trees" dates back to the Bible. For example, Bereshit, *Genesis*, the first book of the Torah, contains extended sections of family listings, and there are numerous classical commentaries on the significance of these genealogies. For the *kohanim*, the priests of Israel, a detailed genealogical list was maintained in the Temple in Jerusalem, which recorded genealogical information on all priestly families; even the *kohanim* who lived in the diaspora provided the genealogical center in Jerusalem with full details of their marriages and offspring (Josephus, *Against Apion*, 1:7).

A priestly tribunal, which convened in a special room in the Temple, was responsible for maintaining the genealogical lists and the verification of genealogical data. The tribunal functioned in accordance with established rules and based its findings on the evidence of witnesses and genealogical documents. One such rule, followed in the Second Temple period, was that families who traditionally performed certain priestly functions were beyond suspicion and their purity of descent required no further examination (*Mishnah Quiddushin* 4:4–5; *Sanhedrin* 4:2; *Arakhin* 2:4).

What began as history in the Bible continued to the present day in our own recorded experiences. Through the pursuit of genealogy in modern times and the charting of generations, we come to the realization that we are links in a great chain that unites the past with the present, as well as the future.

The twentieth century witnessed several massive migrations of Jews. In the early decades of this century, large numbers came from Eastern Europe to America. After World I, significant numbers of European Jews migrated to Palestine. Just prior to and during the Holocaust years, thousands of Jews escaped the Nazi reign of terror in Europe to seek refuge in any country that would accept them, significantly enlarging several Latin American Jewish communities, especially in Mexico, Brazil, Argentina, and Venezuela. Immediately after World War II, many survivors of the death camps made their way to America and Israel. Others, who were unable or unwilling to return to the destroyed communities of Eastern Europe, settled in various communities around the world. There have also been significant postwar migrations of Jews to North America from Eastern European countries, such as Poland, Romania, and the Soviet Union.

With the passage of time, more and more descendants of those modern Jewish migrations have begun to explore their "roots" in an effort to discover and preserve their family history and cultural heritage. For many of these family historians, it is already too late to interview immigrant members of the family.

Interest in "roots" reached a peak at the time of the bicentennial celebrations in 1976, which coincided with the televised version of Alex Haley's book *Roots* (about a black American's search for his roots dating back to a slave from Africa). Genealogical societies were inundated with inquiries from thousands of Americans. To date, the obsession shows no sign of abating.

The motivation for starting a family history comes from a variety of influences. First, there is simply an inquisitive desire to know about themselves. Jewish genealogists and family historians are a growing number of individuals who have recognized the importance as well as the enjoyment of tracing their family history.

Traditionally, genealogists compile a chart of ancestors' names and dates in chronological order, generation by generation. However, the volume of data is far less important than gaining an understanding of who our ancestors were, how they lived their lives, historical events that shaped their decisions, and the legacy to be passed to future generations.

The first step in exploring family history is to conduct interviews with older family members.

These oral histories can be used to chart the "family tree," and as more information is obtained, it can be expanded back through the generations to include, in some cases, thousands of names and their relationships. These interviews are commonly recorded on cassette or video tape, which give the older family members the opportunity to share their own personal experiences of Jewish life and traditions in the "Old Country" and to record their memories. Key questions explored in such interviews are original family names and their origin, location of the family's ancestral town(s), and the existence of family documents and photographs.

Following family interviews, the focus of family historians should be to work back into history in order to develop a broad picture of the life and times of their ancestors. An awareness of the important events of the era in which they lived, such as compulsory military service and the pogroms in Eastern Europe, makes it possible to understand why millions were driven to leave their homes and family members to begin new lives in foreign lands.

The surname, or family name, may reveal the origin of ancestral towns, a trade or profession, the father or mother's name, physical traits, or other characteristics. Family names indicate the country of origin and national ethnology, i.e., Ashkenazi, Sephardi, and Kurdi. In addition, it is not uncommon to discover several different names for the same individual: a Hebrew name, an English name, and a Yiddish name. The use of nicknames and "Yiddishizing" was also common.

For many generations, it has been an Ashkenazi tradition to name a child after a deceased member of the family or a respected member of the community (deceased), such as a teacher or *rebbe*. Sephardim to this day name the oldest son after his paternal grandfather and the oldest daughter after her paternal grandmother, whether deceased or living.

A civil license was not required for the religious marriage ceremony; therefore, many marriages were not registered with civil authorities. In certain circumstances, children assumed their maternal surname without registration and, as a result, are difficult to trace.

Within the last century, special circumstances have developed that make tracing family origins even more difficult. It is not unusual for parents, grandparents, and children in Western countries to live far apart from one another with visits among them relatively rare.

The continuing border changes in Europe due to various wars make it difficult to determine which government currently maintains the vital statistics and other records. When the borders shifted, the language changed and along with it, the geographic names and frequently the location of the records. Documents and reference material appear in many different languages and dialects, some no longer used and difficult to read. The pronunciation of town names varies greatly from conventional spelling with similar-sounding names all located within the same country. Russian archival records have previously been inaccessible to the public, thereby frustrating researchers with Russian roots; however, cooperative efforts between the National Archive of Washington, D.C., and the Soviet Archives have led to an agreement signed in 1990 that established a procedure for processing genealogical research requests in the Soviet Union. Implementation of the agreement, however, has since been put indefinitely "on hold."

PUBLIC RECORDS AND OTHER DOCUMENTS. Nevertheless, surviving public records, archival material, individual and organizational records, and a growing number of published genealogical aids, along with modern technology, make it possible for almost anyone to trace his or her family history back through the generations.

Government offices, libraries, and archives in the United States yield such public documents as naturalization records, ship manifests and photos, city directory listings, census records, voter registration applications, World War I draft registrations, and birth, marriage and death records. With some restrictions, copies of old insurance policies and medical and school records can also be obtained.

Although names frequently changed during the immigration process and thereafter, it is still possible to identify the original family name through existing civil records. For example, the "first papers" (Declaration of Intention to Become a Citizen) of Morris Weiner, the author's paternal grandfather, revealed his date and place of birth, physical description and occupation, date and port of arrival to the United States, name of ship, name, date, and place of birth of his wife. His subsequent "Petition for Naturalization" included a photo and a vital piece of information. In his response to the question "Under what name did you enter this country?" his answer was "Moische Winikur," thereby revealing his name in the Old Country. These documents are available from the court where naturalization occurred (or where transferred for storage) or from the Immigration and Naturalization Service in Washington, D.C.

The National Archives in Washington, D.C., is the largest repository of ship passenger records, census and military records, visa and passport applications, Russian consular records (many dealing with visa applications for Jews), documents relating to the Holocaust, including the Nuremberg files, and a wealth of other information.

All of these documents and records form a chronology of the lives of our ancestors and at the same time weave a unique pattern that expands the knowledge of our Jewish heritage.

Although genealogies have been recorded on an individual basis for centuries, the comparatively recent phenomenon of organized Jewish genealogy owes its origin and a great debt to Rabbi Malcolm H. Stern, a guiding light to those who want to know more about their roots. In Stern's *First American Jewish Families* (1978, 1991), virtually every Jewish family established in the United States by 1840 is traced, where possible, to the present. Additionally, Stern has counseled countless family historians through his lectures, correspondence, and continuing leadership in Jewish genealogy societies worldwide.

Rapidly expanding interest has spurred the growth of Jewish genealogy societies in Canada, England, France, Holland, Israel, Switzerland, and 35 to date in the United States. Over 90 Anglo-Jewish newspapers in North America regularly publish columns on Jewish genealogy. Furthermore, lectures and courses on Jewish family history are offered widely by educational institutions and community-sponsored adult education programs.

One of the major contributions of Jewish genealogical societies has been the sponsorship of publications to aid researchers. For example, a comprehensive publication, *Genealogical Resources in the New York Metropolitan Area*, published by the Jewish Genealogical Society, Inc., in New York, includes detailed descriptions of resources and finding aids in 52 government agencies and courts, 32 libraries, and 20 archives. Each year, a national conference is hosted by a local Jewish Genealogical Society offering seminars, visits to research sites, and access to newly discovered sources.

Computers have opened up access to records that were previously difficult to identify and locate. Another outgrowth of organized Jewish ge-

nealogical research is a computerized index of ancestral names and geographic locations called the "Jewish Genealogical Family Finder." This database links people throughout the world who are seeking information about their ancestors and ancestral towns. It contains over 12,000 entries from more than 1000 contributors. Family and town names that sound alike are grouped together, such as Auerbach, Ohrback, and Uhrback or Vilna, Wilno, and Vilnius, a practical solution to the problems caused by spelling variations. The Family Finder combines the names under a unique system called the Daitch-Mokotoff Soundex Code. To date, there have been hundreds of exact matches among the submitted entries.

RABBINIC SOURCES. Researching rabbinic genealogy is much more than documenting "who begat whom." It is the study of Jewish history by following the lives of generations of teachers, sages, and leaders of the Jewish people throughout the ages. In some rabbinic families, there are as many as 20 generations of scholars, outstanding men and women who persevered physically and spiritually in spite of persecution, repression, expulsion, and ultimately the Holocaust.

Important references include:

Encyclopedia Judaica (Jerusalem: Encyclopedia Judaica, 1972). Biographies and genealogies.

Friedberg, Bernhard, *Bet Eked Sepharim Bibliographical Lexicon* (Tel Aviv: Ha-Mimkhar ha-rashi; M. A. Bar-Yoda, 1951) 4 vols. Massive bibliography of rabbinic literature from 1474 to 1950.

Friedmann, Nathan Zvi, *Otzar Harabinim. Rabbis' Encyclopedia* (Bnei-Brak, Israel: Agudat Otzar ha-Rabinim, 1975). Biographical directory of 20,000 rabbis from the year 970 to 1970.

Gottlieb, Scholom Noah, *Ohole-Schem* (Pinsk: M. M. Glauberman). Directory, including addresses, of rabbis throughout the world to 1912.

Halperin, Raphael, *Atlas Eytz Chayim* (Tel Aviv: Department of Surveys, 1978). Includes a series of 70 chronological and genealogical tables, diagrams, maps, and illustrations for more than 2000 rabbis and scholars from 940 to 1492.

Rosenstein, Emanuel, and Rosenstein, Neil, *Latter Day Leaders, Sages and Scholars: Bibliographical Index* (Elizabeth, N.J.: Computer Center for Jewish Genealogy, 1983).

Rosenstein, Neil, *The Unbroken Chain: Biographi-*

cal Sketches and the Genealogy of Illustrious Jewish Families From the 15th–20th Century (Elizabeth, N.J.: Computer Center for Jewish Genealogy, 1990). 2 vols.

Wunder, Meir, *Meorei Galicia [Encyclopedia of Galician Rabbis and Scholars]* (Jerusalem: Institute for Commemoration of Galician Jewry, 1977–1986). 3 vols.

TOMBSTONE AND CEMETERY RECORDS.

Jewish heritage is reflected in gravestones all over the world dating from the seventeenth century. Tombstones make biographical and historical statements as they reflect family life. In the seventeenth, eighteenth, and nineteenth centuries, the tombstone was very symbolic and included more information than the name and date of death. Often a description of a man's life, his occupation, his town, and other interesting items were included. A woman's tombstone would include such information as name, date, mother/wife, name of father, the words "a woman of valor," and a symbol.

Until the twentieth century, tombstones were written mainly in Hebrew and sometimes in Yiddish. The trend in twentieth-century America is to have bilingual or all English inscriptions, giving an impersonal characterization to the stone. One might see only the word *mother* or *father* with no names or simplified versions of what used to be documentation. There may be a headstone with only a family name and an abbreviated version on a footstone with very little information.

Various symbols have been used over the years. Among them are a pitcher or jug (Levite), blessing hands (Kohen), books or an open book (a learned man or author), an ark with Torah (a rabbinic authority), menorah (female), and a Star of David (male). In some cemeteries, children are buried in a separate section and the symbolism used might be a lamb, a broken tree trunk, or a bed. Animals usually stand for a name: dove (Jonah), bear (Dov), lion (Aryeh, Judah, Leo), fish (Fischel), eagle (Adler), rooster (Hahn). Other symbols include birds (soul), broken lilies (young child), broken candle (early death).

Cemetery records are among the most important genealogical sources. In addition to the valuable data found on tombstone inscriptions, mortuary records, obituaries, and governmental archives for military burials should not be overlooked. Some sources for mortuary names are death certificates, synagogue or burial society records, family interviews, cemetery records, newspaper clippings, and a listing of mortuaries near "the old neighborhood" in the local telephone directory. Mortician's records are indexed in several ways: some by last name, others by date of death, and still others by burial plot.

YIZKOR BOOKS (Memorial Volumes). For survivors of the Holocaust, precious family photos and documents were left behind and ultimately lost forever. Therefore, for both survivors and family historians, a book devoted to the history of an ancestral town can lead to a deeper understanding of the period in which their forebears lived and, in many cases, direct information about family members. Following the tragedy and devastation of the Holocaust, various towns and *shtetlach*, primarily in Poland, but also in Germany, Russia, Hungary, Romania, and Czechoslovakia, were memorialized in *yizker bikher*, the memorial volumes written by survivors and immigrants.

Most of the books are about one community, but some include the surrounding towns as well.

Written by people from all walks of life, these first-person accounts document people, places, and events. The selections describe entire Jewish communities that no longer exist and are written with warmth in the words of those who remember them most vividly.

Each memorial book generally begins with the history of the community up to the Holocaust and includes its Jewish institutions as well as stories about the residents, memoirs, and, in many cases, lists of those who perished and those who survived. Many volumes contain maps and photos of people and places. Memorial books are written in Hebrew and Yiddish, although some have an English section. Few include a name index.

In *From a Ruined Garden* (New York: Schocken, 1981), editors Jack Kugelmass and Jonathan Boyarin recapture the lost world of Polish Jewry as represented in selections from over 100 Yiddish memorial volumes, available for the first time in English. The book's appendices include a geographical index and a comprehensive bibliography of memorial books, compiled by Zachary Baker, librarian at the YIVO Institute in New York.

The largest collection of memorial books (now over 1000 titles in print) can be found in the library at Yad Vashem in Jerusalem. In New York, extensive collections of memorial books are housed at the YIVO Institute, New York Public Library (Jewish Division), Yeshiva University, Jewish Theological Seminary, and the Bund Archives of the Jewish Labor Movement. When these books were originally published, primarily in the 1950s, they were printed in small numbers, mostly for members of landsmanshaftn societies—benevolent societies of Jewish immigrants from the same hometowns who gathered together to remember their towns and seek other community members lost during the war.

U.S. REPOSITORIES. In addition to local historical societies and public libraries, there are numerous organizations, archives, and libraries to assist researchers collecting ancestral data and historical references to ancestral towns.

American Jewish Archives, 3101 Clifton Avenue, Cincinnati, OH 45220 (part of the Hebrew Union College Jewish Institute of Religion)

Congregation histories, extensive Holocaust material from World Jewish Congress Archives, special collection of microfilm reels from other sources, over 10,000 photographs and 1500 sound recordings, thousands of published and unpublished family genealogies.

American Jewish Historical Society, 2 Thornton Road, Waltham, MA 02154 (on Brandeis University Campus)

Over 4 million items including newspapers/periodicals, photographs, Yiddish films, records of Jewish farming communities in New Jersey, Industrial Removal Office records, Hebrew Immigrant Aid Society of Boston documents, family histories and genealogies.

Association of Jewish Genealogy Societies, 1485 Teaneck Road, NJ 07666

International group representing Jewish genealogy societies worldwide. Maintains *Jewish Genealogy Family Finder*, a computer listing of ancestral surnames and place names being researched by individual genealogists. Updated frequently, with copies available at meetings of local Jewish genealogical societies. Three lists are circulated simultaneously: surnames, place names by town, connected by code number to list of individual researchers.

Family History Library, 35 Northwest Temple Street, Salt Lake City, UT 84150 (with extensive worldwide branches called "Family History Centers")

Holdings include microfilmed vital records (births, marriages, deaths) of many European Jewish communities before 1900 in Poland, France, Germany, and Hungary, indexed by present town name. To date, records have not been microfilmed in Romania or the USSR. Microfilms can be brought by request and payment of a small fee to a nearby Family History Center. The Family History Library also has extensive holdings of vital records from virtually every locality in the United States, along with city directories, passenger manifest lists, regional histories, federal and state census returns, and numerous other sources of vital interest to the family historian.

Jewish Theological Seminary, 3080 Broadway, New York, NY 10027

The largest collection of Hebraica-Judaica in the Western Hemisphere—including records of French and Moroccan Jewish communities, yizkor books and vital records of congregations, rabbinic records, communal records books from Europe, 300 Ketubot, mostly from Italy, North Africa, Egypt, Russia, and Syria.

Leo Baeck Institute, 129 East 73rd Street, New York, NY 10021

Extensive collection of Jewish records for German-speaking lands including German Jewish communal histories, biographical dictionaries, deportation lists, and genealogical resources such as circumcision and birth records, marriage and death records.

Library of Congress, Washington, DC 20540 (Local History and Genealogy, Hebraic Division, Map Division, and European Division)

Holdings include extensive collection of worldwide telephone books, yizkor books, maps/gazetteers including detailed towns plans for many Eastern European communities.

National Archives, 8th Street & Pennsylvania Avenue NW, Washington, DC 20408 (regional branches throughout the United States)

United States census (1870–1910), military records, court records, maps, passport and visa applications, index to some ship passenger lists and the Russian Consular Records collection. Also files of aerial and ground-level photos for various cities and towns in the Soviet Union.

New York Public Library, 42nd Street & Fifth Avenue, New York, NY 10018

    Jewish Division: community histories and many yizkor books.

    Map Room: extensive and detailed map collection, gazetteers and maps including pre-nineteenth-century maps of New York City.

    Microform Room: borough directories of New York City, censuses for the Greater New York area, indexes of births, marriages, and deaths in New York City, back issues of the *New York Times*.

    Local History and Genealogy: indexes to federal census records.

Yeshiva University, 2520 Amsterdam Avenue, New York, NY 10033

    Archives: collections of Orthodox Jewish institutions and individuals, records of the Central Relief Committee and rescue efforts, and biographical data on famous American Jews.

    Gottesman Library of Hebraica-Judaica: rabbinic materials, family histories, biographies, Jewish community histories, Sephardic collection, yizkor books, and data from tombstones in Jewish cemeteries.

YIVO Institute for Jewish Research, 1048 Fifth Avenue, New York, NY 10028

    Records of Jews in Yiddish-speaking lands, including yizkor books, landsmanshaftn records, rabbinic encyclopedias, extensive photo collection, HIAS immigration records, regional histories, biographies, and periodicals.

SEPHARDIC RESOURCES.
Sources for the history of Sephardic Jewry in the United States include:

Sephardic Community Center Archives, 1910 Ocean Parkway, Brooklyn, NY 11223

Jacob E. Safra Institute of Sephardic Studies, Yeshiva University, 500 West 185th Street, New York, NY 10033

American Sephardi Federation, 133 East 58th Street #404, New York, NY 10022

Spanish and Portuguese Synagogue, 8 West 70th Street, New York, NY 10023

FOREIGN REPOSITORIES.
Once an American researcher has documented his family history within the United States, it becomes necessary to utilize worldwide sources for the period of time prior to immigration to America. Among the many foreign repositories and institutions with relevant archival material and data are the following:

Archives of the Sephardi Community, Hahavazelet Street 12a, Jerusalem 91000, Israel. Extensive records representing over 80 Sephardic communities throughout the world, including correspondence and organization and congregation records dating back to the sixteenth century.

Arias Montano Institute, Duque de Medinacelli 4, Madrid 28014 Spain. Over 16,000 volumes on Sephardic history and newspaper, manuscript, and photograph collections.

Beth Hatefutsoth, (Museum of Diaspora), P.O. Box 39359, Tel Aviv University, Tel Aviv 61392 Israel. Computer registry of family names and their meanings, database of Jewish communities based upon entries from *Encyclopedia Judaica*, local histories, personal interviews, atlases/gazetteers, and other sources.

Bibliotheque et Archives de L'Alliance Israelite Universelle, 45 Rue la Bruyere, Paris 75009 France. Records dating from 1860 consisting of files of the administration of the A.I.U., photograph collections.

Central Archives for the History of the Jewish People, Hebrew University Campus, Givat Ram, P.O. Box 503, Jerusalem 91004 Israel. Surviving records from Europe and the Middle East including *pinkassim* registers, extensive collections from Germany, France, Poland, and Italy, published genealogies, and family histories.

International Tracing Service, D-3548 Arolsen, Germany. A master card index of 39,700,000 cards representing concentration camp victims, survivors, displaced persons, and inquiries.

Israel State Archives, P.O. Box 1149, Jerusalem 91919, Israel. Holdings include Turkish census, German and British consulate records, and the Mandate Citizenship Index.

Search Bureau for Missing Relatives, P.O. Box 92, Jerusalem 91920, Israel. Index to all residents of Israel, including biographical and immigration data, current address and telephone number.

Yad Vashem, P. O. Box 3477, Jerusalem 91034, Israel. Memorial to victims of the Holocaust, extensive library and archives including more than 2.5 million Pages of Testimony completed by surviving relatives and friends; largest collection of Yizkor books in the world; landsmanshaftn records; extensive collection of victim and survivor lists; thousands of eyewitness accounts from survivors indexed by family name and location.

MIRIAM WEINER

BIBLIOGRAPHY

Manuals and Source Books

Cohen, Chester G. *Shtetl Finder Gazetteer.* Bowie, Md.: Heritage Books, 1989; reprint of 1980 edition.

Grimsted, Patricia Kennedy. *Archives and Manuscript Repositories in the U.S.S.R.* Vol. I: *Moscow and Leningrad* (1972); Vol. II: *Estonia, Latvia, Lithuania and Belorussia* (1981); Vol. III: *Ukraine and Moldavia* (1989). (Princeton, N.J.: Princeton University Press).

Guzik, Estelle M., ed. *Genealogical Resources in the New York Metropolitan Area.* New York: Jewish Genealogical Society, 1989.

Kaganoff, Benzion C., *A Dictionary of Jewish Names and Their History.* New York: Schocken, 1977.

Kurzweil, Arthur. *From Generation to Generation.* New York: Schocken, 1981.

——, and Weiner, Miriam. *The Encyclopedia of Jewish Genealogy.* 5 vols. Northvale, N.J.: Aronson, 1990.

Mogilanski, Roman. *The Ghetto Anthology,* Los Angeles: American Congress of Jews from Poland and Survivors of Concentration Camps, 6534 Moore Drive, Los Angeles, CA 90048 [1985].

Rottenberg, Dan. *Finding Our Fathers: A Guidebook to Jewish Genealogy.* Baltimore: Genealogical Publishing, 1986; paperback reprint of 1977 ed.

Sack, Sallyann Amdur. *A Guide to Jewish Genealogical Research in Israel.* Baltimore: Genealogical Publishing, 1987.

——, and Wynne, Suzan Fisher. *Russian Consular Records Index and Catalog.* New York: Garland, 1987.

Stern, Malcolm H. *First American Jewish Families: 600 Genealogies, 1654–1988.* Baltimore: Ottenheimer, 1991; updates 1978 ed.

Wiesenthal, Simon. *Every Day Remembrance Day.* New York: Holt, 1987.

Yad Vashem, *Pinkas Ha-Kehillot—Romania, Hungary, Germany, Poland, Netherlands, Yugoslavia, Latvia/Estonia.* Jerusalem: Yad Vashem, 1972–1989, ongoing.

Zubatsky, David. *Jewish Genealogy: A Sourcebook of Family Histories and Genealogies.* Vol. 2. New York: Garland, 1990.

——, and Berent, Irwin M. *Jewish Genealogy: A Sourcebook of Family Histories and Genealogies.* New York: Garland, 1984.

Periodicals

Avotaynu: The International Review of Jewish Geneaology, P.O. Box 1134, Teaneck, NJ 07666. Quarterly magazine including articles from contributors worldwide.

Search: The Quarterly Journal of the Jewish Genealogical Society of Illinois, 1981–. Available by subscription from Search, P.O. Box 48102, Niles, IL 60648. Articles on methodology and dates; notable for its series of guides to research in many cities.

Genetic Disorders.

Certain genetic disorders occur at higher frequencies among the Jewish people than in the general population. The reasons why those disorders are found among specific Jewish groups are found in the history, culture and genetic makeup of the Jewish people. Some aspects of these contributing factors are understood, but many intricacies cannot be adequately explained. The majority of these disorders are autosomal recessive, i.e., both parents must be carriers of the disease-causing gene and occur at various frequencies. Most are severely incapacitating and often debilitating, leading to early death in infancy or childhood. The management, treatment, and prevention of these disorders have been greatly aided by advancements in understanding the nature of these diseases and improvements in diagnosis.

Although a few disorders or "Jewish diseases" were described in the 1880s and some of the earliest descriptions can be found in the Bible and the Talmud, the majority of these diseases have been recognized since 1960. The majority of the disorders appear in Ashkenazi Jewish communities, a group that makes up 82 percent of the world's Jewish population. The increased immigration of Oriental and Sephardic Jews into Israel since the 1950s has provided opportunities for the study of genetic disorders in these small Jewish groups. With few exceptions, the pattern of occurrence of genetic diseases in the Sephardic and Oriental Jewish communities is characterized by disorders that are also found in non-Jewish populations and that occur in individual Jewish subgroups rather than dispersed throughout the Oriental and Sephardic communities.

The seven most common disorders occurring in the Ashkenazi Jewish communities are Familial Dysautonomia, Torsion Dystonia, Gaucher disease, Mucolipidosis IV, Niemann-Pick disease, Tay-Sachs disease, and Bloom syndrome. The occurrence, characteristics, and nature of each disease will be explained, and a bibliography for further information on these diseases will be provided.

Tay-Sachs disease is the best-known Jewish genetic disease, afflicting about 1 in every 2500 Ashkenazi-Jewish newborns. It is characterized by the onset of severe mental and developmental retardation during the first 4 to 8 months of life. Basically a biochemical disorder, the disease involves the central nervous system, leading to a state of total debilitation by 2 to 5 years of age. Death usually occurs by 5 to 8. The disease is inherited as an autosomal recessive trait, and no treatment is available.

Familial Dysautonomia is a genetic disease present at birth in males and females, primarily causing dysfunction of the autonomic and sensory nervous systems. The most striking manifestations include relative indifference to pain and the inability to form tears. The disease, an autosomal recessive, so far has only occurred in Ashkenazi Jews with an incidence of 1 in 30 individuals as carriers. The cause is unknown, and there is no prenatal diagnosis or carrier identification test. The Dysautonomia Treatment and Evaluation Center at New York University Medical Center was established in 1970, and the Dysautonomia Foundation, Inc., was founded in 1951 by the parents of afflicted children.

Gaucher disease is the most prevalent Jewish genetic disease, afflicting 1 in every 2500 Ashkenazi Jews of Eastern and Central European ancestry. It is a biochemical disorder occurring in three subtypes, which are distinguished by their clinical severity, course, and neurologic complications. Patients with Type I, the most common, display a wide variety of symptoms. At present there is no specific treatment, and it is estimated that 1 in every 25 Jews is a carrier of recessive Type I Gaucher gene.

Torsion Dystonia, a disease affecting movement control, may occur as an autosomal recessive disease or be brought about from environmental causes, such as drug reaction, encephalitis, or trauma to the head. In its inherited forms, it may occur in the population at large or in Ashkenazi Jews. Approximately 1 of every 70 Jews in the United States carries the gene, and it occurs in about 1 of every 20,000 Jewish live births. Among Jews the disease generally appears between the ages of 4 and 16 and has a rapid rate of progression. It is characterized by severe motor spasms, resulting in physical incapacity while mental capabilities remain normal or even superior. Life expectancy is usually normal. At present there is no genetic screening test.

Niemann-Pick disease, also autosomal recessive, is caused by an abnormal storage of lipids and cholesterol. The first case was reported in 1914. The age at which symptoms first appear varies, but most children exhibit such symptoms as vomiting, poor feeding, abdominal protuberance, and an inability to thrive before they are 6 months old. There are various types of the disease, and the incidence is between 1 in 20,000 and 1 in 30,000 births per year in Ashkenazi Jewish communities. Recent strides have been made in controlling this disease through prenatal diagnosis and identification of carriers.

Bloom syndrome, inherited in autosomal recessive fashion, is very rare in most populations, but the carrier rate in Ashkenazi Jews is greater than 1 in 120. It was first described by Dr. David Bloom in 1954 in New York. Symptoms include small birth size, shortness of stature, and redness of the skin of the face. Victims have increased numbers of respiratory tract and ear infections. Mental ability is normal, but fertility may be reduced. The risk of cancer is also considerably greater than normal. No test is known for the carrier state, nor is there treatment for the growth restriction.

Mucolipidosis IV is the most recently recognized genetic disorder, having been first described in 1974. Only 20 patients have been diagnosed so far, and no specific therapy is available. Children with the disease are normal at birth and develop signs of central nervous system deterioration during the first year of life. Inherited as a autosomal recessive trait, the disease can be diagnosed by amniocentesis early in pregnancy.

PATRICIA LEVIN

BIBLIOGRAPHY

Adams, A. "Genetic Diseases Among Jews." *Israel Journal of Medical Science* 9 (1973):1383.

Goodman, Richard. *Genetic Disorders Among the Jewish People.* Baltimore: Johns Hopkins University Press, 1979.

Gormley, Myra Vanderpool. *Family Diseases: Are You At Risk?* Baltimore: Genealogical Publishing Company, 1989.

Tillem, Ivan L., ed. *Jewish Directory and Almanac.* New York: Pacific Press, 1985.

National Foundation for Jewish Genetic Diseases, Inc. 250 Park Avenue. New York, NY 10017. Contact for literature.

Gentleman's Agreement.

Laura Z. Hobson's 1947 novel, *Gentleman's Agreement*, is one of the few works of literature that can be said to have altered the social and moral fabric of a nation. In dealing with "polite" anti-Semitism, i.e., the restrictive practices of certain hotels and resort areas and the genteel veneer of bigotry that was taken for granted among people who might otherwise be considered enlightened—as well as *inter alia* Jewish self-hatred and the need to hide one's ethnic background—the novel struck a chord in the hearts and minds of the readers of the time. It was hailed by the *New York Times* as "brilliant." The film version won the 1947 Academy Award. Since that time, it can be said to have passed into Jewish-American folklore.

The novel recounts the efforts of a non-Jewish writer, Philip Green, to report on anti-Semitism in American society. Since Philip is new to the magazine where he works, he tells everyone, including his co-workers and society at large, that he is Jewish and thus gains firsthand experience of the myriad ways that Jews are the victims of anti-Semitism in the general workplace. But the real brunt of the novel is focused not on the more general practices of hotel clerks and the like but on the society in which Green moves, including that of the upper-class world of his fiancee. Eventually, even his son is taunted and mocked for being Jewish. Philip learns more than he bargained for. He not only writes an article that causes a furor in the circles in which he had moved, but at the risk of personal loss he rejects the "gentleman's agreement" by which prejudice and bigotry is allowed to run rife in society in general.

Despite its good intentions, the novel may strike the modern reader as somewhat disconcerting, for the novel appeared only two years after the end of World War II and no reference is made to the events in Europe in the work. For this reason alone, its themes may strike the reader as irrelevant and inconsequential.

In her autobiography, *Laura Z.: A Life*, Hobson, who is of Jewish parentage and, like her protagonist, devoted to liberal causes, discusses the roots of the novel. She mentions that she felt that the causes of the support that many pro-Nazi groups had in the United States during World War II was the result of a "longer" war that people like her were losing, the war against bigotry. In many ways, she continues, the Holocaust was "too religious" in thematic material, and she would have greater success in getting her point across if she stuck to the kind of prejudices she had encountered firsthand. This point may not be invalid, for it was not for a decade or more after the Holocaust that American-Jewish literature began to tackle this latter theme in earnest.

Hobson's argument, though, hints at a deeper problem of the novel. Not only are her conclusions too roseate and facile, but her presentation of Judaism and of her Jews lacks depth and dimension. They seem devoid of any "real" life. They are, in fact, Jews in "Protestant face," the obverse of Phil Green. It may be easy to buy her thesis that Jews are just like everyone else because "everyone else" has no real identity beyond the social manners of an era. The novel is really about "passing," denying one's essential familial or ethnic roots in order to be accepted by society. Her Jews want to be accepted because their Jewishness holds no value for them, except the pain of hatred. Rather than being accepted for their differences, they want to be accepted for their sameness. In an age that has seen the emergence of groups that have asserted their rights to be accepted notwithstanding their sexual, religious, and ethnic differences, this novel has the opposite effect. It denies the very points it should be glorifying.

MASHEY BERNSTEIN

BIBLIOGRAPHY
Hobson, Laura Z. *Gentleman's Agreement.* New York: Simon & Schuster, 1947.

Gershwin, George

(1898–1937). Perhaps no other American composer has elicited more respect, love, excitement and admiration from a music-loving public than George Gershwin. The son of Russian-Jewish immigrants, Gershwin was born in Brooklyn, New York. His father, Moshe Gershovitz, Americanized the family name to "Gershvin," which George amended to "Gershwin" after beginning his professional career. Gershwin left high school in 1914 to take a job as a song plugger—a sort of a musical salesman—for Jerome H. Remick & Company. During his three-year stint at Remick, he began composing popular songs and playing for piano rolls. In 1917, he began working as a rehearsal pianist on

Broadway and was hired by the Harms publishing company as a composer. His first hit tune, "Swanee" (1920), launched his career as a composer of popular song, and with the premiere of his *Rhapsody in Blue* for jazz band and piano (1924), he became famous as an inventive and popular force in American music. He collaborated with his brother, Ira (1896–1983), in over 10 Broadway shows (among them, *Of Thee I Sing*, *Strike up the Band*, and *Girl Crazy*), wrote individual songs for inclusion in other theatrical productions, and composed music for films.

Gershwin straddled the popular and classical styles. The *Concerto in F for Piano* (1925), *An American in Paris* (1928), *Preludes for Piano* (1923–1926), and the *Rhapsody* are four examples of his serious composition. All of Gershwin's symphonic compositions utilize popular musical elements. His magnum opus, *Porgy and Bess* (1935), was not unanimously praised at its premiere, but it has come to be recognized as a landmark American opera that helped to evidence the legitimacy of indigenous afro-american culture. It has enjoyed numerous revivals and productions throughout the world, including performances at La Scala in Milan and the Metropolitan Opera in New York. In addition to his popularity as a composer, Gershwin frequently appeared in concerts as a pianist and conductor of his own music and on nationwide radio broadcasts. He and his music were extremely popular, and the royalties that he earned allowed him to live quite lavishly. He died of a brain tumor on July 11, 1937.

Gershwin was not a practicing Jew, but he never tried to deny or hide his family origin. Indeed, he came close to writing two overtly Jewish stage works. In 1915, he was invited by the great Yiddish actor and director Boris Thomashevsky to collaborate with Sholom Secunda in the writing of a Yiddish operetta, an idea that Secunda rejected. Gershwin actually signed a contract with the Metropolitan Opera in 1929 to produce a work based on S. An-Ski's (Solomon Rapaport) play *The Dybbuk*; he even contemplated traveling to Europe to study Jewish musical practice in order to further prepare himself for this undertaking. The entire project collapsed when it became known that the rights to the play had already been assigned to the Italian composer Lodovico Rocca.

One can discern Jewish sounds in a few of Gershwin's works. His song "'S Wonderful" from the broadway show *Funny Face* (1927) has a very obvious similarity to "Noach's Teive," a song from Abraham Goldfaden's opera *Akeidas Yitzchak* (1897). Some sections of *Porgy and Bess* smack of Jewish idioms, such as the beginning of the second act. Associations between Jewish music and other Gershwin works, ranging from "My One and Only," the clarinet opening of *Rhapsody in Blue*, and the second of the Preludes for Piano, have all been suggested (*see* Schwartz, 1973). It is improbable that Gershwin used Jewish musical elements—except perhaps unconsciously—for any other reason than to add to the eclectic makeup of what, during his era, constituted American popular music. What elevated Gershwin to the top of his profession was his innate talent to reflect musically America's cultural diversity. His songs and tunes contain an enduring attractiveness and an ongoing ability to elicit various moods and emotions from a devoted and ever appreciative audience. *See also* Music, Popular.

BRIAN D. ROZEN

BIBLIOGRAPHY

Armitage, Merle. *George Gershwin: Man and Legend*. Freeport, N.Y.: Books for Libraries Press, 1970.

Chase, Gilbert. *America's Music: From the Pilgrims to the Present Day*. Urbana: University of Illinois Press, 1987.

Crawford, Richard. "George Gershwin." In *The New Grove Dictionary of American Music*, edited by H.W. Hitchcock and S. Sadie. Vol. 2. New York: Grove's Dictionary of Music, 1986. Pp. 199–211.

Ewen, David. *George Gershwin: His Journey to Greatness*. Englewood Cliffs, N.J.: Prentice-Hall, 1970.

Gershwin, George. *George Gershwin's Song Book*. New York: Simon & Schuster, 1932.

Gershwin, Ira. *Lyrics on Several Occasions*. New York: Knopf, 1959.

Jablonski, Edward. *Gershwin*. New York: Doubleday, 1987.

———, and Stewart, Lawrence D. *The Gershwin Years*. 2nd ed. Garden City, N.Y.: Doubleday, 1973.

Kimball, Robert, and Simon, Alfred. *The Gershwins*. New York: Atheneum, 1973.

Schwartz, Charles. *Gershwin: His Life and Music*. Indianapolis: Bobbs-Merrill, 1973.

Ginzberg, Louis (1873–1953).

Ginzberg, Louis (1873–1953). The preeminent American Talmudist of the early twentieth century, Louis Ginzberg was born in Kovno into a family of illustrious Lithuanian scholars. He studied at the Slobodka and Telshe yeshivas. He left Lithuania to pursue modern scholarship, concentrating in Semitics, Assyriology, and philosophy at the Universities of Berlin, Strassburg, and Heidelberg. After receiving his doctorate, he emigrated to the United States in 1899. He soon became a writer and editor of the *Jewish Encyclopedia*, contributing 406 articles, many of them definitive. In 1902, Solomon Schechter designated Ginzberg as professor of Talmud at the Jewish Theological Seminary, his first faculty appointment at the newly reorganized Seminary. Ginzberg would retain this position for over 50 years.

Ginzberg was a scholar's scholar, whose primary objective was to create a climate of Jewish learning on American soil. He pursued his goal along three tracks: personal example, expert pedagogy, and the creation of an infrastructure to support Jewish learning. His own area of concentration was rabbinic "law and lore." Building upon his dissertation on Jewish legends, he created the seven-volume *Legends of the Jews* (1909–1938), which combined the manifold *aggadot* (legends) and parables surrounding each central biblical figure into a seamless, continuous narrative.

Because Ginzberg considered Halakah to be the cornerstone of Jewish life and culture, most of his research focused on the origin and development of Jewish law. Applying the philological-historical approach of German *Wissenschaft* and utilizing newly uncovered texts from the Cairo Geniza, he traced the sources of rabbinic law. Like his great collateral ancestor, the Gaon of Vilna, he investigated the Palestinian Talmud, ultimately producing his magnum opus, the three-volume *A Commentary on the Palestinian Talmud*. He tracked the evolution of rabbinic law into the medieval period, demonstrating the significance of the Geonim and illuminating the Karaitic controversy. His pioneering study of the Damascus sect probed an earlier antirabbinic trend. *On Jewish Law and Lore* and *Students, Scholars and Saints*, collections of essays largely directed to a general audience, clarified Ginzberg's philosophy of Judaism and portrayed great Jewish leaders of the recent past.

Ginzberg's Seminary students became scholars and rabbis. The first group, comprising such illustrious figures as Louis Finkelstein, Boaz Cohen, Solomon Goldman, Judah Goldin, and Arthur Hertzberg, became the teachers of the next generation. From pulpit rabbis Ginzberg solicited and received funding that facilitated the publication of the writings of European scholars, e.g., Ben-

jamin Lewin, Chaim Kosovsky, and Abraham Schreiber.

To stimulate Jewish scholarship in the United States, Ginzberg became the founding president and long-time mainstay of the American Academy of Jewish Research. He served the Hebrew University of Jerusalem as academic adviser, visiting professor (1928–1929, 1933–1934), and member of the Hartog Commission, which restructured its administration in 1934. He was also active in the effort to save refugee scholars and find them positions during the 1930s.

The leading Halakist of the Conservative Movement, Ginzberg produced a number of responsa that grappled with the issues of modern life (e.g., artificial insemination and even the permission to use grape juice for sacramental purposes during Prohibition). He was not, however, an innovator, preferring to remain, in his son's words, a "keeper of the law."

BAILA R. SHARGEL

BIBLIOGRAPHY
Boaz, Cohen. "Bibliography of Writings of Professor Louis Ginzberg." *Louis Ginzberg Jubilee Volume*. New York: American Academy for Jewish Research, 1945.

Finkelstein, Louis. "Louis Ginzberg." *American Academy of Jewish Research* 23 (1954).

———. "Louis Ginzberg." *American Jewish Year Book*. 56 (1955): 573–579.

Ginzberg, Eli. *Keeper of the Law: Louis Ginzberg*. Philadelphia: Jewish Publication Society, 1966.

Goldman, Solomon. "The Portrait of a Teacher." *Louis Ginzberg Jubilee Volume*. New York: American Academy for Jewish Research, 1945.

Goldberg, Arthur J. (1908–1990).

Arthur J. Goldberg was born in Chicago. His father, who had immigrated in 1894 to avoid being forced into the Russian army, died of cancer when Goldberg was very young. This loss left a large family with limited resources. Judaism was important to the Goldberg family; Goldberg's father was once a president of an Orthodox congregation, and his grandfather was a rabbi.

Goldberg was the first member of his family to graduate from high school. He then matriculated at a local community college, then attended DePaul University, and finally Northwestern University, where he graduated first in his class with a doctorate in law in 1930.

After graduation Goldberg entered private

practice in Chicago, and he represented major labor unions during the 1930s. His practice was interrupted by World War II, when he served in the Office of Strategic Services, but once peace was restored, Goldberg returned to his duties as a union legal adviser—for the Congress of Industrial Organizations (CIO) and the United States Steel Workers. He took part in the merger of the AFL and CIO in 1955 and was retained as legal counsel for the newly formed organization. In 1957, Goldberg was instrumental in writing the ethical practices code for unions and their workers.

Goldberg's extensive experience working with unions and the trust he earned as a negotiator led President John F. Kennedy to appoint him as secretary of labor in 1961. When Justice Felix Frankfurter announced his retirement from the Supreme Court, President Kennedy chose Goldberg to fill the vacancy. Once again Goldberg's experience was a factor, but so was his religion. President Kennedy realized "the necessity of replacing Frankfurter with a Jew [and] if a Jew was placed on the Court, it should be Arthur Goldberg."

Although Goldberg remained on the Court for only three years, his vote was crucial. During his tenure he defended cases concerning civil rights, personal liberties, and due process. In one such case, *Mendoza-Martinez v. Kennedy*, the Court had to decide whether citizenship could be revoked when an individual evaded the military draft during time of war or national emergency. Goldberg broke the Court's split on the issue by his decision that revoking one's citizenship was not a just punishment.

Goldberg enjoyed his position on the Court and may have considered it the high point of his career, but President Lyndon Johnson had other plans. Johnson wanted to reward his friend and adviser, Abe Fortas, with a seat on the Supreme Court, and with the death of the United States ambassador to the United Nations, Adlai Stevenson, the President saw his opportunity. Prior to Stevenson's death, Johnson had offered Goldberg several political opportunities in the hope of enticing him to resign—the post as the Secretary of Health, Education, and Welfare and the promise of the President's support for a future vice-presidential slot should he accept the assignment. Johnson argued that the only way Goldberg could become the first Jewish vice-president was to become more politically visible, and this required leaving the isolated world of the Supreme

Court. Goldberg turned down the Cabinet position, but when Johnson offered him the UN ambassadorship by appealing to his patriotism, Goldberg, reluctantly, accepted in July 1965. Confident of his ability as a negotiator, Goldberg believed he could make a contribution toward bringing peace to Vietnam. However, Goldberg was aware of the position's limitations. Historically, the ambassador lacked authority to set policy and served at the whim of the President.

In addition to rewarding Fortas, Johnson had other reasons for selecting Goldberg for the UN post. There were few who could match the level of respect and prestige of Stevenson, and Goldberg was one who came very close. Also, Johnson was aware of Goldberg's negotiating skills, which were necessary for the UN position. Goldberg was also prominent in the Jewish community with important liberal friends and connections amongst Johnson's Jewish backers. The only uncertainty in the appointment was if a Jewish ambassador could be effective with the Arab countries.

Goldberg's resignation was a personal mistake. After three gratifying years serving on the Court, Goldberg spent three unfulfilling years at the UN. He became increasingly unhappy with the escalation of the American role in Vietnam and frustrated in not having a stronger voice in peace negotiations with North Vietnam. Citing "personal reasons," Goldberg resigned his post on April 25, 1968.

Goldberg then became active in various political and humanitarian causes. In 1970, he ran unsuccessfully for governor of New York. In 1977, he was the U.S. representative at the Belgrade conference on human rights, and in 1981, he served as chairman of the American Jewish Commission on the Holocaust.

Although Goldberg did not have the opportunity to serve longer on the Supreme Court and make his mark on American judicial history, his rise from a poor Jewish neighborhood and an illiterate family to the front door of the White House is noteworthy. *See also* Law and Lawyers.

SHERRY OSTROFF
HOWARD SHAKER

BIBLIOGRAPHY

Moynihan, Daniel Patrick, ed. *The Defenses of Freedom: The Public Papers of Arthur J. Goldberg*. New York: Harper & Row, 1966.

Murphy, Bruce Allen. *Fortas: The Rise and Ruin of a Supreme Court Justice*. New York: Morrow, 1988.

Shogan, Robert. *A Question of Judgment: The Fortas Case and the Struggle for the Supreme Court.* Indianapolis: Bobbs-Merrill, 1972.

Golden, Harry Lewis (1903–1981). Journalist, humorist, and civil rights advocate, Harry Lewis Golden achieved fame as the publisher of the idiosyncratic newspaper the *Carolina Israelite* (1944–1968) and author of several bestsellers, including most notably *Only in America* (1958). Born Herschele Goldhirsch in Mikulinsty, a village in eastern Galicia (now a part of the Ukrainian Soviet Socialist Republic), Golden came to the United States with his family at the age of 2 and grew up on the Lower East Side of New York City. After failing in various careers and serving time in prison for mail fraud, he moved to Charlotte, North Carolina, in 1941 to sell advertising and write editorials for the *Charlotte Labor Journal*, the newspaper of the Charlotte Central Labor Union. At this time, Golden separated from his family and changed his name from Harry Goldhurst, the name he had taken when he entered the business world, to Harry Lewis Golden.

In February 1944, Golden published the first issue of the *Carolina Israelite*. He modeled his journal on Emanuel Haldeman-Julius's *American Freeman* and issued it at first as a monthly, then a bimonthly in tabloid format. He claimed that the name insulated him somewhat since Southerners could safely ignore it as "another Jew paper." Indeed, one editor described it as a Yiddish newspaper translated into English. Nevertheless, Golden's editorials favoring labor unions and championing racial brotherhood concerned many Jewish Southerners, who feared that he would be perceived as speaking for them all.

Golden's aim in publishing a liberal newspaper in North Carolina was to tell the story that he saw developing in the postwar South, a story he felt other journalists would ignore because it meant describing the condition of blacks. The South, he thought, was on the verge of an industrial revolution that would change its entire social order and swiftly correct the injustices of the past. Golden not only reported this story, but also sought to shape opinion by using humor to point out the folly of segregation. In 1957, *Time* publicized his Vertical Negro Plan. Observing that Southerners had no objection to standing with blacks, Golden suggested that seats be removed from public schools and replaced by stand-up desks. "Since no one in the South pays the slightest attention to a Vertical Negro," this change, he jested, would make school integration acceptable.

From the late 1950s through the mid-1970s, Golden was a national celebrity. In quick succession, he published three collections of essays based on his columns: *Only in America* (1958), *For 2¢ Plain* (1959), and *Enjoy, Enjoy!* (1960). The first two presented such compelling stories of the lives of early twentieth-century Jewish immigrants, the foibles of Southerners, and the general humor and irony of life that they were on the best-seller list simultaneously. He reported for *Life* on the Adolf Eichmann trial (1961) in Israel, wrote an anecdotal biography of his friend Carl Sandburg (1961), chronicled the civil rights program of President Kennedy in *Mr. Kennedy and the Negroes* (1964), retold the story of Leo Frank in *A Little Girl Is Dead* (1965), and published several more collections of essays. A frequent guest on television talk shows, he testified before Congress on civil rights legislation, delivered hundreds of speeches around the country to Jewish and Gentile audiences, and contributed dozens of articles to national magazines.

Golden's popularity and emergence as the "Jewish Will Rogers" depended primarily on his ability to appeal to and influence various audiences through the use of humor. Because of it, he sold millions of books and won praise from Martin Luther King, Jr., who, in his *Letter From Birmingham Jail* (1963), included Golden among a handful of Southerners who had written about the struggle of blacks "in eloquent, prophetic, and understanding terms." Nevertheless, Golden's humor did not please everyone, and some Jewish critics accused him of glamorizing ghetto life and of exaggerating the virtues of upward mobility. Moreover, when he closed the *Carolina Israelite* in 1968, he did so in part because he found that humor no longer had a place in the increasingly militant civil rights movement.

During the 1970s, Golden wrote six more books, including *The Israelis: Portrait of a People* (1971), *The Greatest Jewish City in the World* (1972), and *Our Southern Landsman* (1974). By mid-decade, however, only a few newspapers subscribed to his once popular syndicated column "Only in America," and his writing lacked its earlier verve and wit.

Golden proved to be overly optimistic about the pace of improvement in race relations, and he usually ignored the harsher realities of life on the Lower East Side. Nevertheless, he was an important figure in the early civil rights struggle in the

South, and he had a large following among the immigrant generation of Jews in the North. Within these worlds, he had few peers as a social critic and raconteur.

ROBIN BRABHAM

BIBLIOGRAPHY

Contemporary Authors. New Revision Series, edited by Ann Evory. Vol. 2. Detroit: Gale, 1981.

Current Biography. New York: Wilson, 1959.

Golden, Harry. *The Right Time: An Autobiography.* New York: Putnam, 1969.

"Golden Rule," *Time*, April 1, 1957, 62.

Hohner, Robert A. "The Other Harry Golden: Harry Goldhurst and the Cannon Scandals." *North Carolina Historical Review* 65 (April 1988): 154–172.

Powell, William S., ed. *Dictionary of North Carolina Biography*, edited by William S. Powell. Vol. 2. Chapel Hill: University of North Carolina Press, 1986.

Sides, Margaret N. "Harry Golden's Rhetoric: The Persona, the Message, the Audience," Ph.D. dissertation, Northern Illinois University, 1988.

Solotaroff, Theodore. "Harry Golden and the American Audience." *Commentary* 31 (January 1961): 1–13.

Goldfaden, Abraham (1840–1908). Yiddish playwright, dramatist, poet, theatrical director, producer, stage manager, songwriter, and folksong collector, Abraham Goldfaden was born in Stara-Konstantin, Russia. He was first educated by Abraham Ben Gottlober, a leader of the Yiddish Haskalah (or Enlightenment) and then continued his education at the Rabbinical Seminary of Zhitomir, Volhynia (1857). For 32 years (1876–1908), Goldfaden followed a theatrical career in Romania, Russia, Poland, France, England, and, finally, the United States. All of this experience prepared him for his future role as "the Father of the Yiddish Stage."

It is conventional to place this paternity in Jassy, Romania, in 1876, where, Goldfaden himself remarked, the love for folk singing was highly developed. For this reason, all Goldfaden the theatrical innovator had to do was to present his audiences with songs often adapted from Ukrainian folk melodies and integrate them into a prose plot in Yiddish. He then had to find actors for his musicals who were above all talented at fostering illusion, whether they were professional singers or actors or not. Thus, his first star was a craftsman, Sacher Goldstein, because the latter had a young face, could therefore play female roles in spite of being a male (later to be played by such leading ladies as the East Side's Bertha Kalish), and had the gift for quick repartee. The "Goldfaden formula" was thus a mixture of Thespian versatility and a folkist vaudevillian spirit, resulting in a lyrical, popular, sentimental, and ethnically simplistic archetype for the Yiddish stage and a genuinely Jewish *commedia dell' arte* for the first time in modern Jewish history.

However, there was a serious background to this formula. Goldfaden was raised in a bookish home in which "his father was the only craftsman in town who savored a Yiddish book." Moreover, in addition to Yiddish, this father also taught his son the Hebrew of Abraham Mapu's *Ahavas Zion* (1853), a narrative that later became the basis for his "biblical operetta" *Shulamis* (1880). As such, the young Goldfaden was a good candidate for the kind of enlightenment propagated by the Zhitomir Seminary, an institution for Russifying minorities. While a student there, he starred in *Serkele* (1885?) by Shloime Ettinger, a Yiddish Enlightenment dramatist, and his own *Shmendrik* (1887), the title hero of which became a widespread colloquialism, was a bourgeois comedy in Ettinger's tradition. To those who saw in this play nothing more than a humiliating farce, Goldfaden answered that its "vulgarity" was the "needed bridge" toward the development of a more "refined" understanding, especially among backward Romanian Jewry.

When Goldfaden returned to southern Russia, particularly to Odessa, he founded another theatrical company to embody his purposes. At Odessa, he hired in 1879 the future star of New York's East Side realistic drama, Jacob P. Adler, and thereby initiated the latter's career. The Russian establishment described his company as waging a "fearless war against the fanaticism of the Jewish People." However, this favorable outlook for Goldfaden's reformist program did not last long: local Russian opinion soon denied him permission to play in anything but "literary and musical clubs," thereby returning him to the days before Jassy. In addition, the Orthodox Jewish community was violently opposed to his "frivolity."

In spite of this opposition, Goldfaden's company finally did receive permission to appear throughout the Russian Pale of Settlement. Unexpectedly, however, he met with competition from one of his own former actors, the Romanian Zelig Mogulesco, later an East Side star, and Joseph Lateiner, in future years the perpetrator of

Shund ("trash") on the New York Yiddish stage. At the same time, he saw that his stock types did, in fact, express painful reality, as much later modernist and "folk revivalist" productions realized (the Yiddish Art Theater of 1926 and the Folksbuehne of 1943).

The pogroms throughout southern Russia (starting in April 1881) made him more conscious of this reality, and he began to write serious (albeit somewhat melodramatic) plays about Jewish history, especially resistance: *Doktor Almasada* (1882), *Uriel Acosta* (1883), and *Bar-Kochba* (1883). The latter was so popular that the czar issued an edict on August 17, 1883, that outlawed Yiddish theater. Under such pressures, many Jews decided to emigrate, among them Goldfaden.

He joined the masses of Jews leaving Russia for New York City in 1887. By all rights, he should have been extremely successful. After all, one of his plays had inaugurated the East Side Yiddish stage on August 12, 1882, and even such a devoted realist as Jacob P. Adler had started his American career in Chicago with Goldfaden drawing cards. Moreover, as Morris Rosenfeld, the "Sweatshop Poet," had written, a "masked ball" was just what the downtrodden sewing-machine "operator" needed to restore him/her to life, and Goldfaden was an expert in such "dressing up."

Unfortunately, however, he was met by strife in the forms of a labor dispute with Mogulesco and other actors, commercial competition from the melodramas of Lateiner and "Professor" Hurwitz, and ideological opposition from unionist radicals, who championed the realist playwright Jacob Gordin. Zalman Libin, one of the opponents, wrote that "a well-made play" on the East Side had to be about local conditions (like Gordin's *The Russian Jew in America*) in order to be successful.

Goldfaden tried hard to rehabilitate his reputation. He became more nationalistic and wrote the first Hebrew-language play to be performed on American soil, thereby reverting to his Hebrew Haskalah background (as early as 1865, he had written a collection of Hebrew poetry). With the same "source-minded seriousness," he insisted that his last play in Yiddish be performed without frills; therefore, *Ben-Ami or the Son of My People* (1907) contained no song and dance. However, precisely such attractive "frivolity" was uppermost in the minds of the mourners at Goldfaden's mass-attended funeral in the streets of New York City in 1908, and his rehabilitation remained incomplete in spite of the public honor. *See also* Theater, Yiddish.

ALBERT WALDINGER

BIBLIOGRAPHY

Hapgood, Hutchins. *The Spirit of the Ghetto*. New York: Funk & Wagnalls, 1902.

Howe, Irving. *World of Our Fathers*. New York: Harcourt Brace Jovanovich, 1976.

Sandrow, Nahma. *Vagabond Stars*. New York: Harper & Row, 1977.

Goldman, Emma (1869–1940). A revolutionary anarchist and feminist, Emma Goldman, through her writings, particularly the monthly journal *Mother Earth* (1906–1917), and her magnetic speaking style, popularized radical ideas. She incessantly attacked what she called "institutionalized violence," the making of women into objects, and the coercions of organized government.

Born in Kovno, Russia, to a struggling Jewish couple, Goldman was raised in an era marked by economic dislocation, political violence, government oppression, and virulent anti-Semitism. She managed to get some formal elementary education, but she was mainly self-taught. She came to the United States in 1885 and by 1889 was converted to anarchism. Goldman helped Alexander Berkman plan the attempted assassination of the head of U.S. Steel, Henry Clay Frick, in 1892. The following year she was arrested for inciting to riot. One year in prison did not dampen her spirit, and after her release she continued to participate in radical activities.

Goldman, a pioneer of the birth control movement, attacked the institution of marriage, and celebrated sexuality. She was arrested again in 1917 for obstructing the military draft and was deported to Russia upon her release in 1919. Her initial sympathy for the Soviet experiment turned to disappointment with the authoritarian statism of Lenin. In 1921, Red Emma, as she had come to be known, left the USSR, returning to the United States, and wrote *My Disillusionment in Russia* (1923). Later she said, "I do not criticize Russia because Stalin is too revolutionary, but because he is not revolutionary at all." Goldman remained on the side of progressive, liberating causes her entire life. And in the mid-1930s, she toured several countries speaking for the anti-Franco revolutionaries in the Spanish Civil War (1936–1939).

Emma Goldman's politics were a product not

only of the rapid economic dislocation of late-nineteenth-century Russia, but also of the rich ethical demands of the prophetic strain of Judaism that emphasized community self-help, the ethical obligation of charity in its broadest sense of social justice, and antiauthoritarianism. The issues of *Mother Earth* were filled with Yiddish stories and tales from the Talmud, and her commitment to anarchism and universalism did not divert her from speaking and writing, openly and frequently, about the *particular* burdens Jews faced in a world in which anti-Semitism was a living enemy.

In 1931, Goldman published her autobiography *Living My Life*. It remains startlingly contemporaneous as a testimony to the aspirations of individual freedom, impatience with radical cant, and rejection of the prejudices that destroy the possibilities of individuality and community.

GERALD SORIN

BIBLIOGRAPHY

Drinnon, Richard. *Rebel in Paradise: A Biography of Emma Goldman*. Chicago: University of Chicago Press, 1976.

———, and Drinnon, Anna Maria, eds. *Nowhere at Home: Letters from Exile of Emma Goldman and Alexander Berkman*. New York: Schocken, 1975.

Falk, Candace. *Love, Anarchy and Emma Goldman*. New York: Holt, Rinehart and Winston, 1984.

Goldman, Emma. *Living My Life*. Garden City, N.Y.: Garden City Publishing, 1936.

Shulman, Alix Kates, ed. *Red Emma Speaks*. 2nd ed. New York: Schocken, 1983.

Solomon, Martha. *Emma Goldman*. Boston: Twayne, 1987.

Wexler, Alice. *Emma Goldman in Exile*. Boston: Beacon Press, 1989.

Goodman, Benny (1909–1986). Known to jazz fans throughout the world as Benny, Benjamin David Goodman was one of twelve children born to David and Dora Goodman of Chicago. Both parents had come to the United States in the 1880s; David from Warsaw and Dora from Lithuania. They met in the United States and married in the 1890s. David Goodman, a tailor by trade, seeking to improve his fortunes, moved the family to Chicago from Baltimore in 1903 and worked both in the garment industry and in the stockyards. The family was very poor, and Benny Goodman grew up in dire poverty. His father, however, was someone who put his family

above everything else, and despite pressure to feed a large family he was determined that his children receive every available opportunity to improve themselves. It was under these circumstances that the father enrolled Benny, aged 10, and two of his brothers in the Kehelah Jacob Synagogue band, where Benny was introduced to the clarinet.

Benny Goodman would go on to study classical clarinet, an interest he was to maintain throughout his life. By the time he was 18, he had already performed in a group with Bix Beiderbecke and was working regularly in Chicago's jazz clubs. In September 1926, he made his first recording with Ben Pollack and his Californians.

By 1935, Goodman was leading his own "big band" and with the help of the famous impresario, John Hammond, landed a spot on the popular national radio program, "Let's Dance" on NBC. In 1935, he took the band to the Palomar Ballroom in Los Angeles and received such an enthusiastic response that the crowd gathered around the bandstand and forgot to dance. As one critic remarked, "On that night, the Swing Era began." The Swing Era lasted from 1935 until roughly the end of World War II. During that period Goodman's enormous success as a bandleader, arranger, and instrumentalist earned him the sobriquet, "the King of Swing," a title that stayed with him until his death.

Also beginning in 1935, Goodman started experimenting with small combos. In the summer of 1936, he introduced his first quartet. The group, consisting of Gene Krupa on drums, Teddy Wilson on piano, Lionel Hampton on vibraharp, and Goodman on clarinet, became one of the most popular and most endearing associations in the history of jazz. The group's appearances in the fall of 1936 marked the first time anyone had attempted to ignore the racial taboos that had dictated the strict separation of white and black musicians on the performing stage. Given the temper of the times, Goodman showed not only great musical taste but genuine courage as well. In 1939, the addition of Charlie Christian on guitar and Arthur Bernstein on bass turned the quartet into the equally famous sextet. Goodman continued to experiment with small combos of various sizes throughout his career.

While the Goodman big band remained the leading name in popular music during the late thirties and early forties, perhaps the zenith of the band's entire career was reached in the summer of 1938 at Carnegie Hall in New York City. It was there that Goodman headlined the famous "Spirituals to Swing" concert produced by John Hammond. Goodman brought down the house with his rousing 22-minute version of "Sing, Sing, Sing." While Goodman never sought to deny his religious or ethnic heritage, his music reflects little consciousness of either. There is one justly famous exception, which occurs in the middle of a tune called, "And the Angels Sing." There the Jewish trumpeter, "Ziggy" Elman, plays a traditional Yiddish wedding dance "straight" before he "swings" it back to Martha Tilton's vocals.

Goodman's popularity extended far beyond the Swing Era although his later audiences often were motivated more by nostalgia than genuine appreciation of his artistry. Toward the end of his life he achieved the status of a distinguished Elder Statesman of jazz in much the same way that Louis Armstrong had before him and Ella Fitzgerald after him. His deep respect for classical music remained constant throughout his life, and his sense of place and style is evidenced by the fact that on his classical recordings he always listed himself as "Mr. Benjamin Goodman."

MICHAEL ROTH

BIBLIOGRAPHY

Collier, James Lincoln. *Benny Goodman and the Swing Era.* New York: Oxford University Press, 1989.

Goodman, Benny, and Kalodin, Irving. *The Kingdom of Swing.* New York: Stockpale, 1939.

Simon, George T. *The Big Bands.* New York: Macmillan, 1967.

Gordis, Robert (b. 1908). Rabbi, author, biblical scholar, teacher, and lecturer, Robert Gordis is a leading American Conservative scholar. He was born in Brooklyn. In 1928, he married Fannie Jacobson, and they had three sons. Educated at the City College of New York, Dropsie College (Ph.D. in Bible and Semitics, 1929) and the Jewish Theological Seminary of America (rabbi, 1932). He has been rabbi of Temple Beth El of Rockaway Park, N.Y. (1931–1968); professor of Bible and philosophies of religion, the Jewish Theological Seminary of America (1937–1982); adjunct professor of religion, Columbia University (1948–1957); professor of religion, Temple University (1967–1974); and has also taught Bible and Judaism at other institutions of higher learning.

In his public life, Gordis has served as president of the Rabbinical Assembly (1944–1946) and the Synagogue Council of America (1948–

1949) and has been a board member of important scholarly and communal organizations, including the American Academy for Jewish Research and the New York Board of Rabbis. He founded the *Conservative Judaism Magazine* and *Judaism Magazine*, which he still edits, and served as chairman of the Commission on the Philosophy of Conservative Judaism, which produced the centennial *Statement of Principles of Conservative Judaism.*

A prolific writer in biblical research and Jewish religious thought, his biblical volumes include *Koheleth: The Man and His World* and *Job: Commentary, New Translation and Special Studies.* Gordis's many essays in religious thought include *A Faith for Moderns, Understanding Conservative Judaism,* and *Judaic Ethics for a Lawless World.*

Gordis has followed a conservative path in biblical scholarship, eschewing radical emendations of the text and defending the integrity of biblical traditions. Specializing in Wisdom Literature, Gordis has analyzed the social, cultural and religious background of this genre of Scriptures. In his religious studies, Gordis has eloquently espoused liberalism and modernity while defending traditional laws and values. He has noted that growth is the law of life and law is the life of Judaism; that Jewish law never stood still and that Jewish ethical norms shaped legal decisions toward greater democracy, sensitivity to the needs of the weak and downtrodden, and increased protection of the rights of women. He has argued for the human role in revelation, insisting that revelation consists of *two* active participants: God and man. Gordis has been long regarded as one of the leading spokesmen of Conservative Judaism and one of the most fertile and creative minds in American Jewry. *See also* Conservative Judaism.

GILBERT S. ROSENTHAL

BIBLIOGRAPHY

Faber, Salomon. *Jewish Book Annual* 40 (1982–1983): 139–146.

Gordis, Robert. Speech in *Rabbinical Assembly Proceedings XXXIII* (1969). Pp. 135–146.

International Who's Who, 1987–1988. 51st ed. (1987). P. 541.

Robinson, Jacob. "Gordis Robert." In *Encyclopedia Judaica* (1972), Vol. 7. P. 789.

Gratz College. Gratz College in Philadelphia is the oldest nondenominational college of Jewish studies in the Western hemisphere. Hyman Gratz (1776–1857), banker and member of a distinguished Jewish family in Philadelphia, in his will included a "trust for the establishment and support of a college for the education of Jews residing in the city and county of Philadelphia." Trustee for the fund was Congregation Mikveh Israel, which decided to establish the college as an institution to prepare teachers for Jewish schools.

A board of trustees was constituted in 1895, and a lecture program initiated. The first lectures were delivered by distinguished scholars, among them Solomon Schechter, Marcus Jastrow, and Sabato Morais. The college itself was formally opened in 1897. Moses A. Dropsie, founder of Dropsie College, was the first president of the board of trustees and served until his death in 1905.

In 1928, the trustees of the college, the Hebrew Education Society of Philadelphia (founded 1848), and the Federation of Jewish Charities entered into an agreement providing for joint support and governance of the college under a joint board of overseers.

From 1945 until 1956, among the distinguished educators administering the college were Leo L. Honor, Azriel Eisenberg, and Abraham P. Gannes. In 1951, William Chomsky, a Hebrew scholar who had been a faculty member since 1923, was appointed chairman of the faculty, a post he held until his retirement in 1969. In this period the curriculum was expanded, summer sessions were started, and a special extension division for adults was organized. In 1952, the first academic degree, Bachelor of Hebrew Literature, was awarded under the charter issued to the Hebrew Education Society in 1849. The right to grant degrees under that state charter was confirmed by the Middle States Association of Colleges and Schools, which granted the college accreditation in 1967.

In 1958, the Federation of Jewish Agencies of Greater Philadelphia delegated to the college the administration of the functions of the former Council on Jewish Education. They were carried on by the Division of Community Services until 1987, when a separate Central Agency for Jewish Education was created.

In the 1960s, the present 5-year Gratz College high school program was inaugurated, based on earlier secondary programs; the Samuel Netzky Adult Institute was organized; and the present school building at Tenth Street and Tabor Road was erected.

In 1970, the college published a seventy-fifth anniversary *Festscrift*, which was followed by several annuals, edited by faculty, with contributions from faculty, alumni, and invited scholars. The college's annual Youth Ulpan tours to Israel was also inaugurated. Between 1972 and 1982, new programs were approved, including one for a Bachelor of Arts in Jewish Studies, Master of Hebrew Literature, and Master of Arts in Jewish Music.

In the 1980s, a number of administrative and program changes were introduced, including a Master of Arts in Jewish Education and one in Jewish Studies; joint bachelor's degrees with Temple University and Beaver College; the nation's first Certificate in Judaica Librarianship and Certificate in Sephardic Studies; Certificate in Jewish Chaplaincy for rabbis and cantors; a Certificate in Jewish Communal Studies, which can be combined with a joint graduate program in Jewish communal service and a Master of Social Work degree from the School of Social Work, University of Pennsylvania.

In 1979, a Holocaust Oral History Archive was created. A major grant by the Pew Memorial Trust in 1985 provided funding for a Visiting Distinguished Professorship in the Judaic Humanities, a librarian/cataloguer for the Schreiber Music Library, and library and computer equipment. In the same year, the Rosaline B. Feinstein Chair in Jewish Education, the first college-endowed chair, was established. Branches of the college, Netzky Institute, and high school were established throughout the Delaware Valley region. In 1987, the college published *Community and Culture*, essays in Jewish studies in honor of the college's ninetieth anniversary, culminating a series of major anniversary events.

In the fall of 1988, the college relocated to the 28-acre Mandell Education Campus in Melrose Park, Pennsylvania. A citywide Jewish community high school under the aegis of the college has been established on the Gratz campus.

NORA LEVIN

BIBLIOGRAPHY

King, Diane A. *A History of Gratz College, 1893–1928.* Philadelphia: Dropsie College, 1979.

Greenberg, Irving (b. 1933). Rabbi, thinker, writer, educator, and communal activist, Irving Greenberg was born and raised in Brooklyn, New York. He graduated from Brooklyn College in 1953 and in the same year was ordained a rabbi at Beth Joseph Rabbinical Seminary in Brooklyn.

He earned a master's degree in 1954 and in 1960 a doctoral degree in American history, both from Harvard University. He and his wife Blu, whom he married in 1957, have five children. Blu too is an activist in the Jewish community and is a leading exponent of Orthodox Jewish feminism.

Greenberg has held a number of important positions in American Jewish life. He has served as the Hillel director at Brandeis University (1957–1958), been a professor at Yeshiva University (1959–1972) and the City University of New York Graduate Center (1972–1976), and held several rabbinical positions at influential Orthodox congregations. Since 1974 he has served as president of CLAL, the National Jewish Center for Learning and Leadership, an organization started by Greenberg and Elie Wiesel. The goal of CLAL was to provide Jewish education to the lay leadership—that is, the fund raisers, philanthropists, and administrators of American Jewry. Greenberg was especially successful in his efforts with the leaderhip of the local Jewish federations and councils and its national umbrella group—the Council of Jewish Federations (CJF). By means of weekend retreats, convention programming, special classes, and lectures, CLAL led by Greenberg sought to enrich the Jewish knowledge of the leaders of local federations.

Greenberg has written numerous articles and two books, *Guide to Shabbat* (1981) and *The Jewish Way* (1985). As a thinker and writer, he has sought to deal with problems of modernity from an Orthodox Jewish perspective. He has often taken controversial stands that have increasingly made him an isolated figure in American Orthodoxy, and even in the so-called Centrist Orthodox camp.

Greenberg has posited that Orthodoxy must separate its core, the Halakah (Jewish law)—that is, its traditions and legal framework—from its antiquated "premodern" lifestyle and replace this old framework with a modern one committed, among other principles, to tolerance, universalism, and self-growth and awareness. As such, Greenberg feels that women were rightfully entitled to equality in Orthodox Jewish life. This issue was taken up both in writing and lectures by his wife, Blu. Greenberg contends that Orthodoxy is not the only valid spiritual force in Judaism, but that Reform, Conservative, Reconstructionist, and even secular groups have equal validity. Needless to add, he has found few supporters in Orthodoxy for these positions.

Greenberg adopted an even more controver-

sial approach by offering Christianity the status of a true and valid religion, on par with Judaism. He saw the two religions as equally meaningful for their respective communities.

For Greenberg the events of the Holocaust signaled an end to the covenantal relationship between God and the people of Israel, as it was marked by a period of silence on the part of God. Yet the Jews voluntarily chose to renew this covenant, as shown by the creation of the State of Israel, the renewal of Jewish life in Europe, and the period of Jewish creativity in the United States. Greenberg further felt that in light of the Holocaust, the Jewish people had acquired a "senior status" in the covenant, thus allowing for a reorganization and modernization of Halacha. Here too Greenberg had more influence on non-Orthodox Jewish thinkers than on his own constituency.

Since 1985 and the publication of his essay "Will There Be One Jewish People by the Year 2000?" Greenberg and CLAL have focused on efforts to bring unity to the American Jewish community, which he saw as being on the brink of dividing into two different groups. As Greenberg understood the problem, increasingly radical positions taken both by the Reform and Orthodox movements with regard to the laws of conversion and marriage and other family laws were leading to a time when hundreds of thousands of Jews recognized by the Reform community would not be recognized as Jews by the Orthodox community. Each group would not only be religiously and socially separated from the other, but also would not be able to marry each other. Greenberg has sought to initiate dialogue between the Orthodox and non-Orthodox groups in order to foster a climate of mutual respect and understanding, necessary at arriving at some solutions for the problems at hand. Greenberg's efforts in this area were praised by many Jewish lay leaders as well as non-Orthodox rabbis, but they were not received positively by most of the American Orthodox rabbinate. Thus his efforts in this field have been marked by consciousness raising but little practical results.

Greenberg's importance has been in leadership education. He has familiarized many lay leaders of American Jewry with the fundamentals of Jewish knowledge and traditions. Thus, he has sensitized a large sector of American Jewry to the key concerns of Judaism and to Jewish values as they relate to the issues of the day. He has also expounded a systematic Orthodox approach to modernity by boldly confronting such issues as Jewish unity, pluralism, the Holocaust, intermarriage, and ecumenism. Though this theology has had little or no impact on American Orthodoxy, it has been influential in other sectors of American Jewry.

ZALMAN ALPERT

BIBLIOGRAPHY

Fenyvesi, Charles. "Can Yitz Greenberg Really Bring the Jewish People Together?" *Moment* 12 (November 1987): 26–31, 53–54.

Grodzinsky, Rabbi Zvi Hirsch (1857 or 1858–1947).

From his arrival in the United States in 1891 until his death, Zvi Hirsch Grodzinsky was "chief rabbi" of Omaha, Nebraska. His significance lies in several areas. He may have published more prolifically than any contemporary American Orthodox rabbi, thereby gaining an international reputation among rabbinic scholars of his generation, and he served as an early *posek* (decider) for distinctively American questions of Jewish law. In addition, like other contemporary Orthodox scholars, he sought to transplant intact Eastern European Orthodoxy to America and suffered the concomitant pressures that this conviction aroused in his newly American congregants who wanted an American version of Judaism.

Zvi Hirsch Grodzinsky was a cousin of Rabbi Hayyim Ozer Grodzinsky (1863–1940; *dayyan* [ecclesiastical judge] of Vilnius [Vilna], 1887–1940, and its religious leader until his death), and the two studied together as boys. Direct documentary evidence of Zvi Hirsch's education and ordination is incomplete, but he probably was ordained by Rabbi Yitzhak Elhanan Spektor, chief rabbi of Kaunas (Kovno) and came to the United States with the latter's endorsement. Spektor, generally considered the leading light of Lithuanian Jewry in the late nineteenth century, provided an approbation to Grodzinsky's first book, *Mikveh Yisrael* (1898), a commentary on the laws of building ritual baths.

Grodzinsky's scholarship constitutes his most enduring contribution to Jewish history. He wrote prolifically and well and demonstrably controlled the full range of rabbinic literature. He published four major works, two of them multivolume. In addition to *Mikveh Yisrael*, his works include *Likutei Zvi* (1916), a reference work on the whole of *Orah Hayyim*; *Milei De-Berakhot*

(1923, 1945) a commentary on the first thirty-four pages of Tractate Berakhot; and *Mikraei Kodesh* (1936, 1937, 1941), a three-volume examination of the laws of reading, writing, and qualifying Torah scrolls. These books represent only a fraction of Grodzinsky's publications. He wrote many articles for such leading rabbinic journals as *Ha-Meassef*, *Ha-Pardes*, and *Ha-Mesilah*.

Perhaps even more important are his unpublished works. The most notable among them is *Tiferet Zvi*, a collection of 64 *responsa*, many addressing questions that are distinctively contemporary or American. An early *responsum* on artificial insemination, several addressing the permissibility of modern appliances on the Sabbath, and one discussing the use of American police officers to help enforce *kefiah*, compelling a recalcitrant husband to give his wife a *get*, stand out. Other unpublished manuscripts include a commentary on *Shulhan Arukh*, *Yoreh Deah*; treatises on kosher wine and family purity; a compendium of Talmudic expressions; sermons; and correspondence with leading scholars of the day. Toward the end of Grodzinsky's life, another of his unpublished manuscripts, *Likutei Zvi* on *Even Ha-Ezer*, was utilized as a primary resource in the early volumes of *Otzar ha-Poskim*, a major scholarly project inaugurated by the then Chief Rabbi of Israel, Isaac Herzog.

Grodzinsky went to Omaha in 1891 at the written invitation of the city's two major Orthodox congregations, who had appointed him to serve as a calming force between them. His reasons for accepting the post included a commitment to pursuing his scholarly endeavors without having to contend with the political tension among rabbis that was common in larger cities in Europe. From the time of his arrival, Grodzinsky sought to fulfill two roles: the developing communal responsibilities of the American rabbi and the halakic duties of the Eastern European *av beit din*.

In a locale that, at the turn of the century, was relatively isolated from America's growing centers of Jewish learning and culture, Grodzinsky served as supervising rabbi (*rav ha-makhshir*), overseeing the production of kosher meat and wine; provided training in ritual slaughter; acted as a *dayyan* in civil matters and religious divorces; and ordained at least one rabbi. He also accepted such routine responsibilities as answering individual questions of Jewish practice, leading classes for his congregants, conducting weddings, and preaching weekly (the latter, a concession to American demands).

Grodzinsky's rabbinic activities extended beyond his community. In 1902, he helped found Agudat ha-Rabbanim (later the Union of Orthodox Rabbis of the United States and Canada), the first Orthodox rabbinical organization in North America. His endeavors as supervising rabbi included the production of kosher meat for shipment throughout the United States and the production of Passover wine, which he oversaw annually in California. He also maintained an active correspondence with leading scholars in Europe, America, and Israel.

Grodzinsky fought "modernizing" tendencies in Judaism. Though he knew English, he refused to speak it, preferring to use Yiddish. His views of political Zionism were ambivalent. He consistently opposed the budding Conservative movement and the new, "modern Orthodoxy." In 1916, still in his fifties, lay leaders seeking just such modernity discharged him from his post as head of Omaha's Orthodox community. His dismissal illustrates the challenges that faced Orthodox leaders in America.

Despite this rejection, for some 30 years until his death, Grodzinsky carried on his scholarship, significantly increasing his published output after his "retirement." In addition, he continued to decide questions of Jewish law, taking precedence over younger Orthodox rabbis who deferred to him in his ongoing though no longer official role as "chief rabbi." Such deference was due to his acknowledged learning in both technical and practical questions. His greatest work, his *responsa*, are indicative of this careful scholarship. When published in full, they may play a useful role in the contemporary halakic debates regarding American Jewish life.

JONATHAN ROSENBAUM
MYRON WAKSCHLAG

BIBLIOGRAPHY

Grodzinsky, T. H. "Be-Inyan Hazra'ah Melakhutit [On the Issue of Artificial Insemination]." In *Halakhah U-Ref'ah*, edited by M. Hirschler. Pp. 140–154. Jerusalem: Mechon Regensberg, 1988.

Rosenbaum, Jonathan, and Wakschlag, Myron. "Maintaining Tradition: A Survey of the Life and Writings of Rabbi Zvi Hirsch Grodzinsky," *American Jewish History*, in revision.

———. "Rabbinic Repartee: Rabbi Tsvi Hirsch Grodzinsky of Omaha and the Lights of the Land of Israel." In *Eretz Israel, Israel, and the Jewish Diaspora: Mutual Relations Through the Ages*. Lanham, Md.: University Press of America, in press.

Wakschlag, Myron. "T. H. Grodzinsky: Mi-Toldotav [T. H. Grodzinsky: A Biographical Sketch]" In *Halakhah U-Refu'ah*, edited by M. Hirschler. Pp. 139–140. Jerusalem: Mechon Regensberg, 1988.

H

Hadassah. The largest Jewish women's organization in the United States, Hadassah was founded by Henrietta Szold, the daughter of a modernist rabbi from Baltimore. After visiting Palestine in 1909, Szold became determined to bring modern medical care and standards of hygiene to Palestine. She directed the expansion of her study group, "the Daughters of Zion," into a national organization. Fifteen women met on Purim, February 24, 1912, and founded Hadassah, using the Hebrew name for Queen Esther. Hadassah also means myrtle, a hardy plant used to bind and enrich soil. Hadassah's motto became "the healing of the daughter of my people," taken from the book of Jeremiah. The stated purpose in founding Hadassah was to foster Zionist ideals through education in America and to begin public health and nursing training in Palestine.

In 1913, Hadassah sent two nurses to Jerusalem to set up a clinic for maternity care and for the treatment of trachoma (an eye disease). This was the beginning of Hadassah's continuing involvement in the medical care of the people of Palestine. Henrietta Szold directed much of Hadassah's early work in Palestine.

After World War I, Hadassah, in cooperation with other volunteer organizations, sent much needed medical personnel and equipment to Palestine. Known as "the Unit," this group opened the first modern emergency hospital and clinic in Jerusalem's Rothschild Hospital; similar facilities in other locations were opened later. The Henrietta Szold-Hadassah School of Nursing opened in Jerusalem in 1915. Throughout the Holy Land, Hadassah established hospitals and clinics and turned them over to the local municipalities.

In 1934, Youth Aliyah, an organization initiated by Recha Freier to save Jewish children from Germany by resettling them in Palestine, received its first 43 children. Henrietta Szold, the first director of Youth Aliyah, met the children when they arrived in Palestine and took them to Kibbutz Ein Harod. In 1935, Youth Aliyah became a regular Hadassah project, and Hadassah initially was the sole agency in the United States supporting Youth Aliyah. Today, Youth Aliyah focuses on culturally deprived Israeli children.

In 1939, the Rothschild-Hadassah University Hospital, the first teaching hospital in Palestine, opened atop Mt. Scopus in Jerusalem, thus beginning a series of medical firsts for the region. With the birth of the State of Israel, Hadassah worked to cope with the war emergency and the influx of immigrants. Although Mt. Scopus was established as a demilitarized zone, Jordan violated the agreement and evacuation of the hospital was necessary. In 1950, a building fund campaign was launched for a new Hadassah Hebrew University Medical Center at Ein Karem, Jerusalem. In 1961, all of the Hadassah Medical Organization (HMO) facilities scattered throughout Jerusalem since 1948 moved to Ein Karem.

In 1967, Hadassah returned to Mt. Scopus, as a result of the Six Day War. The Hadassah flag was raised as a pledge to rebuild. October 21, 1975, marked the rededication of the Hadassah University Hospital on Mt. Scopus.

Both Hadassah hospitals have come to represent the best medical care for all people, regardless of race, religion, or nationality. Hadassah's contribution to the medical needs of the region continues to provide the best and most modern medical care possible to the entire Middle East. Hadassah, however, means even more than "just" medical care. In 1942, Hadassah started vocational education with the opening of the Alice Seligsberg Trade School for Girls in Palestine, followed in 1945 by the Brandeis Vocational Center for boys. These programs were subsequently consolidated as the Seligsberg-Brandeis Comprehensive High School. In 1967, Hadassah became the sole sponsor of the Zionist Youth Movement in the United States, known as Hasacher, The Dawn. Hadassah continues to be one of the largest supporters of the Jewish National Fund (JNF), having sponsored more than 20 specific projects.

Hadassah is the largest volunteer organization in the United States. There are over 1500 chapters, and Hadassah boasts over 385,000 members and 22,000 Associates (male members). Its current projects include the Hadassah Medical Organization, Youth Aliyah, Hadassah Comprehensive High School, Hadassah Community College, Hadassah Vocational Guidance Institute, JNF, and U.S. youth programs. It owes its success to America's female Zionists. *See also* Communal Organizations; Szold, Henrietta.

LINDA GLAZER

BIBLIOGRAPHY

Baum, Charlotte; Hyman, Paula; and Michel, Sonya. *The Jewish Woman in America*. New York: New American Library, 1975.

"Hadassah Chronology, 75 years, Dreaming, Daring and Doing." New York: Hadassah, 1986.

Marcus, Jacob Rader. *The American Jewish Woman: A Documentary History*. Hoboken, N.J.: Ktav, 1981.

Halpern, Moyshe-Leyb (1886–1932).

Perhaps the most original of the modern Yiddish poets who wrote in America, Moyshe-Leyb Halpern was born in a town in eastern Galicia (in either Zlotchev or Sosev) into an enlightened Jewish home. His Jewish education consisted only of heder; in 1898, at the age of 12, he was sent by his father, a businessman, to Vienna to study commercial art. He returned to Zlotchev in 1907 and emigrated to the United States in 1908.

After the publication of his first book of poems in 1919, *In nyu york* (In New York), Halpern became widely known in the Yiddish world as a significant and rebellious poet. His second book, *Di goldene pave* (The Golden Peacock), appeared in 1924. The second edition of *In nyu york* came out in Warsaw in 1927.

Halpern married Reyzl Baron in 1919; their son Isaac was born in 1923. He lived with his family in New York City until 1924 and from 1929 until his death. Between 1924 and 1929, Halpern lived in Detroit, Cleveland, Los Angeles, and Boston, sometimes with and sometimes without his family. He earned an unpredictable living as a journalist and peripatetic writer and artist. He died in 1932.

In 1934, the Yiddish poet and critic Eliezer Greenberg edited two posthumous volumes of Halpern's previously uncollected poems, *Moyshe leyb halpern*. The first of these volumes has poems originally published in the New York Yiddish papers, and the second gathers previously unpublished poems. In 1954, Farlag Matones in New York reissued *In nyu york* in its third edition and *Di goldene pave* in its second edition.

Halpern's significance lies in the sharp individuality of his voice that tempered a sweet, quasi-sentimental romantic lyricism with the irony of social criticism turned inward. During his early years in America, Halpern was associated with *Di yunge* (The Young Ones), a movement of Yiddish poets who emphasized the importance of aestheticism and lyrical individualism in poetry. At the same time he also wrote for the "anti-aestheticist satirical magazines" (Howe, 1987) *Der kibitzer* and *Der groyser kundes* (The Big Stick). From 1921 to 1924, Halpern wrote steadily for the Jewish Communist daily newspaper, *Di frayhayt* (Freedom). Such bipolarity—the play between the lyric and the satiric, between the romantic individualist and the communal chastiser—characterizes Halpern's poetry. In fact, the distinctive quality of his poems depends upon his constant undercutting of poetic convention and the reader's expectation.

In his first book, *In nyu york*, the poems embody Halpern's struggle between the Jewish poet's traditional obligation to his people and the modern poet's individual sensibility and vision. Here one finds self-conscious, ironic versions of labor poems; "I. L. Peretz" (1915, 1919), an elegy that reads, in fact, as an anti-Kaddish; and "*A nakht*" (A Night) (1916, 1919), a pogrom narrative in which the Freudian protagonist has a collective, historical dream. Halpern's second collection of poems, *Di goldene pave*, further develops the technique of subverting a convention while using it. This occurs notably in his art ballads, which parody the coherent dialogue between singer and community found in authentic folk ballads. Some of Halpern's other poetic means in this second volume are his allegorical, pseudo folk fables and those poems that rely upon dramatic personae or characters who are themselves poetic objects. This latter type of poem is spoken either entirely by a dramatic persona or to a dramatic character who deflects the subjectivity of the poem. Sometimes these are illusorily "realistic" characters, such as Moyshe-Leyb the poet, "Reyzele" his wife, his toddler son, Aby Kirly, and the old man Zarkhi at the edge of the sea. Or they are fable characters, such as Yohama and Gingele. The personae in these poems give ironic leverage to the poems and Halpern's brilliance comes forth in the inspired, manic colloquialisms with which they speak or are characterized. Some of Halpern's most startling and original poems can be found in the two posthumous volumes, *Moyshe-leyb halpern.*

Halpern's importance to his contemporaries can be measured in part by the more than 50 poems and 400 articles written in Yiddish as a tribute to him from 1932 to 1954 by such diverse poets as Yankev Glatshteyn, Mani Leyb, Kadya Molodowsky, and Itzik Manger and such critics as Sh. Niger, Eliezer Greenberg, and Moyshe Nadir. (See Yeshurin's Bibliography.) The number of translations and scholarly assessments published in English from the 1960s onward (aside from those in Yiddish, Hebrew, French, Spanish, and German) attests to Halpern's continuing appeal to an American poetic and scholarly audience. Ultimately a lone figure, Halpern wrote poetry that boldly joined the solipsistic modern self to those larger forces influencing the lives of Eastern European Jews in America.

KATHRYN HELLERSTEIN

BIBLIOGRAPHY

Greenberg, Eliezer, ed. *Moyshe Leyb Halpern.* New York: Moyshe-Leyb Halpern Komittet, 1934.

——. *Moyshe Leyb Halpern in Ram Fun Zayn Dor.* New York: M. L. Halpern Arbeter Ring Branch 450, 1942.

Halpern, Moyshe-Leyb. *Di goldene pave.* Cleveland: Farlag Grupe Yiddish, 1924.

——. *In nyu york.* New York: Farlag Vinkl, 1919.

Harshav, Benjamin and Barbara, eds. *American Yiddish Poetry: A Bilingual Anthology.* Berkeley: University of California Press, 1986.

Hellerstein, Kathryn. "Moyshe-Leyb Halpern's *In New York*: A Modern Yiddish Verse Narrative." Ph.D. diss., 1980.

——, ed. *In New York: A Selection.* Moyshe-Leyb Halpern. Philadelphia: Jewish Publication Society, 1982.

Kharlash, Yitzkhak. "Moyshe Leyb Halpern." In *Leksikon fun der nayer yidisher literatur*, edited by Sh. Niger and I. Shatsky. 3 (1963): 31–37.

Wisse, Ruth R. *A Little Love in Big Manhattan: Two Yiddish Poets.* Cambridge: Harvard University Press, 1988.

Yeshurin, Yefis. "Moyshe leyb halpern-bibliografye." In *In nyu york*, 3rd ed., by Moyshe-Leyb Halpern. New York: Farlag Malones, 1954.

Hammer, Armand (1898–1990). Industrialist and entrepreneur. Armand Hammer was born on the Lower East Side of New York. His parents, Julius Hammer and Rose Lifschitz, were born in Russia and came to the United States in 1875. In his autobiography Hammer states that he was either named after Armand Duval, the hero in Dumas's *La Dame aux Camelias*, or the symbol of the Socialist Labor Party, the arm and hammer. As a child, Armand's father "weaned" his son on stories of pogroms and czarist anti-Semitism. Julius Hammer was active in the Socialist Labor Party and an admirer of Daniel DeLeon. Many years later, Menachem Begin would intercede on Hammer's behalf with President Ronald Reagan, who believed Armand was a Communist because of his father's reported affiliation with the party.

Armand Hammer earned his millions in many different enterprises. He made his first million while still a student at Columbia University. In 1921, he received his M.D. degree from the Columbia College of Physicians and Surgeons.

Hearing about the typhus epidemic in the Soviet Union, Hammer went to Russia in 1921 with his own mobile hospital unit. While there, he talked with Lenin, who convinced him to help the Russians with his business talent rather than his medical skills. Among his many financial achievements during his stay in Russia was to win sales concessions from Lenin for the Ford Motor Company, United States Rubber, Allis-Chalmers, and Underwood Typewriters. When he left the Soviet Union in 1930, the Soviets allowed him to acquire many of the former royal family's paintings. This was the genesis of his becoming one of the world's most famous art collectors.

By the 1950s, Hammer had not only established himself as one of the world's most successful industrialists but also as an important intermediary between the United States and the Soviet Union. Hammer was often used by the United States government on informal missions to the Kremlin. In 1956, he ventured into oil and became president and chief operating officer of the Occidental Petroleum Corporation, a post he held until 1973. However, despite Occidental's oil interests in Libya, Hammer remained a strong supporter of the State of Israel.

Not an actively practicing Jew, Hammer never hid his Jewishness and contributed to Jewish causes. He used his personal contacts in the Soviet Union on behalf of Soviet Jewry. Hammer argued that the best way to help Jewish dissidents in the Soviet Union is through discreet and quiet work. In his autobiography, Hammer takes credit for persuading Leonid Brezhnev to lift the education tax against Jews wishing to leave the Soviet Union.

Hammer lent his experience in the petroleum industry to help Israel drill for oil in the Negev. In 1989, Hammer used his Soviet contacts to provide Israel with important documents in the trial of John Demjanjuk.

On the eve of his death, Hammer was to be Bar-Mitzvahed, a religious ceremony that his parents denied him as a child.

JACK FISCHEL

BIBLIOGRAPHY
Hammer, Armand, with Neil Lyndon. *Hammer*. New York: Putnam, 1987.
Weinberg, Steve. *Armand Hammer, The Untold Story*. Boston: Little, Brown, 1989.

Handlin, Oscar (b. 1915). American historian Oscar Handlin was born in Brooklyn, the eldest child of Joseph and Ida Handlin, who had immigrated from Russia. At the age of 15, he qualified to enroll in Brooklyn College, and after graduation in 1934 he went to Harvard, from which he received an M.A. in 1935. In 1937 he married Mary Frug, and till her death in 1976 she was a partner in much of his scholarly work. In 1938–1939 he taught at Brooklyn and then returned to Harvard to obtain his Ph.D. (1940) and to teach. Beginning as an instructor, he rose steadily to Harvard's most eminent history professorships, the climax being his appointment as Carl H. Pforzheimer University Professor in 1973. In addition, he organized and directed the Center for the Study of Liberty in America (1958–1967)

and the Charles Warren Center for Studies in American History (1965–1973).

Handlin was highly regarded as a teacher. Additionally, he was productive as a writer. His first book, *Boston's Immigrants 1790–1865* (1941), won the John H. Dunning Prize of the American Historical Association; *The Uprooted* (1951), which is believed to reflect some of his childhood experiences, was awarded the Pulitzer Prize in history. *Adventure in Freedom: Three Hundred Years of Jewish Life in America* (1954) and numerous articles and reviews deal with themes of Jewish interest.

Much of Handlin's writing focuses on the immigrant, and his work has brought fresh light to bear not merely on the physical aspects of the transition from one part of the world to another, but also on the struggle and confusion involved in adapting to a new society.

Handlin has been a leading figure in Jewish studies. He was among the first professional scholars to deal with the whole scope of American Jewish history, and he has had great influence on a whole generation of academics, such as Moses Rischin, whose scholarship stresses the Jewish experience in the United States. *See also* Historiography.

S. D. TEMKIN

BIBLIOGRAPHY
Solomon, Barbara. "A Portrait of Oscar Handlin." In *Uprooted Americans—Essays to Honor Oscar Handlin*, edited by Richard L. Busman et al. Boston: Little, Brown, 1979.

Havurah Movement. The Hebrew word *havurah* means fellowship or friendship group. Since the 1960s it has been used in the United States to designate a variety of informal groups that have become popular in North American Jewish life. In their inception, many havurot (the plural form of havurah) defined themselves as alternatives to the organized structures of North American Jewry. They began as grass-roots expressions of a desire for Jewish renewal rather than as initiatives aimed at creating a new religious movement on the North American scene. The identification of the term "movement" accrued over time as a way of linking the multiplicity of disparate groups and communities that had emerged across the United States, designating themselves as havurah. Few would deny that the havurah phenomenon has had a major impact on the practices and beliefs of thousands of Jews throughout North America and has contributed to a new consciousness among American Jews. The havurah is more a movement of process than of ideology; however, those who identify with it tend to share a common core of beliefs. They value religious pluralism, understand Judaism as an evolving religious tradition, and regard every individual as empowered to participate actively in his or her cultural and spiritual heritage.

THE GENESIS OF THE CONTEMPORARY MOVEMENT. Both the term and the concept have ancient roots. In Jewish Palestine of the Second Commonwealth (first century B.C.E.), small utopian communities were established whose members took upon themselves a commitment to a rigorously observant lifestyle. The contemporary havurah emerged on the American scene in the 1960s. It caught the attention of the establishment Jewish leadership almost from the outset. While most havurah members focused their attention inward toward the group and its pursuits, some individuals began to write and speak in public forums about the challenges that a resurgent Judaism thrust upon American Jewry. In 1969, Hillel Levine, a member of Havurat Shalom of Somerville, Massachusetts, gave a major uninvited address to delegates of the General Assembly of the Council of Jewish Federations in Boston in which he demanded a redirection of communal resources and values.

From the outset there were two major trends in the movement, both identifying themselves as havurot and largely unaware of each other's development. Independent havurot arose in several communities where the (university) student movement was active. They grew out of the widespread unrest in the 1960s of those intellectually and politically turbulent times. At the same time, the Reconstructionist Movement, in particular, articulated a growing awareness of the need to transform the impersonality, formality, and passivity that characterized participation in American synagogue life. A few large suburban synagogues also sought to develop more meaningful and personal connections among their members.

Several factors contributed to the revival of interest in creating models of ideal Jewish communities, though none can be seen as the single catalyst for the emergence and acceptance of the havurah movement. Explorations in new forms of Judaism were given impetus by the political activism and cultural reexaminations that characterized the period. The "counterculture" of the sixties spawned many new experiments in group and communal living, and the independent havurah was a Jewish articulation of the search for a more meaningful community. It was an age where many young Americans were rejecting societal values of individual achievement measured by materialistic acquisitions and were seeking greater spiritual involvements, often within the context of a religious community. The havurah was able to offer a Jewish channel for the spiritual quest that was leading some Jewish seekers to Eastern religious traditions.

The advent of contemporary feminism generated a widespread critique of the male domination of social, religious, and educational institutions. Havurot responded to the challenge by creating opportunities for Jewish men and women to develop egalitarian structures for prayer and social interaction that were unavailable in most Jewish communal institutions and synagogues. Women affiliated with havurot were affected by the empowering voice of the women's movement in American society and brought their heightened awareness to their havurah groups. So, too, the renaissance in the consciousness of black Americans prodded some liberal Jews to look inward to their own heritage and group identity. The havurah was one response that expressed legitimate group differences and represented Jewish authenticity in ways that were creative, serious, and in tune with the cultural style of the generation.

The Vietnam War spurred widespread ferment and protest among a generation of college youth. During this period of breakdown of trust in major educational institutions, young people were emboldened to reject traditional authority and initiated their own peer-led groups for learning, personal growth, and social activism. It was an era known for the "generation gap," wherein young people sought to grapple with life's challenges in a milieu of their age peers, expressing alienation in relation to the generation of their elders.

In addition, sociological shifts in American Jewish life were occurring. The postwar baby boom and the increased access of Jews to higher education led to an enormous increase in the number of young Jews attending universities and traveling easily in intellectual and politically activist circles. While political, cultural, and social issues of the day dominated people's consciousness, less newsworthy factors, such as the increased mobility of young people, also changed the traditional patterns of Jewish life. Whereas holidays and festivals, for example, were traditionally family-centered occasions, by the 1960s young people were often living far from parents and grandparents. Friends replaced relatives as the basis of community, roots were where people chose to strike them, and havurot often became surrogate or substitute families.

THE INDEPENDENT HAVUROT. Havurat Shalom in Somerville, Massachusetts, was founded in 1968 as a community seminary by a number of young Jewish scholars, ordained rabbis, and graduate students. An autonomous group seeking new forms of religious commitment and spiritual expression, it created a context for serious and intensive exploration of Jewish texts and modalities of prayer and the development of an intensely involved community. Some of its members were also seeking a legitimate exemption to military service during the Vietnam War; a religious seminary could provide both spiritual nourishment and a justifiable alternative to the draft.

There was a reluctance to designate formal leaders, and many leadership functions were shared or rotated in the group. Rabbi Arthur Green provided spiritual direction for the community, whose first teachers included Rabbis Zalman Schacter Shalomi and Everett Gendler. Many other members of Havurat Shalom chose careers in fields of Jewish scholarship and have gone on to make distinguished contributions to contemporary Jewish intellectual life through their writings and teachings.

Similar groups soon emerged, such as the New York Havurah, the Fabrengen in Washington, and Philadelphia's Germantown Minyan and B'nai Or community. Havurot groups also formed in Chicago, Cincinnati, and Cleveland during the early 1970s. They varied in their political, spiritual, and communal orientations and their different emphases on study, prayer, personal growth, and group dynamics. The Fabrengen in Washington, for example, was very politically involved in liberal/Left causes, motivated to engage in social activism and protest by the members' understanding of Jewish values and commitment to repair the world (*tikkun olam*). Kibbutz Langdon in Wisconsin was formed a few years later as a residential commune whose members attempted to transfer the ideals of Jewish socialism to an urban, campus setting. Initially, each group arose without specific reference to the others, insisting on its autonomy and integrity as a community, each seeing itself as a timely response to the personal, political, and communal priorities of their individual members. After a few years, occasional regional gatherings took place at Weiss's Farm in New Jersey, attracting members of independent havurot from several East Coast and Midwest communities.

In 1970, the Jewish women's group Ezrat Nashim was established. Although it was not itself a havurah, the group was started by members of the New York Havurah and reflected a Jewish feminist consciousness and a political approach that was developed within it. This collective of women became vocal advocates for the ordination of women as rabbis and for the full empowerment of women in all areas of Jewish life.

The diverse independent havurot were linked by a general consciousness shaped by the student subculture of those times. They rejected the authority of rabbis as the specialists of Jewish experience and the broadcasters of Jewish priorities. The focus was on the individual's responsibility for change and self-definition. Havurah Jews shared aspirations for a less materialistic environment wherein close interpersonal relationships and attention to the spiritual needs of the self would make for a more harmonious world and a Jewish society returned to its own roots and basic values.

THE SYNAGOGUE HAVUROT. Concurrent with the emergence of the independent havurot, but unidentified with them, groups calling themselves havurot were forming within synagogues or as alternative unstructured synagogues in several parts of the United States. In contrast to the independent havurot, whose founding members were primarily unmarried individuals or young couples without children, these groups were usually composed of small clusters of families. The Reconstructionist Movement encouraged small groups of people to come together as "fellowships" and promoted the ideal of self-directed study. In 1960, their association took the name of the Federation of Reconstructionist Congregations and Fellowships, which was changed to Reconstructionist Congregations and Havurot in 1982. Denver, Colorado, was the birthplace of a number of these havurot, which engaged in educational programming for their children, adult study groups focusing on Jewish ethics and values, holiday observances, and Sabbath services. Decision-making was a democratic process, and concern for the welfare of the group and the satisfaction of its members was a valued priority.

In Los Angeles at the large Temple Valley Beth Shalom, under the leadership of Rabbi Harold Schulweis, congregants were grouped into smaller units in order to establish more personal ties among them and engender feelings of familiarity and comfort with each other and with Judaism not possible within a synagogue of well over a thousand members. Participants in the synagogue's 60 havurot learned to take responsibility for their group's activities and to relate to each other's needs and Jewish interests. In other far-flung parts of the country, too, from Savannah, Georgia, to Marblehead, Massachusetts, havurot emerged as a dynamic response to the passivity and indifference that often characterized synagogue affiliation. Some rabbis supported and encouraged havurot to form within their congregations; others felt threatened by the decentralization and independence of the groups and the shift in their leadership role necessitated by the development of synagogue havurot.

COMMONALITIES AND CONTRASTS BETWEEN THE HAVUROT.

Despite their many differences, the havurot share certain common characteristics. What they generally have in common is their small size, the value that they place on a high degree of involvement and personal participation of all members, and a shared, democratic leadership structure. Most are egalitarian, meaning that roles and responsibilities in all spheres of activity are equally accessible to men and women.

In 1990, it cannot be claimed that an ideal model of havurah exists. Several typical paradigms have developed with various regional, age, and lifestyle differences. When havurot are affiliated with synagogues, they tend to identify themselves with a particular branch of religious Judaism in North America. The Reconstructionist, Reform, and Conservative movements have all established havurot or have been in association with havurot that function as unstructured synagogues. The independent havurot generally reject any formal attachment to the denominational allegiances of the synagogue movements. Religious norms for observance in the group setting are usually established by consensus; they may be more stringent than those practiced by individual group members in their home environment. Kashrut or vegetarianism are frequently accepted as binding on the group for meals taken together. Most groups do not articulate expectations for individuals' personal practice. The approach of havurot to prayer, Torah study, and worship tends to be eclectic. They may blend disparate liturgical elements and combine traditional Jewish prayer with innovative additions in both Hebrew and English. A havurah service may borrow freely from Hasidic traditions, Camp Ramah prayer services (an experience shared by many members of the original independent havurot), critical text interpretation feminist conceptions of the Divine, and Eastern meditational techniques.

HAVURAH ACTIVITIES.

A havurah describing itself as an independent Jewish community will seek to fulfill a wide range of religious, communal, and social needs of its members. These will include providing Jewish education for themselves and their children, observing Jewish holy days and festivals together, engaging in prayer services, making joint philanthropic contributions (through *tzedakah* collectives), celebrating communal meals, occasionally participating in weekend retreats, and sharing each other's milestone events—happy occasions, such as marriages, baby namings, and bar and bat mitzvahs, and hard times, such as illness, divorce, death of parents, loss of employment, and so forth. More often, a havurah will engage in some, but not all, of the aforementioned activities. It may constitute itself as an adult study group or a collection of families that meet to celebrate the Sabbath and Jewish holidays, or a "minyan," an assembly of individuals who come together primarily for purposes of communal Jewish prayer. Some of these havurot have continued for more than a decade and attest to strong personal relationships and enduring Jewish commitments in the adult lives of their members.

The early experiments in forging inclusive communities demanded intense involvement, and occasional conflicts and tensions caused some members to leave and others to reformulate their expectations of themselves and the group. Those havurot that continue into the 1990s have tended to moderate the nature of interactions within the group and respond to the changing life issues and concerns of their members as they grow older. Independent havurot of young Jews that have formed or reconstituted themselves through the 1970s and 1980s have defined themselves as alternative communities in light of issues that have risen to prominence during these years. Gay and lesbian Jews, for example, have confronted their communities with their concerns about inherent bias against homosexuals and have challenged prevailing assumptions regarding sexual orientation.

A heightened consciousness about gender concerns has motivated a reconsideration of traditional liturgy composed by men only and the masculine God language in which it is written. For several groups, the emphasis has moved from equal access and equal participation of women and men within the tradition to a critique of the inherent masculine centeredness of concepts and images in Judaism and creative attempts to reformulate them. The National Havurah Summer Institutes have offered a fertile testing ground for the introduction of new prayers and blessings, notably those composed by the feminist poet and writer Marcia Falk.

ORGANIZATIONAL DEVELOPMENT. An informal steering committee of volunteers met throughout 1978 to consider the phenomenon of the havurah in American Jewish life and to ponder what, if anything, the diverse groups across the country had in common. In the summer of 1979, 350 people attended the first National Havurah Conference, which took place at Rutgers University in New Jersey. It brought together a wide range of individuals and groups affiliated with "havurah Judaism" to study, worship, celebrate the Shabbat, examine the ideals and values of the havurah experience, share resources and ideas, and applaud their existence as a new force in North American Jewish life. The following year, the National Havurah Committee (NHC) was formed, with a board of directors drawn from independent and synagogue-based havurot across the United States, though predominantly from New York, Philadelphia, Boston, Washington, and Los Angeles. Michael Strassfeld was the founding chairperson. The creation of the NHC was accompanied by considerable controversy within some havurah groups, for some believed that an organization of havurot was a contradiction in terms.

The NHC defined itself as only one expression of the pluralistic havurah movement, which it explicitly recognized. It committed itself to remain independent of any of the denominational movements. Programming was aimed to appeal to transdenominational concerns for Jewish ideas, ethics, and religious practices. There would be national summer institutes for study and experiential learning, regional outreach activities and networking, and a number of publications, including a weekly Dvar Torah column that appeared in a number of Jewish community newspapers and the NHC's own newsletter, *Havurah*.

The National Havurah Committee has sponsored a week-long residential institute every summer since 1980. It draws both Judaically knowledgeable participants and those who are just beginning to study and explore Jewish texts and tradition. The program has developed over the years and, in addition to courses in classical and contemporary Jewish texts, offers sessions on a wide range of current Jewish issues and interests. "Hands-on" workshops in Jewish crafts, and the arts, "how-to" lessons in synagogue skills, and major participatory symposia on Jewish ethical dilemmas are all an integral part of the program, as is a full schedule of planned activities for the children of adult participants. The event enables people to experience themselves as part of a larger havurah community during the institute and to identify with a national movement upon their return to their home environments. Issues of religious pluralism, tolerance for diversity within the community, feminist and gay demands for a rigorously egalitarian community, questions about authority and Halachic (Jewish legal) standards for the community have all arisen as tensions and challenges for the group at its gatherings.

CONTRIBUTIONS OF THE HAVURAH MOVEMENT. The contribution of havurot to North American Jewry cannot be measured simply in terms of the activities, programs, and initiatives of the groups themselves. It is, indeed, difficult to separate out the explicit and distinct influences of the havurah movement. For many of its adherents their adult Jewish identities have been forged by and through their havurah experiences. Several former members of the independent havurot of the 1960s and 1970s have assumed positions of leadership in the mainstream organizations that they once spurned or in which they had seen no place for themselves. The Reconstructionist Rabbinical College, the American Jewish Committee, the Jewish Theological Seminary of America, YIVO, the Solomon Schechter Day Schools, the National Foundation for Jewish Culture, and the Federation of Jewish Philanthropies are just a few of the institutions in which independent havurah activists currently play important professional leadership roles. Several others have become scholars, teachers, and researchers in fields of Jewish study in major universities throughout the United States and Canada.

Jewish feminist scholarship was given impetus through a range of havurah experiences. Innovations in liturgy and practice emerging from a critique of traditional masculine conceptions of God and experimenting with new God language are frequently tested in havurah communities. It is fair to attribute some of the new initiatives in Jewish family education, such as weekend retreats and Shabbatonim, to the influence of the havurah movement. So, too, the Orthodox women's prayer groups that have developed in various communities borrow in style and approach from havurah services. One can also make the claim that some new directions in rabbinic education and training have been influenced by havurot, where the role of rabbi necessarily moved from that of ultimate authority to one of resource person, teacher, and group facilitator. More emphasis is given to these functions and skills in the current preparation of rabbis than was the case some years ago.

Response magazine, *Menorah* newsletter, and *The Jewish Catalogs* originated in the havurah culture and were edited and contributed to by people involved in havurot and identified with the havurah movement. Several books have been written and published, and scholarly journals have arisen that reflect their authors' havurah-based commitments to reappropriate the value and study of Jewish texts, both classical and contemporary. *Back to the Sources* (ed. B. Holtz, 1984) is one such example, most of whose contributors have long been active within havurah circles. Many Jewish newspapers and magazines have featured stories and articles about the havurah movement, which is widely recognized as a major influence in revitalizing American Jewish life.

What cannot yet be assessed is the viability of the havurah movement to sustain itself as an independent force in American Judaism. Several of its innovations have been appropriated into mainstream Jewish life. Just as the havurah emerged out of a confluence of social and cultural factors, so it has contributed to contemporary Jewish-American history and culture in a variety of ways. The havurah has been responsive to the changing needs of its adherents; indeed, the ability to develop and respond has differentiated these small groups from the formal, highly structured institutions of the Jewish establishment. However, changes have occurred within synagogues, too. It is no longer unusual for havurah members to belong to the local synagogue in the community where they reside in addition to their havurah affiliation. It remains to be seen what Jew-

ish path the children who have grown up within havurot will take. Those who have developed a sense of themselves as Jews through their havurah experiences may feel that their primary Jewish home will always be a small group of caring individuals who share common values and ideals and approaches to celebrating their Judaism. However, they may choose to exercise their leadership skills in the context of the larger American Jewish community and advocate for change in the wider arena. What the lasting impact of the havurah experience on Jewish identification and practice is for the next generation cannot yet be evaluated. *See also* Reconstructionism.

ELAINE SHIZGAL COHEN

BIBLIOGRAPHY

Elazar, Daniel J., and Monson, Rela Geffen. "The Synagogue Havurah—An Experiment in Restoring Adult Fellowship to the Jewish Community." *Jewish Journal of Sociology* XX1 (June 1979).

"Jewish Radical Zionists in the U.S." *Encyclopedia Judaica Yearbook, 1975-1976* (Jerusalem).

Havurah. 1980-. Newsletter. National Havurah Committee, 9315 SW Court, Miami, FL 33156.

Neusner, Jacob. *Contemporary Judaic Fellowship in Theory and In Practice.* New York: Ktav, 1972.

Prell, Riv-Ellen. *Prayer and Community—The Havurah in American Judaism.* Detroit: Wayne State University Press, 1989.

Reisman, Bernard. *The Chavurah.* New York: Union of American Hebrew Congregations, 1977.

Hasidism. *See* LUBAVITCHER REBBE, ORTHODOXY, SATMAR REBBE.

Hebrew Education. *See* JEWISH EDUCATION.

Hebrew in America. The oft quoted adage that "Hebraic mortar has cemented the foundations of American democracy" was undoubtedly coined because of the influence of the Bible on early American society. It was the theological interest in the Bible that led to the study of the Hebrew language at various educational institutions beginning with colonial times when Hebrew was a required subject of study. That the seals of such universities as Yale, Columbia, and Dartmouth still retain Hebrew inscriptions attests to the high regard in which the language was held. The large number of Hebrew grammars and lexicons published in this country over a long period attest to the popularity of biblical and Hebrew learning among non-Jews. Judah Monis, a converted Jew who was professor of Hebrew at Harvard, was the author of the first grammar, entitled *A Grammar of the Hebrew Tongue*, which was published in 1734.

The very first book printed in the American colonies, the *Bay Psalm Book* (1640) consisted of a translation of the Psalms and contained Hebrew type and a preface by Richard Mather on Hebrew poetry and the Hebrew language. There is also the fascinating report quoted by Henry Mencken in his book *The American Language* that at the close of the American Revolution some members of Congress proposed that English be prohibited and Hebrew be substituted for the language of the mother country.

Despite the early interest in Hebrew in America, the fact remains that Hebrew literary activity among American Jews is of comparatively late origin. It was not until the advent of the increased Jewish immigration during the second half of the nineteenth century that we have the beginnings of publication in Hebrew. Until that time, the small Jewish population had few Hebrew scholars, and the use of the language was limited to religious purposes. The few examples of secular Hebrew usage by Jews, such as the Hebrew commencement address delivered in 1800 at Columbia College by Sampson Simson, the first Jewish graduate, remain but oddities.

By the middle of the nineteenth century there was a slow influx of rabbis and religious functionaries who brought with them a knowledge of Hebrew, which they tried to foster here. Such men as Isaac Leeser, Sabato Morais, Benjamin Szold, and Henry Vidaver included Hebrew writing and scholarship among their interests. Gradually the arrival of East European intellectuals widened the audience for Hebrew endeavor. Among the early East European rabbis was Joshua Falk, who in 1860 published *Avne Yehoshua* (The Stones of Joshua), a commentary on the Ethics of the Fathers. His book has the distinction of being the first Hebrew book printed in America.

The American Hebrew press had its inception with the publication in 1871 of *Ha-Zofeh ba-Arez ha-Hadashah* (The Observer in the New Land), which lasted for some five years. Its editor was Zvi Hirsch Bernstein, who sought to provide the new immigrants with a link to the Old World and to create an organ that would help integrate them into their new life. To further these aims, Bernstein solicited contributions from Hebrew writers in Europe and encouraged the publication of material on American life and history. Except for the publication in Chicago of a Hebrew supplement of the Yiddish newspaper *Die Israelitische Presse*, no other journalistic effort was made until the end of the 1880s.

In 1877, there appeared a small volume of verse that is known as the first printed work of both Hebrew and Yiddish poetry. The author, Jacob Zvi Soble, an immigrant from Russia, entitled his book *Shir Zahav li-Khevod Yisrael ha-Zaken* (A Golden Song in Honor of Age-Old Israel). It included a poem about "A Polish Scholar" in America that mirrors the struggles of a learned Jewish immigrant who had to bear the peddler's pack. Three of the four poems in the work were translated by the author into Yiddish.

In 1880, there was founded in New York the *Shohare Sefat Ever* (Friends of Hebrew), which may be considered the first organized society of Hebraists in the world. Its program for fostering Hebrew included the publication of a quarterly magazine, of which only the first number appeared in 1881 under the title *Ha-Meassef ba-Arez ha-Hadashah* (The Compiler in a New Land). The society was the prototype of scores of others that were organized throughout the country in later years. In Chicago, a Hebrew society sponsored the literary organ *Keren Or* (Ray of Light), the first Hebrew monthly in America. In Baltimore, the efforts of local Hebraists were supported by Benjamin Szold, whose scholarly commentary on the book of Job was published in 1886.

The Hebrew writers who arrived as part of the immigrant waves of the 1880s and 1890s voiced their constant complaints about the difficult economic struggle that they faced. Thus, in his book *Ha-Yehudim ve'ha-Yahadut be-New York* (The Jews and Judaism in New York, 1887), Moses Weinberger decried the low state of Jewish cultural and religious life. Nevertheless, the various immigrant authors who settled here persisted in their efforts. In 1889, three weekly publications were launched. Wolf Schur made his first effort to publish *Ha-Pisgah* (The Summit) in New York. Although only 13 issues of the weekly appeared, it was to resume publication in Baltimore, Boston, and Chicago and to continue to appear with interruptions down to 1901. In its last phase in Chicago it went under the name *Ha-Tehiyah* (The Rebirth). Schur also published one of the more important books of the 1890s, *Nezah*

Yisrael (Israel Eternal, 1897), in which he upheld the Jewish religion against missionary attacks and opposed Reform, socialist, and anarchist efforts to weaken it. He was followed by Ephraim Deinard, whose *Ha-Leumi* (The Nationalist) lasted for 23 issues. Michael Levi Rodkinson published *Ha-Kol* (The Voice) for 19 issues, first as a weekly and then as a biweekly. In 1890, he edited *Ha-Sanegor* (The Defender), which appeared irregularly and lasted but for 9 issues.

Kasriel Zvi Sarasohn, who played a central role as a publisher of Yiddish newspapers, also entered the field of Hebrew journalism. After a short-lived partnership with Schur in publishing *Ha-Pisgah*, he launched his own Hebrew weekly, *Ha-Ivri* (The Hebrew) in 1892. Gerson Rosenzweig, the poet satirist who was a regular contributor, eventually assumed the editorship of this publication, which was issued with interruptions during 1892–1898 and again in 1901–1902. In 1899, Rosenzweig also edited the monthly *Kadimah* (Forward) and launched the humorous monthly publication *Ha-Devorah* (The Bee) in 1912. The 1890s saw the debut of several other journalistic ventures, the most important among them being *Ner ha-Maaravi* (The Western Light), issued by the Society for the Advancement of Hebrew Literature in America.

Among the important works that appeared during the last decade of the nineteenth century were the concluding volume of Alexander Kohut's *Ha-Arukh ha-Shalem* (Arukh Completum), the first two parts of Abraham H. Rosenberg's *Otzar ha-Shemot* (Cyclopedia of Biblical Names), and Arnold B. Ehrlich's *Mikra ki-Feshuto* (The Bible According to Its Plain Meaning). Still the general picture of Hebrew literary creativity remained bleak indeed.

Gerson Rosenzweig sought refuge in satire and in well-turned epigrams hit at various ills in American Jewish life. A master of parody, he composed his *Talmud Yankai* (Yankee Talmud) in which he castigated American Jews as a shallow people. The poet Isaac Rabinowitz, who had been part of the literary scene in Europe, fell into decline and made his verse a vehicle for his despair.

Menahem Mendel Dolitzky, who had been touted as the successor to the noted poet Judah Leib Gordon, also succumbed to a spirit of sadness and futility. While still loyal to the romantic dream of Zion restored, he never came to terms with America and remained a lost soul. And Naphtali Herz Imber, author of the national anthem *Hatikvah* (The Hope), led here a vagabond

existence. Rabinowitz and Dolitzky turned to the writing of Yiddish melodramatic novels in order to eke out a living. Imber devoted most of his efforts to the publishing of books and articles in English during his American period.

Were it not for the influx during the 1900s of a new type of Hebraist who was caught up by the spirit of renascent Hebrew, American Hebrew letters might never have entered upon a modern period in which significant writings were produced. The new arrivals joined the *Mefize Sefat Ever* (Disseminators of the Hebrew Language), which was founded in 1902 and which advanced the ideals of Hebraism, which its members had brought with them from Europe. In 1909, Moshe Ben-Eliezer was able to found a modern journal, *Shibbolim* (Ears of Corn), in which the work of a number of new young writers first appeared.

The old-time intellectuals, however, did not relax their efforts to propagate their ideas. Moses Goldman, who edited *Ha-Leom* (The Nation, 1901–1908), first as a monthly and then as a weekly, felt that the time was ripe enough for a Hebrew daily newspaper. He published *Ha-Yom* (The Day) in 1909 and again in 1913.

By this time the number of modern Hebrew-speaking societies had proliferated and had joined together under the aegis of the *Ahiever* (Hebrew Brotherhood). This organization initiated in 1913 the publication of *Ha-Toren* (The Mast), which continued to appear until 1925 and which was to benefit from the editorship of such veteran Hebrew writers as Isaac Dov Berkowitz and Reuben Brainin. Together with *Ha-Ivri* (The Hebrew, 1916–1921), edited by Rabbi Meyer Berlin, it played a vital role in the furthering of creative Hebrew writing. By 1921, the organized Hebraists were able to launch the daily newspaper *Hadoar* (The Post), which became the focal point for American Hebrew writing. It soon became evident that the publication could not continue as a daily. Instead, it became a weekly and has perservered to this day. Its editor, Menahem Ribalow, became a central figure on the Hebrew literary scene. He spearheaded various literary undertakings and headed up the Ogen publishing agency which made available the works of American Hebrew authors.

Conditions were now ripe for the development in America of a new center, albeit a minor one, for Hebrew literary creativity. It was furthered in 1909 with the publication of Benjamin Nahum Silkiner's epic poem *Mul Ohel Timmurah* (Facing Timmurah's Tent), which initated the trend of giving expression to indigenous American themes. Silkiner dealt with the dramatic chapter of the defeat and subjugation of the Indians during the era of Spanish rule. He was to be followed by other American Hebrew poets who took their cue from him and dealt not only with the Red Man but also with the blacks and various other American themes. Silkiner became the central figure of a whole group of poets, who in 1910 issued a collective volume of poetry aptly entitled *Senunit* (Swallow). It ushered in a new era in American Hebrew letters.

While American Hebrew literature may be characterized as largely a literature of immigrants, it does represent an effort to strike roots in American soil. The primary contribution of the writers was to open up Hebrew literature to Anglo-American literary influences. As part of their effort to give expression to their role as American writers, the writers devoted themselves to such projects as the translation of Shakespeare's plays and the rendering into Hebrew of the works of leading English and American poets and prose writers.

Silkiner, who had introduced the Indian motif into American Hebrew poetry, was followed by Israel Efros, who in his *Wigwamim Shotekim* (Silent Wigwams) related a melodramatic tale of the love of the half-Indian Lalari for an Englishman. The most ambitious work dealing with the Indians was Ephraim E. Lisitzky's *Medurot Doakhot* (Dying Campfires). His work made wide use of Indian folklore and legend and depicted the rivalry of two tribes that led ultimately to their decline.

Not only the Indian but blacks as well provided American Hebrew poets with thematic material. Lisitzky was the author of an entire volume entitled *Be-Ohale Cush* (In the Tents of Cush), dealing with the folklore and travail of American blacks. A long-time resident of New Orleans, Lisitzky came to know the black spirit and identified with black spirituals, religiosity, and childlike simplicity. Other poets, like Hillel Bavli and Eisig Silberschlag, turned their attention as well to motifs dealing with blacks.

While a number of the poets who experienced the pangs of acclimitization, like Abraham S. Schwartz, remained detached from reality and sought refuge in the past, the majority did seek to treat various aspects of American and American Jewish life. Efros was the author of an epic poem on the California Gold Rush entitled *Zahav* (Gold). Simon Ginsburg devoted poems to the

city of New York and the Hudson. Bavli was the author of perceptive idylls about New England figures, as well as the Mormons. Lisitzky contributed idylls of small-town American Jewish life, which touched upon the problems of assimilation and intermarriage. Simon Halkin dealt with Cafe Royal types in New York and wrote evocative nature poems, such as "On the Shore of Santa Barbara." He was also the translator of Whitman's *Leaves of Grass*. Abraham Regelson, in his poetic output, manifested a close affinity to the masters of Anglo-American literature. The American influence has been most pronounced in the modernist poetry of Gabriel Preil. It is as natural for Preil to use Whitman or Washington Irving as subjects for his poems as it is for him to refer to the angel Gabriel or his own grandfather. He has identified closely with the American landscape, particularly that of New England, and his imagist verse is widely accepted and dealt with by literary critics in Israel.

If Americanism is the bond of these poets with this country, then the ideal of Zion is their link with the people of Israel and its age-old aspirations. They exhibit strong emotional ties to Zion, which are expressed in feelings of polarity and ambivalence regarding their life in America. The Holocaust, too, has had an impact on their work, and its tragedies are depicted in the poetry of Lisitzky, Bavli, Efros, and others.

Prominent among the subjects that are treated in American Hebrew poetry are biblical themes and characters. Silkiner has dealt with Ruth and with Hagar and Ishmael. Ginsburg was the author of a book entitled *Ahavat Hosea* (The Love of Hosea). Regelson penned a philosophical poem on Cain and Abel. Halkin illumined the character of Baruch ben Niriah, the disciple of the prophet Jeremiah. Moses was the subject of poems by Efros and Schwartz, who also dealt with Ruth and Jeremiah. Moshe Feinstein was the author of an historical poem on the thirteenth-century mystic and Kabbalist Abraham Abulafia. Aaron Zeitlin, who came to this country from Poland in 1939, issued a series of impressive works in which he continued to draw upon mysticism and symbolism for inspiration. For the most part, it was lyrical poetry in which most of the poets found they could best give expression to their feelings of loneliness and isolation.

The Chicago-born poet Reuven Avinoam, who made his home in Israel, was the editor and major translator of two important anthologies which were devoted to English and American poetry respectively. Three leading American Hebrew poets who took up residence in Israel were Efros, Halkin, and Regelson. Indicative of the reception accorded to their work is the fact that they were each awarded the prestigious Bialik Prize for belles lettres. The American-born T. Carmi, who settled in Israel, has achieved recognition as a leading modernist poet. He has several volumes to his credit and is the editor and translator of the *Penguin Book of Hebrew Verse*, as well as the translator of a number of works by Shakespeare and other leading literary figures. Another American-born writer, Reuven Ben-Yosef, who published English poetry here, successfully made the transition to Hebrew poetry.

Among other authors who published collections of their poetry were Moshe Brind, Aaron Domnitz, Israel J. Schwartz, Moshe S. Ben-Meir, Abraham Z. Halevi, Eliezer D. Friedland, Elhanan Indelman, Rena Lee, and George Goren.

American Hebrew prose represents a much later development and is neither as varied nor as extensive as the poetic output. In this area as well we find a progression from immigrant themes to thoughtful and mature treatments of American Jewish life.

The earlier prose writers, like Isaac Dov Berkowitz, Abraham Soyer, and even L. A. Arieli, remained strangers to America and retained a sentimental attachment to the Old World. Samuel L. Blank published a number of stories that were set in America, but his best writing dealt chiefly with Jewish life in Bessarabia. The historical novel was cultivated by Johanan Twersky and Harry Sackler, who was also a dramatist and wrote not only in Hebrew but in Yiddish and English as well. Sackler's novel *Bein Eretz ve-Shamayim* (Between Earth and Heaven) treats American Jewish immigrant life.

A shift in emphasis was heralded by Abraham H. Friedland, who was the first among the prose writers to describe realistically characters on the American scene. Also active as a poet, he recorded with psychological insight incidents from various areas of Jewish life, including religious and communal activity. Bernard Isaacs was among those who in his short stories was able to shift his interest from the Old World milieu to American Jewish life. A keen observer of the American scene, he interpreted the mind of both integrated and ambivalent American Jews. Other writers of short stories and sketches were Aaron D. Markson, Solomon Damesek, and Simha Rubinstein.

By far the most significant contributions to American Hebrew prose writing were made by Simon Halkin and Reuben Wallenrod. Halkin's novel *Ad Mashber* (To the Point of Crisis) is an ambitious effort to depict the inner life of New York Jewry on the eve of the Great Depression. Implied in his psychological treatment of his characters, who run the gamut of Riverside Drive Jews, East Side inhabitants, Greenwich Village radicals, and members of the "lost generation," is a questioning of the direction and viability of American Jewish life.

Wallenrod, like his counterparts among Yiddish and American Jewish writers, illumined various facets of Jewish immigrant life. His novel *Ki Fanah Yom* (The Day Wanes, translated by him into English under the title *Dusk in the Catskills*) depicts the disillusionment of Jewish farmers who turned to hotel-keeping. Several of his stories deal with the adjustment of postwar Russian-Jewish immigrant youth to America.

Hebrew scholarship, which had but few notable representatives in the earlier period, began to be actively cultivated in the twentieth century. This development was furthered by the concentration here of leading scholars and the growth of institutions of higher Jewish learning, including the Hebrew Union College, the Jewish Theological Seminary, Yeshiva University, and Dropsie College. The Hebrew writings of such scholars as Louis Ginzburg, Chaim Tchernowitz, David Neumark, Israel Davidson, Michael Higger, and Samuel J. Feigin, among others, helped enrich Jewish learning. Judah David Eisenstein singlehandedly produced and edited a number of encyclopedic works, including the 10-volume *Otzar Yisrael* (Treasury of Israel) devoted to all aspects of Judaism and the Jewish people. The pioneering efforts of these men were built upon and expanded by a host of other scholars.

Biblical studies were augmented by the contributions of H. L. Ginsberg and Robert Gordis. The field of rabbinics was enriched by the works of Saul Lieberman, Louis Finkelstein, Simon Federbush, Samuel K. Mirsky, Abraham Weiss, Samuel Atlas, and David Helivni-Weiss. Simon Bernstein, Shalom Spiegel, Leon J. Weinberger, and Menahem Schmelzer contributed to the publication of medieval Hebrew poetic texts. Meyer Waxman, the author of the multivolume *History of Jewish Literature*, wrote monographs on important figures in Hebrew literature and Jewish thought. In the area of history, Pinkhos Churgin published studies on the period of the Second

Commonwealth, and Abraham S. Halkin dealt with themes from medieval times. The works of Simon Rawidowicz, who settled in America after World War II, dealt with various aspects of Jewish philosophy. Moshe H. Amishai-Meisels, who served for some years as the editor of *Hadoar*, was the author of a philosophical work entitled *Mahashavah ve-Emet* (Thought and Truth).

Several of the authors who made their mark in belles lettres also cultivated the essay and literary criticism. Among the poets and prose writers who published collections of essays were Bavli, Lisitzky, Halkin, Ginsburg, Efros, Regelson, Silberschlag, and Zeitlin. Wallenrod's book of essays was devoted entirely to American novelists.

Menahem Ribalow was among those who held out high hopes for the growth and development of Hebrew literary creativity in America. In addition to editing the weekly *Hadoar*, the *American Hebrew Yearbook* and the *Anthology of American Hebrew Poetry*, he was the author of five volumes of literary criticism. His last book, *Me'Olam le-Olam*, which was published posthumously, contains a section on New England and its literary figures. Jacob J. Wohl treated both European and Hebrew literature in his *Shte Reshuyot* (Two Realms), while Joshua Ovsay wrote on literary subjects and the world of East European learning in his *Maamarim u'Reshimot* (Articles and Notes). Abraham Epstein included in his critical purview a two-volume work entitled *Sofrim Irvim ba-Amerikah* (Hebrew Authors in America), and Isaiah Rabinowitz, who also wrote short stories, adopted a humanistic approach in his two volumes of critical essays.

Zvi Sharfstein, who enriched Hebrew textbook literature, was the author of a multivolume history of Jewish education and also two volumes of memoirs. The veteran educator Israel Z. Frishberg published a collection of essays on educational and publicist themes. William Chomsky was the author of a book on *Hebrew the Eternal Language*, which appeared in both English and Hebrew versions. A unique role in the fostering of modern Hebrew literary expression was played by Daniel Persky, who for many years contributed feuiletons to *Hadoar*. His literary output includes collections of holiday pieces and a volume entitled *Ivri Anokhi* (I Am a Hebrew), consisting of essays on the Hebrew language and literature. The field of bibliography was enriched by Isaac Rivkind, an authority of the history of Hebrew printing, and Eliezer R. Malachi, who achieved prominence for his expertise on the Hebrew press and the history of the Palestine Yishuv.

A major contribution was made by Abraham J. Heschel with the publication of his two-volume work *Torah Min ha-Shamayim ba-Aspaklariah Shel ha-Dorot* (Theology of Judaism). Nahum N. Glatzer issued studies on Jewish thought, while Moshe Davis and Jacob Kabakoff published volumes on American Jewish history and American Hebrew literature, respectively. Among other scholars who published studies in the fields of history and literary criticism were Yekuthiel Ginzburg, Moses Shulvass, Moshe Carmilly-Weinberger, Moshe Starkman, Moshe Pelli, Ezra Spicehandler, Abraham Holtz, Noah Rosenblum, Aryeh Weinman, and Yael Feldman.

Other essayists who were active on the American Hebrew literary scene and who issued their writings in book form were Abraham Goldberg, Moshe Halevi, Shalom B. Maximon, and Zevi Diesendruck. Abraham S. Orlans, Judah Pilch, and Philip Birnbaum also published collections of articles.

Several factors, including the settling in Israel of a number of leading authors and the death of others, have combined to bring about a decline in American Hebrew literary productivity, which reached its high point in the period between the two World Wars. The publication of the three imposing double volumes of the literary miscellany *Hatekufah* (The Era, 1946, 1948, 1950), under the editorship of Eisig Silberschlag and Aaron Zeitlin, represented a last concerted effort to present the fruits of American Hebrew literary creativity. *Hatekufah* was sponsored by the veteran publisher Abraham Stybel, who had headed the famed Stybel publishing house in Europe. Because few native creative authors have appeared to take the place of the earlier literary figures, American Hebrew writing is now confined largely to scholarship and the publishing of rabbinic tracts. The annual bibliographies of American Hebrew books that appear in the *Jewish Book Annual* bear witness to this fact.

The organized movement for Hebrew in America is represented by the Histadruth Ivrith (Hebrew Language and Cultural Association). It was not until 1916 that the various Hebrew-speaking societies were brought under one banner with the founding that year of this body. At its first convention, held in New York in 1917, the presence of such Zionist figures as Shmarya Levin, David Ben-Gurion, Yizhak Ben-Zvi, and Eliezer Ben-Yehuda served to spark the movement for Hebrew language and culture and to give impetus to its activities.

During its early years the organization engaged in various educational and literary projects. It maintained the Tarbut teacher-training courses and published books and paperbacks through its publication arm, Kadimah. When the Hebrew daily newspaper *Hadoar* became a weekly in 1922, its publication was assumed by the Histadruth Ivrith.

The organization has published more than 60 volumes of belles lettres and research, and for a number of years it issued the *Sefer ha-Shanah l'Yehude Amerikah* (The American Hebrew Yearbook), a literary miscellany. In 1962, it began to publish the monthly *Lamishpaha* (For the Family) in vocalized Hebrew in order to attract beginning readers. Previously it had sponsored for more than a quarter century the children's biweekly *Hadoar Lanoar*, edited by Daniel Persky and later by Simha Rubinstein, and had also issued for several years the biweekly *Mussaf Lakore Hatzair*, edited by Hayim Leaf. Both appeared as supplements to the weekly *Hadoar*.

During the 1930s, the organization fostered the Hebrew youth organization Histadrut Hanoar Haivri, which published the literary journal *Niv* (Expression) and encouraged activities in the fields of dramatics, dance, and choral work. These activities led to the establishment of the Hebrew Arts Foundation, which in 1952 founded the Hebrew Arts School in New York. The Massad Camps, the first Hebrew summer camps for children and youth, were another outgrowth of the enlistment of the youth in the organization's work.

In order to foster the Hebrew language and culture in the wider community, the Histadruth Ivrith sponsors annually a Hebrew Month. It has also issued publications in English that stress the role of Hebrew. It sponsored the publication of *Selected Poems of Hayyim Nahman Bialik* (1945, 1965), edited by Israel Efros. Among those who have served as president of the organization have been Reuben Brainin, Israel Efros, Abraham H. Friedland, Abraham Goldberg, Solomon Goldman, and Judah Pilch.

The weekend editions of the Israeli newspapers *Maariv* and *Yediot Aharonot* are published in the United States by satellite on the Friday that they appear in Israel. In addition, a Hebrew weekly entitled *Yisrael Shelanu* (Our Israel) is published in New York by Israeli expatriates. Nevertheless, a local Hebrew press still persists.

The weekly *Hadoar*, which celebrates its seventieth year of publication in 1991, is edited by Shlomo Shamir and Yael Feldman. *Bitzaron* (Fortress), which was founded in 1940 by Chaim Tchernowitz as a monthly, still appears as a quarterly under the editorship of Chaim Leaf in 1990. The Hebrew educational quarterly *Shevile Hahinnukh* (Paths of Education), which was founded in 1925, has appeared with interruptions down to 1988. The vocalized monthly *Olam Hadash* (New World), is the latest in a long series of children's publications that began to appear beginning in 1915.

The widespread study of Hebrew has been strengthened by the rapid rise of the Hebrew day school movement and the proliferation of programs of Jewish and Hebrew studies in colleges and universities. The National Association of Professors of Hebrew, consisting both of Jewish and non-Jewish members, sponsors publications and conferences to further the cause of Hebrew. An additional factor that has led to an increased awareness of the role of the Hebrew language are the varied study-abroad programs for American Jewish youth conducted by the universities in Israel. In the United States, the Ulpan method for the study of Hebrew, introduced in Israel, has won wide acceptance and has resulted in the establishment of a large number of Ulpan courses.

JACOB KABAKOFF

BIBLIOGRAPHY

Kabakoff, Jacob. *Pioneers of American Hebrew Literature.* (In Hebrew.) Tel Aviv: Yavneh, 1966.
———. *Seekers and Stalwarts: Essays and Studies on American Hebrew Literature and Culture.* (In Hebrew.) Jerusalem: Rubin Mass, 1978.
Mikliszanski, Jacob K. *A History of Hebrew Literature in America.* (In Hebrew.) New York: Ogen, 1967.
Silberschlag, Eisig. *From Renaissance to Renaissance: Hebrew Literature From 1492-1970.* Vol. I. New York: Ktav, 1973.
Waxman, Meyer. *A History of Jewish Literature.* 5 vols. New York: Yoseloff, 1960.

Hebrew Sheltering and Immigrant Aid Society. See HIAS.

Hebrew Union College–Jewish Institute of Religion. The oldest center of higher Jewish learning in America, the Hebrew Union College–Jewish Institute of Religion has four campuses,

located in Cincinnati, New York, Los Angeles, and Jerusalem. The college-institute trains Reform rabbis, religious school educators, cantors, scholars, and communal workers. Its museums, libraries, and archives are repositories of Jewish art, history, and culture that generate research and publications.

In 1875, Rabbi Isaac Mayer Wise founded Hebrew Union College in the basement of a Cincinnati synagogue. It was the first successful attempt to train American rabbis for American Reform congregations. Through its graduates, HUC forged a strong American Jewish consciousness by uniting the American ideal of equality with the Reform Movement's vision of social justice.

With the rise of fascism in Europe in the 1930s the college recognized the need for a political solution to Jewish persecution. Under President Julian Morgenstern, the college embarked upon a program of rescuing as many Jewish scholars as possible, and the Cincinnati campus became known as the Jewish College in Exile.

In 1950, during the administration of Nelson Glueck, HUC merged with the Jewish Institute of Religion in New York. President Glueck then launched the Los Angeles campus and in 1963 inaugurated the first building on the Jerusalem campus.

During the administration of Alfred Gottschalk, the first woman rabbi, Sally Preisand, and the first Israeli Reform rabbis in Jerusalem were ordained. The School of Jewish Communal Service in Los Angeles was founded, programs of study in Jerusalem for all first-year rabbinic and cantorial students were introduced, and the School of Graduate Studies on the Cincinnati campus was implemented. The school has gained renown for its unique Interfaith Fellow Program for Christian scholars. *See also* Reform Judaism.

MAXINE BERKMAN BERNSTEIN

BIBLIOGRAPHY

Meyer, Michael A. "A Centennial History." In *Hebrew Union College-Jewish Institute of Religion at One Hundred Years*, edited by S. E. Karff. Cincinnati: Hebrew Union College, 1976.

Hecht, Ben (1894–1964). A prolific American screenwriter, journalist, playwright, and novelist, Ben Hecht helped create two popular images—the hard-boiled newspaperman and the madcap Hollywood writer. Hecht was a controversial figure who all his life gloried in his role as outsider. He mixed offhanded cynicism with unabashed sentimentality, denouncing standards of public taste and art while creating popular works that brought him money and fame. After ignoring his Jewish origins until middle age, he became a vociferous anti-Nazi propagandist and early supporter in the United States for the creation of Israel. But he became disillusioned with Israeli politics and broke all connections following independence. He remained bitterly anti-British, however, and was denounced and blacklisted there in the 1950s.

Hecht was born on the Lower East Side of New York City to Russian immigrants and grew up speaking Yiddish. But when the family moved to Racine, Wisconsin, he enjoyed a thoroughly American adolescence. He left the University of Wisconsin after three days convinced he would learn nothing and started a career as a sensation-seeking reporter for the *Chicago Journal* in 1910. He developed admiration for the corrupt political bosses and strong men of the city who molded opinion and defied accepted beliefs.

The *Journal* sent him to cover Berlin after World War I; there he soon became involved in the revolutionary trends in the German arts, including Expressionism and Dadaism. His first novel, *Erik Dorn* (1921), brought him fame for its semiautobiographical picture of artistic immortality and ruthlessness. He returned to Chicago and was later sued for offending public morals in his writings.

Hecht moved to New York and began his long collaboration with Charles MacArthur. They wrote and produced both stage and film versions of *The Front Page* (1928 and 1931), featuring the cynical yet romantic newspaperman as antihero, as well as *Twentieth Century* (1932). In Hollywood Hecht wrote the film *The Scarface—Shame of the Nation* (1932), the first great crime movie; he later wrote two of Alfred Hitchcock's most famous films, *Spellbound* (1946) and *Notorious* (1948). Only a fraction of the 70 to 80 films on which he worked are credited to him, although he was the highest paid script writer of his time, sought after for his great speed (he is said to have written the first nine reels of *Gone with the Wind* in a week, without reading the novel).

Hecht claimed that he discovered his "accidental" Jewish identity in 1939 upon learning of Nazi atrocities. Earlier, his novel *A Jew in Love* (1931) was denounced as a prime example of Jewish self-hatred, but in the 1940s he worked tirelessly for American entry into the war, for the creation of a Jewish army to fight the Axis, and for Allied action against the death camps. He wrote about his convictions in *A Guide to the Bedevilled* (1944) and publicized them in full-page newspaper ads involving personalities from Broadway and Hollywood in the mass pageants *We Shall Never Die* (1943) and *A Flag Is Born* (1946) staged in New York (music by Kurt Weill). He supported the Irgun against the Jewish Agency and accused Chaim Weizmann, David Ben-Gurion, and other Jewish leaders of cowardice toward the British. He rejected the partition of Palestine and abandoned Israel entirely when the Labor party suppressed the Irgun. In 1961, his book *Perfidy* accused the Jewish Agency of Nazi collaboration in the Kastner-Greenwald libel trial, a trial that divided Israeli opinion.

Hecht's reputation had faded well before his death in 1964 (his final projects included a life of Marilyn Monroe and an attempt to prove Shakespeare was a Jew). Autobiographical materials are in *A Child of the Century* (1954) and *Gaily, Gaily* (1963). Extensive archives are at the Newberry Library in Chicago. *See also* Zionism.

MARK BERNHEIM

BIBLIOGRAPHY

Fuller, Stephen. "Ben Hecht: A Sampler" (includes filmography prepared with Hecht's widow). In *Film Comment* 6 (Winter 1970–1971): 32–39.

Hecht, Ben. *A Child of the Century*. New York: Fine, reprint 1985.

McAdams, William. *Ben Hecht: The Man Behind the Legend*. New York: Scribner, 1990.

Herberg, Will (1901–1977). When Will Herberg died in March 1977, American Judaism lost one of its most provocative religious thinkers of the post–World War II generation. Like Hermann Cohen and Franz Rosenzweig before him, Herberg came to Judaism from the outside. A Marxist and atheist through much of his young adulthood, who had received no Jewish education or religious training in his youth, Herberg turned to the study of Judaism only after his romance with Marxism ended.

Herberg was born in the Russian village of Liachovitzi. His father, Louis Hyman Herberg, moved his family to the United States in 1904. When his family arrived in America, his parents, whom he would later describe as "passionate atheists," were already committed to the faith that socialism would bring salvation to mankind and freedom from the restraints that had bound Western societies for centuries. Graduating from Boys' High School, in Brooklyn, in 1918, Herberg later attended City College of New York and Columbia University, where he studied philosophy and history, without apparently ever completing the course work for an academic degree.

Herberg inherited his parents' "passionate atheism" and equally passionate commitment to socialism. Entering the Communist movement while still a teenager, Herberg became a regular contributor to Communist journals, such as the *Workers Monthly* and *Modern Quarterly*, during the 1920s and early 1930s. He wrote scores of articles and editorials on an amazingly diverse number of topics, critiquing Edmund Wilson's views on proletarian literature, arguing with Sidney Hook over the textual validity of Marx's ambivalent position on revolution, and explicating the relationship between Freudian psychoanalysis and Communist thought. His attachment to communism was no mere affectation; it reflected intellectual conviction as well as moral ardor. So earnestly did he embrace Marxism that he even sought to reconcile it with Einstein's theory of relativity. Indeed, perhaps his boldest contribution to the radical thought of the period was his effort to reconcile Marxism to the new Einsteinian cosmology, the "second scientific revolution," that had been virtually unnoticed amongst radical writers in America.

As the 1930s progressed, however, Herberg became progressively disenchanted with his earlier Marxist faith. The grotesque Stalinist purges, the Communist "betrayal" of the Popular Front on the battlefields of Spain during the Spanish Civil War, the Russian invasion of Finland, and the Stalin-Hitler Nonaggression Pact of 1939 all contributed to his growing disillusionment. For Herberg, as for so many ex-Marxists of his generation, the cynical, opportunistic Molotov-Ribbentrop agreement of 1939 dispelled any remaining belief, once held, that "only a socialist government can defeat totalitarianism."

As his disenchantment with Marxism was increasing during the late 1930s, Herberg chanced to read Reinhold Niebuhr's *Moral Man and Immoral Society*, a book that was to change profoundly the course of his life. In an autobiographical passage of one of his essays, Herberg said that his encounter with Niebuhr's thought in 1939 was the "turning point," even before he met Niebuhr personally, who was then teaching at Manhattan's Union Theological Seminary. Like Franz Rosenzweig before him, whose writings he began to read during the early 1940s, Herberg went through a wrenching personal struggle over whether to become a Christian. After several soul-searching meetings with Niebuhr, Herberg declared his intention to embrace Christianity. Niebuhr counseled him, instead, first to explore his Jewish religious tradition and directed him across the street to the Jewish Theological Seminary, where Herberg went to study. The professors and students at the Seminary undertook to instruct Herberg in Hebrew and Jewish thought.

Throughout much of the 1940s, while he was earning a living as the educational director and research analyst of the International Ladies Garment Workers Union, Herberg also devoted much of his time and energy to the study of the classical sources of Judaism. He met regularly with rabbis and students at the Seminary, developing and explicating his emerging theology of Judaism. At the same time, he wrote on Jewish theology for journals such as *Commentary* and the *Jewish Frontier*, and he lectured on religious faith and the social philosophy of Judaism to synagogue groups and on college campuses. He met regularly, moreover, at his home, with rabbinical students and others to discuss his theological ideas.

Out of these intellectual encounters, and out of several essays published in *Commentary* and elsewhere in the late 1940s, came Herberg's first major theological work, *Judaism and Modern Man*, which appeared in 1951. At the time, Herberg's existentialist approach to Jewish theology struck a responsive chord among many within the Jewish community who were searching for religious roots and spiritual inspiration. Widely acclaimed as a carefully reasoned and intensely written interpretation of Judaism in the light of the newest existentialist thinking, *Judaism and Modern Man* was highly praised by such Jewish reviewers as Rabbi Milton Steinberg, who went so far as to say that Herberg "had written the book of the generation on the Jewish religion." Reinhold Niebuhr believed that the book "may well become a milestone in the religious thought of America." For some traditional Jews, however, the theology of *Judaism and Modern Man*, which Herberg described "as avowedly Niebuhrian in temper and thought," seemed in crucial respects to owe more to Christianity than to Judaism.

Protestant-Catholic-Jew, which, unquestionably, is Herberg's most famous book, was published in 1955. It remains a work of enduring value to anyone hoping to understand the sociology of American religion. It has become a classic work in American religious sociology, one that Nathan Glazer has called "the most satisfying explanation we have been given as to just what is happening to religion in America." The critical and public acclaim that greeted its publication brought Herberg instantaneous public acclaim as one of the country's best-known sociologists of religion, a reputation that he would enjoy until the end of his life.

The critical acclaim brought Herberg the academic recognition, and position, he had long sought. In 1955, he obtained a full-time academic appointment as professor of Judaic studies and social philosophy at Drew University, a Methodist institution in New Jersey, where he would teach until his retirement in 1976, the year before his death.

During the 1950s and 1960s, while teaching at Drew, Herberg also lectured at numerous universities, synagogues, and churches throughout the United States and Europe. He published scholarly anthologies on the works of Martin Buber, Karl Barth, Jacques Maritain, and other modern existentialist theologians. A collection of some 20 of his articles on aspects of biblical theology, *Faith Enacted into History*, appeared in 1976. During the 1950s and 1960s, moreover, Herberg became part of a remarkable group of ex-Communists and ex-Trotskyists that included James Burnham, Willmore Kendell, Frank Meyer, Max Eastman, and Whittaker Chambers, among others, who transformed *National Review* into the preeminent intellectual journal of American conservatism.

As religion editor of *National Review*, Herberg emerged as one of the leaders of the post-World War II conservative intellectual movement in America. His new conservatism found its most eloquent expression in his views on religion and state. Earlier than most other American Jewish intellectuals, Herberg called for a reassessment of the prevailing liberal Jewish consensus concerning church-state separation and the role that religion should play in American life. His perceptive critique of a public life devoid of religious values is reflected in the thought of a growing number of Jewish leaders who have come to share Herberg's belief that an American political culture uninformed by religious beliefs and institutions itself poses a danger to the position and security of America's Jews. *See also* Interfaith Cooperation, Neoconservatism.

DAVID G. DALIN

BIBLIOGRAPHY

Ausmus, Harry J. *Will Herberg: From Right to Right.* Chapel Hill: University of North Carolina Press, 1987.

Dalin, David G. "Will Herberg in Retrospect." *Commentary* 86 (July 1988): 38–43.

———, ed. *From Marxism to Judaism: The Collected Essays of Will Herberg.* New York: Wiener, 1989.

Heschel, Abraham Joshua (1907–1972).

Through his writings and the force of his personality and image, Abraham Joshua Heschel provided a model of theological, political, and personal leadership for American Jews. Brought to the United States in 1940 by Reform Judaism's Hebrew Union College, he already represented both tradition and modernity, having been born heir to a Hasidic dynasty in Warsaw in 1907. Heschel never forgot his heritage, to which he dedicated much of his scholarship; however, he also engaged in modern studies at the University of Berlin and the liberal *Hochschule fur die Wissenschaft des Judentums*, and he guided Franz Rosenzweig's *Freies Judisches Lehrhaus* in Frankfurt. His combination of traditionalism and openness to modernity proved both a strength and an irritant in the American setting. After teaching at the Hebrew Union College for five years, he joined the faculty of the Jewish Theological Seminary of America, the seminary of Conservative Judaism, where he remained until his death. Theologically, he was a maverick, fitting in neither with Reform's efforts to celebrate accommodation nor Conservatism's traditionalism.

Deliberately polemical, his theological writings seem directed against every established position. He rejected humanism, declaring that God is in search of man, and that religion must serve Divine rather than human needs. At the same time he considered the human need to be a basic religious intuition. His writings on Jewish religious practice are equally divided. He criticizes those who emphasize Jewish "behaviorism" as well as those who claim that only belief, and not practice, is required. His approach to Halakah (Jewish law) reflects his ambivalence. He reproaches those who denigrate that law but admits that "the power to observe depends on the situation."

This maverick stance characterized Heschel's position in the activity that gained him the most notoriety, political activism. From the mid-1950s until his death, Heschel championed various political causes. Testifying to federal commissions, he advocated fair housing, care for the aged, and educational reform. He joined with activists such as Martin Luther King, Jr., Daniel Berrigan, and William Sloan Coffin in protesting against infringements on civil rights as well as American involvement in Southeast Asia. He also fought against Soviet persecution of Russian Jewry as a Jewish representative responsive to the changing concerns of American political life.

Heschel explained his involvement in these political activities as more than mere responses to the modern situation. For him his activities were grounded in the prophetic consciousness, and he claimed that they were expressions of traditional religion. He would refuse to violate such Jewish laws as Sabbath observance or dietary obligations, even in the name of universal humanistic principles. In this way, he united social and religious issues.

He defined his political concerns as what he called "depth-theology," the religious conscientiousness of a sense of God's stake in humanity common to all religion. Theology, on the other hand, he felt, was derived from particular traditions and the response of specific groups to God's demands upon them. Heschel's category of depth-theology provided a common meeting ground with representatives from other religions. His ecumenicalism extended beyond shared political concerns. In 1963, Heschel was instrumental in helping Cardinal Bea shape the statement on the Jews for the Vatican II document. He often spoke to non-Jewish groups about "the God of Israel" and Jewish spirituality. Heschel's conceptualization of two strata of theology captured the tension between universalism and parochialism and sought to dissolve that tension through mutual respect and shared values.

Perhaps Heschel's death on December 23, 1972—occasioned by his vigil awaiting Dan Berrigan's release from prison—and the interfaith outpouring of sorrow it stimulated testifies to the success of his tactics. *See also* Conservative Judaism.

S. Daniel Breslauer

BIBLIOGRAPHY

Heschel, Abraham Joseph. *God in Search of Man: A Philosophy of Judaism.* New York: Farrar, Straus and Young, 1955.

———. *The Insecurity of Freedom: Essays in Applied Religion.* New York: Farrar, Straus and Giroux, 1966.

———. *Man Is Not Alone: A Philosophy of Religion.* New York: Farrar, Straus and Young, 1951.

———. *A Passion for Truth.* New York: Farrar, Straus and Giroux, 1973.

Merkle, John C. *The Genesis of Faith: The Depth Theology of Abraham Joshua Heschel.* New York: Macmillan, 1985.

Sherman, Franklin. *The Promise of Heschel.* Philadelphia: Lippincott, 1970.

Sherwin, Byron. *Abraham Joshua Heschel.* Atlanta: Knox Press, 1979.

HIAS (Hebrew Sheltering and Immigrant Aid Society). Founded in 1880 as the Hebrew Emigrant Aid Society (HEAS), the Hebrew Sheltering and Immigrant Aid Society has aided hundreds of thousands of immigrants and refugees throughout the United States and in more than 53 countries across the globe.

In 1902, members of the Voliner Zhitomir Aid Society, one of hundreds of New York immigrant landsmanschaftn (fraternal associations), founded the Hebrew Immigrant Aid Society to help ease the path of those following them to America. Its first act was to station at Ellis Island a Yiddish-speaking representative, later Alexander Harkavy, the renowned Yiddish lexicographer. In 1909, HIAS merged with the Hebrew Sheltering House Association, founded in 1888, to become the Hebrew Sheltering and Immigrant Aid Society. The organization worked to protect Jewish immigrants on the incoming ships. Its pier service met arrivals at Ellis Island and intervened with the Boards of Special Inquiry to prevent deportations. It provided temporary shelter, food, and clothing; helped the newcomers reach their final destinations; and encouraged their Americanization and acculturation.

During World War I, HIAS grew from an organization concerned primarily with the last stages of immigration into one involved in the entire process. When the war closed off western routes of migration, it opened a shelter in Yokohama, Japan, for those fleeing eastward. Afterward, its European subsidiary, Emigdirect, facilitated the reunification of families. Because the expanded activities overlapped with the work of the Jewish Colonization Association, in 1927 the three organizations merged as HICEM. During the Nazi era, HICEM rescued refugees. Between June 1940 and December 1941, it sent 25,000 people to safe havens from its offices in Lisbon, Casablanca, and Marseilles.

When HICEM dissolved after the war, HIAS took over the work with displaced persons.

In 1954, for economic and practical reasons—including a decreased need for its services—HIAS again merged with other agencies concerned with Jewish emigration. The new organization became the United HIAS Service. Since then, HIAS has rescued refugees from the Hungarian uprising of 1956 and the Prague Spring of 1968. Since the 1970s, its representatives have met Soviet emigrants in Vienna and sheltered in Rome those awaiting visas to the United States and Canada. It has participated with other Jewish organizations in Operation Exodus.

PAMELA S. NADELL

BIBLIOGRAPHY

Dobkowski, Michael. *Jewish American Voluntary Organizations.* Westport, Conn.: Greenwood Press, 1986.

Sanders, Ronald. *Shores of Refuge: A Hundred Years of Jewish Emigration.* New York: Holt, 1988.

Wischnitzer, Mark. *Visas to Freedom: The Story of HIAS.* Cleveland: World, 1956.

Higher Education. See ACADEME.

Hillel. The B'nai B'rith Hillel Foundations serve the religious, cultural, interfaith, social, counseling, and community service needs of Jewish students and faculty on 400 college and university campuses throughout the world. Hillel was founded in 1923 by Rabbi Ben Frankel at the University of Illinois. Frankel was its director until his death four years later, to be succeeded by Abram Leon Sachar. Sachar, the "master builder," became Hillel's national director as the number of foundations increased and later still the chairman of the governing body, the B'nai B'rith Hillel Commission.

B'nai B'rith had assumed responsibility for the Hillel Foundations in 1925, and since then Hillel has been one of B'nai B'rith's major branches. As B'nai B'rith became more internationalized, so did Hillel, expanding beyond the United States to Argentina, Australia, Brazil, Canada, Great Britain, Israel, the Netherlands, South Africa, Switzerland, and Venezuela.

For decades, Hillel alone functioned as the college campus Jewish center, serving students of all religious and cultural and social backgrounds. With the fragmentization of the American Jewish community in the latter half of the twentieth century, however, other groups proliferated on the campus, especially denominational ones. In general, however, Hillel still continues as the umbrella Jewish organization on the campus.

As the Jewish community, notably the federations and welfare funds, recognized the importance of the college years to Jewish survival, there was a trend to establish multiple Jewish student groups and activities at colleges and universities. Hillel responded by setting up a cooperative venture with these groups. Initially under national Hillel sponsorship, the Association of Hillel and Campus Workers was formed to include campus staff unaffiliated with the Hillel movement.

The goals of Hillel have varied little since its founding, but new structures, emphases, and programs have developed in response to Jewish community changes and needs. New areas of activity and service have emerged. Funding by federations and welfare funds, supplementary to that by B'nai B'rith, has made it possible to increase staff at many campuses. Counselorships and extension units (part time) have increased in number, although in the United States alone there are still several hundreds of colleges to be served. A National Student Secretariat was formed and a National Jewish Law Student Association.

The area of social action has received new emphasis at Hillels throughout the United States, especially in relation to Israel and Soviet Jewry. Hillel Foundations have been active supporters of Israel, and Hillel annually sends hundreds of students and faculty to Israel for tours, volunteer service, and seminars, with special groupings of medical, law, and business students. Under Hillel sponsorships, 4000 students went to Washington for a Soviet Jewry protest rally in December 1987. Hundreds arrive every summer for leadership training on behalf of Jewish rights at the Hillel international office in the B'nai B'rith headquarters in Washington, D.C.

BENJAMIN KAHN

BIBLIOGRAPHY

Dobkowski, Michael. *Jewish American Voluntary Organizations.* Westport, Conn.: Greenwood Press, 1986.

Elazar, Daniel. *Community and Polity: The Organizational Dynamics of American Jewry.* Philadelphia: Jewish Publication Society, 1976.

Jospe, Alfred. *Tradition and Contemporary Experience: Essays on Jewish Thought and Life.* Hillel Library Series. New York: Schocken for B'nai B'rith Hillel Foundations, 1970.

Jospe, Alfred, ed. *The Test of Time.* Washington, D.C.: B'nai B'rith Hillel Foundations, 1974.

Kahn, Benjamin M. *History of the Hiller Foundations.* Unpublished Manuscript, 1990.

Moore, Deborah Dash. *B'nai B'rith & the Challenge of Ethnic Leadership.* Albany: State University of New York Press, 1982.

Historiography. The writing of the history of the Jewish experience in the United States dates from the late 1880s, and this telling was restricted primarily to investigators of Jewish origins. It is only since the 1950s that serious work has been done in this youngest of Judaica disciplines. Until the post-World War II period, American Jewish historiography was designed to serve Jewish communal defense purposes. It contributed little toward the advancement of objective scholarly discourse among students of both American and Jewish history. Today, American Jewish historiography, whether written by Jews or Gentiles, Americanists or specialists in Jewish history, has taken its place as a respected discipline in academe. Although the field still has its share of amateur filiopietists and apologists writing their self-serving tracts, the future lies with those writers of American Jewish history who approach their tasks with objectivity and a willingness to explore all aspects of Jewish life in America.

The earliest works on American Jewish history—tracts such as Isaac Markens's *The Hebrews in America* (1888) and suggestive volumes such as Mayer Kayserling's *Christopher Columbus and the Participation of the Jews in the Spanish and Portuguese Discoveries* (1894)—were specifically dedicated and commissioned to answer those who were then questioning the historical role and present-day place of the Jews in the United States. In the nativist and racist 1890s, an era that witnessed the growth of "patriotic" organizations such as Daughters of the American Revolution as well as the rise of social exclusionary anti-Semitism, works that proved that Jews were in America at the time of the Mayflower, that Jews fought and died in the defense of this country, and that they contributed mightily to the building of the United States, were written to counteract popular conceptions of Jews in the United States. If Jews could only show their long association with what was best with America, these findings, as German-American Jewish leader Oscar Straus cogently explained, "would be an answer to all time to come to anti-Semitic tendencies in this country." This defensive, filiopietistic style of writing by Jews dominated the field until the end of World War II.

During these same years, trained historians, Americanists and mostly Gentile historians, showed little interest in dispassionate treatment of Jews, or for that matter such treatment of America's other immigrant and ethnic or racial minorities. During the opening decades of the twentieth century American historiography was preoccupied with political, diplomatic, or military history—the stories, if you will, of the ruling WASP elite. In truth, when immigrants were observed by these chroniclers, they were invariably discussed as a problem that faced America. In their subjective treatments, these historians failed to confront squarely the social history and reality of Jewish and other immigrant life.

Equal treatment for the immigrant—and out of that thoughtful examinations of the American Jew—by American historians awaited the inspired work of Marcus Lee Hansen. Writing in the late 1930s, Hansen, widely acknowledged as the father of immigrant and ethnic historiography, rejected the notion of Anglo-Saxon supremacy that pervaded so much of his colleagues' work. He argued strongly that the immigrant experience had to be studied, without prejudice or apology, as an integral part of a greater American history. Hansen's critique and approach spread slowly through the ranks of American historians as the post-World War II years opened, and by the close of the 1950s American Jewish historiography had become the beneficiary of this new thrust.

Harvard University historian Oscar Handlin, American and American Jewish, was the most influential and instrumental transmitter of Hansen's message to the next generation of historians. In his early work on immigrant adjustment, *Boston's Immigrants* (1949), as well as in his most famous volume, *The Uprooted* (1951), Handlin demonstrated to all how to explore immigrant life without prejudice and how to measure immigrant achievements without apology. Handlin's specific contributions to American Jewish historiography were twofold. He was one of the first Jews, from within academe, to attack the point of view of the amateurs who still dominated the Jewish field. And he educated students, most notably, Moses Rischin, who would write seminally important monographs in Handlin's tradition in the early 1960s.

Needless to say, over the most recent de-

cades, American Jewish historiography has benefitted greatly by communications and cross-fertilization among scholars of both Jewish and other immigrant groups. Comparative works detailing the relationship between the many cooperating and competing minority groups in this country are now a standard part of the scholarly literature.

Concomitant with the postwar Americanists' discovery of the immigrant, the minority and racial group member, and the Jew came a focusing of attention by specifically Jewish historians on the American experience. In this realm, credit for breaking the hold of the antiquarians may be shared by Columbia University's Salo Wittmayer Baron and Jacob Rader Marcus of the Hebrew Union College (Cincinnati). Significantly enough, even as both roundly criticized the defensive passions that colored the writings of the leaders of the American Jewish Historical Society, Oscar Straus's pet organization, then the very institution of apologetics, Baron and Marcus were themselves also motivated, in part, by heartfelt perceptions of communal needs. Writing independent of one another, both argued at the depth of the Holocaust, that with European Jewry on the verge of destruction, American Jewry could no longer look, as it had for three centuries, to the Old World for leadership. For them, the survival of the Jewish people, both within and without the United States, required the raising up of home-grown scholars and knowledgeable leaders. Knowledge and comprehension of what was, in fact, American Jewish history, and not what was legend, was an unqualified communal desideratum.

So motivated, both set out, each in his own way, to rebuild a misused field, to create an American subdiscipline within Jewish history. Marcus, for his part, through his multivolume histories of colonial American Jewry (first published in 1951) more than anyone else undermined the inaccuracies of early American Jewish history. He also articulated, in 1958, a periodization for American Jewish history, which continues to be the starting point for all discussions of dating. His most dramatic and enduring contribution, however, is his organization of two of the most important research centers for the scholarly examination of American Jewish history: the American Jewish Archives (founded in 1947) and the American Jewish Periodical Center (founded in 1956). These institutions plus the library of the American Jewish Historical Society in Waltham, Massachusetts, and the archives of the YIVO Institute in New York (a resource that specializes in immigration, labor, and Jewish socialist history) have become the major scholarly establishments for American Jewish history.

Baron's contributions in the conceptual areas, beyond his early and telling rebuke of the assumptions of the antiquarians, has been in his concrete statements of the needs and priorities of the field. Equally important, through his teaching and mentoring, he produced, starting in the late 1940s, a most illustrious cadre of students who are now the outstanding senior practitioners of this discipline. People like Hyman B. Grinstein, Marshall Sklare, Naomi W. Cohen, Lloyd P. Gartner, and Arthur A. Goren joined Marcus's best—Bertram W. Korn, Stanley Chyet, and Martin A. Cohen—in bringing American Jewish history as a legitimate scholarly discipline, first into America's Jewish seminaries, soon thereafter into Eastern-based municipal and private colleges, and ultimately to many of this country's most elite institutions. By the late 1980s, these scholars and their students—(and, to be sure, also those students of Handlin) were teaching various aspects of the American Jewish experience in over 100 colleges and universities nationwide.

These scholars have advanced the horizons of American Jewish historiography in a number of specific areas. The history of the East European Jewish immigrants' arrival, settlement, advancement, integration, and assimilation during the years 1880-1930 has received the greatest attention. This focus may be attributed to the combination of the availability of primary sources for this one period—from government records to Yiddish newspapers—with the interest and skillfulness of writers of East European heritage in writing empathetically but dispassionately about their ancestors. The second most popular subject area has been the history of anti-Semitism in the United States, particularly the history of America and American Jewry during the Holocaust. Here interest has been sparked by American Jewry's own raised consciousness, in the post-1967 period, of the implications of the Jewish cataclysm of our times and fueled by the desire of major Jewish defense organizations—and their Jewish opponents—to have the story of domestic Jew-hatred and Jewish response well researched and analyzed. Similar types of feelings have led to a proliferation of works over the last generation on the history of Zionism in the United States.

Much less useful work has been done in the area of community history in localities remote from the immigrant hubs. Here a paucity of objective, extant source material and a lack of compelling scholarly interest in these localities have held back the field. In truth, it is precisely in the area of communal history that, all too often, filiopietism still finds its residual expression. Other worthy areas of American Jewish life that demand attention include Jewish women's and family history, denominational history, and the darker sides of Jewish communal experience (i.e., criminality, intra-Jewish conflict, etc.). It may be assumed that in a contemporary era where Jewish scholars are inured to writing about American Jewish history without apology, remorse, or even exaltation, that in time attention will also be directed to these understudied areas of a rapidly developing discipline.

JEFFREY S. GUROCK

BIBLIOGRAPHY

Brickman, William W. *The Jewish Community in America: An Annotated and Bibliographical Guide.* New York: Franklin, 1977.

Handlin, Oscar. *Boston's Immigrants 1790-1880: A Study in Acculturation.* Cambridge: Belknap Press of Harvard University Press, 1959.

Gurock, Jeffrey S. *American Jewish History: A Bibliographical Guide.* New York: Anti-Defamation League of B'nai B'rith, 1983.

Hansen, Marcus Lee. *The Immigrant in American History.* Cambridge: Harvard University Press, 1940.

Marcus, Jacob Rader. *Studies in American Jewish History.* Cincinnati: Hebrew Union College Press, 1969.

Holocaust, America and the. Just how decisive America's involvement in the Holocaust was can be distilled from a single episode in 1945. Standing above a pit containing the remains of countless death camp victims General Dwight D. Eisenhower directed his troops to scrutinize the destruction and the death all around. The "starvation, cruelty, and bestiality were so overpowering as to leave me a bit sick," he later recalled. But Eisenhower insisted on seeing the worst the camp had to offer, and he urged the American government to send reporters and Congressmen because he wanted to "leave no room for cynical doubt."

Everything significant in America's relationship to the Holocaust was symbolized in that scene: (1) the mandate to remember and the resistance to remembering and (2) the deep impression that the Holocaust would make on American (and American Jewish) life and culture.

Americans are not eager to absorb the historical impact of the Holocaust. The reason may be obvious: its central horror is simply too shocking to grasp. Americans are certainly not alone in this respect, but they have devised unique defenses against discussing the subject. Above all is the assertion that the Holocaust occurred on a different continent and in the dim past. Distance, presumably, makes the Holocaust irrelevant. Americans also dismiss the subject as an "old-world" problem, Europe's apocalyptic dance of death. By seeing the Final Solution as an alien phenomenon, the Holocaust is safely relegated to the status of an academic historical curiosity. But as Eisenhower anticipated, America's relationship with the Holocaust could never be casual. The impulse to forget has jostled painfully against a reality impossible to ignore.

During the Nazi era, the American national myth of exceptionalism—a belief in America's special destiny—governed policies and passions. America's struggle with the Depression and its unpleasant memory of having been manipulated into entering World War I promoted an isolationist mood. Few actually lauded the ascendant National Socialist movement in Germany (pro-Nazi rallies in America, though frightening, were marginal), but few actively opposed the Nazis' persecution of German Jews. After the Nazi boycott of Jewish stores in April 1933, for example, American reporters expressed outrage (briefly), but the Roosevelt administration remained indifferent.

In fairness, the signs of sustained anti-Semitic violence in Nazi Germany were not easy for Americans to discern. The boycott was, after all, a failure—an indication that the situation might improve. Decrees in the spring of 1933 forbidding Jews to hold office seemed unimportant during the next two years of relative calm. Even the Nuremberg laws of 1935, prohibiting Germans and German Jews from mixing, seemed innocuous. Interested in projecting a positive image to the rest of the world, especially during the Berlin Olympics in 1936, the Nazis were not eager to risk notoriety by enforcing racial policies.

Events in 1937–1938 drew the concern of the West for the first time. As the Nazis prepared for military dominance, they searched for ways to become self-sufficient—independent, above all, of Jewish participation in the Reich's economy. By "Aryanizing" (confiscating) Jewish businesses, they hoped to pressure Jews into leaving the Reich. Faced with the prospect of refugees seeking political asylum, the Western nations, led by the United States, met in Evian, France, in July 1938. That conference presaged the world's indifference to the worsening situation in Nazi-occupied Europe. No nation was willing to open its doors. There was not even a resolution condemning Nazi anti-Semitic practices. The United States delegation announced only that it would continue admitting German and Austrian immigrants (among others), at the unimpressive rate of about 27,000 per year. (Between 1938 and 1941, the United States accepted a total of 124,000 immigrants.) Sentiments at home were the decisive factor; these reflected the intense support for strict quotas. Americans feared competing with refugees for scarce jobs, and many, prone to anti-Semitism, were especially opposed to admitting Jews. Unintentionally, the Roosevelt administration sent a signal to the Nazis. The Nazis could feel free to find a radical "solution" to the Jewish problem.

The American entry into World War II in 1941 at last mobilized the nation against the Nazis. Although fighting to preserve democratic ideals, and determined to win the war, Americans showed little sympathy for the victims of genocide. Even when reports of the death camps, in 1942–1943, alerted American officials to the horror, no one with any authority budged. They wanted more evidence. At most, Roosevelt promised to rescue European Jews only through an Allied victory. When, for example, it became possible to bomb the death camp Auschwitz-Birkenau, in 1943–1944, the Allies practically went out of their way to avoid doing so. Ways were found only to bomb a synthetic rubber works and SS barracks, a mere 7 kilometers from Auschwitz. With the exception of the War Refugee Board established early in 1944 to spirit Jews away from the Nazis, and the Oswego Project (the relocation of hundreds of Jews to Oswego, New York), Jews were invisible victims of the Nazis. Only when the Allies liberated the death camps in 1945 did a few Americans finally begin to accept the enormity of the Nazi crimes.

Until the late 1970s, Americans were, for the most part, unwilling to grasp fully the facts of the Nazi annihilation of close to 6 million European Jews. But there were several dramatic developments that momentarily did disturb their apathy. First was the prosecution of Nazi criminals before the International Military Tribunal (IMT) in Nuremberg in 1945–1946. In assembling the evidence, the prosecution offered explanations for the carnage that the world first learned about toward the end of the war. However, by focusing attention on Nazi criminals, the IMT maintained the veil that blinded the Western world to the victims of the Nazi inferno.

During the 1950s, concern about the Nazi era receded to an all-time low. Most survivors who managed to start a new life in the United States wanted to return to a "normal" life. Their voices, which would eventually stir people's consciences, were momentarily still. But one event aroused renewed interest—the publication of Anne Frank's diary. That moving testimony of one young girl's life in hiding in Amsterdam fascinated (and still fascinates) readers, especially young students who can easily understand Anne Frank's adolescent struggles. By expressing her ideals and hopes, however, it avoided discussing the suffering endured by so many Jews and other victims in favor of preserving a faith in mankind. Emblematic of the historical amnesia that characterized the 1950s, the *Diary* overshadowed two seminal textual studies from this decade that defined the scope of the Nazi assault: Leon Poliakov's *Harvest of Hate: The Nazi Program for the Destruction of the Jews of Europe* (French edition, 1951; English edition, 1954) and Gerald Reitlinger's *The Final Solution: The Attempt to Exterminate the Jews of Europe, 1939-1945* (1953).

The year 1961 was the first of two major turning points in America's struggle to remember the Holocaust. Tellingly, Americans were still dependent on others for their information and insights. The most dramatic of the events during the year was the trial of Adolf Eichmann in Jerusalem. Eichmann's trial was coincident with the rise of television as a mass medium, and it was covered extensively. Millions of Americans observed the proceedings against a man accused of supervising the deportations of Jews to death camps. The evidence provided by witnesses and documents exposed the full extent of the Nazi plan to persecute and destroy European Jewry, including the prewar Nazi persecution of German Jews (which the IMT ignored). Perhaps the most penetrating analysis of the trial were the reports filed by Hannah Arendt, a German Jewish refugee, for the *New Yorker* magazine. Published in 1963 as a book, *Eichmann in Jerusalem*, the reports offered the lasting observation that a functionary like Eichmann, removed from the field and front lines, could murder without guilt or remorse. Describing Eichmann's antiseptic inhumanity as a new manifestation of evil, evil as "banality," Arendt suggested how aggression could become an integral part of government and, whenever sanctioned, of all society.

Also during 1961 appeared the now-classic historical interpretation, *The Destruction of the European Jews*, by Raul Hilberg. A refugee himself from the Nazis, Hilberg furnished a more meticulous exploration than Arendt's into the Nazi machinery of destruction (a phrase Hilberg created). For years Hilberg could not find a publisher for his impressive study, an indication of the indifference to the Holocaust even in intellectual circles. Eventually, however, it became a standard text, used within only a few years of its publication.

In light of the present explosion of interest in the Holocaust era, it may seem surprising that a generation of Americans was ignorant of the Nazi design against European Jewry. America's intellectual awakening is only a little more than a decade old. In the late 1970s, an American concern for the Holocaust era became more consistent. Survivors, emerging from their self-imposed silence, set the tone. Among the most important testimonies to come to public attention was Elie Wiesel's *Night*, an evocation of the victim's terrible ordeal of family loss and bitter disillusionment.

It is probably safe to say that the NBC-TV four-part docudrama broadcast of "Holocaust" in 1978—the other turning point in America's wrestling with the Nazi past—was the first time Americans fueled the effort to remember. This production, more than any other single incident, shattered the cultural taboo that had limited discussion of the Holocaust. Not only did it arouse interest among Americans, it was also something of a sensation in Germany when it was broadcast there in 1979. Although criticized by some as "trivializing" or exploiting Nazi viciousness and the victims' despair, "Holocaust" at least made the subject suitable for general audiences, i.e., for people not already familiar with the subject, much less committed to remembering it. The broadcast spawned a cottage industry of novels and memoirs, radio plays and docudramas, theater productions and films.

The 1978 broadcast also gave rise to several other influential public programs: the establishment in 1979 of a national Holocaust commission and an Office of Special Investigations (OSI) by the federal government and the grass-roots formation of Holocaust resource and education centers. The commission was charged with enhancing the American memory of the Holocaust, mainly in an ambitious museum in Washington, D.C. The purpose of OSI was to track down and deport Nazi criminals who lied about their backgrounds when they entered the United States. By the end of the 1980s, there were myriad Holocaust resource and education centers (there are roughly 200 local and national ongoing programs, mostly connected with colleges and Jewish federations). They exist to document the Holocaust era or to create educational resources, such as conferences, books, and curricula for the secondary schools.

Propelling the commission (renamed the United States Holocaust Memorial Council) is a desire to commemorate not only 6 million Jews, but also all other victims of the Nazi genocide. In fact, former President Jimmy Carter defined the Holocaust as the Nazi murder of 11 million innocent civilians. As a result, there has been an unfortunate competition among the victims' national or ethnic descendants for historical attention. Because American society is pluralistic and celebrates its social diversity, the Council seeks to recognize a variety of groups and group claims.

The OSI follows a parallel path. Although its authority rests on the statutory question of legal or illegal immigration to the United States (it can deport or extradite Nazis only if they are found to have concealed their Nazi pasts), it carries considerable moral authority as well. It symbolizes the American commitment to serving justice by repeatedly denouncing Nazi injustice and, in the process, proclaiming the value of a fair system of justice. The one legitimate criticism expressed about the OSI deals with its limited jurisdiction. It cannot try Nazis unless they have committed crimes against American citizens. (Recently Canada, through its Deschenes Commission, has taken these critical steps.) As an endeavor late in coming and slow in practice, the OSI reflects the deep ambiguity in America's confrontation with the Nazi past.

The lessons that Holocaust centers strive to teach deal, for the most part, with the consequences of prejudice and discrimination, the virtues of democracy, and how a commitment to democratic practices can help protect future generations from totalitarian temptations. For example, questions for discussion that end a unit in a curriculum typically ask students to consider what they might have done had they observed the persecution of Jews and what they believe are appropriate responses to the worldwide persecution of minorities today. The Holocaust era, therefore, provides ample case studies to sharpen a student's moral and civic self-awareness. This is an important educational objective, but it is not complete. It defines the historical study of the Holocaust era merely as a pretext for an ulterior discussion of issues facing Americans today. As a result, the programs and publications sponsored by most centers give less heed than they should to the Holocaust era itself. Although devoted to remembering the Holocaust, they ironically engage in more than a little avoidance of the subject.

Ambiguity has characterized American reactions to the Holocaust in the past and today. This is true because Americans find themselves in the convenient position of not feeling forced to confront the Nazi past, the way Germans and Austrians are. Having defeated Nazism, Americans, again and again, have been able to affirm their distance. By clinging to the national myths of the democratic experiment and historical exceptionalism, they have succeeded in keeping aloof. (The disclosures of French collaboration with the Nazis and French wartime anti-Semitic initiatives have corroded the governing French-Gaullist myth of a nation that mobilized itself to resist the Nazi yoke.)

But any past, and surely one so deeply resonant as the Nazi past, invades present-day American life in spite of all the cultural defenses erected against it. For American Jewry, the Holocaust has penetrated so completely that one observer, Jacob Neusner (*Stranger at Home*, 1981) has branded the American Jewish community as a "fellowship of victimhood." He and others fear that an intense memory of the Holocaust is crowding out a creative awareness of Judaism as a religion and a heritage. Whether or not these critics are right, there is no doubt that American Jews have always been preoccupied with the Holocaust. During one week each year, the organized American-Jewish community observes the "Days of Remembrance," in Hebrew, *Yom haShoah.*

Less explicit, but at least as potent, is the legacy of the Holocaust era in the lives of other Americans. Is there not, for example, a new awareness that a nation can implement a policy of human extinction, and has not that awareness introduced an urgency to the basic impulse to survive? Has not this dreadful knowledge reinforced an anxiety about the future of humanity? Isn't it now accepted that innocent civilians can be mysteriously deemed an enemy and defined as a target for all-out assault? This is the embryonic logic of modern terrorism and contributes to the terrorism with which we still live. Given the proximity of violence in our time, is it any longer morally defensible to remain an onlooker? Doesn't such proximity confer new responsibilities on individuals as witnesses? After the Munich Pact (the treaty authored in 1938 by British Prime Minister Neville Chamberlain to appease Nazi imperial ambitions), isn't neutrality the moral equivalent of complicity?

Americans like to see themselves as the main purveyors of ideals formed during the Enlightenment, that intellectual revolution promoting faith in reason and progress. But no one the least bit familiar with the Holocaust can doubt that scientific progress can yield destructive as well as productive results. (In the shadow of the Holocaust, such technological hallmarks as the factory and its furnaces, railroad trains, and medical discoveries forebode something deeply ominous.) Religious and legal codes of ethics and the supremacy of the law have also been sullied by Nazi practices and are susceptible to misuse. And because the Holocaust emerged from an advanced civilization, nurtured by the same ideals as those Americans cherish, no American can doubt that as civilization progresses so does its destructive potential.

Traditional American myths and ideals have proven resilient in the face of the Holocaust. But do Americans cling to these beliefs from faith or from doubt? If from faith, it is blind faith, for the Holocaust has irrevocably transformed the postwar world. *See also* Holocaust Survivors in America.

DENNIS B. KLEIN

BIBLIOGRAPHY

Abzug, Robert H. *Inside the Vicious Heart: Americans and the Liberation of Nazi Concentration Camps.* New York: Oxford University Press, 1985.

Feingold, Henry L. *The Politics of Rescue: The Roosevelt Administration and the Holocaust, 1938–1945.* New Brunswick, N.J.: Rutgers University Press, 1970.

Lifton, Robert J. *History and Human Survival.* New York: Random House, 1970.

Lipstadt, Deborah E. *Beyond Belief: The American Press and the Coming of the Holocaust, 1933–1945.* New York: Free Press, 1986.

Lowenstein, Sharon R. *Token Refuge: The Story of the Jewish Refugee Shelter at Oswego, 1944–1946.* Bloomington: Indiana University Press, 1986.

Penkower, Monty N. *The Jews Were Expendable: Free World Diplomacy and the Holocaust.* Urbana: University of Illinois Press, 1983.

Whitfield, Stephen J. *Voice of Jacob, Hands of Esau: Jews in American Life and Thought.* Hamden, Conn.: Archon, 1984.

Wyman, David S. *The Abandonment of the Jews: America and the Holocaust, 1941–1945.* New York: Pantheon, 1984.

Holocaust, Literature of the. The Holocaust (*Shoah*), a disaster of biblical proportions for European Jewry, forced Jewish-American literature to explore its impact on the world's largest Diaspora community. In the process, novelists, both well- and lesser-known, and representing a variety of orientations to Judaism, have come to reflect on the meaning of covenantal existence and Jewish identity.

While the Holocaust is the fundamental orienting event for contemporary Jewish existence, raising in an intense manner questions about God, chosenness, and the nature of evil, Jewish-American novelists were slow to make it the orienting theme of their fiction. Separated by geography, history, and language from the agony of their slaughtered European brethren, Jewish-American novelists, with few exceptions, continued for almost two decades after the Holocaust to display prewar modes of historical and theological innocence. They concerned themselves with issues such as assimilation and suburban Judaism or presented romanticized images of a vanished shtetl world. In the 1960s, however, several events reminded Jews everywhere of their vulnerability: the trial of Adolph Eichmann, the writings of Elie Wiesel, the Six-Day War, and the unceasing diplomatic and political hostility from both the right and left. A plenitude of Holocaust novels and short stories emerged against this background, reflecting a growing awareness of the Holocaust's enormity for Jewish-American life and thought. Unlike earlier Jewish-American fiction, this literature evaluated everything in light of the flames of Auschwitz.

Among the many difficulties confronting the writings of the Jewish-Americans was that they were nonwitnesses. Had they undertaken to depict an event that defies artistic expression? Elie Wiesel, a writing witness, insists "A novel about Auschwitz is either not a novel or not about Auschwitz." The literary critic and novelist Norma Rosen deemed the nonwitnessing writers' confrontation with the Holocaust a fundamental paradox, a "double bind, as nearly impossible to write about as to avoid writing about." Jewish-American writers were "witnesses through the imagination."

Though less successful at depicting the Holocaust experience, Jewish-American novelists successfully posed a plethora of related concerns important for both witnesses and nonwitnesses, European and American Jews alike. How, for example, can one imagine the unimaginable terrors of the death camps? Theologically speaking, does the covenant still exist? What kind of God permitted this tragedy to engulf His chosen people? What constitutes authentic Jewish living and literature after Auschwitz? These are only some of the ineluctable issues confronting Jewish-American novelists.

Problematics aside, Jewish-American novelists have felt compelled to respond to the Holocaust. Among the first to do so was Meyer Levin, whose 1959 novel *Eva* tells the story of an escape from Auschwitz and the heroine's eventual arrival in Israel, where she marries and works in the legal profession. Subsequent Jewish-American writers can be understood as writers of indirection, lacking as they did Levin's historical experience as foreign correspondent during World War II and his Jewish and Zionist commitments. These writers utilized a variety of sources such as survivor testimony (Susan F. Schaeffer's 1974 novel *Anya* is the clearest example), scholarly accounts (Saul Bellow's *Mr. Sammler's Planet*, 1970, and Leslie Epstein's *King of the Jews*, 1979), and the fundamental mythic ethos of biblical, rabbinic, and mystical Judaism in attempting to confront Auschwitz and its aftermath. Novels and short stories treating the complexities of post-Auschwitz Jewish existence constitute in fact a continuum of religious, secular, and symbolic responses. Moreover, not infrequently, works of a single writer may be appropriate to more than one of these categories.

RELIGIOUS RESPONSES. Religious responses to the Holocaust sharply distinguish between Jewish authenticity and American culture. They reflect what Ruth B. Wisse termed Act II of American Jewish writing. The Holocaust novels and short stories of Arthur A. Cohen, Hugh Nissenson, Cynthia Ozick, Chaim Potok, Isaac Bashevis Singer, and Elie Wiesel are uncompromising in their adherence to covenantal Judaism. Singer, a refugee from Poland, wrote several novels directly treating American Jewry and the Holocaust (*Enemies, A Love Story*, 1972; *Shosha*, 1978; and *The Penitent*, 1982). Two of Wiesel's searing novels (*The Accident*, 1962, and *The Fifth Son*, 1985) concern this theme. Taking their cue from the Europeans, the native-born Jewish-American novelists confront the disaster by utilizing mystical and rabbinic motifs, classical teachings, and messianic hopes as normative guides for the Jewish imagination. Issues of faith and doubt are a palpable presence in the lives of their characters. God, the covenant, and the Jewish people are enmeshed in the search for post-Auschwitz meaning.

Three examples illustrate these points. Hugh Nissenson's short story "The Law" (1965) is both an indictment and affirmation of God's presence in history. Nissenson, while differentiating the survivor from American nonwitnesses, casts the former in the role of instructor both for his own American-born son and, by extension, all nonwitnesses. He insists on the validity of the covenantal mythos, distinguishing authentic from spurious forms of Holocaust literature. Cynthia Ozick, beginning with her first novel *Trust* (1966) and in subsequent short stories such as "Bloodshed" (1976), "Levitation" (1979), and "The Shawl" (1980), relentlessly contends that Judaism is lived in constant tension between covenant adherence and the vicissitudes of history. Post-Auschwitz Judaism, in Ozick's fiction, is a critique of both paganism and the lure of American assimilation. In two novels, *The Cannibal Galaxy* (1983) and *The Messiah of Stockholm* (1987), she contends that post-Holocaust Jewish authenticity can be modeled only by those who view history through a covenantal lens or by martyrs of the Holocaust.

The work of the late theologian and novelist Arthur A. Cohen is the model of religious response to the Holocaust. His mammoth novel, *In the Days of Simon Stern* (1973), combines magic, messianism, mysticism, and myth in outlining the continuing post-Holocaust struggle between good and evil. Very much in the kabbalistic manner, Cohen underscores the tension between a diminished God and a mankind impatient to assume the role of diety in overturning evil. Unlike Ozick, however, Cohen was ambivalent about the State of Israel, viewing America as the resuscitator of post-Holocaust Jewry.

SECULAR RESPONSES. Secular Jewish-American Holocaust literature reflects a preoccupation with the mystery of Jewish continuity. In individual works, Saul Bellow, Mark Helprin, Robert Kotlowitz, Bernard Malamud, Jay Neugeboren, and Susan F. Schaeffer distinguish between a Jewish authenticity rooted in Europe and a banalized American Judaism in which neither

Jewish kinship nor covenantal ethics play a role. In *Mr. Sammler's Planet, Anya,* and Cynthia Ozick's "Rosa" (1983), the Holocaust, not the covenant, determines Jewish identity. For example, survivors who were prewar assimilationists are, after the Holocaust, committed to Jewish kinship and a common Jewish destiny.

Saul Bellow's *Mr. Sammler's Planet* portrays the prewar, Holocaust, and post-Holocaust experiences of Artur Sammler, a Polish Anglophile who loses his wife and an eye during the Holocaust. He and his daughter survive and come to America. In New York City Sammler, the physically and psychically damaged survivor, serves as a moral pivot for the assimilated, sexually promiscuous, and Jewishly indifferent relatives surrounding him. His message combines covenantally based ethics and a commitment to human obligation. Bellow/Sammler posits this message as a counter to the culturally fashionable nihilism and apocalyptic mood of post-Auschwitz American life. Susan Schaeffer's *Anya* follows the same biographical structure as Bellow's novel. Schaeffer tells the tale of Anya Savikin and her daughter. Anya is not religious in the traditional sense, although contending that she observes "in her own way." Her survivor's message concerns the post-Holocaust necessity of remaining Jewish.

This normative communal theme is also emphasized in an innovative way by Robert Kotlowitz in *The Boardwalk,* his 1977 novel about Jewish America in 1939. Kotlowitz has written a post-Holocaust critique of pre-Holocaust Jewish-American innocence. The novel's main character is a Hebrew-speaking veteran of World War I who had also lived in mandate Palestine. It is he alone who realizes the isolation of the Jews and the necessity of Jewish community. Kotlowitz also pinpoints the persistence of an ugly Jewish-American anti-Semitism. Three of Bernard Malamud's short stories, "The Loan" (1952), "The Lady of the Lake" (1958), and "The German Refugee" (1963) despite their various settings (Europe and America) all portray the Holocaust as the point of entry into Jewish history for prewar assimilationists and their recognition of the inescapability of Jewish identity and community.

SYMBOLIC RESPONSES. Symbolic literary responses to the Holocaust are perhaps the most complex. Novelists in this category either refrain from engaging the issue of Jewish specificity or highlight rifts within the Jewish community. Emphasis is placed on psychology more than theology. Questions of ethics, morality, and even those with theological overtones are asked outside the traditional covenantal framework. There is history, but little certainty of a Lord of History. There is a definable Jewish behavior, but it is radically attenuated and eludes classical ritual formats. These writers focus on the complicated issue of post-Holocaust Jewish-Christian relations. The Holocaust works of Edward Lewis Wallant, Norma Rosen, and Philip Roth underscore these views.

Wallant's *The Pawnbroker* (1961), though similar in structure both to *Mr. Sammler's Planet* and to *Anya,* differs from them radically in universalizing the theme of human suffering and in portraying the survivor as Jewishly unreflective and indifferent. Sol Nazerman, the Jewish survivor, is, for example, symbolically restored to spiritual wholeness only by the murder of his Christian assistant. Norma Rosen has written a novel with a far different type of universalism. Her *Touching Evil* (1969) boldly attempts to bring non-Jews into the universe of Jewish sensibility by describing the effects of the televised Eichmann trial on two Christian women. Rosen wisely understands that the Holocaust's evil is an enormous poison touching everyone. Philip Roth is the most complex of the writers in this group. His short stories and novels employ the Holocaust as a symbol of Jewish authenticity against which he measures the behavior and attitude of American Jews. Two short stories, "Defender of the Faith" and "Eli, the Fanatic" (both published in 1959), and two novels in particular, *The Ghost Writer* (1979) and *The Counterlife* (1986), treat the issue of the Holocaust and Jewish identity. While admitting no easy summary, these works share a concern for post-Holocaust Jewish identity as it is forged either in the crucible of Jewish-Christian relations or within the Jewish community itself.

Epitomizing symbolic responses are the Holocaust novels of Leslie Epstein, Bernard Malamud, and Hugh Nissenson. Malamud's *The Fixer* (1966) and Nissenson's *My Own Ground* (1976) are symbolic prefigurations of the Holocaust. Malamud's novel is set in Europe and focuses on czarist Russia's blood-libel trial of Mendel Beiliss, an antecedent war against the Jews, emphasizing Jewish vulnerability and the corruption of the modern state. Malamud, a master storyteller, is keenly aware of spiritual complexity, but his main character, Yaakov Bok, seems Jewishly indifferent. Betrayed by a fellow Jew, and rejecting God, Bok is befriended by Christians and seeks meaning in a symbolic community of the oppressed. Nissenson's novel takes place in the early teens of twentieth-century America. He, like Kotlowitz, depicts an American Jewry in process of dissolving its ties with tradition. Mystics, Marxists, and socialists all compete for the soul of America's Jews. A fortune-telling mystic forsees the Holocaust. Unlike Malamud, however, Nissenson has written a novel whose main character, Jake Brody, while attracted by none of these options, is Judaically knowledgeable although he neither practices nor believes in the tradition.

Epstein's *King of the Jews* (1979) is a historical fable concerning the plight of the Jews in the Lodz ghetto and of Mordechai Rumkowski, their mysterious and complex leader. Epstein's highly symbolic work employs gallows humor in fabulizing the historical predicament of the ghetto, thereby enabling his fictional Jews to gain a measure of transcendence over their oppressors that history itself cruelly denied them.

SECOND-GENERATION LITERATURE.

A second-generation Jewish-American literature of the Holocaust has begun to appear. The second-generation phenomenon had received some psychological attention in the late 1960s, but it was brought to public awareness with the appearance of Helen Epstein's journalistic account *Children of the Holocaust* (1979). Elie Wiesel's *The Fifth Son*, dedicated to his son and to all children of survivors, legitimizes this genre. The novel emphasizes the importance of remembrance for American nonwitnesses, those whom Wiesel describes as suffering from a history they never experienced but with which they are intimately acquainted through witnessing parents. In second-generation fiction, children of Holocaust survivors struggle against evil, contend with the problematics of survivor parent-child relationships, and define their own quest for Jewish identity. Significant selected works in this genre include Thomas Friedmann's *Damaged Goods* (1984), Art Spiegelman's controversial *Maus* (1986), and Barbara Finkelstein's *Summer Long-a-Coming* (1987). The issues of witnessing and authenticity remain problematic. Novels such as Robert Greenfield's *Temple* (1982) and Frederick Busch's *Invisible Mending* (1984) use the genre without necessarily penetrating the issues.

This brief survey has by no means included all that has been written about the Holocaust in Jewish-American fiction. It has, however, suggested ways in which such fiction can be intelligently read. There exists, moreover, a threefold red thread uniting the various expressions of Jewish-American Holocaust literature. Such literature takes seriously the search for meaning in history, recognizes that the Holocaust is a continuing trauma both for its survivors and their children, as well as for nonwitnesses, and it serves as a critique of human nature and contemporary civilization. There remains the difficulty of writing about the catastrophe of European Judaism when primary access to the event is through the imagination. But novelists can raise ultimate questions without being required to provide definitive responses. There is as well a recognition that America is increasingly the center of Jewish renewal and creativity, and its literature is, therefore, distinctively positioned to shed light on the continuing quest for authenticity in post-Holocaust Jewish identity.

ALAN L. BERGER

BIBLIOGRAPHY

Abrahamson, Irving, ed. *Against Silence: The Voice and Vision of Elie Wiesel*. 3 vols. New York: Holocaust Library, 1985.

Alexander, Edward. *The Resonance of Dust: Essays on Holocaust Literature and Jewish Fate*. Columbus: Ohio State University Press, 1980.

Alter, Robert. *Defenses of the Imagination: Jewish Writers and Modern Historical Crisis*. Philadelphia: Jewish Publication Society, 1977.

Berger, Alan L. *Crisis and Covenant: The Holocaust in American Jewish Fiction*. Albany: SUNY Press, 1985.

Cohen, Arthur A. "The American Imagination After the War: Notes on the Novel, Jews, and Hope." Nineteenth Annual B. G. Rudolph Lecture in Judaic Studies. Syracuse, N.Y.: Syracuse University Press, 1981.

Knopp, Josephine Z. *The Trial of Judaism in Contemporary Jewish Writing*. Urbana: University of Illinois Press, 1975.

Kremer, S. Lillian. *Witness Through the Imagination: Jewish American Holocaust Literature*. Detroit: Wayne State University Press, 1989.

Ozick, Cynthia. *Art and Ardor*. New York: Knopf, 1983.

———. *Metaphor and Memory*. New York: Knopf, 1989.

Rosen, Norma. "The Holocaust and the American-Jewish Novelist." *Midstream* XX (October 1974): 54–62.

———. "The Second Life of Holocaust Imagery." *Midstream* XXXIII (April 1987): 56–59.

Rosenfeld, Alvin H. *A Double Dying: Reflections on Holocaust Literature.* Bloomington: Indiana University Press, 1980.

Wiesel, Elie. *The Fifth Son*, trans. by Marion Wiesel. New York: Summit, 1985.

Wisse, Ruth R. "American Jewish Writing Act II." *Commentary* 61 (June 1976): 40-45.

Holocaust Survivors in America. On May 8, 1945, the SS *Brand Whitlock*, bearing the very first survivors of Auschwitz to the United States, slipped into the harbor at Newport News, Virginia. Three of the passengers were sisters, Hungarian Jewish women named Katz. They had gone through the hell hole of Auschwitz and survived the whistle and thumb flick of Dr. Josef Mengele, the devastatingly simple means he had employed to decide who would live and who would die.

Forty years later, one of the sisters, as the novelist Isabella Leitner, would write about that sea voyage and what she had felt escaping from one universe into another:

Dr. Mengele, we are on our way to America, and we are going to forget every brutal German word you forced us to learn. We are going to learn a new language. We are going to ask for bread and milk in Shakespeare's tongue. We will learn how to live speaking English and forget how people die speaking German.

She continues:

The ship detaches itself from land and plunges into the waves of the Black Sea. I search the sky to see if I can conjure my mother and my little sister, Potyo. I look in desperate sorrow but can discern no human form. The smoke has vanished. There is not a trace. No grave, nothing. Absolutely nothing.

Our sailor friend, Jack, talks to us about this new world we are about to encounter: skyscrapers, buildings that rise to the clouds in New York; the world's tallest building, the Empire State, Times Square and 42nd Street, the crossroads of the world.

He speaks of Ellis Island and New York harbor, where millions of immigrants have been greeted by a lady holding high a torch of liberty.

He describes a land where the color of people's skin can vary from white to black, from yellow to red; where people can be Protestant, Baptist, Buddhist, or Catholic—even Jewish or atheist—and they all live together in that melting pot called democracy; where people ride in huge automobiles or sweat in the belly of the earth; where there are slums, and estates with private tennis courts, tall Texans and short Mexicans, the very rich and the very poor, and a great many people who are neither rich nor poor, just citizens of a free country, a country very different from those we have known.

Isabella Leitner and her fellow survivors came to America, the *goldene medina*, with the same hopes and dreams that symbolized other Jews from other places who had preceded them to those shores. The same hopes and dreams, but yet different.

In April 1945, the late American Jewish novelist Meyer Levin was a war correspondent traveling with the Fourth Armored Division as it made its way east around the German town of Gotha. He and his companions came upon some "cadaverous refugees" along the road. "They were like none we had ever seen," Levin wrote later. "Skeletal with feverish sunken eyes, shaven skulls." They identified themselves as Poles and asked Levin and the others to come to the site where they had been held prisoner. They spoke of "people buried in a Big Hole and Death Commando." They described a camp, but the Americans did not want to go there during the oncoming darkness for fear of enemy attack. They would wait for light.

What they found the next morning at a camp called Ohrdruf, named for and just outside a small town near Gotha, were scenes that had not been seen before—not in the quantity, not in the form of death, not in the manner of killing.

As Levin drove through the gate, he saw piles of dead prisoners, all in striped uniforms. The corpses were fleshless, and at the back of each skull was a bullet hole. A shack held a stack of stiff and naked men. The bodies were "flat and yellow as lumber" Levin remembered.

This was only the beginning! During the next several weeks, camp after camp was liberated by Americans, English, and Russians. We know best what the American liberators felt at the moment of liberation of such camps as Nordhausen, Buchenwald, Dachau, and Mauthausen in Austria.

"Oh, the odors," wrote one, "well there is no way to describe the odors. . . . Many of the boys I am talking about—those were tough soldiers, there were combat men who had been all the way through on the invasion—were ill and vomiting, throwing up, just the sight of this. . . ."

Another wrote, "These Jewish people were like animals, they were so degraded, there was no goodness, no kindness, nothing of that nature, there was no sharing. If they got a piece of something to eat, they grabbed it and ran away in a corner and fought off anyone who came near them."

Finally, a third wrote, "The prisoners were so thin, they didn't have anything, didn't have any buttocks to lie on: there wasn't any flesh on their arms to rest their skulls on. . . . One man that I saw there who had died on his knees, with his arms and head in a praying position, and he was still there, apparently had been for days." These were some of the physical reactions and impressions of tough American GIs, from boys from Iowa, street-wise New Yorkers, and mountain men from Appalachia. But it took the sensitivity of a literary imagination like Meyer Levin's to give it the perspective, the meaning, that defines the Holocaust for our time. Levin wrote:

> We had known. The world had vaguely heard. But until now no one of us had looked on this. Even this morning we had not imagined we would look on this. It was as though we had penetrated at last to the center of the black heart, to the very crawling inside of the vicious heart.

And during those early weeks of spring 1945, a group of perhaps as many as 100,000 Jewish survivors found themselves among the 11 million uprooted and homeless people wandering throughout Germany and Central Europe. Many of these displaced persons (DPs) sought to return home to rebuild their lives and their nations.

Not so the Jews. As one Jewish survivor wrote, "The Jews suddenly faced themselves. Where now? Where to? For them things were not so simple. To go back to Poland? To Hungary? To streets empty of Jews. To wander in those lands, lonely, homeless, always with the tragedy before one's eyes . . . and to meet again a former Gentile neighbor who would open his eyes wide and smile, remarking with double meaning, 'What Yankel! You are still alive?'"

These Jews, later to be joined by 150,000 others from Russia and Poland, formed the She'erith Hapletah (Hebrew for the Saving Remnant). The term was both a description and a source of identity for those surviving the death camps, those who were partisans in the forests, and those who took refuge from Hitler in the deepest reaches of Russian Siberia. It was an identity that would give birth to a revolutionary ideology created from the inner being and experience of the She'erith Hapletah.

"*Mir szeinen doh*" (we are here) was the phrase that best expressed the resolution of the Jewish DPs to rebuild their shattered lives. It was the unshakable belief of a group of survivors who felt that they had seen in the Holocaust, as one survivor stated, "the end of creation—not only an indelible memory of horror, but a permanent warning," that what he and others had experienced was a pilot project for the destruction of humanity.

"We are here," was expressed in a number of ways. By the end of 1948 the Jewish DP camps had the distinction of having the highest birth rate of any Jewish community in the world. This resolve to say yes to a Jewish future surprised visitors to the camps, who had come there expecting to find a despair-ridden and essentially pessimistic community.

Even more pronounced than the birth rate was the resolve of the She'erith Hapletah to develop a philosophy of survival that would never again allow Jews to experience such a tragedy as the Holocaust.

Writing in April 1946 in the Jewish DP newspapers, J. Nemenczyk related a concentration camp fantasy that he had experienced lying on lice-filled straw in hunger and pain. "I had a vision," he wrote, "that if the world could not give us back our dead brothers and sisters, then it could give us back a moral world."

Even earlier, speaking at the first ceremony in June 1945 marking the liberation from Nazism, Zalman Grinberg, one of the earliest acknowledged spokespersons of the She'erith Hapletah, stressed the moral aspect of its existence.

"Hitler won the war against the European Jews. If we took revenge, we would descend into the lowest depths . . . which the German nation has fallen during the past ten years. We are not able to burn millions of people."

The Free Word, the journal of the Feldafing

camp, echoed Grinberg's message in an article entitled, "We Jews and the World." It stated that "what we, the She'erit Hapletah must do is to show that we, the victims of Nazism, have always been and will always be, the carriers of humanity."

The ideology of the She'erit Hapletah was thus formulated and the conditions for its implementation were set. Emissaries spoke to gatherings of Jewish organizations in America, expecting to become the vehicle for revolutionary change within the Jewish people and within the world. But the encounter with the world was only now beginning, and it was not a positive one. As early as June 1945, Grinberg had expressed the fear that "mankind does not comprehend what we have gone through and what we experienced during this period of time and it seems to us," he speculated, "neither shall we be understood in the future."

Even though the activity associated with the survivor's ideology was an important source of hope, by 1950 a deep sense of disillusion and disappointment was already evident. For one of the last issues of *Undser Veg*, Pesach Pekatsch expressed a sense of that disappointment. "We believed that it was time to conquer evil and humanity," he wrote, "that it would be a long time before bestiality would again be able to conquer the ideas of freedom." Instead, Pekatsch found a different picture, one in which the "specter of hatred" and the forces advocating the call to destruction and murder emerged freely and openly to attack the democracies they so hated.

Slowly but surely, in the late 1940s and early 1950s, the survivors left Germany and left Europe. A quarter of a million went to Israel and nearly 100,000 to the United States. Those coming to America, for the most part, came penniless, physically and emotionally drained, with personal losses that words and numbers could not describe.

Yet they were coming to America, where millions of European Jews before them had found new lives and transformed their existence into the freest and most tolerant of any Jewish society in history.

But survivors were different. Theirs were special lives because they had been participants in history, both Jewish and world. And it was the sense of that history that opened their mouths, not only about the specific tragic experiences they had survived, but about human experience in general. The Holocaust was the central illumina-

tion and the authority for that which they knew about life, a sum of knowledge that was, in their eyes, considerable. The Holocaust had tested them and taught them, taught them to know the nature of men, as they believed, and to know it in a way and a degree it was not given other people to know. Not even in America.

Pesach Pekatsch had realized, even in the DP camps, that the She'erit Hapletah's call for change within the human condition and within the Jewish condition was not being heard. The Double Vision inherent in the human condition took precedence over what the survivors felt was a sacred mission.

Elie Wiesel has put it best: "What the survivors wanted was to transmit a message to the world, a message of which they were the sole bearers. Having gained an insight into man that will forever remain unequaled, they tried to share a knowledge with that world."

But the survivors, according to Wiesel, found themselves in another kind of exile, another kind of prison. People welcomed them with tears and sobs when they stepped off the boats, then turned away. And why not. As one survivor recounted of her first years in this country, "My cousins were American-born Jews—kind, generous people who also shrank from me a little. You understand, the concentration camp experience is nothing that endears you to people."

Shortly after her arrival in America in 1951, one survivor had the experience of being told by her American-born Jewish neighbor in Brooklyn that she should write stories. "You have a terrific imagination," the neighbor told her on hearing a tale about selections and gas chambers.

In New Orleans a truck driver told a survivor, "Don't try to tell people here what happened in Europe: forget about it. I was in the American army. I walked into those camps and I saw all the things the Germans did and people here don't believe it when you tell them." The truck driver had given up mentioning the sights he had seen in the camps to anyone but people who had been there.

In many respects, these attitudes were the beginning of a conspiracy of silence between Holocaust survivors and society, a silence that would characterize the lives of most survivors even 25 years after their arrival in America. For many Americans, they would still be the "refugees" who had come with amazing tales to tell, but who soon stopped talking and interacting with the native American community.

Helen Epstein, whose book on the children of survivors has become the Bible of the "second generation," remembers her mother's tatoo as being "like a mysterious flag. It made some people blush, turn their eyes aside, mumble garbled things."

So the survivors retreated, convinced that tales about starvation, the ghetto, Auschwitz selections, or any other such experiences could not be accepted as the truth or as lessons to change the nature of our world.

Instead, the survivors remained different. They were not like Americans; indeed, the connection between American Jews and themselves was only slightly less remote than the connection between themselves and American Gentiles.

They worked hard, bore children, and found a place for themselves in their adopted homeland. Many became professionally successful, steeled by the experience of survival to endure the slings and arrows of the difficult and uncertain world of trade and commerce.

Yet with a determined consistency certain feelings emerged from within the survivor communities that reflected a long lost echo of that early sense of idealism, of the revolutionary fervor that shook the DP camps. There were those survivors who believed that, for many in their group, material well-being became an end rather than a means. They felt that because survivors saw and suffered, "there should have come forward from among them a better sort of person, less selfish than the ordinary, perhaps; one more sensitive to humankind, one with spiritual goals that were a little higher than those of most people—otherwise, for what had they survived."

At the end of the 1970s, the conspiracy of silence—a scrupulously kept taboo which lasted for decades—broke apart. The genius of the American soul allowed both the survivor and his and her children to occupy a unique role in the evolution of the Jewish presence in history. The Holocaust and its observance became, in its rites and rituals, an American obsession: from the President of the United States, who issued a mandate that its rememberance become a full national memorial museum in our nation's capital, to annual observances of its meaning for Christians and Jews in every state of the Union. The children of the survivors have opened, in the words of Helen Epstein, their "iron boxes," that internal sense of being different, of having grown up in a home with survivors, but without grandparents or aunts and uncles, and what it has meant for their development as Ameri-

cans, as Jews, as members of a community of the second generation is still being evaluated.

Indeed, to some observers, the American Jewish return to Judaism is comprised of the rites and rituals of identification with and fascination about the Holocaust. This allows "ready access to deep feelings and a direct encounter with transcendental experience."

For many, all of this is too much to grasp, almost too unbelievable to accept.

The "in" status of the Holocaust has not found acceptance within the entire range of the survivor community. Its most persistent voice, Elie Wiesel, remains its most persistent critic. As early as the 1970s he wrote that "suddenly everyone began calling himself a survivor. One consequence is that an international symposium on the Holocaust was held recently in New York without the participation of any Holocaust survivors. The survivors didn't count. They never did. They are best forgotten. . . . They are an embarrassment. If only they weren't there, it would be so much easier."

And even in the "decade of the survivor," the 1980s, when they are asked to speak in the classrooms and into the cassette recorder they are, in the words of the late Terence Des Pres, "both sought and shunned: The desire to hear the survivor's truth is countered by the need to ignore him. Insofar as we feel compelled to defend a comforting view of life, we tend to deny the survivor's voice."

Despite all of the surface success, American Jews have not really listened to the voice of the She'erith Hapletah. They have not listened to the prophetic voice that sought to change the direction of Jewish identity and of human destiny, to steer a course toward the moral and social perfection of humanity. They have not listened to a voice that could tell all of us (Jew and Gentile) that the consequences of the Holocaust are all around us in what we see and what we are.

Where is the voice of the She'erith Hapletah? Perhaps it is in the voice of Jacob Felberbaum, who talks about the memories and feelings that haunt the aging survivor:

To no surprise we take our memorabilia.
The fragments saved from the abyss of our tragedy. Photographs of our dear ones grace the walls. And we try to read those sometimes yellowing faces and to recreate their past and with it our own past. Somehow it is not possible. The

time blurred our memory and we stare in the empty space. So when we are talking about loneliness, we are talking about feelings in different dimensions than in the usual meaning of this word.

This is simply the result of absence of generations that are gone and also those generations that were denied to come into being. We are condemned never to see our dear ones, never to listen to our friends, or for that matter to those we did not like so much.

So we lost the world of our fathers. In the smokestacks of devilish camps, in the ravines, in the outskirts of cities, within the ravished ghettos, a deep-rooted credence in the justice of the Higher Power was fundamentally shaken. We remained with the hidden pain of indescribable loneliness.

But perhaps the voice of the She'erith Hapletah belongs to another time, a century or more from now, when Jews will talk of the Holocaust in the same distant, almost metaphysical way in which they describe the Exodus from Egypt or the revolt of the Macabees. One day, the Holocaust will simply be a child's memory, a parent's recounting of a tale that will give meaning to Jewish identity and bring special meaning to being a Jew. But that, after all, is what lay at the very center of the voice of the She'erith Hapletah and all the other prophetic voices that have spoken to the Jewish people and to the world— and which will, no doubt, continue to do so. *See also* Holocaust, America and the; Holocaust, Literature of the.

ABRAHAM J. PECK

BIBLIOGRAPHY

Dinnerstein, Leonard. *America and the Survivors of the Holocaust.* New York: Columbia University Press, 1982.

Epstein, Helen. *Children of the Holocaust: Conversations with Sons and Daughters of Survivors.* New York: Putnam, 1979.

Rabinowitz, Dorothy. *New Lives: Survivors of the Holocaust Living in America.* New York: Knopf, 1976.

Wiesel, Elie. *A Jew Today,* trans. by Marion Wiesel. New York: Random House, 1978.

Howe, Irving (b. 1920). Political, social and sociological essayist and analyst, historian, scholar, literary critic, anthologist editor, and educator, Howe was born in New York City, educated in the city's public schools, and received a B.A. (English) from the City College of New York in 1940. Subsequently, he taught English at Brandeis University (1953–1961), Stanford (1961–1963), and Hunter College (1963–1986), a part of the City University of New York, where he held the title of Distinguished Professor. At the beginning of his career, as Christian Gauss Chair Professor at Princeton (1954), he met such leading creative and critical personalities as Saul Bellow and R. W. B. Lewis.

Howe made his name as a democratic radical of the Trotskyite school, as editor of *Dissent* (an alternative to the *Partisan Review*), and as a critic of English, American, Russian, and continental fiction in such books as *Politics and the Novel* (1957), *William Faulkner: A Critical Study* (1951), and *Celebrations and Attacks* (1979), literary and cultural essays covering 30 years. As a historian and scholar of American Jewry and radical thought, Howe has been the winner of major book awards for *World of Our Fathers* (1976) and *Leon Trotsky* (1978). In his critical activity, he has followed in the intellectually based social criticism of Edmund Wilson and Lionel Trilling, relationships that are detailed in his "intellectual autobiography," *A Margin of Hope* (1982).

This autobiography mentions that the young Howe was prevented by his father from attending a socialist-Yiddishist middle school run by the Workmen's Circle, but this did not stop him from becoming a member of YPSL (Young People's Socialist League) in the very same place. In other words, socialist universalism had to overshadow Jewish particularism at this time. Max Schachtman, the American version of Trotsky, attracted Howe because he offered a key to the mysteries of socioeconomic reality as well as a key to ideals such as equality and justice through the hope of achieving "a significant redistribution of income, wealth and power" and "eradicating racism and poverty in the near future," as Howe wrote in a *Dissent* anthology on *The Seventies: Problems and Proposals* (1972).

In fact, the slightly more mature Howe began to see such democratic participation as the essence of socialism, and, in the sense that the economic strategies of his "militant" days no longer seemed relevant, it was true that "the years of my life coincided with the years of socialist defeat." However, for him socialism remained a potent "moral solution," and he felt obliged to attack the

Soviet Union and all orthodox ideologues (including those of the New Left) who infringed on the freedom to choose democratically. As a result, Howe reinterpreted traditional ideology in *Socialism and America*, first published in 1977 and reissued in 1985: "collective ownership" became "democratic control" and Roosevelt's Welfare State became a "socialization of concern" rather than a mere "capitalistic sop" to the need for community. Other signs of this trend in his thinking were two anthologies that he edited, *Poverty: Views from the Left* (with Jeremy Larner, 1968) and *The World of the Blue Collar Worker* (1972).

In short, Howe began to conceive of "liberal necessities" in a less ideological, more realistic, and even "ethnic" way. For this reason, he edited an anthology with Carl Gershman on *Israel, the Arbas and the Middle East* (1972), in which he quite openly stated a critical "commitment to democratic Israel." In addition, his biography of Trotsky devoted several pages to Trotsky's not widely known understanding that the Jews had the right to a group life of their own.

Howe was on the way to discovering his particular, rather than merely universal, identity. Thus, when he noted in *Socialism and America* that Oklahoma socialists and populists had much in common with East-Side Jews, he was taking a step toward the Jewish populism of the *World of Our Fathers* (1976), a full examination of the Jewish immigrant milieu. Moreover, only a few years earlier (in 1969), he had anthologized modern Yiddish poetry in *A Treasury of Yiddish Poetry* (co-edited with Eliezer Greenberg), and he continued this interest in 1977 in a selection from modern Soviet Yiddish fiction entitled *Ashes Out of Hope* (also with Greenberg). In addition, he selected *The Best of Sholem Aleichem* in 1979. This celebration of Jewish communal creativity

did not completely rule out his status of "partial Jew," as he expressed it. Nevertheless, it did move him to defend his people against Hannah Arendt, whose research tended to present Holocaust victims as "cowards."

Likewise, Howe made an intensive effort to discover America as a literary critic. Passing through the Midwest on his way to army duty in Alaska, he noted how far "Sherwood Anderson's America" seemed from New York City (or the "Eastern Establishment"); the result was a book on Anderson (1951). He then became the spokesman for this New York literary intellectuality and wrote criticism that spread to the South as well as to Middle America (Flannery O'Connor as well as Anderson) and from New York itself (Delmore Schwartz and Bernard Malamud) to England (Thomas Hardy and George Orwell) and the world at large (Stendhal and Ignazio Silone). His aim was to apply Trilling's definition of "authenticity" in such a flexible and humane manner that even the American Jewish "stranger"—the "Jewboy" without a solid Emersonian heritage—could fall into it. *See also* Critics, Literary.

ALBERT WALDINGER

BIBLIOGRAPHY

Dector, Midge. "Socialism and Its Irresponsibilities: The Case of Irving Howe." *Commentary* 74 (December 1982): 25–32.

Howe, Irving. *A Margin of Hope: An Intellectual Autobiography.* New York: Harcourt Brace Jovanovich, 1982.

Pinsker, Sanford. "Lost Causes/Marginal Hopes: The Collected Elegies of Irving Howe." *Virginia Quarterly Review* 65 (Spring 1989): 585–599.

Humor. *See* COMICS AND COMEDY.

I

Imber, Naphtali Herz (1856–1909). Hebrew poet and author of "Hatikvah" (The Hope), the Jewish national anthem, Naphtali Herz Imber was born in Zloczow, Galicia, where he received a traditional Jewish education. He wrote his celebrated "Hatikvah" at the age of 22 while in Romania.

By nature a restless spirit and a semivagabond, while in Constantinople in 1882 Imber met Laurence Oliphant (1829–1888), the Christian Zionist. He accompanied Oliphant to Palestine and served as his secretary until 1887. He then settled in London where he was befriended by Israel Zangwill (1864–1926), who made him the prototype for one of his characters in his volume of stories, *Children of the Ghetto* (1892).

In 1891, Imber migrated to America. For a time he lived in Boston, where he launched his short-lived monthly magazine *Uriel* (1895), which was devoted to "Cabbalistic Science." After years of wandering from coast to coast, he returned to the East Side of New York. There he was a familiar figure at Zionist assemblies and was known for his addiction to liquor.

In addition to three collections of Hebrew poetry entitled *Barkai* (*Dawn—Jerusalem*, 1886; *Zloczow*, 1900; *New York*, 1904), Imber published a Hebrew translation of Edward FitzGerald's *Rubaiyat* (1905). He also contributed Yiddish poems to the press. Unlike other Hebrew-Yiddish immigrant writers, Imber readily adapted to the American scene and published extensively in English. He was the author of two books dealing with folklore and legends, *Treasures of Ancient Jerusalem* (1898) and *Treasures of Two Worlds* (1910). His autobiographical writings and his reminiscences of his experiences in Palestine, the Old World and America are of particular interest.

When Imber died in New York there was a tremendous outpouring by many thousands who paid him homage for his contribution to the movement for the restoration of Zion. The Zionist ideal was the leitmotif of his poetic output. After the establishment of the State of Israel, a movement arose for the transfer of his remains to Jerusalem and he was re-buried there in 1953. His anthem is sung not only at Jewish gatherings everywhere, but it has also the distinction of being included in various editions of the Jewish prayerbook. *See also* Hebrew in America.

JACOB KABAKOFF

BIBLIOGRAPHY

Collected Poems of Naphtali Herz Imber (In Hebrew). Tel Aviv: Committee for the 50th Anniversary of Hatikvah, 1929. With a biography by his brother Shmaryahu Imber.

Kabakoff, Jacob, ed. *Master of Hope: Selected Writings of Naphtali Herz Imber*. Cranberry, N.J.: Herzl Press, 1985.

Immigration, German (nineteenth century). The Jews who migrated to the United States in the nineteenth century from the German-speaking areas of Central Europe made up the second wave of Jewish settlers in America. The earlier Ashkenazi Jews who had settled in the eighteenth century had blended into the dominant Spanish-Portuguese Jewish congregations in New York, Philadelphia, and other East Coast cities. It was not until the 1820s, with the mass migration of Jews from those areas of Europe that either spoke German or were influenced by German culture that German Jews began to form separate communities and institutions in America and ushered in the "German period" in American Jewish history. The German Jewish migration continued through the 1880s, when it was supplanted by the arrival of large numbers of Jews from Eastern Europe.

It is only possible to estimate the number of German Jews who migrated to the United States in these decades since no data was collected on the religious affiliation of immigrants, nor did the United States census ask about such matters. Furthermore, there were no organized Jewish bodies that could have provided this information. One rough calculation puts the number of German Jewish immigrants of this period at approximately 200,000, since in 1820, at the beginning of this wave of settlement, there were fewer than 3000 Jews in the United States, while in 1880 the number topped 250,000. Similarly, the growth in the number of congregations provides a way of measuring the impact of this migration. In 1820, American Jews had formed themselves into a scant 8 congregations. By 1840, the number had climbed to 19, and by 1850, to 77. In 1877, another 200 congregations had been added to the institutions of American Jewish life, thus attesting to the impact of the German Jewish migration.

The term "German Jewish" is an ambiguous one for the nineteenth century. It was not until 1871 that there was a political unit called Germany. Before that a number of independent entities existed in which German was spoken. These were unified under Bismarck. But many of the Central European Jews who came to the United States, who either spoke German or who considered themselves to be linked to German culture, did not necessarily come from those areas that would eventually be incorporated into Imperial Germany. Furthermore, many who migrated from clearly German-speaking areas did not actually have German as their first language; instead, they spoke a Judeo-German dialect. Thus, while the bulk of the immigrants in the period 1820–1880 were from identifiable German provinces, others of the same years migrated from Posen, which was in the German-influenced sector of Poland. Similarly, immigrants from Austria and

Bohemia to the east and Alsace from the west may or may not have considered themselves, or been considered, German Jews. This ambiguity of identity complicates the analysis of nineteenth-century German Jewish immigration.

While the German Jewish immigration spanned some 70 years, it maintained a consistent character and changed little over time. Although starting in the 1840s a number of rabbis and other educated Jews did go to America, the vast bulk of the immigrants throughout this time period were young people, both men and women, who had little hope for the future if they remained in their native towns. In some cases entire families did make the move together, but more typically young people migrated with their peers. The youth of the immigrants is revealed, for example, in the statistics of the archives of Württemberg, which are typical of the migration of the period. They show that out of 206 Jews who departed for America between 1848 and 1865, 61 percent were younger than 20.

Like other "chain" migrants, these German Jewish young people earmarked their earliest savings to bring over other siblings and sometimes parents. In the main, the youthful migrants had few skills and had little education in either secular or religious fields.

The migration was heavily centered in the small towns of the southwestern German states: Baden, Bavaria, Württemberg, as well as Swabia, the Palatinate, and Saxony. While some German Jewish intellectuals, like Leopold Zunz, sought to encourage Jewish immigration out of Europe, the movement of young Jews to America was largely spontaneous and arose in reaction to the worsening of both the political and economic status of Jews in their regions. In post-Napoleonic Central Europe repressive anti-Jewish legislation had limited Jews to a narrow range of trades and occupations at the same time that anti-Semitism was becoming a more salient feature of German every day life. Many of the Jews of southwestern Germany had previously derived a livelihood in the peasant economy as petty middlemen, tradesmen, and cattle dealers. As that economy began to break down with early industrialization, so too the Jewish livelihood was shaken. In addition, those Jews who were artisans were not allowed to practice their crafts. Also the repressive legislation of the period severely curtailed the number of Jews who could marry and start families. Thus, young people had the bleak prospects of poverty and a life of celibacy to look forward to if they stayed at home.

While the German Jewish migration needs to be considered as part of the history of the Jewish migratory experience, it was also intimately connected to the general German migration of the period. At the same time that Jews were leaving the small towns of southern and southwestern Germany, so too were German Lutherans, Catholics, and Evangelicals. In the United States German Jews and German Christians settled in some of the same communities, such as Cincinnati, Milwaukee, and St. Louis, and often in close proximity to one another. In many places Jews participated amiably in German benevolent and recreational institutions, and religious differences were accepted with tolerance in the nineteenth-century German American communities.

German Jews landed in the United States at a time of tremendous economic growth. Their arrival coincided with the beginning of the canal era, spanned the development of the railroad, and the onset of industrialization. Vast opportunities existed in cities as well as in the interior hinterlands.

The kind of economic and cultural adjustments made by these German Jews was shaped in part by the nature of their migration and their massive dispersion around the United States. Because so many of them were unmarried and were not encumbered by either parents or children, they were able to take advantage of economic opportunities wherever they arose. While the small pockets of Jewish settlement that greeted them were limited to a few Atlantic coastal cities, the German Jews fanned out into every state and territory of the United States. They made their way through New England, the Midwest, the Great Plains, the South, and even the Far West.

Although going to primarily agricultural areas, the German Jews who settled in these regions did so not as farmers but as small businessmen ready to serve the needs of the rural population. They came initially as peddlers, an occupation that required little capital for start up and that was less disruptive to the life of a single man than it would have been to one who was married. Peddling was by and far the most frequent occupation for the newly arrived. There were few retail outlets outside of the large cities, and the Jewish peddler played a crucial link in the mercantile chain, bringing supplies of all kinds to the scattered rural population. In the large regional city or depot the immigrants would load themselves up with a pack of goods, weighing sometimes as much as 100 pounds, and would

then embark on a journey by foot, or eventually, if a peddler did well, by horse and wagon. So widespread was Jewish peddling that in 1859, of all employed Jews in the town of Easton, Pennsylvania, 59 percent were peddlers.

While peddling was a grueling, lonely, and often dangerous occupation, it became for many Jews the first step to a more settled and predictable business future and laid the basis for Jewish community formation. Successful Jewish peddlers became suppliers of goods and credit for fresh waves of German Jewish immigrants, more likely than not, relatives ready to take up the pack. As the distributive system became more developed and the need for the itinerant peddler diminished in all but the most isolated areas, the Jewish peddler often became the owner of a dry-goods or general store in a small town.

He was often ready to settle down and not infrequently went back to Germany to find a wife. A few of these petty merchants would open stores in a given locale. They, in turn, would attract other Jews and thus provided the nucleus of what would become a Jewish community. As early as the 1830s the outlines of Jewish communal life could be seen among the former peddlers in Albany, St. Louis, and Cleveland and in Chicago and Milwaukee in the 1840s.

There were regional variations to this pattern. Jews in the South also began their careers as peddlers, but a certain number of the more successful ones became cotton brokers in New Orleans, Montgomery, and Mobile. In the Far West Jewish peddlers made their way alongside the prospectors in the mining areas, supplying them with clothes, tools, and food. They too became the first members of what would develop as small Jewish communities.

The bulk of the German Jews, however, were urban dwellers, even if they had begun in America as peddlers. Some of them became extremely wealthy, and indeed some have been seen as the great princes of American retailing and business. Such wealthy families as the Seligmans, Lehmans, Warburgs, and Schiffs in investment banking as well as such retail merchants as the Bloomingdales, Filenes, Lazaruses, Straus, Gimbels, and Rosenwalds in varying degree created the mystique of the German Jewish immigrants who in a single generation catapulted themselves from poverty to fabulous wealth. The staggering success of the few should not obscure the fact that most of the German Jewish immigrants of the period remained small merchants, and many, indeed, never left the ranks of laborers, working as tailors, cigar makers, and other kinds of skilled craftsmen.

The nineteenth-century German Jewish immigration not only had a tremendous impact on the economic condition of American Jews, but also profoundly changed the nature of Jewish life in the United States. The German Jews were responsible for the creation of many of the basic institutions associated with American Jewish culture. Over the course of the last half of the nineteenth century, they created an elaborate network of social service and philanthropic institutions in every community. It was Jews from Germany who founded the B'nai B'rith in 1843, which would become the single largest Jewish organization in the world. And perhaps most importantly, the German Jews changed the religious complexion of American Judaism.

The arrival of large numbers of German Jews led to the establishment of new congregations in which the German ritual prevailed, one that was a modification of the traditional Orthodox, thus splitting the religious unity that had previously existed in the United States. As more German Jews came, new congregations proliferated, determined largely by the European regional variations. There was also a splintering of established congregations.

It was not only numbers that stimulated the German Jews in America to begin a massive wave of congregation building. Given the freedom of American society and the absence of state interference in religious matters, individual Jews were free to create congregations as they wanted. These Jews who, by and large had little religious knowledge and whose work precluded punctilious attention to the keeping of Halakah (Jewish law), became particularly receptive to the religious reforms that were being tried out in the latter half of the nineteenth century and that formed the basis for Reform Judaism.

The development of Reform Judaism was hastened by events in Germany. Reform of Jewish ritual and tradition had begun earlier there among a new crop of rabbis who had received university training and who began to debate the nature of Jewish life and law. The traditional rabbinical leadership, threatened by this challenge, successfully appealed to the local state authorities to suppress innovations of any kind. This convinced many of the reform-minded rabbis that only in the United States could a serious restructuring of Jewish life take place. A number of these rabbis, for example, Emil Hirsch, Samuel Adler, and David Einhorn, immigrated to the United States. It was this group that was responsible for formally establishing the Reform Movement in the United States. In 1873, under Isaac Mayer Wise, an immigrant from Bohemia, they created the Union of American Hebrew Congregations and in 1875 the Hebrew Union College in Cincinnati, the seminary to train an American Reform rabbinate.

German Jews also provided the earliest spokesman for an Americanized, but still traditional, Judaism. Isaac Leeser (1806–1868), an immigrant from Westphalia, became the chief spokesman for the traditionalists. He launched a number of publications and tried to create a school to spread the message that traditional Judaism could survive in America. The founding of the Jewish Theological Seminary in 1886, also by German Jews, was hoped by its founders to be an antidote to the radical tendencies in the Reform Movement. The traditionalists, however represented only a small percentage of the mass of German Jews in the United States.

By the 1880s as the immigration from Germany slackened to a trickle and as the larger migration from Eastern Europe was beginning, the slight regional variations among the German Jews had blurred, and the German Jews had become American Jews who continued to articulate a strong fondness for German culture, patriotism for their new American home, and a generalized loyalty to the Reform variant of Judaism. *See also* Immigration (1933–1945), German Refugee; Reform Judaism.

HASIA R. DINER

BIBLIOGRAPHY

Birmingham, Stephen. *Our Crowd: The Great Jewish Families of New York.* New York: Harper & Row, 1967.

Cohen, Naomi W. *Encounter With Emancipation: The German Jews in the United States, 1830–1914.* Philadelphia: Jewish Publication Society, 1984.

Korn, Bertram W. "German-Jewish Intellectual Influences on American Jewish Life, 1824–1972." In *The B. G. Rudolph Lectures in Judaic Studies.* Syracuse, N.J.: Syracuse University, 1972.

Strauss, Herbert A. "The Immigration and Acculturation of the German Jew in the United States of America." In *Year Book XVI of the Leo Baeck Institute.* London: The Institute, 1971.

Immigration, German Refugee. (1933–1945).

The approximately 150,000 Jews from German-speaking Europe who escaped from Nazi domination and came to the United States in the 1930s and early 1940s were a relatively small group. Unlike the Jewish immigrants from Eastern Europe who came to America between 1881 to 1924, they did not overwhelm the preexisting American Jewish community by force of numbers. Nevertheless, they have had considerable influence both on American society as a whole and on American Jewry in particular.

These German-speaking immigrants were quite a heterogeneous group. Those born in Germany itself had a different historical experience and often different intellectual traditions than those from Vienna or from German-speaking areas in former Austrian Czechoslovakia or Hungary. Degrees of Jewish identification, levels of education and income, and political attitudes also varied widely.

Despite their wide internal variation, the refugees did have certain features in common that marked them as different from earlier Jewish immigrants. They had not come to the United States out of choice, as had most of their predecessors. They were refugees (although in general they did not like the term "refugee"), coming to save their lives rather than to improve their economic condition. The newcomers of the 1930s were overwhelmingly middle class in background unlike the usually poverty-stricken earlier arrivals in America.

Culturally, they came with a dual identity as Jews and as Germans. They had been far more integrated into German culture than Jews in Eastern Europe had been into the Christian cultures of their home countries. Whereas Jews in Eastern Europe generally saw themselves as members of an independent nationality with its own language and culture, Jews in Germany tended to see themselves as German nationals of the Jewish religion.

The refugee wave of immigration was the last in a number of waves of German Jewish immigration to the United States. The main wave had been between 1820 and 1880, but small numbers continued to arrive after 1880 as well. Estimates of German Jewish immigration between 1918 and 1931 range as high as 30,000.

The persecutions that began in Germany with the rise of Hitler to power in 1933 increased Jewish emigration. This emigration began fairly slowly and was originally directed to European neighbors of Germany rather than to the United States. In 1933, the number of Jewish immigrants to the United States from Germany was a mere 535. Although the number rose in the following years, the bulk of the wave of German Jewish immigrants did not arrive in America until 1938–1940. These three years were marked by increased persecution, the most devastating being the *Kristallnacht* pogrom of November 1938. In the years after 1940, Germany restricted and then cut off emigration, preventing any further influx to the United States.

The position of the refugees when they arrived in America was an anomalous one. Most were relatively well educated and had lived middle-class lives. Many of those who arrived in 1938 or earlier had brought heavy bourgeois furniture and elegant clothing with them. Yet the strict German currency regulations, which after 1937 allowed only 10 marks to be taken out of the country, ensured that they arrived penniless. Because of their generally prosperous appearance and lifestyle, it was often difficult for the new arrivals to convince Americans that they were indeed needy. This often led to tension.

In contrast to the situation for most immigrants to the United States, the refugees experienced a great drop in standard of living upon their arrival, and not all looked upon America with awe. Though all were happy to be out of Germany, many continued to look with nostalgia at certain aspects of their former way of life and former culture. This, too, sometimes led to resentment and accusations of arrogance, even by their co-religionists. (Another source of tension was the refugees' rejection of Yiddish.)

Not only was their economic position anomalous, their cultural situation too was fraught with ambivalence. On the one hand, the great majority of the new arrivals were deeply rooted in German culture. They felt an attachment to the German language and, in many cases, to the art, literature, and music of German high culture. On the other hand, their terrible experiences in Nazi Germany led most of them to sever any sense of attachment to Germany and to its people. The refugee communities were marked by fervent American patriotism during World War II and a strong commitment to the defeat of Germany. They, however, did continue their attachment to aspects of German culture and, in the first generation, most continued to speak German.

The majority of Jews in Germany (contrary

to a popular viewpoint among American Jews) had never given up their Jewish identity. However acculturated the majority was, most still retained some feelings of attachment to the Jewish group, and, in many cases, some level of Jewish religious practice. The Jewish attachments of the refugees were, in general, much strengthened by their experiences in Nazi Germany. Most German refugees surveyed in the 1980s labeled themselves as German Jews or American Jews with only a small minority choosing the label "German-American."

The Jewishness of the refugees expressed itself in a great variety of ways, from the founding of German synagogues and German Jewish burial societies to further German Jewish liturgical practices, to the attachment of most to Israel, to the fact that most of the refugees chose to live in Jewish neighborhoods—in New York City, for example, in Washington Heights, the Upper West Side, and Kew Gardens—rather than in German-American neighborhoods.

Arrival in the United States put a third cultural element into their lives. The refugees now had to balance their German cultural traits, their attachment to the Jewish community, and their desire for integration into American society. The balance was often difficult. On the conscious level the vast majority identified as American citizens and as Jews. However, many German cultural traits that were ingrained in their personalities from their early upbringing remained noticeable. Such traits as formality, punctuality, a respect for musical and literary high culture, and an attachment to the German language were not always consciously recognized by members of the group. Yet they tended to make German Jews recognizable and different from other American Jews. Even the synagogues, the most Jewish institutions founded by the refugees, were marked by German traits in the liturgy, music, and interpersonal style of congregational life. German remained the language of sermons and synagogue bulletins well into the 1960s. Only in the native-born second generation were most of these marks of German culture no longer noticeable.

In general, the children of the refugees merged into the American Jewish scene with little residual sense of Germanness. Marriage patterns of these children show the majority marrying American Jews of East European descent. Various types of evidence show that despite some original reluctance, most German Jews of the first generation have accepted this merger into American

Jewry. A survey in one refugee community shows virtually all wishing their children to remain Jewish, with only a minority considering it important that they preserve a sense of German Jewishness.

Students of the refugee wave of immigration have stressed both the elite character of much of the group and the relatively high level of integration into America. Unlike many other immigrant groups, the refugees of the 1930s did not, in general, remain in immigrant neighborhoods and enclaves. Even the one clearly German Jewish neighborhood in the United States—the Washington Heights section of New York—was only about 10 percent German Jewish and its 20,000 or so German-speaking Jewish inhabitants were barely 25 percent of the German Jews of New York.

Despite their tendency to scatter, however, the refugees did found a complex net of institutions that made for group cohesion. In general, these institutions were much more formalized and carefully organized than were the institutions of most immigrant groups in the United States. The German Jewish institutions ran the gamut of activities from religious, to cultural, to mutual aid, to the press.

At least 30 refugee synagogues are known to have existed, most of them in New York. Some communities without German synagogues founded German Jewish burial societies. The German synagogues have had an influence both on liberal Judaism in America (where they tended to have a traditionalizing influence) and within Orthodoxy (through the Breuer community with its very strict but secularly educated membership). Whatever their ideological tendencies, the German synagogues tended to be large, with formal liturgies and well-organized administrations.

The Breuer community in Washington Heights was also distinctive in its success in transplanting a cradle-to-the-grave organic community to the United States.

In the first 15 years of the German Jewish immigration social clubs played an important role as sources of entertainment, places to meet potential marriage partners, centers for sports activities, and a place to forget the troubles of the times. Foremost among the social clubs were the Prospect Unity Club and the New World Club, both in New York. The latter organization, which still exists, had an extensive program of lectures and cultural activity in addition to social events. In New York there were even special German and

Austrian lodges of B'nai B'rith (the Leo Baeck Lodge and Freedom Lodge).

Although the refugees were helped by a host of American Jewish organizations when they arrived in America (including HIAS and the National Council of Jewish Women), they tended to favor creating their own organizations for mutual aid. One of the first such organizations had the characteristic name Self-Help. Other mutual-aid organizations included Help and Reconstruction, the Blue Card, Gemiluth Chessed (an Orthodox organization), United Help, and the United Restitution Organization (designed to aid refugees in making their claims for restitution from the West German and other governments).

In the field of cultural life, German Jews founded only a few organizations, generally those catering to specific professional interests. However, many refugee organizations whose main purposes were social or even religious devoted an important part of their program to lectures, concerts, or other cultural activities. German Jews also showed an interest in preserving their heritage and studying their history. Among the organizations they created were the Leo Baeck Institute, dedicated to the study of German Jewish history through publication of books, an annual scholarly yearbook, and a host of lectures and other activities. The Research Foundation for Jewish Immigration was dedicated specifically to the study of the German Jewish immigration of the 1930s.

Perhaps the single greatest institution in uniting the geographically scattered German refugees was the press, and especially the New York-based German language *Aufbau*, published by the New World Club. The *Aufbau*, with a peak circulation of some 50,000, represented a viewpoint that was liberal politically and religiously, but also strongly pro-Zionist. The influence of the *Aufbau* was, however, more as a means of communication between the refugees than as an organ of a particular point of view. The newspaper's advertisements played an important role in the economic life of the community during the early years. In later years the family announcements, and especially the obituaries, were read by German Jews around the world.

Despite the initial advantage of relatively good education and middle-class skills, most German Jews had a difficult economic and social adjustment in the first decade or so after their arrival. Many found it difficult to adjust to their new poverty. Since the Depression was not completely

over in the late 1930s, many had difficulty finding work. Often former professionals and business people were forced to take menial positions to survive. Some who had had servants in Europe now found work as butlers and maids. Because it was often easier for women to find service jobs than for men, the traditional patriarchal structure of the German Jewish family was often challenged. Generational conflict was also caused by the greater freedom that young people were given in America.

Certain professions were subject to special obstacles. Physicians usually were forced to seek recertification and to pass examinations before they could practice in this country. Lawyers often found it impossible to apply their skills to the totally unfamiliar Anglo-American legal system.

Although the economic hardships were often severe in the early years, most refugees were able to reestablish themselves financially during World War II and the immediate postwar years. Many set up businesses or returned to some form of professional life. In many cases German Jewish businesses were small-scale retail establishments, some of which began in the owner's apartments before being transferred to a regular store. Other immigrants of the 1930s succeeded in establishing large and successful corporations, some of which merged into even larger conglomorates. Although the level of self-employment among German Jewish refugees was high, not all were in business for themselves. A minority of the first generation worked at skilled labor in factories or were employed as clerks or sales personnel. Whatever the occupation they pursued, the beginning of German reparations payments in the 1950s enabled many who still suffered from hardship to live more comfortably.

Within the German refugee wave there was a very broad spectrum. The ends of the spectrum represented vastly different cultural types. At one extreme were the refugee intellectuals, relatively few in number but very influential within the community and beyond. The other extreme was represented by the much more traditionalist Washington Heights immigrant community of New York with its many former rural Jews and Orthodox and Conservative synagogues.

The refugee wave of 1933–1945 has been made famous by the disproportionate number of intellectuals among those who came to the United States. But, as noted, the intellectuals represented only one of the many different cultural and social types found among the refugees. Only some 17 percent of employed refugees of the 1930s had been professionals in Europe, and most of the professionals were doctors and lawyers rather than intellectuals. The vast majority of the rest of the refugee immigrants were in commercial fields or were skilled workers.

The bulk of the refugees were somewhere in between the intellectuals and the residents of Washington Heights. Many belonged to synagogues, not necessarily German Jewish ones, visited Israel, and supported Jewish causes. Although most German Jewish immigrants living in New York in 1981 had a rather low level of religious observance, over one-fifth considered themselves Orthodox and another one-fourth labeled themselves Conservative. Economically, the former refugees tended to group either in the lower middle part of the American Jewish economic spectrum or near the top. In 1981, 32 percent of German-born New York Jews who arrived between 1934 and 1949 earned over $50,000, while another 30 percent earned the more modest sum of $20 to $30,000.

The Washington Heights immigrant neighborhood represented one end of the refugee spectrum rather than being typical of German Jewish immigrants as a whole. This was because that immigrant neighborhood attracted a particular type of refugee. Unlike the bulk of German refugees from Nazism in America who came from urban environments (66 percent from German cities of over 100,000 inhabitants), those who settled in Washington Heights often came from small towns (37 percent from towns with fewer than 10,000 inhabitants). South Germans (especially Hessians) were much overrepresented in Washington Heights and Berliners very much underrepresented.

Although only about 25 percent of the refugees even in Washington Heights defined themselves as Orthodox (and 41 percent Conservative), levels of religious observance, synagogue attendance and synagogue affiliation were a good deal higher than for New York Jewry as a whole. Nine of the twelve synagogues in the neighborhood founded by refugees were Orthodox. The Hirschian Orthodox Breuer community, headquartered in Washington Heights, had an influence far beyond its 1500 or so actual congregational members. German refugees in Washington Heights contributed to the traditional religious atmosphere of the neighborhood by founding a ritual bath, a network of religious educational institutions, almost a dozen kosher butcher stores, a rabbinical court, burial societies, charity organizations, and in many more informal ways.

The traditionalist small-town atmosphere of the refugee neighborhood in Washington Heights was evident in other ways besides religion. Visiting, greeting, culinary, and linguistic patterns of a distinctly conservative German type were quite noticeable in the daily life of many of the local residents. Among examples of such Old Country patterns in Washington Heights were the custom of making short courtesy calls of a few minutes on happy occasions, the prevalence of formal receiving lines at celebrations, and elaborate patterns of deference of younger persons toward their elders. The German language continued to be used in Washington Heights longer than elsewhere. Although its use in synagogue sermons and congregational bulletins was largely eliminated in the 1960s and early 1970s, German as a spoken language was still widely used in the 1980s.

Economically, the German Jews of Washington Heights were less prosperous than either German Jews in other neighborhoods or New York Jews as a whole. Over 35 percent of male German Jews in the area in 1960 were in managerial or proprietary fields, and almost 30 percent more held clerical or sales jobs. Fewer than one in eight were professionals. Levels of secular education were far lower among refugees in Washington Heights than elsewhere (fewer than 30 percent had any education beyond high school), although levels of religious knowledge and education were probably higher.

The contrast of those in this neighborhood with the refugee intellectuals is striking. Donald Kent, in his study of the *Refugee Intellectual*, found only a minority of his respondents identified as members of the Jewish religion. Most either considered themselves Christians or did not answer his question on religion. Works on the refugee intellectuals often stress the iconoclastic nature of many of the refugee thinkers. A considerable number of refugee writers and thinkers (some of them Jewish) returned to Germany after World War II, a pattern rare in the extreme among nonintellectual refugees.

Although it is true that the intellectual immigrants were an atypical minority within the refugee wave, they had an important influence on American intellectual life. The role of the German Jewish refugees in American culture has been the subject of a much more extensive literature in twentieth-century America than have all other aspects of German Jewish life combined.

The influence of refugee scholars can be seen in a wide spectrum of fields. In some disciplines, especially the social sciences and the humanities, one can detect specific German or Jewish cultural influences in their contributions; in other fields, such as the physical sciences, one can point only to disproportionate numbers. In many areas both Jewish and non-Jewish refugee intellectuals worked together closely, and one would be hard-pressed to find many traits that would distinguish the Jewish and the non-Jewish contributions.

Soon after the massive dismissals of professors of Jewish background from German universities in April 1933, organizations were created to help the victims. Among these were the Emergency Committee in Aid of Displaced Foreign Scholars. The New School for Social Research in New York set up a "university in exile" that employed many former German professors. Many leading German-speaking intellectuals were invited to the Institute for Advanced Studies in Princeton, New Jersey, and another group worked at the experimental Black Mountain College in North Carolina. Some worked at or founded research institutes (for example, the Institute of Social Research or the Princeton Office of Radio Research). A larger percentage of the refugee intellectuals found employment in "mainstream" American universities. In a number of cases they were the first Jews admitted to formerly "restricted" college departments.

It is difficult to discuss the German Jewish intellectuals without lapsing into a catalogue of famous names. Still, the influence of the refugee intellectuals was not based simply on individual famous personalities, but on the new intellectual trends and points of view they brought to the United States. The overall influence of the refugees is often illusive since the German intellectuals represented widely differing political and ideological viewpoints. One common thread mentioned by a number of observers is the fact that many introduced a more theoretical approach rather than the pragmatic approach said to be more common in the earlier American intellectual tradition. Perhaps this would tie together some of their influence in theoretical physics with the introduction of psychoanalytic and Marxist dialectic ideas into the social sciences, although, like all rules, this too has exceptions.

Among the intellectual refugees from Germany were a number of prominent physicists. They were especially well represented in theoretical physics and played an important role in the

development of atomic weapons. Besides the towering figure of Albert Einstein (1879–1955), they included Hans Bethe (b. 1906), James Franck (1882–1964), Victor Weisskopf (b. 1908), and a number of Hungarian Jews who had worked as scientists in Germany (Leo Szillard [1898–1964], Eugene Wigner [b. 1902], and others).

In mathematics there were such important figures as Richard Courant (1888–1972) and (Hungarian-born) John von Neumann (1903–1957).

German and Austrian Jews were extremely influential in the spread and popularization of psychoanalytic ideas in the United States. They also played a leading role in neo-Freudian and non-Freudian forms of psychology. Among the best-known refugee thinkers in the field of psychology were Erik (Homburger) Erikson (b. 1902), Erich Fromm (1900–1980), and Bruno Bettelheim (1903–1990). Many applied psychological ideas to more general problems of social science and politics. Their own personal experiences as Jews and as victims of the Nazis were often included among the subjects of their analyses of society.

German Jews also had considerable influence in other sections of the social sciences. The so-called Frankfurt school of sociology headed by Theodor Wiesengrund Adorno (1903–1980) and Max Horkheimer (1895–1973) was known for its neo-Marxist approach. Their Institute for Social Research pioneered a number of influential studies, including the famous *The Authoritarian Personality* (1950). A very different approach, but perhaps even more controversial, was that of Hannah Arendt (1906–1975). Her analysis of totalitarianism and especially, her book *Eichmann in Jerusalem* (1963) with its thesis of the "banality of evil" infuriated many. Regardless of her stand, she was very active in Jewish affairs.

As the cases of the Frankfurt school and Arendt show, social analysis often shaded over into social criticism and political activity. Many of the German Jewish social thinkers who came to America have been identified with the Left. Some, most notably Herbert Marcuse (1898–1979), became leading intellectual figures in the New Left radicalism of the 1960s. Often the debates of the 1960s pitted one group of influential German Jews against another, as in the foreign policy debates between Hans Morgenthau (1904–1980) and Henry Kissinger (b. 1923).

Refugees played an important role in the study of intellectual history and literature. Among many influential works one can cite *Mimesis* by

Erich Auerbach (1892–1957) with its analysis of comparative literature, Erwin Panofsky (1892–1968) for his work in art history, and Hans Kohn (1891–1971) for his analysis of nationalism.

In philosophy, Jews of German or Austrian descent were to be found in such disparate intellectual positions as the logical positivism of the Vienna Circle, on the one hand, and the Jewish theological writings of Emil Fackenheim (b. 1916), on the other.

German-speaking refugees also were significant contributors to the creative arts. In music they included composers Arnold Schoenberg (1874–1951) and Kurt Weill (1900–1950); conductors Erich Leinsdorf (b. 1912), Otto Klemperer (1885–1973), William Steinberg (1899–1978), and Bruno Walter (originally Bruno Walter Schlesinger) (1876–1962). A number of German and Austrian Jews were prominent in the film industry especially as directors, for example, Otto Preminger (1906–1986) and Billy Wilder (b. 1906).

The German Bauhaus school of architecture and furniture design (some of whose exponents were Jewish) helped to create much of the modern style of American cities with its severely functional lines and absence of ornamentation.

In the field of literature, German refugees had less influence since most wrote in their native language. The most famous of the refugee writers, Thomas Mann (1875–1955) and Bertolt Brecht (1898–1956), were not Jewish, and both eventually returned to Germany. Although Mann wrote some of his major works in America (like *Doctor Faustus*) even these works are more a part of German intellectual history than of American. A few German and Austrian Jewish writers—such as Lion Feuchtwanger (1884–1958), Franz Werfel (1890–1945), and Vicki Baum (1888–1960)—had some following in America, but for most German Jewish writers the great period of creativity took place before their exile from Germany. In most cases their names are better known in Germany where *Exilliteratur* is a major interest.

Although it is true that most members of the immigrant generation were not elite or intellectual, the rapid social mobility of those who came to the United States as children as well as of the American-born second generation insured that many of the American-educated Germans did join the American elite. Virtually all of the second generation is college educated. Few are to be found in the blue-collar or small shopkeeping fields, which were so prominent among the first generation in Washington Heights and other refugee communities. Among those born in Germany but educated in the United States are such well-known personalities as former Secretary of State Henry Kissinger, sex therapist and television personality Dr. Ruth Westheimer, Max Frankel of the *New York Times*, and Henry Kaufmann the stock analyst. This phenomenon of achievement is as much a function of general American Jewish social mobility as of German Jewish cultural influence, however.

With the exception of the influential but atypical German Jewish intellectuals, a large minority of whom did not seem very interested in Jewish affairs of any kind, the vast majority of German Jewish immigrants of the 1930s have integrated into the American Jewish community. The trend in the second generation seems to be toward the elimination of virtually all specifically German traits coupled with the retention of some sort of Jewish ties. It is highly unlikely that many of the grandchildren of the immigrants will continue to consider themselves German Jews.

Most Jewish immigrants who arrived before the 1930s had come as traditional Jews; it was in America that these groups underwent acculturation and secularization. The German refugees from Nazi Germany did not share this experience. They were not as traditional as the earlier groups when they arrived, and they did not change as much as the others after they arrived. For the newcomers of the 1930s much of the decline in traditional Jewishness had taken place before arrival. Those German-speaking Jews who did arrive with a degree of Jewish tradition seem to have had less tendency to abandon it than had earlier immigrants. This was partly because the United States itself underwent a change in the period since the arrival of the refugees. The replacement of the "melting-pot" model (at least in part) by a model of "ethnicity" has helped slow the pressures on German Jews to give up their distinctiveness. The existence of a larger American Jewish community into which the German Jews could integrate allowed them to enter American society without giving up their Jewish identities. *See also* Holocaust entries; Immigration, German (Nineteenth Century); Leo Baeck Institute.

Steven M. Lowenstein

BIBLIOGRAPHY

Davie, Maurice R., et al. *Refugees in America. Report of the Committee for the study of recent immigration from Europe.* New York and London: Harper, 1947.

Fermi, Laura. *Illustrious Immigrants: The Intellectual Migration from Europe, 1930–41.* Chicago: University of Chicago Press, 1968.

Fleming, Donald, and Bailyn, Bernard, eds. *The Intellectual Migration: Europe and America 1930–1960.* Cambridge: Belknap Press of Harvard University Press, 1969.

Heilbut, Anthony. *Exiled in Paradise: German Refugee Artists and Intellectuals in America, from the 1930s to the present.* New York: Viking Press, 1983. (A somewhat popularized and politically engaged study.)

Kent, Donald P. *The Refugee Intellectual: The Americanization of the Immigrants of 1933–1941.* New York: Columbia University Press, 1953.

Lowenstein, Steven M. *Frankfurt on the Hudson: The German Jewish Community of Washington Heights, 1933–1983. Its Structure and Culture.* Detroit: Wayne State University Press, 1989.

Strauss, Herbert, et al., eds. *Jewish Immigrants of the Nazi Period in the USA.* 6 vols. New York: Saur, 1979–1987. (Mainly bibliographic, but Volume 5 consists of oral history excerpts and Volume 6 is a group of essays.)

Immigration, Iranian. On January 16, 1979, the Shah of Iran was forced to leave his country. Two weeks later Ayatollah Khomeini, who had been living in exile for almost 15 years, assumed power. On February 11, for the first time in Iran's history, the government of the Ayatollahs came into being and the kingdom of Iran became the Islamic Republic of Iran. This political phenomenon significantly changed the demographic map of the Jewish community of Iran and that of Iranian Jews in the United States.

Before the Islamic revolution, an estimated 80,000 Jews lived in Iran, about 60,000 in Teheran and the balance in Shiraz, Isfahan, Kermanshah, and other provincial towns. The economic boom of the 1960s and the 1970s in Iran had benefited the Jews; many became rich, which enabled them to provide higher education for their children. The Jews—as well as other religious minorities—were regarded as supporters of the royal regime because it was under the Pahlavi dynasty that they enjoyed prosperity and some measure of freedom. However, when the revolution broke out, it was soon apparent that minorities would lose their religious and cultural autonomy. The situation of the Jews was even more perilous than that of the other minorities because of the anti-Zionist character of the revolution.

The Jews stood accused of being the supporters of the Shah, Israel, Mossad, CIA, and the United States. All were defined as "Satan." A number of wealthy Jews, among them the former head of the Jewish community of Teheran, Habid Elghanayan, were tried by the revolutionary courts and sentenced to death. This alarming situation caused a massive Jewish exodus from Iran.

There are really no firm statistics about the number of Iranian Jews in the United States. It is estimated that during the 1980s about 60,000 Jews fled Iran. Of these, about 35,000 went to the United States, 20,000 to Israel, and the remaining 5000 to Europe, mainly to England, France, Germany, Italy, and Switzerland. Of those who went to the United States, about 25,000 live in California, with approximately 20,000 in the Los Angeles area, 8000 in New York City and on Long Island, and the remaining in other cities, mainly Boston, Baltimore, Washington, Detroit, and Chicago.

The Iranian Jews have set up numerous organizations in Los Angeles to meet the needs of their community, including:

The Iranian Jewish Federation (IJF), formed in 1979, was established officially in the summer of 1981 as an umbrella organization to represent all the Iranian organizations in Los Angeles and collaborate with the other Jewish area organizations, but some Iranian groups refused to join. The IJF is active in fund raising, in settling disputes among persons and groups, in arranging communal celebrations and banquets, in holding seminars on important issues such as intermarriage and assimilation, and in publishing a monthly Persian magazine called *Shofar*.

The Iranian Jewish Cultural Organization of California (IJC) was formed by the Jews of Iran who migrated to the United States before the Islamic revolution. It was officially established in 1978. Among its activities, the IJC sponsors lectures and seminars, organizes social and cultural events, helps in the publication of books and theses on Judeo-Persian subjects, assists needy students and synagogues, and raises funds for Israel and its important organizations.

The Iranian Jewish Women's Organization of Southern California (IJW) has roots in the organization that was founded in Teheran in 1947. IJW was established in 1976 mostly by members of the old organization, notably Mrs. Shamsi Hekmat and Mrs. Maliheh Kashfi. The IJW concentrates on family issues, such as health, welfare, and education. Despite its limited resources, the group is particularly active in helping Iranian students in the United States and Israel. IJW is affiliated with the International Council of Jewish Women.

The Iranian Nessah Israel Congregation (INIC) was established in August 1980. INIC is an Orthodox synagogue offering religious services to the Iranian community in Los Angeles. Its religious, cultural, and social functions are under the guidance of Rabbi David Shofet, a Persian-born and American-educated rabbi. He is the son of Hakham Yedidiah Shofet, the Grand Rabbi of Teheran, who immigrated with his family to the United States immediately after the Islamic revolution. INIC did not possess a building of its own until 1990. This building is also home to the Nessah Hebrew Academy (NHA) which is associated with the Bureau of Jewish Education. NHA is directed by Rabbi David Shofet and offers religious education from kindergarten through the college level.

The Valley Iranian Center (VIC) opened in 1980 to serve the Iranian community of the San Fernando Valley, primarily as an Orthodox synagogue.

The Iranian Jewish Association of California, known by its Iranian abbreviated name SYAMAK, was established in 1979 by a number of Jewish Iranian university graduates. It offers general assistance, for example, concerning visas, doctors, hospitals, lawyers, and the American system and agencies. SYAMAK also organizes religious services, lectures, and social gatherings for the Iranian community.

Four organizations are involved with Jewish Iranian youth: Persian Hillel, Ness, Tekvah Youth, and the Fariborz Group of B'nai B'rith. These youth organizations have similar programs that aim to provide a link between young Iranian Jews and their Jewish heritage and to prepare youth for future leadership. From time to time, they issue magazines in the Persian language. The Ness organization has an Orthodox orientation in its activities.

"The Aged Home" is in the process of being erected in the Los Angeles area. It is sponsored by the Iranian Jewish Senior Center.

As stated earlier, about 8,000 (some estimate as many as 15,000) Iranian Jews settled in the Greater New York area, after the overthrow of the Shah. According to various sources, until 1970 there were only 40 Iranian Jews living in Greater New York. Their number rose to 100 in 1976. In 1978, as the result of a meeting between Ardishir Zehedi, the son-in-law of the Shah and the Iranian ambassador to Washington, and Jan Elghanayan, a wealthy Iranian Jew, a pro-royal Jewish Iranian organization was born, the Iranian Jewish Society of Greater New York (IJSGNY). This organization actually became active in 1978 with the first wave of Iranian Jews leaving Iran because of the political situation to settle in the New York area and on Long Island. IJSGNY's main concern continues to be helping new immigrants, especially the children and youth, acclimate to life in the United States. IJSGNY works closely with religious Orthodox groups in New York and New Jersey as well as United Jewish Appeal (UJA) and the United Jewish Federation (UJF). UJA, UJF, and wealthy Iranian Jews have provided funds for a large-scale rescue operation of children and youth. In general, large sums were donated to the rescue groups sponsored by the Jewish Orthodox organizations in New York. On arrival in New York, the youths were accommodated temporarily in Yeshiva-type centers. Since 1979, IJSGNY has published a monthly magazine in Persian like the youth magazine in Los Angeles, *Shofar*. IJSGNY is also active in helping Israel and Iranian Jews living there.

The Iranian Jewish Society and Great Neck Synagogue, Inc., an affiliate of IJSGNY, in 1990 was in the process of constructing a synagogue on Long Island.

The Paras Jewish Organization (PJO), founded in 1980, has built a synagogue in Queens. PJO publishes a magazine called *Paras*.

Several organizations have been established to continue the home traditions of Iranian Jews so that they will not be assimilated into the non-Jewish American society. Their focus is primarily a religious one.

In general, the Iranian organizations noted in this article were started by a group of friends. In the Iranian community past communal experience is highly valued.

A thorough study of Iranian Jews in the United States remains to be done. One has to be cautious of the label "Iranian Jewish community," which oversimplifies the reality and obscures the wide spectrum of groups, classes, settings, and socioeconomic background that is included within the label. A general observation, however, can be made of the Iranian Jewish community in their "new home" to which many came reluctantly and with little notice.

The assimilating power of American society and culture has already affected the Iranian Jews in different ways, making them something they had not been before. The Iranian Jews brought with them their own mores, which in many ways differ from the land to which they immigrated. Iranians value, in general, individualism, believe in fate, have respect for authority and family, pursue the enjoyment of life. They try to maintain a good social appearance. In general, an average Iranian Jew pays much attention to clothes, an expensive house, and a lavish pattern of living. In Western culture, the emphasis is on efficiency and punctuality. In Iranian culture, life and business are conducted in a leisurely, enjoyable fashion. For instance, an Iranian merchant may frequently serve his customer tea and chat with him for some time before he begins his business transactions. Some Iranian values are transmitted by signs and behavior styles often tailored to the particular encounter. In general, they are not understood by the American society. Because of this, Iranian Jewish migrants cannot perform many of the tasks that they performed in the country of their birth.

In Iran the traditional family unit is patriarchal: father is the undisputed head of the family. The older the migrant the more difficult becomes his adaptation in the new society. The seniors left behind a whole lifetime of experiences, and now they are dependent on others, especially on their children. They fail to gain proficiency in the new language, which impedes their integration into the new society. This setback creates a new situation, which is frustrating: fathers who in the old country had respected their fathers are often humiliated before their sons by failure in their new setting.

Although parents want their children to succeed in America, they want them to do so without losing their Iranian identity and Iranian mores. The open and free American society poses a threat to sexual mores, and intermarriage in particular poses a threat to tradition. Premarital sexual relations are looked upon with disdain and contempt and considered a stigma to the entire family. In Iran, girls were forbidden to date; it was very important for them to keep their virginity. To combat the possibility of premarital sex, parents try to marry their daughters off as soon as possible. As for boys, in Iran they listened to their parents in choices of marriage partners. In America one marries for love.

In Iran divorced women were stigmatized and had almost no chance to remarry. In the United States the rate of divorce, which was almost nonexistent among Jews in Iran, is rising rapidly. The freedom of women in America is creating tensions in the Iranian Jewish family structure. Men are losing their authority, their confidence, and their "virility." The right of women to some type of payment after divorce, coupled with the relative ease and acceptability of filing for divorce in the American society, has pushed the Iranian Jewish divorce rate upward. American laws of common property have become a disruptive cause of difficulties between husband and wife. In Iran the husband did almost whatever he wanted to do with his money and property. In America he has to consult his wife.

In Iran parents were not so much concerned about Judaism; the Muslim society was not open to them. There it was difficult for them to identify openly with Jewishness. Many Iranian Jews state that in America they are "more Jewish" because here they are proud of their religion. More synagogues are available to them, and the number of kosher food markets and restaurants ensure that they and their children will not lose their Jewish identities. As a consequence, Iranian Jews attend synagogues more often in the United States than they did in Iran. But they are confused as to their religious affiliation, since in their country they were "Jews." There was no choice of Orthodox, Conservative, or Reform Judaism.

The Iranian Jewish community in the United States is, for the most part, well-educated and financially stable. It looks forward to making important contributions to the Jewish-American community and to American society as a whole. *See also* Sephardim.

AMNON NETZER

Immigration, Russian (1880–1924). In 1880

close to 6 million of the world's 7.7 million Jews lived in Eastern Europe, more than 4 million confined to the Pale of Settlement, which consisted of the 15 western provinces of European Russia and the 10 provinces of Congress, or Russian-held, Poland. Between 1881 and 1924, approximately 2.5 million Jews emigrated from the Russian empire (78 percent), Austria-Hungary (18 percent) and Romania (4 percent). This was not only one of the largest migrations in world history (one-third of East European Jewry left the lands of their birth), but the vast majority, more than 2 million, went to the United States, eventually generating the most populous (over 40 percent of world Jewry by 1920), most vibrant Jewish community on the globe.

The causes of this mass migration are many and complex. Life in Eastern Europe, and particularly in the Russian empire, was never comfortable for Jews. And between 1750 and 1800, with the conquest of new territories in the south and the partition of Poland, the number of Jews under Russian domination increased greatly. That Jews were guilty of deicide, a pariah people standing in the way of the coming of the millennium, was deeply rooted in Russian official doctrine and popular legend. And the czars, though occasionally indifferent, and even tolerant, more often promoted extended periods of severe oppression. The most zealous of them instituted coercive policies for the "conversion" of the Jews. Nicholas I (1825–1855) under a general program of "modernization" issued more than 600 anti-Jewish decrees, including expulsions from particular areas, censorship of Hebrew and Yiddish literature, and military conscription of young boys for periods of up to 25 years.

Under Alexander II (1855–1881) there was some liberalization, but no real change in general objective. And despite increases in the "right of residence" for "useful Jews" and the increasing enrollment of Jews in Russian secondary schools and universities, legal humiliations and economic harassments continued. Jews, heavily dependent on petty trade and crafts, were generally kept out of the economic centers. Kiev was closed with few exceptions; the same was true for Kharkov and Moscow. And St. Petersburg was open only to the upper bourgeoisie and a handful of students.

Along with anti-Semitism, the restructuring of the East European economy had a negative effect on Jews and proved a powerful force for dislocation. In many areas of Eastern Europe in the late nineteenth century peasant-based economies were slowly eroding. The modernization of agriculture, particularly in the Pale, where Jews in the 1890s constituted approximately 70 percent of those engaged in commerce and 30 percent of those engaged in crafts, led to the displacement of petty merchants, peddlers, and artisans as well as teamsters, factors, and innkeepers. Railroads and peasant cooperatives changed the functional role played by large numbers of Jews in the small market towns, virtually eliminating local fairs. In addition, the emancipation of the serfs (1861–1862) left the peasants heavily in debt, unable to afford the services of Jewish middlemen. By 1880, some sections of Eastern Europe produced one Jewish peddler for every 10 peasant customers. And nobles were left needing fewer stewards and administrators.

In the context of general economic dislocation and spreading Russian discontent, the government, in an attempt to deflect resentment, encouraged anti-Semitism, focusing on the Jews' preeminence as middlemen. The government, in addition, offered loans to a nascent indigenous class of commercial men waiting for businesses to be abandoned by Jews, and native middlemen organized boycotts of Jewish merchants. In Galicia (Austria-Hungary) in the 1880s, 60 percent of the Jews had to be supported by the community, and 5000 were dying annually of starvation or of diseases brought on by malnutrition. Still there was a relatively low death rate for Jews in most of Eastern Europe, and the Jewish population soared from 1.5 million in 1800 to 6.8 million in 1900, greatly exacerbating the decline of economic opportunity.

The pressures on Jews to seek livelihoods elsewhere mounted from year to year. They were intensified by an unsuccessful Polish uprising in 1863, a famine in Lithuania in 1867–1869, and a cholera epidemic in Poland in 1869. Galician Jews migrated toward eastern Hungary and Vienna; Polish Jews overflowed such cities as Lodz, Warsaw, and Vilna. Bialystok drew uprooted shtetl (small town) dwellers, artisans, and laborers. By 1897, 41 percent of the urban population of Russia and Poland was Jewish. But even the cities offered only a precarious existence. Jews, victims of Russian paranoia, patriotism at its most vulgar, and narrowly defined economic self-interest, were excluded from many branches of the economy.

Scapegoating became even more intense after terrorists assassinated Alexander II in 1881. Confusion reigned, and revolutionaries called on the people to rebel. The Russian press, and the government attempting to defend itself, stepped up the accusation that Jews were responsible for the misfortunes of the nation, and pogroms (anti-Jewish riots) broke out in numerous towns and hamlets of southern Russia. Between 1881 and 1882, there were pogroms in 225 communities, including Yelizavetgrad and Kiev. There was a massive pogrom in Warsaw in December 1881; 1500 homes, shops, and synagogues were sacked before troops intervened. An even more bloody and destructive episode took place in the largely Jewish town of Balta in Podolia in late March 1882.

In the immediate aftermath of violence, 13,000 Jews emigrated from Russia to the United

States. This was almost half the number that had arrived in the United States for the entire decade of the 1870s. And Jewish emigrés in 1882 outnumbered those in 1881 by 300 percent. Russian commissions investigating the causes of the pogroms concluded that "Jewish exploitation" was at the root of the violence. Based on this finding, the government published the "Temporary Laws" (May Laws, 1882). These were designed to isolate the Jew from the peasant. They circumscribed movement within the Pale, prohibiting Jews from living in villages. This meant the expulsion of 500,000 Jews from rural areas. No business could be conducted by Jews in the larger towns, nor could any business be conducted on Sunday. Jews were forbidden to purchase real property or even to negotiate mortgages. And in 1886, reacting to the virtual flood of Jews seeking entry to secondary schools and universities, the government limited the number of Jewish students to 10 percent of the student body in the Pale and 3.5 percent outside it.

This quota was part of the administrative harassment of the Jews, which became increasingly worse after the pogroms temporarily halted in 1884. In 1887, over 23,000 Russian Jews immigrated to the United States—the highest total for a single year up to that point. By 1891, 700,000 Jews living east of the Pale were driven into the confined area, and previously privileged Jews were subject to wholesale expulsion from Russian cities; 20,000 were expelled from Moscow alone. The press continued a campaign of unbridled anti-Semitic propaganda and K. Pobedonostev, the head of the governing body of the Russian Orthodox Church, clarified the goals of the government when he predicted that "one-third of the Jews will convert, one-third will die, and one-third will flee the country." Between 1891 and 1892, 107,000 Jews left Russia for the United States.

After a short interregnum (1893–1898), the strict application of the discriminatory laws were continued under Nicholas II (1894–1918). His government subsidized close to 3000 anti-Semitic publications, including the classic forgery *Protocols of the Elders of Zion*. Free reign was given to anti-Jewish agitation, particularly in reaction to the growth of the revolutionary movement, in which a disproportionate number of Jewish youth took part. An explosion of pogroms filled the years from 1903 to 1906. In contrast to those that took place between 1881 and 1884, these involved a steep escalation of violence and mass murder. In the Kishinev pogrom of April 1903, 47 Jews were killed, and hundreds were severely beaten. In Zhitomer in April 1905, 29 were killed; 100 died in Kiev in July, 60 in Bialystok in August, and 800 in Odessa in October. In 1906, pogroms became practically uncountable, with many hundreds dead, robbed, raped, and mutilated. As in the 1880s, the pogroms in the beginning of the twentieth century were followed by a steep jump in the rate of emigration from Russia to the United States. In 1900, 37,000 Jews had emigrated. By 1904, 77,500 left; 92,400 emigrated in 1905 and 125,200 in 1906. A total of 672,000 Jews entered the United States as immigrants between 1904 and 1908, the vast majority from the Russian empire.

While pogroms were clearly a factor in mass emigration, a case can be made that pogroms alone do not explain the extraordinary movement of the Jewish population between 1881 and 1924. The highest rate of emigration was after all experienced in Galicia, where there was economic hardship and some local repression but virtually no pogroms. The Ukraine, the heartland of pogroms in the Russian empire, produced a relatively low rate of emigration before World War I, and Lithuania, with relatively few pogroms, had a very high emigration rate. Also concurrent with the acceleration of the Jewish emigration was an expanded emigration from the Russian empire of non-Jewish Poles, Lithuanians, Finns, and even Russians. Jewish emigration then can be seen as directly related to economic strains and dislocations of Eastern Europe and particularly of pre-Revolutionary Russia. Persecution, however, was critical. Jews, constituting about 5 percent of the population of the Russian empire, made up close to 50 percent of the Russian emigrant stream between 1881 and 1910. And from Romania, where Jews were treated arbitrarily and violently as aliens, over 75,000 (30 percent of the Jewish population) came to the United States between 1881 and 1915.

Mass Jewish migration from Eastern Europe had been gathering momentum throughout the 1870s. After 1881, however, Jews had to face anti-Semitism not simply as a permanent inconvenience but as a threat to their very existence. The Russian government was encouraging pogroms as a matter of policy. This seemed a new and frightening matter, distinct from the government's mere indifference to Jewish victimization in the past. By the time of Alexander III and certainly by Nicholas II the desire was no longer to russify the Jews but to be rid of them. At a conference of Jewish "notables" in St. Petersburg in 1882, a majority continued to maintain that mass emigration would appear unpatriotic and might undermine the struggle for emancipation. But thoughts about emigration soon became pervasive. Anti-Semitism was seen by some, including M. L. Lilienblum and Leon Pinsker, as deeply rooted, not a vestige—a disease incurable in the foreseeable future. And, after 1881, more and more believed that emancipation for Jews was not possible within the intolerable conditions of the Russian Empire.

Fear had become a central factor in Jewish life in Russia. But in itself fear, intensified by new and more violent persecution, dislocation, and deepening poverty, does not account for the stunning uprooting and transplantation of millions of East European Jews. It is necessary to include the ingredients of cultural ferment and renewal. East European Jewish life was based on deeply rooted tradition and for centuries was relatively static. There was a reality too, however, of internal conflict and change. The seventeenth century saw the false messianism of Sabbatai Zevi, which indicated a revulsion against passive waiting for redemption. In the late eighteenth and early nineteenth centuries, Hasidism, an enthusiastic, pietistic movement of religious renewal, challenged rabbinic authority. Later from the West came the Haskalah, or Enlightenment, which strove toward complete and equal citizenship for Jews. East European Jews were turning with religious imagery and the ethical concepts of their tradition to the idea of secular expression and to new forms of intellectual hegemony. This collective resurgence reached its height in the last three decades of the nineteenth century with Yiddishism, the blossoming of a secular Yiddish literature, and the self-education and increasing social awareness of the Jewish masses. There was among city Jews and shtetl Jews, as they struggled to synthesize the forces of modernization with their tradition, a widespread feeling that Jewish culture was experiencing a renaissance. The postliberal movements—Zionism and socialism—and the various blends of the two, initially products of the failure of emancipation and the default of radical Russia during the pogroms, also reflected the cultural renaissance. "To become" was always central to Jewish culture. Modernization redirected and intensified that desire, and increasing East European anti-Semitism frustrated it. For large numbers relocation seemed the only answer.

Without external assault and increasing poverty, the collective energetic resurgence, rather than mass emigration, would more likely have produced a temporary culture of Yiddishkeit for the Jews as they moved toward assimilation. Persecution, pogroms, and poverty without cultural renewal would more likely have produced internal upheavals and perhaps new religious enthusiasms rather than an exodus. The combination, however, of spiritual hope and physical wretchedness proved explosive. Between 1881 and 1910, 1,562,800 Jews came to the United States from Eastern Europe—almost 72 percent from Russia, 19 percent from Austria-Hungary and 4.3 percent from Romania. Another 435,000 would arrive between 1911 and 1914 and a quarter of a million more between 1915 and 1924.

In the 1880s, there was also the pervasive belief that overseas immigration was now indeed a viable alternative. As early as 1817, there existed in Eastern Europe a Yiddish translation of *The Discovery of America*, a popular celebration of the United States. Between 1820 and 1870, there had already been a trickle of Jewish emigration (7500) to America from Eastern Europe. Between 1870 and 1890, however, America would become more clearly the "distant magnet," a place for potential collective renewal for Jews. In these years the American economy experienced a 28 percent growth in the number of industries and a net increase in the value of production of 168 percent. In addition, large-scale scheduled steamship transportation became more available, companies actually sending out agents to solicit travelers from the Old World. At the same time published reports began to appear in Hebrew and Yiddish about the opportunities in the *goldene medine* (golden land). More than 3 million Jews would cross borders in Eastern Europe seeking their fortunes elsewhere. Of these, 7 percent went to Western Europe, 10 to 13 percent to Canada, Australia, Argentina, South Africa, and Palestine, and more than 80 percent ended up in the United States.

Jews from the Ukraine and southern Russia crossed the Austro-Hungarian borders illegally, often to Brody, traveled from there by train to Vienna or Berlin, and regrouped to go to Hamburg, Bremen, Rotterdam, Amsterdam, and Antwerp, where for $34 (by 1903) one could purchase a steamship ticket to the New World. Jews from western Russia came surreptitiously across the German borders, while the Austro-Hungarians could cross legally. And the Romanians arrived at the northern ports mainly through Vienna.

Western Jewish organizations, at first reluctant and even ready to oppose emigration whenever hope arose that the position of Jews in Russia might be improved, began to face the reality of mass Jewish migration from Eastern Europe. A group of German Jewish associations organized as the Hilfsverein der Deutschen Juden in order to help their coreligionists and to avoid being overrun by the mass influx, set up information bureaus, negotiated special rates with railroad companies and steamship lines, and lobbied governments to ease the immigrants' journey and speed them on their way. Between 1905 and 1914, 700,000 East European Jews passed through Germany and 210,000 were directly aided by the Hilfsverein. Baron de Hirsch, scion of financiers to the Bavarian Royal Court, who made a fortune in banking and railway finance, contributed large amounts to improve the conditions of East European Jews. In the late 1880s, however, after the pogroms and mass expulsions, Baron de Hirsch encouraged emigration, and he set up the Jewish Colonization Association in 1891 with vast programs for international resettlement.

The several organized efforts, while important, particularly in terms of making the idea of transplantation viable, played a small part compared to the migration of individuals. The voyage of these individuals was filled with tribulation. In Europe they had to face rapacious peasants and smugglers and often brutal border guards. Even legal travelers had to deal with the bewildering confusion of various bureaucracies and the officious manner of German authorities, who, fearful of plague, among other things, conducted innumerable inspections. There were questions upon questions, disinfections, and the constant fear of being sent back or quarantined. Success meant facing a 13-to-20 day voyage in the most primitive conditions in steerage. The suffering endured by the travelers was real and persistent and was exacerbated by swindlers and unscrupulous steamship agents. By the early 1900s, there was some improvement. Competition among steamship lines led to a modification of steerage into compartments on newer ships; the voyage was reduced to between 6 and 10 days; and the Jewish organizations at various transit points now had more experience and were better able to serve and protect the emigrés.

Between 1899 and 1910, 86 percent of the Jews heading for the United States landed in the North Atlantic states, the vast majority in New York City. Here they faced a grueling ordeal at Castle Garden or, after 1891, Ellis Island. Immigration employees, always overworked (processing 4000 immigrants a day at peak periods) and often insensitive, checked arrivals for "defects," tuberculosis, "dull-wittedness," eye problems, and "contagious and loathsome diseases." Piled into massive halls in dozens of lines, the immigrants underwent incessant pushing, prying, and poking. There were some exceptional officials, including Philip Cowen and Alexander Harkavy, who helped ease the immigrants' predicament; and the Hebrew Emigrant Aid Society (HEAS), a makeshift organization (founded in 1880), despite fear of the consequences of the in-migration of large numbers of Jews and some contempt for the "wild Russians," cared for approximately 14,000 Russian immigrants. HEAS eventually evolved into the Hebrew Sheltering and Immigrant Aid Society (HIAS), which by 1897 combined under one roof employment, training, housing, and legal aid for immigrants. From 1884 to 1892, the aid given Jewish arrivals was sporadic and unsystematic. In 1892, this changed when, with generous funding from Baron de Hirsch, several groups, concerned with the welfare of the immigrant, joined forces.

Aid was often necessary, for the average Jewish immigrant arrived with less money and more dependents than other immigrants. Between 1899 and 1910, 44 percent of the Jewish immigrants were female and 25 percent were children under 14. For other groups in the same period, only 30.5 percent were females and 12.3 percent children under 14. The Jewish migration was much more a movement of families than that of other European nationalities and groups. More dependents meant more burdens, but also more emotional sustenance in a relatively unfamiliar environment. Also sustaining the Jewish immigrants was the fact that they appear to have had better preparation for urban life than did most other immigrants from Eastern and Southern Europe. Before World War I, two-thirds of the Jews specifying occupations were classified as skilled laborers. There is little doubt that this is an exaggerated proportion, but many were craftsmen and artisans who had had at least some experience in living and working in semiurban environments.

Of the skilled Jewish workers between 1899 and 1914, 60 percent were clothing workers. The American garment industry was undergoing a period of rapid expansion precisely at the time of the

East European arrivals, and by 1910 New York City was producing 70 percent of the women's clothes and 40 percent of the men's clothes made in the United States. By the late 1880s German Jews owned more than 95 percent of the clothing factories and shops in the city, and their East European cousins believed that they would find familiarity in those shops and the possibility of *Shabos* (Sabbath) off.

The German Jews already in the United States, out of cultural and class arrogance, fear of anti-Semitism, and anxiety over being burdened by masses of poor dependents, often began with a negative reaction to the large-scale East European Jewish immigration. Their press reflected the general anti-immigration tendencies of the late 1880s and used phrases like "they are lazy and shiftless" and a "bane to the country and a curse to the Jews." But relatively quickly the German Jewish community's position changed. Ultimately, the Germans played an important role in the fight against immigration restriction and provided much philanthropy. In addition to fighting restriction directly, German Jewish leaders like Simon Wolf, Jacob Schiff, and Louis Marshall involved themselves in relocation, agricultural colonization, and diversion of immigrants to ports of entry other than in the Northeast (e.g., Galveston, Texas). Dispersal, it was incorrectly believed, would ward off immigration restriction.

There were several significant anti-immigration bills passed by Congress between 1875 and 1903, but antiforeign sentiment did not seriously impede the flow of immigration until World War I, when Congress passed a literacy bill over President Woodrow Wilson's veto. In 1921 and 1924, highly restrictive quotas were imposed for immigrants from Southern and Eastern Europe. Of the East European Jews who entered the United States in the period from 1881 to 1924, relatively few left. As many as 25 percent, however, did return to Eastern Europe prior to 1900 in response to variations in economic conditions in America and political conditions in Europe. But after 1903 the return rate dropped off radically, and between 1908 and 1914, only 7 percent of the number of entrants left. The rate of return migration for all other groups was higher, ranging from 9.5 percent to 57.5 percent and averaging 33 percent for the entire period of mass migration. Neither hardships upon arrival nor recurrent depression could drive the Jews back to Europe in any significant numbers.

Jews voted with their feet for America, and mainly for its urban centers. By 1920, 45 percent of the Jewish population of the United States lived in New York City. The next two largest Jewish cities, Chicago and Philadelphia, accounted for 13 percent, and seven other cities in the East and Midwest held another 14 percent. Between 1881 and 1920, the United States population experienced a general population increase of 112 percent, while the Jewish population rose 1300 percent, mainly by the immigration of East European Jews. By 1928, of the 4.7 million Jews in the United States, 3 million were of East European origin. Living on the West Side of Chicago, in Boston's North End, Philadelphia's downtown, and especially on New York's Lower East Side (by 1925 one of every three New Yorkers was a Jew!), the Jews from Russia and other parts of Eastern Europe became a "conspicuous minority,"—in factories and stores, in streets and cafes, in landsmanshaftn (regional mutual-aid societies) and labor unions, in synagogues, in Yiddish theater and press, in philanthropic and self-help organizations.

Millions had left the shtetlach and cities in which they had built their lives. Artisans and stewards and peddlers faced with obsolescence and dislocation, socialist militants faced with repression and Jew-hatred, students and the religiously committed faced with grave uncertainties, and above all the innumerable ordinary Jews faced with impoverishment and persecution made the decision to leave Eastern Europe in the late nineteenth and early twentieth centuries. They did not merely flee. With a strength born of cultural renewal, they aspired "to become." The United States in a period of extensive industrial expansion and economic growth, and with its reputation as a land of opportunity, provided the context for fulfillment.

GERALD SORIN

BIBLIOGRAPHY

Frankel, Jonathan. *Prophecy and Politics: Socialism, Nationalism, and the Russian Jews, 1862–1917.* Cambridge, Eng.: Cambridge University Press, 1981.

Howe, Irving. *World of Our Fathers: The Journey of the East European Jews to America and the Life They Found and Made.* New York: Harcourt Brace Jovanovich, 1976.

Joseph, Samuel. *Jewish Immigration to the United States from 1881 to 1910.* American Immigration Collection Series, No. 1. New York: Arno Press, reprint 1969.

Kuznets, Simon. "Immigration of Russian Jews to the

United States: Background and Structure." In *Perspectives in American History* 9 (1975): 35–124.

Taylor, Philip. *The Distant Magnet: European Emigration to the United States of America.* New York: Harper & Row, 1971.

Immigration, Soviet (1964–   ). The American campaign for the migration of Soviet Jews represents a case study of many of the internal dynamics of the American Jewish community in the mid-twentieth century, interesting not only for its international implications but also for its domestic impact. The major players in the campaign were, on the international scene, the Soviet government, the American administration, and the Israeli government. On the domestic scene, the various Jewish groups involved engaged in numerous internal struggles in relation to each other, their constituencies, and the State of Israel. At times, the campaign possessed vague, even conflicting, goals; often external events engaged the participants in a vortex of activity that forced them to react first and think later. Several crises mesmerized the groups involved for diverging spans of time. Sometimes the "movement" led events; more often it followed.

The Soviet government's gradual strangulation of Soviet Jewry intensified in the wake of World War II. The Soviets shut all remaining Jewish schools, murdered Jewish artists, and intimidated most Jews by the Slansky trial, the Doctor's Plot, and various other actions. Soviet Jewry, frightened and cowed, hoped only for a change; yet even Khrushchev's denunciation of Stalin in his 1956 speech did not improve the situation. The government systematically strangled any form of Jewish worship or cultural expression. Western Jewry looked on horrified but, perceiving itself as helpless, did nothing.

For various reasons, American Jewry awoke in the sixties. Perhaps the civil rights movement and the subsequent student activism were the events most responsible for the rapid growth in sentiment to take action to save the remaining Jews in the USSR. Many of the earliest supporters of action had participated in the civil rights struggle of a few years earlier. That struggle demonstrated the efficacy of activism; true, the American and Soviet situations were radically dissimilar, but, nevertheless, many lessons from the former were applied to the latter.

The public movement to save the Soviet Jews began in the early sixties, although there had been some private efforts previously. In 1963, the shortage of matzoth for Passover in the major Soviet Jewish centers precipitated a flurry of activity. The Jewish community attempted to utilize the usual channels of help, such as shipping matzoth from Western states, but with little success. Frustrated by these failures, a group of individuals, eventually led by Herbert S. Caron and Louis Rosenblum, launched the Cleveland Committee on Soviet Anti-Semitism (CCSA) in October 1963. The CCSA set out to educate the American Jewish public as well as the general population about the Soviet Jewish plight. At first, the organization worked primarily within the established Jewish organizational channels, but, eventually, frustrated by the slow movement of the larger organizations, it set out on its own. As a pressure group for Soviet Jewry, the CCSA presented a more assertive agenda on Soviet Jewry at Jewish organizational meetings. It organized numerous demonstrations, endeavoring to attract media attention. And while it often failed to accomplish its stated objectives in convincing other established Jewish groups to adopt a more aggressive stance on Soviet Jewry, it, and various other activist groups of similar inclinations, did succeed in bringing the issue to the forefront of American Jewish consciousness.

Despite the Cleveland efforts, the movement, in order to succeed, would have to galvanize the major centers of American Jewry, both geographically and organizationally. On April 5–6, 1964, 500 delegates from 24 major Jewish organizations met in an American Jewish Conference on Soviet Jewry. The rising scarcity of matzoth as well as other Soviet anti-Semitic actions, such as the publication, by the Ukrainian Academy of Sciences, of the notorious *Judaism Without Embellishment* by Korneyevick Kichko, had catapulted the issue of Soviet Jewry into the forefront of the American Jewish agenda. The conference debated three alternatives: (1) to continue the effort, minimal though it was, on an ad hoc basis, (2) to place the effort under the umbrella of the Conference of Presidents of Major American Jewish Organizations, or (3) to establish a new organization dedicated to this issue. The first alternative had been and would be, most delegates quickly realized, unworkable. It would prevent any unified effort, and most organizations would continue doing what they were so adept at doing—issuing press releases and passing resolutions. The second alternative was also not viable. The Presidents' Conference, as it came to be known, was established in the fifties to promote the safety and security of Israel. Even though nearly all American Jewish organizations agreed on this objective, one of the most prominent, the American Jewish Committee, while willing to cooperate on most issues, refused to be subsumed officially under this umbrella organization. Choosing this alternative would place Soviet Jewry in a clear second-class position vis-à-vis Israel and would ensure that the issue would never attain prominence unless it served the interests of Israel. Besides, placing it under the Presidents' Conference would automatically exclude the American Jewish Committee. As the latter had important contacts within the international community as well as within American governmental circles, such an exclusion could be fatal to the effort. Thus the third alternative seemed the only viable one, and the American Jewish Conference on Soviet Jewry came into being.

While most of the delegates returned home satisfied with the organization they had created, they failed to realize the extent of its handicaps. The new American Jewish Conference on Soviet Jewry possessed no resources; all its needs were to be provided through external sources. Thus, the new organization had no central office, resources, or staff. These functions would rotate among several Jewish organizations each of which would bear the responsibility of administering the conference for six months. Everyone soon recognized that the arrangement was unworkable, so the National Jewish Community Relations Advisory Council (NJCRAC) agreed to provide a staff member to manage the fledgling organization, first Albert Chernin, later Abraham Bayer. Nevertheless, the organization always operated at the mercy of 24 masters.

At the same time, a group of students, encouraged by the indefatigable Yaakov Birnbaum, established an organization of their own, the Student Struggle for Soviet Jewry, or the Triple SJ as it came to be known. Driven by an untiring zeal, Birnbaum scraped, begged, and pleaded for an independent organization for Soviet Jews. He finally succeeded at a meeting at Columbia University on April 27, 1964. Many of the students he attracted had been heavily involved in the civil rights movement, and, indeed, the literature of that period constantly chastises Jews for standing up for the rights of every group except the Jews. Among his earliest adherents was Glenn Richter, who would become the pivot of the new organization. With a shoestring budget, a recalcitrant,

elderly mimeograph machine, no office equipment (indeed, no office outside of Birnbaum's bedroom), the organization busily planned a mass protest outside the Soviet United Nations mission. On May 1, 1964, the SSSJ celebrated its birth with a thousand-student protest. Amazed by their success, Birnbaum, Richter, and a few others threw themselves into a frenzied pace of activity. They quickly became experts at begging, cajoling, even perhaps slightly threatening, other Jewish organizations to provide them with meager resources; an aged typewriter here, a sheaf of yellowed paper there. Driven by activist taunts, the larger Jewish community gradually limped into demonstrations and other activities.

The next three years saw a succession of marches, vigils, and demonstrations that generally centered around the holidays of Passover and Hanukkah with their themes of struggle for freedom. While the demonstrations normally drew from several hundred to, at best, a few thousand demonstrators, the movement's most crucial goal was simply educating the Jewish, as well as the general community, about the Soviet Jewish plight. To the extent that the demonstrations captured headlines, they succeeded. Yet, had there not been a particularly fortuitous cycle of international events, the movement might have eventually dissipated from a sense of frustration and futility. The Soviets seemed determined not to permit Jewish culture or Judaism to survive.

At first glance, the Six-Day War in 1967 seemed to have only peripheral interest for the Soviet Jewry movement. Israel played no official role in the struggle, although its unofficial influence and interest in the issue were well known. Ideologically, it perceived itself as the caretaker of all oppressed Jews. Historically, its founders derived from Eastern Europe and often continued to maintain links with extended family there. Practically, it also saw Soviet Jewry as a potential source for mass immigration.

Nevertheless, Israel's battle for survival mobilized and affected world Jewry as little else had done in the past twenty years. The crisis roused American Jewish consciousness, and this, together with the new sense of confidence engendered by the Israeli victory, provided the Soviet Jewry movement with an impetus that was to carry it through the next several years. Mass demonstrations, legitimized by the concern over Israel's survival, could now be channeled toward Soviet Jewry. Yet, the war had even more crucially affected Soviet Jewry, partially because of gargantuan Soviet miscalculations. Soviet Jews were, undoubtedly, extremely distressed by their government's anti-Israel stance in the days just prior to the war; but in the aftermath of the war, they watched in shock as the Soviet government subjected them to a barrage of anti-Semitic propaganda, the likes of which had not occurred since the Nazi period. The tremendous Israeli victory imbued them with a sense of euphoria. This, combined with the resentment and anger generated by the Soviet hate campaign, forced a few to desperate action. It was now clear that there could be no Jewish survival in the Soviet Union. While the Soviets undoubtedly succeeded in cowing the majority of Soviet Jews into even more deafening silence, some Soviet Jews, the proverbial "Jews of Silence," began to speak—slowly and haltingly at first and then gradually with increasing determination. Boris Kochubiyevsky, the son-in-law of a Ukrainian KGB agent, refused to acquiesce in the "unanimous" denunciation of Israel at his factory. His application for an exit visa to Israel rejected, he and his family visited Babi Yar, the grave site of tens of thousands of Jewish victims during World War II. The KGB responded by arresting and sentencing him to three years of forced labor. Yasha Kazakov renounced his Soviet citizenship on June 13, 1967, and requested an exit visa; the immediate refusal prompted a protest letter by his parents to Israeli Prime Minister Golda Meir. In response to the increasing tempo of exit visa applications, the Soviets completely shut off the trickle of emigration that had been allowed. Tension mounted until, on November 10, 1969, in a dramatic change of policy, Prime Minister Golda Meir released an appeal for exit visas by 18 Soviet Georgian Jewish families, directed to her and the UN Human Rights Commission. Previously, all references to individuals had been masked for fear of reprisals by the Soviet government; now the movement decided that the sheer publicity engendered by the revelation of names might actually serve to protect protestors from Soviet revenge. Inspired by Soviet Jewish courage, the tempo and magnitude of American protests increased. Local organizations, such as the New York Conference on Soviet Jewry, gradually developed; meanwhile the activist groups, such as the Cleveland Committee on Soviet Anti-Semitism, the (San Francisco) Bay Area Council on Soviet Jewry, and others formed the Union of Councils for Soviet Jews to help coordinate national protests.

A major Soviet miscalculation accomplished what the various organizations failed to do—place the Soviet Jewry issue in the forefront of international attention and rivet media attention on their plight. On June 16, 1969, *Leningskaya Pravda* published a short article about an unsuccessful hijack attempt at Leningrad's Smolny airport. On December 15, 1970, the trial of the "Leningrad Eleven," nine of whom were Jewish, opened. Ten days later, the court sentenced Mark Dymshits and Eduard Kuznetsov to death for the attempted hijacking. The timing of the verdict, on Christmas Eve, was deliberate; the court assumed that the Western press would be too preoccupied to notice. It was not. The parallel commutation, by Franco's Spanish government, of Basques only served to increase the pressure. Mass protests erupted all over the world; some even turned quasi-violent as the Jewish Defense League adopted the issue. Soviet diplomats were followed by groups of rough youths who shouted obscenities at them. Numerous Soviet sympathizers such as the British Communist Party and the French left-wing trade union, the C.G.T., protested and the international clamor eventually forced the Soviet government, on December 31, 1970, to reduce the death sentences to terms of imprisonment. Yet this failed to quiet the clamor; the damage had been done, and the Soviet Union never quite recovered from this debacle. Once the subject of exit visas and human rights gained international attention, it could not be safely ignored.

As if to compound its errors, the Soviet government committed a second faux pas barely two months later. An international conference to publicize the plight of Soviet Jewry had been scheduled in Belgium for February 23, 1971. Rather than ignoring it and thus ensuring a minimum of press attention to yet another international conference, the Soviets decided to attack it publicly. On February 15, 1971, *Tass* denounced the meeting as an anti-Soviet provocation. On February 18, 1971, it published an "Open Letter to the Government of Belgium from Soviet Citizens of Jewish Nationality," which condemned the meeting and even hinted at repercussions on Soviet-Belgian relations. The two foremost Soviet Jewish apologists for the regime, Aaron Vergelis, editor of *Sovietish Heimland* (the only Yiddish journal in the Soviet Union) and Col. Gen. David Dragunsky were paraded before Moscow radio and *Pravda*. A team of official Soviet Jews flew to Brussels to extol Soviet Jewish life, and four days before the opening of the conference the Soviet government officially warned the Belgian government of the meeting's negative effects on Soviet-Belgian relations. The Belgian government was not intimidated, and the meeting was held as scheduled. Because of the Soviet paranoia, the international press focused on this meeting.

The renewed focus on Soviet Jewry precipitated further American Jewish organizational modifications. The American Jewish Conference on Soviet Jewry metamorphosed into the National Conference on Soviet Jewry in June 1971. Unlike its older sibling it established offices, staff, and an independent budget of $250,000. From 1971 to 1973, the movement savored its golden age. In 1971, 13,000 Soviet Jews emigrated, 31,600 in 1972, and 34,933 in 1973. National and international demonstrations proliferated, especially Solidarity Day; Soviet Jewish tours drew crowds. On September 27, 1972, Senator Henry Jackson launched the most controversial attempt of those years when, in response to the Soviet attempt to halt the brain drain with an exit tax on educated emigrés, he proposed what would become known as the Jackson-Vanik Amendment. As an amendment to the East-West Trade Relations Act of 1971, it would deny most-favored-nation status as well as credits to any state that prohibited the free emigration of its citizens. The controversy surrounding this amendment is detailed elsewhere; suffice it to say that it split the American Jewish community. Eventually the Soviets "ignored" the exit tax but by this time the Yom Kippur War of October 1973 had cast a shadow on the campaign. The rising international pressure on Israel as well as the political gains of the PLO shifted American Jewish concern from Soviet Jewry to Israel. In addition, the rising tide of *noshrim*, Soviet Jews who opted not to go to Israel, dampened Israeli enthusiasm for the effort to get Jews out of the Soviet Union. Nevertheless, the flow continued until the early eighties when the spigot closed, at least temporarily. The following table traces the rate of emigration of Soviet Jews from the late 1960s through the 1980s, giving the total departing and the number entering the United States.

After 1978 the majority of Soviet Jews emigrating chose to go to the United States. Since Soviet Jews often ignored Jewish communal and fraternal organizations and a large percentage did not observe traditional Jewish laws and customs, this raised the issue of their too rapid assimilation into the American mainstream. In one study of Soviet emigrés in the United States, Rita and Julian Simon concluded that only 12 percent kept

Migration of Soviet Jews, 1967–1989

	Total	To the United States
1967	1,400	72
1968	230	92
1969	3,000	156
1970	1,000	124
1971	13,029	214
1972	31,791	453
1973	34,741	1,449
1974	20,634	3,490
1975	13,229	5,250
1976	14,269	5,512
1977	16,737	6,842
1978	28,868	12,265
1979	51,294	28,794
1980	21,472	15,461
1981	9,450	6,980
1982	2,688	1,327
1983	1,319	887
1984	896	489
1985	1,141	570
1986	913	641
1987	8,011	3,811
1988	19,233	10,576
1989	71,196	36,738
1990	215,000	31,938

Source: Hebrew Immigration Aid Society, New York.

the dietary laws and 20 percent observed Saturday as a special day. About half fasted on Yom Kippur and observed Passover, while 57 percent lit Hanukkah candles. In some areas, this is significantly less than the American Jewish norm. Thus the movement faced the question, Had it merely succeeded in permitting a quarter million Soviet Jews to escape from the Soviet Union only to see them disappear in the United States? Further disillusionment set in when, in contrast to the exceptional leaders of the movement, the vast majority of the emigrés proved to be ordinary people with their ordinary failings. The aura around them gradually dissipated.

Nevertheless, demonstrations continued in support of emigration for Soviet Jews, although an increasing sense of *deja vu* combined with a certain disillusionment and frustration overcame the movement in the early eighties. People tired of going to demonstrations and the spontaneity of the first years evaporated. The Soviets seemed determined to strangle the emigration movement.

In the mid and late eighties under the influence of *Glasnost* and Mikhail Gorbachev the rate of emigration began again to climb; the effect on the U.S. movement to "free" Soviet Jews remains to be seen.

WILLIAM ORBACH

BIBLIOGRAPHY

Orbach, William. *The American Movement to Aid Soviet Jews*. Amherst: University of Massachusetts Press, 1979.

Rass, Rebecca, and Brafman, Morris. *From Moscow to Jerusalem: The Dramatic Story of the Jewish Liberation Movement and its Impact on Israel*. New York: Shengold, 1976.

Interfaith Cooperation.

AMERICAN RELIGION: FROM ESTABLISHMENT TO PLURALISM. At the time of the Declaration of Independence there were about 3.8 million people in the thirteen colonies. The colonies had established churches on the European pattern, with the exception of Rhode Island and Pennsylvania. The latter limited the franchise to Trinitarian Protestants. Officially, the population was Protestant, and as late as 1820, 85 percent were descendants of the peoples of the British Isles. There were about 20,000 Roman Catholics and 1,500 to 2,500 Jews in 1776.

During the nineteenth century, after religious liberty had become the national standard, the states slowly adapted themselves to freedom of religious expression. There were setbacks, notably when Protestant nativist movements, with their high tide in the 1840s and 1920s, erected barriers against Roman Catholic and Jewish immigrants. Intermittently, governorships and legislatures were controlled by "antiforeign" parties in a number of states.

Affirmative support of an approved denomination for the nation declined, even when the change to a pluralistic society was somewhere temporarily and ineffectually resisted. Connecticut ended its tax support of the established church in 1819, Massachusetts in 1834. New Hampshire in 1912 eliminated its longtime restriction of public office to Christians.

National policy has shown itself flexible, however, when some public need could best be served by close cooperation between the government and the churches.

The American pattern has never been radical separationism of the kind that in Europe has often accompanied a radical swing from clerical establishment and privilege to anticlerical policies advanced by a militantly secularist or even atheist regime. The Virginia Bill of Religious Freedom 1784–1786) and the First Amendment to the federal Constitution (1789–1791) were adopted by persons friendly to both religion and representative government and equally opposed to religious or political policies that injured the liberties of loyal citizens. The result is that disestablishment in America has worked to the benefit of both organized religion and organized government.

The general pattern involves a creative tension between two poles: the voluntary support of religious profession and activities, on the one side, and the restraint of limited and secular government from meddling in religious affairs, on the other. On the general scene, to defend religious liberty involves a constant battle against the campaigns of religious groups to get tax moneys for their continuing programs and another constant battle against the efforts of different governmental agencies to undermine the discipline of religious communities and to take over definition and control of religion.

As important as preservation of the general pattern is, there have always been exceptions to it where unusual cases called for common sense exceptions. The military chaplains are a case in point, although equally pointed exceptions can be found in tax support of chaplains at hospitals and prisons and mental institutions, in tax support of chaplains at state universities, in contracts with religious agencies to carry on overseas assistance programs, and so on.

The military chaplain's office is an exception to the general pattern that still preserves the essentials. The chaplains afford in one of the most advanced of American public institutions—the military forces—the acceptance of religious variety and the cultivation of interfaith cooperation. While the public at large has only recently come to accept a trifaith blessing of inaugurations and dedications, the chaplain's office has adapted to a much more complicated task.

At the end of World War II, four-fifths of the chaplains that the services designated as "Protestants and Others" came from just 6 mainline denominations. In 1985, there were 77 different accrediting agencies with which the government had to deal. The chaplains have boldly clung to the affirmation of "Cooperation Without Compromise," which has now extended far beyond the three-faith pattern that Will Herberg—in his 1955 classic, *Protestant-Catholic-Jew*—portrayed as standard and culturally accepted.

By developing new methods of mass evangelism, the Protestant churches during the last century and a half regained the adherents that they had lost through disestablishment. And in spite of the great variety of small denominations, estimated at approximately 1200 varieties by J. Gordon Melton, today a dozen large churches comprise more than 80 percent of all American Protestants.

During the same period of time, through large immigrations the Roman Catholic Church and the Jewish community have become major forces on the American scene. Today the Roman Catholic Church is the largest denomination (ca. 52.5 million), and for two generations it has provided the largest financial support of the Vatican. The Jewish community with 5.8 million is nearly twice the Jewish population of Israel and more than twice the third largest body: Soviet Jewry. The American Protestants since 1938 have been the most vigorous factor in the spread of Christianity on the world map.

All three of the major faith communities—Protestant, Roman Catholic, and Jewish—confront each other in strength, and for the first time in history anywhere they have the opportunity to work out a new set of interfaith interactions and patterns of cooperation.

FORMAL COOPERATION. In the civilian sphere, organized interfaith cooperation in the United States is commonly dated from the aftermath of the 1928 Presidential election. That election marked the last massive political offensive of a once-dominant force in American politics: Protestant nativism. The target of that offensive was Alfred E. Smith, candidate of the Democratic Party and a Roman Catholic. Smith was defeated by Herbert Hoover, a Quaker, who did not personally engage in anti-Papist demagoguery but politically profited by its appeal in a number of states.

After the election as the result of a letter circulated jointly by Charles Evans Hughes (former New York governor, presidential candidate, and the future Chief Justice of the United States), industrialist Roger William Straus, and S. Parkes Cadman (past president of the Federal Council of Churches), a conference was convened to set up an organization to promote the "advancement of amity, justice, and peace" amongst Jews and Christians. Everett Clinchey of Wesleyan University in Connecticut became executive secretary in 1928 responsible for a program to educate for tolerance and brotherhood. Called at first the National Council of Catholics, Protestants, and Jews, the organization adopted the name the National Conference of Christians and Jews because the Roman Catholic Church did not officially permit its members to participate in interfaith dialogue until after the Ecumenical Council: Vatican II (1961–1965). Before then, according to official instructions, interreligious discussion was strictly forbidden.

Nevertheless, by a broad interpretation of certain instructions it was possible for Roman Catholics to participate with Protestants and Jews in specific practical areas: e.g., combatting communism, supporting the public order against destructive forces, etc. During World War II, interfaith activity expanded greatly in civilian life as well as the military chaplaincy, and in the two decades before Vatican II there were extensive private discussions between such leaders as John Courtney Murray and Gustave Weigel, on the one side, and Reinhold Niebuhr, on the other.

Out of Vatican II came what was popularly called "the American declaration": *Dignitatis Humanae*, the Declaration on Religious Freedom (actually a declaration on a generous religious toleration, not Religious Liberty). There was also issued *Nostra Aetate*, the Declaration on the Relationship of the Church to Non-Christian Religions, which laid the foundation for later pastoral instructions on interreligious dialogue. Because of the bitter opposition of Arab League governments—and their intensive lobbying of the Vatican—and some right-wing anti-Semites in the Council itself, a separate declaration on Christian/Jewish relations was aborted. A modified version was incorporated as Section 4 in *Nostra Aetate*. Roman Catholic participation in interfaith agency work has increased greatly since 1965, especially under the direction of Edward H. Flannery and his successor Eugene Fisher in the United States Catholic Bishops Conference.

The *Journal of Ecumenical Studies*, founded at Duquesne University (Pittsburgh) and now affiliated with the Department of Religion at Temple University (Philadelphia), is the chief journal of interfaith dialogue. In 1990, it was still directed by its founding editor, Leonard Swidler, a Roman Catholic lay theologian also known for his authorship of the "Dialogue Decalogue"—explicit rules for effective interfaith discussion.

By the time of Vatican II, the election of a member of the Roman Catholic community as President of the United States—John F. Kennedy in 1960—signaled the emergence of a new style of interreligious and intercommunal relationships on the map of American pluralism.

The year 1960 also marked the emergence of another agency important in interfaith cooperation in the United States: the Association of Coordinators of University Religious Affairs (ACURA). Interfaith cooperation developed on a number of university campuses before it became generally accepted in civic affairs. The pioneer unit was established by Richard Henry Edwards at Cornell University in 1923. The second unit was started by Kenneth W. Morgan at the University of Michigan in 1936.

During and after World War II there was strong pressure on many campuses for consultation and cooperation among the Newman Club, Hillel Foundation, Wesley Foundation, and other faith and denominational groups. By 1946, the interfaith federation at Michigan counted 23 affiliates.

By 1959, a number of universities had professional staff to work with organized religious communities in fostering interfaith dialogue. ACURA, a professional association of interfaith workers, was founded at the instigation of the Consultant on Religion in Higher Education to the NCCJ. It has held annual conventions since then and publishes a newsletter, *Dialogue on Campus.*

Before World War II, the support of the NCCJ was thin and the organizational budget austere. But its work survived the Great Depression and the restrictions set initially by the Roman Catholic hierarchy and grew steadily. Through able leadership and great devotion, three-faith public cooperation became a reality in a number of cities.

National Brotherhood Week has also become a tradition. "Trio" groups of priest/rabbi/minister address schools and public meetings from one end of the country to the other, thus demonstrating that fellow Americans can speak to each other and listen to each other across religious lines.

Clinchey's successors as president of the NCCJ were Lewis Webster Jones, Sterling W. Brown, David Hyatt and Jacqueline G. Wexler. Under David Hyatt the commitment of the NCCJ to Christian/Jewish dialogue was strengthened. He also gave strong support to the growing Christian concern for Israel's survival and well-being, which had been a weak point among his predecessors. Clinchey, in fact, was much under the influence of the American Council for Judaism. There has been a marked slackening off since Hyatt's retirement, although some local and regional offices continue to cultivate the interfaith dialogue in depth. ACURA and the Annual Scholars Conferences, which began with NCCJ encouragement, have for long functioned independently.

EXTENDING INTERFAITH WORK ABROAD. Everett Clinchey led the work of the National Conference of Christians and Jews during the war. In America there was a great expansion in the number of regional offices. Clinchey was also active in the fraternal work which laid the foundations of the International Council of Christians and Jews (ICCJ).

One of the most important undertakings of the national staff of the NCCJ, especially Clinchey, Willard Johnson, and Carl Zietlow, was cooperation with the American occupation of postwar Germany in organizing interfaith seminars, conferences, and societies (*Gesellschaften fuer christlich-juedische Zusammenarbeit*). Initially the work was paid for by the American occupation authorities, but since the founding of the German Federal Republic, the several dozen *Gesellschaften* have been paid for and staffed by Germans.

In the occupation of postwar Germany, the American government, as in other unusual situations of the past, worked closely with the religious communities.

Protestant, Roman Catholic, and Jewish staff and liaison people received extensive logistical support from both the American Military Government and the Office of High Commissioner that succeeded it when policy direction passed from the Department of the Army to the State Department. The staff assignment was to work with reliable German individuals and religious agencies to assist them to give leadership in the recovery of liberty and representative government after the collapse of the Third Reich. Here again the American system of good faith cooperation between government and religious agencies—*neither* establishment with "entanglement" *nor* "a high wall of separation"—showed its value.

President Theodor Heuss addressed the founding conference of the German interfaith work in 1949, with an address that received wide acclaim: "Courage to be Tolerant" (*Mut zur Toleranz*). The American custom of observing Brotherhood Week, with the president of the republic issuing an annual message, was adopted.

With the assistance of the Religious Affairs Staff of OMGUS (Office of Military Government of the United States), and HICOG (U.S. High Commissioner for Germany) and in spite of the small number of Jews remaining in Germany, a national council (*Koordinierungsrat*) was finally brought into being.

Very extensive work was done with publications, including the translation of books by Gordon Allport and others, the preparation of textbooks for the schools reflecting interfaith cooperation, and books interpreting different religious traditions.

The government of the German Federal Republic has been supportive, as has the German public. The international headquarters of the ICCJ is located at Martin Buber Haus in Bensheim, just south of Frankfurt/Main.

INTERFAITH HOLOCAUST EDUCATION. Awareness of the importance of the Holocaust for Christian as well as Jewish history, and of the necessity of rethinking Christian preaching and teaching about the Jewish people in the post-Holocaust setting, has become a fertile source of interfaith dialogue.

In the late 1960s, three institutions of Christian/Jewish cooperation were founded that continue to grow in religious and political importance—the National Christian Leadership Conference for Israel (originally, Christians Concerned for Israel), the Christian Study Group on Israel and the Jewish People (originally, the Israel Study Group), and the Annual Scholars' Conference on the Holocaust and the German Church Struggle (originally, the Conference on the German Church Struggle and the Holocaust). All three agencies have contributed substantially to Christian/Jewish understanding and cooperation. Originally, the three were closely interrelated, but as they have extended their scope, each has developed new leadership and its own style.

Christians Concerned for Israel (CCI) was started in the aftermath of the Six-Day War of 1967, an attack on the Jewish state during which the Arab League threatened to push the Jews into the sea. The possibility of a second Holocaust was met by a thunderous silence on the part of the denominational bureaucracies. To counteract this, some 250 church leaders responded to an invitation by Franklin H. Littell to establish an organization to show more active Christian concern for Jewish survival and Israel's well-being. In 1978, CCI joined with several other organizations to form a federation—the National Christian Leadership Conference for Israel (NCLCI). At the

same time, a working relation was firmed up with the America-Israel Friendship League.

NCLCI issues a newsletter, holds conferences, rallies church lobbying on issues such as Bitburg and billion-dollar arms sales to Arab League regimes, and issues public statements on critical issues affecting Christian/Jewish relations.

The Christian Study Group (previously the Israel Study Group) was originally set up under the auspices of the National Council of Churches and the U.S. Catholic Bishops Conference, with 10 Roman Catholic and 10 Protestant theologians. It is now affiliated with the Baltimore Institute for Christian/Jewish Study. Occasional statements are issued on matters of theological significance to Christian/Jewish relations. The chief work of the group remains, however, preparing and discussing papers on the critical issues confronting post-Holocaust Christian theology. Many of the papers have been published, and several have resulted in books.

The founding Annual Scholars Conference was called by Franklin H. Littell and Hubert G. Locke at Wayne State University in 1970. It was the first conference to bring together the problem of the Holocaust with the issues raised by the Nazi subversion of the churches. Attending were representatives of the Jewish and Christian faiths. Until that time Jewish and Christian scholars had been working in isolation from each other. The conference also set the pattern that has become standard: research and education on the Holocaust and related themes should be *interfaith*, *international*, and *interdisciplinary*. The proceedings were published as *The German Church Struggle and the Holocaust* (Detroit, 1974).

Numerous published articles and several books have come out of the Annual Scholars Conferences. For a time clerical assistance was provided by the National Conference of Christians and Jews. Later the Anne Frank Institute and the Philadelphia Center on the Holocaust has served that function.

The Scholars Conferences have been cosponsored by a number of organizations, including the Philadelphia Center on the Holocaust, Genocide and Human Rights, the U.S. Holocaust Memorial Council, and the International Bonhoeffer Society. Over two decades the conference has attracted the participation of the major scholars in Israel, Europe, and North America who are working on the Holocaust and/or the church politics of the Third Reich.

The Scholars Conference has also played an

important role in encouraging and supporting several affiliated developments. One such was the first Conference on the Church Struggle and the Holocaust on German soil, at Hamburg, June 5–7, 1975, sponsored by the NCCJ and the German Societies for Christian/Jewish Cooperation.

Another was the international conference on the Holocaust held in Oxford and London July 10–17, 1988. This conference, "Remembering for the Future," which brought together 650 scholars from 24 countries, was underwritten by Robert Maxwell. The Maxwell Publishing interests had already launched *Holocaust and Genocide Studies*, a scientific journal under the editorship of Yehuda Bauer of Hebrew University. Over 260 papers were submitted and published in advance, with discussion carried on in 42 workshops.

On fraternal initiative and sometimes in consultation with the leadership of the Annual Scholars Conference, a number of independent Holocaust conferences have become centers of interfaith cooperation. In 1974, a major conference was held under the auspices of the Cathedral of St. John the Divine in New York, which resulted in an important volume edited by Eva Fleischner: *Auschwitz: End of an Era?* (New York, 1977).

In 1977 and 1978, under the direction of the NCCJ, major conferences were held in San Jose, California. The resulting publication edited by Henry Friedlander and Sybil Milton—*The Holocaust: Ideology, Bureaucracy, and Genocide* (New York, 1980)—shows the breadth of the interdisciplinary and interfaith approach.

Important regional conference series on the Holocaust have been held at Kent State University in Ohio and Millersville University and West Chester University in Pennsylvania, the latter being the center of the National Association of Holocaust Educators (NAHE).

Since 1970, the study and teaching of the Holocaust has produced significant advances in the education of the public to the importance of interfaith understanding.

In 1972, "Christians Concerned for Israel" began the publicizing of *Yom Hashoah* observance, which had been set as a calendar day in Israel the previous year. Christian pastors and lay people were urged to hold special services in their churches or to cooperate with Jewish congregations in interfaith events. A decade later the campaign for recognizing the Days of Remembrance was taken up by the U.S. Holocaust Memorial Council, and it is now observed by the President

and Congress, the governors of all 50 states, and the mayors of all major American cities. Although interfaith congregational and campus services continue, the Days of Remembrance celebration has become fixed in the civil calendar and tends in the larger cities and at state and national level to become an expression of civil religion.

In 1986 the Anne Frank Institute issued an award-winning interfaith volume of *Liturgies on the Holocaust* edited by Marcia S. Littell. The volume has been adopted officially by the chaplains in the armed forces, as well as by a number of state and local agencies, for it provides Jewish and Christian and interfaith services and resources.

In 1978–1979, President Jimmy Carter established, under the chairmanship of Elie Wiesel, the President's Commission on the Holocaust. Enacted as a federal agency in 1980, and renamed the U.S. Holocaust Memorial Council, the agency was given the mandate to establish a national memorial museum. The cornerstone of the museum was laid on October 5, 1988 on the Mall in Washington, D.C. The attendant exercises were marked by a powerful message by President Reagan, stating the country's commitment to Holocaust education.

Under the Council several important interfaith projects have developed. In addition to the Annual *Yom Hashoah* observances in April, in 1988 the Council gave special attention to observance of *Kristallnacht* in November. The previous year a *Kristallnacht* Workshop was held in Philadelphia, drawing participants from six nations. Materials were provided for planning fiftieth anniversary interfaith observances.

The following season many hundreds of meetings and ceremonies were held throughout the United States—in congregations and schools and public halls—to recall the memory of *Kristallnacht* on November 9–11, 1938 in Hitler's Third Reich. As *Yom Hashoah* is a time of meditation and mourning, *Kristallnacht* is the time to speak of the lessons to be learned from the failure to heed the early warning signals of that event.

Another significant event sponsored by the council was the September 1984 international conference convened by Elie Wiesel: "Faith in Mankind: Rescuers of Jews During the Holocaust." The organizer was Sister Carol Rittner, a Roman Catholic, and the major financial responsibility was undertaken by a layman, William J. Flynn. During this event, which brought together from around the world 83 living rescuers and the Jews they saved from the Nazi killing program, interviews were filmed that provided the materials for an award-winning film and a fine book: *Courage to Care.* The editors were an interfaith team: Carol Rittner and Sondra Myers. The groundwork was international, with many of the rescuers and rescued being identified and located for the Conference by the staff of the Division of the Righteous of the Nations at Yad Vashem (Jerusalem).

OTHER NATIONAL DEVELOPMENTS. The largest single occasion for featuring the interfaith dialogue itself is the National Workshop on Christian-Jewish Relations. More than a thousand now attend the event, which is held in different cities annually.

Sponsoring organizations include local agencies as well as the National Council of Churches, the U.S. Catholic Bishops Conference, the American Jewish Committee, the American Jewish Congress, the Anti-Defamation League of B'nai B'rith as well as several rabbinical and denominational agencies.

The National Workshop, which is the initial introduction to the interfaith dialogue for most who attend, still has to walk gingerly about the most sensitive issues affecting relations between Christians and Jews. This includes such major issues as religious liberty (including abortion legislation and tax support of religious schools) and especially Holocaust education and the stance of the churches toward Israel.

The most anxiety-producing issues affecting the relations between the faiths are intermarriage and conversion. Jewish communal leadership is especially, after the loss of one-third of the Jewish people during the Holocaust, sensitive on these two issues.

The dissolution of European Christendom and the rapid change in religious and/or ideological alignments on the world map have led to attacks on cults and sects and even against movements within the traditional faith communities that attempt to adapt the cultic practices and doctrinal instructions to the changing scene. These attacks have jeopardized the religious liberty of individuals and groups as well as run contrary to the general movement toward interfaith and interreligious understanding.

In May 1986, the Vatican issued a pastoral instruction calling for the faithful to meet the newer movements with open dialogue rather than with anxiety and repression. In September of the same year a consultation called by the World Council of Churches and the Lutheran World Federation issued recommendations along the same line. In the spring of 1987 the first conference on the churches and new religious movements (NRMs) was held at Catholic University in Washington D.C., resulting in the establishment of the American Conference on Religious Movements (ACRM). Conferences followed at Loyola Merrymount (Los Angeles), Baylor University, Chicago Theological Seminary, and again at Loyola Merrymount. A statement on interfaith dialogue was issued by Loyola Merrymount II, affirming the commitment of participants to the religious liberty of individuals and groups and to the interreligious dialogue as the appropriate method of resolving misunderstanding and hostility on sensitive pressure points between religious communities.

The executive director of ACRM is Marvin Bordelon, a leading Roman Catholic layman, and the executive committee members are evenly divided between Roman Catholic and Protestant officials and leaders of NRMs. Jewish communal leaders have participated in the later consultations, although official Jewish agencies have been slower than Roman Catholic and Protestant officialdom to speak up for religious liberty and interfaith dialogue at this front.

In the United States, with its tradition of religious liberty rather than persecution/toleration (two sides of the same coin), leaders and members of different communities of faith have the opportunity to develop new patterns of interaction, and since World War II they have been active in so doing. *See also* National Conference of Christians and Jews.

FRANKLIN H. LITTELL

BIBLIOGRAPHY

Cargas, Harry James. *Reflections of a Post-Auschwitz Christian.* Detroit: Wayne State University Press, 1989.

"The Dialogue Decalogue: Ground Rules for Interreligious, Interideological Dialogue." *Journal of Ecumenical Studies* 20 (Winter 1983) 1:reprint.

Eckardt, A. Roy. "Can There Be a Jewish-Christian Relationship?" *Journal of Bible and Religion* 33 (1905): 122–130.

Flannery, Edward H. *The Anguish of the Jews.* New York: Macmillan, 1965.

Littell, Franklin H. *The Crucifixion of the Jews: The Failure of Christians to Understand the Jewish Experience.* New York: Macmillan, 1975.

Niebuhr, Reinhold. "The Unsolved Religious Problem

in Christian-Jewish Relations." *Christianity and Crisis* 26 (1966): 279–283.

Ostling, Richard N. "Coming to Terms with Judaism." *Time* 129 (June 29, 1987): 57.

Talmage, Frank. "Judaism on Christianity: Christianity of Judaism." In *The Study of Judaism: Bibliographical Essays.* Vol. 1. New York: Anti-Defamation League of B'nai B'rith, 1972.

Intermarriage. The tremendous increase in intermarriage since 1970 has caused widespread concern in the Jewish community. The facts of intermarriage, though, have turned out to be far more complex than originally thought. Such complicating factors as the retention of Jewish identity by the intermarried Jew, conversion, and patrilineality have made analyses more difficult.

The first problem in analyzing intermarriage is defining the term. There are at least two distinct meanings to the word. By religious definition, an intermarriage in Jewish life involves the marriage of someone Jewish, whether by birth or conversion to Judaism, to someone not Jewish. By sociological definition, a mixed marriage is any marriage between someone born Jewish and someone not born Jewish, whether or not the non-Jew eventually converted. An intermarriage, or conversionary marriage, is one in which the non-Jew did convert. The term must be considered in both senses to understand its importance in Jewish life.

Although intermarriage has only been identified as a serious problem relatively recently, it has occurred almost since the arrival of Jews in America. There were only a small number of Jews in this country during the colonial period and immediately after. Even by 1840, there were only 15,000 Jews, most of whom were of Sephardic origin. Because of the sparseness of the Jewish population and the fact that there were many more Jewish men than Jewish women, there was a large rate of intermarriage. One authoritative estimate is that 28.7 percent of marriages involving a Jew between 1776 and 1840 were intermarriages. The Sephardic Jews involved in these intermarriages did not convert, but their children were raised as Christians, so that the fledgling Sephardic community was numerically depleted.

The American Jewish community grew rapidly in the nineteenth century with waves of German Jewish immigration, especially after the European revolutions of 1848, and East European Jewish immigration, especially after the Russian pogroms in the 1880s. By 1900, there were more than 1 million Jews in America. This increased density of the Jewish population—resulting in communal organization and adequate available marital partners—helped lead to a reduction in intermarriage.

The rise in anti-Semitism was another factor in the decline of intermarriage. In the early years of Jewish life in America, the Protestant population welcomed Jews. By the 1870s, however, a nativist Protestant anti-Semitism emerged. Jews who had once been welcomed as marriage partners were no longer seen as acceptable by many Protestants.

These factors resulted in a very small intermarriage rate. Between 1900 and 1920, for instance, only 2 percent of Jews married non-Jews. In the 1920s, the intermarriage rate was 3.2 percent. In the 1930s, 3.0 percent, in the 1940s, 6.7 percent, and in the 1950s, 6.2 percent.

Suddenly, however, the intermarriage rate soared. The growth was affected both by Gentile attitudes toward marrying Jews and the Jews' own reactions. By ever increasing percentages, Jews were seen by non-Jews not only as acceptable but desirable marriage partners. This atmosphere of acceptance that emerged, especially during the 1960s, was felt in the Jewish community as well. More Jews began to accept intermarriage as part of living in an open society, a society in which love was considered more important than religion in choosing a marital partner. Also, the very economic success of Jews in the more open postwar society and the fact that young Jews were accepted in large numbers at prestigious colleges and left home to study at them led Jews into increasing social contacts with non-Jews. This propinquity led naturally to increasing intermarriage.

The first book on intermarriage sponsored by a Jewish organization, *Intermarriage and Jewish Life*, did not appear until 1963. The *American Jewish Year Book* published its first article on the subject in the same year. In 1971, the National Jewish Population Survey (NJPS) was conducted. The survey was the first attempt to examine the entire American Jewish population. The results were first published in the 1973 *American Jewish Year Book.* In a summary of intermarriage rates, it was claimed that the level of intermarriage had increased considerably. While only 9.2 percent of American Jews were intermarried, according to the NJPS, the number of intermarriages entered between 1956 and 1960 had climbed to 17.4 percent and between 1960 and 1965 to 31.7 percer a 500 percent increase in 10 years. This increasing rate implied that, in time, the overall intermarriage rate would become considerably higher. There was, and is, considerable questioning of the NJPS's methodology and statistics, with a number of Jewish analysts concluding that the intermarriage rate was, in fact, considerably lower. Whether or not the NJPS was accurate, its conclusions were widely accepted as validating the worst demographic fears of the Jewish community.

The American Jewish community was clearly shaken. The demographic situation they faced frightened them. One-third of world Jewry, 6 million Jews, 2 million of whom were children, died during the Holocaust. Additionally, many Jewish communal leaders believed the American Jewish birth rate was below replacement level, although experts disagreed about this. These factors and others—such as the reduction in involvement in Jewish life and the decrease in Jewish literacy among third- and fourth-generation Jews—made the intermarriage problem a major one in their eyes.

There were various attempts through the 1970s to determine the causes of intermarriage. In general, certain specific factors were considered to help determine the rate of intermarriage. Such factors were found to be demographic, social and economic, and cultural. Among the demographic factors were (1) the size and density of the Jewish community, with higher intermarriage rates in smaller and less dense communities, (2) the availability of marital partners within an acceptable age range, and (3) the age at marriage, with intermarriage increasing as the age of marriage increased. Among the social and economic factors were (1) educational achievement, with increasing education often correlating with increasing intermarriage, (2) occupational choice, with higher rates of intermarriage found in higher social occupations, such as among professionals and managers, and (3) the dispersion from urban to suburban areas, accompanied by a lack of Jewish communal institutions. Among the cultural factors were (1) the increasing social acceptance of intermarriage in general and with Jews in particular and (2) the decline in the centrality of religion, religious observance, and communal involvement among those who intermarried.

Attempts to stem the increase in intermarriage usually focused on an increase in Jewish education. Providing Jewish education, however, was often simply an example of how Jewish the child's home was already, so that the effect was not great. Most researchers did not correlate a relationship between the number of years of Jewish schooling and intermarriage, although young Jews who had had some Jewish education seemed to intermarry less than those with no Jewish education.

Seeking to clarify the intermarriage confusion, the American Jewish Committee commissioned a study of the subject by Egon Mayer. The study was summarized in 1979 in *Intermarriage and the Jewish Future*. Mayer's findings were significant. He confirmed that intermarriage posed a real threat to the Jewish community. He also found, however, that the born-Jewish spouse continued to affirm a Jewish identity. Indeed, the commitment to that identity was the key to the Jewishness of the marriage. Additionally, he found that when the non-Jewish spouse converted, the marriage was considerably more Jewish.

The intermarriage picture became more complicated. The fact that Jews in an intermarriage retained some sense of their identity and that many more born-Christian spouses converted to Judaism than born-Jewish spouses converted to Christianity indicated that the relationship between intermarriage and assimilation was far less clear than had been assumed. Assimilation did not seem to be the motive for intermarrying, as the Jewish community, relying on historical precedent, had assumed.

Perhaps the single most intriguing factor in analyzing intermarriages was the increase in the number of conversions to Judaism. Most authoritative estimates are that at least 10,000 non-Jews convert each year, that there are at least 150,000 converts within American Jewry, and that that number will double by the year 2000.

The fact that almost 80 percent of the converts are women and that any child of a Jewish mother is considered Jewish by all movements within Judaism has led some analysts to a startling conclusion: that intermarriage rather than endangering Jewish survival actually will lead only to a modest loss in numbers and could lead to a modest gain.

In 1989 there were about 300,000–400,000 intermarried couples. In 100,000–150,000 of these couples the non-Jewish partner has converted to Judaism, with about one-third of the conversions taking place after marriage. About 400,000–600,000 children have been born in marriages between Jews and non-Jews.

Many questions about intermarriage remain. There are continuing disputes about how to measure it and how to analyze its causes, consequences, and methods of prevention. Perhaps most importantly, questions remain about the place of conversion in Jewish life. In particular, there are at least three important areas of dispute in Jewish life that affect the intermarriage issue.

The first area of dispute is about whether and how to seek and welcome converts. If conversions reduce the threat of intermarriage and increase the chances of the children of intermarriage remaining Jewish, it would seem logical that the Jewish community would encourage conversion. The Reform Movement does have an organized outreach program, while the Conservative Movement currently expresses a willingness to accept converts but not to seek them actively. Their efforts are not as organizationally expansive as are the Reform's. The Orthodox do not encourage conversions. However, even with the efforts underway for conversion, about 60 percent of intermarried couples are not religiously affiliated, and the Jewish community has no organized effort to reach them.

Additionally, the percentage of conversionary marriages is declining. In part, this is due to the fact that more rabbis are willing to perform intermarriages now than they have ever been. Intermarriage is also much more acceptable now than it perhaps has ever been. There are a series of guidebooks to successful Jewish-Christian marriages. There also seems to remain a residue of uncertainty about converts by born-Jews. This uncertainty may, for instance, prevent a born-Jew from even requesting that a potential marriage partner convert.

The second area of dispute is about the Reform Movement's patrilineality ruling. In 1983, the Central Conference of American Rabbis declared that children would be considered Jewish by the Reform movement if either parent was Jewish and if the child publicly and formally identified with the Jewish faith and people. Traditionally, a Jew is defined as someone born to a Jewish mother or who converts to Judaism. This decision has not been accepted by either Orthodox or Conservative rabbis. The problems raised by this dispute include the very definition of who is a Jew and therefore who qualifies as a marriage partner for traditional Jews. Some analysts have even considered patrilineality to be a contributing factor in the proportional decline of conversionary marriages since under it conversion is not seen as necessary for the children potentially to be con-

sidered Jewish. The identity confusion raised by this ruling remains to be resolved.

The third area of dispute involves the definition of who is a Jew. The overwhelming percentage of conversions to Judaism in the United States are performed by Reform and Conservative rabbis. In general, these conversions are not considered to be religiously valid by the Orthodox, so that the converts and their children (if the convert is a male) are not considered Jewish by the Orthodox. As with patrilineality, the whole definition of an intermarriage depends centrally on the definition of who is a Jew. The religious tensions engendered by the question of what constitutes a valid Jewish conversion (and other related religious questions) continue to wait for a resolution. *See also* Assimilation, Conversion.

LAWRENCE J. EPSTEIN

BIBLIOGRAPHY

Berman, Louis A. *Jews and Intermarriages: A Study in Personality and Culture.* New York: Yoseloff, 1968.

Cahnman, Werner J., ed. *Intermarriage and Jewish Life.* New York: Herzl Press, 1963.

Drachsler, Julius. *Democracy and Assimilation.* New York: Macmillan, 1920.

Gordon, Albert I. *Intermarriage: Interfaith, Interracial, Interethnic.* Boston: Beacon Press, 1964.

Gordon, Milton M. *Assimilation in American Life.* New York: Oxford University Press, 1964.

Mayer, Egon. *Children of Intermarriage.* New York: American Jewish Committee, 1983.

———. *Love and Tradition: Marriage Between Jews and Christians.* New York: Plenum Press, 1985.

———, and Avgar, Amy. *Conversion Among the Intermarried.* New York: American Jewish Committee, 1987.

———, and Sheingold, Carl. *Intermarriage and the Jewish Future.* New York: American Jewish Committee, 1979.

Sklare, Marshall. *America's Jews.* New York: Random House, 1971.

Iranian Jews. *See* IMMIGRATION, IRANIAN.

Israeli–United States Relations. *See* UNITED STATES–ISRAELI RELATIONS.

Israel's War for Independence (1947–1949): American Volunteers. World War II had ended in 1945, yet two years later thousands of Jewish displaced persons were still in camps living under conditions little better than under the Nazis. Only a few could find refuge in Western countries. The majority wished to go to Palestine, but the door was barred by Britain's restrictive immigration policy established in the British White Paper of 1939 that set a quota of 75,000 immigrants in the next five years and then a total cessation of Jewish immigration. Due to the war, the immigration slowed to a trickle, and at the end of 1944 there were still some 31,000 unused certificates for immigration. However, by the end of 1945 these had been used. After that time the British allowed the entry of only 1500 people per month. Young Jews from around the world, along with their Christian friends, acted together to help the refugees reach the Promised Land.

The North American volunteers, the result of a spontaneous grass-roots movement, were illegal (at least in the eyes of the British). Hence, secrecy had to be maintained at all times. The United Nations Organization had placed an embargo on the shipment of arms to all countries in the Middle East. All member nations were urged to prevent the influx of personnel of military age into the area. Before their departure from Palestine, the British were still trying to prevent the arrival of displaced persons and the shipment of arms to the Jews. Secrecy about the group was so well maintained that 40 years later most of the Jewish communities of both North America and Israel were still unaware of the very fact that the volunteers had existed.

Most of them were young; many of them became aware of the opportunity to participate through sources on their college campuses. It was not uncommon for the Hillel House, the gathering place for Jewish students on many campuses, to be used as an informal recruiting center. Most volunteers had no military training or experience. Recent research indicates that 1067 volunteers from the United States and 289 from Canada participated in Israel's War for Independence. Few of the young people had Zionist backgrounds, but they knew that they were Jews and they wanted to help.

With the end of World War II, the horrors of the "final solution" were revealed to the world. Finally, the appalling conditions were publicized. Even as late as 1947, however, survivors continued to live in the displaced persons camps under guard and in not much better conditions. One camp resident noted, "We are liberated, but we are not free."

The first to respond to the needs of the survivors were the young rabbis who were chaplains of the U.S. Army of Occupation. That the chaplains were involved at all is undoubtedly one of the best kept secrets up to nearly fifty years later. They used their authority, far beyond its limits, using military transport and supplies in an effort to ease the suffering of their fellow Jews. (Their story has been covered in great detail in the dissertation of Alex Grobman, whose doctorate was obtained at the Hebrew University in Jerusalem. A copy is held in the library of the University of Judaism in Los Angeles, California.) They operated as individuals. At least a dozen of them played major roles in the movement of refugees to the Mediterranean ports where the Aliya Bet ships awaited. The outstanding work of Rabbi Abraham Klausner was justly praised by Rabbi Max Weill: "Klausner is doing one of the most important pieces of work that anyone has ever done. . . . The American community will have to decorate him for what he has done and continues to do, almost completely by himself." Others who played a part were Rabbis Abraham Haselkorn, Yosef Miller, Meyer Abramowitz, Samuel Burstein, and Frank Goldenberg, who died in a jeep accident while escorting refugees through the military lines on the way to Vienna.

The chaplains were aided by a group of young servicemen, including a number of Christians, in their effort to ease the suffering of the refugees. They helped survivors in their flight from Germany and Eastern Europe to the American Zone of Occupation. Thus they became part of the operation known as the *Bricha*, which means "flight." The attempt by the refugees to return to homes in Poland led to pogroms in which in one year alone over 400 Jews were killed while authorities looked on. Polish Jews who had been evacuated into the interior of Russia returned from the east, and on finding the desolation of the Jewish community in their former homes, they continued on into the Western-controlled zones rather than remain in Poland.

The rabbis also used their influence to make secret agreements with the military authorities to "infiltrate" thousands of refugees into the U.S. zone. After infiltration, the *Bricha* then moved them to the shores of the Mediterranean where the ships of the Aliya Bet waited to take them to the Promised Land. This was the so-called "illegal" immigration that had to run the gauntlet of British naval interception in the attempt to enter Palestine.

When it became increasingly obvious that Britain would not ease its immigration quotas, the Jewish Agency, the group recognized by the British as the spokesmen of the Jewish community in Palestine, decided to empty the refugee camps by using the Aliya Bet to get the refugees to Palestine. Initially, small ships were leased to run the British blockade. These had a good chance of avoiding interception but could carry only small groups of passengers. It was then decided that larger vessels must be used. These could be purchased from the postwar surplus ships in America. Furthermore, American crews could be obtained to man them. (Two converted banana carriers of this operation, the *Pan York* and the *Pan Crescent*, later became the first passenger ships of the Israeli merchant marine, the Zim Line.)

A motley assortment of vessels was assembled, as described in the book *The Jews' Secret Fleet* by Joseph Hochstein and Murray Greenfield. While some professional crewmen were hired through the seaman's unions, the bulk of the crews were volunteers. Some were veterans of the U.S. Navy and others of the Merchant Marine. However, the majority had no seagoing experience and had little to offer other than their willingness to learn. While there is little in the way of statistical data, it is estimated that nearly 300 volunteers served in some capacity aboard a ship carrying "illegal" immigrants to the Promised Land.

The dangerously overloaded vessels carried more than 30,000 refugees to the shores of Palestine. There the ships were seized by the British and retained in the harbor at Haifa in northern Palestine. The refugees were interned, either in Palestine or on the Island of Cyprus. The crewmen were hidden amongst the refugees and eventually sent to Palestine as part of the allowable monthly quotas. Some of the crewmen were secretly removed from the convoys on the way to the detention camps. Others were given priority on the quotas in the names of true refugees who surrendered their identities to permit the needed sailors to escape detention.

Continuous pressure was put upon the British to either allow unlimited immigration or to surrender the mandate. Their resources were strained to the limit in the attempt by the Royal Navy to stop the flood of refugees being brought in by the Aliya Bet. The British decided to turn the problem over to the United Nations. The U.N. Special Commission on Palestine (UN-

SCOP) investigated conditions in Palestine as well as the displaced persons camps in Europe and recommended the immediate admission of 100,000 immigrants. President Truman pressed the British to carry out this policy. Instead, they decided to terminate their League of Nations mandate. The final result was the momentous decision to partition Palestine into an Arab state, a Jewish state, and an internationalized Jerusalem.

The Arab refusal to accept partition and the subsequent war that they launched against the Jewish community in Palestine brought forth a new and even larger group of volunteers from America. As a result of the British attempt to disarm the Jews in Palestine during the mandate, it was crucial to bring in arms the instant the British left the country. The only possibility of doing this quickly enough would be by aircraft.

Trained air crews for this mission were being recruited as early as 1947. Al Schwimmer and Sam Lewis had resigned their positions with TWA in order to take on the task. The aircraft that would be needed were already being readied in the United States. The organization created is described in Leonard Slater's book *The Pledge*. Large numbers of World War II surplus planes were available for purchase by air force veterans. Approximately 250 volunteers, veterans of the Canadian and American air forces, came forward to man them. The crews ferried the planes to Czechoslovakia, where the transport planes were used to carry the much needed supplies to the hard-pressed Israeli forces. The timely arrival of the fighter planes that they brought in virtually prevented the early demise of the Jewish state. The three B-17 bomber planes that were flown to Czechoslovakia to be fitted with armament were then flown to Israel via Egypt, where they bombed Cairo and other targets. The Arabs now knew that their own cities were no longer inviolate.

The Israeli Air Force would have to be built from the Aero Clubs that the British had permitted to operate. They had prevented Jews from obtaining anything except light civilian aircraft so it was necessary to acquire military aircraft. Essentially, the volunteers became the Israeli air force. Many non-Jews helped form the air crews and were a noteworthy part of the maintenance personnel. They played a significant role in the victories that finally ensured the security of the Jewish state.

The air force quickly established its superiority over all the attacking Arab forces and soon

controlled the skies over Israel. Its personnel consisted of highly trained crews of volunteers from most of the Allied air forces of World War II. The information published in the world press, wildly exaggerated as to numbers of squadrons of aircraft on their way to the beleaguered state, induced a considerable degree of caution in the Arab air forces.

The arms brought in by the tired and overworked crews who flew the airlift enabled the rapidly expanding brigades of the Israel Defense Forces to hold their ground. During the first truce arranged by the United Nations, the airlift brought in much needed weapons. The heavier equipment, provided by American volunteers, came in by sea. At the end of the truce, the Israeli forces were able to take the offensive. The survival of the infant state was now assured. However, the desperate struggle was not yet over.

The skills needed for the functioning of modern mechanized armies were furnished by additional volunteers, many of whom had already served in other functions. There were enough battle-experienced veterans among them to provide leadership to the youthful volunteers from many college campuses to make them a highly effective fighting force. A group of students from the University of British Columbia manned the first heavy artillery to arrive in Israel. None of them had even seen a heavy weapon before. Yet with only two weeks training they managed to stave off the attack of the Syrian army in the Galilee.

A so-called "Anglo-Saxon" Brigade was formed from the English-speaking volunteers under the command of Col. Ben Dunkelman of the Canadian Army. Col. David "Mickey" Marcus of the United States Army was given overall command of the Israeli Defense Forces. His greatest accomplishment was the construction of the "Burma" Road to Jerusalem, which effectively relieved the siege by the Jordanian Legion. Unfortunately, Marcus was killed by an Israeli sentry when he failed to give the recognition sign when challenged. He was buried with full military honors in the cemetery at West Point, where a memorial service is held for him each year by the veterans organization known as the American Veterans of Israel.

The Anglo-Saxon Brigade eventually drove the Syrian, Lebanese, and Iraqi armies out of the whole of northern Israel. Other volunteers who were in all Hebrew-speaking units participated in virtually every campaign from Dan to Beersheba.

Several of them were in the mechanized units that conducted the final campaign in March 1949. This campaign ensured that Eilat (and with it access to the Red Sea) would be a part of Israel. An American volunteer who was on that expedition was wounded when his jeep struck a mine. He was probably the last wounded casualty of the 1948–1949 war in which 38 volunteers sacrificed their lives.

The two corvettes, which were the first two ships purchased for the Aliya Bet, had been part of the Canadian Navy during World War II. Now renamed the *Hagana* and the *Hashomer*, they became the first ships of the Israeli Navy. Many members of the crews were volunteers and the first navy commander was Paul Shulman, a U.S. Naval Academy graduate. Several of the sailors from Aliya Bet went into the navy and filled the more skilled jobs on the crews.

The most notable naval engagement in the war was the sinking of the Egyptian warship the *Emek Farouk*. (This was another well-kept secret at the time: both by Israel, since it was sunk during a truce period, and by the Egyptians, who did not want their vulnerability known.) The ship was spotted by volunteers in the Israeli Air Force and sunk by frogmen, including several volunteers who were part of that service. While frogmen formed a small unit in the navy, a disproportionate number were volunteers from the United States. Leonard Cohen, a native of California, had gone to Britain as an alternate for the U.S. swim team in the 1948 Olympic Games and had continued on to Israel to join the navy.

Quite a number of young women also volunteered. Many of them were in the medical corp, while others functioned as radio and radar operators and as air controllers. They were recruited in the same manner as the men and underwent the same risks.

The remarkable achievements of the volunteers in that momentous period in modern Jewish history is one of which their countrymen can well be proud. Though their numbers were not large, they played a significant role in the final victory. Each of the volunteers feels that this was the most important period in his or her life. They are proud that they aided in that age-old dream—the re-establishment of a Jewish state in the land of Israel.

I. M. FINEGOOD

BIBLIOGRAPHY

Ben-Ami, Yitshaq. *Years of Wrath, Days of Glory*. New York: Speller, 1982.

Blumberg, Stanley with Owens, Gwen. *The Survival Factor*. New York: Putnam, 1981.

Greenspun, Hank, with Alex, Pelle. *Where I Stand . . . The Record of a Reckless Man*. New York: McKay, 1966.

Grobman, Alex. Doctoral diss., Hebrew University, Jerusalem.

Heckelman, Joseph. *American Volunteers and Israel's War of Independence*. New York: Ktav, 1974.

Hilber, Raul. *The Destruction of European Jewry*. New York: Harper & Row, 1961.

Perl, William R. *The Four Front War*. New York: Crown, 1979.

Slater, Leonard. *The Pledge*. New York: Simon & Schuster, 1970.

J

Jackson-Vanik Amendment (1972). The Jackson-Vanik Amendment to the East-West Trade Relations Act of 1971 prohibited the granting of most-favored-nation (MFN) status and the extension of credit to any nation that did not permit the free emigration of its citizens. Senator Henry Jackson of Washington introduced it in response to the Soviet decree of August 3, 1972, that imposed an educational tax, ranging from $5,000 to $25,000 on all those wishing to emigrate. On October 4, 1972, after negotiations, Jackson with the cosponsorship of 73 senators announced the amendment, which was quickly submitted to the House of Representatives by Representative Charles Vanik. At first the Nixon administration dismissed it as an election year ploy and on October 18, it agreed to extend to the Soviets the status of a most-favored nation and Export-Import Bank credits for Soviet sales. Nixon did not realize the seriousness of the situation in early 1973, when the amendment was reintroduced in the House with 254 cosponsors, including Wilbur Mills, chairman of the House Ways and Means Committee. The White House blundered further by placing the provision for Soviet MFN into the Omnibus Trade Bill, which gave Jackson the opportunity to hold a major piece of legislation hostage. The AFL-CIO, long opposed to the trade bill, announced its support for the Jackson Amendment, perceiving it as a means of defeating that legislation. Administration pressure failed to sway the crucial senators and attempts to influence the Jewish-American leadership backfired because of mass public support for the amendment. Secretary of State Henry Kissinger's efforts against the amendment also failed. A deadlock was inevitable; by early August, Jackson and Kissinger, attempting to break the stalemate without officially involving the Soviet Union, agreed to an exchange of letters on Soviet assurances of relatively free emigration and an end to harassment. The subsequent publicity, the $300-million limit on credits imposed by the Stevenson Amendment, and possible Soviet internal developments and pressures led the Soviets to deny publicly that they had made any commitments on emigration. The amendment became law, and the Soviets failed to gain MFN or credits from the Export-Import Bank. *See also* Immigration, Soviet.

WILLIAM ORBACH

BIBLIOGRAPHY

Albright, Joseph. "The Pact of the Two Henrys: How the Deal to Buy Jews from Russia Grew from a Moral Impulse into the Unwanted Policy of Two Superpowers." *New York Times Magazine*, January 15, 1975, 20.

Korey, William. "The Story of the Jackson Amendment, 1973-75." *Midstream* 21 (March 1975): 8.

———. "The Struggle over Jackson-Mills-Vanik." *American Jewish Yearbook* 75 (1974): 200-210.

Stern, Paula. *The Water's Edge: Domestic Politics and the Making of Foreign Policy.* Westport, Conn.: Greenwood Press, 1979.

Javits, Jacob Koppel (1904–1986). U.S. lawyer and politician, Javits was a tireless worker whose political career spanned over five decades, including 8 years as a U.S. congressman and 24 as a U.S. senator from New York State. He was instrumental in helping to enact legislation involving foreign affairs, urban redevelopment, civil rights, organized labor, and big business. While in the Senate, Javits, a liberal Republican, influenced as much important legislation as any Republican who served in the Senate during the modern era. Javits was outspoken in his support of U.S. aid packages to Israel, a position that he effectively lobbied as a long-time member of the Senate Foreign Relations Committee.

Born to Jewish immigrants in a tenement on New York City's Lower East Side, Javits was educated in New York schools, graduating from Columbia University and the New York University School of Law by working during the day and attending classes at night. He established a law partnership with his older brother, and it was during this period that he first became involved in politics. In 1932, Javits joined the Ivy Republican Club. His affiliation with the Republican Party continued throughout the rest of his life.

After a short stint with the U.S. Army in World War II, during which he reached the rank of lieutenant colonel, Javits returned to New York City and resumed his active involvement in the Republican party, a party that was perpetually outnumbered by the Democrats in the city. To "reward" Javits for his commitment to the party, in 1946 the party nominated him as a candidate in a congressional district that had been strongly Democratic for over two decades. Javits surprisingly won and remained in the House for three more terms until he challenged and defeated Democrat Franklin D. Roosevelt, Jr., in the 1954 race for state attorney general. Of the Republican statewide nominees that year, Javits was the party's only winner.

Two years later Javits successfully ran for the U.S. Senate and remained there until he was defeated in the 1980 Republican primary. Throughout his entire political career he was one of the strongest vote getters in the state because he had large appeal among Jewish and liberal voters, groups who traditionally voted Democratic. As a liberal Republican, Javits's ideology alienated him from many other Republican senators. This estrangement was the primary reason for his failure to capture the party's 1968 vice-presidential nomination, the first time ever that a Jew had seriously been considered for this office.

Even after his electoral defeat, Javits remained active as a college professor, guest lecturer, and author. He was awarded both the Medal of Freedom and the Charles Evans Hughes Gold Medal in recognition of his outstanding contributions to the nation. The memory of Jacob Javits will not soon be forgotten as the federal government's largest office building in New York State and the New York City Convention Center are both named in his honor. *See also* Politics.

BRUCE ARMON

BIBLIOGRAPHY
Javits, Jacob. *Discrimination, U.S.A.* New York: Washington Square Press, 1962.
———. *Javits: The Autobiography of a Public Man.* Boston: Houghton Mifflin, 1981.
———. *Order of Battle: A Republican's Call to Reason.* New York: Atheneum, 1964.

JDC. *See* AMERICAN JEWISH JOINT DISTRIBUTION COMMITTEE.

Jewish Children's Literature. In this article, Jewish children's literature refers to literature written specifically for children from ages 4 to 14, adult literature adapted for or suitable for children, and literature written by children that supplies information about the historic, religious, social, cultural, or economic background of the Jewish people, their ideals, and ethical standards. It also includes Jewish stories and book-length fiction. The latter enable children to experience Jewish history, to see Jewish values in action, and to observe a wider range of Jewish traditions and practices than those of their own group. Besides furnishing information and understanding through vicarious experience, Jewish children's literature is important for the child's psyche. It augments a sense of connectedness to an ethnic/religious group and helps to defeat marginality. Children living in areas where contact with Jews are few or nil can keep emotionally in touch with other Jews, thus providing a stronger sense of Jewish identity and, consequently, a healthier sense of self. This makes it less likely that—should they encounter anti-Semitism—they will convert it into Jewish self-hate. Finally, good Jewish children's literature entertains as it informs.

THE FIRST JEWISH CHILDREN'S LITER-
ATURE. The earliest form of Jewish children's
literature was storytelling—simplified versions of
biblical history and stories told by parents fulfilling the *mitzvot* of "you shall teach them to your
children."

Teaching tales once told by scribes, sages,
rabbis, and later recorded in Talmud and Midrash
still serve as sources for contemporary picture
books, anthologies, and even novels for children.
Until the Haskalah (the Enlightenment) in the
eighteenth century, there was almost a total absence of written literature designed specifically
for children. When boys were old enough, they
went to heder (religious school) where they
studied Torah, Mishnah, etc. according to their
age and ability. Girls remained at home and were
largely illiterate. With the advent of the Haskalah,
some religious materials were translated into the
language of the people, usually Yiddish, and girls
and women began to read. Another consequence
of the Haskalah was the acquiring of the indigenous language of the host country. Jewish boys
and girls surreptitiously began to read secular literature—folktales, myths, legends, and national
histories. These were considered *traife* (unkosher)
and dangerously diverting. To counteract their
baleful influence, rabbis and Jewish educators
began to sponsor nontraditional Judaica (not primary religious materials) that were adaptations
for children of biblical or midrashic nature. Most
were printed in Hebrew, but some were in Yiddish.

A body of Jewish children's literature, written with the understanding that children are not
miniature adults but have perceptions of reality
different from adults', did not occur until the
nineteenth century, when educational philosophy
and Freudian psychology had penetrated Jewish
circles in Western Europe. It would not reach
Eastern Europe until 50 years later.

When the Haskalah reached Eastern Europe,
it inspired a lode of creativity, a veritable treasure
of adult and children's Yiddish stories, so rich that
one of its veins became the Yiddish theater;
another, Yiddish fiction; the third, Yiddish folklore; the fourth, children's literature. To this very
day, Yiddish literature is prospected for its themes
and unique characterizations and, in 1987, YIVO
(YIVO Institute for Jewish Research) and Moyer
Bell Limited published two bilingual facsimiles
of Yiddish children's books: *Little Stories for
Little Children*, told by Miriam Margolin, one

of the first early childhood educators, and illus-
trated by Issachar Ryback; and *Yingle Tsingl
Khvat*, by the famous poet Mani-Lieb and illus-
trated by the equally famous artist, El Lissitzky.
Both have been translated into English by Jeffrey
Shandler.

EARLY JEWISH CHILDREN'S BOOK PUB-
LISHING IN THE UNITED STATES. The
first Jewish children's books published in the
United States were strictly religious materials,
frequently siddurim (prayer books), histories,
and textbooks of Jewish ritual and practice. By
1766, several books of scripture had been translated into English for adults' use, and in 1820,
Isaac Gomez, Jr., using siddurim as an example,
adapted one for his son's use and thus published
the first children's book in the United States. This
book was followed by many others. Some were
translations of previously published children's books
in French and Spanish. Others were original.
Among the writers of religious books for children
between 1829 and 1852 were Isaac Leeser, Simha
C. Peixotto, Benjamin Szold, and H. Pereira
Mendes. Magnus's *Outlines of Jewish History* and
Abraham's *A Manual of Scripture History for Use
in Jewish Schools and Families*, imported from England in the late 1800s, were used in revised editions through the 1940s.

In 1845, Isaac Leeser, who had published a
Hebrew Primer for Children in 1838, helped to
establish the Jewish Publication Society, which
failed, but a Jewish Publication Society was established successfully in 1888. In 1988, the society
celebrated its centennial anniversary and continues to publish quality books for Jewish children, as well as for adults. About this time, a
Bohemian immigrant, Rabbi Isaac Mayer Wise,
who later established the Hebrew Union College
for training Reform rabbis, influenced his
brother-in-law Edward Bloch to establish Bloch
Publishers in New York. The firm subsequently
published many Jewish children's books, and it is
still publishing Jewish books, still run by a
member of the family, Charles Bloch.

In addition to instructional materials, Jewish
children continued to borrow books from adults.
Scott's *Ivanhoe* was considered "Jewish" because
of its Jewish heroine, Rebecca. A popular British
writer of the time, Grace Aguilar, of a Sephardic
family, wrote biographies, histories, and novels
that were eagerly read by adults and children, and
may still be read today.

DENOMINATIONAL PUBLISHING. Jewish children's books in appreciable numbers were not published in the United States until the 1920s. In 1922, the Reform Movement through the Union of American Hebrew Congregations (UAHC) and the Central Conference of American Rabbis (CCAR) established a joint commission on Jewish education. Emanuel Gamoran, the director, and his wife, Mamie, wrote, and also commissioned others such as Rose Lurie, M. Soloff, Lenore Cohen, and the Levingers—Elma Ehrlich Levinger and her husband Rabbi Lee J. Levinger—to write texts needed for Hebrew schools—books on worship, ceremonies, holidays, the Bible, and traditional stories. Their major contribution to Jewish children's literature was to develop a grade-related body of children's works and to have the books illustrated by artists. As much as 25 percent of titles published for children before 1950 were from the UAHC. After a hiatus of many years, UAHC is again publishing lively, attractive Jewish children's books, which, while supporting their curriculum, sell to a broader readership.

The United Synagogue Commission on Education of the Conservative Movement was also active in children's book publishing. Over the years it published a still popular series of Jewish holiday picture books that show a fictional Jewish family celebrating around the year, two picture storybooks by Hyman and Alice Chanover, several books by Lily Edelman, Sol Scharfstein, Morris Epstein, Rabbi Hyman Goldin and Rabbi Abraham Burstein, Deborah Pessin, Bea Stadtler, G. Rosenfeld, Shulamit Ish-Kishor, A. Eisenberg, and Sadie Rose Weilerstein. Most of these books, while possibly out of print, can be found in multiple copies on the shelves of Jewish libraries. Shulamit Ish-Kishor became a prize-winning author, as did Bea Stadtler and Sadie Rose Weilerstein, creator of "Ktonton."

Orthodox denominational publishers have only recently become in-depth publishers for Jewish children. Many of their books, while "Torah-true," are fiction. This is quite a change from the traditional point of view, which held that original texts were the only reading matter sanctioned for Jewish children from religious families. Mesorah/Art Scroll and Merkos L'Inyonei Chinuch (Habad) are representative Orthodox publishers.

Most other Jewish children's books, up to the 1950s, were published by Jewish secular publishers such as Behrman (mainly textbooks), Bloch, Feldheim, Hebrew Publishing Company, Greenstone, the Jewish Publication Society, and Schocken Books.

PUBLISHING IN THE LATTER HALF OF THE TWENTIETH CENTURY. In 1947, Random House, a large trade publisher, published *The Diary of Anne Frank*, and Follet, another trade house, brought out Sydney Taylor's *All-of-a-Kind-Family* in 1965. These books were not only best-sellers, they became classics of children's literature. Both Jews and Gentiles began to write books of Jewish content with sufficiently universal themes to appeal to a nonsectarian readership. From this point on, the majority of Jewish-content children's books were published by trade publishers. And why not? The Holocaust and the establishment of the State of Israel were two singular events. Additional reasons for the shift of publishing of Jewish-content books to trade publishers are the increased demand for ethnic materials in public libraries and public school libraries, a result of the civil rights movement, thus providing a new marketplace for ethnic children's books. Then, too, the establishment of the State of Israel gave Jews a new sense of security and pride. If the outnumbered Israelis could vanquish armies, surely the American Jew could come out of hiding and celebrate his or her Jewishness. This newly found pride was, and is, reflected in the increased writing, publishing, and purchasing of books about Judaism, Jews in politics, examinations of American Jewish life, and Jewish children's books. A new Jewish marketplace!

The move, in the 1950s, of many Jews to the suburbs resulted in the establishment of beautiful new synagogues and Hebrew schools. The demand for all Jewish books grew. Jewish libraries were established in synagogues and Jewish community centers, not only to collect traditional literature, but also to promote and provide popular Jewish nonfiction and fiction. A traditional Jewish education was not essential in order to read these books. The books explained and educated and were written in nonacademic, popular language, a language that appealed to a broad segment of the population.

Many young parents, especially the women, of this generation had not received a Jewish education, but they made sure that their children attended Hebrew school. The children's book collection was a major component of the new libraries. These libraries were first manned by volunteers, and their numbers were few, but with the encouragement and guidance of the Association of Jewish Libraries, professionalism accelerated, and the majority of synagogue librarians today comply with professional standards. Professional librarians have influenced publishers to publish Jewish children's books, as was testified to in a special symposium on Jewish Children's Literature (November 9, 1987), conducted by the JWB Jewish Book Council and hosted by UAHC. Librarians have an enormous influence on the genre and subject content of books published.

The Jewish marketplace for Jewish children's books, especially books for early childhood, has increased dramatically since the latter half of the 1970s and shows no signs of diminishing at the beginning of the 1990s. Two young mothers, Madeline Wikler and Judye Groner, were not satisfied with the didactic, carelessly edited and produced books for children. They found, in addition, that none approached young children at their proper developmental level. Thus was started the firm of Kar-Ben Copies, publishers of books for children from 2 years of age to 10. The UAHC Press also publishes many books for younger children, ages 3 to 6, and 6 to 10.

The publication of books for young Jewish children was an idea whose time had come. The Jewishly educated children born in the 1950s and 1960s were parents, albeit delayed parents. They took the availability of Jewish children's books for granted. They, who put off parenthood until their mid-thirties, absolutely doted on their belated offspring. As financially established, well-educated Jewish career couples, used to the good things in life that double incomes can provide, they are willing to, and have the money to, buy beautiful well-made books for their children. Furthermore, they are sufficiently comfortable in America not to be self-conscious about their Jewishness. Many of these young parents have helped to establish day schools, which will have more extensive Jewish libraries, meaning more Jewish children's books.

To further encourage Jewish children's book publishing, there are six annual Jewish children book awards. The JWB Jewish Book Council grants two National Jewish Book Awards for Jewish children's books—one for older children and one for an illustrated book. The AJL (Association of Jewish Libraries) Sydney Taylor Awards are for the best older children's book, best younger children's book, a "Body-of-Work" award, and an original children's book manuscript award; and the Kenneth B. Smilen Awards include one for a children's book. In addition, the Jewish Book Council sponsors the Jewish Children's Book Conference every two years where editors, publishers, agents, writers, illustrators, and librarians can meet. The Jewish Book Council's *Jewish Book Annual* includes a bibliography of Jewish children's books of the previous year and sometimes an article about Jewish children's literature.

To further encourage Jewish children's book buying, there are Jewish children's book clubs, children's bookstores that issue catalogues of Jewish children's books that can be mail ordered, lists of Jewish children's books, Jewish and trade publishers of such books, and Jewish bookfairs for the general public.

THE JEWISH AMERICAN IN JEWISH CHILDREN'S LITERATURE. It is important for Jewish-American children to read about Jewish participation in the society of their own time and in Jewish-American history. Fortunately, there are several nonfiction histories of Jewish-American life, especially Milton Meltzer's *The Jewish Americans: A History in Their Own Words: 1650–1950* (Crowell, 1982) and *The Jews in America: A Picture Album* (Jewish Publication Society, 1985), which is based on his *Taking Root: Jewish Immigration in America* (Dell, 1974)—all ages 12 and up. Unfortunately, there is very little fiction with Jewish characters set in America from the colonial times to the great immigration from Eastern Europe from the 1890s to the 1920s (when World War I and the McCarran Act effectively closed the doors of America to immigrants from Eastern Europe). This is a gap that should be filled.

Precolonial and Colonial Periods. There is no Jewish children's fiction about the earliest colonies of Jews who first arrived in new Amsterdam, or their coreligionists who followed and participated in international trade (and also set the pattern of civil rights for minorities in this country). The few children's books set in America during the first Jewish immigration (the Sephardic immigration) or in the pre-Revolutionary period and Revolutionary period, including Diana Green's *The Lonely War of William Pinto* (Little, 1968 [10–14]—a biographically based Revolutionary War story with a Vietnam War theme of a conscientious objector) are no longer in print. The story of the ubiquitous patriot and financier of the Revolution, Haym Salomon, is still available in Shirley Milgrim's *Haym Salomon: Liberty's Son* (JPS, 1975 [7–10]) but not in Vick Knight's *Send for Haym Salomon* (Borden, 1976 [8–12]).

Period of Expansion. Jews fought in all the wars of the United States. In the War of 1812, they not only fought, but some were privateers. No children's fiction set during this time includes Jews. There are biographies of Uriah Philips Levy, the first Jewish commodore of the American navy, who fought in the War of 1812 and who stood for patriotism and naval reform, applying Jewish humanitarian values to a cruel navy, where floggings and injustice were commonplace. One is found in Alberta Eiseman's collective biography *Rebels and Reformers: Biographies of Four Jewish Americans* (Doubleday, 1976 [10–14]) and in a fictionalized biography by Harold W. Felton, *Uriah Phillips Levy* (Dodd, 1979 [10–14]), both out of print.

Between 1815 and 1850, many German Jews were among the immigrants from Western Europe who helped settle the central section of America. Jewish Americans fought in the wars against the Indians. In the war with Mexico, there was at least one Jew, Abraham Wolf, who died at the Alamo, another who was among those who were massacred in the surrender to the Mexicans at Goliad, two surgeons, a score of officers, and an entire colony of 5000 German Jews living in Texas. Jewish fiction and nonfiction do not take note of Jewish involvement at this time.

The Civil War Period. Jews lived both North and South of the Mason-Dixon Line in the Civil War period. There were those who were anti-slavery and were active in the Underground Railroad, and those who themselves were slave owners. Jews fought on both sides of the Civil War and figured in one of the most flagrant examples of anti-Semitism in the history of this country—when Major-General Ulysses S. Grant ordered all Jews expelled from the region encompassing western Tennessee, southern Kentucky, and northern Mississippi and negated their permits to trade. Fortunately, this order was canceled by President Abraham Lincoln. Although adult books describe this, there are no children's books about this period in American Jewish life, save for a few textbooks. Jewish participation in the Civil War is portrayed mostly in biographies of Jews living at that time, but not in fiction.

Westward Expansion. By 1880, there were 250,000 Jews in the United States, contributing to its economic development and the establishment of the western frontier. They fanned out across the continent seeking economic opportunity. Jews were present in the California gold field, they were buffalo hunters, ranchers, miners, photographers, and newspaper editors. A comedy film from 1979, *The Frisco Kid*, starring Gene Wilder, is an affectionate spoof of the adventures of a Polish Jewish rabbi who journeys to bring a Torah to a Jewish congregation in San Francisco. But there is no fiction for children about Jews in the gold rush.

Substantial numbers of Jews became peddlers, then shopkeepers; many went on to found great department stores. Adult fiction and nonfiction has heeded this part of Jewish-American history very successfully, but not children's literature. Germans Jews who found work as peddlers traveling the wagon routes going west are represented in only two works of children's fiction. In both, Jews have lesser roles in the story. For instance, in John D. Fitzgerald's *The Great Brain* (Dial, 1967 out-of-print [o.p.]; Dell, 1976, paperback [pb], [8–12]), a Jewish peddler who has been invited to open a store in a small western town starves to death because of the townspeople's image of him as a wealthy Jew who does not necessarily need their business and in Patricia Beatty's *Melinda Takes a Hand* (Morrow, 1983 [8–12]) set in a small western town in the 1890s where the Jewish family is the town's shopkeeper, "spunky Melinda" (a Christian newcomer to town) advertises for more Jews to settle there so her new Jewish friend's father can have a minyan. Anti-Semitism is a subtle part of the plot in the first story, and it is overtly demonstrated in the second, where "spunky Melinda" defends her powerless Jewish friend. These Christian authors are trying to show how destructive anti-Semitism can be.

Jewish Immigration from Eastern Europe. By the 1920s, the great Eastern European Jewish immigration was a fact. Unlike the German Jews before them, these Jews sought employment in the needle trades industries of the Northeastern cities. It is here that American children's literature discovers Jewish Americans. Many stories about this period are written by grandchildren of immigrants, anxious to preserve the family saga and aware of the passing of the immigrant generation.

Some children's fiction and picture books deal with the difficult conditions in eastern Russia that impelled emigration, and others offer a nostalgic glimpse of close Jewish village life. Many books are about the escape from Russia, the voyage across the Atlantic, the arrival in America, the home life and customs of immigrant families, the clash of American culture and economic opportunity with traditional Judaism, and the striving for education and Americanization. The titles below describe Jewish Americans from the 1890s to the 1920s. The books discussed here have been selected because they reflect Jewish-American life from the turn of the century to the present time and for their literary quality.

Anita Heymain's *Exit from Home* (Crown, 1977 [11–14]) shows a religious boy's loss of faith, introduces socialism, Zionism, and the lure of secular literature as the Haskalah penetrates Eastern Europe. *Beyond the High White Wall* by Nancy Pitt (Scribner's, 1986 [10–14]) and *A Russian Farewell* by Leonard Fisher (Four Winds, 1980 [10–14]) describe two prosperous Jewish families, the first in the Ukraine, the second in Russia, who are on excellent terms with local officials until 13-year-old Libby (*High White Wall*) reveals that she has seen a peasant murdered by the overseer of a large estate and persists in accusing him. The second family—because of their good relations with the chief of police—is warned of an imminent pogrom. Both families emigrate to America.

Economic and civil restrictions against Jews, fearful pogroms, furtive escapes, and perilous crossings over Russian and European borders in the exodus of the fleeing immigrants to the point of departure are described in *Birthday in Kishinev* by Fannie Steinberg (Jewish Publication Society, 1979 [9–14]), *D'vora's Journey* by Marge Blaine (Holt, 1979 [8–12]), *The Night Journey* by Katherine Lasky (Warne, 1981 [10–14]), and *Rifka Grows Up* by Chaya Burstein (Hebrew Publishing, 1976 [10–14]).

Barbara Cohen in *Gooseberries to Oranges* (Lothrop, 1982 [6–10]) and Adele Geras in *Voyage* (Atheneum, 1983 [10–14]) describe the ocean voyage—the older people so fearful, the younger full of hope and romance. They also tell of the Ellis Island experience, as does Ricky Levinson and Diane Goode's *Watch the Stars Come Out* (Bradbury, 1986 [7–11]), which carefully refrains from identifying the characters as Jewish.

The heartbreak of family members denied entrance to America because of illness is discreetly handled in *Waiting for Mama* by Marietta Moskin (Coward, 1975 [8–12]). Mama has to return to Russia with the youngest child who has an eye disease. In the meantime, the rest of the family immigrate to America where they are settled in an apartment by one of the Jewish community's immigrant aid societies. The father and older sister get jobs in garment factories, while the youngest is sent to school where she quickly learns to speak English. Mama's family sews her a real American coat, and when she arrives at Ellis Island, they remove her Old World shawl and replace it with the New World coat.

The Immigrant Years: Acclimating to America. The years of Eastern European immigration were marked by hardship—poverty, illness, clashes between those who could not divorce themselves from their shtetl background and those overeager to embrace American ways. There were generational clashes between children and parents—once figures of authority in Europe but who now knew less than their American-educated children. Nowhere is this clash better expressed than in Marilyn Sach's *Call Me Ruth* (Doubleday, 1982 [10–14]). Rifka, encouraged by her adored teacher, announces to her mother, who is unable to adjust to America, that from now on she is to be called "Ruth." Their once warm and loving relationship deteriorates. Not until the mother becomes involved in the labor movement is she drawn out of her shell. Another story of intergenerational conflict, this time between father and son, is *Our Eddie* by Shulamith Ish-Kishor (Pantheon, 1969 [10–14]).

Marilyn Hirsh's *Ben Goes Into Business* (Holiday, 1973 [6–10]) and Brett Harvey's *Immigrant Girl: Becky of Eldridge Street* (Holiday, 1987 [7–11]), a fictionalized history of the period, describe the economic activities of Jewish immigrants, even of the children. Sheilah Greenwald's *The Hot Day* (Bobbs-Merrill, 1972 o.p. [4–8]) portrays how the immigrant family took boarders into an already crowded apartment to help pay the rent. The best nonfiction books about this period are Milton Meltzer's *World of Our Fathers: The Jews of Eastern Europe* (Farrar, 1974 [11 up]) and *Taking Root: Jewish Immigrants in America* (Farrar, 1976 [11 up]).

A Nostalgic, Romanticized View of Settling Down in America. Sydney Taylor's *All-of-a-Kind Family* (the first by Wilcox and Follet, 1951 [8–12]) series is a veritable social chronicle of a Jewish family's upward migration. The father already has a business, a junk and scrap yard. The family is not rich, but neither is it poor. By the end of the series, the oldest sister's fiancé is a U.S. soldier in World War I. Carol Snyder's equally regarded *Ike and Mama* (Lothrop, 1981 first book [8–12]) series are set in the same period as the Taylor books. All the children go to school. They no longer work in sweat shops, although they continue to work in the needle trades. Both the Taylor and Snyder books have brotherhood as a prevalent theme. Once they are established in America, both families take in relatives newly arrived from Russia.

Taylor's autobiographical *All-of-a-Kind Family* books demonstrate Jewish living much more than the *Ike and Mama* books, which are ethnically Jewish. Taylor's family is a large, extended one that celebrates the Jewish holidays, observes Jewish life-cycle ceremonies, has its share of illnesses, accidents, and tragedies but is buoyed by warmth, love, and a celebration of life. Both series include books about the move to places of second settlement, as Jewish immigrants leave New York's Lower East Side and begin their upward economic, educational, and social climb. Here is where they feel the brunt of anti-Semitism, largely absent in a multinational immigrant community described by Taylor and Snyder in their series and by Myron Levoy in *The Witch of Fourth Street* (Harper & Row, 1972 [7–11]).

"Moving up" and being a minority in the community is the theme of books by Mina Lewiton—*Rachel;* and *Rachel and Herman* (Watts, 1954 o.p. [8–12]; 1957 o.p.); Lorraine Beim—*Carol's Side of the Street* (Harcourt Brace, 1951 o.p. [8–12]); Anne Emery—*Dinnie Gordon, Jr.* (McCrae Smith, 1964 o.p. [12 up]); Lois Hobart—*Strangers Among Us* (Funk and Wagnalls, 1957 [12 up]); and Emily Neville Cheney—*Berries Goodman* (Harper & Row, 1965 [10–14]). Books written in this period soon after the Holocaust dwell on the evils of anti-Semitism and encourage "tolerance" of differences and acceptance by Christians of Jews in their midst.

The Great Depression and the Pre-Holocaust Years. The period of the Great Depression, 1930–1939, is clearly described in Gil Rabin's *False Start* (Harper & Row, 1969 o.p. [10–14]) about a cruel alcoholic unemployed father; in Nora Simon's *Ruthie* (Meredith, 1968 o.p. [8–12]); and Barbara Brenner's *A Year in the Life of Rosie Bernard* (Harper & Row, 1971 [8–12]). The Great Depression and the rescue of their persecuted relatives in Europe forms the central theme of *Becky's Horse* by Winifred Madison (Scholastic, 1975 [8–12])—where Becky forgoes her contest prize of a horse and accepts its alternative, money, which the family uses to pay for the passage to America of a young cousin in Vienna—and in *The Crystal Nights* by Michele Murray (Seabury, 1973 o.p.; Dell, 1975 [10–14]). Here the Jewish father's

sister and her family, fleeing from Vienna, are provided with passage money by Jewish organizations. When they arrive, they are warmly welcomed into the home of the brother, his Christian wife, their children, and her mother. Instead of being grateful and making the best of things, the refugee family complains. The host family, in financial peril because of the Depression, worries how to make ends meet and the children do not get along; but when anti-Semitism threatens one of the refugees, the two families coalesce in defense.

Jewish children were especially sensitive to their Jewish refugee classmates from France, Germany, and Belgium and not quite sure how to play with them. In *Finders, Weepers* by Miriam Chaikin (Harper & Row, 1980, second in a series of four, [8–12]), Molly finds a ring in the playground, puts it on and cannot remove it from her finger to return it, even when she finds out that its rightful owner is a little refugee girl. The enormity of her "crime" is compounded in Molly's mind because the ring belongs to a refugee child, someone to whom special compassion should be shown—and here she, Molly, has "stolen" her ring. In *Benny* by Barbara Cohen (Lothrop, 1977), Benny befriends his "mischling" refugee cousin and knowing the boy's interests is able to find him when he runs away.

After 1939, American Jews fretted and worried about their families in Europe, stayed glued to the radio, but felt powerless to do anything to help, misguidedly putting their faith in President Franklin D. Roosevelt to save the Jews of Europe. This is shown in Chaikin's first Molly book, *I Should Worry, I Should Care* (Harper, 1979), and in Charlotte Herman's *The Difference of Ari Stein* (Dial, 1976).

The Jewish leadership and the community were fearful of anti-Semitism in the United States. Father Coughlin, the arch anti-Semite, was broadcasting. Until the nation entered the war, the Bund held marches up and down the neighborhoods of America. Some Jews went underground out of fear, the theme of *The Turning Point* by Naomi J. Karp (Harcourt Brace, 1976 o.p. [8–12]).

Impact of World War II on American Jewish Life. There are several books where Jews are in uniform during World War II. *Introducing Shirley Braverman* by Hilma Wolitzer (Farrar, 1975 o.p. [10–14]) is a story of a Jewish family living in the Bronx during the World War II years that discusses friends and relatives killed in action; *Make*

Me a Hero by Jerome Brooks (Dutton, 1980 [10–14]) has two of the family's three sons in uniform; and in *The Last Mission* by Harry Mazer (Delacorte, 1979 [10–14]), the younger brother uses his older brother's birth certificate in order to volunteer because he wants to do something about helping the Jews of Europe—the only one that connects World War II and the Jews. *My Sister's Wedding* by Richard Rosenblum (Morrow, 1987 [7 up]) is an amusingly illustrated nostalgic memoir of the author/illustrator sister's wartime wedding.

Bette Greene's provocative book, *Summer of My German Soldier* (Dial, 1973 [10–14]; Dell pb) is atypical of this period. It is about a young Jewish girl, abused by her father and belittled by her mother, who falls in love with a German prisoner of war billeted in a camp on the outskirts of the southern town in which she lives. Although the book purports to be about how ordinary citizens get caught up in events beyond their control, and also how decency cuts across all boundaries, the author's choice of a German soldier as a symbol of what is decent and her Jewish parents as a symbol of what is abhorrent, may be an example of anti-Semitism turned inward—the result, perhaps, of the author's childhood spent in a small southern town where her family were the only Jews in town.

No discussion of American children's literature would be complete without noting the outpouring of books about the Holocaust, set in Europe, but published in America; so here we digress from our theme of American Jews portrayed in children's literature to discuss books about the Holocaust read by American Jewish children. The two best histories of the Holocaust for children are *A Nightmare in History: The Holocaust 1933–1945* by Miriam Chaikin (Clarion, 1987 [10–14]) and *Never to Forget: The Jews of the Holocaust* by Milton Meltzer (Harper, 1976 [12 up]; Dell, 1977). Many Holocaust books are personal narratives; others barely fictionalized personal narratives or fiction based on true stories. Among the best personal narratives for children from age 10 and up are *I Am a Star* by Inge Auerbacher (Prentice-Hall/Simon & Schuster, 1986 [10–14])—a child's perspective of life in the concentration camp, Terezin; *The Cage* by Ruth Sender (Macmillan, 1986 [12 up])—a teenager's efforts to keep her remaining family (two brothers) together in the Warsaw Ghetto and her subsequent internment in Auschwitz, where her poetry arouses sparks of humanity in her captors;

and Rose Zar's *In the Mouth of the Wolf* (Jewish Publication Society, 1983 [11 up])—a Jewish nursemaid to a Nazi officer's child. Among the best fictionalized personal narratives are Aranka Siegal's *Upon the Head of a Goat* (Farrar, 1981 [11 up])—the author's account of her family's disintegration after the Nazi incursion into Hungary, despite the valiant efforts of her courageous mother to protect them. Two of the best stories based on true incidents are Arnost Lustig's *A Prayer for Katerina Horovitzova* (Harper, 1973 [12 up])—one of many novels about teenagers in the Holocaust by this survivor-author—and Yuri Suhl's *Uncle Misha's Partisans* (Four Winds, 1973 [10–14]; Shapolsky, 1987).

The best Holocaust books for children from age 6 up are Chana Abells's *The Children We Remember* (KarBen, 1983; & Greenwillow, 1986) and David Adler's *The Numbers on my Grandfather's Arm* (UAHC Press, 1987).

Survivors and Second Generation in the United States. The effect of the Holocaust on survivors in America and their children is told in many personal narratives, but there are a few novels that envelop the reader in the reality of these experiences. *Alan & Naomi* by Myron Levoy (Harper & Row, 1977 o.p. [8–12]) is a heartbreaking story of Naomi, a survivor, and her failed attempt to regain her sanity after the horrors of her experiences in the Holocaust. *Daughters of the Law* by Sandy Asher (Beaufort, 1980 [10–14]) shows how support by American friends—both Jewish and Christian—by family, and by a supportive rabbi finally drives away the demons that haunt a bitter survivor and her nearly deranged daughter, Ruth. Anti-Semitic incidents in America cause Naomi to take her life and to drive Ruth of *Daughters of the Law* nearly insane. Another survivor tries to relive her lost childhood vicariously through her daughter in Deborah Hautzig's *Second Star to the Right* (Greenwillow, 1981 [12 up]) which is indirectly blamed for her daughter's anorexia. *Maus: A Survivor's Tale* by Art Spiegelman (Pantheon, 1986 [12 up]) is a serious cartoon-strip treatment by a son of his father's ordeal and of his own relationship with his father. Despite the medium, and the fact that the Jews are portrayed as mice and the Nazis as rats, this book is for adults and young adults.

The Establishment of the Modern State of Israel. During the 1960s and 1970s, a few novels were published about American teenagers' experiences in Israel, but none are currently in print. Far fewer books have been written about Israel than about the Holocaust. Among those involving American children are *The Year* by Hope Lange (S. G. Phillips, 1970 [10–14]); *One More River* by Lynne Reid Banks (Simon & Schuster, 1973 [12 up]); *The Time of Anger* by Thelma Nuremberg (Abelard, Schuman, 1975 [12 up]); *That Summer With Ora* by Rusia Lampel (Franklin Watts, 1967 [8–12]); and *Lori* by Gloria Goldreich (Holt Rhinehart, 1979 [12 up]; Dell 1979 pb). These books demonstrate the differences between American Jewish youngsters and Israelis. The Israelis are credited for having a beneficial influence on lessening the American teens' materialism and suffusing them with idealism. The stories show the diversity of Israelis, kibbutz life, and frequently, death from war or terrorism. A different type of book is *Joshua's Dream* by Sheila Segal (UAHC, 1985 [6–10]), which shows that the Zionist dream of his aunt, an early settler, is alive and well in her young American nephew who dreams of planting a tree in Israel. The best nonfiction book about an American teen in Israel has been written by American Josh Clayton-Felt—*To Be Seventeen in Israel: Through the Eyes of an American Teenager* (Franklin Watts, 1986 [12 up]). It is a series of interviews with Israeli teens by the author and includes his reflections on their remarks.

There have been many passages about the "idea of Israel" in books about the Holocaust. The goal of starting a new life in "Israel" gave courage to Jews in concentration camps and, after the war, in displaced persons camps. Encounters between assimilated Western European Jews with Zionist Jews during the abnormal times preceding and during the Holocaust often resulted in renewed sparks of Jewish feeling in Western Jews.

Although there are books about the struggle for Palestine, illegal immigration, and life in the new state, about the Israeli-Arab Wars, and the relations between Israelis and Arabs, they do not involve American Jews who have made aliyah. There is one photo essay, *Alina: A Russian Girl Comes to Israel* by Mira Meir (JPS, 1972 [7–10]), that describes a Russian child trying to get used to Israel, one about an Argentinian family who has settled on a northern Kibbutz and who benefit from Syrian shelling that opens up the side of their second floor flat, allowing their daughter's piano to be placed there—Miriam Chaikin's *Aviva's Piano* (Clarion, 1986 [7–11])—and three books have been published about "Operation Moses," the rescue of some of Ethiopia's Jews from Sudanese camps and their transport to Israel—*The Return* by Sonia Levitan (Atheneum,

1987 [12 up]), *My Name is Rachamim* by Jonathan P. Kendall (UAHC, 1987 [10–14]), and *Falasha No More* by Arlene Kushner (Shapolsky, 1986 [8–14]).

At Home in America: A Paradox—More Jewish, Less Jewish. By 1980, Jewish families had begun to return to their religious roots, and at the same time one out of every three marriageable Jews were intermarrying—some of these intermarriages resulted in the couple becoming more Jewish, as Rachel and Paul Cowan, photographer and author of *A Torah is Written* (Jewish Publication Society, 1986 [6–14]), but more often, they did not. Another book on this issue is Barbara Cohen's *People Like Us* (Bantam, 1987 [12 up]).

As American Jews become more like the majority population, they are heir to the same problems—drugs, suicide, divorce, overaffluence, etc. There are books that address these problems, suicide, for instance. Gloria Miklowitz's *Close to the Edge* (Delacorte, 1984 [12 up]) is about a teen having too much money and material goods and not enough inner riches, who almost becomes suicidal. *When Living Hurts* by Sol Gordon (UAHC, 1985 [12–adult]) is a nonfiction treatment of the subject. Barbara Pomerantz's *Who Will Lead Kiddush?* (UAHC, 1986 [6–10]) is a fictional treatment for young children of life after divorce.

The increasing interest in Judaism and Jewishness has resulted in the publication of many delightful books about celebrating the holidays, life-cycle events, and stories about a return to stronger Jewish identification. Holiday House has published a Jewish holiday series by Malka Drucker, one for younger children by Marilyn Hirsh, a book of Jewish children's holiday poetry selected by Myra Cohen Livingston and beautifully illustrated by Lloyd Bloom. Clarion has published a Jewish holiday series by Miriam Chaikin, and most recently her history of the Holocaust discussed previously. KarBen Copies has a long list of children's fiction and nonfiction for all Jewish holidays, and the UAHC press publishes books about Judaism, belief in God, life-cycle books about death, marriage, divorce, and bar mitzvah in fiction and nonfiction that are of high literary quality. David Adler, Peninnah Schram, and Barbara Cohen have been kept busy writing holiday stories, adaptations of Jewish tales, and stories about the Jewish family experience in contemporary America. Lodestar/Dutton has published an excellent Jewish Biography Series. The return to a stronger religious identification is exemplified by themes of Johanna Hurwitz's *Once I Was A Plum Tree* (Morrow, 1980 [8–12]) and Charlotte Herman's *What Happened to Heather Hopkowitz?* (Dutton, 1981). In *Plum Tree*, Gerry Flamm feels foolish staying home from school on Jewish holidays that she and her assimilated family do not celebrate or know anything about. Gerry senses that some part of herself is missing. She is nothing. While taking piano lessons from a refugee neighbor who lives a traditional Jewish life, Gerry learns about Judaism and participates in Shabbatim, eventually reclaiming her heritage. In *Heather Hopkowitz*, the daughter of assimilated parents becomes observant after spending two weeks with family friends who are religious, but Heather hides her "conversion" from her parents so as not to upset them.

As if to counterbalance the number of intermarriages, the traditional Jewish community has grown stronger and more numerous. With the increase in numbers comes an increase in public awareness. Miriam Chaikin has introduced an American Hasidic hero, little Yossi, who gets into trouble with his evil urge, with the angels, and even with God (tongue-in-cheek) in a series of three books, beginning with *Yossi Fights the Evil Urge* (Harper & Row, 1985), *Yossi Asks the Angels for Help* (Harper & Row, 1986 [7–11]), and *Yossi Tries to Help God* (Harper & Row, 1987 [7–11]). Judaica Press publishes stories about traditional American and Israeli Jewish life in the form of entertaining mysteries featuring the exploits of "EMES." The heros are two boys, one a son of an Israeli intelligence officer, the other the son of an American Orthodox rabbi. Most stories are set in Israel, but Miriam S. Zakon's *The Floating Minyan of Pirate's Cove* (Judaica Press, 1986 [12 up]) is set in a small town in the American South. Feldheim published June Leavitt's *The Flight to Seven Swan Bay* (Feldheim, 1985 [12 up]) about the ingenuity needed to keep kosher on an island in the Northeast after an emergency landing of an airplane carrying observant Jews.

In other words, the publishing of Jewish children's literature in America has never been better.

MARCIA W. POSNER

BIBLIOGRAPHY
Davis, Enid. *A Comprehensive Guide to Children's Books with Jewish Themes.* New York: Schocken, 1982.

Posner, Marcia W. *Juvenile Judaica: The Jewish Value's Book Finder.* New York: Association of Jewish Libraries, continually updated.

——. *Selected Jewish Children's Books.* New York: Jewish Book Council, annual update.

Jewish-Christian Relations. See INTERFAITH COOPERATION, NATIONAL CONFERENCE OF CHRISTIANS AND JEWS.

Jewish Daily Forward (*Yiddish*, **Forverts**). This most important of the American Yiddish newspapers was founded as a daily by Louis Miller and Abraham Cahan as an ideological statement following the orthodox marxist paper *Tsaytung di arbeter* ("The Worker's Paper," 1890–1897). The first issue was published on the Lower East Side of New York City on April 22, 1897. It represented the unionist, "revisionist," and democratic socialism of Morris Hillquit and a generation of garment industry workers and their sons "on the make" in a mobile society. Under the policy guidelines of Cahan, who led the paper (except for 1898–1902) until his death in 1951, and the managerial direction of Baruch Charney Vladeck, it reached a peak of 200,000 readers during World War I. However, as its readers became Americanized, its circulation declined, and in 1983 it became a weekly—the *Jewish Forward*. The weekly contained a supplement in English, and in 1990 an independent English-language edition of the *Jewish Forward* (regarded as a "child" of the Yiddish paper) was published in New York City, and plans were made to go national. Meanwhile, the commitment to publish a Yiddish-language version of the *Jewish Forward* remains undiminished, and the newspaper will presumably continue for as long as there are Yiddish readers who want it.

Cahan took a leave from the paper only eight months after founding it and went to work as an East Side reporter for Lincoln Steffen's *Commercial Advertiser*, the prestigious "grandma" of muckraking but mainstream journalism. However, he continued as a contributor to the *Forward*. At this time he wrote a story on night school classes in which a Russian Jewish grandfather expressed his idea of fulfilled citizenship as the opportunity to read a newspaper. The aim of the *Forward*, to which he returned full time in March 1902, was to realize this ambition. During its most influential period the *Jewish Daily Forward* not only performed a necessary function in the education of the immigrant masses, but its pages also presented a large enclosing mirror of the Yiddish world, one that in Irving Howe's words reflected "its best, its worst, its most ingrown, its most outgoing, soaring idealism, its crass materialism, everything."

The devotion to being a reflection of its readership was behind the *Forward's* unionism; after all, as Cahan said to the Amalgamated Clothing workers in 1918, his paper owed a debt to the underpaid and overworked sweatshop workers who had built it. Moreover, Western Social Democratic (as opposed to Russian Revolutionary) morality dictated that every "exploited" man had the right to achieve complete humanity through a relevant and interesting education. Consequently, a socialist and democratic newspaper (rather than a party organ) had to be flexible and "populist" (rather than "Russian Populist").

To this end, the *Forward* offered general information as well as enlightenment in the popularization of the literature of Tolstoy, Dreiser, and the classics of Realism. At the same time, it encouraged Yiddish literary creation, provided that this be expressive and despite the widespread feeling that Yiddish was doomed to make way for English. It fought for a high-quality Yiddish theater and published Sholem Asch and, most recently, Isaac Bashevis Singer, no doctrinaire realist.

It also realized that the Americanization of the Jewish immigrant was a special matter. Thus, Cahan's series of sketches in the *Forward* of 1900, *Di neshome yeseyre* (The Special Soul), at once suited the religious background of the immigrant and stated that only an elevated socialist (and secular!) morality could see him through the trials of the New World, which in the *Forward's* "Gallery of Allrightniks" was seen as premature success and in its "List of Missing Husbands" as a threat to family life.

Even more popular was its *Bintl Brief* (Bundle of Letters), a highly popular column started on January 20, 1906, in which Cahan and his staff gave advice to the culture-shocked. Likewise reducing trauma was the *Forward's* pictorial memorial to destroyed Jewish communities in the Holocaust, later published in book form as *Di farshvundene velt* (The Vanished World).

The *Jewish Forward* thereby took on the charisma of the *magid* or "folk preacher and comforter," as Gus Tyler, assistant president of the International Ladies Garment Workers Union, expressed it. Of course, over the years the daily's programmatic radicalism and anti-Zionism were out of touch with the philosophy of its readership; however, its editor could still attack Israeli policy in Lebanon at times in front-page editorials. After all, the most important thing on the *Forward's* mind was the American future, just as in the past. Thus, when Abraham Cahan was burned in effigy by Communists after publishing a series of articles critical of the Soviet Union (written by Harry Lang in the 1930s), this gesture may be understood as a sign of the paper's uncompromising American stand and its opposition to Russian autocracy, whether czarist or Bolshevik. *See also* Journalism; the Left, Yiddish Literature, Yiddish.

ALBERT WALDINGER

BIBLIOGRAPHY

Howe, Irving. "The *Forward* Fades." *New Republic* 188 (February 21, 1982): 10–11.

———. *World of Our Fathers.* New York: Harcourt Brace Jovanovich, 1976.

Rischin, Moses. *The Promised City.* Boston: Houghton Mifflin, 1962.

Tyler, Gus. "Looking Back to the 'Forward.'" *New Leader* 70 (April 20, 1987): 9–10.

Jewish Defense League. In 1968, Meir Kahane, Bertram Zweibon, Morton Delinsky, Irving Calderon, and Chaim Bieber founded the Jewish Defense League (JDL). Kahane, an Orthodox rabbi from the Mirrer Yeshiva, emerged as the leader of the JDL.

The roots of the JDL can be found among its founders who were dissatisfied with the quality of Jewish life in the United States. Jews were increasingly the victims of urban crime, and the rise of black anti-Semitism reawakened fears that were once associated with European pogroms and Nazi street violence. The belief was prevalent among the founding members that police protection was concentrated unfairly on other minorities, especially in the safeguarding of black civil rights. In addition, they felt that Jewish life and its tradition in the United States was disintegrating and that Jewish organizations such as B'nai B'rith, the American Jewish Congress, and the American Jewish Committee had failed the Jewish community because their agendas included non-Jewish causes (e.g., civil rights). The JDL believed these Jewish organizations and their activities diluted Jewish life and had "sold out" to Christian America. The JDL hoped to solve these problems and to restore Jewish life and community to a Jewish people.

In 1968, the JDL received wide publicity during a New York City teachers' strike. The work stoppage was instigated when 19 teachers, mostly Jews, were dismissed because of their opposition to an experiment in decentralization of the New York City schools. When Superintendent Bernard Donovan rehired the teachers, their way was barred from entering the school by angry black parents. The teachers had to be escorted by the police, but the situation remained unresolved and led to a strike that 95 percent of the city educators supported.

The strike centered on racial and anti-Semitic issues because the teachers were mostly white and Jewish and their adversaries were black students and the black community. The subsequent introduction of decentralization and discriminatory hiring practices that were directed against Jewish teachers brought the JDL into the strike. They claimed that Jews were penalized when a merit system is replaced with the quota system in hiring. The JDL soon mobilized its resources to combat what it perceived as prejudice directed against the Jewish teachers. The teachers' strike marked a turning point in JDL's history as a force in the Jewish community. Soon it would become known throughout the country for its combativeness in the form of demonstrations and its willingness to encounter physically those perceived as threats to Jews, such as the attempt of Nazis to march in Skokie, Illinois.

Starting with 30 members at the first meeting, the JDL grew steadily, reaching its largest membership of 15,000 in 1972. The JDL placed offices in major American cities and college campuses and eventually in other countries: Canada, France, England, and Belgium. Jewish protection became an international concern.

In 1969, the JDL focused on the issue of Soviet Jewry and attracted national exposure by demonstrating at the Soviet Mission to the United Nations, Soviet travel agencies, the Soviet News Agency Tass, and the interruption of Soviet air service at Kennedy Airport. The JDL equated the treatment of Soviet Jews to European Jews during World War II, and the motto, "Never Again," became the JDL slogan. To bring national attention to their cause, the league announced a plan to help Soviet Jews by agitating against the ongoing American and Soviet exchange programs in sports and cultural and the trade negotiations between the United States and the Soviet Union.

In 1971, the JDL promoted Aliyah as part of its agenda. Only by returning to Israel, argued the leadership, could the Jews in Diaspora recapture their religious fervor and fight anti-Semitism effectively. If Jews stayed in America, they would be spiritually lost. In addition, the JDL believed, Jews throughout the world were needed in Israel to secure their ancient homeland from the ever growing Arab enemy. This fear of the Arabs and the safety of Israel led the JDL and Meir Kahane to call for the expulsion of all Arabs from Israel. In 1981, Kahane explained his expulsion policies in the book, *They Must Go.* Subsequently, Kahane and his family moved to Israel. He became the JDL's international chairman and was eventually elected to the Knesset in 1984. Bertram Zweibon became the new national chairman.

Undoubtedly, Kahane's move to Israel removed a charismatic leader from the American scene and hurt JDL's efforts to recruit followers. But the decline in JDL's membership had more to do with changes in its philosophy as well as accusations of extreme militant tactics, including bombings and other illegal aggressive tactics. As long as JDL addressed itself to the issues faced by Jews living in vulnerable communities, especially among the aged, the organization was able to generate membership and support. The shift to Middle East politics and the extreme ideology of Kahane's KACH party apparently cost the JDL many of its followers.

On November 5, 1990 Kahane was assassinated after making a speech at a New York City hotel. Thus, the JDL lost its most influential leader.

Sherry Ostroff

BIBLIOGRAPHY

Dolgin, Janet L. *Jewish Identity and the JDL.* Princeton, N.J.: Princeton University Press, 1977.

Friedman, Robert I. *The False Prophet: Rabbi Meir Kahane.* New York: Hill Books, 1990.

The Jewish Defender. 1981–(the JDL newspaper).

Kahane, Meir. *Never Again!* Los Angeles: Nash, 1971.

——. *Our Challenge: The Chosen Land.* Radnor, Pa.: Chilton, 1974.

——. *The Story of the Jewish Defense League.* Radnor, Pa.: Chilton Books, 1975.

——. *They Must Go.* New York: Grosset & Dunlap, 1981.

——. *Time to Go Home.* Los Angeles: Nash, 1972.

Mayer, Martin. *The Teachers Strike: New York 1968.* New York: Harper & Row, 1969.

Orbach, William W. *The American Movement to Aid Soviet Jews.* Amherst: University of Massachusetts Press, 1979.

Jewish Education. The education of Jews in America is a twofold tale: one of transplanting Judaism to the new world, adapting it to its new context and sustaining it as a living force in successive generations. The other, parallel history, is of an emerging American educational system and the evolving relations of Jews to it.

In the seventeenth and eighteenth centuries Jews were largely responsible for the Jewish and general education of their own children. By the mid-nineteenth century primary responsibility for the education of Jews had shifted to the emerging American system of public schools, and with that shift instruction for Jewish children became predominantly secular. Jewish education, if provided, was assigned a secondary, supplementary role. At present, a substantial majority of American Jewish youth attend public and secular private schools where, as a group, they have recorded high levels of achievement in their studies. A majority also receive supplementary Jewish schooling. A minority of Jewish children, however, are now receiving general and Jewish studies in Jewish day schools.

COLONIAL AND EARLY FEDERAL PERIOD.

The first Jewish settlers to North America, Sephardim from the Caribbean, arrived in New Amsterdam in 1654. Numerous restrictions were imposed on this small community, and religious and educational activities were carried on in the privacy of their homes. Throughout this period education was considered a private function, not a public responsibility. In addition, instruction in religion and in general subjects were inseparable in the popular imagination. Thus it was common practice for each church to provide religious and secular instruction to the children of its congregants. Further, churches in the colonial period, especially in towns with heterogeneous immigrant settlers, such as New Amsterdam (New York), tended to be religious-national institutions (Dutch and Dutch Reform, English and Anglican, Scots and Presbyterian, German and Lutheran, French and Huguenot, etc.). Thus the early association of the education of Jews with Jewish congregations was within the established religious-national-educational pattern. America had yet to arrive at the "common" school.

During the colonial period and well into the nineteenth century, education was not considered to be a Jewish communal responsibility in the same way as cemeteries, synagogues, and support of the Jewish poor. Parents were expected to pay for their own children's schooling (the general American practice of the period) by engaging tutors or sending them to private schools for both general and Jewish instruction. Some congregations, however, made some provision for the education of impoverished children.

Tutors and teachers of Jewish subjects were in short supply in the colonies, especially in light of a sparse and scattered Jewish population that numbered about 1200 by 1790. This led to intermittent instruction at such prominent congregations as Mikveh Israel in Philadelphia and Shearith Israel (the Spanish and Portuguese Synagogue) in New York.

The earliest known school under Jewish auspices was established in 1731 at Shearith Israel. A fee-paying school that focused on Hebrew studies, its first recorded teacher was the congregation's *hazzan* (rabbi-cantor). Later a *shamash* (teacher) was engaged. The school, although attached to the synagogue, was a separate entity with its own board. The congregation, however, did reserve a small number of places for the children of the poor.

In 1755, Shearith Israel established a "publik school" to teach Hebrew, Spanish, English, and secular subjects. The school functioned intermittently until the Revolutionary War, resuming its precarious existence in 1793. Reorganized as the Polonies Talmud Torah School in 1808, it functioned as a day school until 1821 and received New York State funds as part of New York's hybrid common school system to enable poor Jewish children to receive a common school education. This followed a similar practice at Protestant church schools, a practice that ended in 1842.

In 1821, the Polonies Talmud Torah was reorganized as a supplementary school, meeting in the late afternoons after "regular" school and confining its curriculum exclusively to Jewish studies. This school remained in existence until the Civil War.

There is no record that other eighteenth-century congregations such as Beth Elohim (Charleston, S.C.), Yeshuat Israel (Newport, R.I.), or Mikveh Israel (Philadelphia) organized instructional programs prior to the nineteenth century. To the extent that Jewish studies were pursued, the small American Jewish communities seemed to rely on private tutors, including tutoring by the *hazzan*. The level of Jewish learning was modest, and there was no instruction beyond the elementary level. But apparently it was adequate to provide the knowledge and skills necessary to participate in Jewish religious and communal life.

The earliest period of Jewish settlement in America left few "institutional" legacies to later immigrants. Several significant precedents were established, however, many of which persist to our day. Most significant, Jewish education had to mold itself to the American environment. It tacitly acknowledged the primacy of general studies and came to accept the time schedule of American education. Jewish education was adapted to fit within time not otherwise preempted by secular schooling, and English became the language of instruction for Jewish studies.

There was a general acceptance that secular and religious studies were divisible, and instruction for each could be offered in different institutions. Jews came to accept nonsectarian schools that eventually allowed Jewish children to prepare for full economic and political participation in American life. Jewish education was closely correlated with prevailing American educational practices, pedagogical as well as philosophical.

Elementary levels of Jewish learning came to be accepted as adequate for Jewish living, with "higher" learning provided for largely by relying on the immigration of more learned Jews from Europe. Early experience suggests an ambivalence regarding the congregation's role in the education of the young. In the early years most Jewish communities were small and functioned as a single congregation. Even then, relatively homogeneous communities did not perceive of education as a collective function. As the number of Jews increased by successive migrations, and communities became more heterogeneous, and as different religious tendencies and political ideologies emerged, it became even more difficult to foster the concept of community responsibility for the Jewish education of all its children.

Finally, with Jewish education cast as part time and supplementary, it contributed to the low status of the Jewish teacher, and, since instruction was confined to the elementary level, only a low level of skill was required to enter the field. This had a severe dampening effect on the quality of Jewish instruction and on the status of instructors.

ARRIVAL AND ESTABLISHMENT OF GERMAN JEWS, 1820s–1870s.

Ashkenazic Jews from German lands started arriving in the United States in appreciable numbers in the early nineteenth century and rapidly surpassed in size the small but long-settled and well-assimilated Sephardic community. By 1840, there were approximately 15,000 Jews in America, a substantial majority of whom were of German background, and by 1877 over 230,000.

When few in number, Ashkenazim shared religious and educational institutions provided by the Sephardic community. They were dissatisfied, however, with the quality and intensity of Jewish studies and were unfamiliar with the prevailing Sephardic *minhag* found in the synagogues. As their numbers grew they established congregations and schools to perpetuate their concept of Judaism and practice their own *minhag*.

The great educational innovation of the German-Jewish community, with the participation of other immigrant Ashkenazim, was the establishment of congregational day schools that offered secular and religious studies. Day schools were opposed by the settled, American-born Jewish community, which had largely been assimilated into the lifeways of American society.

B'nai Jeshurun, New York City's first Ashkenazic synagogue (1824), was the first to organize a day school (1842), which survived for five years. Three other New York German congregations were more successful: Ansche Chesed founded a school in 1845, which lasted 12 years, and shortly thereafter Rodeph Shalom and Shaarey Hashamayim. In 1849, Isaac M. Wise founded the Talmud Yeladim in Cincinnati, and in 1851 the Hebrew Educational Society was established in Philadelphia. By the early 1870s, however, the once burgeoning Jewish congregational day school movement had collapsed.

The 1840s and early 1850s were a time of rapid growth in the German Jewish population. It was also an era during which there still was virtually no public education in New York City, the site of America's largest Jewish community. A public board was created in 1842 to establish public schools, a time when the common school movement was already well advanced throughout much of the United States. Most schools in New York were still church related, and the Public School Society, a philanthropy organized early in the century to provide instruction to the city's poor, had a decidedly Protestant cast. Recently arrived German Jews lacked the resources to hire private tutors for their children's education, lacked funds to pay for middle-class private schools (which were, in any event, considered too Christian in character), and were not willing to send their young to Christian charity schools where the level of instruction was minimal. The Public School Society's schools were also free but employed the monitorial system where one teacher instructed a hundred and more children, using student monitors to do most of the direct teaching. German Jews were also concerned with providing Jewish studies, which were lacking in the city's established schools. The congregational-sponsored day schools thus met a real need in the German Jewish community. These schools all became coeducational, with girls making up about one-third of enrollments.

The rapid proliferation of day schools in New York City led to efforts at coordination. Rabbi-educator Max Lilienthal was brought to New York in 1845 to head Ansche Chesed, Rodeph Shalom, and Shaaray Hashamayim. He succeeded in getting them to merge their schools in 1847. This "Union School," however, lasted but a year when bonds were dissolved, and each congregation went its separate way.

The inability to coordinate efforts has been a persistent feature of Jewish education in America. With schools based in congregations, institutional particularism and loyalties ultimately have risen to the surface and inhibited interinstitutional collaboration. Even when the Jewish population seemed adequate to support intensive educational efforts, especially beyond the elementary level, existing institutional affiliations balkanized the population, no one segment of which was capable of the required effort nor commanded adequate resources. The weakness of community integration was a natural corollary of the voluntary nature of religion and religious institutional affiliation in America.

The constant in-migration of Jews from various lands to New York, Boston, Philadelphia, Baltimore, the Ohio and Mississippi valleys and beyond insured an increasingly heterogeneous and transient population and made the process of building voluntary communitywide organizations arduous and never ending. Especially with regard to education, the larger and more heterogeneous the community, the less likely one school program, encompassing both religious *and* secular instruction, would be acceptable to all.

Private Jewish day schools unattached to congregations also arose in this period. They were modeled after American private schools but with the inclusion of Jewish studies. The most prominent of these was established in New York City by Lilienthal in 1849, after leaving his congregational post. He moved to Cincinnati in 1855 and established another school, while his New York school was continued by the Rev. Mr. Henry. Wealthy Jews from New York and

other towns sent their boys and girls to these single-gender schools, most of which had boarding facilities, through most of the remainder of the century.

Most Jewish parents, however, could not afford high school fees. The public schools, which developed rapidly in New York City in the 1840s and 1850s, were attractive but the persistence of strong Protestant Christian influences in textbooks, prayer, Bible readings, and holiday celebrations dissuaded most Jews (and most Catholics as well, who objected strongly to the schools' anti-Catholic bias) from sending their children to these public institutions.

Changes in New York State education laws in the 1850s, however, addressed many of the concerns of Jewish parents. In 1855, local school boards were granted the powers to choose instructional materials, and reading from the Scriptures was made discretionary. As a result, overt Christian religious influences were considerably diluted. These changes, coupled with the demise of the monitorial system of instruction, were sufficient to win over many Jewish parents, who enrolled their children in record numbers. Jewish parents apparently were ready to accept the division of secular and religious instruction for their children, a step most Catholics were then not willing to take. While Jews reacted favorably to secularization of public education, Catholics were not prepared to split religious from general instruction. As a result, Catholics continued to develop their own parochial schools, while Jews rapidly abandoned congregational day schools. Before the end of the 1850s, all seven of New York City's congregational schools had closed their doors for lack of students, although private Jewish schools continued to function. There was an added incentive in the city for attending public school. Graduating from the public schools became a prerequisite for entering the Free Academy (1847), later the City College of New York.

The demise of the day school was not universally lamented in the Jewish community. By this time many German Jews were well assimilated into the American world, and there was growing concern that Jewish day schools acted as a wall separating the Jewish and Gentile communities. The movement of Jewish youth to the public schools, it was believed, would hasten the full incorporation of Jews into the American mainstream. Jews would henceforth be Americans in nationality and Jews in religion.

The separation of nationality and religion was an important aspect of mid-nineteenth century Reform Jewish thought and served to permit, and perhaps to encourage, the division of education between two agencies: public schools for secular studies, Jewish schools for supplementary religious instruction.

The rapid desertion of Jewish youth from Jewish day schools to the public schools created the need for supplementary Jewish schooling. Some synagogues started afternoon programs, but the most common form such schooling took was the Sabbath or Sunday school, which experienced rapid growth among the growing number of Reform congregations.

The first Sunday school was organized by Rebecca Gratz (1781–1869) at Philadelphia's Mikveh Israel, fashioned after the Protestant Sunday school, which had originated in the same city. At about the same time a Jewish Sunday school was opened in Richmond, Virginia. Many at the time acknowledged the limited instruction that could be offered in such schools. The development of Reform Judaism, which stressed Judaism as a universalistic rather than a particularistic religious lifeway of the Jewish people, permitted a paring down of the curriculum. Hebrew was generally excluded, as was the study of classical texts, except for the Bible in translation. The ethical monotheism of Judaism was stressed, especially in the resounding tones of the prophets. Acknowledging time limits and poorly prepared volunteer teachers, catechisms of the Jewish religion were prepared and published for use in the Sunday schools.

While Jews with even modest means had several educational options available to them, there was little or no provision for the Jewish education of the children of poor Jews. The opening of a Christian mission school on New York's Lower East Side in 1864 spurred the established Jews to act. Eleven congregations met and organized the Hebrew Free School Association, which opened Hebrew Free School No. 1, a day school teaching general and Jewish subjects, in 1865. Many in the community opposed separate day schools for the Jewish poor, preferring that they be educated in the American public school. School No. 1 closed in 1872 as a result of this opposition. Additional Hebrew free schools were opened, starting in 1866, but all were supplementary schools offering Hebrew and religious instruction, and attendance at public school became a precondition for enrollment. With time these schools, which enrolled more girls than boys, came to stress morality and were expected to exert a refining influence on their young scholars.

ARRIVAL OF EAST EUROPEAN JEWS. East European Ashkenazic Jews began arriving in small numbers after the Civil War. They were unhappy with available Jewish education. In New York City some of the more observant, who rejected the Hebrew Free School both in terms of its subject matter and its religious spirit, gravitated to Rabbi Pesach Rosenthal's Talmud Torah, which the rabbi had founded in 1857 to promote Torah learning and to provide assistance to impoverished youth. Yiddish served as the language of instruction, and the school, while supplementary, focused on traditional learning of Torah and Talmud.

Established Jews opposed the Talmud Torah for the very reason that its goal was to sustain East European religious practices and lifeways. They supported a Jewish education that facilitated assimilation: Americanization, vocational preparation, and cultural refinement.

East European Jews also established hederim as part of their effort to establish educational institutions they had known back home. Rabbis of small congregations would gather together 40 to 50 children, often in wretched physical quarters, after public school hours to learn mechanical reading of Hebrew, Sidur, Chumash, and Mishnah. Hundreds of hederim existed in New York City by 1890.

Rosenthal's school eventually became the Machazikai Talmud Torah (1883), and in 1886 New York's first yeshiva, Etz Chaim, was organized. While East Europeans struggled to establish institutions that they felt were needed to sustain Judaism in America, settled "uptown" Jews continued to expand mission social-work efforts among the ever growing population of "downtown" immigrant poor. The Down-Town Sabbath School is an example of such outreach efforts. Organized in the early 1880s by Mrs. Minnie Louis as a charitable venture of the Sisterhood of Temple Emanu-El, it became the Louis Down-Town Sabbath School in 1884, expanded to daily technical-vocational instruction for girls in 1887, and, passing through several changes, eventually became the Hebrew Technical School for Girls in 1899. Religious education, in effect, was displaced by what was considered the more pressing need for assistance in adapting immigrants to America.

The Hebrew Free School, whose enrollments had grown to 5000 by 1899, was forced to close due to lack of support, although religious instruction for the children of impoverished Lower East Siders was ostensibly assumed by the Educational Alliance.

The Educational Alliance, founded in 1889, became the prime institution through which established Jewish philanthropy sought to assist and transform immigrants. By the turn of the century New York had already become the largest Jewish city in the world and would become the residence for more than 1.5 million Jews by 1920. A substantial majority of New York's Jews had arrived within the past generation from Eastern Europe and lived in densely settled ethnic enclaves. It was the goal of the alliance to Americanize these immigrants, integrate them into America, and thereby to "dissolve the ghetto." Its extensive educational and social programs, however, were directed toward secular learning and rapid assimilation rather than to Jewish studies and maintenance of traditional lifeways (including "Halakic" observance).

By the end of the nineteenth century, settled American Jews had come to embrace American culture and integrated schooling, although two generations earlier they themselves had established separate schools and sought to preserve their inherited lifeways. The newly arrived immigrants were at the initial stage in their climb into America. They wished to preserve some of their Old-World ways and beliefs and wished to establish a form of Jewish education consistent with their vision of Judaism, the lifeways of Jews, and the place of Jews in America. Thus the clash was not just between the *minhag* of American Jews and newcomers, nor differences in "Halakic" interpretations, but a confrontation between old settlers at home in their American world and greenhorns recently cut from their ancestral moorings seeking a new equilibrium in a radically altered world.

Established Jews viewed Jewish education intended for immigrants as part of a larger strategy to transform them: modernize, secularize, Americanize, "enlighten" religiously, teach vocational skills for contemporary occupations, teach English, rid them of "Oriental" beliefs and lifeways, and thus facilitate their successful integration into American society. Settlement houses and mission schools would play a role, but enrollment of the children of immigrants in American public schools was critical to their design. The public schools were perfecting their curricula and practices to transform greenhorns into the model of

Americans and Jewish education was to complement that effort.

The education of Jews in Eastern Europe had functioned for centuries as a means of transmitting Jewish beliefs, knowledge, and lifeways. The traditional education of Jews showed signs of change in the second half of the nineteenth century under the combined influences of the Haskalah, urbanization, and industrialization. But for most Jews, education was a "conservative" force. In the New World the established Jews now wished to use Jewish education as an agent of "transformation." While immigrants, as a group, sensed the need to adapt to the American environment, religion and religious education were compartments of their lives to which, initially, they were least open to radical change.

From the very outset, however, East European Jewish immigrants accepted changes in secular instruction and overwhelmingly accepted the public schools for the general education of both their boys and girls. In part because of compulsory education laws (although these were in reality poorly enforced), the absence of Jewish day schools acceptable to traditionally observant Jews, the lack of immigrant community cohesion and organization necessary to establish a day school that offered traditional religious studies and simultaneously satisfied state education requirements, the strong encouragement and direction of established Jews and their social agencies to enroll children in public school (a majority of the children of established Jews already attended such schools), the lack of negative associations regarding public schools (as had been the case with government schools in Russia), the high reputation of many modern urban school systems, the participation of Jews in the public schools (Jacob Schiff, noted philanthropist who was held in high esteem by the immigrant community, was himself a member of the New York City Board of Education for most of the 1880s), and a strong desire on the part of immigrant parents and their children to learn the language and lifeways of their new land, Jewish children attended public schools in record numbers. In 1917, in New York City, for example, 277,000 Jewish children were enrolled in public schools and less than 1000 in the three existing Jewish day schools (Orthodox yeshivas).

Parents seek to prepare their children for adult life. In traditional societies, such as the Pale of Settlement, the education of the parent is usually appropriate for the child. In a rapidly changing world, parents—immigrant parents in particular—find it difficult to anticipate the adult world that their children will inhabit and the education that is appropriate. Jewish immigrant parents in this period let the public school take responsibility for secular education, preparing their young for an unknown American adult life. Immigrants themselves took responsibility for religious education, choosing Old-World practices with which they were familiar. Heder or private tutor (what one Jewish educator called a "peddler *melamed*") would provide the skills and knowledge needed to fulfill the role of a Jewish adult. They assumed that traditional beliefs and practices could be learned in traditional ways and that participation in the religious and secular Jewish community would be effectively the same in America as in Europe.

The children of immigrants, however, lacking Old-World consciousness and affective associations, did not always wish to recapitulate the lifeways of their parents. Jewish education, presented in Old-World garb, purveyed by a peddler *melamed* or heder *rav*, could only prepare them for a world they hoped to escape. Thus, in New York City in 1917, when virtually all school-aged Jewish children were attending public school, less than one-fourth were receiving any form of Jewish education.

The challenge to Jewish educators was to present a desirable adult Jewish world that was compatible with life in America and in which the young would wish to participate. The child who could be attracted to a Jewish school had been changed by the public school. The schools gave children American personae and helped to shape their interests and values. Secular school experiences also shaped their image of what a school was and how it functioned. They created in the minds of the children a model of "teacher" and of teacher-student relations and legitimized "women" teachers. They made English the functional language of the children and discredited Yiddish as a medium of communications. Schools also established standards of dress, personal hygiene and environmental cleanliness, and established models of school building design.

THE NEW JEWISH EDUCATION. Samson Benderly (1876–1944), the father of modern Jewish education in America, was born in the Levant, raised in Safed, and studied medicine in Baltimore, where he became professionally involved in Jewish education. Called to New York City in 1910 to organize and head the Bureau of Jewish Education, part of the recently founded Kehillah of New York City, he set forth the bureau's agenda in a letter to the Kehillah's president, Judah Magnes. Jews, he argued, were integral members of the American republic, and thus the task confronting Jewish educators was twofold: to Americanize in the best sense and to build a viable Jewish culture in America. "As the great public school system is the rock bottom upon which this country is rearing its institutions, so we Jews must evolve here a system of Jewish education that shall be complementary to and harmonious with the public system."

Benderly and Rabbi Mordecai Kaplan (1881–1983), founding head of the Teachers Institute at the Jewish Theological Seminary of America, set out to identify the best and brightest college graduates of the day, and attract them to the field of Jewish education. Education, rather than serving to transmit traditional knowledge and beliefs, would become the moving force behind the enlightenment of Jewish immigrants and the reconstruction of Judaism in America. The settled Jewish community had also sought to create a "transformative" educational system to assimilate rapidly immigrant Jews into American society. But the transformation that the new Jewish educators wished to bring about did not posit an assimilated Anglo-American future, but a bicultural world, with Jews actively living and participating in both. The Jewish world was represented by Cultural Zionism: a modern, enlightened Judaism, proud of its classical roots but aware of itself as an active cultural force in the contemporary world, a culture that embraced Hebrew as its living language. The Cultural Zionists, strongly influenced by Ahad Ha'Am, infected by the worldwide rise in nationalism and the movement for the self-determination of peoples, perceived the possibility of a Jewish renascence under liberal democratic regimes. Here in America was an opportunity to merge the best of modern Western and Jewish thought and practice.

There was a need, at the very outset, to build up Jewish self-esteem, especially among the children of immigrants, to increase the level of Jewish knowledge, especially modern Hebrew, and to create authentic opportunities to participate in contemporary Jewish life. Their programs reinforced modernization efforts of schools and settlement houses but ran counter to extreme Americanization goals. The intention of the new Jewish educators was not to facilitate complete assimilation into American society, retaining only a limited self-contained Jewish religion. They wished to nurture a Jewish cultural life in America, parallel to and compatible with American culture, and teach Jewish youth how to participate in both to the mutual enhancement of each.

The new Jewish educators were not opposed to religious instruction, and they included study of religious practice in their curricula, but their interests were more broadly directed at Judaism as a civilization—with a history, a culture, and a language along with a religion. They hoped to offer a community-based education, serving all segments of the Jewish population: all religious denominations, secular Jews, politically radical Jews, Yiddishists, nationalists, and Zionists. Their intention was to strengthen community-wide allegiances and to raise ethnic consciousness rather than to reinforce "Halakic" practice.

The Bureau of Jewish Education was the institutional manifestation of the new Jewish education. Through it Benderly and his disciples intended to raise the relevance and quality of instruction, increase the distressingly low proportion of Jewish children receiving Jewish education, and support "modernization." In the words of Alexander Dushkin (1890–1976), Benderly and Kaplan's first recruit, it was to play a major role "in the solution of the fundamental problem in the creation of a wholesome Jewish life in America—the problem of identifying the Jewish child with the Jewish people. . . . Education has probably never meant as much to the preservation of any group life, as Jewish education means at this moment to the continued life of our people" (*The Jewish Teacher*, inaugural issue, 1916).

Coupled to the mission of Jewish survival in America was the bureau's stress on community responsibility for Jewish education. Individual religious denominations and ideological and philosophical schools, each offering its own education, would divide and segment the Jewish community. What was needed, the bureau's leaders believed, was a Jewish "common" school to serve all factions, to promote a sense of *k'lal Yisrael*, and to transmit the cultural and historical, as well as religious, heritage common to all Jews.

Lacking the financial resources to found a school system of their own, they chose to work with the eight largest Talmud Torahs (community- and not congregation-based supplementary schools) in New York City. The bureau worked to improve the efficiency of school organization and to rationalize finances. The staff worked at improving and enhancing the curriculum, especially by promoting the Direct Method of Hebrew instruction (*Ivrit b'Ivrit*) that was gaining ground in such cities as Baltimore and Detroit. They also tried to include materials related to modern Jewish history, contemporary Jewish events, and the Jewish arts.

Benderly recruited a corps of exceptionally talented college men and women to the field. The original disciples represent a "who's who" of twentieth-century Jewish educators. In addition to Dushkin, they included Isaac Berkson (1891–1975), Emanuel Gamoran (1895–1962), and Albert Schoolman (1894–1980). Also recruited were Israel S. Chipkin, Rabbi Bernard Brickner, Rebecca Aronson Brickner, Samuel Dinin, Jacob Golub, Leo Honor, Mordecai Soltes, Libbie Suchoff Berkson, David Rudavsky, and Samuel Citron.

The recruits were educated at both the Teachers Institute and Teachers College, Columbia University. At the Jewish Theological Seminary they were imbued with the mission of Jewish education, Cultural Zionism and the zeal and intellectual acumen of Kaplan, Benderly, and Israel Friedlaender (1876–1920). At Teachers College they were exposed to the new American progressive education as they worked under John Dewey, Edward Thorndike, and their colleagues.

The need to put Jewish learning into practice, to demonstrate that Judaism was a living culture, melded exceedingly well with Dewey's pedagogical philosophy of "learning by doing." The American educated professionals that the bureau sought to develop were to serve as living models of ideal Jewish life in the contemporary age. They were the pioneers who would demonstrate the strength, vitality, and value of a bicultural world, of the inestimable value of Judaism as a living religion and dynamic culture, and of Judaism's real potential for enhancing American life.

The active new Jewish education went beyond the classroom to weekend events and retreats, to clubs and organizations, to vacation programs, and, perhaps its most innovative idea, to the Jewish camp. Jewish camping featured learning and living in a modern Jewish lifestyle, including the arts, intellectual study, social comaraderie, learning and use of modern Hebrew, as well as ritual observances. In 1919, Albert Schoolman, then director of the innovative Central Jewish Institute, a supplementary Jewish school and social center serving the Yorkville

(N.Y.C.) neighborhood, founded Camp Cejwin. Dushkin and Berkson participated in this venture, which was supported by Rabbi Kaplan. A second camp, Modin, followed in 1922. Eventually all denominations and most secular branches of the Jewish community organized camps to provide authentic experiences in Jewish living.

The New York Kehillah failed at the time of World War I. The bureau continued in various institutional forms, but its ambitions were greatly reduced. The young people it had recruited and trained could not be retained. New York's loss was to become American Judaism's gain as these people scattered across the nation, helping to establish and run city bureaus of Jewish education. Between 1915 and 1938 bureaus were started in Minneapolis, Pittsburgh, Detroit, Baltimore, Boston, Chicago, Cleveland, Indianapolis, Cincinnati, Saint Louis, Buffalo, Los Angeles, Essex County (N.J.), Washington, D.C., and Omaha. An important outgrowth of several bureaus was the founding of Hebrew teachers colleges to train modern Jewish educators (as in Chicago, Cleveland, Boston, and Baltimore).

RISE OF THE CONGREGATIONAL SCHOOL. Bureaus across the United States attempted to promote the idea of community-based schools. But the Talmud Torah did not readily translate to the new communities where Jews were settling. Jews were moving out of areas of initial immigrant settlement to newer urban neighborhoods and suburbs. Whereas the densely settled and homogeneous Jewish neighborhoods were able to support an array of Jewish institutions (from burial societies to free loan associations), these function-specific organizations, including Jewish schools, found it difficult to reestablish themselves in more sparsely settled and heterogeneous communities. The synagogue as Jewish center took on much greater prominence than in older, more Jewishly homogeneous neighborhoods and gathered up the separate functions into itself.

The Jewish centers became, in effect, Jewish department stores, attempting to meet all of the Jewish needs of their congregants, including education. In addition, the competition for membership among denominations was a strong argument for a congregation to organize a school. In most communities congregations were unwilling to abdicate this responsibility or to share it with an independent community-based Talmud Torah.

The return to congregational schools, the nineteenth-century practice, and the move away from the Talmud Torah, heder and private tutor had the effect of reinforcing sectarian differences within the Jewish community. Against the backdrop of a volatile, heterogeneous, and rapidly growing Jewish population in early twentieth-century America, it is not surprising that each religious denomination and ideological group (Yiddishists, nationalists, and radicals organized their own schools) wanted to safeguard and transmit their point of view and gain new adherents. Education was central to their ends and could not be abdicated to a third, presumably "neutral," party. The congregational schools helped to define and promote the views of each denomination and establish a common *minhag* within each and to transmit it to successive generations. But it did not reinforce the sense of community and commitment to *k'lal Yisrael* that the new Jewish educators had sought.

The return of the congregation school as the norm for Jewish education meant that the focus of instruction was religion, with less attention devoted to other than religious aspects of Cultural Zionism. Following the Holocaust and the establishment of Israel, these two seminal events have been incorporated into the supplementary schools' curriculum.

The Yiddishists, nationalists, and radicals were far less successful than denominational Judaism in surviving the move to the suburbs. The economic mobility associated with moves to new neighborhoods undercut the ideological bases of radical programs, and the geographic mobility to English-speaking environments undermined Yiddish cultural efforts. In diminished form and altered shape, however, Yiddishist programs continue to this day. The nationalist's message became incorporated within Zionism and attached to the State of Israel, and it became part of the life of Jewish centers.

CONTEMPORARY JEWISH EDUCATION. From the 1930s to the present, congregational schools have dominated supplementary Jewish education. Enrollments in all forms of Jewish education peaked in the mid-sixties at over 550,000 and have declined since, largely due to the end of the baby boom and other demographic changes within the American Jewish community. By the mid-eighties enrollments stood at about 375,000, of which 90 percent were in congregational schools. Approximately 80 percent of all Jewish children (about 900,000 of school age in the mid-

1980s) received some Jewish education during their school years, although at any one time only about 40 percent of preschool through high school students are actually enrolled. Enrollments are highest for those aged 10–12 (nearly 70 percent) and decline precipitously after bar/bat Mitvah age (35 percent of 13–15 year olds, and 12 percent of 16–17 year olds). In relative terms, however, these proportions are substantially higher than those encountered earlier in the century.

For most youth, Jewish school is confined to the elementary level and lasts for only a few years. In recent years, however, secondary enrollments have grown.

One of the major changes in Jewish education over the last half-century has been the growth of Jewish day schools. Once again, as in the colonial period and the mid-nineteenth century, both the general and Jewish education of a number of Jewish children is offered under Jewish auspices.

The growth of the small day-school sector was spurred initially by the arrival of ultra-Orthodox Hasidim, refugees fleeing Europe before and after World War II. Unlike previous Jewish immigrants, the ultra-Orthodox had no wish to be integrated socially into American society. They preferred living in a separated community shielded from secular and Gentile life. They were never interested in placing their children in American public schools, nor did they wish to separate general from religious instruction, both of which had to conform to Orthodox precept and practice. To prepare their children for their adult roles, they had to provide them with a Jewish education under strict religious control. They developed schools for their boys and separate schools for their girls in order to prepare them for life as observant, ultra-Orthodox Jews.

Other Orthodox groups also fostered day schools, albeit with more emphasis on secular studies and on seeking a constructive synthesis of general and Jewish worlds. Yeshiva University in New York, and its affiliated day schools for boys (founded 1916) and girls (1948), served as models for such schooling.

In the recent past the Conservative Movement has established Solomon Schechter day schools in over 60 communities, and the Reform Movement has also begun to found day schools. An increasing number of Jews, most of whom were born and educated in America, no longer feel that they have to send their children to public schools to make them Americans.

At present over 100,000 Jewish children attend day schools, approximately 75 percent of whom are enrolled in Orthodox-related schools, 12 percent in Conservative, 2 percent in Reform, and 11 percent in interdenominational or independent Jewish schools. Day school enrollments account for about 20 percent of all children receiving Jewish education, but these figures still represent only a modest proportion of all Jewish youth.

Even though day schools represent a growing sector in Jewish education, they do not represent a coherent movement. The motives, means, and goals of the various day schools and their sponsors are extremely varied.

The growth of Jewish studies on American university and college campuses is the second significant change in the Jewish education of Jewish youth since World War II. Over 300 schools offer Jewish studies programs, and more than 150 have professorial chairs in Jewish studies. The sometimes elementary level of Jewish education often has been criticized. At present, however, there is a growing number of Jewish young adults enrolling in university-level Jewish-content courses, at the most intellectually active period in their lives. Although many take introductory-level courses, significant numbers continue to higher academic levels, including graduate study.

The future of Jewish studies on American campuses will be of great interest. The potential to become knowledgeable and to live in two worlds and seek a creative interaction of the two, the goal of the new Jewish educators early in the century, may see its realization at the American college at the end of the century. In addition, for the first time the study of Jewish subject matter has been extended to the non-Jewish community, as many non-Jews enroll in classes. Jewish thought, beliefs, values, and culture have begun to be infused into the general education of Americans. The creative interaction of two cultures, another goal of the new Jewish educators, may find its realization within American higher education. *See also* Jewish Studies.

STEPHAN F. BRUMBERG

BIBLIOGRAPHY

Berkson, Isaac. *Theories of Americanization.* New York: Arno Press, 1969.

Berman, Jeremiah. "Jewish Education in New York City, 1860–1900." *YIVO Annual of Jewish Social Science* 9 (1954): 247–275.

Brumberg, Stephan F. *Going to America, Going to School: The Jewish Immigrant Public School Encounter in*

Turn-of-the-Century New York City. New York: Praeger, 1986.

Dushkin, Alexander M. *Jewish Education in New York City.* New York: Columbia University Press, 1918.

Friedlaender, Israel. "The Problem of Jewish Education in America and the Bureau of Education of the Jewish Community of N.Y.C." In *Report of the Commissioner of Education for the Year Ending June 30, 1913.* Vol. 1. Washington, D.C.: Department of the Interior, Bureau of Education, 1913. Pp. 365–393.

Gamoran, Emanuel. *Changing Conceptions in Jewish Education.* New York: MacMillan, 1924.

Grinstein, Hyman B. *The Rise of the Jewish Community of New York, 1654–1860.* Philadelphia: Jewish Publication Society, 1945.

Honor, Leo. "Jewish Elementary Education in the United States (1901–1950)." *Publication of the American Jewish Historical Society.* 42 (September 1952): 1–42.

Pilch, Judah, ed. *A History of Jewish Education in America.* New York: American Association for Jewish Education, 1969.

Skirball, Henry. *Isaac Baer Berkson and Jewish Education.* Ph.D. dissertation, Teachers College, Columbia University, 1977.

Sklare, Marshall, ed. *The Jewish Community in America.* New York: Behrman House, 1974.

Winter, Nathan. *Jewish Education in a Pluralist Society.* New York: New York University Press, 1966.

Jewish Encyclopedia

Jewish Encyclopedia (1901–1906). The 12-volume *Jewish Encyclopedia* was the first comprehensive collection of all available material pertaining to Jews—their history, literature, philosophy, rituals, sociology, and biography. Published in English in New York and compiled by an editorial board of prominent Jewish scholars in America, the work marks the emergence of Jewish scholarship in America.

The *Jewish Encyclopedia* was designed to combat growing anti-Semitism by demonstrating the worth of the Jew and his religion throughout the ages. It was also meant as a summary and continuation of *Wissenschaft des Judentums* (the Science of Judaism). Finally, American Jewry was coming of age, with cultural and religious life emerging in their own right. Some Jewish leaders hoped the encyclopedia would promote this flowering while also establishing the scholarly credentials of American Jewry.

Unable to publish a Jewish encyclopedia in Europe, Isidore Singer, managing editor of the *Jewish Encyclopedia*, came to the United States (1895). A promoter of outlandish and largely unrealizable schemes, Singer was also committed to combatting anti-Semitism and furthering ecumenism and universalism. Isaac Funk, a Lutheran minister and chairman of Funk & Wagnalls, shared Singer's goals, and his company agreed to publish the work. After protests concerning the motives and qualifications of Singer, an editorial board of prominent Jewish scholars was constituted. Volume I appeared in 1901, at which time it became apparent that the project was too costly and inefficient. Publication was suspended for several months until several wealthy Jews, including Jacob Schiff and Cyrus Sulzberger, guaranteed the project.

The editorial board, including Cyrus Adler, Gotthard Deutsch, Louis Ginzberg, Richard Gottheil, Emil G. Hirsch, Joseph Jacobs, Marcus Jastrow, Morris Jastrow, Kaufmann Kohler, Herman Rosenthal, Solomon Schechter, and Isidore Singer, supervised the work's content. They were aided by hundreds of world-renowned scholars. Collaborators disagreed on many religious and communal issues, yet they decided to present critically and objectively the results of modern scholarship, including critical Bible scholarship. They also agreed to describe Judaism without promoting any particular viewpoint. While these decisions did not always work out as hoped, a shared commitment to underlying goals held the editors together.

The *Jewish Encyclopedia* is an important record of the state of Jewish knowledge and the views and priorities of Jewish leaders at the turn of the twentieth century. Entries reflect the influence of Reform and tensions over higher biblical criticism. Articles poignantly illustrate both the insecurity of Jews as well as their fundamental optimism that education could dispel prejudice. The work is also testimony of the efforts of Jewish leaders to promote American Jewish scholarship and culture.

The *Jewish Encyclopedia* was a crucial link in the transference of Jewish scholarship from Europe to America and its language from German to English, thereby endowing the American center with needed respectability. Young scholars, such as Louis Ginzberg, honed their skills on the encyclopedia and then went on to make major contributions to Jewish scholarship. The project provided a successful model of cooperation that inspired subsequent efforts. Finally, the *Jewish Encyclopedia* stimulated new research and other encyclopedias of Judaica. It became the standard against which subsequent reference works were measured, and it was not eclipsed until the publication of the *Encyclopaedia Judaica* (1971).

SHULY RUBIN SCHWARTZ

BIBLIOGRAPHY

Brisman, Shimeon. *A History and Guide to Judaic Encyclopedias and Lexicons*. Hoboken, N.J.: HUC, Ktav, 1987.

Schwartz, Shuly Rubin. *The Emergence of Jewish Scholarship in America: The Publication of the Jewish Encyclopedia*. Cincinnati: HUC Press, 1991.

Jewish Publication Society of America.

On June 3, 1888, the Jewish Publication Society of America (JPS) was formally constituted for the third time in Philadelphia by Rabbi Joseph Krauskopf (1858-1923) and Solomon da Silva Solis-Cohen (1857-1948) as an annual membership organization. Its purpose from the very beginning was to publish and disseminate quality works of Jewish literature, history, and religion. It had been established twice before as the American Jewish Publication Society—the first time in 1845 by Isaac Leeser, lasting until 1851, and the second time by a New York group in 1873, lasting only until 1875.

The JPS has grown from a membership of 882 in January 1889 to approximately 15,000 in 1988. By 1988, it had published over 820 books and distributed over 8 million volumes all over the world.

From the beginning, the editorial board of the JPS enriched the average Jewish reader with rich and varied traditions of Judaism through historical scholarship. The first book to be published was *Outline of Jewish History* by Lady Katie Magnus. Between 1891 and 1898, the society published the six-volume English edition of Heinrich Graetz's monumental eleven-volume *History of the Jews*. Another major undertaking was the publication of Louis Ginzberg's seven-volume work *Legends of the Jews* (1903-1938). In 1952, the society arranged with noted historian Salo Baron to reissue *A Social and Religious History of the Jews*. The first two volumes were brought out in 1952 and the eighteenth in 1983. Over the years the society has published several briefer histories, such as *A History of the Jewish People* by Alexander Marx and Max Margolis, and many monographs, including Cecil Roth's *Venice* (1930) and *A History of the Marranos* (1932,

1947), *The Pharisees* (1938) by Louis Finkelstein, *The Jews of Georgian England, 1714-1839* (1979) by Todd M. Endelman, *Mandarins, Jews, and Missionaries* (1980) by Michael Pollak and *Tsar Nicholas I and the Jews* (1983) by Michael Stanislawski.

From 1919 to 1950, the society operated as a Hebrew-English press, through gifts of Jacob H. Schiff. Since 1899, it has annually issued the *American Jewish Year Book* (AJYB), which since 1908 has been a joint venture with the American Jewish Committee. The AJYB provides demographics and developments within the Jewish community through an annual survey and analysis of significant sociological and cultural trends.

A major undertaking by the society was the English translation of the Old Testament or Tanach (1917-1925). A second translation to accommodate changes in language and new findings in biblical research appeared in three volumes: *The Torah* (1962), *The Prophets* (1978), and *The Writings* (1981).

The JPS does not limit its publications to works of scholarship. It has also published a number of important works of fiction, art, poetry and children's literature by such authors as Israel Zangwill, Sholem Asch, Joseph Opatoshu, Ludwig Lewisohn, Charles Resnikoff, C. N. Bialik, Linda Heller, and Mira Meier. In 1979-1980, it inaugurated a series of English translations of contemporary Hebrew poetry.

The JPS has been involved in sending books to Soviet Jews through Project Sefer in hopes of encouraging the continuation and growth of Jewish culture in the USSR. It has also cooperated with the Jewish Braille Institute of America and has prepared a large-print edition of the Torah for the visually handicapped.

No publishing house has been as dedicated to the furtherance of Jewish publishing and the cultivation of Jewish scholarship and literacy as has the Jewish Publication Society. *See also* Publishing.

MICHAEL N. DOBKOWSKI
JANET L. DOTTERER

BIBLIOGRAPHY

Dobkowski, Michael N., ed. *Jewish American Voluntary Organizations*. Westport, Conn.: Greenwood Press, 1986.

The Jewish Publication Society of America Twenty-Fifth Anniversary. Philadelphia: Jewish Publication Society, 1913.

Madison, Charles. *Jewish Publishing in America*. New York: Sanhedrin Press, 1976.

Sarna, Jonathan. *JPS: The Americanization of Jewish Culture, 1888–1988.* Philadelphia: Jewish Publication Society, 1989.

Jewish Studies. Jewish Studies—research and teaching of postbiblical Jewish history, literature, and thought—are now part of many college curricula in the United States. These are recent developments due to heightened Jewish self-awareness after the Six-Day War of 1967, the African-American and ethnic consciousness that emerged during the late 1960s, growing awareness of the losses of the Holocaust, a diversification of the curriculum during the 1970s, and intensive support by individuals, communities, and faculty members during the 1980s. However, this growth was facilitated by the long-standing receptivity of American colleges to the study of Hebraica and Judaica as well as the presence of strong academic institutions established by the American Jewish community.

After several centuries as an academic endeavor developed by Christian scholars in Europe, often for conversionary purposes, during the seventeenth century Jewish studies reached the new colleges in the American colonies along with Jewish colonists. Hebrew was required at Harvard from the school's beginning; many students wrote theses about Hebrew and attempted to prove that it was the original language. Nevertheless, to teach Hebrew at Harvard, Judah Monis (1683–1764), a rabbi of obscure origins, had to convert before he could receive his appointment in 1722. Ezra Stiles (1725–1795), a minister who had studied Hebrew and Kabbalah in Newport with Raphael Hayyim Carigal, an itinerant rabbi and kabbalist, made Hebrew a required subject at Yale when he was president there, 1778–1795. Chairs in Hebrew were established at Princeton and the schools that would later be called Columbia and the University of Pennsylvania. These classes were taught primarily for Christian divinity students by Christian instructors. Despite these early efforts, the study of Hebrew began to wane because, as colleges shifted from training clergy to providing general education for the young men of the new nation, the curriculum became more practical and less classical. In 1787, Hebrew became an optional subject at Harvard, and the professor of Oriental languages switched to teaching English. The swan song for colonial Semitics study was the last Hebrew oration delivered at the Harvard commencement of 1817.

Despite attempts made by European Jewish scholars of *Wissenschaft des Judentums* (the scientific study of Judaism) to introduce their field into the curriculum of the universities there, it was in America that the first Jewish scholar with modern training was appointed to a university position in Semitics.

Isaac Nordheimer (1809–1842), the first avowedly Jewish professor in the United States, taught, for no salary, at the new New York University from 1836 until 1842 in addition to the Union Theological Seminary, inaugurating a long tradition of Semitic study there. It has been suggested that Nordheimer flirted with Christianity, but this can be validated neither in the reminiscences of a Christian colleague used for proof of such an assertion, nor in accounts of his life written by other Christian contemporaries. In 1871, Rabbi Abram Isaacs, an alumnus of New York University who had received further training in Breslau, was appointed to teach at his alma mater, rising to the professorship of Semitics in 1889. In 1874, the newly opened Cornell University hired Felix Adler (1851–1933), the son of a prominent New York Reform rabbi, as a professor of Hebrew and Oriental languages. At the time, this arrangement, financed by members of his father's synagogue, was unique for an American college. When, a few years later, Adler left academe, Jewish studies would remain divided between Christian Hebraists (usually clergymen) at the universities and European-trained Jewish scholars at Jewish community institutions. In 1875, Isaac Mayer Wise (1819–1900), once offered the help of Senator Daniel Webster to secure a position at Boston University in 1849, founded Hebrew Union College in Cincinnati to train Reform rabbis, and in 1885, Sabato Morais (1823–1897) opened the Jewish Theological Seminary in New York to train more traditional rabbis. These seminaries would attract many European Jewish scholars and rabbis to the United States.

At the end of the nineteenth century some American Jews, largely from the Reform Movement and often sons of leading pulpit rabbis, having earned doctorates in Europe, began to teach Semitics and rabbinics at major American universities, such as Columbia [Richard Gottheil (1862–1936), in 1886], Johns Hopkins [Cyrus Adler (1863–1940), in 1888; William Rosenau (1865–1943), in 1902], the University of Pennsylvania [Morris Jastrow, Jr. (1861–1921), in 1892], the University of Chicago [Emil G. Hirsch (1851–1923), in 1892], Temple [Joseph Levy (1865–

1917), in 1893], Berkeley [Max Margolis (1886–1932), in 1897; William Popper (1874–1963), in 1905], and the University of California [Jacob Voorsanger (1852–1908), in 1894]. These men, who sometimes taught for no pay or for a subsidy provided by the Jewish community, attracted both Jewish and Christian students, but they did not produce any widespread dissemination of Jewish studies on American campuses.

The important work in Jewish studies was done at institutions developed by the Jewish community. In 1888, the Jewish Publication Society was founded to help publish basic Hebrew texts, English translations of important works, and new scholarship. In 1892, the American Jewish Historical Society was established to promote research in American Jewish history. From 1901–1906, *The Jewish Encyclopedia*, the first systematic presentation of Jewish scholarship, was published in the United States, by Isaac Funk, a Christian minister.

In 1902–1903, three men who would do much to promote Jewish studies in America received appointments at important institutions. As president of the Conservative Jewish Theological Seminary, Solomon Schechter (1847–1915) would gather there some of the finest Jewish scholars in America and Europe, eventually including Israel Davidson (1870–1939), Louis Ginzburg (1873–1953), Israel Friedlaender (1876–1920), Alexander Marx (1878–1953), and Mordecai Kaplan (1881–1983). Similarly, as president of Hebrew Union College, Kaufmann Kohler (1843–1926) assembled a distinguished faculty, including Gotthard Deutsch (1859–1921), Moses Buttenweiser (1862–1939), David Neumark (1866–1924), Henry Malter (1864–1925), Jacob Lauterbach (1873–1942), Julian Morgenstern (1881–1976), Jacob Mann (1888–1940), Jacob R. Marcus (b. 1896), and, for a short time, Max Margolis (1886–1932). George Foote Moore (1851–1931), professor of religion at Harvard, developed the academic study of religion by combining German scientific standards with an American openness for Jews and the study of Judaism.

During this period of expansion of the field, Dropsie College, an institution devoted exclusively to postgraduate study of Hebrew, Semitics, and rabbinics, opened in Philadelphia in 1907. The mantle of Jewish scholarship unofficially passed from the old world to the new in 1910 when the *Jewish Quarterly Review* moved from England to Dropsie College. Institutions devoted to Jewish studies continued to emerge in the United States, Europe, and Palestine. Local Hebrew colleges in many major cities offered preparatory programs for high school students and courses for college credit, while several new Jewish seminaries, such as the Chicago Hebrew Theological College (1922) and the Jewish Institute of Religion in New York (1922), provided opportunities for faculty and made graduate courses available. Important Judaica and Hebraica collections continued to grow at major universities, at the Jewish seminaries, and at public institutions such as the New York Public Library and the Library of Congress. In 1915, the Alexander Kohut Memorial Foundation was established to support the publication of Jewish scholarship. In 1916, Bernard Revel (1885–1940), a Dropsie graduate and head of what would later be called Yeshiva University, tried to establish a Society of Jewish Academicians of America. Because Revel announced the provision that "scientific truth will have to be sacrificed to tradition," his plan came to naught until the idea was revived in 1920 and the American Academy of Jewish Research was established to promote Jewish scholarship in the United States.

Despite the slow acceptance of Jews into the ranks of American faculties, Jewish studies continued to emerge at secular colleges, and prominent scholars in areas of Jewish studies received appointments. In 1924, David Blondheim (1884–1934), a pioneer in the study of Judeo-Romance dialects, began to teach Romance languages at Johns Hopkins. In 1925, a chair in Jewish studies at Harvard was established by Lucius N. Littauer. This was the first chair in Jewish studies in the United States; until 1958, this position was occupied by Harry A. Wolfson (1887–1974), a student of Moore's who had been teaching Jewish studies at Harvard since 1915. In 1930, a chair in Jewish history was endowed by Linda Miller at Columbia; it was held until 1968 by Salo W. Baron (1895–1989). Wolfson and Baron produced graduate students who would determine the contours of the field for a long time.

During the 1930s, influenced by the renaissance of Hebrew language and literature in Eastern Europe and Palestine, there was a growing interest in the study of Hebrew in the United States. As a result, Hebrew was introduced in the New York City public high schools. This movement soon reached the colleges and, in 1934, New York University (the institution that had the largest Jewish student body in the world but not a single Jewish instructor until 1930) began to offer modern Hebrew, taught by Abraham Katsh (b. 1908), in the Division of General Education. Although there was a course in Jewish history at this time at City College, Hebrew was not introduced there until 1948. By the 1940s, about a dozen colleges offered modern Hebrew, in addition to the 77 colleges and 47 seminaries that taught biblical Hebrew. Some of the schools that introduced modern Hebrew included standard bastions of Semitics such as Pennsylvania, Hopkins, Chicago, Harvard, Columbia, and Yeshiva, as well as large universities, often with sizable Jewish enrollments such as Buffalo, Boston, Brooklyn, Colorado, Missouri, Wayne State, and Houston.

Courses in modern Hebrew and Jewish studies were also offered during the 1930s and 1940s at Smith, a small but prominent women's liberal arts college with few Jews. For a year or two the Hebrew course, which included "readings from Modern Hebrew schoolbooks," was taught by Cyrus Gordon (b. 1908). Beginning in the academic year 1940-1941, S. Ralph Harlow (1885-1972), a minister and scholar who received an honorary doctorate from Hebrew Union College, taught a course in Contemporary Judaism.

Although by 1945 some schools had let their Semitics programs lapse (including New York University, Cornell, and Buffalo), there were now about a dozen full-time positions around the country in Jewish studies. After the establishment of the State of Israel in 1948, Jewish studies, especially courses on Israel and Hebrew, were introduced at schools with both large and small Jewish enrollments, such as Vanderbilt, Illinois, Texas, Maryland, Iowa, Wisconsin, Wayne State, Cornell, Pennsylvania, Temple, Yale, Kentucky, the New School, Teachers College (Columbia), Alabama, Miami, Rutgers, Western Reserve, and Omaha. Also at this time Brandeis University, opened in 1948 as a secular university supported by the American Jewish community, developed a Department of Near Eastern and Judaic Studies. The first chair was Simon Rawidowicz (1896-1957) who, as the Philip Lown Professor of Jewish Philosophy and Hebrew Literature, taught courses in Jewish thought and literature. At most schools, however, courses in Jewish studies were mainly taught by Hillel directors, leaders of Jewish educational agencies, and special appointees. By 1956, 48 colleges and universities offered modern Hebrew, and 133 colleges and 112 seminaries taught biblical Hebrew. In 1958, the National Defense Educational Act gave added impetus to the study of foreign languages, including modern Hebrew. By 1966, throughout the country, there were 54 professors and 34 Hillel directors who offered Jewish studies at 92 colleges and universities. Despite this growth, in 1966, Jewish students still were not turning out in large numbers of courses in Jewish studies and non-Jewish participation was dismissed as negligible—one notable exception being the presence at Smith College of Jochanan H. A. Wijnhoven (1927-1988), an expert in Kabbalah and Jewish religious thought who had degrees from Hebrew University and Brandeis. Because there were more positions than trained candidates, questions were raised about the qualifications of many people who were hired to teach during this period of expansion. Also at this time, on the undergraduate level, the number of women students equaled or exceeded that of men, but at the graduate level, most of the students were men and faculty members were routinely referred to as men.

In 1969, the year that the Association for Jewish Studies was established, there were over 80 full-time positions and another 200 part-time appointments. During the 1970s, interest in the study of modern Hebrew continued to grow while national trends indicated decreased participation in language courses. During the 1980s, after a period of recession in university growth, important programs in Jewish studies have thrived at major research universities, such as the Ivy League schools and leading state university systems, while new chairs in Jewish studies are still being established at small colleges such as the Seven Sisters schools. In addition, most major academic presses publish works in Jewish studies.

Jewish studies have succeeded in providing unprecedented opportunities for widespread exposure to serious, creative, critical scholarship of the Jewish experience by Jews and non-Jews. Despite the great strides made by Jewish studies programs on secular campuses, the intensive, specialized, textual training offered by Jewish seminaries and Israeli institutions still remains an essential component of serious preparation in the field. As Jewish studies becomes more sophisticated as an academic calling, in addition to generalized training in the field and particular expertise in an area, practitioners must demonstrate skill in a traditional academic discipline. Despite the growing interdisciplinary nature of Jewish studies programs, students and professors are called upon to exercise rigorous methodological control in their work. The varying strengths of Jewish studies programs reflects their abilities to make interdisciplinary connections with departments representing all the disciplines of study relevant to the Jewish experience, their support by students and faculty of all backgrounds and faiths, and their insight at striking a balance between the emotional and intellectual needs of the students involved. *See also* Academe, Jewish Education.

HOWARD ADELMAN

BIBLIOGRAPHY

Adelman, Howard. "Is Jewish Studies Ethnic Studies?" In *Ethnicity, Women, and the Liberal Arts Curriculum.* Johnella E. Butler and John C. Walter, eds. Albany: State University of New York Press, 1991.

Band, Arnold. "Jewish Studies in American Liberal Arts Colleges and Universities." *American Jewish Yearbook* 67 (1966): 3–30.

Gordis, Robert, ed. "Jewish Studies in the University." *Judaism* 35 (1986): 134–197.

Jick, Leon. *The Teaching of Judaica in American Universities: The Proceedings of a Colloquium.* New York: Ktav, 1970.

Katsh, Abraham I. "Growth of Modern Hebrew in American Colleges and Universities." *Jewish Education* 21 (1950): 11–16.

———. "The Teaching of Hebrew in American Universities." *Modern Language Journal* 30 (1946): 575–586.

Neusner, Jacob. *The Academic Study of Judaism.* 2 vols. New York: Ktav, 1975 and 1977.

Rosenau, William. "Semitic Studies in American Colleges." *Central Conference of American Rabbis Yearbook* 6 (1986): 99–113.

Rudavsky, David. "Hebraic & Judaic Studies in American Higher Education." *Congress Bi-Weekly* 41 (1974): 8–10.

Waxman, Mordecai, ed. "A Symposium on Jewish Studies in the University." *Conservative Judaism* 27 (1973): 3–48.

Wechsler, Harold, and Ritterband, Paul. "Jewish Learning in American Universities: The Literature of a Field." *Modern Judaism* 3 (1983): 253–289.

Jewish Theological Seminary of America, The.

The academy for advanced Jewish studies and the founding institution of the Conservative Movement, the Jewish Theological Seminary was established in 1886 under the presidency of Rabbi Sabato Morais (1886–1897) as a school for the training of English-speaking American rabbis, in reaction to the increasing radicalization of American Reform Judaism as reflected in that movement's Pittsburgh Platform (1885). The Seminary's purpose, in the words of its original charter, was "the preservation in America of the knowledge and practice of historical Judaism." This translated into a program for American Jewry that stressed a more "conservative" approach to Jewish practice than that of Reform Judaism, while encouraging an open, scientific, and historical stance to Jewish scholarship, in contrast to the traditionalism of American Orthodoxy.

During the twentieth century, the Seminary's Rabbinical School has ordained over 1200 rabbis. In addition to the Rabbinical School, it now encompasses the Albert A. List College of Jewish Studies which cosponsors undergraduate programs with Columbia University's School for General Studies and Barnard College, the Graduate School, which offers masters and doctoral degrees in Judaica, the Cantors Institute/Seminary College of Jewish Music, and the Prozdor, a high school division. The University of Judaism, the Seminary's West Coast affiliate in Los Angeles, was founded in 1947.

The Seminary sponsors a range of academic programs in Israel including the Seminary of Judaic Studies. The Jewish Museum, which now occupies its own home in the former Warburg mansion on New York City's Fifth Avenue and which houses the most comprehensive collection of Jewish ceremonial art and objects in the world, was initially launched by the Seminary in 1904.

In contrast to the history of American Reform Judaism where the movement's congregational arm (the Union of American Hebrew Congregations) preceded and founded its academic center (the Hebrew Union College), it was the Seminary that spawned the various arms of the Conservative Movement. It began by launching the United Synagogue of America, 1913, under the Seminary's second president Solomon Schechter (1902–1915). Upon Schechter's death, the presidency of the Seminary was assumed by the eminent communal leader and Semitics scholar, Cyrus Adler (1915–1940).

The most notable of the Seminary's nonacademic programs is Camp Ramah, a network of Hebrew-speaking, educational sleep-away and day camps in the United States, Canada, Argentina, and Israel, created in 1947 by Louis Finkelstein, the Seminary's fourth president (1940–1951). Finkelstein, who became the Seminary's first chancellor (1951-1972), was also responsible for launching the Seminary's prize-winning Eternal Light radio and television programs and its Institute for Religion and Social Studies. He also sponsored a Conference in Science, Philosophy, and Religion, which pioneered efforts to establish communication between representatives of various American religious communities and academicians in the sciences and the humanities.

The Seminary's formal doctoral program in Judaica dates from 1969, but its reputation as America's preeminent academic center for higher Jewish studies was in place decades before. Most of this century's foremost Judaic scholars including Schechter and Finkelstein, the late Talmudists Louis Ginzberg and Saul Lieberman, the historian Alexander Marx, the theologian Abraham Joshua Heschel, the philosopher Mordecai M. Kaplan, the Bible scholar H. L. Ginsberg, and two eminent authorities in medieval Hebrew literature, Israel Davidson and Shalom Spiegel, among others, served on its faculty. Other living Seminary faculty include the Bible scholar Robert Gordis and the historian Gerson D. Cohen (Seminary chancellor, 1972-1986).

The Seminary's reputation as a major academic center was enhanced by its library, which now occupies a new state-of-the art facility on the Seminary campus. This world-renowned collection of books, manuscripts, incunabula, archives, and graphics serves as a resource for scholars from around the world.

The Seminary's more traditionalist posture within Conservative Judaism was sharply modified by the faculty's decision to admit women to the Rabbinical School (1983). In 1987, Chancellor Ismar Schorsch (1986-) extended that policy to the Cantors Institute. Though clearly controversial, these decisions brought the Seminary's religious posture into line with the more dominant position of the other arms of the Conservative Movement, the Rabbinical Assembly (the association of Conservative Rabbis), and the United Synagogue.

The Seminary celebrated its centennial in the academic year 1986-1987 with a wide-ranging series of public programs dealing with issues in American religious and specifically Jewish life. As it enters its second century, the overriding challenge on the Seminary's agenda is the tension inherent in its dual role as a Western, academic institution, on the one hand, and the spiritual center of an American religious movement, on the other. *See also* Conservative Judaism, Louis Finkelstein.

NEIL GILLMAN

BIBLIOGRAPHY

Bentwich, Norman. *Solomon Schechter: A Biography.* Philadelphia: Jewish Publication Society, 1938.

Davis, Moshe. *The Emergence of Conservative Judaism: The Historical School in 19th Century America.* Philadelphia: Jewish Publication Society, 1963.

Schechter, Solomon. *Seminary Addresses and Other Papers.* New York: Burning Bush, 1959.

Sklare, Marshall. *Conservative Judaism: An American Religious Movement.* Lanham, Md.: University Press of America, 1985.

Waxman, Mordecai, ed. *Tradition and Change: The Development of Conservative Judaism.* New York: Burning Bush Press, 1958.

Joseph, Jacob (1848-1902). Talmudic scholar, preacher, and "Chief Rabbi" of New York City, Jacob Joseph was born in the town of Krozhe in the Kovno district of Lithuania. After studying at the Volozhiner Yeshiva under the tutelage of Rabbi Hirsch Berlin, he held a number of rabbinic positions in Lithuania, culminating in his election as *magid* (communal preacher) and rabbinic judge in Vilna. In 1888, he was chosen by a number of Orthodox congregations in New York to act as their Chief Rabbi. Although the title gave Joseph no official status, it accorded him a great deal of influence, especially in the first years of his rabbinate. Yet his title and position were contested from the start, and as a result of internecine rivalries between rabbis, lay leaders, and synagogue, Joseph's position was so weakened that he was unable to achieve little of lasting importance. He died in 1902, and his large funeral was marked by an anti-Semitic riot on the part of some Christian onlookers and the New York Police Department. Joseph was a brilliant Yiddish preacher, and his sermons in New York were always well attended. Some of his sermons in Vilna were published under the collective title *Le Beit Yakov* (To the House of Jacob) in Vilna 1888.

Rabbi Jacob Joseph was the first major rabbinic figure of world status to settle in the United States. He was preceded by numerous competent Orthodox rabbis, but none had achieved his reputation in Europe or had held an important rabbinic post there.

Although he was referred to as "Chief Rabbi of New York," in fact his actual jurisdiction was limited to the several dozen Lower East Side synagogues that had united and accepted him as their Chief Rabbi. Yet his sphere of influence and moral authority went beyond the narrow confines of his own community. As such, Joseph and his lay supporters attempted to create the framework for a traditional European-style Orthodox community in New York City. Thus Joseph established a rabbinic hierarchy with a rabbinic court (Beth Din) consisting of important Orthodox rabbis who came to the United States on Joseph's invitation. He attempted to reorganize New York's antiquated system of Jewish religious education and at the end of his life (1900) did establish a Jewish day school, which after his death was named in his honor.

However, it was Joseph's attempt to bring order to the chaotic state of the Kosher meat trade in New York that proved to be his downfall. By attempting to impose even an insignificant tax on Kosher meat, especially poultry, Joseph aroused the anger of not only the men and women of the street, but also powerful sectors of New York's Jewish community who opposed such a tax. The fact that the income of the tax was to be used to support the Chief Rabbi and his rabbinical court only further compounded their anger at Joseph.

His attempt to license the *Shohetin* (ritual slaughterers) and to ban the incompetent among them led to a frontal assault on the authority of the Chief Rabbi by the slaughterers, many of whom were rabbis themselves. Other rabbis feared that Joseph aimed to monopolize kashrut (kosher) supervision in New York City, thereby depriving them of their chief source of livelihood. They too became his opponents and were joined by many of the retail kosher butchers and wholesalers.

Compounding this problem was the question of Jewish geographic rivalry. Joseph and his court were all Lithuanian Jews. Thus the large Jewish population hailing from Poland, Hungary, and Galicia felt slighted and in no time competing "Chief Rabbis" established themselves in New York City. By the early 1890s, Joseph's authority and influence had evaporated, and even his early supporters abandoned his cause.

After struggling for a number of years to carry out his rabbinic mandate, Joseph was felled by a serious stroke in 1895. He was an invalid from thereon. He made only rare public appearances and no longer carried out any rabbinic functions.

Rabbi Jacob Joseph's contribution to American Jewry was his presence as the first Talmudic scholar of note to settle in the United States. His arrival paved the way for the coming of other well-known rabbis after him. His well-meaning

attempt at establishing a kashrut system in New York was a failure, yet he defined the issue clearly and helped in finally bringing order to this controversial issue. *See also* Orthodoxy.

ZALMAN ALPERT

BIBLIOGRAPHY

Karp, Abraham J. "New York Chooses A Rabbi." *Publication of the American Jewish Historical Society* 44 (1955): 129–198.

Journalism. The subject of the Jewish influence in journalism—newspaper, magazine, radio, and television—has captivated the adversaries of the Jews far more than it has fascinated either Jews themselves or independent scholars. In a biography of Mordecai M. Noah (1785–1851), the first significant journalist of Jewish origin in the New World, Jonathan D. Sarna states categorically: "There is no history of Jews in American journalism." The researcher is therefore required to begin with specialized monographs, such as biographical portraits of individuals appearing in encyclopedias and reference works. One journalist's book, Stephen D. Isaacs's *Jews and American Politics* (1974) does include a chapter speculating on the apparent overrepresentation of such journalists on the contemporary political landscape. But the topic is not treated in a historical—much less in a general scholarly—way; nor is the overview on the subject of journalism in the *Encyclopedia Judaica* interpretive. It too is primarily biographical in orientation, tracking the careers and achievements of reporters, editors, and publishers in various countries—one of whom, Theodor Herzl, even became the prophet and father of the Zionist state. The rest is "no comment."

In breaking this silence, a scholar must weigh without apology the validity of the claim of Jewish overrepresentation in the media. However exaggerated or unwarranted the beliefs of bigots may prove to be, the conspicuous attractiveness of journalism for many Jews merits analysis and explanation, within the context of the modern Jewish experience.

Over 1700 daily newspapers are currently published in the United States. Jews own about 50, or less than 3 percent, which is the proportion of Jews in the general American population. Even when the circulation of these newspapers is taken into account (8 percent of all papers circulated), it is evident that newspaper publishing is hardly an awesome sign of Jewish entrepreneurship. There are nearly 9000 radio stations and 1000 television network affiliates, but no data on the ethnic and religious identification of their owners appear to be extant. According to the only published figures on the percentage of Jews among American editors and reporters, the 3.3 percent so identified is only slightly above their proportion in the general population.

The two most newsworthy American cities, however, do seem to be covered by a large fraction of journalists of Jewish birth. According to a 1976 study, a quarter of the Washington press corps was of Jewish background. A volume of Jewish economic history published a year earlier claims that "it has been estimated that . . . 40 percent of . . . [New York's] journalists are Jews." The author of this study, Marcus Arkin, fails to disclose the basis of this estimate or even its source. But since New York City is the media capital of the country, as well as the most populous concentration of Jews on the planet, the proportion of Jews in the general population is more relevant than their percentage in the city itself. Arkin's estimate is therefore almost certainly too high, perhaps much too high.

Numbers do not, of course, correlate with influence, nor participation with impact; and the prestige of certain papers cannot be quantified. However, analogues in European history can be instructive. In the Weimar Republic, as earlier in the Second Reich, special distinction was conceded to the Jewish-owned *Frankfurter Zeitung* and the publishing houses of Ullstein and Mosse. And the Jewish editorial control of the *Berliner Tageblatt* and the *Vossische Zeitung* typified the Jewish presence across the spectrum of the liberal and leftist press, even though the conservative and right-wing press (dominated by the Hugenberg trust) enjoyed greater circulation. The most prestigious newspaper in Central Europe was undoubtedly Vienna's *Neue Freie Presse*, which Jews published and to which they contributed *feuilletons*.

In the United States as well, some news organizations are more respected and important than others. According to one survey, the reporters whose beat is Washington, D.C., acknowledge the supremacy of the following influences: (1) television networks, (2) weekly news magazines, (3) the wire services, and (4) four daily newspapers—the *Washington Post*, the *New York Times*, the *Washington Star* (now defunct), and the *Wall Street Journal*.

With the exception of the wire services (the Associated Press and United Press International),

these branches of the Fourth Estate are institutions in which Jews have tended to congregate. A 1979 survey revealed that 27 percent of the employees of the *Times*, the *Post*, the *Wall Street Journal*, *Time*, *Newsweek*, *U.S. News and World Report*, the three networks, and the Public Broadcasting System were of Jewish origin. At the American Broadcasting Company, for example, 58 percent of the producers and editors were Jews. The survey revealed that Jews were conspicuous at the top. The Sulzberger family retains its ownership of the *New York Times*, of which, in 1990, the executive editor was Max Frankel and the editorial page editor, Jack Rosenthal. Eugene Meyer had bought the *Washington Post* at an auction in 1933; and it was under the leadership of his daughter, Katherine Graham, raised as a Lutheran, and executive editor Benjamin C. Bradlee, a Brahmin, that the newspaper became the chief rival to the *New York Times*. For the *Post's* Pulitzer Prize-winning exposure of the Watergate scandal of 1972–1973, Carl Bernstein and Bob Woodward, the reporters who broke the story, benefitted from the support of editors Howard Simons, Harry Rosenfeld, and Barry Sussman. "More than any other editor at the *Post*," they claimed, "Sussman became a walking compendium of Watergate knowledge, a reference source to be summoned when even the library failed." The city editor was essentially "a theoretician. In another age, he might have been a Talmudic scholar."

Other Jews who have occupied pivotal positions in the media should also be mentioned. Warren Phillips, chairman of the board in 1990, was editor of the *Wall Street Journal*, whose current managing editor is Norman Pearlstine. Marvin Stone was editor of *U.S. News and World Report*, long the extended shadow of David Lawrence; it is now owned by Morton Zuckerman. Edward Kosner was editor of *Newsweek*. The managing editor of *Time* was Henry Anatole Grunwald, who began his career at the magazine as its part-time copy boy. William Paley was chairman of the board of CBS, while Fred Friendly and Richard Salant were presidents of its new division. The Sarnoff family was long dominant at the National Broadcasting Company, whose news division was headed by Richard Wald. Leonard Goldenson was president of ABC, while the executive producer of its evening news was Av Westin. The president of the Public Broadcasting System was Lawrence Grossman. The president of National Public Radio has been

Frank Mankiewicz, the son of the coscenarist of Hollywood's brilliant film, a portrait of a press lord, *Citizen Kane* (1941).

Statistical measurement cannot convey the impact that Jews have exerted upon American journalism. How can the prestige of the *New York Times* be tabulated? In its authoritativeness as the newspaper of record, in its reputation for accuracy and comprehensiveness, the *Times* is in a class by itself. It has a news staff of 550 in New York alone, where its Times Square news room covers 1.3 acres. But what does it mean for its editors and reporters to realize that their words will be read and pondered in the White House and in the Kremlin, in City Hall, and in the libraries and archives of posterity?

Or how does the scholar measure the impact of Walter Lippmann (1889–1974)? He was one of the most admired American journalists of the twentieth century, and one reputable historian considered him "perhaps the most important [American] political thinker of the twentieth century" as well. Because Lippmann's approach to journalism was oriented to interpretation, he made little impression on the process of news gathering. But it was said in Washington during his prime that foreign governments formally accredited their ambassadors to the President and by private letter to Lippmann, who seemed to stride above the norms of diplomacy when it suited him. His regular pilgrimages to Europe were so rigorously arranged that, in 1961, Nikita Khrushchev's request to delay Lippmann's Soviet visit by a few days, due to an unanticipated political crisis, was rejected. The Russian dictator then rearranged his *own* plans so that he could meet the American journalist. (The resulting interviews earned Lippmann a second Pulitzer Prize.) Quantification of his stature can sometimes be attempted. When Lippmann spoke at the National Press Club to celebrate his seventieth birthday, more correspondents were in attendance than had come to hear Khrushchev speak in the same room a little earlier.

Or how is the impact of Herbert Bayard Swope (1882–1958) to be assessed? He won the first Pulitzer Prize for reporting (in 1917) and gained fame as the executive editor of the *New York World* in its heyday, the 1920s (when Lippmann ran the editorial page). He coined the term "op ed" page, a feature for which he was primarily responsible. From a Roosevelt campaign speech of 1932, Swope singled out the phrase "new deal," thus labeling an administration and

also an era. When both were over, he coined the phrase "the cold war" (which Lippmann gave currency). Swope instituted the newspaper practice of capitalizing the word "negro"; and under his direction the *World* won a Pulitzer Prize for a series exposing the Ku Klux Klan. Lord Northcliffe of London's *Daily Mail* considered Swope the finest reporter of his time. The editor's mansion on Long Island had so impressed F. Scott Fitzgerald that it was the inspiration for the East Egg home of Tom and Daisy Buchanan in *The Great Gatsby*. Swope brandished so much *chutzpah*, RCA's David Sarnoff once remarked, "that if you wanted to meet God, he'd arrange it somehow." Swope was so famous that he became one of the first *Time* magazine cover subjects, so arrogant that he listed among his favorite books not only the Bible and the *World Almanac* but also any volume containing a reference to himself, so imperious that he could scoop other reporters by dressing exactly like a diplomat and getting a front-row seat at the Versailles Peace Conference. Swope's written legacy is surprisingly sparse and brittle, but his "hellzapoppin'" personality made him into a formidable newsman.

One other biographical illustration will further suggest the elusiveness of measuring the Jewish role in American journalism. If Swope lived the myth of American journalism, Ben Hecht (1894–1964) not only enjoyed it as fully but also, more than anyone else, created it. It is from Hecht that Americans learned that newspapermen could be corrupt, cynical, wenching, dissolute, coarse, drunken rogues, insensitive to anyone's privacy, oblivious to puritanical codes—and therefore have more fun than anyone else. Born on New York's Lower East Side, Hecht began his professional career in Chicago at the age of 16. His first assignment, which the publisher of the *Chicago Journal* gave him, was to write obscene verses for a stag party. Over a decade of such intimacy with the vulgarities of his profession and the raunchiest features of city life gave Hecht material for *1001 Afternoons in Chicago* (1922), for later autobiographical novels like *Gaily, Gaily* (1963) and for his spirited memoir, *A Child of the Century* (1954). But Hecht's greatest achievement as a myth maker was *The Front Page* (1928), in collaboration with Charles MacArthur. Newspaper experiences were the capital that Hecht drew upon for writing fiction and films, and his recounting became the standard against which the vicissitudes of the profession came to be measured.

Since such examples could be multiplied, the

limitations of space make it impossible to "read all about it." It is preferable to elucidate such impact rather than illustrate it.

History must be appealed to in accounting for the special responsiveness of many Jews to opportunities in professions such as journalism. There has to be some sort of "fit" between skill and milieu, between potentiality and circumstance. That is why the *Encyclopedia Judaica* dates the Jewish contribution to European journalism at the beginning of Emancipation itself, conjecturing that a people already relatively urban and literate found itself "in the right place at the right time." Moreover, the encyclopedia asserts, the "gift of adaptability permitted the Jew to act as an intermediary, the link between the event and the reader, as the journalist has often been called." The press offered "brightness and novelty," an outlet for a people that felt little if any devotion to pre-modern tradition. Also pertinent here are the speculations of sociologist Arthur Ruppin that "city life forces people into intensive interaction, into an exchange of goods and ideas. It demands constant mental alertness. . . . The great mental agility of the Jews . . . enabled them to have a quick grasp and orientation in all things."

Such comments get us closer to the truth, though they would appear to be more applicable to the nineteenth century than to the twentieth. They are more useful in explaining the initial attraction that journalism might have exerted on the newly emancipated, not why, if anything, the Jewish involvement has persisted without noticeable loss of intensity. By the twentieth century, especially long past its midpoint, the relative historical advantages that literacy and urbanity might have conferred should have become quite marginal. The conjectures of the encyclopedia and of Ruppin undoubtedly apply more directly to Europe than to the United States, which was postemancipation from its inception as an independent nation and has imposed no official restrictions upon Jews.

This theory, like others, suffers from the disadvantage of blurring or ignoring the distinction between journalists themselves and their employers. With some important exceptions, Jews often achieved prominence on the business side before the expressive side. This distinction was put most cogently by A. J. Liebling, who realized early on that he "did not belong to a joyous, improvident professional group including me and [publisher] Roy Howard, but to a section of society including me and any floorwalker at Macy's. Mr. Howard, even though he asked to be called Roy, belonged in a section that included him and the gent who owned Macy's. This clarified my thinking about publishers, their common interests and motivations." Liebling himself wrote primarily for the *New Yorker*, where there was publisher Raoul Fleischmann.

But the persuasiveness of the generalization depends in part on what one makes of Joseph Pulitzer (1847–1911), certainly among the most inventive and spectacular figures in journalism at the turn of the century. The format and style of the two newspapers he owned, the *St. Louis Post-Dispatch* and the *New York World*, established the rules for layouts, features, and photography that still govern the modern newspaper. In the late nineteenth century, as American anti-Semitism was peaking, Pulitzer bore the handicap of being considered a Jew, without enjoying the spiritual advantages that adherents of Judaism can cultivate. His father was part-Jewish, his mother was a Catholic. He was at least nominally an Episcopalian, and his children were not raised as Jews. In the haunted, afflicted years of his greatest wealth and fame, Pulitzer employed a series of secretaries to read to him the news that his failing eyesight prohibited him from following. There is some grandeur in his insistence that his secretaries be capable of literate and sparkling conversation. There is nothing admirable in the advice that the young men were given not to speak to the publisher on the topic of Jews.

Adolph S. Ochs (1855–1935), who bought the *New York Times* in 1896, harbored his own sensitivities on the topic of *am-echad* ("a certain people"). But his identity as a Jew was not in doubt. He married the daughter of the most innovative of nineteenth-century rabbis, Isaac Mayer Wise; and he and his descendants, the Sulzbergers, remained members of the flagship Reform synagogue, Temple Emanuel of New York City. "Religion is all that I stand for as a Jew," Ochs announced in 1925. "I know nothing else, no other definition for a Jew except religion." So constrained a classification exhibited a logic of its own. Faith was so private and minor a feature of family life that his descendants and relatives generally were informed that they were Jewish on the eve of their departure for boarding school. Having severed the bonds of peoplehood, the Sulzberger family through its foundation gave a pittance to Jewish philanthropies: $1800 to the United Jewish Appeal in 1973, $900 the year after the Yom Kippur War.

But limiting Jewishness to religious belief did not keep the family that has owned the *Times* from realizing that others might be troubled by Jewish "clannishness" and cohesiveness in their newspaper empire; therefore, much effort was expended to limit the perception of the *Times* as a "Jewish" newspaper. If the business side preceded the expressive and editorial side, that was because it was undoubtedly a matter of *Times* policy. Under Ochs, his son-in-law Arthur Hays Sulzberger and *his* son-in-law Orville Dryfoos, no Jew rose to the position of managing editor. That barrier was finally scaled by A. M. Rosenthal, but only after the chief foreign correspondent, Cyrus L. Sulzberger, had kept him from covering a UN conference in 1948 by announcing the following quota: "One Jew in Paris is enough." In 1952, when Daniel Schorr, then a *Times* stringer in the Low Countries, asked for a staff position, C. L. Sulzberger rebuffed him with the observation that "we have too many Jews in Europe." It is commonly believed that Theodore Bernstein, the newspaper's authority on usage, the "technical genius" of the bullpen, could have risen to the post of managing editor had he been a Gentile. It is also widely assumed that *Times* policy once disguised the given names of Jews, so that bylines were given to A. (for Abraham) M. Rosenthal, A. (for Abraham) H. Raskin, et al. The current editor of the editorial page, Jacob Rosenthal, forced the *Times* to break its rule against informality; the masthead lists him, rather incongruously, as Jack Rosenthal.

The history of American journalism cannot exclude Jews whose interest was not in deadlines or headlines but merely in the bottom line. Terms like "brightness and novelty," or bridging the gap "between the event and the reader," make little sense in evaluating the career of Samuel I. Newhouse (1895–1979). He took charge of his first newspaper, the *Bayonne* (New Jersey) *Times*, at the age of 17. By the time of his death, Newhouse owned 31 newspapers, 7 magazines, 6 television stations, 5 radio stations, 20 cable-TV stations, and even a wire service. Only two other newspaper chains were larger; none was more profitable. But profit was all that mattered to Newhouse; no publisher was less interested in the editorial policies—which varied—of the newspapers he owned. He did not bother to read his own products, preferring to peruse the *Times* instead. Newhouse's credo was simple: "Only a newspaper which is a sound business operation can be a truly free, independent editorial enterprise." His sons now direct his empire.

Entrepreneurship having nothing to do with expressiveness also characterized the career of Moses Annenberg (1878–1942), the immigrant who founded Triangle Publications (the *Daily Racing Form*, the *Philadelphia Inquirer*, and the *New York Morning Telegraph*). His son Walter founded *Seventeen* magazine as well as the magazine with the second greatest circulation in the United States, *TV Guide*, which has over 17 million readers. Dorothy Schiff (1903–1989), the former publisher of the *New York Post*, whose grandfather was the venerable communal leader and banker Jacob Schiff, undoubtedly spoke for her peers when she confirmed an axiom that, "once you reach a certain financial level, people don't think of you as anything but very rich." Unpredictable and frivolous, she ran the *Post* from 1939 till 1976 in a style akin to the very last line in *Citizen Kane*: "I think it would be fun to run a newspaper!" They belong to the history of American business, not in the *Oxford Companion to American Literature*.

Other explanations for the Jewish predilection for journalism also merit scrutiny and criticism. In *Jews and American Politics*, Stephen Isaacs argues that the intellectual and verbal resourcefulness that Jews have historically cherished is rewarded in the mass media. By now Isaacs's explanation smacks of a commonplace—which does not mean that it is false, only that it is familiar. Truisms are often hard to separate from truths, and this one at least has the virtue of identifying the core of values that may be the matrix of a Jewish occupational proclivity as well as a contrast with other values stressed among Gentiles. If the Jewish encounter with modern society does differ from the experience of others, the explanation may well be connected to alternative beliefs.

But Isaacs's theory is also quite restricted. Almost no publishers or network executives have been intellectuals. The celebrated journalists who grew up ignorant of the Judaic religion and its stress upon the Word would make a long list. Nor does the explanation incorporate those journalists whose success has been visual rather than verbal. The most prestigious award of the National Cartoonists Society, for example, is called the "Reuben," in honor of the first president of the society, Rube Goldberg. The most honored of political cartoonists is the *Washington Post*'s Herbert Block ("Herblock"). Al Capp (né Caplin) created the Dogpatch of *Li'l Abner*, which was syndicated in 500 newspapers and has entered the mainstream of popular culture. Verbal resourcefulness had nothing to do with the photojournalism of Erich Salomon in Germany, Alfred Eisenstaedt in Germany and then with *Life* Magazine, or Robert and Cornell Capa, Budapest-born brothers whose original name was Friedmann. Probably the most famous shot ever taken by an American photojournalist was Joe Rosenthal's depiction of the four U.S. marines raising the flag on Iwo Jima—an icon of heroism and patriotism. And since President Reagan himself was a former sports announcer, it would be patronizing to ignore such figures as Mel Allen and Howard Cosell, or Nat Fleischer of *Ring* magazine, whose approach to subjects like the New York Yankees and Muhammad Ali has shown little trace of Talmudic learning.

Stephen Isaacs also notes the Jewish representation in a field that, "like all forms of mass education, prizes the nonethnicity of universalism" and especially the ideal of objectivity. Those opting for journalism as a career might therefore hope to be judged by their merit, not their religious or national origin.

This generalization is partially valid, for the Jews attracted to it have usually been quite assimilated and "deracinated," eager or anxious to blend into civil society. This would include the star foreign correspondent of the *New York Daily Tribune* from 1852 till 1862, Karl Marx. His parents having converted, Marx was formally baptized as a Lutheran; and he grew up into an atheist. It is less well-known that the only occupation for which he was ever paid was journalism. When Marx edited the *Rheinische Zeitung*, he depended on Jewish businessmen in Cologne for support; but his greatest success was writing for the American newspaper that Horace Greeley edited. Marx submitted 350 articles that he himself wrote, plus another dozen in collaboration with F. Engels. The *Tribune*'s managing editor, Charles A. Dana, once announced that Marx was "not only one of the most highly valued, but one of the best-paid contributors attached to the journal." The contributions ceased in 1862, however, when Greeley fired Dana, who had permitted anti-Semitic material to be published in the *Tribune*. Several articles infected with such material had been submitted by Marx.

Perhaps the epitome of the "non-ethnicity of universalism" was Walter Lippmann. In the more than 10 million printed words of wisdom and counsel that he imparted in his lifetime, Jews were seldom mentioned. But he did write an analysis of anti-Semitism for the *American Hebrew* in 1922,

blaming the growth of bigotry primarily on the vulgarity and ostentatiousness of nouveaux-riches Jews themselves. No one was more anxious to sever whatever bound him to the community of Israel. He agreed that his alma mater, Harvard College, was correct in imposing a limit on Jewish admissions. More than 15 percent of the student body, Lippmann suspected, would generate a *Kulturkampf*; and his own "sympathies are with the non-Jew[, whose] . . . personal manners and physical habits are, I believe, distinctly superior to the prevailing manners of the Jew." From 1933, no column by the most influential pundit of his time mentioned the persecution of Jews in the Third Reich, though two columns in 1938 did suggest that the "surplus" population of Europe should be sent to Africa—the very continent that the Zionists had rejected four decades before. During the Holocaust Lippmann wrote nothing about the Nazi death camps; afterward he wrote nothing either. Though he never converted to any version of Christianity, Lippmann went to ludicrous proportions to obscure his own origins. Ronald Steel's excellent biography records the nervousness that one friend experienced in playing Scrabble with Lippmann. She worried that the letters forming the word "Jew" might come up, perhaps upsetting the champion of disinterested reason, the Apollonian savant who wrote in 1915: "Man must be at peace with the sources of his life. If he is ashamed of them, if he is at war with them, they will haunt him forever. They will rob him of the basis of assurance, will leave him an interloper in the world."

A. J. Liebling (1904–1963) constitutes a final case of how fiercely many journalists tried to bleach out their origins. A crack reporter for the *New York World* under the direction of Swope, he became the inventor of modern criticism of the press and was among the most savvy monitors of its performance. Liebling bragged that he could "write better than anyone who could write faster, and faster than anyone who could write better." Both of Lippmann's wives were Gentiles; so were all three of Liebling's. Identifying with the Irish toughs among whom he was raised, attending Dartmouth when it was perhaps the most religiously restrictive of Ivy League colleges, Liebling became a *New Yorker* war correspondent who was more pained by the devastation that Nazi Germany was wreaking on France than by the Holocaust itself. His third wife commented: "Even Hitler didn't make him an intensely self-conscious Jew." Liebling once declined to attend a literary salon on Manhattan's Upper West Side because "sheenies who are meanies will be there." He was an eccentric as well as a witty and facile craftsman who suffered the strangest of deaths, because he was a gourmand who became a glutton. Devouring the "forbidden" foods (like lobsters, clams, and oysters), Liebling simply ate himself to death.

There are, of course, exceptions to Isaacs's generalization; a few American journalists did not propel themselves furiously from their Jewish origins for the sake of a neutral or abstract universalism. Although Mordecai Noah (1785–1851) was a "restorationist" rather than a genuine forerunner of Zionism (before the term had been coined), he was an advocate of Jewish rights as well as an adept polemical journalist who helped usher in the form of mass communications associated with the liveliness and sensationalism of the penny press. Ben Hecht, for whom a boat transporting refugees illegally to Palestine was named, was certainly the most fervent Jewish nationalist to emerge from American journalism. He became a leading champion of the Irgun and an indignant critic of the first prime minister of Israel, David Ben-Gurion. But Hecht's blazing opposition to Nazism and commitment to Jewish rights came after his newspaper career had essentially been abandoned. Swope's support of the Jewish Telegraphic Agency, his presence at the creation of the Overseas News Agency, and his fund raising for the United Jewish Appeal also took place after he had ceased working for the *World* or for any other newspaper. He had nothing to do with the astonishing decision of his brother, Gerard, once the president of General Electric, to bequeath the bulk of his estate (nearly $8 million) to Israel's leading engineering institute, Haifa's Technion, in 1957. A younger example of comfort with Jewish identity is Martin Peretz, who edited the campus newspaper as an undergraduate of Brandeis University and in 1974 became the editor-in-chief of *The New Republic* (which Lippmann had helped to found six decades earlier). Peretz has presumably been responsible for the considerable interest that the magazine has shown in the Middle East, primarily from a Labor Zionist perspective.

If the rarity of such figures tends to corroborate Isaacs's point, an even more striking phenomenon invalidates it. For if objectivity and universalism are supposed to endow the profession with so much appeal, the influx of Jews to journals of opinion and to partisan organs would not be so large. Neutrality would hardly characterize The

New Republic from Lippmann and Walter Weyl through Gilbert Harrison to Peretz, nor *The Nation* under Victor Navasky, nor *Dissent* under Irving Howe, Lewis Coser, and Michael Walzer, nor *The Progressive* under Morris Rubin, nor *Partisan Review* under Philip Rahv and William Phillips, nor *The New York Review of Books* under Robert Silvers and Barbara Epstein, nor *The Public Interest* under Daniel Bell, Irving Kristol, and Nathan Glazer. The Nixon administration's "enemies list," which was provided to the Senate's Watergate investigating committee in 1973, included CBS's Daniel Schorr ("a real media enemy") and Marvin Kalb; NBC's Sander Vanocur; and columnists Sydney Harris, Joseph Kraft, Max Lerner, and Frank Mankiewicz. The underground press that surfaced in the 1960s also made no pretense of reaching for the asymptote of objectivity. A short list of its luminaries would include Paul Krassner (*The Realist*), Marvin Garson (*The Berkeley Barb*), Jeff Shero (*Rat*), Allan Katzman (*The East Village Other*), and Jesse Kornbluth and Marshall Bloom of the Liberation News Service. Like other radical journalists beginning at the dawn of the twentieth century, their writing was a direct extension of their politics and was indistinguishable from it—and, indeed, was often a substitute for political action.

Even within the context of American media, objectivity is not universally prized, quite apart from the growing suspicion that it may be impossible to attain. Lippmann and David Lawrence largely invented the syndicated column of opinion and interpretation. Its eminent practitioners in recent years have included David Broder, Anthony Lewis, and the late Joseph Kraft. Moreover, the career of William Safire suggests how misleading it would be to remove the study of journalism from cognate fields. Safire began as a public relations counsellor (once called "press agent"), became a speech-writer for Richard Nixon in particular, then a lexicographer, a novelist and primarily a columnist—honored with a Pulitzer Prize—for the *New York Times*, all without breaking stride. Swope saw no conflict between his role as an editor and his services as a publicity flack for Bernard Baruch.

There is another possible explanation for the disproportionate impact that Jews have exerted in the American media. It is advanced tentatively because it is at best only partly satisfactory; it cannot cover all the cases or withstand all objections. No theory on this subject can. But it enjoys the advantage of taking into account the experience of other countries in the Diaspora and applies especially well to the particularities of the American framework. The speculation allows one to acknowledge the historical singularity of the Jewish people without requiring for its theoretical validity the journalists' knowledge of or fidelity to Judaic tradition and values.

This thesis holds that the press has been a key instrument in the recognition that we inhabit one world—not one village or valley or province or nation. Journalism is not only a bridge between reader and event, as the *Encyclopedia Judaica* avers, but between people and people. And a certain dispersed and vulnerable minority might be especially sensitive to the recalcitrant problems that human diversity and plurality can pose. Exile made the Jews aware that the world is larger than parochial and even national boundaries, and some Jews became hopeful that those borders might be transcended. Positioned as outsiders, they were vouchsafed the knowledge of relatives and other coreligionists abroad, were given at least a glimmering sense that there *was* an abroad, a life elsewhere. Jews were therefore responsive to cosmopolitanism, or transnationalism; they tended to want to see the world as one.

Such a marginal situation and such an international spirit have commonly been appreciated by scholars explaining the Jewish penchant for trade, even though the Biblical Hebrews were not famous for their business acumen. In describing the comparatively large number of Jews working for American newspapers prior to the Civil War, Sarna has observed that "journalism . . . permitted the kind of independence and mobility that Jews have often looked for in their occupations. . . . Commerce on a large or small scale," he added, "depends on information. Jewish merchants, travellers, peddlers and, of course, relatives served as 'reporters' long before the public press had any interest in printing the news." But other scholars have not extended or tested Sarna's claim that "Jews had the kind of cosmopolitan outlook which journalism demands." Too little curiosity has been piqued by this explanation for the Jewish attraction to journalism.

It was not necessary to be an immigrant to seize the possibilities of communicating to newly literate, increasingly enfranchised and empowered masses. Of course, the case is complicated by the obvious fact that the United States has been a nation of immigrants; and a thesis that is scientifically elegant would have to demonstrate that immigrant Jews, or immigrants generally, were represented in journalism more fully than in the American populace. Such validation is probably impossible, and impressionistic evidence will have to be substituted.

It is striking that Adolph Ochs of the *Times* and William Paley of CBS were the sons of immigrants; David Sarnoff of RCA/NBC was born in Russia. Lippmann had made many trips to Europe as a child and was attuned to advanced European thinkers like Bergson, Wallas and Freud. Swope, Hecht, and Liebling were also the sons of immigrants; and Liebling's dying words could not be understood because they were uttered in French. The closest American equivalent of the *feuilleton* was undoubtedly "Topics of the Times," whose anonymous but much-admired author was Simeon Strunsky, born in Russia. Even today, long after the era of mass migration of Jews is over, the executive editor of the *New York Times* is Max Frankel, born in Germany. His predecessor, Abe Rosenthal, was born in Canada to immigrants from Russia. Henry Anatole Grunwald, who became the chief of all Time, Inc. editorial enterprises, was born in Vienna.

Complications will continue to bedevil the study of Jews in American journalism. Even though the subject cannot be studied in isolation, confined to the 12-mile limit of the shores of the United States, it must also be fixed within the compass of a society in which an independent press has flourished and in which the talented, the ambitious, and the lucky could often be handsomely rewarded. Freedom of the press has occupied a central place in the democratic design; and even wayward pressmen could point out that their occupation is one of the few businesses (along with religion, firearms and liquor) that is granted Constitutional protection. Jefferson idealized liberty of the press so fervently that he once committed the logical flaw of the excluded middle term when he expressed a preference for "newspapers without a government" over "a government without newspapers." But his extravagant tribute to journalism was to echo for nearly two centuries of the Republic, even though individual journalists have been hated and vilified (some by Jefferson himself), lost duels, been beaten up and tarred and feathered and murdered. Their power has been respected even when it has not always been exalted. It failed to strike Americans as odd that one of the legendary lawmen of the Old West, "Bat" Masterson (1853–1921), ended up as an editor of the *New York Morning Telegraph*. It was also natural for the comic book creators of

Superman, Joe Shuster and Jerome Siegel, to provide the man of steel and righteousness with the earth-bound identity of a newspaper reporter, Clark Kent of the *Daily Planet*. Jews could succeed as journalists in part because journalists could succeed in America.

Finally, what will continue to render this topic enigmatic is the larger question of Jewish identity in modern times. This essay is not the place to explore the definition of who a Jew is. But it is certainly fair to assert that *at most* only a segment of ethnic identity or religious heritage has ever been implicated in what journalists have done, and therefore the task of determining a distinctive Jewish contribution is complicated when so many Jews have blended so successfully into the structure of social organization. What they have achieved as individual journalists betrays only the most tenuous link to their sensibility as Jews, but that is why any study of their influence and motivations promises to shed further light on the elusive meaning of Jewish modernity in mass society. During a historical period when it is hardly a disability and indeed something of an asset to be a Jew in America, journalism is among the indices of full participation in the host society. The press badge is a certificate of "making it." Far from signifying a cabal or a conspiracy, disproportionate representation in the mass media demonstrates the hospitality of the American environment, the congruence of American values— and the benign challenge that is thereby posed to Jewish singularity and survival. *See also* Press, Jewish.

STEPHEN J. WHITFIELD

BIBLIOGRAPHY

Cooney, John E. *The Annenbergs*. New York: Simon & Schuster, 1982.

Kelly, Tom. *The Imperial Post: The Meyers, the Grahams, and the Paper That Rules Washington*. New York: Morrow, 1983.

Liebling, A. J. *The Wayward Pressman*. Garden City, N.Y.: Doubleday, 1947.

Reichley, A. James. "Moe's Boy Walter at the Court of St. James." *Fortune* 81 (June 1970): 88–93.

Steel, Ronald. *Walter Lippmann and the American Century*. Boston: Little, Brown, 1980.

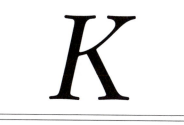

Kaplan, Mordecai Menahem (1881–1983).

A highly systematic and influential thinker, Mordecai Kaplan was the spiritual founder of the Reconstructionist Movement. In his quest for a way to be both authentically Jewish and American, Kaplan played pivotal roles in the forming of many major American Jewish institutions. His ideas and actions were seminal in shaping Jewish life in America.

Born in Lithuania, Kaplan was the son of an Orthodox rabbi. He came to New York when he was 9 years old. His early training was Orthodox, but Kaplan had heterodoxical ideas from an early age. He earned his B.A. at the City College of New York in 1900 and was ordained at the Jewish Theological Seminary in 1902. He then became the spiritual leader of Kehillath Jeshurun in New York City while continuing his graduate studies at Columbia University.

He left Kehillath Jeshurun in 1909 to become the principal of the newly created Teachers Institute at the Jewish Theological Seminary, where he taught homiletics and theology until 1963, wielding a profound influence over three generations of Conservative rabbis. He was one of the founders in 1913 of the United Synagogue, thereafter constantly advocating change within the Conservative Movement. While active in the New York Kehillah, he was also the founding rabbi of the Jewish Center (an Orthodox congregation) on New York's Upper West Side. There his emerging ideas about the need for the synagogue to serve as a center for Jewish living were first put into practice in a building with fine athletic and social facilities. This model provided the paradigm for hundreds of congregations. His ideas also influenced the Jewish settlement house movement, which was beginning the transition into Jewish community centers.

Kaplan left the Jewish Center in 1921, when it became clear to the Orthodox congregation that their rabbi was unwilling to accept the infallibility of inherited tradition. In 1922, some families who remained loyal to Kaplan joined with him to form the Society for the Advancement of Judaism (SAJ) a short distance away from the Jewish Center on New York's Upper West Side. There over the next few decades the Reconstructionist platform evolved, the Reconstructionist liturgy emerged, and the national Reconstructionist institutions were built. The SAJ provided Kaplan the opportunity to experiment freely. On a Shabbat morning in 1922, his daughter Judith became the first bat mitzvah in America there.

In 1934, when he was 53 years old, Kaplan published his *magnum opus, Judaism as a Civilization,* to wide national acclaim. In it he defined Judaism as "the evolving religious civilization of the Jewish people," describing the Jewish people rather than the doctrine of monotheism as the central force in Jewish life. The book's success led to the emergence of the *Reconstructionist* magazine in 1935; it was an expanded national version of the biweekly *SAJ Review* that gave Kaplan an ongoing national voice beyond his frequent lectures and consultations around the country. From this point on, Kaplan had to resist pressure from many of his disciples to make Reconstructionism a separate movement. Kaplan hoped that he could influence the Conservative Movement—and for that matter the rest of the American Jewish community—to accept his vision and did not fully acquiesce in the development of Reconstructionism as a separate movement until the founding of the Reconstructionist Rabbinical College in 1968.

Kaplan's commitment to liturgical innovation resulted in the co-editing of *The New Haggadah* with Rabbis Ira Eisenstein and Eugene Kohn. Published in 1941, it met with sharp criticism from Kaplan's colleagues at the Jewish Theological Seminary but achieved substantial popular success. Its changes included omission of references to chosenness, elimination of the ten plagues, and inclusion of historical references to Moses. The responses of his colleagues did not deter Kaplan, who never stopped making liturgical changes at the SAJ. In 1945, he and his disciples (now including Milton Steinberg) published the *Sabbath Prayer Book*. When representatives of the Union of Orthodox Rabbis (UOR) burned the prayerbook and put Kaplan in *herem* (the ban of excommunication), their action was on the front page of the *New York Times*. While the methods of the UOR were decried by the JTS faculty, the disapprobation of Kaplan's faculty colleagues was no less vehement. With his customary determination, Kaplan proceeded to publish without delay. In 1948, he and his co-editors issued a prayerbook for the High Holidays; in 1958, a prayerbook for the Pilgrimage Festivals; in 1963, a daily prayerbook.

Kaplan was the author of hundreds of articles and a series of important books. His range of mind was extraordinary, as a description of some of his books indicates. He edited and translated the *Mesillat Yesharim* by Moses Hayyim Luzzatto (1937); suggested fresh interpretations of the Jewish holidays and of the Sabbath in *The Meaning of God in Modern Jewish Religion* (1937); outlined a program for revitalizing American Jewish life in *The Future of the American Jew* (1948); co-created liturgies for such American holidays as Thanksgiving in *The Faith of America* (1951); dissected the dilemmas and prospects of the State of Israel in *The New Zionism* (1955); traced the development of modern Jewish ideologies in *The Greater Judaism in the Making*; described and analyzed the thought of Hermann Cohen in *The Purpose and Meaning of Jewish Existence* (1964); and attempted to show the universal values upon which human survival depends in *Religion of Ethical Nationhood* (1970).

Kaplan taught at the Reconstructionist Rabbinical College after its founding in 1968. A devoted Zionist who participated in a number of Zionist congresses, Kaplan lived in Israel for several of his latter years, returning to the United States to celebrate the centennial of his birth.

Kaplan was deeply influenced by disparate intellectual trends, from the pragmatist philosophies of John Dewey and William James to the emerging field of sociology; from the spiritual Zionism of Ahad Ha-Am to the approach to ethics of Felix Adler. All of these were balanced by deep immersion in traditional Jewish texts and modern scholarly study of them.

The core of Kaplan's thought lies in an understanding of the Jewish people as having a civilization with its own languages, art, literature, dance, poetry, political culture—its own experience. For Kaplan, the uniqueness of the Jewish people lies in their history. This has resulted in the unique merging of religious and national consciousness. Whereas all religion must be concerned with the transcendent, with salvation, with ultimacy (all words that Kaplan utilized at different times in his long career), only for Jews is this concern lifted to a central place in their national culture. This fact explains why Judaism is a *religious* civilization.

Having defined Judaism as one civilization among many, Kaplan saw attempts to see any one nation or religion as "chosen" as nothing more than chauvinism. He saw every people as having its own character and saw the Jewish people as having the vocation of promoting righteousness in the world. He saw this vocation as having evolved out of the Jewish historical experience.

Like all civilizations, Jewish civilization is evolving in response to changing social and technological conditions. It is also struggling toward a fuller understanding of the implications of moral precepts and daily practice for salvation. For Kaplan, therefore, Judaism is not only changing but improving over time. This process is the only way to move in the direction of perfecting the world.

Kaplan defined God as "the Power that makes for salvation," describing God in transnatural rather than supernatural terms. The unifying and vivifying force in Kaplan's universe, God is not a Being who interferes through personal judgment in individuals' lives but is rather the unifying and harmonizing force in the cosmos that allows us to move toward higher spiritual levels. Thus, Kaplan did not see God as a dispenser of reward and punishment either in this life or an afterlife.

One consequence of this changed definition is that God does not reveal in any simple and infallible fashion. In a postemancipation world, rabbis should not have binding authority; neither political power nor claims of exclusive access to the divine will should be sources of rabbinic authority. This permits a fresh understanding of how authentic Jewish communities can function under the changed conditions of modernity. Central to Kaplan's fresh understanding is the necessity of creating democratic, pluralistic organic communities. The current UJA/Federation structure was deeply influenced by this aspect of Kaplan's thought, but he was never satisfied with that degree of community and lobbied for a democratically elected world Jewish legislature.

In a rapidly changing world, Kaplan advocated moving beyond Halakah in order to respond to changing moral, spiritual, and aesthetic sensibilities. He recognized that the tradition should have "a vote but not a veto" and worked to provide examples of ways to preserve and reinterpret Jewish tradition. This explains, for example, his decision to add the bat mitzvah ceremony rather than dispensing with bar mitzvah as had the Reform Movement of his time.

Kaplan's understanding of Jewish sociology has been almost universally accepted. It is his theology that has been the subject of most frequent criticism. His ideas about God are often portrayed as making God remote and inaccessible. Kaplan's demand that each individual search anew for the divine and play an active role in determining the Jewish future is seen by many critics as overly optimistic. The contemporary success of the Reconstructionist Movement attests, however, to the continued appeal of the intellectual and social framework Kaplan created for growing numbers in the American Jewish community. *See also* Conservative Judaism, Reconstructionism.

DAVID A. TEUTSCH

BIBLIOGRAPHY

Cohen, Gerson D. "Bibliography 1909 to 1952." In *Mordecai M. Kaplan Jubilee Volume*, Moshe Davis, ed. 2 vols. New York: Jewish Theological Seminary, 1953. Pp. 9–33.

Eisenstein, Ira, and Kohn, Eugene, eds. *Mordecai M. Kaplan: An Evaluation.* New York: Reconstructionist Press, 1952.

Goldsmith, Emanuel S., and Scult, Mel, eds. *Dynamic Judaism: The Essential Writings of Mordecai M. Kaplan.* New York: Schocken, 1985.

Kaufman, William E. *Contemporary Jewish Philosophies.* Lanham, Md.: University Press of America, 1986. Pp. 175–216.

Kazin, Alfred (b. 1915). Critical essayist, literary anthologist and writer of memoirs, Alfred Kazin is best known for New York City-centered reminiscences such as *A Walker in the City* (1951) and *New York Jew* (1978) and for his study of modern American prose literature, *On Native Grounds* (1942). He is also the author of six other books. Kazin has, in addition, edited the works of Ralph Waldo Emerson, Nathaniel Hawthorne, F. Scott Fitzgerald and William Blake. Born in Brownsville, then a section of Brooklyn similar to Manhattan's Lower East Side, to Russian immigrant parents, Kazin attended City College of New York during the early 1930s and received his M.A. at Columbia University. He has taught at many universities, among them C.C.N.Y., Amherst College, and the University of California at Berkeley, and was literary editor of *The New Republic* 1942–1943 (a period he examines extensively in *New York Jew*). At one time Distinguished Professor of English at the State University of New York at Stony Brook and William White Professor of English, University of Notre Dame, Kazin currently teaches at City University of New York Graduate Center and Hunter College, where he is Emeritus Professor. During the spring of 1988 he was the first holder of the Newman Chair in American Civilization at Cornell University. He is a member of the National Institute of Arts and Letters and the American Foundation of Arts and Sciences. In all, he has been awarded six honorary degrees.

As a literary critic, Kazin reacted strongly against the aridity of "new criticism," the close, technically oriented reading of literature that he calls, in the "Preface" to *On Native Grounds*, a purely textual-esthetic approach. In its stead Kazin offers in the concluding pages of *On Native Grounds* a paean to pluralist, human-centered, socially situated criticism. In other works, such as "The Happy Hour" (*Esquire*, October 1980), he calls on the critic to speak for literature beyond the professional interpretation that contemporary university criticism was, he felt, advocating. In doing so, he provides a way of teaching classical, but remote, and modern, but demanding, literature to students who do not necessarily share similar cultural experiences. Clamourous, prodigious New York, which has drawn such diverse people together, is one of Kazin's muses.

Kazin is a humanist who, nonetheless, retains strong ties to his lineage and heritage, about which he writes richly in *New York Jew*. Here he remarks on his markedly different engagement with Jewish culture than that of Lionel and Diana Trilling, whose life and writing merge much less visibly with that milieu. Saturating his work is a recognition of the horror and incomprehensibility of the Holocaust, which looms over such a seemingly academic and literary enterprise as *On Native Grounds*. *A Walker in the City* provides loving vignettes of his Jewish upbringing in Brownsville. There he also enunciates his credo that it is unthinkable to go one's own way, to try to elude one's Jewish identity. *New York Jew* engages all aspects of his life as a New York Jew and intellectual: from his shock at the discovery of Ezra Pound's anti-Semitic broadcasts on Italian Fascist radio to his portrayals of those Jews associated with *Partisan Review* during the 1940s to a visit to Israel and his response to a speech by Elie Weisel. In an essay written in the mid-1960s, "Introduction: The Jew as Modern American Writer," from *The Commentary Reader*, Kazin chronicles the growing stature in the United States of Jews as intellectuals and literary figures. *See also* Critics, Literary.

STANLEY FOGEL

BIBLIOGRAPHY

Wald, Alan. *The New York Intellectuals*. Chapel Hill: University of North Carolina Press, 1987.

Kehillah Experiment. *See* COMMUNAL ORGANIZATIONS.

Kissinger, Henry Alfred (b. 1923). The elder son of Louis Kissinger and Paula Stern Kissinger, Henry Kissinger was born in Fürth near Nuremberg, Germany. A year later his only sibling, Walter Bernhard, was born. Louis Kissinger and his family belonged to one of several Orthodox synagogues in Fürth. Louis was a teacher at several public schools prior to 1933. The family emigrated from Germany in 1938, via England, to the United States to New York City, where Louis found employment as a bookkeeper and Paula as a cook and, later, as a self-employed caterer.

Shortly after his arrival, Kissinger enrolled at George Washington High School, but a year later he had to shift to night school and work during the day to help with the family finances. Upon completion of high school, he enrolled in night courses at City College of New York. In February 1943, he was drafted and, later that year, became a citizen. Under the Army Specialized Training Program, he was enrolled in a special engineering program at Lafayette College. After reassignment to an infantry company in 1944, Kissinger was sent to Europe, where he was assigned to Army Intelligence and Counterintelligence. In June 1945, he was promoted to the rank of staff sergeant and received the Bronze Star. Earlier in that year he was appointed military administrator at Krefeld and became a Counter Intelligence Corps (CIC) agent. Other similar assignments followed. Upon demobilization in 1946, Kissinger remained in Germany as a civilian instructor of German history at the European Command Intelligence School at Oberammergau. In 1947, he returned to the United States and enrolled at Harvard College. Here he would remain for the next 20 years as an undergraduate and graduate student and as a member of the faculty.

In 1950, he married Ann Fleischer, the daughter of Conservative German Jews. In 1951, while still a graduate student, Kissinger was appointed director of the Harvard International Seminar and editor of the quarterly journal, *Confluence, An International Forum*, which was published until 1958. In 1954, Kissinger was awarded the Ph.D. degree, and the following year he joined the Council on Foreign Relations in New York as study director. During the same year he was appointed lecturer on government at Harvard. In 1957, he published *Nuclear Weapons and Foreign Policy*, which became a Book-of-the-Month Club selection. During this period he also established his warm relationship with Nelson Rockefeller, which was to be of paramount importance to his future. Thereafter, his career advanced rapidly. In 1958, he was appointed co-director of the Harvard Center for International Studies (he resigned in 1960) and director of the Defense Studies Program. In 1960, he attained the rank of full professor. Dedicated and hardworking himself, he expected total commitment from his students, as he did later from his subordinates.

After the publication of his second book, *Necessity for Choice*, in 1961, he was introduced by Arthur Schlesinger, Jr., to President John

Kennedy. Shortly thereafter Kissinger was appointed consultant to the Rand Corporation, the National Security Council, and the Arms Control and Disarmament Agency. However, he was not happy with the Kennedy administration and barely hid his disappointment. When Nelson Rockefeller was seeking the Republican nomination for president in 1964, Kissinger served as his foreign policy adviser. At this time he was also completing his third book, *The Troubled Partnership.* (His fourth and, perhaps, most controversial book, *A World Restored,* dealing with the Congress of Vienna and the Metternich era, was published in 1973.)

Kissinger and Ann had had two children, Elizabeth (1960) and David (1962). But their marriage had not been a happy one, and they were divorced in 1965. Eight years later Kissinger married Nancy Sharon Maginnes, whom he had met earlier while a member of the Rockefeller circle.

Kissinger first met Richard Nixon in December 1967. With the approval of Rockefeller, in 1969 Kissinger accepted the position of special assistant on foreign affairs to the President. He exercised his authority via the National Security Council, which now, essentially, became his "instrument." During the ensuing "Nixon Years" Kissinger identified himself totally with the President's foreign policy regarding China, Southeast Asia, the Middle East, and other spheres. His influence upon President Nixon was much greater than that of Secretary of State William Rogers, whom Kissinger did not hesitate to circumvent when he wanted to see the President. In his position Kissinger was instrumental in negotiating the SALT I Agreement with the Soviet Union in May 1972. He was also given responsibility for conducting the negotiations in that year to bring U.S. involvement in Southeast Asia to an end. For this successful effort, Kissinger was awarded the Nobel Peace Prize in 1973.

In August 1973, Kissinger was appointed secretary of state to help shore up the sagging Nixon administration during the catapulting Watergate crisis. He remained in his post on the National Security Council. In October 1973, Egypt and Syria initiated the Yom Kippur War against Israel. A month later Kissinger met for the first time with President Anwar Sadat of Egypt, whose armies had suffered defeat. The two men took an immediate liking to each other, and Kissinger would engineer an improvement in U.S.-Egyptian relations that would bring him his greatest triumph and for which he is best remembered. His efforts continued into the Ford administration and laid the groundwork for the signing, during the Carter administration, of the accords by which Egypt and Israel established formal diplomatic relations.

Kissinger resigned as secretary of state in 1977. Since that time he has given public lectures and heads two consulting firms that advise clients, both domestic and foreign, on government contacts.

REYNOLD KOPPEL

BIBLIOGRAPHY
Graubard, Stephen R. *Kissinger: Portrait of a Mind.* New York: Norton, 1973.
Kalb, Marvin and Bernard. *Kissinger.* Boston: Little, Brown, 1974.
Landau, David. *Kissinger: The Uses of Power.* Boston: Houghton Mifflin, 1972.
Mazlish, Bruce. *Kissinger: The European Mind in America.* New York: Basic Books, 1976.

Kosinski, Jerzy (1933–1991). Jerzy Kosinski was born in Lodz, Poland, in 1933, the only child of wealthy Jewish parents. After the Nazi invasion of Poland, Kosinski's parents sent their six-year-old son into the countryside, where he suffered the experiences that are detailed in his first and most famous novel, *The Painted Bird* (1965). This autobiographical volume tells of the horror and grotesque behavior witnessed by a nameless child wandering through Holocaust-ravaged Europe. Rather than speaking directly of the Holocaust itself, the author focuses on the savagery of the peasants among whom the boy travels. Kosinski's unrelenting and graphic portrayal of gratuitous violence embody the human condition during this period when all pretense of civility vanished. *The Painted Bird* made Kosinski a controversial figure inasmuch as his depiction of brutality in his native land earned him the ire of the Polish government, which accused him of slandering the Polish people. The book, nevertheless, quickly became a classic in the genre of Holocaust literature, and it won the French Best Foreign Book Award. In the United States *Steps* (1969), Kosinski's second novel, won the National Book Award for Fiction.

Kosinski received an M.A. in sociology and history from the University of Lodz in 1953; in 1957 he immigrated to the United States and in 1965 was naturalized. His first two books, consisting of political essays, *The Future is Our Comrade* (1960) and *No Third Path* (1962), were published under the pseudonym Joseph Novak.

Although Kosinski is not perceived as an American Jewish writer, insofar as his novels do not include Jewish characters or themes, his personal travails during the Holocaust is evident in many of his works, which deal with the themes of horror and deception, the legacy of his nightmare childhood. In addition to his six subsequent novels, none of which achieved the prominence of the first two, Kosinski wrote literary criticism and books on the phenomenon of collective behavior. He taught literature and criticism at several universities, including Princeton, Yale, and Wesleyan.

Kosinski was the recipient of many honors including an honorary Ld.H. from Albion College in 1988 and from SUNY in 1989. He also received an honorary Ph.D. in Hebrew letters from Spertus College in 1982.

Kosinski's other novels include *Being There* (1971), made into a film in 1979, *The Devil True* (1973), *Cockpit* (1975), *Blind Date* (1977), *Passion Play* (1979), *Pinball* (1982), and *The Hermit of 69th Street* (1988).

ALAN L. BERGER
JACK R. FISCHEL

BIBLIOGRAPHY

Lavers, Norman. *Jerzy Kosinsky*. Boston: Twayne, 1982.

LuPack, Barbara Tepa. *Plays of Passion, Games of Choice: Jerzy Kosinski and His Fiction*. Bristol, Ind.: Wyndham Hall Press, 1988.

L

Labor Movement. Jewish participation in the American labor movement includes several distinct but related types of experiences. The core of that involvement came through the Jewish labor movement of the 1890s through the 1930s. However, a significant number of Jewish workers also labored in trades that were not predominantly nor significantly Jewish, and this constitutes a second major contact point between Jews and the American labor movement. Finally, some Jewish labor leaders have achieved prominence in unions that were not part of the Jewish labor movement. These leaders shared the general socialist orientation of those Jews who headed the Jewish labor movement, but differences in time and place led them into a separate arena.

Prior to 1890, Jews concerned about the American labor movement were uninvolved as Jews. Usually their interest flowed from a political base—socialism—not from any ethnic affinity to their fellow Jews. Samuel Gompers (1850–1924) entered the American labor movement in the 1870s through his activity in the Cigarmakers' Union. He quickly extended his work in the early 1880s to the fledgling national organization of trade unions. In 1886, with the formation of the American Federation of Labor, Gompers became its first president, a position he was to hold, except for 1895, until his death. Thus a Jewish immigrant from a Dutch and English background became the leader and spokesman for much of the American labor movement.

Gompers never identified personally as a Jew, and Jewish concerns were of little impor-

tance to him. His objective was to create an American trade union movement, and he tended to disparage any ethnic basis for organization. In this he reflected a fundamental belief of many Socialists in the late nineteenth century.

This same stress on class consciousness rather than ethnic affinity also can be seen in the activities of the Jewish Socialists in New York City in the 1880s. Morris Hillquit (1869–1933) is an excellent representative of this group. Although he and Gompers were to become bitter enemies once Gompers gave up his socialist beliefs in favor of a pragmatic, bread-and-butter type of unionism, the two agreed that workers should be regarded as a united class, not as a set of distinct ethnic groups. They should be organized into a single American labor movement, not into several ethnic labor movements. Hillquit even eschewed Yiddish, preferring Russian initially and later English. Yiddish connoted an inward-looking, self-contained group of workers, and Socialists committed to universal class values could not accept this.

Hillquit also shared Gompers's lack of identification as a Jew. In Hillquit's case, it became open hostility to Jewish practices, as seen in his support during the 1880s of parties on Yom Kippur. Hillquit later gave up such attacks on Jewish religious practices because he recognized that they alienated many Jewish workers from the Socialists.

Although Jewish immigrants entered a wide array of occupations, they concentrated in the garment trades. This resulted from several factors, including the rapid expansion of the use of ready-made clothing, which provided the immediate work needed by the newcomers; the experience of many Jewish immigrants with either needle work or jobs in small shops in their home towns; the subdivision of the work that took place at the time, thereby allowing even the unskilled to enter the garment shops; and the presence of Jewish employers in the industry, drawn mainly from the older German Jewish group. As with other immigrants, once Jews began to enter an industry, they became the base for networks that reached those who came later. Newcomers then gained employment through family members or *landsleit* already at work in the garment industry.

The Jews who worked in the garment trades came to America for several reasons. Most came to escape poverty and seek economic gain, but others wanted to flee from the Russian army draft or the czar's police. Some came to join members of their family, while for those weary of the limited horizon of traditional small-town life, the modernism of America exerted a powerful pull. As with other groups of immigrants, most Jews had no intention of shedding their ethnic identity or group practices. For Jews this identity was defined by their distinctive language, Yiddish, by a palpable concern, if less intense and central than in Europe, for certain religious practices, and by a continuing linkage to family in the Old Country. A major objective of most Jews in America was to bring family members to this country. Other immigrants shared this desire, but unlike some other groups of newcomers, the Jews had no great interest in a return to Europe. They were in America to stay and to build a new life.

Among the mass of Jewish immigrants was a small number of socialists who quickly undertook the task of organizing Jewish workers for political and trade union action. Many originally shared Hillquit's vision that Jewish workers should become part of the American working class. However, this notion quickly lost out to a more realistic understanding that Jewish immigrant workers measured their lives in terms of both their Jewish identity and their class position. Neither could be slighted. After 1905, this position was reinforced by the emigration to the United States of many Bundists from Russia. Their brand of socialism was based less on a universal working class than a recognition of the cultural autonomy of the Jewish worker and the necessity to build socialism on this base. Key Jewish labor leaders, such as David Dubinsky (1892-1982), Sidney Hillman (1887-

1946), and Max Zaritsky (1885-1959), came from Bundist origins.

The task of organizing Jewish workers was frustrating. Even with the formation of the United Hebrew Trades in 1888 to coordinate and encourage the formation of unions, many Jewish workers either failed to join unions or left them after bitter strikes. Benjamin Schlesinger (1876-1932), the long-time leader of the International Ladies Garment Workers Union, complained bitterly in 1906 that only 2500 of the 40,000 cloakmakers in New York City had joined the union. The nonjoiners were the temporary workers, those who feared retaliation from the boss, those who were the favorites of the boss, and those with their sights on an exit from wage labor—something not uncommon among the low-capital, small shops that proliferated with the growth of a contracting system in the garment trades.

Many of the early unions organized by the Jewish Socialists collapsed. Those that survived were hardly robust. The tailors in the men's clothing industry were organized within the United Garment Workers, established in 1891. However, the leadership of this union came from the men's work-clothes segment of the trade, depended on the union label for influence with employers, and had little interest in risking its modest gains to try to organize the new immigrants who labored elsewhere in the industry. The workers in the ladies' garment industry were represented by local unions that usually lasted only a short time. The cloakmakers in New York City were the major exception. In 1900, this group took the lead in establishing the International Ladies Garment Workers Union (ILG). In addition to slow growth, the ILG was beset in its early years by internal conflicts. Particularly severe were those between the highly trained and indispensable cutters and other less skilled workers. The weak union also had to bear a struggle between socialists and advocates of a less ideological approach to unionism. In 1908, the ILG was close to dissolution.

The situation changed abruptly beginning in 1909. By 1916, national unions had been established in all areas of the garment trades. By 1920, they had won further tests against the employers, and they were now a stable and increasingly important element in trying to control the poor conditions and cutthroat competition that marked the industry. The change occurred through a series of highly publicized strikes. The first of these in 1909 was a spontaneous "Uprising of the Twenty

Thousand" among the young women who made shirtwaists in New York City. Although not a total success, the strike rallied the public behind the immigrant workers. This support was critical in the Cloakmakers' Strike of 1910 in New York City. After a bitter and protracted walkout, the largely Jewish employers entered into a Protocol of Peace with the workers and their union. This came after continued public support for the strikers led prominent Jewish business leaders to intervene on behalf of a settlement. Louis Brandeis (1856–1941) played a key role in negotiating the final agreement with its provisions for conciliation and arbitration. Although the Protocol of Peace only lasted until 1915, it established the de facto presence of the ILG in the industry, and it set the principle of the third-party umpire that has survived in the industrial relations of the garment trades to the present.

Workers in the men's clothing industry, led by Jewish Socialists, also created their union on a firm basis in this period. A highly publicized strike in Chicago at the well-known firm of Hart, Schaffner and Marx not only attracted widespread public support, but also exacerbated tensions between the leaders of the United Garment Workers and the mass of the immigrant strikers. Relations between the two groups within the union grew worse over the conduct of a strike among the men's clothing workers in New York City in early 1913. By 1914, the conflict became an open break. The leaders of the United Garment Workers, including a number of Jews, refused to turn over control to the majority within the union, now composed of new immigrants led by Jewish Socialists such as Sidney Hillman. It was less an ethnic struggle than one of personalities and power. When the leadership refused to seat delegates to the 1914 convention chosen by the new Socialist-led locals, these delegates, who clearly represented a majority of the membership, walked out and founded their own union, the Amalgamated Clothing Workers of America.

The new union not only had to battle with the employers to establish itself, but also had to resist efforts by the United Garment Workers, through the American Federation of Labor (AFL), to brand the Amalgamated an illegitimate dual union. This campaign ultimately failed, in part because other unions led by Jewish Socialists, such as the ILG and the Cloth Hat, Cap and Millinery Workers Union, supported the Amalgamated. The Amalgamated did not join the AFL until 1933.

The garment workers secured the critical public support needed to establish their unions firmly because of the progressive reform spirit of the period; the clearly exploitative conditions in the industry, whose impact was heightened by the fact that the many young women in the work force were widely regarded as defenseless; and the marginal nature of the garment industry within the American economy. The strikes did not affect the public greatly, and the employers' often were either newcomers themselves or from German Jewish origins. Thus attacks on these employers could draw on the widely felt disdain in the nation for immigrants. The basic nonunion character of American labor relations would remain untouched. Jewish workers and labor leaders benefitted from this unusual set of circumstances, rarely repeated in other sectors of the American economy.

With the establishment of Jewish-led unions in the cap and millinery trades and among the furriers, the basic structure of the unions in the garment industry was set by World War I. However, what emerged was not merely another segment of the larger American labor movement. While all the Jewish-led garment unions sought to join the AFL and participate in the American labor movement, they also developed a distinct character.

The Jewish labor movement was defined by the influence of Jewish identity and concerns on a work force that recognized its distinctiveness and on the leaders and organizations that represented these workers, and by the creation of a subculture that recombined elements of the Jewish heritage and socialism into a new amalgam. The Jewish labor movement was more than the trade unions. It also comprised the Socialist Yiddish literature and press, led by Abraham Cahan's (1860–1951) *Forward*. Publicists, editors, and writers produced a secular view of the Jew's place in the world that could be an alternative to the traditional religious outlook. In addition, the Jewish labor movement included the Workmen's Circle, and later other fraternal bodies, that not only provided insurance benefits, but also sponsored secular and socialist schools, conducted in Yiddish.

All elements of the Jewish labor movement reinforced each other. Thus the unions protected Jewish workers in their basic economic needs, but they then joined the Jewish labor press in support of socialism as the ultimate solution for the problems faced by these workers. The Workmen's Circle helped workers protect themselves against the ravages of premature death or sickness, which Socialists in the Jewish labor movement attributed to the excesses of capitalism, and which the Jewish-led trade unions sought to overcome through adequate wages and decent working conditions. None of these elements of the Jewish labor movement were unique to Jewish immigrants in America, but because of the large number of Jews in the garment trades, and their geographical concentration in several urban areas, but principally in New York City, they came together more fully and with greater impact than among other ethnic groups.

The Jewish labor movement had a strong socialist base that defined its character in several ways. It clearly separated the Jewish labor movement from the traditional communal leadership, drawn largely from among businessmen. Jewish labor leaders also were distant from the synagogues. Despite their personal and ideological hostility to Jewish religious institutions and practices, most Jewish Socialists accepted the religious practices of Jewish workers so as not to alienate them. However, Jewish Socialists ultimately sought to replace the religious messianism that had supported Jews through so many trials with a secular millennialism that offered the victory of the proletariat instead of the ultimate victory of God. The Jewish labor movement thus became organizationally and ideologically an alternative to the traditional Jewish community and its values.

The Jewish-led unions also pioneered in providing services to the membership. The garment unions developed a wide array of programs and services not normally available in other American unions. This resulted in part from the socialist ideology of the leaders, who viewed the unions as more than a bargaining tool, and in part from the imprint on Jewish labor leaders of the traditional Jewish communal responsibility for the members of the group. The ILG developed extensive educational programs and recreational opportunities, including Unity House, which allowed members to enjoy a summer vacation in the country at reasonable cost. Both the Amalgamated Clothing Workers and the Cap and Millinery Workers had more modest but similar programs. The ILG also stressed improved health care. As early as 1913, it established a union health center, which expanded over the years in scope and complexity. All the garment unions stressed various forms of sickness benefits at a time when few unions had such programs. Finally, the Amalgamated established successful banks in Chicago in 1922 and in New York City in 1923. During the 1920s, the same union built housing for its members. Following World War II, other garment unions also subsidized housing projects.

The socialistic and Jewish-led garment unions seem at first to have little in common with the AFL and its affiliates. Certainly they differed over socialism and industrial unionism, which marked the garment unions, but were opposed by most of the craft unions that dominated the AFL. There also were differences on more specific issues, such as support for the American war effort in World War I—which was strongly favored by the AFL but initially opposed by most Jewish labor leaders—and the troublesome matter of dual unionism, either on the issue of the legitimacy of the Amalgamated or over jurisdictional conflicts between the United Hebrew Trades and AFL affiliates. There is even the anomaly of the AFL supporting Zionism and the Balfour Declaration as a means of enlisting the support of Jewish workers for the American effort in World War I while the Jewish Socialists, heavily influenced by Bundist ideology, equivocated or opposed Zionism.

Despite the differences, the garment unions joined the AFL, and they remained loyal to it until the split in the American labor movement in the 1930s produced the Congress of Industrial Organizations (CIO). There were several basic points of agreement that bound together the Jewish and the American labor movements. First, the Jewish Socialist labor leaders believed some type of unionization was a prerequisite to the ultimate victory of radicalism among American workers. The AFL was far from ideal in this respect, but it was better than nothing. Second, as is true for all successful Socialist labor leaders in America, Jewish labor leaders after 1900 generally gave trade union concerns top priority. This agreed with the approach of nonsocialist leaders of American unions. The Jewish labor movement never sought isolation, nor did it become the enemy of the more conservative American trade unions. Even with the differences, there was a continuing relationship of cooperation.

Within the garment industry, Jews comprised a majority or a sizable portion of the work force. However, Jewish workers also labored in many other industries in which they constituted a distinct minority. When they attempted to organize, it was within unions dominated by non-Jews, who could be hostile for a number of reasons. Most basic was the antipathy among many American unionists to adding new members no matter who they were. This attitude turned on the fear that immigrants, women, or black workers would accept lower wages or turned on a desire to keep the number of good jobs and unionists able to fill them in balance. These trade considerations were widespread among American craft unionists, and they could lead to the strange situation of local unions that avoided organizing.

Jewish workers also faced possible anti-Semitism. Although it could operate as an independent factor, anti-Semitism often was used as a justification or cover for trade considerations. Finally, some Jewish workers outside the garment industry also were led by Socialists. In such cases, those American unions that opposed socialism generally were all the more hostile when Jewish immigrants sought to extend its influence within their trades.

Even in the face of such problems, Jewish workers made concerted efforts to join unions. A union card often meant access to the best jobs in the trade. However, entry often was difficult. In some cases, it could only be achieved through self-organization by the Jewish workers outside the established union. This dual union then became a threat to the control of the trade by the existing labor organization. To avoid a destructive competition, the newcomers were accepted into the older union. Using such means, Jewish workers entered Local 1 of the bookbinders' and the painters' unions, both in New York City, as well as the United Hatters of North America. In the latter case, the "Hebrew Hatters" threatened to become strikebreakers in a major strike undertaken by the United Hatters in order to convince the established union that the Jewish workers were less of a problem inside the union than outside of it.

Trade considerations also could override the antipathy of American unionists to Jewish Socialists. Thus the International Cigarmakers' Union accepted a group of largely Jewish workers from Chicago into the union in 1920 because exclusion promised to threaten the union's continued control of the trade. The inclusion of the Jewish workers took place despite open hostility by the Cigarmakers' Union to the Socialist leaders of the newcomers.

Some American trade unions had a policy that encouraged widespread organization. This was true for industrial unions or craft organizations, such as the United Brotherhood of Carpenters, which faced a breakdown of the skill level in the trade, combined with an excess of workers ready to perform the easier tasks. As a result of this situation, the Carpenters used ethnic and racially based locals to encourage organization among nonunion workers. Clearly, this policy was based purely on trade considerations since the Carpenters were one of the American unions that by the early 1890s favored the closing of immigration. Sixteen Jewish locals were organized in addition to the significant number of Jews who joined regular locals. The Jewish locals were not led by Socialists, and they played no role in the affairs of the union. The Jewish hat workers and bookbinders also lacked Socialist leaders. Those Jewish workers who operated in the larger American environment, rather than that of the Jewish labor movement, clearly had less attraction to socialism. These workers responded more often to the sentiments found in American unions.

The Amalgamated Meat Cutters and Butcher Workmen had become an industrial union by World War I. It welcomed Jews into its ranks, both through separate locals and as members of established ones. In this case, however, the newcomers came into conflict with a major demand of the non-Jewish workers. The union favored Sunday closing laws, but for the Jewish workers in the kosher meat trade, this would mean two days of closure each week. The issue remained unresolved despite a sympathetic attitude toward the position of the Jewish workers by the union's national leaders. Socialism was not a factor. In this case, it was the traditional practice of the Jewish community that came into conflict with American imperatives.

While Jewish workers increasingly had won entry into a variety of trades and unions by the 1920s, that decade proved to be a near disaster for the many Jewish workers who still labored in the garment industry. A bitter conflict between the old-line Socialist leadership and a new body of Communist leaders divided all the garment unions, but it came closest to destroying the ILG and the International Fur Workers' Union.

The Bolshevik Revolution of 1917 led ultimately to two splits within the American Socialist Party, including the Jewish Socialists. Those who became Communists, or who were willing to work with the Communists, soon focused on the garment unions as appropriate targets for a takeover. Through ardent organizing, and by exploiting long-standing problems in the industry that had persisted despite the stabilization of the garment unions in the 1909–1920 period, the Communists made rapid headway in the ILG and the Fur Workers' Union. In both unions bitter conflict developed between the Socialists, who controlled the national leadership, and the Communists, who gained ascendancy in the locals in New York City.

In 1926, the Communists sought to gain a decisive victory in the ILG by leading a victorious strike in the New York City cloak trade. Against the objections of the national leaders, the Communists rejected a reasonable compromise before the strike began, and on orders from the Communist Party they maintained the strike long after it could have been settled. The objective was a smashing victory that would have enhanced the Communists' position in the ILG and increased their prestige in other garment unions. However, the result was defeat, the financial collapse of the entire ILG in the wake of the strike, a substantial loss of membership, and renewed control by the older Socialist leaders as the Communists were blamed for the debacle. The ILG was seriously weakened, and it remained so through the early years of the Depression.

Communists in the International Fur Workers' Union also gained control over the locals in New York City—the heart of the union. They also called a strike in 1926 to solidify control. Unlike the situation in the ILG, the Communists in the fur industry were able to win at least a partial victory. Continued militant unionism on behalf of the membership allowed the Communists to retain control of the union despite the efforts of the AFL to dislodge them.

The attempt of the Communists to win power in the Amalgamated Clothing Workers and the Cap and Millinery Workers failed as did their effort to take over the Workmen's Circle. Although ultimately the Communists were defeated in all but the Fur Workers, their challenge to the established Socialist leaderships weakened the Jewish labor movement and diverted its attention from the many problems in the garment trades. The depression that began in 1929 further weakened union standards.

Yet the 1930s proved not to be a continuation of the setbacks of the 1920s. Instead, the garment unions immediately took advantage of the New Deal legislation, including Section 7A of the National Recovery Act. Even more, they shared in the spirit of renewed hope that encouraged workers nationwide in the first years of the New Deal. The losses of the 1920s were reversed in 1933 and 1934, and the unions emerged even stronger within their trades.

The 1930s also witnessed decisive changes in the policies of the Jewish Socialist labor leaders. First, the appeal of the New Deal led to a significant political decision: lifelong Socialists decided to support Franklin Roosevelt in 1936. To do so in New York, without falling under the control of the machine politicians who controlled the Democratic Party, made necessary the establishment of a new political organization—the American Labor Party. Fueled by the votes of garment workers, the new party quickly became a major force in New York politics. Second, the rise of Hitler threatened European Jewry in a clear way. Older concepts of universalism gave way to the present danger, and many Jewish labor leaders significantly increased their involvement in specifically Jewish concerns. This led initially to their support for the Jewish Labor Committee, which was committed to the defense of Jewish interests worldwide, and then, with the added impact of the Holocaust, to an unprecedented acceptance of and support for the State of Israel.

Jewish labor leaders also played a major role in the effort to establish industrial unionism within the AFL during the 1930s. David Dubinsky, Sidney Hillman, and Max Zaritsky were among the eight labor leaders who created the original CIO in 1935. They believed the industrial unionism so long practiced in the garment trades should be available to all American workers. Dubinsky and Zaritsky ultimately returned to the AFL as they opposed the conversion of the CIO from a goad to the AFL into a permanent second labor federation.

By the 1930s, the Jewish labor movement was rapidly dissolving. The number of Jews in the garment trades was falling steadily; the Yiddish language that had been the medium of political and intellectual discourse rapidly declined as the second generation discarded it for the English they needed to make their way in new occupations; and the socialist ideology that had provided direction for the leadership, and had offered an explanation of their lives to many in the rank and file, was replaced by New Deal liberalism and a renewed interest in the concerns of the Jews as Jews.

The Jewish labor leaders had created a distinctive blend of universal socialism and ethnic identity. American-born labor leaders who happened to be Jews were still attracted to socialism, but without the linkage to the identity and needs of a specifically Jewish work force. Thus younger labor leaders, such as Albert Shanker (b. 1928) of the teachers and Victor Gotbaum (b. 1921) of the state and local government employees, shared the ideology of socialism and the Jewish origins of the older generation of Jewish labor leaders. They also led unions that contained significant numbers of Jewish workers. However, these second-generation Jewish labor leaders had less concern than their forebears with the ethnic character of the work force, nor did they have a substantial impact on these Jewish workers as Jews. As with Samuel Gompers, they became Jewish labor leaders in an American labor movement. Thus had Jewish participation in the American labor movement returned to its starting point.

The Jewish labor movement reflected specific historical conditions for Jews in America. With the end of a concentration of Jews in the garment trades, and the decline of a discrete, isolated Jewish community that focused as much on its European origins as its American existence, the distinctive labor movement that emerged to serve the needs of this community also declined. American Jews now participate in the labor movement more as Americans than as Jews. The Jewish labor movement is gone, but Jews in the American labor movement will continue. *See also* Left, Jews on the.

IRWIN YELLOWITZ

BIBLIOGRAPHY

Dubinsky, David, and Raskin, A. H. *David Dubinsky: A Life with Labor*. New York: Simon & Schuster, 1977.

Dubofsky, Melvyn. *When Workers Organize: New York City in the Progressive Era*. Amherst: University of Massachusetts Press, 1968.

Epstein, Melech. *Jewish Labor in the U.S.A.* 2 vols. New York: Ktav, 1969.

———. *Profiles of Eleven*. Lanham, Md.: University Press of America, 1965.

Herberg, Will. "Jewish Labor Movement in the United States: Early Years to World War I." *Industrial and Labor Relations Review* V (1952): 501–523.

———. "Jewish Labor Movement in the United States: World War I to the Present." *Industrial and Labor Relations Review* VI (1953): 44–66.

Howe, Irving. *World of Our Fathers*. New York: Harcourt Brace Jovanovich, 1976.

Josephson, Matthew. *Sidney Hillman: Statesman of American Labor*. Garden City, N.Y.: Doubleday, 1952.

Rischin, Moses. *The Promised City: New York's Jews, 1870–1914*. Cambridge: Harvard University Press, 1962.

Yellowitz, Irwin. "Jewish Immigrants and the American Labor Movement, 1900–1920." *American Jewish History* LXXI (1981): 188–217.

Landsmanshaftn. This Yiddish term (singular, *landsmanshaft*) refers to benevolent societies formed by European Jews newly arrived in the United States. Landsmanshaftn are Jewish ethnic voluntary associations based on members' shared origins in an East European city or town. Beginning in the 1800s, immigrants created landsmanshaftn in order to pray together, to provide financial assistance and insurance benefits, to supply burial services, and to raise money to send aid to the hometown. These organizations also serve as social centers for landslayt people sharing loyalty to a common birthplace.

In the United States, landsmanshaftn were originally immigrant synagogues. With the mass migration of East European Jews after 1880, this trend shifted. Not only was there an increase in the number of these associations generally, but both religious and secular landsmanshaftn of immigrants from the same hometown operated simultaneously and as autonomous groups. There were synagogue societies, independent men's associations, women's sections, relief organizations, and branches of national fraternal orders, such as the Workmen's Circle, the Jewish National Workers Alliance (Farband), and Brith Abraham.

Newcomers from both larger urban centers and smaller towns of Eastern Europe generated multiple and heterogeneous landsmanshaftn. Immigrants and their descendants organized themselves into locality-based associations that also reflected their diverse occupations, political allegiances, religious views, as well as gender and age differences. For example, the city of Bialystok was represented by over 40 separate landsmanshaftn in America from 1868 to the present, including such groups as Bialystoker Somach Noflim, Bialystoker Bricklayers Benevolent Association, Bialystoker Young Mens Association, Bialystoker Ladies Aid Society of Harlem and the Bronx, and the Bialystoker Center. In addition to the New York societies, Bialystok lodges were also active in Detroit, Chicago, Philadelphia, Newark, and Milwaukee and in Canada.

The height of landsmanshaft activity peaked in the early decades of the twentieth century. These organizations proliferated during World War I, and they actively helped finance relief work in their respective birthplaces in Europe.

Particularly in connection with these efforts during crisis periods, namely World War I and World War II, federations of landsmanshaftn were formed to coordinate fund-raising campaigns on a regional basis. As a result, coalitions such as the United Bessarabian Relief and the American Federation for Polish Jews were created.

In the years prior to World War II, one of every four Jews in New York City belonged to a landsmanshaft. The results of a survey of 2500 societies in that city, where landsmanshaftn were most prolific, were published in 1938 by the Federal Writers' Project of the Works Progress Administration. This pioneering study outlined categories of organizational bodies that utilize the landsmanshaft structure. Family circles were identified in this typology as an outgrowth of the landsmanshaft community in America.

Modifications of the landsmanshaft model of affiliation emerge as the needs and circumstances of immigrant Jews and their American-born offspring change. For example, today membership is not delimited solely by geography, Yiddish is replaced by English as the primary language of communication, and responses to issues and events change. What remains at the core of all groups, however, are the principles of mutual aid and social fellowship.

Another central tenet of landsmanshaft life is philanthropy and charitable work. Contributions are made locally to Jewish and non-Jewish-American causes. As for the native country, this concern has largely been abandoned, understandably, although some landsmanshaftn still maintain ties with the few Jews that remain in their European communities. Since World War II, Israel's enterprises and institutions are almost universally accepted by American landsmanshaftn as primary recipients of organizational giving.

As members learned of the destruction of European Jewry and witnessed the rise of the State of Israel, landsmanshaftn shifted their focus from hometown to homeland. After World War II, landsmanshaftn joined various campaigns on behalf of Israel. They also worked to locate and aid survivors of the Holocaust, some of whom joined landsmanshaftn after reaching America.

The post-World War II refugees infused the landsmanshaft community with new spirit and new purpose, yet their arrival also highlighted the differences between them and previous waves of immigrants. While some joined existing societies, other initiated new landsmanshaftn to represent their unique bond. Despite their common link to a community of origin, the earlier settlers had become distanced from the European hometown as the course of adjustment to America progressed. Minute books and meeting records reflect the evolution of priorities and goals.

Survivors of the Holocaust initiated new features of landsmanshaft activity in the postwar period, including annual commemoration ceremonies to honor the memory of the 6 million Jews who perished in Europe. The survivor landsmanshaftn also work to document the achievements of their communities, as well as how they were destroyed under Nazism, by publishing memorial (yisker) books. Over 400 of these volumes trace the history of the hometown and also the accomplishments of landslayt in different countries. Counterparts to the landsmanshaft societies in the United States and Canada are found in Latin America, Australia, South Africa, Europe, and Israel.

In existence for over a century, landsmanshaftn were a vital and creative grass-roots response on the part of a transplanted population. As a result of the outpouring of communal energies in the early decades of the twentieth century, there were more of these associations than other institutions created to aid immigrants in their accommodation to American life.

The landsmanshaft sector has been reduced in size, and the profile of the leadership has changed. Societies have disbanded because their membership declined when the flow of immigrants dwindled. Yet, despite predictions of their virtual disappearance in the second and third American-born generation, there are signs of landsmanshaft continuity. The traditional model of community and belonging is borrowed and adapted by the American generation.

Throughout their history, landsmanshaftn modified their structure and purpose. These ethnic organizations offer members a context in which to discern the rules of American society, while affirming their unique bonds as Jews of East European heritage. *See also* Communal Organizations.

HANNAH KLIGER

BIBLIOGRAPHY

American Jewish History. LXXVI, No. 1 (September 1986).

Kugelmass, Jack, and Boyarin, Jonathan. *From a Ruined Garden: The Memorial Books of Polish Jewry*. New York: Schocken, 1983.

Mitchell, William E. *Mishpokhe: A Study of New York City Family Clubs*. The Hague: Mouton, 1978.

Schwartz, Rosaline, and Milamed, Susan. *Guide to the Landsmanshaftn Archive*. New York: YIVO, 1978.

Weisser, Michael R. *A Brotherhood of Memory: Jewish Landsmanshaftn in the New World*. New York: Basic Books, 1985.

Law and Lawyers. Jewish immigrants to the United States abandoned an ancient legal culture. Ever since Sinai, the Jewish sacred law of divine revelation had left its distinctive imprint upon the Jewish people. Its recurrent affirmation had enabled Jews to survive a succession of national disasters, culminating in the destruction of the Second Temple (C.E. 70) and exile from the land of Israel. Thereafter, rabbinical legal interpretation created a living legal system (Halakah) that sustained the autonomy of the Jewish people for nearly 2000 years after their national sovereignty had ended.

The Jewish legal tradition was a sacred-law tradition. Because the sole source of authority for Torah, and for the legal system that emanated from it, was divine command, the unity of religion and law was its distinctive feature. From their common source in divine revelation, ethics and ritual merged into legal obligation. A single paragraph in one of the most ancient of the legal codes found within the Torah (*Ex.* 22:24–23:19) provides a vivid example of this commingling. It combines guidelines for loans and pledges, justice in legal proceedings, and Sabbath observance, with injunctions not to revile judges, curse rulers, or boil a kid in its mother's milk (the legal foundation of Jewish dietary observance). Guided by rabbis (the law men of Judaism) after the first century of the Common Era, Jewish law retained its inherently religious character; and Judaism, insofar as it was a religion, remained intrinsically legalistic. Although, according to talmudic doctrine, the law of the state where Jews lived was the law, Jews retained their own autonomous legal system throughout eighteen centuries of exile. Rabbinical courts assured the transmission and enforcement of the basic principles of Jewish law.

Neither Jewish judicial autonomy nor rabbinical legal authority could be transplanted to the United States. By the nineteenth century, emancipated European Jews rejected their sacred-law tradition for the privileges of national citizenship. As the Jewish communal structure fragmented, rabbinical authority was restricted to exclusively "religious" issues, primarily ritual observance. In the United States, the enticements of individual opportunity and legal equality were irresistible. While Orthodox Jews struggled, in vain, to preserve a measure of rabbinical legal authority, most Jewish immigrants looked to the American legal system, in which judges and lawyers, not rabbis, defined the meaning of law and justice.

Although Jewish immigrants entered an American culture that was as legalistic as the one they had abandoned, the differences were conspicuous. The Torah revealed to Israel instructs Jews how to live a holy life, while the Constitution ratified by "We the People" is a charter of governance. The Torah defines a covenantal relationship between God and Israel, demanding submission to divine authority (God, in Jewish liturgy, is King). The Constitution, by contrast, reflects an abiding suspicion of power (especially royal power), the legacy of the American colonial relationship to England. The Constitution has nothing to say about such intimately personal aspects of behavior as diet, sexual relations, dress regulation, or ritual observance. Expressing the secular values of the Enlightenment, it separated religion and nationality, so closely conjoined in the Jewish legal tradition and historical experience. The cherished Jeffersonian metaphor of a "wall of separation," so fundamental to American constitutionalism, is completely foreign to Jewish law, which is predicated upon the obligation of holiness, defined biblically as loyalty to God.

Reform Jews were the first to confront the challenges posed by American life to Jewish law. Their initial focus on liturgical change broadened into a sweeping rejection of what Rabbi Kaufmann Kohler (1843–1926), their leading theoretician, described as the "dry legality" of Judaism. Reformers found legitimacy, instead, in a synthesis of Hebrew prophecy, American patriotism, and Protestant social gospel. The Pittsburgh Platform (1885) repudiated Jewish law as the normative framework of Jewish life in the United States. Once severed from its own sacred-law tradition, Judaism could be accommodated to the dominant religious and social norms of Protestant America. By the end of the nineteenth century, the demise of Jewish legal authority was all but complete. In the United States, law—historically the source of Jewish autonomy—became an instrument of Jewish acculturation.

In urban industrial American society, by the end of the nineteenth century, the legal system beckoned invitingly to Jews, with promises of religious freedom and civil equality, while the legal profession served as an important channel of social mobility and political influence. German Jews quickly capitalized upon these opportunities. A generation of commercial experience, in banking and manufacture, had created a flourishing business and institutional clientele that was increasingly dependent upon the advice of legal counsel. By the turn of the twentieth century a handful of German Jewish lawyers had begun to emulate, and even join, the corporate elite of the legal profession.

In the major cities of Jewish commercial activity, German Jewish lawyers achieved professional distinction, which quickly translated into public influence. In Louisville, Lewis N. Dembitz (1833–1907) achieved renown as a practitioner and as a scholar of American and Jewish jurisprudence. In Boston, his nephew Louis D. Brandeis (1856–1941) developed a lucrative corporate practice before turning his energies toward progressive causes. In Philadelphia, Mayer Sulzberger (1843–1923) participated in a wide range of philanthropic activities as a judge and community leader. Especially in New York, the center of American commerce, German Jews established their own law firms to represent a prospering Jewish corporate clientele. Outstanding among them was Guggenheimer, Untermeyer & Marshall, whose newest partner, Louis Marshall, (1856–1929), converted his varied legal talents into three decades of personal dominance in American Jewish affairs.

Marshall's accession to power, through an association with wealthy German Jewish philanthropists, led to his presidency of the American Jewish Committee, his institutional power base. From it, he redefined the nature of Jewish legal authority in the United States. Before 1900, the major issues in American Jewish life were largely the subject of rabbinical debate and decision. Thereafter, as authority slipped from the rabbinate in a secular society, lawyers came to dominate Jewish affairs. "Marshall law" defined a new conception of American Judaism, grounded in the American constitutional tradition, oriented around the obligations of citizenship, and emphasizing concepts of legal equality and civil rights. As a lawyer, Marshall enjoyed privileged access to the special language and symbolism of law, which defined American identity and purpose. As a Jew, he insisted upon a religion of Judaism that was compatible with American patriotism. Respect for law was consistent with the ancient traditions of the Jewish people, just as it was consonant with their modern obligations as American citizens. In his most re-

vealing metaphor, suggesting his personal fusion of two legal traditions, Marshall described the Constitution as the "holy of holies, an instrument of sacred import." Perhaps his most significant achievement was to begin the process of reconciling the disparate traditions of Judaism and Americanism in secular legal terms.

Marshall and Brandeis jointly defined an American Judaism that drew upon the concepts of law and justice that were central to both traditions. Marshall, a conservative Republican, emphasized the rule of law; Brandeis, a liberal Democrat, fused social justice to his understanding of the New England Puritan tradition. Both men attracted lawyers to Jewish communal affairs and empowered them to articulate American Jewish policy. Marshall, Sulzberger, and Julian W. Mack (1866–1943), a prominent reformer and federal judge, guided the American Jewish Committee, established in 1906 as the organizational voice of German Jewry; while Brandeis, after his surprising identification with Zionism in 1914, assigned the most important Zionist tasks to his trusted legal associates, especially Mack and Felix Frankfurter (1882–1965), recently appointed to the Harvard Law School Faculty. By World War I, German Jews had secure positions in the legal profession, as private practitioners in corporate firms, on law-school faculties, and on state and federal benches (where the eminence of Benjamin N. Cardozo [1870–1938], author of *The Nature of the Judicial Process*, added to the lustre of Jewish professional achievement). With the appointment of Brandeis to the United States Supreme Court in 1916, the process was complete: for the first time in American history, a Jew was empowered to interpret and declare the meaning of the supreme law of the land.

Despite their conspicuous success within the legal profession, German Jews were the privileged exceptions. The emergence of the modern legal profession coincided with the era of mass immigration. The immigrants' quest for social mobility was quickly translated into demands for professional access. But the bar, organized, stratified, and dominated by a Protestant elite, resisted. Immigrants, especially Jews, were blamed for the transformation of a dignified profession into a commercial pursuit. Immigrant aspirations were obstructed by the racism, nativism, and anti-Semitism of the organized bar. Jews were repeatedly targeted by the professional elite for their ethical and character deficiencies, including their "Oriental" minds, acquisitive tendencies, and "Jewy" attitudes.

At every stage of professional access, Jews confronted high walls of discrimination. Law-school barriers were surmounted with relative ease, at least for those who could afford the cost of college education upon which admission depended. But professional entry and opportunity were more tightly restricted. With corporate firms at the apex, and solo practice at the base of the professional opportunity structure, Jewish lawyers, all but excluded from the elite firms, were overwhelmingly confined to the least lucrative and least prestigious sectors of professional life. Although Jews ultimately comprised the most successfully mobile group of immigrants, whose professional success fulfilled the Horatio Alger opportunity myth, this was a protracted process. Eastern European Jews did not finally gain access to form the privileged sectors of professional life until after World War II.

The Depression of the 1930s compounded the dire professional plight of aspiring Jewish lawyers. Economic retrenchment, reinforced by professional anti-Semitism, decimated opportunity in the private sector; economic hardship drove many Jews from the profession. Even the most academically distinguished Jewish law-school graduates, from elite law schools, were not hired by law firms or law faculties. For a talented few, however, the curse of hard times was transformed into the blessing of New Deal opportunity. Government regulatory agencies, linked to the political reforms of the Franklin D. Roosevelt administration, offered positions that attracted ambitious Jewish lawyers to Washington. The New Deal offered a unique opportunity for professional fulfillment, in novel areas of the law like securities regulation and collective bargaining. In effect, the New Deal provided a parallel opportunity ladder for Jewish lawyers, whose government experience later certified them for positions in the elite sectors of professional life.

A talented group of younger professionals quickly capitalized upon their opportunities in what became known, to enemies of the administration, as the "Jew Deal." At the center of these developments was Felix Frankfurter, combining the functions of social critic, teacher, and job broker with the conviction that lawyers were uniquely qualified for the tasks of governance. Frankfurter, who had long since converted law into his surrogate religion, cherished the demonstration of patriotic loyalty that attached to government service. His own appointment to the Supreme Court in 1939 was the crowning symbol of the achievements of Jewish lawyers in the New Deal years.

Government service attracted many Jewish lawyers who left their mark on the New Deal, and subsequently at the bar and on the bench. Among them were Jerome Frank (1889–1957), author of *Law and the Modern Mind* (1930), a significant contribution to legal realism, who served in a variety of government legal positions before his appointment to the federal bench; Charles E. Wyzanski, Jr. (1906–1986), solicitor to the Labor Department and then a Justice Department lawyer before his elevation to a judgeship; and Abe Fortas (1910–1982), who moved from New Deal service to professional eminence to the Supreme Court. Fortas, along with Simon Rifkind (b. 1901), legislative assistant to Senator Robert F. Wagner (N.Y.) when national labor policy was formulated, and Samuel Rosenman (1896–1973), special counsel to Roosevelt, all capitalized upon their government experience to build successful law firms once the reform energy of the New Deal subsided. Concentrated within the financial and political power centers in New York and Washington, their firms enabled Jewish lawyers to reach the pinnacle of professional stature in the years following World War II.

Even labor law, once a marginal area of practice, blossomed into professional legitimacy during the 1930s. It was especially attractive to Jewish lawyers, enabling them to fuse their professional aspirations with liberal political commitments during a momentous era in American labor history. In time, one of them, Arthur J. Goldberg (1908–1990), became secretary of labor and (in 1962) the first labor lawyer to sit on the Supreme Court. Goldberg, with Fortas, symbolized the triumphant passage of Jewish lawyers from the rags of immigrant origins, through the New Deal, to the riches and robes of the nation's most prestigious law firms and its highest court.

Success culminated the process that had begun, more than half a century earlier, in professional ostracism and stigmatization. Not only had Jews come to be disproportionately represented in the elite sectors of professional activity; they were also conspicuous in the public service sectors of the bar. Fervently attached to American constitutionalism, they were as likely to be found in civil liberties and civil rights litigation on behalf of disadvantaged minorities as among the senior partners of corporate firms. Their distinctive conjunction of professional success and liberal activism enabled them to fuse their own self-interest with prevailing conceptions of the public interest. That alliance endured until the political turbulence of the 1960s, when liberal activism began to cut against Jewish interests, especially on issues of affirmative action and preferential hiring. While the prominence of Jewish lawyers in American public life was undiminished, the writings of constitutional scholar Alexander Bickel (1924–1974), and the public advocacy of lawyer Morris Abram (b. 1918), demonstrated that they were increasingly likely to defend legal order at the expense of liberal activism. The identification of Judaism with American legalism, the formative ideological contribution of Louis Marshall, still retained its power more than half a century after his death.

In the United States, where lawyers and judges (not rabbis) monopolized legal authority, Jews rooted their identity in the secular legal system. Their boundless love affair with American law surely reflected their appreciation of the protection it afforded them and, not incidentally, the opportunities it provided for professional status in American society. It has often been claimed that the commitment of Jews to the American rule of law expresses their fidelity to venerable Jewish legal principles (law, covenant, social justice), which are also deeply embedded in American constitutionalism. That theme was first expressed more than a century ago by Oscar Straus (1850–1926), lawyer, businessman, and the first Jew to serve in the Cabinet (during Theodore Roosevelt's administration). Its frequent reiteration still reveals the yearning of American Jews to root their identity in two traditions and to merge them into a unitary Judeo-American legal tradition. But the transfer of Jewish allegiance from the Torah to the Constitution, a characteristic expression of modern Jewish secularism, also constitutes a paradigm of the acculturation process. As Jews identified with the American legal and constitutional system, they erased the stigma of dual loyalty and secured their acceptance as Americans. The erosion of Jewish tradition, not fidelity to its norms, accounts for the fervent Jewish attachment to American law.

The role of law and lawyers in American Jewish acculturation remains one of the distinctive aspects of the American Jewish experience. Once lawyers assumed communal leadership, they defined the terms of Jewish identification with the United States. Indeed, their ability to identify Judaism with American principles, as Marshall and Brandeis were the first to demonstrate, accounted for their ascent to leadership. But as lawyers struggled to resolve the tension between competing American and Jewish loyalties, they reexperienced the classic dilemma of the medieval court Jew, caught between his Jewish responsibilities and his dependence upon the favor of his Christian princes. Consequently, just when Jewish lawyers assumed leadership in communal affairs, and began to articulate the compatibility of the American and Jewish legal traditions, Zionist statements of Jewish national aspirations compounded their task. Marshall's opposition to Zionism, and even Brandeis's belated embrace of it, expressed overriding American priorities. Similarly, during the Nazi era when Jewish lawyers reached the peak of their public influence in the Roosevelt administration, the Jewish lawyers in the New Deal acquiesced in American policies that severely restricted the admission of Jewish refugees, virtually ignored the Holocaust, and displayed little enthusiasm for Jewish statehood. During World War II and after, Joseph M. Proskauer (1877–1971), the influential leader of the American Jewish Committee, would not tolerate an independent Jewish position (for or against Zionist aspirations) that contradicted American government policy. Since 1948, as lawyers have continued to play a conspicuous role in Jewish organization affairs, they have functioned as mediators between the Jewish community and American society, invariably locating Jewish aspirations securely within American constitutional norms. Indeed, this has become their most distinctive leadership function.

The striking success of Jewish lawyers in American society is without parallel in American immigrant history. Jews, long confined to the lowest levels of professional activity, achieved such distinction that for half a century after 1916 there was a "Jewish seat" on the Supreme Court. The tantalizing question remains: to what extent was their success within the American legal culture attributable to their Jewish legal heritage? It is difficult to imagine the fervent identification of American Jews with law without locating its origins in ancient Jewish norms, in the rabbinical tradition of legal exegesis, or in the compatibilities between Jewish and American law. To be sure, several of the most distinguished American Jewish lawyers of this century (among them Marshall, Brandeis, Frankfurter, and Fortas) came from families where familiarity with Jewish law was expressed in the Orthodoxy of at least one family member. But the alacrity with which Jewish lawyers (like other American Jews) abandoned their sacred-law heritage suggests that it was not Jewish tradition, but the repudiation of it, that pulled so many Jews toward the American legal profession. Their identification with the legal culture of their new homeland secured their credentials as loyal Americans.

The constitutional bicentennial celebration in 1987 prompted fervent Jewish proclamations of the continuities between the Jewish and American legal traditions. Like seventeenth-century New England Puritans, whom they often emulated, Jews diligently advanced biblical typologies for American constitutionalism. Indeed, it has become all but impossible for American Jews to understand themselves without reference to the origins of American constitutional principles in the Hebrew Bible. Whether Jews actually find biblical precedents, or imaginatively invent them, they still use law to merge altogether disparate traditions. By now the transition from Halakah, rabbinical legal interpretation rooted in divine revelation, to constitutional jurisprudence, the province of lawyers and judges, seems uncomplicated, inevitable, and an unmitigated blessing. But an immense cultural reorientation was required of Jewish immigrants before they could complete their successful journey from Jewish sacred law to American constitutionalism.

JEROLD S. AUERBACH

BIBLIOGRAPHY

Auerbach, Jerold S. *Justice Without Law?* New York: Oxford University Press, 1983.
———. *Rabbis and Lawyers.* Bloomington: Indiana University Press, 1990.
———. *Unequal Justice.* New York: Oxford University Press, 1983.
Burt, Robert A. *Two Jewish Justices: Outcasts in the Promised Land.* Berkeley: University of California Press, 1988.
Cohen, Naomi W. *Encounter with Emancipation: The German Jews in the United States 1830–1914.* Philadelphia: Jewish Publication Society, 1984.
Felix Frankfurter Reminisces: Recorded in talks with Harlan B. Phillips. New York: Reynal, 1960.
Hirsch, H. N. *The Enigma of Felix Frankfurter.* New York: Basic Books, 1981.
Irons, Peter H. *The New Deal Lawyers.* Princeton, N.J.: Princeton University Press, 1982.
Reznikoff, Charles, ed. *Louis Marshall: Champion of Liberty.* 2 vols. Philadelphia: Jewish Publication Society, 1957.
Strum, Philippa. *Louis D. Brandeis: Justice for the People.* Cambridge: Harvard University Press, 1984.

Lazarus, Emma (1849–1887). Best remembered for the sonnet "The New Colossus" inscribed at the base of the Statue of Liberty, Emma Lazarus was a minor American poet but a pioneering figure in the history of Jewish-American verse. A resident of New York since birth, she was regarded as a promising poet in the transcendental school while yet in her teens. Critics of the day commented on the "inner heat and glow" that characterized her early odes in *Century* and *Lippincott's.*

But it is the Jewishness of her later poetry that distinguishes Lazarus's work. For example, a Rosh Hashanah poem for 1883 describes the tensions of "rushing sunward" toward assimilation and "homeward" to the synagogue. Although she was not particularly observant, Lazarus remained proud of her Sephardic heritage, one that could be traced to the earliest beginnings of Jewish settlement in the seventeenth century.

Lazarus's poem "In a Jewish Synagogue at Newport" (1868) so moved Rabbi Gustav Gottheil of New York's Temple Emanu-El that he induced her to translate some Jewish hymns from the German. The project had much larger ramifications than he could have imagined, for Lazarus discovered the poetry of Heinrich Heine, and by 1881, she completed the definitive English translations of Heine's work.

The year 1881 proved to be a fateful one, both for Lazarus and the mass of 4 million Jews struggling to survive in the Russian Pale. The assassination of Czar Alexander II resulted in 167 Jewish communities being ravaged by pogroms. When a thinly veiled anti-Semitic apologia by a Russian aristocrat appeared in *Century,* Lazarus responded decisively: "It is not that it is the oppression of Jews by Russians which Americans need consider or act upon," she wrote in April 1882. "It is that it is the oppression of men and women by men and women; and we are men and women."

Lazarus was both shaken and energized by the specter of hundreds of thousands of broken, humiliated people from Eastern Europe who entered America through Castle Garden, New York. American Jews, she argued, could not be indifferent to the cries of their "barefoot, beggared brothers and sisters." These sentiments are repeated, and amplified, in "The New Colossus" (1883), clearly her most famous poem.

In addition, she helped to establish a technical institute for Jewish immigrants, contributed money to Am Olam, an organization that attempted to set up agricultural settlements in New Jersey, Louisiana, Oregon, and the Dakotas, and joined Hoveve Zion, a Zionist organization that predated Herzl by more than a decade. For her Zionist sympathies, Lazarus earned the rebuke of Cyrus Sulzberger, Abraham Isaacs, and Sabato Morais.

In the spring of 1882, *The American Hebrew* magazine began to publish a series of Lazarus's poems that would eventually become *Songs of a Semite* (1882). The work addresses the central question, "Where is the Hebrew fatherland?" and speaks to the plight of Jews in the Diaspora. For Lazarus, the denial of basic human rights to the Jew was all the more ironic because the Jewish people had not asked that much from Providence or their fellowmen. In a poem entitled "Gifts," she notes the Egyptian had asked for wealth, the Greek for beauty, the Roman for power. By contrast, the Jew had asked only for "Truth." However, when his prayer was answered, "he became the slave of the Idea, a pilgrim far and wide."

Sixteen more essays to *The American Hebrew* followed from November 1882 through February 1883. In these "Epistles to the Hebrews," Lazarus tried to refute widely held beliefs that Jews were excessively tribal, that they could never produce statesmen or artists, and that they could never become agriculturalists.

But it was in an article entitled "The Jewish Problem" published in *Century* (February 1883) that Lazarus put her position most forcefully. After providing her readers with a survey of Jewish history, she concludes on the following note:

> The melancholy and disgraceful fact being established that, in these closing decades of the nineteenth century, the long-suffering Jew is still universally exposed to injustice proportioned to the barbarity of the nation that surrounds him . . . blind intolerance and ignorance are now forcibly driving them into that position which they have so long hesitated to assume. They must establish an independent nationality.

A year after writing these words, Lazarus fell ill with cancer. She died, on November 19, 1887, while working on a poem to Rembrandt. Ten years later, her "Banner of the Jew" was reproduced at Basel in the form of the Mogen David standard. Fifty years later, after the Holocaust, it became—as she had predicted—the symbol of the resurrected bones of Ezekiel. The devo-

tion she expressed in her ode to Bar Kochba was reciprocated by Walt Whitman, who said of Lazarus's passing: "Since Miriam sang of deliverance and triumph by the Red Sea, the Semitic race has had no braver singer. . . . Among the mourning women at her grave, the sympathizing voice of Christian daughters will mingle with the wail of the daughters of Jerusalem." *See also* Poetry.

SAUL FRIEDMAN

BIBLIOGRAPHY

Cohen, Rachel. "Emma Lazarus." *The Reform Advocate* LXXIV (September 24, 1927): 184–189.

Frank, Murray. "Emma Lazarus-Symbol of Liberty." *The Chicago Forum* 6 (Summer 1948): 251–256.

Jacob, H. E. *The World of Emma Lazarus*. New York: Schocken, 1949.

Merriam, Eve. *Emma Lazarus: Woman with a Torch*. New York: Citadel Press, 1956.

Pauli, Herta. "The Statue of Liberty Finds Its Poet." *Commentary* I (November 1945): 56–64.

Leeser, Isaac (1806–1868). Rabbi, editor, and translator, Isaac Leeser was the leading proponent of American Jewish traditionalism in the United States prior to the Civil War. Leeser was born in the tiny Westphalian village of Neuenkirchen and was orphaned at an early age. He received his early education at a traditional Jewish school in nearby Dulmen and later studied at a Jesuit-run gymnasium in Muenster. In Muenster, he was also strongly influenced by Abraham Sutro, the district rabbi and an outspoken opponent of the emerging Reform Movement.

In 1824, with few prospects for the future, Leeser accepted the invitation of a maternal uncle, Zalma Rehine, to resettle in Richmond, Virginia. Shy, studious, and religiously observant, the young immigrant attached himself to the local hazan (cantor), Isaac B. Seixas, learned the Sephardic rites of the early American synagogue, and familiarized himself with a variety of English-language texts on Judaism. In 1828, Leeser published two letters in Richmond's *Constitutional Whig* defending Jews and Judaism against the calumnies of an apostate missionary, Joseph Wolff. His reputation as a defender of the faith and skilled synagogue officiant spread quickly. At his uncle's urging, he reluctantly accepted the invitation of Philadelphia's prestigious Mickveh Israel Congregation to serve as its hazan and abandoned his plans to become a pharmacist.

Leeser arrived in Philadelphia in 1829 and spent the rest of his life in the "city of brotherly love." Unfortunately, his relationship with Mickveh Israel was stormy from the outset and progressively worsened over the years. Intellectually oriented and highly energetic, Leeser sought to upgrade the office of hazan against the wishes of his congregational leadership. Nearly blind and badly scarred on his face from a near fatal bout with smallpox in 1833, Leeser never married and poured himself and his personal resources into his work: the creation of a unified, vital Jewish community in North America. His congregation, on the other hand, viewed him as a hired religious functionary.

During his first few years in Philadelphia, Leeser wrote prolifically. He published a catechism, *Instruction in the Mosaic Law* (1830) and an antideistic essay, *The Jews and the Mosaic Law* (1834). Instrumental in helping Rebecca Gratz launch the Jewish Sunday school movement in 1838, he wrote a second educational text, *Catechism for Younger Children*, in 1839. Moreover, beginning in 1830, at the suggestion of "several ladies" in his synagogue, Leeser began giving regular sermons at Saturday morning services. The pioneer preacher of the American synagogue, Leeser published ten volumes of *Discourses* (1837, 1841, 1867). He also published a six-volume, bilingual edition of *The Form of Prayers According to the Custom of the Spanish and Portuguese Jews* (1837–1838).

In 1840, Leeser gained national prominence. Outraged by the revival of the medieval blood libel in Damascus, Syria, he organized a major interfaith demonstration in Philadelphia and encouraged similar activities in other cities. However, he was less successful in using the Damascus affair as the occasion for permanently organizing the American Jewish community on a national basis. Leeser's 1841 Plan for Union, the first comprehensive attempt to unify American Jewry, was modeled after the French consistory system, but it failed to gain the support of a variety of subgroups within the chaotic American Jewish community.

Undaunted by the failure of his plan, Leeser began publishing *The Occident and American Jewish Advocate* in 1843, the first successful Jewish "newspaper" in the United States. He served as the editor and chief correspondent of the popular monthly for 25 years and through its pages became the best-known Jewish religious leader in antebellum America. Published in English, the *Occident* advocated unifying American Jews under the banner of a modernizing, Sephardic orthodoxy. It included both national and international Jewish news and provided a forum for Jewish writers, including women, to publish their works.

In addition to his work as editor of *Occident* and hazan of Mickveh Israel during the 1840s, Leeser expanded his work as a writer, translator, and communal leader. He published an original translation of the Pentateuch in 1845 and two books in 1848: a *Biblia Hebraica*, the first vocalized biblical text to appear in the United States, and *The Book of Daily Prayers According to the Custom of the German and Polish Jews*. In 1845, Leeser organized the first American Jewish Publication Society, and in 1849, under the auspices of the Hebrew Education Society, he established the first Hebrew high school in the United States.

In 1850, following a scandalous controversy, Leeser permanently severed his ties with Mickveh Israel. To support himself, he embarked on a national railroad tour to increase the readership of the *Occident* and rally support for his most important literary project, an English translation of the entire Hebrew Bible. Leeser's *Twenty-Four Books of the Holy Scriptures* (1853–1854) remained the standard Jewish translation of the Bible in North America for over 60 years. Hoping to find common ground with moderate reformers, he also attended a rabbinic conference in Cleveland in 1855. Organized by his arch rival, Isaac Mayer Wise, Leeser was disappointed in the meeting's final decisions. Two years later, in 1857, a group of loyal supporters in Philadelphia organized Congregation Beth El Emeth and named the 51-year-old Leeser hazan for life. In 1859, he was elected vice-president of the Board of Delegates of American Israelites, the first Jewish defense organization in the United States.

Typical of most American Jewish leaders of the period, Leeser did not participate in the great political debates prior to the outbreak of the Civil War. Still strongly tied to Richmond and the South, he was principally interested in preserving the union and did not oppose slavery on either moral or religious grounds. Appalled by the war's carnage, Leeser worked diligently to establish a Jewish chaplaincy corps in the North and a Jewish hospital in Philadelphia (1866).

The final achievement of Leeser's life was the opening of Maimonides College in Philadelphia, the first rabbinic school in the United States, in

1867. Leeser was named provost but fell ill soon thereafter and died on February 1, 1868. His funeral was the largest Jewish public event in the United States up to that time. Without Leeser at the helm, Maimonides quickly failed and only graduated four students before closing.

Mayer Sulzberger, one of Leeser's leading disciples, was correct when he eulogized his teacher and observed that more than any other American Jewish religious leader of the period, Isaac Leeser had "interwoven himself into the whole system of American Judaism." Leeser was claimed by both Conservatism and modern Orthodoxy as a forerunner of their respective movements. Leeser was also a leading proto-Zionist and a believer in "Catholic Israel," a phrase he coined that was later popularized by Solomon Schechter. Simultaneously a religious traditionalist and a cultural accommodationist, Leeser played a major role in the transformation and perpetuation of the Jewish heritage in North America.

LANCE J. SUSSMAN

BIBLIOGRAPHY

Korn, Bertram W. "Isaac Leeser: Centennial Reflections." *American Jewish Archives* 19 (November 1967): 127–141.

Seller, Maxine S. "Isaac Leeser's Views on the Restoration of a Jewish Palestine." *American Jewish Historical Quarterly* 58 (September 1968): 118–135.

Sussman, Lance J. "Another Look at Isaac Leeser and the First Jewish Translation of the Bible in the United States." *Modern Judaism* 5 (May 1985): 159–190.

Whiteman, Maxwell. "Isaac Leeser and the Jews of Philadelphia." *Publications of the American Jewish Historical Society* 48 (June 1959): 207–244.

Left, The. Jews have been disproportionately represented in virtually all American radical movements since the 1890s. Although the vast majority of American Jews have not been radicals, giving their allegiance to mainstream political parties, a significant minority has helped to shape American radicalism.

American anarchism briefly flourished around the turn of the century. Its two most prominent figures, Emma Goldman (1869–1940) and Alexander Berkman (1870–1936), were both Jewish. Berkman, who was arrested in 1892 for attempting to assassinate steel magnate Henry Frick, and Goldman were deported to Russia during the Palmer Red raids in 1919. They quickly became disillusioned by Bolshevism but remained committed anarchists. One of the largest and longest-lived anarchist periodicals was the Yiddish *Frei Arbiter Shtimme* (the Free Voice of Labor), which continued to publish into the 1970s, although the Jewish anarchist movement had largely disappeared by the 1920s.

The first substantial socialist party in the United States, the Socialist Labor Party (SLP), was dominated by German immigrants from its founding in the 1870s, but Jews were the second largest ethnic group in the SLP. SLP members played the leading role in organizing the United Hebrew Trades in 1888. The SLP's most prominent leader and the dominant figure on the American Left before the turn of the century was Daniel DeLeon (1852–1914), a Sephardic Jew born on the island of Curacao. DeLeon denied his origins, claiming to be a Castillian Spaniard, and falsified much else about his background.

DeLeon, whose theoretical writings on Marxism earned the praise of Lenin, gained control of the SLP in the early 1890s and ruled it with an iron hand until his death, driving dissidents and critics out of the organization. One such rupture took place during a fight for control of the weekly *Arbeiter Zeitung*, a Yiddish-language paper put out by the SLP's East European Jewish members. Dissidents, including Abraham Cahan (1860–1951) and Morris Winchevsky (1856–1932), established in 1897 a new independent socialist newspaper, the *Forward*, destined to become the dominant voice of Jewish socialism on the Lower East Side. Other prominent Jewish members of the SLP, including future congressman Meyer London (1871–1926) joined Cahan and Winchevsky in Gene Debs's newly organized Social Democracy Party.

Torn by internal feuds and smothered by DeLeon's heavy hand, the SLP slowly withered into insignificance. By the turn of the century it had been replaced as the largest socialist organization in the United States by the Socialist Party of America (SP), founded in 1901, and identified for the next half-century with its frequent presidential candidates, Eugene Debs and Norman Thomas. Jews played a major role in the SP. Two of the Socialist Party's three most prominent early leaders were Jewish—Morris Hillquit (1869–1933) of New York, another refugee from the SLP, and Victor Berger (1860–1929) of Milwaukee. Because Debs shunned party organizational issues, these men exercised enormous influence over the actual operation of the party. Although Berger was most often regarded not as a Jew but an ethnic German, Hillquit's leading role in the party did occasion grumbling from some party members concerned that its identification with a Jewish, foreign-born constituency in New York limited its appeal to other Americans. Both men served as national chairman of the party after World War I. The only two Socialists ever elected to Congress—Berger, from Milwaukee, and Meyer London, from New York's Lower East Side—were Jewish.

Although Jews at first constituted a very small percentage of Socialist Party membership, over the years their numerical and proportional strength grew. The Jewish Socialist Federation, formed in 1913 and led by J. B. Salutsky Hardman (1882–1968), was the third-largest of the foreign-language federations affiliated with the Socialist Party; its membership in 1916 reached 8000 of a total party membership of some 80,000. Many Jews, however, were also members of other language federations, particularly the Russian one, while others preferred to affiliate directly with the Socialist Party's English-language branches.

Many of the party's most successful and prosperous institutions were located in New York City, where the Socialist ethos was overwhelmingly Jewish. The largely Jewish needle unions, the ILGWU, Amalgamated Clothing Workers, and Cap and Hat Workers, were strongholds of support for the Socialist Party and its causes. Many of their leaders, including David Dubinsky (1892–1982) and Sidney Hillman (1887–1946), were either affiliated to or closely allied with the Socialist Party. The Workmen's Circle, a Socialist fraternal organization, reached a membership of more than 80,000 in the 1920s. The *Forward*, an avowedly Socialist newspaper, had a circulation of 200,000, the largest of any Socialist paper in the United States and was a major financial supporter of party causes and campaigns.

Jewish voters in New York also became one of the major sources of the Socialist Party's voting strength. Not only did they elect London to Congress in 1914, 1916, and 1920, but several Jewish-dominated assembly districts consistently gave Socialist candidates more than one-third of their votes between 1914 and 1920. In 1917, the voters in overwhelmingly Jewish wards in New York elected 10 Socialist state assemblymen, 7 aldermen, and 1 municipal judge. That same year, Hillquit garnered 22 percent of the vote in a los-

ing mayoral race. After 1920, New York consistently provided the Socialist Party with from 20 to 40 percent of its national vote; most of it came from Jews.

The Communist Party (CPUSA), which displaced the Socialist Party as the largest and most important radical organization in the 1930s, has throughout its history had a disproportionate number of Jews. In the 1920s, they comprised about 15 percent of the party (Finns were then about 50 percent of the CPUSA). In the 1930s, when the party achieved its greatest successes in the United States, about 40 percent of its members were Jewish.

Throughout its history, many of the party's leading figures were Jewish. Between 1921 and 1961, one-third of the members of the Central Committee were of Jewish background. During the last half of the 1920s, the party's general secretaries were both Jewish, Benjamin Gitlow (1891–1965) and Jay Lovestone (1898–1990), born Jacob Liebstein. Deposed by direct orders of Stalin in 1929, Lovestone went on to become a fierce anti-Communist, adviser to the AFL-CIO on international affairs and consultant to the CIA on combatting Communist unions abroad. Beginning in the 1930s, the CPUSA made a conscious decision to "Americanize" and no Jew ever again led the organization, although Jews were plentiful at the second level of leadership.

Other evidence of the Jewish presence in the party is abundant. The party's Yiddish-language newspaper, the *Freiheit*, was the first Communist daily published in the United States and for many years had a larger circulation than the *Daily Worker*. The Jewish People's Fraternal Organization, created to compete with the Workmen's Circle, reached a membership of 60,000 in 1947 and was by far the largest ethnic bloc in the Communists' fraternal organization, the International Workers Order. The only union led by an avowed Communist was the largely Jewish Fur and Leather Workers Union, whose fiery president was Ben Gold (1898–1985). Other unions where Communist influence was considerable, like the Distributive Workers and the Social Service Employees, the American Federation of Teachers, and United Public Workers, were largely Jewish and concentrated in New York.

The radical student movement of the 1930s was strongest on campuses with large numbers of Jewish students—City College of New York, Columbia University, New York University—and a large percentage of its leaders were Jewish. In a mock presidential election in 1936, Communist candidate Earl Browder got 25 percent of the vote at City College.

In some sections of the Jewish community, in fact, support for communism was not deviant behavior but the norm. Under party sponsorship, the United Workers Cooperative Colony, or Coops, a cooperative housing project with 750 apartments on Allerton Avenue in the Bronx (New York City), was modeled after a Soviet community. The renters were almost entirely Jewish and Communist. Children went to school on Yom Kippur, stayed home on May Day, and even the athletic teams sported party slogans.

Although Communist candidates for electoral office rarely got significant numbers of votes, they frequently did best in largely Jewish precincts. The American Labor Party, a third party formed in New York to enable Socialists and radicals to support Franklin Roosevelt without voting for him on the Tammany Hall-dominated Democratic ticket, was closely allied with the Communists in the 1940s. Its candidates did best in heavily Jewish areas, and one, Leo Isaacson, was elected to Congress from the Bronx in 1948. In 1948, Jews gave Progressive Party presidential candidate Henry Wallace, backed by the Communists, 10 to 15 percent of their votes while he got 2 percent from non-Jews. One-third of Wallace's 1.1 million votes probably came from Jews.

Many of the dissident Communist sects also had a disproportionately high Jewish representation. Leaders of the Lovestoneites included not only Lovestone and Gitlow, but also Bert Wolfe (1896–1977) and Will Herberg (1909–1977), both of whom later achieved renown as academics. Among the key leaders of the Trotskyists was Max Shachtman (1904–1972). A number of Jewish intellectuals writing in *Partisan Review*, sympathetic to the Trotskyist movement, made a major impact on American cultural life. They included William Phillips (b. 1907), Philip Rahv (1908–1973), and Sidney Hook (1902–1989).

The New Left of the 1960s was also heavily Jewish. The percentage of Jews in SDS, Students for a Democratic Society, ranged from 30 to 50 percent over the years. At its 1966 convention, 46 percent of the delegates who gave a religious background were Jewish. A number of its founders and national officers were Jews. Both Abbie Hoffman (1936–1989) and Jerry Rubin (b. 1938) of the Yippies were Jewish. A substantial proportion of the white students active in

SNCC, the Student Non-violent Coordinating Committee, were Jewish. One study of student activism in 1966–1967 found that the most important indicator of participation in antiwar or other protests was Jewish background. In a 1970 survey, Louis Harris found that 4 percent of Catholic students, 2 percent of the Protestants, and 23 percent of the Jews called themselves radicals.

Clearly, without Jews the American radical movements of the past century would have looked very differently and been far smaller. Jewish radicals, however, comprised only a small proportion of the entire American Jewish community. At its height in 1939, for example, there were about 100,000 members of the Communist Party, of whom perhaps 40,000 were Jewish. In a Jewish population of some 4.8 million, this was a tiny proportion. Similarly, far more Jews supported the Democratic Party in New York than the Socialists.

It is also important to note that most Jews who became radicals did not remain radicals. The Socialist Party lost virtually its entire mass base in 1936 when Socialist union leaders like Dubinsky and Hillman took the lead in forming the American Labor Party in New York. Many one-time Jewish Socialists soon became liberal Democrats. The Socialist movement itself gradually abandoned the notion of a radical transformation of American society. Today, the political views of many prominent Socialists like Irving Howe (b. 1920), one of the leaders of the Democratic Socialists of America, emphasize support for liberal Democrats. And, DSA itself is a tiny organization with less than 5000 members.

What happened to the Jewish Communists is more complicated. Many Jews were attracted to the CPUSA in the 1930s because they believed it to be an effective enemy of fascism. Of the 3000 Americans who went to Spain to fight in the Communist-recruited Abraham Lincoln Brigade against the Nazi-backed forces of General Franco, for example, some 40 percent were Jewish. The Nazi-Soviet Pact in 1939 thus proved to be a serious blow to the Communist Party. Surprisingly, few prominent Jews dropped out of the party in 1939, but party membership dropped by at least a third and many of those who quit were probably Jewish.

A larger number of Jewish Communists became disillusioned after 1955 when stories about Soviet anti-Semitism became widespread. The myth of the Soviet Union as a place where anti-

Semitism had been eliminated was replaced with grim news that only Hitler had murdered more Jews than Stalin. Many Jewish Communists were also shocked by the Soviet invasion of Hungary in 1956 and Nikita Khruschev's 1956 speech admitting Stalin's crimes. By 1961, the CPUSA had shrunk to 3000 members.

Finally, in 1973, another purge of Jewish Communists took place when the CPUSA expelled Paul Novick (1891–1989), charter member of the party and editor of the *Freiheit*, for adopting a pro-Zionist policy during the Yom Kippur War. Shortly before, Morris Schappes (b. 1907), editor of *Jewish Currents*, a magazine long close to the CPUSA, also left the party.

An indication of the Communist Party's virtually negligible influence among its one-time Jewish supporters is that its appeal in the mid-1970s to the 6000 *Freiheit* subscribers to oust Novick as editor was decisively rejected. A handful of old-time Jewish Communists remain in the party, which serves as a comfortable old-age home. A few thousand other party members are Jewish by birth, but they have no ties or identification with the Jewish community or any Jewish cultural institutions.

The United States is not the only country in which Jews have played a prominent role in radical political movements. In a number of European nations, in Argentina, South Africa, Tunisia, and other places, they have been disproportionately represented in radical political movements. A variety of theories have attempted to explain why.

The least credible explanation focuses on the economic situation of Jews. Anyone might have found the argument that economic exploitation causes radicalism plausible in the early part of this century when the overwhelming majority of the Jewish population lived in squalid slums and labored in sweatshops. Jews, however, were also the only ethnic group to contribute large numbers of middle-class members to the Communist Party. Nor were the upper-middle-class Jewish New Leftists crying for economic redress. If economic distress led directly to political radicalization, other American groups would have contributed far more to American radicalism than they in fact have. One of the tasks of anyone trying to understand Jewish political activities is to explain why, unlike most other groups, their economic status is so poor a predictor of their politics. While economic distress was undoubtedly a contributing factor in Jewish support for socialism at the turn of the century and during the Great Depression, it

clearly cannot be the only or even the major reason.

Other scholars have suggested that Judaism accounts for the attraction of radicalism for Jews. Socialism, it is suggested, is a secularized form of Judaism. The Torah had stressed that Jews were God's chosen people; Marx wrote a new code in which the proletariat was chosen to lead the world to redemption and build the Kingdom of God—a chosen class instead of a chosen people. In this argument, Marx's messianic vision led him to create a theory that proved attractive to Jews precisely because it spoke to some of their most fundamental values. The practices of Judaism were allegedly in conformity with socialist ideas. Such values as justice, caring for one's neighbors, respect for labor, concern for the needy, and improving and living in this world, core values of socialism, were Jewish injunctions. Unlike Christianity, whose stress on sinfulness and the other world is at odds with socialism, Judaism supposedly encouraged social activism. Additionally, it is argued, certain themes in Jewish history have made Jews particularly sensitive to oppression and supportive of efforts to eradicate it. The Exodus story, for one, has been a source of inspiration for centuries to those seeking to overthrow an unjust social order. Socialism, then, became a secular substitute for Jews who had shed their religious roots.

Whatever virtues there are in this explanation, there are also severe problems. Most Jews have not been radicals. This hypothesis does not explain why some Jews were and most were not. It also unfairly suggests that Jews who were not radicals were somehow not true to the ethical and moral values of Judaism. Moreover, many Jewish leftists knew nothing of Judaism; others rejected it. Marx himself bitterly attacked Judaism as a religion glorifying greed and looked forward to the disappearance of Jews in a socialist society.

Benjamin Disraeli, another Jewish apostate, years ago suggested another explanation for Jewish radicalism, chastising European governments for their anti-Semitic policies. Because of their heritage, his argument went, Jews faced economic, educational, social, and political limits on their opportunities. This discriminatory treatment resulted in a sense of injustice and a commitment to changing society to prevent inequality. Hence, it led Jews into radical movements.

One of the virtues of this explanation is that it suggests that certain Jews—those with significant talents or abilities who are excluded from society's rewards—are most likely to be radicalized. Unfortunately, it also has flaws. Most Jews affected by anti-Semitism did not become secular radicals. Many became Zionists. Others opted for assimilation. Moreover, in certain radical movements, there was intense anti-Semitism and that did not stop Jews from joining such movements. Marx himself savagely attacked Jews. Russian socialists defended pogroms on the grounds that attacks on Jewish capitalists by peasants was a sign of their increasing class consciousness. Socialist attacks on Jewish bankers had reached such a level by the 1880s that a leading German Socialist had to warn his comrades against anti-Semitism, calling it the socialism of fools. More recently, Jewish Communists for many years turned away from, found excuses for, or denied that Soviet anti-Semitism existed.

A variant of this argument hypothesized that radical groups provided an attractive option in societies suffused with anti-Semitism. Their universalistic values offered an escape from the restricted, medieval, Jewish ghetto into the modern, scientific world without the need to convert to Christianity. Socialism promised a rational world in which religion and ethnicity would no longer matter, where heritage would not leave one an outsider in the society.

In the United States, joining a radical movement offered some Jews an opportunity to become more "Americanized." They interacted with young people from a variety of ethnic backgrounds. They could also escape from their own ethnic communities to work among "real" Americans. Many young Communists adopted new names to facilitate their work among the masses; invariably, they chose non-Jewish ones.

For other Jews, however, radical movements in the United States offered a comfortable and comforting cultural home amidst the chaos of a new world. The Jewish federations in both the Socialist and the Communist parties provided a rich cultural milieu—clubs, newspapers, singing groups, sports—through which members were able to build a network of friends and activities.

A full explanation for Jewish radicalism needs to take into account the particular historical experience of East European Jews and American Jews in the last 100 to 150 years. In Russia and Eastern Europe, the home of the largest concentration of the world's Jews in the late 1800s, intense economic, political, and religious repression had created a substantial radical community. By the turn of the century, Russian Jews had created a secular, left-wing cultural world that competed with the religious world. It included press, fraternal associations, unions, political parties—like the Jewish Bund—that all built and reinforced radical values. These Jews, their emigrant brethren, and their children formed the core of the radical Jewish communities of a number of countries, including the United States.

The Jewish radical movement in America was largely a product of several generations of Russian immigrants. Subjected to intense economic pressures, living in dire poverty, uprooted from a traditional way of life and exposed to a powerful left-wing cultural world, a substantial number of immigrants and their children gravitated to the radical movement. Feeling themselves marginal figures in American society, they joined organizations fundamentally dissatisfied with American life.

This account emphasizes the transient nature of Jewish radicalism; it was the product of the experience of a few generations and with the passing of those generations, it ceased to be an important factor in the Jewish community. Changing economic conditions, suburbanization, and, most importantly, the greater acceptance of Jews in American society, have largely destroyed the radical Jewish community and its institutions and, with them, the potential for a mass radical base in the Jewish community.

Jewish history since the 1940s has not borne out the predictions of radicals. They had preached that the end of capitalist society would solve the ills of the Jews. In the United States, however, the Jewish condition improved dramatically without a fundamental alteration of the economic system. At the same time, the Jewish working class upon which Jewish radicalism had been built largely disappeared. Communist regimes meanwhile not only did not ease the plight of Jews, but persecuted them.

The growth of Jewish nationalism also had a dispiriting impact on the Jewish Left. Although socialist Zionism has always had support in the United States, many, if not most, Jewish radicals have been hostile to Zionism and Jewish nationalism. Many Jewish Socialists, veterans of the European Jewish Bund, were indifferent to early efforts to build Palestine. After the Holocaust, however, their Jewish identity became more important as their socialist faith waned.

The Communist Party and the *Freiheit* actually supported the Arab riots in Palestine in 1929. Except for a brief interlude around the time of Israel's founding, the Communist Party has resolutely opposed Zionism. As the American Jewish community has become more and more identified with Israel, the radical Left's isolation in that community has grown.

The Jewish presence in the New Left seems to belie the prediction that Jewish radicalism will largely disappear. However, a substantial percentage of Jewish New Leftists were in fact "red diaper babies," as the children of 1930s radicals were sometimes called. As the New Left began to embrace the Palestinian cause and attack Israel as a racist, imperialist power after the Six-Day War, it lost many of its Jewish adherents. A few were so divorced from their Jewish backgrounds that the issue of Israel had no impact on them. Moreover, many New Leftists were radicalized only because of the Vietnam War; with its end their short-lived radicalism disappeared.

A small Jewish radical remnant may well continue to exist in the United States, but it will probably never again be a significant factor on the American Left. Jews are no longer marginal figures in American society or culture. While anti-Semitism has not been eradicated, it is nowhere near as pervasive in this country as it was fifty years ago. Moreover, the deep-seated hatred for Israel that exists among many American radicals minimizes the chances that many Jews will be attracted to their ranks, at least so long as the survival of Israel remains important to American Jews. Rather than heralding the revival of the Jewish radical tradition, Jewish New Leftists may have been nothing more than the last remnants of a dying movement. *See also* Labor Movement, New Left.

HARVEY KLEHR

BIBLIOGRAPHY

Howe, Irving. *World of Our Fathers: The Journey of the East European Jews to America and the Life They Found and Made.* New York: Harcourt Brace Jovanovich, 1976.

Johnpoll, Bernard, and Klehr, Harvey, eds. *Biographical Dictionary of the American Left.* Westport, Conn.: Greenwood Press, 1986.

Klehr, Harvey. *The Heyday of American Communism: The Depression Decade.* New York: Basic Books, 1984.

Levin, Nora. *While Messiah Tarried: Jewish Socialist Movement, 1871–1917.* Paperback edition. New York: Schocken, 1979.

Liebman, Arthur. *Jews and the Left.* New York: Wiley, 1979.

Sanders, Ronald. *The Downtown Jews: Portrait of an Immigrant Generation.* Paperback edition. New York: Dover, 1987.

Lehman, Herbert Henry (1878–1963). Banker, politician, and philanthropist, Herbert Lehman won more statewide elections than any other person in New York's history. He was elected lieutenant governor in 1928 and 1930, governor in 1932, 1934, 1936, and 1938, and United States senator in a special election in 1949 to fill the last year of an unexpired term. In 1950, Lehman was reelected to the Senate for another 6 years. Prior to his first run for office at age 50, he was very active in the affairs of the state's Democratic Party and in the family vocation, which enabled him to amass his great wealth, the investment firm of Lehman Brothers.

Herbert Lehman was born in New York City. Upon his graduation from Williams College, he joined the family investment company until the outset of World War I. Deeply disturbed by the devastation suffered by Jewish communities in Europe, he helped found the American Jewish Joint Distribution Committee, which became the major source of American aid for Jews around the world. Lehman's affinity to the plight of his own people continued throughout his lifetime, as he was instrumental in the creation of a number of financial institutions that helped to establish a Jewish homeland in Palestine.

In 1926, Lehman managed the reelection campaign of New York Governor Al Smith, a close friend. By 1928, he was the chairman of the Democratic national finance committee and had been nominated to run for lieutenant governor alongside Franklin D. Roosevelt. For two terms he ably served in this capacity and was affectionately referred to by Roosevelt as "my good right arm." When Roosevelt was elected president in 1932, Lehman was elected to serve the first of his four consecutive terms as governor of New York. As governor, he effectively lobbied for numerous pieces of legislation that called for broad social reform. He is widely regarded as one of the best governors New York has ever had.

Lehman did not seek reelection in 1942; he instead concentrated on humanitarian causes. He was named head of the newly formed United Nations Relief and Rehabilitation Administration, which served to help war-torn populations.

After World War II, he publicly urged the establishment of a Jewish state in Palestine. Lehman reentered politics in a special U.S. Senate election in 1949, which he won. He remained in the Senate for seven years. He became a major antagonist against Senator Joseph McCarthy and passionately argued for civil rights and civil liberties. When Lehman returned to New York in 1956, he undertook his last major political crusade, the successful reformation of the Democratic Party organization of New York City.

Throughout his entire life, Lehman sought to serve the public interest. He was an active participant in over 25 philanthropic organizations and was extremely generous with his great wealth. His political career is a testament to his altruistic nature. Herbert Lehman was awarded the Medal of Freedom by President Lyndon Johnson, but Lehman died one day before the ceremony was to take place. President Johnson awarded it to him posthumously. *See also* Politics.

BRUCE ARMON

BIBLIOGRAPHY
Alden, Robert. "Herbert Lehman, 85, Dies: Ex-Governor and Senator." *New York Times*, December 6, 1963, 1, 29.

Glazer, Nathan. "Herbert H. Lehman of New York." *Commentary* (May 1963): 403–409.

Nevins, Allan. *Herbert H. Lehman and His Era*. New York: Scribner, 1963.

Leo Baeck Institute. An academic center whose subject is the life and history of German-speaking Jewry, the Leo Baeck Institute has its main research facility and repository in New York City. Founded in Jerusalem in 1954, the institute's three centers (New York, London, and Jerusalem) publish, support scholars, and offer exhibits and conferences to its members and the public. Among the founders were Martin Buber (1878–1965), Gershom Scholem (1897–1982), Ernst Akiba Simon (1899–1988), Siegfried Moses (1897–1974), and Rabbi Max Gruenewald.

The institute bears the name of Rabbi Leo Baeck (1873–1956), who served as its first president during the last year of his life. Rabbi Baeck was a leading figure in German life. He was active in many areas, including membership in the Centralverein deutscher Staatsbuerger Juedischen Glaubens and founding president (1933) of the Reichsvertretung der Deutschen Juden. He continued in this office after the Nazis changed the name (1938) to Reichsvereinigung der Juden in Deutschland until his deportation to the Theresienstadt Concentration Camp in 1943. After 1945, Baeck resided in London, taught in British and American Jewish institutions (including Hebrew Union College, Jewish Institute of Religion), and published several books.

The collections and scholarly work of the Leo Baeck Institute were originally planned for the period between the beginning of the Emancipation and Hitler's seizure of power (1933). However, many of its collections and publications deal with the period of National Socialism and the Jewish response, including emigration from Germany. Over 125 books and nearly 1000 articles—in English, German, and Hebrew—have covered diverse aspects of life among German-speaking Jews in Europe and as dispersed after 1933. The institute has an extensive collection of over 30,000 photographs.

The library collections (about 60,000 volumes), including many rare books and periodicals, were outlined in the *Leo Baeck Institute New York Bibliothek and Archiv Katalog Band*, Volume I (1970). Volume II, cataloguing archival holdings, slated for publication in 1990, details the literary estates, personal papers, genealogical and organizational records held by the New York institute.

Indexes are also available for the *Year Book*, published annually in London, which features an annotated bibliography.

The institute's *Bulletin*, a German-language serial, published by LBI Jerusalem since 1957, became a quarterly in 1989.

Other publications include the *Schriftenreihe*, a series of basic historical studies (Volume 46 published in 1988), and a collection of excerpts from the more than 1200 memoires in the archives as well as biographies and translations. The LBI *News* and the *Library and Archive News* appear semiannually. The Leo Baeck Memorial Lecture, presented annually since 1957 by a recognized scholar, is published separately.

Fellowship assistance is available through the Fritz Halbers and David Baumgardt funds, as well as the LBI/DAAD program. Younger scholars are invited to participate in the Fritz Bamberger Faculty Seminars. The library, archive, and lecture programs are available for public use.

ROBERT A. JACOBS

BIBLIOGRAPHY
Baker, Leonard. *Days of Sorrow and Pain: Leo Baeck and the Berlin Jews*. New York: Macmillan, 1978.

Levin, Meyer (1905–1981). Meyer Levin was born in Chicago to Eastern European parents, Joseph and Goldie Batiste Levin. He began his career as a reporter for the *Chicago Daily News* in 1923 while a student at the University of Chicago. He visited Palestine in 1925 and eventually made his home there, with frequent visits to the United States. Similarly, his career spanned the two worlds of the emerging nation of Israel and the teeming metropolis of Chicago. Chicago brought him his greatest commerical success, the *roman à clef, Compulsion* (1957). But it was his love for Israel and the Jewish people that became his central credo as an artist. He stated this best in his autobiography *In Search* (1950) when he noted that he could accept the messianic ideal as long as he could embody it "in the people" instead of an individual Messiah.

A writer for over 50 years, Levin never received the critical or popular acclaim that was bestowed on many of his contemporaries. He was a consistent writer who produced a wide variety of works touching on almost every aspect of Jewish and American Jewish life in the twentieth century. Nonetheless, his novels failed to capture the imagination of the public. A reason for this lack of interest may have been that stylistically Levin never escaped his days as a newspaper reporter; his prose style had a certain blandness and was flooded with details. Overall, he wrote in a realistic quasi-documentary style with a highly moralistic frame of reference. Thus, his characters, especially his Jewish characters, were presented in affirmative and optimistic tones, and they lacked the more universal implications that Saul Bellow and Bernard Malamud were able to elicit from their Jewish backgrounds.

Ironically, Levin's greatest successes were centered in Chicago, while his bitterest defeat concerned a subject close to his heart, the Holocaust. In 1937, he published *The Old Bunch*, a broad and comprehensive novel, in the manner of Dos Passos and the proletarian novels of the era, that followed the lives of a dozen Jewish boys and girls over a 13-year period. Each of these youths, different from one another in emotional makeup, is never able to escape those aspects that have always defined his limitations—his Jewishness and his Americanness.

Levin's documentary novel *Compulsion* brought him his greatest popular and critical success. The work retold the Leopold and Loeb abduction and murder of Bobby Franks in 1924, a notorious case involving some of Chicago's finest Jewish families. Levin also re-created the subsequent trial, which he had covered as a young reporter. Levin divided the book into two main sections: the first part probes deeply into the psychological aspects of the crime, and the second is devoted to the trial. The acclaim for the novel was universal. It was compared to *An American Tragedy*. In 1959, *Compulsion* became an equally acclaimed feature film.

Prior to this success, Levin had been locked in a bitter dispute with the producers and writers of a play based on *The Diary of Anne Frank*. Levin had played a large part in bringing the work to the attention of the American public and had written his own version for the stage. It was initially accepted by the producers and then on the advice of the playwright Lillian Hellman was rejected in favor of a version by the writing team of Goodrich and Hackett. Contending that their version emasculated the Jewish elements, Levin sued all the parties involved. After years of litigation he won a pyrrhic victory that gave him monetary compensation but forbade him from ever producing his version. Levin never got over his sense of having been wronged and never reconciled himself to his defeat.

His later works—which ranged from the Holocaust-based *Eva* (1959) to two historical novels that depict life on the early settlements in Palestine, *The Settlers* (1972), and its sequel, *The Harvest* (1978)— show a serious lack of imaginative power.

Only in his last work, the posthumously published novel *The Architect* (1981), based on the life of Frank Lloyd Wright, did he reveal a talent for creating a sense of place and character, and once again one cannot escape the ironic fact that the novel is based in Chicago and has no Jewish characters.

Ultimately, with the exception of the works mentioned in the body of this text—and even though he wrote nearly 30 works of fiction and autobiography—Levin's value as a writer lies in the realm of history and sociology rather than in the creation of enduring works of fiction.

MASHEY M. BERNSTEIN

BIBLIOGRAPHY

Halperin, Irving. "Meyer Levin's *The Harvest* and *The Settlers*." *Studies in American Jewish Literature* 2 (1982): 191-198.

Levin, Meyer. *The Architect*. New York: Simon & Schuster, 1981.

———. *Compulsion*. New York: Simon & Schuster, 1957.

———. *In Search: An Autobiography*. New York: Horizon Press, 1950.

———. *The Old Bunch*. New York: Viking, 1937.

Liptzin, Sol. *The Jew in American Literature*. New York: Bloch, 1966. Pp. 218–221.

Varon, Benno Weiser. "The Haunting of Meyer Levin." *Midstream* 22 (1976): 7–23.

Levinson, Salmon O. (1865–1941). Lawyer and peace publicist Salmon O. Levinson was born in Noblesville, Indiana. His father was a poor Jewish tailor who came to the United States from Germany. Levinson, an 1888 graduate of Yale, was a prominent lawyer in Chicago and peace activist who called for the outlawry of war. He attempted to start an international peace movement during World War I and opposed the terms of the Versailles Treaty, pointing out that the terms were not conducive to world peace. He also opposed the League of Nations. In 1920, he backed Warren G. Harding for president because Harding spoke favorably of Levinson's ideas concerning world peace.

Levinson established the American Committee for the Outlawry of War in 1921. The committee published his "A Plan to Outlaw War" that called for a three-step process for all nations to follow. First, the institution of war was to be made illegal; then an international law was to be codified; this was to be followed by the establishment of an effective world court (in 1925 he advocated the entry of the United States into the World Court). His plans for outlawing war were backed by Senators Philander Knox and William E. Borah, both of whom were also against the League of Nations, reformer Raymond Robins, philosopher John Dewey, progressive preacher John Haynes Holmes, and Charles Clayton Morrison, editor of the *Christian Century*.

In February 1923, Senator Borah introduced a resolution to Congress making war an international crime. Levinson believed that the signing of such an agreement by all nations would keep peace on moral grounds. He proposed using debt cancellation as an inducement for international acceptance of the outlawry of war.

In 1927, he presented the Levinson Plan, advocating the readjustment of German reparations and allied and interallied debts, as well as world peace. Levinson was a principal sponsor of and one of the drafters of the Kellogg-Briand Pact, which was eventually signed by 64 nations, including all the great powers but the Soviet Union.

Levinson continued his prolonged fight for world peace into the 1930s. He supported Indiana Congressman Louis Ludlow in his attempts to secure an international agreement that would limit the defense establishment and reduce the executive use of force in diplomacy. In 1931, he received the Rosenberg Medal from the University of Chicago for his work in improving international relations. In 1937 and 1938, he donated 50,000 documents to the University of Chicago documenting his national and international activities and descriptions of his meetings. He also established the W. E. Borah Outlawry of War Foundation at the University of Idaho. With the outbreak of World War II, all efforts to outlaw war were brought to a bitter end.

JANET L. DOTTERER

BIBLIOGRAPHY

Bolt, Ernest C., Jr. *Ballots Before Bullets: The War Referendum Approach to Peace in America, 1914–1941*. Charlottesville: University Press of Virginia, 1977.

Caridi, Ronald J. *20th-Century American Foreign Policy: Security and Self-Interest*. Englewood Cliffs, N.J.: Prentice-Hall, 1974.

Josephson, Harold. "Salmon Oliver Levinson." In *Biographical Dictionary of Modern Peace Leaders*, edited by Harold Josephson. Westport, Conn.: Greenwood Press, 1985.

Lewisohn, Ludwig (1883–1955). Novelist, critic, polemicist, teacher, and translator, Ludwig Lewisohn wrote over 30 volumes in a literary career spanning half a century. In this production of uneven merit, his best work included three volumes in which an assimilated Jew discovers or deepens his knowledge of himself as a Jew. *Upstream* (1923), an autobiography of his early years, traces his turnabout from absorption into Southern Christian culture to his identification of himself as a Jew and a critic of the American scene.

Israel (1925), a book of travel and comment, his best nonfictional study of Judaism, marks Lewisohn's disillusionment with the German civilization he had once ardently admired. He sees anti-Semitism at work in Germany and the blinders German Jewish writers wore in its presence. In *Israel*, too, he witnesses the piety of Polish Jews despite their poverty, and, as he travels through Palestine, he voices his affirmation of Zionism, perhaps the first by an American man of letters. The book seems almost prophetic of later events in the century. *The Island Within* (1928), his most popular novel, outlines with wit and irony the destructive effects of intermarriage upon several generations of a Jewish family, first in Europe and then in America. The last in this family's line, the psychiatrist, Arthur Levy, divorces his Gentile wife and turns to Jewish observance out of psychological need. Here Lewisohn allies his interest in Freud and psychoanalysis with his affirmation of Judaism.

His best work also included books of non-Jewish content: *The Case of Mr. Crump* (1926), a naturalistic novel of hideous marital discord, based on his own first marriage; a book of drama criticism, *The Drama and the Stage* (1922), a penetrating collection of reviews and articles that he had written from the drama desk of the *Nation* magazine; *Cities and Men* (1927), literary and travel sketches advocating moral and rational standards in literature; and *Expression in America* (1932), a literary history of the United States, often lively and insightful but flawed by Freudian misreadings of Romantic writers, notably of Emerson, Thoreau, Poe, and Melville.

Lewisohn's best work covered one decade, from 1922 to 1932. His subsequent decline as a writer and his marital embroilments, publicized in the press and in his own writings, did much to damage his literary reputation. But his best books transcend this damage.

Lewisohn was born in Berlin. At the age of 7 he moved with his parents to South Carolina, where they settled in Charleston. His parents, reared in German culture, provided no Jewish commitment. In *Upstream*, Lewisohn wrote, ". . . at the age of fifteen I was an American, a Southerner, and a Christian." This assumed identity proved merely a facade when, as a graduate student at Columbia University, he was told, in 1903, that he could not get a job teaching college English—his persistent dream—because he was a Jew. Despite this shock, his sense of himself as a Jew was insignificant. (It was not to become a major factor until the 1920s in Europe.) In 1906, he married a Gentile, Mrs. Mary Crocker, 20 years his senior, a misalliance not formally dissolved until 1937.

He often conveyed in his later work the feeling that he was being persecuted. In 1917, he tells us in *Upstream*, he had to leave his post in German literature at Ohio State University because of the anti-German feeling on campus during the war. In 1922, he fled to Europe with Thelma Spear, a young singer, since he could not get a divorce from his wife. *The Case of Mr. Crump* could not be published in the United States until 1947, for publishers feared libel suits instigated by his wife. But out of adversity rose opportunity; in Europe, he wrote *Israel, The Case of Mr. Crump, The Island Within,* and *Cities and Men.*

His life and writings were often intertwined. His career illustrated Edmund Wilson's theory of the wound and the bow, of psychic trauma leading to creative energy. The blow suffered at Columbia University and his subsequent need for redefinition led to his best autobiography; his first marriage, contracted without adult preparation and knowledge, led to *The Case of Mr. Crump*, an engrossing exposure; and his sense that as a Jew he had been sidetracked out of his normal course led to *The Island Within*, in which he extrapolated upon his own experience.

In 1940, he began a regular column for *The New Palestine*, a Zionist journal; in 1943, he assumed its editorship. In 1948, he was appointed Professor of Comparative Literature at Brandeis University, his first academic post in 30 years. Lewisohn wished to be a Jewish advocate and an American man of letters at the same time, and, in large measure, he succeeded.

SEYMOUR LAINOFF

BIBLIOGRAPHY

Gillis, Adolph. *Ludwig Lewisohn: The Artist and His Message.* New York: Duffield and Green, 1933.

Lainoff, Seymour. *Ludwig Lewisohn.* Boston: Twayne, 1982.

Libraries and Archives in the United States and Canada, Jewish.

Throughout the United States and Canada there are 39 major Jewish libraries and archives. They are housed in community, public, college and university libraries, museums, archives, research institutes, the National Library of Canada, and the Library of Congress. The following information has been divided so that the United States is covered first, followed by Canada. The libraries and archives are further divided according to states, provinces, and cities. All of the following information regarding the size of the collections was provided by the libraries themselves.

UNITED STATES

Arizona

Bloom Southwest Jewish Archives
    University of Arizona
    1052 North Highland Avenue
    Tucson, AZ 85721
    10,000 documents
    Research center for pioneer Jewish history of
Arizona, New Mexico, and west Texas. Contains
an extensive collection on Southwest pioneer
Jewish history and related background material
on Jews in America. Currently creating a database
of historical material on pioneer Jewish history of
the Southwest.

California

Berkeley

Judah L. Magnes Museum
    Western Jewish History Center
    2911 Russell Street
    Berkeley, CA 94705
    1500 volumes, over 325 archival collections,
        and more than 100 oral history tapes
        and transcripts
    Covers western American Jewish history, in-
cluding Alaska and Hawaii.

University of California at Berkeley Library
    Berkeley, CA 94720
    45,000 volumes
    A well-rounded basic research collection
with special emphasis on various periods of Hebrew literary activity.

Los Angeles

Hebrew Union College-Jewish Institute of Reli-
        gion, Frances-Henry Library
    3077 University Avenue
    Los Angeles, CA 90007
    80,000 volumes
    Covers every aspect of Jewish intellectual en-
deavor. Strong holdings in biblical studies, American Jewish history, Jewish communal studies,
and Jewish education. Also serves as the West
Coast branch of the American Jewish Archives
and the American Jewish Periodicals Center.

Peter M. Kahn Jewish Community Library
    6505 Wilshire Boulevard
    Los Angeles, CA 90048
    30,000 volumes

Covers all aspects of Jewish history, thought,
culture, and life. Special features: the history of
the Jews of Los Angeles, Yiddish works, Jewish
education, rare edition of Pirke Aboth. Audio-
visual department serving schools and the community.

Simon Wiesenthal Center Library and Archives
    9760 West Pico Boulevard
    Los Angeles, CA 90035
    20,000 volumes, 300 serial subscriptions,
        1000 individual archival collections in-
        cluding 10,000 photographs
    Subject strengths: the Holocaust, anti-Semit-
ism (both historical and contemporary), pre-
World War II Jewish life, Nazi war crimes and
criminals, racism, and human rights. Special collections of primary anti-Semitic and Holocaust
revisionism.

University of California at Los Angeles
    Jewish Studies Collection
    University Research Library
    Los Angeles, CA 90024
    170,000 volumes
    Covers all areas of Jewish studies. Includes
numerous rare Hebraica and Judaica, Judeo-
Arabic, and Ladino works and early Italian Hebrew books. Very large Yiddish collection. Significant microform holdings of Jewish periodicals.
Collections of Jewish music, art, and civil law
housed in the UCLA library branches (Music,
Art, Law).

University of Judaism Library
    15600 Mullholland Drive
    Los Angeles, CA 90077-1599
    100,000 volumes and several hundred micro-
        forms
    Research-level Judaica collection. Particular
strengths: rabbinics, modern Hebrew literature,
books on Israel and the Middle East. Unique collection of Russian-Jewish publications of the
early twentieth century. Strong in periodicals
published in Israel.

San Francisco

Holocaust Center of Northern California
    639 14th Avenue
    San Francisco, CA 94118
    10,000 volumes, 1200 pamphlets, 1000 ar-
        chival collections
    Strengths: memorial books and German
works on the rise of Nazism through the end of

World War II. Videotape collection, including 300 interviews with local Holocaust survivors, and slide collection documenting primarily the liberation of World War II concentration camps.

Stanford

Stanford University Libraries
    Cecil H. Green Library
    Stanford, CA 94305
    35,000 volumes
    Covers all areas of Jewish history and culture. Houses private library of Salo Wittmayer Baron, with its strong collection on the legal status of Jews and Jewish communal and social history, and including approximately 1000 volumes printed before 1800.

Colorado

University of Denver
    Penrose Library
    Denver, CO 80208-0292
    20,000 volumes
    A good basic collection of Judaica. Includes religious and secular materials as well as a valuable rare-book collection.

University of Denver
    Ira M. Beck Memorial Archives of Rocky Mountain Jewish History
    Denver, CO 80208-0292
    Over 1 million documents
    Includes manuscripts, photographs and memorabilia relating to Jews in the Rocky Mountain region, with special emphasis on Colorado.

Connecticut

Yale University Library
    P.O. Box 1603A Yale Station
    New Haven, CT 06520
    90,000 volumes, 156 Hebraic manuscripts, 45 Judaic incunabula
    A comprehensive collection of Jewish history, as well as significant collections on the Jewish religion, law, ethics and philosophy, rabbinics, talmudica, Hebrew and Yiddish literature and translations, and Hebrew and Aramaic philology and linguistics. Special features: manuscripts, incunabula, the Sholem Asch collection, and extensive papers on the Palestine Statehood Commitee and related manuscripts.

District of Columbia

Library of Congress
    Hebraic Section, African and Middle Eastern Division
    Washington, D.C. 20540
    1.3 million volumes, extensive microform holdings
    Extensive Hebraic collection covering such topics as the Bible, the cultures and languages of the ancient Near East, Jews and Judaism throughout the world from biblical times to the present, Palestine and Israel, and Ethiopia. Special collections housing cuneiform tablets, manuscripts, incunables, kettubot, micrographies, miniature books, and amulets. Also maintains union catalogs of Hebrew and Yiddish in major collections in the United States and Canada. In addition, books in Western languages, numbering in the hundreds of thousands, in the library's general collections.

Florida

University of Florida Libraries
    Isser and Rae Price Library of Judaica
    406 Library East
    Gainesville, FL 32611
    42,500 volumes
    The largest collection of Judaica and Hebraica in the southeastern United States. Collects extensively in virtually all subject areas pertinent to Jewish studies with holdings concentrated in late nineteenth-century and twentieth-century publications.

Illinois

Chicago

Spertus College of Judaica
    Asher Library
    618 South Michigan Avenue
    Chicago, IL 60605
    75,000 volumes
    Represents all areas of Jewish religion, history, and culture. Special features: a rare-book collection with many sixteenth- and seventeenth-century imprints and extensive periodical holdings, including publications from the nineteenth century. Primarily documents of Chicago Jewish history, with papers of congregations, social and welfare organizations, and individuals in its archives.

University of Chicago
    Department of Special Collections
    University of Chicago Library
    1100 East 57th Street
    Chicago, IL 60637
    22,000 volumes (Ludwig Rosenberger Collection of Judaica), 55,000 volumes (general collections of the Joseph Regenstein Library)

The Ludwig Rosenberger Collection of Judaica covers Jewish social and intellectual history from the Middle Ages to the present. Strongest concentrations in German, French, and English eighteenth- and twentieth-century works. Thematic areas of greatest depth: emancipation, anti-Semitism and Jewish responses to it, Zionism, Marxism, and socialism.

Skokie

Hebrew Theological College
    Saul Silber Memorial Library
    7135 North Carpenter Road
    Skokie, IL 60077
    64,000 volumes

Subject strengths in the Bible, rabbinical literature, Jewish law, Judaism, Zionism, Holocaust literature, and Hebrew language and literature.

Massachusetts

Brookline

Hebrew College Library
    43 Hawes Street
    Brookline, MA 02146
    100,000 volumes

Covers all areas of Jewish studies. Special collections of incunabula, rare books from the sixteenth, seventeenth, and eighteenth centuries, Russian Judaica and Japanese Judaica, and 70 manuscripts, the earliest from the late fourteenth century. Particularly strong in modern Hebrew literature and Jewish medical ethics.

Cambridge

Harvard College Library
    Cambridge, MA 02138
    200,000 volumes

A comprehensive collection covering all areas of Jewish history and culture. Consists primarily of printed materials, but also includes a large collection of microforms, sound recordings, videotapes, and a small manuscript collection.

Waltham

American Jewish Historical Society
    2 Thornton Road
    Waltham, MA 02154
    80,000 volumes and a large archival collection

Collection devoted to American Jewish history in all its ramifications. Includes large American Yiddish theater collection, early American Jewish printed books, and a very complete collection of American Hebraica.

Brandeis University Library
    P.O. Box 9110
    Waltham, MA 02254-9110
    100,000 volumes

A comprehensive collection of Judaica, Hebraica, and Yiddica covering all areas of Jewish history, language and literature, philosophy, and rabbinic literature. Also includes extensive microfilm holdings of periodicals and manuscripts.

Michigan

University of Michigan
    Graduate Library
    Ann Arbor, MI 48109-1205
    55,000 volumes

A comprehensive collection, with emphasis on modern Hebrew literature, Jewish history and culture, and Judaism in general.

New Jersey

Princeton University Library
    Nassau Street & Washington Road
    Princeton, NJ 08544
    20,000 volumes of Hebrew books

A research-level collection in all areas of Jewish history and culture. Particularly strong in modern Hebrew literature, rabbinic literature, and the history and literature of Jews under Islam. Extensive collection of books printed by the Jews of Jerba and the S.D. Goitein Genizah Archive.

New York

Ithaca

Cornell University Library
    Ithaca, NY 14853
    60,000 volumes

Covers the principal areas of Jewish history and culture. Stronger in European and North American titles than in Hebrew/Yiddish titles. Includes holdings in Jewish-American labor history in the library of the School of Labor and Industrial Relations.

New York City

American Jewish Committee
    Blaustein Library
    165 East 56th Street
    New York, NY 10022
    35,000 volumes
    Primarily concerned with contemporary American Jewish life, intergroup relations, civil rights and civil liberties, and the position of religious and ethnic minorities in American society. Includes a special collection of propaganda issued by domestic and foreign extremist groups.

Columbia University Library
    535 West 114th Street
    New York, NY 10027
    43,500 volumes in Hebrew and Yiddish
    A comprehensive collection covering all areas of Jewish history and culture, except rabbinics. Includes over 1000 Hebrew manuscripts and many rare books from the Temple Emannuel collection.

Hebrew Union College-Jewish Institute of Religion
    Klau Library
    1 West 4th Street
    New York, NY 10012-1186
    130,000 volumes
    A comprehensive collection of Judaica.

Jewish Theological Seminary of America Library
    3080 Broadway
    New York, NY 10027
    270,000 volumes
    Rich collection of primary sources for research in the Bible, rabbinics, philosophy, liturgy, history, and medieval and modern Hebrew literature. Also manuscripts, archives, graphics, and a large segment of the Cairo Genizah.

Leo Baeck Institute
    129 East 73rd Street
    New York, NY 10021
    60,000 volumes and archives
    Devoted to the life and history of German-speaking Jewry. Archives including 600 memoirs and over 30,000 photographs.

New York Public Library
    Jewish Division
    Fifth Avenue & 42nd Street
    New York, NY 10018
    230,000 volumes
    Collection strengths in Judaism, Jewish history, literature and traditions in all languages, and

Jewish periodicals and newspapers in Hebrew, Yiddish, and other Jewish languages.

World Zionist Organization-American Section
    Zionist Archives and Library
    110 East 59th Street
    New York, NY 10022
    50,000 volumes, archives on microfilm
    An information center for all aspects of life in Israel and other Middle Eastern countries, as well as for Zionism and Judaism.

Yeshiva University
    Mendel Gottesman Library of Hebraica/Judaica
    500 West 185th Street
    New York, NY 10033
    198,000 volumes
    A comprehensive Judaica research library with particular strengths in rabbinics, the Bible, and Jewish history. Special collections: rare books, manuscripts, archives, and the Jacob E. Safra Institute's Sephardic colection.

YIVO Institute for Jewish Research
    1048 Fifth Avenue
    New York, NY 10028
    320,000 volumes in the Library and 22 million documents in the archives, including 100,000 photographs
    Covers all areas of Jewish history and culture, with particular emphasis on the Jewish experience in Eastern Europe. Areas of special interest: Yiddish language and literature, theater and folklore, anti-Semitism, Nazism and the Holocaust, Jewish migration patterns and the consequent growth of Jewish communities throughout the world, including above all the American Jewish community.

Ohio

Cincinnati

American Jewish Archives
    3101 Clifton Avenue
    Cincinnati, OH 45220
    8 million pages of documents
    Manuscripts, microforms, videos, and tape recordings on the Jewish experience in the Western Hemisphere.

Hebrew Union College-Jewish Institute of Religion Library
    3101 Clifton Avenue
    Cincinnati, OH 45220
    375,000 volumes

A comprehensive collection covering all areas of Jewish history and culture. Among its special collections: Hebrew manuscripts, incunabula, sixteenth-century Hebrew printing, Jewish Americana to 1875, Jewish music, broadsides, Yiddish theater, the Inquisition, Spinoza, and Josephus.

Columbus

Ohio State University Library
    Columbus, OH 43210
    60,000 volumes
    A research collection with a special interest in Jewish history and Hebrew language and literature.

Pennsylvania

Annenberg Research Institute
    420 Walnut Street
    Philadelphia, PA 19106
    150,000 volumes
    Comprehensive Judaica and Semitics library, including manuscripts, early printed books, archives, Genizah material, Americana, and microfilms of Hebraica manuscripts in other collections.

Gratz College
    Tuttelman Library
    Old York Road & Melrose Avenue
    Melrose Park, PA 19126
    100,000 items
    A comprehensive collection of Judaica, with special strengths in the Holocaust, Hebrew literature, Israel studies, and modern Jewish history. Includes also the Schreiber Jewish Music Library and the Holocaust Oral History Archives.

Texas

University of Texas
    Perry-Castañeda Library
    Box P
    Austin, TX 78713-7330
    75,000 volumes
    General coverage of Jewish culture, especially of the contemporary period, with emphasis on Israel and the United States.

CANADA

Montreal

Jewish Public Library
    5151 Côte Ste Catherine Road
    Montreal, Quebec H3W 1M6
    110,000 volumes

Covers all areas of Jewish history and culture, including books in English, French, Hebrew, and Yiddish. Among its special features: the archives of Canadian Yiddish writers and Jewish Canadiana.

Ottawa

National Library of Canada
    395 Wellington Street
    Ottawa, Ontario K1A 0N4
    15,000 volumes
    Hebraica-Judaica collections including the Jacob M. Lowy collection of 2000 rare Hebraica and Judaica (incunabula and early European printed Hebraica), as well as the Hayes Collection of oriental (mostly Yemenite) Hebrew manuscripts. The modern Judaica collection especially strong in Canadiana, reflecting every area of Canadian Jewish history, literature, and culture.

Toronto

University of Toronto Library
    Toronto, Ontario M5S 1AS
    60,000 volumes
    A research collection covering all aspects of Jewish studies. Areas of strength: rabbinics, medieval Judaism and Jewish literature, and East European Jewish history.

Information regarding the size and scope of the collections was provided by the libraries themselves. Volume designations refer to the Judaica collections as described, not necessarily to the collections as a whole.

STEPHEN LEHMANN
EVA SARTORI

Lippmann, Walter (1889–1974). Walter Lippmann, born in New York City, was the only child of German Jewish parents. Lippmann's family managed a successful business and resided in what was referred to as the gilded Jewish ghetto off Lexington Avenue. As an offspring of a wealthy family, he received a prized education, which included a diploma from Sachs Collegiate High School and an undergraduate degree from Harvard. At these institutions Lippmann was able to develop his considerable intellect.

Once out of college, he wrote for the *Masses*, a radical socialist publication. Lippmann's radical politics was swiftly pushed aside as he gained acceptance and recognition for his writing and as establishment publications showed a willingness to publish his articles. Fortifying his growing conservatism was a skepticism that questioned all forms of idealism. Idealism at best was judged to be romantic and impractical. Such romantic sentiments ran counter to Lippmann's temperament, which compelled him to take a detached and undogmatic view of the world. How these sentiments led to Lippmann's conservatism is clarified by examining his thoughts on democracy. He distrusted mass democracy, which he categorized as mob rule. Lippmann believed that the masses lacked the knowledge, interest, and inclination to govern and that the most effective government was one in which an elite ruled within representative democratic institutions. With the increasing conservatism of his political views, the stage was set for Lippmann to become one of the most influential journalists in American history. What distinguished his writing from that of most other journalists was his ability to combine deep learning and scholarly interests with reporting the weekly news. The *New Republic*, a liberal centrist publication of which Lippmann was a founding member, provided Lippmann with a forum in which to observe and influence the world. Lippmann also became a columnist for several New York papers, including the *World* and the *Herald Tribune*. The extent of Lippmann's influence is best illustrated by the fact that it was Lippmann who authored Wilson's fourteen-point peace plan. He hoped that this proposal would lead to lasting peace among nations.

A troubling aspect in Lippmann's life was his Jewish identity. His grandparents had come to America in the 1840s. Growing up in a milieu and era that extolled cosmopolitanism and eschewed ethnicity and religion, Lippmann wished to sever his ties to Judaism. Though he wanted others to believe Judaism was of no consequence to his life, the reality was otherwise. Buried beneath Lippmann's indifference toward his background were elements of self-hatred. In his personal letters, he attacked Jews as being clannish and vulgar. The degree of Lippmann's antipathy toward his own people comes to light in viewing his relationship with former Supreme Court Justice Felix Frankfurter. Two decades of friendship between these men ended abruptly after Lippmann wrote a column in 1933 advocating a policy of tolerance toward Germany after Hitler came to power. This was too much for Frankfurter. Lippmann's promulgating "tolerance toward Hitler's policies" was accompanied by not a single protest against Germany once the details of the Holocaust were revealed.

After World War II, Lippmann's career and reputation continued to grow unabated. Lippmann traveled widely and wrote prolifically. In addition to his column syndicated throughout the country, Lippmann published several books. It was on the issue of Vietnam that the maverick trenchant and critical voice of Lippmann, quiescent since his days with the *Masses*, began to reassert itself. To his credit, Lippmann was willing to sacrifice his influence and prestige by stridently attacking the Southeast Asian policy of the Johnson administrations. Lippmann, a writer who used words precisely and gingerly, employed adjectives such as ignorant and foolish in describing Johnson's policy. According to Lippmann, this policy diverted the United States from dealing with critical domestic issues and was leading the nation toward imperialism, which would have ruinous consequences. As Lippmann wrote incessantly on Vietnam, he alienated himself from the Washington establishment. His growing distance from the establishment is illustrated by the people he chose to associate with during this period. Rather than inviting people such as McGeorge Bundy (Johnson's national security adviser) to his dinner parties, I. F. Stone, a radical journalist, and others with similar political leanings were in attendance. By taking a strong and vociferous stance on Vietnam, Lippmann subjected himself to attacks. Moreover, several valued friendships were lost because of differences on this matter. Despite the toll the Vietnam War extracted from Lippmann, he remained an optimist to the end of his life. To quote Lippmann "The need to be civilized and the capacity are inherent in men's nature, and are reborn with each new generation." Lippmann died from cardiac arrest at the age of 85. *See also* Journalism.

HOWARD B. SHAKER

BIBLIOGRAPHY

Childs, Marquis William, ed. *Walter Lippmann and His Times*. New York: Books for Libraries Press, 1968.

Steel, Ronald. *Walter Lippmann and the American Century*. Boston: Little, Brown, 1980.

Literature. *See* FICTION; HOLOCAUST, LITERATURE OF THE; JEWISH CHILDREN'S LITERATURE; LITERATURE, YIDDISH; POETRY; POETRY, YIDDISH.

Literature, Yiddish. By the middle of the nineteenth century, in the Pale of Settlement in Eastern Europe, the central fact for the Jew was the recognition that to be a Jew was the fundamental environing condition on one's life. All values arose from where one was forced to live, that is, in the shtetl. All traditions were bound up in the shtetl. The shtetl was the embodiment of the Jewish community, and from it came one's prestige (or *yikhus*). To be a Talmud *Khochem* or a *Yeshiva Bokher* was the one sure way to gain status. After several hundred years of constraint and pogroms and despair, however, broken only by the influence of the Hasidic movement and the importation of the Haskalah (the Jewish Enlightenment), it was clear that aspirations could only be satisfied within the shtetl. What more natural for Jews, who were not and could not be citizens, than to turn their energies inward? They lived in a world of their own. They were innocent, free of the Sins of the Fall, and though good and evil existed and it was believed that man was free to choose which, he would always choose what was morally and ethically right.

In the grip of reality, all Jews were potential victims of the repressive governments that surrounded them. Thus, in view of the Jewish tradition of learning, of testing and self-examination, it is not surprising that these conditions would be reflected in the literary tradition. After all, the Eastern European Yiddish writer had an identity crisis. The result, expressed by I. L. Peretz, is that the notion of a shared historical consciousness created a new type, a Jew from Eastern Europe: "Is there a people, a wander-folk without fixed borders . . . that lives, suffers, and does not perish; that is weak, attacked by the greatest and the strongest and does not surrender—then must such a people see differently, feel differently, have a different view of life, a different conception of the future of the world, of life, and of man." The result was a literary reflection of this culture that bore the weight of the past and gave values to what Matthew Arnold called "sweetness and light." Where there were no dominant or heroic figures in the present, the writers turned to a biblical and/or mythical past or to a present saturated with the personalities of those who existed, "as they could." The most sensitive and perceptive voices in the nineteenth century were Mendele Mokher Seforim, I. L. Peretz, and Sholem Aleichem.

All three of these classic Yiddish writers were involved with the people they wrote about. Characteristically, they felt a bond of sympathy with the downtrodden, the helpless. Caught up in a community without leverage and forced to struggle against external temptation, they were drawn to the heroism of the anti-heroic hero, the little man, the schlemiel, poor but proud. Their stories and novels, criticizing the old of medieval Judaism, the corruptions within and the dangers from without, reflected the voice of the people. Therefore, they were terribly popular and loved until well into this century.

Among the disciples of Peretz were David Pinski, Abraham Reisin, and Sholem Asch. It was through Peretz that the Jewish intellectual was brought back to his heritage. Sholem Asch, one of the most talented of Peretz's disciples, was known primarily as the writer of plays and novels sympathetic to the Jewish community. Suddenly, in mid-career, he wrote a trilogy of Christological novels: *The Nazarene* (1939), *The Apostle* (1943), and *Mary* (1949). According to Asch, his purpose was to enrich the accepted Jewish tradition with the usually unacceptable teachings of Jesus of Nazareth. That Asch fell out of favor with the people was to be expected. That he returned to their good graces is testimony to the lasting power of his plays *The Messianic Age* and *God of Vengeance* and his novels *Motke the Thief* and *America*. More important was David Pinski, writer, poet, and playwright, also influenced by Peretz, who published first in Poland and then, from the turn of the century on, in New York. Oscillating between his need to foster socialism as a panacea and his later conviction that Jews had to struggle for personal and national dignity, he carved out a career rich in Yiddishkeit; but he is remembered today chiefly as the author of *The House of Noah Edon* (1929), written in English, a genealogical novel of three generations. That he wrote in English after three decades of writing in Yiddish indicates his realization that Yiddish was no longer as universal a language as it had been. That Noah, at the end, was left with no one to continue the ancestral ways points to Pinski's central metaphor, that of Noah adrift in the flood. With one of his children dead, amidst a ruined marriage, and two grandchildren dead in a suicide pact, Noah was left with death, despair, and no hope. Other Yiddish writers, while not prone to the melodrama that marked *The House of Noah Edon*, shared Pinski's sense that the Yiddish writer's days were numbered in America.

With the onset of large-scale immigration to the New World of millions of Eastern European

Jews, from the 1880s to the 1920s, the Old Country began to crumble. With the destruction of 6 million Jews in the Holocaust, the United States became the stronghold of Yiddish culture. Unfortunately, even as the forces of acculturation whittled down the strength of Yiddishkeit, so the later creation of the State of Israel and its choice of Hebrew as *the* official language dealt Yiddish another blow. Yiddish, since the tenth century the language of the Diaspora, was finally engaged in its greatest trial as a living language.

The environment of America during the 1880s and 1890s proved to be a mixed blessing, both conducive and not conducive to the development of American Yiddish literature. On the one hand, the writers, having been uprooted from their Eastern European home, were suffering the effects of culture shock. For some, the shock would prove to be a paralyzing obstacle, even a fatal one; for others, the culture shock became a continuing—indeed, often the sole—source of their works. On the other hand, as with most immigrants, many writers were eager to adjust, no matter what the cost. The popular song "Un brivele der mamen" (A Letter to Mama) was a reflection of that yearning. Meanwhile socialist and anarchist writings duplicated the political patterns established in Eastern Europe. But out of these tensions came the first American Yiddish writers, Morris Rosenfeld, Yehoash, Abraham Reisen, Mani Leyb, Abraham Liessin, H. Rosenblatt, and David Pinski. In them was the essence of generations past, mixed with the sweat and joy of Jewish America. They went into the factories and on the farms, they wrote of their experiences, and in the process they created a new Yiddish literature.

The first major literary movement was called Di Yunge. As a self-conscious movement against their literary "fathers," it soon became a protest against the sentimentalized Yiddish still being written and spoken in Eastern Europe. An affirmation of love for America, this movement also provided a united stand against the mediocrity and irresponsibility then existing in the Jewish community. Whatever else one may say about it, the literature of the Di Yunge was true to itself. In the works of H. Leivick, writing of Siberia in New York City, Jewishness suffused every line. The same was true of the work of Isaac Raboy, who wrote of farms and cows and horses and prairies, and of works of M. L. Halpern, Mani Leyb, Aaron Leyeles, Jacob Glatstein, and others. It was a question of content and form and

rhythm, especially rhythm. America has a rhythm, of course, as does every country. The inner rhythm comes from feeling at home in America, of feeling the streets and buildings, the people, the wood, the concrete, the distances, the breadth and beat of life, the ideas Americans hold sacred. The inner rhythm also comes from a people's spiritual resources, and it comes from an individual's attempts to liberate himself, to find himself, to find a justification in Jewish life. The writers mentioned all sought and found these depths. Based on the pillars of Yiddish literature, they flourished. They carried on their shoulders the past and the present, the accumulation that has made a consummate body of epics, novels, poems, plays, and stories about life and people that we call Yiddish literature in America.

Coming on the heels of Di Yunge were two movements that proved congenial to the young immigrant intellectuals. One, called the Introspectivists (the Inzichisten) arose in 1919 following the lead of Aaron Leyeles, N. B. Minkoff, and Jacob Glatstein (Yankev Glatshteyn) in founding a magazine titled *In Sich*. Unlike the Di Yunge group, the Inzichists emphasized poetry as the means by which one interpreted the environment, in accord with one's individual *Weltanschauung*. As they collectively put it in 1920, "The world exists for us only insofar as it is mirrored in us, insofar as it touches us. The world is a non-existent category, a fiction, if it is not related to us. It becomes a reality only in us and through us." In short, they believed only in what the inner will created, as seen in their innovative style. Their content was wedded to their form.

Of the Inzich group, Glatstein was the most talented. Although he began to write when he was 14, a few years before he arrived in America, and published his first story in 1914, it was not until 1921 that his first volume of verse came out. Called simply *Jacob Glatstein*, it invoked Buddha, Brahma, and Nirvana. In *Free Verses (Frei Versen*, 1926), he began to deal with Jewish themes, and in the 1930s, after a return visit to his home in Lublin, Poland, he became preoccupied with the misery and suffering of the Jews. Indeed, the more he tasted the New World and felt the shadow of Hitler, the more he believed that Jews might as well have remained in the ghetto. For what he had in mind, as he put it in *Homecoming at Twilight* (1940), was the almost unchanging attitudes he had experienced: "They hate us for observing the Sabbath," he wrote, "and they hate us for violating the Sabbath. They hate pious Jews and they hate free-thinking Jews who eat lobster. They hate our capitalists and they hate our beggars. They hate our reactionaries and they hate our radicals. They hate Jews who earn bread and those who die three times a day from starvation."

Through it all Glatstein, realizing that his audience was becoming ever smaller, wrote in Yiddish because it was a personification of the fate of his people, the secret of the relation between meaning and reality. His lot was to be a major poet in a minor language, and for a whole range of complicated reasons, Glatstein—who was educated in American universities and who could write English fluently—accepted his destiny. In his poem "1919," he speaks of the disappearance of Yankel (presumably himself), and yet he also saw the future, what was to be. "How much destruction can a people suffer," his speaker asks, "and still believe in rebuilding?" Glatstein's life and his poetry, so intertwined as to be virtually the same thing, provide a kind of answer to the unanswerable: his words reflect a life filled with the recognition that it was his fate to suffer.

Independent of the Introspectivists but also following on the heels of the Di Yunge group were a group of independents. Head and shoulders above all others in this category was H. Leivick, who was born Leivick Halpern. Influenced early by socialist ideas, he spent four years in Siberia but escaped and somehow got to New York in 1913, where he supported himself by working as a paperhanger. His first volume of poetry, *Locked In* (*Hintern Schloss*, 1918) speaks of the nature of pain.

In 1920 *The Golem*, Leivick's most famous poetic drama, was published. Using an historical legend of the Frankenstein monster, the man-made robot, he detailed the price necessary for a messianic age. With the realization that the sheer mechanical power of the robot was too inhuman for a Messiah, and thus not appropriate, he made the Messiah a young beggar traveling with Elijah the prophet. In short order, several more plays appeared, capped by *Chains* (*Kehten*, 1929), which marked his break with communism and his questioning of bad means to get to good ends. And then midway through the 1930s he wrote "Ballad of the Denver Sanatorium," and after visiting the death camps, *I Was Not in Treblinka*, *A Wedding in Fernwald*, and *In the Days of Job*. Near the end of his life, in *The Father's Shadow* (*Dem Tatens Shuttn*, 1953), he pleaded with God: "Save yourself, O God, return with us to our little land, become once more the Jewish God." He realized that unbelief and skepticism were dangerous. At least when he was within the community, even in a Hasidic community, he would pray with a handful of genuine old-fashioned Jews and sense a breath of God's nearness. He knew the dark side, and yet he saw the possibilities.

Although the Yiddish theater is largely dormant today, with only occasional "revivals" mounted for the nostalgia crowd, it was a thriving medium until the 1940s. Its traditions dated back to the 1870s, where Abraham Goldfaden's first musical presentations took place in Jassy, Romania. As with the earlier writers, he too took his work seriously, in social terms. "Every true, loyal Jew," he wrote in the 1880s, "must strive to help with thoughts and deeds, with propaganda and organization, to save his people, to work for its liberation and independence, to rescue it from discouragement, and to pour into its bitter cup at least a few drops of faith in a better future." In the New World, to which he and Boris Tomashefsky, Joseph Lateiner, Jacob Adler, Jacob Gordin, David Kessler, and I.J. Singer came, their work was appreciated. They were celebrated as if they were but a little lower than God. But gradually, as they and their audiences became Americanized, the plays and musicals showed the influence. *Shund* (i.e., junk) would no longer suffice, and thus the unsophisticated days in which broad comic farce, a bit of song-and-dance, spectacle, and "four-hanky" sentimentality were shoveled into a single play came to an end. In its stead was serious art, in a distinctly Yiddish idiom. As a result, when *The Jewish King Lear* (*Die Yiddishe Kenig Lear*, 1892) became an enormous success, a sequel was written, the Jewish Queen Lear, called *Mirele Efros* (1890), which was equally successful. With the rise and fall of Maurice Schwartz's Yiddish Art Theater, Yiddish theater took its last major plunge, never to recover.

On the eve of World War II, a new movement called Young Vilna arose. Coming out of a tradition in which Vilna had been the intellectual and cultural center of Eastern Europe, the Jerusalem of Lithuania, the major voices were Isaac Meier Dick, Eliakhum Zinser, Abraham Cahan, and Abraham Reisin; more recently, we have Abraham Sutzkever (now living in Israel) and Chaim Grade. Grade is known to Americans for *The Synagogue Courtyard* (1958), *The Well* (1962), and especially *The Agunah* (1961), a novel about a woman whose husband is missing but she cannot get a Jewish divorce because it cannot be established that he is dead. In the process, Grade unveiled a rich panaorama of Jewish religious life in

Vilna and the struggle between traditionalists and innovators in the 1930s. Sutzkever, whose poems date from the inception of World War II, has been concerned with the advantages of liberty for which he and his family yearned. Failing to find light, beauty, and freedom, however, he conjured them up. The problem is that Sutzkever is in Israel, and those Yiddish poets still writing in America are not well known. Cynthia Ozick's wickedly satirical story, "Envy, or Yiddish in America" is often taken as a statement of their sad, embittered condition, although Yiddishists vigorously deny its vision. Still, the fact remains that American Yiddish poets labor in something of a self-generated obscurity. Eliezer Greenberg and Ephraim Auerbach, for example, should be better known, but their renown bears a direct relation to their availability in English translations. And as for all translations, especially of poetry, something is lost in the translation. Yiddish, influenced by the environing culture, by the fate of Jewishness, and, in addition, being essentially plebian, a culture of *folkmessen*, is held by the tension between the traditional and secular forces that gave it life. In this context, Yiddish literature is part of the Western tradition, especially in the works of Abraham Cahan and Isaac Bashevis Singer.

Abraham Cahan more than anyone else has best dramatized the losses and gains of the transition to the New World. Arriving in this country from Vilna in 1882, he wrote stories and novels that were classic accounts of the crisis of ethnic identity confronted by the Eastern European Jews as they poured into New York from the 1880s through World War I. At an early age his mother told him, "You have a mirror before your eyes." Taking this seriously, he embraced Russian culture, atheism, and socialism only to find that they effected a transformation that influenced his entire life. Because of his passion for humanity he overlooked the pogroms in the Ukraine; he could not see the forest for the trees. His solution then was socialism. Only later did he realize that there was a difference between a revolutionary who mouthed universal-sounding platitudes and one who really cared for the welfare of the people, his people.

In the 1880s, New York City was moving uptown, as a new breed of millionaires, roughnecks, political leaders, and ethnics emerged. At the same time, sweatshops and cold-water flat tenements proliferated. In this milieu Cahan became a worker, a political activist, and a writer

and editor. Realizing that Yiddish papers at that time appealed to readers in a kind of literary Yiddish, he decided to write Yiddish as it was spoken. His decision not only transformed the *Jewish Daily Forward* (the *Forverts*), but made it the most popular Yiddish daily in the world. He encouraged a letters-to-the-editor column, known as the *Bintele Brief*, and he wrote a thinly disguised socialist sermon each week under the pen name of the "proletarian preacher." His first essay on literature, "Realism," in 1889, dealt with man's nature and Herbert Spencer's social Darwinism and asserted that sensations are a form of cognition. He rejected the idea that the sole end of art is to afford pleasure. In this he was a link from the past, but he was also true to his own convictions. From 1891, when his first fiction appeared, it was clear that he was a "realist" and that he was involved with his people and their problems. When his first novel was to appear, *Yekl the Yankee* (1896), W. D. Howells, the dean of American letters, liked it enormously but suggested the name be changed to *Yekl: A Tale of the New York Ghetto*. His collection *The Imported Bridegroom and Other Stories* (1898) was also well received. But it was with the appearance of *The Rise of David Levinsky* (1917), written in English, that Cahan's rise to maturity was established in literary terms. It is still considered the best immigrant novel ever written. It is, as John Higham points out, a novel in which Cahan successfully combines the distinctively American theme of success with a Jewish subject and a Russian artistic sensibility.

All through these years Cahan was editor of the *Forverts* and an active Socialist. Caught up with the idea that the old spirit of idealism (the *neshomah yeseroh*) was gone, he wrote a number of tales at the turn of the century exploring this concept. In "Fanny and Her Suitors," written in English and later translated into Yiddish, he wrote of a socialist editor's talks with a worker named Fanny. In the same year his "Autobiography of an American Jew" was published serially in *McClure's*. From these two tales, especially from the "Autobiography," came *The Rise of David Levinsky*. Concerning a young man's business success, and the cost of that success, the novel relates David's Americanization to his unsuccessful love life and his loneliness. At the end David laments his present station, power, and worldly happiness, because he can never forget "the days of his misery." In David's words, "I cannot escape from my old self. My past and my present do not comport well. David, the poor lad swinging over a Talmud volume at the Preacher's Synagogue, seems to have more in common with my identity than David Levinsky, the well-known cloak manufacturer."

Was David really unhappy? Did he regret the choice of a career? Of course, David was unhappy. But he relished his unhappiness; he would have made the same decision had he to do it all over again. The fact is that David, egotistical, aloof, reserved, controlled, powerful, was the man he wanted to be. He had chosen success; he had pursued the American dream. He was also enmeshed in a schizophrenic existence, caught between the realization of what he had lost and what he had wanted to gain.

What had Cahan accomplished? Editor of the *Forverts* from 1903 till his death, he played a crucial role in the acculturation of the Jews in America. Author of novels and short stories, almost always dealing with the problems of acculturation, he is remembered today as the author of *The Rise of David Levinsky*. Realizing, as he wrote in *The Education of Abraham Cahan*, that "America lives more in one day than Russia does in ten," he transmitted that celebration of America to his people. As a socialist, he believed that to influence people you must first become a man (a *mensch*). To do this, he popularized Yiddish and taught his people how to grow. He realized, as it is said in "Rabbi Eliezer's Christmas," "This isn't Russia . . . it's America, the land of machines and of 'hurry up. . . and there you are.'" In short, he made his peace with America. He adapted. And in doing so he became a fine writer who influenced several generations of Americans, in part because he wrote *The Rise of David Levinsky* in English and because adaptation was an essential message. The primacy of an audience and accommodation were as important as felicity to Jewish life. In more recent times Isaac Bashevis Singer has taken the same path, although he continues to write in Yiddish.

When I. B. Singer was a child he recalled his father's warnings against reading the works of Peretz. "Everybody who reads such books," his father said, "sooner or later became a worldly man and forsook the traditions." He was right. When his older brother, I.J. (Israel Joshua) Singer, moved out and into the Bohemian life, Isaac was entranced, but he managed to hold onto the duality of Bohemia and tradition for himself. "Even in my stories," Singer has written, "it is one step from the study house to sexuality and back again." From age 13 to 17 he lived with his mother in the little town of Bilgoray, a town that had remained unaltered since the Middle Ages. From this experience came his feeling for and belief in demons, spirits, magic, and the like. While he studied Torah and Talmud, he also dipped into the Cabalah. While he pored over Spinoza, he hummed a Hasidic tune. While he read Dostoyevsky, he delved into mysticism. While he pursued free inquiry, he resisted Orthodoxy. In short, as his life became saturated with that special apocalyptic and messianic flavor that gave to *Satan in Goray* its urgent fervor and fever, so he fed on the tension that it built. In that little town he had a chance to see the past as it really was. "Time," he says, "seemed to flow backward." He "lived Jewish history."

Composed in 1933, published in 1935 in Yiddish, and translated into English in 1955, *Satan in Goray* was impelled into being by the closeness of Hitler, Singer's unsuccessful marriage to a woman who chose communism in Russia over Singer, and the international success of his brother's play *Yoshe Kalb*. In 1935, Singer followed his brother to America. When he first arrived, Singer felt that he had no roots, that Yiddish had no future, that the existence of the Jewish people was imperiled. Abraham Cahan, who had given I.J. Singer a job on the *Forverts*, refused initially to do the same for Isaac. After all, how many Yiddish readers would there be in the next decades? As a result, Singer had what he calls "a real case of literary amnesia." He could not write for a number of years. Looking back, he realized that "one has to get a very great blow to act in such a way." After his second marriage, and particularly after his brother's death in 1944, he was able to write again. Since then he has poured forth an unending stream of short stories and novels, all in Yiddish, which have invariably been translated into English. Thus, in English, he is known to those who read the *New Yorker, Esquire, Harper's, Cosmopolitan, Partisan Review, Commentary, Playboy, Saturday Evening Post, Chicago Post,* and many more of our nation's most influential magazines.

More important, it must be said that Singer uses the past: he dwells in the past, a past replete with demons and devils who vie with men and women and God. But Singer uses the devil both as the alter ego of God and, psychologically and artistically, to credit and to release another secret sharer, man's secret and unconscious desires. At base, the devil is used to revive moral choice, to give added dread and urgency to moral dilemma, and to make personal choice a mode of self-creation and self-destruction. But whether clothed in modern American dress or in the framework of the past, Singer's concerns have proved attractive to American readers. For example, in a 1975 *New Yorker* story entitled "Tanhum," Singer's protagonist berates himself for not praying fervently enough or devoting himself sufficiently to Jewishness, "and he [Tanhum] warred eternally with evil thoughts." At the same time, the questions, "What was the sense of robbing one person to give to another?" and "Had the greed for money and honors so blinded him that he didn't know the wrongs he committed?" sound suspiciously contemporary, despite the story's nineteenth-century context. Singer is a highly moral man, interested in moralism in literature. Certainly, as Gimpel the Fool discovers, there is a difference between a world that deceives him and a life without complications, without ridicule, and without deception. Having been sinned against so much, Gimpel sees clearly that his faith and innocence are ways to measure the corruption and meanness surrounding him. So with Tanhum. At least in that way everything is still possible.

For all that, as Irving Howe has written, Singer is really not in the mainstream of Yiddish literature. "It's hardly a secret," says Howe, "that in the Yiddish literary world Singer is regarded with a certain suspicion. . . . One reason is that 'modernism' signifies a heavy stress upon sexuality, a concern for the irrational, expressionist distortions of character, and a seeming indifference to the humane ethic of Yiddishism." Singer, according to Milton Hindus, "is utterly at variance with the warmhearted humanitarianism characteristic of the fathers of Yiddish literature, I. L. Peretz, Sholem Aleichem, and others."

Ironically, Singer, the only living Yiddish writer who is known to millions, is not in the mainstream, as judged by those in the mainstream. The question then arises, What is the direction of Yiddish and Yiddish literature? This question becomes especially apparent if those who are most popular are known only in translation and those who are known to the few are known only in Yiddish. Is it time, as in Singer's "The Little Shoemakers," for Jews to celebrate the fact that they have not become idolators? Is it time, with Jacob Glatstein, to find security "With a bit of fence/Not a ghetto, God forbid/Just a quiet wall?" Or is it time to affirm what has happened, and revel in the positive, recognizing that nothing stands still, that Yiddish literature in America is like nothing else in the history of the Jews?

As early as 1928, and probably much earlier, the future of Yiddish and Yiddish literature was being debated. Some commentators prophesied the imminent demise of the culture. Certainly, there are facts to support this thesis, if one looks at the number of those in each census who put down "Yiddish" as their mother tongue or considers the declining number of Yiddish publications. As Samuel Goldenberg, a well-known actor, put it in 1928, the cause of the decline was the "merciless grinding of the wheels of American industrialism." The immigrant, for whom Yiddish was his first language and an economic asset, has disappeared, replaced by the need to hold English to be supremely important.

Will Yiddish survive? In the universities, Yiddish is now being taught, and its appeal is on the rise. In the Hasidic communities, Yiddish is still the first language and will remain so. But considering how clearly the Hasidim are cut off from the mainstream Jew and the American culture, it is virtually certain that Yiddish will not survive as the carrier of culture in the way it was. And certainly the romanticized version of the past seen in presentations like *Fiddler on the Roof* will do little to help. The fact is that nothing can compete with the pressures generated by the need to be American.

In the end, then, one has to admit that most of the great figures who wrote in Yiddish were born and brought up in Eastern Europe but moved here and died here, and most of what is now known to the general public is known through translation. A *few* remember Mendele, Sholem Aleichem, and Peretz, but *many* know Cahan and Isaac Bashevis Singer—and precisely because one wrote in English and the other is known in English. Yiddish, of course, has a great deal to give to the world. Indeed, the poets and writers *if* adequately translated *would* be discussed with the intensity that students of literature now reserve for European, English, and American writers. That is the point! Yiddish literature must be translated—and translated well. After all, our "Western" tradition includes Egypt, Greece, and Rome, and our literary tradition includes Dostoyevsky, Turgenev, Cervantes, Balzac, Mann, Freud, the Bible, and so on, all through translation. Rather than lament the passing of Yiddish and Yiddish literature, it is perhaps time to anticipate its arrival and to celebrate the virtues and the values that will be known to all in English. Seen with this perspective, we can look forward to the time when, as part of our Western heritage, general readers will be as familiar with Mendele, Sholem Aleichem, Peretz, and Glatstein as they now are with Cahan and Singer. That day is long overdue. *See also* Poetry, Yiddish; Theater, Yiddish.

DANIEL WALDEN

Adapted from Daniel Walden's article "The American Yiddish Writer: From Cahan to Singer," in *Ethnic Literatures Since 1776: The Many Voices of America, Part 2,* edited by Wolodymyr T. Zyla and Wendell M. Aycock (Lubbock: Texas Tech University Press, 1978). Reprinted by permission.

BIBLIOGRAPHY

Howe, Irving. *World of Our Fathers.* New York: Harcourt Brace Jovanovich, 1976.

Liptzin, Sol. *History of Yiddish Literature: Its Scope and Major Writers.* New York: Ungar, 1968.

Madison, Charles. *Yiddish Literature.* Middle Village, N.Y.: Jonathan David, 1973.

Literary Criticism. See CRITICS, LITERARY.

London, Meyer (1871–1926). Lawyer and Socialist leader Meyer London was born in Poland. He came from a background that embraced both rabbinic learning and radical politics. He settled in New York in 1891, living and working in the immigrant milieu of the Lower East Side. Despite his poverty, he secured a law degree from New York University Law School and was admitted to the New York bar in 1898. In the practice of the law, London devoted himself to the interests of his clients, usually poor workers or struggling unions, without regard to material reward.

London became an active propagandist for the Socialist Party. His political career reflected his personal individuality and the often conflicting currents among the Jewish voters of the Lower East Side. The Twelfth Congressional District was a fiefdom of Tammany Hall, having been enlarged to nullify the influence of Jewish Socialists. London ran unsuccessfully for the seat in 1910 and 1912; finally, in 1914, he ousted the Tammany nominee and became the sole Socialist in the United States Congress.

London was reelected in 1916, but controversies arising out of his stand on World War I weakened his position. He opposed American intervention, but once the United States had entered the war, declined to follow the Socialist Party's policy of continuing the opposition. He was aloof to specifically Jewish issues, such as the establishment of a Jewish national home advocated by the Zionists or the securing of cultural rights for the Jewish minority in Eastern Europe advocated by the Bundists. In 1918, he lost his seat.

By 1920, however, the tide of personal affection for London had swept past these differences, and he was again victorious. Realizing the hold he had on the voters, the older parties secured the redrawing of the boundaries of the Twelfth District so as to make his reelection in 1922 impossible. London's career was cut short when he was killed in 1926 by a passing motor car.

The setting in which London strove for human improvement has disappeared—not least through the "embourgeoisement" and the Americanization of the Jewish community—so as to make it difficult to trace the influence of such individuals. It may be suggested that his work for social reform, even when it conflicted with personal interest, may be reflected in the continuing Jewish sympathy with liberal causes.

S. D. TEMKIN

BIBLIOGRAPHY

Epstein, Melech. *Jewish Labor in U.S.A.* New York: Ktav, 1969.

Gorenstein, Arthur. "A Portrait of Ethnic Politics." *Publications of the American Jewish Historical Society* 50 (1960): 202–238.

Rogoff, Hillel. *An East Side Epic: The Life and Work of Meyer London.* New York: Vanguard, 1930.

Los Angeles. With a population of 3.5 million that includes a substantial majority of Asians, Latinos, and blacks, Los Angeles, California is regarded as the Ellis Island of the Pacific. Its half-million Jews, the second largest Jewish community in the world, have become functionally the "WASPs" of the community.

It was not always so. In the first census after California was admitted to the Union (1850), of the 1610 residents, only 8 were Jews. By 1854, the numbers had grown sufficiently to warrant a Jewish cemetery. By 1862, the first congregation was founded, which still exists under the name Wilshire Boulevard Temple. Jews, until the latter part of the nineteenth century, were comfortably integrated into the civic, political, and economic life of the community and were proportionally listed with the other social elites in the Los Angeles Blue Book.

All this changed when a migration boom in the 1880s added fivefold to the population figures. The city now reflected the flavor of Midwest provincialism. The result was that no Jew was elected to public office for 60 years, and Jewish marriages were no longer reported in the social sections of the daily newspaper. The Blue Book, which had 44 Jewish names in the 1894 edition, was free of Jewish listings by 1921.

The influx of Eastern European Jews into the community at the turn of the century was stimulated by health seekers, many of them from the garment industry in New York. The Hebrew Consumptive Relief Association was formed to help tuberculars by establishing a tent city called a "Town of Hope." Today, the City of Hope Hospital is Los Angeles Jewry's largest single national institution.

Numerous independent institutions, serving the aged, the infirm, the orphaned, and the newcomers, were consolidated in 1911 into the Federation of Jewish Charities, which 40 years later became the Jewish Federation Council.

Two major waves of Jewish population growth after each world war changed the character of the community from an outpost of 2500 Jews in 1900 to the sophisticated Jewish society it is today.

In recent years, the Jews of Los Angeles have reasserted a dominant position in the philanthropic, cultural, political, and economic life of the community.

The Jewish Federation Council attained distinction as a progressive, democratically administered, umbrella organization with strong planning and research components. Its Council for Jewish Life was established in the late 1970s to build links to the religious and secular communities by supporting efforts to raise the quality of Jewishness and Judaism. Its expanded services also included grants to synagogues for innovative programs, sponsorship of the Los Angeles Board of Rabbis, and sponsorship of a commission on spirituality.

The Friends of Simon Wiesenthal Center for Holocaust Studies is centered in Los Angeles, and its outreach is worldwide. Within the center is the Documentation Center and the Museum of Tolerance. From the Documentation Center, the Holocaust is investigated and analyzed and Nazis throughout the world are tracked down. The center also investigates and analyzes anti-Semitism worldwide.

The Museum of Tolerance simulates critical events and places through the use of video and interactive computer devices during a guided tour of a history of intolerance and the Holocaust.

Synagogue life, which in 1900 was represented by two congregations, had grown to several hundred congregations by 1980. These ranged from ultra Orthodoxy to a wide variety of experimental religious forms, such as private minyanim and hundreds of Havurah groups, office, and home study groups. After World War II, all the denominational groups established major schools in Los Angeles: Hebrew Union College, University of Judaism, and Yeshiva University.

The largely Jewish entertainment industry was linked from its inception to Jewish community life. In recent years two synagogues for the performing arts were established for Jews in the industry. Increasingly, fund-raising events for Israeli universities and hospitals utilized the talents of Hollywood. Chabad established an annual telethon, enlisting the support of a wide and enthusiastic array of movie and television personalities.

All, nevertheless, was not glitter. Even though the numbers of Jews settling in Los Angeles continued to grow, many Jews disassociated themselves from the community and the tradition. Only 50,000 contributions were given to the Welfare Fund in 1986. By contrast, 75,000 Jews in Cleveland and in Detroit gave that year. Also one of every two marriages in Los Angeles involved a non-Jewish partner, only 60 percent of Jewish children were receiving any form of Jewish education, and 75 percent of the city's Jews were not affiliated with any Jewish organization.

The major challenges facing Los Angeles Jewry, as of all Jewish communities, will be the retention and enrichment of Jewish identity. If it is true that as Los Angeles goes so goes the nation, then the Jews of Los Angeles will bear close watching in the years ahead.

MAX VORSPAN

BIBLIOGRAPHY

Rand, Christopher. *Los Angeles: The Ultimate City.* New York: Oxford University Press, 1967.

Russell, James S. "Bearing Witness in Bricks and Steel." *Architectural Record* 176 (April 1988): 65–66.

Vorspan, Max. *History of the Jews in Los Angeles.* San Marino, Calif.: Huntington Library, 1970.

Lubavitcher Rebbe: Menachem Mendel Schneerson (b. 1902).

Hasidic leader and the seventh Lubavitcher Rebbe, Menachem Mendel Schneerson has been the spiritual leader of the

Chabad branch of Hasidim since 1950, with headquarters in Brooklyn, New York. He is popularly referred to as the Lubavitcher Rebbe.

Schneerson was born in the Ukrainian town of Nikolayer to Rabbi Levi Isaac (d. 1944) and Channah Schneerson (d. 1964). His father, a direct descendant of Rabbi Schneur Zalman of Lyady (d. 1813), the founder of Chabad Hasidism, served as chief rabbi of the Ukrainian city of Dnepropetrovsk. In 1929, Menachem Schneerson wed his distant cousin, Chaya-Musiah Schneersohn, second daughter of the sixth Lubavitcher Rebbe, Rabbi Joseph I. Schneersohn. Following his marriage, Schneerson followed an unusual course of study for a Hasidic rabbi, studying in Berlin and Paris and reportedly attaining an engineering degree in the late 1930s in Paris. In 1942, he and his wife arrived in the United States to join his father-in-law, who had settled in Brooklyn in 1940. In 1944, Schneerson was appointed the director of Lubavitch publishing and educational activities, known as the Merkoz L'Inyon El Chinuch. Following Rabbi Joseph I. Schneersohn's death (1950), Schneerson was the victor in a struggle for the succession with his brother-in-law, Rabbi Samarius Gourary (d. 1989) and in 1951 was formally installed as the seventh Lubavitcher Rebbe.

As rebbe, Schneerson built a loyal cadre of followers, many from non-Hasidic, and even non-Orthodox, homes. With their support, Schneerson launched an ambitious program of disseminating Orthodox Judaism, and specifically Chabad Hasidism, among all sectors of American and world Jewry. He set up Hebrew day schools in various cities in the United States and Canada. More importantly, by the early 1970s Schneerson's followers were establishing so-called Chabad houses throughout the United States. Typically, these centers served as synagogues, schools, drop-in centers, and counseling centers. Their activities were aimed primarily at college-age youth, but they also had activities for other age groups. In 1990, there were over 250 such houses throughout the United States. In addition, the Lubavitch movement launched an extensive media campaign to spread their message. They published textbooks, periodicals, and broadcast the rebbe's speeches over radio and cable TV. The Lubavitch movement under Schneerson's leadership achieved a great deal of success, and the Lubavitch community increased in size as newcomers joined. Thus, Schneerson was in the vanguard of the so-called Baal Teshuva movement,

the loosely organized movement that saw tens of thousands of American Jews become Orthodox Jews. Schneerson stressed such outreach activities, and his emissaries traveled throughout the world to spread his message.

Schneerson, as Lubavitcher Rebbe, delivers lengthy weekly discourses on a diverse range of subjects, among them Hasidism, rabbinic thought, and political issues. These talks, lectures, and speeches, as well as his correspondence, have been published in various editions and in various languages, including English. Schneerson is a highly regarded rabbinic scholar whose opinion on Jewish law is widely sought.

He has often adopted controversial stands on public and political issues. He opposed public demonstrations on behalf of Soviet Jewry, favoring instead private government intervention on their behalf. Considering the fact that the Lubavitch movement operated an organized underground movement in the Soviet Union, this opinion carried weight among American Orthodox Jews.

Schneerson favored federal aid to religious schools, as well as a "Moment of Silence" in public schools. He also advocated the obligation of non-Jews to observe the seven Noahide Commandments, believing that the Jews were ultimately responsible for the moral welfare of their Gentile brethren.

Schneerson has been a firm supporter of the State of Israel. Although never admitting to being a Zionist, he adopted a rigid position on the question of Israel's occupied territories, believing that the Bible and Jewish law prohibited the return of these lands. Thus, he was a vocal opponent of the Camp David Accords, which saw Israel returning the Sinai to Egypt as part of a general peace accord.

Among Schneerson's most controversial campaigns was his move to have the Israeli parliament—the Knesset—change Israel's Law of Return, so that conversions performed by non-Orthodox rabbis would be invalidated. But he has been unable to prevail on this issue. The opposition has been led by many Reform and Conservative Jewish leaders in the United States, many of whom were financial backers of Lubavitch activities. In all but name, Schneerson's campaign to amend the Law of Return was dropped in the face of this strong opposition.

In the 1980s, Schneerson came under attack by an array of Orthodox rabbinical leaders, chief among them Rabbi E. M. Shach of Israel, for fostering a cult of personality and for implying that he was the Messiah. By the 1980s, Schneerson's campaigns and speeches had become marked by a messianic fervor. Indeed, the semiofficial Lubavitch motto was "We Want Messiah Now." Schneerson's followers denied that they regarded the Rebbe as the Messiah. Even more controversial was Schneerson's involvement in the spring 1990 Israeli elections when he urged select Orthodox members of the Knesset not to help the Labor Party form a government that would have supported the Baker Plan, which called for a peace conference to negotiate the question of Palestinian autonomy.

In recent times, Schneerson's leadership has been marred by an intense struggle between himself and his only nephew Rabbi Barry S. Gourary over ownership of the library of Rabbi Joseph I. Schneersohn. Although Schneerson achieved a clear-cut court victory, the feud continues, and it has focused public attention on relations within the Schneersohn family.

As Schneerson grew older and suffered a heart attack (1976), speculation grew as to who should succeed the childless rebbe and as to the future of the Lubavitch movement. Schneerson has given no indication as to how the problem of succession is to be handled.

In 1990, he continued to be the leading figure of the Hasidic movement in the United States. Although not the largest group, Lubavitch is the most influential Hasidic group in the United States. Under Schneerson's leadership it has not only grown in size, but also in importance. By virtue of Schneerson's charisma, knowledge, aura of piety and administrative talent, Lubavitch has become a major force in American Jewish life.

ZALMAN ALPERT

BIBLIOGRAPHY

Harris, Lis. *Holy Days: The World of a Hasidic Family.* New York: Summit Books, 1985.

Shaffir, William. *Life in a Religious Community: The Lubavitcher Chassidim in Montreal.* Toronto: Holt, Rinehart and Winston, 1974.

M

Malamud, Bernard (1914–1986). Novelist and short-story writer, Bernard Malamud was born in Brooklyn to Russian immigrant parents. After graduating from Erasmus Hall High School in Brooklyn, he attended the City College of New York (B.A., 1936), and Columbia University (M.A., 1942). In 1945, he married Ann de Chiara, an Italian-American. Malamud taught high school in Brooklyn and Harlem before joining the staff of Oregon State College (1949–1961). He then taught at Bennington College (1961–1986) and Harvard University (1966–1968). His novel *The Assistant* (1957) and short-story collection *The Magic Barrel* (1958) established his reputation as a Jewish writer. *The Fixer* (1966), winner of a Pulitzer Prize, was a searing probe of anti-Semitism. Recipient of two National Book Awards (1959, 1967), Malamud was elected to the American Academy of Arts and Sciences (1967) and served as president of the PEN American Center (1979–1981).

Malamud, with Saul Bellow and Philip Roth, secured a place for Jewish writers at the center of American literature in the 1950s. His first novel, *The Natural* (1952), deals with the rituals of baseball and lacks any overtly Jewish subject matter. In *The Assistant* Malamud focuses on the immigrant Jews of his father's generation, impoverished shopkeepers imprisoned in their stores. The grocer Morris Bober symbolizes the Jewish ethical values of goodness, humility, and self-sacrifice. The plot concerns the love of the Italian-Catholic Frankie Alpine, a criminal, for Bober's daughter Helen, an aspiring college student. In the end Alpine redeems himself, undergoing a circumcision that marks his acceptance of the Jew's ethical burden. In *A New Life* (1961) Sy Levin, a self-confessed failure, journeys from New York to a college-teaching job in the Pacific Northwest. Levin's Jewishness is hardly mentioned, but his comic pratfalls type him as a schlemiel. After battling the college McCarthyites, Levin achieves manhood by rescuing Pauline Gilley, a colleague's discontented wife, and becoming a father to her children.

The Fixer, set in czarist Russia, describes a Jew's struggle with peoplehood. The handyman Yakov Bok flees the shtetl's narrow world, but he finds himself unjustly accused of a ritual murder. Confronted by the tyranny of the state and savagely persecuted by anti-Semites, the imprisoned Bok dons a prayer shawl and composes a prayer. Based on the historical Mendel Beiliss case, *The Fixer* also draws upon the Holocaust, the Dreyfus affair, the Sacco-Vanzetti trial, and the civil rights revolution. The Jew is portrayed as the symbolic sufferer, history's archetypal victim.

Pictures of Fidelman: An Exhibition (1969) comprises six short stories loosely composed into a novel, a comedy on the tenuous relations of art and life. The first story, "The Last Mohican," treats a frequent Malamud theme: the Jew who seeks freedom only to confront his identity. Arthur Fidelman, artist and scholar, travels to Italy to immerse himself in the grandeurs of Western culture, but his pretensions are comically deflated by the schnorrer Susskind, who returns him to the ghetto. *The Tenants* (1971) marks a darker, pessimistic turn in Malamud's fiction. The novel focuses on black–Jewish relations in New York City as Harry Lesser, a novelist, and Willie Spearmint, "Soul Writer," fight over turf, women, and literature in a New York tenement. Though examining a topical social issue, Malamud elevates the story to a fable with dream visions, tribal rituals, and a double ending. *Dubin's Lives* (1979) describes an aging Jewish intellectual, a biographer of Thoreau and D. H. Lawrence. Dubin is less the ethical Jew than a man obsessed with sexual liberation. After seducing the student Fanny Bick, Dubin confronts his guilt when he sees old Jews praying in a synagogue.

God's Grace (1982), Malamud's last complete novel, is inspired by biblical and rabbinic literature. The paleontologist Calvin Kohn, a rabbi's son, is the sole survivor of a nuclear holocaust. After a second flood, the shipwrecked Kohn seeks a new covenant with God for a new chosen people, a society of talking primates. Kohn advocates obedience to the Law, but the Christianized chimp Buz argues that God is love. The novel ends with a reenactment of the sacrifice of Isaac as a gorilla recites kaddish over Kohn.

The People and Uncollected Stories (1989), published posthumously, includes an unfinished novel that describes the immigrant peddler Yozip Bloom, who ventures into the western frontier and transforms himself into a Jewish Indian, the adopted chief of a persecuted tribe.

Malamud was a master of the short story, and he published collections alternately with his novels: *The Magic Barrel, Idiot's First* (1963), *Rembrandt's Hat* (1973), and *The Stories of Bernard Malamud* (1983). Malamud's prose style, spare and evocative, owes both to the fractured rhythms of Yiddish immigrant speech, with its genius for irony, and to the minimalist prose of literary modernism. Malamud is at once a traditional storyteller and an artistic experimenter. In "The Loan," "The Mourners," "Take Pity," "Idiot's First," "The First Seven Years," and "The Cost of Living" Malamud writes of urban, immigrant Jews surviving, without love, in reduced circumstances. Malamud borrows characters from the rich stock of Jewish folklore and Yiddish literature. Like Peretz and Aleichem, Malamud creates antiheroes, humble and long-suffering. "Talking Horse" and "The Jewbird," with their animal dybbuks, are otherworldly fables written in an earthy tone. "Angel Levine" deals with a black Jewish angel who helps a suffering storekeeper. "The Silver Crown," about a wonder-working

rabbi, and "The Magic Barrel," about a rabbinic student's search for love, ironically explore old-world customs and superstitions. Malamud never directly confronts the Holocaust, though in "The Lady of the Lake" and "The German Refugee" he draws themes and characters from it. Like Kafka, Malamud writes stark, haunted tales but with a humor and compassion for his characters that undercut the sadness.

Though his subjects are typically Jewish, Malamud reworks the grand themes of American and European literature. He writes moral fables in the manner of Hawthorne, and his nature imagery, even in his urban stories, evokes the romanticism of Emerson and Thoreau. His Americans abroad recall those of Henry James. Malamud's obsession with guilt and redemption echoes the Russian masters Tolstoy and Dostoevski. As a Jewish writer, Malamud is frequently linked with Roth and Bellow, though each has found the association confining. Malamud's work is more symbolic and less philosophical than Bellow's. Roth objects to Malamud's tendency to portray good, passive Jews and corrupt, violent Christians. Malamud writes of lapsed, alienated Jews who journey to strange lands. Malamud's Jews are metaphors for what is universal in humanity, and his dictum is that "all men are Jews." Some critics regard Malamud's moralism as Christian in its emphasis on suffering and redemptive love. Other critics view his universalism as a Jewish humanism and seek its roots in prophetic Judaism or even Hasidism. The struggle of a typical Malamud character is, in Jewish terms, to rise from a schlemiel to a mensch, to redeem personal failure by assuming responsibility for others. Malamud's work achieved both critical and popular success. *The Fixer, The Natural*, and "Angel Levine" were made into motion pictures. At his death, Malamud was eulogized as a master of twentieth-century American literature.

LEONARD ROGOFF

BIBLIOGRAPHY

Astro, Richard, and Benson, Jackson. *The Fiction of Bernard Malamud.* Corvallis: Oregon State University Press, 1977.

Field, Leslie, and Field, Joyce. *Bernard Malamud and the Critics.* New York: New York University Press, 1970.

———. *Bernard Malamud: A Collection of Critical Essays.* Englewood Cliffs, N.J.: Prentice-Hall, 1975.

Helterman, Jeffrey. *Understanding Bernard Malamud.* Columbia: University of South Carolina Press, 1985.

Hershinow, Sheldon. *Bernard Malamud*. New York: Ungar, 1980.

Pinsker, Sanford. *The Schlemiel as Metaphor: Studies in the Yiddish and American Jewish Novel*. Carbondale: Southern Illinois University Press, 1971.

Richman, Sidney. *Bernard Malamud*. Boston: Twayne, 1966.

Roth, Philip. *Reading Myself and Others*. New York: Penguin, 1975.

Salzberg, Joel. *Bernard Malamud: A Reference Guide*. Boston: Hall, 1985.

Marcus, Jacob Rader (b. 1896). Historian and Reform rabbi, Jacob Rader Marcus was born in Connellville, Pennsylvania. He entered Hebrew Union College in Cincinnati at the age of 15 to become a Reform rabbi. His entire career has been associated with the college. After active service with the U.S. Army during World War I, the college sent him to Germany to pursue postgraduate study. He obtained his doctorate (in history) from the University of Berlin in 1925 and returned to Cincinnati to teach.

He taught courses in many fields, but since the forties, he has made American Jewish history his specialty, doing much to establish it as a recognized academic discipline. In 1947, he embarked on an original enterprise by establishing the American Jewish Archives. The college assigned it a disused library building, and under Marcus's direction it has come to house a full documentary record of American Jewish life. Accessibility was enhanced by an efficient catalogue, interest was stimulated through a biannual publication, and the provision of fellowships helped to make it a research center in American Jewish history.

As the teacher of more than one generation of Reform rabbis, Marcus became unofficial adviser to his pupils throughout their careers. In 1949–1950, he served as president of the Central Conference of American Rabbis and, in 1986, became its honorary president—an office usually reserved for the president of Hebrew Union College. From 1956 to 1959, he was president of the American Jewish Historical Society.

Marcus's many writings (to 1958) are listed in a bibliography by Herbert C. Zafren in *Essays in American Jewish History. A Bicentennial Festschrift for Jacob Rader Marcus*, ed. Bertram Wallace Korn, appeared in 1976. Through his established position in Hebrew Union College and his association with the American Jewish Archives, Marcus has created effective roles in both the broader reaches of American Jewish history and the narrower domain of Reform Judaism.

S. D. TEMKIN

BIBLIOGRAPHY
Essays in American Jewish History; To Commemorate the 10th Anniversary of the Founding of the American Jewish Archives; Under the Direction of Jacob Rader Marcus. New York: American Jewish Archives, 1958.

Korn, Bertram Wallace. *A Bicentennial Festschrift for Jacob Rader Marcus*. New York: Ktav, 1976.

Marshall, Louis (1856–1929). Born in Syracuse, New York, to German Jewish immigrants, Louis Marshall became the most influential Jewish communal leader of his generation. In 1876, he entered Columbia Law School, where he completed the two-year law school class in one year. Between 1878 and 1894, Marshall argued over 150 cases before the New York State Court of Appeals, evidence of his growing stature and reputation in the legal profession. At the same time, Marshall took a prominent role in the Syracuse Jewish community and by 1891 was important enough to be included in a national delegation that visited President Benjamin Harrison on behalf of Russian Jewry.

In 1894, he became a partner in the New York City law firm of Guggenheimer, Untermeyer and Marshall, with which he remained associated to the end of his life. Recognized as one of the country's leading authorities on constitutional law, he argued many landmark cases affecting workmen's compensation, alien migration, child labor laws, segregation of blacks, inheritance taxes, and church-state relations. His most famous legal victory was won before the United States Supreme Court, which upheld his contention that an Oregon law denying Catholics the right to send their children to parochial schools was illegal. He was appointed or elected to three constitutional conventions in New York State (1890, 1894, and 1915), the only New Yorker to be so honored. Although he never sought public office, he was at one time considered for appointment to the United States Supreme Court.

Marshall was considered by many to be the preeminent Jewish communal leader of his time. He served, at various times, as president of Manhattan's Temple Emanu-El, the most important Reform Congregation in the United States, as president of the American Jewish Relief Committee, and as chairman of the Board of Directors of the Jewish Theological Seminary, which he had helped to reorganize in 1902. One of the founders of the American Jewish Committee, he served as its president between 1912 and 1929. Together with Jacob Schiff, Mayer Sulzberger, and other Jewish leaders, Marshall played a key role in the successful campaign to abrogate the 1832 U.S. Commercial Treaty with Russia, because of the czarist government's refusal to recognize the passports of American Jews. In so doing, he helped ensure the religious liberty of American Jews traveling abroad. As the official president and spokesman for the Committee of Jewish Delegations to the Paris Peace Conference in 1919, Marshall played an instrumental role in securing minority rights for the Jews of Eastern Europe through the formulation of the minority rights clauses eventually incorporated into the constitutions of the newly created Eastern European states. During the 1920s, Marshall helped expose and publicize the forged and slanderous nature of the Protocols of the Elders of Zion. With others, he successfully pressured Henry Ford to admit his error in publishing them and to make a public apology to American Jews for the anti-Semitic agitation in his *Dearborn Independent*. *See also* Law and Lawyers.

DAVID G. DALIN

BIBLIOGRAPHY

Reznikoff, Charles, ed. *Louis Marshall: Champion of Liberty*. 2 vols. Philadelphia: Jewish Publication Society, 1957. Selected papers and addresses.

Rosenstock, Morton. *Louis Marshall: Defender of Jewish Rights*. Detroit: Wayne State University Press, 1965.

Rosenthal, Jerome C. "The Public Life of Louis Marshall." Ph.D. dissertation, University of Cincinnati, 1983.

Marx Brothers. The famous comedy team of the Marx brothers were of French-German Jewish ancestry. The team was principally three brothers—Leonard, known as Chico (1887–1961), Adolf (later Arthur), known as Harpo (1888–1964), and Julius, known as Groucho (1890–1977). At times two lesser-known brothers were also part of the act—Milton, known as Gummo (1897–1977), who dropped out in 1918, and Herbert, known as Zeppo (1901–1979), who dropped out after 1933. The Marx Brothers began in show business in the era of vaudeville, entered the legitimate theater in 1923, and began making films at the beginning of the sound era in 1929. It was through their films that they became famous throughout the world for a zany style of comedy that depended on both sight gags and verbal wit. The combination made them perfect for the sound film. At the same time, their genius helped to define the possibilities of the medium much as the genius of Charlie Chaplin or Buster Keaton had defined silent comedy.

Although many facts of the Marx Brothers' lives are difficult to fix, because of their penchant for fantasy and their admirers' hopes to outdo each other in their stories about the fabulous five, certain parts of the story are clear. Their father, Simon Marrix (1861–1933), was born in the province of Alsace annexed by Germany in 1871 after the Franco-Prussian War. He emigrated to the United States in the aftermath of that conflict, arriving in New York in 1881. Soon afterward, at the advice of a cousin, he adopted the name of Marx, in deference to the German Jewish families of that name who were already prominent on the Lower East Side, and began to ply the trade of a tailor. Minna Schoenberg (1865–1929), the future wife of Simon and mother of the Marx Brothers, had arrived in the same city the previous year, where she also resided on the Lower East Side with her parents and two younger brothers. Minna was no sooner in the United States than she changed her name to Minnie in honor of a leading child actress of the day. Minnie and Simon met at a dancing school in their neighborhood and married in 1884. By 1895, when the Marxes moved to 179 East Ninety-third Street, where they were to live for the next 15 years, the first three of the brothers had been born and the pattern of their family life set. That pattern was dictated by two major factors: the poverty of the family, with Simon earning only a marginal income, and the constant presence of relatives from the Schoenberg side of the family, in particular Minnie's parents. The authority in the family rested mainly with Minnie and her mother.

Because of their poverty, the brothers had little formal schooling. Groucho stayed in school through the eighth grade; Harpo, on the other hand, dropped out after several years in second. None of them completed high school. Gradually, in search of a living, the brothers, following the example of their Uncle Al, entered show business. Chico, the oldest, was first, and Groucho soon followed. With talent as a singer, Groucho ultimately became part of an act, managed by his mother, known as the Nightingales. By 1908, when Harpo joined Groucho and Gummo in the act, they had considerable success on the competitive and grueling vaudeville circuit.

Their ups and downs in vaudeville form a fascinating story, with both amusing and touching moments. By the early twenties, however, the direction of entertainment was clearly toward the movies, and it was time for the Marx Brothers to strike out on a new path. Largely through the encouragement of Chico, they entered into an agreement to open in Philadelphia in June 1923 in a revue called *I'll Say She Is*; this marked a major transition in the career of the brothers, taking them from the four or five turns a day of vaudeville and the incessant travel it required to the world of the legitimate stage. It was only a short step from there to the movies, and entertainment history was made. By this time the brothers were known by their own family name and had already acquired the nicknames by which they became famous.

Chico's name was derived from "chicken," a slang term for "girl" (Chico's prowess with women was legendary); Harpo's name, of course, came from the instrument he played; Groucho, the most serious of the brothers, was also somewhat short-tempered, hence his name; and Zeppo's was an invention of Chico's, a take-off on "Zeb," a favorite vaudeville name for a hick. (Gummo's came from "gumshoes.") The comic personae of the big three also became fixed: Chico, the Italian, who was not too bright and played piano; Harpo, the silent one; and Groucho, the wise-cracking con man.

With *The Cocoanuts* (which opened in December 1925 in New York) they truly arrived. This satire on the Florida land boom had a book by George S. Kaufman and music by Irving Berlin. In performance, it followed the Marx Brothers practice of improvisation on a given theme; Kaufman later said that he did not recognize his own work. It ran for 377 performances in New York and later (1929) became the first film the Marx Brothers made. *Animal Crackers* (1928), with a book by Kaufman and Morrie Ryskind and music by Bert Kalmar and Harry Ruby, was the second Marx Brothers Broadway show and their second film (1930). It was followed by a long and dazzling list of movies, as the brothers moved to Hollywood to pursue their new career and make their name synonymous with film comedy: *Monkey Business* (1931), *Horsefeathers* (1932),

Duck Soup (1933), *A Night at the Opera* (1935), and *A Day at the Races* (1937). With *Room Service* (1938) (not really a Marx Brothers comedy, but a comedy starring the Marx Brothers), their films entered into a decline. None of their later films— *At the Circus* (1939), *Go West* (1940), *The Big Store* (1941), *A Night in Casablanca* (1946), or *Love Happy* (1949)—is on a level with their earlier successes. What the Marx Brothers needed most was carte blanche; what they often got in their later films was material more appropriate for the Three Stooges.

The great film comedians—Chaplin, Keaton, Fields, the Marx Brothers—all managed to appeal to highbrow and lowbrow audiences alike; they managed to kick their audience in the pants and at the same time make them laugh. Of all the great comedians, however, the Marx Brothers were the most anarchistic in comic style; for that reason their best comedies are virtually plotless, giving them the greatest freedom for invention. When that freedom was curtailed by poor scripts or when the brothers simply began to burn out, the interest of their films declined.

Only Groucho continued into the age of television. Beginning on radio in the late forties, where he had only modest success, Groucho took the quiz show "You Bet Your Life" to television in the fifties, where it became very popular. With George Fenneman as his straight man, Groucho became famous to a whole new generation for his caustic wit and verbal improvisation. *See also* Comics and Comedy.

ARCHIE K. LOSS

BIBLIOGRAPHY

Adamson, Joe. *Groucho, Harpo, Chico, and Sometimes Zeppo.* New York: Simon & Schuster, 1973.

Arce, Hector. *Groucho.* New York: Putnam, 1979.

Marx, Groucho. *Groucho and Me.* New York: Simon & Schuster, 1989.

Marx, Harpo. *Harpo Speaks!* New York: Limelight Editions, 1985.

Marx, Maxine. *Growing Up with Chico.* New York: Limelight Editions, 1980.

Medicine. The history of Jews in American medicine begins with the voyage of Columbus, who is said to have had two Jews in his crew: Bernard, the ship's physician, and Marco, the surgeon. The first practicing physician in the new land was Jacob Lumbroso, a native of Portugal, who enjoyed a lucrative practice in Maryland

(1656). Another early physician, also born in Portugal, was John di Sequera (1712-1795), who came to Williamsburg, Virginia, in 1745. His portrait hangs in the Winterthur Museum in Delaware, and an exhibit in Williamsburg illustrates his career as physician to the first American hospital for the insane. Samuel Nunez Ribiero came to Savannah in 1733, a month after the colony was founded. David D'Isaac Nassy (1748-1806) was the first physician in Philadelphia. Moses Sheftal (1769-1835) served as private in the Revolution and as a surgeon in the War of 1812. Jacob de La Motta (1789-1845), Nathan Levy (b. 1722), David Sarzedas (1760-1841), Levi Mayers (d. 1872), Isaac Levy (b. 1779), and Joel Hart (1784-1842) were other early physicians. During the Revolutionary period a Doctor Siccary (1712-1795) was praised by Jefferson for his professional qualifications.

In early New York we find the recorded names of Elias Woolin, A. Nunez, Jacob Isaacs, Barnet Cowan, Saul Israel, Hyman Levy, Leo Wolf and Isaac Abrahams (the first Jewish graduate of Columbia University, then Kings College) as Jewish physicians. Woolin, Nunez, and Abrahams were members of Congregation Shearith Israel. In the tiny Jewish cemetery near the Bowery, across from the Chinese section, is the grave of Walter J. Judah, a student at the medical school of Columbia College who died while caring for victims of yellow fever.

Better-known physicians of the early period were father and son, Abraham de Leon (1790-1847) and David (1813-1872). The father practiced in South Carolina until he became an army doctor. The son was also a career army doctor. He served in the Seminole and Mexican wars. When the Civil War broke out, he resigned his commission and became the first surgeon-general of the Confederate Army. A colorful character was Moses Albert Levy (1800-1848), who was surgeon-general in Sam Houston's army at the Alamo.

Three Jews were dominant figures in the field of medicine of the nineteenth century. Isaac Hays (1796-1879), in addition to being a noted clinician, was editor of the *Journal of Medical Sciences*, "the Yellow Journal," which for decades was the leading journal of clinical medicine. He was a founder and first treasurer of the American Medical Association and the author of its first Code of Ethics. Jacob Mendes DaCosta (1833-1900) wrote *Medical Diagnosis*, one of the earliest textbooks for students. It was published in nine

editions and was regarded as a leading text in the field. Abraham Jacobi (1830-1919), a refugee from Germany, was the "father of American pediatrics." He was the first American chairman of a department of pediatrics, holding the chair at New York University and later at Columbia. He was president of the American Pediatric Society and of the American Medical Association and received at least six honorary degrees. His medical writings have been published in eight volumes.

In addition to these "giants" of the nineteenth century, there was a substantial increase in the number of important Jewish physicians. Among these were the Friedenwalds. Aaron (1836-1901), the father, was an organizer of the prestigious Association of American Medical Colleges. Harry (1864-1950) was an opthomologist active in many local and national Jewish organizations and is best known for his classic, two-volume *Jews and Medicine*. Julius (1866-1941) was a professor of gastroenterology and a prolific writer in the field.

Medical educators we have already mentioned are three great teachers and authors: Hays, DaCosta, and Jacobi. Abraham Flexner (1866-1959) was not a physician, but his importance in medical education in this country cannot be overestimated. One of his articles, "The American College," attracted wide attention and led to his recruitment to undertake a survey of medical schools. His report, published in 1910, reported "sordid, hideous, unintelligent, and so little that is even honest" in the schools and affiliated hospitals. The sensation created a demand for reform. Consequently, the number of medical schools fell from 155 to 35. His *Medical Education in the United States and Canada* introduced the concept of full-time, paid professors instead of the men who depended on income from patients referred by their students. More than anyone else, Flexner made the American medical school a world leader in medical education and research.

Morris Fishbein (1889-1976) was a physician whose impact on American medicine rests on his editorship for 25 years of the *Journal of the American Medical Association*. Under him the *Journal* became the most influential voice in the field of medicine and the first to report many medical innovations, both scientific and social. In addition, he wrote numerous articles, and made public appearances to educate the public on health and social problems. He pioneered books for laymen on self-help for medical problems. Toward the end of his career his staunchly conservative views diminished his position as spokesman for American medicine.

Joseph B. De Lee (1869–1942) and Marion B. Sulzberger (1896–1983) stand out as physicians and teachers who had an important impact on the status of their specialties. De Lee, a professor of obstetrics at Northwestern University and later at the University of Chicago, wrote three textbooks that became the classical texts for doctors and nurses. He edited the *Yearbook of Obstetrics and Gynecology*, which provided an annual update for practitioners. Sulzberger served as professor and chairman of the Department of Dermatology at New York University, became director of dermatological research at the Letterman Army Research Institute, and was technical director of research for the U.S. Army Research and Development Command. He wrote 438 scientific articles and edited, wrote, or contributed to 26 medical texts. He was a founder of the Society for Investigative Dermatology and editor of its journal. In 1983, a chair was established in his name at the Uniformed Services University of Health Sciences.

Joseph Goldberger (1894–1929) and Milton Joseph Rosenau (1869–1946) were two giants in the field of preventive medicine. Goldberger served in the U.S. Public Health Service from 1899 to his death. He made important contributions to the diagnosis and prevention of infectious diseases and was particularly interested in the influence of economic factors in health. However, his important contributions, and those which brought him international fame, were his demonstration that pellagra resulted from vitamin deficiency and could be prevented by administration of nicotinic acid.

Milton Joseph Rosenau was not only a distinguished investigator in preventive medicine, a collaborator in some studies with Goldberger, but was the foremost teacher in the field. Returning from study in Europe, followed by a spell in the U.S. Public Health Service, he became, in 1922, professor of epidemiology at the Harvard School of Medicine. Among his important contributions were his standardization of tetanus-antitoxin, his work on serum sickness and hypersensitivity, and his papers on dental caries prevention. His claim to fame rests on his massive *Preventive Medicine and Hygiene*, which went through several editions and was the standard text for generations of doctors. Upon his retirement from Harvard in 1935, he became director of the School of Public Health at the University of North Carolina. The building that now houses the school is named in his honor.

Bela Schick (1877–1967), chief of the Department of Pediatrics at Mt. Sinai hospital in New York, is included here because of his development of the test for diphtheria. The test permitted early diagnosis, hence early treatment, of the often fatal disease. His discovery led to the development of similar tests for childhood diseases, and to interest in formulating antitoxin and vaccine treatment and prophylaxis.

Two laymen deserve mention. Nathan Straus (1848–1931) was a wealthy financier and philanthropist. One of his most important achievements was his role in the control of infant mortality. In 1900, in New York City, of 100,000 infants, 140 died in the first year of life. Convinced by several studies that milk was the cause, Straus established six milk stations at which pasteurized milk was sold at a penny a quart. Infant mortality dropped precipitously and by 1925 reached 10 per 100,000. Straus extended this project to the cities of Chicago, Philadelphia, Jerusalem, and Tel-Aviv and to the state of California.

Adolphus Simeon Solomons (1826–1910), together with Clara Barton, was a founder of the American Red Cross, and was its first vice-president. With Clara Barton he represented the United States at the International Red Cross Congress in 1887, where he was elected vice-president of the international organization. He also organized the first fund raiser (at Niblo's Garden) that helped start Mt. Sinai Hospital in New York City.

In the twentieth century the number of Jewish physicians approached 35,000 and account for about 10 percent of the total. Many have achieved distinction; more have become eminent. The following names constitute a sample of those who have made important contributions.

Isaac Arthur Abt (1867–1955) was a prominent pediatrician who from 1923 to 1926 edited the eight-volume *Abt's Pediatrics* and wrote much of it. It still continues in publication.

Simon Baruch (1840–1921) served in the Confederate Army and wrote *Bayonet Wounds*, which was used as a reference work until the 1920s. Moving to New York, he became professor of hydrotherapy at Columbia, a specialty that has become an area of rehabilitation medicine. His was the first reported case of successful surgically treated ruptured appendix.

Abraham Arden Brill (1874–1948) was head of the psychiatry clinic at Columbia. More than anyone he introduced Freud and Freudian psychiatry in the United States.

Max Einhorn (1862–1953) was professor of medicine at New York Post-Graduate Medical School and Hospital, inventor of many surgical instruments, and author of a number of books dealing with the gastrointestinal system. He was the world-renowned "inventor" of stomach relining. He was also consulting physician at Lennox Hill Hospital.

Moses Einhorn (1862–1966) was the author of several texts on diseases of the gastrointestinal system.

Charles A. Elsberg (1871–1948) was the author of several texts on disease and treatment of diseases of the spinal cord.

Vladimir G. Eliasberg (1877–1969) was a noted psychiatrist, a pioneer in the field of forensic psychiatry.

Maurice Fishberg (1872–1934) was a professor of medicine at New York University and author of the popular, standard text *Pulmonary Tuberculosis*.

Simon Flexner (1863–1946) was able to isolate a common strain of dysentery bacillus (1899). As director of the Rockefeller Laboratories (1903–1935) and Institute (1920–1935), he led the research team that produced a nonfatal form of poliomyelitis in monkeys. He was able to pass the virus from one monkey to another, thus enabling him to trap a poliovirus for study in the laboratory. He is the author of over 350 medical and scientific articles and recipient of 14 honorary degrees here and abroad.

Harry Goldblatt (1891–1977) was a pathologist best known for his demonstration that disease of one kidney can cause hypertension and that removal of the kidney results in a cure.

Max A. Goldstein (1870–1941) was an otolaryngologist who founded, in St. Louis, the first school for the deaf where modern pedological methods were used.

Leo Kanner (1894–1981) wrote the first, and, for a long time, the authoritative text on child psychiatry.

Naomi M. Kanof (1912–1988) was the chairman of the Department of Pediatric Dermatology at the Children's Hospital in Washington, D.C. She was editor of the *Journal of Investigative Dermatology* (1948–1967), the *Journal* of the American Medical Woman's Association (1972–1976), and the dermatologic section of Stedman's *Medical Dictionary*.

Benjamin Kramer (1882–1972) was famous for his development of micromethods for examination of blood, facilitating such studies in infants. He utilized these methods in pioneering studies on the calcium and phosphorus content of the blood, leading to fundamental understanding of the pathogenesis of rickets and tetany.

Philip Levine (1900–1987) was a protegé of Karl Landsteiner with whom he demonstrated the blood groups M, N, and P. His work led to the discovery, with Albert Wiener, that disease can be caused by autoimmunization, the reaction of the body to its own normal tissues.

Leo Loeb (1869–1959) was professor of pathology at Washington University in St. Louis. A member of numerous scientific societies and recipient of many honors, his published work covers an extensive field of medical and pathology research.

David Israel Macht (1882–1961) was professor of pharmacology at Johns Hopkins Medical School, where he studied the pharmacology of a variety of drugs, particularly the opium alkaloids and snake venoms.

Frances Pascher (1905–1983), professor of dermatology at New York University, pioneered in descriptions of the skin manifestations of lupus erythematosis and demonstrating its relationship to lupus vulgaris. She was the first to demonstrate the importance of skin absorption of drugs. She elaborated a system of scientific study of the efficacy of drugs for the skin. In recognition of her distinguished teaching, she received the Clark Finnerad Award from the American Academy of Dermatology and distinguished alumni awards from New York University and the State University of New York, Downstate Medical Center. The library of the National Education Center of the Academy of Dermatology, as well as a research fund of the Dermatology Foundation, are named for her.

Max Thorek (1880–1960) was the author of a text on surgical methods, founder of the International College of Surgeons, and editor of its journal.

Israel Wechsler (1886–1962) was the author of a textbook, *Clinical Neurology*, which was printed in many editions and was the standard for generations of medical students.

Albert Wiener (1907–1976) assisted Karl Landsteiner in the work leading to the discovery of the blood groups. Wiener went on to discover the Rh blood factor, at the same time as Levine developed the concept of autoimmunization. With his Rh discovery as the basis, he developed the use of exchange transfusion in the treatment of erythroblastosis fetalis, caused by the agglutination of Rh fetal cells in the mother's blood.

The list of Jewish Nobel Prize winners for medicine and physiology that follows is quite large considering the number of Jews in the overall population. Those with an asterisk received their awards before immigrating to the United States.

Julius Axelrod (b. 1912), for studies of the mechanism that regulates the formation of noradrenalin in nerve cells. Awarded 1970.

David Baltimore (b. 1938), for discoveries concerning the interaction between tumor viruses and the genetic material of the cell. Awarded, with Howard Temin, 1975.

Baruj Benacerraf (b. 1920), for work with genes and the regulation of immunological reactions. Awarded 1980.

Konrad Bloch (b. 1912), for discoveries in the mechanism of cholesterol and fatty acid metabolism. Awarded 1964.

Baruch Samuel Blumberg (b. 1925), for studies that led to a test and a vaccine for hepatic diseases. Awarded 1976.

Stanley Cohen (b. 1922), for discoveries concerning natural substances that influence growth cells and the orderly development of tissues. Awarded, with Rita Levi-Montalcini, 1986.

Gerald Maurice Edelman (b. 1929), established the structure of gamma globulin that carries the body's defense mechanism against disease. Awarded 1972.

Joseph Erlanger (1874–1965), for basic discoveries in both cardiovascular and neurologic systems. Awarded, with Herbert Gasser, 1944.

Herbert S. Gasser (1888–1963), a leading neurophysiologist who shared the prize with Erlanger in 1944.

Joseph L. Goldstein (b. 1940), for researches that drastically widened our understanding of cholesterol metabolism. Awarded 1985.

Arthur Kornberg (b. 1918), for researches in the chemistry of DNA, which forms the genetic units in cells, which, in turn, determine heredity. Awarded 1959.

Joshua Lederberg (b. 1925), for fundamental work in genetics. Awarded 1958.

Rita Levi-Montalcini (b. 1909), for discoveries concerning natural substances that influence growth cells and the orderly development of tissues. Awarded, with Stanley Cohen, 1986.

Fritz Albert Lipmann (1899–1986), for his discovery of coenzyme and its importance for intermediary metabolism. Awarded 1953.

Otto Loewi* (1873–1961), for discoveries relating to the chemical transmission of nerve impulses. Awarded 1936.

Salvador Luria (1912–1991), for work on the replication and the genetic structure of viruses. Awarded 1969.

Otto Meyerhoff* (1884–1951), for discoveries relating to the production of heat in muscles. Awarded 1922.

Hermann Joseph Muller (1890–1967), for studies in the effect of x-rays in producing congenital defects and mutations. Awarded 1946.

Daniel Nathans (b. 1928), for researches in the virus-cancer program. Awarded 1978.

Marshall Warren Nirenberg (b. 1927), for the discovery that a code equivalent exists between a nucleic acid component and an amino acid; this laid the groundwork for solution of the genetic code. Awarded 1968.

Howard Temin (b. 1934), with David Baltimore. Awarded 1975.

Selman Abraham Waksman (1888–1973), for isolation of streptomycin, a powerful antibiotic valuable in combating several diseases, especially tuberculosis. Awarded 1952.

George Wald (b. 1906), for discovering vitamin A in the retina, showing that retinene is a light-sensitive pigment, a fact that underlies the visual process. Awarded 1967.

Rosalyn Sussman Yalow (b. 1921), for developing with others a radioimmunoassay to measure tiny amounts of various substances in the blood. Awarded 1977.

In regard to the general public, perhaps, the two most famous Jewish names associated with the profession of medicine are Jonas E. Salk (b. 1914) and Albert B. Sabin (b. 1916). Salk received his greatest recognition for developing the first effective vaccine in the prevention of poliomyelitis (1954). Sabin, a medical researcher, developed the oral polio vaccine in 1960. The widespread use of both vaccines has nearly eliminated polio in many parts of the world.

THE JEWISH HOSPITAL. The idea of a Jewish hospital had its origins in medieval Europe when buildings or rooms were set aside for the purpose, often adjoining the synagogue—the *hekdesh*, in Yiddish. The first Jewish hospital in the United States was the Jew's Hospital in New York, later Mt. Sinai (1852). The second, the Touro Infirmary, opened in 1853 in New Orleans. In 1868, there were hospitals under Jewish sponsorship in Philadelphia, Cincinnati, Baltimore, and Chicago. A century later there were over 60 Jewish hospitals in the country. Many of them have become important research and teaching institutions, and two have become the core of prestigious medical schools, Albert Einstein Institute (1955) and the Mt. Sinai School of Medicine (1968). Two of the earliest hospitals for rehabilitation of the chronically ill, Montefiore in New York and the National Hospital for Consumptives, in Denver, have become important in research and teaching.

Jewish physicians have made an inordinate contribution to medicine when one considers the small percentage of Jews that have historically resided in the United States. It would be a mistake, however, to attribute the propensity of Jews to enter medicine to Judaism or other aspects of Jewish cultural life. Rather, for historical reasons and circumstances that have to do with the Jewish experience of persecution in Europe, Jews found the medical vocation one of the few occupations open to them. Not until Jews began to feel the sting of prejudice and quotas in American medical schools in the twentieth century did Jews feel uncomfortable about the prospects of a career in medicine.

The triumph of tolerance over prejudice in the latter part of the twentieth century made it easier for Jews to reenter a profession that historically had become part of their experience. A career in medicine was perceived as a profession that advanced the social and economic mobility of the individual and not necessarily of the peoplehood. The history of Jews in medicine, therefore, is the study of significant contributions made by physicians to medicine who also happen to be Jewish. *See also* Mental Health, Science.

ABRAM KANOF

BIBLIOGRAPHY

Elzaz, B. A. *The Jews of South Carolina.* Philadelphia: Lippincott, 1905.

Kagan, S. R. *Jewish Contributions to Medicine in America.* Boston: Medical Publishing, 1934.

Marcus, Jacob Rader. *United States Jewry, 1776–1985.* Vol. 1. Detroit: Wayne State University Press, 1989.

Mendes, Henry Pereira (1852–1937).

A communal leader, scholar, and author, Henry P. Mendes was a leading Orthodox rabbi in the United States, serving the historic Congregation Shearith Israel—the Spanish and Portuguese Synagogue—in New York City from 1877 through 1920 as preacher and reader.

He was born in Birmingham, England. His father, Abraham, was minister of the Jewish congregation there. Indeed, on both his father's and mother's side, there was a notable tradition of family members who served as religious leaders. He was educated in London at Norwick College, a boarding school founded by his father, where he studied rabbinics. He also studied at University College in London for two years. In 1885, he graduated from the Medical School of New York University. In 1890, he was married to Rosalie Rebecca Piza. Prior to coming to Shearith Israel, Mendes had served as hazan and minister of a congregation in Manchester, England.

Mendes served Shearith Israel with singular zeal and was a leading voice for Sephardic Judaism in the United States. He was proud to be the religious head of the oldest Jewish congregation in North America, and he used his prestigious position to promote communal and social causes that he espoused.

Although he was Sephardic, he was recognized as an Orthodox rabbinic leader even by Eastern European, Yiddish-speaking Jewish immigrants. He worked with all segments of the Orthodox community, with the goal of organizing and uniting Orthodoxy. He was a founder and the first president of the Union of Orthodox Jewish Congregations of America (1898). He was one of the founders of the Jewish Theological Seminary (1887), which he hoped would produce modern Orthodox rabbis for the Jewish communities of the United States.

Although he was a forceful and energetic leader of Orthodoxy, Mendes worked with and was respected by non-Orthodox Jews as well. When the New York Board of Jewish Ministers (later to be called the New York Board of Rabbis) was founded in the early 1880s, Mendes was among the founders and was one of the early presidents of the organization. In 1885, he organized a branch of the Alliance Israelite Universelle and served as an officer. He was also involved in the founding of the Young Women's Hebrew Association in New York, and Mendes worked to establish the Montefiore Hospital and the Lexington School for the Deaf.

Mendes was an avid spokesman for Zionism. Theodore Herzl asked his cooperation in organizing the Zionist Movement in the United States, and Mendes was elected vice-president of the Federation of American Zionists and a member of the Actions Committee of the World Zionist Organization. He expounded what he called "Bible Zionism" or "Spiritual Zionism."

Mendes was a prolific author, utilizing a variety of literary genres. He wrote essays and editorials, children's stories, textbooks, sermons, prayers, dramas, poems, and commentaries. His writings were infused with deep religious conviction and attachment to the Bible. Among his books were *Jewish History Ethically Presented* (1895), *The Jewish Religion Ethically Presented* (1895), and *Jewish Life Ethically Presented* (1917).

Bernard Drachman, a colleague of Mendes, described him as "an ideal representative of Orthodox Judaism." He praised Mendes's "absolute freedom . . . from anything approaching narrowness of sectarian bias within the Jewish community."

Throughout his career Mendes was a major Orthodox figure in American Jewish life who was instrumental in organizing and strengthening Orthodox interests. Yet, he fostered a love of the entire Jewish people and worked with non-Orthodox Jews to promote Jewish causes. His humanitarian concerns led him to help found institutions for the ill and disabled.

MARC D. ANGEL

BIBLIOGRAPHY

Markovitz, Eugene. "Henry Pereira Mendes: Architect of the Union of Orthodox Jewish Congregations of America." *American Jewish Historical Quarterly* 55 (1965): 364–384.

Pool, David and Tamar. *An Old Faith in the New World: Portrait of Shearith Israel, 1654–1954.* New York: Columbia University Press, 1955.

Mental Health: Psychoanalysis, Psychiatry, and Psychology.

Jews have played an important role in the broad arena of American mental health services, both as providers and consumers. As providers, all studies have noted the high percentage of Jews who are psychoanalysts, psychiatrists, and clinical psychologists, the figures ranging up to nearly 50 percent in major urban settings. As consumers, surveys have shown that in communities such as New York and Los Angeles Jews comprised nearly half the clientele of psychoanalysts and psychiatrists. The famous Midtown Manhattan Study, published in 1962, found that more than three times as many

Jews as Protestants and Catholics sought outpatient treatment.

The important demographic and epidemiological studies of mental illness and treatment were carried out around mid-century, and the Jewish populations they tapped were predominantly Eastern European immigrants and their offspring. It is likely that the high prevalence rates they catalogued for emotional distress among Jews were due both to generic issues of Jewish socialization and the specific sociological strains to which these generations had been subject. As early as 1924, the Jewish-American psychiatrist, Isadore Wechsler (1896–1962) attributed the psychological stresses of Jews to social pressures, an overemphasis on educational success, overly close family ties, with their intimate links to guilt feelings, and stern religious values, which provided few of the escapist avenues found in the more mystical promises and rituals of Christianity. Jews were seen as locked in a struggle between their overdeveloped conscience and their reality situation, which called for a tenacious will to survive against tough environmental odds. The specter of assimilationist conflicts hung heavy over this cohort of Jewish Americans.

In later studies, Jews have been found to admit more freely to psychological pain and to be willing to talk over their worries, an attitude seen as part of their pace-setting orientation to life.

These mid-century figures have probably declined over the past three decades, but more current research has been unduly circumspect about assessing religion or ethnicity in examining patterns of mental health care or patienthood.

As providers of service, and theoreticians, there is no question as to the seminal contributions made by Jewish mental health professionals to the development of theory and practice in these fields. The reasons for this have been attributed to factors such as Jewish marginality, the Jewish tradition of intellectual exegesis, and Jewish upward mobility. The psychological rationale has been best summed up by the American psychiatrist Karl Menninger, himself not a Jew, who ascribed the "genius" of Jews in the mental health field to their identification with the suffering of others, their separatism that has invoked a curiosity about people, their detachment that allows for a more objective, analytical stance toward all phenomena, their sensitivity to insecurity that produces a dubiousness about human motives, and their intense love of the verbal expression of emotions.

In what follows, the roles Jews have played in the development of American psychoanalysis, psychiatry, and psychology will be discussed.

PSYCHOANALYSIS. The complex connection between psychoanalysis and Judaism is embodied in the personality of its creator, Sigmund Freud (1856–1939). The role of Freud's Jewishness in the development of psychoanalysis has occasioned much debate. The psychologist David Bakan (b. 1921) suggests that Freud was a secret Jewish mystic, profoundly, if unconsciously, influenced by Kabbalistic wisdom. Others interpret Freud's theories as a covert attack on the fabric of European Christian culture and society, exposing its duplicity through the uncovering of hidden sexual and aggressive tendencies.

Whether Freud's psychoanalysis is a transmutation of Jewish teachings into a universal theory, a masked response to Viennese anti-Semitism, or an expression of inner ambivalence about his own Jewishness, the fact remains that Freud's personal ties to his heritage were deep and abiding. These are cogently summed up in his 1926 letter to the members of the Vienna B'nai B'rith Lodge, of which Freud had been a member for 30 years.

> What tied me to Jewry was—I have to admit it—not the faith, not even the national pride, for I was always an unbeliever, have been brought up without religion, but not without respect for the so-called ethical demands of human civilization. . . . But there remained enough to make the attraction of Judaism and the Jews irresistible, many dark emotional powers all the stronger the less they could be expressed in words, as well as the clear consciousness of an inner identity, the familiarity of the same psychological structure.

Beyond creating an enduring link of emotion and community, Freud went on to postulate a theory of how his Jewish identity influenced the development of his revolutionary theories.

> Because I was a Jew I found myself free of many prejudices which restrict others in the use of the intellect: as a Jew I was prepared to be in the opposition and renounce agreement with the compact majority.

The role of Jews in the early days of the psychoanalytic movement is noteworthy. Between 1902 and 1906, for example, all the members of the nascent Vienna Psychoanalytic Society were Jewish. Freud's concern that psychoanalysis was in danger of becoming a Jewish national affair led him to embrace the Swiss pastor's son Carl Jung (1875–1961) as his "Crown Prince," the Joshua to Freud's Moses who would possess the promised land of psychiatry, which Freud could only view from afar. Jung's theoretical apostasy and abandonment of the Freudian movement shattered these dreams, but Freud continued to seek support for his ideas in the larger Gentile world of academic psychology and psychiatry.

It was this desire to broaden the base of interest in his discoveries that brought Freud to accept an invitation to speak at Massachusetts' Clark University on the occasion of its twentieth anniversary in the fall of 1909. In his lectures at Clark, Freud presented the basic tenets of his early theorizing, including the key concepts of the unconscious and psychic determinism.

At Clark, Freud found another Gentile spokesman for psychoanalysis, James Jackson Putnam (1846–1918), a distinguished professor of neurology at Harvard Medical School. It was, however, a young Hungarian-born Jew, also in the audience at Clark, who was to become the leader of the American psychoanalytic movement. Abraham A. Brill (1884–1948), Freud's first American translator, was the founder, in February 1911, of the New York Psychoanalytic Society, the earliest psychoanalytic group in this country.

Brill's compatriots included several Jews, among them the first historian of American psychoanalysis, Alabama-born Clarence B. Oberndorf (1882–1954). By 1913, some 25 percent of the membership of American psychoanalytic associations were of Jewish origin. One of the founders, in 1914, of the Boston Psychoanalytic Association was the Philadelphia-born, Sephardic Jew Isador H. Coriat (1875–1943).

During its earliest phase, from the 'teens through the early 1930s, psychoanalysis in America was allied with the avant-garde movement in art and culture, and its adherents stressed Freud's psychological conceptions more than the clinical practice of psychoanalytic therapy. Brill contributed to this popularization as an ardent propagandist, also writing on the adjustment of Jews to the American world, stressing their adaptability and flexibility. Brill, at Columbia, and Oberndorf, who in 1913 established a psychiatric outpatient clinic at New York's Mount Sinai Hospital, were influential in proselytizing for psychoanalysis among young physicians.

Psychoanalytic education during this period in America was a hit-and-miss affair, and the early generation of American analysts went abroad for their training. Among these sojourners were many Jewish psychiatrists who were to play central roles in the professionalization of psychoanalysis: Bertram Lewin (1896–1971), Ruth Mack Brunswick (1897–1946), M. Ralph Kaufman (1900–1977), Monroe Meyer (1892–1939), Abram Kardiner (1891–1981), and Laurence Kubie (1896–1973).

By the 1930s, the younger generation of American analysts had successfully medicalized psychoanalysis, much against Freud's wishes, opening their newly developed training institutes only to psychiatrists. This new elite moved away from an avant-garde image to one of cosmopolitan liberalism. Routinizing the charisma of the earlier generation, for the next 30 years psychoanalysts became influential spokesmen for American ideals of cultural pluralism and adaptation.

The Jewish cast of American psychoanalysis was dramatically accentuated by the influx of European refugee analysts fleeing Nazi persecution. This group included the most important and influential names in subsequent American psychoanalysis: Rene Spitz (1887–1974), Margaret Mahler (1897–1985), Heinz Hartmann (1894–1970), Rudolf Loewenstein (1898–1976), Sandor Rado (1890–1972), Ernst Kris (1901–1957), Helene Deutsch (1884–1982), Otto Fenichel (1897–1946), Franz Alexander (1891–1964), Frieda Fromm-Reichmann (1890–1957), Erich Fromm (1900–1980), Theodore Reik (1888–1969), Bruno Bettelheim (1903–1990), Erik Erikson (b. 1902), David Rapaport (1911–1960), and Ruth Jacobson (1897–1978).

In a 1980 survey of over 400 analysts, 8 of these refugees were named as the leading psychoanalysts in America. Among the 10 most often named, the only native-born leaders were Chicagoan Phyllis Greenacre (b. 1894) and Bertram Lewin (1896–1971).

The American experience, however, blunted the pessimistic thrust of Freud's work. The development of psychoanalysis in this country paralleled the broader social views of the Jewish-American social elite. As psychoanalysis became an established part of the American landscape, its emphasis shifted from a concern with Freud's id, with its striving for immediate instinctual gratification (and akin to the concept of the mystic evil impulse, the *yetzer harah*), to that of the ego, the aspect of mental activity that became synonymous with moralistic American notions of control and postponement of gratification.

The 25-year reign of the adaptational and conformist American view of psychoanalysis was sharply challenged by the countercultural rebellion of the 1960s. New-old heroes were resurrected from psychoanalysis, most dramatically the pariah, Wilhelm Reich (1897–1957), whose madcap theories of sexuality and exhibitionistic Marxism had led to his expulsion from the psychoanalytic movement as early as 1934. And, as if in response to the dramatic attack on psychoanalysis by the generation of the 1960s and 1970s, the current emphasis in psychoanalytic theory has centered on the theme of narcissism and its vicissitudes, as exemplified in the work of Otto Kernberg (b. 1928) and Heinz Kohut (1913–1981).

The years since 1970 have witnessed dramatic changes in the American psychoanalytic establishment. There has been a proliferation of training institutes that have challenged the medicalization imposed by the earlier generations, so that many of the new spokespeople for psychoanalysis have come from backgrounds in psychology and social work. This new constituency of analysts, which includes large congeries of Jews, will ensure the Jewish presence in the future development of psychoanalysis in this country.

PSYCHIATRY. From the Revolutionary period until after the Civil War, there were no Jews in American psychiatry. The founders, in 1844, of the American Association of Medical Superintendents, the precursor of the American Psychiatric Association, included no Jewish representative. One can, however, sense the philosophical presence of Maimonides (1135–1204) in the nineteenth-century American movement toward more humane and enlightened moral treatment of the mentally ill.

The two basic strands of psychiatry, in the United States as elsewhere, have been the organic and the psychological. The organic approach seeks the causes of mental illness in a dysfunctional brain, while the psychological explanation looks toward the role of faulty socialization in the etiology of emotional and behavioral disturbance. The latter approach is most closely identified with Freud's psychoanalysis (*see* above).

The first Jewish-American psychiatrists were allied to the neurological-organic model.

These included Sidney Kuh (1866–1934), professor of nervous and mental diseases at Rush Medical College in Chicago, Sidney Schwab (1871–1947), who had studied with Freud in Vienna, at Washington University Medical School in St. Louis, and Bernard Sachs (1858–1944), professor of nervous and mental disease at Columbia and the discoverer of Tay-Sachs disease, who was a caustic opponent of the Freudian influence on psychiatry.

Even before Freud made his 1909 journey to America, however, psychiatrists like Boris Sidis (1867–1923) in Boston were evidencing interest in this new psychotherapeutic approach to mental illness. Other early psychiatric interest in the new psychology can be found in the works of Samuel Tannenbaum (1874–1948) and Meyer Solomon (1887–1953).

Early-twentieth-century American psychiatry was, like its European counterpart, equally divided on the question of whether there was some specific form of "Jewish psychopathology." The arguments, pro and con, had been bandied about in Europe since at least the eighteenth century. They took on new saliency with the massive Eastern European immigration into the United States at the turn of the century. Although the American Psychiatric Association did not officially endorse the more blatant elements of immigration restriction, many of its most influential members adopted the prevailing racist attitudes, asserting that Jews were more prone to insanity than other "races" and were eugenically tainted.

The Jewish psychiatrist Aron Rosanoff (1879–1943) challenged the idea of a high prevalence of immigrant insanity, but, as late as 1920, other Jewish psychiatrists, such as Abraham Meyerson (1881–1948), were still commenting on Jewish "nervousness," now seen as due to their mythical inactivity and excessive cerebration.

By the 1930s, Jews had entered further into the mainstream of American culture, and increasing educational opportunities allowed their numbers to expand exponentially in the world of psychiatry. The generation of Jewish Americans that came of age in the 1930s produced most of the important names in the psychiatry of that period and for the next thirty years: Harold Wolff (1898–1962), Roy Grinker, Sr. (b. 1900), Lawrence Kolb (1881–1972), Manfred Guttmacher (1898–1966), Frederich Redlich (b. 1910), Lauretta Bender (1897–1989), Jules Masserman (b. 1905), Morris Schwartz (1913–1976), Leo

Kanner (1894–1981), Lewis Wolberg (1905–1988), William Malamud (1896–1982), Erich Lindemann (1900–1974), David Levy (1893–1977), and Nathan Ackerman (1908–1971).

In the 1960s, and for the next 20 years, at least in the major urban centers of America, Jews comprised nearly 50 percent of the psychiatric profession, and a significant number of university departments of psychiatry and other training centers were headed by Jews, such as Milton Rosenbaum (b. 1910), Milton Miller (b. 1927), Seymour Halleck (b. 1929), and Milton Greenblatt (b. 1914). It was during this same period that Fritz Perls (1893–1970) introduced Gestalt therapy into the American mainstream of psychotherapy.

Psychiatry, as a profession, continues in its attempt to integrate the organic and psychological approach to the problems of mental disorder. Modern Jewish psychiatrists of note represent both approaches: Robert Lifton (b. 1926), whose extensive writings on the subject of survivorhood are well known; Aaron Beck (b. 1921), who has developed an important cognitive approach to the problem of depression; Daniel Offer (b. 1929), a prolific researcher on issues of adolescent development; and Nathan Kline (1916–1983), a controversial figure in the field of drug therapy and one of the key figures in the introduction of tranquilizers into psychiatric treatment.

PSYCHOLOGY. Jewish contributions to psychology, as the general science of human and animal behavior, have been many. The first American doctorate in psychology was awarded by Johns Hopkins University in 1886 to Joseph Jastrow (1863–1944), who went on to establish the psychological laboratory at the University of Wisconsin. Another of the important early experimental psychologists was Hugo Munsterberg (1863–1916), who came to Harvard in 1892 to direct the laboratory founded by William James. Both Jastrow and Munsterberg were prolific publicists for psychology, writing on a variety of applications of the new science. Jastrow authored one of the early syndicated self-help columns, "Keeping Mentally Fit," while Munsterberg, in 1916, produced the first study of the psychological impact of the movies (*The Film: A Psychological Study*).

The first half century of American psychology saw its movement away from the purely laboratory science methodology inherited from its German predecessors to a more broadly conceived enterprise concerned with complex human functions embedded in everyday life. Nevertheless, the locus of psychological work remained in the universities. This meant that the formal and informal *numerus clausii* of American academia prevented any large-scale growth among the ranks of Jewish psychologists.

The second generation of American Jewish psychologists, however, includes many professionals of renown: Samuel Fernberger (1887–1956), known for his work in psychophysics and the study of facial expression in emotion; Irving Lorge (1905–1961), statistician and educational psychologist; Carl Pfaffman (b. 1913), physiological psychologist; David Krech (1909–1977), a polymath who did important research in both neuroanatomy and social psychology; Otto Klineberg (b. 1899), pioneer in the study of the interconnection between culture and personality and race relations; Morris Viteles (b. 1898), America's first industrial psychologist; Herman Witkin (1916–1979), who made significant contributions in the field of cognitive processes; Herbert A. Simon (b. 1916), brilliant cyberneticist and mathematical psychologist; Howard Schlosberg (1904–1964), coauthor of the classic textbook on experimental psychology; William N. Schoenfeld (b. 1915), noteworthy behavioral psychologist; Isidor Chein (b. 1912), social psychologist and for several years director of research on community relations of the American Jewish Congress; Solomon Asch (b. 1907), important for his work on social influences in perception; and Abraham Roback (1890–1965), a Harvard Ph.D. who wrote on Yiddish and Hebrew literature.

Psychology, too, had its influx, in the 1930s, of European refugees. The presence among them of noted psychologists working in the field of developmental processes gave an impetus to the study of child development and social interaction. Two of the most important of these refugees were Kurt Lewin (1890–1947) and Max Wertheimer (1880–1943). Together with Kurt Koffka (1886–1941), who had arrived in America in the 1920s, these men were the founders of the Gestalt school of psychology, with its emphasis on the impact on an individual of their total psychological reality at any given moment.

Lewin's work, at the Iowa Child Welfare Station, was of great significance for a whole generation of researchers in the world of childhood. Fellow refugees Charlotte Buhler (1893–1974), William Stern (1871–1938), and especially Heinz Werner (1890–1964), were also of central importance in enriching the field of developmental psychology. Jewish psychologists have continued to be in the forefront of research in developmental processes. Notable names include Jerome Bruner (b. 1915), Jerome Kagan (b. 1929), Joseph Adelson (b. 1925), David Ausubel (b. 1918), Urie Bronfenbrenner (b. 1917), David Elkind (b. 1931), Jacob Gewirtz (b. 1924), William Goldfarb (b. 1915), Bernice Neugarten (b. 1916), and Edward Zigler (b. 1930).

It has been the area of clinical psychology, the professional specialty specifically concerned with mental health issues, that has attracted the largest contingent of American Jews in psychology. In a 1971 large-scale study of mental health professionals (W. E. Henry, J. H. Sims, and S. L. Spray, *The Fifth Profession*), almost 50 percent of the clinical psychologists surveyed were Jews. Jews had taken a pivotal role in the post-World War II development of clinical psychology. As a relatively new profession, it was less hidebound by tradition and offered upward mobility. It also provided an interesting blend of intellectual challenge and dedication to humanitarian impulses. And, in its early days, being very much influenced by psychoanalytic conceptualization, it maintained a direct tie to Freud's "Jewish science." All of these factors helped reinforce the Jewish-American commitment to clinical psychology.

The three areas of clinical psychology—research, assessment, and service—have all been enriched by Jewish contributions: David Shakow (1901–1981), for many years the chief psychologist at Worcester (Massachusetts) State Hospital, initiated basic research on schizophrenia; Joseph Zubin (b. 1900), Kurt Salzinger (b. 1929), and Sarnoff Mednick (b. 1928), are well known for their work on experimental psychopathology, as are Leonard Ullmann (b. 1930), Carl Zimet (b. 1925), and Leonard Berkowitz (b. 1926); Hans Strupp (b. 1921) and Lester Luborsky (b. 1920) are leaders in the field of psychotherapy research; and Emory Cowen (b. 1926) and Seymour Sarason (b. 1919) are central figures in the fields of the early prevention of psychological disorders and community psychology.

In the field of psychological testing and assessment, Bruno Klopfer (1900–1971) and Samuel Beck (1896–1980) were the first to foster interest in projective tests in America. They were joined by the exemplary David Rapaport (1911–1960) who, at the Menninger Clinic and the Austin Riggs Foundation, influenced a stellar coterie of psychologists. His intellectual heirs include Roy Schafer (b. 1922) and Martin Mayman (b. 1924). Saul Rosenzweig (b. 1907), the developer of the Picture-Frustration Test, is another key figure in psychological evaluation. Sidney Blatt (b. 1928), Irving Weiner (b. 1933), and the Lerners, Howard (b. 1945) and Paul (b. 1937) have continued to demonstrate the importance of assessment in clinical work.

The largest number of members of the American Psychological Association are in the field of clinical service. As the variety of psychological forms of treatment have proliferated, Jews have been central figures in all the important modalities: Arnold Lazarus (b. 1914) and Marvin Goldfried (b. 1936) in behavioral therapies; Alan Gurman (b. 1945), Gerald Zuk (b. 1929), and Neil Jacobson (b. 1949), in family therapy; Nathan Farberow (b. 1918) and Edward Shneidman (b. 1918) in the field of suicidology; and Abraham Maslow (1908–1970) in existential and humanistic forms of psychotherapy.

The field of clinical psychology has grown apace over the past two decades. It is no longer as dramatically Jewish in its constituency as it was for the first 30 years of its development, but it still remains an appealing profession to Jewish young men and women. It is significant, moreover, that a *Journal of Psychology and Judaism*, now in its second decade, continues to devote itself to the interrelationship of psychology and Judaism in all its variegated facets.

LESLIE Y. RABKIN

BIBLIOGRAPHY

Alexander, F. G., and Selesnick, S. T. *The History of Psychiatry*. New York: Harper & Row, 1966.

Hale, Nathan G., Jr. *Freud and the Americans*. New York: Oxford University Press, 1971.

Henry, W. E.; Sims, J. H.; and Spray, S. L. *The Fifth Profession*. San Francisco: Jossey-Bass, 1971.

Hersen, M.; Kazdin, A. E.; and Bellack, A. S., eds. *The Clinical Psychology Handbook*. New York: Pergamon Press, 1983.

Midwest, The. Jews have lived in the Midwest ever since the region was open to English settlement. Their experience has been an urban one, similar to but also different than that of their coreligionists on the East Coast. An understanding of the particular circumstances of this history is necessary in order to comprehend the total record of Jews in America.

The earliest Jews in the region were traders. Chapman Abraham, for example, opened a trading post in Detroit in 1762. He sold munitions to the British as well as wine and brandy to other residents. Other Jewish traders could be found in frontier villages as whites pressured Indians to move further west. But Jewish settlement in the Midwest was sparse. The first congregation in the region was formed in Cincinnati, begun in 1824. The congregation did not build a synagogue until 1836, but this early start helped make the town an important center of Reform Judaism. Jews in other cities also created congregations: St. Louis had one in 1836; Louisville, in 1842; Chicago, in 1847; Detroit, in 1850; and Indianapolis, in 1856. By the Civil War, Jewish communities existed in Akron, Columbus, and Dayton, Ohio; Ft. Wayne, Lafayette, and Evansville, Indiana; Keokuk, Iowa; and Milwaukee, Wisconsin.

The tide of Jewish immigration to America rose from 1820 to 1860, bringing the total population to 150,000 from 4000. Most of the new arrivals came from German states torn by political strife. Many became peddlers, and a pattern of mobility soon emerged. Starting as pack peddlers, these Jews sold goods on the frontier. As they became successful, they bought horses and wagons and then opened dry-goods stores. Such was the career path of Jacob Gottlieb, Chicago's first Jewish resident in 1838. Another in the same mold was Adam Gimbel, who migrated from Bavaria in 1832, peddling in the Midwest for a time before settling in Vincennes, Indiana. Not all peddlers were as successful as Gimbel, who saw his sons found Gimbel Brothers and Saks Fifth Avenue in New York City.

Jews in the Midwest, particularly in smaller towns, faced many obstacles to maintaining traditional religion and culture. In these communities often too few Jews resided to form a congregation. In those large enough to possess the requisite number, quite frequently only a minority would join a synagogue, if built, while the majority might keep kosher and attend services irregularly. The pressures of American society led to an attempt to modify traditional practices in order to adjust better to the new situation. Among the leaders of Reform Judaism was Rabbi Isaac Mayer Wise, an immigrant from Germany, whose move to Cincinnati to lead Ben Jeshurum in the 1850s made that city the center of that movement in America. Wise compiled a revised prayer book, *Minhag Amerika*, and helped form the Union of American Hebrew Congregations in 1873, Hebrew Union College in 1875, and the Central Conference of American Rabbis in 1889.

American Judaism received an influx of new members in the years after 1880 down to World War I. These Jews came from Eastern Europe, primarily from Russia. While many settled in East Coast cities, not a few swelled the population of such Midwestern cities as Chicago, Cleveland, and Detroit, bringing with them a commitment to Orthodox Judaism. Although living in ghettos in such cities, their economic and physical mobility was such that they soon moved out. Their social mobility was less rapid, however. Because they lacked the acculturation of the second-generation German Jews and were less inclined to Reform Judaism, they did not easily enter that community. Ethnic and religious differences continued to cause problems for those trying to unite the Jewish population. In 1903, Orthodox Jews in Chicago tried to appoint a chief rabbi but failed; and while attempts in Detroit to create a *kekilla* (an association of all Jewish institutions in the city) succeeded in 1913, the organization proved disappointing.

Zionism and socialism were two ideas brought to the Midwest by Eastern European Jews. Although they were divisive, major Midwestern cities had groups supporting both ideas. The Knights of Zion, a national organization, was based in Chicago and attracted many traditional Jews. On the other hand, Hebrew Union College was a center of anti-Zionist sentiment in the region.

The integration of Jews into full participation in American life increased in the twentieth century as a few individuals successfully entered larger communities. Among these persons was Henry Horner of Chicago, who, after being elected probate court judge for five terms beginning in 1914, successfully ran for governor of Illinois in 1932 and 1936.

External events also helped bring an end to earlier divisions. World War II, the Holocaust, and the establishment of a Palestinian homeland helped to promote Zionism as support for such organizations as the American Council for Judaism lessened. In Indianapolis, for example, only the Indianapolis Hebrew Congregation led by a Reform rabbi retained elements of anti-Zionism after 1945. Moreover, there appeared to be a return to greater ethnic identity and more religious participation.

But this return was countered by increasing assimilation into the larger society through inter-

marriage. This was particularly evident in small towns in the Midwest. In Indiana, one of the few states where questions of religion are asked of those marrying, 34.5 percent of Jews intermarried in the years 1960 to 1963 in Indianapolis, but in the state's smaller towns, the percentage was 63.5.

Thus Jews in the Midwest are threatened with extinction by the very success they have had in joining American society.

DWIGHT W. HOOVER

BIBLIOGRAPHY

Endelman, Judith E. *The Jewish Community of Indianapolis: 1849 to the Present.* Bloomington: Indiana University Press, 1985.

Glazer, Nathan. *American Judaism.* Chicago: University of Chicago Press, 1957.

Holli, Melvin G., and Jones, Peter d'a. *The Ethnic Frontier: Essays in the History of Group Survival in Chicago and the Midwest.* Grand Rapids, Mich.: Eerdmans, 1977.

Learsi, Rufus. *The Jews in America: A History.* Rev. ed. New York: Ktav, 1972.

Raphael, Marc L. *Jews and Judaism in a Midwestern Community: Columbus, Ohio, 1840–1975.* Columbus: Ohio Historical Society, 1979.

Rockaway, Robert A. *The Jews of Detroit: From the Beginning, 1762–1914.* Detroit: Wayne State University Press, 1986.

Waxman, Chaim I. *America's Jews in Transition.* Philadelphia: Temple University Press, 1983.

Military, The. The revelation that one half of the first graduating class of the United States Military Academy at West Point was Jewish is surprising. The surprise is only somewhat mitigated by the knowledge that the class consisted of two students, one of whom was a Jew. This interesting statistic, moreover, points to the fact that American Jews have been involved in the defense of their country from the beginning and in greater numbers than their proportion to the general population would lead one to expect.

Jews arrived in New Amsterdam—later New York—in 1654 and on August 28, 1655, Peter Stuyvesant and the New Amsterdam Council voted to exclude Jews from military service and impose a special tax upon them because they could not serve. This discriminatory decision was challenged by two Jews, Jacob Barsimson and Asser Levy, who requested that they be given the right to stand guard with other burghers. Although their petition was denied, the right was won later.

A number of Jews fought in the French and Indian War. David Harp, Jr., served under George Washington in that war. Aaron Hart was responsible for the formation of a battalion of troops and was a member of the staff of General Amherst when Montreal was captured from the French in 1760. Isaac Isaacs was a captain in the campaign against the French in Canada, while Isaac Myers led a company in an expedition against the Indians. Two other Jews were under his command. The privateer ship, the *Duke of Cumberland*, was captained by Judah Harp.

There were only some 2500 Jews in America at the outbreak of the Revolutionary War, and they joined the ranks as officers and soldiers out of all proportion to their numbers. Jewish merchants volunteered their ships to sail as privateers. Francis Salvador, a member of the General Assembly of the new state of South Carolina, and the first Jew to hold state office in the newly declared United States, died fighting a Cherokee Indian uprising instigated by the British within days after the Declaration of Independence. Mordecai Sheftall, whom the British considered "a very great rebel," was commissary general for Georgia troops, later deputy commissary of Issues for the Southern Department, and was captured at the fall of Savannah. Also active in the revolutionary cause in Georgia was David Emanuel. The leader of a patriot community known as Rebel Town, located near Augusta, Emanuel and several others were captured by the British at McBean's Creek. After escaping and making his way to the American lines, Emanuel served in the Continental Army under General Truggs. Emanuel was later to become a Governor of Georgia.

Isaac Franks enlisted at the age of 17 and fought in the Battle of Long Island under Washington's command. Isaac Nunez Cardozo was a member of a company made up almost completely of Jewish soldiers who fought to defend Charleston harbor. His brother, David Nunez Cardozo, led the attack to recapture Savannah in 1779. The Jewish company was led by Major Benjamin Nones, a Jew born in France, who had served on the staffs of Lafayette and Washington. Lewis Bush, because of his bravery, was rapidly promoted to the rank of major and was fatally wounded at the Battle of Brandywine in 1777. His brother, George Bush, also reached the rank of major, and Solomon Bush, deputy adjutant general of the Pennsylvania militia, was seriously wounded by the British. Colonel David S. Franks was on the staff of General Benedict Arnold. He was honorably acquitted of all connection with Arnold's treason.

Dr. Phillip Moses Russel served as a surgeon's mate and was praised in a letter by General Washington for the doctor's "assiduous and faithful attention to the sick and wounded." Russel attended to the Continental Army at Valley Forge during the winter of 1777–1778 (Fredman and Falk, 1943).

The best-known Jew of the war is Haym Salomon, brother-in-law of Colonel Franks. Salomon rendered extraordinary financial service to the young American government, depleting his own wealth for his country's cause and acting as a broker for loans from Holland and France for the support of the Revolution. He also helped officers of the army meet their personal expenses. Born in Lissa, Poland, in 1740, Haym Salomon immigrated to New York after the partition of his native country. Well-educated and remarkably talented, he immediately became successful as a broker. Although New York was the seat of British power in America, Salomon cast his fortunes with the Sons of Liberty, was arrested after the revolutionary outbreaks of 1776, and was sentenced to prison as a spy. The British, recognizing that he could speak ten languages, put him to work as an interpreter until his release, after which he went back into his business, aiding the American cause with his mounting fortune. For his repeated revolutionary activities Salomon was arrested again, and this time tortured and condemned to be hanged. With the aid of friends he managed to escape to Philadelphia, where he quickly opened up a business as a broker again, purchasing food with his profits for the starving Continental Army. Washington, Lafayette, von Steuben, and others came to him for aid.

Another patriot, David Hays, drove cattle from his Westchester farm through the British lines to hungry American troops. In reprisal, British troops burned down his farm house while he was serving with Washington's troops.

Between the American Revolution and the War of 1812, the American merchant fleet was asserting itself across the seas. When pirates from Tripoli sought to levy tributes on American commerce, the United States Government used force to suppress this threat to its commercial trade. When the United States Navy launched a "suicide sortie" into Tripoli harbor by loading a small boat with explosives and combustibles to attack the pirate fleet, Midshipman Joseph Isreals was one of ten American seamen from the frigates

Nautilus and *Constitution* who volunteered for the successful mission that destroyed the bulk of the pirates' ships.

Jewish soliders participated in the War of 1812. Among them was Major Mordecai Myers, who was badly wounded at the Battle of Chrysler's Farm. He had earlier been instrumental in saving 200 American soldiers and marines from wrecked ships off Sackett's Harbor on Lake Ontario. Abraham, Moses, and Solomon Seixas were captains in the infantry. Jewish soliders were among the successful defenders of Fort McHenry and the city of Baltimore in 1814. Many of the sons of the Revolutionary generation fought in the War of 1812. Haym M. Salomon, son of Haym Salomon, was captain of the Tenth Brigade, 115 Regiment. In Georgia, several sons of Mordecai Sheftall served in the army. The son of Benjamin Nones was a navy midshipman and served as secretary to Henry Clay, who represented the United States at the peace negotiations in Ghent. Major Abraham A. Massias fought the British in Georgia. His men repulsed numerous attempts by the British to enter Georgia from the sea. In the words of one historian, "the enemy attacked Point Peter on the St. Mary's, sending 1500 men in boats up the river for that purpose, but the fortifications were good and the garrison under Major Massias made so brave a show that the English concluded the post was too strong to be carried, and withdrew" (Fredman and Falk).

Judah Touro served under the command of General (later President) Andrew Jackson. While in the ranks of Jackson's army, Touro, son of a rabbi, established a strong friendship with fellow soldier Rezin Shepherd, a Christian who saved Touro's life during the defense of New Orleans. Touro later became a great benefactor of the city of New Orleans. Aaron Levy reached the rank of lieutenant colonel. Bernard Hart was quartermaster of an infantry division. Jewish officers included Brigadier General Joseph Bloomfield, who commanded the district of Pennsylvania, Delaware, and Western New Jersey; Lieutenant Benjamin Gratz, a Pennsylvania volunteer; Lieutenant Isaac Mertz, of the Pennsylvania Regiment; Adjutant Isaac Myers of Pennsylvania; Lieutenant David Metzler; Captain Meyer Moses; and Colonel Nathan Myers.

The most prominent Jewish officer in the War of 1812 was Commodore Uriah P. Levy. After the war, he was to achieve fame for abolishing punishment by whip in the United States Navy. At the age of 14, Levy left his Philadelphia home to sign on a merchant ship; the next year he was mate of the brig *Polly and Betsy*. At 20, he became master and part owner of the brig-of-war *Argus*, which ran the British blockade to France with William Crawford, American minister to France, aboard. On the return voyage, the *Argus* destroyed 21 British merchantmen and captured a number of other vessels that Levy armed for battle against the British men-of-war. Meeting the heavily armed British frigate *Pelican*, Levy found himself outmatched but fought until the *Argus* was sunk and he himself was taken prisoner. Levy subsequently spent 16 months in Dartmoor Prison in England.

The feats of Captain John Ordroneaux, a victorious privateer, are described by William Maclay, historian of the U.S. Navy: Ordroneaux was "so diminutive in stature as to make it appear ridiculous in the eyes of others even to think of him enforcing authority among a hardy, weather-beaten crew." But he commanded respect through his courage and ability. Once he halted retreat by his men in the face of a British boarding party by standing at the powder magazine with a lighted match and threatening to destroy his ship (the *Prince de Neufchatel*). Maclay writes, "One of the most remarkable actions of the war was between the British forty-gun frigate *Endymion* and the armed ship *Prince de Neufchatel*." The extraordinary feature of this affair lies in the fact that a vessel fitted out at private expense actually frustrated the utmost endeavors of an English frigate of vastly superior forces in guns and men. The commander of the *Endymion* observed that he lost as many men in his efforts to seize the *Prince de Neufchatel* as he would have done had his ship engaged a man of war of equal force, and he generously acknowledged that the people in the privateer conducted their defense in the most heroic and skillful manner. Captain Ordroneaux himself fired some 80 shots at the enemy. It was well understood that Ordroneaux had avowed his determination of never being taken alive and that he would blow up his ship with all hands before striking his colors. As the British gained the advantage on the *Prince de Neufchatel* Ordroneaux's threat at the magazine had the desired effect, and "at the end of 20 minutes the English cried out for quarter, upon which the Americans ceased their fighting" (Fredman and Falk, 1943).

Jews continued to serve in the navy and army after the War of 1812. They participated in the Texan War of Independence and the Mexican War. The surgeon who accompanied General

Sam Houston through the war in Texas was Moses Albert Levy. Abraham Wolf was killed in the Battle of the Alamo. Adolphus Sterne was captured by the Mexicans and sentenced to be shot but subsequently was released. He was later elected to the legislature of the Republic of Texas. Davis S. Kaufman, aide-de-camp to General Douglas, was wounded at the Battle of Neches. He was later chosen speaker of the Texas Assembly and supported the movement for annexation by the United States. Following the entry of Texas into the Union, Kaufman was elected a representative from that state in Congress.

Perhaps the most famous Jewish officer of the Mexican War was Surgeon General David de Leon of South Carolina. Twice he took the place of commanding officers who had been killed or wounded and both times acted with such courage and ability as to merit expressions of gratitude from Congress. He won the title "the fighting doctor" in the Battle of Chapultepec. Twice he led cavalry charges into the mouths of enemy cannons. In 1861 de Leon resigned as surgeon major in the Union Army and was appointed first surgeon general of the Confederacy. Others in the Mexican War included Colonel Leon Dyer, who was quartermaster general for General Winfield Scott; Lieutenant Henry Seligson, who fought with such distinction that he was summoned by General Zachary Taylor to receive personal commendation; and, among the first killed in action in the war, Sergeant Abraham Adler of the New York Volunteers. Altogether, 57 Jewish soldiers have been prominently mentioned in the records of the Mexican War.

During the Civil War proportionately large numbers of Jews fought on both sides and many received high honors. It is estimated that 10 percent of all Jewish men saw service. Over 2000 entered the Union Army from the state of New York and over 1000 volunteered from Illinois. Altogether about 7000 Jews served in the Union forces and approximately 3000 in the Confederate forces. Among the Jewish officers there were 9 generals, 18 colonels, 8 lieutenant colonels, 40 majors, 205 captains, and 325 lieutenants. Seven Jews won the Congressional Medal of Honor, the highest military distinction.

The first Jew elected to the United States Senate, David Yulee (Levy), resigned his seat during his second term to join the Confederate Army in the field. Judah P. Benjamin, called by historians "the brains of the Confederacy," was also a member of the Senate but with the outbreak of the war he became the attorney general of the Confederacy. Later Jefferson Davis appointed him secretary of war, and finally he became the secretary of state for the Confederacy.

In the South the name of a Jewish Confederate soldier, Max Frauenthal, became synonymous with courage. His name became corrupted to "Fronthall" and when southerners wished to refer to someone as courageous, they would call him a "regular Fronthall." Frauenthal won this unique distinction through his bravery in battle. Among the Jews in the Confederate forces were General David de Leon, "the fighting doctor" of the Mexican War who served as surgeon general of the Confederate Army, and Captain L. G. Harby, another veteran of the Mexican War, who became a commodore in the Confederate fleet and commanded the defense of Galveston. Approximately 336 Jews were killed in the war and 272 were wounded.

In the West, after the Civil War, the Indians generated their last gallant resistance against the white man's advance. At Arickaree Fork, a greatly outnumbered United States Army detachment fought against the Sioux Indians. One of the 50 men under General G. A. Forsyth's command was Samuel Schlesinger, a 19-year-old Jewish soldier who had been only reluctantly accepted to complete the volunteer unit. Of Schlesinger, Forsyth wrote that he seemed to be "inferior and in all respects unfit for service, with small, narrow shoulders, sunken chest, quiet manner, piping voice and little knowledge of firearms or horsemanship." Of the ensuing battle, fought in September 1867, Forsyth wrote that it was "the hardest ever fought on the western plains," and of Schlesinger's performance the general wrote: "I can accord him no higher praise than he was equal in manly courage, steady and persistent devotion to duty, and unswerving and tenacious pluck of any man in my command. He behaved with great courage, cool persistence and a dogged determination that won my unstinted admiration" (Golden and Rywell, 1950).

The Spanish-American War was the shortest war in American history and the first in which American troops left the North American continent. About 5000 Jews served in the army and approximately 100 in the navy. They represented 0.5 percent of the Jews in the country at that time, while the total number of Americans in the armed forces constituted 0.4 percent. There were 30 Jewish officers in the army, 20 in the navy. Fifteen Jews went down with the *Maine*, whose sinking precipitated the war. The executive officer of the *Maine*, and later a vice-admiral of the navy, was Adolph Marix. He was appointed chairman of the board of inquiry to investigate the *Maine* disaster and wrote a notable report on the mysterious sinking.

Half a dozen Jewish privates and a Jewish lieutenant served in the Rough Riders, Theodore Roosevelt's famous regiment. The first casualty in the attack at Manila was Sergeant Maurice Joost of the First California Volunteers, a regiment that included over 100 Jews. The accomplishments of Corporal Ben Prager won him the Silver Star for his performance in the Philippines.

Colonel Joseph M. Heller, the first American volunteer accepted by the War Department in the Spanish-American War, left a successful medical career to become acting assistant surgeon in the United States Army. He served in the field as regimental surgeon in charge of a smallpox hospital and after the war headed the mission to combat the cholera epidemic in Manila. General Elwell Otis commended Heller by cable—the only medical officer in the Philippines to receive such recognition. He also was awarded the Silver Star with a citation that extolled his "gallantry in action against Insurgent forces at Naguilian, Luzon, Philippine Islands, December 7, 1899, in attending the wounded under fire." Jewish casualties numbered 104.

About 250,000 Jews served in the United States Army during World War I, 40,000 volunteering. Jews numbered 3 percent of the American population but more than 4 percent of the army and navy. The proportion of Jews in the fighting units of the American Expeditionary Forces was far greater than in the noncombatant branches. Approximately 3500 Jews were killed in action or died of wounds—5 percent of the entire death roll; 12,000 were wounded. In the Marine Corps, some 2500 Jews enlisted, and more than 100 were commissioned as officers. Approximately 10,000 Jews served as officers in the army, most having received battlefield promotions. Major General Julius Ochs Adler, Brigadier Generals Milton J. Foreman and Abel Davis won the Distinguished Service Medal, and Brigadier General Charles H. Laucheimer of the Marine Corps was awarded the Navy Distinguished Service Medal. In the navy over 900 Jews were commissioned officers, with the highest rank that of Rear Admirals Joseph Strauss and Joseph K. Taussig. More than 3000 Jews served in the air corps. In the army over 100 Jews were promoted

to colonel and lieutenant colonel, over 500 to major, 1500 to captain, and 6000 to lieutenant. The Seventy-seventh Infantry Division, which was heavily engaged in the Meuse-Argonne Battle, was 40 percent Jewish. At least 1100 citations for bravery were bestowed upon Jewish fighting men, 723 by the American command, 287 by the French, 33 by the British, and 46 by other Allied commands. The Congressional Medal of Honor was awarded to 6 American Jews, one of whom was killed in his act of heroism. Twenty-three Jewish chaplains served their country, one of whom, Michael Aaronson, was blinded in action.

Stories abound of Jewish heroism during World War I. Sergeant Benjamin Kaufman on October 4, 1918, was out on his company's advance in the Argonne when, after finding himself separated from his patrol, he alone faced a German machine gun placement. He advanced on the machine gun, had his one arm shattered, and with his other arm threw hand grenades until all the Germans scattered but one, whom he took prisoner with use of an empty weapon. Kaufman received the Congressional Medal of Honor as well as awards from nine other governments.

Sergeant William Sawelson, killed in action, received the Medal of Honor posthumously. On October 26, 1918, at Grand Pré, he left his shelter to administer aid to a wounded friend when he was hit by machine gun fire. Sergeant Sydney Gumpertz, on September 26, 1918, advanced alone on a machine gun placement at Bois de Forges and silenced it after jumping into the gun fortification itself. He also was awarded the Medal of Honor.

Corporal Barney Salner was credited by Major Jesse Wooldridge with saving the major's battalion from disaster during a battle along the Marne.

World War II saw the largest number of Jewish men and women serving in the American military forces. Incomplete records show that 550,000 Jews, the equivalent of 37 divisions, defended their country. Of the Jewish population of the United States, this represented between 11 and 12 percent; of the total armed forces, Jews constituted about 3.5 percent. All Jewish casualties—dead, wounded, captured, and missing—totaled 35,157, of whom 10,500 died in the service, 8000 in combat. More than 36,000 Jews in uniform received awards for valor, winning 61,448 medals, from the Medal of Honor to the Purple Heart (over 26,000 of the latter). They served in every branch of the service, over 80 percent in the army. Twenty-three reached flag rank: 6 major generals, 13 brigadier generals, 1 admiral, 2 rear admirals, and 1 commodore. More than a third of all Jewish physicians were in uniform, 60 percent of those under 45.

Perhaps the best-known story out of World War II to signify the common faith in freedom of Americans is that of the four chaplains—the Reverends John Washington, George Fox, Clark Poling, and Rabbi Alexander Goode—who voluntarily gave away their needed life preservers to crew members of the torpedoed and fast-sinking cargo transport *Dorchester* in the North Atlantic. All four chaplains died. In Goode's last letter to his wife is an appropriate commentary: "We are fighting for the new age of brotherhood, the age of brotherhood that will usher in at the same time the world of democracy we all want" (Golden and Rywell, 1950).

Admiral Ben Moreell created and organized the Seabees, an important development in the history of the United States Navy. Under his direction this force grew during World War II from an original authorization of 3300 personnel to an organization boasting more than 10,000 officers and 240,000 men. Moreell was also a brilliant engineer and author.

In like mode, Commander Edward Ellsberg, number-one graduate of his 1914 United States Naval Academy class, was recognized by the navy as "the foremost expert in the world on deep-sea rescue work." Within 9 days during World War II he raised 26 ships and docks scuttled by the fascists in East Africa. Ellsberg was also an inventor and prolific author.

Brigadier General David Sarnoff served in the office of the chief signal officer and on General Eisenhower's staff. Sarnoff's earlier work with the wireless telegraph had enabled him to be instrumental in the dramatic rescue operation of survivors of the *Titanic*.

Major General Maurice G. Rose was killed on March 30, 1945. He had led the Third Armored Division through block-by-block fighting in Metz and Cologne, and into the Ruhr Valley. It was Rose's practice personally to lead reconnaissance patrols—entering potentially dangerous territory before his men. On his last reconnaissance, Rose was hit with machine gun fire from a German tank.

Master Sergeant Meyer Levin was killed in action on January 7, 1943. Before his death, Levin had received the Distinguished Flying Cross, the Silver Star, and the Oak Leaf Cluster.

He was the bombardier on the plane responsible for the destruction of the Japanese battleship *Haruna*. He also fought in the Battle of the Coral Sea and served on General MacArthur's staff. When his plane was forced down at sea, Levin was last observed putting together a life raft and yielding his place in it to his comrades. His name now marks a room at West Point in his honor.

Major Arthur E. Hoffman, holder of the Distinguished Flying Cross, the Silver Star, and a Purple Heart, was a member of General MacArthur's escort group on the general's epic evacuation from the Philippines to Australia. Before the Japanese attack on Pearl Harbor, his squadron, in the first mass flight of its kind, crossed the Pacific Ocean. In less than two weeks of fighting in the Philippines, his squadron engaged in 41 combat missions, achieving a remarkable record of enemy damage, including the sinking of a battleship. In 600 hours of combat flying during 11 months, Hoffman covered some 120,000 miles.

Lieutenant Commander Solomon S. Isquith received the Navy Cross for bravery at Pearl Harbor. According to Admiral Nimitz, commander of the United States Pacific Fleet, Isquith saved 90 percent of the sunken *Utah*'s crew on December 7, 1941, by "his cool and efficient manner of directing abandonment during the bombing attack."

Perhaps exemplifying the uncommon valor of the common soldier is the story of Private First Class Jack Sugarman, of the United States Marine Corps. His Navy Cross citation for action in Guadalcanal reads as follows: "For extraordinary heroism during action against enemy Japanese forces in the Solomon Islands area [in October] 1942. Serving with the First Marine Division, during a mass frontal attack by a numerically superior enemy force, P.F.C. Sugarman, with his gun temporarily out of action and his position threatened by hostile troops, removed the weapon and with the aid of a comrade, repaired and placed it back in action under heavy fire. On four separate occasions he saved the gun from capture, repaired it under fire, and continued to maintain effective resistance against masses of attacking Japanese. By his skill and determination, he inflicted heavy casualties upon the enemy and helped prevent a breakthrough in our line, which at that time was weakly held by a small group of riflemen."

American rabbis enlisted—they could not be drafted—311 serving in the army and navy, including the air corps and the marines. More than three-quarters saw action overseas. A precedent in the history of the American armed forces was set when General Dwight D. Eisenhower, commander of American troops in Europe, appointed a Jewish chaplain, (Major) Judah Nadich, as his adviser on Jewish affairs. Jewish chaplains played a significant role in helping Jewish survivors after the liberation of the German concentration camps.

Admiral Hyman G. Rickover, almost single-handedly, was responsible for the transition of the United States Navy from its reliance on conventional power to the employment of nuclear power in the propulsion of its vessels. The achievements of Admiral Rickover's more than 60-year naval career include assignment to the Manhattan Project in 1946, lobbying for his nuclear propulsion program between 1946 and 1948; heading the Nuclear Power Branch BuShips and appointment to the Division of Reactor Development in the Atomic Energy Commission in 1948; his involvement in the building of the USS *Nautilus*, the first nuclear submarine, in 1951; heading the Shippingport, Pennsylvania, power reactor program in 1953; and an advocate of President Eisenhower's decision to build a nuclear merchant ship in 1955. Among the long list of awards received during his career, perhaps the most prestigious was his receipt in 1980 of the Presidential Medal of Freedom for the development and application of nuclear propulsion for the United States Navy (Polmar and Allen, 1982). However, Rickover throughout his tour of duty downplayed his Jewish roots.

Jews were to be found in significant numbers in the U.S. forces during the Korean and Vietnam wars. Although statistical research remains to be done, available data shows that about 150,000 saw service in Korea and almost 30,000 in Vietnam. There were 25 Jewish chaplains in Korea and 47 in Vietnam. Rabbi Sholem Singer was killed in action in Korea, and Rabbi Meir Engel died of a sudden heart attack in Vietnam. Among Jewish officers in Vietnam, Ben Sternberg served as a major general. Colonel Jack Jacobs, recipient of the Congressional Medal of Honor, was one of the most decorated soldiers of the war in Vietnam.

A recent controversy over one veteran's war record may illustrate that anti-Semitism in the American military was not an absent factor with regard to Jews serving their country. The case involved David S. Rubitsky, a retired merchant seaman who, along with his supporters, claimed

that in December 1942, in the New Guinea jungles, he killed over 500 Japanese soldiers attempting to overrun his machine gun nest. In affidavits written by his former commanders, it is stated that not only did Rubitsky perform his act of heroism, but that he was denied decorations because a superior officer did not believe the Congressional Medal of Honor should be awarded to a Jew. Rubitsky was denied his appeal for the medal in 1990, but 70 members of the United States House of Representatives did sign a letter that urged the army to recommend Rubitsky for the honor.

During the conflict in Iraq and Kuwait in January–February 1991, eight Jewish chaplains served with the U.S. armed forces. The JWB Jewish Chaplains Council estimates that Jews are proportionately represented in the U.S. army, navy, air force, and the marines. *See also* American Revolution, Civil War.

JUDAH NADICH
MICHAEL WITMER

BIBLIOGRAPHY

Ausubel, Nathan. *The Book of Jewish Knowledge.* New York: Crown, 1974.

Duker, Abraham G. *Jews in World War I.* Reprinted from *Contemporary Jewish Record* II (September 1939): 6–29.

Fredman, J. George, and Falk, Louis A. *Jews in American Wars.* Hoboken, N.J.: Terminal Printing and Publishing, 1943.

Golden, Harry L., and Rywell, Martin. *Jews in American History: Their Contribution to the United States.* Charlotte, N.C.: Stalls, 1950.

Korn, Bertram W. *American Jewry and the Civil War.* Philadelphia: Jewish Publication Society, 1951.

Meyer, Isidore S., ed. *The American Jew in the Civil War.* Reprinted from the Publication of the *American Jewish Historical Society* 50, No. 4 (June 1961).

Nadich, Judah. *Eisenhower and the Jews.* Boston: Twayne Press, 1953.

Plesur, Milton. *Jewish Life in Twentieth-Century America: Challenge and Accommodation.* Chicago: Nelson-Hall, 1982.

Polmar, Norman, and Allen, Thomas B. *Rickover: Controversy and Genius.* New York: Simon & Schuster, 1982.

Schappes, Morris U., ed. *A Documentary History of the Jews in the United States.* New York: Citadel Press, 1971.

Wiernik, Peter. *History of the Jews in America: From the Period of the Discovery of the New World to the Present Time.* New York: Hermon Press, 1972.

Wolf, Simon. *The American Jew as Patriot, Soldier and Citizen.* Boston: Gregg Press, 1972.

Miller, Arthur (b. 1915). Along with Eugene O'Neill and Tennessee Williams, Arthur Miller has achieved lasting recognition as one of America's most important dramatists. The author of many critically acclaimed plays and stories, Miller is best known for two works that are destined to be remembered as classics of the modern theater: *Death of a Salesman* (1949) and *The Crucible* (1953).

Miller was born in New York City to moderately wealthy parents; however, the Great Depression of the 1930s ruined his father's business and left his family in near poverty conditions. This economic crisis and the impact it had on his family strongly affected Miller and contributed to his depiction of personal relations in plays such as *No Villain* (1936), *They Too Arise* (1936), *The Grass Still Grows* (1939), *All My Sons* (1947), *Death of a Salesman* (1949), *After the Fall* (1964), *The Price* (1968), and *The American Clock* (1980). Miller believes that his parents' reverence for family values based on the Jewish tradition shaped his outlook on life and made it impossible for him to write "a totally nihilistic work."

A playwright-philosopher who generally relies on the traditional form he inherited from Henrik Ibsen, Miller adjusts his structure to the content and shifts comfortably from the realism of *All My Sons* and *The Crucible* to the expressionism of *Death of a Salesman* and the impressionism of *A View from the Bridge* (1956), *After the Fall*, and *The American Clock*. Though he covers a wide spectrum of subjects in his plays, in almost all of his work Miller explodes the myth of private life in America and emphasizes the value of social responsibility. He respects the sanctity of individuality and upholds liberal democratic principles that provide moral solutions to the problems of his age. Throughout his career, Miller has written extensively about a number of concerns chiefly affecting the modern era: social dislocation is the subject of *Death of a Salesman* and *The Misfits* (1961); the effect of betrayal and guilt on both the individual and his society is examined in *All My Sons*, *The Crucible*, *A View from the Bridge*, and *The Price*; anti-Semitism, the Holocaust, and the link between public and private acts of cruelty are explored in his novel *Focus* (1945) and plays *After the Fall, Incident at Vichy* (1964), and *Playing for Time* (1980)—Miller's adaptation of Fania Fenel-

on's memoirs about her internment at Auschwitz; and questions involving the nature of reality are raised in *The Archbishop's Ceiling* (1977), *Fame* (1978), *Elegy for a Lady* (1980), *Some Kind of Love Story* (1980), *Clara* (1987), and *I Can't Remember Anything* (1987). More universal concerns can be found in all of Miller's work, but specific metaphysical issues such as the problem of fate and free will and the nature of good and evil are dealt with directly in *The Creation of the World and Other Business* (1972) and *Up from Paradise* (1974).

Also the author of numerous essays and short stories, Miller will always be remembered for his notable achievements in the theater. Winner of the Pulitzer Prize (1949) and other prestigious awards, Miller has made an indelible mark on the American theater with his technical innovations and enlightened vision of the human condition. His timeless tragedies about eternal conflicts between parents and children, men and women, and the individual and society will serve as universally significant reminders of the need for personal integrity and moral and social responsibility. *See also* Theater.

STEVEN R. CENTOLA

BIBLIOGRAPHY

Bigsby, C. W. E. *A Critical Introduction to Twentieth-Century American Drama.* Vol. 2. Cambridge, Eng.: Cambridge University Press, 1984.

Carson, Neil. *Arthur Miller.* New York: Grove Press, 1984.

Martin, Robert A., ed. *Arthur Miller: New Perspectives.* Englewood Cliffs, N.J.: Prentice-Hall, 1982.

——. *The Theater Essays of Arthur Miller.* New York: Penguin, 1978.

Martine, James J., ed. *Critical Essays on Arthur Miller.* Boston: Hall, 1979.

Miller, Arthur. *Arthur Miller's Collected Plays.* 2 vols. New York: Viking Press, 1957, 1981.

——. *Salesman in Beijing.* New York: Viking Press, 1983.

Nelson, Benjamin. *Arthur Miller: Portrait of a Playwright.* New York: McKay, 1970.

Welland, Dennis. *Miller: The Playwright.* London: Methuen, 1983.

Minnesota. German Jews were among the early fur buyers and peddlers who came to Minnesota from New York and the South to trade with the Indians. By 1881, 600 had settled in as merchants, manufacturers of clothing, furniture, and leather goods, dealers in scrap metal or hides and furs, doctors and attorneys, etc. Patterns of accommodation were already being established. In St. Paul, the state capitol, Jews had considerable wealth, high social status, and public acceptance from German and Irish Catholic neighbors. In small towns the pattern was similar. Only in Minneapolis, the state's largest city, was there significant anti-Semitism from both the working class (Scandinavian and Central European) and the Protestant establishment, Easterners amassing great wealth in lumber, milling, railroads, retailing, and wholesaling.

On July 14, 1882, 200 impoverished, Yiddish-speaking Russian refugees arrived in St. Paul. More came subsequently, and by year's end, Minnesota's Jewish population had doubled to about 1200. By 1900, St. Paul had 4000 Jews, Minneapolis 5000, northern Minnesota and Duluth some 3000 as the Mesabi Range iron mines opened. The Jewish population of the state peaked in 1937, with 43,700, including 4000 in Duluth. Out-migration after World War II, much of it to California and the Southwest, has reduced Minnesota's Jewish population to about 31,000, less than 1 percent of Minnesota's 4.2 million people. There are about 500 in Duluth, 500 in Rochester (many doctors at the Mayo Clinic), 600 more in small towns, including Hibbing, Eveleth, Chisholm, St. Cloud, Austin, Albert Lea, Mankato, and Virginia (where 40 members support a 1908 synagogue listed on the National Historic Register as the oldest in the state). The rest are in the seven-county Minneapolis–St. Paul metropolitan area, where half the state's population lives; 22,000 in greater Minneapolis (2.3 percent of the population), and about 7000 in greater St. Paul.

The East Europeans did not reproduce New York's pushcart jungle. They were peddlers, but they were also carpenters, tailors, printers, ironworkers, butchers, bakers, teachers, grain traders, scrap dealers, and manufacturers of leather items, clothing, furs, and cigars. Several thousand were "HIAS farmers" who soon moved into town. Their sons and daughters attended the University of Minnesota in Minneapolis and became doctors, lawyers, social workers, and school teachers. Their integration into Jewish life locally and nationally was typified by I. S. Joseph, a Romanian, the first East European elected president (1933–1944) of Minneapolis's Temple Israel (Reform), and Fanny Fligelman Brin, who graduated from the University of Minnesota in 1907, Phi Beta Kappa, and became national president (1932–1938) of the National Council of Jewish Women.

Minneapolis alone had 94 Jewish organizations by 1930, including socialist groups like Workmen's Circle, which built the Labor Lyceum, and active Zionists who established an achsherah (its "graduates" were founders of Kfar Blum, Israel). Early synagogues were Minneapolis's Temple Israel (Reform, founded as Shaarai Tov, 1878), Adath Jeshurun Synagogue (Conservative, 1884), Kenesseth Israel (Orthodox, 1891), and St. Paul's Sons of Jacob (Orthodox, 1872) and the state's oldest congregation, Mount Zion (Reform, 1856). In 1962, Rabbi Moshe Feller came from New York to spread the tenets of Lubavitch Hasidism; the Lubavitch Center and Bais Chana women's institute are in St. Paul. Today there are six congregations in St. Paul, eight in Minneapolis, and one in Duluth, which shares its rabbi with neighboring Superior, Wisconsin. Minneapolis Talmud Torah opened in 1894, St. Paul's Capitol Center Hebrew School (now Talmud Torah) in 1912, Duluth Talmud Torah in 1905. Minneapolis and St. Paul organized federated fund campaigns in the 1930s; Minneapolis traditionally ranks first nationally in per capita donations (e.g., over $525 per capita in 1987–1988).

In the 1930s anti-Semitism increased markedly in Minneapolis. Fascist leaders and evangelizing clergy preached anti-Semitism from pulpits and on the radio. A whispering campaign about then-Governor Elmer Benson's alleged "Jewish connections" helped elect Harold Stassen governor in 1938. Jews were discriminated against in jobs, housing, admission to hospitals and the University of Minnesota's professional and graduate schools. Banks, major corporations like 3M and Honeywell, retailers like Dayton-Hudson, and smaller businesses as well had few, if any, Jewish employees. Even some Jewish entrepreneurs hesitated to hire Jewish receptionists or sales clerks for fear of "offending" clients or customers. Jews were not even permitted to join the local branch of the American Automobile Association because they might want to use the organization's suburban clubhouse. However, by the time Minneapolis was dubbed the "anti-Semitism capital of the U.S." by journalist Carey McWilliams in 1948, change was already underway, led by a local chapter of the B'nai B'rith Anti-Defamation League and the Minnesota Jewish Council, founded in 1938, and by men like young Hubert H. Humphrey, elected mayor of Minneapolis in 1945. Humphrey immediately established a Mayor's Council on Human Relations and pushed through pioneering Fair Employment and Fair Housing ordinances. Postwar prosperity also helped. The Jewish community-financed Mt. Sinai Hospital opened in 1948, and Jews took leadership roles in funding the Variety Club Heart Hospital at the University of Minnesota and a wide variety of civic and cultural buildings and programs.

As recently as 1986, rural Minnesotans blamed farm foreclosures on "Jewish bankers." Yet Minnesotans have elected two senators who are Jewish, Rudy Boschwitz (1978-1990) and Paul Wellstone (1990-   ), and have elected Jews to state and local office, and even Minneapolis elected a Jewish mayor (Arthur Naftalin, 1961-1969), as has St. Paul (Lawrence Cohen, 1972-1976) and Austin (George Hirsh, 1924). Jews are, or have been, directors or presidents of formerly Protestant preserves: Minneapolis Art Institute (Samuel Sachs, Alan Shestack, and Evan Maurer, director; Marvin Borman, president), Walker Art Center (Martin Friedman, director; Erwin Kelen, president), Greater Minneapolis Chamber of Commerce (Jay Phillips, president), United Way (Marvin Borman, chairman), St. Paul Chamber Orchestra (Pinchas Zukerman, conductor), Minnesota Orchestral Association (Luella Goldberg, president).

Significant Minnesota contributors to Jewish life include Rabbis David Aronson, Kassel Abelson, and Arnold Goodman, all of Minneapolis (the only three pulpit rabbis west of the Mississippi to be elected president of the international Rabbinical Assembly), Rabbis Albert G. Minda and Gunther Plaut (presidents, Central Conference of American Rabbis), Marver Bernstein (president of Brandeis University), Rabbi Kassel and Shirley Abelson (founders, United Synagogue Youth, 1948), Miriam Freund Rosenthal (past national president, Hadassah), and Viola Hymes (past national president, National Council of Jewish Women).

Other prominent Minnesotans have included Geri Joseph (U.S. ambassador to the Netherlands during the Carter administration), her husband, grain trader Burton Joseph (national chairman, Anti-Defamation League), theater entrepreneur Ben Berger (founder of Radio Free Europe and Amicus), humorist Max Shulman (author and creator of "Dobie Gillis"), Irving Shapiro of E. I. DuPont (first practicing Jew elected president of a Fortune 500 company), and Thermo-King founder Joseph Numero (who revolutionized truck transportation of refrigerated products). Melvin Calvin of St. Paul received the Nobel Prize for chemistry in 1961 for research in physical organic theory. Celebrities in the entertainment field include singer Bob (Zimmerman) Dylan, baseball player Morrie Arnovich (New York Giants, Philadelphia Phillies), and Minnesota Vikings founder and owner Max Winter.

RHODA G. LEWIN

BIBLIOGRAPHY

Berman, Hyman. "Jews in Minnesota." In *They Chose Minnesota: A Survey of the State's Ethnic Groups*, edited by June Drenning Holmquist. St. Paul: Minnesota Historical Society, 1981.

Gordon, Albert I. *Jews in Transition*. Minneapolis: University of Minnesota, 1949.

Kramer, Judith R., and Leventman, Seymour. *Children of the Gilded Ghetto: Conflict Resolutions of Three Generations of American Jews*. New York: Archon Books, 1961.

Plantz, W. Gunther. *The Jews in Minnesota*. New York: American Jewish Historical Society, 1959.

Morgenthaus—Henry, Sr., Henry, Jr., and Robert.

A philanthropic and involved Jewish family, the Morgenthaus have been prominent in American culture as well as Jewish-American affairs. Henry Morgenthau, Sr. (1856-1946), was born in Germany and came to the United States at the age of 10. He attended Columbia Law School and went on to earn his fortune in real estate. He was the Democratic National Committee's treasurer during the 1912 presidential campaign and actively worked for Woodrow Wilson. He was rewarded with the ambassadorship to Turkey, but returned to the United States to campaign for Wilson's reelection in 1916.

During World War I, Morgenthau was concerned with the protection of Christian missionaries, Armenians, and Jews living in Turkey. At the end of World War I, he headed a commission investigating the treatment of the Jews in Poland. Some felt that because he was Jewish he was so concerned with appearing objective that he minimized the pogroms. He subsequently chaired the League of Nations' Refugee Settlement Commission and was also an incorporator of the Red Cross.

Henry Morgenthau, Jr. (1891-1967), was born in New York City. He attended Cornell University for three semesters between 1909 and

1913. After leaving Cornell he served an apprenticeship at the Henry Street Settlement. Eventually he was to become a successful farmer. His agricultural knowledge and his interest in social welfare made him an excellent candidate for many important state and national positions. In 1928, Governor Franklin Roosevelt appointed him chair of the New York Agricultural Advisory Commission. Morgenthau developed reforestation and soil conservation state works projects that were used as models for national programs during the Depression.

Under President Franklin Roosevelt, Morgenthau served as head of the Federal Farm Board and the Farm Credit Administration in Washington, D.C. In 1934, Morgenthau was named secretary of the treasury, the highest political appointment attained by a Jew. He revamped the department, restoring confidence in the nation's banking system. Believing that the United States would become involved in World War II, he initiated the policy of selling United States savings bonds directly to the public as a means of financing the war effort.

Morgenthau was instrumental in forcing a public awareness of Hitler's plan to exterminate the Jewish people. During World War II, the Treasury Department and the State Department were often at odds over war policies. The State Department tried to delay public recognition of the organized mass extermination of the Jews. Morgenthau was the official who finally brought the problem to President Roosevelt's attention. After attempting to work with the State Department, Morgenthau received a copy of a memorandum about the State Department's obstruction entitled "Report to the Secretary on the Acquiescence of This Government in the Murder of the Jews." Within days of receiving this report, Morgenthau went to President Roosevelt, proposing to take the rescue and refugee problem away from the State Department. Roosevelt issued executive order 9417, establishing the War Refugee Board.

The War Refugee Board was composed of the secretaries of state, treasury, and war, under the direction of John W. Pehle of the Treasury. It was responsible for rescuing and assisting war victims. The State Department and England continued to show indifference or hostility to the board's plans, and military policy was always the first consideration. The board never lived up to its potential, coming too late to really be effective.

Toward the end of the war, Morgenthau proposed a very controversial peace plan that suggested partitioning Germany and making it an agrarian society. The concept of an agrarian country in the middle of Europe was considered too radical and was unacceptable to the policy makers.

After the death of President Roosevelt, Morgenthau resigned his position of secretary of the treasury and went on to become active in the United Jewish Appeal (UJA). The UJA was a controversial organization. Some American Jews believed that the UJA had stepped beyond philanthropical work and was too involved in politics. They did not want the organization to appear to represent a Jewish political point of view that was different than the national government's policies. Because Morgenthau had just come from the highest political appointed office held by a Jew, his UJA involvement gave the organization the prestige it needed to unite the American Jews. In 1947, Morgenthau was the first person to hold the job of chairman of UJA; until then, UJA was chaired by a committee.

Between 1950 and 1954, Morgenthau served as the first chair of the Bonds for Israel Campaign. Once again, his name helped to unite the Jewish community when they were afraid that there might be a conflict between Zionism and patriotism to the United States.

His son, Robert Morgenthau (b. 1919), continues the family's commitment to public service. In 1962, he ran unsuccessfully for governor of New York. He was the United States attorney for New York State from 1961 to 1970 and is presently district attorney for New York County, a position he has held since 1975.

LINDA GLAZER

BIBLIOGRAPHY

Cohen, Naomi W. *Not Free to Desist.* Philadelphia: Jewish Publication Society, 1972.

Fishman, Priscilla, ed. *The Jews of the United States.* New York: Quadrangle/New York Times Books, 1973.

Karp, Abraham J. *Haven and Home. A History of the Jews in America.* New York: Schocken, 1985.

Madison, Charles A. *Eminent American Jews, 1776 to the Present.* New York: Ungar, 1970.

Morganthau, Henry, III. *Mostly Morganthau: A Family History.* New York: Ticknor & Fields, 1991.

Silberman, Charles E. *A Certain People.* New York: Summit Books, 1985.

Wyman, David S. *The Abandonment of the Jews. America and the Holocaust, 1941-1945.* New York: Pantheon, 1984.

Motion Pictures. *See* FILM, FILM STARS,
MOVIE MOGULS.

Movie Moguls. Although Jews did not invent
the motion picture apparatus, a relatively small
group of Jewish immigrants to America built a
massive motion picture industry whose impact on
American life and thought was profound. Called
the "movie moguls," these men built large personal fortunes on their way to creating companies
whose film entertainments provided much more
than mere enjoyment to generations the world
over. Yet their own attitudes toward being Jewish
in America reveal important tensions at the core
of American Jewish life.

Exactly who first used the term "mogul" to
describe a small group of successful businessmen
involved in the making of motion pictures is lost
in the myths surrounding Hollywood. That this
should be so is hardly surprising. Yet why precisely the term mogul? Beyond the alliteration of
movie mogul, it seems odd to use a term associated with the Middle Eastern world of Muslim
rulers. The term was never applied to the great
nineteenth-century industrialists John D. Rockefeller and Andrew Carnegie, for instance. Nor to
twentieth-century giants like Henry Ford and
Thomas Edison. No, the term mogul was, and is
still, reserved for less than a dozen men who made
a living making movies in the period from about
1908 until well into the 1950s.

That virtually all of these moguls should
have been Jewish may or may not have something
to do with the odd appellation applied to them.
Was it something about the movie business itself,
the glamor, the exoticism, the vaguely artificial
aura of the enterprise that inspired the term? Or
was it that these men, these immigrants or children of immigrants, were somehow foreign, falsely grandiose, different from other American
business magnates? The answers to these questions cannot be known with certainty, but it is
undeniably the case that the image of the movie
business and of the men who invented and perfected it is shrouded in ambivalence, and the admiration felt for these moguls is combined with
more than a degree of condescension and amusement.

That the movie moguls were virtually all
Jewish is something much more than a coincidence, whether or not the term itself contains a
hint of WASPish bemusement. For the growth
and development of the motion picture industry is
intimately tied in with the great wave of Jewish
immigration from Eastern Europe in the late nineteenth century. The invention of the motion picture camera and attendant technologies is surely
coincidental with this mass migration, but the
subsequent growth of the movie business surely is
not. The movie business was primarily an urban
phenomenon and even beyond that, an immigrant
and working-class phenomenon. A number of
factors conspired to make this so. Among the
middle class, popular leisure pursuits included
mass-market books and magazines. Beyond the
fact that many of the magazines, in particular, had
an overt appeal to "genteel" values was the fact
that many immigrants could not read, or if they
could they could not read English. The "high
culture" of opera or the middle-class culture of
the theater were not only beyond the interest of
the immigrant classes, among whom were many
Eastern European Jews, but also beyond their
price range. The immigrant groups formed their
own culture and their own leisure activities,
among which were vaudeville, Yiddish theater
(for the Jews), cafes, and saloons. As the motion
picture invention was perfected around the turn of
the century, movies, too, became part of the new
urban immigrant culture. Films had many of the
advantages of magazines and theater but without
the disadvantage of having to read, or even speak,
English. The silent "flickers," as they were
known, were short and simple, not only without
dialogue but frequently without written titles of
any kind. Admission to these nickelodeons was
only five or ten cents, while the theaters themselves were often little more than storefront operations with folding chairs and a cotton sheet for a
screen. Their appeal to immigrant audiences is
undeniable and the growth of the movie business
quite spectacular: By 1908, there were over 400
small theaters in New York City alone. A prestigious journal of the day estimated in 1910 that
there were at least 20,000 nickelodeons in northern cities from Chicago eastward.

From the Jewish standpoint, the invention of
the motion picture was an even happier coincidence. In addition to movies being produced and
exhibited virtually in their own (tenement) back-
yard, and the fact that linguistic barriers were
nonexistent, other factors enabled Jews to enter
the movie business. Not the least of these factors
was that there was no one there before them to
keep them out. Moreover, as the nickelodeon was
cheap to enter, it was cheap to operate. Lack of
regulation (considering that the business was

new) meant that anyone with a little capital and a lot of foresight could own and operate theaters. It is definitely no coincidence that every major movie mogul got into the business via exhibition. Beyond this, though, the particular backgrounds, experiences, and ethnic characteristics of the Jews conspired to bring about their spectacular success in the movies. In general terms, Jewish success in America has been near miraculous. The movie moguls are in this sense just part of the larger picture of Jewish success in the United States. The qualities of hard work, literacy, family bonding and values, and a certain "democracy" in religious practices enabled many Jews to escape the urban tenements in one generation or less. The movie business, in particular, also had attractions for the Eastern European Jews in that not only did it require little initial capital, it was also not primarily dependent on land or other solid property. It also involved selling, in knowing what the customer wants, and how to give it to him. Again, it is no coincidence that most of the movie moguls had backgrounds in selling, in furs, the garment trade, even in junk. Family bonding and a certain mistrust of others (non-Jews) led to a spirit of cooperation in the early days. What little capital was needed was secured from family members, from in-laws as well as uncles, aunts, and cousins. Although later such family bonding would be a source of jokes among those on the fringes of the movie business, this early practice had firm roots in ethnic background and economic necessity.

Arguably, however, the most significant factor in the Jewish dominance of the motion picture industry is the way in which Jews possessed or adopted primarily middle-class values of a particularly American sort. Community and country came first and foremost. Jewish culture in the New World paid respect both to rugged individualism and staunch family values and to the hard work of men. There was also respect for women as wives and mothers. The myth of the melting pot was played out in the films, in the lives of the moguls, and in the theaters themselves, which eventually attracted a wider diversity of racial, ethnic, and class representatives and which earned the movies the epithet, "the democratic art."

Who, then, in specific were these dozen or so men who rose to such fame and fortune that they have been compared to Oriental potentates? They were Louis B. Mayer, Adolph Zukor, Carl Laemmle, William Fox, the Warner Brothers (Harry, Jack, Sam, and Albert), Harry Cohn. And there was Nicholas and Joseph Schenck, Marcus Loew,

Jesse L. Lasky, Samuel Goldwyn, Irving Thalberg, and David O. Selznick. The only non-Jew who earned the designation mogul was Darryl F. Zanuck, who formed Twentieth Century Pictures (in partnership with Joe Schenck, with capital from Louis B. Mayer).

Of all the moguls, Louis B. Mayer could stand as a paradigm: an immigrant from Russia whose exact year of birth is in doubt (1882 or 1885 have been given, while the date of July 4 was Mayer's fanciful tribute to his adopted homeland when he was granted U.S. citizenship); whose first name was changed as was the family name (the middle initial was added some years later); and whose success was undreamt of. The films he made as head of Metro-Goldwyn-Mayer (MGM), formed in 1924, were among the most successful of the period through the 1950s. They were glossy productions with the brightest stars of the era, solidly middle class, patriotic, and "moral." Mayer himself was active in the Jewish communities in which he lived and, following his business success in the 1920s, in Republican politics, a great friend and supporter of Herbert Hoover. His crass, uneducated manner, violent temper, nepotism, shrewd practicality, and business sense were also held to be paradigmatic, both of the movie moguls and of Jews in general. The love-hate relationship people felt for Mayer contains elements of anti-Semitism and, among Jews, self-hatred. Mayer's own attitudes about himself and his country similarly reflect the Jewish desire to make it in America and the price that was paid to achieve that goal.

Initially, there seemed not to be much price to be paid in making it in America. By the late 1920s, the Jewish film producers who had started their careers modestly enough in exhibition had a virtual lock on the motion picture industry, which combined mass production with mass distribution. The studios formed by these emerging moguls have come to be known as the "Big Eight": MGM, founded by Marcus Loew and Louis B. Mayer and run by Mayer and Irving Thalberg (until the latter died in 1936); Warner Bros.; Universal, founded by Carl Laemmle; 20th Century-Fox, an outgrowth of Fox Film Co., started by William Fox; Paramount, started by Adolph Zukor and Jesse Lasky; Columbia, founded by Harry Cohn following a stint in the employ of Carl Laemmle; United Artists, which, though it was founded by filmmakers Charlie Chaplin, D. W. Griffith, Mary Pickford, and Douglas Fairbanks, was headed by Joseph

Schenck, whose brother Nicholas succeeded Marcus Loew as head of Loews, Inc., the parent company of MGM, when the latter died in 1927; and R.K.O., which emerged out of the Jewish-owned Keith-Orpheum vaudeville circuit and the Radio Corporation of America (RCA), headed by David Sarnoff.

At the same time that the Jewish businessmen were securing their virtual monopoly on film production and exhibition, the production center shifted to the once sleepy Los Angeles community of Hollywood, with which the movie moguls are intimately linked. A bifurcated structure soon emerged with corporate and financial headquarters remaining in New York. But the glamor and exoticism of the movies all belonged to Hollywood. The reasons for the move to Hollywood are many and complex. Certainly, the good weather year round was initially a necessity for the primitive technology of the film stock and camera lenses, which relied strongly on sunlight, while the variety of the landscape—ocean, mountains, desert, and city—made for interesting film backgrounds. As important as the climate was, of even greater importance was the political climate favorable to large companies. Favorable real estate prices enabled studios to acquire relatively large tracts of land at prices impossible in the urban centers, and inexpensive housing encouraged the migration of a new, primarily young work force. Of greater importance, but more difficult to define, was the lure of the Golden West, that fundamental American myth, which no doubt appealed immensely to the Jewish immigrants and urban dwellers.

Whatever the reasons for Hollywood's emergence as the dream factory, the movie moguls found themselves living dreams come true, fantasies beyond their wildest imagination; success that not even the movies would dare portray had come their way. Yet there was even in the 1920s an unease on their part that may be attributable to fears of anti-Semitism, fears that would have tragic ramifications in the 1930s and again in the 1950s. However, as far as films were concerned, almost 50 features overtly focusing on Jewish characters were released in this first decade of monopolistic gains by companies controlled by the moguls. *The Jazz Singer* (1927), credited for ushering in the era of "the talkies," was an archetypal Jewish-American story, with Al Jolson's screen character experiencing the tension between Jewish assimilation and alienation.

Yet off screen some uneasiness could be detected. The first such sign was the appointment of former Republican National Chairman and Postmaster General William Hays as head of the Motion Picture Producers and Distributors Association (MPPDA). Although the MPPDA had many functions, including lobbying against export tariffs on American films and securing loans from major banks for individual film companies, its primary task was to ward off the fury of citizen reform groups clamoring for regulation of the content of motion pictures in the wake of the star scandals of the early twenties. The moguls feared that their urban cosmopolitanism, that is, their Jewish backgrounds, would surface amidst the clamor for censorship. This was not a new nor unjustified fear, to be sure. Censorship pressures had been put on the movie makers even before the rise of the Big Eight. In fact, as early as 1908, a major campaign was mounted to close down every movie theater in New York, some 550 of them! Censorship and regulation of the movies was part and parcel of the major Progressive movements in the first two decades of the twentieth century, and almost without exception they were Protestant run and inspired. Expressed fears about increased prostitution, white slavery, drunkenness, and a general decline of the family could not disguise the antiethnic character of much of the invective, along with an attempt to resist industrialization and urbanization in general.

Movies, as initially the entertainment form of the ethnic immigrant masses, were linked to the decline in moral standards and to fears of women's debauchment. Thus, the first watch-dog organization, the National Board of Review, was established in 1909. Although it had the expressed cooperation of many film companies, its leadership was drawn from outside film-producing circles, its all-male board consisting primarily of wealthy Protestant industrialists, such as Andrew Carnegie. In the case of the MPPDA and Will Hays, however, the censorship board came from within the film industry itself. While the Hays Office, as it came to be known, did not especially clamp down on the content of the films themselves in the 1920s, it did establish a bureaucracy that later would, in fact, severely curtail the content of movies. The appointment of Hays, with his roots in the Progressive movement and his ties to the Republican establishment, to an internal organization indicates the kind of paranoia that movie makers felt. This paranoia expressed itself in greater form in the 1930s, first with the appointment of Joseph Ignatius Breen to administer the Production Code Administration (as the censorship board came to be known) in 1934 and later in the decade with the virtual banishment of overtly Jewish characters from American movies.

The 1930s in Hollywood has been characterized as its Golden Age, the term reflecting both the gold of box-office receipts and the luster of artistic achievement. With the major studios distributing at least one film per week, their stranglehold on the major movie houses, the brightest stars ever to grace a movie screen under contract, and a vast array of talented directors, writers, cinematographers, editors, costume designers, and composers equally bound by their signatures on the bottom line, the motion picture industry emerged as the most influential medium of art, entertainment and information the world had ever seen. Yet the owners of this means of artistic and commercial production continued to demonstrate a clear, if inchoate, sense of unease with their power and prestige. There is an overdetermined celebration of all-Americanism in their films (the Jewish mogul Harry Cohn of Columbia financing and distributing the films of the Italian-immigrant Frank Capra, for instance) and a clear avoidance of too many overtly political or controversial issues. This dual attitude had the tragic effect of banishing Jewish characters from American screens precisely at the same moment European Jewry was being imperiled by the rise of Nazism in Germany. As the Nazis began persecuting the Jews within Germany and Austria, Hollywood avoided the issue entirely. Fears of alienating both the lucrative overseas German-language circuit and America's ethnic Germans partly accounts for this attitude. Yet even as war with Germany loomed ever more certain, the moguls were careful to avoid any overt references to Jewish persecution and imprisonment, lest, they felt, the movies be taken as propagandizing for America's entry into the war on the Allied side in order to save European Jewry. This attitude led to much contorting, with a world of things implied to those already knowledgeable, but little onscreen to educate the lowest common denominator.

Two examples from the period will illustrate the odd twists and turns the moguls imposed upon the filmmakers. In 1939, Warner Bros. produced *Confessions of a Nazi Spy*. It was inspired by a series of articles by Leon Turrou, an FBI agent who had investigated the activities of Nazi supporters in the United States. Neither Jack nor Harry Warner were really supportive of making

the film, fearing attacks from the American Right, German Americans, and a rise of anti-Semitism. However, it is possible that the memory of Joe Kaufman, Warner's chief salesman in Germany beaten to death by Nazi thugs in 1936, helped to overcome their reluctance. As it documents the activities of American Nazis, the film avoids acknowledging the actual anti-Semitic programs in Germany. But it does allude to the Nazi racial program in the speeches of the American Nazis with their vague calls for "racial unity" and the like. Moreover, while the FBI agent who stands in for Turrou is called Inspector Renard, he is played by the Jewish-American actor Edward G. Robinson (née Emmanuel Goldberg). So that while the film does little to make explicit the virulent anti-Semitism that formed the foundation of Nazi ideology, it does draw attention to Nazism as a threat to American life.

Hold Back the Dawn (1941) demonstrates the lengths Hollywood films would often go to to repress the underlying issues. On the surface, this soap-operaish tale of a gigolo (Charles Boyer) hoping to marry a spinster (Olivia de Havilland) in order to enter the United States from Mexico seems little linked to Nazism and its anti-Semitic nightmare. Yet we must ask of the film: Who are these European refugees? Why are they in Mexico, unable to legally enter the United States? And the answer is that many of them were Jews fleeing persecution, and many (most, in fact) were unable to enter the United States due to strict immigration quotas imposed in the 1920s in an anti-Semitic fervor. In fact, one of these refugees who spent time in Mexico awaiting a visa was Billy Wilder (born in Vienna in 1906), who fled the Nazis in 1933 and who would later become a major Hollywood filmmaker, partly on the strength of screenplays like *Hold Back the Dawn*. Perhaps if both Wilder and the movie moguls had realized that Wilder's entire family would perish in the death camps, the underlying issues might have been made more explicit.

The moguls perhaps should not be completely condemned for their fears of anti-Semitism nor their belief that America would not enter the war to save European Jewry. The latter contention is certainly inarguable—the fact that the restrictive immigration policies enacted in the 1920s were not repealed is only one index among many that this is so. American isolationist feelings still ran high, and certain powerful senators, like Burton K. Wheeler of Montana and Gerald P. Nye of North Dakota, threatened the film industry with government censorship. Moveover, it is a fact that Warner Bros. experienced a wave of protests in the wake of *Confessions of a Nazi Spy*. The German consul raised a cry as did American businessmen trading with Germany. Studio executives received threats, and theater managers were similarly terrorized. Worst of all, perhaps, from the studio's point of view, was that the film was a box-office flop.

If the moguls generally avoided having overtly Jewish characters on screen, or mitigated Jewishness by casting non-Jewish actors in Jewish roles (Ricardo Cortez playing the lead in *Symphony of Six Million*, 1932, or John Barrymore in *Counsellor-at-Law*, 1933), out of fears of anti-Semitism, there was, nevertheless, a tradition of the social-problem film. This genre is often overlooked in the glossy, soft-focused image of Hollywood's Golden Age, but it does demonstrate a degree of awareness on the moguls' part of America's problems and a degree of willingness to confront them. That America was always shown to be fundamentally sound, that the political and economic system was fundamentally fair and just, should not necessarily be taken as an index of contorted all-Americanism, of pandering to popular beliefs in an effort to detract attention from oneself. The moguls had succeeded in America, had grown rich and powerful, and had no reason to doubt the virtues of such a society. A certain tradition of Jewish concern for the welfare of others, and an almost instinctual siding with the underdog, accounts for the social-problem film. This was especially prevalent at Warner Bros., whose support of Franklin Roosevelt and the New Deal was made manifest in many films. But the social-problem film did not necessarily mean the overtly political, controversial film, and this was where the moguls found themselves pitted against another group of Jews in Hollywood.

At the time the moguls actively campaigned against overtly Jewish portrayals in Hollywood films, and against anti-fascist, anti-Nazi works, another group of younger Jews attempted just the opposite. On the one hand, a number of European Jewish emigré filmmakers found their way to Hollywood. They had firsthand experience of the Nazi terror combined with a more sophisticated political and cultural sense. The moguls who had emigrated a generation earlier did not. On the other hand, the younger group was a second-generation Jewish-American clique, of writers primarily, with ties to the American Communist Party. They lobbied hard for films about the Spanish Civil War, for anti-fascist films, and for films that detailed class and racial injustice in this country. While a very small number of such films were, in fact, produced (more as the 1930s gave way to the 1940s), the moguls were more troubled by the unionizing activities of these men, especially the formation of the Screen Writers Guild in 1933. Its most active founder and vocal supporter was John Howard Lawson, an American Jew and Communist, whose labor activities earned him the enmity of the antiunion movie moguls. Many of these politically motivated directors and writers would find their careers ruined in that second severe sop to anti-Semitism on the part of the moguls, the Blacklist era. In the 1940s, however, with America at war, the moguls and their irksome politically active employees cooperated to ensure the movies a height of political and social glory unseen before or since.

America's entry into World War II provided the movie moguls with their greatest opportunity yet to demonstrate their own "America-first" attitude. They willingly produced war films of all kinds at an incredible pace. Even the vaunted Hollywood musical went to war; star actors and directors were either released from contracts or lent to the armed forces to make outright documentary and propaganda films (Frank Capra's *Why We Fight* series and John Ford's and John Huston's documentaries are the best-known examples). The studios even cooperated with the government via its Office of War Information, which not only provided updated information on the progress of the war to the studios, but actually had a hand in story and script development. The moguls, however, remained acutely conscious of Jewishness within this context. The by-now clichéd formula of the combat film seems always to have had a Jewish member of the platoon—he was either the wise-guy comic or the serious intellectual type, but in any case was always the most patriotic, typically sacrificing his own life for the sake of his (non-Jewish) buddies. The celebration, in this instance, of ethnicity was a tribute to American diversity, juxtaposed to the Nazi and Japanese claims of "racial purity." However, it was always made abundantly clear that the Jewish soldier was there to fight for America, not for his fellow overseas Jews. Thus it is important to realize, although not yet frequently noted in film histories, that during the war more combat films were produced that focused on the Pacific theater, as if to guarantee the idea that Jews fought for America, not for Judaism.

It is ironic that the previously politically engaged writers and directors who so troubled the moguls should have proven extremely valuable to them in producing effective war propaganda. Men like Alvah Bessie, Lester Cole, Edward Dmytryk, Albert Maltz, Sam Ornitz, and John Howard Lawson, not to mention Dalton Trumbo, were responsible for such effective war-related dramas as *Hitler's Children* (1942), *Action in the North Atlantic* (1943), *Sahara* (1943), *Destination Tokyo* (1944), *Thirty Seconds Over Tokyo* (1944), *Objective Burma* (1945), *Pride of the Marines* (1945), and *Back to Bataan* (1945). It is further ironic that films like *Mission to Moscow* (1943), *Song of Russia* (1943) and *North Star* (1943, with a script by Lillian Hellman), made with U.S. government cooperation to help inspire support for our Soviet allies, should return to haunt the movie moguls when a less friendly U.S. government sought to find alleged Communist influences in the film industry in the postwar period.

As the war ended, the movie moguls must have felt secure in their positions: America had won the war, the film industry had clearly helped the cause, and 1946 marked the biggest year to date in ticket sales. But this was to be a bitter calm before the storm as the film industry was rocked from within and without at U.S. government urging. In one instance, the movie moguls were blameless, if shortsighted; in the other, they again caved in to fears of anti-Semitism and to overt anti-Semitic tirades launched against them.

In 1939, the government initiated an antitrust suit against the Big Eight companies. The suit was put on hold to secure the industry's cooperation in the war effort. After the war, however, the suit was reinstituted, and in 1948 the Supreme Court ruled against the film industry. The resulting Paramount decision, or Consent Decree, forced the movie moguls to divest themselves of their theater chains. This might not have proven to be so damaging to the industry, except an even greater factor had entered the postwar world: television. Here the movie moguls attempted to respond much as the first generation of film companies had treated them, by trying to ignore and/or destroy this upstart form. This strategy was, of course, a disaster, and by 1957 attendance had fallen by half from its 1946 peak.

The antitrust suit and the rise of television are bitter coincidences to the legacy of the movie moguls when combined with the more insidious, but preventable rise of the Blacklist. The House UnAmerican Activities Committee (HUAC) investigation into Communist influences in the motion picture industry was, of course, just part of the disgraceful period known as McCarthyism. The movie moguls' cowardice in the face of political pressure was no more manifest perhaps than the Truman Administration's and, after it, Eisenhower's. But given the overtly anti-Semitic nature of the committee, led by Mississippi Congressman John Rankin and Representative J. Parnell Thomas, the moguls should have taken a firmer stand. That anti-Semitism had a large part in the attack on Hollywood seems inarguable: it is the case that 10 out of the first 19 witnesses called by HUAC in 1947 were Jews; and 6 of the 10 later indicted by the committee (the so-called Hollywood Ten) were Jews: Alvah Bessie, Herbert Biberman, Lester Cole, John Howard Lawson, Albert Maltz, and Sam Ornitz. With the revelations of the Holocaust fresh on the minds of all Americans, the moguls might have regretted their "de-Semiticization" of the thirties' films. Here, then, was a chance to take a stand, to speak out against anti-Semitism under the guise of anti-Communism. Again, tragically, they did not. Instead, they diligently worked, once again, to prove their patriotism and instituted a house cleaning in excess of what all but the most rabid right-winger would have demanded. In this respect, the moguls' response to the witch hunts mirrors the death penalty meted out to the Rosenbergs by Jewish Judge Irving Kaufman and the nationwide attempt by Jewish organizations to disassociate Jews from communism. The response to McCarthyism is thus perhaps more revealing of how the Jews felt about living in America than any indication of the movie moguls' unique attitudes and responses. Nevertheless, the Blacklist was perpetrated against Jews far in excess of any other group—perpetrated against Jews by fellow Jews.

It can be claimed that the witch hunts provided the moguls with a chance to seek revenge against many of the union and guild organizers of the thirties. Thus the moguls will be seen as small minded and petty rather than cowardly—an image of the moguls made popular by the genre of the anti-Hollywood novel that arose in the 1930s. So much of the popular mythology surrounding Hollywood has been derived in some ways from this genre, itself overwhelmingly produced by Jews (Nathanael West's *Day of the Locust*, 1939; Budd Schulberg's *What Makes Sammy Run?* 1941). Similarly, tales of the moguls' crassness, their vulgarity and bad taste, their classlessness has been spread through novels, short stories, and newspaper columns equally disproportionately written by Jews. Even stories of how the moguls mangled the English language, many attributed especially to Sam Goldwyn and immortalized as "Goldwynisms," were spread by Jews. These tales of vulgarity and ignorance on the moguls' part (even if true, why should one have expected anything different from self-taught, uneducated immigrants?) smack of Jewish self-hatred, of an embarrassment on the part of Jews about the behavior of fellow Jews. Like the actions of the moguls themselves who wished to divert attention from Jewishness, so, too, many second- and third-generation American Jews went out of their way to deride the moguls. It may be taken as indicative of this attitude that the fairest, most intriguing Hollywood novel of all was produced by a non-Jew, F. Scott Fitzgerald, who fictionalized the life of Irving Thalberg for *The Last Tycoon* (1941).

In the end, however, it was certainly not the anti-Hollywood novel, nor the Consent Decree, nor the rise of television that ended the reign of the movie moguls; nor, despite the enmity it produced, was it the Blacklist that humbled the moguls. It was rather, their mere mortality that did them in. Carl Laemmle, first of the great moguls, was first to go in 1939; Louis B. Mayer, king of the moguls, died in 1957; Harry Cohn, the most hated, apparently, of them all, followed shortly thereafter in 1958; David O. Selznick, the classiest of them, passed on in 1965; Joseph and Nicholas Schenck, perhaps less famous than their peers, but no less powerful, died in the 1960s, Joseph in 1961 and Nicholas in 1969; Samuel Goldwyn saw his company stay alive into the new era, but he passed away in 1974; Adolph Zukor lived to an amazing 103 years old, but 1976 saw his demise; Jack Warner survived all of his brothers and the rest of the moguls, too, but 1978 saw his passing. Changing times and old age slowed them down, but nothing, not even their deaths, has erased them from the popular consciousness. They created more than an industry, these immigrant Jews, they created a national image and way of life. *See also* Film.

DAVID DESSER

BIBLIOGRAPHY

Basinger, Jeanine. *The World War II Combat Film: Anatomy of a Genre.* New York: Columbia University Press, 1987.

Erens, Patricia. *The Jew in American Cinema.* Bloomington: Indiana University Press, 1984.

Friedman, Lester. *Hollywood's Image of the Jew.* New York: Ungar, 1982.

Gabler, Neal. *An Empire of Their Own: How the Jews Invented Hollywood.* New York: Crown, 1988.

Koppes, Clayton R., and Black, Gregory D. *Hollywood Goes to War: How Politics, Profits, and Propaganda Shaped World War II Movies.* New York: Free Press, 1987.

May, Lary. *Screening Out the Past: The Birth of Mass Culture and the Motion Picture Industry.* New York: Oxford University Press, 1980.

Navasky, Victor. *Naming Names.* New York: Viking Press, 1980.

Wyman, David S. *The Abandonment of the Jews: America and the Holocaust, 1941–1945.* New York: Pantheon, 1984.

Music, Cantorial. Cantorial music always interacts with its host culture in the Diaspora. Among the various waves of Jewish immigration to America, however, Eastern Ashkenazic ethnicity has exerted the strongest influence. Its Slavic/Oriental song pervades even the Protestantized Reform ritual, in the form of neo-Hasidic refrains. These, plus indigenous American folk motifs, are opening new paths to a younger generation.

SEVENTEENTH AND EIGHTEENTH CENTURIES. American cantorial music got its start in 1654, when the Inquisition drove 23 Brazilian Jews to Dutch New Amsterdam in what is now the state of New York. The synagogue song of these early settlers and their descendants mirrored their Western European Sephardic heritage, specifically the Amsterdam-London rite that survived the 1492–1498 expulsions from Spain and Portugal. That rite—known as the London minhag—is austere and measured, sung with precision by the entire congregation. Congregational prayer is normally chanted less formally than solo synagogal Bible reading (called cantillation), which follows neume signs (called *te'amim* in Hebrew or *trop* in Yiddish), printed above or below each word. Of the musical motifs assigned to various neume signs, two—*dargä* and *tevir*—are universally used in the reading of either the Five Books of Moses (Torah) or the Scrolls (*Megillot*) of Ruth-Ecclesiastes-Song of Solomon.

Example 1a shows the neume motifs for *dargä* and *tevir* (bracketed in the music), here used in London-minhag congregational prayer. The text, from Moses's Song at the Sea (Exodus 15:1–21), appears in daily *Shacharit* or morning worship.

EXAMPLE 1

The Sephardic London-Minhag, Incorporating Neume Motifs *Dargä* and *Tevïr* in Shacharit Prayer

a. Isaac Levy, *Antología de Liturgia Judeo-Española* (Jerusalem: Ministry of Education and Culture, 1975), Vol. VII, pp. 21–22. Reprinted by permission.

b. Emanuel Aguilar, David Aaron de Sola, and E. R. Jessurum, *Sephari Melodies* (London: Oxford, 1930), p. 30.

. . . et hashirah hazot ladonai . . .

1. [Then Moses . . . sang] this song . . .

. . . ozi vezimrat yah

2. The Lord is my strength and my song.

Example 1b, another London-minhag congregational song, is from a liturgical poem on the Binding of Isaac, by Judah Samuel Abbas (died in Aleppo, Syria, 1167). It, too, uses the universal *dargä* and *tevïr* neume motifs (bracketed).

Al har asher kavod . . .

Upon a mountain radiant
with God's glory,
stand the binder [Abraham],
the one who is bound [Isaac],
and the altar!

Early Sephardic congregations include Shearith Israel (New York City, 1654), Jeshuath Israel (Newport, R.I., 1658), Mikveh Israel (Savannah, Ga., 1735), Mikveh Israel (Philadelphia, Pa. 1747), and Beth Elohim (Charleston, S.C., 1749). After 1700, the Ashkenazic (Northern and Eastern European) component of Jewry grew in America, leaving Sephardic Jews a proud but isolated minority. But Ashkenazic practice treats music less rigidly than the Sephardic London minhag, allowing worshippers to recite most prayers in an undertone, with the cantor improvising paragraph openings and closing blessings.

Such dependence upon improvisation—in the absence of a well-trained cantorate—left no musical trail of early Ashkenazic practice in America.

Religious denominations during the late seventeenth and early eighteenth centuries followed the egalitarian congregationalist structure of all denominations in this country, but especially that of the dominant group, Protestantism. Instead of a governmentally organized religious community to which local branches might be held accountable, as in Europe, Jewish immigrants encountered a system of separately autonomous sects. For the first time in the long history of the Diaspora, individual synagogues in America determined their own rites free of a hierarchal superstructure.

NINETEENTH CENTURY. The nineteenth-century pattern is one of minorities within congregations resigning over ritual issues—Ashkenazic versus Sephardic at first, Reform versus Orthodox later on. At the time of the early splits (1801–1825) there were about 10,000 Jews scattered throughout the United States. Each community still constituted an independent congregation that set its own religious standards, much like the isolated towns of colonial New England. Synagogues had no pulpits and did not employ preaching rabbis. The office of spiritual leader was filled by a cantor who functioned as a minister. Gershom Mendes Seixas (1745–1816), the first American-born hazan (as the cantor is still called in Sephardic congregations) was a trustee of Columbia University as well.

But a cantor functioning as minister proved at best a stopgap. Although communities required a *Sheli'ach Tsibbur*, or Messenger-in-Prayer, to hold worship services, most qualified cantors refused to leave Europe for an uncertain life in the New World. Those who came were generally unversed in Jewish law; the only Talmudic requirement they fulfilled was possessing "a pleasant voice" (Taanit: 16a). As public worship suffered, critics began blaming cantor ministers for all the evils that beset American synagogues, from lack of decorum to lack of spiritual content.

In 1840, the first ordained rabbi, Abraham Rice (1802–1862) of Bavaria, came to Nidche Israel in Baltimore. His arrival heralded a steady immigration of German Jews who would eventually transform American Jewish society from isolated congregationalist communities into nationally organized religious denominations. The process began in 1848 with modifications in ritual: spoken prayer took the place of chant; a rabbi reader took the place of the cantor; services were shortened; and liturgical poetry—in the form of laudatory hymns (*piyyutim*) and penitential laments (*Selichot*)—was eliminated.

Progressive congregations associated themselves with the emerging Reform Movement. Begun in Sessen, Westphalia, in 1810, Reform Judaism flourished in the United States; American tolerance for all religious groups meshed with the Reformers' program of multiple Judaisms, i.e., liberal along with traditional. The Union of American Hebrew Congregations organized in 1873, and Hebrew Union College opened its doors in 1875.

Synagogues not yet ready to discard their traditionalist image formed the Conservative Movement, founding the Jewish Theological Seminary in 1877 and the United Synagogue in 1913. Orthodoxy established the Isaac Elchanan Theological Seminary in 1897 and the Union of Orthodox Jewish Congregations in 1898.

In the middle of the nineteenth century, regular choirs began to supplant the occasional ones that had earlier appeared only at synagogue consecrations, such as that of Shearith Israel (New York City, 1818). Unaccompanied synagogue music for cantor and choir typically came from Vienna (Example 2a), and Paris (Example 2b). The twelfth-century text of Example 2a imitates Arabic *hazag* meter (half-short-short-long syllables), yet its nineteenth-century tune is in ¾ time, Vienna-waltz style.

Adon olam asher malach . . .

Eternal God who antedated
every living thing,
acclaimed by all which he created
to be the sov'reign King.

The text of Example 2b is biblical (Psalm 29:2–3), linking parallel ideas of 21 syllables (congregation) and 14 syllables (cantor) into a proportion of 3:2. However, its symmetrical, French-operetta-style melody equalizes the two uneven verses. The Hebrew 21-to-14 ratio, unfortunately, vanishes in translation.

Havu ladonai kevod shemo . . .

2. Ascribe to the Lord the glory
   of his name,
   worship the Lord in holy array.
3. The voice of the Lord is
   upon the waters,
   the God of glory thunders.

Pursuit of economic opportunity swelled the Jewish population to 200,000 by 1860. Mostly Germans, their aim was to Americanize themselves as rapidly as possible. It was an easy step to equate Americanism with its dominant religious denomination, Protestantism. By 1870, an industrial-age elitism prevailed throughout the reunified nation's Northeastern cities. This two-tiered social structure was anything but egalitarian: factory-owner church trustees imported well-known ministers who preached to masses of worker parishioners. Soon synagogues followed church architecture in emphasizing the preaching pulpit, and Jewish services aped the Protestant practice of stressing the sermon. Congregational participation consisted of hymn singing, which, in many synagogues, was supported by newly installed organs, following the lead of Beth Elohim in Charleston (1838).

The German-Romantic melody of Example 3, with organ accompaniment, comes from Berlin's Jewish religious community. Using a call-and-response between cantor and congregation, it is typical of late-nineteenth-century American synagogue hymnody as well.

Ein Keiloheinu, ein kadoneinu . . .

None is like our God, none like our Lord;
none like our King, none like our Redeemer.

THE CANTORATE: NINETEENTH CENTURY.

The first full-time professional cantors

EXAMPLE 2
Nineteenth-Century Synagogue Music from Vienna and Paris

a. Salomon Sulzer, *Schir Zion* (Vienna: Published by the author, 1839), No. 18.
b. Samuel Naumbourg, *Chants religieux des Israëlites* (Paris: Published by the author, 1847), No. 42.

EXAMPLE 3
Call-and-Response Treatment of a Hymn, with Organ Accompaniment

Louis Lewandowsky, *Todah W'simrah* (Berlin: Published by the author, 1876), No. 83.

brought over from Europe were G. M. Cohen (Emanu-El, New York, 1845), Jacob Fraenkel (Rodeph Sholom, Philadelphia, 1848), Leon Sternberger (Anshe Chesed, New York, 1849), Ignatius Ritterman (B'nai Jeshurun, New York, 1855), Samuel Welsh (Ahavas Chesed, New York, 1865), Alois Kaiser (Ohev Sholom, Baltimore, 1866), and Moritz Goldstein (B'nai Israel, Cincinnati, 1881).

The American cantor's role would change radically during the century's second half. In 1849, the cantor was still required "to chant in the ancient traditional style," according to the minutes of New York City's Congregation Emanu-El. Two years later Rabbi Isaac Mayer Wise (1819–1900), the "father" of American Reform, abolished the office of cantor at Anshe Emeth Temple in Albany, New York. Instead, Rabbi Wise read both prayer and Scripture, a radical departure that put cantorial music on hold in American Reform temples for the better part of a century.

Cantorial music stems from the ancient first fruits of Israel's religious awakening. The classic texts, codified into Scripture and prayer book and Bible as the written record of living speech, were always sung, never read. The form that this singing took—sacred chant—evolved over two millenia and perfectly suited its Hebrew liturgy.

When Rabbi Wise excised cantorial music, he effectively changed the language of prayer in American Reform temples. To replace Hebrew chant, he and other Reform rabbis published a series of hymnals, using predominantly German and English texts. Since no music existed for the newly created hymn texts, the *Union Hymnal* of 1897 borrowed melodies from oratorio, folksong, and Christmas carols: "I Know That My Redeemer Liveth" (hymn #3), "Auld Lang Syne" (hymn #80), "Deutschland ueber alles" (hymn #95), and "Hark! The Herald Angels Sing" (part II, hymn #8).

Two Reform organist choirmasters composed their own music, borrowing freely from operatic themes: Sigmund Schlesinger (1835–1906) of Mobile and Max Spicker (1856–1912) of New York City. Three Reform cantors—Alois Kaiser (1840–1908) of Baltimore, Samuel Welsh (1835–1901) of New York City, and Moritz Goldstein (1840–1906) of Cincinnati—collaborated in producing a four-volume liturgical anthology, *Zimrath Yah* (New York, 1871–1886). It did not take root, nor did the efforts of Edward Stark (1863–1918) of San Francisco.

THE CANTORATE: EARLY TWENTIETH CENTURY. In the wake of Russian persecutions after 1880, an influx to the United States of 2 million largely traditional Eastern European Jews to the United States began. This served as counterweight to some of American Reform's liberal excesses. Among the first Orthodox cantors to take up synagogue posts in New York were Boruch Schorr (Mogen Avrohom, 1891), Alter Karniol (Ohab Zedek, 1893), Pinchos Minkowsky (Adath Jeshurun, 1897), and Israel Cooper (Kalvarier, 1900).

After World War I, with the impoverishment of European communities, more top-notch traditional cantors fled to the United States, prompting claims of a Golden Age: Zeidel Rovner and Yossele Rosenblatt (1912), Aryeh Rutman and Berele Chagy (1913), Samuel Malavsky (1914), Jacob Beimel (1916), David Roitman, Zavel Kwartin, Herman Semiatin, Joseph Shlisky, and Abba Weisgal (1920), Mordechai Hershman and Adolph Katchko (1921), Samuel Vigoda (1923), David Steinberg and Israel Schorr (1924), Pierre Pinchik (1925), and Leib Glantz (1926).

Cantorial recitatives of that era are typically virtuostic. Phonograph recordings "froze" immensely popular prayer interpretations, encouraging every would-be cantor to parody salient features, stifling potential for variant treatments of the same texts. Moreover, cantors recorded only set pieces—those rare static moments during the service—while neglecting the fluidity that was the hallmark of their practice.

One such static set piece, *Hashkiveinu* (excerpted in Example 4), was published in 1927 by the celebrated "King of Cantors," Yossele Rosenblatt. To maintain listener interest, it combines neume motifs, harmonic sequences, motivic sequences, Middle Eastern stepwise motion, operatic cadenzas, vocal-register shifts (e.g., upper/lower), and a lullabylike folk refrain (all bracketed below the music). These elements—plus choice of prayer mode (a sacred vocal pattern of traditional motifs that retains its identity even though melody, rhythm, and note intervals and note sequences change, according to where in the liturgy the text is sung)—combine to form what cantors call the *nusach* (literally, formula) of the chant. The *nusach* of Rosenblatt's *Hashkiveinu* opens in the didactic or teaching mode, *Magein Avot* (Our Forbears' Shield; first two phrases) and then enlists the devices listed above to create a varied musical tapestry.

EXAMPLE 4
"Golden Age" Set Piece

Yossele Rosenblatt, *Tefiloth Josef* (New York: Metro, 1927), No. 4.

Unfortunately, Rosenblatt never recorded this piece, to which he surely would have brought the same beautiful tone and agile delivery exhibited in the 122 other compositions that he did record.

Hashkiveinu adonai eloheinu, leshalom . . .

Cause us, O God, to lie down in peace, and raise us up, O our King, to life . . . Shield us from every enemy . . .

Shelter us beneath thy wings . . .
Spread over us thy tabernacle of peace.

BETWEEN THE WORLD WARS. The 1932 *Union Hymnal*, while including new settings by European refugees Joseph Achron (1886–1943), Heinrich Schalit (1886–1976), and Jacob Weinberg (1879–1956), also quotes Mozart (hymn #10), Haydn (hymn #60), Rossini (hymn #140), and Handel (hymn #175).

The 1933 *Sacred Service* of Ernest Bloch (1880–1959), commissioned by a Reform group in San Francisco, is a high-water mark of twentieth-century synagogue song. Example 5 shows the seventh part of a doxology, known as the *Kedushah*, that is sung during the Amidah (Standing Devotion).

Echad hu eloheinu . . .

One is our God, our Father, our Saviour;
and He in his mercy will again proclaim to us,
in the presence of all living . . .

Cantor and choir alternate in developing a melody reminiscent of a synagogue motif so old that Jewish tradition categorizes it—as it does most ancient practices—under the heading *Misinai* (literally, from Mount Sinai), as if God had handed it down to Moses with the other commandments in the Torah. Since *Misinai* motifs, or "tunes," are musical themes subject to endless variations, Bloch was correct in successively varying this one, based on the cantor's chant as he asks Divine permission (*reshut*) to approach God during the High Holy Day liturgy. Be it coincidence or the unconscious recapturing of a traditional melody heard in childhood, the fact is that Bloch succeeded in evoking something from deep within snyagogal tradition. He treated the elusive strain as only a composer familiar with cantorial practice could—responsively.

In addition to Bloch, composers Lazare Saminsky (1882–1959), Frederick Jacobi (1891–1952), Abraham Binder (1895–1967), and Lazar Weiner (1897–1982) also helped reshape the Re-

EXAMPLE 5
Development of a Melody Reminiscent of a *Misinai* Tune

From *Sacred Service* by Ernest Bloch. Copyright © 1934 by Summy-Birchard Publishing Company. Renewal, 1962, assigned to Broude Brothers. Copyright © 1962 by Broude Brothers. Reprinted by permission of Broude Brothers Limited.

EXAMPLE 6
Biblically Inspired Reform Settings

a. Lazare Saminsky, *Sabbath Evening Services* (New York: Bloch, 1930), pp. 26–27. Reprinted by permission.

b. Frederick Jacobi, *Ahavas Olom* (New York: Bloch, 1952), p. 7. Reprinted by permission.

c. Abraham W. Binder, *Morning Service for the New Year* (New York: Transcontinental, 1957), p. 38.

d. Lazar Weiner, *Likras Shabos* (New York: Mills, 1954), p. 3. Copyright © 1954 (renewed 1952) by Mill Music, Inc. All rights reserved. International copyright secured.

Neume-motif parallels. HAF—Haftarah; LAM—Lamentations; RES—Ruth, Ecclesiastes, Song of Solomon. Solomon Rosowsky, "Neume Motifs for the Yearly Cycle of Biblical Chant, According to the Lithuanian Tradition," unpublished manuscript, Jewish Theological Seminary, New York, 1958. In Joseph A. Levine, *Synagogue Song in America* (Crown Point, Ind: White Cliffs, 1989), Appendix B.

form service, choosing thematic material from Bible reading.

Example 6a, by Saminsky, is from the conclusion of every Amidah:

> May the words of my mouth
> and the meditations of my heart
> be acceptable unto thee, O Lord,
> my Rock and my redeemer, Amen.

Example 6b, by Jacobi, is from the second blessing preceding the evening Shema or Declaration of Faith, *Ahavat Olam* (With Everlasting Love):

> *nasi'ach bechukecha . . .*

> We rejoice in thy laws.

Example 6c, by Binder, introduces the shofar ritual, that portion of the Rosh Hashanah liturgy in which a ram's horn is sounded.

> The Lord reigneth (Psalm 47:8).

Example 6d, by Weiner, is from *Lechah, Dodi* (Come, My Beloved), a Sabbath-welcoming hymn from the *Kabbalat Shabbat* service.

> *Sof ma'aseh bemachashavah techilah . . .*

> Sabbath was first in God's scheme,
> but the last to be wrought.

Neume-motif parallels to the right of each musical illustration follow Solomon Rosowsky's codification of the Lithuanian Bible-reading tradition, the one most heard in America.

Among the mid-twentieth-century Orthodox cantors of repute were Benzion Kapov-Kagan (1899–1953), Moishe Oysher (1907–1958), Leibele Waldman (1907–1969), and Moshe Ganchoff (b. 1905). Their recordings attest to an accomplished vocalism devoted more to rehashing the prior generation's proven formulas than to serious attempts at originality. Conservative cantors followed Orthodox practice except that they avoided the improvisation crucial to Orthodox style.

POST-WORLD WAR II. As a result of the decimation of European Jewry during World War II, American cantorial music was finally on its own. Joining Eastern European immigrants Moshe Koussevitsky (1899–1966), Israel Alter (1901–1979), Jacob Koussevitsky (1903–1959), David Koussevitsky (1911–1985), and Sholom Katz (1919–1982) were two native American cantors, Jan Peerce (1904–1984), and Richard Tucker (1914–1975). With European cantorial music in decline, the Reform, Conservative, and Orthodox movements launched American cantorial schools, including the School of Sacred Music (1948), the Cantors Institute (1952), and the Cantorial Training Institute (1954). Their alumni graduated into professional cantorial organizations of the three movements: Cantors Assembly (Conservative, 1947); American Conference of Certified Cantors (Reform, 1953), and Cantorial Council (Orthodox, 1960).

In 1954, the School of Sacred Music reissued *25 Out of Print Classics of Synagogue Music*, documenting continuity in nineteenth-century European practice. Volume 6, for instance, a 1905 edition of 1839 material from Vienna, offers the Call to Prayer, *Barechu*, from the Friday-night evening service, or Maariv. The chant is written in a "plagal"-major mode, whose characteristic range is from a fourth below its final note to a fifth above (Example 7a). Its mood is optimistic: God reigns on high; man below; all's right with the world. Volume 24, from Czestochowa, Poland, 1908, treats *Barechu* in like manner (Example 7b).

Cantor's call: *Barechu et adonai hamevorach . . .*

Bless ye the Lord who is to be praised.

Congregation's response: *Baruch adonai hamvorach le'olam va'ed*

Blessed is the Lord who is to be praised forevermore.

Eastern European immigrants to America modified this Friday-night Maariv tradition, preferring a "plagal" minor mode. The shift to minor—in the *congregation's response*—surfaced in 1951 (Example 7c). By 1968, the transition to "plagal"-minor was complete (Example 7d); American Jewry preferred this prayer mode—associated with penitence—until very recently. Example 7e shows two parallels to American Friday-night practice, in the Yom Kippur prayer that asks forgiveness from all personal vows: Kol Nidre. The two Kol Nidre "forgiveness" motifs parallel *et Adonai* (the Lord) and *hamvorach* (who is to be praised), bracketed in Friday-night Example 7d.

What was there about the Eastern European experience that warranted welcoming the Sabbath with a forgiveness chant, as if it were a weekly Day of Atonement? Under the czar, evidently, Shabbat (Sabbath) *was* like Yom Kippur, so the same tune fit. And when—in desperation—Russian Jews emigrated to America, their life was still a struggle; initially, they had no reason for modulating to a more joyous mode. Later, their cantorial music brightened along with their economic and social environment.

Following World War II, thousands of Jewish servicemen, returning from overseas, belatedly started families. Conservativism saw its greatest growth at that time, attracting young couples who had grown up in city tenements and now pursued the American dream of owning their own home in suburbia. The Jewish Theological Seminary provided copies of heretofore unpublished music manuscripts for its cantorial graduates to sing at Conservative services.

An "authentic" minor mode, whose characteristic range is from its final note to an octave above, and which seems openly to lament the calamity that had overtaken all of European Jewry, typifies the Conservative approach to cantorial music of a generation ago. Example 8a, composer unknown, is for chanting the Psalms of Praise (113–118) known as Hallel.

Lo hameitim yehalelu yah . . .

The dead do not praise the lord, nor do any that go down into silence (Psalm 115:17).

It quotes music from the lovers' betrothal duet, "Ot, Der Brunem" (There, The Well), from the 1880 biblical Yiddish operetta, *Shulamis* (Example 8b).

EXAMPLE 7
Progression of Mode for Friday-Night Maariv:
"Plagal" Major to "Plagal" Minor; Parallel in *Kol Nidre*

a. Salomon Sulzer, *Schir Zion* (Vienna: Published by the author, 1839), No. 20; 1905 reissue No. 25.

b. Abraham Ber Birnbaum, *Amanut Hachazanut* (Czestochaw, Poland: Published by the author, 1908), No. 30.

c. Abraham Zvi Idelsohn, *The Jewish Song Book*, edited by Baruch Cohon (Cincinnati: Publications for Judaism, 1951), p. 17.

d. Israel Alter, *The Sabbath Service* (New York: Cantors Assembly, 1968), pp. 11–12. Reprinted by permission.

e. Fabian Ogutsch, *Der Frankfurter Kantor* (Frankfurt, Ger.: Israelitischen Gemeinde, 1930), No. 23.

The operetta's composer, Abraham Goldfaden (1840–1908), in turn, paraphrased Violetta's aria, "Ah, fors'e' lui" (Ah, Perhaps He Is The One), from Verdi's *La Traviata* (1853, Example 8c).

POST-VIETNAM. Within the past 25 years American congregations have attempted to recapture the fervor of traditional prayer. In 1968, a semistaged review of Hasidic tales—*Ish Chasid Hayah* (Once There Was a Hasid)—interspersed with *nigunim* (melodies without words), so fired the imagination of its Tel Aviv audience that an annual Hasidic Song Festival ensued. Winning entries swept American Jewish communities via recordings, sheet music, and touring troupes.

EXAMPLE 8
"Authentic"-Minor Mode in Hallel; Its Derivation from Yiddish Operetta and Italian Opera

a. Hallel, *Festival Kit*, compiled and edited by Max Wohlberg (New York: Jewish Theological Seminary, ca. 1950).

b. Abraham Goldfaden, *Shulamis* (New York: Hebrew Publishing, 1912), No. 9.

c. Giuseppi Verdi, *La Traviata, Seven Verdi Librettos*, edited by William Weaver (New York: Norton, 1975), p. 185. Reprinted by permission. Copyright © Doubleday, a division of Bantam, Doubleday, Dell Publishing Group, Inc.

Hasidic-style tunes borrowed liturgical texts like the final strophe of the Amidah for every service.

Oseh shalom bimromav . . .

He who makes peace in the heavens,
grant peace unto us and unto all Israel,
and let us say, Amen.

At first (1968), the tunes were in "authentic" minor (Example 9a). A later (1975) version of the same text—*Oseh Shalom*—shifted to "plagal" minor (Example 9b). The American trend toward Hasidic-style "plagal"-minor prayer in the Selichah, or forgiveness, mode continued in this country (1978) with the concluding Kedushah refrain:

Ledor vador nagid godlecha . . .
All Generations Recount Thy Greatness.
    (Example 9c.)

Of late, guitar-playing Reform cantors are *de rigueur*, and informal dress and demeanor have entered Conservative Judaism through the Havurah (Fellowship) Movement. Amateur groups have deposed professional choirs in some Reform congregations, while choral music of any kind is fast disappearing from Conservative and Orthodox synagogues.

In all three movements of American Judaism, unison congregational singing of neo-Hasidic *nigunim* is the norm, bypassing *davenen*, an untranslatable term connoting the historically lively give-and-take between cantor and congregation, during which worshippers preceded the cantor in reciting each paragraph, just as he summed up their collective effort before leading them into the next one. Bible reading, the motivic source of cantorial music, is being relegated to an untutored laity. Prayers have increasingly been replaced by English readings that bypass or subvert their original meanings.

INFLUENCE OF AMERICAN FOLK AND POPULAR MUSIC. One by one, the European-born cantors who carried on their synagogal tradition amid the strange surroundings of a secular America are retiring from the scene. The baton is now passing to a younger generation of American-born cantors, men and women, preoccupied with survival in a nuclear age. They were raised

EXAMPLE 9
Hasidic-Style Tunes in "Authentic"-Minor and "Plagal"-Minor Modes

a. Nurit Hirsch, "Oseh Shalom," *Hassidic Song Festival*, Hed Arzi recording BAN 1421, Side 2, Band 1 (Tel Aviv, 1968). Transcribed by Joseph Levine. Reprinted by permission. Copyright © by Nurit Hirsch, Israel.

b. Reuven Sirotkin, *Hassidic Festival Songbook* (Tel Aviv: Or-Tav, 1975), p. 18. Copyright © by Or-Tav Publishers, Israel.

c. Sol Zim, *The Joy of Shabbos Songbook* (Cedarhurst, N.Y.: Tara, 1978), p. 52. Reprinted by permission.

to believe in the American Way of Life, "the operative faith of the American people," as Will Herberg puts it. Based on democratic ideals (life, liberty, the pursuit of happiness), boasting saints (Washington and Lincoln), symbols (stars and stripes), festivals (Fourth of July), holy writ (Constitution and Bill of Rights), and songs (rock and roll), the American Way of Life summarizes our society's drift toward what might be called "national secularism."

Songs particularly pervade America's national-secularist existence, influencing attitudes and behavior. Contemporary songwriters, including synagogue cantors, have had to look no farther than American folksong for music expressive of the American Way of Life. One melodic/cadential pattern is so common that it might be called the American-Way-of-Life motif. It resembles a biblical neume motif, i.e., its absolute pitches vary according to the occasion and type of song, yet it is always recognizable: optimistic and sure of itself.

Example 10 cites the motif in nine songs that span almost a century and a half (1845–1981). They cover the gamut of American life: children (Example 10a), patriotic (Example 10b), work (Example 10c), leisure (Example 10d), winter holiday (Example 10e), hymn (Example 10f), spiritual (Example 10g), peace (Example 10h), and love (Example 10i). All the songs appear in D

EXAMPLE 10
The American-Way-of-Life Motif in Synagogue Song, 1845–1981

a. **Children** ...Pol-ly wol-ly-doodle all the day.

b. **Patriotic** ...to the shores of Tri-po-li.

c. **Work** ...let the wheel-er roll!

d. **Leisure** Hal-le-lu-jah, I'm a bum!

e. **Winter Holiday** ...in a one-horse o-pen sleigh.

f. **Hymn** ...from this day be...

g. **Spiritual** ...rock and reel,

h. **Peace** Where have all the flo-wers gone?

i. **Love** Well, we're all in the mood for a me-lo-dy.

a. Anne and Max Oberndorfer, *New American Song Book* (Chicago: Hall & McCreary, 1941), p. 120 ("Polly Wolly Doodle").

b. Joseph E. Maddy and W. Otto Miessner, *All-American Song Book* (New York: Robbins, 1942), p. 30 ("Marine Hymn").

c. John W. Work. *American Negro Songs and Spirituals* (New York: Bonanza, 1940), p. 37 ("O, Captain").

d. Margaret Bradford Boni, *Fireside Book of Folk Songs* (New York: Simon & Schuster, 1947), p. 102 ("Hallelujah, I'm a Bum").

e. Katherine Tyler Wells, *Golden Song Book* (New York: Simon & Schuster, 1945), p. 73 ("Jingle Bells").

f. Boni, *op. cit.*, p. 282 ("My Faith Looks Up to Thee").

g. Work, *op. cit.*, p. 66 ("A'int You Glad").

h. Pete Seeger, "Where Have All the Flowers Gone?" In *Great Songs of the Sixties*, edited by Milton Okun (New York: Random House, 1961), p. 310. Copyright © 1961 (renewed) by FALL RIVER MUSIC INC. All Rights Reserved.

i. Billy Joel, "Piano Man." In *100 Giant Hits of the 60's and the 70's* (New York: The Big Three, 1981), p. 139. Words and music by Billy Joel. © 1973, 1974 JOEL SONGS. All Rights Controlled and Administered by EMI Blackwood Music Inc. All Rights Reserved. International Copyright secured. Used by permission.

"authentic" major to facilitate comparison; the motif itself describes a descent from *A* to *D*, with *B*, *G*, *F#*, and *E* serving as passing tones.

Synagogue cantors of the 1980s have fused recent folk and popular practices because their musical formulas echo American Jewry's current rock-and-roll environment. Borrowing the American-Way-of-Life motif observed in Example 10, contemporary American cantors have applied it to lyrics that talk of peace (Example 11a) and related

EXAMPLE 11

The American-Way-of-Life Motif in Synagogue Song, 1981–1986

a. Jeff Klepper and Daniel Freelander, "Shalom Rav." In *Yehi Shir* (New York: North American Federation of Temple Youth, 1981), p. 22.

b. Gordon Lustig, "Hineh Tov Me'od." In *A Sourcebook of Jewish Songs for Peace* (New York: Jewish Educators for Social Responsibility, 1986), p. 10.

c. Steven Schiller, "Livrachah." In *Yehi Shir, op. cit.* p. 28.

concerns such as ecology (Example 11b) and life (Example 11c).

11a—*Shalom rav al yisra'eil amcha . . .*

Grant lasting peace to thy people, Israel;

11b—*Vayar elohim . . .*

And God saw all his work, and it was good

11c—*Lechayim, velo . . .*

May God renew this month for life.

Phrased in a rock rhythm, Examples 11a–c "push the beat," i.e., sing an eighth note ahead of time and tie it to the following note on which the actual beat occurs. Thus, an iambic Hebrew prayer text like *Shalom Rav* (Example 11d) is made to resemble colloquial American speech (Example 11e). These kinds of rhythms and stresses, reminiscent of "black English" (Example 11f, same as Example 10c), have pervaded American popular music for over a century. Cantorial music is now following suit.

Ironically, the American-Way-of-Life motif used in the synagogue melodies of Example 11 is similar to the "authentic"-major pattern of worship shared by every Diaspora community. It parallels the opening of a prayer mode common to all branches of world Jewry, called the *Tefillah* mode by Sephardic communities, and the *Adonai Malach* mode by Ashkenazic ones. Secure in its freedom, American Jewry, predominantly Ashkenazic, is now choosing praise over petition. Increasingly, prayers are sung in the laudatory *Adonai Malach* mode rather than in the penitential Selichah (forgiveness) mode of Kol Nidre (see Examples 7d and 7e).

Example 12a shows opening and closing motifs [1] and [4] of the *Adonai Malach* mode.

Adonai Malach . . . / / . . . bal timot

The Lord reigns [robed in majesty] . . . / / [The world] shall never be moved.

Equivalent neume motifs (from Torah reading) for *Adonai Malach* motifs [1] and [4] appear in Example 12b.

EXAMPLE 12
Adonai Malach Parallels
with the American-Way-of-Life Motif

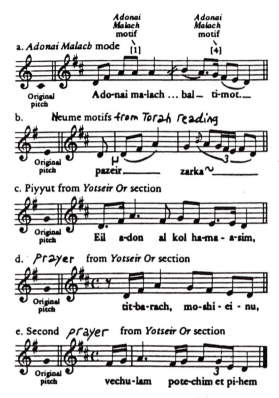

a. Abraham Zvi Idelsohn, "The Traditional Song of the South German Jews," *Thesaurus of Hebrew Oriental Melodies* (Leipzig: Hofmeister, 1933), Vol. VII, p. xx.

b. Salomon Sulzer, *Schir Zion* (Vienna: Published by the author, 1839), 1905 reissue, No. 108, neume motif 14 (Torah reading).

c. *Idem.*, 1905 reissue No. 64.

d. Louis Lewandowsky, *Kol Rinnah U't'fillah* (Berlin: Published by the author, 1871), No. 32.

e. Glantz, Leib, *Rinat Hakodesh* (Tel Aviv: Israel Music Institute, 1968), p. 69.

Such widespread usage of the laudatory mode finds precedence in the nineteenth-century Shabbat Shacharit practice of many European Ashkenazic communities, East and West. Example 12c (a Piyyut), as well as Examples 12d and 12e (both prayer texts), all portray the heavenly hosts' echoing of God's praise in the *Yotseir Or* (Creator of Light) section that heralds the Shema and Amidah in the morning Shacharit service.

12c—*Eil adon al kol hama'asim . . .*

God, the Lord over all creation;

12d—*Titbarach, moshi'einu . . .*

Be thou blessed, our Redeemer;

12e—*Vechulam potechim et pihem . . .*

The angels declare God's holiness.

All of this helps to explain the recent blending of Ashkenazic tradition with American environmental influence. Even Orthodoxy does not escape the Americanization process. A final musical example offers a recent Orthodox setting of a liturgical text. This type of setting was popularized as a *Ruach* (sing-along) song for all occasions during the 1970s. Although Orthodoxy prefers to elevate derivative material from the realm of "profane" to that of "sacred," it too has lately opted for melodies in the "authentic"-major *Adonai Malach* style. Example 13, *Achas Sho'alti* (One Thing Have I Asked Of The Lord, Psalm 27:4), echoes the American-Way-of-Life motif but in four-square rhythm.

> *. . . kol yemei chayai*
>
> [that I may dwell in the house of the Lord] all the days of my life.

CONCLUSION. Cantorial music represents all segments of an American Jewry still unpacking the cultural baggage of its many earlier host countries. That baggage includes stately congregational Sephardic hymns (Example 1); Viennese waltzes and Parisian-operetta melodies (Example 2); German Romantic call-and-response (Example 3); cantorial recitatives, unaccompanied or with choral commentary (Examples 4 and 5); settings thematically based on Biblical neume motifs (Example 6); lyric airs from Italian opera and Yiddish theater (Example 8); American-Way-of-Life-inspired anthems that coincide with the universal prayer mode, *Adonai Malach* (Example 12); and *Ruach* songs for all occasions (Example 13).

EXAMPLE 13
American Influence on
an Orthodox *Ruach* Song of the 1970s

S. Mernick, "Achas Sho-alti." In *Hassidic-Style Hits of the 70's*, edited by Velvel Pasternak (Cedarhurst, N.Y.: Tara, 1975), p. 9. Reprinted by permission.

Until recently, cantorial music preferred the penitential sound of forgiveness as expressed in the "plagal"-minor Selichah mode of Kol Nidre and Eastern European Friday-night Maariv. Lately, it seems to be forging its own link between the optimistic "authentic"-major sound of the universal Jewish praise-saying mode (Ashkenazic *Adonai Malach*), indigenous folk song (American-Way-of-Life motif), popular rhythms (rock and roll), and colloquial speech patterns ("black English"). In short, the long-awaited Americanization process has begun.

JOSEPH A. LEVINE

BIBLIOGRAPHY

Avenary, Hanoch. "The Concept of Mode in European Synagogue Chant." In *Yuval*. Jerusalem: Hebrew University, 1973.
——. "Music," "Nusach," "Psalms," "Shtayger." *Encyclopedia Judaica*. Jerusalem: Keter, 1972.
Idelsohn, Abraham Zvi. *Jewish Music in its Historical Development*. New York: Tudor, 1929.
——. "Songs of the Babylonian Jews." In *Thesaurus of Hebrew Oriental Melodies*. Vol. VII. Berlin: Hartz, 1923.
Levine, Joseph A. *Synagogue Song in America*. Crown Point, Ind.: White Cliffs, 1989. *See* Appendix B for "Neume Motifs for the Lithuanian Tradition of Bible Reading according to Solomon Rosowsky."
Slobin, Mark. *Chosen Voices*. Urbana: University of Illinois, 1989.
Werner, Eric. *A Voice Still Heard*. State College: Pennsylvania State University, 1976.

Music, Classical. Jews should be extremely proud of their enormous contribution to music in the United States; the Jewish share in shaping and realizing the American musical consciousness has been central out of all proportion to numbers, in both quality and quantity. There have been major twentieth-century Jewish composers embracing the entire spectrum of advancement and styles, from the dadaists to the cerebral, from the most conservative to the most avant-garde, from the romantic to the intellectual, from the jazzy to the square (with some composers representing several of the above characterizations)—and also from the most consciously Jewish in style (taking elements from sacred and secular traditions) to those who ignore any kind of Jewish music. In fact, this topic is so enormous that—given space limitations—its scope can only be suggested.

There are inherent problems with this topic that should be addressed at the outset.

What is American music, and what is an American composer? These are exceedingly difficult questions to answer. Is American music that which is written within the geographical boundaries of the United States, or does it utilize specific stylistic traits? For example, is Milton Babitt an American composer? He is certainly a distinguished, influential composer who lives in America, but his music by no stretch of the imagination has the jazzy, jaunty rhythms and syncopations, the soaring melodic qualities, the open and expansive harmonies and forms that have come to be associated with American style. Was Darius Milhaud American? Well, no, but he spent a considerable amount of time in the United States; also, he composed some extremely American music. For example, his ballet, *La Création du Monde* (1923), is the earliest example of the use of jazz in a symphonic score, antedating Gershwin's *Rhapsody in Blue* (1924).

Another question for the purposes of this article: What is a Jew? This is a serious, substantial question, on which there is profound disagreement both in the American Jewish community and in Israel. Of most of the composers covered in the following discussion, there could be no question about Jewishness. However, in other instances, the present writer offers a liberal solution to this question. In any case, the wide range of styles mentioned is quite impressive, as almost a microcosm of American music. If there is to be a connecting stylistic thread through the majority of composers mentioned, it could concern the mysterious and subjective questions of spirit and tonality—of inflection, timings, emphasis, imagery, sorrow, and optimism. In many cases folk song and/or biblical nuances abound. Although often there is a musical pull toward the interval of the augmented second, exceptions prove the rule.

There is a striking parallel between works of Jewish composers and black composers, but this has to do with spirit—the spirit of exclusion and pain, expressed in Block's *Schelomo* as well as in a black spiritual.

The American Jewish classical music style vacillates between the universal and the provincial. What the writer Irving Howe wrote about Yiddish writers can also be applied to American Jewish composers: ". . . even as they seek and receive the impress of surrounding cultures, they cannot break past the visible and invisible boundaries."

The following list of composers, chronologically organized, is hardly comprehensive. Nevertheless, a picture emerges of great accomplishment and thriving artistic activity.

Louis Moreau Gottschalk (1829–1869) was the son of a celebrated Creole beauty of aristocratic French lineage; his father was an intellectual English Jewish businessman. During his lifetime, Gottschalk was famous as both composer and concert pianist. Indeed, his career was comparable to those of Liszt, Chopin, and Thalberg. He was, in addition, an imaginative writer, and his *Notes of a Pianist* provides a fascinating chronicle of nineteenth-century American musical life. In a creative sense, however, "the American Chopin," as he was called, remained a lonely figure. After his death most of his finest works were completely forgotten, only the more sentimental pieces remaining popular. It was not until 100 years later that Gottschalk's significant works were rediscovered and his true value as an important composer made widely known.

The unique feature of Gottschalk's music lies in its fusion of European and American materials, an achievement that foreshadows the later works of Ives, Gershwin, Copland, and others in the twentieth century. In a formal sense, Gottschalk's style shows the influence of Chopin and Berlioz, but his melodic and rhythmic ideas often derived from Spanish and Latin-American sources and from American folk, patriotic, and popular tunes. Gottschalk was the first to introduce moods and colors of the new world into serious music, but beyond this historical fact, there remains the freshness and fascination of his best compositions.

Rubin Goldmark (1872–1936), the American composer who taught such luminaries as Aaron Copland, Abram Chasins, and Frederick Jacobi, stemmed directly from the late romantic tradition. Especially fine is Goldmark's *A Negro Rhapsody* (1923).

Ernest Bloch (1880–1959) is an American Swiss composer whose music contains unmistakable Jewish accents. Perhaps his masterpiece is *Schelomo* (1915–1916), a "Hebrew rhapsody" for cello and orchestra, which is still enormously popular on concert programs. Bloch also composed *Israel* (a symphony), *Suite hébraïque* (1951), for viola and orchestra, *Méditation hébraïque* (1924), and *From Jewish Life* (1924), both for cello and piano.

Artur Schnabel (1882–1951) is another musician whose nationality is perhaps in dispute. Born in Austria, he divided his time between Europe and the United States; however, he became an American citizen in 1944. Additionally, he contributed much to the musical life of this country. Schnabel was one of the great pianists and pedagogues, especially in works of Mozart, Schubert, Beethoven, and Brahms. As a composer, he was uncompromisingly modernistic, in works marked by dissonance and atonality. He wrote many chamber works, a symphony, and a piano concerto.

Mana-Zucca's (1887–1981) hundredth year was celebrated on December 25, 1987, at least according to Baker's *Biographical Dictionary of Musicians*. (*The New Grove Dictionary of American Music* reveals her birthdate as 1885.) She studied with Lambert and then took lessons with Godowsky and Busoni. Her lively descriptions of Carreno, Busoni, Godowsky, and others were published in American music magazines. A piano child prodigy, she lists among her published works approximately 390 titles; she claimed to have actually published 1100 works and to have written 1000 more. Mana-Zucca became known for her lyrical songs, including those in Yiddish. Her song, "I Love Life" was quite popular. Many of her songs were sung by the leading vocalists of the 1920s and 1930s. She personally gave the impression of great enthusiasm in an elflike, almost phantasmal appearance—at least to the present writer, who met her on a number of occasions.

Darius Milhaud (1892–1974) was descended from an old Jewish family from Provence, France. He composed expertly and voluminously in a dazzling variety of styles. As noted above, he composed some extremely American music, such as his ballet, *La Création du Monde* (1923). Other works using jazz include *Scaramouch* and *Le Boeuf sur le toit* (1920). His works on Jewish themes include *8 Poemes juifs* (1916), *Kaddisch* (1945), *Sabbath Morning Service* (1947), and *Ode pour Jérusalem* (1972); there are many more.

Leo Ornstein (b. 1892), the son of a cantor, was born in Russia. He left Russia in 1907 (at the age of 15) because of anti-Semitic disturbances and settled in the United States. Ornstein was an exponent of what he called "futuristic" music. Much of his music is both percussive and dissonant and also extremely energetic.

Nicolas Slonimsky (b. 1894), the Russian-American musicologist and composer, has done Herculean labor as the editor of and prime contributor to several editions of Baker's *Biographical Dictionary of Musicians*; he has also written several significant books, such as *Music Since 1900, Music of Latin America*, and *Lexicon of Musical Invective*. Slonimsky is also a witty, sparkling composer. His fifty *Minitudes* (1971–1977), a collection of delightful, short piano works, are among his best pieces.

Abraham Wolfe Binder (1895–1966) was an American composer, author, and conductor who taught liturgical music at the Jewish Institute of Religion in New York. His many compositions include an opera and a choral ballet; especially recommended is Binder's *The Legend of Ari* (1963) for small orchestra.

Lazar Weiner (1897–1982) was a composer, conductor, pianist, teacher, and father of the composer Yehudi Wyner (one of many omitted from this survey). A leading advocate of Jewish music and the Yiddish art song, Weiner also composed musical comedies and many Yiddish art songs. In his opera *The Golem* (1957) (produced at the New York 92nd Street Y in 1981 and in White Plains in 1957), as well as in many other works, Weiner tried to express the inflections and the richness of Yiddish culture.

George Gershwin (1898–1937) was an immensely gifted American composer of European Jewish background. Gershwin reinvigorated American music with his unique, authentic blend of jazz, blues, and Jewish inflections in a classical/romantic framework. His ethnic background is evident in his music. (*See also* Gershwin, George; Music, Popular.)

Aaron Copland (1900–1990), one of the really important twentieth-century composers, wrote "Study on a Jewish Theme" (1928) for piano trio and other works that indirectly suggest Jewish consciousness. His body of work represents an invaluable legacy of American music. (*See also* Copland, Aaron.)

Kurt Weill (1900–1950), a German American who began his career as a composer of avant-garde music, eventually became best known for his musical comedies and musical plays. Before he fled Nazi Germany in 1933, he had collaborated with playwright Bertolt Brecht in writing *The Rise and Fall of the City Mahogony* (1930) and *Die Dreigroschenoper* (*The Three Penny Opera*) (1928). In the United States he became a successful composer of Broadway musicals. In 1947, he wrote *Down in the Valley*, a folk opera noted for its thoroughly American folk songs.

Marc Blitzstein (1905–1964) was a significant composer who combined a cabaret music style with classical structures. The social message

in many of his works—such as *The Cradle Will Rock* (1937), play in music; *Sacco and Vanzetti* (1959–1964, incomplete) opera; *The Magic Barrel* (1963, incomplete), an opera after Mamamud—is analogous to that of Bertolt Brecht and Kurt Weill.

Elie Siegmeister (1909–1991) is a prolific composer whose musical language is communicative, often lyrical, and recognized as representative among the best of modern romanticism. His 40 orchestral works have been performed by major orchestras throughout the world, and his operas have been performed in four nations. He has also written scores for Broadway and films, ballet, chamber music, chorus, and piano, as well as over 100 concert songs. The recipient of many distinguished awards and commissions, Siegmeister is author of *The New Music Lover's Handbook* and *A Treasury of American Songs* as well as the textbook *Harmony and Melody*. Among Siegmeister's compositions with Jewish stylistic or thematic content are his operas *Angel Levine* (1984–1985) and *The Lady of the Lake* (1984–1985), both after short stories by Malamud, and his *String Quartet No. 3* (1973), in which the composer incorporates three chants—Yemenite, Hasidic, and Ashkenazic—weaving them into the fabric of the music.

Hermann Berlinsky (b. 1910), a celebrated organist, composer, and musicologist, has been an invaluable force for Jewish music in his three fields of expertise. According to Vernon Gotwals in *The New Grove Dictionary of American Music*, "his widely-performed organ toccata *The Burning Bush* (1957) fully succeeds in fusing Hebrew imagery with sacred musical media. He is a gifted recitalist and his recordings reflect an international Jewish background coupled with brilliant technical achievement."

William Schumann (b. 1910) has been a distinguished American composer, educator, and administrator. He had extremely successful tenures as president of the Juilliard School of Music and of Lincoln Center in New York City. As a prolific composer, he has written an impressive body of works of every size and description. A master of technique, orchestration, form, and proportion, he employs many ways of modern composition, without losing reference to tonality. Above all, his music always has rhythmic energy.

Arthur Berger (b. 1912) divides his time between composing and writing for many journals and periodicals. For many years he has been a distinguished critic. As a composer, he has received numerous awards, grants, and honors. Although Berger's music is original in style, perhaps Stravinsky especially influenced his early music; in his later music, Berger might be described as a serial or post-Webern composer. He has always been concerned with musical space—both vertical and horizontal—in a lean, spare texture.

Hugo Weisgall (b. 1912) has served for many years as chairman of the faculty of the Seminary College of Jewish Music in New York and is now president of the National Academy of Arts and Letters; he has also served with distinction on the faculties of the Juilliard School of Music and Queens College. In addition to being an authority on Jewish music, Weisgall is important in his incorporation of Jewish materials into his many compositions. Especially to be recommended is *The Golden Peacock*, (1960, rev. 1976, rev. 1978), in which Weisgall uses well-known Yiddish folk songs.

Morton Gould (b. 1913), an extraordinarily fine and versatile composer and conductor, is also the president of ASCAP (American Association of Composers and Publishers). He composed the highly successful *Concerto for Tap Dancer* (1953) and many other virtuoso works with jazz orientation. Gould also wrote music for the television miniseries "Holocaust" (1978).

Henry Brant (b. 1913), an American composer who was born in Montreal, wrote the symphony *The Promised Land* (1947). He has experimented in direction music, and when he performed his composition *December* (1954) in Carnegie Hall, the musicians were scattered throughout the auditorium.

Irving Fine (1914–1962) at first wrote neoclassical music reminiscent of Stravinsky or Hindemith; however, he later wrote works of the highest melodic and contrapuntal quality, in a style distinctly his own.

George Perle (b. 1915) is an influential composer and theorist of Russian Jewish immigrant parents. Most of his music is squarely in the post-Webern school, but his *Songs of Praise and Lamentation* (1974) reflects his Jewish heritage.

Milton Babitt (b. 1916), a theorist and composer of inestimable influence on younger colleagues and students, is extremely gifted in the mathematical and organizational aspects of music; therefore, he tries to apply the serial principle to all aspects of his pieces—pitches, dynamics, rhythm, timbre. He has been honored by the Pulitzer Committee for "his life's work as a distinguished and seminal American composer."

Peter Paul Fuchs (b. 1916) is a conductor and composer who divides his time between Europe and Greensboro, North Carolina. Fuchs has written operas, orchestral music, and chamber music.

Leonard Bernstein (1918–1990) is undeniably one of the most important musical figures in the twentieth century, in many different aspects of music—as composer, conductor, instrumentalist, and lecturer in both the classical and popular worlds. He wrote much strikingly effective music in what may be called the American style, both popular and abstract. He also wrote music on Jewish themes—for example, Bernstein's *Halil* (Hebrew for "flute") is a nocturne for flute, string orchestra, and percussion dedicated to the memory of an Israeli soldier killed in the 1973 war. It was first performed in Tel Aviv in 1981. (*See also* Bernstein, Leonard; Music, Popular.)

George Rochberg (b. 1918), a composer of significance who has been honored with the Pulitzer Prize, used to write 12-tone music suffused with lyricism; now he draws from various diverse sources of the past for recognizable quotes, fragments, and stylistic imitation. His craftsmanship is superb in any style. Among his best pieces are a violin concerto and several major piano pieces.

Leon Kirchner (b. 1919), a major American composer of Russian Jewish parents, studied with (among others) Ernest Bloch in San Francisco. He has produced an enviable body of tightly knit contemporary works of high quality. Kirchner was given the New York Music Critics Award in 1950 and in 1960; he also received the Pulitzer Prize in 1967, as well as many other prestigious honors.

Harold Shapiro (b. 1920) is a composer who has won numerous prizes and awards. His works adhere to a classical contemporary pattern and show contrapuntal skill; they also contain long, emotional lines.

Irwin Bazelon (b. 1922) is an especially outstanding orchestral composer, whose style ranges from simple to exceedingly complex structures. Jazz syncopation is a central ingredient in his style, and he is outstanding in his use of percussion instruments.

Lukas Foss (1922), a thoroughly brilliant composer, conductor, and pianist, was born in Germany, of a father who was a professor of philosophy, and a mother who was a fine painter. With the advent of Nazism in Germany, the family moved to Paris, finally arriving in the United States in 1937. Thereafter, although he has an international career, Foss has been based in the

United States. His music represents a compendium of contemporary styles and techniques, from incorporation of American and jazz materials to neo-Classicism to advanced avant-garde ideas, always expressed with sparkling intelligence.

Ezra Laderman (b. 1924) has received three Guggenheim grants and has served as director of the music program of the National Endowment for the Arts. Among his best works are the cantata *And David Wept* (1971) and the opera *Sarah* (1958).

Benjamin Lees (b. 1924) is an outstanding American composer who was born in Manchuria. A prolific writer, he creates music that is effective, idiosyncratic, by turns energetic and lyrical. His harmonic vocabulary is discreetly dissonant and attractive to both performers and audience.

Robert Starer (b. 1924), born in Vienna, studied at the Vienna State Academy, the Jerusalem Conservatory, and the Juilliard School of Music, where he taught for many years after his graduation in 1949. He is Distinguished Professor of Music at Brooklyn College and the Graduate Center of the City University of New York. Among his honors are two Guggenheim fellowships and an award from the American Academy and Institute of Arts and Letters. His stage works include ballets for Martha Graham, and three operas, two with libretti by novelist Gail Godwin. His symphonic works have been performed by major orchestras in the United States and abroad, with such conductors as Mitropoulos, Steinberg, Bernstein, and Mehta. Although Starer is definitely an American composer using American materials in many of his works, he also incorporates Near Eastern and Arabic melodies and scales in his music.

Morton Feldman (1926–1987) was one of the leading figures of the avant-garde. His many works are mostly notated on graphs with rhythmic and tonal indetermancy. For most of his life he was a miniaturist; in his last years he was given to creating works lasting longer than an hour— and some are considerably longer.

Meyer Kupferman (b. 1926) was taught to sing Romanian folk songs by his father, an immigrant from Romania; his mother, from Russia, taught him old Yiddish songs. He incorporated these materials into his music, along with jazz elements. One of his many successful pieces is *In My Father's Image* for violin and piano. He said of this work that it is "a creative reminiscence about my father, who played all of the instruments without lessons—his favorite was the violin—and taught himself twelve languages—he had this 'ear' thing. As a young man he traveled with a gypsy band—there was also his Jewish side—the old Hebrew mysteries and rituals I remember as a child, the melodies he used to play and improvise on. The form of his work is totally new and reached out toward the perception of those aesthetic and philosophical thoughts of the future, while utilizing the memories and feelings of the past."

Jacob Druckman (b. 1928) has won many prestigious prizes and grants and has achieved considerable recognition in the music world, especially for his orchestral music. Although he combines the full measure of contemporary techniques with contrapuntal mastery, he does not adhere to any specific school of composition.

Donald Keats (b. 1929) is a lesser known composer who is highly recommended. He is disciplined in form and techniques, and his works are slowly and carefully realized. His best compositions, nevertheless, contain expansive and lyrical sonorities. Concerts of his music were well received in Tel Aviv in 1973.

Andre Previn (b. 1929), the pianist, composer, and conductor, is of Russian Jewish descent. Accepted at the Berlin Hochschule für Musik, he was compelled to leave school in 1938. His music combines jazz elements with classical forms. Previn has written many orchestral works and ensemble pieces.

Jack Gottlieb (b. 1930), a student of Aaron Copland and Robert Palmer (among others), was music director of the Congregation Temple Israel in St. Louis and composer-in-residence at the School of Sacred Music, Hebrew Union College in New York. In addition to being a fine composer who blends the classical with different varieties of popular music, he is also a witty and informative lecturer on Jewish music, jazz, and popular music.

Abraham Kaplan (b. 1931) was born in Tel Aviv. Dividing his time between conducting, teaching, and composing, he has written a *Sanctification* symphony as well as works for chorus and orchestra.

Aaron Blumenfeld (b. 1932) is especially expert in his use of authentic blues and barrelhouse music in his works; he is also extremely knowledgeable in the field of Jewish music, having studied cantorial music at the Jewish Theological Seminary of New York and the Cantorial Institute of Yeshiva University. His *Symphonic Song for the Ingathering and Redemption of the Jewish People* was performed in 1980, and his *Holocaust Memorial Cantata for Chorus and Orchestra* has been performed. His compositions are in the romantic vein. They can be characterized as a blend of classical, jazz, and Judaic musical traditions, with both an intense spirituality and a strong sense of humor.

Eric Salzman (b. 1933), composer, writer, and musicologist, worked with Stockhausen at Darmstadt, Ussachevsky at Columbia, and Babitt at Princeton. His music, in which he follows the most advanced techniques in mixed media, reflects these influences.

Richard Wernick (b. 1934) worked with such teachers as Kirchner, Toch, Copland, and Bernstein. He is a member of the music faculty of the University of Pennsylvania. In 1977, he was awarded a Pulitzer Prize for his *Visions of Terror and Wonder* (1976), to texts from the Bible and the Koran, in Hebrew, Arabic, and Greek. Wernick has an individual style, one of seeming improvisation. His music characteristically has sensuousness and advanced techniques. Among his works reflecting Jewish consciousness are *Prayer for Jerusalem* (1971), *Kaddish Requiem* (1971), and *The Oracle of Shimon Bar Yochai* (1982).

Peter Schickele (b. 1935) rose to fame as the creator of P. D. Q. Bach, the mythical, last son of J. S. Bach, composing such pieces as *Schleptet*, *Fuga Meshuga*, *Fantasie-Shtick*, and *Iphigenia in Brooklyn*. Although P. D. Q. Bach is presumably not Jewish, Peter Schickele is.

Elliot Schwartz (b. 1936) is a composer and teacher who has worked with numerous composers of the avant-garde of the older generation. He is chairman of the music department at Bowdoin College. In *Baker's Biographical Dictionary of Musicians* Nicolas Slonimsky states: "In his compositions he develops the Satiesque notions of unfettered license in music leading to their completely unbottoned state."

Philip Glass (b. 1937) is the grandson of Orthodox Jewish immigrants from Russia. His intense, minimalist style, involving hypnotic repetition, stems from the mysterious world of Hindu ragas and North African (or Moroccan) melorhythms with a dash of Eastern modes and robust rock music.

Anton Kuerti (b. 1938), the Viennese-born pianist, lived in the United States before moving to Canada in the 1960s. Kuerti is especially brilliant in German and Austrian traditional masterworks (Mozart, Schubert, Beethoven, Schumann, etc.); what is not known, however, is that he is also a fine composer, in the conservative and communicative mode.

Harvey Sollberger (b. 1938), who is a virtuoso flutist in addition to being a composer, has been one of the moving forces behind the New York avant-garde. In his compositions Sollberger uses the serial method.

Stephen Albert (b. 1941), an especially fine composer whose music excites enthusiasm in both colleagues and audiences, has worked with Elie Siegmeister, Bernard Rogers, Roy Harris, and George Rochberg. He has received such awards as the Prix de Rome, a Guggenheim fellowship, and a Pulitzer Prize. Although he is completely at home with advanced modern techniques and concepts, he molds tonality into an individual style.

Warren Cytron (b. 1944) writes finely proportioned and constructed works in a contemporary idiom. Having studied with Stefan Wolpe, Cytron wrote *Between Bridges* (1984), for the oboe and a chamber orchestra and dedicated this work to the great oboist Joseph Marx, who came from a long line of Jewish scholars.

This short synopsis of Jewish-American classical music only touches the highlights of the profession. The Jewish-American composer has had a profound influence on American classical music and most certainly will continue to do so.

ALAN MANDEL

BIBLIOGRAPHY

Baker's Biographical Dictionary of Musicians. 7th ed. Revised and edited by Nicholas Slonimsky. New York: Schirmer, 1984.

Ewen, David. *Modern Music: A History and Appreciation—From Wagner to the Avant-Garde.* Rev. ed. Philadelphia: Chilton, 1969.

Fromm, Herbert. *On Jewish Music: A Composer's View.* New York: Bloch, 1978.

Heskes, Irene. *Studies in Jewish Music: Collected Writings of A. W. Binder.* New York: Bloch, 1971.

New Grove Dictionary of American Music. Edited by H. Wiley Hitchcock and Stanley Sadie. New York: Grove's Dictionary of Music, 1986.

Nulman, Mary. *Concise Encyclopedia of Jewish Music.* New York: McGraw-Hill, 1975.

Ruben, Bruce, and Clurman, Judith. *Seasons of Our Lives: A Resource Guide of the Music, Books, Films, and Videos of Jewish Life Cycle Occasions.* New York: Jewish Music Council, 1966.

Siegmeister, Elie. *The New Music Lover's Handbook.* Irvington-on-Hudson, N.Y.: Harvey House, 1973.

Music, Popular.

American popular music would not exist as we know it today without the contribution made by the Jews. Beyond mere entertainment, popular songs mirror the history, lifestyle, mores, religious beliefs, and interests of those about and for whom they were written and by whom they were sung. These songs played important roles in educative and political processes, emphasizing major social issues, such as slavery and abolition, prohibition, women's suffrage, immigration, emancipation, religious freedom, and national patriotism. Popular songs allowed the lower and middle class to fantasize about travel to far-off places filled with romance, places that would rarely be visited in the lifetime of most Americans. These songs taught and exemplified American family values. They portrayed the "American dream" and would export that dream to countries around the world.

Prominent Jewish contribution began in the 1840s, with John Howard Payne (1791-1852), and Henry Russell (1812-1900), although the Jewish presence in America was small indeed, numbering no more than 15,000 in a population of some 17 million. However, with the opening of America by transportation links and wider communication, the popular song's role fostered both education and entertainment. Soon after the inception of burlesque and vaudeville, Jews gained prominence in the show business world. David Braham (1838-1905) wrote the songs for the first great Gentile vaudeville team, Ned Harrigan and Tony Hart, to poke fun at immigrants. Joe Weber and Lew Fields, two Jews, continued their comedic tradition with special slapstick emphasis on the "greenhorns," the new Jewish immigrants coming to America. Vaudeville fostered the beginnings of many of the early great American composers of popular music, including Irving Berlin (1888-1989), Jerome Kern (1885-1945), Irving Caesar (b. 1895), and Charles K. Harris (1867-1930).

If no one could hear the songs, then these songs could not be appreciated. The music publishing business was largely controlled and totally dominated by immigrant Jews. Isidore and Julius Witmark, the "sons" of M. Witmark & Sons, Charles K. Harris, Joseph Stern, Lew Shapiro, Maurice Bernstein, Harry and Albert von Tilzer, Leo Feist, Alex and Tom Harms of T. B. Harms, and Irving Berlin were the vanguard of the publishing business that came to be known as Tin Pan Alley, a name coined by the Jewish lyricist-journalist Monroe Rosenfeld (1861-1918), when vis-

iting Harry von Tilzer in the Flat Iron Building in New York City. To Rosenfeld, the sound of so many pianists playing pianos in small cubicles reminded him of the dropping of coins on a tin collection plate, hence the name Tin Pan Alley.

Before Charles K. Harris, a Milwaukee Jew who could neither read nor write music, there had never been a "million seller," a song that sold a million copies of sheet music. Harris's masterpiece, "After the Ball" (1892), sold over 10 million copies in approximately 7 years. A Detroit Jew was the most prolific composer on Tin Pan Alley (he claimed to have written 8000 songs); Harry Gumm (1872-1946) changed his name to honor his mother's home town of Tilzer, Germany, adopting the pen name Harry von Tilzer. In a brief time, the songs of these men became part of our American cultural fabric. What summer would be without "Take Me Out to the Ball Game" (1908) by Albert von Tilzer (Harry's brother), so September would be without "School Days," by Gus Edwards (1878-1945).

Jerome Kern's insistence on the unity of script and song paved the way for those who followed in the American musical theater, including Irving Berlin and George and Ira Gershwin. Berlin, a Russian immigrant born Israel Baline in Temun, Siberia, revolutionized the popular music field, and, in the process, became as all-American as the songs he wrote. His songs called men to serve their country in two world wars. They symbolized two secularized Christian religious holidays, Christmas and Easter. They provided numerous romantic interludes for numerous couples, and portrayed both tragedy and celebration in the lives of men and women around the world. Berlin wrote what many consider to be our second national anthem, "God Bless America" (1939) as a song to be shared by soldiers in his World War I musical, *Yip, Yip Yaphank* (1918), a show written to raise money for a soldiers' social center at Camp Upton on Long Island, N.Y. Berlin, feeling that a song proclaiming the soldiers' love of country was at best redundant, put the song away until 1938 when songstress Kate Smith requested a patriotic ballad to counteract the emotions created by the war brewing in Europe. Jerome Kern said of him, "Irving Berlin has no place in American music, he is American music." George Gershwin (1898-1937), born Jacob Gershovitz, and Ira Gershwin (1896-1983), born Israel Gershovitz, broadened the scope of the popular music industry by showing that theatrical and popular songs could stand side by side with the more serious music of the orchestra hall. Jazz, a truly American musical idiom, was made all the richer because of George Gershwin's fulfillment of a request by Paul Whiteman to write a formal work suitable for the concert hall; Whiteman inspired Gershwin's writing of the symphonic jazz classic *Rhapsody in Blue*, for the Aeolian Theater concert of February 12, 1924, an event that electrified the audience, if not the critics. In 1935, Gershwin's opera *Porgy and Bess* opened on Broadway.

Other contributors to the Tin Pan Alley days included wordsmith and German immigrant, Gus Kahn (1886-1941), lyricist for such songs as "Memories" (1915), "Pretty Baby" (1916), "Yes Sir, That's My Baby" (1922), and "Carolina in the Morning" (1925). Composers Harry Ruby (1895-1974), with such hit songs as "I Want To Be Loved by You" (1928) and "Who's Sorry Now" (1923); Sammy Fain (1902-1989) with "Let a Smile Be Your Umbrella" (1927), "I'll Be Seeing You" (1938), and "April Love" (1957); and Joseph Meyer (1894-1987), with such songs as "If You Knew Susie" (1925), the signature song for Eddie Cantor, and "California, Here I Come" (1921)—written with vaudeville and Broadway star, songwriter, and "plugger," Al Jolson (1884-1950)—are among the most prominent.

Others began their careers in Tin Pan Alley and went on and expanded to theatrical and film careers. The son and grandson of two great New York musical-theater leaders, Oscar Hammerstein II (1885-1960) was the lyricist for many of our most treasured musicals, including *Showboat* (1925), *Oklahoma* (1943), *Carousel* (1945), and *South Pacific* (1949). The grandson of opera impresario and theater builder Oscar Hammerstein I, an early competitor of the Metropolitan Opera and builder of Harlem's famous Apollo Theater, and father William Hammerstein, theater producer and entrepreneur, Hammerstein worked with numerous composers, but his two most long-lasting relationships were with Jerome Kern and Richard Rodgers (1902-1988).

Although most commonly remembered for his hugely popular musicals with Oscar Hammerstein, Richard Rodgers wrote with many lyricists. Other than Hammerstein, his most prolific partner was Lorenz Hart (1895-1943), the lyricist for such songs as "With a Song In My Heart" (1929), "The Lady Is a Tramp" (1937), and "This Can't Be Love" (1938). Their relationship deteriorated because of Hart's unsuccessful bout with alcoholism and depression ending a brilliant and creative career.

Although not as caustic as Hart in everyday life events, a great political lyricist of the day, E. Y. "Yip" Harburg (1898-1981) is well known 60 years later for having written the Depression classic, "Brother, Can You Spare a Dime" (1932) and the pre-World War II movie musical *The Wizard of Oz* (1939), based on the L. Frank Baum novels, with its classic "Somewhere Over the Rainbow" (1939), a thinly veiled political commentary on Europe and the Far East of that troubled time. With Russian-born composer Vernon Duke (1903-1969), born Vladimir Dukelski, Harburg wrote "April in Paris" (1932).

World War II brought a new generation of composers and lyricists to the American popular music scene. Following on the World War I tradition of great patriotic songs, as well as songs that would allow the singers and listeners to forget the trials and tribulations of war, Frank Loesser (1910-1969) gained wide popularity with his song, "Praise the Lord and Pass the Ammunition" (1942). His fame was guaranteed through such musicals as *Guys and Dolls* (1950), a musicalization of the Damon Runyon short stories caricaturing the seamy side of New York, and *The Most Happy Fella* (1956), an American light opera that portrayed the lives of immigrant Italian-American and local farmhands in the California wine country. English-born Jule Styne (b. 1905) composed such hit songs as "Diamonds Are a Girl's Best Friend" for *Gentlemen Prefer Blondes* (1949), which catapulted Carol Channing into Broadway stardom, "People," from his musical *Funny Girl* (1964), a fictionalized story of comedienne and vaudeville headliner Fanny Brice and his most acclaimed score, *Gypsy* (1959), written with Stephen Sondheim (b. 1930), including such songs as "Everything's Coming Up Roses" and "Some People."

While the original production was a personal tour de force for Ethel Merman, *Gypsy* was brought back to Broadway in two later revivals: one starring English-born actress Angela Lansbury, and the most recent starring Tyne Daly, a popular television actress who toured with *Gypsy* for more than a year until bringing it to Broadway in a triumphant return in 1989.

Stephen Sondheim served as lyricist for *Gypsy*, *West Side Story* (1957), and *Do I Hear A Waltz* (1965). He was composer/lyricist for many milestone Broadway musicals, including *Company* (1970), the story of relationships in the fast track of New York; *Follies* (1970), recounting the history of a theater soon to be torn down and the reunion of former follies' dancers and their spouses, visually merging the spectrum of the past and the reality of the present; and *A Little Night Music* (1973), taken from the Ingmar Bergman film *Smiles of a Summer Night* set in Sweden at the beginning of the twentieth century, for which his most popular song, "Send In The Clowns," was written. In the writing of *West Side Story*, a modernization of Shakespeare's Romeo and Juliet set in the tenements of New York, pitting Puerto Rican against "Anglo" gang members, Sondheim was teamed with composer-conductor Leonard Bernstein (1918–1990) whose early musicals, written in the 1940s, included *On The Town* (1944), with its outstanding song "New York, New York," and *Wonderful Town* (1953), starring Rosalind Russell. *West Side Story* (1957) had such gigantic hits as "Tonight," "I Feel Pretty," and "Maria." Parts of *West Side Story* were reproduced in the 1989 Broadway show *Jerome Robbins' Broadway*, a self-created tribute by that noted director-choreographer.

Sammy Cahn (b. 1913), the lyricist for *Funny Girl*, also wrote the lyrics for such famous songs as "Bei Mir Bist Du Schoen" (1937), setting new English words to the Sholom Secunda masterpiece; "Papa, Won't You Dance With Me" (1947) from Cahn's first musical *High Button Shoes*, which starred vaudevillian and comedian Phil Silvers; "Three Coins in a Fountain," which Cahn wrote with his favorite partner, Jule Styne; and "Love and Marriage" (1955), which was popularized by Frank Sinatra from the original TV musical version of "Our Town."

The 1940s and early 1950s saw several other composers and lyricists who went on to great success. Alan J. Lerner (1918–1986), the son of the founder of the Lerner clothing stores, and Frederick Loewe (1904–1989), the son of a prominent Viennese opera singer and cantor, wrote such Broadway musicals as *Brigadoon* (1947), with songs "Almost Like Being In Love" and "Heather On The Hill" and their worldwide favorite musical version of George Bernard Shaw's "Pygmalion," *My Fair Lady* (1956), which starred Rex Harrison and Julie Andrews. *My Fair Lady* contained numerous standards, such as "Get Me to the Church On Time," "A Hymn to Him," and "On the Street Where You Live." Other Lerner and Loewe musical successes include *Camelot* (1960), the story of King Arthur and the Knights of the Round Table, which

starred *My Fair Lady* favorite Julie Andrews with Richard Burton and Robert Goulet; and both the film and stage versions of the Collette novel, *Gigi*.

Richard Adler (b. 1921) and Jerry Ross (1926–1955) began as popular music writers with their hit "Rags to Riches" but completed their careers writing the Broadway shows *Pajama Game* and *Damn Yankees* with hit songs "Hey There" (1954) and "You Gotta Have Heart" (1955).

Cy Coleman (b. 1929), a well-known jazz musician, also wrote several Broadway musicals, ranging from *Wild Cat* (1960) to *Sweet Charity* (1966). His 1990 musical entitled *A City of Angels* combines the spy novel and "who dunnit" with the conventions of the Broadway stage. Included among Coleman's popular songs are "Witchcraft" (1957), "Hey, Look Me Over" (1960), sung by Lucille Ball in her Broadway musical starring debut, and "Big Spender" (1966). His several-time lyricist, Dorothy Fields (1905–1974), the daughter of Lew Fields of the vaudeville team Weber and Fields, was a renowned songwriter before collaborating with Coleman. Among her many famous songs are "I Can't Give You Anything But Love, Baby" (1928) and "On the Sunny Side of the Street" (1930). With Coleman, she wrote one of her standard songs, "If My Friends Could See Me Now" (1966), which was for *Sweet Charity*.

The music scene in the 1950s and 1960s experienced an enormous growth of songwriters in several musical fields. Hal David (b. 1921) and Burt Bacharach (b. 1928) wrote popular songs such as "One Less Bell to Answer" (1967), "I'll Never Fall in Love Again" (1968), "Raindrops Keep Falling on My Head" (1969), and "Close to You" (1970), as well as their successful Broadway musical *Promises, Promises* (1968). Among the great popular songwriters of the 1950s were Max C. Freedman (1893–1962) and James Myers (b. 1919), whose 1953 classic "Rock Around the Clock" contributed to the "rock-and-roll" music of that decade. The most widely known Jewish songwriters of the '50s, with a profound impact on American and world culture of that day, were Jerry Leiber (b. 1933) and Mike Stoller (b. 1933), who wrote such classics for Elvis Presley as "You Ain't Nothin' But a Hound Dog" (1956), "Lovin' You" (1957), "Treat Me Nice" (1957), and "Jail House Rock" (1957). American popular music would never be the same after Presley's and his colleagues' collaboration.

If the 1950s were known for escapist, almost silly music, the 1960s saw a return to the political, social, and cultural upheavals of the decades after

World War I. With this growth of political content songs came an explosive growth in the meaningful contribution by Jewish songwriters and performers. Among the most important was Bob Dylan (b. 1941), born Robert Zimmerman, with such songs as "Mr. Tambourine Man" (1964), "Blowin' In the Wind" (1962), "Like a Rolling Stone" (1965), and "The Times, They Are a Changin'" (1964). Neil Diamond (b. 1941) contributed such songs as "I Got the Feelin'" (1966), "I'm a Believer" (1966), "Song Sung Blue" (1972), and the remake of the early Al Jolson film, *The Jazz Singer*, with Diamond as both composer/lyricist and star. Neil Sedaka (b. 1939), who began writing in the 1950s, had numerous song hits but enjoyed his greatest impact in the early 1960s with such romantic ballads and love songs as "Breakin' Up Is Hard to Do" (1962) and "Calendar Girl" (1962). Sedaka's career stretched over three decades with his ability to update his hits of the 1950s and 1960s into the different stylized versions of the 1970s and 1980s.

Considered by many to be the most influential songwriters since the 1960s, Paul Simon (b. 1942) and Art Garfunkel (b. 1942) are responsible for some of the most beautiful songs and meaningful ballads in recent American popular music, including "The Sound of Silence" (1966), "Scarborough Fair" (1966), "Bridge Over Troubled Waters" (1969), "My Little Town" (1975), and "Forty Ways to Leave Your Lover" (1976). After they dissolved their partnership in 1969, each went on to creative and profitable solo careers in the music and entertainment fields. Garfunkel also starred in several successful Hollywood films in non-singing roles. Simon created much controversy when he collaborated with a large group of black South African musicians and performers to record several albums and tour the world. Even at their young age, Simon and Garfunkel have made meaningful contributions to American music in four different decades.

Two women of note are performer-songwriters Carole King (b. 1942) and Carly Simon (b. 1945), of the Simon and Schuster publishing family. King's songs, some of which she introduced and performed, include "Go Away Little Girl" (1964), "I Feel the Earth Move" (1971), "You've Got a Friend" (1971), and her most popular song, "You Light Up My Life" (1974). Carly Simon's hits include "You're So Vain" (1971) and "Anticipation" (1973), the appeal of which fostered a television advertising campaign.

Even with the growth of the record, video, and compact disc industries, which have fostered numerous talented composers and lyricists, some of our most popular songs were created for Broadway musicals. Jerry Herman (b. 1932), the University of Miami-trained composer/lyricist, was responsible for many hugely successful musicals as well as several that broke new ground in creative themes and sensitive issues. Among these were *Milk and Honey* (1961), a tribute to the then 13-year-old State of Israel, which starred Yiddish theater actress Molly Picon and opera star Robert Weedes; *Hello Dolly* (1964), starring the irrepressible Carol Channing and succeeding her, a "who's who" of prominent Broadway stars portraying the role of Dolly Levi, the "matchmaker" based on Thornton Wilder's play; *Mame*, starring Angela Lansbury as the outrageous, iconoclastic offbeat, yet ingratiating Auntie Mame of the Patrick Dennis novel; and *La Cage Aux Folles* (1983), based on the French movie of the same title, a truly innovative show that made musical comedy history by using a homosexual couple as its protagonists. These shows provided such songs as "Shalom" (1961), the title songs "Hello Dolly" (1964) and "Mame" (1966), and the so-called "gay anthem," "I Am What I Am."

Charles Strouse (b. 1928) joined with several partners to write such popular shows as *Bye, Bye Birdie* (1960), the humorous tribute to an Elvis Presley-like singer whose popularity sweeps and overturns a midwestern "typical" home-town; *Applause* (1970), a musicalization of the Oscar-winning Bette Davis film *All About Eve*, and the musical *Annie* (1977), a Broadway version of the famous comic-strip characters found in Little Orphan Annie. Among the song successes of those shows were "One Last Kiss" from *Bye Bye Birdie*, the title song in *Applause* and "The Sun Will Come Out Tomorrow" from *Annie*, which became a world famous saccharine hymn to the future, enjoying huge success.

John Kander (b. 1927) and Fred Ebb (b. 1932) were responsible for such meaningful theatrical presentations as *Cabaret* (1966), which dealt with pre-Nazi Germany; *Zorba* (1968), taken from the Kazantzakis novel *Zorba the Greek*; and *Chicago* (1975), which satirized the gangster days of the 1920s in Chicago. The hit songs from these shows included the title song "Cabaret," "Life Is" from *Zorba* and "Mr. Cellophane" from *Chicago*. Kander and Ebb have written several other musicals and contribute prominently to the "specialty-music" field, writing and producing one-person shows, especially for Liza Minnelli.

Jerry Bock (b. 1928) and Sheldon Harnick (b. 1924) collaborated on the Pulitzer Prize show *Fiorello* (1959) and two musicals that dealt with Jewish themes, *Fiddler on the Roof* (1964) and *The Rothschilds* (1970).

Finally, Marvin Hamlisch (b. 1944), the now famous Broadway composer and film arranger who has earned huge success with Academy Award winning contributions to the film *The Sting*, adapting music by Scott Joplin, and his Pulitzer Prize first Broadway musical, *A Chorus Line* (1975), which surpassed 6000 performances on Broadway, becoming by far the longest running play or musical in the history of the American theater. Hamlisch's songs include the standard from *A Chorus Line*, "What I Did for Love," and his equally popular film song and Academy Award winner, "The Way We Were." After the success of *A Chorus Line*, Hamlisch wrote several undistinguished musicals and will strive for years to achieve the acclaim of his Antoinette Perry (Tony) Best Musical Award winning classic story of "gypsies"—the dancers in a Broadway Show.

The enormity of the contribution by Jews to American popular music can only be understood when realizing that the names and songs included herein are but the peak of a creative mountain, containing hundreds more names and thousands more songs that have, in the past 150 years, contributed profoundly to American culture and the American psyche.

Jerome Kern wrote, "Irving Berlin has no place in American music; he is American music." This statement might be paraphrased accurately by saying, "American Jews have no place in American music; they are American music." *See also* Music, Classical; Music, Rock and Roll.

KENNETH A. KANTER

BIBLIOGRAPHY

Ewen, David. *All the Years of American Popular Music.* Englewood Cliffs, N.J.: Prentice-Hall, 1977.

Green, Stanley. *The World of Musical Comedy.* South Brunswick, N.J.: Barnes, 1976.

Hamm, Charles. *Yesterdays.* New York: Norton, 1979.

Kanter, Kenneth A. *Jews On Tin Pan Alley.* New York: Ktav, 1982.

Levy, Lester S. *Give Me Yesterday.* Norman: University of Oklahoma Press, 1975.

Music, Rock and Roll.

Almost a half century after British playwright Israel Zangwill described the United States as "God's crucible, the great Melting Pot" where a new man, "the fusion of races" would live, a new music emerged from urban America that seemed to fulfill Zangwill's prophecy. A history of rock and roll music could well be called the electric melting pot since the music brought together in amplified form the musical traditions of many cultures.

Jewish Americans have played an important role in every stage of the history of the music, although not all Jewish performers, record company executives, disc jockeys, songwriters, promoters, critics, and fans who shaped and championed the music brought distinctively Jewish sensibilities to the music. Nonetheless, their sheer numbers speak to the crucial role Jewish Americans have played in the shaping of contemporary popular culture.

Perhaps more than anything else, the disproportionately large number of Jews who have made their mark in rock and roll reflects the respect and affinity Jewish people feel for Afro-American culture. Perhaps this alliance reflects the common historical experience of two peoples who have often been made to feel their marginality in American society. Does this kinship perhaps speak to common musical roots? More than one artist has answered the question in much the same manner that rhythm and blues talent scout Ralph Peer once did when he told an interviewer: "I hear the blues in a minor key, and, hey, baby, I'm back in synagogue."

When Elvis Presley first went to Sun Records in Memphis in 1953 for an audition, his family was so poor that when the secretary asked him to leave his phone number, Presley left the number of the rabbi who lived downstairs from his parents' apartment. That rabbi probably did not know that he was helping to inaugurate a revolution in musical taste, but even before the advent of Elvis, it was clear that young people were hungering for music more relevant to their lives than Perry Como and Patti Page.

Disc jockey Alan Freed (1922–1965) popularized the phrase "rock and roll" to describe the new sound emerging in the early 1950s, defended the integrity of the music against those who wished to censor it or water it down, and, some say, was among the music's first martyrs.

Freed was the host of a classical program until he began to notice that every time he went into a local record store, the young shoppers went wild whenever the owners put on a record featuring a driving beat and a honking saxophone. Convinced that there was much untapped potential in rhythm and blues, in 1951 he convinced radio station WJW in Cleveland to let him host a new program, "Moondog's Rock 'n' Roll Party." Freed promoted several teen dances at various midwestern arenas and armories that stunned locals by attracting overflow crowds of allegedly rampaging teens drawn to the sounds of predominantly black artists.

Freed's popularity grew proportionately when he moved his show to WINS in New York in 1954. His name practically became synonymous with rock and roll thanks to his presence as an M.C. at many rock and roll reviews, his starring role in several hastily thrown together films designed to cash in on the rock and roll "fad," and his outspoken defense of the music in the face of a barrage of criticism. Freed refused to play records by white artists who "covered" songs originally recorded by black artists because he felt that they were inferior and sanitized versions of the originals.

In the early 1960s, Freed's career was destroyed by his close association with the heavily publicized "payola" scandals. The payment of cash in exchange for radio play was common in the industry then and now, but politicians, sensing that there were votes in investigating rock and roll, subpoenaed Freed to appear before a congressional committee. It is true that Freed received payoffs as well as royalties for songs he did not write, but his punishment hardly fit the crimes. Broke, hounded by the IRS, and suffering from alcoholism, Freed lived a nightmarish existence in his final days. His story is told in fictionalized form in the 1978 film *American Hot Wax*.

Before Alan Freed helped create a national market for rock and roll, several savvy businessmen also sensed that there was a growing market for urban rhythm and blues. Among the best-known record company owners were Phil and Leonard Chess of Chicago, who came to America from Poland in 1928 as part of the last wave of immigrants from Eastern Europe. For many years, the Chess brothers operated a nightclub for predominantly black patrons on Chicago's South Side that featured an electrified blues appealing to migrants from the rural South. Eventually, the Chess brothers began to record some of the acts appearing in their club and distributed the records on various labels until they adopted the name "Chess Records" in 1949. Chess quickly achieved enormous success in the rhythm-and-blues market, issuing classic sides by Muddy Waters, Howlin' Wolf, and numerous other wizards of the South

Side. In 1951, Chess recorded Jackie Brenson's "Rocket 88," which is generally considered to be the first rock-and-roll record.

When rock and roll began to dominate the airwaves in the mid-1950s, Chess enjoyed success with Bo Diddley and arguably the most influential guitarist songwriter in the history of the music, Chuck Berry. Most Chess Records were produced by Leonard, who is recognized as one of the finest producers in the business as well as a shrewd businessman. An eccentric and superstitious man, Leonard represented a peculiar amalgamation of the shtetl and the urban ghetto. One might think of Leonard Chess as the one and only "shtetl cat."

Legend has it that Syd Nathan was told by his doctor to get into a less stressful occupation than the furniture business, so in 1945 he formed King Records in Cincinnati. King Records was one of the few companies to market black and white artists on the same label, and Nathan enjoyed success in both markets. He recorded popular country artists, such as Moon Mullican, Grandpa Jones, and the Delmore Brothers. In 1954, King gained notoriety for issuing Hank Ballard and the Midnighters' raunchy classic "Work With Me Annie," sales of which were no doubt boosted by the refusal of respectable stations to play it. Later, King Records also included on its roster such notable performers as blues guitarist Albert King and the inimitable James Brown.

While an older generation of record moguls might have viewed rock and roll as another fad to be cashed in on for a fast buck, a younger generation of artists who came of age with the music demonstrated a considerable amount of empathy for the music's sources. Jerry Leiber (b. 1933) and Mike Stoller (b. 1933) were the master craftsmen of rock and roll songwriting. Leiber grew up in a racially mixed neighborhood, where he presumably gained some of the fluency in street language that would later characterize his lyrics. He met his collaborator, Mike Stoller, when he moved to California. The duo began to write songs and peddle them to various artists in the Los Angeles area.

Leiber and Stoller had a number of minor hits in the rhythm-and-blues market before they got their first big break when they signed a distribution deal with Atlantic Records in 1953. Atlantic was the dominant label in rhythm and blues in the 1950s and had an impressive stable of artists. Leiber and Stoller enjoyed their greatest initial success writing songs for the Coasters, a slapstick Los Angeles vocal group whose series of quasi-novelty songs such as "Yakety Yak" (1958), "Charlie Brown" (1959), and "Shoppin' For Clothes" (1960) offer a schlemiel's perspective on the world.

It was a song that Leiber and Stoller had originally written for "Big Mama" Thornton in 1953, "Hound Dog," that would provide Elvis Presley with his second national hit in 1956. Writing several more hits for Presley (including the title song for his 1957 film *Jailhouse Rock*) gave Leiber and Stoller added prestige. They wrote moving and innovative songs, which they produced, for the vocal group the Drifters, beginning with "There Goes My Baby" in 1959.

It would be impossible to list even a fraction of the groundbreaking songs this duo is responsible for, but among their many standouts are Wilbert Harrison's "Kansas City" (1959), the Coasters' civil rights anthem "What About Us" (1959), and Ben E. King's remarkable "Stand By Me," a stunning ballad that went to the top of the charts when it was released in 1961 and again 25 years later when it was used as the title song to a highly successful film.

Leiber and Stoller, like a generation of Tin Pan Alley songsmiths before them, never seriously considered recording their own material. This tradition was continued by the songwriters associated with the Brill Building, a legendary songwriting factory located at 1619 Broadway in New York City.

Don Kirshner (b. 1924) had already tried his hand at every aspect of the music business when he rented office space in the Brill Building in 1958 to house Aldon Music, a publishing company he cofounded in the hopes of developing some hit songs. He began to hire young songwriters, most barely out of their teens, and in just a few years he put together one of the most remarkable arrays of talent anywhere.

One of Kirshner's first discoveries was songwriter-pianist Neil Sedaka (b. 1939). Classically trained as a youngster, Sedaka was already composing when at 13 years of age he met his songwriting partner Howard Greenfield, whose family lived in the same apartment building in Brooklyn as the Sedakas. Eventually, the two would collaborate on some 500 songs, but in the early days they played in various bands hoping to get some recognition. Sedaka scored his first hit with "The Diary" (1958) and followed it with a string of hits, most notably "Calendar Girl"

(1960), "Happy Birthday Sweet Sixteen" (1961), and "Breaking Up Is Hard to Do" (1962). Like many of the careers of the Brill Building artists, Sedaka's career sagged in the aftermath of the British invasion of 1964, but Sedaka enjoyed a major resurgence of popularity with his light pop tunes in the mid-1970s.

He was principally known for his recordings of his own compositions, but most Brill Building artists were apparently content to avoid the spotlight. Such was the case with a teenager of whom Neil Sedaka later recalled his mother initially disapproved. This chain-smoking 16-year-old "would follow me around every time I appeared at a wedding or bar mitzvah" Sedaka once said, but in truth Carole King (b. Carole Klein, 1942) was already a precocious college freshman and the leader of her own band, the Cosines.

King began putting melodies to lyrics written by her boyfriend and future husband Gerry Goffin (b. 1939). Beginning with the Shirelles' groundbreaking 1960 hit "Will You Still Love Me Tomorrow?" Goffin and King became one of the most astonishingly prolific and successful songwriting teams in rock-and-roll history. The couple wrote songs that ranged from eloquent hymns to urban music like the Drifters' much covered "Up on the Roof" (1962), to songs that inspired dance crazes like Little Eva's "The Loco-Motion" (1962), and eventually even to the Byrds' counterculture classic "Wasn't Born to Follow" and "Goin' Back" (1966).

King and Goffin ended their musical partnership when they divorced. Carole King had recorded a few minor hit versions of her own songs, but it would not be until the release of her second solo album, "Tapestry," that she would become a star in her own right. Released in 1971, "Tapestry" stayed on the album charts an unbelievable three years and established a new record for album sales.

Barry Mann (b. 1939) and Cynthia Weil were also a husband and wife team in the Brill Building workshop. Their best-known songs include "Uptown" (1962), a subtle affirmation of black pride recorded by the Crystals. The duo seemed to enjoy their greatest success collaborating with producer Phil Spector to create some of the most memorable rock-and-roll records of the 1960s, including the Ronettes' "Walking in the Rain" (1964) and "You've Lost That Lovin' Feeling" (1964), which was the biggest hit of the Righteous Brothers' career.

In 1966, Mann and Weil wrote an unusual

gritty antidrug song, "Kicks," which was a hit for Paul Revere and the Raiders. Mann and Weil enjoyed occasional successes in the 1970s and 1980s, and in 1986 helped to do the score for Steven Speilberg's mouse-eyed view of the Jewish-American immigrant experience, *An American Tail*.

Jeff Barry (b. 1938) had written and recorded several minor hits when he began collaborating with Ellie Greenwich (b. 1940), an English major in college who had recorded a few songs under the name Ellie Gay. Amidst the highly competitive environment of the Brill Building, Greenwich and Barry more than held their own with such standards as the Ronettes' "Be My Baby" (1963), the Dixie Cups' "Goin' to the Chapel" (1964), and the Crystals' "Then He Kissed Me" (1963). In 1964, the pair began to compose for various artists appearing on Leiber and Stoller's Red Bird label. For Red Bird they penned a series of melodramatic hits for the Shangri-Las.

Greenwich and Barry also played an important role in launching the career of singer-songwriter and actor Neil Diamond (b. 1941). Like many of his peers, Diamond earned his spurs working at Aldon Music writing songs for others. He wrote the Monkees' 1966 hit "I'm a Believer" and landed a recording contract of his own when Greenwich and Barry recommended him to Bang Records. Beginning with "Cherry, Cherry" (1966), Diamond had an enormous run of hits and developed a wide following both for his music and his starring role in a 1980 remake of *The Jazz Singer*. Like singer-actress Barbra Streisand (b. 1942), Diamond's appeal is largely to a nonrock audience, hence a fair assessment of his or Streisand's work lies outside the parameters of rock and roll.

Many of the Brill Building's most memorable songs were written for singers in girl groups, a genre that seemed to give producers and songwriters as much prestige and possibly more wealth than the singers themselves. One teenage vocalist who attained success belting out Brill Building tunes was Lesley Gore (b. 1946), who liked to refer to herself as an average girl to whom other teens could relate. At 17 she topped the charts with "It's My Party" (1963) and went on to record a number of successful and energetic versions of songs written by Mann and Weil, Greenwich and Barry, and others. In late 1963, she recorded her most intriguing record, the protofeminist anthem "You Don't Own Me."

But of all the artists to emerge from the Brill Building/New York scene, none topped the legendary status attained by musician, songwriter, and producer Phil Spector (b. 1940). He set the standards for the production of rock-and-roll records that heavily influenced the Beatles, the Beach Boys, and later Bruce Springsteen.

Spector was born in the Bronx but moved to California with his mother Bertha (for whom he would later name his publishing company) after his father's death. By all accounts, Spector was the consummate outsider as a kid, and he was viewed by his southern California peers as something of a weirdo.

In 1958, he took the inscription on his father's tombstone in a Jewish cemetery on Long Island and used it as the title of a song he'd written, "To Know Him Is To Love Him" (1958). He formed a band with classmates Annette Bard and Marshall Lieb, and billing themselves as the Teddy Bears, the teenagers found themselves with a number-one song and an appearance on national television. Unfortunately, the Teddy Bears did not receive a fair share of the royalties owed them, and in the process Spector learned some harsh lessons. After briefly abandoning the music business, he moved back to New York, where, in effect, he apprenticed himself to Leiber and Stoller. He co-wrote the much covered "Spanish Harlem" (1961) for Ben E. King, and by the following year he was a widely respected freelance producer.

At the ripe old age of 21, Spector formed his own record label, Philles, and from 1962 until 1966, he fashioned a string of memorable and highly distinctive records. Spector devoted an immense amount of studio time to the creation of each 45 RPM, processing drums, pianos, guitars, percussion, and background singers to create what was widely referred to as the Spector Wall of Sound. A Phil Spector record called attention to itself by its sheer energy and noise. Spector liked to describe his records as "pocket symphonies for the kids," and no one ever has made records that sound quite like "Be My Baby," "Da Doo Ron Ron" and "You've Lost That Lovin' Feelin.'"

Spector's fame increased considerably after the Beatles and Rolling Stones praised his work, and he was the subject of a myth-making essay by New York journalist Tom Wolfe, but he also made many enemies with his arrogance and unpredictability. After the commercial failure of Ike and Tina Turner's "River Deep, Mountain High"

(1966), an embittered Spector retired from the business and went into seclusion. Lured out of retirement by the Beatles (John Lennon called him "the greatest record producer ever"), he pulled together an album from the fractious "Let it Be" sessions and eventually produced solo albums for Lennon and George Harrison.

In part the victim of his own legend, Spector worked sporadically in the 1970s and 1980s, and with increasingly limited commercial impact. The music business is now a big business, and few artists or labels can afford to hire the musicians and studio time necessary for the creation of a Phil Spector record.

Prior to the British invasion in 1964, two of the biggest trends in popular music were the surf music craze and the folk revival, the latter, in turn, giving way in 1965 to folk-rock. The surf instrumental sound—a raunchy guitar over a pumped-up beat—was originated by Dick Dale, a Lebanese-born southern Californian whose recording career never equaled the impact of his live performances. Dale reworked a traditional Middle Eastern folk tune, "Miserlou" (1961) and turned it into a regional hit, and later he laid down a truly memorable surf-rock version of "Hava Nagila."

When folk music enjoyed one of its periodic resurgences of popularity in the late 1950s, Ramblin' Jack Elliott (b. Elliott Charles Adnopoz, 1931) was one of the links between the protest singers of the Depression era and the new generation of folkies. Elliott had attached himself to legendary balladeer and topical songwriter Woody Guthrie in the late 1940s and played an important role in preserving and popularizing Guthrie's music in the 1950s, particularly through his spirited recordings of Guthrie's songs for children.

One of the young singers who came to hear Elliott perform in Greenwich Village was Phil Ochs (1940-1976), the son of an army doctor and an aspiring journalist who was one of the more original talents to come out of the folk scene. His tune "I Ain't Marchin' Anymore" (1965) became a staple of the antiwar movement of the 1960s and typifies Ochs's iconoclastic left-wing patriotism. Beset with personal problems, Ochs's career seemed to lose its focus by the late 1960s, and his life deteriorated rapidly in the years prior to his suicide in 1976.

Singer, songwriter, and generational hero Bob Dylan (b. Robert Allen Zimmerman, 1941) emerged from the folk scene to become the dominant figure in rock and roll in the 1960s. Dylan grew up in a solidly middle-class family in Hibbing, Minnesota, where according to some of his contemporaries there were strong undercurrents of anti-Semitism. Initially attracted to rock and roll as a teenager, in his high school yearbook he claimed his greatest ambition in life was to play in Little Richard's band. After spending an unhappy year at the University of Minnesota, where he briefly joined Sigma Alpha Mu, a Jewish fraternity, he made his way to New York City in 1961. By then, Dylan had been transformed into a folk singer, thanks to the influence of his "first and last idol," Woody Guthrie.

Dylan quickly gained attention as a traditional folk singer with a penchant for creating topical songs similar to those of Guthrie and Pete Seeger. His first album, "Bob Dylan" (1962), flopped, but his reputation as a songwriter gained him increasing respect. In 1963, Peter, Paul, and Mary scored a hit with Dylan's "Blowin' in the Wind," which they later sang with Dylan at the Lincoln Memorial in August 1963 just before Martin Luther King's famous "I Have a Dream" speech.

From 1963 until his motorcycle accident in 1966 caused a retreat from stardom, Dylan enjoyed his greatest period of productivity. He penned a series of classic protest songs in 1963–1964 that revealed that he had taken the Guthrie tradition of topical songwriting and merged it with, among other things, the black humor of the atomic age, the rhythmic sense of the beat poets of the 1950s, and the contempt for authority that is the basis of rock and roll. He composed several songs in response to the civil rights movement: "The Times They Are A-Changin'," "Oxford Town," and "Only a Pawn in Their Game" (1963). He also offered several satiric and cutting comments on the Cold War including "Masters of War," "With God on Our Side" (which included the lines "When the Second World War came to an end/ We forgave the Germans and we were friends. Though they murdered six million/ In the ovens they fried. The Germans now too/ Have God on their side") and the apocalyptic "A Hard Rain's Gonna Fall," written amidst the Cuban missile crisis of 1962.

In 1964, Dylan signaled an end to his explicitly political work and turned to more personal concerns. The following year he shocked and angered many of his friends in the folk community by returning to the music he played as a teenager, rock and roll. In 1965-1966, he released three albums—"Bringing it All Back Home," Highway 61 Revisited,'' and ''Blonde on Blonde''—that are perhaps his finest. He gained increasing respect as a uniquely talented poet who not only had a biting sense of irony, but also knew how to rock.

In the late 1960s, Dylan explored country music and clearly seemed intent on retreating from the mass adulation he had gained in the mid-1960s. He became increasingly reclusive and for a time was reported to have rediscovered his Jewish roots. He made at least three trips to Israel and was photographed at the Wailing Wall.

Thus it came as a shock when it was revealed in 1979 that Dylan was calling himself a born-again Christian. Other more perceptive critics, however, noted that Dylan's work had always reflected an interest in spiritual concerns in general, Jewish and non-Jewish. In 1962, after all, he had recorded a traditional tune called ''Gospel Plow.''

By 1983, Dylan apparently abandoned Christianity and once again began to record secular material, although his work was neither critically nor commercially successful. Critics on the left were particularly appalled by ''Neighborhood Bully,'' a strident defense of the State of Israel that appeared on his ''Infidels'' album.

Dylan is a contrary figure, but he has probably inspired more people to take up the guitar than any artist other than the Beatles and Elvis Presley. He retains the respect of his peers. He headlined the Live Aid benefit that raised millions for starving Africans in 1985. After suggesting during his performance that something ought to be done to help American farmers, the first of a series of Farm Aid benefit concerts was held later that year. In 1986, he appeared on a national television special devoted to the first national observance of the holiday honoring the birthday of Martin Luther King, Jr.

Dylan's work is replete with references to Jewish theology and mystical traditions, and this is most movingly evident in ''Forever Young,'' a song written for his 1974 ''Planet Waves'' album. ''May God bless and keep you always/ May your wishes all come true. May you always do for others/And let others do for you'' Dylan sang in phrases that clearly echo the priestly blessing known as *Y'vorech'cho*. More than any other artist discussed in this entry, Dylan's work reflects a lifelong search for spiritual fulfillment.

Guitarist and vocalist Mark Volman (b. 1944) and vocalist Howard Kaylan (b. 1945) were among the many artists during the 1960s to score a commercial breakthrough with a pop version of a Bob Dylan song. Their version of Dylan's ''It Ain't Me Babe'' (1965) gave Volman and Kaylan's band, the Turtles, the first of numerous top ten hits featuring their piercing, falsetto harmonies. The duo later reemerged billing themselves as Flo and Eddie, first as the lead singers of Frank Zappa and the Mothers of Invention, and later as rock-and-roll satirists. It is perhaps easy to imagine Kaylan and Volman, witty and irreverent, as stars of vaudeville or the Yiddish theater if they had come of age in the 1920s or 1930s.

The Mamas and Papas were also part of the folk-rock movement of the mid-1960s, and while songwriter John Phillips was the vocal group's dominant figure, on stage and occasionally on record the spirit of these West Coast refugees from Greenwich Village was best exemplified by vocalist Cass Elliot (1943–1974). Between 1964 and 1968, the group had 14 top ten hits, and after the band split up Elliot inaugurated a successful solo career until her accidental death in 1974.

Like Phil Spector, singer, guitarist, and songwriter Paul Simon (b. 1941) and vocalist Art Garfunkel (b. 1941) had their first taste of the big time as teenagers, when billing themselves as Tom and Jerry they scored a modest hit with ''Hey Schoolgirl'' (1957). Simon and Garfunkel began singing together as grammar school students in Forest Hills (Queens, N.Y.), and both recorded a couple of unsuccessful solo records in the early 1960s. The duo got their break when producer Tom Wilson, sensing the growing popularity of folk rock, added strings and other electric instruments to an acoustic version of a song that had been recorded a few months earlier. The record, ''The Sounds of Silence'' (1965), immediately shot to the top of the charts, and Simon and Garfunkel were on their way.

Over the next five years, Simon and Garfunkel had a dozen top ten singles. The songs were written by Simon and were unusually self-conscious for rock-and-roll lyrics; generally, their records were carefully produced. The two went their separate ways in 1970 just after the release of what turned out to be their most successful album, ''Bridge Over Troubled Waters.''

Art Garfunkel has recorded several albums of pop standards since 1970 and appeared in several feature films. He joined Simon briefly for a reunion single in 1975 and a subsequent tour.

Paul Simon continued to enjoy a steady stream of hit albums and singles in the 1970s and 1980s while exploring a number of musical genres. His career briefly floundered in the 1980s, but he enjoyed a major comeback in 1987 with the critically acclaimed and politically controversial "Graceland" album.

The 1960s truly were a renaissance period for rock and roll, as the music panned out and explored one musical vein after another. The popularity of the Rolling Stones in particular helped to spawn an awakening interest in the blues. Mike Bloomfield (1944–1981) and Al Kooper (b. 1941) also played important roles in reviving the popularity of the urban blues.

Mike Bloomfield grew up amidst the Chicago club scene and learned the blues guitar while sitting at the feet of the masters. He joined Paul Butterfield's Blues Band in 1965 and that same year accompanied Bob Dylan on stage and on record. Eventually, he was a founding member of the Electric Flag and recorded several solo albums. To his admirers, Bloomfield was America's answer to British blues' guitarist hero Eric Clapton. Tragically, his career was overtaken by drug abuse, and he died from an overdose of heroin in 1981.

Bloomfield's greatest commercial success came in 1968 when he cut the "Super Session" album with Stephen Stills and producer, songwriter, and organist Al Kooper, already a seasoned veteran of the music business. Kooper began his recording career at 15 when his band the Royal Teens enjoyed a novelty hit with "Short Shorts" (1958). In the 1960s, he free-lanced as a songwriter and played the organ on several Dylan albums. He helped organize the Blues Project in 1965 (a virtually all-Jewish blues band) and the highly successful jazz-rock fusion band Blood, Sweat, and Tears in 1968. In the 1970s and 1980s, Kooper continued to produce hit records and wrote an autobiography, *Backstage Passes* (1976).

Inspired by the example of Carole King, the 1970s saw the advent of the singer-songwriter. Carly Simon (b. 1945) emerged in the early 1970s with a series of hits based on loosely autobiographical concerns, most notably "You're So Vain" (1972).

Bette Midler (b. 1945), on the other hand, was clearly in a class by herself with her Sophie Tucker-style Red Hot Mama stage act and her successful reworking of old torch songs. Midler, who had a minor part in the Broadway version of *Fiddler on the Roof* before delving into her recording career, never lost her bent for theatrics. Her records, while usually a good deal of fun, never quite captured the vitality and presence of her live act. By the 1980s, she seemed intent upon devoting more time to her increasingly successful film career and seems likely to remain a major film star for many years to come.

Midler's musical director in the early 1970s was pianist-composer Barry Manilow (b. 1946), who launched his solo career with the chart-topping "Mandy" (1975) and became one of the biggest selling artists of the decade. Although he was classically trained, Manilow's enormous popularity probably owed more to his background as the composer of numerous advertising jingles in the early 1970s.

It has been said that rock-and-roll musicians made records in the 1960s and made money in the 1970s. The industry came increasingly to be dominated by arena rockers who recycled old formulas. Glitter and heavy metal placed particular importance on theatrics, and the public loved it. Among the most successful bands in this genre was Kiss, a band that wore makeup and carefully guarded their true appearance. Kiss included bassist and vocalist Gene Simmons (b. Gene Klein, 1949) and guitarist and vocalist Paul Stanley (b. Paul Eisen, 1952), who have both pursued solo careers in the 1980s.

Punk rock emerged in the early 1970s to challenge the excesses of the superstar mentality that had overtaken the music. Like many reform movements, the punks sought to change things by returning to basics. Such was the objective of the pioneer punk band, the Ramones, who began playing in seedy New York bars in 1974. Although the Ramones never enjoyed much commercial success, they were widely imitated here and in Europe and were critically acclaimed for their humor and originality. Lead singer Joey Ramone (b. Jeffrey Hyman, 1952) wrote many of the band's utterly irreverent songs.

When punk was being widely hailed (at least in some quarters) for purging rock and roll of many of its excesses, chroniclers seeking to trace the origins of the movement invariably cited the work of songwriter-guitarist Lou Reed (b. 1943). After an unhappy childhood on Long Island, Reed attended Syracuse University, which he did not like much either. He learned to play the guitar and also studied with the tormented poet Delmore Schwartz, later the subject of two Reed compositions, "The European Immigrant's Son" (1967) and "My House" (1982).

Reed played with several bands in the 1960s but did not get much attention until 1967 when, amidst the "summer of love," his band, the Velvet Underground, shocked the rock-and-roll world with songs reflecting Reed's unusually dark vision.

After the band fell apart in 1970, Reed launched a rocky solo career that somehow saw him move to the brink of stardom only seemingly deliberately to back away. In the 1980s, apparently more at ease with himself, Reed resumed his recording career and enjoyed modest success. While Reed is best known as the author of a series of rock-and-roll classics, particularly on his solo albums, he has written with unnerving realism about the internal dynamics of Jewish family life.

The 1980s also saw the belated commercial success of pianist-songwriter Warren Zevon (b. 1947), who, while best known for his 1978 "Werewolves of London," has written a number of songs reflecting his biting wit and social concerns.

Rock and roll has always been accused of being vulgar and tasteless, and perhaps no band in the 1980s honored this tradition in a more orthodox fashion than the Beastie Boys. Their second album, "Licensed to Ill" (1986) suddenly cast this trio of Jewish boys in the limelight, and they responded by putting on their worst behavior.

Beneath their often crude poses, however, the Beastie Boys' music revealed them to be one more group of white boys who had hammered together a new synthesis of contemporary black and white music, which the band called rap-metal. The trio shares vocals and consists of Mike D. (Michael Diamond, b. 1967), MCA (b. Adam Yaunch, 1965) and King Ad-Rock (b. Adam Horovitz, 1967). Upon closer inspection, it is also worth noting that Ad-Rock is in real life the son of playwright Israel Horovitz.

The Beastie Boys are in many respects representative of many of the Jewish Americans who were attracted to rock and roll. In the past, the entertainment field provided Jews with an avenue to succeed, even at a time when many other routes were closed to them because of anti-Semitism and poverty. These concerns, while certainly still a factor, have become less pervasive in recent times. One suspects that the substantial presence of Jews in rock and roll is representative of the restlessness and yearning for a legitimate vehicle for self-expression that has characterized youth culture in general over the past few decades. For Jewish Americans, the history of our people in rock and roll reflects the increasingly assimilationist tendencies within American society since the end of World War II.

RICHARD TASKIN

BIBLIOGRAPHY

Baker, Robb. *Bette Midler*. New York: Popular Library, 1975.

Belz, Carl. "The Role of the Disk Jockey: Alan Freed." In *The Story of Rock and Roll*. 2nd ed. New York: Harper & Row, 1972. Pp. 49–52.

Bloomfield, Michael, with S. Summerville. *Me and Big Joe*. San Francisco: Re/Search Production, 1980.

Burt, Rob, and North, Patsy. *West Coast Story*. Secaucus, N.J.: Chartwell, 1977.

Clapton, Diana. *Lou Reed and the Velvet Underground*. New York: Proteus, 1982.

Darzin, Diana. "Carly Simon on Men, Motherhood and Music." *Rock Magazine* 2 (December 1983): 46–47.

Finnis, Rob. *The Phil Spector Story*. London: Rockon Books, 1975.

Garofalo, Reebee, and Chapple, Steve. "From ASCAP to Alan Freed: The Pre-History of Rock 'N' Roll." *Popular Music and Society* 6 (1978): 72–80.

Helander, Brock, comp. *The Rock Who's Who*. New York: Schirmer, 1982.

Humphries, Patrick. *Bookends: The Simon and Garfunkel Story*. New York: Proteus, 1982.

———. *Paul Simon, Still Crazy After All These Years*. Garden City, N.Y.: Doubleday, 1989.

Kienzle, Rich. "The King Records Story." *Pickin'* 6 (October 1979): 9–11.

Kooper, Al, with Ben Edmonds. *Backstage Passes*. New York: Stein & Day, 1977.

Morse, Ann. *Barry Manilow*. Mankato, Minn.: Creative Educational Publications, 1978.

Palmer, Robert. *Baby, That Was Rock & Roll: The Legendary Leiber & Stoller*. New York: Harcourt, 1978.

Ruppli, Michel, comp. *The Chess Labels: A Discography*. 2 vols. Westport, Conn.: Greenwood Press, 1983.

Sedaka, Neil. *Laughter in the Rain: My Own Story*. New York: Putnam, 1982.

Williams, Don. *Bob Dylan: The Man, The Music, The Message*. Old Tappan, N.J.: Revell, 1985.

Music, Yiddish. Yiddish music can be described as the informally accumulated history of the Jews of Eastern Europe and America. Within its numerous forms, from folk songs to fiddle tunes, a clear picture emerges of the Jewish people through their music.

The Yiddish language and its culture sprang from the Western European Jewish communities that had settled and grown during the Middle Ages along the Rhine River in what is modern-day Germany (Ashkenaz). It was the success of

Moses Mendelssohn's Haskalah (Enlightenment) movement in the late eighteenth century that gradually ended Yiddish and its attendant culture in Germany. However, it continued to grow and thrive in Eastern Europe.

The most influential form of musical expression within the Jewish community was the singing of the khazn (cantor). No aspect of Jewish music remained unaffected by the performance and content of this principal form. After the destruction of the Second Temple in Jerusalem (70 C.E.), the rabbinate, in mourning, banned instrumental music. Now, the only officially sanctioned music was unaccompanied liturgy. The cantor, though not seen by the community as ritually indispensable as was the rabbi, was still required to maintain an "above-average" character. Even with the cantor's commitment to the content of the prayers, there are examples of rabbinical reprimands against cantors because of their beautiful voices, which, as it was claimed, distracted the worshippers from the piety of the prayers. In addition to his role as a leader in the dynamic of community prayer, the khazn was also responsible for training the future generations of khazonim. The apprentices (*meshoyr'rim*) would learn the rudiments of the special prayer modes to accompany the cantor; some of them might later become cantors themselves. By the end of the nineteenth century trained *meshoyr'rim* would also go on to help create the Yiddish musical theater in both Europe and the United States as both composers and performers. In smaller towns that had no *khazonim* prayers were led in the synagogue by talented "amateurs" such as the *ba'al tfile* and the *ba'al k'riah* or had their services led by one of many traveling *khazonim*. Religious music also thrived in the *kheyder* and yeshiva (primary and secondary schools), where the whole of Jewish law and traditions were taught to students with the help of specific mnemonic melodies.

Also influential were the myriad forms of unaccompanied folk songs that reflected the broad diversity of East European Jewish life. These included songs of love and marriage, lullabies and children's songs, work songs, and ballads detailing natural and national disasters. Sung in a plain style, they would, by the beginning of the twentieth century, form a rich source for music of the Yiddish theater. Most of these songs were learned via the "oral tradition," that is, from family and friends and later by attending theater performances or hearing records or radio.

It was the Hasidim, and their charismatic interpretation of piety, who encouraged song and dance as a valid approach to prayer. Their fervor accorded a great value to compositions called *nigunim* (wordless songs). These melodies bypassed the "burden" of words in the quest of a oneness with God. The tunes, meant to be sung on holidays and celebrations, would build in intensity as they progressed, accompanied by clapping, stamping, and enthusiastic dancing. Because of the religious mandate of separation of men and women, there was no mixed dancing. This created specific men's and women's dance traditions.

The influence of vocal stylings and inflections could also be heard in the music of the klezmer. The term "klezmer" is a Yiddishized contraction of two Hebrew words, *klei* and *zemer*, meaning vessel of melody. Though looked down upon by the rabbinate for promoting "frivolousness," instrumental music was an important part of both sacred and secular events in Jewish life. Using instruments popular in their particular region, klezmorim played such instruments as the fiddle, flute, bass, *baraban* (drum), *tsimbl* (hammered dulcimer), and *tats* (cymbals). By the nineteenth century other instruments—clarinet, trumpet, tuba—were added. Music was heard at weddings, balls, and other celebrations, on market days, and in village inns. More than any other social situation in the Jewish world, Jews and non-Jews could share their art and their economics through the forum of klezmer music.

In addition to playing dance music, the musicians would accompany the improvisatory rhymes and songs of the *badkhn*. The *badkhn* combined the talents of a poet, satirist, Talmudist, and social critic. His pithy and sly insights into the nature of life and religious responsibilities made him an integral part of any Jewish wedding. The vocal style used by the *badkhn* was also derived from the religious chanting heard in the synagogue, while the klezmorim, in accompanying him, adapted a Romanian musical form called doina, favored by star soloists as a showcase for their virtuosity.

Up until the mid-nineteenth century, the only way that Jewish musicians could obtain a place in conservatories or orchestras was through conversion. This period saw the eventual erosion of the many socially restrictive measures against Jews and the rise of a new generation of Jewish prodigies. These included Mischa Elman (1873–1967), Jascha Heifitz (1901–1988), and others, who for the first time were able to make the transition from klezmer band to concert hall without the humiliating necessity of conversion.

During the 1870s a new development was taking place in the burgeoning Yiddish world. From the wine cellars of Jassy, Romania, came the Yiddish theater of Abraham Goldfaden (1840–1908). Until Goldfaden's time, the rabbinate discouraged any kind of theater as antithetical to proper Jewish behavior and only tolerated amateur plays, which were presented on certain holidays (Purim, for example, when *purimshpilers* —schoolboy actors—presented the story of the foiling of a plot against the Jewish community of Persia through song, dance, and skit.) By borrowing from all the sources available to him in the late nineteenth century from grand opera to biblical anecdote, Goldfaden crafted a musical theater whose future influence was little imagined in its humble birthplace.

Within a few years of the theater's inception, a number of traveling companies had sprung up, bringing Yiddish variants of everything from the works of Shakespeare to contemporary plays based on the pages of daily newspapers, as well as episodes from the annals of Jewish history. Singers, comics, composers, artists and musicians joined the growing numbers of these traveling theater troupes. Like their fellow performers the klezmorim, acting companies too suffered at the hands of belligerent local and national governments who instituted restrictive measures against their performances.

Motivated by social, political, and economic upheavals in Eastern Europe, some 3 million Jews emigrated between 1880 and 1924. The ultimate destination for many of these Jews was to be the United States, and among them were numerous musicians, composers, singers, actors, and dancers. They and their children would soon provide the creators, performers, and audiences for the Yiddish-American cultural experience.

The America to which the Jewish musicians immigrated was one of great possibilities and diversity. Popular entertainment was in its awkward growing stages and afforded many opportunities for those who had the skills to take advantage of it. By the mid-1840s, America had already tentatively embarked on the establishment of a native popular theater with the rise of the minstrel show. These grotesque, stereotyped depictions of "Negro" life in America were the foundation of the soon to emerge variety shows, vaudeville, and burlesque, which continued the older black depictions but added a new cache of ethnic and national peoples: the "depictable types" who were at that moment streaming off

the boats at New York's Castle Garden and, by 1892, Ellis Island. It is ironic that Jewish musicians seeking employment in vaudeville theater orchestras could find themselves accompanying singers who were parodying them with such songs as "Sheenies in the Sand" or "Yiddle On Your Fiddle Play Some Ragtime." More ironic was the fact that Jewish composers themselves, as well as other minorities who were eager to succeed in the highly competitive world of Tin Pan Alley, wrote racist novelty songs about their own people. Add to these musical outlets the myriad number of hotel and cafe orchestras, roof garden restaurants, circuses, Wild West shows, parties, picnics, political rallies, records, and silent movie houses, and one gets the picture of an emerging leisure class finding numerous outlets for its free time.

Nowhere was this new-found entertainment more evident in the immigrant Jewish community than in the rise of the Yiddish theater. The theater along with the lyceum lecture hall now join the synagogue as a meeting place where the powerful beliefs, devotions, and loyalties of the Jewish community were publicly expressed. It was not uncommon for Jews who religiously attended *shul* Saturday mornings to attend the Yiddish theater on Saturday afternoons. From the rough and energetic offerings of Joseph Lateiner (1853–1935) and "Prof." Moishe Hurwitz (1844–1910) of the late 1890s to the more sophisticated and influential presentations of Jacob P. Adler (1855–1926) Boris Thomashefsky (1868?–1939), and Maurice Schwartz (1888–1960) of the 1920s, the Yiddish theater offered theatergoers (both Jewish and non) a colorful and occasionally innovative experience. Rising together with the young actors was the new generation of composers. Many, like Joseph Rumshinsky (1881–1956), Herman Wohl (1877–1936), and Sholem Secunda (1894–1974) received their musical training as *meshoyr'rim* back in Europe and, once in New York, augmented it with studies in both classical and popular composition.

While the Yiddish theater presented a wide variety of popular entertainments, this so-called *shund* (trash) was looked down upon by a growing Yiddish intelligentsia. Championing the rise of Yiddish art music, the *kunst* tradition emphasized a more literary and sophisticated content and performance style. Among the great figures in this tradition were the composers Leo Low (1878–1962) and Lazar Weiner (1897–1982), singers Sidor Belarsky (1900–1975) and Isa Kremer (1885-1956), and musicologists Abraham Zvi Idelsohn (1882-1938), Eric Werner (1901-1986), and Albert Weisser (1918-1982).

Parallel to the rise of political and labor movements were their attendant cultural groups, manifested in both worker's choruses and mandolin orchestras. From Zionists to Communists the choruses sang the anthems (and the praises) of their particular political perspective. Among the most active political people's choruses were those of the militant pro-Soviet Freiheit Gezangs Ferain, the more moderate Arbeiter Ring chorus, and the labor Zionist Paole Zion Singing Society. Though they all might be singing the glories of a workers' state, the Paole Zionists would be doing it in Hebrew while the others would be singing in Yiddish and other languages, including English. Groups like the Arbeiter Ring benefitted from its national network of affiliated chapters in its ability to disseminate these songs to a far-flung constituency.

Many of these political and labor groups also fostered the involvement of their nonsinging members by supporting mandolin orchestras. Based on the popular turn-of-the century trend of college, community, and vaudeville mandolin orchestras, the Yiddish labor and political groups adapted the widely available instrumentation to fit the needs of their cultural/political mandate. The instrumental repertoire reflected the same political perspective as that of the choruses (with the groups sometimes performing together) while also featuring traditional folk melodies and classical music.

Within a short time, the marketing of Yiddish music was in full swing. Downtown New York Yiddish publishers expanded beyond their usual fare of sacred and secular books and began giving over part of their press time to printing Yiddish sheet music. Via early journeyman publishers, such as Katzenellenbogen, S. Schenker, A. Teres, and Joseph Katz, to the larger Hebrew Publishing Company and later, Metro Music, thousands of songs found their way onto the pianos of Lower East Side music devotees. Beginning in the 1880s, Yiddish music publishing peaked in the era around World War I and declined rapidly after World War II. Many of the published pieces tended to be simplified piano arrangements of Yiddish theater, liturgical, socialist, and Zionist songs with a smattering of klezmer music. The publishers Jack and Joseph Kammen printed a collection of Yiddish dance tunes, the *Kammen International Dance Folio* in 1924 that is still used by many Jewish wedding bands.

Many of the musical comedy stars who popularized the music of Rumshinsky, Wohl, and Secunda were not only performing it on the stages of the numerous Yiddish theaters but also in recording studios. Talents like Aaron Lebedeff (1873-1960), Molly Picon (b. 1898), Ludwig Satz (1891?-1944), Morris Goldstein (1889-1938), Gus Goldstein (1884-1944), and Jenny Goldstein (1896-1960), among many others, were hard at work in the fledgling recording studios, producing 3- and 4-minute versions of their popular songs. Cantors as well as theater stars were sought out by the competing recording companies. Yosele Rosenblatt (1880-1933) (called by some "The Jewish Caruso"), Berele Chagy (1892-1952), and Mordechay Hershman (1888-1940) were among the most popular. The cantors, many of whom were brought to America by synagogues eager to add to their prestige of having a European cantor, were very well suited to the limited recording abilities of the primitive equipment, by dint of their powerful voices. Klezmorim were also recorded: Abe Schwartz (ca. 1880-1950), Naftule Brandwein (1884-1963), Dave Tarras (1897-1989; ironically called by some "the Jewish Benny Goodman"), and Harry Kandel (1890-1940). They preserved a repertoire that was gradually changing Jewish-American life. Even the great Yiddish novelist Sholem Aleichem (1859-1916; promoted as "the Jewish Mark Twain") made his way into a studio in 1915 to record excerpts of some of his short stories.

Begun at almost the same moment as the arrival of the East European immigrants, the new recording technology soon grew into a full industry. Record companies vied for the opportunity to sell the music of the immigrants back to them. In doing so, they took on the work of documentors by preserving the traditional music of a culture in transition years before professional ethnomusicologists did. Maintaining separate catalogues of classical, popular, and ethnic music, the companies thought little of issuing records that accurately portrayed the minority communities in one series while badly maligning them in another. There were some 50,000 Jewish discs made in the United States between 1894 and 1942, the vast majority of them before 1925. An interesting side note to the recording of ethnic music by outsiders is the founding of perhaps the first ethnic-owned, operated, and marketed record company. The United Hebrew Disc & Cylinder Record Company (UHD&C) was founded in 1905 by two partners, H. W. Perlman and S. Rosansky. Perlman had already established a piano factory on the Lower East Side, making him one of the first Jewish piano builders in New York, when he entered into business with Rosansky a few blocks from his piano factory. Perhaps because of the competition of the larger uptown record manufacturers or because of UHD&C's inferior quality, the company did not see out its 1906 season.

Radio was the medium that successfully competed with the recording business. By the middle 1920s, this new technology afforded the listener a truer fidelity than the 78 rpm records, and once the playing apparatus was purchased, the music was free. In addition, the radio offered news, advice, drama, and sports. In fact, with just a twist of the dial, the radio emerged as a preeminent entrée to the understanding of the world surrounding the Yiddish-speaking population and helped as much as night school to bring English into a Yiddish speaker's world. Though there were several stations that had some Jewish programming (New York's WHN, WBBC, WMCA, Philadelphia's WHAT, Cincinnati's WLW, among those) perhaps the best known of the radio stations that pioneered Yiddish language broadcasts was WEVD. Founded in 1928 and owned by the socialist Yiddish newspaper the *Forward*, this station (whose call letters memorialized twice unsuccessful Socialist presidential candidate Eugene Victor Debs) emerged in response to the needs of both Jewish and Gentile immigrant populations. Because of its diversity of programming, musicians, singers, composers, and arrangers were kept busy meeting the needs of an enthusiastic constituency.

Another outlet for the creative talents of Jewish performers began quietly outside of New York City. Immigrant workers seeking a temporary respite from the oppression of the urban slums began to vacation in the Catskill region of upstate New York. Small farms taking in "roomers" gradually developed into larger and more sophisticated hotels catering to the cultural and culinary needs of the vacationing community. There were numerous hotels, such as the Majestic, the Normandy, the Concord, and the Gradus, but the best known, opened in 1914 by Zelig and Malke Grossinger, was Grossingers. At hotels like these, performers in Yiddish theater, radio, and recording could vacation and perform during the months when the regular venues in the city were closed.

With the passage of restrictive emigration laws in 1924, the flow of potential new East European Yiddish writers, musicians, and actors, as well as audiences, was halted. This, coupled with the more assimilated children of the American-born Jewish population, saw the appreciative population for Jewish music shrink. Attempts were made by enterprising impresarios to capitalize on the shift of American-born Jews toward American-born music. One of these was the premiere in 1938 on radio station WHN of "Yiddish Melodies in Swing" featuring the Barry (née Bagelman) Sisters, Jan Bart, and the swing arrangements of Sam Medoff with the "Yiddish Swingtette" featuring Dave Tarras. The show, sponsored by the B. Manishewitz Company, proved popular for a number of years and was syndicated throughout the United States. Though Tarras was featured in this more popular venue, the younger Jewish population preferred the clarinet playing of Benny Goodman to him. Goodman, (1909–1986), never at home with the klezmer style, would defer to his star trumpeter Harry (Ziggy Elman) Finkelman (1914–1968) when he needed something played that sounded "Jewish." Based on the success of Elman's 1938 Bluebird recording of "Frailach in Swing," an arrangement of the traditional tune "Der Shtiler Bulgar," Goodman had Johnny Mercer write words to the modern version and recorded it the next year as "And the Angels Sing," featuring Martha Tilton as vocalist. In 1942, Goodman tried to repeat the formula of a Jewish crossover hit by reworking the 1917 Abe Schwartz hit "Di Grine Kuzine" into "My Little Cousin," this time with vocalist Peggy Lee.

A major contribution to the mix of klezmer and jazz was made by clarinetist/saxophonist Sammy Musiker (1922–1963). Musiker had vast experience in the two musical worlds as a reed player in the orchestras of both Gene Krupa and Dave Tarras. In the late 1940s, Musiker arranged for the Savoy jazz label to record Tarras and his band. Though the discs were musically outstanding, the resulting sales were bitterly disappointing. Musiker's fusion attempt came at a time when Jewish audience interest in both Yiddish music and big band was in decline. His innovative instrumentations also failed to develop into a real stylistic trend among mainstream Jewish or jazz players. A more popular mixed genre form was pursued by clarinetist/comedian/band leader Mickey Katz (1909–1985). Fresh from his success with the Spike Jones orchestra, Katz used his experience with Jones to concoct "Yinglish" parodies of Top 40 songs. Employing the finest L.A. recording musicians (including Ziggy Elman and Manny Klein) Katz's records and subsequent tours clearly demonstrated his ability to move seamlessly from *freylekhs* to pop.

What assimilation had begun, the ravages of the subsequent Holocaust seemed to complete. At once, the vital birthplace of Yiddish was destroyed, and New York became the major world center of this culture. This situation was reinforced by New York being the destination of the remnants of the East European Jewish population. Except for the Hasidic communities and the remaining secular Yiddish organizations, Yiddish and its attendant culture was not uppermost in the minds of the post-Holocaust American Jewish community. The creation of the State of Israel in 1948 came with a linguistic, political, and cultural agenda, none of which sought to look back to the Old World. Hebrew replaced Yiddish; Israel replaced Eastern Europe as a Jewish center.

However, almost as gradually as the postwar interest in Yiddish culture faded, a renewed interest in it began in the 1970s. This was stimulated in part by the success of Alex Haley's TV program and book *Roots* and by a younger Jewish post-Holocaust generation eager to find a context for its family and group history. Perhaps nothing represents this search better than the revitalization of klezmer music. From the mid 1970s, the klezmer renewal has inspired both young and old Jewish and non-Jewish musicians to begin learning this repertoire. However, the interest has not focused merely on the melodies. The language, history, and folklore of the rich Eastern European experience have all been recalled in an attempt to reinvest the community with its nearly discarded culture. Musicians trained in Appalachian country music, jazz, classical, rock, and East European folk music forms were drawn into playing a music thought to have become passé even by those musicians and the audiences who loved it most. The revival that began with three klezmer bands in the United States in 1979 grew in less than a decade to more than 80 groups across North America. Noteworthy, too, is the reemergence of older, experienced klezmer stylists who have been sought out by younger players eager for musical role models.

For the first time in years record companies are producing albums of traditional Yiddish music as more and more radio stations have begun playing them. In 1990 the recording of *Partisans of Vilna: Songs of World War II Jewish Resistance* was nominated for a Grammy Award, the first time a Yiddish recording was thus honored. Klezmer bands are now performing in concert series, which, until recently, comprised primarily classical and jazz and folk revival groups. Even Hollywood, in its attempt to infuse its films with more "authentic atmosphere" sought out the services of klezmer bands in the production of such films as *The Chosen, Over the Brooklyn Bridge* (Kapelye), *Brighton Beach Memoirs* (New York Klezmer Ensemble), and the third remake of *The Jazz Singer* (The Klezmora). In 1982, the New York-based YIVO Institute for Jewish Research opened its Max and Frieda Weinstein Archives of Recorded Sound. This open-access sound archives, the largest of its kind in the world, has enabled numerous musicians, scholars, researchers, and composers the chance to study and listen to thousands of rare 78 rpm discs, classic Yiddish radio shows, and unique field recordings of Yiddish music.

In 1985, YIVO sponsored the first Yiddish Folk Arts Institute. Dubbed "KlezKamp" this five-day event brought together 120 teachers and students of Yiddish language, literature, folklore, song, klezmer music, dance, and the visual arts. By 1990, its sixth year, some 2,000 people from North America, Europe, and Israel attended "KlezKamp" to study these vital Jewish genres.

It is possible that Yiddish culture will never again achieve the popularity it enjoyed at the turn of the century. However, this current revitalization demonstrates that reports of its demise are, to paraphrase Mark Twain's famous quip, highly exaggerated. *See also* Music, Cantorial; Theater, Yiddish.

HENRY SAPOZNIK

BIBLIOGRAPHY

Mlotek, Eleanor Gordon. *Mir Trogn A Gezang.* New York: Workman's Circle, 1972.

———, with Malke Gottlieb. *We Are Here: Songs of the Holocaust.* New York: Workman's Circle, 1983.

Rubin, Ruth. *Voices of the People.* New York: McGraw-Hill, 1979.

Sapoznik, Henry. *The Compleat Klezmer.* Cedarhurst, N.Y.: Tara, 1987.

———, ed. "A Resource Guide to Yiddish Music." *The Book Peddler.* Amherst, Mass.: National Yiddish Book Center, 1988.

Slobin, Mark. *Chosen Voices: The Story of the American Cantorate.* Chicago: University of Illinois Press, 1989.

———. *Old Jewish Folk Music: The Collections of Moshe Beregovski*. Philadephia: University of Pennsylvania Press, 1982.

———. *Tenement Songs: The Popular Music of the Jewish Immigrants*. Chicago: University of Illinois Press, 1982.

Spottswood, Richard. *A Discography of Ethnic Recordings Produced in the United States 1895–1942*. Chicago: University of Illinois Press, 1989.

Discography

Belarsky, Sidor. "Songs by M. Gebertig." LP B115. Cedarhurst, N.Y.: Tara.

———. "Songs of the Holocaust." SB 1001. Cedarhurst, N.Y.: Tara.

Kapelye. "Chicken." Shanachie 21006. Newton, N.J.

Kirshenblatt-Gimblett, Barbara, ed. "Folksongs in the East European Tradition from the Repertoire of Mariam Niremberg." Global Village GVM 117, New York.

Klezmer Conservatory Band. "A Touch of Klez." Vanguard 79455. New York.

Rosenblatt, Joseph. "Art of Cantor Joseph Rosenblatt: Masterpieces of the Synagogue." Vols. 1 and 2. RCA TDK 1003/4. Cedarhurst, N.Y.: Tara.

Rubin, Ruth, ed. "Jewish Life: The Old Country." Folkways FG-3801. Washington, D.C.

Sapoznik, Henry, ed. "Jakie, Jazz'em Up: Old Time Klezmer Music 1912–1926." Global Village GVM 101. New York.

———. "Klezmer Music 1910–1942: Recordings from the YIVO Archives." Folkways FSS 34021. Washington, D.C.

———, with Josh Waletzky. "Partisans of Vilna: The Songs of World War II Jewish Resistance." Flying Fish FF450. Chicago.

———, with Zalmen Mlotek. "Pearls of Yiddish Song." Workman's Circle, New York.

Schwartz, Martin, ed. "Klezmer Music 1910–1926." Folk Lyric FL 9034. El Cerito, Calif.

Weiner, Lazar. "Musical Settings of Yiddish Poetry." Tambour 597. Cedarhurst, N.Y.: Tara.

Various Artists. "Golden Voices of Israel: Gerson Sirota, Zavel Kwartin, Yosell Rosenblatt, Pierre Pinchik, Ben Zion Kapov-Kagan, Samuel Vigoda, Leyb Glantz." Eastronics Ltd. K 530248. Cedarhurst, N.Y.: Tara.

N

National Conference of Christians and Jews.

The years immediately following World War I were characterized by a resurgence of organized hate groups as intense as the nation had ever experienced. This blatant exploitation of religious and racial prejudice aroused the apprehension of thoughtful Protestants, who felt that the outrages being committed against other fellow Americans were a challenge to themselves and determined that something had to be done about it.

At a meeting of the Home Missions Council of the Federal Council of Churches in 1923, Executive Secretary Alfred Williams Anthony proposed that a Committee on Good Will between Jews and Christians be established to take action on this matter.

John Herring of the Federal Council Staff was assigned the responsibility of directing this new effort. He enlisted the support of such persons as Alfred M. Cohen of B'nai B'rith, Rabbi David de Sola Pool, New York's Monsignor Lavelle of St. Patrick's Cathedral, and others. In a series of small private meetings these persons planted the seeds for the creation of an emerging national movement in the following five years.

In 1927, S. Parkes Cadman, past president of the Federal Council and then chairman of the Committee on Good Will, conducted an anti-Klan tour throughout the Midwest. As America's first well-known radio preacher, Cadman drew crowds of up to 10,000 in cities such as Indianapolis and Lima, Ohio, where the Ku Klux Klan had made significant inroads.

Later that same year, former New York governor and 1916 presidential candidate (later Chief Justice of the Supreme Court) Charles Evans Hughes, Cadman, and industrialist Roger Williams Strauss circulated a letter to potential sponsors proposing the creation of what became the National Conference of Christians and Jews.

On December 11, 1927, the formal organizational meeting of the National Conference of Jews and Christians for the Advancement of Amity, Justice, and Peace was held. On that occasion, Cadman stated that "the intergroup problem of the nation rises like a specter in the path of democracy and dares her to come on." He also noted that the conference was not merely a sentimental organization formed to preach brotherly love between Jews and Christians, but "it is Jewish, Protestant, Catholic, Park Avenue, Long Island City, whites, Negroes, Italians, Irish, Russians, Chinese." The new conference, he said, "recognizes a vast need for color harmonizing in our national life."

In the spring of the following year, Everett Clinchy, campus minister of Wesleyan University in Middletown, Connecticut, was employed as executive secretary. One of his early responsibilities was to guide the fledgling movement through the severing of its institutional ties with the Federal Council of Churches into an autonomous civic organization.

Roger Williams Strauss and Newton D. Baker, former secretary of war under President Wilson, were installed as Jewish and Protestant co-chairmen, respectively. They were joined the following year by Charlton J. H. Hayes, distinguished professor of history at Columbia, who accepted the position as Catholic co-chairman.

From these beginnings the NCCJ has grown to be an organization with regional offices in 75 American cities. Over the more than six decades of its history, the conference has played a significant role in the development of the Jewish-Christian dialogue, promoted innovative materials and methods in multicultural education, pioneered in the development of police and community relations efforts, and participated in many other kinds of community interventions within the educational framework of the mandate of its founders. *See also* Interfaith Cooperation.

DONALD MCEVOY

BIBLIOGRAPHY

Kraut, Benny. "Towards the Establishment of the National Conference of Christians and Jews: The 1920s." *American Jewish History* 77 (March 1988): 388–412.

Ryan, Michael D. *Bernard E. Olson Scholars' Conference on the Church Struggle and the Holocaust.* New York: Mellen Press, 1981.

National Council of Jewish Women.

Founded in 1893 by Hannah Greenebaum Solomon, the National Council of Jewish Women is the oldest Jewish women's volunteer organization in America.

At the 1893 Chicago World's Fair a special building for women's exhibits was planned. Hannah Greenebaum Solomon was chosen to represent Jewish women; however, she wanted to present a Jewish Women's Congress as part of the Parliaments of Religions, which meant working in cooperation with the Jewish men. The men set up a program that did not include the women in any position except as "hostesses." Not believing this amounted to "joint collaboration," Hannah Solomon rejected their offer and organized the First Congress of Jewish Women.

She contacted 95 women from 29 cities. Those women formed the core of the Jewish Women's Congress that met in September 1893. This represented the first attempt by Jewish women to assemble as an entity. The excellent program included such notable speakers as Henrietta Szold and Josephine Lazarus (Emma's sister). Believing that social injustice was the concern of women as well as men and that women should work to correct those problems, Solomon organized programs for the congress emphasizing women's roles in correcting social injustices.

At the congress's conclusion, a new organization, the National Council of Jewish Women (NCJW), was formed. Solomon was elected its first president. In 1895, the council adopted the motto "Faith and Humanity."

The council's programs consisted of aid to destitute immigrant families; promotion of child labor laws; support for public health regulations, Jewish education, and advancing Jewish culture. The first activity of the New York Council was to help immigrant women establish themselves safely in this country. In 1904, the council hired a Yiddish-speaking woman to assist women and children at Ellis Island. Eventually, the council had representatives in over 250 cities in Europe and the United States to help women immigrate to the United States.

As many other Jewish women's charities began to form, it became clear that some umbrella organization was needed. In 1910, under the auspices of the National Council of Jewish Women a meeting was held to reestablish the National Conference of Jewish Women. The conference's purpose was to unite all Jewish women to make contributions to Jewish religious, educational, and philanthropic work. The National Conference of Jewish Women is still in existence today, acting as a clearing house for Jewish women's groups.

NCJW organized Sabbath schools in communities throughout the United States, even in those without a rabbi or a synagogue. It urged women to serve on religious committees.

NCJW was the first to arrange to broadcast the Jewish holiday services to Jewish farmers who had no access to synagogues. In 1926, through an arrangement with RCA, radios were placed in central locations in rural communities so that farmers could gather to hear services.

The council has helped all factions of the Jewish community. It was the first organization to work for the Jewish blind; it established golden age clubs; and it offered rehabilitation services to mental patients. During the Depression, it helped with job training and placement. During World War II, it rescued German Jewish children and placed them in private homes through the German Jewish Children's Aid.

The National Council of Jewish Women has taken many political positions. It worked to promote the League of Nations and the World Court; it supported the founding of the United Nations; it fought anti-Semitism and supported civil rights; it launched the Freedom Campaign in 1952, becoming the first membership organization to undertake the battle to protect civil liberties; and it launched the Freedom-to-Read project to oppose censorship in public libraries.

To stimulate research in American Jewish culture, the National Council of Jewish Women established fellowships. It undertook the building of a campus for the Hebrew University High School in Jerusalem; it worked to develop program materials and teaching methods for educationally disadvantaged students and, based on this, became a consultant for Head Start.

The council continues to work for the social needs of the Jewish people. It is dedicated to advancing human welfare and the democratic way of life through social legislation, social welfare, and activity in community and international relations.

LINDA GLAZER

BIBLIOGRAPHY

Baum, Charlotte; Hyman, Paula; and Michel, Sonya. *The Jewish Woman in America.* New York: New American Library, 1977.

Graziani, Bernice. "Where There's A Woman." New York: National Council of Jewish Women, 1967.

Kenvin, Helen Schwartz. *This Land of Liberty.* New York: Behrman House, 1986.

"National Council of Jewish Women—Provides . . . Hope for Israel's Disadvantaged." New York: National Council of Jewish Women.

"The Promise, The Promise." New York: National Council of Jewish Women.

Solomon, Hannah Greenebaum. *Fabric of My Life, the Autobiography of Hannah Greenebaum Solomon.* New York: Bloch, 1946.

Yoffe, James. *The American Jews.* New York: Random House, Paperback Library Edition, 1969.

Neoconservatism. The term "neoconservatism" was coined by Michael Harrington in the early 1970s to discredit those who had "abandoned" socialist ideals by turning "sharply to the Right." Though Harrington used the term quite narrowly, others soon employed it to describe something far more meaningful in American political life: the demise of the New Deal Democratic coalition. For several years, that coalition had been unraveling under the combined pressures of black power, feminist protest, antiwar demonstrations, and political "reform." At stake, it seemed, was not only the future of the Democratic Party, but of liberalism itself.

A backlash was inevitable. The neoconservatism of the 1970s grew out of the struggles of the 1960s, when radical movements swept the land. The first neoconservatives included national labor leaders who opposed minority hiring quotas and supported the Vietnam War, mainstream Democratic leaders who resented the reform-minded McGovernites now in charge of their party, and prominent intellectuals who looked askance at an "alternative culture" marked by anti-American sloganeering and plain bad taste. What all of these groups had in common was a fear of radical change, caused by "left-wing militants" whose influence seemed to be growing everywhere—in the arts, the media, the academic world, and the political arena.

The neoconservative intellectuals were a unique group, bound together by their common backgrounds, grievances, and beliefs. Most were Jewish former radicals from New York City, steeped in the heritage of the Talmud and the writings of Karl Marx. They had begun their political lives in the 1930s as avid Communists, switched briefly to the anti-Stalinist radicalism of Leon Trotsky, and moved rightward in the 1940s and 1950s to become loyal Truman Democrats—a position that Arthur Schlesinger, Jr., then defined as Cold War liberalism of the "vital center." Not surprisingly, their political journey had left them fearful of *all* radical movements, but especially those on the Left. As good Democrats, they supported both the New Deal welfare state and the containment of communism abroad. That support would not waver, despite the ugly battles to come.

By the 1960s, these intellectuals formed the backbone of America's literary and scholarly elite. They ran the small but powerful journals of high culture and informed opinion, such as *Commentary* and *Partisan Review*, and they dominated the social sciences at key universities, such as Harvard and Columbia. But then, quite suddenly, it all seemed to come apart. Their hard-earned status and authority, their well-crafted opinions, their deepest feelings about politics and culture were now being challenged by a new generation of radicals, their spiritual children. For these intellectuals, noted Sidney Blumenthal in *The Rise of the Counter-Establishment,* "two decades matter most: the one in which they were student radicals, the 1930s, and the one in which they reacted against student radicals, the 1960s. At the moment of their arrival at their properly tenured stations, when they believed they had earned deference for their accumulated wisdom, hordes of longhairs screamed that they belonged in the dustbin of history."

These screams did not go unnoticed. For some, they signaled the beginning of national chaos and decline. According to Hilton Kramer, an early neoconservative who worked as chief art critic for the *New York Times*, the resurgence of left-wing radicalism in the sixties had terrible consequences for American culture, highbrow, middle, and low. "As political standards came to replace artistic standards," says Kramer, "the net effect was to make the life of culture more and more hostage to the influence of the Left." Everything was affected, "from the writings of textbooks to the reviewing of trade books, from the introduction of kitsch into the museums to the decline of literacy in the schools." The more the Left railed against racism, sexism, and elitism in our cultural institutions, the "harder these institutions worked to satisfy the Left's political criteria and the more respectable and established these criteria became." Needless to say, the results were "catastrophic."

Other intellectuals were appalled by the hatred they saw directed at their own country—a country that had overcome the Great Depression and won a world war against fascism without compromising its democratic values. "We were shaken up," wrote Norman Podhoretz, the editor of *Commentary*, "by the anti-Americanism that by the late 1960s had virtually become the religion of the radical movement in which we ourselves had actively participated in . . . earlier years. . . ." This anti-Americanism manifested itself in many ways: an opposition to the Vietnam War that *included* a call for a Communist victory, a belief that American imperialism was responsible for all the misfortunes in the Third World, a mindless solidarity with leftist police states around the globe, and a personal identification with the foreign and domestic "victims" of a "selfish," "corrupt," and "racist" American society. "Somewhat to our surprise," added Podhoretz, "we found that we simply could not stomach the hatred of 'Amerika' that increasingly pervaded the New Left and the counterculture. And this revulsion led to a process of reflection and reconsideration that gradually brought us to a new appreciation of the virtues of the American political system and of its economic and social underpinnings."

These feelings came to a head in the presidential election of 1972, when a few prominent intellectuals, led by Irving Kristol, the so-called "godfather of neoconservatism," supported Richard Nixon's reelection campaign. This was hardly surprising, for the Democratic candidate, George McGovern, was an ardent "dove" who opposed not only the Vietnam War, but also the fundamental assumptions behind America's anticommunist foreign policy. Following McGovern's disastrous defeat, a number of important intellectuals joined with more traditional Democratic leaders, such as Senators Hubert Humphrey, Henry (Scoop) Jackson, and Daniel Patrick Moynihan, to found the Coalition for a Democratic Majority. Its goal, quite frankly, was to free the Democratic Party from "the new leftist liberalism" of the McGovernites.

By 1976, these intellectuals were openly describing themselves as neoconservatives. In addition to Kramer, Podhoretz, and Kristol, their ranks included prominent scholars such as Nathan Glazer, Robert Nisbet, Gertrude Himmelfarb, Seymour Martin Lipset, James Q. Wilson, and Daniel Bell. Glazer, a Harvard sociologist, defined a neoconservative as "someone who was never a conservative"—someone, like himself, who had moved from socialism to liberalism to a centrist position within the Democratic Party. Glazer emphasized his firm support for racial equality, the welfare state, and the tough anti-Communist foreign policy of Democratic presidents from Harry S Truman to Lyndon Baines Johnson. Like many Democrats, he believed that his party had abandoned the first and last of these goals in order to appease radicals and minorities of every kind. Glazer was particularly opposed to the new concept of affirmative action, designed to overcome the long history of racial and sexual discrimination in America by giving special preference to women and minorities in college admission, employment, and the like. Affirmative action was un-American, Glazer argued. By practicing "reverse discrimination" against white males, it violated the sacred concepts of meritocracy and equal treatment for all.

In 1976, the neoconservatives supported Jimmy Carter for the presidency after Henry Jackson, their favorite son, was defeated in the primaries. When Carter took office, the Coalition for a Democratic Majority submitted a long list of names to the White House as possible appointees. Virtually all of them were rejected. The list included prominent neoconservatives like Jeane

Kirkpatrick, Richard Perle, and Nathan Glazer. In their place, wrote one angry Democrat, Carter appointed "people identified with George McGovern's views on foreign policy and Ralph Nader's views on domestic [affairs]."

Before long, the neoconservatives were dismissing President Carter as another left-wing McGovernite. Everything he did or tried to do—from his human rights campaign in Latin America to the hostage debacle in Iran—was viewed as weak, naive, or sometimes both. Norman Podhoretz described the president as a pawn of those who were undermining America's will to resist the Communist enemy. The radical movements of the sixties were fading, wrote Podhoretz, but their ideas are "more entrenched in bowdlerized form than they ever were in the past, all over the liberal culture. Obviously, it is in the universities, certain sectors of the media, in the publishing industry. The incessant harping on the danger of confrontation and nuclear war, all of this is part of a culture of appeasement."

When Ronald Reagan defeated Jimmy Carter in 1980, he did so with the public support of Kristol, Podhoretz, and Kirkpatrick, among others. Though most neoconservatives still considered themselves to be Democrats, their affinity for Reagan's anticommunism and "evil empire" rhetoric was quite compelling. For his part, the new president welcomed these neoconservatives with open arms. Indeed, he seemed to accept the notion, put forth by Podhoretz, that he could not have won the election without them. "If the grip of the conventional liberal wisdom and leftist orthodoxies in the world had not been loosened by [our] criticism . . . ," said Podhoretz, "[then] Ronald Reagan would in all probability have been unable to win over the traditionally Democratic constituencies (blue-collar workers, white ethnic groups like the Irish and the Italians and a surprisingly high percentage of Jews) whose support swept him into the White House."

That few of these people had ever heard of Podhoretz, that most of them were quite capable of rejecting "leftist orthodoxies" without his assistance, did not seem to matter. Ronald Reagan was impressed. His administration did not turn its back on neoconservative job seekers, as Jimmy Carter's had done. Dozens of them—including Richard Perle, Max Kampelman, and Richard Pipes—were appointed to important posts in the State and Defense Departments. Jeane Kirkpatrick wound up as United Nations ambassador. Elliott Abrams, Podhoretz's son-in-law, became

assistant secretary of state for human rights. Podhoretz himself took a seat on the advisory board of the United States Information Agency. William Kristol, son of Irving Kristol, received a key post in the Department of Education. The list went on and on.

Significantly, however, these appointments were limited to the fields of education, foreign policy, and defense. Few, if any, neoconservatives were given positions dealing with economics, welfare, or public health. The reason was simple: most of them still supported the domestic programs of the old Democratic Party. There was little enthusiasm for "supply side" economics or the theories of Milton Friedman. Even Irving Kristol—by now a registered Republican, a columnist for *The Wall Street Journal*, and a fellow at the American Enterprise Institute—defined neoconservatism as something quite different from the traditional conservatism of Russell Kirk, William F. Buckley, Jr., and *The National Review*. "Neoconservatism," said Kristol, "is not at all hostile to the idea of the welfare state. . . . In general, it approves of those social reforms that, while providing needed security and comfort to the individual in our dynamic, urbanized society, do so with a minimum of bureaucratic intrusion in the individual's affairs." Those reforms included social security, unemployment insurance, some form of national health insurance, some kind of family assistance plan, etc.

Such statements did not sit well with the Old Right or the New. The former, staunchly Republican, is devoted to small government and free market ideas. The latter, staunchly Christian, is devoted to social issues like preventing abortion and legalizing school prayer. Both groups viewed the neoconservatives as alien intellectuals who either opposed or ignored their basic ideals. And both groups suspected these intellectuals of using the Reagan landslides to re-create the Democratic vision of the pre-McGovern years, with its emphasis on containment of communism and a vigorous welfare state.

By the end of the Reagan years, however, neoconservatism seemed to be on the wane. *Glasnost*, the missile reduction treaty, the pullout in Afghanistan—all served to undercut the vital neoconservative belief about the static nature, the irreversible evil, of the Soviet state. At home, meanwhile, the Democratic Party appeared to be inching back toward the center of the political spectrum after five defeats in the past six presidential elections. That signaled, some thought, a reconciliation between neoconservatives and party leaders, an end to the warfare. Finally, the neoconservatives did not seem to be gaining new adherents, especially among the young. This was not surprising, said Seymour M. Lipset, for "the common link" among neoconservatives "is past involvement against Communism as anti-Stalinists"—a link unique to the largely Jewish intellectuals who came of age during the Great Depression in New York City. "In any case," he concluded, "the concept of neoconservatism is irrelevant to the further developments within American politics."

Not everyone agreed. Norman Podhoretz argued that neoconservatism was still very much alive, fighting the good fight against leftists at home and abroad. "Just when [people are] saying that neoconservatism has become irrelevant," he wrote, "we are confronted with the spread of an updated and repackaged version of leftist attitudes toward America that neoconservatism was originally born to fight. Far from being played out and ready to die, then, neoconservatism is being given a whole new set of jobs to do and a whole new lease on life."

DAVID OSHINSKY

BIBLIOGRAPHY

Blumenthal, Sidney. *The Rise of the Counter-Establishment: From Conservative Ideology to Public Power.* New York: Random House, 1986.
Draper, Theodore. "Neoconservatism History [Reevaluating Yalta Conference]." *New York Review of Books* 32, No. 21-22 (January 16, 1986): 5-15.

New Jewish Agenda. New Jewish Agenda (NJA or Agenda) was founded at a conference convened in late December 1980 in Washington, D.C. Seven hundred participants had gathered to discuss a "Jewish Agenda for the 1980s." By the mid-1980s, NJA had grown to a national membership organization with 48 local chapters and over 5000 members. The organization defined itself as liberal or leftist politically, seeking to work within two communities as a "Jewish voice among progressives" and a "progressive voice within the Jewish community."

The impetus for NJA's creation was the disillusionment of some younger Jewish intellectuals with the parochialism of organized Jewish life. Many had been participants in the Jewish counter-culture of the 1960s. Others attracted to NJA had been alienated by the inhospitable and sometimes anti-Semitic nature of the American Left. Gerald Serotta, a Hillel rabbi who had been active in the Havurah (Jewish Communalist), anti-Vietnam, and Civil Rights movements, convened a meeting in May 1979 at the New York Havurah, during which a precursor, the Organizing Committee for a New Jewish Agenda, was formed. A "Statement of Purpose," ratified in 1980 stated:

> We are Jews concerned with the retreat from social action concerns and open discussion within the organized Jewish community. As Jews who believe strongly that authentic Jewish life must involve serious and consistent attention to the just ordering of human society and the natural resources of our world (Tikun Olam), we seek to apply Jewish values to such questions as economic justice, ecological concerns, energy policy, world hunger, intergroup relations and affirmative action, women's rights, peace in the Middle East, and Jewish education.

NJA proved to be a highly controversial organization. Politically conservative Jewish groups attacked its positions on Israel, gay rights, and sanctuary for Central American refugees. Some localities refused to allow NJA chapters to participate on local Jewish community relations councils. However, many local chapters were involved in stimulating Jewish community coalitions in civil rights work, black-Jewish cooperation, education against apartheid, disarmament activities on the holidays of Sukkot and Tisha B'Av, and support of women's liberation and gay rights.

NJA was an early and persistent critic of Jewish organizational deference to Israeli government positions, particularly during the war in Lebanon and with respect to Palestinian rights. On a national basis, NJA influenced major Jewish organizations to take positions in support of nuclear disarmament and in opposition to the Reagan administration's positions on Central America. In addition to its political involvement, NJA consciously sought to offer a cultural haven for many otherwise unaffiliated Jews attempting to harmonize Jewish and progressive political conceptions. NJA created and published new or revised rituals based on religious and secular sources, including a haggadah with three separate seders focusing on liberation, disarmament, and Middle East peace themes.

GERALD SEROTTA

BIBLIOGRAPHY

Serotta, Gerry. "For the Sake of Tikun Olam." *Jewish Spectator* 46, No. 2 (Summer 1981).

The Shalom Seders. Compiled by New Jewish Agenda (various authors). New York: Adama, 1984.

New Left. The New Left was a loose label applied to a youthful radical movement of the 1960s and early 1970s. It was born out of the ashes of the Old Left, that is, the American Socialist and Communist parties, which virtually collapsed in the 1950s. By the end of that decade, these parties played virtually no important role in affecting American politics.

Galvanized by its strident opposition to American military involvement in Vietnam and its intense involvement in the civil rights movement, the New Left was primarily a student-led movement whose early organizational core was the Students for a Democratic Society (SDS) and the Student Non-Violent Coordinating Committee (SNCC), a militant black-led civil rights organization. The "Movement," which was what the New Left was also called, attracted numerous Jewish students and intellectuals. Jewish reaction to the New Left, as it evolved, had a profound effect upon Jewish political attitudes in the years that followed its rise and fall.

Jewish involvement focused largely upon SDS. Founded in the early 1960s, SDS attempted to revive a left movement dispirited by the Cold War and intimidated by McCarthyism. Its leaders were from the affluent middle-class and elite state universities such as Wisconsin, California at Berkeley, and Michigan. Its most important document, the Port Huron Statement, written at the 1962 SDS convention, underscored the self-consciousness of its leaders as a new and distinct radical generation. The statement read, "We are people of this generation bred in at least modest comfort, housed now in universities, looking uncomfortably to the world we inherit."

From its beginnings, SDS leadership was disproportionately Jewish, including such national officers as Al Haber, Richard Flacks, Steve Max, Bob Ross, Mike Spiegel, Mike Klonsky, and Mark Rudd. Soon its membership was as well. At the 1966 SDS convention, 46 percent of the delegates who recognized a particular religious background were Jewish. In the mid-1960s, when SDS membership rose to about 30,000, Jewish students constituted between 30 percent and 50 percent of the total.

SDS was not, however, the only focus of Jewish involvement in the New Left. Young Jewish intellectuals played a prominent role on the editorial boards of the leading New Left journals, such as *Studies on the Left, Ramparts,* and *New University Thought.* The works of two prominent Jewish writers, Paul Goodman (*Growing Up Absurd*) and Herbert Marcuse (*One-Dimensional Man*), had a profound effect upon the thinking of the New Left.

The civil rights movement, particularly in the early 1960s, also attracted a high proportion of Jews. Of the white Freedom Riders, who in the summer of 1961 traveled to the South to challenge the segregated transportation system, two-thirds were Jewish. The two martyred white students, Michael Schwerner and Andrew Chaney, murdered during the Mississippi Summer voter registration campaign in 1964, were Jewish. Surveys indicate that from one-half to two-thirds of the Mississippi Summer volunteers were Jewish.

By no means was the New Left leadership exclusively Jewish. Many of its best-known leaders and personalities, such as Tom Hayden, Timothy Leary, Carl Oglesby, David Dellinger, and Staughton Lynd, were not. Radicalism did not attract the vast majority of Jewish college students, who numbered over 300,000 in the 1960s. Only a modest percentage participated in the New Left. Jewish students did, nonetheless, represent the most numerous and visible ethnic group. Three members of the "Chicago 7," who were charged with conspiracy to riot at the 1968 Democratic convention, were Jewish (Jerry Rubin, Abbie Hoffman, and Lee Weiner) as well as their attorney (William Kunstler). It became the most publicized political trial of the period.

How then was this phenomenon of extensive Jewish participation in the New Left explained? Some scholars trace it to the Jewish experience in nineteenth-century Europe. Then, the Right was identified with monarchy, hierarchy, nationalism, and anti-Semitism and was perceived as the enemy of Jewish survival. The Left, on the other hand, stressed rationalism, individual rights, personal freedom, and social equality and seemed a more compatible political home for most Jews, particularly in the emancipated environment of Western Europe. This attitude was brought to America, for many Jews played leading roles in the radical movements of the early twentieth century. Although the majority of American Jews were not radical, they did vigorously support the liberal New Deal reforms of Franklin D. Roosevelt.

Even second- and third-generation American Jews, a large proportion of whom attended college after World War II, displayed the same tendency. For example, a survey of college students in the 1950s showed that Jewish students were more likely than non-Jewish students to have liberal views on civil rights, civil liberties, and economic issues. Thus, there was a greater receptivity to New Left appeals among Jewish students than among others. Traditional Jewish concerns with social equality that found expression in left-wing politics in the 1930s and 1940s found similar compatibility with the New Left. This was especially true during the early and mid-1960s when civil rights was the major focus of New Left activity.

Jewish activists of the Old Left and the young leaders of the New Left had established a close bond that was crucial to understanding Jewish participation. There was the phenomenon of "red-diaper" babies, the children of parents who had been active in the Socialist and Communist parties. These children of older Jewish radicals provided leadership and brought organizational skills and an ingrained political orientation to the New Left. There was also the relationship between the New Left and the Jewish-led and socialist-oriented needle trade unions. SDS was originally subsidized by the League for Industrial Democracy (LID), an organization of the garment unions and whose leaders were largely Jewish socialists.

Throughout the early and mid-1960s, Jewish involvement in the New Left provided little public discomfort in the Jewish community. Questions of civil rights and economic equality were not incompatible with issues of Jewish concern. The 1967 Six-Day War in Israel brought an issue of primary Jewish concern to the public agenda and made it impossible for the New Left to ignore the Arab-Israeli conflict. From that time on serious strains developed between the New Left and much of the Jewish community. The relationship was never the same.

The chaotic National Conference for New Politics held in Chicago during the 1967 Labor Day weekend provided the first visible indications of the split. Initially held to provide an umbrella organization for the New Left and to meld the black power and anti-Vietnam movements closer together, the conference was rife with conflict between militants and moderates. Much of the conflict focused upon the New Left position toward Israel after its military victory that previous June. After a long and acrimonious debate, the conference adopted a policy statement, drafted by the black caucus, denouncing Israel for the "imperialist Zionist War."

After the 1967 Chicago conference, it became more difficult to be an active member of the New Left and a supporter of Israel. The New Left became more strident in its support of radical Third World liberation movements against the West. Israel was considered an integral part of the so-called Western World. Black radicals in particular were outspoken in their criticism of Israel. The Black Panther Party, for example, featured many articles in its newspaper supporting Al Fatah, one of the most militant Palestinian guerrilla groups, and frequently referred to Zionism as a racist doctrine. New Left rhetoric in general became more militant and Marxist, while Israel was frequently associated with Western imperialism. In turn, the 1967 war only strengthened the ties between the American Jewish community and Israel, deepening the discomfort of many Jewish participants in the New Left Movement.

Other issues also increased the alienation among the radical black leadership. The black power movement asserted that civil rights organizations should be controlled by black leadership. The brunt of this policy fell upon many Jews, who had been active in these organizations and had moved into positions of influence. They felt repudiated by their former political allies.

The 1968 teachers' strike in New York City's Ocean Hill–Brownsville area put the largely Jewish teachers' union against the black community leaders, who desired greater control over their neighborhood schools. The New Left interest in black power and neighborhood control were in vivid conflict with Jewish unionism, which in the 1960s had focused upon organizing teachers.

By the end of the 1960s, the New Left was stressing youth culture, radical individualism, psychedelic experience, and romantic violence. The Movement had moved away from the perspective it had shared with the Old Left. SDS at its 1969 convention had split into two factions: the Maoist Progressive Labor Party, which was explicitly Maoist, and the even more militant Weatherman faction, which extolled outlaw violence. Increasingly, the New Left identified the American Jewish community with the establishment and felt that anti-Semitism was no longer a major issue. Few in the New Left raised a voice against the anti-Semitic rhetoric of some black nationalist leaders and even found a rationale for such stridency. On the college campuses Jewish students began to drift away from the New Left organization. By 1970, Jewish participation in the leadership of SDS was at its lowest ebb.

This New Left evolution had a profound impact upon Jewish political and intellectual leadership. Many, alarmed by what they felt was growing anti-Semitism within the New Left, turned to the political right. For example, Norman Podhoretz, editor of *Commentary*, published by the American Jewish Committee, turned that magazine from a one-time left-liberal voice into an important vehicle for neoconservatism. Other Jewish intellectuals, such as Irving Kristol, the editor of *Public Interest*, felt that Jews would find a more compatible home in a conservatism that stressed order and stability. With greater frequency many American conservatives, in sharp contrast to the New Left, stressed their strong support for Israel.

Jewish disillusionment with the New Left also affected Jewish–black relations. In mayoralty elections in Philadelphia, Los Angeles, and New York in the 1970s many Jews supported the candidates strongly opposed by the black community. This split became more pronounced in the late 1970s and 1980s.

In 1980, as the New Left faded from view, American Jews drifted somewhat to the right, granting Ronald Reagan 38% of their vote. Although George Bush received only 29 percent of the Jewish vote in 1988, there was little doubt that some Jews and many Jewish leaders had moved distinctly to the right. In December 1988, a conference of left Jewish intellectuals, sponsored by the progressive Jewish magazine *Tikkun*, was held in New York City. The conference was an explicit attempt to revive the progressive Jewish tradition and to rekindle the spirit of the early New Left. As the 1990s opened, it was difficult to forecast how much of that spirit and tradition had been permanently affected by the divisive struggles of the late 1960s and 1970s. *See also* Black–Jewish Relations; Left, the.

ROBERT J. BRESLER

BIBLIOGRAPHY
Rubenstein, W. D. *The Left, the Right, and the Jews*. London: Croom Helm, 1982.

New York City. The first Jewish community established in North America in 1654, New York City, remains the foremost American Jewish community to this day. New York contains a Jewish population of just under 2 million, the largest urban Jewish concentration in history and roughly a third of the total American Jewry. Most national and international Jewish organizations locate their headquarters in New York City. The city achieved this preeminence through its position as the major port of entry for immigration to the United States, including over 4 million Jews. Of the Jewish immigrants who entered the port, approximately 75 percent remained, attracted by the city's economic opportunities. The critical mass of Jews concentrated in New York has influenced the character of the city and fostered a recognizable Jewish cultural style. New York Jews share a cosmopolitan elan and a vigorous parochialism nourished by the extraordinary diversity of Jewish city life. Since 1945, New York Jews have migrated throughout the United States so that the city's particular Jewish style can be seen in the sunny environs of Los Angeles and Miami as well as on the streets of Brooklyn and the Bronx.

As the largest Jewish community in the United States, New York Jews shelter many Jewish minority groups, ranging from multiple sects of Hasidic orthodoxy to numerous fragments of the secular Jewish Left. The city's Jewish population derives from a wide array of immigrant sources and from such countries as Syria, Greece, Cuba, Iran, and even Ethiopia. The city's size allows these Jews to develop their own independent collective life. However, the predominant population stems from the descendants of Eastern European Jews, who arrived during the era of mass migration from 1880 to 1924. During the preceding century, Jews from the German lands constituted the majority of the city's Jewry. They established the pattern of Jewish communal life that subsequent immigrants modified, elaborated, and enriched. The Jewish community of the colonial era, identified with Sephardic Jews, left only a faint imprint upon enduring institutional structures despite the continuity of Jewish settlement in the city.

Since the turn of the twentieth century, New York Jews have sustained a rich and diverse Jewish culture as well as contributing significantly to the city's artistic and intellectual milieu. As New York City became the national and then the international cultural capital in art, classical music, theater, dance, and publishing, Jews eagerly participated as producers and consumers of the books, paintings, shows, and concerts. The city is also the home of Yiddish secular culture, including literature, the press, theater, and popular music. Jewish scholarship flourishes in New York, supported by Reform, Orthodox, and Conservative rabbinical schools as well as by major institutions of advanced learning, Yeshiva University, the Jewish Theological Seminary of America, and the YIVO Institute for Jewish Research. Jewish intellectuals within and without academe contribute to a diverse cluster of magazines and journals of opinion published in the city. The city's cosmopolitan culture and its multiple ethnic cultures have thrived synergistically. Although the attraction of the city for Jews corresponds to a historical pattern of Jewish migration to centers of international influence, the intensity and mutuality of Jewish interaction with New York City remains unique.

Jewish settlement in New York City, then New Amsterdam, began under less than auspicious auspices given its subsequent history. The first group of 23 Jews to arrive on the North American mainland fled persecution and upheaval after the Dutch colony of Recife, Brazil, fell to the Portuguese, and entered the harbor destitute. The bigoted governor of the ethnically and religiously varied colony requested permission to expel the "deceitful race" from the Dutch West India Company. But the Jews obtained the intervention of their brethren on the company board who successfully secured permission for the group to reside, trade, and worship quietly in the colony provided they took care of their own poor. Additional rights, including the right to bear arms and to conduct kosher slaughtering, were granted after vigorous protest by Asser Levy [d. 1681]. When the British arrived in 1664, they did not challenge the fledgling Jewish community. However, transiency characterized the community and not until 1730 did the congregation established in 1654, Shearith Israel (Remnant of Israel), acquire sufficient security and capital to build a synagogue on Mill Street.

The slow growth of Jewish population in the eighteenth century reflected the character of the colonial New York Jewish community as primarily a trading outpost that attracted Jews who migrated as individuals. Most of the 100 Jews in New York, or 1% of the 4,500 population in 1700, were related to each other. They engaged in trade with overseas relatives, or with farmers and Indians up the Hudson River. In the second half of the eighteenth century the community

achieved stability, and many Jews left trade for work as artisans. The naturalization act of 1740 secured the rights of citizenship for colonial Jews after seven years residence. New York permitted them to vote and hold office, modifying or eliminating the required Christian oath, if they met the requisite property qualifications. New York Jews thus obtained political equality before Western European nations began to debate Jewish emancipation.

The Jewish community was largely coextensive with the congregation and self-sufficient for its internal needs. In addition to worship services led by a hazan (the congregation was too poor and uneducated to support a rabbi), Shearith Israel provided its members with a school, a mikvah, burial grounds, charity, kosher meat, and matzos for Passover. It supported these services through contributions, tuition charges, fines, and a tax for seats in the synagogue. Exceptional expenses, like exceptional knowledge, were solicited from better situated Jews abroad, especially in London. The members of the congregation included both Ashkenazi and Sephardi Jews, although the synagogue ritual followed the more prestigious Sephardi *nusach*. In 1729, Jacob Franks (1688–1769), an Ashkenazi Jew, assumed the leadership of Shearith Israel, indicating the spirit of cooperation that prevailed.

A similar spirit animated Jewish relationships with Gentiles. Jews lived among their Christian neighbors, many sent their children to Christian schools, and by the 1740s Jews enjoyed intimate friendships with Christians. Jews formed business partnerships with Christians, and Christians witnessed over half of the 41 extant wills of Jews. Increasing numbers of Christians and Jews intermarried. Sanctions imposed by Shearith Israel in the early decades of the century—refusing burial or a seat to a Jew who intermarried—were quietly overlooked. Although Jews remained apart from Christian New Yorkers in matters of religion, their successful occupational and social assimilation revealed the difficulties of sustaining Jewish life in an open, cosmopolitan frontier society.

The American Revolution unleashed a process of dynamic social change fostered by the rapid expansion into the frontier lands. New York City recovered quickly from the isolation of the war years when it served as British headquarters and began the decades of continuous growth that transformed the modest trading town into a major commercial metropolis of over 800,000 in 1860. The Jewish community split during the war;

many fled the city for Philadelphia as patriots while others stayed as Tories and supported the British. After the war a partial reunification occurred under the energetic leadership of the hazan, Gershom Mendes Seixas (1746–1816). As more Jews migrated to the city, they filled the places of those who had returned to London with the British. The new arrivals from the German lands substituted religious dissension for political disagreement. The first congregation to emerge by secession—Congregation B'nai Jeshurun—initiated in 1825 the process of congregationalism that severed New York Jewish communal life from the synagogue.

The establishment of two congregations in New York City anticipated a new Jewish community. By 1843, a dozen Jewish men turned away from the incessant squabbling they identified with the synagogue and proposed instead a new form of association, Jewish fraternalism. When they established the Independent Order of B'nai B'rith as an alternative to the congregation, there were in the city eight synagogues, two separate charitable organizations, and one women's benevolent society. The New York innovation soon spread throughout the United States, wherever German Jewish immigrants congregated. But the contours of a new Jewish communal life did not become visible until the migration of Jews from German lands reached substantial proportions after 1848.

By 1840, there were 7000 Jews in New York City, and on the threshold of the Civil War their numbers reached 40,000. The Jewish population started to grow at a faster rate than the burgeoning city population; Jews increased from 2 percent to 5 percent of the total population. The character of Jewish immigration also changed to a family chain migration led by youths. Jewish immigrants turned to peddling and petty crafts to establish an economic foothold in the city, and they clustered their residences in a section of the predominantly German neighborhood on Manhattan's east side. In the growing immigrant city, filled with Irish and Germans, Frenchmen and Englishmen, Jewish immigrants preferred to associate with those who spoke their language, shared their homesickness, and understood their ambition. As their numbers increased, Jews encountered prejudice, job discrimination, and exclusion from fraternal groups. Stimulated by the spirit of reform and self-improvement that flourished in the 1830s and 1840s and in response to expressions of anti-Jewish sentiment, Jews elaborated an extensive communal structure before the Civil War.

New York Jews organized literary societies (Hebrew Young Men's Literary Society, 1852), a hospital (Jews' Hospital, later Mt. Sinai, 1852), social clubs (the Harmonie became the most prominent), landsmanshaftn, a library (Maimonides, 1850), and an orphan home (Hebrew Orphan Asylum, 1859). Several independent charitable organizations separated philanthropy from the synagogue (the Hebrew Benevolent Society in 1822 was the first). When the first ordained rabbis arrived in the 1840s, they stimulated Jewish cultural activity and ideological diversity, especially the growth of Reform Judaism in the city. Robert Lyon (d. 1858) started the first successful Jewish paper, *The Asmonean* (1849–1858); in 1857, Samuel M. Isaacs (1804–1878) began editing *The Jewish Messenger*, an influential conservative Jewish weekly.

Jews continued to be active in local politics. Mordecai Manual Noah (1785–1851), a native-born Jew, achieved the most influence, first as a Jacksonian Democrat and Grand Sachem of Tammany Hall and later as editor of the Whig paper *The Evening Star* and supporter of the anti-Catholic Native American Party. He also espoused Jewish causes, and his abortive plan to rescue and resettle European Jews in an upstate colony, Ararat, in 1825 attracted much attention.

By the Civil War, German Jews had established a pattern of congregationalism in religion, communalism in philanthropy and Jewish political and cultural affairs, cooperative individualism in economic and social activities, and integration in politics and education. Religious congregationalism encouraged the growth of Reform and Orthodox synagogues and their mutual toleration. Philanthropic communalism enabled New York Jews to draw upon the expanding resources of the community to solve social problems of poverty and immigration adjustment, to support an array of cultural and social events, and to speak out with unanimity on international issues involving Jews, such as the Mortara Affair in 1859. Cooperative individualism provided a network of *landslayt* and family to assist immigrants in establishing petty retail shops through loans and credit as well as offering solace and sympathy in the context of congenial social groups. Political integration implied participation in the Democratic, and increasingly in the Republican, parties. Educational integration involved gradual acceptance in the 1850s and 1860s of public schools as they slowly lost their most prominent Protestant features. These patterns endured after the Civil War when New York Jews acquired greater wealth, leaving a concentration in petty retailing for merchandising, garment manufacturing, wholesaling, and banking.

The Civil War tore apart the social fabric of New York City, epitomized in the Draft Riots of 1863, but Jews remained largely insulated from the bitter passions of the war despite divisions within the city's Jewish community over slavery, the Union, Abraham Lincoln, and the social cost of the war. The majority supported the war, as registered in enlistment figures, bonds sold, monies raised at the 1864 Sanitary Fair, and political support of the Republican Party. The industrialization stimulated by the war, especially in the area of garment manufacture, speeded the embourgeoisement of many New York Jews and firmly anchored the needle trades in New York City. This proved to be the critical legacy of the Civil War for Jews. Beginning in the 1870s and expanding during the subsequent decades, ever increasing numbers of Jews from Eastern Europe immigrated to the city and entered its garment industry. In the process they radically transformed the communal pattern established by German Jews.

East European Jews came to New York City in such large numbers that the rate of growth of the city's Jewish community exceeded the city's own enormous population growth. Jews rose from 4 percent of the population in 1870 to 17 percent in 1900 to 29 percent by 1920. The early arrivals followed the German Jews to the Lower East Side and into the needle trades where they found work. Soon the newcomers overwhelmed the established community, which beat a steady retreat to the new uptown neighborhoods. By 1900, most German Jews had also left the needle trades factories to the East Europeans, only maintaining their positions as wholesalers. The physical and economic segregation and succession bred two separate Jewish societies, interrelated and interdependent but often in conflict. The "uptown" Jews were affluent, acculturated, politically integrated, and identified with Reform Judaism. Downtown Jews were poor, Yiddish-speaking immigrants, often inclined to radical politics, and Orthodox if religiously observant. After 1897, a growing number were Zionist.

The heart of the downtown Jewish settlement was the Lower East Side. At its peak in 1910, the Lower East Side—south of 14th Street, north of Catherine Street, and east of the Bowery and Third Avenue—housed 540,000, concentrating 25 percent of Manhattan's population on 5 percent of its land. The most congested sections, the center of the Jewish district, reached densities of 701 persons per acre, greater than found in Bombay, India. The rapid construction prior to 1901 of dumbbell tenements, designed to use between 75 and 90 percent of a lot, contributed to the overcrowding. The six-story buildings squeezed four apartments of three rooms each onto a floor, although only one room received any light or air from the street. The widespread acceptance of boarders, often recently arrived *landslayt* or relatives who helped pay the rent, added to the mass of humanity. The prevalence in the needle trades of the sweatshop system, in which apartments were used during the day as workshops, sustained the concentration.

Most immigrant Jews found work within a day of their arrival, and a majority entered the burgeoning women's and men's clothing industry where the simplification of tasks allowed for a brief apprenticeship. Women, close to 50 percent of the Jewish immigration to New York City, flocked to work in the needle trades if they were unmarried. Married women took in boarders, worked as peddlers, or helped their husbands run a small retail store. The building trades employed the second largest number of Jewish workers, although Jews worked in many of the city's trades, including printing and processing of cigars and food. The concentration of their brethren on the Lower East Side encouraged Jews to enter a variety of retail occupations, some of which, like kosher butcher shops, bakeries, and restaurants, catered to Jewish tastes. The confluence of work and residence, mediated through kinship and *landslayt* networks, transformed the Lower East Side into a separate Jewish world. The average of 10 to 15 years spent in the neighborhood facilitated the process of acculturation and often encouraged social mobility.

After the consolidation in 1898 of the city of Brooklyn and Queens and Richmond counties with Manhattan and the Bronx into the present city of New York, immigrant Jews rapidly moved out of the Lower East Side to new neighborhoods. The construction of rapid-transit facilities brought Brownsville, in eastern Brooklyn, and Harlem, in northern Manhattan, within reach. These neighborhoods offered better quality housing built to conform with the 1901 tenement law, moderate rents, and less overcrowding. The gradual migration of the garment industry north of 14th Street and the increasing restrictions against sweatshops weakened the Lower East Side's economic advantages. However, Harlem attracted a disproportionate number of Jews in the building trades, and Brownsville imported sweatshops, as did the older Brooklyn neighborhood of Williamsburg. The physical mobility of Jewish immigrants also measured their acculturation, economic success, and rising expectations for their children.

Although the Jewish population of the Lower East Side began to decline after 1910, the quarter of a million Jews remaining sustained a rich and diverse Jewish life and ignited a cultural explosion of major proportions. Russian, Romanian, Hungarian, and Galician Jews clustered on separate streets, as did a small colony of Levantine Jews. Each group supported an array of religious organizations, social groups, charitable societies, and landsmanshaftn. Jewish ethnic diversity also influenced occupational patterns; Jews from one district in Europe often monopolized a particular occupation—in the 1890s 90% of the pants makers were Romanian. As the dominant group, Russian Jews established the leading organizations that sought to unite the fractured downtown community. These included the Hebrew Sheltering and Immigrant Aid Society (1890), the United Hebrew Trades (1888), the Beth Israel Hospital (1889), and the Hebrew Free Loan Society (1892). The first Yiddish newspapers appeared in the 1880s. By 1905, there were four major dailies competing: the socialist *Forward*, the conservative *Tageblatt*, the religious *Morgen Journal*, and the radical *Warheit*. A flourishing Yiddish press gave employment to scores of Yiddish writers and helped to nourish the city's first group of intellectuals. Periodicals, journals, books, and poetry found an audience among immigrant Jews. The Yiddish theater also blossomed along the Bowery as did vernacular songs, the Yiddish equivalent of Tin Pan Alley. Nickelodeons offered immigrants a taste of fantasy and a way of looking at themselves. The popularity of these early motion pictures started several enterprising East Side Jews on careers that shaped the budding movie industry.

The creation of a Jewish world sustained by an ethnic economy facilitated the growth of Jewish secularism. In the 1880s, Jewish anarchists and socialists engaged in lively debates. Although both groups supported the 1886 mayoral campaign of Henry George (1839–1897), they subsequently became bitter rivals. The anarchists attacked all social institutions, including religion,

New York City Jewish Population, 1700–1990

Year	Jews	Total Population	Percent Jewish
1700	100	4,000	2.5
1750	300	13,300	2.3
1820	450	123,700	0.4
1840	7,000	312,700	2.2
1850	16,000	515,000	3.1
1860	40,000	814,000	4.9
1870	60,000	942,000	6.3
1880	80,000	1,206,000	6.6
1890	225,000	2,515,000	8.9
1900	580,000	3,437,000	16.8
1910	1,100,000	4,766,000	23.0
1920	1,640,000	5,620,000	29.1
1930	1,830,000	6,930,000	26.4
1940	1,950,000	7,454,000	26.1
1950	2,100,000	7,892,000	26.6
1960	1,936,000	7,782,000	24.8
1970	1,840,000	7,895,000	23.3
1980	1,133,000	7,072,000	16.0
1990	1,130,000	7,323,000	15.4

and held Yom Kippur balls to prove their point. Emma Goldman (1869–1940), through her monthly *Mother Earth* (1906), called for the liberation of women, the end to government and capitalism, the creation of a free society. The socialists, led by Abraham Cahan (1860–1951), turned to Yiddish-language propaganda, to the formation of a socialist fraternal order (Workmen's Circle, 1900), to unionization, and after 1910 to Yiddish socialist schools, to complement their efforts to build a socialist party. After many abortive strikes, they established the International Ladies Garment Workers Union on a firm foundation, following the 1909 uprising of the 20,000 women workers in the shirtwaist industry and the men's cloakmakers strike of 1910. The agreements hammered out between the Jewish workers and Jewish owners reflected the growing cooperation of uptown and downtown Jews and their awareness of belonging to a larger Jewish community of New York. Socialist victories at the polls followed successful unionization. In 1914 the Lower East Side elected New York's first Socialist Congressman, Meyer London (1871–1926).

Not all immigrant Jews supported socialism or other secularist movements. Many adhered to the religious traditionalism characteristic of the intense communal culture of Eastern Europe. These Jews attempted to transplant such institutions as the *hevra kadisha* (burial society), Talmud Torah (school for indigent boys), yeshiva, and even a communal rabbinate. But the social disorganization of immigrant life precluded an easy transference of East European traditions to New York City. Instead, some immigrant Jews created several new institutions adapted to American conditions that established modern Orthodoxy in the United States. These included a yeshiva for advanced study that also taught secular subjects, first on the high school and then on the college level, the Rabbi Isaac Elchanan Theological Seminary (1896) and Yeshiva College (1925), the Young Israel congregational movement (1912), and the Union of Orthodox Congregations (1898), which united uptown and downtown rabbis. A similar joint effort of uptown and downtown, the New York Kehillah (1908–1922), led by Reform Rabbi Judah L. Magnes (1877–1948), successfully, albeit briefly, brought representatives of more traditional organizations into a forum to cooperate with uptown leaders to confront such problems as the dearth of Jewish education, absence of kashrut supervision, Jewish criminality on the Lower East Side, and the coordination of Jewish charity.

Uptown Jews also tried to influence directly the Americanization of Jewish immigrants by establishing organizations that catered to Lower East Side Jews. These included a number of schools and settlements, such as the Educational Alliance (1889), the Hebrew Technical Institute (1890), the Jewish Theological Seminary of America (1886, reorganized in 1902). Through its sponsorship the Educational Alliance introduced into the public schools special English classes for foreigners, a kindergarten program, physical education classes, and lectures in Yiddish and English for adults. It also nourished the first circle of Jewish artists in the United States. The Jewish Theological Seminary (JTS) trained rabbis and teachers for what became Conservative congregations. Supported by wealthy uptown Jews, many of whom were Reform, JTS drew its students from the immigrant Lower East Side. Other organizations sponsored by uptown Jews sought to alleviate the suffering caused by poverty and dislocation. These included Lillian Wald's (1867–1940) Henry Street Settlement (1893) with its nursing service, the Jewish Big Brother program for juvenile delinquents, the Lakeview Home (1909) for unwed mothers, and the National Desertion Bureau (1911) to locate missing husbands.

The special problems of women received attention from women's organizations that reached out across class lines. The National Council of Jewish Women (1893) established its headquarters in New York and focused its efforts to help single immigrant women who traveled alone to New York City. The council also tried to raise the Jewish community's consciousness regarding the problem of Jewish prostitution. The Zionist Movement also attracted women, especially after the organization of Hadassah (1912), which enlisted women to provide health services in the land of Israel. The Women's Trade Union League assisted union organizers in the needle trades, despite differences in class and religion between the wealthy members of the league and the poor Jewish women workers. Immigrant women also established their own organizations to help each other, ranging from day nurseries and baby hospitals to landsmanshaftn and free loan societies. In 1915 and again in 1917, New York Jewish women took the lead in the women's suffrage struggle, marching in parades, organizing rallies, and soliciting the support of their husbands, brothers, and sons.

Although successful in winning the vote for women in New York State in 1917, New York City Jews increasingly found themselves out of step with the mood of the nation and the city. World War I promoted a virulent nationalism that did not tolerate ethnic diversity. New York Jewish Zionist intellectuals, including Mordecai Kaplan (1881–1983), Judah Magnes, and Israel Friedlaender (1876–1920), articulated the vision of cultural pluralism, but they failed to stem the tide of Americanization. The Bolshevik Revolution had a similar disastrous impact upon Yiddish socialism, splitting its ranks and fracturing its organizations. The Red Scare of 1919 decimated the New York Socialist Party and in 1920 the New York State legislature expelled its Socialist members, many of whom represented Jewish districts. But congressional restriction of immigration in 1924 struck the worst blow to New York Jewish life. Without immigrants to fill the places of those who moved to new neighborhoods, the Lower East Side entered a period of steady decline. The future lay with the children of the immigrants, the second generation.

New York Jews of the second generation rooted their lives in a variety of new neighborhoods located primarily in Brooklyn and the

Bronx. Differentiated by class and ideology, each neighborhood boasted modern apartments with space, light, and air, located often near broad streets or large parks. Less varied and densely populated than the immigrant quarters, such neighborhoods as Flatbush, Crown Heights, Brighton Beach, and Boro Park in Brooklyn and Morrisania and the Grand Concourse in the Bronx sustained intense, provincial Jewish communities. On average, Jews constituted between 40 to 60 percent of the population. Jews' occupational mobility fueled their physical mobility. The second generation moved into white-collar jobs as salesmen, insurance agents, clerks, government employees and into the professions of teaching, social work, pharmacy, dentistry, law, and medicine. Many also entered their own businesses in building, advertising, publishing, electricity, dry cleaning, and automotive dealerships as well as in the older Jewish retail fields. The diversity of occupations paralleled the variety of residential neighborhoods and contrasted with the immigrants' concentration in the needle trades and on the Lower East Side.

Second-generation Jews crafted a middle-class Jewish way of life that embraced American culture. In fact, many Jews contributed to New York's material culture so eagerly consumed by the millions of New Yorkers. From the motion picture palaces built by Jewish movie moguls to the art deco apartment buildings constructed by Jewish builders, from the popular tunes on the radio to the Broadway musical theater, Jews helped to shape the exuberant culture of New York City. Jews also supported less popular art forms, including opera, theater, classical music concerts, publishing—both books and journals of opinion—and continued to create vibrant works in Yiddish. In 1928, there were 11 Yiddish theaters in New York, and in 1931, the *Forward* established the world's only full-time Yiddish radio station, WEVD. Quotas limited Jewish enrollment at colleges, universities, law and medical schools, but Jewish men flocked in such large numbers to the tuition-free City College of New York while Jewish women went to Hunter College that Jews made up well over a majority of the students. The establishment of Brooklyn College in the 1930s was designed to accommodate constant Jewish pressure for higher education. Heavy Jewish enrollment in public high schools where many Jewish teachers taught facilitated the introduction of Hebrew language instruction in 1929, symbolic recognition of the legitimacy of a distinct American Jewish ethnic identity. New York Jews also incorporated American values into Jewish religious life by creating a new American form of congregation, the synagogue center, which catered to Jewish families and provided education, recreation, and worship under one roof.

Second-generation Jews not only influenced New York culture, they helped to shape its politics. In the 1920s, many supported the liberal Democratic governor, Al Smith and his successor, Franklin D. Roosevelt. When Roosevelt entered the White House, New York Jews abandoned the Socialist Party for the liberalism epitomized in the New Deal. Immigrant Jewish unionists created the American Labor party in 1936 to vote for FDR when they could not in good conscience vote Democratic. But New York Jews also continued the radical tradition through many social and cultural, as well as political, groups. In the 1920s, the Communist, Socialist, and Yiddishist left each built innovative cooperative housing in the Bronx for their members. These buildings with their schools, libraries, and meeting rooms filled with collective spirit nourished radical Jewish traditions in the city. The economic difficulties of the Depression of the 1930s eroded Jewish affluence, but other New Yorkers suffered greater deprivation. Jewish politics included helping some of these dispossessed, such as the growing black population of Harlem. The rise of Nazism in Germany and fascism in Italy and the Spanish Civil War (1936–1939) fomented ethnic and religious tensions on the streets of New York between Jews and Germans, Italians, and Irish. But the United States entry into World War II in 1941 encouraged New Yorkers to bury their intramural hatreds against a common enemy.

Although New York Jews reached a consensus supporting democratic liberalism, they failed to agree upon a united response to the Nazi "final solution," the destruction of the Jews. The city served as a center for ideological dissension promoted by the national Jewish organizations with ideological constituencies that located their headquarters in New York. These included the four major defense organizations, the American Jewish Committee (1906), the American Jewish Congress (1922), the Jewish Labor Committee (1934), the Anti-Defamation League of B'nai B'rith (branch office 1937, headquarters 1946); the coordinating organizations, National Jewish Welfare Board (1917), American Jewish Joint Distribution Committee (1914), Council of Jewish Federations and Welfare Funds (1932); the

Zionist organizations, Zionist Organization of America (1897), Hadassah (1912), Labor Zionists (1902), Mizrachi (1901); and the United Jewish Appeal (1939). In the context of the fragmented neighborhood structure of New York City Jewish life, coordination and cooperation proved impossible. The Federation of Jewish Philanthropies (1917) only managed to consolidate with the separate Brooklyn Federation (1912) in 1937 after years of negotiation, so it was not up to the task of unifying New York Jews. New York City also absorbed over 100,000 refugees from Nazism and many of them formed a visible enclave in Washington Heights.

The postwar prosperity ushered in a period that allowed New York Jews to forget the difficult war years. Even the 250,000 refugees who arrived after the war were encouraged to forget their pasts and remake their lives through the American pursuit of happiness. Chafing at the restrictive covenants, college quotas, and executive-suite discrimination that hampered their prospect for mobility, New York Jews allied themselves with blacks to dismantle the barriers erected to equality in employment, housing, and education. Within a decade after World War II they achieved legislative and court victories that permitted many Jews to enter exclusive colleges and graduate schools, hold executive positions, and move out of the city to suburban homes in Westchester and Nassau counties or across the Hudson River to New Jersey. Others chose elegant apartments in previously restricted sections in Queens and Riverdale and on Manhattan's Upper East Side. These moves separated third-generation Jews from the city's newest Puerto Rican immigrants, its growing black population, and older Jews who declined to move. The Jewish population of New York peaked at just over 2 million in 1950, dropping steadily in the succeeding decades (although the metropolitan area population remained stable).

Jewish involvement in New York City's cultural life remained high, although Jews no longer supported both a rich ethnic culture in Yiddish and a vernacular culture in English. Jewish contributions to popular American culture yielded to blacks and immigrants, but Jews sustained active involvement in the artistic, musical, theatrical, and publishing worlds. The Jewish Museum sponsored shows of Jewish abstract expressionist artists, helping to popularize the New York School. The 92nd Street Young Men's Hebrew Association (1870) encouraged avant-garde Jewish poets, dancers, and musicians by providing a stage and an audience for their art. Jews made up an estimated 70 percent of the theater and concert audiences in New York during the 1950s. Both the Broadway and Off-Broadway stage accommodated Jewish talents.

In contrast to the virulent anticommunism of the Cold War that decimated the Jewish left in New York City, Orthodox Jews were reinvigorated by the arrival of many Hasidic sects, refugees from Nazism. Most settled in declining Brooklyn neighborhoods and built institutions to ensure their survival. The second generation developed an aggressive form of ethnic interest-group politics that departed from the reigning liberalism of New York Jews. In the late 1960s, after bitter Jewish clashes with blacks over education, housing, and jobs, the new ethnicity of the ultra-Orthodox appealed to wider circles of Jews. The 1973 election of Abraham Beame [b. 1906], the first Jewish mayor of New York City, reflected a shift in Jewish politics that has continued with Jewish support for Edward Koch [b. 1924], mayor from 1977 to 1990. The 1970s brought a fiscal crisis to many Jewish institutions, which had lost their population base. Synagogues on the Upper West Side closed, others in Brooklyn transferred their assets to Hasidic groups, while a few revived with the support of alternative Jewish Havurah groups. The major Jewish educational institutions, however, survived the fiscal crisis and resisted the impulse to leave New York City.

Jewish confidence in New York, despite periods of pessimism, always revived. The city has offered Jews a unique milieu in which to live, work, consume, and create; it has provided unmatched opportunities for Jews to achieve their personal and collective goals, to live as Jews and as Americans, to influence the shape of a common American culture. New York Jews have found the reality of the promise worth the cost.

DEBORAH DASH MOORE

BIBLIOGRAPHY

Goren, Arthur A. *New York Jews and the Quest for Community: The Kehillah Experiment, 1908–1922.* New York: Columbia University Press, 1970.

Grinstein, Hyman B. *The Rise of the Jewish Community of New York 1654–1860.* Philadelphia: Jewish Publication Society, 1954.

Gurock, Jeffrey S. *When Harlem Was Jewish 1870–1930.* New York: Columbia University Press, 1979.

Howe, Irving, and Libo, Kenneth. *World of Our Fathers.* New York: Harcourt Brace Jovanovich, 1976.

Mayer, Egon. *From Suburb to Shtetl: The Jews of Boro Park*. Philadelphia: Temple University Press, 1979.

Moore, Deborah Dash. *At Home in America: Second-Generation New York Jews*. New York: Columbia University Press, 1981.

"New York City." *Encyclopedia Judaica*. 1062–1124.

Poll, Solomon. *The Hasidic Community of Williamsburg: A Study in the Sociology of Religion*. New York: Schocken, 1962.

Rischin, Moses. *The Promised City: New York's Jews, 1870–1914*. Cambridge: Harvard University Press, 1962.

92nd Street Y (New York City). The 92nd Street Young Men's and Young Women's Hebrew Association is a major cultural center in New York City and among the oldest, largest, and most renowned Jewish community centers in the United States. Founded in 1874, it is best known simply as the 92nd Street Y, located on Manhattan's Upper East Side. The 92nd Street Y nurtures the cultural, educational, recreational, and spiritual growth of a diverse constituency that includes more than 300,000 users a year, from infants to senior adults. They partake of a huge array of concerts, readings, lectures, classes, and programs in all the arts and social services. A comprehensive Jewish lecture, education, and outreach program attracts large numbers from all Jewish denominations, as well as the unaffiliated.

The Y presents a full-scale classical music season of some 100 concerts a year in resonant, wood-paneled Kaufmann Concert Hall, where talented musicians from all over the world perform and are regularly noticed by New York's music critics. The Y's resident orchestra, the New York Chamber Symphony, under the direction of Maestro Gerard Schwarz, presents three annual series; records on the Nonesuch, Delos, and Angel-EMI labels; and will have its first international tour in 1992. In addition to its classical music, the Y programs jazz series in the summer and winter, a spring musical theater series, "Lyrics and Lyricists," and other popular and jazz concerts.

The Y has a wide audience for those who care about the spoken word. For more than 50 years, its poetry center has been America's principal forum for writers worldwide who read from their own work on most Monday nights September through May. Each year the Y also schedules more than 100 lectures and panel discussions

led by experts in art, architecture, politics, science, film, and theology.

Since 1966, Elie Wiesel has been giving a four-part lecture series on Jewish literature at the Y as part of the Y's Jewish Omnibus program, which includes a wide variety of lectures and all-day study institutes on subjects of particular scholarly interest. In addition to Wiesel, Abba Eban, Stuart Eizenstat, Gerson D. Cohen, Norman Podhoretz, Lucy Dawidowicz, Elie Kedourie, David Hartman, and Teddy Kollek are among those who have delivered the Y's prestigious annual State of World Jewry address.

The Y's educational offerings include a 700-student school of music, an art center, and a dance center. The latter helped launch many of the country's great dance pioneers, such as Martha Graham, Agnes de Mille, Merce Cunningham, Awsa Sokolow, and Alvin Ailey.

The Y's many other offerings include a 400-room residence, a state-of-the-art health and fitness center, a highly respected parenting center, a full-scale senior adult program, a teen division, and classes for persons with special needs. The Y's tours and talks program offers guided walking and bus tours to points of historic interest in and beyond New York, hostel groups, and international travel with cultural themes to Europe, Israel, and Latin America. *See also* Communal Organizations.

HENRY NIGER

BIBLIOGRAPHY

Celazar, Daniel. *Community and Polity*. Philadelphia: Jewish Publication Society, 1976.

Sklare, Marshall, ed. *The Jewish Community in America*. New York: Behrman House, 1974.

Noah, Mordecai Manuel (1785–1851). Early American diplomat, journalist, playwright, and Zionist, Mordecai Manuel Noah was born in Philadelphia to German immigrants. Noah and his sister were raised by grandparents after his father abandoned the family and his mother died when he was 9 years old. Shuttling back and forth between Philadelphia and New York City, Noah picked up what formal education he could while working as a peddler and engaging in local politics. In his early twenties he worked feverishly on behalf of Simon Snyder, the Jeffersonian-Republican candidate for governor of Pennsylvania. Snyder was elected, and Noah received the first of many patronage favors in his long career as a political activist.

Noah's reward for his efforts on behalf of Snyder was the post of major in the Pennsylvania militia. He held the job only briefly, but forever after he was known as "Major Noah."

A restless and combative personality, Noah sought a career as a diplomat. His strong polemical efforts on behalf of President James Madison in 1812 during a brief sojourn in Charleston, S.C., gave him a claim on a consulship in Tunis. In Tunis for less than two years, Noah emphasized his Sephardic origins in his relations with political leaders of the region. He was relieved of duties in 1815 because of his involvement in a complex rescue mission in Algeria, though Secretary of State James Monroe, seeking not to worsen relations with the Tunisian dey, emphasized Noah's religion and unspecified financial irregularities as the basis for his recall. Noah turned this disingenuous public explanation to personal advantage, portraying himself as a victim of prejudice.

By 1817, Noah was back in New York City, working as an editor of the *National Advocate*, an influential newspaper. Writing was his strong suit. A vivid writer with wide ranging interests, he provided the reams of copy necessary in the small-shop newspaper common to the era. Noah excelled in the word wars between rival editors. He had a talent for invective and a relish for directing it at political targets. Not surprisingly, such qualities proved attractive to politicians seeking aid from the press. One such politician, Martin Van Buren of New York, was then building a political machine known as the Albany Regency, which would dominate New York politics for nearly two decades.

Noah served the Albany Regency well for several years, though he chafed at party discipline. He turned to independent journalism before joining the coalition in New York backing Andrew Jackson for President in 1828. When Jackson was elected, Noah was again in line for an appointment. Over Van Buren's objections, he was named surveyor and inspector of New York Port, a position attractive for the lucrative fees it generated.

Noah did not abandon journalism during the years as an officeholder. In 1829, he sold his *Enquirer*, which he had established in 1826, to James Watson Webb and became an increasingly close associate of the more prominent New York editor on the latter's *Courier and Enquirer*. This association ultimately led Noah out of the Jacksonian party. In 1832, when the New York Jacksonians joined the President's assault on the Bank

of the United States, Noah and Webb, with financial obligations to the bank, refused to go along. Noah was forced into opposition.

By 1833, Noah was back running his own paper, the *New York Evening Star*. The *Star* was a quality newspaper, emphasizing solid reporting and writing. It was not geared, however, as Webb's and James Gordon Bennett's papers increasingly were, to the technology or the tastes of the new age of journalism. Noah's paper survived with a relatively small readership because he was patronized by the wealthy merchants of the city and the conservative wing of the Democratic Party, which grew increasingly disenchanted with the hard-money policies of the Jackson and Van Buren administrations.

Noah's increasing conservatism manifested itself in other ways as well. He was virulently antiabolitionist, generally supportive of southern political interests, and was one of the relatively few northerners who openly defended slavery. This "dough-face" ideology contributed to the *Star's* demise in 1840. Noah undertook a number of other journalistic ventures, including a weekly newspaper, but none was particularly successful. His renown derived from other endeavors.

Noah has been called "the most fascinating American Jew of the first half of the nineteenth century." This appraisal may have less to do with his success in journalism or politics—in these fields he was well recognized but hardly in the first rank—than with the variety of Noah's interests and the deftness of his self-promotion.

In addition to his mainline career as a journalist and political hanger-on, Noah was, by turns, a dramatist, theater critic, travel writer, and Zionist. His plays, which were largely derivative in plot and language, were nonetheless popular in the United States and in England. His account of life in North Africa, published in 1819, is today considered a noteworthy primary source.

But Noah's leading claim to fame lay in his proto-Zionism. Always loyal to his heritage in a society where assimilation was attractive to the socially and politically ambitious, Noah publicly advocated Jewish traditions, a Jewish college, and Jewish agricultural settlement. In the 1820s, he purchased land—Grand Island on the Niagara River—and promoted it as a haven for Jews, a "night's lodging" until their eventual restoration to Palestine. Public response to Noah's proselytizing was surprisingly favorable, but not among American Jews. European Jews, the real focus of Noah's promotion, were equally uninterested in moving to this American "Ararat," and the idea faded. But Noah had earned a reputation as a man of considerable moxie and some vision. He was one of the best-known American Jews in the early republic. *See also* Journalism.

MICHAEL J. BIRKNER

BIBLIOGRAPHY

Goldberg, Isaac. *Major Noah, American Jewish Pioneer*. Philadelphia: Jewish Publication Society, 1936.

Gordis, Robert. "Mordecai Manuel Noah: A Centenary Evaluation." In *The Jewish Experience in America*, edited by Abraham J. Karp. Waltham, Mass.: American Jewish Historical Society, 1969.

Sarna, Jonathan D. *Jacksonian Jew: The Two Worlds of Mordecai Noah*. New York: Holmes & Meier, 1981.

Nobel Prize Winners. Although the number of Jews in America has never exceeded 3 percent of the population, American Jews have received a disproportional share of the prizes in the six categories that were first awarded in 1901. Those with asterisks received their awards before migrating to the United States.

World Peace
1973—Henry Kissinger (b. 1923)
1986—Elie Wiesel (b. 1928)

Literature
1976—Saul Bellow (b. 1915)
1978—Isaac Bashevis Singer (b. 1904)
1987—Iosif Brodsky (b. 1940)

Physiology and Medicine
1922—Otto Meyerhoff* (1884–1951)
1936—Otto Loewi* (1873–1961)
1944—Joseph Erlanger (1874–1965)
1944—Herber Spencer Gasser (1888–1963)
1946—Hermann Joseph Muller (1890–1967)
1952—Selman Abraham Waksman (b. 1888)
1953—Fritz Albert Lipmann (1899–1986)
1958—Joshua Lederberg (b. 1925)
1959—Arthur Kornberg (b. 1918)
1964—Konrad Bloch (b. 1912)
1967—George Wald (b. 1906)
1968—Marshall W. Nirenberg (b. 1927)
1969—Salvador Luria (1912–1991)
1970—Julius Axelrod (b. 1912)
1972—Gerald Maurice Edelman (b. 1929)
1975—David Baltimore (b. 1938)
1975—Howard Martin Temin (b. 1934)
1976—Baruch S. Blumberg (b. 1925)
1977—Rosalyn Sussman Yalow (b. 1921)

1978—Daniel Nathans (b. 1928)
1980—Baruj Benecerraf (b. 1920)
1984—Cesar Milstein (b. 1927)
1985—Michael Stuart Brown (b. 1914)
1985—Joseph L. Goldstein (b. 1940)
1986—Stanley Cohen (b. 1922)
1986—Rita Levi-Montalcini (b. 1909)
1988—Gertrude Bell Elion (b. 1918)

Chemistry
1961—Melvin Calvin (b. 1912)
1972—William Howard Stein (b. 1911)
1979—Herbert Charles Brown (b. 1912)
1980—Paul Berg (b. 1926)
1980—Walter Gilbert (b. 1932)
1981—Roald Hoffmann (b. 1937)
1983—Henry Taube (b. 1915)
1989—Sidney Altman (b. 1949)

Physics
1907—Albert Abraham Michelson (1852–1931)
1921—Albert Einstein* (1879–1955)
1944—Isidor Isaac Rabi (1898–1988)
1952—Felix Bloch (b. 1905)
1959—Emilio Segré (b. 1905)
1960—Donald A. Glaser (b. 1926)
1961—Robert Hofstadter (1915–1990)
1965—Richard Phillips Feynman (1918–1988)
1965—Julian Schwinger (b. 1918)
1967—Hans A. Bethe (b. 1906)
1969—Murray Gell-Mann (b. 1929)
1975—Benjamin R. Mottelson (b. 1926)
1976—Burton Richter (b. 1931)
1978—Arno Allan Penzias (b. 1933)
1979—Steven Weinberg (b. 1933)
1979—Sheldon L. Glashow (b. 1932)
1988—Leon M. Lederman (b. 1922)
1988—Melvin Schwartz (b. 1932)
1988—Jack Steinberger (b. 1921)
1990—Jerome I. Friedman (b. 1930)

Economics
1970—Paul A. Samuelson (b. 1915)
1971—Simon Kuznets (b. 1901)
1972—Kenneth J. Arrow (b. 1921)
1976—Milton Friedman (b. 1912)
1978—Herbert A. Simon (b. 1916)
1980—Lawrence R. Klein (b. 1920)
1985—Franco Modigliani (b. 1918)
1987—Robert M. Solow (b. 1924)
1990—Harry Markowitz (b. 1927)
1990—Merton Miller (b. 1923)

DAVID ZUBATSKY

O

Odets, Clifford (1906–1963). Playwright Clifford Odets was the son of East European immigrants Louis and Pearl Geisinger Odets, who moved from Philadelphia to New York when he was 6 years old. He starred in drama and debate at Morris High School in the Bronx, but dropped out of school in November 1923 at age 17 and went to work for his father. Odets wanted to be an actor and soon quit working for his father's printing business to become the Roving Reciter, presenting dramatic poems by Kipling and other writers. He acted with small theater groups and the Theater Guild, was an announcer and writer for radio station WBNY (1925–1927), where later he claimed to have been the first disc jockey, and was a charter member of the Group Theatre (1931). He joined the Communist Party late in 1934 but resigned after eight months. In testimony before the House Committee on Un-American Activities (HUAC) in 1952, he said he joined because "there were perhaps 16 million unemployed people in the United States, and I myself was living on ten cents a day" but resigned because the Party believed "art is a weapon." "I couldn't be given a theme and handle it," Odets said. "I could only write out of my own experience, my own incentive."

In 1933, Odets wrote *Waiting for Lefty*, in just three days, as his entry in a *New Theatre Magazine* competition for a short play of "social significance." *Lefty* is a series of vignettes of jobless and hungry Americans trying to make a living as taxi drivers during the Depression. Staged by the Group Theatre in January 1935, it was an instant hit; as the play ended, the audience spontaneously rose to their feet and joined with the actors in shouting "Strike! Strike! Strike!" Odets became the foremost playwright of the decade, with *Awake and Sing!* (1935), *Till the Day I Die* (1935), *Paradise Lost* (1936), *Golden Boy* (1937), and *Rocket to the Moon* (1939). His other plays included *Clash by Night* (1941), *The Country Girl* (1950), and *The Flowering Peach* (1954). His movie scripts included *Humoresque* (1942), *None But the Lonely Heart* (1943), *It's a Wonderful Life* (1945), *Notorious* (1947), *Sweet Smell of Success* and *The Way West* (1957), *Walk on the Wild Side* (1961), and *Wild in the Country* (1960). In 1962, Odets wrote, "While you were looking ahead for something to happen, that was it! That was life! You lived it!" He was writing an NBC-TV dramatic series when he died of cancer in August 1963 in Los Angeles.

Although Odets made theater history in 1936 with three hit plays running concurrently on Broadway, theater critics and scholars tend to dismiss him as a playwright who "failed to live up to his promise" because he "disappeared" from the Broadway stage in the 1940s. Like the hero in *Golden Boy*, however, he had chosen to become a "prizefighter" instead of a "violinist" to win fame and fortune. In Hollywood, Odets earned a six-figure income writing for the 80 million Americans who went to the movies each week. His immigrant mother had worked in a sweatshop at age 11 for pennies a day, but he lived the "American dream" in a Hollywood mansion with a swimming pool. He wrote and directed the film

None But the Lonely Heart (1943), for which Cary Grant and Ethel Barrymore won Academy Awards. His film adaptation of his play, *The Country Girl*, starred three of the greatest film stars of the era, Grace Kelly, Bing Crosby, and William Holden (1954). Columbia University's Drama Committee voted the Pulitzer Prize for Drama (1955) to *The Flowering Peach*, although the university's trustees vetoed their decision. He received the Gold Medal of the American Academy of Arts and Letters (1961). His work has also passed into nonliterary history; *Waiting for Lefty* is frequently cited in social histories of the 1930s.

Before Odets, the Jew in American drama was a vaudeville comic, a caricature (*Abie's Irish Rose*), or a minor, sentimentalized background character (the Jewish student in *Street Scene*). However, the Group Theatre's members were mostly first- or second-generation Jewish Americans from lower-middle-class backgrounds, and they had developed a new style of acting in which the players moved about, embracing and recoiling from each other, using what we now call "body English" but what was really "body Yiddish." It was an ideal acting style for Odets' portrayal of the psychological adjustments people have to make to other people and to the world they live in and for his focus on the Jewish middle-class family and its dominant matriarch, on male chauvinists and independent, searching women, and on love in all its manifestations—youth's yearning for independence, the problems and fulfillment in marriage, and the economic motif in love, especially the financial impossibility of marriage during the Depression. Odets was the spokesman for the Depression era, but he captured the essence of the immigrant experience and described it in figurative language that was typically and historically Jewish. Statements like "Life shouldn't be printed on dollar bills" or "New art works should shoot bullets" could lift his plays out of social realism into the realm of allegory. He prepared the way for playwrights like Arthur Miller and Paddy Chayefsky and novelists and autobiographers like Alfred Kazin, Bernard Malamud, Saul Bellow, and Philip Roth. Black playwrights like Lorraine Hansberry and Lanford Wilson also echo his influence. Odets wrote that "We live in a time where you say something in one decade, and a decade later you're old fashioned." But his plays and films are peopled by men and women filled with passion and loneliness, who struggle to achieve fulfillment, and he still is relevant to those who believe that "life shouldn't be printed on dollar bills." *See also* Theater.

RHODA G. LEWIN

BIBLIOGRAPHY

Brenman-Gibson, Margaret. *Clifford Odets, American Playwright: The Years from 1906 to 1940.* New York: Atheneum, 1981.

Cantor, Harold. *Clifford Odets: Playwright-Poet.* Metuchen, N.J.: Scarecrow Press, 1978.

Mendelsohn, Michael J. *Clifford Odets: Humane Dramatist.* LeLand, Fla.: Evrett/Edwards, 1969.

Weales, Gerald. *Clifford Odets, Playwright.* New York: Praeger, 1974.

ORT: Organization for Rehabilitation Through Training.

ORT, Organization for Rehabilitation Through Training, is a worldwide network of vocational and technical schools that originated in Russia in 1880. The original goal of a small group of Russian Jewish businessmen and financiers was to petition Czar Aleksandr II to establish a fund for needy Jews. It was hoped that the necessary funds, privately donated, would create a Society for the Promotion of Handicrafts and Agriculture to provide economic relief for Jews living in the Pale of Settlement. Permission was granted on March 22, 1880, and thus ORT came into being.

ORT established a foothold in the United States on June 22, 1922, through the efforts of ORT leaders Leon Bramson and Aron Syngalowski, whose appeals enlisted American Jews who wanted to help friends and relatives still living in Eastern Europe. From April 1923 to 1924, the ORT organization that they set up in America disbanded, reorganized, and merged with other Jewish relief organizations to emerge as the American ORT of today. The first order of business was to raise capital ($300,000) through the ORT Reconstruction Fund and establish a sense of freedom to raise funds independently.

The ORT Tool Supply Corporation, originally called the People's Tool Campaign, encouraged interested American Jews to purchase the tools, machinery and raw materials for their Eastern European brethren in the United States to enhance their work as farmers and artisans. Assistance was offered rather than charity, and 10,000 Americans applied between 1928 and 1931. The successful ORT Tool Supply Corporation combined with American ORT in 1932 and was renamed People's ORT Federation.

Additional support from American ORT was needed in 1940 for Eastern European Jewry when their situation changed because of the Nazi occupation of their lands. The increase of European refugees to the United States called for ORT to meet new challenges. A new school, named for Abraham C. Litton, an early ORT activist, opened its doors in New York City in 1940. The school focused on technical crafts and eventually moved to Israel in 1957. A second ORT school, the Bramson School, opened in 1942 to introduce the needle trades to its students. To meet the needs of the 900 refugees interned at the Fort Ontario Emergency Refugee Shelter, 1944–1945, eight workshop camps were set up in Oswego, New York.

ORT was also part of the American labor scene. Initially known as Labor ORT in the 1920s and then as American Labor ORT in 1938, ORT over the years has numbered 100 unions within its organization, including the International Ladies Garment Workers Union, the Amalgamated Clothing Workers of America, the Restaurant Workers Union, the Plastics and Novelty Union, to name only a few. These unions had many Jews as members.

Women's American ORT (WAO) was founded in 1927. WAO supported school buildings, training programs, and scholarships. Early goals were expanded to include economic independence and freedom for its students while strengthening Jewish identity and community. WAO has continued to expand to meet new demands: career education, anti-Semitism awareness, and involvement in Jewish as well as non-Jewish affairs, including the abortion issue, human rights, and peace and security for the State of Israel.

Through the support of WAO, the second Bramson ORT Technical Institute opened in New York City in 1977. It was the first Jewish junior college in the United States. Courses are offered in modern technology, business management, and Jewish studies, and certificates are awarded in computer programming, electronics, secretarial skills, and ophthalmics. In 1985, another ORT Technical Institute was opened in Los Angeles (LAOTI) with branches in the San Fernando Valley. Jewish immigrants, in the 1980s mostly those from the Soviet Union, can receive English instruction, introduction to American society and culture, and financial aid at ORT institutions. The Zarem Golde ORT Technical Institute, which opened in January 1991 in Chicago,

will continue the tradition of training students in the Chicago area. In Miami ORT operates the Computer Department of a Jewish high school.

It is not the intention of ORT to provide charity but to offer an opportunity for people to improve themselves. Over 2 million students have benefitted from ORT programs. Today, ORT is located on five continents and includes programs in developing countries to provide the technical expertise so desperately needed by those disadvantaged nations. ORT trains 195,000 students annually from all over the world; 2,077 are in the United States.

Currently, Women's American ORT has 145,000 members in 1,150 chapters nationwide, but the American presence exerts a global influence because it is the largest contributor to the World ORT Union.

SHERRY OSTROFF

BIBLIOGRAPHY

"Close-Ups." *Women's American ORT* 3, No. 1 (Fall 1989).

"Milestones in the History of ORT." New York: Women's American ORT, n.d.

"Ort in Brief." New York: Women's American ORT, n.d.

Shapiro, Leon. *The History of ORT: A Jewish Movement For Social Change.* New York: Schocken, 1980.

Orthodoxy. Orthodox Judaism is the oldest of the three major branches of Judaism as established in the United States. It is committed to the maintenance of the Mosaic Code, as outlined in the Torah (Bible), the Oral Law (Talmud), and Jewish law as interpreted throughout the ages by the major rabbinic figures of their times and codified in the Shulhan Arukh (the Code of Jewish Law).

The first congregations in the American colonies were established in accordance with Orthodox ritual. Thus Shearith Israel, the oldest congregation in the United States, founded in New York in 1654, was Orthodox. The ritual used by most of the colonial congregations was the Western European version of the Sephardic rite. Besides congregations, the early Jews also established mikvahs (ritual baths), set up kosher meat slaughtering facilities, and closed their stores on the Sabbath. Yet the New World with its professed policy of religious freedom posed many obstacles to traditional Jewish living. There were no rabbinic authorities, and the small numbers of Jews made intermarriage a problem. Indeed, while the congregations were organized on traditional basis, only a small number of their members were in fact completely observant. The fact that America was not looked upon favorably by the European rabbinic authorities encouraged most observant European Jews not to come to America. (This attitude only changed in the mid-twentieth century with the rise of Nazism in Germany.) The United States did not have a fully ordained resident rabbi until 1840, when Rabbi Abraham Rice (1802–1862) arrived from Germany. Until 1881, few other Orthodox rabbis followed suit.

Yet until the 1840s, Judaism in America was based on Orthodox ritual, although there were few outstanding leaders or scholars. Gershom Mendes Seixas (1746–1816), the cantor and spiritual leader of New York's Shearith Israel Synagogue, was perhaps the period's best known Orthodox leader, but he was largely self-educated and hardly a scholar.

The arrival of thousands of central European Jews in the United States in the late 1830s and 1840s not only increased the Jewish population in the United States, but also saw the start of the Reform Movement. Among the arrivals were influential Reform leaders such as Isaac M. Wise (1819–1900), David Einhorn (1809–1879), and Samuel Adler (1809–1891). They and other Reform rabbis led a spirited and often bitter struggle to break the Orthodox hold on Judaism and establish Reform Judaism. While they were largely successful in this struggle, they faced vehement Orthodox opposition in their bid to reform Jewish ritual and synagogue practice. Isaac Leeser (1806–1868) stands out as the most prominent among the important Orthodox Jewish leaders in mid-nineteenth-century America. From his pulpit in Philadelphia and his newspaper, *The Occident* (1843–1868), he led the battle against the Reform Movement. Among his achievements was the establishment of the first American rabbinical college, Maimonides College (1867) in Philadelphia. Other Orthodox leaders were the previously mentioned Rice, who was the chief authority on Jewish law in the United States, Bernard Illowy (1812–1871) and Morris J. Raphael (1798–1868) of New York.

By the end of the Civil War, Reform had come to dominate the Jewish religious scene in the United States and Orthodoxy found itself on the defensive. Orthodoxy was limited to several dozen synagogues in the United States. One group of Orthodox Jews were the old-line Sephardic and German congregations who chose to remain loyal to their traditions. These "Western" Orthodox loyalists were led by Sabato Morais (1823–1897), Henry Pereina Mendes (1852–1937), Bernard Drachman (1861–1945), and Henry Schneeberger (1848–1916) of Baltimore. Another group of Orthodox Jews were the recent immigrants from Eastern Europe centered in New York City. Their spiritual center was the Beth Medrash Hagadol Synagogue on New York's Lower East Side. Its rabbi, Abraham J. Ash (1813–1888), was regarded as the group's senior spiritual leader. The Western and Eastern groups, although sharing a common allegiance to Orthodoxy, differed on many points, such as the modernization of synagogue services, use of English, and religious liturgical ritual. Thus there was little cooperation between them, and, ultimately, the Western Orthodox group developed what later became Conservative and Modern Orthodox Judaism. The Eastern European Orthodox group evolved into a more fundamentalist Orthodoxy.

The mass immigration of hundreds of thousands of Jews to the United States from czarist Russia starting in 1881 reinforced Orthodoxy. Within 10 years, hundreds of new Orthodox synagogues and prayer houses were established. What had been perceived as a dying Orthodoxy suddenly underwent a revival. Besides synagogues, traditional Orthodox institutions evolved, such as kosher butcher stores, ritualariums (mikvah), religious schools, and the like. However, leadership and organization was lacking because there were no prestigious scholars among the newcomers and hardly any English-speaking Orthodox rabbis. Thus, each group of Orthodox Jews developed its own way of solving these problems.

The "Western" Orthodox group, with the financial support and moral encouragement of prominent reform lay leaders such as Louis Marshall (1856–1929) and Jacob Schiff (1847–1920), established the Jewish Theological Seminary (1886) as a rabbinical seminary to train English-speaking, secularly educated rabbis for all segments of American Orthodoxy. Indeed, until its reorganization in 1902, the Seminary was an Orthodox school, whose faculty consisted of men like Morais, Mendes, and Druchman. Yet the Eastern European Orthodox population and rabbinate looked down on the Seminary because of its inferior level of Talmudic study.

The Western group also established the Union of Orthodox Jewish Congregations of

America in 1889 as a means of solving the leadership and organizational problem of American Orthodoxy. This organization, however, failed to attract any significant following among the Eastern European Jews until well into the twentieth century.

The Eastern European Jews sought to solve the problem of rabbinic leadership by setting up a Chief Rabbinate for New York. In 1888, they installed a well-known Lithuanian rabbi, R. Jacob Joseph (d. 1902), as Chief Rabbi of New York. Although this experiment failed, the fact that a man of Rabbi Joseph's stature would come to America encouraged other Eastern European rabbis to immigrate to the United States. By the twentieth century, there were a number of competent rabbinical authorities residing in the Northeast. Following Rabbi Joseph's death in 1902, these recognized Eastern European rabbis formed an organization called Agudath Ha-Rabbonim—the Union of Orthodox Rabbis of the United States. This group sought to set standards for the rabbinate and exert leadership on behalf of Orthodox Jewry in the United States, and it remained the most significant Orthodox tribune until the 1950s. Among its leaders were Rabbis Eliezer Silver (1882–1968), Israel Rosenberg (1875–1956), Moses S. Margolies (1851–1936), Bernard Levinthal (1865–1952), and Tobias Geffen (1870–1970). The problem of producing future generations of native rabbis for the United States did not generally concern the Eastern European Orthodox leaders, as they could always import European rabbis. This attitude greatly hurt Orthodoxy in its efforts to pass its traditions on to the second-generation, American-born Jewish successors. Yet, in 1897, a small traditional yeshiva, or Talmudic academy, was started in New York on the Lower East Side. It was not designed as a rabbinical college but rather as a place of study for young European rabbinical scholars who had come to America. Even so, a number of these refugee scholars did eventually become rabbinical and educational leaders in the United States. This small school, named for the late Chief Rabbi of Kovna, Isaac Elhanan Spektor (1817–1896), eventually grew to become Yeshiva College and later Yeshiva University under the leadership of Bernard Revel (1885–1940).

By the beginning of World War I, a full-scale Orthodox Jewish life existed in most Jewish communities in the United States with 500 or more Jews. These communities had synagogues, rabbis, teachers, ritual slaughterers, and schools among other institutions. The heart of Orthodox Jewish life was located in major cities such as New York, Philadelphia, Chicago, and Baltimore. But Orthodoxy could not hold the second-generation American Jew. The powerful forces of assimilation, secularization, socialism, upward mobility, and Americanization in general made Orthodoxy look "Old World," primitive, foreign, and associated with the poverty of the first-generation immigrants. Orthodoxy had failed to produce an English-speaking rabbinate and had not set up any meaningful effective school system to teach its beliefs to the younger generation. Yet, it must be added that a small number of American-born or educated youth did remain Orthodox and attempted to build an American version of Orthodoxy.

With the end of World War I, Orthodoxy faced new challenges. As mass emigration from Eastern Europe to the United States declined, Orthodoxy found its future dependent on attaining the loyalties of second-generation American Jews. As a religious group, Orthodoxy was challenged by Conservative Judaism, an outgrowth of the previously Orthodox Jewish Theological Seminary. Conservative Judaism asserted its loyalty to tradition, yet was in favor of significant change in ritual, liturgy, and practice. In its battle with Orthodoxy, it held the upper hand until well into the 1960s.

However, the small group of second-generation Orthodox followers took steps to build a new and more attractive Orthodoxy, which was organized in New York City.

The Rabbi Isaac Elhanan Rabbinical School was reorganized as a high school (1916) and a college—Yeshiva—(1925), and a formal rabbinic program was established in the 1920s to produce American-trained, English-speaking, Orthodox rabbis. Under the leadership of Bernard Revel, Yeshiva College became the undisputed center of Talmudic scholarship and Orthodox Judaism in the United States until well into the 1970s. By the late 1920s, a small cadre of English-speaking Orthodox rabbis were in place. The Hebrew Theological College, an institution similar to Yeshiva College, was founded in Chicago in 1922 with Rabbi Saul Silber (1881–1946) as its president. Several smaller rabbinical schools also existed in Brooklyn and the Lower East Side at this time. Graduates of these schools, as well as other English-speaking Orthodox rabbis, founded the Rabbinical Council of America in 1935. Among the prominent members of the Rabbinical Council were Rabbis Joseph H. Lookstein (1902–1979), rabbi of New York's fashionable Kehillah Jeshurun Synagogue and founder of the Ramaz Day School (1936). Herbert S. Goldstein (1890–1970) of the West Side Institutional Synagogue, Leo Jung (1892–1987) of New York's Jewish Center, Samuel Rosenblatt of Baltimore (b. 1902), and David de Sola Pool (1885–1970) of New York's Shearith Israel Synagogue.

Together with the Union of Orthodox Jewish Congregations and the newly created National Council of Young Israel Synagogues (1912), a loose alliance of English-speaking Orthodox congregations, aimed at second- and third-generation Americans, was created, and thus, the institutional framework for what was to be called Modern Orthodoxy was put in place. With the appointment in 1939 of Rabbi Joseph B. Soloveitchik (b. 1903) as head of the Talmud faculty of Yeshiva College, Modern Orthodoxy gained a respected and influential leader who was to dominate Modern Orthodoxy well into the present.

As Modern Orthodoxy emerged, there was also the corresponding development of a new American-style traditional Orthodoxy. This movement was centered in the Williamsburg section of Brooklyn, around the Mesifta Torah V'daath (f. 1917), directed by Rabbi Shraga Feivel Mendelowitz (1886–1948). Under Mendelowitz's leadership this school had grown from a small elementary school to include a rabbinical program with prominent scholars on the faculty. What separated Torah V'daath from Yeshiva College was a more restrained attitude toward secular education, the Western culture, as well as a stricter interpretation of Jewish law. Yet at that point (the 1930s) all were part of the same Orthodox grouping.

During this time, one could also detect the beginnings of a home-grown American Hasidic Movement. Although tens of thousands of Hasidim (mostly Lubavitch) had arrived in the United States prior to World War I, few if any were able to pass their traditions on to a second generation. Following a year-long visit to the United States in 1929, the sixth Lubavitcher Rebbe, Rabbi Joseph I. Schneersohn (1880–1950), revived interest in Hasidism among American Orthodox youth. Several small Lubavitch groups were established in New York, and several dozen young men traveled to Poland to study under Schneersohn's tutelage.

The 1930s also saw the establishment of a number of Orthodox Jewish high schools, which eventually grew into rabbinical colleges. Among the better known were Yeshivah Chaim Berlin in Brooklyn (1939), under the leadership of a charismatic scholar from Europe, Rabbi Isaac Hutner (1907–1980); Yeshivah Tifferth Jerusalem (1937), in Manhattan, under the leadership of Rabbi Moses Feinstein (1895–1986), who was eventually to become the leading authority on Jewish law in the United States; and the Ner Israel Yeshiva in Baltimore (1933), under the leadership of Rabbi Jacob I. Ruderman (1901–1987). Yet, until World War II, Orthodoxy in the United States was still dominated by the old-line Yiddish-speaking rabbi, synagogue, and laymen. The voice of Orthodoxy was still predominantly the voice of the poor, the refugee, and the uneducated.

With the rise of Nazism in Germany and later in Austria, a new stream of Jewish immigrants arrived in the United States. Among them were a small group of highly dedicated and educated Orthodox Jews. A group of Orthodox Jews from Germany reorganized themselves in the Washington Heights section of New York under the leadership of Rabbi Joseph Brever (1892–1980). This group, known as Khal Adas Jeshurun, built a full-scale Orthodox community with a synagogue, a school system, and a kashruth network. This group played an important role in proving that Orthodoxy could be transplanted to the United States, with its strict standards intact.

Austrian refugees included a large number of Orthodox Jews who belonged to the strict separatist tradition of Hungarian Orthodox Jewry. They set up a number of schools and synagogues in New York under the leadership of scholars like Rabbi Samuel Ehrenfeld (d. 1970) of Mattesdorf, Austria, and Rabbi Levi Y. Grunewald (d. 1980) of Deutsch-kreutz, Austria. Grunewald was responsible for raising the standards of kosher milk and meat in the United States and laid the groundwork for the post-World War II Hasidic influx to New York.

The onset of World War II brought tens of thousands of Orthodox Jews to the United States in the period between 1939 and 1951. Among these were prominent rabbis, yeshiva deans, Hasidic leaders and their followers, and lay Orthodox Jews. As a rule, the new immigrants were better educated in Judaism than their American counterparts and more concerned about Jewish education for their children.

Prominent among the yeshiva deans to arrive

was Rabbi Aaron Kotler (1892–1962) of Kletzk, Poland. Kotler, a universally recognized Talmudist, immediately reorganized his yeshiva in Lakewood, New Jersey (1941). Upon his death, his school had 250 advanced students, and in 1988 it numbered over 1000 students. Kotler inculcated American Orthodox Jews with a love for Torah study and preached that the highest form of Jewish life was the study of Torah. Thus, together with his European colleagues, he set up various rabbinical schools and kolels (advanced institutes for rabbinic studies) across the United States. By the 1960s, these schools, and their deans, had become a major force in American Orthodox life. This group of American Orthodoxy, known as the Yeshiva World, was organized around the Agudath Israel of America, whose dominating figure was Rabbi Mushe Sherer. The Agudah was governed by a Council of Torah Sages consisting primarily of yeshiva deans. Since 1945, it membership has included Rabbi Aaron Kotler, Moses Feinstein, Shneur Kotler (d. 1982), Jacob Kaminetsky (1891–1986), Israel Spiro (1897–1989), Isaac Hutner, and Jacob Ruderman. The organ of the Agudath was the *Jewish Observer*.

The Modern Orthodox camp, the Yeshiva World, and Rabbi Mendelowitz joined forces to organize the Torah U'Mesorah Movement (f. 1944), the National Council of Jewish Day Schools, which sought to establish Orthodox day schools across the United States. By the 1960s, the movement came under the domination of the Yeshiva World. Schools were established in cities with 5000 or more Jews, and a number of high schools and seminaries were also established.

A large number of Hasidic Jews, primarily from Hungary, arrived after World War II. The two most prominent Hasidic rabbis were the Satmar Rebbe, Rabbi Joel Teitelbaum (1886–1979), and the Lubavitcher Rebbe, Rabbi Joseph I. Schneerson (1880–1950) from Russia via Poland.

Teitelbaum and other rebbes like him, chiefly from Hungary and Romania, sought to reestablish their communities here exactly as they were in Europe. They sought to preserve the dress, Yiddish language, and customs of Eastern Europe. As such, they were very successful. They established schools, synagogues, and a kosher food industry. It has been estimated (1988) that there are over 100,000 Hasidim in the United States, centered primarily in metropolitan New York, and their numbers are growing. Other prominent Hasidic leaders who built communities similar to Teitelbaum's were the Bobover Rebbe, Rabbi Solomon Halberstan (b. 1908), the Poper Rav, Rabbi Joseph Grunwald (d. 1984), the Kluzenberger Rebbe, Rabbi Y. Y. Halberstam (b. 1904), and the Skverer Rebbe, Rabbi Jacob Twersky (d. 1968).

Under the leadership of Rabbi Joseph I. Schneersohn, and his American-born disciples, a massive outreach program aimed at bringing Orthodox Judaism to the Jewish masses was launched by the Lubavitcher Hasidim. Day schools were established as were afternoon schools, summer camps, and youth groups. After 1945 Schneerson was joined by 1000 or so of his followers who managed to escape from the Soviet Union. Succeeded by his son-in-law, a Western-educated engineer and rabbi, Menachem M. Schneerson (b. 1902) fine-tuned the outreach program. These were the beginnings of what came to be known as the Repentance Movement (Baal Teshuva Movement). It reached its peak during the Six-Day War (1967) and the Vietnam War (1960s) and saw tens of thousands of young American Jews from non-Orthodox backgrounds become Orthodox Jews. Although the Lubavitch pioneered this approach, by the 1970s almost all Orthodox groups were active in outreach work. Among the prominent figures were Rabbi Shlomo Riskin (b. 1940), Grand Rabbi Levi I. Horowitz of Boston (b. 1921), Rabbi Shlomo Carlebach (b. 1925), and Rebbetzin Esther Jungreis. A number of special schools for the newcomers to Judaism were also established.

Modern Orthodoxy was also growing. Its flagship school, Yeshiva College, expanded into Yeshiva University. Under the leadership of Rabbi Joseph B. Soloveitchik and Norman Lamm (b. 1927), hundreds of Orthodox young men were ordained as rabbis. In general, there were by the 1980s thousands of Orthodox doctors, lawyers, teachers, college professors, and even a practicing Orthodox Jewish United States Senator, Joseph Lieberman (Democrat, Connecticut, elected in 1988). The majority of these professionals and intellectuals were associated with Modern Orthodoxy, others were of the Baal Teshuvah group, and still others were affiliated with the Yeshiva World.

Yet by the late 1960s, American Orthodoxy was divided. Clear distinctions could be made between the right and left wings of American Orthodoxy. Left-wing, or Modern Orthodoxy, held a positive outlook with regard to Israel, Zionism, and aliyah (Jewish immigration to Israel) and saw religious significance in the State of Israel. Modern Orthodoxy, while upholding the strong role of Torah study, was also firmly committed to Western culture, secular education, and pluralism. In addition, it supported an increased role for Jewish women in Orthodox Jewish life. It believed that Orthodox Jews may and should cooperate with their Reform and Conservative colleagues on such bodies as the Synagogue Council of America and the New York Board of Rabbis.

The so-called "right-wing," or Yeshiva World, Orthodoxy, while not actively opposed to the State of Israel, held a negative attitude toward aliyah, were anti-Zionist, and saw no positive religious significance in Israel. They believed that the only justification for secular studies was for professional and occupational purposes but saw no value, per se, in modern culture and secular education. They believed that women's primary role was in the context of the Jewish family, as mother and wife, and were firmly opposed to all manifestations of the feminist movement. In addition, they were firmly opposed to cooperation with non-Orthodox Jewish religious bodies and refused to consider the Reform and Conservative movements as legitimate expressions of the Jewish religion. This group adhered to a stricter interpretation of Jewish law or Halakah.

The Hasidic groups, by and large, were similar in orientation to the Yeshiva World, except that they were opposed to secular studies under any circumstances (except as mandated by state law). Many Hasidic groups were also actively anti-Israel, such as the Satmar, Popa, and Skver. These Hasidim were also very concerned with the retention of the East European way of life, in contrast with the Yeshiva World who were generally Americanized.

In addition, Modern Orthodoxy was having its authenticity questioned by the right-wing Orthodox. Right-wing standards on secular studies, kashruth supervision, outward manifestations of religious observance, and stricter standards of interpretation of Jewish religious law were becoming the accepted norm for the Orthodox community.

However, by the 1980s, the various Orthodox communities were affected by the death or illness of their senior religious leadership. Modern Orthodoxy had to make do without the leadership of its long-term leader and Halachic authority, Rabbi J. B. Soloveitcheik, who (afflicted by Parkinsons disease) was forced to retire from pub-

lic life in 1984. His retirement left a gap in Modern Orthodoxy, which continues to go unfilled. Indeed, Modern Orthodoxy is pulling in several directions. One approach takes an intellectual approach to Judaism, is sympathetic to feminism and ecumenical theology, and supports mild changes in Jewish law. This group is led by rabbis such as Emanuel Rackman (b. 1910), Shlomo Riskin (b. 1940), Walter Wurzburger (b. 1920), Irving Greenberg (b. 1933), and Haskel Lookstein (b. 1932). On the other hand, there are those in Modern Orthodoxy who seek to link it to the Yeshiva World. This group is led by various members of the Talmud faculty at Yeshiva University. Finally, there are those committed to the classical synthesis as developed over the years at Yeshiva University. The spokesman for this view is Norman Lamm (b. 1927), president of Yeshiva University. *Tradition* magazine continues to serve as the forum for this exchange of opinion among Modern Orthodox thinkers.

The Yeshiva World lost its spiritual leadership between 1982 and 1984, as the senior Yeshiva deans—Rabbis Feinstein, Kaminetsky, Hutner, and Ruderman—passed away. Feinstein's death was a particular blow as he had been accepted by all sectors (except the Hasidic community) as the binding authority on Halakah in America. Presently, there are no leaders with the reputations or the mantle of authority that characterized these older scholars. Currently, the trend in the Yeshiva World is in the direction of full-time Torah study and at the same time a move toward accepting Hasidic norms in the areas of dress and Zionism. At the same time, an increasing number of Yeshiva World graduates are college educated and in secular professions, which invariably links them to the Modern Orthodox in some areas of lifestyle.

The Hasidic world too has lost much of its senior leadership since the death of Rabbi Joel Teitelbaum in 1979. Although his nephew Rabbi Moses Teitelbaum (b. 1916) officially succeeded him, he has not been able to act as the senior spiritual leader of the Hungarian Hasidic community. Presently, only Rabbi Menachem M. Schneerson, the Lubavitcher Rebbe, continues as a senior rabbinic leader in the Hasidic world.

Other current trends in Orthodoxy show a revival of commitment to Orthodoxy of the Syrian and other Sephardic communities in America. As such, Sephardic lay leaders and even rabbis are again playing an active role in Jewish life.

Orthodox Jewish life remains centered in

New York and several other metropolitan areas, such as Baltimore, Los Angeles, and Miami Beach. Orthodoxy is clearly on the decline in most towns with Jewish populations under 20,000. Thus old Orthodox centers such as Portland, Maine, Waterbury, Connecticut, and Omaha, Nebraska, are rapidly dwindling in numbers. How the centralization of Orthodox Jews in several dozen major metropolitan areas will affect the future of Orthodoxy remains to be seen.

The kashruth-kosher industry has been growing at a rapid rate. Whether this indicates a trend toward keeping the laws of koshruth, on the part of American Jews, only time will be able to tell.

Orthodox Judaism has clearly established itself in America. It has a viable infrastructure of schools, synagogues, and other religious institutions. It is rapidly shedding its refugee image and has become very acculturized. Its committed and learned laity, as well as its educated and effective rabbinical leadership, promises that Orthodoxy will continue to be a vital force in the American Jewish community as we approach the twenty-first century.

ZALMAN ALPERT

BIBLIOGRAPHY

Bernstein, Louis. *The Challenge and Mission: The Emergence of an English-speaking Orthodox Rabbinate.* New York: Shengold Press, 1982.

Bernstein, Saul. *The Renaissance of the Torah Jew.* Hoboken, N.J.: Ktav, 1985.

Bomzer, Herbert W. *The Kolel in America.* New York: Shengold Press, 1985.

Gurock, Jeffrey S. *The Men and Women of Yeshiva.* New York: Columbia University Press, 1988.

———. "Resistors and Accommodators, Varieties of Orthodox Rabbis in America, 1886-1983. *American Jewish Archives* 35 (November 1983): 100-187.

Helmreich, William B. *The World of the Yeshiva.* New York: Free Press, 1982.

Klapperman, Gilbert. *The Story of Yeshiva University.* New York: Macmillan, 1969.

Kranzler, Gershon. *Williamsburg.* New York: Feldheim, 1961.

Liebman, Charles. "Orthodoxy in American Jewish Life." *American Jewish Year Book* 66 (1965).

Rothkoff, Aaron. *Bernard Revel: Builder of American Orthodoxy.* Philadelphia: Jewish Publication Society, 1972.

———. *The Silver Era in American Jewish* Orthodoxy: *Rabbi Eliezer Silver and His Generation.* Jerusalem: Yeshiva University Press, 1981.

Sharfman, Harold I. *The First Rabbi: Origins of Conflict.* Malibu, Calif.: Pangloss Press, 1988.

Ozick, Cynthia (b. 1928). One of the most significant, and most self-consciously "Jewish," literary voices to emerge in the past three decades is Cynthia Ozick, who was born in New York City, received a B.A. in English from New York University and her M.A. from Ohio State. Equally at home with fiction and the literary essay, she has published three novels, *Trust* (1966), *The Cannibal Galaxy* (1983), and *The Messiah of Stockholm* (1987); four collections of short fiction, *The Pagan Rabbi* (1971), *Bloodshed* (1982), *Levitation: Five Fictions* (1982), and *The Shawl* (1989); and two collections of essays, *Art and Ardor* (1983), and *Metaphor and Memory* (1988).

Ozick is the case of a writer who blossomed late (she blames her long, fruitless apprenticeship on an early fascination with the fiction of Henry James) but who has gradually emerged as the dominant voice for new directions in Jewish-American writing. If contemporary Jewish-American literature often seems to be dominated by those either estranged or downright hostile to Judaism, Ozick is a noteworthy exception: she is a tireless student of Jewish ideas, and a fierce supporter of the State of Israel. As she puts it in a famous essay entitled "Toward a New Yiddish": "If we blow into the narrow end of the shofar, we will be heard far. But if we choose to be Mankind rather than Jewish, we will not be heard at all."

For Ozick, it is essential that the Jewish-American writer think, and even *dream*, in centrally Jewish ways; and she goes on to define the "centrally Jewish" as "whatever touches on the liturgical." In her case, the result has been a series of fictional works that pit Pan against Moses, unbridled passions against the fences of law. Moments in her first long, and largely unsuccessful novel, *Trust*, intimate this theme; the stories in *The Pagan Rabbi* make it breathtakingly clear.

For many years Ozick so worried about the idol-making character of fiction—in the essays collected as *Art and Ardor*—as well as in fictional works—ranging from *Bloodshed* and *Levitation* to *The Cannibal Galaxy* and *The Messiah of Stockholm*—that critics began to worry about her obsessive self-abnegation. Not since Hawthorne has writer seemed so fatally attracted to the demonic, to the "pagan." However, her 1988 collection of essays, *Metaphor and Memory*, makes it clear that at least some imaginative works can be numbered on the side of the angels and that literature itself need make no apology for its potential as an abiding, even necessary, moral force.

SANFORD PINSKER

BIBLIOGRAPHY

Lowin, Joseph. *Cynthia Ozick*. Boston: Hall, 1988.

Pinsker, Sanford. *The Uncompromising Fictions of Cynthia Ozick*. Columbia: University of Missouri Press, 1987.

P

Philadelphia. The Greater Philadelphia area contains the fourth largest Jewish population in the United States, 139,000 living in the city proper, 117,000 in the nearby suburbs of Lower Bucks, Montgomery, and Delaware counties. Across the Delaware River in adjacent New Jersey counties, another 30,000 Jews make their residence. The region is also home for 6000 Russian Jews and 6000 former Israelis.

The Philadelphia community has a vital tradition within American history. There were Jewish fur traders combing the woods before William Penn, as early as 1652. The Philadelphia Jewish community of less than 300 helped to create a new nation. Heroes include David Salisbury Franks (1749–1812), Haym Salomon (1740–1785), Bernard Gratz (1738–1801), Benjamin Nones (1755–1825), and Jona Phillips (1736–1803). All of them saw active service in the American Revolutionary army. Franks was also a diplomat, helping Thomas Jefferson arrange peace in Paris. Haym Salomon is best known. He was an intelligence agent, a spy, persuading a number of Hessians (German mercenaries) to desert, before he became a broker for the Revolutionary army. His generosity with the Founding Fathers impoverished himself and his family. Bernard Gratz, a trader, helped open up areas west of the Alleghenies; he ran vital supplies through the British blockade. Benjamin Nones risked his life in battle to save others and achieved the rank of major. In the postwar period he was a well-known pro-Jeffersonian writer and publisher, also an essayist who attacked anti-Semitism. Jona Phillips fought as an enlisted man. At the Constitutional Convention in Philadelphia he influenced the delegates to place a no-religious-oath clause in the Constitution. Like his fellow Philadelphia Jewish patriots, he was an officer in America's fourth oldest synagogue, Mikvah Israel (1782).

In the 100 years from just before the Civil War to 1940, Philadelphia Jews greatly influenced American Jewish life, creating model local institutions and founding national Jewish organizations. Isaac Leeser (1806–1868), an immigrant from Germany, became hazan (reader-leader) of Mikvah Israel, a post from which he made many innovations. He introduced the first English sermon, wrote the first American edition of the Hebrew Bible, started the first Anglo-Jewish periodical, the *Occident* (1843–1868), and was behind the first nationwide union among congregations, the Board of Delegates of Israelites. Leeser was the driving force behind the first American rabbinic training school, Maimonides College (1867–1873), and a Jewish Publications Society (1845–1851). His ideas for organized protests for Jewish rights both on a national and international level led later to the creation of Jewish defense agencies.

Leeser was a great influence on Rebecca Gratz (1781–1869), a Mikvah Israel congregant. With Leeser's guidance and fellow members, Gratz started a number of institutions that other cities copied: the first nonsynagogue communal charity called the Female Benevolent Society (1819) and the first communal religious school, the Hebrew Sunday School Society (1838). She was the driving force behind the Jewish Foster Home (1855).

A few decades later, Gratz's tradition of organizing women to aid the poor was followed by Fannie Binswanger (1862–1928) who founded the Young Women's Union in 1885. This organization added some "firsts" to help the large influx of Eastern European Jewish women. They included the first day care center, the first nursery school, the first kindergarten, and the first juvenile aid committee; the latter was to provide foster care and more humane court treatment for delinquents. These institutions were taken over later by city government.

Hazan Sabato Morais (1823–1897), successor to Leeser at Mikvah Israel, was initiator of the Jewish Theological Seminary (1886) in New York. Although a Philadelphian, he urged placement of the rabbinical training institution in New York because of the folding of Maimonides College in Philadelphia. New York had the vast Jewish population and very wealthy Jews needed to sustain such an institution. Morais backed friendship and social justice for the masses of Russian Jewish immigrant factory workers. He personally arbitrated a crucial strike in the clothing industry. Morais backed congregant Louis Levy (1846–1919), head of the Philadelphia Association for the Protection of Jewish Immigrants and founder of the National Liberal Immigration League, in all of Levy's efforts to welcome and aid brethren from Eastern Europe.

Mayer Sulzberger (1843–1923), a student of Isaac Leeser and close to Sabato Morais, was the first Jew to hold the position of judge in Philadelphia's Common Pleas Court. Sulzberger, a bachelor, was the patron of literary figures who stayed awhile in the city, such as Naftali Imber (1856–1909), author of "Hatikvah," now the Israeli national anthem. Sulzberger was a major figure in creating the American Jewish Committee and became its first president. Although a member of Orthodox Mikvah Israel in Philadelphia, he and fellow congregants Solomon Solis-Cohen (1857–1948) and Cyrus Adler (1863–1940) were instrumental in establishing the Conservative Movement in the United States. The Jewish Theological Seminary in New York was almost bankrupt and of little influence. The Philadelphia group convinced banker Jacob Schiff (1847–1920), a Reform Jew and New York millionaire, that the way to arrest the assimilation of East European Jews was to find a middle way between Reform and Orthodox, both denominations viewed by the newcomers as too "foreign." Conservatism, with its historical approach of adjustment to changing times, with customs and rituals familiar to the immigrant, was the answer. The Philadelphia group persuaded Schiff to donate money, and persuaded Solomon Schechter (1850–1915), renowned scholar of the Historical School, to head the Seminary in 1902, and were instrumental in founding the United Synagogue (1912), the parent body of Conservatism.

Sulzberger's cousin and good friend was Cyrus Adler. A scholar, he was the first American-trained Ph.D in Semitics. Adler founded the American Jewish Historical Society (1893). With Moses Dropsie (1821–1915), a philanthropist, he started Gratz College (1897), a Philadelphia religious teacher-training school, the first in the Western Hemisphere. He launched the *American Jewish Yearbook*, the almanac of American Jewish life, and was its first editor (1900), a job he soon shared with Henrietta Szold (1860–1945), when the City of Brotherly Love's Jewish Publication Society took her on as co-editor in 1903. Adler, as a charter member of the American Jewish Committee, followed Louis Marshall as president of that organization. From that position, Adler was a major force behind the creation of the Joint Distribution Committee, the overseas Jewish relief agency; also he initiated the National Jewish Welfare Board, which oversees community centers.

At the same time, Adler headed two learning institutions he helped start, Dropsie College, the doctorate-granting school in Semitics and Jewish Studies, located in Philadelphia, and the Jewish Theological Seminary in New York. He was the *eminence gris* behind most Philadelphia philanthropic activities until his death in 1940.

Rabbi Bernard Levinthal (1862–1952) came to Philadelphia in 1891 from Lithuania to head the Russian Jewish synagogue, B'nai Abraham, and stem the assimilationist tide among East European Jews. An indication of the size of that immigration is reflected in Jewish population statistics, which jumped from 15,000 (mainly German-Jewish) in 1880 to 70,000 in 1904, to 200,000 in 1920. Levinthal created a kosher governing body, a free burial society, communal afternoon religious schools (free or inexpensive), a Jewish high school, and an academy for advanced Jewish studies.

On the national level, Levinthal was a founder of the Union of Orthodox Rabbis (1902) and played a major role in establishing Yeshiva College in New York. The first head of that institution, Bernard Revel (1885–1940), lived at Levinthal's house for some time. Levinthal was among the founders of the Federation of American Zionists, Mizrachi (religious Zionists), and Esras Torah, a worldwide organization to aid needy rabbis and scholars. He was one of the fathers of the American Jewish Congress, and in 1919 he attended the Peace Conference at Versailles, representing Jewish interests. Very ecumenical, Levinthal was a charter member of the American Jewish Committee, working with German Jews, Mayer Sulzberger, Cyrus Adler, and Solomon Solis-Cohen. He helped to launch the United Palestine Appeal with Reform Rabbi Stephen Wise (1874–1949).

Bernard Levinthal's son, Louis (1892–1976), was a community leader like his father. He was appointed to the "Jewish seat" of Philadelphia's Common Pleas Court after Mayer Sulzberger died. Judge Levinthal was an ardent Zionist, a founder of the Jewish National Fund, the worldwide agency to reclaim land in Palestine. He was president of the Zionist Organization of America (1941–1943) and an important figure at the Biltmore Conference when that body, in 1942, formally proclaimed the need for an independent Jewish state. Levinthal initiated Philadelphia's Allied Jewish Appeal (1937), a parallel federation to the Federation of Jewish Charities started in 1901. The FJC had been stripped of its Jewish content. Allied allotted funds for Jewish education, the United Palestine Appeal, the Joint Distribution Committee, which was aiding the growing number of refugees from Hitler in 1938, and Jewish defense organizations. One year later, Judge Levinthal cochaired the newly formed United Jewish Appeal, the national body of federations such as Allied.

Reform rabbis from two of Philadelphia's oldest congregations helped to evolve national institutions. David Einhorn (1809–1879), during his short ministry just before the Civil War at Kenesseth Israel (founded 1846), composed a prayer book, the ideas and contents of which were adopted by the Reform Movement. However, it was under Rabbi Joseph Krauskopf (1858–1923) that the Reform Movement made its complete break with Orthodoxy. Krauskopf was the vice-president of the conference that set up the Pittsburgh Platform of 1885, the major statement of Reform principles that lasted until 1937. He and Einhorn eliminated the skull cap, prayer shawl, use of Hebrew, two-day holidays, and the reliance on Halakah (Talmudic law). Krauskopf's major thrust, a national farm school for Russian Jewish immigrants, did not find favor with his coreligionists. However, his sermons on vital issues of the day and concern about urban problems fixed a tradition of such interest in the Reform movement to this day.

Rabbi Krauskopf and Dr. Solis-Cohen are credited with regenerating the Jewish Publication Society in 1888. It had ceased functioning for the second time in 1875. This Philadelphia institution still publishes milestone Judaica such as English versions of the Bible and other holy books.

Three rabbis from Rodeph Sholom, the city's second synagogue (1810), were innovators and founders. Rabbi Morris Jastrow (1861–1904) was provost of Maimonides College and editor-in-chief of JPS projects including the new English Bible and the *Jewish Encyclopedia*. He was also involved with the start of the Young Men's Hebrew Association. Rabbi Henry Berkowitz (1852–1924), Jastrow's successor, introduced the practice of the junior congregation; established and was first chancellor of the Jewish Chautauqua Society, a national organization designed to educate religious leaders, college students, and laity; and was the guiding hand behind the formation of the Central Conference of American Rabbis. Rabbi Louis Wolsey (1877–1953) launched the American Council for Judaism in 1942, an anti-Zionist, anti-Jewish "peoplehood" national organization headquartered in Philadelphia and financed by Sears magnate Lessing Rosenwald (1891–1979). Wolsey recanted after World War II and became pro-Israel.

About 25 percent of Philadelphia Jews polled by the Federation of Jewish Agencies (FJA), the umbrella group for most Philadelphia philanthropy, call themselves Reform Jews. The 1988 Reform Handbook for the tristate area lists temple affiliation at 9000 families. In the Greater Philadelphia region, FJA recorded 15 Reform congregations, while another survey counted 5000 students in Reform congregational schools, 1000 of whom were studying above the Bar/Bat Mitzvah level.

The only Reconstructionist College in America is located in Philadelphia's northwestern suburbs. Founded in 1968 by followers of Mordecai Kaplan (1881–1983), it has flourished, graduating over 120 rabbis. In 1990, it had a faculty of 22 and a student body of 60. Graduates serve as area rabbis and educational directors in Conservative and Reform congregations. They are also guides to the Havurah movement—small friendship, innovative clusters of study groups, prayer quorums, and holiday observance gatherings, some of which are attached to local synagogues.

In Greater Philadelphia there are 46 Conservative congregations supporting 5600 in their schools. As with Reform, many nursery schools and kindergartens, even day care centers are run by these congregations, providing religious content.

Conservative congregations support Camp Ramah in the Pennsylvania Pocanos, a summer program of intense religious training. They also sponsor United Synagogue Youth, an adjunct to each synagogue that makes up the largest youth group in the area with over 1000 members. Two Solomon Schechter Day Schools are Conservative in orientation. Another day school, while nondenominational, Akiba Hebrew High School, has largely Conservative students.

Conservative and Reform have moved closer in practice. Many Conservative synagogues have mixed choirs, use women hazanim (cantors), even women rabbis, and grant women full participation in all aspects of the service. About 40 percent of Philadelphia's Conservative congregations do not grant women full participation; however, only a few rabbis and lay leaders are part of the Union for Traditional Conservative Judaism, an organization that views Conservatism as moving too far toward Reform practices.

Many synagogues have left the city proper following their congregants. Adath Jeshurun and Har Zion, long bastions of Conservative practice and membership, are no longer in the city. The Germantown Jewish Center, which chose to remain, has encouraged regentrification of the Mount Airy/Germantown neighborhood, attracting younger members and hosting Havurah worship groups and activities.

The Orthodox component of the Philadelphia Jewish community is a fast growing one. During the 1960s, a number moved into Philadelphia. The spiritual hunger manifest today by young people disillusioned with secular materialism has led to the phenomenon of *baale teshuvah* (return to Orthodox Judaism). About 10,000 live in the Greater Philadelphia area, concentrated in the Overbrook-Merion section, Elkins Park in the western suburbs, and the Rhawnhurst neighborhood of the Great Northeast. The Orthodox support four day schools enrolling 1000 students— Abrams Academy, Torah Academy, Philadelphia Yeshiva, and Northeast Hebrew Academy. In 1988, there were 21 Orthodox congregations on record, most of them within the city proper. Mikvah Israel flourishes, now in the Independence Mall area and in the same building with the National Museum of American Jewish History.

Rhawnhurst has seven Orthodox congregations varying from Modern Orthodox to Strictly Orthodox to Sephardic Orthodox to the Hasidic Lubavitch Center.

Closely associated with the Orthodox are the Traditional. Eight in number, they retain rabbis from Yeshiva University, hold an Orthodox service, but have mixed seating. Some do have *minyons* (prayer quorums) with separate seating for women. Traditionals support a three-day congregational religious school program enrolling 650 students.

Jewish intellectual, cultural, and artistic needs are serviced by a number of organizations, many of which are supported by the Federation of Jewish Agencies. The Anglo-Jewish newspapers— the *Jewish Exponent* (circulation 78,000) and the *Northeast Jewish Times* (circulation 35,000)—are Federation owned and controlled. Federation also publishes a quarterly magazine, *Inside*.

Gratz College, now located in a 12 acre educational park along with the Solomon Schechter Day School, and the Central Agency for Jewish Education, continues to grant a Hebrew teachers diploma. The Mandell Campus site in the northeast suburbs also offers college-level programs, an undergraduate degree in Jewish studies and Jewish education and a graduate program in Jewish music, Jewish Communal studies and Judaic librarianship. It houses a Hebrew High School, an advanced after-secular-school program. Gratz's outreach extends to courses at various sites of Jewish concentration in the Greater Philadelphia area.

Dropsie College, started in 1907, was granted a charter in 1909 as a doctorate-granting institution in Semitics, but it ceased in 1984. It has been reborn by a grant from former Philadelphian, publisher Walter Annenberg (b. 1908) as a research institution, located in Center City in Philadelphia. It still publishes its scholarly journal, *The Jewish Quarterly Review*.

Philadelphia Jews can visit the Jewish Archives center housed at the Balch Institute for Ethnic Studies or tour the National Museum of

American Jewish History at Independence Mall or view artifacts of the Rodeph Sholom museum in center city or the Holocaust Awareness Museum. They can join 5000 to 7000 people, including 1000 Holocaust survivors, at a memorial statue in center city for the annual observance in memory of the Six Million every April.

Philadelphia Jewry is aging with 27 percent in the city proper over 65 and only 17 percent under 15 years old at the start of the 1990s. Programs for the elderly exist in most congregations and through Federation. The latter supports three low-rent apartment houses for senior citizens in the Great Northeast. The Young Mens/Womens Hebrew Associations, now called Jewish Community Centers, have five locations, two of which are exclusively for the elderly.

All JCCs are committed to promoting Jewish identity and are friendly to all denominations. They serve the needs of the entire community from infants to the elderly.

Philadelphia Jewry is beset with problems common to other older communities. Hebrew school enrollment is down, intermarriage is up (36 percent for those under 30), a low birth rate, late marriage, many singles and divorced people, and about 60 percent unaffiliated with a synagogue. In the race against assimilation, however, there are encouraging signs: college Jewish activities are increasing; Jewish day schools are growing; a new spiritual hunger has developed for Jewish content as disillusionment with secular hedonistic values has increased. Interest in Jewish studies is growing in all groups, and all Jewish organizations are enriching their programs with Jewish content and have instituted outreach programs. In Philadelphia's past the fear of the disappearance of Jews by assimilation was great, but today innovative, concerned leaders and institutions seem to be turning the tide.

PHILIP ROSEN

BIBLIOGRAPHY

Friedman, Murray, ed. *Jewish Life in Philadelphia, 1830–1940*. Philadelphia: ISHI, 1984.

Friedman, Murray, ed. *Philadelphia Jewish Life, 1940–1985*. Ardmore, Pa.: Seth Press, 1986.

Goldman, Alex J. *Giants of Faith: Great American Rabbis*. New York: Citadel Press, 1964.

Morais, Henry Samuel. *The Jews of Philadelphia, Their History from the Earliest Settlements to the Present Time*. Philadelphia: Levytype, 1894.

Seventy-Five Years of Continuity and Change. Philadelphia: Federation of Jewish Agencies, 1976.

Summary Report of the Jewish Population Study of Greater Philadelphia. Philadelphia: Federation of Jewish Agencies of Greater Philadelphia, 1984–1985.

Wolf, Edwin, 2nd. and Whiteman, Maxwell. *The History of the Jews of Philadelphia from Colonial Times to the Age of Jackson*. Philadelphia: Jewish Publication Society, 1975.

Podhoretz, Norman (b. 1930). New York literary critic of controversial reputation, Norman Podhoretz has been editor of *Commentary* since 1960. His strong political views made the journal a major forum of neoconservatism. He graduated with a B.A. from both Columbia University (1950) and Cambridge University (1952) and has a B.H.L. and an honorary Doctor of Letters from the Jewish Theological Seminary (1950, 1980). He has written six books, contributed to many periodicals, and edited *The Commentary Reader: Two Decades of Articles and Stories* (1966).

Podhoretz was born in Brooklyn, the son of European Jewish immigrants. He and his older sister Mildred grew up in a humble environment. From an early age he was bookish, and he aspired to become a famous poet. He graduated from high school, where he had edited a student's newsletter, in 1946, and that same year enrolled in Columbia College. His personal experience as a young Jewish intellectual is described in his first autobiographical volume, *Making It* (1967). In this work he mixes self-examination with social, historical, political, and cultural analysis. His drive for success pushed him far: in college, he began working intensively to achieve high grades. To be rich, to be talked about, and to create constant controversy were his goals. After a course in creative writing with Mark Van Doren, he realized poetry was not his point of strength. He then decided to become a teacher and a literary critic. He admired acclaimed intellectuals such as Lionel Trilling and F. W. Dupee. With a Kellett fellowship and a Fulbright scholarship, he went to Cambridge. There he developed a close alliance with F. R. Leavis, and it was Leavis who published his first piece of literary criticism in *Scrutiny* (1951). Other articles followed in *Harper's, Partisan Review, New Republic, New Yorker*, and others.

On a summer visit to New York in the early 1940s, Podhoretz first came in touch with *Commentary* and began reviewing books for the journal. It was then being edited by Elliot Cohen, and its pages, with a hard-line anti-Communist policy, were devoted to contemporary issues and Jewish affairs.

After Podhoretz's return from England, he planned to pursue a Ph.D., but his interest in academia had diminished. Instead, he was dominated by an overwhelming desire to see his name in print. He served a two-year stint in the United States Army, and when he returned from Germany in 1955, he became assistant editor of *Commentary*. He received attention for his unfavorable reviews of Saul Bellow's *The Adventures of Augie March* and Nelson Algren's *A Walk on the Wild Side*. But the author, whose views were more liberal than the acting editor's, began to feel dissatisfaction, and so he resigned.

In 1959, when Elliot Cohen died, Podhoretz accepted the editorship of *Commentary*. He transformed the journal by dissolving its anti-Communist policies. Contributors such as Alfred Kazin, Irving Howe, Lionel Trilling, Hannah Arendt, and others began to appear more regularly, while others who symbolized predictability of argument and mediocrity were no longer asked for articles. Perhaps Podhoretz's most important stroke in revitalizing the journal was to serialize in three parts Paul Goodman's *Growing Up Absurd*, a book about America's failure to give hopes to young people. It was a triumph. Podhoretz's first article in the new epoch was "My Negro Problem—and Ours" (1963), in which he advocated an integrationist perspective that had marriages of mixed race as the solution to racism in America. The piece was the source of much controversy and gave Podhoretz the great success and recognition that he had been waiting to achieve.

In the 1970s, he became disappointed with radicalism and the New Left and moved toward a neoconservative ideology. In *Breaking Ranks: A Political Memoir* (1979), his candid second autobiographical work, he explains in an opening letter-prologue to his son John how he grew to abhor liberal views. He came to think that propaganda was damaging future generations and believed that the New Left was castigating American democracy and was ignoring the power of the middle class. With his change in philosophy *Commentary* became the forum of what is now known as neoconservatism, a mode of thought that was sharply criticized but spread among Jewish intellectuals during the late 1970s and in the early 1980s. Podhoretz affirmed in *Breaking Ranks* that indifference toward money seems snobbish and

that political messianism based on social activism had lost its strength.

Since the early years of his career, Podhoretz has moved away from literature into politics. *Doings and Undoings: The Fifties and After in American Writing* (1964) suggests that instead of considering literature as an end in itself, one should regard it as a mode of public discourse that either illuminates or fails to illuminate the common ground on which we live. During the 1970s, Podhoretz devoted almost all of his writing to social issues, and the results, besides scattered pieces in different magazines, are two books: *The Present Danger: Do We Have The Will to Reverse the Decline of American Power* (1980) and *Why We Were in Vietnam* (1982). In the first he argues that the United States politically and socially subordinated to the Soviet Union, an empire with the desire to dominate the world. The conquest of America, according to Podhoretz, may not be the result of a military defeat but of an increasing debilitation of culture, the economic system, and the standard of living. He then calls for resistance, for a reverse in the "retreat" of American power initiated in the Nixon era.

Dealing with social issues, *Why We Were in Vietnam*, is perhaps the most controversial of Podhoretz's works. In it he alleges that the Vietnam War was moral because it was fought to free the Vietnamese from communism. He rejects all liberal and moderate critics that have viewed Vietnam as a national mistake.

Podhoretz considers the critic to be a guardian of culture whose responsibility is to expose the fraudulent in society. In the mid-1980s, his attention returned to literary authors such as Milan Kundera, George Orwell, Aleksandr Solzhenitsyn, Albert Camus and F. R. Leavis. First published in *Commentary* and other journals, pieces were collected in *The Bloody Cross-Roads: Where Literature and Politics Meet* (1986). Here Podhoretz explains that he has given up literary criticism because contemporary novels for him seem less worth writing about. They deal with the author's biography and not with the world we live in, giving nothing to the reader. For Podhoretz, Western civilization is witnessing a devastating deterioration of culture and morality.

After 30 years as editor and writer, Norman Podhoretz is regarded as having a fine interpretative and analytical eye for understanding contemporary culture. He remains a critic with a brilliant mind and a first-rate intelligence who is often driven to pessimistic judgments. Podhoretz's political arguments and artistic taste have left a mark on an entire generation of intellectuals. *See also* Neoconservatism.

ILAN STAVANS

BIBLIOGRAPHY
Podhoretz, Norman. *Breaking Ranks: A Political Memoir.* New York: Harper, 1979.
———. *Making It.* New York: Random House, 1967.

Poetry. The critical issue for twentieth-century Jewish-American poetry is whether, and to what degree, it can be perceived as separate from twentieth-century American poetry itself and whether, whatever peculiarities the Jewish-American poets can be construed as having, taking them as a group, those "peculiarities" are the result of their *Jewishness* rather than other factors, such as age, geographic locations, aesthetic or philosophical commitment, and such—or another way of putting it is to ask whether those very commitments (age, philosophy, etc.) are more overriding for those poets than their Jewishness.

The answer must be that in some cases it is one and some cases the other; that some poets are more "Jewish" than others; that in the case of some (Jewish) poets the overriding concern might be the Jewish experience itself, while in the case of other (Jewish) poets the overriding concern might be the issue of form or politics or language or some other thing that that poet shares with like-minded non-Jewish poets, and that obsesses him more than his Jewishness, and that it varies from book to book and poem to poem.

In addition, American poetry in general was moving through several periods of variety and diversity just at the time when the Jewish presence had begun to be felt, say from 1930 to the present, and the Jewish poets responded, partly perhaps because they were Jews and had a great tradition of "adjusting" to new ideas. In a certain year, say 1962, it is more likely than not that there would be Jewish-American poets on both sides of the argument that divided American poets at that time, formalist versus organicist, closed verse versus open.

Howard Nemerov, for example, and Allen Ginsberg, both Jews, would have had little to agree upon, and Nemerov's aesthetic, his poetic, world, would have been defined not by his religious and cultural bonds but by his aesthetic ones, and of course the same is true of Ginsberg.

Thus, there are poets in all the traditions who are Jews. Some are committed to traditional (English) form, some are projectionists; some write in the tradition of William Carlos Williams, some of Wallace Stevens. Since most (or almost all) Jewish-American poets lived and wrote in urban areas, there would probably be none, or certainly very few, who would write, say, in the tradition of Robert Frost, though there have been lovely pastoral moments in Paul Goodman, Louis Zukofsky, and others; and though there would be Jewish-American poets who would be deeply influenced by both Ezra Pound and T. S. Eliot, and might even be (slightly) affected by their hieratic values and priestly concepts, it is more likely that they would be interested in the innovations in form than in the philosophic orthodoxy and pathetic regressions of those masters.

The hatred, and nostalgia, of Pound and Eliot would make little sense to Jewish poets—and not only because so much of it was directed against the Jewish presence: Jews, as poets, could not, except through the most tenuous lines of adoption, have felt the loss as those two poets felt, or pretended to feel, of a Saxon and Norman past that was abandoned for a "mongrel" democratic present, nor would they grieve in the same way, if at all, the replacement of the feudal world with the modern. There would indeed be, and there always was, an interest in Walt Whitman, one that perhaps anticipated and predated the passion for him that flowered in the 1950s and 1960s, even if that interest was for the more popular aspects of his work as well as for the more profound and formal aspects, that is, Whitman the democrat, Whitman the optimist. Because the prophetic, and particularly the political, impulse has been so strong in late-nineteenth- and twentieth-century Ashkenazi Jewry, there was, and is, an unusual emphasis on political and social issues. There is, therefore, a kind of "cumulative" difference between Jewish and non-Jewish poets in this area; and, given the Jewish culture in America in the first decades of this century, its poverty, its idealism, its overwhelming dislocations, and the sudden terrifying removal from the religious base, there was an emphasis, in the poetry, on loss, ruin, social malaise, and isolation that was perhaps even greater than the emphasis on those things by non-Jewish poets. It has been said that the Jew has become the symbol—perhaps the image—of the alienated person of this century, that the alienated personage *is* a Jew. In this connection, the Jewish experience, if fully realized, becomes the most appropriate subject for poetry itself, if the Jewish experience can be defined as one of loss, regret, ruin, mourning, even if the non-Jewish poet experiences those things from a different cultural and psychic viewpoint. Stevens stands apart and so does Goodman. It is the difference I am exploring. Maybe John Berryman's "Imaginary Jew" is the closest coming together of the two consciousnesses; maybe Berryman, as a poet, incorporates the two consciousnesses more than anyone else.

There is, of course, another strain in Jewish-American consciousness and Jewish-American poetry, and that is the assimilationist strain. Assimilation is radically different in American poetry than it is, for example, in Russian or French poetry, simply because the process, and the significance, of assimilation itself is different. American Jews are, by assimilating, following a complicated but subtly defined course that other ethnic or minority groups—in America—choose to follow (or not) in various degrees. To examine the *difference* between Jews and others is to address the very agony of Jews, both in America and in the Diaspora at large. Certainly, other groups have similar agonies. As far as poetry is concerned, the issues are the relationship to the English—and American—language, the influence and inspiration of classic English literature, the content of that literature in terms of English culture, including religious culture, the identification with the American literary position in its relation to England and English literature, and the relative freedom of choice in America. A Jew who writes poetry in America is subject to the very same pressures—and opportunities—as other Jews. At this point—1990—she or he seems to have immense economic, social, and intellectual freedom, and the pressures are overwhelmingly internal—psychological and philosophical—rather than external. This has generated an enormous variety in the kind of poetry that is being written by American Jews. At the same time, the relative prosperity in America, the huge explosion in the arts, and the university workshop phenomenon have produced a large number of poets, including Jewish poets, and these poets vary enormously in the expression of their Jewishness.

John Hollander, a Jewish-American poet himself, seems to dispute the very idea of Jewish-American poetry, which is perhaps a way of disputing the idea of Jewishness itself. He says there is no Jewish-American "subject," not to mention Jewish-American "form," that the American poet of Jewish descent is not essentially involved in a *Jewish* experience in the act of writing, that there is no Jewish way of writing, that an overwhelming number of American poets of Jewish descent do not reveal their Jewish identity in their poems, that the poet whose language is English must come to grips with the great poets in that language—who are not Jewish—and a literature that is informed and inspired by non-Jewish, indeed by Christian, ideas, including, especially, the Protestant Bible. He also claims there is not a great Jewish literary culture in English, as there was, presumably, in German, a claim similarly made by the critic Harold Bloom. There is ambivalence in Hollander's stance, for he does talk about Jewish-American poets even as he disclaims them, and he refers repeatedly to Paul Celan as a great—indeed in his eyes, the greatest—modern Jewish poet, even though he lived in Galut and wrote in German. He attributes to Celan a wisdom, perhaps a knowledge, that only Jews—Jewish poets—could attain.

Bloom, for his part, treats the idea of Jewish-American poetry almost with contempt. He says there are no Jewish-American poets of the order of Frost, Stevens, Williams, Pound, Moore, Eliot, Crane, Roethke; that no Jewish-American poet of undoubted major status has established himself in this century. He further states that it is no accident. He says that the Yiddish poetry written in America is far superior and alludes to the "uneasiness" and the "inhibiting and poetically destructive excessive self-consciousness" of Jewish-American poetry. He is particularly hard on Allen Ginsberg, whom he calls "mock-bardic," and he has praise for Irving Feldman, John Hollander, Richard Howard, Allen Grossman, Edward Field, Robert Mezey, and Harvey Shapiro (whom he prefers to Karl). Jewish-American poets, according to Bloom, found themselves, in this century, face to face with a modernism that was inimical to their visions, presumably their inherited visions, as Jews. They lacked, he said, a language—perhaps a form—appropriate to their desired stance. The "idiom" bequeathed to them, as Bloom puts it, by the various modernist and postmodernist masters, is essentially "hostile." This is an interesting, if awkward, idea that takes into account neither the complexity of influence nor the enormous variety among the writers themselves. He even applied his well-known theory of poetic influence to account for the lack of important Jewish-American poets, a theory that involves a kind of "killing of the father." According to Bloom, young Jewish poets cannot identify with, and worship (and later kill), the Gentile precursors, since they are not truly "fathers." He even finds the process alien to Judaism, which makes the plight of the young Jewish poet doubly hopeless—that is, for Bloom.

Jerome Rothenberg, in *Sulphur 2* (1981) denounces Bloom's deconstructionist strategy as well as his taste, and dubs him an "exterminating angel," in memory of Joseph Mengele, for his deliberate and rather formal decisions of "which poets shall live and which shall die." In Rothenberg's own *A Big Jewish Book* (1978) there is an extensive selection of Jewish poets, American and otherwise, and though the poems do seem to have a certain direction—experimental, esoteric, mythic; Poundian and Olsenian; religious, politically radical, antiacademic, sacred, secret—the volume, nonetheless, is a rich book and begins to indicate the enormous scope of contemporary Jewish-American poetry. Some of the poets represented are Jackson Mac Low, Allen Ginsberg, Armand Schwerner, Jack Hirschman, Nathaniel Tarn, David Meltzer, Cid Cormen, Harvey Shapiro, Rochelle Owens, David Antin, Larry Eigner, Louis Zukofsky, Gertrude Stein, George Oppen, Charles Reznikoff, Denise Levertov, Edward Dahlberg, David Ignatow, Howard Schwartz.

A Jewish poem can be defined as one written by a Jew or one with a Jewish subject. But it is more in the way of *accumulation* that Jewish poetry can be perceived. This or that individual poem can be seen to be Jewish, perhaps, when in the company of other poems of a similar nature. Jewish poetry tends to be deeply emotional, concerned with family, obsessed with the past, ritualistic, concerned with the problem of injustice and inequality. But not all poetry that concerns itself with these things is Jewish poetry, and not all Jewish poets have these interests. Furthermore, a poet can be most Jewish when he or she is least deliberately trying to be. Stephen Berg's deeply moving poems about his father's death and Philip Schultz's poems of fear and isolation are more to the point, more Jewish, than the set pieces. Allen Ginsberg's "From Aether," a poem about the secret name of God, is Jewish both in its subject matter and its voice, whereas "1st Light Poem: For Iris—10 June 1962," by Jackson Mac Low, which appears with Ginsberg's poem in *A Big Jewish Book*, could only be construed to be Jewish in its devotion to the ideas of "light," but that is not a concern that is exclusively Jewish. The Persians, the Christians—now the whole world—light candles and are devoted to light.

Ginsberg's poem, which is terse and abstract as many of his religiopolitical poems are, is written almost like a telegram, in caps and leaving out unnecessary pronouns and articles for economy's sake. It is also full of both humor and pathos, as it shows both the physical and metaphysical distance between the poet and God—and smacks of the absurd. It is Jewish in its humor, in its intimacy (to God), in its self-avowed and slightly mock helplessness, in its formalisms and ritual, in its mocking, in its utter loneliness.

In Mac Low's "1st Light Poem" there is something Jewish—or at least biblical—about his use of repetition, but other than that, the poem is not necessarily Jewish, at least in this reviewer's eyes. The ultimate question, and one that we have been exploring in different ways so far in this essay, is: "Is there an essence to Jewish poetry?" This is also, at the same time, asking, Is there an essence to Judaism? Although it may be easier to answer the second question than the first, perhaps it can be said that if one identifies with a Jewish past—if one identifies as a Jew—then his or her poetry will be Jewish and perhaps it will be the more Jewish the more he or she moves in that direction. What it means in the poet to be Jewish, what it means in poetry to be Jewish, is something that cannot, except in the most obvious ways, be predicted. My own guess is that there is a driving force in the poetry that is Jewish, and it will become more and more manifest, rather than less, as a body of Jewish-American literature, of Jewish-American poetry, develops.

It is customary to begin the study of contemporary Jewish-American poetry with Emma Lazarus (1849–1887), who turned her attention almost exclusively to Jewish subjects and to the translation of Jewish poets after reading George Eliot's *Daniel Deronda*, but the first Jewish-American poet of any note was Gertrude Stein (1874–1946), who, though principally a novelist and a playwright, also wrote important poetry and contributed significantly to the psychological and aesthetic development of twentieth-century American poetry, even if she has not been sufficiently acknowledged. Lazarus, of course, is best known for "The New Colossus," which is engraved on the base of the Statue of Liberty. She wrote other poems, some of them moving, in a style and with an aesthetic attitude that reflected the minor poetry of her time. This style was excessively discredited with the advent of the modern in the first decades of this century. Stein's poetry makes use of repetition, juxtaposition, and deliberate naiveté, qualities also found in her prose. She clearly was made use of by Robert Duncan, Robert Creeley, and the second-generation Objectivists and was a parallel influence, along with George Oppen and Louis Zukofsky. The whole range of Jewish-American poetry, from the conventional, familiar, and bourgeois, on the one hand, to the radical and experimental on the other is reflected in the work of these two poets.

The first extended generation of Jewish-American poets was born in the first decade of the twentieth century, George Oppen in 1908, Carl Rakosi in 1903, Louis Zukofsky in 1904, and Stanley Kunitz in 1905, which means that, by and large, the first exposure, the first "surfacing," would occur in the middle and end of the second decade, or later, after modernism had been established and after Pound, Williams, Eliot, Frost and Stevens had made their respective breakthroughs. Those poets would therefore, along with their non-Jewish contemporaries, be in a situation to *react*, in various ways, to the first efforts of modern poetry. Three exceptions are Charles Reznikoff (1894-1976), Samuel Greenberg (1893-1916), born in Vienna, and Walter Lowenfels (1897-1965), although Reznikoff, to the degree that he was an Objectivist—in the sense that that word was defined by Louis Zukofsky and the others—was really associated with the "later" generation. In my eyes, Reznikoff is not an Objectivist, but an imagist, if we have to give him a label, and though influenced by Pound and the other imagists, he was a true loner, a great original. If anyone remained true to the *credo* of the imagists throughout his life it was Reznikoff.

Samuel Greenberg died of tuberculosis at the age of 23, in 1916, after a life of anguish and poverty. He is remembered today only because Hart Crane was so moved by some of his poems that he actually took lines and structures from them. Most of his poems are new-romantic and late Victorian, deriving in part from Emerson's essays and poems, as well as from Shelley, Keats, and Thoreau. But a few of his poems are absolutely remarkable, and it is fascinating to conjecture what would have happened to his poetry had he survived and been exposed to the poetry of this century. Allen Tate, who edited a *Selected Poems*, praised him highly and identified "Elegy," "Soul's Kiss," and "To Dear Daniel" as his best poems. But I believe "The Tusks of Blood" and his prose autobiography are his most interesting pieces. "The Tusks of Blood" is one of the great poems of the century.

Reznikoff is one of the simplest, most transparent poets of history; and it may be, ironically, that his reputation suffered the way it did simply because of this. His poetry is so elemental, so committed to detail, so connected to the scene that it is involved with, that it seems almost always as if he is engaged in mere *descriptions*. Some of the more famous short poems of William Carlos Williams are, as it were, nothing compared to the dozens and dozens of pages of perfect realization that Reznikoff achieved. Here he is describing a loose girder lying on the ground.

> Among the heaps of brick and plaster lie
> a girder, still among the rubbish.

The very weight of this girder can be felt, as well as its hopelessness, even—at risk—its loneliness. It is an object that causes us to see. It is, perhaps, the poet himself. Oppen praises these lines, and Reznikoff's poetry in general. He said, "Line upon line of his perfect poems have been with me for the fifty-eight years since I first came upon them. If we had had no other poetry, I think we could nevertheless live by virtue of these poems, these lines, these overwhelming gentle iron lines and images of all that is and our love and pride and our small life which is immeasureable as these lines which are still themselves among the rubble."

Essentially Reznikoff, like Oppen and Williams, was trying to discover the beautiful in mean objects, usually in an urban setting. Here are some other vignettes from the same poem ("Jerusalem the Golden," 1934):

> This smoking winter morning—
> do not despise the green jewel shining
> among the twigs
> because it is a traffic light.

> ***

> My hair was caught in the wheels
> of a clock
> and torn from my head, see I am
> bald!

He moves from description into apothegm, into proverb. He is Blakeian.

The other side of Reznikoff is his strong Jewishness, his obsession with Jewish life and history. Nor is it something that is implied or inferred. It is quite explicit. He wrote with specific reference to the biblical history of Israel, to the Jewish experience in America, and to the Holocaust. He was bitter about anti-Semitism and full of guilt at his own "straying." More than the others of his generation, he was a "Jewish" poet.

What is most amazing is how Reznikoff has been ignored by the academics. It is all but scandalous. The obvious reasons are his lack of obscurity and the avoidance of allusion and reference we have come to expect from the moderns, and perhaps his enduring respect for traditional narrative—perhaps also his direct confrontation with the subject, the lack of any suspension or distance, almost the lack of art. Yet there would be such a rich subject—if the critics only knew how to reach him. He is, in spite of them, read, and his reputation grows. Reznikoff is a profound and subtle poet.

The Objectivists came to light nationally in 1932 when *Poetry* published a selection on their work plus a manifesto of their beliefs. It is rather amazing that the Objectivists are all Jewish—unless W. C. Williams could be considered one of them. It is equally amazing that so much of their work is derived from the theory, and to some degree the practice, of Ezra Pound, a fascist and anti-Semite. The relationship of Jewish-American poets in this century with Ezra Pound is complex, sometimes astonishing. Many of them were friends of his, or admirers and followers, and some are apologists for his ideas and words. The simplest things that can be said are that Pound was not, at all times, a fascist, that he was generous to young poets, that he loved followers, that he was a brilliant poet and an extraordinary teacher, and that he made his initial contacts with Jewish poets—or they with him—before the anti-Semitic and fascist ideas obsessed him. Also he had a denunciatory, prophetic voice that was not at all unfamiliar to Jews and Jewish poets. Olsen rejected him, Frost and MacLeish were embarrassed by him, but none of the Jewish poets publicly turned against him, except Karl Shapiro. Ginsberg's embracing him and forgiving him is a well-known event. We creatures of justice knew much love here.

Louis Zukofsky was the leader, the originator, of the Objectivists, but George Oppen was the more important poet. Objectivism could have been an excuse for a movement rather than a movement. Zukofsky talked about "the desire for what is objectively perfect," and the emphasis was on exactness, simplicity, and sincerity, with no superfluous words or sentiments. Oppen often quoted a twelfth-century Chinese poet in defining the movement. "Poetry," he said, "should be precise about the thing and reticent about the feeling."

It is difficult to speak critically of Oppen's poetry. One critic said that "the sole purpose of his poetry was to show a sense of awe." This emphasizes the religious base. Another emphasized his "Cezanne-like poetry." Another emphasized the moral, the ethical, "pressure" of his words and lines. Perhaps the last lines of his tribute to Reznikoff, "to write/in the great/world small" sum up the theory of Oppen as much as anything else. He was a passionate, generous, brilliant, ironic, complex soul, and uncompromising humanist; many think a great poet.

Zukofsky's poetry tended to be obscure, arcane, hermetic, in comparison with Oppen's. It is intellectual and learned. There is a certain excitement in the very obscurity, in the implication of a setting, but perhaps the lack of drama, as well as the lack of coherence, finally limits the poetry, though occasionally there are beautiful extended clear passages. Here is the ending of a section from *A-12*. Stein is there, and Pound, the French painters, and the Talmudists:

> A shop bench his bed,
> He rose rested at four.
> Half the free night
> Befriended the mice:
>   Singing Psalms

Stanley Kunitz (b. 1905) is the first Jewish poet of this century to incorporate fully the high-modern sensibility that Pound and Eliot—and after them Tate, Ransom, MacLeish, Cummings, and Crane—first developed. He was a close contemporary and dear friend and neighbor (in Pennsylvania) of Theodore Roethke, and though their poetry is quite different, there is a common ground in the lucidity, the elegiacal note, and the great personal sadness. I see the poetry of these two men as the third stage in the development of the sensibility I describe, if Pound, Eliot, Williams, and Stevens were the originators and Cummings, Crane, et al represented the second stage. Kunitz, who was not only a great poet, but also a great teacher, had a profound—an overwhelming—influence on the generation of poets that followed him, and though there was a "companion" or "parallel" line that occurred in American poetry in general, as well as Jewish-American poetry, the line of objectivism (in all its diverse manifestations), it was Kunitz's poetry, I believe, that had the greater influence, again in American poetry in general as well as Jewish-American poetry.

Kunitz's Jewishness can be seen in his isolation and separation, in a particular tenderness and even commitment to the lost, in his passion for and search for the father, even if it has overwhelming personal meaning, and in his strong moral and prophetic stance. I think he has a profound Jewish soul, even if he does not write about Jewish aunts and bar-mitzvahs, even if he does not make Jewish history and mythology his central subject. In "An Old Cracked Tune" he writes of Solomon Levi dancing "on the edge of the road":

> My name is Solomon Levi,
> the desert is my home,
> my mother's breast was thorny,
> and father I had none.

This poem typifies his Jewish mode. He is stripped of everything, alone, yet still exulting, still dancing. And in "The Quarrel," another aspect of his Jewishness is realized in his terrible compassion, regret, guilt, and understanding—what shall I say?—a knowledge of existence itself, that is almost unbearable:

> *Liebchen,*
> with whom should I quarrel
> except in the hiss of love,
> that harsh, irregular flame?

In his more recent poems, Kunitz continues, and even expands, his vision. One of his profoundest poems is "The Wellfleet Whale," which is, it seems to me, simultaneously an invocation of the lost and powerful God and a paean to the monstrous, alien, and abused whale foundering on our shore (the Jews?). It is a great poem, one of the finest of this century, and the distinction between it and Moby Dick, say, is the very distinction between a Jewish and a non-Jewish sensibility. "The Raccoon Journal," also recent, is just as great. Though seemingly casual, it invokes not only the connection between the speaker and animals, but the connection between all things. It is full of humanity, and wisdom.

Eli Siegel (b. 1902) is another poet from this generation. Again, his subject matter is not specifically Jewish, but his rhythms, his tone, his very celebration are directly from the Scriptures. W. C. Williams saw him as an astounding original when his poems first appeared in the late 1920s. That odd combination of factual obsession and elegiac loss would not be lost on a Jewish reader.

The second great concentration of Jewish poets in this century centers around the work of Delmore Schwartz, Paul Goodman, Chaim Plutzick, Muriel Rukeyser, David Ignatow, and Karl Shapiro. These were the sons and daughters, and the language they used, the poems they wrote, tended not to be experimental in the sense that the generation of 1905 was. They were in their twenties and early thirties when some of the terrible events of this century occurred—German destructionism, Stalinism, the murder of the Jews, the dropping of the bomb—perhaps for this reason—at least in part—the appropriate mode for them seemed to be elegy and simplicity. In a certain sense, they were a stunned and bitter generation, as far as their poetry was concerned, or a wise and ironic one, even though they sometimes expressed the redemptive hope of the political Left.

Delmore Schwartz (1913–1966), a *wunderkind*, seemed, more than any of the others, as if he were going to be the first major poet that American Jewry produced. He was New York based, one of the editors of the *Partisan Review*; and a well-known poet and short story writer when he was in his twenties, but he did not continue to develop in the last decades of his life. There was a revival of interest in Schwartz in the 1970s, but it was more the romance of his life and his bitter failure that attracted readers. He seemed to be the classic melancholic poet, doomed even by his own brilliance, wit, and passion. Many of his poems are quite lovely, deeply musical, and profoundly intelligent, but there is not a substantial body of work. There is no question that if he had remained "healthy" and continued to produce, we would have witnessed a deeply important contribution to American poetry.

Paul Goodman (1911–1972) is better known as an educator, analyst, and even novelist, but he is a moving poet and his reputation may finally rest more on his poetry than on anything else. There is in Goodman the use of language that can only be described as humane, liberal, and intellectual, and he brings to bear a profound social conscience in his poetry, for example, in his poem on the New York Port Authority Bus Terminal or in the "Lordly Hudson." His elegy to his son Matty, killed in a rock-climbing accident, is, in my eyes, one of the great elegies in the English language. Interestingly enough, there is in Goodman a great and continuous sense of the presence of English literature, of the masters as well as the classics, especially Latin, that takes the form of a certain eloquence and even monumentality.

Chaim Plutzik (1911–1962) is a distinguished poet who lived in Rochester, New York. His poetry shows strong traces of W. H. Auden, T. S. Eliot, and Robert Graves. In addition, there is a strong biblical influence that is reflected not only in his subject matter, but also in a certain dignity and formality that is reminiscent of the scriptural voices. This formality—a kind of eloquence—keeps repeating itself in Jewish-American poetry. Part of it stems from the Scriptures, and Talmud, and part of it from a sense that "English" (and English poetry) is to a degree alien, and there is a constant need to "prove oneself" in the foreign language. Plutzik, for example, who was deeply learned, grew up in his early years speaking Yiddish more than English.

Muriel Rukeyser (1913–1980), who won the Yale Younger Poets Prize at the age of 22, is an important American poet whose full recognition did not come until the last decade of her life, when appreciation for her merged with a newly awakened feminism. She was a profound social critic, stemming directly from the prophetic and socialistic tradition. Her themes are both historical and personal; her language is tender yet passionate, moving toward the sublime, and her mood is always one of pity—for the unacknowledged and the despised and the oppressed. Her Jewish vision is strongest here.

Karl Shapiro (b. 1913) is both a critic and a poet. His poetry received early recognition, and he won many awards. His earlier poetry is realistic, witty, and formal, strongly influenced by Auden. Many of those poems, "The Drug Store," "The Jew," "The Southerner," have been anthologized, but in middle life he abandoned his early mode in favor of a freer, more ecstatic poetry, in the style of Whitman and the Beats. He is a strong force in American poetry. Both "opposing" modes represent the Jewish vision: urbanity, wit, wisdom, on the one hand; ecstasy, iconoclasm, on the other.

David Ignatow (b. 1914) is, in my view, the most important poet of this generation. There are no single great brilliant poems, as one finds in Schwartz, but there is a lifetime of careful and beautiful writing. Ignatow's poetry seems to be a plea for kindness, for justice, for decency, for sanity. It starts, as it were, in the absolute confusion and ambiguity that is our lives, and if it sometimes ends up in just another bewildering place, it is not that there has not been an agony of trying. Kafka comes a little to mind, but K., in this case, is never totally defeated. There seems in Ignatow's poems to be a presence, or a memory, of Yiddish. The intonations, the rhythms, are Yiddish. There is nothing of the English in Ignatow, no heroics, no grandeur, even very little sublimity. He is quite different from Kunitz. What we get, in Ignatow, is a voice arguing, gesturing, a voice from the Talmud. Finally, it is a pessimistic voice, an angry and bitter voice based in reality, with no false hopes. The connection is more with W. C. Williams than with anyone else.

The Jewish poets of the twenties, in general, are comfortable with the prevailing poetic modes and, with few exceptions, they are fairly indistinguishable from the non-Jewish poets, except occasionally for subject matter. Three poets, Theodore Weiss, Gil Orlovitz, and Howard Nemerov, all born just before or during the year 1920, anticipate the mode of the decade. Howard Nemerov (1920–1991), a brilliant critic and an urbane and witty, if sometimes bitter, poet has very little of the specifically Jewish in him, except for a certain sense of pessimism and hopelessness that is not at all alien to the Jewish spirit. Theodore Weiss (b. 1916), like Nemerov, is a formal poet, though one might prefer the word "civilized." He is brilliant, earnest, thoughtful, and passionate. In him there is always a sense of the outsider, and it seems to me that this is his most characteristic Jewish touch. The sense of the outsider is present even in those poems that have a nominally literary, an "English" subject matter. Gil Orlovitz (1918–1973) is a passionate, outrageous, even ecstatic, poet. There is social satire and personal anguish combined. He had a unique voice, related as much as anything else to Joyce, Cummings, and the French surrealists. His Jewish poems are very powerful. There is a series called "M'sieu Mshigu," and some almost terrifying poems in "Numbers" that deal specifically with the Holocaust. Here is a passage from NUMBERS: 35:

> I don't know where we are now. Post-
> card, Dead Sea Scrolls.
> I could use Weinstein's eyes as mucilage
> to affix a stamp—six
> million judenmarks
> —the cost is minimal due to the inflation
> of the dead.
> Or Goldberg's. Or Cohen's. Or Rabin-
> ovitz's. Or Lotka's.

Over two dozen Jewish-American poets were born in the 1920s: Harvey Shapiro (1924), Anthony Hecht (1923), Ruth Whitman (1922), Alvin Fineman (1929), Leonard Nathan (1924), Louis Simpson (1923), Shirley Kaufman (1923),

Constance Urdang (1922), Howard Moss (1922), Richard Howard (1929), Adrienne Rich (1929), Donald Finkel (1929), Philip Levine (1928), John Hollander (1929), Gerald Stern (1925), Irving Feldman (1926), Nathaniel Tarn (1928), Larry Eigner (1927), Allen Ginsberg (1926), Kenneth Koch (1925), Denise Levertov (1924), Jackson Mac Low (1922), Armand Schwerner (1927), Maxine Kumin (1925), Cid Corman (1924), L. E. Sissman (1928), Stanley Moss (1925), Dan Hoffman (1923), Jack Lindemann (1924).

There are different ways of explaining these poets. It is convenient to talk of poets as belonging to schools, but finally, they are each an individual struggling with his or her own vision. Hollander, Feldman, Hecht, Moss, all work in a tradition related to the work of Richard Wilbur and the other formalists. They came of age when a reaction against the radicalism, the experimentalism, of the first part of the century had set in and when there was a move toward the university and toward what can only be called polite or mannered verse. In my view, the best of these poets is Irving Feldman, for he retains passion and personal sensibility even as he succumbs in part to a more formal muse. I like in particular the muscularity, the wit, the East Coast sensibility, the nervous mind, the memory of Coney Island. There is a lovely poem called "The Golden Schlemiel" in which an Egyptian cab driver named Dief receives a Fiat from the President of the United States for returning some money he found in the back seat of his cab, while his own daughter, Jasmin, is dying of an illness and needs the money for an operation. All of Feldman's ruthless honesty, his raging irony, his wisdom are contained in this poem.

Philip Levine, Adrienne Rich, Allen Ginsberg, and myself are the Jewish poets born in the 1920s who are the more personal, the more passionate and expressive, perhaps the more romantic, more to the Left politically. Rich's early work, which was in the style of the poetry of the fifties and early sixties—formal, indirect, learned—changed radically as she moved into her principal subject matter and passion, the situation of women in the American culture. Her poetry became one of anger and vision, yet delicate and lovely withal. In some of her more recent poems, she has identified strongly as a Jew, invoking Jewish memories. In "Sources" she writes of "Yerushalaym, the Zion of hope and fear/and broken promises/this promised land." In the beautiful

poem "Yom Kippur 1984" she speaks out of the profoundest knowledge to ask forgiveness from those she has separated from—she speaks as a Jew, as a lesbian; she is one of our great poets.

Allen Ginsberg is Jewish, as the term has come to mean in its twentieth-century European and American expression, in his fierce prophetic utterances, in his wild humor, in his irreverence, in his sense of social justice, in his uncanny location of "persecution," in his affection and tenderness, in his urban identification, in his rebellion, in his paradisical vision, in his passion for knowledge. "Howl," "America," "Sunflower Sutra," "Kaddish" are Jewish poems, even as they are partially derived from Whitman, Blake, and the French surrealists. Ginsberg is a wild figure—a bit of the con artist, but a beautiful, a major, poet.

Philip Levine is a poet of family, of urban loss, of individual desperation—and courage—of bitter humor, of tenderness, of memory. He is a quintessential Jewish poet, without self-consciously insisting on it. It may be, indeed, that the route Levine has plotted, or stumbled onto, is the route that the Jewish poets after him have taken more than any other; that is, that his experience—his Jewish experience—is the most typical, or characteristic. Many of his poems are about relatives (grandfathers, uncles, his father), but a poem about a streetcar conductor on Joy Road fingering his new knotted hat "with the twin wool lappets/that closed perfectly on a tiny metal snap" is as Jewish as any because of the memory of "the hosts of the dead." The whole issue of memory in Levine, whether of Belle Isle in 1949 or of Joe Louis in 1936, is what makes him most Jewish as a poet. But is it more than memory that makes Levine a Jewish poet. It is his fierce honesty, his stubborn loyalty, his *belief*. He, more than anyone else, is our prophet, our spokesman. He expresses our bitter hopes, even if we are reluctant to speak them. And it has finally happened, after nine decades, that a Jewish-American poet is the spokesperson, whether he is heard or not, not just for the Jewish community, for us all.

Denise Levertov, Maxine Kumin, and Louis Simpson are poets of mixed sensibility, as far as their Jewishness is concerned. Levertov, whose mother was Welsh and whose father was a Russian Jew who converted to Christianity, is one of the great poets of this century, but her vision is not predominantly "Jewish." Critics have remarked that her mother was descended from a Welsh mystic and her father was descended from the founder of Chabad Hasidism (albeit he ultimately became an Anglican minister), and there may be a connection here, by way probably of deliberate identity. Levertov has been connected with Williams and with the Black Mountain poets, Creeley and Olsen, and her theories of organic poetry are related to their work, but it is an awareness of, an interest in, the invisible, the spiritual, just as it connects with the visible, that—characterizes much of her poetry, and this certainly can be called mystical, particularly, I would like to think, *Jewish* mystical. In addition, one could mention her denunciatory and prophetic voice, her rage at injustice, her political poems, but I would claim this not as a Jewish vision but as a *poetic* one, steeped as it is in a Judea-Christian ethos.

Maxine Kumin is most at home in the woods and the garden, waiting for her wild moose to come, dreaming of her young horses, yet sometimes she has Jewish family memories, and sometimes she writes out of an agony of self-identity or out of pain and curiosity concerning Israel as at the end of "In the Absence of Bliss":

> Bliss is belief, what where's
> the higher moral plane I roost on?
> This narrow plank given to splinters.
> No answers. Only questions.

Louis Simpson, whose mother was Jewish and whose father was Jamaican-Scottish, is, it seems, a little Jewish in his complaining and his almost Talmudic arguing. His voice, which is reasonable, intelligent, sane, and a little sarcastic, is certainly Jewish and his poems about the suburbs and his memories of proverbial Russia are very Jewish.

Most Jewish-American poets born in the 1930s are significantly more removed both from the immigrant experience and from the Jewish life in Eastern Europe, and that is probably what defines them as Jewish poets—although already there are a solid number of such poets who have assimilated not only into the culture but into the language itself and whose memories, so to speak, do not reach back to a Jewish "condition." The very oldest of these, after all, were only ten years old when the horror began, and the youngest of them was barely born. As for the Jewish-American poets born in the 1940s, and into the 1950s, there is already the beginning of a different kind of Jewish awareness, a persistence, a cultural definition that, though taking account of the European and the Euro-American experience, has a certain coloration, an acceptance, a confidence,

even a pride, that is altogether new. The younger of the Jewish-American poets were born without much Yiddish in the house; they were hardly stoned, and they would have been able to enter medical school with relative ease. Judaism was becoming one of the cultures of America. All this, unhappily, could easily change in a new birth of anti-Semitism but, as of this writing, though there is much ignorance about Jews in America, there is relatively little in the way of organized hatred. Jews have entered the suburbs and beyond, and the poetry reflects this.

The nature of Jewish-American poetry, in terms of numbers, in terms of variety of styles, in terms of the state of poetry itself in America, is such that it is possible to overlook or not yet to have discovered significant poets. And this is truer of the poets born in the 1940s. Of the Jewish-American poets born in the 1930s, I would identify Milton Kessler (1930), Neil Myers (1930), Joel Oppenheimer (1930-1988), Jerome Rothenberg (1931), Allen Grossman (1932), Linda Pastan (1932), Jack Hirschman (1933), Grace Schulman (1933), Marge Piercy (1936), Stephen Berg (1934), Robert Mezey (1935), Paul Zweig (1935-1982), Morton Marcus (1936), C. K. Williams (1936), Jack Marshall (1937), Alicia Ostriker (1937), Marvin Bell (1937), Stephen Kowit (1938), Larry Lieberman (1935), Carol Berge (1934), Rochelle Owens (1936), David Meltzer (1937), Philip Corner (1933), Robert Winner (1930), Michael Heller (1938), S. J. Marks (1935), Mark Strand (1934), Stuart Friebert (1931), Frederick Seidel (1936), L. S. Asekoff (1938).

It is actually becoming an extraordinary decade, as far as the poetry is concerned; there is a wide diversity of style and attitude, and a great richness. The poetry ranges from Rothenberg's revived Yiddish vision and his underground and tribal chants, to Grossman's mystic and mythological visions, to Hirschman's lucid and powerful personal and political recollections, to Pastan's family memories, to Marshall's dramatic and biblical poems. Joel Oppenheimer carries on the tradition of Oppen and Zukofsky, mellowed by Williams and Olsen, a realistic poetry based on the New York experience, full of sadness and wry knowledge. Milton Kessler writes in what can only be described as the ecstatic mode, a lovely poetry full of the memories of his father and the past. Alicia Ostriker writes of another past and the emergence of a new sensibility, governed by her sense of feminism as a political idea and her deeply felt sense of the role of the woman, the female, in our culture. Paul Zweig writes of death and memory and the beautiful place in a brilliant language that was just coming into its own before his untimely death. Marge Piercy directs her feminism to a strong political vision that more and more includes us all, in a language that is reminiscent of Allen Ginsberg. Robert Winner writes with a precision and a grace that redeems the pain of his vision. Morton Marcus writes of the journey of the immigrants in a mode and in a language that avoids the tell-tale sentimentality. He redeems that lost world in a poetry full of feeling and grace. Mezey merges a Jewish East Coast sensibility with the measures of Yeats and Hardy in poems that are often clear and powerful. Grace Schulman brings humor, irony, deep intelligence, a passion for order. Lieberman writes with a precision and a delicacy and an attention to details that is reminiscent of Oppen and seems absolutely characteristic of the Jewish-American poets. It is a kind of Jewish realism. Kowit writes in a passionate jazzy mode that is zany and melancholy at the same time. It is a post-Ginsbergian music. Stuart Friebert incorporates Eastern European poetry and an Eastern European sensibility—which is already partly Jewish—into American verse in an entirely natural way. He is a profound, tender, elegiac poet who is also an extraordinary translator, particularly of Hungarian and German poetry. Frederick Seidel is a poet of great complexity and beauty. He is difficult, learned, cosmopolitan, Baudelarian, and mock-prophetic. He speaks the secrets of our time—political and personal—in profound, outrageous, lovely verse. He is powerfully Jewish.

The three most important poets of this decade are Marvin Bell, Stephen Berg, and C. K. Williams. Berg is essentially an elegist, a poet of grief. In fact, one of his most important volumes is called *Grief*. Much of that book was taken up with the then recent death of his father. There is poem after poem that explores, weeps, rages, pleads for an understanding of the father and for an understanding of their connection. Berg is a passionate, even a wild, poet, yet his subject is not myth—it is the daily life of the urban dweller. In this daily life, this almost bourgeois daily life, there is a penetration of the whole range of emotions that constitute this life, from the most banal to the most sublime. Berg, born in 1934, came of age during the Eisenhower era, and he reflects the official ethos of obedience, domesticity, cooperation—even as he rages against it. One sees the

Spanish surrealists and W. C. Williams in his work. His language is moving, and in spite of the abrasiveness, the key element is affection.

Bell combines irony, although a gentle irony, with a pastoral vision that, nonetheless, takes the city into account. His world is the world of Long Island, Iowa, and, recently, the Pacific Northwest. In a way, Bell is a poet of ideas: it is as if the poetry were generated in ideas, but it is the complex laying out of the idea, the lovely—almost delicate—language, that is appealing. He is a realist (another Jewish realist) stemming from W. C. Williams—and James Wright. At his best, Bell catches the very essence of a moment in time like almost no one else. It is the voice that does this, the honest human voice. That is what is most Jewish. In "Late Naps" he says: "There is a dead part of the day/when the soul goes away—the late afternoon, for me, or else why is it/that sleep starts up in the stomach/in the late afternoons? . . ." He is a poet of the ordinary moment; and he makes that moment extraordinary.

Williams is a political poet, in the largest sense of the word "political." He expresses amazement, outrage, and sadness at the stupidity, smallness, and cruelty of institutions, the state, and individuals. Several of his "Jewish" poems have been widely anthologized, particularly "Spit," which relates how an SS man spits into a rabbi's mouth so that the rabbi could continue himself to spit on the Torah, and "A Day for Anne Frank." The anger and grief that are present in those poems are equally present in his other works. It is not even so much that he (Williams) rails when justice is absent, as the prophets did; it is the absence of sheer decency, of honesty, of plain kindess, that upsets him. And these things—kindness, decency, honesty—are elevated to a powerful, to a metaphysical, reality. His language is plain; his mode is deeply serious; he has, it seems, no time for the cuteness and the niceties of poesy; his message is urgent. This is his art. He is a major poet with a heartbreaking sensibility—and the vision is Jewish, as Isaiah was Jewish and Amos. In his more recent poems he lightens up, as it were, but even in his lighter moments, his pen is terrifying. He has been called a poet with a dark vision, but what we encounter is neither mask nor myth nor manner; neither Swinburne nor Kafka; but Everyman, walking through our hell, with our sensibility, our language, our soul.

As for Mark Strand, he is not a Jewish poet as that term is ordinarily understood. Nowhere, to my knowledge, is there "Jewish subject matter," or an interest, as such, in Jewish tradition, or a deliberate attempt to continue and to develop the Jewish poetic tradition. Yet he is connected with Judaism through birth and through association, and so is his poetry. Perhaps the Jewish quality in Strand's poetry exists in its very concentration on emptiness and its sense of helplessness; in its sense of isolation and dislocation; in its eerie distance from things; in its confrontation with darkness. These are universal characteristics, of course, but I am not unconvinced that the particular directions they take in Strand's poetry do not have something to do with a Jewish sense, even as it is a "modern" sense. Perhaps it is a modern sense we have come to associate particularly with the Jewish vision.

It is certainly too early to evaluate the work of the poets born in the 1940s, let alone those born in the 1950s. We know from experience that though some of the important poets of that decade have already surfaced, and some of them quite early, some have only begun to make their mark, and some will not appear for years. Some of their names are: Robert Pinsky (1940), Hugh Seidman (1940), James Reiss (1941), Steve Orlen (1942), Louise Glück (1942), Lyn Lifshin (1944), Daniel Halpern (1945), Ira Sadoff (1943), Roger Weingarten (1945), Philip Schultz (1946), Leslie Ullman (1947), David Shapiro (1947), Diane Ackerman (1948), Albert Goldbarth (1948), Mark Rudman (1948), Michael Blumenthal (1949), Marcia Falk (1941), Edin Shomer (1944), Charles Fischman (1942), Jack Meyers (1941), Lynn Emanuel (1949), Barbara Goldberg (1943), Judith Kroll (1943), Kenneth Rosen (1942), Stan Rubin (1942), Jane Miller (1949), Frederick Fierstein (1945), Ralph Angel (1948), Marilyn Hacker (1942), Rachel Hadas (1948), D. A. Levy (1942), Erica Jong (1942), Marcia Falk (1941), Kenneth Rosen (1942), Susan Mitchell (1944).

Pinsky, Hacker, Glück, Schultz—recently Jane Miller—have perhaps received the most attention. Louise Glück's *Jewish* spirit is hard to describe. Glück is the perfect example of a poet who is the product of a number of cultural expressions, *one* of which is Jewish (perhaps I should say a certain kind of Jewish) and this is true of others as well as her, as the Jewish presence and contribution become more and more varied and complicated. In the poem "The Gift," she speaks directly to "Lord" in a manner reminiscent of the prophets and even the patriarchs. For, she says, "You may not recognize me/ speaking for some-

one else./ I have a son. He is/ so little, so ignorant." It is a kind of prayer in which she asks for protection, in which she believes—for one awkward minute—in goodness, and sense. And in "Legend" she writes of her grandfather, an immigrant from Hungary, a wanderer remembering his *shtetl*:

> in such a world to scorn
> privilege, to love
> reason and justice, always
> to speak the truth—

Jane Miller has a voice that argues and reasons, that both pleads and praises. She is, in her way, a kind of stand-up comedian, like Lenny Bruce. It is a trait shared by other despised people (Irish, blacks) but one likes to think of it as preeminently a Jewish trait. In addition, she speaks for the situation of women in a voice that is both deeply informed and poignant.

Philip Schultz is one of the most "Jewish" of the new poets, whether he is writing of his mother sending a gift from Israel, or updating the *Guide to the Perplexed*, or talking to his "Guardian Angel Stein," or addressing *goyishe* Isaac Babel. He is a passionate and moving poet, but sometimes, as in "Pumpernickel," as in "Mrs. Appelbaum's Sunday Dance Class," he is too indulgent, perhaps too easy, in various invocations of the "Jewish mystery." The language of "I'm Not Complaining" is typically Schultz:

I didn't go hungry as a kid & I'm not constantly
oppressed by fascists, what if my apartment
never recovered from its ferocious bearing,
no one ever said city life was easy. . . .

Robert Pinsky is a poet who more and more reaches into his sources and, as he does so, comes more and more into contact with his Jewishness. "History of My Heart" is an example, as is the beautiful poem "The Questions," where he takes up the overwhelming issue of charity and, in a complicated tableau, shows us what we do, what we think, of this issue. His more recent poems move into profound ecstasy and vision.

Marilyn Hacker combines political radicalism with poetic formalism. She is a gifted lyric poet who awakens our sensibilities to experiences that have heretofore been mostly hidden, including lesbian life. She spends part of her time in France, and some of her best poems take place in her adopted country, but she retains the sensibility of a "Bronx Jew," as she calls herself in one of her poems. She is an important poet.

Four important poets of the 1940s who will probably be receiving wider attention in time to come are Ira Sadoff, Jack Myers, Susan Mitchell, and Mark Rudman. Myers's voice is as much a transliterated Yiddish, second or third generation, as it is updated French surrealism. He is like Jane Miller in his nervous quick take and reversals, although he is less fragmented than she is. Noteworthy examples of this fine poet's work are "The Diaspora," "Like Trees in the Desert," and "The Discovery of Peanut Butter," from *As Long As You're Happy*.

Rudman is another monologist, only the language is more complex and the vision is less peaceful. There is, in Rudman, a search for the lost father, which always brings up the subject of God. Here are some lines from "The Mystery in the Garden":

Would anyone listen, much less believe?
The sun I love, warming my heart,
warming my hands.
Can't hoard the fire. . . .

Rudman says he is interested in "describing the indescribable." He is one of our most brilliant and moving poets.

Sadoff brings deep intelligence, toughness, and a lovely delicacy, into his poetry. He seems to be identifying as a kind of exile; it is interesting that he has lived so much of his adult life away from his New York sources. His Jewishness is realized, in particular, by his search for "connection" and his fascination with separation. The beautiful "My Father's Leaving" is an example of this, a boy writing the father who just left— apparently forever—a "note" and continuing to write it in spite of his mother's admonitions. It is a note he has been writing (singing) all his life.

Mitchell is a poet of tremendous power and originality. Her dark personal vision moves her through a tableaux rich in imagery and music. The "literal" in her poetry is the literal world of mysticism, so that the *occasions* of her poems— family memories, walks, bar scenes—are never there for their own sake but for a deeper reason. She is able to take on the most terrifying of experiences. She is becoming an important force in American poetry.

Of the other poets born in the 1940s, I would like particularly to mention Barbara Goldberg, Diane Ackerman, Albert Goldbarth, and Lynn Emanuel. Goldberg, as a child of the Holocaust, grew up not only in fear but, literally, with the notion that she might have to make a sudden quick getaway. Her poems reflect an unnamed menace, quick journeys, a certain obliquity. Ackerman writes in a kind of glittering exoticism that reflects the idea of journey and escape as well as exile. Goldbarth's sprawling canvas and word play and wit and intelligence are, as I see it, pure Jewish. Emanuel in her search for a father, and for peace and stillness, embodies another Jewish vision.

Jorie Graham (1950), Edward Hirsch (1950), Michael Blumenthal (1949), Charles Bernstein (1950), Jane Hirshfield (1953), Liz Rosenberg (1952), and Allen Shapiro (1953) are some of the new poets. Graham's dialogue with the *other*, her social consciousness, her particular sense of a wilderness, her *journey*, indicate a Jewishness to me in spite of a certain concentration on Christian and Greek mythology and ritual. Blumenthal's Jewishness is in his deep humanism, his almost practical intelligence, and a kind of Talmudic arguing. Hirsch, in his tender grief-stricken memories, in his going over old hurts, in his affections, in his sense of loss, is the most Jewish of the new poets. His is a remarkable voice. There is in him a continuation of the great tradition.

Jewish-American poets will continue to write in all the modes that characterize American poetry in general. They will be conservative and radical, experimental and traditional, and they will continue to be assimilationist and separatist. It will continue to be as hard to define Jewish-American poetry as it will be to define and describe Judaism in America, as it takes its expected, and unexpected, turns. But that strange combination of culture, religion, and memory, which constitutes Jewishness, will not disappear nor will the poetry that, above all else, describes its spirit. That spirit will endure.

GERALD STERN

BIBLIOGRAPHY

Alter, Robert. *After the Tradition: Essays on Modern Jewish Writing*. New York: Dutton, 1969.

Bloom, Harold. "The Sorrow of American-Jewish Poetry." *Commentary* 53 (March 1972): 69–74.

Gershator, Phillis. *A Bibliographic Guide to the Literature of Contemporary American Poetry, 1970–1975*. Metuchen, N.J.: Scarecrow Press, 1976.

Guttman, Allen. *The Jewish Writer in America, Assimilation and the Crisis of Identity*. New York: Oxford University Press, 1971.

Lipzin, Solomon. *The Jew in American Literature*. New York: Bloch, 1966.

Malin, Irving, ed. *Contemporary American-Jewish Literature: Critical Essays*. Bloomington: Indiana University Press, 1973.

Pinsker, Sanford. "Great Expectations/Nagging Disappointment: Towards a Definition of American-Jewish Poetry." *Studies in American-Jewish Literature* 2 (Spring 1976): 14–23.

Rosenfeld, Isaac. "The Situation of the Jewish Writer." In *An Age of Enormity, Life and Writing in the Forties and Fifties*, edited by Theodore Solotaroff. Pp. 67–69. Cleveland: World, 1962.

Poetry, Yiddish. The century-long history (1880–1990) of Yiddish poetry in America can be divided into movements and individuals. Only a treatment of both the diverse, short-lived movements and the works of individual poets, who may or may not have been part of the group endeavors, can sketch the complexity of this literature.

A general trend characterizes the first six decades of Yiddish poetry in America: poetic voices develop from representations of collective concerns to expressions of the individual poet. This development can be explained by the shift in the role of poetry from a convention-ridden tool of political and national ideology to an art form embracing and embellishing upon versions of modernist notions of aestheticism, symbolism, and expressionism. However, the destruction of European Jewry during World War II interrupted and bankrupted this movement, and many Yiddish poets writing in America from 1939 onward have returned to the spokesman stance, writing poetry that speaks for the Jewish people, although the collective intention is enhanced and informed by the previous lessons in modernism.

Yiddish poetry arrived in America with the first wave of Yiddish-speaking immigrants in the 1880s. Initially, it became an expressive medium for the nascent Jewish labor movement, influenced by Romantic poetry as well as by socialist political ideologies. Concurrently, several prominent poets transcended this utilitarian poetry in a turn-of-the-century effort to reconnect Yiddish poetry with traditional Jewish culture. In 1907, Di Yunge (The Young Ones), the first of two modernist movements, established itself in Yiddish poetry in America, with the publication of a journal that exemplified these poets' new aestheticism, and in 1919, the second, Di Inzikhistn (The Introspectivists), published a collection of poems with a manifesto outlining its precepts of high

modernism. These two modernist movements, though relatively short-lived, as such, were the touchstones for a number of major poets who developed in the subsequent decades, although the course of history altered the fate of Yiddish poetry after 1939.

THE LABOR POETS. According to Irving Howe, the first book of Yiddish poems published in America was by an enlightened rabbi, Jacob Sobel, in 1877. In contrast to this stilted Haskalah writer, another early American Yiddish poet was Eliakum Zunser (1840–1913), a popular wedding bard from Eastern Europe, whose lyrics echo their folk origins. But the early period was best known for the poets who wrote poetry to express the plight of the Yiddish-speaking working masses. N. B. Minkoff divides the poetry of this period into "the labor poem" and "the revolutionary poem" and finds in these subgenres five basic categories of motifs: (1) social-sentimental poetry expressing the terrible need experienced by those being exploited by the sweatshops and the difficult conditions of the impoverished immigrants and the compassion for them; (2) poems of struggle; (3) satirical poems unmasking the enemies of humanity: capital, state, and the powers that support them; (4) social lyrics characterized by their symbolic despair; and (5) poems combining social ideas with elements of high romanticism—tones of heroism and pathos—through themes of sacrifice and martyrdom. The poetry of this period is characterized by highly conventionalized rhetoric, both political and personal, standard symbols, and predictable meters and rhymes. The general thrust of this poetry comes out of the sense of the poet as spokesman for the collective interests of the "folk" or the working-class immigrants.

The major poets of this period are Morris Winchevsky, David Edelstadt, Joseph Bovshover, and Morris Rosenfeld.

Morris Winchevsky (1856–1932) was born in a Lithuanian village, lived in Kovno and later Koenigsburg, Prussia, before settling in London, where he was active in Yiddish socialist journalism. He came to America in 1894, where he wrote for the Yiddish daily *Morgen Frayhayt*. Considered by later critics to be the central figure among the Labor Poets, though perhaps not the greatest poet, Winchevsky was the first socialist to develop Yiddish into a literary tool. Joining socialist thought with sentimental lyricism, Winchevsky's poetry became more than didacticism in rhymes, for his poems included compassion and sorrow as well as ideology. Winchevsky influenced other poets of his generation with his sentimental constructs and with his meter and rhyme. He developed a sentimental realism in his poems that depicted the pathetic and terrible conditions of life of the poor, as in the well-known "Dray shvester" (Three Sisters), from his series "London Silhouettes." He also wrote rousing songs of protest, such as "A Kamf-Gezang" (A Song of Struggle). Ten volumes of his collected writings were published in New York in 1926.

David Edelstadt (1866–1892), a Russian-born Jew (from Kaluga), came to the United States in 1882, after witnessing the Kiev pogrom of 1881, and worked in a Cincinnati clothing factory. Radicalized by his experiences in the sweatshop and by the 1886 Haymarket Affair in Chicago, Edelstadt, whose native language was Russian, began writing polemical verse in his acquired Yiddish and soon became a popular poet spokesman for the anarchist movement. He moved to New York, where he wrote for and was an early editor of *Di Fraye Arbeter Shtime*. At age 25, in a Denver sanatorium, Edelstadt died of tuberculosis. Many collections of his poems appeared in book form after 1892 in London, New York, Warsaw, and Moscow.

Two of Edelstadt's best-known poems are "Mayn Kamf" (My Battle, 1889) and "Mayn Tsavoe" (My Testament, 1889). Typical of Edelstadt, these poems, written in ballad strophes, are noble and grandiose, filled with catchwords of revolutionary propaganda, cliches, rhetoric, assumptions of agreed-upon values and goals, and simplified dualisms in opposition, such as good versus evil, the workers versus the capitalists. Although these poems strike the contemporary reader as lacking subtlety, they still exhibit the poet's control of limited terms. These poems tend to romanticize the poet as the spiritually powerful though physically enervated source of inspiration for the working masses.

Joseph Bovshover (1873–1915) had a career truncated by the onset of mental illness at age 22. During his boyhood in Lyubovitsh, Mohiliver Province, White Russia, Bovshover received a strong traditional Jewish education in heder and from his father, but at age 14 he left for Riga, where he became involved in anarchist circles. He learned German and read the German literary classics. Four years later he arrived in America in 1891, and began publishing poems pseudonymously in September 1892. That year he became

known for his elegy for Edelstadt. Over the years, he failed to hold down numerous jobs in furriers factories, in a grocery store his brothers bought him, in his brothers' business, and as a private tutor of German, but he did manage to read classical and contemporary English and American poetry in the library of Yale University, when he found himself in New Haven for a period of time in 1895. Bovshover's earliest poems show the strong influence of Winchevsky, Rosenfeld, and especially Edelstadt. By 1894, he had begun to develop his own direction, writing poems celebrating love, spring, and poetry itself, as well as continuing in a vein of revolutionary poems, inspired by Walt Whitman. In 1896, he published 11 poems in English in the anarchist publication *Liberty*. In 1898 and 1899, he experienced a crisis, and his poems became extremely embittered; in these years, too, he published a critical edition of his verse translation of Shakespeare's *The Merchant of Venice*. The play was staged, under the direction of Jacob Adler. In 1899, he wrote an essay, "Vegn Poezye," including treatments of Goethe, Heine, Milton, and Petrarch; he also wrote critical biographies of Heine, Emerson, Whitman, and Markham, accompanying his translations of their selected works. He began or projected work on other dramatic translations of Goethe's *Faust*, Schiller's *Kabalah and Love*, and Hauptman's *Furman Henschle*. In October 1899, Bovshover published his poetic credo, "Naye un Alte Lider" in *Di Fraye Arbeter Shtime*.

Financial problems and his egomania led to the onset of his mental illness, and finally he was committed to a mental hospital, the Hudson River Street Hospital, in Poughkeepsie, New York, where he lived for 15 years, until his death. His poems were published in book form in London (1903, 1907), in Petrograd (1918), Moscow-Kharkov-Minsk (1931), and the collected writings, *Gezamlte Shriftn*, in New York (1911, 1916). Bovshover's poems are more subtle, complex, and poetically sophisticated than those of either Winchevsky or Edelstadt. In them one hears echoes of Blake, Wordsworth, and Whitman. Mastering a variety of verse forms, including the ballad stanza, blank verse, and rhymed pentameter and Alexandrine couplets, Bovshover enriched Yiddish poetry.

Morris Rosenfeld (1862–1923) was born in a small town in Poland into a family of fishermen, who were forced out by government decree. Rosenfeld lived in Warsaw after the age of 9, where he attended heder. He married at 18 and lived in

Holland and England before coming to America in 1886. He began writing poetry in the sweatshops of London. Working in the garment factories in New York, Rosenfeld wrote of the lives of immigrant workers. He became known for these, his best poems, not so much a spokesman for the battle, like Edelstadt, but as a depictor of the pathos in the lives of urban workers. What distinguishes his career from those of the other Labor Poets is that he achieved brief fame outside the Yiddish world. In 1898, a Harvard professor of Slavic languages, Leo Weiner, translated a selection of his poems into English in a volume called *Songs of the Ghetto*, and Rosenfeld was taken up by American literati. The taste for his brand of exoticism passed, however, and Rosenfeld later earned a meager living as an assistant at *Der Forverts*, resentfully blaming his humbled circumstances for his depleted poetic abilities.

Critics concur that his later poetry, which relies upon the standard themes of protest and calls-to-arms, as well as upon Jewish national themes, is more bombastic and less compelling than his earlier work. Like Bovshover, he also wrote nature poems, but they are more stilted and conventional. He is best known for such poems as "The Sweatshop," "The Teardrop Millionaire," and "My Little Son," poems that make personal and particular the universal sufferings of the workers. In "My Little Son" a father tells of how much he loves his young son, whom he sees only asleep when he returns from work late at night. Rosenfeld draws on generalized characters, like the shtetl types in Yiddish fiction by Mendele Moykhr Sforim and Sholem Aleichem (but here they are city types)—the factory worker father who has to punch the time clock, working 16 hours a day for meager wages, the exhausted wife and mother, the innocent son who is victim to his parents' circumstances. The poet tells us little about these characters besides what is relevant to their situation—their financial poverty that makes necessary the terrible working hours and results in the depletion of their only source of pleasure and sustenance: the emotional life of the family.

Early Yiddish poetry in America draws upon traditional Jewish conventions of representation to present human predicaments that are not expressly Jewish: these writers substitute the problems of class for those of religious life. The protest poem secularizes the collective voice of religious liturgical poetry. Such poems maintain the same values of historical continuity of peoplehood and community but shift from God-or-iented to human-oriented hopes of salvation. Edelstadt's poems secularize the liturgical collective voice and politicize messianic hope. In Rosenfeld's poems the portrayal of characters as "types," a convention borrowed from classical Yiddish fiction, shifts away from the problems that people with roles defined by a stable, enclosed society face when changed by modern influences. Rosenfeld's "types" are deracinated, cut off from any community but that of the anonymous city defined by grueling work and the nuclear family, in contrast to the fictional characters of Mendele Moykhr Sforim and Sholem Aleichem, whose dilemmas are woven into the problems of the Jewish people and entangled in the social structure of Eastern European Jewish life.

POETS OF YIDDISHKAYT. Contemporary with the Labor Poets were three poets whose work came to maturity after they migrated to the United States at the turn of the century. Irving Howe (in *World of Our Fathers*, 1976) groups together Abraham Liessen, Yehoash (Solomon Bloomgarden), and Abraham Reisen as "Poets of Yiddishkayt," for he argues that their poetry, in bringing together socialist and Jewish nationalist themes in response to the difficulties of Jewish life, healed the rift between the Old World and the New. These poets do share an explicit concern with bringing to the surface of Yiddish poetry the elements of Jewish tradition, but each of them does so in a distinctive way that contradicts the attempt to group them.

Abraham Liessen (Valt, 1872–1938) was known in Minsk and better in New York as a journalist and a writer of verse essays that emphasized the link between the nationalist and socialist hopes for alleviating the suffering of Jews. His poems do so by drawing analogies between the triumphs of the Jewish past and the problems of his times, finding heroes in the Jewish martyrs of Talmudic and rabbinic literature.

Yehoash (Yehoash-Solomon Bloomgarden, 1872?–1927) had his origins in Verzshbolove, near Suvalk, on the Russian-German border, and came to New York in 1890. He contracted tuberculosis and, from 1890 to 1909, resided in a Denver sanatorium. He returned to New York in 1909, where he continued to live, except for a visit to Palestine and Egypt in 1914–1915. Commonly considered an intellectual poet, Yehoash was more concerned with aesthetic problems and less explicitly political in his works. He attended to the art of poetry on its own terms, combining in his lyrics the influence of traditional folk song and modern speech. Like Bovshover, Yehoash wrote nature poems, although his were unencumbered by Romantic conventions. Yehoash's main contribution lies in his attempts to bring Yiddish poetry up-to-date by importing the themes, forms, and language of world literature. He experimented with exotic subjects in his poems—writing of experience completely outside of the Jewish world, such as Chinese personages—and anticipated the cosmopolitan interests of Di Yunge poets (and also, strangely, of American modernists, such as Ezra Pound). He was the first to translate European and American poetry for the sake of enriching the poetic and prosodic vocabulary of Yiddish. His translation of Longfellow's verse narrative *The Song of Hiawatha* (1910) brought native American mythology into Yiddish. As early as 1891, the first year his work appeared in print, Yehoash published his translations of Byron's "The Gazelle" and Psalm 18. This early biblical translation was a harbinger of Yehoash's greatest literary achievement, his translation of the entire *Tanakh*, a lifelong project that appeared in full only posthumously in 1941. The translating interests of this prolific writer indicate the two simultaneous developments of Yiddish literature that Yehoash sought—the cultivation of Yiddish as a medium that both reflects the world's literatures and expresses its deeply Jewish origins. For his concern with the aesthetic and multicultural enrichment of Yiddish poetry, Yehoash was one of the few older poets that the rebellious modernist Di Yunge poets respected.

Abraham Reisen (1876–1953) was born in Koydenev, White Russia. He had established himself as a literary presence in Warsaw, published or helped by I. L. Peretz, Sholem Aleichem, and M. Spektor and closely affiliated with H. D. Nomberg and Sholem Asch, well before he settled in America in 1914. His first book of poems appeared in 1902, in Warsaw, and a four-volume collected writings appeared in 1908, in Krakow. His numerous short stories were noted for their understated, muted depictions of ordinary events and characters in European shtetl life and in immigrant life in America. Although he was a sophisticated reader of poetry, Reisen in his poems deliberately echoed Yiddish folk lyrics in prosody and tone, with an understated modesty, simplicity, and accessibility. This folklike quality accounts for why the Yiddish-speaking masses adopted many of Reisen's lyrics, set to music, as folk songs. Howe considers Reisen's work to be the culmination of YiddishkAyt, for it expresses a harmonious naturalness, at home with the inner workings of Yiddish-speaking Jewish life and sharing the ethic of that culture.

DI YUNGE. The major change in American Yiddish poetry occurred when, in 1907–1908, a group of younger poets and writers gathered to publish an earnest little magazine, *Di Yungt* (Youth). In contrast to the prevailing ideological and utilitarian orientation of the Yiddish press, *Di Yungt* eschewed the issues of nationalism and socialism in order to focus on a program of aestheticism. The poets who contributed to this short-lived journal and to its successors, *Shriftn* (Writings), *Literatur* (Literature), and *Inzel* (Island), sat for hours in literary cafes and cafeterias on the Lower East Side when not working in sweatshops, painting or papering houses, or looking for employment. They were young, mostly male, and new immigrants to New York. They were avid readers of recent and contemporary poetry in German, Russian, French, and Polish, and they sought to transcend the spokesman role of the Yiddish poet by exploring the poet's individual sensibility, the doctrine of art for art's sake, and the relationship between image and word. Abraham Cahan of the *Forverts* and other established members of the Yiddish press reacted to the social irrelevance of these poets by labeling them derogatorily as "di yunge" (the young upstarts). To the Yiddish world, the Yunge seemed radical in their adherence to a poetry that "spoke" for no one but the individual poet.

The central poets of Di Yunge were Mani Leyb (Brahinsky, 1883–1953), Reuven Iceland (1884–1955), Zishe Landau (1889–1937), and Joseph Rolnick (1879–1955). The works of these poets embodied the principles of musicality and romantic understatement, conveying mood or eroticism through quotidian detail. Their experimentation was not formal, for most of their poems were written in conventional rhyme and stanza forms. Rather, their poetry appeared radical in subject, approach, and language as it played upon idiomatic Yiddish diction for unexpected melodious effect, excised rhetorical grandiosity or Germanic poeticisms, and relied on direct, sparse, concrete imagery.

Of these four writers, Landau (from a Hasidic dynasty in Plotsk, Poland) was something of a theorist, spelling out the general terms guiding their writing in manifestos. In such an introduction to a 1919 anthology, Landau defined the achievements of "pure" poetry (illuminating ordinary experience and puncturing overblown claims of false messianism) against what he scornfully called that of "the rhyming departments" of the socialist and nationalist movements. Landau's poems are characterized by ironic wit that plays against the blur of romantic idealization.

Rolnick (from Zhukhovitz, White Russia) was the first American Yiddish poet to write a body of poems dealing with memories of Eastern Europe. Reuven Iceland (born in Great-Radomish, West Galicia) edited the journals *Literatur un lebn* (Literature and Life) and *Inzel*. His poems are characterized by an elegant spareness, as in a series of "Still Lifes" that exemplify his descriptive powers.

Mani Leyb (from Niezhin, in the Ukraine) developed into perhaps the most interesting of this core of Di Yunge poets. His earliest poems became a touchstone for the heightened sound play and artificiality of Yiddish symbolism, but he branched out by reinventing or adapting pseudo folk-forms, such as the ballad, in order to gain access to the folk imagination to enrich the individualism of Yunge poetry. In this folklike vein, he wrote poems that later became famous as children's poems in the Yiddish schools. During his last two decades, Mani Leyb's poetic powers came to full expression in a sonnet sequence (see Ruth R. Wise, *A Little Love*, 1988), where he joined the public and private voices of the individual man and the anonymous poets of the folk and of liturgy.

Other poets, briefly associated with the group, set out in their own directions and developed into major poetic voices. Most noted of these were the acerbic, complex ironist Moyshe-Leyb Halpern (1886–1932) (see article herein), the visionary H. Leivick (Leyvik Halpern, 1888–1962), and the writer of the epic poem *Kentucky* (1925), Yisroel-Yankev Schwartz (1885–1971). Leivick, who came from White Russia, was arrested in 1906 for his activities in the Bund, imprisoned and sentenced to hard labor, and, in 1912, exiled to Siberia. When he escaped in 1913, he made his way to America, where he became the most prominent Yiddish poet. Harshav characterizes Leivick's poetry as filled with themes of suffering, messianic fervor, mysticism, and humanism, which he couched in musical verse lines that show the influence of Russian symbolism. To express these themes, Leivick appropriated traditional Jewish motifs, such as the stories of Job, the binding of Isaac, the golem of Prague, and the Messiah in chains. He is perhaps best known for his verse drama, *The Golem* (1921). Y.-Y. Schwartz, who came to New York from Lithuania in 1906, taught Hebrew school and published his translations of Bialik and his own poetry. In 1918, he moved to Lexington, Kentucky, where he ran a clothing store until 1928. *Kentucky* appeared in 1925, the first sustained narrative poem in modern Yiddish, which was innovative, too, because it depicted an American subject at such length.

The Yunge publications consistently included few of the many women poets writing at the time. Among these stand out Fradl Shtok (1890–1930?), Anna Margolin (Rosa Lebensbaum, 1887–1952), and Celia Dropkin (1888–1956). Shtok's lyrics were noted for their shockingly original imagery; although she did not introduce the sonnet into Yiddish, as was popularly assumed (Winchevsky did), she was innovative in developing that form for modernist expression. Anna Margolin is a major modernist voice, although her poetic career was relatively truncated, like Shtok's. Her poems in *Lider* (Poems, 1929) are extremely complex, relying upon dramatic personae that defuse the personal voice. Celia Dropkin's poems are characterized by their explicit eroticism from a female point of view. The poems in her book *In Heysn Vint* (In the Hot Wind, 1935, 1959) subtly undermine accepted assumptions about women and poetry.

Di Yunge not only contributed their individuality to Yiddish poetry, but also were avid translators and expanders of the literary medium. Inspired by Yehoash's example, they filled their journals and anthologies with translations from European and American languages, as well as from Classical Greek, Arabic, and Chinese. Zishe Landau translated English ballads and Russian and German poems into Yiddish. Reuven Iceland translated Heine's prose and poems, as did Moyshe-Leyb Halpern. Mani Leyb translated a Scottish ballad and other poetry. Y.-Y. Schwartz translated Whitman, as well as Bialik, classical Hebrew poets, Shakespeare, and Milton. This flurry of translations indicated the stepped-up effort of the Yunge to invent a tradition for their poetry. Even as they rebelled against their immediate poetic predecessors, they sought to find roots for their poetry in world literature. The ballad form, consciously imported from other literatures, proliferated in their works (especially in Mani Leyb's and Halpern's) as an illusory artifice of folk poetry.

THE INZIKHISTN. Inzikhism (Introspectivism) was a trend launched in 1919 as a theoretical and practical revolt against the dominance and the overly "poetic" quality of the Yunge. In 1918, Yankev Glatshteyn (1896–1971, born in Lublin) and Nakhum-Borekh Minkoff (1893–1958, born in Warsaw), who had met in law school at New York University, brought poems to A. Leyeles (Aaron Glanz, 1889–1966, from Lodz), whose first book, *Labyrinth*, had just appeared, and raised the idea for a new poetic movement that would take Yiddish poetry beyond the Yunge, whose innovations now seemed stalemated. Publishing their poems in the Yiddish journal, *Poezye* (Poetry), they struck a chord with American and European modernism. Unlike the Yunge, these poets did not labor in factories and even had the advantage of American higher education. They read English and American poetry of the day, as well. In 1919, these three poets formulated their principles as the introduction to an anthology, *In Zikh*. This introduction became known as the Introspectivist manifesto, and the anthology soon evolved into a journal, although the two words of its title were contracted into one, which came to refer to the name of their movement. The journal *Inzikh* appeared from January 1920 to December 1940.

The poetic principles of the Inzikhistn opposed mimesis as the purpose of art and argued that poetry reflects an internalized social world rather than acting as a vehicle for expressing a political mood or "man" in general. As expressed in the manifesto, the theory is characterized by apparent paradoxes, such as (1) the emphasis on individual experience that makes the historical and political aspects of the world as personal as erotic sensation, (2) the idea that poetry should present the chaos of the psyche's experience through a technique of synthesis they called "kaleidoscopic," (3) an "individuality of expression" that meant not the relative or the personal but the poetic methods of association and suggestion, discontinuous composition and alogical devices of poetic language, through which "individuality" the poet expresses a universality of the contemporary person. Although the Inzikhistn divorced themselves from any national or social mission, they proclaimed that "because it is art, it is Jewish anyway" (Chronicle, No. 5) or, conversely, "A Jew will write about an Indian fertility temple and Japanese Shinto shrines as a Jew" (Manifesto). To these poets, Jewishness was the Yiddish language. Finally, the paradoxes pervade even their sense of poetic form, for although "rhythm makes the poem" (Leyeles), a poem that is "rhythm only" has no value. The Inzikh poets had the freedom to shift rhythmic devices from free verse to traditional stanzas, from poem to poem and even within a poem, in order to avoid monotony, which they considered as poetically fatal. In sum, the theories of the Inzikhistn called for introspection that reflected the social and political world, an individual poetic language that allowed for the expression of "modern man," and the idea of art for art's sake, which at the same time was art that authentically expressed life. According to Harshav, *Inzikh* published 100 poets and writers, including European Yiddish modernists, such as Dvorah Fogel and Avraham Sutskever, poets from the West and Midwest, such as Malka Heifetz Tussman, and American-born New York poets, such as Hasia Cooperman.

Of the three founding Inzikhistn, Yankev Glatshteyn is the best-known poet. In an ironic turn, this prolific poet and journalist was viewed after the Holocaust as a "national" Yiddish spokesman, although the later poetry of *Shtralndike Yidn* (Radiant Jews, 1946) and *Dem Tatns Shotn* (My Father's Shadow, 1953) seems in retrospect to have developed quite naturally from the earlier, modernist work of *Yankev Glatshteyn* (1921), *Fraye Ferzn* (Free Verse, 1926), and *Yidishtaytsh* (Exegyddish, 1937) and to embody in perhaps more subtle forms the verbal play and experimentation with idiom and metaphor of his earlier poems. Along with a body of poetry, N.-B. Minkoff produced major scholarly studies of Yiddish literature and culture. A. Leyeles, who was also a journalist and a political writer, published six volumes of poetry between 1918 and 1957, in which his style evolved from one derivative of Yunge aestheticism to a bold experimental style that combined classical strophes with free verse and architectural urbanism with sophisticated poems of alienation.

OTHER POETS. In this brief entry there is space only to mention, but not to discuss, the many other excellent poets who wrote in Yiddish in America. Although the focus has been on the most clearly identifiable "movements" within Yiddish poetry from 1880 through 1940, it would be unfortunate if the reader turned away with the impression that these were all. In fact, the trends in poetry discussed here simply offer a convenient way to simplify the task of writing an extremely complex history. More validly, perhaps, they also indicate the general tenets of poetry, which in one way or another touched almost every poet writing in Yiddish in America as the language developed into a medium for increasingly more sophisticated expression of individual experience within the context of Jewish destiny. What has been left out of this account is a discussion of poets who wrote outside of the "center" of New York, in Chicago (Shloyme Schwartz), California (Malka Heifetz Tussman), and especially in Canada (Rokhl Korn, Melekh Ravitsh). There are other important figures on the New York scene who for one reason or another evade classification, such as Kadya Molodowsky, Berish Vaynshteyn, J. L. Teller, A. Lutzky, Aaron Zeitlin, Gabriel Preil. And then there is the question of the many women poets, such as Rochelle Weprinsky, Rosa Goldshteyn, Anna Rapport, Esther Schumiatcher, Malka Lee, Berta Kling, Rajzel Zychlinsky, and others, whom the anthologist Ezra Korman sought to classify on their own terms in 1928 and who, in varying degrees of visibility and invisibility, continued to rise and fall with the larger waves of Yiddish literary development.

In the aftermath of the Holocaust, Yiddish poetry in America took on a new force of national purpose, even though there has been a sense of dispersal due to the diminishing number of new readers and writers. This new national purpose has none of the unity of the earlier "labor poetry," for the Yiddish language and the idea of poetry in Yiddish were radically transformed by the early modernist movements. Nonetheless, there are poets who continue to write in Yiddish, some European-born, such as Beyle Schaechter Gottesman, and others American-born and of the postwar generation.

KATHRYN HELLERSTEIN

BIBLIOGRAPHY

Aaron, Frieda W. *Bearing the Unbearable: Yiddish and Polish Poetry in the Ghettos and Concentration Camps.* Albany: State University of New York, 1990.

Feldman, Yael S. *Modernism and Cultural Transfer: Gabriel Preil and the Tradition of Jewish Literary Bilingualism.* Cincinnati: Hebrew Union College Press, 1985.

Glatshteyn, Yankev. *Selected Poems of Yankev Glatshteyn.* Edited and translated by Richard J. Fein. Philadelphia: Jewish Publication Society, 1987.

Hadda, Janet R. *Yankev Glatshteyn.* Boston: Twayne, 1980.

Halpern, Moyshe-Leyb. *In New York: A Selection,* edited and translated by Kathryn Hellerstein. Philadelphia: Jewish Publication Society, 1982.

Harshav, Benjamin and Barbara, eds., *American Yiddish Poetry: A Bilingual Anthology,* co-translated by Kathryn Hellerstein, Brian McHale, and Anita Norich. Los Angeles: University of California Press, 1986.

Hellerstein, Kathryn. "A Question of Tradition: Women Poets in Yiddish." In *Handbook of American-Jewish Literature: Analytical Guide to Topics, Themes, and Sources,* edited by Lewis Fried. Pp. 195–237. Westport, Conn.: Greenwood Press, 1988.

Howe, Irving, and Greenberg, Eliezer, eds. *A Treasury of Yiddish Poetry.* New York: Schocken, 1969.

———; Wisse, Ruth R.; and Shmeruk, Khone, eds. *The Penguin Book of Modern Yiddish Verse.* New York: Viking, 1987.

———, with Kenneth Libo. *World of Our Fathers: The Journey of the East European Jews to America and the Life They Found and Made.* New York: Harcourt Brace Jovanovich, 1976.

Leksikon fun der Nayer Yidisher Literatur. (Biographical Dictionary of Modern Yiddish Literature.) 8 vols. 1956–1981.

Liptzin, Sol. *The Maturing of Yiddish Literature.* New York: Jonathan David, 1970.

Madison, Charles. *Yiddish Literature: Its Scope and Major Writers.* New York: Ungar, 1968.

Minkoff, N. B. *Pionirn fun Yidisher Poezye in Amerike: Dos Sotsiale Lid.* (Pioneers of Yiddish Poetry in America: The Social Poetry). 3 vols. New York: N. B. Minkoff, 1956.

Novershtern, Avraham. "'Who Would Have Believed That a Bronze Statue Can Weep': The Poetry of Anna Margolin." *Prooftexts* 10, 3 (September 1990): 435–467.

Pratt, Norma Fain. "Culture and Radical Politics: Women Yiddish Writers, 1890–1940." *American Jewish History* 70 (September 1980): 68–90.

Roback, A. A. *The Story of Yiddish Literature.* New York: Yiddish Scientific Institute, 1940.

Rosenfeld, Morris. *Songs from the Ghetto,* edited and translated by Leo Wiener, 1898. New York: Irvington Publishers, rpt. 1970.

Schwartz, I. J. *Kentucky.* Translated by Gertrude W. Dubrovsky. Tuscaloosa: University of Alabama Press, 1990.

Tabachnick, A. *Dikhter un Dikhtung* (Poets and Poetry). New York: A. Tabachnick, 1965.

Wisse, Ruth R. *A Little Love in Big Manhattan: Two Yiddish Poets.* Cambridge: Harvard University Press, 1988.

Politics. Perhaps no other ethnic group in the United States has been so intensely and widely involved in national politics as Jewish Americans have been in the twentieth century. Few other groups have been so preoccupied with issues and causes. Certainly, no other relatively economically successful group has been as consistently liberal, voting and lobbying for civil liberties for unpopular groups and individuals, civil rights for blacks and other minorities, and social justice for the economically disadvantaged. And probably no other group has so extensively defined its own ethnic identity through its political behavior.

The enthusiasm of Jews for American politics began early, stemming from a deep appreciation of their position in the new American republic. Detachment from politics had been the appropriate posture in Europe for a people who felt themselves to be in exile, but that was not the way most American Jews felt about the United States. There was a remarkable exchange of mutual admiration between the Jewish congregations in Savannah, Newport, Philadelphia, New York, Charleston, and Richmond and President George Washington. Washington set two basic themes that no European leader had done before. Like so many of his contemporaries, he spoke of Egyptian oppression and the "spiritual blessings of that people whose God is Jehovah." More significantly, he explicitly repudiated the Enlightenment concept of tolerating Jews by insisting that in the United States "all possess alike liberty of conscience and immunities of citizenship." He went on, "It is now no more that toleration is spoken of, as if it was by the indulgence of one class of people, that another enjoyed the exercise of their inherent natural rights."

Here was a new concept of rights—not privileges—and of citizenship, which was defined solely by obedience to a noncoercive set of rules established to permit and encourage the free exercise of religion, speech, enterprise, and political action. Washington told the Jews of Newport, "For happily the government of the United States, which gives to bigotry no sanction, to persecution no assistance, requires only that they who live under its protection should demean themselves as good citizens."

Many Jews wondered at their good fortune in the new republic. One of them, a 31-year old physician, speaking on the occasion of the consecration of a new synagogue in Savannah on July 21, 1820, praised the Constitution as the "palladium of our rights." He sent his address to ex-

Presidents Thomas Jefferson and James Madison, each of whom wrote back to thank him. Jefferson urged that Jews soon take their positions in politics and government. But Jews already had become active in politics in several communities in the United States by 1820, as one state after another abandoned its religious qualifications for voting and holding office.

No religious or ethnic group was more fired by the controversy between the Jeffersonians and the Federalists over the French Revolution and the Napoleonic regime that followed, siding with the pro-French Jeffersonians, partly because the revolutionaries had abolished discriminatory laws against Jews. Jews were especially outraged by the Alien and Sedition Acts of 1789, which were aimed at France and foreigners. When President Adams proclaimed a national fast day on May 9, 1789, most Christian clergymen used the occasion to denounce the French republicans. Not so with Rabbi Gershon Mendes of Shearith Israel in New York, who defended the principles of republicanism and democracy to his congregation.

No prominent Jew opposed Jefferson and the republican cause. Jefferson had written the Disestablishment Act in Virginia, and Madison, soon to become the fourth president of the United States, had introduced the First Amendment to the United States Constitution prohibiting the establishment of a national religion, having also attempted to pass an amendment to prohibit individual states from interfering with freedom of conscience.

Wherever the followers of Jefferson organized political clubs, Jews could be found in their midst, especially in New York, where the Jewish population had been stabilized for 70 years at about 400. This was also true in Maryland, South Carolina, and other places where there were Jewish communities. Since their entrance into American politics sometimes raised ugly anti-Semitic attacks from the opposition, Jews reacted by being more strongly supportive of the Jeffersonian party. Responding to an anti-Semitic attack in a Federalist newspaper, one of the Jewish leaders of the Democratic Society of Philadelphia said, "I am a Jew, and if for no other reason than that I am a Republican." One Republican paper in Pennsylvania was labeled by the opposition as "the Jew Press." Usually when Jews were disparaged, they found Republicans defending them, as in Pennsylvania, where the so-called "Jew Bill" to enfranchise the Jews was made an issue of the campaign of 1819, and, as in Maryland, where two prominent Jews were elected to the City Council of Baltimore immediately following passage of the bill although there probably were fewer than 200 Jews in the state at the time.

New York City was fast overtaking Charleston as the leading Jewish city in the United States. Jewish influence in the Democratic Party grew rapidly there. Emanuel B. Hart was a power in Tammany Hall for almost half a decade after enthusiastically campaigning for Jackson in 1832, eventually being elected to Congress and serving in the national government in various capacities. Foremost of the Jews who were active in politics was Mordecai M. Noah, playwright, mystic, Zionist, and politician, who had been appointed by Madison as consul-general in Tunis in 1813 and who later became an editor and publisher of a series of pro-Democratic newspapers and surveyor of the Port of New York under Jackson.

Though small in number—perhaps no more than 15,000 by 1840—Jews were probably one of the most solidly Democratic groups in the country from the election of Jefferson in 1800 through the election of dark-horse James K. Polk 40 years later. In the South, a majority remained Democrats throughout the Civil War and during the antebellum period, but in the North a series of developments dissipated Jewish affection for the party of Jefferson and Jackson. Perhaps as many as 100,000 German Jews immigrated to the United States between 1848 and the beginning of the Civil War. Some, having fought in the abortive revolution of 1848, brought with them principles of political liberalism that led them to be dissatisfied with the national leadership of both major parties. While the Democrats compromised with slavery in domestic affairs, the Whigs in many states were allied with nativist movements, which, although not always anti-Semitic, were antiforeign. An anti-Semitic commercial treaty with Switzerland that had been negotiated during the Whig administration of Millard Fillmore was consummated in 1855 under a Democratic president, Franklin Pierce. By the fall of 1857, Jewish communities were protesting throughout the nation. A national protest convention was held in Baltimore with representatives coming from as far west as Chicago and St. Louis, but President James Buchanan refused to renegotiate the treaty, which permitted Swiss cantons to expel American Jews in accordance with their law.

In the Italian city of Bologna, papal guards kidnapped a Jewish boy alleged by papal authorities to have been secretly baptized four years earlier by a Catholic maid servant. Mass meetings of American Jews were held in a number of cities protesting the affair. In New York, where the Jewish population probably was not larger than 40,000, about 2000 Jews attended a meeting that demanded that President Buchanan intervene with the pope, but Buchanan, through his secretary of state, replied that the United States could do nothing.

While some Jews feared the influence of the Catholic Church, few joined the anti-Catholic nativist movement, although one of them who did so—an ardent champion of alcoholic temperance—was elected to Congress three times from Pennsylvania. The general view of Jews was expressed by one candidate for the state senate from Charleston in 1855, who declared that Jews themselves would not be safe if bigotry against Catholics should prevail.

The political choices confronting German Jewish immigrants as they arrived in the United States made them ripe for a third-party movement, and a large proportion of them welcomed the new Republican Party, whose very name was attractive to the German immigrants. In New York, Philadelphia, and Chicago (where four out of five persons who organized a Republican mass meeting were Jews), Jews were disproportionately active in the formation of the new party. Although many older Democrats remained faithful to their party in New York even though several of them were active abolitionists, by 1860 Democrats were the exception among Jews, except in the South. Wherever southern influence was strong, most Jews acquiesced in the southern point of view, but in New Orleans several prominent Jews opposed slavery. In the North and the Middle West, Jews found a champion in Abraham Lincoln, whose deep humanitarianism became quickly apparent to them and whose actions on issues of specific concern were consistently sympathetic. When Congress passed a law providing that chaplains be Christians, Lincoln promptly responded to the pleas of Jews and intervened to have the law changed. When General Ulysses S. Grant issued an anti-Semitic order giving all Jews in the state of Tennessee 24 hours to leave the area as an awkward and bigoted way of dealing with tradesmen, Lincoln, who learned of the order from a small shopkeeper in Paduka, Kentucky, immediately wrote a message directing its cancellation.

A disproportionate number of Jews in both

the North and South supported the Union and the Republican Party at the war's end. President Grant gave assurances that he regretted his wartime anti-Semitic order, and during his administration went out of his way to be friendly to Jews, even offering one of them a Cabinet post for the first time in history and making several other appointments of Jews. Although relatively small in numbers, Jews became increasingly active in politics, running for and being elected to office in the 1870s, not just in New York and Illinois, but in places as far away as Utah and the Territory of Washington.

Between 1860 and 1890, when the American Jewish population increased from somewhere between 200,000 and 300,000 to approximately 900,000, with more than half of the newcomers coming from Eastern Europe, Jews became more active in politics. Some received diplomatic and administrative posts. Others became leaders in party organizations, serving widely in both parties, but most of them probably voted Republican in most presidential elections, as did the country as a whole. Their activity in both political parties led to the election of some of them to high office, even from places where there were relatively few Jewish voters. In the late eighteenth century, Jewish congressmen were elected from New Orleans, Gloversville (New York), and Baltimore. In 1900, the two opposing candidates for mayor in Cincinnati were Jews. One was elected for two successive terms, and the other was nominated by his party for governor in 1911.

At the turn of the century, Jews had no pronounced political party loyalty. While most of the English Jewish periodicals tended to be Republican, the growing Yiddish press was sharply divided. In New York City, the *Tagblatt* and the *Morning Journal* were Republican; but the *Warheit* and the *Day* supported the Democrats, while the important *Daily Forward* was Socialist. Between the election of William McKinley and the beginning of World War I, nearly 2 million Jewish immigrants came to the United States. Most of them were refugees from the anti-Semitism and poverty of Eastern Europe. Crowding the tenements of the slums of New York and to a lesser extent Boston, Chicago, and Philadelphia, a large number of them found the parties of the radical left to be sympathetic. Of the rest, probably more chose Republican than Democratic presidential candidates in every election from 1900 to 1928 with the exception of 1916.

As immigrants arrived from cities, towns, and villages in Russia and Poland, some of them attributed their good fortune to Republican presidents usually in power. They could not help but be awed when President William McKinley appeared on September 16, 1897, with his Cabinet for the laying of a cornerstone for a Washington synagogue. And they were buoyed by actions taken by philo-Semitic Presidents Theodore Roosevelt and William Howard Taft. As far back as 1895, when he was police commissioner in New York, Roosevelt won the loyalty of many Jews when he assigned only Jewish policemen to protect a notorious German anti-Semite who arrived in New York to address a large public meeting. Roosevelt, whose humanitarianism was neither as broad nor as deep as Lincoln's, went out of his way to praise Jews. He was the first president to invite the Rabbinical Conference of the United States to visit him in the White House. Twice, he predicted that a Jew would be elected president. In 1902, he appointed Oscar Straus to succeed ex-President Benjamin Harrison as American representative to the arbitration court at The Hague and four years later brought Straus into his Cabinet as secretary of commerce and labor, stating "I want to show Russia what we think of the Jews in this country." When prominent American Jews drew up a petition to send to the czar protesting the massacre of Jews in the Kishinev pogrom of 1903, Roosevelt endorsed the document before forwarding it to the czar.

By the 1904 election, there were about 700,000 Jews in New York City alone. Although perhaps not more than one-tenth of those were eligible to vote, the immigrants from Eastern Europe embraced American politics vigorously. By 1910, the Jews of New York represented about 13 percent of the eligible voters in the city and were courted by politicians. There, in Boston, Chicago, Philadelphia, and other places, Jews organized a variety of political clubs, taking stands on candidates and issues. The Jews from Eastern Europe did not frown on the use of Jewish names or specifically Jewish appeals at mass meetings, as did many of their German coreligionists. Congressmen who took strong stands against a Russian trade treaty that gave the imperial government the right to screen and deny visas to American Jews on a selective basis or who advocated liberal immigration were rewarded with Jewish votes. The tendency to support Republican candidates for the presidency was reversed by Woodrow Wilson, whose idealism and professorial background commended him to Jewish voters, whose loyalty was reinforced by his appointment of Louis D. Brandeis to the Supreme Court. After Wilson's election in 1916, the *American Hebrew* glowed with editorial praise, and for the first time since 1856 it was clear that more Jews voted for a Democratic candidate for president than for the Republican nominee.

Wilson's victory was paralleled by the success of a growing number of Democrats elsewhere. Two of the three Jews in the New York State Senate in 1916 were Republicans, but there were nine Democrats in the Assembly to five Republicans and two Socialists. Of the two Jewish congressmen elected from the city, one was a Republican and the other a Socialist. In Chicago, rapidly becoming the second largest Jewish city in the nation, the major Jewish political figures were Republican, but a rising group of young Democrats was gaining influence. In the Congress itself, the two most influential Jews were Republicans, including the senior Republican on the Military Affairs Committee, Julius Kahn of California.

In 1920, the number of Jews elected to Congress increased from 6 to 11, all Republicans, except for Socialist Meyer London from New York. In the 1920s, it probably seemed to most Jews that there were no crucial issues dividing the major parties. For the confirmed Socialist, the choice was easy. For others, it was more convenient to stick to the Republican Party than to change. The country was prosperous. Jews were moving ahead. Republican politicians, supported by occasional addresses from Republican presidents praising American Jews, continued to recruit the Jewish vote. Although the administration of Warren Harding was lackluster (and Harding himself had voted against the appointment of Brandeis to the Supreme Court), he was saluted after his death by the B'nai B'rith for having been free of prejudice, and his successor, Calvin Coolidge, was welcomed as "a sturdy protector of law and order." His address at the laying of a cornerstone for the Jewish Community Center in Washington, D.C., was called by the *Jewish Advocate* in Boston "the most remarkable tribute to the Jewish people in America ever expressed by any president."

But change was impending in the loyalties of American Jewish voters, who sent one of their own, a Democrat, to Congress from Rochester, New York, in 1922. Despite the election of Coolidge in 1924, three new Jewish Democrats went

to Congress from New York City. Each election brought more Jews to high public office, and most of the new figures were Democrats. In 1926, five Jewish Democrats were elected to Congress, three Republicans, and one Socialist. For New York Jews, the turning point came in 1924. Alfred E. Smith ran for governor, cutting into the usually high Jewish Socialist vote despite the popularity of candidate Norman Thomas. And Thomas ran ahead of Theodore Roosevelt, Jr., the Republican candidate, in some of the most heavily Jewish assembly districts. The enthusiasm of Jews for Al Smith in New York, where almost half of the country's Jews lived, was shared in other large cities during the 1928 campaign for the presidency, where analysis of wards and assembly districts showed that Smith, a liberal Irish Catholic from the Lower East Side of New York, won an overwhelming majority of Jewish voters. The trend was definitely against the Republicans. In 1930, six of eight Jews elected to Congress were Democrats. Of the three Jewish governors elected, two were Democrats, from New Mexico and Illinois, and the third an independent from Oregon. In New York State, where Franklin D. Roosevelt was elected governor, his running mate for lieutenant governor, the Jewish Herbert Lehman, had the largest plurality of any candidate on the ticket.

The election of Franklin D. Roosevelt in 1932 marked the beginning of a 56-year period in which Democratic presidential candidates captured a large majority of the Jewish vote, a phenomenon unparalleled in the history of American politics. In voting districts that were overwhelmingly Jewish, the Democratic vote often went over 80 percent in 1932, the first of 15 presidential elections in which Jews, regardless of their socioeconomic status, provided Democratic candidates with a higher percentage of votes than any other voting group in the population, with the exception in just a few of those years of American blacks. The long-range switch from Republican allegiance in the 1920s to the predominantly Democratic loyalties of the mid- and late-twentieth century of American Jews was dramatically expressed in the party enrollment figures for Ward 14 in the city of Boston, a consistently heavy Jewish area from 1924 until the 1960s. In 1928, 78 percent of the voters there were registered as Republicans, compared to only 14 percent by 1952. In 1926, 75.2 percent of Ward 14's electors voted in the Republican primary; in 1952, only about 10.1 percent, a drop of 65.1

percent. It was a pattern that prevailed in other cities. By 1942, the head of the Democratic Party in the Bronx, the most Jewish county in the United States, claimed that it was also the most Democratic county north of the Mason-Dixon line. Wherever Jews have lived in great concentration since 1936, they have been heavily Democratic. The results of national opinion surveys in 1940 and 1944 showed that more than 90 out of every 100 Jews in the nation voted for Franklin Roosevelt.

The Jewish shift to Roosevelt in 1932 and 1936, while it was enthusiastically large, paralleled the tendency in the nation as a whole. A core element in the great coalition that Roosevelt had forged to win sweeping victories were the children of the great turn of the century immigration, and Italian and Polish Americans also warmed to the prospect of a New Deal. But Jews persisted in the Democratic attachment long after large numbers in other minority groups became disenchanted, and Jews alone among the better-paid and best-educated denominational groups voted Democratic. Jews were the only group in which differences in Democratic and Republican strength could not be correlated with differences in occupational prestige, income, or education.

It was a singular phenomenon. Jews returned massively to the party of Andrew Jackson just at the time they began to climb the class ladder rapidly. So far had the Jewish swing gone to the liberal party, that one study in 1952 showed that a mere 6 percent of Jewish college graduates called themselves Republican, whereas the overwhelming majority of college graduates in all other denominations were Republican.

The high point of the Jewish Democratic vote came in 1944. Whatever the type of city or neighborhood, wherever Jews were concentrated, marginal voters and habitual nonvoters voting for the first time joined activists in casting ballots for Franklin Roosevelt, partly to express their thankfulness to the architect of the New Deal at home and victory over Nazism in Europe. In middle-class neighborhoods, in upper-class neighborhoods, in big cities, in the suburbs, the Jewish vote for Roosevelt was overwhelming, often going over 90 percent. Jewish Democratic strength had to come down from its zenith in 1944, but it diminished only slightly in 1948. The combined vote for Harry S Truman, the Democratic candidate, and Henry Wallace, the Progressive candidate, was almost as high in Jew-

ish assembly districts and wards as the vote for F. D. R. had been four years before, despite the fact that the war was over, anti-Semitism had subsided, the survival of world Jewry was no longer an issue, and American Jews were prosperous. Zionism may have been a factor, since it was Truman who prior to the 1948 election recognized the new State of Israel. But both parties had adopted pro-Israel platforms, and some Jews were critical that Truman had stalled too long before helping Israel.

In 1952, General Dwight D. Eisenhower, the popular hero who had distinguished himself in the war against Nazism and as a benefactor of the Jews, swept the nation off its feet as the Republican candidate in 1952. There were many reasons why Jews might have been influenced, as other voters were, by such factors as income, occupation, and education. Roosevelt had been dead seven years, Israel was no longer a partisan issue, both candidates were united in their opposition to Stalinism. Many Jews were disillusioned with the Wallace movement and other radical causes. The Republican nominee and the wing of the party that had nominated him accepted the main outlines of the New Deal. Eisenhower had little to say against the liberal welfare state, only promised to run it more efficiently. Yet, about 75 percent of the American Jewish voters chose his erudite and liberal opponent, Governor Adlai E. Stevenson of Illinois.

One detailed study of Jewish voting behavior in the 1952 election revealed patterns that would go far toward explaining the persistence of Jewish Democratic voting for the next 36 years. It was found that it was not the poorer Jews, the older Jews, the East European Jews, or even the more Jewish Jews (religiously identified) who voted for the Democratic candidate. Those Jews who were most Democratic were preoccupied with liberal political issues. And they were the Jews who had replaced ritual Orthodox Judaism with a strong Jewish psychological and cultural identification. Jewish voters were beginning to think of themselves as liberals because they were Jewish and as Jews, in part, because they were liberals. Since they identified liberal issues with Democratic candidates, they supported Stevenson and other Democratic candidates who followed him.

Survey after survey showed not only that Jews were well informed about politics, but also that they were extraordinarily active in politics, mainly because of their interest in liberal issues.

More than any other group, they disapproved of the witch hunts of Senator Joseph McCarthy against alleged Communists and supported civil liberties generally. More than any other white group, they supported the Fair Employment Practices Commission and other civil rights legislation and the Supreme Court decision in 1954 desegregating the public schools. More than any other well-to-do white group, they supported economic programs to transfer income to the disadvantaged. Wherever liberal Republicans ran for the Senate or other offices, they tended to enlist Jewish support, but the large majority of liberal candidates in the 1950s, 1960s, and 1970s were Democrats.

The tendency of Jews to support Democrats was not an indication of mere party loyalty. It was clearly an identification with a cluster of issues that Jews identified as questions of fundamental liberalism. The focus on issues went back to the early part of the century, when Jews formed educational clubs to influence voters without regard to party affiliations. Politicians noted repeatedly that Jews frequently split their tickets between major party candidates or even voted for minor party candidates because of their preoccupation with issues. In the early decades of the twentieth century, Jews in the cities were disproportionately involved in efforts to reform city governments. Socialists, who often were in the forefront of local reform movements, attracted Jewish voters for that reason as well as their position on national and international issues. The large minority of Jews—many of them working class—who discussed anarchism, socialism, and other radical movements created a tradition of preoccupation with political issues from a liberal perspective that persisted to the time of their grandchildren and great-grandchildren. The tradition of voting for Socialist candidates continued, as Jews supported liberal third-party candidates much more than other groups, particularly in New York City, where they were influential in the formation of the American Labor Party and the Liberal Party.

In 1956, when Eisenhower was reelected by an even larger landslide than he had achieved four years earlier, more than two out of every three Jews still voted for Stevenson, who opposed him once more. Four years later, a larger proportion of Jews voted for John F. Kennedy, the Democratic candidate and the first Catholic to be nominated for the presidency, than did Catholics, in some districts by more than 75 and 80 percent.

Lopsided victories also were won by Democrats Lyndon Johnson in 1964 and Hubert H. Humphrey in 1968, the candidates most clearly identified as liberals, against the more conservative Republicans, Barry Goldwater and Richard M. Nixon. The Democratic candidate for the presidency in 1972, Senator George McGovern, was seen as much too liberal by most Americans, who preferred to reelect Richard Nixon in a landslide victory. Although McGovern won less than one-third of the white Gentile vote, two out of every three Jews chose him. Johnson did better among the Jews of Chicago than he did among all voters in his home state of Texas; Humphrey won a higher proportion of Jewish votes in Los Angeles than he did from the voters of the state he had represented with distinction in the United States Senate, Minnesota; McGovern was more enthusiastically endorsed by the Jewish voters of New York than in his home state of North Dakota, where he had been enormously popular; and in 1976, Democratic candidate Jimmy Carter did much better among the Jews of Philadelphia than he did in Georgia, where he had been a successful governor, winning slightly more than 70 percent of all Jewish votes in the country.

What made the persistence of Jewish Democratic loyalty so striking was that Jews as a group had become more affluent and presumably had a vested interest in the success of Republican candidates, who tended to favor less spending and lower taxes, and that Republican presidents had shown a strong tendency to support Israel in their foreign policies toward the Middle East. The willingness of Jews to vote for third-party candidates was revealed in the 1980 campaign, when President Jimmy Carter ran for reelection against the extremely popular governor of California, Ronald Reagan. Even though Carter was a southern Democrat, a born-again Christian, and seen by many Americans as a failed president destined to defeat, he received more Jewish votes than Governor Reagan (about 44 percent to 39 percent) as the candidate perceived to be the more liberal of the two. But Congressman John Anderson of Ohio, also a born-again Christian, running on an independent liberal platform, received 15 percent of the Jewish vote, compared to only 7 percent of all votes. Since Anderson had positioned himself to the liberal side of Carter, almost 60 percent of the Jewish vote went to either the Democratic or the independent liberal candidate, compared to only 46 percent of the vote as a whole.

The vote in 1984 once again showed the Jewish penchant for liberal issues. Ronald Reagan, president during one of the most prosperous times in American history, was extremely popular in the nation. The Reagan administration had been staunch in its support of Israel. The Republican Party targeted about $2 million in a specific campaign to win Jewish votes, probably about four times as much as spent by the Democrats.

The attention paid by the Republican national party to Jewish voters was remarkable on the surface, since Jews constituted less than 3 percent of the population in 1984. Yet, they made up 6 percent of the electorate and much higher proportions in urban states, where they constituted a pivotal voting group because of the system by which the winner in each state takes all of its Electoral College votes. Jews were important in American politics far out of proportion to their numbers for other reasons, too. They voted heavily in primaries, contributed generously to campaign funds, participated actively in campaigns as volunteers and expert advisers, and had a 90 percent turnout in presidential elections, compared to less than 60 percent for the population as a whole. By 1984, Jews were the most active of all groups in the American national political system in proportion to their numbers, playing important roles in the federal bureaucracy, in the court system, and in many state and local governments. Eight of them were United States senators and 30 were members of the House of Representatives. Given President Reagan's pro-Israel stance and the domestic economic recovery attributed to his fiscal and tax policies, the Republican decision to woo Jewish voters particularly seemed like a good investment at the time.

Once again, Jews were preoccupied by liberal issues. Surveys showed that more than any other group of whites, they strongly identified with Mondale in his advocacy of civil liberties, civil rights, health care, and the separation of church and state. They were repulsed by the support given to Reagan from fundamentalist religious leaders and Reagan's seeming indifference to the plight of the extremely disadvantaged. Reagan improved his percentage of the vote of all white voters between 1980 and 1984 from 55 to 66 percent, but he actually slipped a point among Jews, who voted overwhelmingly (66 percent) for the liberal Democratic candidate, former Vice-President Walter F. Mondale.

Four years later, the gap in the Democratic vote between Jewish Americans and other whites was greater than it had been since 1944. Whereas white voters generally gave Michael Dukakis, the governor of Massachusetts, only 40 percent of their vote, Jewish Americans, now more affluent and therefore supposed to be more likely to vote conservatively, gave the liberal Democratic candidate 70 percent of their vote in a contest against Vice-President George Bush. Once again, the Republicans claimed correctly to have supported Israel strongly. Bush's campaign promise of no new taxes should have appealed to more affluent voters. Although more than two-thirds of all voters who earned more than $30,000 a year voted for the Republican candidate, more than two-thirds of all Jewish voters who earned more than $30,000 a year voted for the liberal Democrat. Jews voted for the man who was more likely to raise taxes to help the disadvantaged, strengthen the inner-city schools, and support a costly health insurance program. This was consistent with their positions on the issues as revealed by surveys showing that a significantly higher proportion of Jews than non-Jews favored spending more money to help the poor, supported government programs such as welfare and food stamps, were willing to raise taxes, and supported the American Civil Liberties Union. Compared to other whites, Jews were highly favorable toward the National Association for the Advancement of Colored People and the National Organization for Women. They strongly supported civil liberties and civil rights for all persons and opposed the mixing of religion and politics. In presidential politics, preoccupation with those issues made them Democrats.

When asked to identify themselves as liberals or conservatives, the number of Jewish liberals was twice the number of Jewish conservatives in the 1980s, with liberals outnumbering conservatives by 11 percentage points in 1988. Among other whites, conservatives exceeded liberals by 17 percentage points, and party identification was split evenly between Republicans and Democrats. But among Jews, Democrats outnumbered Republicans by a four-to-one margin (60 percent to 15 percent).

That Jews continue to vote overwhelmingly not just for liberal candidates for president but for liberal candidates for Congress and governor, too, probably stems in part from the secularization of Jewish life in the United States. The vast majority of Jewish voters are disposed to oppose any candidate who seems sympathetic to breaching the wall between church and state. Although most third- and fourth-generation American Jews gave up the ritual commandments of Torah, they clung to a Jewish ethnic consciousness that emphasized ethical commandments. Even as they left ritual life behind, they focused on their Jewish identity in the celebrations of Passover and Hanukkah by connecting them to important contemporary political issues, in the case of Hanukkah to the celebration of religious freedom and the separation of church and state in the United States and with Passover to the contemporary struggle to free Soviet or Ethiopian Jews, or as was commonly done in the 1960s, to the fight of black Americans for civil rights and social justice.

In the United States, Passover, the commemoration of a particular tribal experience, has been universalized as a call to justice for the liberation of the poor and the oppressed everywhere, and many Jews hold seders calling for the liberation of women or minority groups. One of the most interesting studies to emerge from the 1984 National Survey of American Jews authorized by the American Jewish Committee was that more Jews (86 percent) attended a Passover seder than attended Yom Kippur services (68 percent). Jews who celebrated only one of four holidays specified in the survey (usually Passover) were much more liberal than those who practiced at least two of them, but Jews who were not involved in Jewish life at all—not even Passover—were much less liberal than the others. The noninvolved Jews had no way of relating their Jewish heritage to politics. The more ritually involved Jews were less likely to apply their Jewishness to a universal liberal politics. Passover-only Jews were most liberal of all. Such Jews were unlikely to know which prophet (Isaiah) in the Torah enjoins Jews to "seek justice; oppose oppression, defend the orphan; plead for the widow" or in what book (Deuteronomy) they are commanded to "execute justice for the fatherless and widow and loveth the stranger,'" but they had a general idea that such Jewish values confirmed their Jewishness in their political actions.

The tendency for American Jews to express their Jewishness by activity in the community and in American politics was reinforced at election time by mainline rabbis who often linked their advice on the candidates to the ideal of *tzdekah* (justice). Perhaps the attitude of well-to-do secularized Jews toward *tzdekah* in American politics was not just an expression of altruism against self-interest, as Conservative Jews sometimes argued. By voting for a politics of *tzdekah*, Jews may still have identified with the historic position of Jews as relatively powerless outsiders. Although non-Jews in the United States may regard Jewish doctors, lawyers, professors, or corporate executives as persons of power and status, such Jews still may feel somewhat insecure in American society, as indicated by surveys in the late 1980s that showed them to be concerned about anti-Semitism.

The selective secularization of certain Jewish values, mainly *tzdekah*, as applied to American politics, became a way in which Jews identified themselves in the decades following World War II. Even as they began to drink and eat like non-Jews, divorce as frequently as non-Jews, and play sports and attend sporting contests as much as non-Jews, they continued to vote in a different way, especially those whose education, occupations, and income were most similar. Nothing quite like it had ever happened with respect to Jews in any other society; nothing like it had happened with respect to any non-Jewish group in American society. A persistently large proportion of American Jews displayed an inordinate preoccupation with liberal issues in American politics, which they tied to their Jewish identity and in a vague way to Jewish values. Perceptive non-Jews sometimes noticed the connection between American political issues and Jewish values, as when the abolitionist Republican Senator Ben Wade told the pro-slavery Senator Judah P. Benjamin that he was an "Israelite with Egyptian principles" or when President Woodrow Wilson, responding to someone who had sympathized on the difficulty that nominee Louis D. Brandeis was having in being approved by the Senate as a Supreme Court justice because he was Jewish, replied, "but he would not be Mr. Brandeis if he were not a Jew." *See also* Left, The; Neoconservatism; New Left.

LAWRENCE H. FUCHS

BIBLIOGRAPHY

Cohn, Werner. "The Politics of American Jews." In *The Jews: Social Patterns of an American Group*, edited by Marshall Sklare. New York: Free Press, 1958. Pp. 614–626.

Fuchs, Lawrence H. *The Political Behavior of American Jews*. New York: Free Press, 1956.

———, ed. "Jews and American Politics." Special edition of the *American Jewish Historical Quarterly* 66 (December 1976).

Rothman, Stanley, and Lichter, S. Robert. *Roots of Radicalism: Jews, Christians, and the New Left*. New York: Oxford University Press, 1982.

Singer, David. "American Jews as Voters: The 1986 Elections." New York: American Jewish Committee, December 1986.

Weyl, Nathaniel. *The Jew in American Politics*. New York: Arlington House, 1968.

Whitfield, Stephen J. *American Space: Jewish Time*. Hamden, Conn.: Archon Books, 1988. Chaps. 5 and 6.

Pool, David de Sola

Pool, David de Sola (1885–1970). From 1907 until 1956, David de Sola Pool served as rabbi of Congregation Shearith Israel, the historic Spanish and Portuguese Synagogue of New York City. He then served as rabbi emeritus until his death in 1970. A leading voice for the Sephardim of the United States, he was an active communal and civic leader and also a prolific author.

Born in London, Pool pursued his rabbinic studies at Jews' College and then at Hildesheimer Rabbinical Seminary in Berlin. In 1917 he married Tamar Hirshenson, who was also to become a leader in the Jewish community. She served as national president of Hadassah from 1939 to 1943, among other positions of leadership in Jewish and Zionist organizations.

During the first decades of the twentieth century, Pool worked actively to assist the influx of Sephardic immigrants, many of whom settled in New York's Lower East Side. He encouraged existing Jewish organizations to take a more active interest in assisting the Sephardim. The Sisterhood of Shearith Israel established settlement houses downtown for the benefit of the Sephardic newcomers.

Pool served in positions of leadership in numerous Jewish and communal endeavors. He was the president of the New York Board of Rabbis (1916–1917), field organizer and director of army camp work of the Jewish Welfare Board during World War I (1917–1918), regional director for Palestine and Syria of the Joint Distribution Committee (1920–1921), president of the Synagogue Council of America (1938–1940), and president of the American Jewish Historical Society (1955–1956). He was founder and president of the Union of Sephardic Congregations (1928) and served as its president for over three decades. He was a United States delegate to the NATO Atlantic Congress in London (1959).

A scholar of Jewish liturgy, de Sola Pool wrote a study of the Kaddish (1909; reprinted in 1964). He edited and translated the Sephardic liturgy, the prayer books published by the Union of Sephardic Congregations, and the Ashkenazic liturgy, under the auspices of the Rabbinical Council of America.

As rabbi of the oldest congregation in North America, Pool took special pride in the history of his congregation. He authored *Portraits Etched in Stone* (1952), a comprehensive study of the ancient cemeteries of Shearith Israel, together with biographies of those individuals interred in them. In honor of the 300th anniversary of Shearith Israel, he and his wife wrote *An Old Faith In The New World* (1955), which offered a thorough historical study of the congregation. Over the course of his life, he published many studies in the fields of American Jewish history, contemporary religious issues, general Jewish history, Jewish literature, education, Jewish thought, Sephardica, and Zionism as well as numerous sermons and addresses.

A man of dignity and deep spiritual sensitivity, David de Sola Pool was a great spiritual leader of Shearith Israel. Through his communal activity and his writings, he provided inspiration and guidance to many thousands of people throughout the United States and—indeed—throughout the world.

MARC D. ANGEL

BIBLIOGRAPHY

Angel, Marc D., ed. *Rabbi David de Sola Pool: Selections from Six Decades of Sermons, Addresses and Writings*. New York: Union of Sephardic Congregations, 1980.

Pool, David and Tamar. *An Old Faith in the New World*. New York: Columbia University Press, 1955.

Potok, Chaim

Potok, Chaim (b. 1929). Brought up in the Bronx, author Chaim Potok remembers that he was "Hasidic without the beard and earlocks." His father was a Hasidic rabbi; his mother was a descendant of Hasidism. When he read *Brideshead Revisited* (as a student in a Jewish high school), he was intrigued by Evelyn Waugh's craftsmanship and the upper-class British world that was described; but what fascinated him most was the play of the imagination, the exotica of the world he was entering, the style, the writing itself, the language with which the imagination and that world was somehow presented. With that under his belt, the whole secular world was opened to his curiosity. Rebellion emerged. He broke with the formal forms of Judaism. Internalizing his rebellion, he moved into the world of the novel, into an aesthetic rebellion. At this time he realized that the rabbinic Judaism of the Talmud was rational; imagination was pagan, imagination was Greek. Although he did not become an iconoclast and did not break with his past, he did move from one area of it to another, that is, from fundamentalism to a more Western reading of the Jewish tradition, through his experience at the Jewish Theological Seminary. He now used the novel as the Greeks used tragedy, "to explore conflicts of good and bad. . . . And . . . between good and good that enabled me to open up the juices of creativity, as it were, with the novel."

By the time he was 18 or 19, young Potok had begun to experience what would later be called a core-to-core culture confrontation. Significantly, all the disciplines he encountered that were alien, exciting ideas were from the core of Western culture; he and the people he came from were in the core of the subculture. In his case, having been formed by his very urban, very Jewish world of the Bronx, but meeting with the umbrella culture, his urban and intellectual and literary wanderings produced a *zwischenmensch*, a "between-person."

In his novel *The Chosen* (1967), set in the urban Crown Heights and Williamsburg sections of Brooklyn, a baseball game brings together Danny, son of the *rebbe* and thus heir to the Hasidic dynasty, and Reuven, son of a modern Orthodox Talmudic textual scholar. Reb Saunders, the *tzaddik* (the Hasidic sect's spiritual leader), believing that there is a danger that his gifted son's soul might be dominated by the mind, communicates to him through silence; in this way he feels he will foster the values of the heart and soul. Each was combining two cultures. Each was reflecting his and Potok's own attempts as a "between-person" to explicate the role of Judaism in a secular society. The point is that Danny and Reuven symbolize the two poles within Orthodox Judaism, and lead to the confrontation between secular humanism and Orthodoxy.

In *The Chosen* and *The Promise* (1969), Potok's emphasis was on Jewish scholarship and study in an Orthodox milieu in Brooklyn. Family, neighborhood and synagogue were beautifully drawn; they were a necessary environment. True, physical poverty was present, but spiritually there was richness. Only from outside the ghetto did the influences impinge. Whether from the radio or the newspaper, or from friends or acquaintances, the news of World War II, the Holocaust, the Senator Joseph McCarthy charges all came through; from liberal and progressive Jews, like Rachel Gordon (who learned to appreciate James Joyce at Brooklyn College), further cracks in Hasidism appeared. Potok was trying to explicate the role of Judaism in a secular society.

Probably as a direct result of his interest in the tensions of faith and scholarship in his first two books, Potok's third book, *My Name is Asher Lev* (1972), concentrates on the tensions between members of one Orthodox family, and, in particular, on the possible aesthetic dimensions. Asher must become an artist, from within or without a society that does not recognize art for art's sake or its Western cultural (including Christian and pagan) antecedents. The point, as Potok has explained, is that "for Asher Lev, the cross is the aesthetic motif for solitary, protracted torment." Potok believes that any artist functioning in the secular world who has used the cross "has emptied the cross of its christological vicarious atonement content and uses it as a form only."

In *In the Beginning* (1975), Max Lurie, a Jew impressed into the Polish army, who realized he was not a full citizen, is the vehicle for David Lurie's story. At issue is anti-Semitism. At the end, having felt the suffering of the Holocaust, David, walking along the Hudson River, recognizes that the death camps have become a part of him.

Not rage but profound moral questions and guilt are the principal effects generated by the atom bomb and explored by Potok in his next novel, *The Books of Lights*, published six years later. The atom bomb becomes the "death light," and, as such, it constitutes one side of each of the many contrasts by which the several major themes are held together in a dynamically integrated whole. It may be seen to represent the side of dehumanized science against man and nature, death against life, darkness (paradoxically, as a *death* light) against light, evil against good, human pride against Divine mystery, destruction against creation, and hate against love.

Finally, in *Davita's Harp* (1988), we see a confrontation between a young woman and Orthodoxy, especially between two kinds of orthodoxies, Jewish Orthodoxy and communism, represented by her parents. In *The Gift of Asher Lev* (1991), Asher is a mature artist faced with the need to choose between order and disorder, equal and competing truths, and an artist's necessity to follow his own truth and yet not violate the traditional Orthodox way in which truth is found in the interpretation of Torah.

As a witness, Potok feels that his people are now engaged in an attempt to create for themselves a third civilization. What is needed is for Judaism to rebuild its core from the treasures of its past, fuse it with the best in secularism, and create a new philosophy, a new literature, a new world of Jewish art, a new community and take seriously the meaning of the emancipation. As a rabbi, as a religious scholar, as a secular intellectual in the Western tradition, as an American, as a *zwischenmensch*, and as a novelist, Chaim Potok is involved in the struggle to maintain the viability of Judaism as a living civilization. *See also* Fiction.

DANIEL WALDEN

BIBLIOGRAPHY
Abramson, Edward A. *Chaim Potok*. Boston: Twayne, 1986.
Walden, Daniel, editor. "The World of Chaim Potok." *Studies in American Jewish Literature* 4 (1985) (special issue).

Press, Jewish. The Jewish press, in all of its linguistic, ideological, and religious diversity, constitutes a major reservoir of Jewish-American cultural history reflecting, for better or for worse, the life and times of the communities it serves. In the several decades since the appearance of the first Jewish periodical in the United States (*The Jew*, New York, 1823–1825), approximately 2500 dailies, weeklies, monthlies, quarterlies, bulletins, and annual reports in English, German, Hebrew, Yiddish, and Judezmo have been published in most of the 50 states. Many of these serials, to be sure, failed to gain public acceptance and were short-lived; a larger number, while qualitatively inferior by today's commonly accepted canons of journalism, were moderately successful despite their establishment as purely commercial enterprises by Jewish businessmen or as vanity publications by rabbis with little or no preparation in professional journalism, while another small number of periodicals today enjoy a high circulation sustained by organizational memberships or subsidies from the local Jewish community federation.

With the rapid growth of the Jewish population in the nineteenth century through immigration from Europe, Jewish communities increasingly provided a sufficient numerical base beginning around 1870 to sustain competing weeklies in the same city, an unthinkable situation just 30 years earlier. Isaac Leeser's *Occident and American Jewish Advocate* (Philadelphia, 1843–1869), a monthly, and the *American Israelite*, a weekly founded in 1854 by Isaac M. Wise in Cincinnati as *The Israelite*, were but two of the most respected Jewish periodicals upon which readers relied for international and domestic Jewish news, entertaining short stories, sermons, and theological essays, often in the form of vituperative personal attacks on rabbinical colleagues, on doctrinal and liturgical concerns in an era when the course of Reform Judaism was being charted by Rabbi Isaac M. Wise. Wise, in turn, was countered in the eastern Jewish press by traditional spokesmen for traditional Judaism led by Isaac Leeser and later by Sabato Morais or Henry Pereira Mendes. Significantly, the *Occident* and the *American Israelite* enjoyed a national circulation and each maintained a network of correspondents who contributed local community news, even from the southern states during the Civil War, from towns as far away as the Pacific coast, from the Midwest, and from the Northeast, where the Jewish press was all but nonexistent. Together with Robert Lyon's *Asmonean* (New York, 1848–1858), "a family journal of commerce, politics, religion, and literature devoted to the interests of the American Israelites," these three organs are indispensable to historians for primary source material on Jewish communal activity and attempts at defending Jews against slanders and civil disabilities in the formative years of the United States prior to the Civil War when numerous congregations, Jewish hospitals, benevolent societies, and fraternal orders were established by American-born Jews or newly arrived German-speaking Jews from Germany, Prussia, and Central Europe. The *American Israelite* is still published in Cincinnati, making it the oldest Jewish periodical in the United States.

The earliest Jewish newspaper to be established in the South was the *Corner Stone*, started by Solomon Jacobs in New York in 1858 but later moved by him to New Orleans, where it had but a brief existence in 1860. T. K. Lyon of Richmond, Virginia, had proposed the publication of the *Hebrews' Magazine and Jewish Miscellany*, but nothing came of this beyond the issuance of a prospectus in 1842, shortly before Isaac Leeser first announced his plans for the respected and successful *Occident and American Jewish Advocate*. The inception of Jewish journalistic activity in California can be traced to the *Voice of Israel* (San Francisco, 1856–1857), co-edited by Herman M. Bien and Henry J. Labatt; no issues of this paper can be found today. Julius Eckman's *Weekly Gleaner* (San Francisco, 1857–1865) is a frequently consulted chronicle of the post-Gold Rush communities of the time. Interestingly, the earliest Jewish paper to appear in Chicago was a postconflagration latecomer on the American scene, the *Occident* (1873–1896?), variously edited by Henry Gersoni and Julius Silversmith. St. Louis was the site of the first paper for Jewish readers west of the Mississippi with its *Jewish Sentinel* (1868–1869). As with the bulk of the nineteenth-century Jewish press in the United States, no complete file of these papers exists owing to a combination of factors: namely, human carelessness, natural disasters in the form of fire, flood, and insects, or the regrettable lack of foresight by American libraries to collect Jewish Americana in decades past when ethnic studies lacked the academic respectability it enjoys today.

Although Isidor Busch's *Israels Herold* (New York, 1849) is frequently cited as the first German-language Jewish periodical (only 12 issues appeared), it was in fact preceded by *Der Israelite* (Philadelphia, 1843), a short-lived weekly edited by Julius Stern, of which only two issues were published. In 1845, another German paper, *Jedidiah* (Philadelphia), was proposed by Herman Felsenheld but never published; only following the revolutions of 1848 in Europe were there enough German Jews in America to justify the creation of a sustainable German-language press. Although the *Asmonean* of New York often contained sections in German, the first successful German Jewish weekly was *Die Deborah* (Cincinnati, 1855–1902), originally intended by its founder, Isaac M. Wise, then personally in debt with not one but two unprofitable papers, as the *Israelite's* supplement for Jewish women.

Some of the most significant and longlived Jewish newspapers of the nineteenth century were the *Jewish Messenger* (New York, 1857–1902) and the *American Hebrew* (New York, 1879–1956). Stressing the compatability of Americanization and traditional Jewish values, these papers were well patronized by non-Jewish advertisers who shrewdly cultivated an increasingly lucrative middle-class Jewish market. Each paper republished credited articles from the general press and the Jewish press in Europe and America, each ac-

cepted gossipy out-of-town social communications from local stringers dispersed throughout the country, and both papers covered the local Jewish scene, i.e., synagogal and social affairs as well as news of the fraternal and masonic orders. The poetess Emma Lazarus contributed to the *American Hebrew*, and this paper and the competing weekly *Jewish Messenger* remain invaluable primary sources for gauging the willingness of the American Jewish community to support the absorption of impoverished East European Jews beginning in the 1880s. In time, the *American Hebrew*, a stock company usually identified with the name of Philip Cowen, absorbed the *Jewish Chronicle* of Baltimore in 1880, the *Jewish Reformer* (New York) in 1886, and the *Jewish Messenger* in 1903.

Then, as now, people criticized the Jewish press for its vapidness, its lack of originality, its failure to promote creative Jewish literature and to enlighten the public, and its unwillingness to attract controversy by taking a firm editorial stand on the burning issues of the day. One anonymous critic 100 years ago bemoaned that, with few exceptions, a subscription to any of the Jewish papers, all but a few of them unprofitable business ventures, was really a form of charity as "they are not strikingly original, able or brilliant. ... There is scarcely one of them that combines literary worth with true journalistic enterprise" (*American Israelite*, July 22, 1887).

Hebrew periodicals in the nineteenth century, while few in number, can be traced to Zvi Hirsch Bernstein's *ha-Tsofeh ba-Arets ha-hadashah* (New York, 1871–1873?), a weekly publication aimed at readers in the small but growing immigrant community of intellectual Hebrew *maskilim* (lit. "enlightened ones") from Eastern Europe. With so few American contributors to call upon, Bernstein reprinted extensively from the Hebrew press in Russia, patterning his paper closely after those familiar sources. The next journalistic attempt to serve a Hebrew reading public was *Heikhal ha-'ivriyah* (Chicago, 1877–1879?), a weekly supplement to the Yiddish *Izraelitishe prese* (Chicago, 1877–1884); no issues of this Hebrew supplement can be traced today. Although Yiddish was quite understandably the vernacular language of the new immigrant arrivals in this period, various attempts to establish a Hebrew press came to fruition in the late 1880s with none of them having an obvious expectation of a profit in the absence of a popular base of support: Michael Levi Rodkinson's *ha-Kol* (New York, Chicago, 1889–1893), Ephraim Deinard's *ha-Leumi* (New York, Newark, 1888–1889), Leon Zolot-koff's literary *Keren-Or* (Chicago, 1889), and Wolf Schur's *ha-Pisgah* (New York, Baltimore, Boston, Chicago, 1889–1899). The latter publication is notable for its contributions from European Hebraists and its ardent promotion of the Zionist cause.

In marked contrast to the Hebrew press, Yiddish journalism in America catered to the public taste and reached its greatest circulation in 1916; the decrease in Jewish migration from Europe during World War I and the highly restrictive immigration acts of 1921 and 1924 doomed the Yiddish press to an irreversible decline with an aging readership. The first Yiddish paper (New York, 1870–1873) was J. K. Buchner's sporadic *Nuyorker yidishdaytshe tsaytung* (later issues were shortened to *Di yidishe tsaytung*), produced lithographically on an intermittent basis because there were presumably no printers in New York at the time capable of Yiddish printing. The second Yiddish newspaper, this edited by Zvi Hirsch Bernstein and Henry Gersoni (the latter doubling as the typesetter), was *Di idishe post* (New York, 1870–1871); although no issues have survived, it is known that before its demise it enjoyed a momentary circulation of 4000 issues owing to intense reader interest in the Franco-Prussian War. When New York's Jacob Cohen ran for a Democratic alderman post in 1871, he established with Zvi Hirsch Bernstein's financial backing a campaign paper, the *Hebrew News* (1871), noteworthy for the fact that in order to reach the multilingual Jewish public regardless of class or country of origin, it appeared with columns in Yiddish, Hebrew, English, and German. It is believed that upon his defeat at the polls, Cohen's Hebrew type passed into Bernstein's possession to be reused in the latter's *ha-Tsofeh ba-Arets hahadashah*, this country's first all-Hebrew newspaper.

Although Yiddish journalism in America is most frequently associated with the *Forverts* (the *Jewish Daily Forward*) founded in 1897 and still published as a weekly, the real success story involves the pioneering labors of the not easily discouraged Kasriel Zvi Sarasohn a quarter of a century earlier. In 1872, his first paper, the *Nu-yorker yidishe tsaytung*, ended in failure after a few months. Two years later, he met success with his *Yudishe gazetten* (New York, 1874–1928), a weekly for most of its existence except for short periods in 1881 and 1883 when the enterprising Sarasohn converted it into a daily (*Di teglikhe gazetten*) hoping to capture the expanding readership resulting from the Jewish exodus from Russia fleeing outbreaks of pogroms and discriminatory legislation following the assassination of Czar Alexander II. The immigrants, impoverished and unaccustomed to buying a Yiddish daily (none existed in all of Europe at this time), were not receptive to Sarasohn's efforts until 1885 when he again met success with the *Yidishes tageblatt*, or *Jewish Daily News* (New York, 1885–1928).

Sarasohn's Orthodox and politically conservative papers were not the only Yiddish papers; by the 1890s, as the immigrant population swelled, newspapers representing Jewish anarchists and socialists appeared in profusion with Abraham Cahan's socialist *Forverts* (New York, 1897–), containing the popular "Bintel Brief" personal advice column, being the most prominent and most enduring. With hundreds of thousands of East European immigrants arriving every year, there was not only a regional Yiddish press in Chicago (e.g., the *Yidisher kuryer*, 1887–1947) and in other major cities such as Baltimore, Boston, Philadelphia, and Providence, there was also a profusion of papers catering to specialized interests: Zionism represented by *Shulamis* (New York, 1889–1890), edited by Joseph A. Bluestone for the "Chebra Chob'bei Zion"; Nahum Meir Shaikewitz's humorous *Der land hokhem* (New York, 1893–1894); or farming as in *Der yudisher farmer* (New York, 1891–1892), published on behalf of the Baron de Hirsch Fund's Agricultural Bureau. Although the popular imagination associates Yiddish journalism with socialism and secularism, this portrayal fails to account for papers such as the *Morgen zhurnal* (New York, 1901–1928), published by Jacob Saphirstein, an Orthodox Jew politically aligned with the Republican Party, or *Di yidishe velt* (New York, 1901–1904), bankrolled by Americanization-minded German Jews led by Louis Marshall to be "everything that the existing Yiddish papers are not, namely, clean, wholesome, religious in tone; the advocate of all that makes good citizenship, and so far as politics are concerned, absolutely independent."

Regrettably, complete files of all but a few papers are nonexistent; an even sadder reality is that numerous nineteenth-century serials are known only by references to them in other papers and are not to be found in any repository. Several dozen Yiddish papers are no longer extant, and not a few Anglo-Jewish papers have completely vanished and evade consultation by regional historians, e.g., the *Northwestern Jewish Advocate* (Minneapolis-St. Paul, 1894), or two of the very early papers for women, Morris Wechsler's *Di vaybershe tsaytung* (New York, 1888) or the *Jewish Woman* (Philadelphia, 1892–1893).

Sephardic Jews in the United States, though numerically small, also sustained a Judezmo (Judeo-Spanish) press, represented by Moise Gadol's *La America* (New York, 1910–1925), Alfred Mizrahi's short-lived *La Aguila* (New York, 1912), *La Boz del Pueblo* (New York, 1915–1919), *El Luzero* (New York, 1926–1927), and the most enduring Judezmo paper in America, Albert Levy's *La Vara* (New York, 1922–1948).

The *Aufbau* (New York, 1934–), founded by and for refugees from Hitlerism, maintains a high cultural standard and is widely read in the German Jewish community. The burgeoning population of Russian Jews in the United States has led to the newly-established Jewish weekly in Russian, *Alef* (New York, 1981–), while Israeli expatriates support the Hebrew weekly *Israel shelanu* (Brooklyn, 1979–).

There is no shortage of Jewish periodicals in the form of newspapers and magazines serving a broad spectrum of Jews of varying Zionist ideologies, cultural interests, and belief systems within the denominational spectrum of the organized Jewish community represented by the Reform, Reconstructionist, Conservative, Orthodox, or Humanist traditions. The periodicals with the greatest circulation are those published by Jewish organizations for their membership as seen in *Hadassah Magazine* reaching 374,900 readers, exceeded only by the Los Angeles-based Simon Wiesenthal Center's publicity-oriented house organ, *Response*, with a circulation of 375,500 copies as of January 1990.

Circulation figures as of late 1989 for representative Jewish papers, journals, and yearbooks with the year of their founding shown in parentheses follow:

Response (Simon Wiesenthal Center, Los Angeles, 1978)	375,500
Hadassah Magazine (New York, 1921)	374,900
Reform Judaism (New York, 1972)	287,200
United Synagogue Review (New York, 1949)	260,000
Algemeiner Journal (New York, 1972)	210,000
Jewish Press (Brooklyn, 1950)	200,000
ADL Bulletin (New York, 1943)	155,000
B'nai B'rith International Jewish Monthly (Washington, D.C., 1886)	148,100
Women's League Outlook (New York, 1930)	140,000
Jewish Week (New York, 1875)	119,000
Jewish Veteran (Washington, D.C., 1933)	100,000
National Jewish Post and Opinion (Indianapolis, 1933)	96,000
Jewish Action (New York, 1950)	70,000
B'nai B'rith Messenger (Los Angeles, 1897)	67,000
Forverts/The Forward (New York, 1897)	65,000
Jewish Exponent (Philadelphia, 1887)	65,000
American Zionist (New York, 1910)	45,000
Commentary (New York, 1945)	45,000
Present Tense (New York, 1973–1990)	40,000
Tikkun (Oakland, 1986)	40,000
Workmen's Circle Call (New York, 1932)	40,000
Der Yid (Brooklyn, 1951)	34,500
Moment (New York, 1975)	30,500
Aufbau (New York, 1934)	30,000
Na'amat Woman (New York, 1926)	30,000
Jewish Floridian (Miami, 1928)	29,500
Congress Monthly (New York, 1935)	26,200
Sentinel (Chicago, 1911)	25,000
Jewish Advocate (Boston, 1902)	24,300
Martyrdom and Resistance (New York, 1974)	22,000
Bitzaron (New York, 1939)	18,800
Judaica Book News (New York, 1970)	18,000
Jewish Spectator (Santa Monica, Calif., 1935)	18,000
Olomeinu/Our World (New York, 1945)	17,000
Jewish Observer (New York, 1963)	16,000
Wellsprings (Brooklyn, 1984)	15,000
Jewish Frontier (New York, 1934)	12,500
Midstream (New York, 1955)	12,000
Kultur un lebn (New York, 1967)	11,000
Reconstructionist (New York, 1935)	10,500
Jewish Guardian (Brooklyn, 1974)	10,000
Keeping Posted (New York, 1955)	10,000
Lilith (New York, 1976)	10,000
Sh'ma (Port Washington, N.Y., 1970)	8,500
Issues (American Council for Judaism, New York, 1958)	8,000
Yivo News/Yedies fun Yivo (New York, 1943)	6,500
Judaism (New York, 1952)	5,500
American Jewish Archives (Cincinnati, 1948)	5,000
American Jewish Year Book (New York, 1899)	5,000

Hadoar (New York, 1921)	5,000
Journal of Jewish Communal Service (New York, 1924)	4,500
Tradition (New York, 1958)	4,000
Jewish Currents (New York, 1946)	3,800
American Jewish History (Waltham, Mass., 1893)	3,550
Journal of Halacha and Contemporary Jewry (Staten Island, N.Y., 1980)	3,250
Unzer tsait (New York, 1941)	3,000
Yiddishe kultur (New York, 1938)	3,000
Humanistic Judaism (Farmington Hills, Mich., 1967)	2,500
Zukunft (New York, 1892)	2,500
Journal of Reform Judaism (New York, 1953)	2,200
Response; A Contemporary Jewish Review (Flushing, N.Y., 1967)	2,200
Genesis 2 (Boston, 1970)	2,000
Pedagogic Reporter (New York, 1949)	2,000
Yivo Annual (New York, 1946)	2,000
Yugntruf (Bronx, 1963)	2,000
Prooftexts (Baltimore, 1981)	1,800
Modern Judaism (Baltimore, 1981)	1,700
Conservative Judaism (New York, 1945)	1,600
Jewish Education (New York, 1929)	1,500
Afn shvel (New York, 1941)	1,200
Jewish Book Annual (New York, 1942)	1,200
Jewish Social Studies (New York, 1939)	1,150
Jewish Quarterly Review (Philadelphia, 1909)	1,000

Opinion is divided within the American Jewish community over the Anglo-Jewish weeklies' state of health, unaffectionately termed by their critics the "weaklies." In the absence of a reportorial staff, not a few of the typical urban weeklies rely almost exclusively on the unaltered copy distributed by the Jewish Telegraphic Agency syndicate in New York for national and international Jewish news and Israeli affairs; more often than not, local "news" is a bland potpourri of self-congratulatory press releases prepared by institutional public relations specialists and social announcements of weddings and bar-mitzvahs. As an increasing number of weeklies become subjugated to the local Jewish federation's fundraising priorities either through outright ownership, editorial control, subsidization, or, indirectly through the placement of advertising, the Anglo-Jewish weeklies increasingly fail to attract the readership of the younger, college-educated reader seeking an enlightened analysis of interfaith and social justice concerns, probes of accountability for the millions of dollars raised by the United Jewish Appeal, or critical examinations of Israeli policies toward the occupied territories or the Israeli intrusion in the Lebanese civil war. To survive, the dwindling number of independently owned papers have experimented with color printing and have been forced to hire staff writers for local investigative reporting. In recent years, some independent papers have begun to purchase Jewish papers in other cities or to form cooperative networking arrangements, all in a cost-saving effort to share original news stories and limited resources by exploiting electronic and satellite transmissions.

Papers such as *Genesis 2* (Boston, 1970–), "An Independent Voice for Jewish Renewal" begun as a Jewish student newspaper, routinely publishes signed articles on peacemaking in the Middle East or timely essays concerning gay and lesbian Jews, Soviet anti-Semitism, Jewish feminism, the Jewish poor, or Israel–South Africa relations. The Jewish Student Press Service, founded in 1970 and based in New York, serves its constituency with monthly packets of articles and features.

Attempts to publish a national Jewish newspaper have met with varying success; the popular *Jewish Post and Opinion* (formerly the *National Jewish Post and Opinion*) has a circulation of some 133,000 copies. Founded in 1943, the American Jewish Press Association, a national voluntary trade organization of editors and journalists, represents dozens of papers with a combined readership of more than 4.5 million.

The Jewish press in the United States is very much an integral part of educating successive generations of American Jews and uniting Jews with Israel and other communities of co-religionists at home and abroad. From the mass-appeal weeklies to the professional and scholarly monthlies, quarterlies and annuals, Jewish solidarity and cultural identity are reaffirmed through the informed medium of the printed word. *See also Jewish Daily Forward*, Journalism.

ROBERT SINGERMAN

BIBLIOGRAPHY

Brody, Fannie M. "The Hebrew Periodical Press in America, 1871–1931; A Bibliographical Survey." *Publications of the American Jewish Historical Society* 33 (1934): 127–170.

Brown, Michael Gary. "All, All Alone: The Hebrew Press in America from 1914 to 1924." *American Jewish Historical Quarterly* 59 (1969/70): 139–163.

Cohen, Naomi W. "Pioneers of American Jewish Defense." *American Jewish Archives* 29 (1977): 116–150.

Goren, Arthur A. "The Jewish Press." In *The Ethnic Press in the United States*, edited by Sally M. Miller. Westport, Conn.: Greenwood Press, 1987. Pp. 203–228.

Howe, Irving. "The Yiddish Press." In *World of Our Fathers*. New York: Harcourt Brace Jovanovich, 1976. Pp. 516–551.

Lippman, Jerome W. "The Jewish Press—Chronicle of the Contemporary Scene." *Conservative Judaism* 36 (1987): 238–242.

Novak, William, and Goldman, Robert. "The Rise of the Jewish Student Press." *Conservative Judaism* 25 (Winter 1971): 5–19.

Singerman, Robert. "The American Jewish Press, 1823–1983; A Bibliographical Survey of Research and Studies." *American Jewish History* 73 (1983/1984): 422–444.

Psychiatry, Psychoanalysis, Psychology. *See* MENTAL HEALTH.

Publication, Jewish. The primary languages of the Jews who settled in the American colonies in the 1700s were Spanish, German, Yiddish, and Hebrew. Gradually, Spanish and German gave way to Yiddish and Hebrew. Hebrew, however, was never much of a spoken language in America, and its use was confined to prayer and scholarship. But because of the pervasive influence of the Old Testament among Protestant Christians, the influence of Hebrew was strongly felt among the Puritans. Therefore, while there was almost no English literature until the early 1800s, there was a great deal of Hebrew literature, and Hebrew was taught and studied at Harvard, Yale, and Columbia. This love of Hebrew influenced which of the early books were published. *The Whole Booke of Psalms* appeared in Cambridge in 1640. Josephus's *War of the Jews* was first published in 1719, and reprints of the Bible as well as histories of ancient Jews began appearing from England.

At the time of the American Revolution there were probably only about 3000 Jews in all the colonies so there was no great need for books and periodicals in languages other than Hebrew. Through the first quarter of the nineteenth century, Jewish publishing in America therefore was confined mostly to prayer books, books on Judaism, and some books published in reaction to Christian proselytizing efforts.

CONTEMPORARY ANGLO-JEWISH MAGAZINES. There are probably about 100 Anglo-Jewish monthlies, bimonthlies, and quarterlies being published in the United States today. What follows is a brief description of some of the most important ones.

The *American Zionist* is the official organ of the Zionist organization of America. Established in 1910 as a monthly, it reported on Zionist events and expounded on the ideals and principles of Zionism. Today, it exists as a bimonthly.

Hadassah Magazine began in 1914 as a three-page newsletter published by the Women's Zionist Organization of America. It has become a monthly magazine with a circulation in excess of 300,000. Its format is that of a popular general publication with features, articles, columns, and stories of relevant Jewish interest in America and Israel.

Important to the history of Jewish journalism in America is the *Menorah Journal*, founded in 1916 by 16 Jewish students at Harvard. Under the editorship of Henry Hurwitz (1886–1962), it became "a seminal event in the cultural life of American Jewry." In Hurwitz's first editorial he declared: "*The Menorah Journal* is under the compulsion to be absolutely nonpartisan, an expression of all that is best in Judaism and not merely of some particular sect or school or locality or group of special interests; promoting constructive thought rather than aimless controversy; animated with the vitality and enthusiasms of youth; harking back to the past that we may deal more wisely with the present and the future; recording and appreciating Jewish achievement and not to brag; but to bestir ourselves to emulation and to deepen the consciousness of *noblesse oblige*; striving always to be sane and levelheaded; offering no opinion of its own, but providing an orderly platform for the discussion of mooted questions that really matter, dedicated first and foremost to the fostering of Jewish 'humanities' and the furthering of their influence as a spur to human service."

Until it ceased publication in 1962, *Menorah Journal* offered some of the most interesting discussions of problems concerning world Jewry contributed by leading thinkers and writers. Hurwitz encouraged new writers to submit their work and promoted Jewish artists by reproducing their work. About 200 writers, artists, and musicians appeared in the magazine.

Another influential magazine founded by

students is *Response*, which first appeared in 1966. Under the original editorship of William Novak, this was one of the first magazines to write about the search by young Jews for religious alternatives. Still in existence today, its articles concern itself with the emergence of Havurah, critiques of the Jewish establishment, the Soviet Jewry movement, alternatives in Jewish education, and Jewish feminism. Each issue also features the work of emerging writers, poets, critics, and artists.

In 1955, the Theodor Herzl Foundation, part of the American Zionist Federation, started *Midstream*, a magazine devoted to Zionism, Israel, and Jewishness. The quarterly's platform was to provide "a critical interpretation of the past, a searching examination of the present, and afford a medium for considered independent opinion and for creative cultural expression." Under the original editorship of Shlomo Katz *Midstream* established itself as a serious literary and cultural periodical containing articles on current problems, Israeli issues, and poems and stories by leading American Jewish writers.

In 1965, it became a monthly under the editorship of Ronald Sanders. In the 1970s, it was taken over by Joel Carmichael, who turned it into a much more conservative magazine. In 1988, Murray Zuckoff became the editor. He saw the magazine as a forum for "Jewish Zionist intellectuals to present political and aesthetic attitudes and points of view." The articles he sought present principles of Zionism as well as a description of life in the Diaspora. Basically, he hoped to return the magazine to a place where "nothing human is alien to Jewish life." Joel Carmichael is presently the editor.

In 1906, the American Jewish Committee was formed to defend Jews from being politically attacked or maligned in the United States. To promote its cause, it decided in 1938 to issue a bimonthly magazine called the *Contemporary Jewish Record*. Its first editors stated that "For some time, the need has been felt also for a regular publication in which important magazine and newspaper articles and significant documents and enlightening editorial comment could be preserved and notices of pertinent books, pamphlets, and articles recorded."

The magazine was intended to be read mainly by Jews, but it was to appeal also to interested Christians. In 1945, the committee decided to issue the *Contemporary Jewish Record* monthly and to change its name to *Commentary*—"in the tradition of the commentaries written by the ancient scribes and sages . . . on the revelation which was the Law."

Commentary gradually developed into a journal of "significant thought and opinion on Jewish affairs and contemporary issues." No longer distinctly Jewish, it sought "diverse points of view and belief" and to "enlighten and clarify public opinion on problems of Jewish concern." Under the editorship of Norman Podhoretz, the magazine has grown more and more conservative.

In 1973, the American Jewish Committee decided to establish another magazine more specifically devoted to Jewish life—*Present Tense*. Going into 1990, *Present Tense* was a bimonthly, under the editorship of Murray Polner, and was largely devoted to reportage about the conditions of Jews in countries around the world. It was probably one of the only Jewish magazines that focused on overseas Jewish communities while trying to remain as objective as possible. While it originally presented all points of view, the magazine developed a distinctly liberal orientation before its demise in early 1990. At that time *Present Tense* ceased publication as a result of budget cuts made by the American Jewish Committee.

In the spring of 1975, Leonard Fein and Elie Wiesel started *Moment* magazine, named after a Yiddish daily that had appeared in prewar Poland. Under Fein's editorship, it remained a lively and provocative independent magazine committed to speaking to and about American Jews. In 1987, Fein sold the magazine to Hershel Shanks, the editor of the *Biblical Archeology Review*. Under its new editorship, the magazine changed its format and has been open to a larger range of features that reflect a whole spectrum of opinion. It tries to offer an "interplay of ideas within a framework of responsible thinking." An interesting aspect of the magazine is that it sometimes runs an article advocating one perspective and then runs another alongside it offering an opposing point of view.

JEWISH BOOK PUBLISHERS. The Jewish Publication Society, after two previous attempts, was founded in 1888 by 100 prominent Jews who met in Philadelphia. The purpose of this new organization, an educational institution devoted to Jewish culture, was to publish for the first time in English books, sermons, and lectures relating to Judaism.

Since that time, the society has published nearly 9 million volumes covering more than 900 titles. Under the aegis of Henrietta Szold, its first editor, its first offering was Lady Magnus's

Outlines of Jewish History. Aware that the society was established to be a major force in scholarly publishing, Chaim Potok, the society's fifth editor, decided in 1973 to publish a controversial book intended for the broader Jewish population—*The Jewish Catalogue*. It became the society's best seller.

The publishing of *The Jewish Catalogue* touched off a controversy about whether the society should publish popular, scholarly, or literary books. A literary book that achieved much recognition was *Shifting Landscape* published in 1987, by Henry Roth, author of *Call it Sleep*.

During times of financial crisis, what has kept the society afloat has been the Bible—its two translations. The first appeared in 1917, and *Tanakh* appeared in 1985. Richard Malina, the society's executive director/publisher until 1989, saw the new commentary, based on the society's translation, as the society's most important current publishing project. Under the editorship of Nahum Sarna and Chaim Potok (literary editor), the project has taken 15 years to complete. *Genesis*, its first offering, appeared in 1989. According to Malina, this is the first full-blown commentary on the Bible to appear since the 1930s, with an eager audience of rabbis and scholars waiting for its much heralded appearance. Mike Munson is now executive director of the society.

Jason Aronson is a publisher of books in psychiatry and psychoanalysis offered through its own psychotherapy book club. In 1983, the company decided to enter into Jewish publishing, and realizing that book club sales could support its intended projects, it bought the Jewish Book Club from *Commentary* magazine, which it continued.

In 1985, under the guidance of Arthur Kurzweil, editorial vice-president, Jason Aronson began to publish Jewish books under its own imprint. Today, it publishes about 25 books a year with two goals in mind, "to restore yesterday's classics and to create tomorrow's."

Salman Schocken, a German Jew (1877–1959) founded Schocken Verlag in Berlin in 1931. From 1933 until 1938, it was the only Jewish publishing company in Nazi Germany. Schocken emigrated to Palestine in 1933 and eventually established Schocken Publishing Company of Tel Aviv. He emigrated from Israel to the United States at the end of World War II and founded Schocken Books in New York. He and his son Theodore began to publish English translations of books by eminent scholars such as

Baeck, Franz Rosenzweig, and Gershom Scholem. They also started the moderately priced Schocken Library, which formed the basis of Schocken paperbacks—books of Jewish interest. Until 1961, the house devoted itself solely to the Jewish book—the "most relevant and excellent in Jewish and Hebrew culture." Slowly, however, they moved into non-Jewish publishing, branching out into various areas of the social sciences.

The firm, however, was still committed to Jewish publishing and Schocken continued to reissue its back list of Jewish authors—S. Y. Agnon, Martin Buber, Gershom Scholem. In 1982, under the editorship of Bonnie Fetterman, it began to add about 10 new Jewish books a year. In 1987, Schocken Books was sold to Random House as a unit of Pantheon Books. Fetterman, who was named Director of Judaica, oversees the publication of 10 original books and 10 reprints—new translations and new books of scholarship.

There are a number of Jewish publishers who publish for the religious Jewish community. These include Behrman House, Soncino, Mesorah, and Ktav. Ktav, one of the largest of this group, began as a storefront business on the Lower East Side. The owner of the store, Asher Scharfstein, became a publisher when he bought Maimon Publishing Company and added its list of Bibles and prayerbooks to his stock.

Ktav started its own list of original books with a title written by one of Asher's sons. Sol Scharfstein's *Haveri*, written in 1947, is a student notebook for writing Hebrew and is still the company's best-selling book.

Sol Scharfstein describes his firm's list as a "supermarket of Judaica." It has a scholarly list, launched in 1965 with the publication of *The Jewish Encyclopedia*, a list of novelty books, and a comprehensive list of textbooks. Many of their textbooks have been revised so that they are appropriate to all of the major branches of Judaism.

COMMERCIAL PUBLISHERS OF JEWISH BOOKS. A number of publishers of distinction have been Jewish and in the course of their publishing careers have published Jewish books. Alfred A. Knopf (1892–1984) began his career at Doubleday and was the first Jew to join a non-Jewish publishing house. He built the firm into one of the most respected publishing houses in America. For many years, Robert Gottlieb, one of Knopf's most distinguished editors, and in 1990 editor of the *New Yorker*, edited some of

America's most important Jewish authors including Cynthia Ozick and Chaim Potok.

From 1981 until 1987, Summit Books, a branch of Simon & Schuster, was probably the premier publisher of Jewish books. Arthur Samuelson, a young enterprising editor, published about 10 Jewish books a year—all of which had large sales. His authors included Elie Wiesel, the late Primo Levi, and Charles Silberman. Samuelson left Summit for Harper & Row (which has become Harper Collins), where he still does some Jewish publishing. Summit still publishes a few Jewish books a year.

Since the 1940s, Farrar, Straus & Giroux has been publishing Jewish authors, largely due to the interest of Roger Straus, one of the firm's prominent Jewish partners. Philip Roth, I. B. Singer, and Bernard Malamud are three of its most noted Jewish authors.

Today, among the 50,000 books published each year in the United States, there are about 450 new titles on Jewish themes or by Jewish authors. Every commercial house, and a growing number of academic presses, publishes some of the titles. These books and authors find a wide readership among readers of all backgrounds. *See also* Press, Jewish.

DIANE LEVENBERG

BIBLIOGRAPHY

Madison, Charles. *Jewish Publishing in America.* New York: Sanhedrin, 1976.

Sarna, Jonathan. *Jewish Publication Society: The Americanization of Jewish Culture 1888-1988.* Philadelphia: Jewish Publication Society, 1989.

R

Rabi, Isidor Isaac (1898–1988). An American physicist, Isidor Isaac Rabi developed nuclear magnetic resonance measurement and theory, for which he was awarded the Nobel Prize in Physics (1944). He also discovered the quadrapole moment of the proton, helped develop essential radar applications during World War II, and was an advocate of arms reduction and of the peaceful use of atomic energy.

Born in Rymanow, Poland, Rabi was brought as an infant to New York City, where his father supported his family with earnings as a sweatshop garment worker and on the meager profits from the family grocery store. Rabi was raised within the traditions of Orthodox Judaism. He was especially fascinated by the biblical account of creation. After his family moved from the Lower East Side of Manhattan to the Brownsville section of Brooklyn, Rabi explored the wonders of the local branch of the Brooklyn Public Library; an encounter with a book on astronomy (he was proceeding alphabetically) determined him to seek to substitute scientific for theological explanations of the universe. For his Bar Mitzvah speech, Rabi offered an explanation of "How the Electric Light Bulb Works."

Rabi entered Cornell University (1915), where he majored in chemistry and was graduated in three years. During graduate study at Columbia University, he developed an elegant new method of measuring the magnetic susceptibilities of substances; the degree to which a substance can be made to assume magnetic properties in a magnetic field provides important information about the atomic content and the arrangement of atoms in the material. He was awarded his Ph.D. from Columbia in 1927.

After applying the new approaches of quantum theory to the energies of molecular systems, Rabi studied quantum theory with its leading developers in Munich, Leipzig, and Hamburg in Germany, in Leeds, England, and in Copenhagen, Denmark.

In 1929, Rabi began a lectureship in theoretical physics at Columbia University (52 years later he received the Oersted Medal, the highest award of the American Association of Physics Teachers); at Columbia he created a magnetic beam laboratory for the measurement of nuclear magnetic properties (1931). Rabi developed nuclear magnetic resonance theory (1932), which became the basis for one of the most important tools both of basic physics research and of modern analytical chemistry, biology, and medicine.

In 1939 and 1940, Rabi's group measured magnetic moments of protons and deuterons. The discovery of the quadrapole moment of the deuteron caused a fundamental reassessment of ideas concerning the atomic nucleus and nuclear forces. Rabi received a prestigious award from the American Association for the Advancement of Science (1940) for a paper contributing to our fundamental knowledge of atoms and molecules by application of the method of radiofrequency spectroscopy.

Rabi joined the MIT Radiation Laboratory (1940), where his Advanced Development Division played a major role in the development of radar for military purposes. The work of this laboratory was essential to the Allied victory in World War II. Rabi also served as an adviser to the nuclear program at Los Alamos headed by J. Robert Oppenheimer.

Recognition of Rabi's fundamental contributions, in particular the nuclear magnetic resonance theory, culminated in the award of the Nobel Prize in Physics (1944).

Although Rabi returned to Columbia University (1944), only part of his energies was devoted to physics. He was instrumental in the development of the Brookhaven National Laboratory, a major cyclotron facility for nuclear research. He helped mold United States policy toward the peaceful use of atomic energy and served on the General Advisory Committee of the Atomic Energy Commission (1946–1949). Rabi consistently opposed the development of thermonuclear bombs.

Serving as a delegate to UNESCO, Rabi helped establish the very important cyclotron facility of CERN (Conseil Europeen Pour La Recherche Nucleaire). He chaired a committee (1944) that planned for the Conference on the Peaceful Uses of Atomic Energy held the next year in Geneva.

Rabi served on the President's Science Advisory Committee (1957–1961). In the latter part of his life he became an important advocate of arms reduction.

Rabi's fundamental contributions to our understanding of how the universe works and his passionate involvement in the guidance of the social and ethical uses of scientific applications place him in the grand tradition of Jewish-American scientific minds. *See also* Science.

IRA FEIT

BIBLIOGRAPHY

Kevles, Daniel J. *The Physicists: The History of a Scientific Community in Modern America.* Cambridge: Harvard University Press, 1987.

Rabi, Isidore I. *My Life and Times as a Physicist.* Claremont, Calif.: Claremont College, 1960.

———. *Science, the Center of Culture.* New York: World, 1970.

Rigden, John S. *Rabi: American Physicist.* New York: Basic Books, 1987.

———. *Rabi: Scientist and Citizen.* New York: Basic Books, 1989.

Rackman, Emanuel (b. 1910). Orthodox rabbi and university administrator, Emanuel

Rackman was born in Albany, New York. He studied at Columbia University and the Rabbi Isaac Elhanan Theological Seminary, where he was ordained as a rabbi in 1934. He served several congregations on Long Island in Glen Cove, Lynbrook, and (after a period as a chaplain in the U.S. Air Force) Far Rockaway. In 1967, he was appointed to succeed Immanuel Jakobovitz, who had become Great Britain's Chief Rabbi, as rabbi of the Fifth Avenue Synagogue in Manhattan. From 1947 to 1970, he taught at Yeshiva University and from 1962 to 1970 was provost and assistant to the president. In 1971, he became professor of Jewish studies at City University, retiring when he took up the leadership of Bar-Ilan University. Rackman also served as president of the New York Board of Rabbis (1955–1957) and the Rabbinical Council of America (1958–1960). In 1977, his standing as a leading Orthodox rabbi received wider recognition by virtue of his appointment as president of Bar-Ilan University, Jerusalem.

Rackman is acknowledged to be a leading exponent of what is known as "modern Orthodoxy," which has some intellectual affinities with the combination of religious and secular learning advocated in Germany by Sampson Raphael Hirsch but opposed to the separatist outlook advocated by the right wing of American Orthodoxy. His position legitimizes cooperation with the non-Orthodox through such bodies as the Synagogue Council of America and local boards of rabbis; it also involves an interpretation of Halakah which takes account of changes in social conditions.

Rackman has published *Israel's Emerging Constitution* (1955) and *One Man's Judaism* (1970) and has been a regular contributor to the Anglo-Jewish press.

S. D. TEMKIN

BIBLIOGRAPHY

Liebman, Charles S. "Orthodoxy in American Jewish Life." *American Jewish Year Book,* 66 (1965): 3–92.

Radio. Two Jewish men were significantly responsible for the development of the form that radio took in the United States—David Sarnoff and William Paley.

With the development of television and the superb special effects of the motion picture industry, Americans have become so accustomed to the visual that it is difficult for many to understand the impact of radio on the people who lived during radio's infancy and development. Voices were brought into people's homes from great distances. When people listened to radio, their imaginations were being used since each listener had to conjure a visual image in his or her mind of what was happening. Therefore, the description of some people's contributions to radio will include the words and sounds of such contributions.

David Sarnoff (1891–1971) was born in Russia. He started his association with the communications business as a messenger boy. His second job was with the Marconi Wireless Telegraphy Company as an office boy. He rose rapidly within the company. After six years, in 1912, he became the operator and manager of the Marconi telegraph station on top of the Wanamaker Department Store in New York. It was the most powerful in the commercial field at that time. That was the year the word "radio" displaced the word "wireless" in popular American usage. The word "radio" came from the fact that signals from the transmitters radiated in all directions.

In 1912, the *Titantic*, the largest, fastest and newest ship in existence, hit an iceberg on its maiden voyage. The New York Marconi station picked up a message that stated the *Titantic* was sinking fast. Most books on the subject indicate that the operator at Wanamaker's at the time was young David Sarnoff, who stayed at his post for 72 hours. Huntington Williams in his book *Beyond Control: ABC and the Fate of the Networks* (1989) claims that the tale was "concocted" and a "myth."

Myth or not, Sarnoff was the operator and manager of the Wanamaker station at the time. The reporting of what was happening and the tragedy of over 1500 people who were drowned in that disaster dramatically highlighted the importance of radio. As the government stepped up military preparations right before World War I, the Marconi Company and others were receiving large orders from the U.S. Navy for radio equipment. David Sarnoff was then made head of the Marconi Commercial Department. He became second in command of the American Marconi Company.

Sarnoff's importance to radio was reflected by his imagination and the ideas he had concerning what could be done with that wonderful invention. His work and his reputation were based on dozens of ideas and predictions he made ahead of their time. As early as 1915, at the age of 24, Sarnoff wrote a memorandum to his superiors

projecting a plan for what he called the "Radio Music Box." The plan would make radio a "household utility" in the same sense as the phonograph. He predicted the possible earnings of such a radio music box, and history proved him correct. In 1922, he predicted what he called the "radiolette," what we call the portable radio today. He also predicted the radio-phonography and car radios and in 1923 predicted television.

The Marconi Company was a European-owned company, and because of World War I many Americans questioned allowing a foreign company to control American communications facilities. General Electric held the rights to a high-speed generator developed by E. F. W. Alexanderson, called the Alexanderson alternator. The Marconi Company realized the problem of foreign ownership, and an agreement was reached between GE and the Marconi Company whereby the Marconi Company divested its ownership of its American division and in return could use the Alexanderson alternator for its own stations in the British empire. GE bought out the holdings of the American stockholders of American Marconi. The new company was given the name of the Radio Corporation of America (RCA).

RCA's major competitor was Westinghouse, which built a number of radio stations including KDKA in Pittsburgh. Westinghouse, therefore, beat RCA in broadcasting since the board of RCA was more interested in the international market and in selling radio receivers. Sarnoff was a prophet and a visionary, but he was an employee and not the boss at the time. By the middle of 1921, Westinghouse had become a participant in RCA. During the reorganization, David Sarnoff became general manager of RCA.

The next battle during this hectic period was between what became known as the "radio group"—RCA, GE, and Westinghouse—and the "phone group"–AT&T and its manufacturing subsidiary, Western Electric. AT&T maintained that it had the exclusive right to sell time for advertising, which was called "toll broadcasting," similar to the concept of the telephone toll call. It also maintained that AT&T had the exclusive right to interconnect stations by wire for broadcasting. AT&T's station in New York, WEAF, had been linked to a "toll station" in Washington, D.C., in 1923. AT&T then licensed selected other stations to become "toll stations." By 1924, a large number of sponsored programs were being broadcast over the AT&T network of "toll stations."

In 1925, both groups agreed to binding arbitration to settle their dispute. After months of arguments and hearings, the arbitrator decided nearly all issues in favor of the radio group. The final settlement assured the use of telephone lines for linking RCA and affiliated stations.

With the radio group's victory, the ingredients for a national network were available to RCA. The National Broadcasting Company, NBC, was incorporated in the fall of 1926. A gala banquet at the Waldorf-Astoria Hotel in New York City inaugurated the network on November 15, 1926, with a 4-hour program featuring many of the best-known movie and theater stars at the time. The hookup included 25 stations as far west as Kansas City. WEAF, now WNBC, the former AT&T New York station, was the flagship for the network.

RCA and NBC took over operation of the former Westinghouse New York area station, WJZ, now WABC, and it became the base for a second network. On January 1, 1927, the second network joined with the first to broadcast the Rose Bowl game between Stanford and Alabama universities. The WEAF-based network became known as the Red Network, and the WJZ-based chain became known as the Blue Network. There are several stories as to why those colors came to symbolize the two different networks. One story has it that the AT&T engineers kept the network routings straight on a map by coloring the circuits for one network red and the other network blue.

Unlike David Sarnoff, William Paley (1901–1990) was born in the United States. Like Sarnoff, he was the son of immigrants. After much hard work, his father started the Congress Cigar Company, which operated out of Chicago. The business expanded and a new factory was opened in Philadelphia. Paley worked for his father's company in Philadelphia. While Paley's father was in Europe on a business trip, Paley bought an hour program on a Philadelphia station, WCAU, to advertise La Palina Cigars, which led to Paley's interest in radio.

A close friend of Paley's father asked him to advertise on a small radio network that had been recently organized. The friend, Jerome Lochheim, had purchased a controlling interest in the network, the United Independent Broadcasters (UIB). UIB did not have a great amount of financial backing, but it did receive the backing of the Columbia Phonograph Company. The name of the network was then changed to the Columbia Phonograph Broadcasting System. The network

had made its debut on September 18, 1927, 10 months after the NBC debut. The program was not as star studded as that of the NBC debut, but it did include "The King's Henchman" featuring artists from the Metropolitan Opera.

Eventually, the Columbia Phonograph Company withdrew its participation and the word "phonograph" was dropped from its name, and the network continued as the Columbia Broadcasting System. Because of the continuous financial problems, Jerome Lochheim approached William Paley's father about buying out his share of the network. The younger Paley had become very intrigued with radio and eagerly purchased 50.3% of the network.

The first thing Paley did after becoming CBS president was to assure a continuous cash flow and the second was to bring the network into stronger competition with the two NBC networks. Paley reorganized the affiliated stations' relationship to the network in a way different from NBC. NBC was charging its affiliates for what were called sustaining programs, i.e., unsponsored network programs. Paley made the entire schedule of sustaining programs *free* to the CBS affiliates. In exchange, Paley asked and received an option for any part of the affiliates' schedules, for *sponsored* network programs. This meant that CBS could sell time to a sponsor and practically assure coverage on the entire network. NBC eventually followed the CBS plan.

Paley believed that eyewitness reporting was a basic function of broadcasting. Although the regular broadcasts of comedies, music, and drama assured a continuous audience loyalty, the impact of on-the-spot news emphasized the uniqueness of what broadcasting could do. It could bring the world to the average person's home. Based on that vision, one day in 1930 all affiliates were asked to clear the time for an emergency program. The listeners heard ambulance bells, crackling flames, the shouts of firemen, screaming, and sobbing. The sound of human grief was being brought into people's homes as CBS broadcast the disastrous Ohio State Penitentiary fire. This was the forerunner of what was to identify CBS as the leader of news broadcasting for three decades.

In developing the CBS News Department in 1930, Paley and his associates determined that the people they hired to broadcast the news should be newsmen and not people who necessarily had good voices for radio. Therefore, it is ironic that the galvanizing broadcast directly from Vienna in 1938 describing the takeover of Austria by Adolf

Hitler was made by Edward R. Murrow, who was not a newsman but the CBS "Director of Talks." Paley should be given credit for hiring Murrow as well as William L. Shirer and creating the first of the famous CBS "radio roundups."

Network radio developed in three phases. This was especially exemplified by the comedians who originally became part of the radio scene. The first phase in radio was the trial-and-error phase, which lasted until about 1935. The second phase was what has been called "the golden age of radio," which lasted from 1935 until the advent of television. The third phase is represented by the reaction of the networks as they tried to keep network radio viable and develop television at the same time.

During the first phase, many of the original radio comedy stars were famous Jewish vaudeville and stage stars. The networks correctly guessed that people would tune in to famous stars, and they rushed to get them on the air. However, the most successful people on radio were those who realized that what was good in vaudeville, which was visual, was not good on radio. Ed Wynn (1886–1966) was the first performer to bring his entire stage show to radio. The Westinghouse station WJZ had Wynn bring his Broadway production *The Perfect Fool* to its studio in 1922. Wynn's reaction was almost a prophecy to future comedians. He told his jokes to the microphone and, of course, there was no applause or laughter. He turned to the announcer and told him he could not continue. Legend has it that the announcer raced into the hall and collected an audience of scrubwomen, telephone operators, secretaries, and visitors and hastily brought them into the studio.

A decade later, a Texaco official saw Wynn performing in another Broadway show and offered him a contract for a radio program. Wynn refused at first because he felt that his performances relied too heavily on visual material, including silly hats and oversized clothing. Texaco finally persuaded Wynn with a sizable sum of money for the Depression years and "The Texaco Fire Chief" premiered on April 26, 1932. Wynn insisted that his contract include the clause that he would have an audience for his programs. Wynn was a link between the first phase of network radio and the more sophisticated second phase. His show finished a strong third that year and ran until 1935. Texaco also brought a former vaudevillian to television. That vaudevillian, Milton Berle, was not very successful on radio, but

his visual style was perfect for TV, and he subsequently became the man identified as "Mr. Television."

Eddie Cantor (1892–1954) was in first place in the ratings in 1932 when Ed Wynn was third. Cantor's show was the most successful of the early radio shows. He started his own show almost a year ahead of Ed Wynn, Al Jolson, and Jack Benny. As Ed Wynn did, Cantor found out in the early days of radio that audiences were frowned on. Cantor changed all that, not because he was fearful of the microphone with no live feedback but because he believed laughter was contagious. His high ratings proved him correct. Cantor's show also included Bert Gordon (Barney Gorodetsky), the Mad Russian, a character with a thick slavic accent whose salutation, "How dooo you dooo?" would have the audience in gales of laughter. Harry Einstein introduced his character of Parkyakarkas on the Cantor show, which was also a character with a dialect. Cantor was proud of discovering new talent and went out of his way to do so. Among those who went on to stardom was a Jewish girl from Tennessee, Dinah Shore. Cantor supported many worthy causes privately and on his radio program. His idea for a "March for Dimes" in the battle against polio launched the final success against the dreaded disease. Cantor was able to go from radio's first phase to its second phase and be part of the golden age of radio with his program always getting high ratings.

Jack Benny (1894–1974) epitomized what could be done with audio. His program premiered in 1932. Although he relied on his writers, he knew what was funny. More importantly, he understood what was funny for radio. His program spanned 23 years and was always a success. That success was based on the gradual refinement of the Benny character and his superior sense of timing. Benny could imply more with his "hmmmmmm" than some comedians did with pages of script. He was a master of the running gag, which was really part of his sense of timing. His running gags included his stinginess, his violin, his vanity about his age, and his old car, the Maxwell. He also included the show's middle commercial as part of the program and the Sportsmen's Quartet singing about Lucky Strike cigarettes was hilarious. The other famous running gag was based on a Mel Blanc (1908–1989) characterization. That was the train station sequence where Mel Blanc as the station master announced, "Train now loading on track three—all aboard for Anaheim, Azusa and Cuc------amonga." The longer the pause between "Cuc" and "amonga," the more the audience would laugh. You could feel the audiences leaning forward in their seats in anticipation of the final syllable.

Among other successful Jews in the early years of radio were Joe Penner (1904–1941), whose popularity waned after 1935. Arthur Tracy (b. 1903), known as The Street Singer, was an instant success after his appearance on CBS in 1931. His identity was kept a mystery similar to another tenor before him, "The Silver Masked Tenor" of the 1920s. Once pictures of him appeared and the mystery was gone, his ratings fell. He performed in England where he was very popular. It was Tracy's version of the song "Pennies From Heaven" that was played in the film of the same name.

George Burns (b. 1898), like Jack Benny and Eddie Cantor, was able to move successfully from the first phase to the second phase and perform through the golden age of radio. Burns changed his show into what we today call a situation comedy, which also brought success to him and his wife Gracie Allen (1905–1964) on television. Fanny Brice (1891–1951) made the transition to radio by playing the role of a child called Baby Snooks. Her program developed along the line of a situation comedy as well.

The unexpected surprise in radio's second phase was the popularity of what have become known as soap operas. Network radio first concentrated on its evening schedule, and some radio dramas were broadcast in the early evening. As network schedules expanded, the soap operas became the major staple of daytime radio. One of the popular soap operas was "The Goldbergs" created and written by Gertrude Berg. It was originally called "The Rise of the Goldbergs." Gertrude Berg (1899–1966) played the starring role of Molly Goldberg. The show opened with Mrs. Goldberg calling out of the window of her tenement with her Jewish accent, "Yoo-hoo, Mrs. Bloom." The program's portrayal of working-class life struck a chord in everyone who listened, especially people who were living through the Depression. The program started on the air in 1929, one month after the stock market crash. The audience could identify with the characters since the characters changed and grew older. Mrs. Berg carried reality to the sound effects. When the script called for the daughter in the family to have a shampoo, Mrs. Berg gave the actress playing her daughter a shampoo. When the family was eating breakfast, Mrs. Berg would fry eggs in the studio.

Comedians, soap operas, variety programs, and Jewish personalities such as Mel Allen (b. 1913), Walter Winchell (1897–1972), Ben Bernie (1891–1943), Gabriel Heatter (1890–1972), and Dinah Shore (b. 1921) were the staple of the golden age of radio, radio's second phase. But both NBC and CBS, Sarnoff and Paley, and their staff members did work to bring other kinds of programs to the networks.

The biggest disappointment in Paley's early years with CBS was his unsuccessful attempt to get the Metropolitan Opera on the network. He tried many things to persuade Otto Kahn, the president of the Metropolitan, to broadcast the opera. Kahn felt that radio would distort the beautiful operatic music. To show them otherwise, CBS put microphones into the opera house and piped a performance by closed circuit to Paley's office. Kahn and several other people from the Met listened to the music and changed their minds. Paley started to arrange broadcasting details with the opera when several weeks later he was informed that Kahn, while visiting Paris, had met the head of the law firm that handled RCA legal matters who convinced Kahn that the Met should broadcast on NBC instead of CBS.

Sarnoff personally scored another cultural victory for NBC when Arturo Toscanini, the director of the New York Philharmonic, who had retired and returned to Italy in 1936, was induced to return to America and perform on NBC. Toscanini agreed to ten radio concerts, but only if he had a veto power over the orchestra's personnel. It was the first orchestra ever assembled for radio. After the first year, the maestro agreed to a three-year contract. He was 71 at the time, and he stayed on until 1954 when he retired for the final time. Toscanini's many years on the air were regarded by many as a high-water mark in American musical history.

CBS won its cultural battles with its dramatic, educational, and news programs. Just as Edward R. Murrow is identified with CBS News, Norman Corwin (b. 1910) is identified with CBS drama and creativeness in the arts. Corwin was one of the most versatile writers and directors on radio. Beginning in 1938, he was given a challenge and worked on a half-hour program called "Words Without Music." The program featured dramatizations of his own works interspersed with modern classics. Some of the works included poetry. Some of the poets whose works he used sent original poems to him to be produced on the program.

On Christmas Day 1938, Corwin aired what has come to be regarded as his masterpiece, the engaging drama of "Satan's Plot to Overthrow Christmas." The drama was presented several times. "They Fly Through the Air with the Greatest of Ease," produced in 1939, was an attack on fascism. It was chosen by the Ohio Institute for Education by Radio as the outstanding broadcast of the year. Eight days after the attack on Pearl Harbor, Corwin's "We Hold These Truths" was broadcast on CBS, NBC-Red, NBC-Blue, and the Mutual Network. It was a dramatic appeal for unity based on the principles America stood for, using historical vignettes as part of the program's thrust. The largest audience ever to hear a drama listened that day. When the war in Europe ended, Corwin's presentation "On a Note of Triumph" was praised by many writers, including Carl Sandburg, who said it was "one of the all-time great American poems." Some people called it pretentious, but no one could question the overall productivity and creativity of Norman Corwin.

CBS was willing to back Corwin as it did other dramatic programs. "The Columbia Workshop" was one of the early experimental theaters of the air that started in 1936. The program was known for its innovations in sound effects to enhance the program's production, and many techniques that would later be taken for granted were developed on that program. Norman Corwin worked with the workshop as well as his own programs. "The Mercury Theater," which produced the famous "War of the Worlds" was originally a sustaining program on CBS opposite the NBC favorite Edgar Bergen/Charlie McCarthy program.

The third phase of radio was the transitional phase between the development of television and the end of radio's golden years. Several Jewish individuals were involved in that phase as well. Henry Morgan (b. 1915) became nationally known after World War II, which was the beginning of the end of the golden era. Corwin described Morgan as "the first radiogenic comedian of stature. . . . His technique is too intimate, too sleight-of-mike for anything but radio." His program is a "daily dose of anarchy."

The creator of "Stop the Music" was Louis G. Cowan (1910–1976), who was later to become famous for the "$64,000 Question" television quiz show. Cowan had developed one of the most popular radio quiz programs, "The Quiz Kids," which featured children of genius and near

genius proportions delightfully answering some of the hardest questions available from algebra to classical music. He left the production of that program during World War II and worked for the public relations division of the War Department. One less publicized aspect of his life was an assignment he had for the War Department. He held a meeting with Frank and Anne Hummert, producers of some of the most popular radio serials of the day, to discuss the subject of the black soldier. If we were fighting for democracy, then blacks had to be understood by mainstream America. Beginning in the summer of 1942, black characters were introduced to the world of the soap opera beginning with "Our Gal Sunday" and "The Romance of Helen Trent." As radio audiences declined in favor of network television, Cowan still developed programs for radio. It is ironic, since he was to become so well known for television. He produced a program called "Conversation." It featured a small group of well-known conversationalists who would discuss any subject without any inhibitions. Another program Cowan developed featured Mahalia Jackson on CBS.

The most successful attempt at bringing back old-time radio was made by a man who had been through all phases of network radio, Hyman Brown (b. 1910). Brown had helped sell, create, write, direct, and produce many radio programs. He sold "The Goldbergs" to NBC and played the role of the father on the program during the program's first several months. He was responsible for radio's first daytime drama, "Marie, The Little French Princess." He produced and directed afternoon serials based on famous comic strips, such as "Dick Tracy" and "Terry and the Pirates." Many of his programs clearly showed his recognition that sound was important to radio. "Inner Sanctum Mysteries" started each week with the opening of a loud creaking door, followed by a welcome by its mysterious sounding host. The creaking door sound was so important to the program that it was trademarked along with the NBC chimes, two of the first sounds ever trademarked. "Bulldog Drummond," a detective show, opened with the sound of hollow footsteps intermingled with the blast of a foghorn, followed by two gunshots and three sharp sounds of a police whistle. Another show which used sound to advantage was "Grand Central Station."

The last quality drama program on network radio went off the air in 1959. It was produced and directed by Hyman Brown. For 14 years

Brown fought, cajoled and beseeched radio executives to return drama to radio. He was finally successful when "The CBS Radio Mystery Theater" went on the air in January 1974. It stayed on the radio for almost a decade and went off the air in 1983 for lack of sponsor support. Brown was inducted into the Emerson Radio Hall of Fame in 1989.

The largest Jewish community in the United States, New York and its environs, produced a unique radio station in 1927. Station WEVD was founded in 1927 by the *Jewish Daily Forward*. Its call letters bore the initials of Eugene V. Debs, who ran for president several times as the candidate of the Socialist Party. The station pioneered in bringing quality educational and cultural programs to its public. During its years it presented the University of the Air. Music, philosophy, psychology, history and literature were covered by famous lecturers, including Fanny Hurst. Some programming reflected the social philosophy of the owners of the station, which was a combination of socialism and a strong Jewish belief in the importance of education, although that belief may have been more secular than religious.

The station not only developed such educational programs in English, but also presented programs in Yiddish. Although Yiddish is the language most people identified WEVD with, since the *Forward* was printed in Yiddish, the station consciously based its programming on the demographic immigrant mix that seemed to predominate in New York at the time. In the 1930s, the station broadcast programs in Italian and Polish in addition to Yiddish and English. Its most famous personality perhaps was the Yiddish Commentator, Zvee Scooler (1899–1985).

The motto of the station became, "WEVD, the station that speaks your language." By 1990, programs were broadcast in Portuguese, Greek, Albanian, and Japanese. As the Jewish population of New York included more second- and third-generation Jews who spoke English and very little Yiddish, the time spent on Jewish topics and concerns continued, but the language used was English. Art Raymond hosted the "Jewish" show for over a quarter of a century. It was broadcast Monday through Friday from 10:00 A.M. to 3:00 P.M. and on Sunday from 8:00 A.M. to 2:00 P.M. The program featured songs in Yiddish and Hebrew and provided information of Jewish concern. Programs strictly in Yiddish included 15 minutes of the news Monday through Friday, a Sunday review of the news, "The Forward Hour," for an hour on Sunday, and a weekly Workman's Circle program.

The station's ability to adapt to changing needs reflects two things that many Jewish organizations and communities have had the brilliance to do in the Diaspora. One is the continuing need to adapt to the changing environment. The second is that most Jewish organizations that deal with the public, although set up to serve Jews, usually do not discriminate against non-Jews and include services to the general community. Jews have been sensitive to the fact that they faced discrimination and therefore have tried not to discriminate against other people. There was also a need to survive, and offering programs for other ethnic groups provided not only a service, but revenue as well.

Many theories have been discussed in trying to determine how and why Jewish people have become involved in certain occupations and in this case intellectual and artistic endeavors. In Europe, depending on which country the Jews lived in and at which time, Jews were prevented from entering certain enterprises. The nobles and upper classes were more interested in political and economic survival. Writing, music, libraries and research were left to the middle classes. Henry L. Feingold in *American Jewish Biographies* (1982) states that to the German Jewish immigrants, "success meant simply achieving a firm foothold in the middle class."

From a sociological viewpoint, Jews have been regarded as "marginal men," being a part of the society they lived in, but viewed as separate because of their religious or ethnic identity. Although marginality can be seen as stressful to deal with, it also allows marginal people to look at the world around them in a different way from other members of society, thereby providing innovation and creativity. The Jewish intellectual tradition of the Talmudic scholar is hundreds of years old, and scholarship has held great status in the Jewish community. After the emancipation in the early nineteenth century, the religious intellectual tradition was also applied to the secular world.

In addition, because of discrimination, Jewish people wanted to work for themselves instead of having to rely on other people. Feingold quotes an historian who ascribed the commercial success of newly immigrated Jews and their families to "courageous enterprising." They were willing to take risks in their new country. The establishment of what we know as Hollywood today was based on the risk taking of many immigrants, including Italian bankers and Jewish film-makers. In addition, the new inventions and the openness of American society to such creativity because of the expansiveness of the developing country allowed such interaction to occur.

Who is to say which factors were mixed in what ways to develop David Sarnoff and William Paley or Jack Benny and Norman Corwin. The interaction between the dynamism of America at the beginning of the twentieth century, new inventions, and a society that encouraged such developments, the marginality of Jewish people, the Jewish intellectual tradition and a history of discrimination against the Jewish people affected each person in different ways. The creativity derived from each unique mixture helped develop radio broadcasting in the United States. *See also* Comics and Comedy.

EARL YAILLEN

BIBLIOGRAPHY

Barnouw, Erik. *The Golden Web: A History of Broadcasting in the United States, 1933–1953.* New York: Oxford University Press, 1968.

———. *A Tower in Babel: A History of Broadcasting in the United States, Volume I to 1933.* New York: Oxford University Press, 1966.

Buxton, Frank, and Owen, Bill. *The Big Broadcast, 1920–1950.* New York: Avon, 1973.

Dunning, John. *Tune in Yesterday: The Ultimate Encyclopedia of Old Time Radio, 1925–1976.* Englewood Cliffs, NJ: Prentice-Hall, 1976.

Gabler, Neal. *An Empire of Their Own: How the Jews Invented Hollywood.* New York: Anchor, 1988.

Gross, Ben. *I Looked and I Listened: Informal Recollections of Radio and TV.* New York: Random House, 1954.

Landry, Robert J. *This Fascinating Radio Business.* Indianapolis: Bobbs-Merrill, 1946.

Lyons, Eugene. *David Sarnoff: A Biography.* New York: Harper & Row, 1966.

Paley, William. *As It Happened: A Memoir.* Garden City, N.Y.: Doubleday, 1979.

Rand, Ayn (1905–1967). Author Ayn Rand, best known for her novels *The Fountainhead* (1943) and *Atlas Shrugged* (1957) was born Alissa Rosenbaum in St. Petersburg, Russia in 1905. She was the oldest of three daughters born into a thoroughly assimilated Russian Jewish family. The Rosenbaums' attachment to Jewish life was almost nonexistent; consequently, the future Ayn Rand received no formal religious training. Early in life, she declared herself an atheist, a conviction she held her entire life.

In 1921, Alissa Rosenbaum entered St. Petersburg University, from which she graduated in 1924 with a degree in history. Years after graduation, she would recall her university days in *We the Living* (1936). In 1926, Ayn Rand migrated to the United States and became a citizen in 1931. Her early years in the United States were spent working as a movie extra and scriptwriter in Hollywood. However, her first love, going back to childhood, was to become a writer, and much of her fame rests on the novels already cited, as well as *Anthem* (1938).

Ayn Rand used her novels as a vehicle to expound on her philosophy of objectivism, which attracted a small but loyal following among intellectuals. Objectivism is the belief that universal concepts or ideas have an objective reality in nature. According to Rand, "Objective reality exists independently of any perceiver or the perceiver's emotions, feelings, wishes, hopes, or fears." In addition, the human mind is capable of perceiving and interpreting these concepts. Rand saw herself in a direct line of early rationalists beginning with Aristotle, Thomas Aquinas, and leading up to herself. Her writing, both in fiction and philosophy, stress the theme of rationalism and is closely linked with individualism. The man or woman of reason is always an individualist, eschewing society's values and following only the dictates of his or her mind. In *Atlas Shrugged* the book's hero, John Galt, broadcasts to the American people the message that each person should take responsibility for his own life and be a rationalist, an individualist, and a producer. Conversely, one's greatest enemy is the temptation to irrational thought, collectivist morality, altruistic ethics, and mystical metaphysics. Galt's speech represents the essence of Rand's philosophy of objectivism.

Other works by Ayn Rand include *For the Intellectual* (1961), *Capitalism: The Unknown Ideal* (1966), and *Introduction to Objectivist Epistemology* (1967).

JOSHUA FISCHEL

BIBLIOGRAPHY

Baker, James T. *Ayn Rand.* Boston: Twayne, 1987.

Branden, Barbara. *The Passion of Ayn Rand.* New York: Doubleday, 1986.

Branden, Nathaniel, and Branden, Barbara. *Who Is Ayn Rand?* New York: Random House, 1962.

O'Neill, William. *With Charity Toward None: An Analysis of Ayn Rand's Philosophy*. New York: Philosophical Library, 1971.

Reconstructionism. A religious ideology and a fourth movement that has emerged in twentieth-century American Jewish life, Reconstructionism was initiated by the teaching and writing of Rabbi Mordecai M. Kaplan. Reconstructionism views Judaism as the evolving religious civilization of the Jewish people and seeks, therefore, to adapt inherited Jewish belief and practice to the needs of the contemporary world. It was initially a school of thought that sought to influence and bring together the existing Jewish movements. Since the 1950s, however, it has emerged as a movement with the establishment of the Federation of Reconstructionist Congregations and Havurot (FRCH), the Reconstructionist Rabbinical College (RRC), and the Reconstructionist Rabbinical Association (RRA).

HISTORICAL DEVELOPMENT. The beginning of Reconstructionism can be dated to 1922 when Kaplan founded the Society for the Advancement of Judaism (SAJ), a synagogue in New York City. At the SAJ, Kaplan developed his approach to Judaism with a group of Jews who were disaffected with other forms of Judaism but committed to reconstructing it in a way that spoke meaningfully in the twentieth century. The congregation experimented with changes in the traditional liturgy, with the inclusion of women, including the introduction of the bat mitzvah ceremony in 1922, and with the "revaluation" of Jewish ritual. Jewish intellectuals from all sectors gathered to hear Kaplan's sermons and talks, in which he continued to develop his new interpretation of Judaism. The *SAJ Review* was published as a means of disseminating the ideas of Kaplan and others.

In 1934, Kaplan published *Judaism As a Civilization*, a comprehensive analysis of the condition of modern Judaism and a program for its reconstruction. The book had an immediate and significant impact in the Jewish world and is regarded as one of the major works of Jewish thought in the twentieth century. In 1935, in the aftermath of the book's enthusiastic reception, the *Reconstructionist* magazine was established. Thereafter, under the editorship of Kaplan and then Rabbi Ira Eisenstein, Kaplan's son-in-law and preeminent disciple and exponent, it became an important forum for forward-looking and controversial ideas and programs. It continues to be read widely beyond the circle of those who define themselves as Reconstructionists.

In 1940, the Jewish Reconstructionist Foundation (JRF) was established to support works that promoted the Reconstructionist program. Kaplan and his disciples, Ira Eisenstein and Eugene Kohn, then published a series of liturgical texts. Both *The New Haggadah* (1941) and *The Sabbath Prayer Book* (1945) created a storm because they altered the wording of the traditional Hebrew text. The latter, which was burned by several Orthodox rabbis in a public ceremony of *herem* in 1945, substituted alternate wording for phrases referring to the chosenness of Israel, the resurrection of the dead, and the messiah. In subsequent years, prayer books for the High Holy Days, the pilgrimage festivals, and daily services were also published.

In 1954, the SAJ joined with three other synagogues to form the Reconstructionist Federation of Congregations as the synagogue arm of the foundation. (Only later was the phrase "and Havurot" added.) In 1960, the idea of *havurot*—small, lay-led, participatory groups of Jews who met for study, worship, and celebration—was introduced. The FRCH grew gradually in the 1960s and 1970s under the direction of Eisenstein and Rabbi Ludwig Nadelmann. Then in 1982, developing as an independent organization under the leadership of Rabbi David Teutsch, it expanded rapidly, doubling in size in five years. Teutsch was succeeded in 1986 by Rabbi Mordechai Liebling. In 1989, the FRCH published a new siddur for the Friday evening service, *Kol Haneshamah*, and plans to publish a complete Shabbat prayer book in the 1990s.

In 1968, the Reconstructionist Rabbinical College was founded in Philadelphia by Eisenstein, who served as its first president. The decision to found the college marked a definitive turn in the establishment of the movement—the initiative of those, led by Eisenstein, who had given up on the idea of influencing other movements and who thus advocated the full development of an institutional structure for a fourth alternative in North American Jewish life. In 13 years as president, Eisenstein established a program to train rabbis in accord with the movement's philosophy—to present Judaism as ever evolving, to encourage lay participation and decision making, to pioneer new ritual and theological innovations, and to lead in contexts other than the synagogue.

As a result, the movement has since been infused with the energy and perspectives of a new generation of leadership. Its graduates are trained in a way that has created a demand for them also among nonmovement congregations. In 1981, Ira Silverman succeeded Eisenstein as president of RRC; in 1986, Arthur Green became president. Under the Silverman and Green administrations, RRC has expanded rapidly because of the generosity of benefactor Aaron Ziegelman. Under Green in particular, the college's academic reputation improved dramatically.

The Reconstructionist Rabbinical Association was founded in 1974 by RRC alumni and had grown by 1989 to a membership of 165 that also includes rabbis trained at other seminaries. It has pioneered in its conversion, divorce, and intermarriage guidelines, has emerged as part of the movement's leadership, and is now a voice that is heard on the American Jewish scene.

KAPLAN'S PHILOSOPHY. *Evolving Civilization.*

In defining Judaism as the evolving religious civilization of the Jewish people, Kaplan embraced the perspective of modern Jewish historians. He rejected the traditional claim that Written (the Bible) and Oral (the Talmud) Torah had literally been revealed by God at Sinai and the consequent claim that Halakhah was binding as a set of divine commandments. Rather, he viewed the development of Jewish belief and practice as having undergone a process of continuous evolution as successive generations of Jews adapted to ever changing social circumstances, political challenges, and cultural influences. Thus, Jewish traditions are to be treasured because evolution has distilled the most lasting and compelling insights reached by previous generations about the ultimate meaning and sanctity of life.

Civilization. By defining Judaism as a civilization, Kaplan rejected the widespread tendency to define it as a religion in accordance with modern Protestant-influenced categories. While the religious component has always been one primary factor in Jewish civilization, Judaism is an all-embracing way of life that has developed organically in self-governing Jewish communities and that includes languages, literature, customs, civil and criminal law, art, music, food—the full range of phenomena that grow out of any civilization but which in modern terms are defined as secular.

This definition had several important consequences. Kaplan argued, particularly against classical Reform Judaism, that an exclusively religious definition is inimical to Jewish survival. This is because Jews' religious commitments cannot be sustained if not grounded in the wider civilizational context. In addition, the definition validated and encouraged modern Jews alienated from traditional Jewish theology and practice who, nevertheless, have strong cultural ties to Jewish lifestyles and community.

Peoplehood. Underlying the ever evolving nature of Jewish beliefs and practices, according to Kaplan, is a constant: the Jewish people. It is the people collectively who weathered the vicissitudes of history and who is the source of all aspects of the Jewish heritage. Even in its encounters with God, the revelation heard and the practices developed as commandments are best understood as human refractions of divine imperatives that reflect the social, cultural, and historical context of the people involved in the encounters.

Out of the primacy of peoplehood came the Reconstructionist teaching that belonging is prior to belief or behavior. Traditionally, Jews were acculturated to belief and practice through their family upbringing and participation in Jewish communities. Kaplan maintained that it was essential to develop new forms of community that would serve as an acculturating context in the modern era.

Need for Reconstruction. As Kaplan understood Jewish history, Judaism has always evolved as Jews have adapted to unprecedented circumstances. He argued that a major, self-conscious reconstruction is now urgent because of the radical dislocations in Jewish life caused by the Enlightenment, the political emancipation of the Jewish people, and the technological revolution. Prior to 1800, Jews lived in autonomous Jewish communities that were granted sovereignty by Muslim and Christian rulers to govern their members in accordance with Jewish law. People were born into Jewish communities that established enforceable norms and provided them with the full range of social, economic, educational, and cultural services, for which there were no alternatives. They had no choice, short of apostasy, but to live as members of the Jewish community. Moreover, for 13 centuries, the competing surrounding cultures were of a piece with traditional Judaism in their assertions of a divinely revealed Scripture, a divinely commanded way of life, the primacy of religion and the authority of the clergy, the existence of a God who intervenes supernaturally to reward and punish, and the promise of an other-worldly recompense for one's deeds in this life.

Kaplan was the first to observe that the Jewish crisis of modernity is a direct result of the loss of these social and cultural circumstances. Socially, since the beginning of the nineteenth century, Jews in various places have undergone political emancipation that has granted them citizenship as individuals in their nations of residence. They participate fully in the surrounding society and thus now have a *choice* their ancestors lacked about whether and how to identify and participate as Jews. Halakah is no longer the law by which they are governed, and it is therefore no longer functional as a legal system. Thus, a new mode for establishing community norms is needed, one that does not depend on the authority of rabbinic decisions.

Culturally, the world view accepted in the societies in which Jews now live is no longer supportive of traditional Jewish teachings. In its belief in natural causes, modern science undercuts traditional supernaturalism. The primacy of individual autonomy conflicts with the traditional virtue of obedience to mitzvot and of following communal norms. The teachings of democracy make Jews reluctant to have decisions made by those with the authority of Halakic learning. Ecumenicism renders archaic traditional notions of separatism and chosenness. Secularism renders counterintuitive the traditional view that God's presence is everywhere. Because Jews are fully integrated into their surrounding cultures, Kaplan thus argued that many traditional teachings required reconstruction if they were to continue to influence the hearts and minds of Jews.

Theology. In response to modern naturalism, Kaplan sought to depart from personal and supernatural descriptions of God, whom he defined as the Power or Process, inherent in the world, that makes for salvation (see his *The Meaning of God in Modern Jewish Religion* [MGMJR]). In this he was influenced by such process theologians as Alfred North Whitehead. Also influenced by the pragmatism of John Dewey, he focused more on the function of belief in God than on the nature of God, emphasizing how one's belief affects the way one lives.

Though often criticized by detractors as a closet atheist, Kaplan possessed, both in his writings and his life, a passionate faith in the existence of an impersonal God-Force, not identical with nature, that is the source of the human impulse to virtue. His God, however—like that of such medieval philosophers as Maimonides—does not intervene supernaturally to reward and punish; God

rather underlies existence, serving as a fount of energy and inspiration to those who seek divine ends. God does not literally answer prayers; prayer serves as a means for reinforcing communal values and as a mode of spiritual discipline. Worship services at the SAJ have followed a somewhat abbreviated but largely traditional Hebrew service, interspersed with contemporary English readings related to service themes and a heavy reliance on teaching and discussions, designed to revivify traditional themes and interpret their contemporary meaning.

Ritual Practice. This view of God entails a rejection of the traditional belief that the Torah and its subsequent interpretations are literally divinely revealed, thus eliminating the belief that all the mitzvoth are God's commandments and that Jews are rewarded and punished for their level of obedience. The rationale for ritual observance is found rather in the civilizational definition of Judaism. Since Jewish civilization is the result of the collective quest of Jews through the generations to live a godly life, Jewish texts, insights, values, and practices are of inestimable value to any Jew or Jewish community on a similar quest. And since insights and values cannot be acquired or transmitted as abstract, disembodied principles, Jews can best mine the treasures of Jewish tradition by entering the Jewish universe through ritual practice and study of traditional texts. By thus structuring their lives to see the world through Jewish lenses, they gain access to cultural, psychological, and spiritual treasures that are largely absent from secular Western culture.

While there is much in Jewish tradition worthy of recovery, there is also a great deal that requires reconstruction based on contemporary criteria. The Reconstructionist motto here is "Tradition has a vote but not a veto."

For example, based on the moral value of equality, it is imperative to include women in roles and practices from which they have been excluded by Jewish law.

Culturally, the traditional, supernaturalist rationales for most rituals and prayers must undergo what Kaplan termed "revaluation"—explaining the meaning of a practice in contemporary terms. Thus, while Sabbath rest was described as "a foretaste of the World to Come," Jews today ought to observe it as an expression of the ultimate value of spiritual rest in a goal-oriented world; while Jews may not believe literally in God's supernatural rescue of the Israelites from Egyptian slavery, the celebration of a revaluated Passover serves as an opportunity to stress the transcendent importance of contemporary meanings of freedom.

Socially, the traditional Jewish emphasis on separation from non-Jews runs counter to the desirable reality of life in the post-Emancipation West. Thus, observance of kashrut, for example, may sometimes require modification when strict adherence to traditional norms obstructs important social intercourse.

Kaplan advocated a process of collective study of traditional sources and their rationales for mitzvoth so that communities could reach norms for public practice together. In line with this approach, each Reconstructionist is individually and communally engaged in study and experimentation with the aim of incorporating an increasing level of ritual observance into his or her daily life. As a result, the degree of Jewish study and ritual practice among Reconstructionists tends to be high.

Living in Two Civilizations. Kaplan parted ways with those who lament the corrosive effects of political emancipation on Jewish life. While noting the problems, he embraced the political culture of Western democracy as a welcome advance over a past in which Jews lived in forced segregation. He was at peace with the reality that Jews in Western democracies live primarily in the civilization of their surrounding cultures and only secondarily in Jewish civilization. For him, the best of American and Jewish values coincide. He believed that the modern West has much to offer Jews in the enterprise of reconstructing Jewish civilization in accord with democratic values and that working for a vital Jewish community is entirely in harmony with the goals of pluralism.

The Chosen People. Because a nonsupernaturalistic God could not literally choose one people over another and because the claim of privileged access to God promotes, however unintentionally, odious feelings of superiority, Kaplan sought to dispense with the idea that the Jewish people are chosen by God, going so far as to eliminate all references to chosenness from the liturgy. In traditional Jewish teaching, this teaching had, in large part, focused on the superiority of Torah rather than on the distinctiveness of Jews. When it is adopted, however, by Jews who do not accept the revealed, binding nature of the commandments, it is transformed into an undesirable chauvinism. Instead, Kaplan taught that all peoples and civilizations have equal access to the Divine, and that each, like Judaism, should be encouraged to evolve in ways that approximate the Divine will more closely. Speaking of Judaism as "the religion of ethical nationhood," he urged Jews to continue Judaism's development as a civilization devoted to the ethical treatment of individuals. He wrote and preached widely on the need for modern Jews to develop a consensus about ethical standards, so that Judaism would be more than a nostalgic relic with little influence over the way one lives one's life.

Social Activism. Because of their commitment to living in two civilizations and to the benefits to be derived from the mutual influence of Western and Jewish cultures, Kaplan and his collaborators on *Reconstructionist* editorials were unrestrained critics of social and economic injustice in capitalist societies. They utilized traditional rabbinic teachings as ideological bases for decrying economic exploitation, unfair labor practices, and militarism.

The New Zionism. Out of the definition of Judaism as a civilization came a strong commitment to the upbuilding of the *Yishuv* in the Land of Israel, since it is only in Israel that Jews can live primarily in a Jewish civilization. Kaplan followed Ahad Ha'am in seeking a cultural and spiritual center in which Jewish civilization can flourish fully, developing new, modern forms of expression in accord with the highest Western liberal ideals. He was early in foreseeing that Jewish life in the Diaspora would continue, picturing Israel as the primary and radiant center of Jewish civilization that would influence and be influenced by other Jewish communities.

After 1948, Kaplan continued to distinguish between the ideal of Zion and the State of Israel, holding the latter up to elevated Jewish standards. He criticized lovingly the secular/religious dichotomy in Israeli society, Israel's foreign policy, and the lack of attention paid to the development of an indigenous and new Jewish culture. He made aliyah late in his life and lived in Jerusalem.

Organic Community. For Jewish civilization to thrive in the modern world, Kaplan believed that the traditional, preemancipation community would have to be reconstituted. He proposed and advocated the formation of an organic community, a super-kehillah, to nurture the development of functioning Jewish communities in North America. The community, which Jews would join by payment of dues, would include all religious and secular Jewish organizations and would have a monopoly on providing Jewish services—life cycle rituals, kosher food, worship services, social and educational programs. His ideal kehillah would be pluralistic and administered democratically. It would have the power to regulate the lives of Jews by insisting on ethical standards and educational commitments that could be arrived at democratically because Jews would have to listen or face loss of membership. On a local level, he proposed geographically based Jewish community centers that would provide religious, cultural, social, and educational services for all Jews, thus bringing diverse Jews together under one roof, eliminating the separation between religious and secular activities. While Kaplan's global proposal has not been accepted, his promotion of Jewish community centers had a major impact on the institutional development of U.S. Jewry.

RECONSTRUCTIONISM AFTER KAPLAN. While Reconstructionism was long identified with Kaplan and Eisenstein alone, a dynamic and diverse movement has emerged since the 1960s with a variety of voices, each seeking to follow the imperative to continue the ongoing reconstruction of Jewish life.

Theology. Kaplan's discussion of God has always been controversial. As early as the 1940s, Milton Steinberg, one of his chief disciples, broke with him and affirmed the need for a personal God. More recently, Harold Schulweis has developed "predicate theology," which seeks to locate God in predicates (*when* God is present) rather than in subjects (*what* God is). Harold Kushner has expanded on Kaplan's theology in his *When Bad Things Happen to Good People* (1982). William Kaufman and Jacob Staub have sought to refine Kaplan's process theology.

Arthur Green has pursued another path in religious naturalism, utilizing Hasidic teachings that speak of God within us rather than above us and that use more traditionally Jewish imagery for describing God in the spiritual experiences of human beings. Green has reclaimed much of the traditional God imagery by regarding it as myth, relying on recent research in religious studies and the social sciences, not available to Kaplan, about the functions of myth and metaphor.

Feminists within the movement have sought to base a gender-neutral God language upon Kaplan's rejection of personal God imagery, which has always been exclusively masculine.

Similarly, Kaplan's teaching on the idea of chosenness has also come under discussion.

Feminism. Jewish feminists have found the Reconstructionist movement an environment hospitable to experimentation. It was here that the

bat mitzvah ceremony was introduced (1922). Women were accorded full equality in the synagogue service at the SAJ in the 1940s, were early accepted as rabbis (in 1968, at the founding of RRC), and were accepted as witnesses and as equal partners in divorce proceedings (RRA decision, 1978). Brit ceremonies for baby girls, prayers and ceremonies for pregnancy, birth, and miscarriage, women's Rosh Hodesh rituals, and feminine God language that alternates with traditional masculine metaphors have all been developed. The effect of women on the rabbinic role has been explored. The RRC curriculum includes the study of the history of Jewish women, and educators have developed curricula and programs that seek to promote egalitarianism from an early age.

Ritual and Prayer. With the development of myth and ritual studies in the social sciences and with a loss of faith in strict rationalism and science in the general culture, Reconstructionists now tend to understand Kaplan's rationalism and pragmatism as reflecting his historical context and thus as subject to further development. Less likely to have been exposed to Old World Orthodox Judaism, they are now less cautious about reclaiming traditional modes of worship and practice, which they understand in naturalistic ways. Hershel J. Matt, who taught at RRC until his death in 1987, advocated the use of contemporary *kavvanot* (meditations) designed to enhance *davvening*, and Green's neo-Hasidic teachings have convinced many to explore more traditional modes of spiritual practice. While more veteran members of the movement remain concerned about the reintroduction of supernaturalistic imagery, the "Statement of Reconstructionist Principles," passed by the FRCH (1985) and the RRA (1986) reflects another attempt to develop a new consensus.

The new siddur, *Kol Haneshamah* (1989), edited by Teutsch, is a collaborative effort of a Prayerbook Commission composed of lay leaders and rabbis and of a group of distinguished scholars that included Green and Joel Rosenberg. The siddur thus reflects many of these new trends and breaks new ground in translating Reconstructionist theory into practice.

Ethics. Kaplan's emphasis on the primacy of ethics in Jewish civilization has led to a movement emphasis on making the study of Jewish teachings an opportunity for contemporary ethical living. Areas of primary concern have been biomedical ethics (in which a curriculum for the education of theological students has been published by Arnold Eisen, Stephen Lammers, and Rebecca Alpert), sexual ethics, and moral education.

Outreach. The growth of the movement, spurred by Teutsch's leadership of FRCH in the early 1980s, has led to many new challenges. *Exploring Judaism: A Reconstructionist Approach*, by Rebecca T. Alpert and Jacob J. Staub (1985), is now the widely used introduction to Reconstructionism. *Dynamic Judaism: The Essential Writings of Mordecai M. Kaplan*, edited by Emanuel S. Goldsmith and Mel Scult (1985), excerpts from Kaplan's writings. Taking over as editor of the *Reconstructionist* (1983–1989; Joy Levitt succeeded him), Staub transformed it into a magazine that reflects new movement developments and promotes intramovement sharing of programs and ideas.

The movement has also led on Jewish identity issues. The JRF pioneered in its adoption of patrilineal descent in 1968, a position that was reaffirmed by RRA in 1978 and FRCH in 1984. The RRA adopted Conversion Guidelines in 1978. It adopted Intermarriage Guidelines in 1983, the FRCH in 1984. While warmly welcoming intermarried couples, Reconstructionist congregations have sought to involve them in the movement program of increasing involvement, study, and practice of all its members.

The RRC also pioneered with its 1984 decision to admit qualified students who are open about their gay or lesbian sexual orientation. The decision has since been affirmed by the RRA and the FRCH, whose affiliates emphasize the inclusion of sectors of the Jewish people who have been disenfranchised or alienated.

Despite the friction caused by these innovative positions, Reconstructionists have continued Kaplan's devotion to Klal Yisrael and have been involved prominently in efforts to reduce gratuitous acrimony that divides segments of the Jewish community.

Education. Jack J. Cohen first led in applying Reconstructionist principles to education, which he outlined in his *Jewish Education in a Democratic Society* (1964). More recently, Jeffrey L. Schein has led in developing the theory and practice of the movement's educational programs. He founded the Temin Center for Education at RRC and serves as the director of education for the FRCH.

Social and Political Action. Kaplan's example has made the movement hospitable to those who seek to combine social and political activism with their Jewish commitments. The editorials of the *Reconstructionist* magazine continue the tradition

established by Kaplan and Eisenstein, regularly taking stands on political and social issues from a Jewish perspective. The FRCH has adopted environmental issues as a main focus of its social action, and Shomrei Adamah, a Jewish environmental organization, was formed under its sponsorship. The RRC was the first home of the Shalom Center, which, under the leadership of Arthur Waskow, focuses on a Jewish approach to nuclear arms issues, and Waskow's influence as an activist on a whole range of issues has been pivotal in the movement's development as a strong voice for social and political change.

Community. The movement has responded to the failure of Kaplan's organic community proposal by fostering the development of smaller communal units. After the movement's introduction in 1960 of the notion of Havurot, most affiliated groups have begun as participatory, intimate, lay-led Havurot for study, worship, and celebration. As groups grow into larger congregations, participation and intimacy remain preeminent values. This has led to the development of support system networks within congregations and to careful thinking about lay-rabbinic relations and democratic governance. Under Teutsch's leadership, FRCH, the lay arm of the movement, developed as an equal movement partner; this includes a process for democratic, movement-wide decision making, in which each affiliated group discusses an issue and sends delegates to the annual convention, where decisions are made by majority vote.

There has thus been much success in increasing the commitments of members and heightening their involvement in the study and thinking required by decision-making processes at the local and international levels. The problem initially posed by Kaplan, however—how to create real communities in which norms, arrived at democratically, can be established—has yet to be addressed adequately. By way of circumventing the obstacles to community formation posed by voluntarism, some are now suggesting that Jews voluntarily join groups whose collective decisions will be regarded as binding on all members.

Future Studies. Following Kaplan's orientation to the future, the RRC is developing an Institute for the Jewish Future, which will attract scholars who will serve as planning consultants for Jewish communities and who will develop position papers on issues faced by the Jewish people. An initial conference in 1988, "Imagining the Jewish Future," assembled an exciting group of scholars and community leaders who sought to anticipate the state of Jewish civilization in a generation.

FUTURE PROSPECTS. After an initial period of slow growth, due in large part to Kaplan's reluctance to abandon his hope of uniting the Jewish community and his consequent reluctance to build a separate movement, Reconstructionism is now experiencing accelerated expansion. Long a source of new ideas adopted by other movements, the movement is now in a position to respond to the current challenges facing North American Jewry—to involve alienated and disaffected Jews, to provide a setting for committed liberal Jews to develop compelling modes of Jewish study and practice, to integrate Jewish political activists, Jewish feminists, and Jews seeking a more satisfying form of Jewish spirituality. Its principle of "Unity in Diversity" will allow it to serve as an umbrella to a variety of liberal Jews, and its commitment to increasing the study and practice of members should enable it to pursue a program of "maximalist Judaism." It is likely to continue to be seen as too radical by some segments of the established Jewish community threatened by its innovations; as it grows and becomes better known, however, the healthy balance the movement seeks to maintain between reclaiming tradition and reconstructing it is likely to attract increasing numbers of thinking Jews. *See also* Havurah Movement.

JACOB J. STAUB

BIBLIOGRAPHY

Alpert, Rebecca T., and Staub, Jacob J. *Exploring Judaism: A Reconstructionist Approach.* New York: Reconstructionist Press, 1985.

Eisenstein, Ira. *Judaism under Freedom.* New York: Reconstructionist Press, 1956.

———. *Reconstructing Judaism: an Autobiography.* New York: Reconstructionist Press, 1987.

Goldsmith, Emanuel S., and Scult, Mel, eds. *Dynamic Judaism: The Essential Writings of Mordecai M. Kaplan.* New York: Schocken, 1985.

Green, Arthur. *See My Face, Speak My Name: A Contemporary Jewish Theology.* In press.

Kaplan, Mordecai M. *Judaism as a Civilization.* New York: Schocken, 1934.

———. *The Future of the American Jew.* New York: Reconstructionist Press, 1981.

———. *The Meaning of God in Modern Jewish Religion.* New York: Behrman House, 1937.

Schein, Jeffrey L. *Reconstructing Jewish Education: A Process Guide.* New York: Reconstructionist Press, 1989.

Teutsch, David A., and Green, Arthur, eds. *Kol Haneshamah: Sabbat Eve.* New York: Reconstructionist Press, 1989.

Reform Judaism. Also known as Liberal or Progressive Judaism, Reform Judaism is one of the principal branches of Judaism in the United States and Canada. It is also the largest and longest-lived movement in "liberal religion" in world history. Developing first in West European Jewish communites, most importantly in Germany during the early and middle decades of the nineteenth century, Reform's greater institutional success in North America was predicated on the broad appeal of both its belief in Jewish cultural accommodation and its highly adaptive religious program, especially its reduction of ritualism, its attempt to link Jewish religious values with American political liberalism, and its emphasis on the aesthetics of worship.

For most of its first 100 years, with the exception of the original Reformed Society of Israelites (1825–1833), which was led by a handful of Sephardic Jews, American Reform Judaism almost exclusively attracted Jews of Central European origin or descent. During the 1920s, East European Jews and their descendants began to join Reform temples in steadily increasing numbers and by the 1940s constituted a majority in the movement. Following World War II, subethnic differences diminished in general among American Jews and thus played virtually no role in the shaping of postwar Reform Judaism. The social structure of the Reform Movement began changing again during the 1970s as the rate of mixed and conversionary marriages soared. From its inception, the American Reform Movement has largely maintained a middle-class social base. It has also been appealing to a significant portion of the socioeconomic elite of the American Jewish community.

Reform Judaism was the first religious movement among American Jews to organize itself on a denominational basis. It pioneered a three-track system of national, or federal, governance in American Judaism, that subsequently was adopted by all the branches of modern Judaism in North America. Reform's institutional superstructure includes an umbrella organization of independent synagogues (the Union of American Hebrew Congregations [UAHC]), a seminary system (the Hebrew Union College/Jewish Institute of Religion [HUC-JIR]), and a professional association of rabbis (the Central Conference of American Rabbis [CCAR]). By the beginning of the 1980s, over 750 American synagogues with more than a million individual members were affiliated with the Reform Movement. Outside of North America, Reform congregations are represented by the World Union for Progressive Judaism.

The basic mode of governance in the American Reform Movement is congregationalist. Power is principally vested in the board and officers of the individual synagogue. However, since World War II the federal institutions of the movement have dramatically widened the scope of their operations. The UAHC presidency, a professional position held by a rabbi since 1943, is the most visible and, perhaps, most influential leadership role in the movement. On the other hand, the authority of the congregational rabbinate, inherently weak because of the Reform Movement's tradition of trusteeism, its liberal theology, and, more broadly, the constitutional separation of the institutions of state and religion in the United States, which has generally limited the power of the American clergy, has been a topic of considerable discussion within the movement. In part, professionalism and traditional respect for the rabbinic office function as mitigating factors. However, Jewish scholarship, the traditional basis of rabbinic power, has largely given way to the individual rabbi's powers of persuasion, personal warmth, and pastoral skills as the basis for his or her authority at the local level.

IDEOLOGY. Unlike their counterparts in Europe, early American Reformers did not initially seek Halakic justifications as part of their effort to adapt Judaism to the American cultural milieu. Rather, influenced by the American belief in the sovereign self, they began with their own religious present and then drew eclectically both from contemporary culture and the cumulative Jewish tradition to express and validate their understanding of Judaism. Subsequently, the American Reform Movement generally remained more radical than its counterpart in Germany. Although currently more favorably inclined toward a number of traditional practices than in the past, the overall religious ideology of the movement remains as liberal as ever. For example, the CCAR's 1983 endorsement of patrilineal descent can be seen as one of the most radical policies ever adopted by an official body of the Reform Movement.

The initial theology of the American Reform Movement was deistic. Although popular religious thought in Reform largely remains in line with that of general American civil religion, an elitist theology, first articulated in Germany and subsequently brought to the United States and Canada by immigrant rabbis during the middle decades of the nineteenth century, is usually presented as the official "religion" of the movement. Two doctrines—Progressive Revelation and the Mission of Israel, derived from classical Jewish sources and Romantic German (Hegelian) philosophy—shaped the ideological character of American Reform during its formative years. In the Reform tradition, revelation was understood in terms of neither a historical theophany at Sinai nor philosophically determined truths. Rather, it was redefined as an ongoing process of individual and collective inspiration in Jewish history. Not only did Progress Revelation account for the development of the written (Bible) and oral (Talmud) law, but it also sanctioned the work of the reformers themselves. In short, it held that religious change was divinely sanctioned and that the Reform Movement and the Jewish people were God's vanguard on earth.

The second concept, the Mission of Israel, proved more problematic and was gradually abandoned by the Reform Movement. Basically, it maintained that the dispersed Jewish people were a "light to the nations" and that they served as the apostles of ethical monotheism with the goal of creating a just society on earth. "Mission" theology thus helped justify and define the continued existence of the Jewish people in the postemancipatory era.

However, the mission concept was more than a mere universalistic reinterpretation of Judaism's ancient theological view of history. It was a radical reformulation of the idea of the chosen people. It committed Reform Judaism to the maintenance of Jewish endogamy and also provided the movement with a buttress against Christian missionary activity. Universal salvation, mission theology taught, was a Jewish obligation.

In its heyday, the mission idea not only complemented the more enduring notion of progressive revelation, but also gave the American Reform Movement a triumphalistic edge. Closely allied to the nineteenth-century belief in infinite human progress, Reform's mission theology was shaken by the terrible carnage of World War I.

Subsequently, it was all but abandoned as Reform reconciled itself with Zionism and embraced Jewish particularism during the 1930s.

An echo of the mission doctrine remains in the movement's commitment to social justice and political action. For the most part, however, contemporary Reform Judaism has lost much of its messianic urgency, and its religious program increasingly serves as a handmaiden to American Jewry's "civil religion" and its Darwinian-like theology of "sacred survival." In limited circles, especially among rabbis and select intellectuals, attempts to redefine Reform theology in terms of religious existentialism with an emphasis on personal spirituality have been highly successful.

PRACTICE. While Reform Judaism remains theoretically committed to a program of open-ended religious innovation and theological reevaluation, fundamental changes in its liturgical life tend to be controlled carefully at both the congregational and national levels. The potential for religious anarchy within Reform is essentially checked by the widespread respect Reform Jews hold for the normative religious principles and practices sanctioned by their movement. Historically, Reform's early and frequently radical antinomianism slowly relaxed during the course of the twentieth century. A new openness toward Jewish legal traditions developed as the movement turned inward in search of new sources of religious guidance. Currently, the CCAR issues a number of guides to Reform observance as well as several collections of Reform responsa. At the same time, the movement continues to respect and engender the individual Jew's freedom of choice.

Current Reform practice is characterized by the slow, eclectic restoration of numerous traditional customs along with the preservation of more radical Reform practices. Although only a tiny percentage of Reform Jews regularly attend services on a weekly basis, the vast majority annually worship at temple during the High Holy Days. Reform does not celebrate the "second day" of Jewish festivals. Many nonliturgical activities, both social and educational, attract large numbers of Reform Jews to their synagogues, which they generally refer to as "temples."

The main Sabbath service in Reform is held on Friday night after dinner, an innovation that can be traced back to the late 1860s but was not widely adopted by Reform congregations until the Depression of the 1930s. Men and women sit together during worship. The reading of the liturgy is usually supplemented with organ music and choral singing. The Reform choir is usually made up of non-Jewish semiprofessional singers. Many congregations also employ a cantor. The music of the Reform synagogue no longer is as heavily indebted to nineteenth-century German liturgical traditions as it was before World War II. Israeli, Hasidic, and folk-style American tunes have been introduced, especially in youth services and at the movement's summer camps. Following Israeli practice, most Reform synagogues have switched from the Ashkenazic to the Sephardic pronunciation of Hebrew. The amount of Hebrew read in the service has also increased steadily since World War II. However, the extensive use of the vernacular continues to distinguish the American Reform service as does its decorum and, compared to either Orthodoxy or Conservativism, its relative congregational passivity.

Outside the synagogue, Reform Jews tend to maintain a modicum of ritual practices. The vast majority of Reform homes have mezuzahs. Passover and Hanukkah are widely observed, and in a large percentage of households, Sabbath and memorial candles are lit. Observance of the dietary laws, not required by the Reform tradition, is rarely maintained in full, although in some homes certain restrictions are respected, based on the particular individual's predilection. Reform Jews tend to maintain strong ethnic identities as American Jews and consider education and ethics to be of paramount importance in one's personal life. In recent years, a large number of Reform males have returned to wearing ritual head covering (kippah or yarmulke) during worship at home and in Temple. Many Reform synagogues provide kippot for those who want to wear them. Prayer shawls, on the other hand, are generally only worn by the rabbis, cantors, and other regular participants in morning services.

Most Reform Jews send their school-age children to supplementary Jewish education programs on the weekends and after regular school during the week. A Reform day school movement is emerging in several large cities and, after considerable debate, has received UAHC sanction. The majority of Reform children remain in religious school through tenth grade and confirmation. Since World War II, bar and bat mitzvah have also been widely observed by American Reform Jews. Adult education programs are increasingly popular. Distinguished speaker series and seminar-style study groups, in particular, have both proven to be successful formats for Reform congregations.

In response to the soaring rate of exogamy and pressure from congregants whose children have chosen to marry non-Jews, many Reform rabbis now officiate at the weddings of religiously mixed couples in contravention of CCAR guidelines. The vast majority of these rabbis, however, insist that the children of such unions be raised as Jews and that the couple receive either premarital counseling or some instruction in Judaism. Few Reform rabbis will co-officiate at a wedding with either a minister or a priest.

Reform policy on conversion has been another source of increasing controversy in the larger Jewish community in recent years. Reform's outreach program, on the other hand, representing a significant softening of traditional Judaism's attitude toward prospective converts, has positively influenced both Conservatism and some segments of Modern Orthodoxy. Reform rabbis continue to be generally interested in both Jewish and general communal affairs and are often active in interfaith circles, civic organizations, and social welfare activities.

HISTORY. Constantly seeking to create a mode of Judaism compatible with contemporary culture, American Reform Judaism has experienced six distinct periods in its development:

1. Beginnings, 1824–1865
2. The Golden Age of Liberal Judaism, 1865–1900
3. Reform Judaism and Uptown Progressivism, 1900–1920
4. Reorientation, 1920–1945
5. Reform on the Suburban Frontier, 1945–1965
6. Reform Since 1965

During the interwar years, the Reform Movement experienced a fundamental shift in its basic ideology from a primary emphasis on theological universalism to a greater appreciation of Jewish particularism. The "reorientation," however, did not result in either a permanent institutional schism or an abandonment of the movement's essential religious liberalism.

Beginnings, 1824–1865. During its initial period of devlopment in North America, the Reform Movement generated a considerable amount of religious controversy among American Jews even though the movement was numerically small and internally divided. By the Civil War, no more than 8 of the 200-plus synagogues in the United States and Canada were either openly Reform or

had Reformistic tendencies. On the other hand, the Reform Movement had several outstanding rabbinic champions, including its indefatigable brick-and-mortar builder, Isaac M. Wise (1819–1900) and the brilliant, radical reformer, David Einhorn (1809–1879).

The first attempt to organize a Reform Movement in American Judaism occurred in Charleston, South Carolina, one of the great cultural centers of the old South and the site of continuous Jewish settlement since the 1670s. Led by young, highly Americanized Jews, many of Sephardic descent, who had only a faint knowledge of the European Reform Movement, a group of nearly 50 members of Charleston's Kehillah—Congregation Beth Elohim—petitioned the synagogue community's board and requested the reading of select prayers in the English language, a weekly "discourse" in the vernacular, and greater decorum and dignity in a variety of congregational activities including worship and fund raising. When Beth Elohim's trustees refused to discuss the group's proposals, the dissidents decided to organize an independent Reformed Society of Israelites (1825–1833). The society flourished for a few years, held annual dinners for its male members, and produced its own liturgy. The untimely death of its principal leader, Isaac Harby (1788–1828), and heavy communal and family pressure resulted in the society's decline. The Charleston Reform Movement experienced a resurgence at the end of the 1830s. Led by a young attorney, Abraham Moise, who received the unforeseen support of Beth Elohim's hazan, Gustavus Poznanski (1805–1879), the Reformers succeeded in having an organ installed in the community's new synagogue building as well as winning custody of the building in a protracted and bitter legal action against the Orthodox members of the congregation. The latter subsequently withdrew from Beth Elohim and formed a synagogue of their own, Shearith Israel.

A second line of development in the American Reform Movement also began in the early 1840s with the arrival of Central European immigrants who quickly became the new majority of American Jews. The Jewish population of the United States grew geometrically from 2700 to 3000 in 1820 to 15,000 in 1840. By 1860, the total U.S. Jewish population approached the 150,000 mark. Included were a small number of Reform Jews and rabbis who laid the foundation for the development of an indigenous American movement. Typical of all immigrant faiths, Reform Jews debated the merits of cultural accommodation. By the 1870s, the Americanizers had clearly gained the upper hand. The first immigrant Reform groups were organized in Baltimore, the Har Sinai Verein, in 1842 and in New York, Congregation Emanu-El, three years later. Both groups' activities were essentially molded by the Reform Movement in Germany. Emanu-El, in particular, quickly prospered and attracted many of New York's most successful immigrants to its pews. It hired Leo Merzbacher (1809 or 1810-1856), who had studied both with the renowned Orthodox scholar, Moses Sofer, and at several German universities, to serve as its spiritual leader. In 1855, Merzbacher published his own prayerbook, *Seder Tefillah*, in Hebrew and English, although he preached exclusively in German. Essentially still a traditional prayerbook, it was sharply criticized by the Orthodox.

Isaac M. Wise, a native of Bohemia, and the leading organizer of nineteenth-century American Reform Judaism, arrived in the United States in 1846. Committed to Americanizing Judaism, Wise, whose personal education was considerably more modest than he publicly claimed, was a highly industrious, pragmatic leader, prodigious reader and writer, and, above all, a practical Reformer. Sent to Albany to Congregation Beth El in 1846, at the age of 27, by his friend, Max Lilienthal (1815-1882, who was then serving as the "Chief Rabbi" of New York's three traditional German congregations), Wise immediately began introducing reforms, including a mixed choir. Tensions mounted and Wise, refusing to be dismissed, insisted on leading services on the Jewish New Year in 1850. Following a melee in the temple, Wise and his followers withdrew and organized Congregation Anshe Emeth. Established as a Reform congregation, Anshe Emeth was the first synagogue in the United States to permit men and women to sit together during services.

In 1854, Wise was called to the pulpit of B'nai Jeshurun (Bene Yeshurun) in Cincinnati, where he remained for the rest of his life. The following year, Lilienthal, who also was moving in the direction of moderate Reform, also relocated in Cincinnati accepting the rabbinic position at Congregation Bene Israel, the oldest in the city. Of the two, Wise quickly emerged as the superior leader. He founded a monthly newspaper, the *Israelite*, which served as a platform to circulate his views on American Judaism on a national basis. Hoping to unite American Jewry under one banner, Wise, along with his arch rival, Isaac

Leeser (1806-1868), the leading Orthodox religious leader in antebellum America, unsuccessfully attempted to convene a conference of American "rabbis" in 1848. Seven years later, however, the relentless Wise organized a rabbinic conference in Cleveland, which was reluctantly attended by Leeser.

Wise hoped to use the Cleveland conference to establish a single mode of American Judaism, a common prayerbook (*Minhag America*), and a Cincinnati-based Zion college. In conceding the authority of the Talmud to his Orthodox colleagues, however, Wise offended the religious sensibilities of numerous radical reformers, especially Rabbi David Einhorn, who vigorously and publicly attacked Wise. Einhorn's protests not only dashed Wise's hopes for a common American Judaism, they also were indicative of the serious religious divisions growing within the American Reform Movement.

Einhorn actually differed from Wise on a number of issues. A Bavarian rabbi who had studied at several German universities, Einhorn was a rigorous and systematic thinker, an uncompromising reformer and a political liberal. Arriving in the United States in 1855 to serve Baltimore's Har Sinai Congregation, he published his own prayer book, *Olat Tamid*, an original German work that later became the basis for the CCAR's *Union Prayer Book*, and a monthly German language journal, the *Sinai*. Despite his unpopular stand in favor of abolitionism, Einhorn emerged as the leading theologian of the Reform Movement in the years prior to and immediately after the Civil War. Ironically, in the postwar period, his ideology dominated the Reform Movement, while Wise's federal institutions and organizations reshaped the character of the Reform polity.

The Golden Age of Liberal Judaism, 1865-1900. The complex period between the end of the Civil War and the death of Isaac M. Wise in 1900 witnessed the transformation of the Reform Movement in America into an American-style denomination. Several factors contributed to this development: the general economic success and cultural accommodation of the German Jew in America, the widespread flowering of "liberal religion" in American Protestantism, and, finally, toward the end of the century, the double displacement of German Jews in American society as the result of the rise of indigenous American anti-Semitism and the mass immigration of East European Jews, which rendered German Jews, in general, and Reform Jews, in particular, a distinct minority in their own communities. This period also witnessed the near complete domination of the radical or "classical" branch of the movement and the vast expansion of Reform, in general, in American Judaism. By 1880, when East European Jews began arriving in large numbers, most of the older German synagogues had become Reform institutions.

Einhorn took the first step to define the character of American Reform Judaism in the postwar period. In November 1869, at the Philadelphia home of a distinguished colleague, Samuel Hirsch, Einhorn convened a small rabbinic conference. Among other things, the Philadelphia conference, animated by the doctrines of Progressive Revelation and the Mission of Israel, rejected the idea of Jewish restoration to Palestine and the Orthodox belief in physical resurrection as the attendees also attempted to strengthen the role of women in various Jewish life-cycle occasions. Ten years later, in his last sermon, Einhorn, who was never fully at home in America, cautioned his followers that "if you sever Reform from . . . the German language, you will have torn it from its native soil and the lovely flower must wilt." While his theology prevailed, his struggle to preserve the German character of American Reform Judaism proved to be a lost cause.

Wise, who attended the Philadelphia conference but contributed little to it, had plans of his own to rally moderate Reform rabbis under one banner. A series of meetings inspired or organized by Wise early in the 1870s proved highly divisive and pitted the East Coast "Einhornians" against Wise's group. To rescue their rabbi, a lay group, led by Moritz Loth, the president of Wise's congregation, organized the Union of American Hebrew Congregations in July 1873. Thirty-four congregations joined, mainly from the Midwest and South. By the following year, the number of affiliated synagogues jumped to 55, and another 17 congregations joined in 1875. By the end of the decade, 118 congregations, more than half of all the identified synagogues in the United States, were affiliated with the UAHC. Almost unwittingly, the Reform Movement had taken the decisive step toward becoming an American-style denomination.

One of the principal purposes of the UAHC was to serve as the patron of a rabbinic school. In 1875, the Hebrew Union College was established in Cincinnati, and Wise was named its president, thus fulfilling one of his lifelong dreams. Hoping that the college could serve all sectors of American Jewish religious life, Wise carefully controlled the curriculum so that ideas and methods repugnant to traditionalists were not offered. However, Wise's nondenominational approach to the rabbinic proved to be a pipe dream. At the dinner honoring the college's first four ordainees in 1883, attended by representatives of over 100 UAHC congregations, shell fish (prohibited by Jewish law) was inadvertently served by the hosts. The "Trefa Banquet" quickly became a symbol of the differences between the Reform Movement and the more traditional schools of Judaism in America. While the college survived the incident, Wise's dream of a common American Judaism had been dealt a fatal setback.

Two years later, a controversy between two scholarly pulpit rabbis in New York set the stage for the promulgation of a platform for "classical" Reform Judaism in America. Alexander Kohut (1842–1894), a Hungarian rabbi recently arrived in the United States, initiated the debate by giving a series of lectures attacking Reform's rejection of Jewish law. Kohut's charge that "Reform is a Deformity" was answered by German-born Kaufmann Kohler (1843–1926), a son-in-law of David Einhorn as well as the late radical's successor at Congregation Beth El. The debate attracted wide attention, filled the two rabbis' synagogues with partisan crowds and clarified many of the differences between Reform and traditional Judaism.

At the same time the Kohler–Kohut debate was raging, Reform Judaism was also being attacked by Felix Adler (1851–1933), founder of the Ethical Culture Society (est. 1876) and son of Samuel Adler, a distinguished Reform rabbi. The young Adler, who had rejected both theism and Jewish ethnicity, charged that Reform, even at its most radical, had failed to liberate itself completely from religious orthodoxy and embrace a universal code of ethics. Adler's views appealed to many Reform Jews and thus elicited strong replies from a number of leading Reform rabbis, including the intellectually adroit Kohler.

Seeking a middle ground between Kohut's positive-historical approach to Judaism and Adler's ethical atheism, Kohler convened a conference of Reform rabbis in Pittsburgh in 1885. Labeled a "Declaration of Independence" by Wise, the eight planks of Kohler's Pittsburgh Platform were unequivocally modern in spirit. However, in its subtext, the platform also preserved Reform's emotional connection to historical Judaism. Thus, it described the Bible as "reflecting the primitive ideas of its own age," rejected all Jewish customs "not adapted to the views and habits of modern civilization," and declared that the Jews are "no longer a nation but a religious community." On the other hand, it also proudly affirmed that "Judaism presents the highest conception of the God-idea" and that Jews continue to exist as a "religious community" with a messianic mission.

While the Pittsburgh Platform again stirred Reform's critics, on both the left and the right, to renewed remonstrations, it was also defended by a number of leading Reform Jews. Most importantly, a Conference of Southern Rabbis, organized in New Orleans later in 1885, strongly endorsed Kohler's work. A quasi-professional organization, it planned to meet on an annual basis. Not to be outdone, Wise responded by organizing a parallel Central Conference at a UAHC convention in Detroit four years later and successfully recruited rabbis from the central or midwestern states as well as his former students.

An organizational success, the CCAR emerged as the third federal branch of Reform's national polity and quickly sought to strengthen the religious authority and improve the professional standing of the average Reform rabbi. It also set out to standardize religious policy and practice in the Reform Movement. In 1892, the conference issued its first *Union Prayer Book*, which was followed two years later with a liturgy for the High Holy Days. Both works, as noted above, were essentially Einhornian in theology and literary style but written principally in English with some Hebrew but no German. In 1897, the CCAR also published the first *Union Hymnal*, modeling it after an Episcopalian work, in an effort to standardize the music as well as the words used in the Reform liturgy. That same year, led by its aging president, the rabbis of the Central Conference declared that "we totally disapprove of any attempt for the establishment of a Jewish state" in anticipation of the first Zionist congress in Basel, Switzerland. "Classical" Reform had reached its highwater mark.

Reform Judaism and Uptown Progressivism, 1900–1920. The changes that occurred in the American Reform Movement during the first two decades of the twentieth century were deeper than the emergence of new leaders in the wake of Isaac M. Wise's death in 1900. Immigration had already radically altered the profile of American Jewry, which had quadrupled in size from 250,000 in 1880 to approximately 1 million peo-

ple at the end of the nineteenth century and nearly 3.5 million by 1920. The Reform Movement, by contrast, could only claim 99 congregations with 9800 members in 1900 and 200 congregations with 23,000 members 20 years later. Even more important than the demographic marginalization of the movement (its members were overwhelmingly prosperous Americanized Jews of German ancestry) was the diminution of its leadership role in the American Jewish community. In 1906, the elite of the German Jewish community formed the oligarchical American Jewish Committee and thereby signaled a major structural change in American Jewish life. Hereafter, defense and philanthropic agencies—and still later, Zionist organizations—would represent the broadest consensus in American Jewish life and not the older religious and fraternal groups like the UAHC and B'nai B'rith. Similarly, the independent National Council of Jewish Women, founded in 1892, won an increasingly widespread following among German Jewish women as did Hadassah in Zionist circles after its formal organization in 1914.

The demographic and political challenges faced by Reform did not shake the movement's confidence in itself. A new synthesis, however, was needed. A variety of new positions were adopted and old, religiously radical ideas modified. Beginning in 1902, when the CCAR voted to maintain the historical Sabbath, Reform's ties to many aspects of traditional Judaism were reestablished as a response to the development of an East European majority in American Jewish life, in general, and, perhaps, the reorganization of the Conservative Movement's rabbinic seminary under the guidance of the scholarly and vigorous Solomon Schechter. In 1906, the conference rejected a proposal to establish, under its auspices, a general synod for American Jews and, instead, established a Responsa Committee the following year. In 1909, it also declared that "mixed marriages are contrary to the Jewish religion." Although the majority of Reform Jews remained "classical" in their orientation, the movement as a whole was slowly abandoning its program to recast Judaism in terms of mainstream American Protestantism, except in the critical area of progressive political activism.

Already challenged during the nineteenth century by both David Einhorn and his Chicago-based son-in-law, Emil G. Hirsch, to incorporate "social justice" into the core of Reform doctrine, the American Reform Movement largely remained reticent about the massive social problems caused by industrialization and urbanization in the United States until the early 1900s. Following the lead of the Social Gospel movement, which culminated in the organization of the Federal Council of Churches in 1908, the CCAR spoke out against child labor that same year but did not formulate a Declaration of Principles on the rights of workers in general for another decade. By contrast, at the urging of its president, Joseph Krauskopf, in 1904, CCAR actively campaigned to strengthen the "wall of separation" between the institutions of government and religion.

Reform's ambivalence toward organized labor was paralleled by its qualified support of the suffrage movement. After 1900, women were increasingly accepted as members of Reform synagogues but were generally not allowed to serve on temple boards and thus remained outside the power structure in the movement. Similarly, the National Federation of Temple Sisterhoods (NFTS), founded in 1913, stressed the role of Jewish women in the home and the virtues of feminine piety. At its inception, NFTS was administered by Rabbi George Zepin, secretary of the UAHC. The CCAR rejected two resolutions in favor of women's suffrage prior to passing a motion of support in 1917. Finally, in the years following World War I, both the faculty of the Hebrew Union College and the CCAR voted in favor of ordaining women as rabbis but were overruled by the college's powerful board of governors in 1923.

Reorientation, 1920–1945. The alliance between uptown progressivism and American Reform Judaism continued during the interwar period as concern for social justice evolved into a hallmark of the movement. Reform, however, true to its mandate, continued to redefine itself and by the outbreak of World War II had changed its theological direction.

By the mid-1930s, under pressure from domestic Zionists and in response to the sharp increase in international anti-Semitism, the movement found itself reevaluating the place of Jewish particularism in Reform religious thought. The CCAR adopted a pro-Zionist platform in 1937, widely viewed as the great turning point in the history of the American Reform Movement, and thereby paved the way for a fundamental reorientation in the ideology of Reform Judaism in North America. Reform's liturgical practices, on the other hand, did not change as dramatically.

Reform's theological reorientation clearly

had a social basis. American isolationism and xenophobia in the wake of World War I led to the severe tightening of American immigration laws during the course of the 1920s and accelerated the pace of the Americanization of the East European Jews already in the United States, many of whom began to join Reform temples. These new Reform Jews, especially in rabbinic circles, often maintained a warm feeling for Old-World Jewish traditions and Zionist ideology. In 1930, the movement peaked at 285 congregations with more than 60,000 members at a time when less than one-third of all American Jewish families were affiliated with a synagogue. Reform, like liberal religion in general, did not flourish during the 1920s and 1930s, although a significant number of new and costly temples were built prior to the Depression. One American church historian even referred to the period beginning in the latter half of the 1920s as the beginning of a "religious depression." Weakened by numerous changes in popular American culture, including the expansion of the automobile market and the development of new entertainment industries, Reform temples often found themselves serving as little more than "ornaments" of middle-class Jewish culture. Symptomatic of its religious decline, the movement helped foster a number of inter- and intrafaith organizations.

The most significant change in the Reform Movement during the interwar years, however, was in its attitude toward Zionism. The CCAR's original hard-line opposition to political Zionism was never unanimous and began to soften after the Balfour Declaration of 1917. In 1922, Rabbi Stephen S. Wise (1874–1949, and no relation of Isaac M. Wise), an outstanding orator, social activist, and Zionist leader, founded the Jewish Institute of Religion in New York, which largely produced pro-Zionist rabbis who served in Reform synagogues until it merged with HUC in 1948. In 1924, the UAHC hired a pro-Zionist director, Emanuel Gamoran (1895–1962) to head its education commission, a position that he held until his death. Finally, the CCAR, after some debate, agreed to include "Hatikvah" in the 1932 *Union Hymnal.*

The great debate over Zionism in the American Reform Movement, however, was yet to come. Sparked by the ascendance of Nazism in Germany in 1933, a parallel surge in domestic anti-Semitism, and the publication of Mordecai Kaplan's *Judaism as a Civilization* in 1934, which advocated both Jewish peoplehood and theological naturalism, the CCAR agreed, in 1935, to reevaluate the theology and antinationalism of the 50-year-old Pittsburgh Platform. The Zionist faction in the conference was led by the militant Abba Hillel Silver (1893–1963), but it was Samuel S. Cohon (1888–1959), a professor of Jewish theology at HUC, who actually drafted the new set of Guiding Principles of Reform Judaism, which was overwhelmingly adopted by the CCAR at its annual convention in Columbus, Ohio, in 1937. Expanding on Reform's traditional theism and reaffirming its commitment to social justice, Cohon's Columbus Platform also spoke of "the obligation of all Jewry to aid in [the] upbuilding [of Palestine] as a Jewish homeland" and the positive role of ceremonialism and Hebrew in Jewish worship. That same year, the UAHC also adopted a resolution calling for "the establishment of a Jewish homeland in Palestine."

Reform opposition to Zionism, however, did not end in 1937. As late as 1942, the movement split over the twin issues of raising a Jewish army in Palestine and the demand for immediate statehood. An anti-Zionist group, the American Council for Judaism, brought American Reform Judaism to the brink of schism. However, news of the destruction of European Jewry and the establishment of the State of Israel sapped the council of its strength and influence. Reform's anti-Zionism was now a thing of the past, and the movement, theologically redefined and institutionally reinvigorated, refocused itself on the rapidly changing religious and social realities of postwar America.

Reform on the Suburban Frontier, 1945–1965. The massive expansion of organized religious life in America in the years immediately following World War II transformed the Reform Movement into a major American denomination by any standard. In 1940, the UAHC could claim 265 affiliate congregations with a total of 59,000 members. Just 15 years later, in 1955, it could boast of 520 congregations with 255,000 members representing perhaps as many as a million people. Although Reform's growth curve began to slow thereafter, the UAHC continued to expand and reported a total of 660 member temples in 1964.

The reasons for the movement's immense growth were unexceptional and largely followed trends in the sociology of religion in general in postwar America. Suburbanization, the vast social process that resulted in the development of huge rings of single-house tracts around established urban centers as well as the creation of entirely new suburban cities, especially in the Southwest, had an enervating effect on both extended family networks and ethnic neighborhoods that had supported much of prewar Jewish life. To retain a modicum of ethnic Jewish culture in their lives, maintain social contacts with other Jews, and, above all, instill a Jewish identity in their children, hundreds of thousands of otherwise secular and highly Americanized Jews joined synagogues for the first time. Thus, while the clergy, academics, and the press debated the depth and religious quality of the postwar revival, new synagogue construction soared, and temples became remarkably busy social centers for suburban Jewry.

If the underlying causes for the Reform Movement's rapid institutional growth were typical of the American religious scene, its postwar leadership was remarkable. Two rabbis in particular, Maurice Eisendrath (1902–1973) and Nelson Glueck (1900–1971), were responsible for reshaping the movement. Eisendrath was named the executive director of the UAHC in 1943 and became its president in 1946. Determined to revitalize the UAHC and invigorate the Reform Movement, Eisendrath successfully campaigned to move UAHC's headquarters from Cincinnati to New York and built an impressive "House of Living Judaism" on Fifth Avenue across the street from Temple Emanu-El. Glueck, a world-renowned archeologist, succeeded Julian Morgenstern as president of HUC in 1947 and, shortly thereafter, oversaw the college's merger with Stephen Wise's Jewish Institute of Religion. An energetic president of the two-campus HUC/JIR, he established a third branch in Los Angeles in 1954 and dedicated a fourth campus in Jerusalem in 1963. CCAR was also transformed by the dramatic growth of the Reform Movement. Run entirely on a volunteer basis since its inception, the Central Conference opened a national office in New York in 1954 and hired its first executive director, Rabbi Sidney Regner (b. 1903). Ten years later, the CCAR began regulating rabbinic placement, heretofore a process largely controlled by powerful individuals at HUC/JIR, and thereby greatly enhanced the conference's position in the overall polity of the Reform Movement. The professionalization of CCAR as well as the Reform rabbinate was also reflected in the decision to begin publishing a quarterly journal of opinion, currently called the *Journal of Reform Judaism*, early in the 1950s.

The Reform Movement of the 1950s and

early 1960s focused much of its energies on social justice issues, including civil liberties, civil rights, and the American peace movement. After a bitter debate, the UAHC resolved to develop a lobby in Washington, D.C., and, with the financial help of Kivie Kaplan, a Reform Jew and prominent civil rights activist, opened a Religious Action Center in 1961 in the former Ecuadorian embassy on Connecticut Avenue. Although many southern rabbis and congregations urged caution on civil rights issues and numerous other voices challenged Eisendrath's and others' increasingly vocal opposition to American military involvement in Vietnam after 1964, Reform Jews broadly favored their movement's liberal political agenda. Reform rabbis, mostly from the North, marched with other civil rights leaders in the Deep South and, a few years later, in mass antiwar demonstrations. By mid-decade, the movement had regained much of its earlier messianic zeal. However, the enthusiasm was short-lived and by the end of the 1960s, the Reform Movement, like many liberal and mainstream religious groups, found itself wallowing in a deep religious malaise.

Reform Since 1965. A combination of at least three different factors accounted for the sudden dramatic change in the mood of American Reform Judaism. By 1965, the direction of the civil rights movement began to change, away from integration and toward black power. Two years later, in the wake of Israel's stunning Six-Day War victory, many Reform Jews found themselves torn between their opposition to the war in Vietnam, which in many cases was undistinguished from antimilitarism in general, and their elation over Israel's success on the battlefield. Furthermore, they felt betrayed by the failure of the Christian clergy to rally behind Israel in its most perilous hour and were angry at much of the American political left, which quickly adopted an anti-Zionist position after June 1967. Finally, a specifically religious crisis also developed, especially within the Reform rabbinate, and, as in American religion in general, led to greater personal spirituality and a broad rethinking of the place of tradition in worship and practice.

Tensions in the movement during this period focused on several key issues. First, the congregational rabbis successfully campaigned for curricular changes at HUC/JIR with a new emphasis on "social and practical relevance." Second, a debate over Diaspora–Israeli relations was opened but to a large extent was muted in the wake of the expansion of local Jewish federations and UJA

(United Jewish Appeal) in American Jewish life in the wake of the 1973 Yom Kippur War. The most bitter fight in Reform Judaism during this period, however, was over the question of rabbinic officiation at mixed marriages. A deeply divided Central Conference debated the issue at its 1973 meeting in Atlanta and by a three-to-two margin reaffirmed its "opposition to participation by its members in any ceremony which solemnizes a mixed marriage." Ironically, the number of Reform rabbis who did solemnize such marriages continued to rise; according to information gathered by the Rabbinic Center for Research and Counseling, founded by Rabbi Irwin H. Fishbein in 1970, over 500 Reform rabbis officiated at the marriage of religiously mixed couples "under specified conditions" just 10 years after the Atlanta vote.

Neither the fight over rabbinic officiation at mixed marriages or the movement's religious crisis, however, led to a schism, and by the mid-1970s, the Reform Movement had regained its equilibrium. The sources of renewal were diverse. Women played an exceptionally important role in raising the movement out of its malaise. First, by the 1970s, they had gained access to the board rooms of most Reform synagogues, and, in 1972, HUC/JIR conferred rabbinic ordination on Sally Priesand. Second, women made up the vast majority of the wave of converts to Reform Judaism during the 1970s, many of whom became highly involved in the affairs of their congregations. Finally, a new group of national leaders, all male and mostly German-born, emerged as the new stewards of the movement.

In 1971, both the CCAR and HUC/JIR hired new chief executives. American-born Rabbi Joseph Glaser (b. 1925) was named first executive vice-president of the CCAR and immediately launched a massive campaign to revise the entire liturgy of the Reform Movement and reflect its growing religious diversity. Four years later, Central Conference published the *Gates of Prayer*, a prayer-book anthology of services and readings ranging from "traditional" to nontheistic, and, in 1978, a parallel volume was published for the High Holy Days. The CCAR also issued numerous guides to Reform practice as well as a few inspirational works. Also, to help "heal the wounds" in the movement, Central Conference sponsored the writing of a "Centenary Perspective" in 1976. Authored by Rabbi Eugene Borowitz, a professor at the New York school of HUC/JIR and a noted existentialist theologian, the San Francisco Platform labeled "diversity . . . the hallmark of Reform." The new platform is nondirective and nondogmatic, although it warmly discusses traditional theological themes and talks of the religious "obligations" of the individual Reform Jew. Its core teaching, however, remains linked to the doctrine of Progressive Revelation.

A second national leader to emerge during the early 1970s was Rabbi Alfred Gottschalk (b. 1930). Gottschalk fled Nazi Germany as a child and resettled in the United States. Rising quickly in the college's ranks after his ordination, he became president of HUC/JIR in 1971. An exceptional fund raiser, he expanded his predecessor's program to enlarge the institution physically and programmatically. The two largest projects involve the expansion of the Jerusalem campus and the building of a "cultural center" in Los Angeles.

The third and final major national leader to emerge in the Reform Movement during the 1970s was Rabbi Alexander Schindler (b. 1925), a German-born Jew and the first Reform religious leader to head the prestigious Conference of Major American Jewish Organizations. A dramatic speaker, Schindler helped launch the Reform Movement's Outreach Program, which has greatly softened much of modern Judaism's approach to proselytism and subsequently challenged the CCAR to adopt a resolution on "patrilineal descent." Passed in 1983, the CCAR resolution has played a significant role in escalating the highly divisive "Who is a Jew?" debate throughout the Jewish world, especially in the weeks following the 1988 Israeli general election. Eleven years earlier, in 1977, the American Reform Movement created the Association of Reform Zionists of America (ARZA) to promote Jewish religious pluralism in Israel and give American Reform Jews a voice in the World Zionist Organization.

Assessments of the current health and prognostications of the Reform Movement's future well-being vary widely. The most sanguine position is held by the movement's premier historian, Michael A. Meyer, who, in a 1978 essay, wrote that "with all its diversity, [Reform Judaism] alone offered [its adherents] a religious expression of Judaism both intellectually attractive and emotionally satisfying." At the other extreme, Rabbi Jakob J. Petuchowski, a colleague of Meyer's at HUC/JIR (Cincinnati), wrote in the *Journal of Reform Judaism* in 1986 of "the process of Reform Judaism's self-dissolution, which is already well under way, seeing that Reform Judaism keeps changing not only its outward forms, as might indeed be expected, but even its theological contents and its demographic make-up." The reality of Reform's current religious and institutional situation probably lies somewhere between these two extremes and is undoubtedly more complex than most analyses of the movement suggest.

LANCE J. SUSSMAN

BIBLIOGRAPHY

Greenstein, Howard R. *Turning Point: Zionism and Reform Judaism.* Brown Judaic Studies 12. Ann Arbor: Scholars Press, 1981.

Heller, James G. *Isaac M. Wise: His Life, Work and Thought.* New York: Union of American Hebrew Congregations, 1965.

Jick, Leon A. "The Reform Synagogue." In *The American Synagogue: A Sanctuary Transformed*, edited by Jack Wertheimer. New York: Cambridge University Press, 1987. Pp. 85–110.

Meyer, Michael A. "A Centennial History." In *Hebrew Union College—Jewish Institute of Religion: At One Hundred Years.* Edited by Samuel F. Karff. Cincinnati: Hebrew Union College Press, 1976.

———. *Response to Modernity: A History of the Reform Movement in Judaism.* New York: Oxford University Press, 1988.

Philipson, David. *The Reform Movement in Judaism.* New York: Macmillan, 1907, rev. 1931, rept., 1967.

Plaut, W. Gunther. *The Growth of Reform Judaism: American and European Sources to 1948.* New York: World Union for Progressive Judaism, 1965.

Polish, David. "The Changing and the Constant in the Reform Rabbinate." *American Jewish Archives* 35 (November 1983): 263–341. Reprinted in *The American Rabbinate, Century of Continuity and Change, 1883–1983.* Hoboken, N.J.: Ktav, 1985.

Raphael, Marc Lee. *Profiles in American Judaism: The Reform, Conservative, Orthodox, and Reconstructionist Traditions in Historical Perspective.* New York: Harper & Row, 1984.

Retrospect and Prospect: Essays in Commemoration of the Seventy-fifth Anniversary of the Founding of the Central Conference of American Rabbis, 1889–1964, edited by Bertram W. Korn. New York: Central Conference of American Rabbis, 1965.

Temkin, Sefton. "A Century of Reform Judaism in America." *American Jewish Yearbook* 74 (1973): 3–75.

Richman, Julia (1855–1912). Julia Richman was born in New York City and was educated at Normal College, now Hunter College, and New York University. She served as a teacher and a principal in the New York public school system and was the first woman appointed to the position of district superintendent.

In her district of Manhattan, Richman introduced several educational innovations that are still practiced in American public schools today. For example, she is credited with setting up the first parent association in public schools. Through her influence, eye examinations and vision correction in her school district was instituted. After an extensive study of learning-disabled children, she organized the first classes tailored especially for their needs. She established an employment agency for children who were forced to leave school and look for work.

In Manhattan, the Julia Richman High School is named for her in recognition of her dedication and contributions to public education in New York.

Richman also had a deep dedication to the Jews of New York. She was a leader in the Jewish Chautauqua Society, director of the Hebrew Free School Association of New York, charter member of the National Council of Jewish Women, and first president of the Young Women's Hebrew Association. She also gave much time and attention to the Hebrew Education Alliance of New York and was founder and editor of *Helpful Thoughts*, a magazine for Jewish children.

In a 1908 controversy concerning New York pushcart vendors, she (even though a person known for her sympathy for and dedication to the underprivileged) publicly came out for the enforcement of licensing for vendors. The cost of the license was $15, and the city had made provisions to issue 4000 licenses. This meant that there were about 10,000 illegal pushcart vendors doing business in the streets of New York.

Richman stated that the law should be strictly enforced and violators should be turned over to the immigration authorities to be deported. The police commissioner, General Theodore Bingham, opposed her view and protected the vendors. He felt that they had to make a living somehow.

The people of the East Side were incensed and started a petition to have Richman transferred to another school district. However, their anger was quickly transferred to the man who initially protected them from prosecution after a statement Bingham made was published in an article titled "Foreign Criminals in New York" for the *New York Review*. He contended that 50 percent of the criminals in New York were Russian Jews, who numbered only 25 percent of the population. "They are burglars, pickpockets, fire bugs, and highway robbers when they have the courage." Bingham's anti-Semitic statement drew a severe reaction from East Side residents and Richman's stance on pushcart vendors was forgotten.

Julia Richman died in Paris after a long and distinguished career dedicated to the New York public school system and the well-being of the Jewish populace of New York. *See also* Women.

RICHARD K. GERLITZKI

BIBLIOGRAPHY
Finkelstein, Louis. *The Jews: Their History, Culture and Religion.* New York: Harper, 1949.
Himmelfarb, Milton. *The Laws of Modernity.* New York: Basic Books, 1973.
Kransdorf, Martha. "Julia Richman's Years in the New York City Public Schools, 1872–1912." Ph.D. dissertation, University of Michigan, 1979.
Landman, Isaac, ed. *The Universal Jewish Encyclopedia.* New York: Universal Jewish Encyclopedia, 1943.
Manners, Ande. *Poor Cousins.* New York: Coward, McCann & Geoghegan, 1972.

Rickover, Hyman George (1900–1986). The father of the nuclear navy, Hyman Rickover, was born in Macow, Poland, a community about 50 miles north of Warsaw. His father, Abraham, a tailor, left his family to try his fortune in the United States. By 1903, he had saved enough money to bring his wife, Rachel, and their two children, Fanny and Hyman, to America.

The Rickovers settled in the Lawndale section of Chicago, where Hyman attended the local schools. After graduating from high school, he took the entrance examination and was admitted to the United States Naval Academy in 1918. Being a first-year plebe midshipman at the Naval Academy is an extremely difficult period in any young man's life. Being a plebe who was also Jewish was doubly difficult. There was a definite anti-Semitic atmosphere at the academy, and the hazing of Jewish midshipmen was widespread. But in Rickover's case, it would appear that the hazing he was subjected to had less to do with his being Jewish than it did with his reputation as a "grind" and a loner.

Rickover graduated in the class of 1922. He was 106th in a class of 539. He earned his master's degree in electrical engineering from Columbia University in 1929 and became a qualified submariner in 1930.

In 1946, Rickover went to Oak Ridge, Tennessee, to work on adapting nuclear energy as a fuel source for naval vessels. During the ensuing years, until the U.S.S. *Nautilus* was launched in 1954, he fought a continuous battle with the navy's apathy and Congress's indifference to the building of a nuclear-powered fleet. As a result of his position, there was a great deal of conflict between Rickover and his superiors as well as with some members of Congress. He was referred to as ''that little Jew'' in some navy and congressional circles. Thus, Rickover fought not only the navy's reluctance to develop nuclear-powered ships but anti-Semitism as well.

Thus his outspokenness, as well as his ancestry, combined to prevent him from being promoted in the early 1950s. However, his allies in Congress and the pressure of public opinion forced the navy to promote him to rear admiral in 1953 and to vice-admiral in 1958.

That anti-Semitism may have prevented Rickover from being promoted is ironic inasmuch as he had distanced himself from his Jewish antecedents. In 1932, he married Ruth Masters and shortly thereafter declared himself an Episcopalian. Ruth Masters Rickover died in 1972, and two years later, Rickover married Eleanore Ann Bednowicz, a naval officer, in a Catholic ceremony. Despite his efforts to separate himself from his Jewish upbringing, Rickover was always perceived as a Jew by the anti-Semites in the navy.

After the launching of the *Nautilus*, Rickover continued the struggle for a nuclear navy. Through his efforts, nuclear-powered surface warships and cargo ships were put into production, and in 1960, the first nuclear-powered aircraft was launched.

In 1964, he was retired from the navy but remained on active duty by Presidential order. Rickover was presented with the Fermi Award by the Atomic Energy Commission for his work in atomic science in the same year. In 1973, while still on active duty, he was promoted to full admiral. He retired in 1982 after 63 years of naval service. Rickover served his country longer than any officer in the history of the United States Navy and actually retired against his will. He died at his home in Arlington, Virginia while recovering from a stroke. *See also* Military.

RICHARD GERLITZKI

BIBLIOGRAPHY
Polmar, Norman, and Thomas B. Allen. *Rickover*. New York: Touchstone Books/Simon & Schuster, 1982.

Rock and Roll. *See* MUSIC, ROCK AND ROLL.

Rose, Billy (1899–1966). Impresario, theatrical producer, newspaper columnist, nightclub owner, and songwriter Billy Rose was born on the Lower East Side of New York City as William Samuel Rosenberg. He rose to prominence in the 1920s as a songwriter, writing over 400 songs, including 50 hits. Some of his most famous songs were ''That Old Gang of Mine,'' ''Without a Song,'' ''Me and My Shadow,'' and ''Barney Google.''

Rose soon moved on to running a number of successful nightclubs in New York City, as well as a few flops. The best known of his nightclubs were the Casino de Paree, opened in 1933 and reportedly a front for gangsters, Billy Rose's Music Hall, and the Diamond Horseshoe.

At the same time Rose became involved in theatrical productions. His first hit was *Jumbo*, a musical set at the circus and based on the book by Ben Hecht and Charles MacArthur, which opened in 1935 at the Hippodrome in New York. It was seen by over 1 million people but was never able to make money because it was such a huge production.

In 1943, Rose produced the Broadway hit *Carmen Jones*, an all-black production of Georges Bizet's opera *Carmen*. It ran three seasons and eventually was made into a movie.

Rose was married five times, twice to the same woman, with all of his marriages ending in divorce. The most famous of his wives was comedienne Fanny Brice.

Rose, a multimillionaire, used his money to invest in real estate, sculptures, and paintings, as well as in stocks. When he died in 1966, he was the major stockholder in AT&T and was heavily invested in IBM as well.

In 1958, he organized the Billy Rose Foundation, a trust established for religious, charitable, and educational purposes. The foundation's special interest was making available works of music, drama, painting, and sculpture to the public. For this reason at his death the bulk of Rose's estate went to the foundation. This did not include the 105 sculptures that he had donated to the National Museum of Israel in Jerusalem in 1965, valued at the time at over $1 million. Included were works by Rodin, Daumier, Sir Jacob Epstein, Ellie Nadelman, Maillol, William Zorach, Richard Hunt, Jose de Creft, and Ossip Zadkine. The pieces were placed in the Billy Rose Garden of Sculpture, which covers seven acres at the museum. The sculptures not given to the museum were bequeathed to the American-Israel Culture Foundation in New York.

Rose was a showman, in life and after. His funeral was held at the Billy Rose Theater in New York to accommodate the 500 mourners who attended.

Rose followed many interests in his lifetime. His career was a varied and intense one. He even became a syndicated newspaper columnist, though it is doubtful that he actually wrote the column but simply lent his name to it. He lived life to its fullest, enjoyed every moment, and shared with the world his love of art and music.

JANET L. DOTTERER

BIBLIOGRAPHY

"Billy Rose." Obituary. *New York Times*, February 11, 1966, 1, 30.

"Bulk of Estate Left to Rose Foundation." *New York Times*, February 12, 1966, 16.

Green, Abel, and Laurie, Joe, Jr. *Show Biz from Vaude to Video*. New York: Holt, 1951.

"Israel Museum to Open in May." *New York Times*, February 28, 1965, 3.

Mitchell, Loften. *Black Drama: The Story of the American Negro in the Theatre*. New York: Hawthorn Books, 1967.

"105 Sculptures Given by Rose Being Packed." *New York Times*, March 16, 1965, 41.

Rose, Ernestine Louise Siismondi Powtowski

(1809–1892). A feminist and abolitionist, Ernestine Rose was born in Poland. Her father, an Orthodox rabbi, provided her with an excellent Jewish education, an unusual background for women in the early 1800s. She rebelled against her father and his religious ways when he attempted to arrange a marriage for her at the age of 16. She fought and won her case against her father in a Polish court.

After this confrontation, she left her family and Poland, traveled throughout Europe and settled in England. There she studied under Robert Owen, a utopian socialist, and married a fellow student, William E. Rose, a non-Jew. They held the very unorthodox view that marriage was for companionship; they had no children. The couple came to the United States in the 1840s.

Rose aligned herself with the feminist Susan B. Anthony. She argued for the right of women to hold property in their own name and for women's suffrage. Few people within the Jewish community took notice of her activities because feminism was an issue only among Reform Jews, who were interested in raising the status of women to an acceptable social level.

Rose also was devoted to the cause of abolitionism, another issue not critical to most of the American Jewish community of the mid-1800s. She felt that slaves could not be "happy and carefree" as the popular propaganda suggested. Rose is most famous for her definition of slavery:

> Even if slaveholders treated their slaves with the utmost kindness and charity; if I were told they kept them sitting on a sofa all day, and fed them with the best of the land, it is none the less slavery; for what does slavery mean? To work hard, to fare ill, to suffer hardships, that is not slavery; for many of us white men and women have to work hard, have to fare ill, have to suffer hardships, and yet we are not slaves. Slavery is not to belong to yourself—to be robbed of yourself.

Rose was noticed by the Jewish community when she began to debate Horace Seaver, the editor of the *Investigator*, a liberal Boston newspaper. Seaver claimed that Judaism was inferior to Christianity and that Jews, by nature, were corrupt and exploited other people. While Rose was not a defender of any religion, she strongly believed that an individual should have the right to choose or reject a religion. She argued that Judaism was no worse than any other religion and that Jews were no worse than other groups and perhaps American Jews were better citizens because of their appreciation of the United States.

Rose was a brilliant and very popular speaker. She was arguably the most famous Jewish woman in the United States during the mid-1800s. She returned to England in 1869 and lived there until her death.

LINDA GLAZER

BIBLIOGRAPHY

Baum, Charlotte; Hyman, Paula; and Michel, Sonya. *The Jewish Woman in America*. New York: New American Library, 1977.

Feldstein, Stanley. *The Land That I Show You*. Garden City, N.Y.: Anchor Press/Doubleday, 1978.

Kenvin, Helene Schwartz. *This Land of Liberty*. New York: Behrman House, 1986.

Marcus, Jacob R. *The American Jewish Woman*. Hoboken, N.J.: Ktav, 1981.

Suhl, Yuri. *Ernestine L. Rose: Women's Rights Pioneer*. New York: Biblio Press, 1990.

Rosenberg Case. In the summer of 1949 an American spy plane returned from Asia with photographs revealing strong traces of radioactive material. The conclusion was obvious: the Soviet Union had exploded an atomic device. America's nuclear monopoly had come to an end.

On October 23, President Harry S Truman broke the news in a one-sentence statement to the press. "We have evidence an atomic explosion occurred in the USSR." Domestic reaction was one of shock. Ever since Hiroshima, Americans had been taught to depend on nuclear superiority, to assume that the technology was uniquely their own. The new finding could mean only one thing: espionage. The Russians had stolen the biggest secret of all.

The news quickly got worse. On January 22, 1950, a New York jury found Alger Hiss guilty of perjury. (The statute of limitations on the real charge—diplomatic espionage—had run out.) February brought the arrest of a British scientist, Klaus Fuchs, for passing atomic secrets to the Russians. March, April, and May were filled with congressional testimony about Communist influence in the State Department. June witnessed the North Korean attack across the 38th parallel. July saw the arrest of Julius Rosenberg. In August, his wife, Ethel, and his friend Morton Sobell joined him in prison. Throughout the autumn months, Congress debated and finally passed the Internal Security (McCarran) Act, an extraordinarily repressive measure. In December, word reached home that American troops in Korea were in full retreat before an advancing Communist Chinese army.

The Korean War, coupled with the loss of America's atomic monopoly, sent shock waves through the nation. Air raid drills became the order of the day, with "simulated" Russian bombings in large metropolitan centers. The sheriff of Kansas City inspected the surrounding quarries and found they could accommodate 840,000 people—or bodies. In New York City, school officials began distributing metal "dog tags" and holding practice drills in which youngsters were taught to dive under their desks. In Washington, D.C., real estate agents put ads in local papers reading, "Small farm—out beyond the atomic blasts" or "An estate in Belle Meade, Virginia—a safe 58 miles from Washington."

Early in 1951 the Rosenbergs and Morton Sobell were convicted of conspiring to commit espionage. The trial judge— Irving R. Kaufman, a master of hyperbole—accused them of "putting" the A-bomb "into the hands of the Russians." Sobell was sentenced to 30 years in prison, the Rosenbergs to death by electrocution. In 1953, following numerous appeals, the Rosenbergs were executed at Sing Sing Prison, just north of New York City.

An overwhelming majority of Americans applauded the outcome, yet some nagging questions remained. Was a fair trial really possible in the prevailing atmosphere of anger and fear? Why had the British sentenced Klaus Fuchs to only 14 years in prison? Was it a coincidence that the defendants, the witnesses, the chief prosecutor, and the judge were all Jewish? Was it possible—just possible—that the Rosenbergs were framed?

Almost four decades later, these questions are very much alive. Hardly a year goes by without a new book, a play, or a documentary on the Rosenbergs. They may well be the most studied Jewish-American couple of this century. They surely are the most controversial.

Julius Rosenberg was a Communist, deeply committed to the Soviet cause. Describing himself as "a soldier of Stalin," he wanted to help the Russians modernize their economy and their military machine. In 1943, he apparently began his own spying operation without the encouragement of Soviet authorities. His recruits included several of his former classmates from the City College of New York—Joel Barr, Alfred Sarant, and Morton Sobell among them—who were then working for the U.S. Navy, the U.S. Army Signal Corps, and defense-related industries. In 1944, quite by accident, Julius learned that Ethel's brother, an army sergeant named David Greenglass, had been assigned to a machine shop at Los Alamos, New Mexico, site of the famed Manhattan Project, where the first atomic bomb was researched, assembled, and successfully tested. From that point forward, Rosenberg centered his attention on obtaining material about the atomic bomb.

In *The Rosenberg File*, published in 1983, authors Ronald Radosh and Joyce Milton demolish Greenglass's self-serving portrayal of himself as a naive and unwitting accomplice, "sucked into" the process by his overbearing brother-in-law. Indeed, Greenglass's private correspondence showed him to be a devoted Communist, willing and anxious to serve his cause. In June 1944, for example, Greenglass wrote to his wife:

> Darling, I have been reading a lot of books on the Soviet Union. I can see how farsighted and intelligent those leaders are. They are really geniuses, every one of them. . . . I have come to have a stronger and more resolute faith and belief in the principles of Socialism and Communism. . . .

In November, Greenglass added these words:

> My darling, I most certainly will be glad to be part of the community project that Julius and his friends have in mind. Count me in dear, or should I say it has my vote.

The arrest of Klaus Fuchs in England eventually led authorities to Greenglass, who readily confessed to the theft of atomic secrets from Los Alamos and then named Julius and Ethel Rosenberg as the masterminds of the spy ring. Greenglass claimed to have given Julius a number of things, including some sketches of the top-secret lens mold used in the Nagasaki bomb. In return for his cooperation with federal authorities, Greenglass avoided both the electric chair for himself and the prosecution of his wife Ruth, who admitted to knowledge of the spying operation.

Like her husband and her brother-in-law, Ethel Rosenberg was a Communist. Like them, too, she lied boldly about her political convictions in public. "Neither [Julius] nor I have ever been Communists, and we don't know any Communists," she told reporters on the eve of her arrest. Caught between the accusations of her brother and blind loyalty to her husband, Ethel performed dismally on the witness stand. The government's case against her was based

on the recollections of Ruth and David Greenglass, nothing more. Radosh and Milton contend that "Ethel probably knew of and supported her husband's endeavors," but they do not portray her as an active co-conspirator. On the contrary, it appears that she was arrested in order to pressure Julius into confessing. This was part of the government's "lever strategy"—a strategy that would lead an unyielding woman directly to her death. When Ethel was arrested in 1950, one of the prosecutors said privately that "the case is not too strong against Mrs. Rosenberg." It did not get any stronger as time passed. A death-house questionnaire, prepared by prosecutors in the event that Julius would break down at the last moment, had this startling question attached: "Was your wife cognizant of your activities?"

The case against Julius was far stronger. Besides Ruth and David Greenglass, damaging testimony about his activities was given by Harry Gold, a convicted Soviet spy, and by several of Rosenberg's former friends and associates. Furthermore, FBI documents released under the Freedom of Information Act have shredded Julius's various denials, including the crucial one that he knew nothing about the atom-bomb project until after the Hiroshima explosion. Finally, evidence gathered recently demonstrates that Joel Barr and Alfred Sarant fled behind the Iron Curtain following the arrest of David Greenglass in 1950 and that both men wound up working for the Soviet defense establishment.

To this day, scholars still debate the significance of the information that Greenglass and Rosenberg allegedly passed on to the Soviets. One group contends that Greenglass was a true novice, whose lens mold sketches were of no value whatsoever. Others disagree. Indeed, a number of top scientists who *opposed* the death sentence admitted privately that these crude sketches were, indeed, of potential value to the Soviets. Why? Because they corroborated the information provided by Klaus Fuchs, reinforcing the fact that America had abandoned the original (Hiroshima) bomb in favor of a plutonium, implosion-type model. As a result, the Soviets may well have avoided the time and expense involved in producing the inferior bomb.

The most controversial part of the Rosenberg case, however, is not the verdict, or the quality of the information, but rather the sentence of death. From the very outset, the government was determined to send Julius to the electric chair. But resistance arose over the sentence that Ethel should receive. The prosecutors—especially Irving Saypol and Roy Cohn—wanted the maximum penalty; others urged compassion for a number of reasons. Some officials worried that the execution of a woman with no previous criminal record would damage America's standing in the world. And FBI Director J. Edgar Hoover, a bachelor who lived with his mother until her death, complained that a double execution would leave two small children orphaned. (He eventually changed his mind after receiving a preposterous FBI report that "Ethel was not a good mother after all.")

At the center of this battle was Judge Irving R. Kaufman, an astute young jurist with barely disguised ambitions to sit one day on the U.S. Supreme Court. On April 5, 1951—judgment day for the Rosenbergs and Sobell—Kaufman dramatically portrayed himself as a man alone, doing the work of God, the soldiers in Korea, and freedom-loving people everywhere. "I have deliberated for hours, days, nights," he said, adding that much of that time had been spent in his Park Avenue synagogue.

Kaufman's speech that day was a masterpiece of Cold War rhetoric. He told the Rosenbergs: "I consider your crime worse than murder. . . . I believe your conduct caused . . . the Communist aggression in Korea, with the resultant casualties exceeding 50,000, and who knows but that millions more of innocent people may pay the price for your treason. Indeed, by your betrayal you have undoubtedly altered the course of history to the disadvantage of your country." Lost in the emotion that day was the fact that the alleged espionage had occurred during World War II, when the Soviet Union and the United States were allied against the Nazi war machine.

Judge Kaufman then sentenced the Rosenbergs to death by electrocution. How can one explain his behavior? Certainly Kaufman understood the correlation between public opinion and his own career. He knew that most Americans were demanding the death sentence, and perhaps he gave them what they wanted. Or perhaps he truly believed that the Rosenbergs had dealt a severe blow to national security. Or perhaps he wanted to show the Gentiles that a Jew could be tough on traitors; after all, the Rosenbergs had embarrassed the "respectable" Jewish community. The irony, of course, is that Irving R. Kaufman—a Jew, a Democrat, a New Yorker, a liberal—imposed a sentence far harsher than even J. Edgar Hoover thought proper at that point.

There are very few heroes in the Rosenberg story. President Eisenhower denied clemency without ever understanding what the case was about. (He believed that Ethel was the ringleader and that the Rosenbergs had spied for money.) The Supreme Court majority, led by Chief Justice Vinson, resembled a lynch mob in the days preceding the execution. The American Civil Liberties Union ignored the case entirely. And the American Jewish Committee "not only declined to join in the call for clemency," note Radosh and Milton, "but became an open advocate of the death penalty." In private, "the AJC leadership did not doubt that there was an anti-Jewish current underlying much of the Red-baiting [of that era]. But their public reaction was to disavow the victims as in no way typical of the patriotic and anti-Communist American Jewish community."

On the other side, the American Communist Party acted with predictable hypocrisy. At first its publications ignored the Rosenbergs. Then, in 1952, the party reversed itself and launched a sickening campaign to exploit the suffering of the couple and their children. The reasons were transparent. First, the Rosenbergs had made it plain that they were willing to go to their deaths without informing on their colleagues, so they were no longer a danger to the party. Second, the Communists needed something, anything, to deflect attention from the outrageously anti-Semitic purges and executions then taking place in Czechoslovakia and in Russia itself. Put simply, the Rosenbergs had become pawns in a sordid propaganda war between the Communists, on the one hand, and American cold warriors, on the other.

The Rosenberg case did violence to America in a number of ways. It damaged our national security; it compromised our system of justice; and it made us look frightening—and vengeful—in the eyes of the world. It tarnished the independent Left while strengthening the radical Right. It allowed opportunists to masquerade as patriots and zealots to pose as martyrs. The crimes of the Rosenbergs were very real indeed. But their fate, as Radosh and Milton accurately put it, "remains a blot on America's conscience . . . an ominous footnote to the first decade of post-nuclear history."

DAVID OSHINSKY

BIBLIOGRAPHY

Radosh, Ronald, and Milton, Joyce. *The Rosenberg File: A Search for the Truth*. New York: Holt, Rinehart and Winston, 1983.

Schnier, Walter, and Schnier, Miriam. *Invitation to an Inquest*. New York: Penguin, 1973.

Roth, Henry (b. 1906). American novelist, Henry Roth wrote *Call it Sleep* (1934), a novel neglected after it first appeared and rediscovered 30 years later with great acclaim. Born in Tysmenicz, Galicia (then a part of Austria), he came to New York with his mother when he was 18 months old.

The experience of growing up Jewish became the material for his expressionist, autobiographical novel. Herman and Leah Roth, the author's parents, lived on the Lower East Side until 1914, when they moved to East Harlem. The change of environs had a tremendous impact on the child, who felt himself among strangers and became timid and introspective. Roth was registered in DeWitt Clinton High School in Manhattan and graduated in 1924, immediately enrolling in City College of New York, with the hope of becoming a zoologist or biology teacher. During his freshman year he had an assignment for an English course to write a paper "in expositional prose" about building something. He submitted the story "Impressions of a Plumber," which surprised the professor and was published in *The Lavender*, the student literary magazine. It was the door to a strange literary career.

At that time, Roth met Eda Lou Walton, a poet and New York University professor, and moved with her to Greenwich Village. She became his lover, literary agent, and patron and introduced him to artists and poets. In 1930, when she was invited to a workshop in Peterborough, New Hampshire, Roth went with her and it was there, in a nearby inn, where he started *Call it Sleep*. It took Roth three years to finish the first draft, and one more to edit it and have the final manuscript ready. He sent it to publishers, but it was rejected. David Mandel, another lover of Walton at the time, finally sent it to his partner, Robert O. Ballou, who published it.

Call it Sleep is the psychological study of David Schearl, an 8-year-old Jewish boy living on the Lower East Side who plays in the streets and in rat-infested cellars as he deals with his mother's overprotectiveness and his father's unstable image. Some critics consider David's story to be the adventure of a sensitive child in search of a pedagogical guide, while others see it as an esoteric pilgrimage. Death, guilt, and physical corruption permeate the book. The protagonist

seems to gravitate in darkness, among negative images. Sexual, geographic, and geological symbols are everywhere, but redemption is the ultimate goal. In a final section, David is knocked unconscious, and it is here where a dream enables him to transcend reality.

When the novel appeared, it was favorably received but early criticism was polarized: a review in *The Masses*, a Communist periodical, considered it too introspective, long, and febrile, but others believed it was powerful and extremely well structured. At first it was considered a proletarian book concentrating on family life and childhood. Comparisons with James T. Farrell's *Studs Lonigan*, the representative trilogy of social protest of the period, emerged. Roth's political views were thought to be anticapitalist and not until the 1970s, with Bonnie Lyons's literary analysis, were the symbolic and spiritual attributes fully understood. *Call it Sleep* asks for many readings, and interpretations vary.

The author experiments with language in *Call it Sleep* by articulating English in such a way that it reproduces the cadence and musical rhythm of Yiddish, without caricaturing it. The novel ceased to command public attention after its second printing in 1935. Alfred Kazin and Leslie A. Fiedler brought it back from obscurity in a symposium entitled "The Most Neglected Books of the Past 25 Years"; in 1960, it was reissued in a paperback edition, immediately becoming a bestseller.

During the 1930s, Roth was an open sympathizer of communism. In this period, he started a second novel about the American Midwest. It was meant to have Dan Loem, an illiterate worker, as a protagonist who is slowly driven to economic and personal despair in a Cincinnati setting. According to the author, some 75 to 100 pages were written and submitted to Scribner, who accepted it and forwarded an advance payment of $1000 to Roth. But unable to unify his artistic expectations with his left-wing ideology, Roth felt blocked and burned the manuscript. Only a chapter under the name "If We Had Beacon," published in the small magazine *Signatures: Works in Progress* (1936), survives. Since then, Roth has never finished a novel. A handful of scattered stories and segments of unfinished books have been collected in *Shifting Landscapes. A Composite 1925–1987*. Roth felt success made him a celebrity too soon, and he could not keep up with it. He believed himself to be a member of a whole generation of writers, among them F. Scott Fitzgerald, Nathanael West, Daniel Fuchs, and John Steinbeck, who failed to develop and came to age in the thirties, some before, some after, with the blight of the one-book or one-trilogy syndrome.

Roth's political ideas have gone from euphoria to silence, from engagement to disinterest. He joined the Communist Party in 1933, but grew disenchanted and came to believe his liaison was a sentimental and forced act. He remained a militant until 1953, when Stalin died. For a time he supported the existence of Jewish life in the Diaspora, but he changed his mind during the Six-Day War. As a result of the Israeli victory, he identified with Zionism; finally, the Jewish people had regained power, becoming a part of history again.

His literary activities during and after the 1940s were opaque as a result of his block. In 1938, in an artist colony in Saratoga, he met Muriel Parker, a musician, and married her one year later. He taught at night in Theodore Roosevelt High School in New York, and worked in the machine industry in New York and Boston. In 1946, he moved to Montville and then to Augusta, Maine, where he got a job in the state mental hospital. He finally settled in Albuquerque, New Mexico.

Roth's work today is considered a classic in Jewish-American literature. His contribution is peculiar in that it has a style of its own, it is the product of first-generation immigrants, and it appeared before World War II when Jewish-American culture was strengthening its roots. Roth was never an intellectual, nor did he have links with foreign literary movements, as did many subsequent Jewish authors.

His other important pieces are a short story about the Spanish Inquisition in Seville, one on black people, a critical approach to the playwright Lynn Riggs, and a contribution to a do-it-yourself magazine. Thanks to Mario Materassi, a close friend, Italian translator of *Call it Sleep* and editor of *Shifting Landscapes*, Roth's reputation in Italy is equal to that in the United States. He is the recipient of the Italian Nonino International Prize 1986. *See also Call it Sleep*; Fiction.

ILAN STAVANS

BIBLIOGRAPHY

Ferguson, James. "Symbolic Patterns in *Call it Sleep.*" *Twentieth Century Literature* 14 (January 1969): 211–220.

Redding, Mary Edrich. "Call it Myth: Henry Roth and *The Golden Bough.*" *Centennial Review* 18 (Spring 1974): 180–195.

Samet, Tom. "Henry Roth's Bull Story: Guilt and Betrayal in *Call it Sleep.*" *Studies in the Novel* 7 (Winter 1975): 569–583.

Roth, Philip Milton (b. 1933). Prominent American novelist and short-story writer, known for his ambivalent relation toward his Jewishness, Philip Roth was born in Newark, New Jersey. He received his B.A. from Bucknell University and his M.A. from the University of Chicago. His prose is characterized by a versatile, rich and audacious style.

Roth's first book of short stories, *Goodbye, Columbus* (1959), which revealed the influence of F. Scott Fitzgerald, won the National Book Award and gave its 26-year-old author a reputation for successfully exploring the problems of contemporary Jewish life. A satirical description of the Jewish community's materialism and a devastating eye for realistic detail made him the target of a polarized controversy: some critics felt strongly attracted to Roth while others accused him of self-hatred, lack of imagination, and misanthropy. "Defender of the Faith" is perhaps the most acclaimed and anthologized story of the collection because of its theological and social implications. Roth received national recognition with its publication, but international acclaim came with his third novel, *Portnoy's Complaint* (1969), about a troubled analysand, and his sexual repression and guilt generated by his Jewish mother. After it, some critics suggested that Roth was the inventor of the Jewish novel of manners.

Before *Portnoy's Complaint*, two other novels were published, *Letting Go* (1962), whose prose closely resembles that of Henry James, and *When She Was Good* (1967), with a plot set in the Midwest similar to Gustave Flaubert's *Madame Bovary* and in which Roth tried to prove he could write about non-Jewish themes. Neither received the critical and popular triumph of *Portnoy's Complaint*—a book where the writer seems to find his ideal form.

Roth has made a career of portraying unhappy Jewish young men engaged in a perennial search for their identity and masculinity. In *Portnoy* the protagonist, Alexander Portnoy, a 33-year-old assistant commissioner of human opportunity for the City of New York, desperately wants a normal existence, without mother and father, where sexual life can be guiltless. Instead, he has overwhelming feelings of shame and the dread of castration. The character's mother, Sophie Portnoy, incarnates the myth of eternal protection and rejection. The tension and conflicts between them are recounted with a humor typical of the cultural and social life among Jews.

Some critics went as far as proclaiming *Portnoy's Complaint* the apotheosis of American Jewish literature, the culmination of a fictional quest since the end of World War II. It was followed by *Our Gang* (1971), a never quite coherent novel or, better, a series of sketches about the indignation generated by politics. Then came *The Breast* (1972), a mixture of Franz Kafka's *Metamorphosis*, Nikolai Gogol's story "The Nose," and other ingredients from Jonathan Swift. The central character, Alan David Kepesh (in Yiddish, *kep* means brain or head), turns into a female breast and goes on to live out adventures of black humor involving women and science.

Next came *The Great American Novel* (1973), also a low point in Roth's career. Baseball, a longtime interest for the writer, becomes here a parody of American society. A parade of schlemiels and other characters flourish, but their profundity is unappealing. Too many gags about the game and training make the text long and difficult to follow.

My Life as a Man (1974) is the debut of Nathan Zucherman's odyssey. In its form, it is also an interesting experiment that relates Roth to modern European culture. After reading Thomas Mann during the 1950s, the fictional character Peter Tarnopol dreams of writing a "Big Book" one day. The second part of Roth's book is Tarnopol's creation. Tarnopol and Roth in the same fit of creativity have created a fictional character named Zucherman to confess their all too desperate search for personal meaning.

David Kepesh returns in *The Professor of Desire* (1977) to lecture about Chekhov, Flaubert, and Kafka (three decisive figures in Roth's career) while talking simultaneously about his chaotic life and his will to become himself. The novel is set before *The Breast*, and it captured the attention of critics because of Roth's repetition of characters, a phenomenon that recalls Balzac and his "autonomous imaginary reality."

The most important reappearance is Zucherman in *The Ghost Writer* (1979): as an emerging young writer, Zucherman visits his admired maestro, Emanuel Isidore Lonoff, in order to talk about literature. Lonoff and Zucherman develop a father-son relationship. The young man gets to meet the maestro's mistress, who turns out to be Anne Frank. *The Ghost Writer* displays one of Roth's frequent interests: literature referring to literature.

The Ghost Writer is the first part of a trilogy, which was later published with an epilogue. The entire work is called *Zucherman Bound* (1985). The second entry is *Zucherman Unbound* (1981), an account of the character dealing with richness and fame that came after the publication of his novel *Carnovsky* (clearly a reference to I.J. Singer's novel *The Family Carnovsky*), and the third is *The Anatomy Lesson* (1983), about Zucherman's despair and inability to create another good novel. *Epilogue: The Prague Orgy* (1985) follows the protagonist's trip to Czechoslovakia to rescue a treasured Yiddish manuscript long lost. The trilogy about Zucherman's ordination as writer may be considered Roth's most accomplished work. Less interested with scandal than perfection, the author brings together his ever present ghosts and makes allusions to Eastern European literature, a field that he helped introduce to the American readership during the early 1980s with the Penguin series "Writers From The Other Europe."

The Counterlife (1987), an experiment of style and on the act of reading, brings Nathan Zucherman once more to life, describing his relationship with his brother Henry, his search and encounter with death, modern Israel, contemporary Jewish issues, and himself. With *Deception* (1990), Roth began a new business contract with the New York publishing house Simon and Schuster. Highly influenced by Czech and Latin American literatures, *Deception* is an account of the erotic affairs between an author named Philip and his own fictitious female characters.

Roth's novels have been loosely adapted into movies: in 1969, a film of *Goodbye, Columbus* (Paramount) was released with mixed reviews; in 1972 *Portnoy's Complaint* (Warner Brothers), an extreme disappointment, was released. Twelve years later, in 1984, *The Ghost Writer* was made for television (PBS American Playhouse) with actress Claire Bloom, Roth's companion since 1976, playing the maestro's wife. It attracted little interest. Three of the writer's short stories have been dramatized for the theater by Larry Arrick and produced under the title *Unlikely Heroes*.

His 1991 *Patrimony* is the story of his relationship with his father, Herman, who lived to the age of 88 before succumbing to a brain tumor.

Roth's sardonic portraits of American-Jewish life have won him a national and worldwide reputation. His fecundity and meticulous style have secured his place as a model for future writers. *See also* Comics and Comedy, Fiction.

ILAN STAVANS

BIBLIOGRAPHY

Bloom, Howard, ed. *Philip Roth*. New York: Chelsea House, 1986.

Finkielkraut, Alan. "The Ghosts of Roth." Interview. *Esquire* 96 (September 1981): 92–97.

Jones, Judith, and Nance, Guinevera. *Philip Roth*. New York: Ungar, 1981.

McDaniel, John. *The Fiction of Philip Roth*. Haddonfield, N.J.: Haddonfield House, 1974.

Pinsker, Sanford. *The Comedy That "Hoits": An Essay on the Fiction of Philip Roth*. Columbia: University of Missouri, 1975.

Rogers, Bernard F., Jr. *Philip Roth*. Boston: Twayne, 1978.

Roth, Philip. *A Philip Roth Reader*. New York: Farrar, Straus & Giroux, 1981.

———. *Reading Myself and Others*. New York: Farrar, Straus & Giroux, 1975.

Rubenstein, Richard L. (b. 1924).

Lawton Distinguished Professor of Religion at Florida State University, Richard L. Rubenstein was among the earliest of the nonwitnesses to recognize the devastating impact of the Holocaust on the assumptions of covenantal Judaism. He argued that the covenant had been overwhelmed by both the death camps and the establishment of the modern State of Israel. His 1966 book *After Auschwitz* articulated a radical theological position in contending that Judaism's covenantal deity was among the victims of the Shoah. Rubenstein's consequent "death of God" position is as much a cultural as a theological statement. He writes in *The Cunning of History* (1975), for example, that humans live in an age that is "functionally Godless."

Rubenstein, who is married and the father of three, was born into a nonobservant New York family. He did not become a bar mitzvah and, at one point, seriously thought about converting to Unitarianism. Eventually, he was ordained by the Jewish Theological Seminary, which awarded him an honorary doctorate in 1987, and received his Ph.D. at Harvard. Rubenstein, who writes movingly of his early life and the impact of the Holocaust on his theological position in the autobiographical *Power Struggle* (1974), has been a pulpit rabbi, a Hillel director, a civil rights activist, and a leading theorist of twentieth-century religious thought. His books have been translated in ten languages.

His assessment of the human condition is based on psychoanalytical social science models, especially Freudian psychology and Weberian sociology of religion. As applied by Rubenstein, these models stress the role of power and the diminished worth of the individual. He views modernity as having produced both surplus people and the technology to dispose of this surplus. State-sponsored population control culminates in annihilation (*The Age of Triage: Fear and Hope in an Overcrowded World*, 1983). Rubenstein views the demonic as being embedded in the very process of modernization. Deeply pained by his own personal inability to believe, he compares his position to that embraced by the Talmudic heretic Elisha ben Avuyah, who contended that there was "neither Judge nor Judgment."

Rubenstein attests that the primary task of the post-Holocaust theologian is "dissonance reduction," by which he means the necessity of affirming the claims of classical paradigms of Jewish theology in the face of the massively disconfirming event of the Holocaust. His rejection of the covenant and his replacement of theological language with the language of social science has found no resonance as a faith option, although more recently Rubenstein confides that theologically he is moving in the direction of a cosmic mysticism (*Approaches to Auschwitz*, 1987).

Rubenstein's impact on Jewish-American culture is seen in his having placed on the theological agenda recognition that the Holocaust is a watershed event in Jewish and Christian history that radically challenges normative conventions, in his demonstrating the relationship between power and religion, and in his stressing that the event has profound intergenerational implications for Jewish identity. *See also* Holocaust, Literature of the.

ALAN L. BERGER

BIBLIOGRAPHY

Rubenstein, Richard L. *After Auschwitz: Radical Theology and Contemporary Judaism*. New York: Macmillan, 1966.

———. *The Age of Triage: Fear and Hope in an Overcrowded World*. Boston: Beacon Press, 1983.

———. *The Cunning of History*. New York: Harper & Row, 1975.

———. *Power Struggle: An Autobiographical Confession*. Lanham, Md.: University Press of America, 1974.

———. *The Religious Imagination*. Lanham, Md.: University Press of America, 1968.

———, and Roth, John. *Approaches to Auschwitz: The Holocaust and Its Legacy*. Louisville, Ky.: Westminster/John Knox Press, 1987.

S

Sabin, Albert B. (b. 1906). Born in Russia, Albert B. Sabin came to the United States at 15 years of age. He attended New York University Medical School where in his senior year he served as an assistant in the bacteriology department. After graduation from medical school he spent two years (1932–1934) as a fellow at the Lister Institute in London. He returned to New York City in 1934 to an appointment at the Rockefeller Institution.

At the outbreak of World War II, Sabin became a member of the U.S. Army Epidemiological Board's Commission on Neurotropic Virus Disease. As a medical officer on active duty, he gained detailed knowledge of a variety of viral diseases in the South Pacific, the Philippines, and the Middle East. His war duty gave him unique experience in conducting large-scale clinical trials with viral vaccines on human subjects. At a March of Dimes Foundation meeting in 1954 he strongly advocated trials of live, attenuated vaccines against poliomyelitis. However, the foundation could not support broad clinical trials with both killed vaccine (that developed by Jonas Salk) and live vaccine (that developed by Sabin), and Salk carried the day. The foundation did continue to support Sabin but on a limited scale.

Today, however, the Sabin vaccine is the one of choice. Vaccination with the live vaccine is given by mouth and is permanent, unlike the Salk vaccine. Thus the need for multiple needle injections is avoided. Immunity is prompt, unlike that of the killed material, which may require months to take effect. Unhappily, this scientific difference became an acrimonious and public personal dispute between Salk and Sabin. While Salk won popular acclaim, with his name becoming a household word, Sabin's recognition came in more traditional ways, with honors and honorary degrees. Sabin was invited to become a member in practically every scientific body in the world. He has received the highest medals the United States Government awards to its civilians and has been the recipient of 31 honorary degrees in the United States and abroad. Today the Sabin vaccine is the universal choice throughout the world.

ABRAM KANOF

BIBLIOGRAPHY

Paul, J. R. *History of Poliomyelitis*. New Haven: Yale University Press, 1971.

Weaver, H. M. *The Research Story of Infantile Paralysis*. Publication No. 42. White Plains, N.Y.: National Foundation for Infantile Paralysis, December 1948.

Salk, Jonas Edward (b. 1914). Physician, scientist Jonas Salk was born in the Bronx, New York. He graduated from City College in 1934 and matriculated at the New York University Medical School. At the end of his first year, Salk took a leave of absence for a year to become acquainted with the world of science. When he received his M.D. in 1939, academic medical research was his logical choice. His entire career has been concerned with two basic biological questions. Can immunity to a viral disease be attained with killed virus material, as is possible in bacterial disease with bacterial substance? Or, can viral disease be prevented only by the administration of live but attenuated virus? On April 12, 1955, the world learned Salk's answer: the viral disease poliomyelitis can be prevented by immunization with killed virus. After massive field testing in 1953 and 1954, his vaccine for poliomyelitis came into wide use in 1955.

Salk's experience with virus immunization began during World War II when he was a member of the Commission on Influenza of the Armed Services Epidemiological Board. This experience, his reputation as an innovative experimenter, combined with the ability to organize a large-scale clinical trial and the energy to see it through, enabled him to win the March of Dimes financial and administrative support in the struggle to end the perennial polio threat. The fundamental prerequisite for this task, the ability to grow the virus in artificial media rather than in monkeys, was accomplished by Dr. John F. Enders, for which he received the Nobel Prize in 1954. Salk owed much to his mentor, Dr. Thomas Francis, under whom he worked for five years at the University of Michigan School of Public Health. As in most scientific breakthroughs, his success was foreshadowed by earlier experiments on monkeys.

Salk's triumph was clouded by the bitter animosity that developed between him and Albert Sabin, who successfully produced immunization with live attenuated virus. It is said that the men did not receive the Nobel Prize because of their loud and acrimonious dispute. However, Salk's popular fame and adulation did not suffer. He became the hero of numerous radio and television programs; his parents represented him as the leaders in the annual New York City loyalty parade. He received over a dozen honorary degrees here and abroad and as many national and international honors, including the Presidential Citation (1955), the Congressional Gold Medal (1955), and the Presidential Medal of Freedom (1977). This frenzied adulation was capped by the establishment by the March of Dimes of a research institute at La Jolla, California, with an annual endowment of a million dollars for research. At La Jolla he has gathered a coterie of brilliant scholars. His present research includes experimental medicine and mechanisms of delayed hypersensitivity. He is also involved in the contemplation, study, and writing on scientific-philosophical matters. He is the author of over 100 publications and was most recently involved in working on an AIDS vaccine. He is adjunct professor of health sciences at the University of California in San Diego, a position he has held since 1970.

Abram Kanof

BIBLIOGRAPHY

Paul, J. R. *History of Poliomyelitis.* New Haven: Yale University Press, 1971.

Smith, Jane S. *Patenting the Sun: Polio and the Salk Vaccine.* New York: Murrow, 1990.

Weaver, H. M. *The Research Story of Infantile Paralysis.* Publication No. 42. White Plains, N.Y.: National Foundation for Infantile Paralysis, December 1948.

Samuelson, Paul Anthony (b. 1915). Nobel Prize winner economist Paul Anthony Samuelson was born in Gary, Indiana, and educated at Chicago and Harvard universities, where he studied with such famous economists as Frank Knight, Jacob Viner, and Joseph A. Schumpeter. When he received his Ph.D. at Harvard in 1941, the young scholar, who had published pathbreaking articles while in his early twenties, was not offered an appointment there. Instead, he was welcomed at the neighboring Massachusetts Institute of Technology, where he has taught since 1940. The failure to appoint Samuelson marks the relative decline of the Harvard economics department, which no longer has a single Nobelist among its members, while at MIT there are three.

Samuelson was elected president of the American Economic Association in 1961 and won the Nobel Prize in Economic Science in 1970. In his doctoral dissertation, and in hundreds of periodical articles that cover virtually all phases of economic theory, he transformed the formerly verbal statements of that theory into mathematical propositions. This transformation of economics has since become conventional—or orthodox—and turned economics into a quasi-natural science. While widely accepted, the approach, nevertheless, has been criticized as unduly rigorous, overly formalistic, and reductive. In his substantive economics (but not in his approach as characterized in the preceding sentences) Samuelson was an early follower of John Maynard Keynes. His great gifts of analytical power at the highest level of abstraction are paired with similarly great gifts of verbal exposition. He is, perhaps, best known as the author of an introductory economics textbook that in the course of time has sold over 4 million copies.

HENRY W. SPIEGEL

BIBLIOGRAPHY

Feiwel, George R., ed. *Samuelson and Neo-Classical Economics*. Boston: Kluwer Nijhoff, 1982.

Samuelson, Paul A. *Collected Scientific Papers*, edited by Joseph E. Stiglitz. Vols. 1–5. Cambridge: M.I.T. Press, 1966–1986.

——— . *Economics*, 11th ed. New York: McGraw-Hill, 1980.

——— . *Economics from the Heart: A Samuelson Sampler*. San Diego: Harcourt Brace Jovanovich, 1983.

——— . *Foundations of Economic Analysis*. Cambridge: Harvard University Press, 1947.

——— . *Microeconomics*, 13th ed. New York: McGraw-Hill, 1989.

——— , and Nordhaus, William D. *Macroeconomics*, 13th ed. New York: McGraw-Hill, 1989.

Sarnoff, David (1891–1971). The "Father of American Television," David Sarnoff was the eldest of five children born to a poor itinerant merchant, Abraham Sarnoff, and his wife Leah, in Uzlian, a Russian village in the province of Minsk. At the age of 5, David was placed in the care of his granduncle, a rabbi, who instilled in the boy a strong love of learning. Under his tutelage, David studied the Prophets and the Talmud to the degree that the Sarnoff family anticipated that he would become a *Lamdun*—a man of great learning.

In 1900, however, the Sarnoffs migrated to the United States, rejoining their father who had preceded the family in 1896. David Sarnoff had many different jobs in his new home on New York's Lower East Side. He sold newspapers, ran errands for a butcher, and made extra money singing in Cantor Kaminsky's choir on the High Holy Days. Many years later, Sarnoff would attribute his support for radio's "Music Appreciation Hour," the Metropolitan Opera Broadcasts, and the airing of the Toscanini concerts to the love of music that this choir experience had instilled in him.

Sarnoff also attended classes at the Educational Alliance, a nonsectarian settlement house on East Broadway. In 1906, however, David left school and became a messenger boy for a cable company. With his wages, he bought a telegraph instrument and learned the Morse code. What followed was a series of jobs that culminated with his appointment as a radio operator for John Wana-

maker of Philadelphia in 1912. It was at this job that Sarnoff picked up the message "SS *Titanic* ran into iceberg, sinking fast." It was Sarnoff's masterful handling of the news during this disaster that led to his appointment as a radio inspector and an instructor at the Marconi Institute.

An avid reader of technical manuals, Sarnoff had mastered the intricacies of the wireless communications industry. In 1915, he submitted to the Marconi Company the idea of a "radio music box," the forerunner of the modern radio. When the newly formed Radio Corporation of America (RCA) absorbed the American Marconi Corporation in 1919, Sarnoff was appointed general manager (1921). He again submitted his "music box" idea, which, after being tested during the Dempsey-Carpenter fight, created a sensation, and in 1922, RCA began the manufacture of receiving sets. In the same year, Sarnoff was elected vice-president of RCA; in 1926, he was responsible for the founding of a subsidiary company, the National Broadcasting Company.

Sarnoff was also aware of the potential of the iconoscope, invented in 1923 by Vladimar Zworykin, and he set up a special NBC station in 1928 to experiment with what is now "TV."

During World War II, Sarnoff served on General Dwight Eisenhower's staff as a communication consultant. RCA was soon producing radar, shoran, and loran and the proximity fuse and sniperscope for the war effort. For his services, Sarnoff was promoted to brigadier general and was decorated with the Legion of Merit in 1944. In 1946, he was also the recipient, as president of RCA, of the Medal of Merit.

Back in civilian life, Sarnoff began the effort to convince radio stations to join him in the television venture. He was able to persuade radio entrepreneurs that successful as radio was, TV would be even more lucrative.

Sarnoff also pioneered in color television, and in the 1950s convinced the Federal Communications Commission to adopt industry-wide standards for color television that were based largely, though not entirely, on the RCA system.

In 1966, Sarnoff relinquished his position as chief executive officer of RCA but continued as board chairman until his death in 1971. He was the recipient of many awards, including the First World Brotherhood Award of the Jewish Theological Seminary of America in 1951. In 1946, he had received an honorary doctoral degree from the Jewish Theological Seminary.

JACK FISCHEL

BIBLIOGRAPHY

Lyons, Eugene. *David Sarnoff*. New York: Harper & Row, 1966.

Satmar Rebbe: Joel Teitelbaum (1886–1979).

The Satmar Rebbe Joel Teitelbaum was a Hasidic leader, rabbinic scholar, and anti-Zionist religious leader. He was the world leader of the ultra-Orthodox Satmar Hasidic community.

Teitelbaum was born in the city of Sighet in Hungary. His father, Rabbi Lipa Teitelbaum (d. 1904), was chief rabbi of Sighet as well as *rebbe* (spiritual leader) of the Sighet Hasidic dynasty, the largest Hasidic group in Hungary and Romania, whose founder was Rabbi Moses Teitelbaum of Ujhely (1759–1841). Following his father's death, Teitelbaum served as rabbi in a number of Romanian towns. Following the death of his brother Rabbi Chaim Zvi Teitelbaum of Sighet (d. 1926), a large proportion of Sighet Hasidim regarded Joel Teitelbaum as their new leader. In 1934, he was elected chief rabbi of Satmar. At Satmar he also headed a large yeshiva-rabbinical seminary.

By the late 1930s, he was considered one of the leading rabbis in Hungary and Romania and was the leader of the ultra-Orthodox anti-Zionist faction in those countries. As chief rabbi of Satmar, he embarked on an aggressive campaign to crush all rabbinic opposition to him. At the same time he tried to establish harmony within the region by placing relatives and disciples in the rabbinic slots. In his drive to become the dominant leader, he clashed, often violently, with competing Hasidic groups, such as the Vishnitz, Spinka, and Munkatch Hasidim.

Despite his stand on Zionism, in 1944, Teitelbaum was rescued by his Zionist opponents from deportation to Auschwitz and certain death by being included in the famous Kasztner train, which carried 1600 Jews from Hungary to safety in neutral Switzerland and then on to Palestine. Teitelbaum migrated to the United States in 1947, settling in the Williamsburg section of Brooklyn, New York. In 1952, the ultra-Orthodox anti-Zionist EDA-Ha-Charedith in Jerusalem chose him as their chief rabbi. Teitelbaum eagerly accepted the appointment but acted as chief rabbi from his seat in the United States, visiting Israel from time to time. In 1956, he organized many of the Hungarian refugee anti-Zionist rabbis to be a unified body, the Central Rabbinical Congress. At the same time he set up a weekly Yiddish newspaper, *DEDYID*, to be the organ of his community. The paper promulgated his anti-Zionist and anti-Israel views. In 1977, he set up Kiryat-Joel in Monroe, New York, as an independent Satmar community, and Monroe became his official residence until his death.

Although married twice, he left no descendants (his three daughters died in his lifetime). Following a short but intense struggle for power involving followers of his widow Mrs. Feiga Teitelbaum and his nephew Rabbi Miske Teitelbaum (b. 1916), the latter was chosen as the new chief rabbi of the Satmar Hasidim.

Teitelbaum was a multifaceted personality who was acknowledged, even by his opponents, as being one of the great Talmudic authorities of the twentieth century. As such, he led the ultra-Orthodox anti-Zionist faction of Orthodoxy in an intense and often violent struggle against Zionism and the State of Israel.

According to Teitelbaum's teachings as outlined in his chief words *Va-Yoel Moseh* (Brooklyn, N.Y., 1959) and *Al Ha-Geulah-V'al Ha-Temurah* (Brooklyn, N.Y., 1967), Jews were forbidden to create their own sovereign state prior to the coming of the Messiah. Teitelbaum emphasized that he not only was opposed to a secular Jewish state, but also would be as opposed to a Jewish state run according to Orthodox Jewish principles. Teitelbaum regarded the Zionist Movement as the devil incarnate and the State of Israel as the work of the devil, whose chief function was to ensnare religious Jews in the web of secularism. According to Teitelbaum, no good could come from the work of the Zionists, and certainly no miracle would ever occur on their behalf. His most heated criticism was saved for the religious Zionists and other Orthodox and Hasidic groups who supported Israel, such as Agudath Israel and the Lubavitch, Klausenberg, and Vishnitz Hasidic groups. He accused them of cooperating with the State of Israel.

Although he achieved fame in the wider world for his anti-Israel stance, above all, Teitelbaum was a classical East European rabbi, Talmudic scholar, and Hasidic guide. Under his leadership his community, known as Yitav Lev of Satmar, grew to be the largest Hasidic group in the United States. The community runs a network of synagogues, schools, welfare organizations, and other religious facilities in various centers in metropolitan New York.

Teitelbaum stressed the importance of rebuilding East European Jewish life in America without making any accommodations to the American lifestyle and to modernity. He stressed the importance of retaining the classical East European Hasidic clothing for men and women. He insisted that Yiddish be the chief language of daily usage with Hebrew reserved for prayer and English for communication with the Gentile world. All East European manners and customs were to be preserved and were regarded as sacred. As such, Teitelbaum and the Satmar community became the yardstick by which other Hasidic communities, and even non-Hasidic Orthodox groups, measured their own commitment to the law and customs of Orthodoxy.

Rabbi Joel Teitelbaum was the prime mover and ideological force behind the successful transfer of the "shtetl" of Eastern Europe to the United States following the Holocaust. By virtue of his rabbinic scholarship, aggressive personality, and leadership ability, not only did he establish himself as an important leader of American Orthodoxy, but also his community became the largest Hasidic community in the United States and the model for similar communities in the United States and Canada. *See also* Orthodoxy.

ZALMAN ALPERT

BIBLIOGRAPHY

Kranzler, George. *Williamsburg: A Jewish Community in Transition.* New York: Phillip Geldheim, 1961.

Nadler, Allan L. "Piety and Politics: The Case of the Satmar Rebbe." *Judaism* 31 (Spring 1982): 135–153.

Poll, Solomon. *The Hasidic Community of Williamsburg.* New York: Free Press, 1962.

Rubin, Israel. *Satmar: An Island in the City.* Chicago: Quadrangle, 1972.

Schechter, Solomon (1847–1915).

Solomon Schechter was a renowned rabbinic scholar whose reputation was established primarily through his recovery of the Cairo Genizah (the place in a synagogue for storing books, ritual objects, or documents that have become unusable). Schechter was born in Foscani, Romania, the son of a Habad Hasid. Already known as a gifted Talmudist in his youth, Schechter studied at the Beth-Midrash in Vienna and received his rabbinical ordination from Rabbi Isaac Hirsch Weiss (1879). He also studied at the Universities of Vienna and Berlin and at the Berlin Hochschule fuer des Wissenschaft des Judentums. In the United States he became president of the Jewish Theological Seminary of America from 1902 until his death and was instrumental in fostering the growth of Conservative Judaism in the States.

In 1882, Claude Goldsmid Montefiore, then a promising fellow student at the Hochschule (and later a leader and theologian of Liberal Judaism in England), invited Schechter to be his tutor in rabbinics in London. Schechter accepted. In London he met and married (1887) Matilde Roth. Schechter was appointed lecturer in Talmudics (1890) and then reader in rabbinics (1892) at Cambridge University. He also became professor of Hebrew at London's University College (1899). Schechter was part of a circle of bright young scholars (which included Israel Abrahams, Lucien Wolf, and Israel Zangwill) that was instrumental in ushering in a revival of Jewish culture in England. His critical edition of *Abot de-Rabbi Nathan* (published in 1887) put him in the front rank of Jewish scholars. This renown was further enhanced by his discovery of the Cairo Genizah. By bringing these historic findings to Cambridge, Schechter preserved the collection for generations of scholars. He himself began the enormous task of identifying manuscript fragments and comparing them with previously known versions. His publication of part of the long-lost original Hebrew text of Ben Sira, *The Wisdom of Ben Sira* (1899), first signaled to scholars the significance of the Genizah find.

Schechter's magnetic personality and brilliance coupled with a philosophy of Judaism that focused on the importance of Torah, learning, observance, and historical development, made him a desirable choice to head the newly reorganized Jewish Theological Seminary of America. Schechter wanted to leave Cambridge because, though it was congenial to scholarship, it was Jewishly unsatisfactory. After 12 years of intermittent negotiations with members of the Jewish Theological Seminary Association, Schechter moved to New York to assume the presidency (1902). Schechter wanted to fashion a school that would embrace all areas of Jewish learning and maintain the highest standards of scientific thoroughness. He assembled a young faculty that included Louis Ginzberg, Alexander Marx, Israel Friedlaender, Israel Davidson, and Mordecai M. Kaplan, all individuals who rose to prominence in their chosen fields. In attracting these men, Schechter revitalized the Jewish Theological Seminary, transforming it into an important center for Jewish scholarship.

He was also instrumental in making the

Seminary into the center of a distinct religious movement. It was Schechter who first used the term "Conservative Judaism" regularly. Though he tried to avoid denominationalism, he was unable to unite traditionalists and Reformers, partly because of his own vehement opposition to Reform Judaism. Instead, his view of Judaism became the underpinning of a distinct movement. Schechter also worked to establish a network of congregations that would promote Conservative Judaism, correctly anticipating the importance of such a group for the future of the movement. This organization was founded as the United Synagogue of America (1913).

Schechter's conception of Judaism was based on that of the Positive Historical School of Zechariah Frankel. Schechter characterized his attitude toward Judaism as an "enlightened skepticism with a staunch conservatism which is not even wholly devoid of a certain mystical touch." His most distinctive contribution to the understanding of Conservative Judaism was his notion of "catholic Israel." In his view, what is significant for the Jew is the revealed Bible "as it repeats itself in History, in other words, as it is interpreted by Tradition." Thus, the center of authority in Judaism is removed from the Bible and placed in some "living body" that by virtue of being in touch with the religious needs of the age is best able to determine the interpretation of Scripture. This living body is "the collective conscience of catholic Israel as embodied in the Universal Synagogue."

Much of Schechter's scholarly research, theological views, and conception of Conservative Judaism can be found in his *Studies in Judaism* (3 vols., 1896-1924), *Some Aspects of Rabbinic Theology* (in book form 1909, based on essays in the *Jewish Quarterly Review*), and *Seminary Addresses and Other Papers* (1915).

Though Schechter devoted himself primarily to the Seminary and the emerging Conservative Movement, he also lent his expertise to other projects devoted to deepening Jewish knowledge and commitment. He served as editor of the department of Talmud for the *Jewish Encyclopedia* (1902-1904) and was involved in the Bible translation project of the Jewish Publication Society.

Most important, Schechter became a fervent supporter of the nascent Zionist movement (1905) despite the strong opposition of influential Seminary board members to Zionism. Convinced that "you cannot sever Jewish nationality from Jewish religion," Schechter also believed that Zionism would serve as a "mighty bulwark against the incessantly assailing forces of assimilation." His view of the spiritual importance of Zionism was close to that of the great Zionist thinker Ahad ha'Am (Asher Zvi Ginsberg). Schechter attended the 11th Zionist Congress in Vienna (1913). As a result of his commitment, the Conservative Movement was strongly pro-Zionist practically from the beginning.

Schechter was instrumental in the emergence of Conservative Judaism as the leading denomination of American Judaism in the twentieth century. His elaboration of the concept of "catholic Israel" and his pro-Zionist position provided the ideological underpinnings of the movement, while his faculty appointments and commitment to scholarship transformed the Jewish Theological Seminary into one of the foremost Jewish scholarly institutions in the world. Schechter's foresight in founding the United Synagogue of America helped ensure the future of the Conservative Movement. *See also* Conservative Judaism.

SHULY RUBIN SCHWARTZ

BIBLIOGRAPHY
Adler, Cyrus. *American Jewish Year Book*. Philadelphia: Jewish Publication Society, 1916-1917. Pp. 24-67.

Ben-Horin, Meir. "Solomon Schechter to Judge Mayer Sulzberger." *Jewish Social Studies* 25 (1963): 249-286; 27 (1965): 75-102; 30 (1968): 262-271.

Bentwich, Norman. *Solomon Schechter: A Biography*. Philadelphia: Jewish Publication Society, 1938.

Fierstein, Robert E. "Solomon Schechter and the Zionist Movement." *Conservative Judaism* 29 (Summer 1975): 3-13.

Karp, Abraham J., ed. *The Jewish Experience in America*. Vol. 5. New York: Ktav, 1969.

Marx, Alexander. *Essays in Jewish Biography*. Philadelphia: Jewish Publication Society, 1947.

Oko, Adolph K. *Solomon Schechter: A Bibliography*. New York: Macmillan, 1938.

Parzen, Herbert. *Architects of Conservative Judaism*. New York: Jonathan David, 1964.

Schick, Bela

Schick, Bela (1877-1967). Bela Schick is considered the first great pediatric practitioner and a world-famous immunologist. He was born in Bolgar, Hungary, and received his medical degree in 1900 from the Karl Franz University in Austria. From 1900 to 1923, he worked for the University of Vienna at the famous Vienna Children's Clinic. His work and research in immunology included the publication of a 1905 treatise on serum sickness, written with Dr. von Pirquet, and a 1912 monograph on scarlet fever, written with Theodore Escherich. Von Pirquet discovered the scratch test for tuberculosis, and Schick used some of von Pirquet's techniques to develop a test to determine an individual's susceptibility to diphtheria. The procedure, widely known as the Schick test, was first announced in 1913 and led to the worldwide conquest of the disease.

Diphtheria was a dreaded disease, striking and frequently killing children between the ages of 2 and 5. German researchers had developed a serum for diphtheria, but the serum's side effects prevented it from being widely used as a preventative measure. The Schick test determined if an individual had an immunity to diphtheria. The test involved injecting under the skin of the arm a small amount of diluted diphtheria toxin and seeing if the area became inflamed. Through the widespread use of the test, doctors discovered that most people did not have an immunity; a safer serum for immunization was needed. By the mid-1920s, such a serum for immunization was developed, and the Schick test was no longer needed for its original purpose. The test was later used to find out if a patient was still immune to diphtheria or if reimmunization was needed.

Von Pirquet and Schick described serum sickness and coined the word "allergy" in their 1905 treatise. The Schick test continued to be used as a way to provide antibodies to people with allergies.

In 1923, Schick accepted a position as head of pediatrics at Mount Sinai Hospital in New York City, and remained at Mount Sinai until 1942, when he reached the mandatory retirement age.

Schick married Catherine C. Fries in 1925. The childless doctor became known as the Father of TLC (tender loving care). His views on child care and child rearing were considered revolutionary. He did not believe in corporal punishment. He believed in playing with children and in getting to know them before examining them. He believed people underestimated the mental capacity of infants. He was a strong advocate of breast feeding. In 1932, he and William Rosenson wrote *Child Care Today*, a book for the general public.

Bela Schick became a naturalized U.S. citizen in 1929. He espoused many liberal causes. He also assisted in the Russian war relief effort during World War II and was the editor of the *American Review of Soviet Medicine* until 1948.

Schick was one of the founders of the U.S. Academy of Pediatrics, and he received numerous awards and honors. Many hospitals named their pediatric wards for the pediatrician who treated an estimated 1 million children during his long and distinguished career. Until his death, he remained active in pediatrics, doing consulting, teaching, and research in the field.

LINDA GLAZER

BIBLIOGRAPHY
Life, October 20, 1957, 77–78.
New York Times, December 7, 1967, 1, 47.
New York Times Magazine, November 24, 1963, 109.
Rothe, Anna, ed. *1944 Current Biography*. New York: Wilson, 1944.
Time, December 8, 1952, 79.

Schneerson, Menachem Mendel. See LU-BAVITCHER REBBE.

Science. In the twentieth century, science has been one of the preferred occupations pursued by American Jews. Jews are numerous among scientific elites, including the Nobel laureates. They show some preferences of discipline and approach that may be attributed to their Judaic cultural background, e.g., inclination to more theoretical rather than experimental work. While before World War II scientists desirous to teach in the science field tended to hide, even negate, their Jewishness, since the 1960s it has become common and socially acceptable even for the conspicuously observant Jews to join the staff of prominent American universities. While social barriers appear all but eliminated, recent data suggest that science may be losing its appeal for American Jews.

Jewish interest in scientific inquiry is not new. Jews displayed scientific curiosity well before the emergence of modern science. A census of prominent medieval savants revealed that one in ten in the sample was a Jew. This phenomenon is directly linked with the higher incidence of literacy among male Jews, with their early socialization to intellectual pursuits, such as the study of Talmud with its emphasis on abstraction and reasoning. The Talmud contains numerous pieces of scientific information even though advancement of specifically scientific knowledge was not among the main objectives of the Talmudic sages. The pursuit of truth, according to traditional Judaic scholars, usually encompassed all domains of knowledge.

Several scholars ascribe the prominence of Jews in science to the cultural and even genetic vestiges of this millennarian tradition. However, the recent ascent to scientific prominence by Chinese and Japanese immigrants in the United States and other countries suggests a sociocultural rather than genetic explanation. Sociocultural factors account for a large part of the Jewish influx into science: they were concentrated in the upwardly mobile middle class in urban centers within easy reach of significant scientific and cultural institutions. Adjusted for these factors, the concentration of Jews in science may appear less unusual or surprising.

The initial entry of Jews in the modern scientific profession dates back to mid-nineteenth century and is a consequence of their emancipation in Western and Central Europe. Their entry happened in the atmosphere of positivism and, later, scientism, which transposed on Judaism the largely Christian history of the conflict between science and religion. It is important to realize that it was also in the nineteenth century that the very term "religion" was introduced into Jewish usage. For Jews who cast aside normative Judaism, science offered an alternative and attractive world view, which contained more than a few reminders of the traditional Jewish culture (such as emphasis on pure knowledge, reliance on abstract theoretical thinking, reverence for the scholar).

Science was a new occupation with few anti-Jewish impediments or traditions. It also carried prestige and attraction to serve as an avenue of social ascendance for the Jews. The settlement of middle-class Jewish families in major urban centers of the United States facilitated the entry into science. In Germany, science offered a legitimately cosmopolitan refuge from the romantic nationalism permeating German intellectual life of the period. Even though conversion to Christianity advanced the scientific career, the occurrence of conversions in natural and exact sciences was less frequent than in the humanities. Similarly, the influx of Jews and other ethnic groups actively or potentially alienated from the official Soviet ideology into science is another example of sociopolitical uses of science by populations perceiving themselves as marginal. Conversely, in France, where the liberal atmosphere has prevailed since the nineteenth century, Jews are significantly more numerous in the arts and humanities than in the natural and exact sciences. French Jews did not seek a refuge in a transnational intellectual occupation but were active and largely accepted in the mainstream of French culture. While the incidence of anti-Semitism (real or perceived) on the occupational choice of the Jews is quite pronounced in the case of the scientific profession in Germany, its significance was less pronounced in the United States.

Indeed, the entry of Jews into American science happened in different circumstances. Emancipation was not an issue, even though science was occasionally seen as a refuge from an inhospitable spiritual environment. Anti-Semitic prejudice in industry and continuing entry quotas at medical and law schools directed Jews toward academic science. This was an inverse of the German situation in the late nineteenth century when Jews opted for medical and legal occupations, for these offered more accessible alternatives to the public sector's university. Anti-Semitic prejudice made American Jews who were entering science in the 1920s and 1930s unwelcome at many campuses, but the intensity of prejudice in the relatively new scientific profession was lower than in the more established occupations. Another factor facilitated Jewish entry into American science. American science was on its way to the dominant position that it finally occupied in the aftermath of World War II. Consequently, it became a "floodgate for social advancement," replicating, albeit in a minor manner, the social consequences of the Jewish entry into German science.

Distribution of Jews among scientific disciplines, in the United States and elsewhere, is skewed in the direction of more theoretical and abstract rather than experimental fields. One historical cultural factor—the traditional mental occupation of the Jews with the Talmud—may provide part of an explanation. The validity of this explanation should not be discarded simply because anti-Semites were among the first to advance it. In the mid-1970s, the last period for which this information is available, the concentration of Jews varied among academic scientific disciplines in the following way: bacteriology, 21 percent; biochemistry, 14 percent; physics, 14 percent; physiology, 9 percent; mathematics, 9 percent; chemistry, 6 percent. While in the physical and life sciences Jews constitute, respectively, 8 and 10 percent, in the social sciences their share is 15 percent, in medicine 22 percent, and in law 25 percent. Thus even among the university faculty the proverbial Jewish preference for medicine and law remain quite pronounced.

It is also noteworthy that social sciences, which are more directly relevant to the ethical issues of social justice and social reform, continue to be attractive to many Jews. The Jewish contribution to American science, when compared to that of other ethnic groups (e.g., the Chinese) supports the existence of cultural variables in the distribution of scientific talent.

The entry of newcomers into new or just emerging scientific fields is easier because of the lack of entrenched power structures in such new endeavors. Breaking old scientific paradigms becomes less difficult when a scientist has no stake in the perpetuation of the old one. The prominence of Jews in interdisciplinary, border areas of science, which are often the most innovative at any given time, also offers an explanation of their overrepresentation in the scientific elite.

Both in Germany in the late nineteenth and early twentieth centuries and in the United States several decades later, Jews were entering a *central* scientific community. Conversely, Russia and Hungary, where Jewish entry into science was relatively more massive, were peripheral to the then established centers of science. This placed Russian and Hungarian Jewish scientists in a more complex position with respect to local cultures. They developed a species of dual loyalty: toward the local national culture and toward a distant, ostensibly cosmopolitan culture of science carrying characteristic traits of the countries central to the development of science. This remained true for those Russian and Hungarian emigrés who moved to the United States in the middle or by the end of their scientific careers.

At the turn of the century, German language and, inevitably, elements of German culture were *de rigueur* in the world scientific community. Since World War II, the cosmopolitan culture of science adopted the English language and several distinctive traits of American civilization. The issue of split cultural loyalties has remained important, perhaps less for Jews who are no longer novices in science, but rather for scientists in peripheral Third World countries aspiring for cultural self-affirmation.

Entering the center rather than the periphery of world science, American Jews had an easier access to world recognition. The fact that American science has been in the center of scientific activity all through the second third of this century has made it attractive for thousands of Jewish scientists immigrating to the United States from the four corners of the world. Using Nobel Prizes as a criterion of success, American Jews are outstandingly prominent; they (i.e., those who have at least one Jewish parent) received nearly one-third—41 out of 134 as of 1989—of all Nobel Prizes awarded to American scientists. It is significant that prior to World War II there were only two Jews among the 13 American Nobel laureates, even though the first American to receive a Nobel Prize was a Jew: physicist Albert A. Michelson in 1907.

It was natural that one of the first institutions to open its doors to Jewish scientists was the City College of New York. The influx of Jewish refugees from Europe in the 1930s, even though it provoked a significant anti-Semitic reaction on many campuses, resulted in substantial acceptance of Jews in American scientific institutions. But even then the bulk of American Jewish scientists came from Eastern European immigrants who had instilled in their children an almost religious respect for science and scholarship.

Jews distinguished themselves in war-related scientific activities, including the Manhattan Project. Subsequently, many Jews among the demobilized soldiers used their veteran privileges to enter America's best scientific schools, and many became faculty members. This largely signified the end of restrictions on access of Jews to American science. The opening of the Jewish access to science was not due to what would later be called "affirmative action," a means of increasing the access of other American minorities to science and education.

Correlations between ethnic or religious characteristics and prominence in American science before World War II point first of all at Mormons and Quakers. Jewish entry into science led to a spectacular rise of the Atlantic coast region—from the seventh to the second place—in terms of concentration of scientific talent. Similarly, while only 1 university from New York was among the 50 best in terms of scientific productivity between 1920 and 1939, there were 11 from New York in the same list for 1950–1961.

There exists a disproportionate concentration of Jewish scientific talent at the elite universities of the United States (31 versus 9 percent for non-Jewish faculty). This is particularly significant since access of Jews to higher education used to be restricted in many American universities. This automatically impeded their entry into science. Just as a century earlier at the Ecole normale supérieure in Paris, the argument against accepting Jews to American universities was circular: why accept them if they cannot find a suitable position later? Some Jews became exceedingly discreet about their origins. For example, the cybernetician Norbert Wiener, whose father Leo was a professor at Harvard, discovered his Jewishness by chance only at the age of 16. Some resorted to the old-country method of entering the university, namely, to convert to Christianity, but these were relatively few. Karl Landsteiner (Nobel Prize in physiology for 1930) went so far in negating his Jewish origin that he took to court a biographical directory that had mentioned his provenance.

According to the Lipset and Ladd data (1960), twice as many Jews among university faculty were indifferent or opposed to religion compared to their Catholic and Protestant colleagues. This reflected the dichotomy between "science and religion" perceived as inevitable by Jews in the nineteenth and the first half of this century. The ethos of science, with its emphasis on moral integrity and a selfless pursuit of truth, was long considered as a substitute for Judaism. This dichotomous perception of science and normative Judaism has been declining since the 1970s.

Indeed, another Nobel laureate, Baruch Blumberg (physiology for 1976), overtly ascribed his scientific eminence to the traditional Jewish education he had received at Flatbush Yeshiva (Brooklyn): "We spent many hours on the rabbinic commentaries on the Bible and were immersed in the existential reasoning of the Talmud at an age when we could hardly have realized its impact." Arno Penzias, Nobel Prize in physics for 1978, also mentioned his Jewish background in the solemn Nobel lecture.

This assertiveness, or at least openness, appears to be in step with the general trend toward ethnic pride in the 1970s. More significantly, however, Jews who used to shed their identity upon admission to an Ivy League university have come to acquire a Jewish identity there since the 1970s. Noncredit courses in Jewish civilization proliferate alongside the regular curricula, and at least one prominent university—Princeton—runs a rabbinically supervised kosher kitchen. While only a few years ago it would have been difficult for an observant Jewish student to have examinations rescheduled should they fall on a Sabbath or a Jewish holiday that forbids work, in the 1980s it is not uncommon for an entire university to reschedule the opening day of classes in order not to conflict with the Jewish New Year.

It was also since the early 1970s that Judaic observance has significantly increased among Jewish faculty and students, particularly in the Ivy League universities. The proliferation of synagogues and kosher cafeterias on American university campuses in the 1970s and the 1980s can be seen as an indicator of this trend. This phenomenon is part of a more general return to tradition which has affected the three monotheistic faiths since the 1970s.

These changes on the American campuses happened in spite of, rather than thanks to, the older Jewish scientific elite. Many scientists educated in the 1930s and 1940s viewed their Jewishness as a birth defect that warranted excision rather than recognition, let alone praise. The attitude of younger scientists to their Jewishness varies from benign indifference to overt affirmation.

Jewish scientists exhibit a stronger self-image as intellectuals than their non-Jewish colleagues (82 vs 70 percent). This happens against the background of lower academic status of their parents, compared to parents of non-Jewish scientists. This further accentuates the predominance of cultural rather than socioeconomic factors in the entry into the scientific profession even though these cultural factors were only historically linked with the Jewish tradition.

Politically, Jewish scientists situate themselves significantly more to the left of the norm in their profession: 75 percent of Jews, compared to 46 percent among their colleagues, consider themselves liberals and leftists. But, unlike the Soviet Union, natural scientists are known to be more conservative than specialists in the social sciences and the humanities. While correlations exist between leftist views and irreligious attitudes, the latter do not seem to encourage higher academic productivity.

The meritocratic character of science tends to favor Jewish scientists. More Jewish Nobel laureates come from New York than the concentration of Jews in that metropolis would suggest, and they come more frequently than non-Jewish laureates from the Ivy League campuses. The cumulative advantage, another important characteristic of the scientific profession, becomes therefore quite tangible when it comes to Jews in American science.

Analyzing the remarkable prominence of Jews among the Nobel prize winners, sociologist Harriet Zuckerman observes that "each phase of the selective process involves an increasing proportion of Jewish scientists appearing in given sectors of the scientific community and thus a decreasing disproportion of Jewish laureates to their number in that sector." But she disagrees with Lipset and Ladd, who claim the Jewish excellence in life and medical sciences might reflect the high numbers of Jews who "did not make it" to become physicians.

A comparative perspective on the prominence of Jews in different fields of science can be gained from the following table. Although based on the Lipset and Ladd, and Zuckerman, studies of the 1960s in percentages of the total, the table figures still held true in 1990:

Denomination	Faculty	Nobel prize	Nobel per faculty
Life Sciences (excluding medicine)			
Protestants	68	54	0.78
Catholics	16	7	0.43
Jews	15	39	2.55
Chemistry			
Protestants	74	84	1.14
Catholics	19	5	0.28
Jews	7	11	1.58
Physics			
Protestants	68	59	0.86
Catholics	16	0	0
Jews	16	41	2.64

In all of these fields the prominence of Jews is felt more strongly in theoretical subfields, which may reflect the traditional emphasis put in the Jewish culture on conceptualization and speculation. Modest social origins of Jewish scientists, and particularly of Jewish Nobel laureates in science, suggest that science has been a more important avenue of social mobility for Jews than for non-Jews. Jewish scientists tend to come from lower classes than their non-Jewish colleagues.

The theory of Thorstein Veblen continues to explain Jewish scientific prominence. He puts emphasis on the role of the Jew as an "outsider." Even though in the United States a Jew has had fewer disabilities and restrictions than in Europe, the outsider status, whether imposed or chosen, has not entirely disappeared. Science values nonconventional, original approaches, and the outsider, whatever the definition of the term, has therefore an advantage of being outside the consensus. Impartial, detached attitudes characterize an outsider's vision and enhance his scientific achievement.

The entry of Jews into the scientific profession, which began in the mid-nineteenth century, has largely come to a close. Specific anti-Semitic hindrances may still obtain in a few countries, but the preference given by Jews to scientific pursuits is no longer salient. With the emergence of a largely Jewish society in the State of Israel a qualitatively new situation has come to obtain: Jews live under the conditions of preferential treatment. It remains to be seen how this new situation affects the preeminence of Jews in science. The fact that Israel is yet to produce a local Nobel laureate in science may have to do more with the objectively peripheral situation of Israel and budgetary limitations than with the new social circumstances of "being a free people in its own land." Substantial evidence suggests a slow decline in the proportionate contribution of Jews to science in the United States. *See also* Medicine, Nobel Prize Winners.

YAKOV M. RABKIN

BIBLIOGRAPHY

Feuer, L. S. *The Scientific Intellectual*. New York: Basic Books, 1963.

Fleming, D., and Bailyn, B., eds., *The Intellectual Migration*. Cambridge, Mass.: Belknap Press, 1969.

Frazier, Kendrick. "Israel: Oasis for Science." *Science News* 107 (January 11, 1975): 28.

Himmelfarb, M. *The Jews of Modernity*. Philadelphia: Jewish Publication Society, 1973.

Hoch, P. "The Reception of Central European Refugee Physicists of the 1930s: USSR, UK, and USA." *Annals of Science* 40 (1983): 217–246.

Kevles, D. *The Physicists*. New York: Knopf, 1978.

Lipset, S. M., and Ladd, C. L. "Jewish Academics in the United States." In *The Jews in American Society*, 1960.

Roback, A. A. "The Jew in Modern Science." In *The Hebrew Impact on Western Civilization*, edited by D. Runes. New York: Philosophical Library, 1951.

Zuckerman, H. *Scientific Elite. Nobel laureates in the United States*. New York: Free Press, 1977.

Sephardim. The foundations of Jewish life in North America were established by the Spanish and Portuguese congregations that flourished in colonial times. Sephardic culture was dominant through the early nineteenth century. During the twentieth century, many thousands of Sephardim migrated to America from Turkey, the Balkan countries, the Middle East, North Africa, and Europe. Sephardic communities are scattered throughout the United States, representing an estimated population of 175,000 to 200,000 people.

Congregation Shearith Israel of New York was founded in September 1654 (New York was then known as New Amsterdam). It was the only Jewish congregation in New York until 1825. Thus, for over 170 years, all the Jews of the city—whether Sephardic or Ashkenazic—were part of this Sephardic congregation. Other Spanish and Portuguese congregations developed later in Newport, Philadelphia, Savannah, and Charleston. All were part of the Western Sephardic tradition, stemming back to the Spanish and Portuguese communities of Europe, notably Amsterdam. Although these congregations functioned according to the Western Sephardic *minhag* (custom), as noted, they were composed of Sephardic and Ashkenazic Jews. Indeed, Ashkenazim soon came to outnumber the Sephardim.

The Sephardic tradition continues to be maintained today by Shearith Israel in New York and Mikveh Israel in Philadelphia. The congregation in Newport presently functions as an Ashkenazic Orthodox synagogue, while the congregations in Savannah and Charleston have become Reform congregations, no longer following the Sephardic tradition.

The historic Spanish and Portuguese congregations provided for the religious, social, and educational needs of their communities. They provided care and assistance to the living and burial to the dead.

During the nineteenth century, large waves of Ashkenazic Jews poured into the United States. Numerous new congregations and institutions sprouted up, and the old Spanish and Portuguese congregations lost their exclusive or central roles in their communities. These congregations, though, continued to participate actively in the vastly expanded and changed Jewish community.

During the first quarter of the twentieth century, 25,000 to 30,000 Sephardim arrived in the United States, most settling on the Lower East Side in New York City. The largest group among these was composed of Judeo-Spanish speaking Jews from Turkey and the Balkan countries. There was also a sizable number of Arabic-speaking Syrian Jews and a smaller group of Greek-speaking Jews from cities in Greece. Most of the Sephardic arrivals, like their fellow Ashkenazic immigrants, were poor and had received only limited formal education in their countries of origin.

They came to America in search of better lives for themselves and their families.

Sephardic communities also were established in Seattle, San Francisco, Los Angeles, Atlanta, Montgomery, Portland (Oregon), Rochester, Indianapolis, Cincinnati and other cities. But these communities accounted for less than one-third of Sephardim in the United States between 1913 and 1946.

The Sephardim were divided among themselves by their linguistic and cultural differences. The Ashkenazic community was largely oblivious to the existence of the relatively small number of Sephardim among them. Indeed, the Sephardim were often not thought to be Jews altogether since they did not speak Yiddish. Congregation Shearith Israel, and especially its sisterhood, expended considerable effort on behalf of the Sephardic newcomers in New York City. The sisterhood operated settlement houses on the Lower East Side, which included synagogue facilities, classrooms, youth programs, classes in American citizenship, etc.

The turbulence and turmoil of the Sephardic immigrants during the early twentieth century are reflected in a Judeo-Spanish weekly newspaper, *La America*, edited by Moise Gadol. Gadol was a Bulgarian-born Sephardic Jew who founded the paper in New York in 1910. It generally appeared every Friday, until it closed in 1925. Gadol was a colorful, fiery communal leader and intellectual. Other Judeo-Spanish publications emerged among the Sephardim, the most successful of which was the newspaper *La Vara*.

Sephardic immigrants tended to set up self-help groups based on their cities of origin. Generally, each group held synagogue services on the High Holy Days. Several groups operated Talmud Torah schools for children, as well as regular services throughout the course of the year.

A host of efforts were made to organize and unify the Sephardic community. The first such attempt in 1912 was the Federation of Oriental Jews. This federation hoped to serve as an umbrella organization for the various Sephardic congregations and societies—to employ a Sephardic chief rabbi and to strengthen Sephardic cultural, religious, and social life in New York. This venture was short-lived. In 1924, the Sephardic Jewish Community of New York, Inc. was established, with practically the same goals as the Federation of Oriental Jews. The new organization purchased a community house on 115th Street, but it too failed within a few years. In

1928, Rabbi David de Sola Pool envisioned the establishment of a Union of Sephardic Congregations to deal with many problems facing the Sephardic synagogues in the United States. Representatives of the historic Shearith Israel in New York, Mikveh Israel in Philadelphia, and Shearith Israel of Montreal met and took the lead in establishing the union. Sephardic congregations throughout the country agreed to participate in this new venture. Its main accomplishment has been the publication of Sephardic prayer books, translated and edited by Rabbi David de Sola Pool. It continues to provide these prayer books to congregations throughout the United States, and indeed throughout the English-speaking world.

In 1941, the Central Sephardic Jewish Community of America, Inc. was founded through the leadership of Rabbi Nissim J. Ovadia. This organization did have some notable successes, but it too was unable to function as effectively as the founders had hoped.

In 1972, the American Sephardic Federation was organized as a national Sephardic umbrella group organization. In the mid-1980s, it took on a more aggressive leadership role, providing increased communal involvement and service to the Sephardic communities.

The Sephardic immigrants of the early part of this century were diligent and hard working. As their economic condition improved, Sephardim moved to new areas, built new synagogues, provided advanced education for their children. They worked together with Ashkenazic Jews in communal and philanthropic organizations.

Sephardim of Judeo-Spanish and Greek backgrounds established the Sephardic Home for the Aged in Brooklyn, New York, in 1951. The home publishes a monthly newsletter with a national circulation of about 10,000.

In 1964, Yeshiva University established a Sephardic studies program under the direction of the Haham Dr. Solomon Gaon, who in 1990 held the chair in Sephardic studies at Yeshiva.

In 1978, the Sephardic House at Shearith Israel of New York City was established under the direction of Rabbi Marc D. Angel. It has grown into a national organization, dedicated to fostering Sephardic history and culture through an active publication program and promoting classes and programs relating to Sephardic topics.

The Syrian Sephardic community, whose largest center is in Flatbush (Brooklyn), has built a number of day schools, yeshiva high schools, and other institutions of Jewish learning. This community's numerous synagogues are active and vibrant. Its community center in Flatbush offers a wide variety of programs and also houses a Sephardic archive of the Syrian Jewish community in the United States.

During the 1960s and 1970s, a new wave of Sephardic immigrants arrived in the United States from North Africa. In recent years, there has been a large influx of Iranian Jews. For the most part they have tended to settle in large Jewish communities, e.g., the New York and Los Angeles metropolitan areas.

Although the term "Sephardic" refers literally to Jews of Iberian origin, the term has popularly been used to refer to Jews of non-Ashkenazic background. By this more general definition, Sephardim in the United States form a very diverse group. Within the diverse community are Jews of North African, Middle Eastern, and Asian backgrounds, as well as Sephardim who arrived here from Europe during the World War II era. *See also* Iranian Jews.

MARC D. ANGEL

BIBLIOGRAPHY

Angel, Marc. "The Sephardim of the United States: An Exploratory Study." *American Jewish Year Book* (1973): 77–138.

Hacker, Louis. "The Communal Life of the Sephardic Jews in New York City." *Jewish Social Service Quarterly* 3 (December 1926): 32–40.

Marcus, Jacob R. *The Colonial American Jew, 1642–1776.* Detroit: Wayne State University Press, 1970.

Pool, David de Sola. "The Immigration of Levantine Jews into the United States." *Jewish Charities* (June 1914): 12–27.

———. "The Levantine Jews in the United States." *American Jewish Year Book* (1913–1914): 207–220.

———, and Pool, Tamar de Sola. *An Old Faith in the New World.* New York: Columbia University Press, 1955.

Settlement Houses.

Settlement Houses. Although other institutions concerned themselves with social reform in general and with improving the lot of New York City's immigrant Jewish population in particular, none was more committed, more visible, than New York's settlement house movement. In most cases its founders and staff people took up full-time residence in the tenements where they confronted the problems of urban squalor firsthand.

Thus, their understanding of "reform" encompassed everything: health and home care, schooling and recreation, culture and politics.

The major settlement houses differed from the earlier institutional churches, not only because they were deliberately nonsectarian, but also because they were specifically designed to bring the estranged together into something approaching community. This was true of the Educational Alliance (formerly the Hebrew Institute), the Jewish Temple Emanu-El sisterhood settlement on Orchard Street, and even the Episcopal House of Aquila, which taught classes in both kosher and American cooking to Jewish housewives.

The first settlement house in the United States, modeled on London's Toynbee Hall, was founded on New York's Lower East Side in 1886. Stanton Coit, an Ethical Society leader, described its ambitious mission this way: "Irrespective of religious belief, or non-belief, all the people . . . shall be organized into a set of clubs . . . to carry out all the reforms, domestic, industrial, educational, provident, or recreative, which the social ideal demands."

In 1891, the Neighborhood Guild became the University Settlement; in 1893, Lilian Wald instituted a class in home nursing for Lower East Side women that would become the impetus for the Henry Street Settlement; and in 1889, the College Settlement (founded by Smith College women) joined with the Educational Alliance. By the turn of the century these settlement houses would become established as the most widely known, and most effective, examples of this important movement.

Although their task was enormous, and no doubt the settlement workers must have often found themselves overwhelmed by sheer numbers and diverse problems, their accomplishments were great. They had a deep influence on their clients. Second only to the public school system, the settlement houses served to Americanize a generation of immigrant children—to give them valuable lessons in civics, in the arts, in organized sport and recreation, in cultural exposure, and in thousands of other smaller ways that made an enormous difference. *See also* Educational Alliance.

SANFORD PINSKER

BIBLIOGRAPHY

Howe, Irving. *World of Our Fathers*. New York: Harcourt Brace Jovanovich, 1976.

Rischin, Moses. *The Promised City*. Cambridge: Harvard University Press, 1962.

Shearith Israel Congregation. Congregation Shearith Israel, popularly known as the Spanish and Portuguese Synagogue of New York City, is the oldest Jewish congregation in North America. It was founded in 1654 by 23 Jews, most of whom were of Spanish and Portuguese descent, who had fled Portuguese rule in Recife, Brazil. Shearith Israel was the sole congregation in New York until 1825 and served the needs of all the Jews of the city—Sephardim and Ashkenazim alike. Over the generations, it has played an active role in New York and American Jewish life and continues to flourish today.

Shearith Israel is representative of the Western Sephardic tradition, having its origins in the traditions of the Portuguese Jewish community of Amsterdam. Its services are conducted according to the Western Sephardic custom and are marked by dignity, formality, and reverence. Although the custom of the congregation is Sephardic, Shearith Israel, as when it was first organized, is composed of Sephardic and Ashkenazic members.

Until 1730, the congregation met for services in rented quarters. In that year the first synagogue building was built on Mill Street. The building was enlarged in 1818. In 1834, the congregation built a new building on Crosby Street. In 1860, the congregation continued its move uptown, to a site on 19th Street, just off Fifth Avenue. In 1897, Shearith Israel completed the building it presently occupies on 70th Street and Central Park West on Manhattan's West Side. The building was designed by Arnold Bruner and has been designated a New York City historic landmark.

The congregation maintains three historic cemeteries, as well as its current cemetery. The oldest is located at Chatham Square on the Lower East Side and includes the remains of members of the community going back to 1683.

From 1654 until 1825, Shearith Israel provided all the Jewish services for New York City. It operated a school, mikvah, and health and welfare societies. It provided kosher food and all the religious needs of Jews from birth to death.

With the large migration of Jews to New York from the 1820s and onward, many new congregations emerged. Shearith Israel continued to play an active role in communal life, and its individual members were leaders in many areas of civic, political, commercial, and intellectual life. The Nathan, Seixas, Gomez, Hendricks, Phillips, and other families were prominent at Shearith Israel over many generations.

Members have served in the United States military since the days of the American Revolution. The congregation or individual congregants were active in the establishment of a number of New York's leading institutions, such as Mount Sinai Hospital, Montefiore Hospital, Columbia University, Barnard University, New York University, Jewish Theological Seminary, the Union of Sephardic Congregations, Sephardic House, and the New York Stock Exchange. Among its members in past generations have been Emma Lazarus, the poet; Benjamin Nathan Cardozo, the United States Supreme Court justice; Cecil Roth, the famed historian; Edgar J. Nathan, Jr., president of the Borough of Manhattan (1942–1945) and a justice of the Supreme Court of the State of New York.

Shearith Israel is the headquarters of the Union of Sephardic Congregations, which distributes Sephardic prayer books to English-speaking communities throughout the world. It also serves as the base of Sephardic House, a national organization dedicated to fostering Sephardic history and culture. In maintaining its historic serenity and dignity, Shearith Israel continues to be an active, vibrant institution. *See also* Sephardim.

MARC D. ANGEL

BIBLIOGRAPHY
Angel, Marc D. *La America: The Sephardic Experience in the United States*. Philadelphia: Jewish Publication Society, 1982.
Pool, David and Tamar de Sola. *An Old Faith in the New World*. New York: Columbia University Press, 1955.

Silver, Abba Hillel (1893–1963).

Abba Hillel Silver was born in 1893 in Lithuania. When he was a youth, his family migrated to the United States. He received his undergraduate degree from the University of Cincinnati and studied for the Reform rabbinate at Hebrew Union College. As a political conservative, Abba Silver cultivated ties to the Republican Party both nationally and in Ohio where he became a close ally of Senator Taft.

Silver used his considerable oratory and organizational skills on behalf of Zionism. It was toward the Zionist cause more than any other enterprise that Abba Hillel Silver directed his energies. Silver's tactics were often controversial, and his prickly, domineering, and ruthless manner

alienated many. Stephen Wise and Chaim Weizmann were among Silver's antagonists within the Zionist Movement. Silver's demand for the immediate creation of a Jewish commonwealth after World War II clashed with Zionists who believed that political necessity demanded compromise and possibly delay in creating a Jewish homeland in Palestine. President Truman referred to Silver and his followers as extreme Zionists.

Whatever the merits of Abba Silver's tactics, his views usually prevailed. He was elected to head the Zionist Organization of America, the United Jewish Appeal, and the American Zionist Emergency Committee, and he served on the Jewish Agency. Rabbi Silver was also active in the debate in the United Nations on the eve of its decision to partition Palestine in 1947. In addition to his political activities, Abba Silver authored several books on Judaism. *See also* Reform Judaism, Zionism.

HOWARD SHAKER

BIBLIOGRAPHY
Fischel, Jack R. "Rabbis and Leaders: Silver and Wise," *American Zionist* (April–May 1983): 5–8.
Ganin, Zvi. *Truman, American Jewry and Israel*. New York and London: Holmes & Meier, 1979.
Raphael, Marc Lee. *Abba Hillel Silver: A Profile in American Judaism*. New York and London: Holmes & Meier, 1989.

Simon, Neil (b. 1927).

Playwright Marvin Neil Simon was born in New York City, the son of Irving and Mamie Simon. He grew up in the Bronx in a middle-class milieu, which he has memorialized in his writings. During World War II, he served in the U.S. Army Air Force Reserve, and in 1946, after his discharge, he attended New York University. In 1948, he began his writing career by joining his brother Danny in writing for acts given at Borscht Circuit hotels and for radio and television comedy shows. In 1953, he married actress Joan Bain, later deceased, by whom he had two daughters, Ellen and Nancy. In 1973, he married actress Marsha Mason, from whom he was subsequently divorced. He resides in New York and in California.

A prolific and highly successful writer, Simon has written for all the major entertainment forms. His early work for such radio and TV personalities as Sid Caesar, Imogene Coca, Phil Silvers, and Garry Moore led to Emmy awards in 1957 for his work for "The Sid Caesar Show" and in 1959 for "Sergeant Bilko." With his brother Danny he wrote sketches for *Catch a Star* (1955) and *New Faces of 1956*, revues that gave him a start in the legitimate theater. His first full-length play, *Come Blow Your Horn* (1961), was a success, running for 677 performances. With the even greater success of his second play, *Barefoot in the Park* (1963, 1530 performances), also a comedy, Simon's place in the commercial theater was established.

These early successes were followed by a long list of plays, books for musicals, and film scripts. His plays include, in addition to the above, *The Odd Couple* (1965), *The Star-Spangled Girl* (1966), *Plaza Suite* (1968), *Last of the Red Hot Lovers* (1969), *The Gingerbread Lady* (1970), *The Prisoner of Second Avenue* (1971), *The Sunshine Boys* (1972), *The Good Doctor* (1973), *God's Favorite* (1974), *California Suite* (1976), *Chapter Two* (1977), *I Ought to Be in Pictures* (1980), *Fools* (1981), *Brighton Beach Memoirs* (1983), *Biloxi Blues* (1984), *Broadway Bound* (1986), and *Rumors* (1988). Musicals include *Little Me* (1962), *Sweet Charity* (1966), *Promises, Promises* (1968), and *They're Playing Our Song* (1979). His work for the screen includes original screenplays—*After the Fox* (1966), *The Out-of-Towners* (1970), *The Heartbreak Kid* (1972), *Murder by Death* (1976), *The Goodbye Girl* (1977), *The Cheap Detective* (1978), *Seems Like Old Times* (1980), and *Only When I Laugh* (1981)—and adaptations of his own stage plays—*Barefoot in the Park* (1967), *The Odd Couple* (1968), *Plaza Suite* (1971), *Last of the Red Hot Lovers* (1972), *The Sunshine Boys* (1974), *The Prisoner of Second Avenue* (1975), *California Suite* (1979), *Brighton Beach Memoirs* (1986), and *Biloxi Blues* (1988).

Among the most memorable of the adaptations are *The Odd Couple*, later a successful TV series, which deals with two incompatible men who share an apartment following their divorces (Simon later did a female version of the same story); *Plaza Suite*, which tells three separate stories all set in the same suite of the famous New York hotel; *Last of the Red-Hot Lovers*, about a man experiencing a middle-age dilemma and three women with whom he has relationships; *Prisoner of Second Avenue*, with its snapshot images of contemporary urban life; *The Sunshine Boys*, which is a kind of septuagenarian *Odd Couple* and one of the first plays in the 1970s to deal with the subject of old age; and *California Suite*, which repeats the scheme of *Plaza Suite* on the West Coast, with three different couples occupying the

same suite of rooms in the Beverly Hilton Hotel. Of the original film scripts, two of the best are *The Heartbreak Kid*, a comedy in which anti-Semitism plays an important part, and *The Goodbye Girl*, starring Simon's second wife, Marsha Mason, in a story about a love affair between a divorcee and an aspiring young actor. Both of these films are notable for their characterization and for comedy that grows out of the personal situations of their major characters.

Simon's writing for both the theater and film is notable for its dialogue, its quick characterization, its surefire comic effects, and its generally optimistic view of the human condition. While the subject matter of his work and the age and disposition of his principal characters vary somewhat, Simon is concerned primarily with the experiences of urban, middle-class people, similar to those in his audience, confronted by typical problems of life. They meet these problems as adroitly as they can under the circumstances, usually with a sense of humor.

These same qualities of Simon's work are turned around by his critics, however, who argue that his writing tends to be slick, his characters superficial, his comedy predictable, and his view too optimistic. There is no denying that he is almost wholly a writer for the commercial theater, with his eye constantly on the audience and how it will react. At the same time, there is also no denying that he knows what he is doing with the forms in which he works and in his best work can bend them skillfully to his dramatic needs.

His trilogy of plays—*Brighton Beach Memoirs*, *Biloxi Blues*, and *Broadway Bound*—has led him into terrain traveled only once before in his work, in the autobiographical *Chapter Two*. In *Chapter Two*, Simon dealt with his own experience of losing his first wife and falling in love with the woman who became his second; his brother Danny figured in the plot of the play, which apparently stuck close to what he had personally experienced in the death of his first wife. In his trilogy he has gone back to his Jewish-American roots to tell the story of what it was like to grow up in the Bronx during the Depression years, enter the army during World War II, and then become a writer for the legitimate stage. In these plays, especially the final one in the trilogy, Simon has reached a depth of characterization rare in his work. In dealing with Jewish-American life during this period of American history, Simon's trilogy compares with recent work in other media—E. L. Doctorow's novel *World's*

Fair (1985) and Woody Allen's film *Radio Days* (1986). In 1991, Simon won the Pulitzer Prize in drama for *Lost in Yonkers.*

Simon has never said much in print about his writing except casually in prefaces to his collected plays and in various interviews over the years. There is to date no biography. *See also* Theater.

ARCHIE K. LOSS

BIBLIOGRAPHY
Johnson, Robert K. *Neil Simon.* Boston: Twayne, 1983.
McGovern, Edythe M. *Neil Simon: A Critical Study.* New York: Ungar, 1979.
Simon, Neil. *The Collected Plays of Neil Simon.* Vol. 2. New York: Random House, 1979.
────. *The Comedy of Neil Simon.* New York: Random House, 1971.

Simon Wiesenthal Center. In 1977, the Simon Wiesenthal Center was founded in Los Angeles by Rabbi Marvin Hier. It was named in honor of the famed Vienna-based Nazi hunter. By 1989, the center had gained a national constituency of some 370,000 member families in the United States.

In 1979, the center opened a Holocaust museum at its Los Angeles campus. During its initial decade of operation, the museum and associated national outreach programs have serviced hundreds of thousands of American students. From its inception, the Wiesenthal Center has sought to impact on social issues related to the lessons of the Holocaust, including the pursuit of Nazi war criminals, worldwide anti-Semitism, neo-Nazism, and international terrorism. The center has played a key role in encouraging the governments of Australia, Canada, and Great Britain to take action against Nazi war criminals living in their countries. Its research efforts in this area, led by its •Israeli director, Efraim Zuroff, and Canadian representative, Sol Littman, have led to the opening of over 500 new cases involving Nazi war criminals and collaborators.

The Simon Wiesenthal Center has also made a significant contribution through film, media, publications, and exhibitions. In 1981, the center began producing "Page One," a weekly radio program on Jewish affairs broadcast by dozens of stations and the National Public Radio satellite throughout North America. In 1982, the Wiesenthal Center's documentary *Genocide* earned an Academy Award for best documentary. The center also helped produce a documentary on the life

and fate of Raoul Wallenberg, and it has videotaped more than 400 hours of testimony by Holocaust survivors and liberators.

Among its publications are its membership magazine, *Response*; the *Simon Wiesenthal Center Annual* (begun in 1984), a scholarly journal of Holocaust research; the studies, *Egypt—Israel's Peace Partner: A Survey of Antisemitism in the Egyptian Press, 1986–1987* (Los Angeles, 1988), and *The Poison Gas Connection: Western Supplies of Unconventional Weapons and Technologies to Iraq and Libya* (commissioned by the Simon Wiesenthal Center in 1990); "Portraits of Infamy," an exhibition on the similarities between Nazi and Soviet anti-Semitism; and "The Courage to Remember," an exhibition on the history of the Holocaust prepared by Gerald Margolis, the Wiesenthal Center's director. The latter was exhibited in Vienna in 1988 in commemoration of the fiftieth anniversary of the *Anschluss*, and three months later it became the first Holocaust exhibition ever displayed in the Soviet Union. It was placed on permanent loan in the Solomon Mykhoels Jewish Cultural Center in Moscow.

The Simon Wiesenthal Center has offices in Israel, France, and Canada, in addition to five regional offices in the United States. In 1991, the center plans to open its new Beit Hashoah–Museum of Tolerance on a 165,000-square-foot complex adjacent to its current facility in Los Angeles. One of the features of the museum will be a comprehensive interactive computer study center that will access text, films, photographs, and documents on all topics related to the Holocaust.

ABRAHAM COOPER

BIBLIOGRAPHY
Chandler, Russell. "First Center for Holocaust Studies to be Established in Los Angeles." *Washington Post*, August 26, 1977, C8.
Miller, Judith. *One By One By One.* New York: Simon & Schuster, 1990.
Teitelbaum, Sheldon, and Tom Waldman. "The Unorthodox Rabbi." *Los Angeles Times Magazine.* July 15, 1990.

Singer, Isaac Bashevis (1904–1991). Recipient of the 1978 Nobel Prize for Literature and two National Book Awards, Yiddish writer Isaac Bashevis Singer achieved international recognition for his portrayal of Eastern European Jews confronting pogroms, false Messiahs, assimilation, and the Holocaust. Though written in Yiddish, a dying language, about a vanished world, his fiction, uniquely blending realism and the supernatural, has wide appeal, depicting characters tormented by real and imagined demons. Serialized since the 1940s in the *Jewish Daily Forward*, Singer's works included novels, short-story collections, memoirs, and children's tales. Critically acclaimed for *Satan in Goray* (1955), *The Magician of Lublin* (1960), *The Slave* (1962), *Gimpel the Fool and Other Stories* (1957), and *Short Friday and Other Stories* (1964), Singer was also known for the stage and screen adaptations of his story, "Yentl, the Yeshiva Boy." While he signed his major translated works Isaac Bashevis Singer, he used Isaac Warshofsky or Isaac Bashevis for publications limited to the *Forward*.

In his memoirs, *In My Father's Court* (1966), *A Little Boy in Search of God* (1976), *A Young Man in Search of Love* (1978), and *Lost in America* (1981), Singer, born in Leonicin, Poland, recalls four impressionable adolescent years in the shtetl of Bilgorarj, two decades in Warsaw, and his harrowing 1935 escape to America, where for several alienated years he was unable to write. Son of Hasidic Rabbi Pinchos Mendel Singer and Orthodox rationalist Basheva (Zylberman) Singer, and younger brother of the worldly novelist, Israel Joshua Singer, the author (who was named Isaac Hirsch but adopted his mother's name) was torn between the traditional and the secular, between faith and skepticism, conflicts that dominate his works. Although he was a long-time resident of New York and Miami, most of his fiction centers on pre-Holocaust Poland. Even the translated American novels, *Enemies, A Love Story* (1972) and *The Penitent* (1983), revolve about troubled immigrants unable to forget the past. An anomaly amongst contemporary writers, Singer believed in God, the Jewish people, and free will, which, he once quipped "we have no choice" but to accept. Politically and artistically conservative, Singer distrusted all movements, particularly those on the Left masquerading as friends of the masses. He criticized modern authors such as Kafka, Joyce, and Proust for abstraction and experimentation, while he praised Dostoevski, Tolstoy, and Chekhov for vivid storytelling.

From his first novel, *Satan in Goray*, located in seventeenth-century Poland, to *The Penitent*, set in twentieth-century America and Israel, Singer pitted passion against reason, chaos against order, the surreal against the real, polarities rooted in turbulent environments and vulnerable characters. Thus the people of Goray, recovering from the sixteenth-century Chmielnicki massacres, turn from the scholarly Rabbi Benish to the fanatic Reb Gedalyia, a Sabbatian who violates the innocent Rechele and Jewish law to hasten the Messiah's coming. Replete with dybbuks, the deranged, and the desperate, Singer's first novel explores good and evil, fate and free will, theological and psychological conflicts whose resolutions require faith, discipline, and repentance. In *The Magician of Lublin*, Yasha Mazur, a tightrope performer, balances a wife and several mistresses before being transformed from a profligate into a puritan, from an adulterer into a celibate. Though the scene shifts from late nineteenth-century Poland to post–World War II America, *Enemies, A Love Story* also centers on a libertine, Herman Broder, a Holocaust survivor hopelessly entangled with two wives and a mistress. In *The Penitent*, Joseph Shapiro tires of New York promiscuity and seeks refuge in Meah Shearim, an Israeli ultra-Orthodox community. Despite his depiction of sin's wages, Yiddishists have criticized Singer for defaming Yiddish life by stressing sexuality and irrationality instead of social issues. Feminists have also complained about the author's portrayal of women as victims or shrews, charges that Singer rejected, refusing to paint "every woman a saint and a sage, every man a cruel exploiter."

Irving Malin has categorized Singer's novels, though thematically similar, as either open or closed. The latter, tightly constructed, focusing on a limited setting and few characters, includes *Satan in Goray*, *The Magician of Lublin*, *The Slave*, and *The Penitent*. The former, sprawling in landscape, chronology, characters, and plot, describes *The Family Moskat* (1950), *The Manor* (1967), and *The Estate* (1969). Epic in design, the "family" novels represent the disintegration of nineteenth- and twentieth-century Jews through materialism, immorality, political movements, and loss of faith. In *The Family Moskat*, set between the two world wars, the death of Reb Meshulam, the family patriarch, weakens traditional values, encouraging dissension, adultery, and spiritual decay. *The Manor* and *The Estate*, a two-part novel, centers on those who trade their Judaism for politics, science, or universal values and allow wealth to erode their family and communal loyalties.

Widely praised as Singer's most lyrical novel, *The Slave*, tautly written, biblical in imagery and references, depicts the love and loyalty of Jacob and his wife Wanda-Sarah, a convert to Judaism.

Against the harsh background of seventeenth-century Poland, the two succeed in remaining devoted to each other and to their religion but are betrayed by nature and human ignorance.

Not surprisingly, as his more compact novels suggest, Singer wrote superb short stories, as evident in "Gimpel the Fool" (1953), which Irving Howe compares to I. L. Peretz's classic "Bontsha the Silent." Though both revolve about humble, exploited protagonists, Gimpel, more aware of his condition, more a participant in his fate, illustrates Singer's skillful blending of traditional and modern materials.

In the same collection, "The Little Shoemakers" (1954), Singer's most loving tribute to Jewish survival, reconciles the old world and the new, the Yiddish father and his assimilated American sons. Realistic and poetic, the story emphasizes the interdependence of generations. Without the children, the father would have perished in Europe; without the father, the children would have lost their Jewish identity. Optimistic, "The Little Shoemakers," is atypical of Singer's fiction, which at the other extreme includes "Blood" (1945), a frightening portrait of unbridled sexuality that quickly develops into blood lust when Reuben, a ritual slaughterer, and Risha, a rapacious housewife, violate dietary laws and the commandments against adultery and killing. "Any single sin invites and encompasses all the others," Singer wrote of Reuben who must flee and Risha who converts and is later killed as a werewolf.

Rooted in Eastern European shtetls, the stories illustrate Singer's range of characters, his concrete, earthy style, and attention to Jewish tradition and superstition. In contrast to many current writers, Singer avoided literary theories, complex styles, and avant-garde movements. Unlike most American Jewish writers, including Saul Bellow and Bernard Malamud, who occasionally focus on Eastern European Jewish history, Singer relived the Yiddish experience in every work, invoking memories of Frampol, Lublin, or Warsaw even in his American fiction. According to most critics, he is not a Jewish-American author but a Yiddish writer whose universal concerns are steeped in distant settings, fantastic plots, and memorable characters that contribute to his widespread popularity. His understanding of human nature, appreciation of tradition and memorial to Yiddish culture assure his fiction a permanent position in world literature. *See also* Fiction; Literature, Yiddish; Theater.

EVELYN AVERY

BIBLIOGRAPHY

Alexander, Edward. *Isaac Bashevis Singer*. Boston: Hall, 1980.

Buchen, Irving. *Isaac Bashevis Singer and the Eternal Past*. New York: New York University Press, 1968.

Kresh, Paul. *Isaac Bashevis Singer: The Magician of West 86th Street*. New York: Dial, 1979.

Malin, Irving. *Critical View of Isaac Bashevis Singer*. New York: New York University Press, 1969.

———. *Isaac Bashevis Singer*. New York: Ungar, 1972.

Miller, David Neal. *Fear of Fiction: Narrative Strategies in the Works of Isaac Bashevis Singer*. Albany: State University of New York Press, 1985.

Singer, Isaac Bashevis. *An Isaac Bashevis Singer Reader*. New York: Farrar, Straus & Giroux, 1971.

Singer, I.J. (Israel Joshua) (1893-1944).

Born in Bilgoraj, Poland, I.J. Singer was the second child of Basheva Zylberman and Rabbi (Reb) Pinchos Mendel Singer. Reb Pinchos was the Hasidic rabbi of Leoncin and later, Radzymin, before moving to Warsaw, where he served as a sort of unofficial rabbi. Singer's mother was the daughter of the powerful rabbi of Bilgoraj. His parents' marriage in 1889 represented the union of two of the most important rabbinical lines in Poland.

Of the four children born to Reb Pinchos and Basheva, three became writers. Hinde Esther (b. 1891) published two novels and a collection of short stories under the name Esther Kreitman. Isaac Hirsch (b. 1904) adopted his mother's name as a matronymic and under the name of Isaac Bashevis Singer became the internationally celebrated writer and, in 1978, Nobelist in literature. The fourth child, Moshe (b. 1906), perished with his mother during World War II. And, of course, Israel Joshua became a renowned author.

At 18 Joshua gave up his rabbinical studies—and religion itself—to seek a modern education. He worked at a variety of manual jobs, as a photographer, an artist's model, and even attempted to paint. In 1914, he was drafted into the Russian army, from which he later deserted.

In 1917, Joshua moved to Kiev, where he married Genia Kupferstock (1892-1962), worked as a proofreader on a Yiddish newspaper, and began to write short stories. In 1919, the couple's first son, Jacob (Yasha), was born. A second son, Joseph, was born in Warsaw in 1923.

In 1921, when Warsaw became the capital of the independent Polish Republic, Singer returned there to publish his first collection of short stories—*Pearls*. When the title story was reprinted by Abraham Cahan, editor of the *Jewish Daily Forward*, in New York, Singer's career was launched in America. Singer became a regular contributor to the *Forward* both as a writer of fiction and a news correspondent, an association Singer maintained throughout his lifetime.

In 1923, his symbolist play *Erd-Vey* (Earth Cry) was produced by the Yiddish Art Theatre in New York. Singer was a founding member of a group of modernist Yiddish writers who called themselves Di Khaliastra—the Gang. This group, which included such figures as Peretz Markish, Melech Rawitch, Uri Zvi Greenberg, Mendel Elkin, and Peretz Hirschbein, shared an interest in literary expressionism and a common distrust of religion, the Establishment, and all "isms" in general.

Before leaving Poland for good in 1934, Singer published four more volumes: *On Alien Soil* (stories, 1925), *Steel and Iron* (novel, first published in America as *Blood Harvest*, 1927), *The New Russia* (nonfiction, 1928), and his celebrated novel *Yoshe Kalb* (1932). *Yoshe Kalb* was produced to great critical and popular acclaim by Maurice Schwartz of the Yiddish Art Theatre. Another play, *Savinkoff*, was produced in Polish in Warsaw in 1933.

Singer's elder son Yasha died in 1933. After preliminary visits to the United States, Singer, his wife, and son Joseph migrated to America in the winter of 1934.

In 1936, Singer published his most important novel, *The Brothers Ashkenazi*, which was also produced on the stage to great acclaim. It was this novel that secured his lasting reputation as a master of the modern Yiddish novel. His last works include *Comrade Nachman* (published in English as *East of Eden*, novel and play, 1937), *The River Breaks Up* (stories, 1938), and *The Family Carnovsky* (novel and play, 1943). There have been many posthumous editions of Singer's works, including new English translations by his son, the painter Joe Singer. Among these translations is the first English edition of *Of A World That Is No More* (1970), a memoir of life in Leoncin that Singer had planned to expand into a three-volume work.

As Irving Howe has said in his introduction to *The Brothers Ashkenazi*, I.J. Singer's "deepest persuasion emerges as a distrust of all classes and programs, a creeping suspicion of all worldly projects, a bleak skepticism about the very history he has brought into Yiddish literary consciousness." Not only in his masterpiece, *The Brothers Ashkenazi*, but in general, it seems fair to say that Singer was, as Howe suggests, a writer whose "imagination [was] fruitfully at war with itself." *See also* Literature, Yiddish.

BRETT SINGER

BIBLIOGRAPHY

Singer, I.J. *Blood Harvest*. London: Sampson Low, Marsten, 1935.

———. *The Brothers Ashkenazi*. New York: Knopf, 1936.

———. *The Family Carnovsky*. New York: Vanguard Press, 1969.

———. *Of a World That Is No More*. New York: Vanguard Press, 1971.

———. *Steel and Iron*. New York: Funk & Wagnalls, 1969.

———. *Yoshe Kalb*. New York: Harper & Row, 1965.

Soloveitchik, Joseph Dov (b. 1903). Talmudic scholar, religious thinker, educator, and professor of Talmud at Yeshiva University in New York City, Joseph Dov Soloveitchik is a member of one of the leading Lithuanian rabbinic families. His grandfather Rabbi Hayyim Soloveitchik (1853–1918) developed an analytic method that revolutionized Talmudic study in most Lithuanian yeshivot known as the Brisker method. Soloveitchik received his Jewish education from tutors under his father's guidance in his birthplace Przuhan and in Hasloviz, in Poland. As a young man he became a master of his grandfather's analytic method of Talmudic study. In 1922, he left Poland for Germany to study at the University of Berlin, where he received his doctorate in 1931 for his dissertation on Herman Cohen's philosophy.

In 1932, Soloveitchik arrived in the United States to serve as rabbi for a large segment of Boston's Orthodox Jewish community. He became embroiled in numerous battles with other Orthodox leaders centering over kashruth supervison and eventually resigned his rabbinic position. In Boston, in the late 1930s, he established an Orthodox day school, the Maimonides School, which in 1990 was still under the guidance of the Soloveitchik family.

In 1941, Soloveitchik was appointed professor of Talmud at Yeshiva University in New York, succeeding his father Rabbi Moshe Soloveitchik (d. 1941). Soloveitchik has educated hundreds of American rabbis and acted both as spiritual and Halakic adviser to his students. The bulk of America's Orthodox pulpit rabbis have been his students.

In addition to his post at Yeshiva, Soloveitchik was chairman of the Halakah Commission of the Rabbinical Council of America. In this capacity, he took strong positions on many communal issues in American Jewish life. He set strict guidelines for cooperation with non-Orthodox Jewish religious groups. He opposed in general any ecumenical dialogues with their leaders on matters of dogma.

As the honorary president of the American Religious Zionist Movement, Soloveitchik took a strong pro-Zionist stance, yet he never visited the State of Israel. In 1959, he refused an offer to become the Ashkenazi Chief Rabbi of Israel. Thus although Soloveitchik is a religious Zionist, he retains strong reservations about certain manifestations in Israel.

Before his retirement from public life, Soloveitchik was a noted orator, both in Yiddish and English. His speeches were marked by a richness in style and content. His discourses, usually given in New York or Boston, were always well attended and were regarded as important communal events. Many have been published.

As a Talmudic and religious authority, Soloveitchik was accepted, albeit begrudgingly, by the so-called "right-wing" Orthodox community. As such, Soloveitchik lent a great deal of legitimacy to "modern" or "centrist" Orthodoxy, whose leader he was. He is one of few Talmudic authorities who can be identified with the modern Orthodox camp.

Soloveitchik is unique in that he is the only Talmudist of note in the United States who is also a philosopher and theologian. Many of his philosophic essays have been published. Chief among them are *The Halakhic Man* (1983), *The Lonely Man of Faith* (*Tradition* 7:2, 1965), and the *Halakhic Mind* (1986). In these essays he sets forth his very personal views on the nature of Halakah, its place in the community, and its place in the larger context of man's relationship to God. Soloveitchik was clearly influenced by the Existentialist school of philosophy. Many of his essays continue to be published, and his reading audience includes non-Jewish as well as Jewish readers.

In 1984, Soloveitchik was forced to relinquish his position at Yeshiva due to illness. He was succeeded by his younger brother, Rabbi Aaron Soloveitchik (b. 1918) of Chicago.

Soloveitchik's chief influence on the American scene has been as a role model for the modern Orthodox community. He could and would be pointed to as someone who was not only one of the world's great Talmudists, but also the holder of a doctorate of philosophy. He was a scion of the famous Brisker rabbinic family, who dressed modern, spoke English, and used academic terminology in their speech. For an American Orthodox community seeking to acculturate, Soloveitchik was a perfect role model. Yet, in fact, Soloveitchik is more East European-oriented than he is perceived to be. He views the study of the Talmud as preeminent. He retains the Yiddish language as his mode of expression in private life and remains greatly influenced by his Brisker legacy. He is clearly a complex figure, although known simply as the "Rav."

Joseph B. Soloveitchik, through his students teachings, writings, and discourses and by dint of his powerful personality is clearly one of the dominant figures in American Orthodoxy in the second half of the twentieth century.

ZALMAN ALPERT

BIBLIOGRAPHY

Besdin, Abraham R. *Reflections of the Rav: Lessons in Jewish Thought, Adapted from lectures of Rabbi Joseph D. Soloveitchik.* Hoboken, N.J.: Ktav, 1981.

Soloveitchik, Joseph B. *Halakhic Man*, translated by Lawrence Kaplan. Philadelphia: Jewish Publication Society, 1984.

———. *The Halakhic Mind: Rabbinic Judaism and Modern Thought.* New York: Free Press, 1986.

———. *Soloveitchik on Repentance*, translated by Pinchas Peli. New York: Paulist Press, 1984.

South, The. Jews have been living in the South since the middle of the seventeenth century—the first group settling in Charleston. Jews settled throughout the region in a myriad of cities, towns, villages, and hamlets. Sephardic Jews came first and then some German Jews. Generally, they concentrated in and around the three coastal cities in which congregations were established: Beth Shalom in Richmond, Beth Elohim in Charleston, and Mickve Israel in Savannah. During the colonial period, these southern Jewish communities not only constituted the majority of the Jewish population in America, forming three of the six colonial Jewish congregations, but established many of the religious and social patterns that American Jewry as a whole would follow in the years to come. Moreover, during this period and not least in the South, Jews experienced their first religious, political, and social emancipation in over 1000 years.

Between 1840 and the late 1870s, the southern Jewish community was eclipsed numerically by its northeastern counterparts. At the same time a unique southern Jewish consciousness emerged as Jews adopted southern cultural ways and the full range of political opinions and passions of their Gentile neighbors. While the size of the Jewish population in the coastal cities remained fairly constant, Jewish immigrants, mostly German or German-Polish, moved along the coast of the Gulf of Mexico and inland, following the region's rivers and overland trails as well as the few railroads in service at that time. In the last quarter of the nineteenth century until the mid-1920s, East European Jews arrived in the area. However, compared to the millions who remained in the Northeast, their migration to the South was hardly a trickle.

Like Jews elsewhere in the country, the Jews who arrived in the South were burdened with personal memories of civil oppression, physical isolation, and religious persecution. As they overcame their natural suspicions of Gentiles, they discovered that they no longer had to live in fear. To the contrary, they found the Gentiles generally were genuinely receptive to their presence. They discovered that it was often easier than in other areas of the country to make the transition from Old World pariahs to New World citizens. Seizing the opportunity offered in the region they often described as a "New Canaan" or "New Jerusalem," Jews pioneered, lived, loved, built, fought, played, and sustained themselves alongside their southern Gentile neighbors. Though the Jews never amounted to more than 4 percent of the South's population, there are few phases of the southern experience, and few places in the South, that are exempt from the influence exerted by their activities.

Jews such as Mordecai Sheftall of Savannah and Francis Salvador of Charleston were among the southern leaders during the American Revolution. In some instances, Jews helped blaze new trails into the new territories of the young nation. Abraham Mordecai, for example, established what was to become Montgomery, Alabama. Jews may have been among Texas's founding "Old Three Hundred," while Jews such as Henri Castro later fought in and helped finance the Texas War of Independence. David Yulee of Florida and Judah P. Benjamin of Louisiana were in-strumental in bringing their territories into the Union and were no less influential in taking their states out of it as part of the Confederacy.

Indeed, Jews shared with their Gentile neighbors a determination to perpetuate a way of life to which they had become attached. They supported the ideas of states' rights and nullification; they defended the institution of slavery, in which they had fully participated; and they unhesitatingly took up arms in defense of what Rabbi James Gutheim of New Orleans described as "our beloved country, the Confederate States of America." Large numbers of Jews fought in the ranks and officer corps of the Confederate regiments during the Civil War. A few held positions within the Confederate military and political leadership, including the surgeon general, judge advocate, quartermaster general, and perhaps the most famous, Judah P. Benjamin, secretary of state.

Since the Civil War, Jews have been counted among the "new moss" and "new pioneers" of the South who have contributed significantly to the political, economic, and cultural recovery of the region. Many assumed an active role as leaders of their communities' social and civic life. Some Jews, such as Samuel Ulman of Memphis, were newspaper editors; some, such as Georgia's David Loveman and South Carolina's Ludwig Lewisohn, were famous poets and writers; some, such as John Bandeman, were renowned actors. Throughout the South they joined a variety of men's and women's social clubs and community civic groups. A few were elected presidents of these organizations. They belonged to the Masonic Lodge, often rising to the position of lodge masters; a few even attained the exalted rank of state Grand Master.

As leaders, Jews became involved in all branches of government. Florida sent David Levy to the United States Senate as the country's first Jewish senator (1841–1845), while Georgia's David Emanuel was the country's first Jewish state governor (1801). Throughout the South, Jews have been elected state and congressional legislators, councilmen and aldermen, mayors, sheriffs, and fire and police chiefs.

Many Jews joined the ranks of the most prominent and influential businessmen. The innovations of Raphael Moses and Sam Sommers laid the foundation for the growth of the peach and pecan industries, while the inventions of Benjamin Ehrlich were essential to the success of soft-drink companies, such as Coca Cola. Merchants such as the Riches in Georgia, the Sangers, Marcuses, and Sakowitzes in Texas, the Maas brothers in Florida, the Psitzes in Alabama, and the Godeaux in Louisiana began a tradition that has been continued by such chain stores as North Carolina's Family Dollar, Tennessee's Service Merchandising, Virginia's Circuit City, and Texas's Zales.

As the Jews entered into southern Gentile society they had to forgo their old ways and adopt southern lifestyles. This process of acculturation did not mean accepting the offer of Gentile southern society "to belong." What many Jews did was redefine Judaism in such a way that it introduced flexibility into ritual performance and emphasized ethical commitment and charitable activity for the entire community, not only for one's coreligionists. Most Jews, nevertheless, retained their Jewish identity. As they established themselves in the few urban centers and the great number of "outposts in the boondocks," they joined together and formed communities, purchased land for cemeteries, developed social service and charitable organizations, organized congregations, built houses of worship, and sought out rabbis. Today, the approximately 500,000 southern Jews live in over 150 communities with 100 members or more and worship in more than 200 Reform, Conservative, and Orthodox temples and synagogues.

That Jews took root successfully in the southern landscape does not preclude the existence of anti-Semitism. Such prejudice, ingrained in the Christian cultural psyche, reared its head sporadically in the form of quotas, social restrictions, strong words, and, on rare occasions, serious action. Nevertheless, the continued success and contribution of southern Jews could only occur if the Gentile majority consciously and overwhelmingly had extended a welcoming hand of acceptance and had allowed the willing Jews access to its society. As such, southern society should be seen as a far more complex entity than hitherto pictured by derogatory and simplistic imagery when it comes to Jewish history in the South.

LOUIS SCHMIER

BIBLIOGRAPHY

Ashkenazi, Elliott. *The Business of Jews in Louisiana, 1840–1875.* Tuscaloosa: University of Alabama Press, 1988.

Berman, Myron. *Richmond's Jewry, 1769–1976.* Charlottesville: University Press of Virginia, 1979.

Dinnerstein, Leonard, and Palsson, Mary, eds. *Jews in the South.* Baton Rouge: Louisiana State University Press, 1973.

Hertzberg, Steven. *Strangers Within the Gate City.* Philadelphia: Jewish Publication Society, 1978.

Kaganoff, Nathan, and Urofsky, Melvin. *Turn to the South: Essays on Southern Jewry.* Charlottesville: University Press of Virginia, 1979.

Proctor, Samuel, and Schmier, Louis, eds. *Jews of the South: Selected Essays.* Macon, Ga.: Mercer University Press, 1984.

Spanish and Portuguese Synagogue of New York City. *See* SHEARITH ISRAEL CONGREGATION.

Sports. In the United States sports have provided Jews with a means to express Americanism as well as physical prowess, ethnic pride, and social status. Although many athletic activities are trivial in themselves, they frequently take on significance through the symbolism invested in them.

Sport is organized, competitive, physical play. The ancient Hebrews, unlike the Greeks, lacked a strong sporting tradition. During the Maccabean rebellion, Jewish traditionalists successfully opposed Seleucid Greeks and Jewish assimilators who sought to impose upon them an Hellenic culture that emphasized athletics. Nonetheless, the Jews of antiquity appreciated bodily strength and stamina. For the Hebrew worker or warrior, physical prowess yielded utilitarian rewards. Jewish tradition valued the health, cleanliness, and vitality of the body.

With the destruction of the Second Temple in 70 CE and the Diaspora, Jewish life turned inward. No longer did Jewish soldiers safeguard an ancestral homeland. During the Middle Ages, anti-Semitic canards accompanied the ghettoization of European Jewry. Vulnerability and isolation encouraged Gentile aggressors as well as Jewish victims themselves to doubt the physical strength and courage of the latter. The stereotyped image of the studious, physically inept Jew began to take shape.

The eighteenth century brought some improvement in the status of European Jewry. Daniel Mendoza, the English boxing champion from 1791 to 1795, was the first Jew to acquire great fame through modern sport. The post-1815 Metternichian reaction reversed some of the gains made by European Jewry, however, and immigration appeared increasingly attractive.

Approximately 2500 Jews arrived in America during the colonial period, and there is little evidence to suggest that they were prominent either in the elite sports of the southern gentry or the folk games of the common people. Largely due to nineteenth-century German immigration, the Jewish population reached 250,000 by 1880. It was during the nineteenth century that modern sport emerged in America, and assimilating, religiously liberal, upwardly mobile German Jews used athletics to confirm their newly acquired status. The wealthiest among them, such as August Belmont, purchased thoroughbred horses. Others owned major league baseball teams. Emulating the Muscular Christianity movement, German Jews established Young Men's Hebrew Associations.

The great majority of contemporary American Jews are descended from the mass migration of East European Jews to the United States between the 1880s and 1920s. East European immigrants took little part in American sport. Their children, however, used sport to feel at home in the physical world that their parents feared, to foster Americanization, and to assert group pride. Numbers of immigrant parents opposed the athletic aspirations of their progeny due to either cultural-religious assumptions about purposeful behavior or the need for children to earn money through work. Many immigrants were merely indifferent to the sports interests of the second generation provided their children engaged in noncontact activities that posed little risk of injury and did not let recreation interfere with education. Despite a lack of parental enthusiasm for American sport, the children of East European immigrants produced more athletic champions than any other generation of American Jews. Boxing, basketball, and handball were city games dominated by Jews who came of age between the two world wars.

The third generation and beyond grew up in more secure, tolerant, and comfortable circumstances in post-World War II America. Movement to suburbia and increased prosperity led to a precipitous decline of the Jewish presence at the highest echelons of boxing, basketball, and other inner-city sports. Yet overall Jewish rates of participation at lower levels of athletics may have increased. Participation in athletics, particularly of one's children, signified possession of the leisure and financial resources that confirmed suburban social status. Indeed, the democratization of country club sports led to the emergence of Jewish tennis and golf champions. Proportionately, contemporary Jews are well represented among the spectators, chroniclers, and entrepreneurs of American sport. Although American Jews still express ethnic pride through identification with famous Jewish athletes, support for the Maccabiah movement, affiliation with physical education programs at Jewish community centers, and sending their children to sport-oriented Jewish summer camps, they also continue to emphasize their American identities through sport. In 1948, for example, when Brandeis University, the first secular university established by American Jews opened, the establishment of a varsity athletic program was used by founders to underline that this was an American institution. As a microcosm of national values, aspirations, perceptions of the hero, and social practices, sport provides contemporary Jews with a means of expressing their participation in a distinctively American culture.

MACCABIAH. The Maccabiah Games are, in essence, a Jewish Olympics. Jews from all over the world gather for athletic competition. In contrast to the Olympics, however, ethnic affirmation is at least as important as the Maccabiah sports program. The games honor the heroic spirit of Judas Maccabeus and his followers, who ironically battled the forced imposition of an Hellenic culture that emphasized sport. Although some world records have been bettered in Maccabiah competition, most participants are not of Olympic caliber. For Diaspora communities with small Jewish populations, the mere fielding of a national team requires much effort. With the largest Jewish population in the world, the United States, however, has produced more medalists than any other nation. Several American Jews, including track and field phenomenon Lillian Copeland, weightlifter Ike Berger, and swimmer Mark Spitz, won both Maccabiah and Olympic medals. Other Americans, such as basketball standouts Larry Brown, Art Heyman, Ernie Grunfeld, Joel Kramer, and Dan Schayes, reached the major league level of professional sports subsequent to their Maccabiah appearances.

Zionism, Jewish self-defense groups, and existing Maccabi clubs provided impetus for the first Maccabiah games. In 1932, 390 athletes from 22 nations, including 13 Americans, descended upon the Palestinian city of Tel Aviv for the first Maccabiah. The American contingent won more gold medals, 13, than any other team. After the second Maccabiah in 1935, a number of European athletes, cognizant of the growing Nazi menace, remained in Palestine. Due to the Holocaust and its aftermath, a third Maccabiah, the first held in an independent Israel, was not held until 1950. After the fourth Maccabiah in 1953, subsequent games were held every four years, always in Israel. By 1985, the Maccabiah, grown to 450 events, attracted 4000 athletes from 42 countries. Through the United States Committee Sports for Israel, American Jews provided generous financial and logistical support for the Maccabiah games. American athletes who competed in the Maccabiah frequently experienced heightened Jewish consciousness.

OLYMPICS. In 1896, amateur athletes gathered for the first modern Olympics. Since 1896, aside from the 1980 Moscow games boycotted by the United States, Jews have won medals at each festival, attaining a peak figure of 30 at the 1968 Olympics. Weightlifters Frank Spellman (1948) and Ike Berger (1956, 1960, 1964), wrestler Henry Wittenberg (1952), judo expert Jim Bergman (1964), track and field stars Steve Seymour (1948), Jim Fuchs (1948, 1952), and Gerald Ashworth (1964), yachtsman Bob Halperin (1960), fencers Norman Armitage (1948) and Albert Axelrod (1960), basketball player Larry Brown (1964), swimmers Marilyn Ramenofsky (1964), Mark Spitz (1968, 1972), and Wendy Weinberg (1976), and ice dancer Judy Blumberg (1984) were among those American Jews who have won medals in the years since World War II.

Undoubtedly, the most significant Olympics for America, Jewry, and the world was the 1936 Berlin games. Despite attempts by Jews and their Gentile allies to protest the anti-Semitic and totalitarian practices of Nazi Germany by organizing an American boycott of the Berlin festival, the United States participated in the 1936 Olympics. In Berlin two Jewish-American sprinters, Marty Glickman and Sam Stoller, were unexpectedly and unfairly removed from the 400-meter relay team by Dean Cromwell, an American coach who apparently shared some of the bias of his German hosts. Nevertheless, the Nazi Olympics impressed many contemporaries as the most lavish festival yet held. The 1936 games provided Adolf Hitler with a forum to don the false guise of benevolent leader and, tragically, further encouraged Western appeasers to view him as a reasonable figure.

In 1972, Germany again hosted the Olympics. At the Munich games Germany appeared eager to atone for its Nazi past. During the opening ceremonies, spectators reserved their most enthusiastic applause for the Israeli team. An American Jew, swimmer Mark Spitz, won an unprecedented seven gold medals. Spitz's triumph and the tolerance of the new Germany, however, were sullied by tragedy. Palestinian terrorists murdered 11 Israeli athletes in Munich.

BASEBALL. From the 1871 founding of the National Association, the first professional baseball circuit, on, there has been a Jewish presence, albeit usually modest, on the major league level. Over 100 players, several owners, 4 managers, and a number of coaches with Jewish antecedents reached the major leagues. The number of Jews playing in a given major league season has varied, but compared to boxing, which Jews once dominated and then virtually disappeared from, the demands of major league baseball have neither featured many Jews nor excluded them. Even during the era of mass immigration when most Jews lived in the inner city, Jewish baseball players have typically come from small towns, suburbs, or outer boroughs. In contrast to the poverty, violence, and crowded tenements that marred the youth of most Jewish boxers, Jewish baseball players frequently grew up in middle-class, culturally assimilated families. As the national pastime, baseball often transformed Jewish players into both symbols of Americanization and group pride to their fellow ethnics.

Lip Pike (1845–1893) was the first Jew to play major league baseball and the first to manage on that level. Primarily an outfielder, he played in the inaugural seasons of both the National Association (1871) and National League (1876). The fastest player of the 1870s, Pike had a career batting average of over .300. He briefly managed National Association (1871, 1874) and National League (1877) teams.

During the Progressive era, the few Jewish big leaguers hailed from backgrounds quite different from that of the East European Jews who peopled the immigrant slums of the urban North. Barney Pelty, George Stone, and Erskine Mayer, for example, were natives of Missouri, Nebraska, and Georgia, respectively. Nicknamed "the Yiddish Curver," pitcher Pelty won 91 games in a 10-year career. In 1906, outfielder Stone, who came from a mixed ethnic background, had the highest batting average (.358) in the American League. Twice (1914, 1915) Mayer, a right-handed pitcher, registered more than 20 victories in a season. The most innovative of the early

Jewish baseball magnates was Barney Dreyfus, longtime owner of the Pittsburgh Pirates (1900–1933), who helped promote the building of a new generation of safer steel and concrete ball parks. In 1903, a challenge by Dreyfus's Pirates, champions of the National League, to Boston, their American League counterpart, led to the first World Series. Unfortunately, at the end of the Progressive Era, the "fixing" of the 1919 World Series by the Jewish gambler Arnold Rothstein helped reinforce anti-Semitic canards about conspiratorial un-American Jews.

Many children of East European immigrants came of age in the generation following World War I. They were often ardent baseball fans. Cognizant that the second generation would flock to the park in record numbers to cheer one of their own, John McGraw, manager of the New York Giants, spent years searching for an authentic Jewish star. In 1928, Giant second baseman Andy Cohen hit well early in the season. New York Jews lionized Cohen, and McGraw thought he had at last found his Jewish sensation. Soon, however, Cohen tailed off, and, by 1930, he was sent down to the minor leagues, where he toiled for years as a player and manager. In 1960, Cohen returned briefly to the majors as acting manager and coach of the Philadelphia Phillies. More Jews reached the major leagues in the interwar period than had in the Progressive era, but most, such as Moe Berg, Morrie Arnovich, Harry Danning, Phil Weintraub, Jimmy Reese, and Goody Rosen, rarely rose above journeyman status. In 1929, Emil Fuchs, Jewish owner of the Boston Braves, named himself manager, guiding the team to a last-place finish. Buddy Myer, a half-Jewish second baseman, did win the American League batting title with a .349 mark in 1934 and recorded a career batting average of .303 over the course of 17 seasons. And baseball produced its first authentic Jewish superstar, Hank Greenberg.

Hank Greenberg (1911–1986) may or may not have been the greatest Jewish-American athlete of all time, but he was the most significant. His major league career (1933–1947) coincided with the second generation's need to resolve the tension between its American and Jewish identities. More so than boastful boxers, the success of the refined and intelligent Greenberg in America's premier sport made him the first Jewish athlete to cross over from ethnic to national favorite. Save for his final season as a Pittsburgh Pirate, Greenberg spent his entire career with the Detroit Tigers.

A 6-foot-4-inch first baseman–outfielder, Greenberg was one of the greatest power hitters in the game's history. No right-handed batter ever surpassed his 1938 season total of 58 home runs. His 183 RBIs (runs batted in) in 1937 was only one short of the American League record. Four times Greenberg led the American League in home runs. He also paced the league in RBIs four seasons, and twice he was the circuit's Most Valuable Player. Had Greenberg not lost four and one-half years to World War II military service, he would have recorded far more than 331 home runs and 1276 RBIs over the course of his career. Even so, only four men in the game's history exceeded his lifetime slugging percentage of .605 and none his career average of .92 RBI per game. A .313 lifetime batting average shows that Greenberg leavened his power with consistency.

Greenberg's importance as an ethnic standard bearer peaked on September 19, 1934, when he refused to play on Yom Kippur despite his team's pursuit of the American League pennant. Given the rising anti-Semitism of the Depression decade, Greenberg's decision took on much importance for young coreligionists. Greenberg provided a role model that suggested successful pursuit of the American dream did not necessitate a denial of ethnicity.

Post-World War II baseball produced a number of Jewish stars. Between 1948 and 1952, National League outfielder–third baseman Sid Gordon hit 25 or more home runs five times. Chicago pitcher Saul Rogovin's 1952 earned run average (2.78) was the best in the major leagues. A .336 batting average, 43 home runs, and 145 RBIs made Cleveland third baseman Al Rosen the American League's 1953 Most Valuable Player. Relief pitcher Larry Sherry was the dominant force behind the Los Angeles Dodgers' triumph in the 1959 World Series. Washington Senator first baseman Mike Epstein accumulated 30 home runs in 1969. That same season Art Shamsky's .300 average contributed to an unexpected pennant for the New York Mets. In 1973, Oakland pitcher Ken Holtzman, who previously notched two no hitters, won 21 games. Norm Sherry, Larry's brother and a former reserve catcher, managed the California Angels during parts of the 1976 and 1977 seasons. In a career (1969–1978) curtailed by injuries, designated hitter–first baseman Ron Blomberg recorded a career batting average of .293. A 25–7 won–lost record brought Baltimore Orioles pitcher Steve Stone a 1980 Cy Young Award.

Undoubtedly, Sandy Koufax, Brooklyn and Los Angeles Dodgers left-handed pitcher, was the outstanding Jewish baseball player of the years since World War II. He and Greenberg are the only Jewish members of the Baseball Hall of Fame. Despite serious physical ailments that forced him to retire at age 30, Koufax's career (1955–1966) totals speak for themselves: 165 victories, 87 losses, a 2.76 earned-run average, 40 shut outs, and 2396 strikeouts in 2324.1 innings. He led the National League in victories three times, earned-run average five times, and strikeouts four times. Winner of three Cy Young Awards (1963, 1965, 1966), Koufax was one of the few pitchers to receive the Most Valuable Player designation (1963). Although the relative tolerance of the era in which he pitched made him a less significant ethnic standard bearer than Greenberg, Koufax, who refused to pitch the first game of the 1965 World Series because it fell on Yom Kippur, was a source of pride to fellow Jews.

FOOTBALL. Relatively few Jews have reached the top echelons of either college or professional football. Parental opposition to football, based on concern with injury, as well as the sport's origins at elite colleges that practiced ethnic discrimination, long limited Jewish participation. Upwardly mobile, Jewish families that sent their children to college were more successful at deterring the gridiron aspirations of sons than the parents of Jewish boxers, who grew up amidst ethnic violence in the inner city. Nevertheless, several Jews made significant contributions to football.

Benny Friedman, Marshall Goldberg, and Sid Luckman have been the three most famous Jewish football players. An All-American quarterback at the University of Michigan in 1925 and 1926, Friedman subsequently starred for several National Football League teams, including the New York Giants. He later served as head football coach at City College of New York and Brandeis University. An explosive running back and twice an All-American (1937, 1938) for powerful University of Pittsburgh teams, Marshall Goldberg played well for the generally weak Chicago Cardinals (1939–1943, 1946–1948) in the National Football League. An outstanding tailback at Columbia University (1936–1938), Sid Luckman was the first successful T-formation quarterback in National Football League history (1939–1950). Luckman, a great passer and signal caller, led the Chicago Bears to four championships. In 1943, he was the Most Valuable Player in the league.

Although offensive end Randy Grossman, an All-American at Temple University (1974) and subsequently a member of Pittsburgh Steeler teams that made multiple Super Bowl appearances, and the half-Jewish Lyle Alzado, a ferocious defensive end of the 1970s and 1980s, achieved notoriety, the only Jewish football player of the years since World War II to approach the status of Friedman, Goldberg, and Luckman was Ron Mix, a bruising offensive lineman for the San Diego Chargers (1960–1970) who won election to the Pro Football Hall of Fame. Despite the decline of Jewish athletes in professional football during the last generation, Jews continued to be represented among coaches and owners. Allie Sherman, Sid Gillman, and Marv Levy were respected coaches. Carroll Rosenbloom and Sonny Werblin owned successful franchises. And the formidable Al Davis, coach-general manager and subsequently principal owner of the Oakland, later Los Angeles, Raiders, took a brief sabbatical from the team in the mid-1960s to serve as commissioner of the American Football League.

BASKETBALL. Unlike many modern sports that evolved from preindustrial folk games, basketball was literally invented by James Naismith, an instructor at the Springfield (Mass.) YMCA Training School. Given the limited space and equipment requirements of basketball, ghetto youth found this fast-paced sport accessible. Basketball became the quintessential city game. For years the best basketball was played in New York City. Jewish settlement houses produced championship teams, and their performance on high school, college, and professional teams made Jews the dominant group in basketball during the first half of the twentieth century. Max Friedman and Barney Sedran were early Jewish stars. Even St. John's, a Catholic university, recruited Jewish players, producing seven Jewish All-Americans. While only two Jews have won election to the Baseball Hall of Fame, several are members of the Basketball Hall of Fame.

Nat Holman, a son of the Lower East Side, was perhaps the most influential figure in basketball history. He introduced many innovations, such as placing the tallest man in the pivot. During the 1920s, he played brilliantly for the New York Whirlwinds and the original Celtics, the two outstanding teams of that era. From 1919 to 1960, Holman was head basketball coach at City College of New York, consistently turning out outstanding squads. His clinics and writings influenced other coaches, and Holman won the sobriquet "Mr. Basketball." In 1950, City College became the first and only team to win both the National Invitation and National Collegiate Athletic Association tournaments. Although Holman personally was cleared of wrongdoing, several of his players were involved in the 1951 basketball scandals. A number of Jewish athletes participated in the fixing of basketball games. Nevertheless, in addition to coaching for several more years, Holman devoted considerable energy to promoting Israeli basketball and the Maccabiah games. He served as president of the United States Committee Sports for Israel.

As players, coaches, referees, entrepreneurs, and league officials, Jews have left a decisive imprint on basketball. In 1927, Abe Saperstein founded the Harlem Globetrotters, an all-black team that combined comedy and outstanding basketball skills. The SPHAs (South Philadelphia Hebrew All-Stars) were one of the premier professional teams of the 1920s and 1930s. Pioneer commissioner of the National Basketball Association (NBA), from 1949 to 1963, Maurice Podoloff presided over the first professional basketball league to acquire fan recognition comparable to that of major leagues in other sports. Eddie Gottlieb, Ben Kerner, and Max Winter owned successful NBA teams. Max Zaslofsky, Sid Tannenbaum, Ralph Kapolwitz, Leo Gottlieb, Sonny Hertzberg, Nathan Militz, Leonard Rosenbluth, Barry Leibowitz, Rick Weitzman, Art Heyman, Barry Kramer, Neal Walk, Ernie Grunfeld, and Joe Kramer were post-World War II collegiate stars who subsequently played professionally. A 6-foot-8-inch forward, Dolph Schayes, an outstanding collegiate at New York University, established himself as the greatest Jewish player in the professional ranks (1948–1964). At one time Schayes held the all-time NBA career records for points scored, rebounds, consecutive games played, field goals, and free throws. As coach of the Boston Celtics (1950–1966), Red Auerbach won an unprecedented nine NBA championships in his last ten seasons. Red Holzman coached the New York Knicks to two NBA titles (1970, 1973).

Today, Jewish coaches, entrepreneurs, and officials remain visible. David Stern, the incumbent NBA commissioner, for example, is Jewish. Nevertheless, Jewish players, once the preeminent group in the game, have virtually disappeared from the top echelons of collegiate and professional basketball over the past generation. During the 1985–1986 season, Ernie Grunfeld and 7-foot Dan Schayes, son of the great Dolph, were the only Jews on NBA rosters. Changes in the style of the game that favor great height, racial integration, and the continued upward mobility of American Jews explain this phenomenon.

BOXING. More than any other sport, boxing reflects ethnic succession in the inner city. In sequence, the Irish, Jews, Italians, and blacks were the dominant group in boxing. Most boxers come from urban slums whose mean streets breed fights and ethnic antagonisms. Joe Choynski, a top heavyweight of the late nineteenth and early twentieth centuries, was the first outstanding Jewish-American boxer. Other Jewish boxers who attained their chief prominence prior to World War I include bantamweight Harry Harris, featherweights Joe Bernstein and Abe Attell (Albert Knoehr), lightweight Leach Cross (Louis Wallach), middleweight Al McCoy (Harry Rudolph), and light heavyweight Battling Levinsky (Barney Lebrowitz). Harris, Attell, McCoy, and Levinsky were world champions.

It was between the world wars, however, that the Jewish presence in boxing peaked. During these years no ethnic group produced more champions and top contenders than the Jews. Sons of East European immigrants sought to escape ghetto poverty with their fists. With the Star of David emblazoned on their trunks, pugnacious Jewish boxers were ethnic standard bearers who intensified group pride and possessed potent gate appeal. Partisan fans of the second generation saw Jewish fighters as surrogates who brought new respect for the group by defeating the physical Gentile on his own terms. Although Jews fought in all weight classifications, tenement conditions produced more candidates for the lighter divisions. Featherweights Louis "Kid" Kaplan and Benny Bass, lightweights Benny Leonard (Benjamin Leiner), Ruby Goldstein, Al Singer, Lew Tendler, Joe Benjamin, Joe Leopold, Phil Bloom, Charlie White (Charles Anschowitz), and Barney Ross (Barnet Rasofsky), welterweights Jackie Fields (Jacob Finklestein), Tendler, and Ross, middleweight Solly Krieger, light heavyweights Maxie Rosenbloom and Bob Olin, and heavyweights Abe Simon and Max Baer were amongst the more notable Jewish boxers of the interwar years. Kaplan, Bass, Leonard, Ross, Fields, Krieger, Rosenbloom, Olin, and Baer (only one of whose grandparents was Jewish) were titleholders.

As the lightweight, junior welterweight, and welterweight champion, Ross was the first fighter simultaneously to hold three divisional titles. In his own time, Leonard, the lightweight champion from 1917 to 1925, was a legend to coreligionists who told apocryphal stories of how he defended Jewish neighborhoods and synagogues from anti-Semitic vandals. A number of boxing authorities called Leonard, pound for pound, the greatest fighter of all time. Many of the most successful promoters (Mike Jacobs, Jack Begun, Irv Schoenwald, Maurice Feldman), managers (Al Weill, Sam Pian, Frank Bachman, Max Waxman), trainers (Izzy Klein, Whitey Blimstein, Charley Goldman), and referees (Davey Miller, Ruby Goldstein) of the era were Jewish. In the next generation, however, upward mobility transformed the Jewish boxer into an anachronism. Comfortable suburbs do not produce lean and hungry fighters. Since 1939, the only Jewish titlist has been the half-Italian Mike Rossman, who briefly held the light heavyweight championship in 1978.

COUNTRY CLUB SPORTS: GOLF AND TENNIS.
Before World War II, golf and tennis were largely the domain of Anglo-Americans from the upper echelons of society. They often played at private country clubs that excluded Jews, Catholics, and blacks. Since 1945, Jewish participation in golf and tennis has increased dramatically. Upward mobility gave Jews, like other new suburbanites, the resources and leisure to participate in formerly inaccessible activities. Newly affluent Jews organized country clubs of their own, and growing tolerance removed social barriers at some of the older clubs. Comfortable postwar communities built and enlarged public recreational facilities. Increasingly, golf and tennis were incorporated into the varsity programs at public schools. President Dwight Eisenhower's fondness for golf and the eventual demise of the genteel amateurism that formerly surrounded tournament tennis also helped democratize the once exclusive country club sports. Although most of the Jewish presence in golf and tennis occurred at the recreational level, some Jews attained stardom with club and racket.

Herman Barron (1909–1976) was the first Jewish golfer of note. He won several tournaments, including the Canadian Open. In 1946, only Ben Hogan won more prize money than Barron. Following the path blazed by Barron, Arnold Blum, Andrea Cohn, Roger Ginsberg,

Gail Denenberg, and other coreligionists later competed professionally.

In Dick Savitt (b. 1927) Jews found their most significant tennis standard bearer. His spectacular, upset victory at Wimbledon in 1951 earned Savitt celebrity status and a *Time* magazine cover. He won the National Indoor Singles Championship three times. Subsequent to capturing gold medals in singles and doubles competition at the 1961 Maccabiah, Savitt's fund raising and instruction contributed to a significant improvement in Israeli tennis.

Another prominent tennis star was E. Victor Seixas, Jr. (b. 1923) of Philadelphia. He was United States Tennis Association (USTA) champion in 1951, 1954, and 1957 and was ranked number three in the world in 1953. In 1953, Seixas won Wimbledon men's singles and the French and Australian men's doubles with Tony Trabert. He was inducted in the National Tennis Hall of Fame in 1971. Harold Solomon, Brian Teacher, Eliot Teltscher, Brad Gilbert, Aaron Krickstein, Jay Berger, and Andrea Leand have also acquired tennis celebrity.

WOMEN. The lingering resonances of American Victorianism and the patriarchal nature of traditional Judaism long combined to circumscribe the activities of Jewish women. Although generalizations about shrewd, domineering Jewish mothers and the so-called Jewish-American princess were usually exaggerated and unfair, the stereotype at least recognized the considerable strength of Jewish women. Nevertheless, prior to the renewed feminist movement of the 1960s, neo-Victorianism and Jewish mores emphasized domesticity, rooted in marriage and motherhood, as the primary sphere of feminine endeavor. Thus, until recently Jewish women, like their Gentile counterparts, found barriers that limited their access to competitive activities outside the home, including sports.

Despite formidable obstacles, some American women, both Jewish and Gentile, challenged the conventional wisdoms of the past. Indeed, several Jewish-American women achieved athletic prominence prior to the contemporary feminist movement. Aquatics promoter-administrator Charlotte Epstein, swim champion and coach Doris Kelman Dannenhirsch, tennis stars Ena Marcus, Helen Bernhard, and Barbara Breit, golfers Elaine Rosenthal, Jane Selz, and Andrea Cohn, fencer Helene Mayer, bowler Sylvia Wene, and track and field stars Sybil Koff and Claire Isicson provided role models for Jewish women who followed. Lillian Copeland, perhaps the greatest Jewish woman athlete of all time, established numerous records while neo-Victorianism still reigned. Winner of six national championships in the shot put, two in the javelin, and two in the discus, Copeland was also an excellent sprinter. She won Olympic silver and gold medals at the 1928 and 1932 Olympics, respectively.

Since the feminist revival of the 1960s, women—Jewish and Gentile—have participated in sport with greater frequency and intensity. Women are no longer a novelty on the track or even in the weight room. College and professional basketball phenomenon Nancy Lieberman, swimmers Jane Katz, Marilyn Ramenofsky, Nancy Spitz, and Wendy Weinberg, divers Debby Lipman and Barb Weinstein, tennis players Julie Heldman, Nadine Metter, Stacy Margolin, Renée Richards, and Andrea Leand, golfers Judy Cooperstein, Gail Denenberg, Barbara Mizrahie, Amy Alcott, and Nancy Rubin, gymnasts Sharon Shapiro and Marcy Levine, water polo All-American Deborah Lee, Olympic figure skater Vivian Joseph, Olympic ice dancer Judy Blumberg, weightlifter Nancy Ostroff, and karate champion Pamela Glaser are among the top Jewish sportswomen of the past generation. (Lieberman converted to Christianity while in college, and Alcott is half-Jewish.) The upsurge in the participation of Jewish women in sports mirrors social change in America. The milieu that produced more outstanding Jewish women athletes also produced more Jewish women lawyers, politicians, physicians, engineers, and professors as well as Judith Resnick, the first Jewish astronaut.

MISCELLANEOUS SPORTS. Although Jewish athletic achievements have varied according to activity and generation, American Jews have reached the top ranks of virtually all sports. Lon Myers, Myer Prinstein, Abel Kiviat, and Gary Gubner established track and field records. Handball, a sport of the crowded inner city, was dominated by Victor Hershkowitz, Jimmy Jacobs, Harry Goldstein, and other Jews. Jews have also earned election to the Soccer Hall of Fame and they have won golf and tennis championships. Larry Zeidel and Bernie Wolfe ensured that the National Hockey League was not bereft of a Jewish component. Shep Messing plays goalie for the New York Cosmos. And Sidney Franklin, a Brooklyn Jew, achieved fame as a bullfighter.

NOVELISTS, JOURNALISTS, SPORTSCASTERS. A number of Jewish novelists, playwrights, and essayists have written about sports. Some wrote parochially about athletics. Others used sports to illuminate Jewish-American life or more universal concerns unrelated to ethnicity. Bernard Malamud's *The Natural* (1952) and Philip Roth's *The Great American Novel* (1973), neither of which overtly employs Jewish themes, are among the better-known works of baseball fiction. In contrast, the baseball diamond provides a forum for antagonisms between Hasidic and secular Jews in *The Chosen* (1967) by Chaim Potok. One of the finest nonfiction works about baseball, *The Boys of Summer* (1971) by Roger Kahn, combines autobiography and an examination of the lives of the men who integrated major league baseball. Clifford Odets's play *Golden Boy* (1937), Budd Schulberg's novel *The Harder They Fall* (1947), Harold Robbins's novel *A Stone for Danny Fisher* (1951), and Rod Serling's teleplay "Requiem for a Heavyweight" (1956) confront the corruption and degradation of professional boxing. Perhaps the best play ever written by an American, *Death of a Salesman* (1949) by Arthur Miller, comments on the destructive and transitory celebrity of a high school football star.

Journalism produced many fine Jewish sportswriters, including Jacob Morse, Stanley Frank, Bernard Postal, Jesse Silver, and Dan Daniel. Longtime editor of *Ring Magazine*, Nat Fleischer, for decades, was recognized as boxing's most authoritative commentator. Sportscasters Mel Allen, Marty Glickman, Bill Mazer, Warner Wolf, and Marv Albert attained prominence on radio and television. And Howard Cosell (b. 1920) redefined sports journalism.

From the mid-1960s to the mid-1980s, Howard Cosell of ABC television was the nation's most influential sports commentator. Cosell was ubiquitous at major boxing bouts, Monday night football games, and Olympic competition. His notoriety reflected the victory of the electronic media over the printed word in American culture. A former lawyer, Cosell brought new standards of analysis and research to sports reporting. He consistently placed athletics within the political, social, and economic context of the larger society. Critical of racism, violence, drug abuse, rapacity, and unfair labor practices in sports, Cosell, possessed of a large ego and a fondness for multisyllabic words, polarized listeners. His admirers praised his courage, integrity, and incisive intelligence. Critics found Cosell pretentious, spiteful, and un-American. Few were able to ignore him.

CONCLUSION. The record of Jewish participation in American sports is significant because it contradicts the widespread image of the Jew as a timid, physically underdeveloped intellectual. Many Americans, both Jews and Gentiles, fallaciously view the cerebral, physically inept character that the celluloid Woody Allen usually portrays as the quintessential American Jew. A stereotype that denigrates the physical qualities of American Jewry perpetuates anti-Semitism by casting the Jew in the role of the perennial victim who lacks the strength and courage to defend himself. It is true that the educational attainments of Jewry significantly exceed the American mean, but it is also true that Jews have been gangsters, soldiers, and athletes. For a generation Jews were the dominant group in boxing, perhaps the most brutal of all sports. If upward mobility has led to the near demise of Jews in boxing and the top ranks of certain other sports, such as basketball, it has allowed Jews to emerge as world-class athletes in other sports, including golf and tennis. Moreover, the limited number of Jews at the highest echelons of many contemporary sports obscures the presence of many good Jewish athletes at lower levels of competition. For every Jew who stars in professional, collegiate, or Olympic sports, thousands participate with vigor and enthusiasm through youth programs, schools, community facilities, clubs, summer camps, Jewish community centers, and the Maccabiah movement.

WILLIAM SIMONS

BIBLIOGRAPHY

Auerbach, Arnold "Red," and Fitzgerald, Joe. *Red Auerbach: An Autobiography*. Foreword by John Havlicek. New York: Putnam, 1977.

Cosell, Howard, with Mickey Herskowitz. *Cosell*. New York: Pocket Books, 1973.

Goodman, Cary. *Choosing Sides: Playground and Street Life on the Lower East Side*. New York: Schocken, 1979.

Guttman, Allen. "Out of the Ghetto and On to the Field: Jewish Writers and the Theme of Sport." *American Jewish History* LXXIV (March 1985): 274–286.

Kaufman, Louis; Fitzgerald, Barbara; and Sewell, Tom. *Moe Berg: Athlete, Scholar, Spy*. Boston: Little, Brown, 1974.

Mandell, Richard. *The Nazi Olympics*. New York: Macmillan, 1971.

Postal, Bernard; Silver, Jesse; and Silver, Roy. *Encyclopedia of Jews in Sports*. New York: Bloch, 1965.

Ribalow, Harold, and Ribalow, Meir. *The Jew in American Sports*, 4th rev. ed. New York: Hippocrene, 1981.

Rosen, Charles. *The Scandals of '51: How the Gamblers Almost Killed College Basketball*. New York: Holt, Rinehart and Winston, 1978.

Ross, Barney, and Abramson, Martin. *No Man Stands Alone: The True Story of Barney Ross*. Philadelphia: Lippincott, 1957.

Shannon, Bill, ed. *United States Tennis Association Official Encyclopedia of Tennis*. Centennial ed. New York: Harper & Row, 1981.

Simons, William. "The Athlete as Jewish Standard Bearer: Media Images of Hank Greenberg." *Jewish Social Studies* 44 (Spring 1982): 95–112.

Slater, Robert. *Great Jews in Sports*. Middle Village, N.Y.: Jonathan David, 1983.

Steinberg, Milton (1903–1950). An American Conservative rabbi and author, Milton Steinberg is perhaps best known for his lucid and popular book *Basic Judaism* (1947) in which he presented Judaism's most fundamental ideas in a carefully organized, highly readable fashion.

Steinberg, born in Rochester, New York, was ordained by the Jewish Theological Seminary in 1928 prior to heading his first congregation in Indianapolis, Indiana. By 1933, he had married Edith Alpert and been invited to become rabbi at the prestigious Park Avenue Synagogue in New York City. In New York, Mrs. Steinberg gave birth to two sons, Jonathan (1934) and David (1937).

Two of his teachers greatly influenced Steinberg. Philosopher Morris Raphael Cohen, his college instructor, made Steinberg take a rigorously philosophic approach to Judaism. Rabbi Mordecai M. Kaplan, one of his instructors at the Jewish Theological Seminary, took Steinberg on an exciting intellectual odyssey, for Kaplan was then developing the ideas that would lead to the Reconstructionist Movement.

In New York, Steinberg published his first book, *The Making of the Modern Jew*, in 1934. This book, an outgrowth of articles written for the *Atlantic Monthly*, was meant to explain the miraculous survival of the Jewish people through-out history. During the 1930s, Steinberg was very active in Jewish life. He was one of the founding editors of *The Reconstructionist* (1934), taught homiletics at the Seminary (1938), and chaired the Cultural Activities Committee of the 92nd Street YMHA. In addition, he was an ardent Zionist and spent much of his time advancing the Zionist cause.

In 1939, his second book, *As a Driven Leaf*, was published. It was a novel set in the Talmudic period. Steinberg used the story of his protagonist, Elisha ben Avuyah, to dramatize the conflict between philosophical and religious thinking. Previously, Steinberg had believed that philosophical reasoning alone was capable of bringing a person to God; *As a Driven Leaf* represented a change in his thinking. Steinberg now saw both philosophy and religion as relying on a more basic faith that combined with reason and led to a religious outlook.

In the 1940s, Steinberg served as a lieutenant colonel in the New York State National Guard, served on a wide variety of committees, and especially pressed his Zionist work and his writing. His next book, *A Partisan Guide to the Jewish Problem* (1945), discussed the contemporary Jewish situation in a way that made the book a companion volume to *The Making of the Modern Jew*. *Basic Judaism*, written simply to reach the widest possible audience, was Steinberg's next book. It was a great success and won for the rabbi an increased measure of fame.

Steinberg's theological beliefs reached full maturity during the last years of his life. At one point, he had believed that evil would evolve into good. Later, he came to understand the world and God in a new way. Steinberg had a traditional theistic conception of a personal, caring, powerful God, but a God who chose to limit His own power to give humans more freedom. That is, by choice, God is all-good but not all-powerful. Such a view of the world enabled Steinberg to come to terms with the concept of the continuation of evil by a good God and simultaneously to define a human task—to work with God in creating a good world.

Steinberg's untimely death in 1950 was followed by a series of posthumous books containing many theological essays: *A Believing Jew* (1951), *From the Sermons of Milton Steinberg* (1954), and *Anatomy of Faith* (1960).

Steinberg's legacy to Jewish-American culture, beyond the beauty and logical force of his works, lies in his challenge to define a Jewish world view and live by it. His contribution to the revival of philosophical theology has proved an important counterweight to the merely pragmatic, which he thought was too often substituted for the substantive Judaism that could attract and retain young Jews.

LAWRENCE J. EPSTEIN

BIBLIOGRAPHY

Cohen, Arthur A. "Introduction." In Milton Steinberg, *Anatomy of Faith*. New York: Harcourt, Brace, 1960.

Noveck, Simon. *Milton Steinberg: Portrait of a Rabbi*. New York: Ktav, 1978.

Stern, Edith Rosenwald (1895–1980). Philanthropist, political reformer, and patron of the arts. Edith Rosenwald Stern followed the pattern set by her philanthropist father, Julius Rosenwald, to use the enormous fortune that he had built as head of Sears, Roebuck, and Co. to contribute more than $63 million to various charities. She would later recall that her family "always regarded wealth as a trust to be invested judiciously in humanity."

She was born in Chicago. Her education came more from her surroundings than from schools. She attended a progressive school in Chicago, "one of those schools where you learn nothing," she said. Then she attended (but did not graduate from) high school and a finishing school in Germany. In 1921, in what she would later call "my finest hour," she married Edgar Bloom Stern and moved with him to New Orleans, where the couple built their magnificent house, Longue Vue, named after the Hudson River estate in New York where they had become engaged.

Soon they had three children, two boys and a girl, and as the children matured the Sterns constructed modern institutions in New Orleans to care for their needs and for the needs of many others. When her eldest child, Edgar B. Stern, Jr., was two, Edith Stern started the New Orleans Nursery School (later the Newcomb Nursery School) so that he could attend a school like those she had seen in the East. Then when Edgar, Jr., was ready for elementary school, she established the Metairie Park Country Day school, a progressive coeducational school in a rural atmosphere just outside urban New Orleans.

Meanwhile, the Sterns were carrying on the

Rosenwald family tradition of supporting educational opportunities for blacks. In 1930, Edgar Stern founded Dillard University and became the first president of its board of trustees, and Mrs. Stern succeeded him in that position after his death in 1959. One building on the Dillard campus is named for Mrs. Stern's husband and one for her father.

Always interested in politics, Edith Stern led a march of women carrying brooms through the streets of New Orleans to dramatize mayoral candidate deLesseps S. Morrison's promise to sweep New Orleans clean. Mayor Morrison appointed her to the New Orleans Parkway and Park Commission. She was also named executive secretary of the housing projects in New Orleans, and, in 1951, she was named the representative from Louisiana on a 48-woman commission (one woman from each state) to advise the Defense Department on matters relating to women in the armed forces.

Her favorite project during those years was the Voters Registration League, Inc., which attempted the Herculean task of reforming electoral politics in Orleans Parish. The parish registrar of voters, William S. Farrell, was also the leader of the Regular Democratic Association (the "Old Regulars" political machine) in the second ward. In November 1951, Stern accused Farrell of systematically eliminating political opponents of the Old Regulars from the voting lists while favoring voters in his own wards. She said that he was running the registrar's office "like a country club." Furthermore, many able-bodied, literate voters were being listed as "disabled" so that poll workers could enter the voting booths with them and "help" them to vote. The ensuing struggle with the Old Regulars took persistence and courage: one registration office told the Voters' Registration League that it could not locate its voting rolls and thus could not furnish them to Edith Stern's assistants. Finally, the rolls were discovered stuffed into the sling of an office worker who was pretending that he had a broken arm. One by one, the Stern group challenged the "disabled" status of voters who worked as house painters and at other hard physical jobs, thereby furnishing the local newspapers with juicy stories exposing corruption and reducing the number of voters registered as "disabled" from nearly 10,000 to 4,075 in 1951. The Voters' Registration League also compiled lists of local residents and contacted them, urging each of them to register and vote. It sold lists of registered voters at $5 per precinct,

thus helping independent political candidates who would have no other way to get such information. "The vote is something so precious," Edith Stern said in a speech in 1956. "It should not be tampered with." She backed up her words by paying the $20,000 annual deficit of the Voters' Registration League out of her own pocket.

She was equally effective in supporting the arts. In 1957, she and her husband saved the New Orleans Symphony with a gift of $300,000. She also supported the New Orleans Museum of Art, to which she contributed several major works, including paintings by Kandinsky and eventually including Longue Vue, her own house, which she willed to the museum along with $5 million to maintain it. She built a new wing to the art museum, which included the Stern Auditorium. In 1961, President Kennedy appointed her to the National Cultural Center Advisory Committee on the Arts.

The Stern Fund, set up by Edgar and Edith Stern, contributed more than $10 million to various causes. It helped consumer advocate Ralph Nader's campaign for a federal "sunshine" law and for a Freedom of Information Act. It helped the work of biologist Barry Commoner (later the Citizens Party candidate for U.S. President in 1980), it funded studies on the side effects of nuclear energy, and it helped to establish the Fund for Investigative Journalism, which paid part of the expenses of Seymour Hersh for his research into his Pulitzer Prize-winning story of the My Lai massacre. The Stern Fund gave more formal structure to the family's earlier eclectic acts of largesse, such as engaging a little-known black singer named Marion Anderson, whom Mrs. Stern had heard at a black Baptist Church, to sing at her home to an audience of the Stern family and their friends.

After the death of her husband in 1959, she took over full responsibility for the family's good works. She was awarded the New Orleans *Times-Picayune* Loving Cup in 1964, the same award that her husband had received in 1930. She also received, among many other awards, the Weiss Brotherhood Award from the National Conference of Christians and Jews. The New Orleans *States-Item*, in its centennial issue in June, 1977, named the Sterns the city's outstanding philanthropists during that newspaper's first century. Her son, Philip, said at her memorial service, which was held in the great hall in Longue Vue after her death in New Orleans in 1980: "Mother lives on through her philanthropy—not so much in what she gave but in how she gave it." David M. Hunter, the executive director of the Stern Fund, put it more simply, "She really was a great lady."

EDGAR LEON NEWMAN

BIBLIOGRAPHY

New Orleans *Item*, November 29, 1951, 15.

New Orleans *States*, November 29, 1951, 8; December 19, 1951, 4.

New Orleans *Times-Picayune*, November 29, 1951, 1, 5; December 4, 1951, 1, 2.

New Orleans *Times-Picayune/States-Item*, September 12, 1980, Section I, 26; editorial, Section I, 16.

Stieglitz, Alfred (1864–1946). Known as the father of photography, Alfred Stieglitz was primarily responsible for the acceptance of photography as a valid form of artistic expression. He also played an important role in discovering and exhibiting works by previously unknown artists who were pioneers in abstract expressionism, cubism, and futurism. He was a major innovator and collector in photography, art, and sculpture, especially working for the recognition of American arts on their own native merits. Essentially a proponent of abstraction in the arts as distinct from detailed fidelity to nature in photography, Stieglitz strove in all he did for purity and simplicity, avoiding all ornamentation and sentiment: "All art, all living work . . . life itself, is abstract in the deepest sense."

Alfred Stieglitz was born in Hoboken, New Jersey, the eldest of six children of prosperous German Jewish parents. Although their ancestors had been observant in Europe, his parents gave Alfred no Jewish upbringing and were thoroughly assimilated. They returned to Germany, when Alfred was young, to further the children's education but continued to spend summers at a family estate in Lake George, New York, which became the setting for many of his later pictures. Stieglitz studied history and sciences in Berlin and developed a great interest in the emerging practice of serious photography. He broke with his teachers by using simple new techniques and materials and by concentrating on natural elements rather than stilted poses and portraiture.

He returned to New York in 1890 and continued experimenting with scenes of everyday urban life, buildings, machines, and, principally, the play of light and shadow in nature. He founded the influential magazine *Camera Work* in 1903 (it lasted until 1917) and held exhibitions of both art and photography at his 291 Gallery (which took its name from its Fifth Avenue address). Stieglitz is credited with introducing modern art to America years before the 1913 Armory Show: he exhibited early works by Matisse, Rousseau, Picasso, Picabia, Braque, Cézanne, Toulouse-Lautrec, Brancusi, Rodin, and others. He showed African and Mexican folk art and supported many struggling American artists as equals to their European counterparts: Marin, Hartley, Dove, Demuth, and O'Keeffe. He is best known for his discovery of Georgia O'Keeffe (1887–1986), whom he married in 1924. He photographed her thousands of times, and these portfolios, along with his "Equivalents" (scenes of clouds, trees, weather, skies), were the first photos to be exhibited at major museums as art.

Stieglitz associated himself with writers and critics (Gertrude Stein, Sherwood Anderson, William Carlos Williams, Van Wyck Brooks, Paul Rosenfeld) who worked to develop a distinctive and original American voice in the arts. He rejected all material concerns and devoted his life to expressing in photos the truth and simplicity of elemental forces. Dressing solely in black and white, he lived out his days at his last New York gallery, An American Place, summing up his principles in numerous pronouncements: "I was born in Hoboken. I am an American. Photography is my passion. The search for truth my obsession. . . . Art or not art that is immaterial. There is photography. I continue on my way seeking my own truth, ever affirming today."

Stieglitz's real faith was in art and the purity of the photographic image: the artist had to open himself, express what was within and "see all." This was as close as Stieglitz came to religion.

MARK A. BERNHEIM

BIBLIOGRAPHY

Abrams, Edward. *The Lyrical Left: Randolph Bourne, Alfred Stieglitz, and The Origins of Cultural Radicalism in America.* Charlottesville: University Press of Virginia, 1986.

Bry, Doris. *Alfred Stieglitz: Photography.* New York: October House, 1965.

Eiseler, Benitta. *O'Keefe and Stieglitz: An American Romance.* New York: Doubleday, 1991.

Frank, Waldo, et al., ed. *America and Alfred Stieglitz: A Collective Portrait.* New York: Literary Guild, 1934.

Greenough, Sarah, and Hamilton, Juan. *Alfred Stieglitz, Photographys and Writings.* Washington, D.C.: National Gallery of Art, 1983.

Homer, William Innes. *Stieglitz and the American Avant-Garde*. Boston: New York Graphic Society, 1977.

Morgan, Ann Lee, ed. *Dear Stieglitz, Dear Dove*. Newark: University of Delaware Press, 1988.

Norman, Dorothy. *Alfred Stieglitz, An American Seer*. New York: Random House, 1960, 1973.

The Stieglitz Archives are at Yale University.

Straus, Oscar Solomon (1850–1926), **Straus, Isidor** (1845–1912), and **Straus, Nathan** (1848–1931). The Straus brothers were born in Otterburg Rhenish Bavaria (Germany). They came to America in 1854, along with their mother, to join their father, who had immigrated earlier in 1852 and settled in Talbotton, Georgia.

Oscar attended Columbia College and the Columbia Law School in New York City. He was associated for a time with the law firm of Ward, Jones and Whitehead and then established his own law firm in partnership with James A. Hudson and Simon Strarne. In 1881, he gave up law to become a partner in L. Straus & Sons, a crockery firm organized in 1865 by Isidore and his father, Lazarus, in New York. Nathan became a partner in 1866. L. Straus & Son grew quickly and in 1888 purchased full ownership of Macy & Co. The brothers also developed Abraham & Straus department store in Brooklyn, New York.

The greater part of Oscar Straus's life, however, was devoted to public service. From 1887 to 1889, he served his first Turkish ministry post. In Turkey he succeeded in reopening American schools, which had been closed for six years, and in securing permission for the American Bible Society to distribute Bibles. He enjoyed good relations with the sultan and arbitrated a major railroad dispute for him. In his second Turkish mission (1898–1900), he was principally concerned with the protection of American Armenians. During the administration of Theodore Roosevelt, he was a frequent consultant to the federal government. In 1902, Straus was appointed a member of the Permanent Court of Arbitration of the Hague Tribunal, a position to which he was reappointed three times. From 1906 to March 1909, he was secretary of commerce and labor in Roosevelt's Cabinet, the first Jew to serve in the Cabinet. In 1909, he returned to Turkey but this time as the first U.S. ambassador to Turkey. During the mission he achieved greater benefits for American schools and missionaries, freeing them from Turkish supervision and winning

for them the right to own land. He opposed the State Department's policy of actively encouraging United States commercial enterprise in Turkey, however, which contributed to his resignation from his post in 1910. After an unsuccessful try for the governorship of New York on the Progressive ticket in 1912, Straus toured Europe and Africa for the Department of State. From 1915 to 1918 he served as chairman of the New York Public Service Commission, and following World War I he returned to diplomacy, assisting President Wilson at the Versailles Treaty talks. He was active in the affairs of the League to Enforce Peace, attending the Paris Peace Conference as its chairman in 1919.

Like his brothers, Isidor and Nathan, he was a benefactor of Jewish charitable and cultural organizations. He was a founder of the American Jewish Historical Society in 1892, of which he was the first president. He supported the Zionist Movement, and after World War I he used his influence to help win guarantees of the rights of Jewish minorities in several European countries.

Straus married Sarah Laranburg in 1882 and had three children, two daughters and a son.

Straus published a number of books, including *Reform in the Consular Service* (1894); *The American Spirit* (1913); and the autobiographical *Under Four Administrations: From Cleveland to Taft* (1922).

His brothers were also active in public life. Isidore served as a member of the United States House of Representatives (1894–1895). He died in 1912 aboard the *Titanic*.

Nathan was New York City park commissioner (1889–1893), president of the board of health (1898), and led the campaign for pasteurizing milk (1892).

SAYEEDA YASMIN SAIKIA

BIBLIOGRAPHY
Cohen, Nathan. *A Dual Heritage*. Philadelphia: Jewish Publication Society, 1969.

Syrkin, Marie (1899–1989). Educator, author, editor, and a leading Labor Zionist intellectual in the United States, Marie Syrkin was the daughter of Nachman Syrkin, ideological founder of Labor Zionism, and his first wife, Basya (an anti-Tsarist activist during the 1905 Russian revolution). Marie, who was born in Bern, Switzerland, was brought to the United States in 1907 and raised in New York City. She graduated from Cornell

University (B.A., 1920 and M.A., 1922). From 1925 to 1950 she taught English in New York City high schools. In 1944, she published her first book, *Your School, Your Children: A Teacher Looks At What's Wrong With Our Schools*. In 1950, she joined the faculty of Brandeis University as an associate professor of English, a position she held until 1966, when she became professor emerita.

Greatly influenced by her father's ideology, she first became associated, in 1934, with the *Jewish Frontier*, the monthly organ of American Labor Zionism, which covered a wide range of Jewish, Zionist and general political, philosophical and intellectual issues from the Socialist Zionist vantage point. In 1950, Syrkin succeeded her mentor, Hayyim Greenberg, as editor of the *Frontier*, serving in that capacity until 1971. Syrkin's writing was brilliant, incisive, and witty; her debating and lecturing style, candid and scholarly. Under her guidance, the *Jewish Frontier* made Labor Zionist ideas articulate to a new generation of American-educated Jews. Along with such other periodicals as the *New Republic*, *Commentary*, and *Midstream*, the *Frontier* served as Syrkin's platform for debates with such controversial figures as Arnold Toynbee, Hannah Arendt, and I. F. Stone on questions relating to Zionism, the Holocaust, and the Arab problem. An anthology of her articles and essays on modern-day Jewish problems, *The State of the Jews*, appeared in 1980.

Soon after World War II Syrkin visited European displaced persons camps in search of young students who could benefit from scholarships for study in the United States. This tour, and her interviews with Holocaust survivors in pre-Israel Palestine, provided the foundations for her book, *Blessed Is the Match: The Story of Jewish Resistance*, which appeared in 1948.

Syrkin was a close friend and confidante of Golda Meir, whom she first met when Meir stayed in the United States during the 1930s. In 1955, Syrkin published *Way of Valor: A Biography of Golda Meyerson*, which was subsequently republished in two updated editions: *Golda Meir: Woman with a Cause* (1963) and *Golda Meir: Israel's Leader* (1969). *A Land of Our Own: An Oral Autobiography by Golda Meir*, edited by Syrkin, appeared in 1973.

During the period immediately preceding the establishment of the State of Israel, Syrkin was in Palestine, where she made broadcasts for Haganah, the anti-British underground army. She was a sharp opponent of Irgun, the underground force

led by Menachem Begin, and equally outspoken in her opposition to the government formed by Begin three decades later. In the United States, she was a member of the Executive of the World Zionist Organization from 1965 to 1968. From 1971 to 1976, she was editor of the Herzl Press, the publishing house of the American Section of the World Zionist Organization. She was on the editorial board of *Midstream*, the monthly of the Theodor Herzl Foundation in New York City, continuing her association with the magazine, also as a contributing author, until her death in retirement at Santa Monica, California.

Following her divorce from a college instructor, with whom she had two sons (one of whom died tragically in infancy), Syrkin married the poet Charles Reznikoff, a union that ended with Reznikoff's death in 1976. She herself became known as a translator of Hebrew and Yiddish poetry into English. Some of her translations are included in Mark Van Doren's *Anthology of World Poetry* (1928) and Hubert Creekmore's *Little Treasury of World Poetry* (1952). A slim volume of her own original poetry, *Gleanings: A Diary in Verse*, with some moving reflections on her personal life, was published in 1979.

In 1960, Syrkin published a biographical memoir of her father, *Nachman Syrkin: Socialist Zionist*, which includes some of his essays and recollections of her own childhood and youth.

At the time of her death, Nahum Guttman, one of her close associates, wrote (*Jewish Frontier*, March–April 1989) that "only Henrietta Szold and Golda Meir could be rated as her peers among the authentic American Jewish women of this century."

GERTRUDE HIRSCHLER

BIBLIOGRAPHY

"Marie Syrkin: A Tribute by Her Friends, Colleagues and Students." *Jewish Frontier* (January–February 1983): 3–46.

Syrkin, Marie. *Gleanings: A Diary in Verse*. Santa Barbara, Calif.: Black Sparrow Press, 1979.

——— . *Nachman Syrkin: Socialist Zionist*. New York: Herzl Press, 1960.

——— . *The State of the Jews*. New York: Simon & Schuster, 1980.

Szold, Henrietta (1860–1945).

Henrietta Szold was born in Baltimore. Her parents, Hungarian Jews, had settled in America in 1859 after Benjamin Szold was offered a job as a rabbi there.

From an early age, all facets of Jewish learning absorbed Szold's attention. She was exposed to Jewish history, literature, ethics, and philosophy. Her education also included the classics of Western literature and philosophy. Szold was a person of varied interests. A lover of nature, she spent time gardening and taking long walks in the woods. When she was ready to enter college, her family lacked the means to finance her education. As a consequence, she never obtained a university degree. Not having a degree, however, did not keep her from utilizing her knowledge and intelligence. Szold gave classes to high school students in English, Latin, German, French, Hebrew, mathematics, botany, and philosophy. By the age of 17, she was publishing articles for Jewish journals under the pen name Sulamith. So adept were her writing skills that, in 1902, the London *Jewish Chronicle* described Henrietta Szold as the leading Jewish essayist in America.

What would prove pivotal in her life was her activities in Zionist groups, which began in 1893. At this time she joined the Zionist Association in Baltimore, America's first Zionist group. Before devoting her time to predominantly Zionist activities, Szold served as an editor of the Jewish Publication Society, where she edited, proofread, and translated books, including Graetz's epic volume *History of the Jews* (1891–1898). During this period, Szold became active in the Federation of American Zionists (later to be renamed the Zionist Organization of America). Here, she served as a member of the executive committee, honorary vice president, and secretary. She was also active in creating a library that would house all publications on Zionist activities relating to Palestine. This endeavor evolved into what currently functions as the Zionist Archives of America.

More than any other organization, Szold would be identified with Hadassah. She joined the organization in 1907 when Hadassah was comprised of 17 women who met periodically to discuss Zionist and Jewish related subjects. After a trip to Palestine in 1909, she returned with renewed energy and insight on how Hadassah should represent Jewish interests. Due to her efforts, Hadassah became a national women's organization. Its aim was to impart practical skills and knowledge to Palestine's Jewish residents, which still is a priority of the national organization. In the United States, Hadassah emphasized Jewish education. The priority Hadassah placed on education, whether learning practical skills or Jewish history, ensured the organization would not simply be another charity group.

On her trip to Palestine Szold had been appalled by the unsanitary conditions, poverty, and poor health that pervaded the area. As a consequence, she sought to establish a health care system to meet the medical needs of the community. In addition to this, having extensively read on what was at the time a new profession, she used principles gleaned from texts on social work to build a system of social welfare there. Poverty would be combated and self-sufficiency taught. Thus education, health, and social welfare (in large measure the result of Szold's efforts) became foundations that helped to make Israel a viable state when it was established in 1948.

One of Henrietta Szold's most notable achievements was the creation of Youth Aliyah. Youth Aliyah was a project to assist young Jews to immigrate to Palestine. After Hitler's ascent to power, Szold traveled to Germany to help those interested to leave Germany and make Palestine their new home. By 1947, 22,000 young Jews, mostly from Central Europe, who would have perished in Nazi concentration camps were saved through Aliyah.

Culture and its attendant virtues were values Szold prized highly. Just as passionately, Szold disdained and eschewed materialism, which she equated with vulgarity. *See also* Hadassah, Women.

HOWARD SHAKER

BIBLIOGRAPHY

Dash, Joan. *Summoned to Jerusalem: The Life of Henrietta.* New York: Harper & Row, 1979.

Fineman, Irving. *Woman of Valor: The Life of Henrietta Szold.* New York: Simon & Schuster, 1961.

Lowenthan, Marvin. *Henrietta Szold: Life and Letters.* New York: Viking Press, 1942.

Zeitlin, Rose. *Henrietta Szold: Record of a Life.* New York: Dial Press, 1952.

T

Teitelbaum, Joel. *See* SATMAR REBBE.

Television. The Jewish presence in American television, both before and behind the camera, has been noteworthy since the beginnings of the industry in the late 1940s. During the past four decades, television has served as an important forum for American Jewish creativity. Moreover, it has emerged as a major means of shaping as well as generating and disseminating images of Jewish life in the contemporary American context.

The considerable involvement of Jews in the various aspects of American television programming is in part a consequence of the large number of Jews working in American film, theater, vaudeville, print journalism, advertising, and radio at the time of television's emergence as a national broadcast medium in the years immediately after World War II. In addition, the newness of the television industry in the rapidly expanding postwar economy provided opportunities for a wide variety of talents—writers, performers, producers, designers, technicians—regardless of their social or professional pedigrees, a situation not unlike the birth of the film and radio industries earlier this century into which Jews also entered with ease. The concentration of early American television production in New York City, the world's largest Jewish population center and home to a major Jewish intellectual and cultural community, also proved a significant factor, as has the expansion of much of the industry in Los Angeles, the site of the second largest Jewish community in the United States.

To date, there has been no contributional history of Jews in American television (though this exists for Jews in the Hollywood film industry), nor are Jews given much, if any, explicit attention in general histories of the medium. There are, however, a number of memoirs and biographies of Jews who either have appeared on television or who worked behind the scenes that constitute an important resource for understanding the role Jews have played in the medium. Likewise, though there have been several works that analyze the Jewish presence in American movies, there has thus far been no published book-length work attempting a comprehensive examination of the Jewish presence on the small screen, whether it be Jewish characters and themes in dramatic programs or the presence of Jews and Jewish issues in television journalism and documentary.

THE EARLY YEARS. Indeed, one of the most remarkable features of the Jewish presence in the early years of American televison is its low visibility. Jews who appeared on television were rarely explicitly identified as such on the air, and few plots of television dramas dealt specifically with Jewish life. This may be due in part to the particular structure of this broadcast medium. While radio in post-World War II America boasted hundreds of independent local stations throughout the country, the Federal Communications Commission has licensed fewer television stations, and the medium has, until recently, been heavily dominated by the three national commercial networks. Thus, whereas for decades the plethora of radio stations have been able to serve an array of specific audiences distinguished by such factors as ethnicity, musical taste, and religious or political ideologies, the American television industry could not create extensive programming for Jews, a group perceived as a specialized market, until the advent of cable and satellite transmission in the 1980s.

Another important factor explaining the low profile of Jews as Jews in the first decades of American television is the problematic nature of ethnicity in modern American life. Television inherited a good deal of Hollywood's gallery of ethnic stereotypes as well as that industry's specific concerns over provoking anti-Semitic sentiments through their representations of Jews on the screen, along with the personal ambivalence of many Jews in the industry toward their Jewishness. In post-World War II America, new intolerances, forged during and immediately after the war, joined old ones. Of particular concern for American Jews in the Cold War era was the suspicion that they were, as a group, sympathetic to communism—witness the large number of Jews in radio and television denounced in *Red Channels*, an inflammatory anti-Communist publication of 1950.

In fact, the majority of American Jews were emblematic of those Southern and Eastern Europeans who crossed the Atlantic during the period of mass emigration from the Old World (1880–1924), or who were the children of these immigrants, in their zealous efforts to Americanize culturally and socially, often at some cost to their ethnic consciousness and pride. The diluted ethnicity in "The Rise of the Goldbergs," the first series on American television to feature a family of Jewish protagonists, epitomizes the ambitions of postwar mainstream American Jewish culture. This successful situation comedy (1949–1954, 1956–1957) was written by its star, Gertrude Berg. Following a format she established successfully in the long-running radio program of the same name (1929–1948), Berg presented a series of comic adventures of an immigrant Jewish family and their neighbors in a Bronx apartment building. The family's Jewish identity, indicated by their last name, remained otherwise unmentioned in the course of the series; much like the menorah and samovar on the sideboard in their dining room, the Goldbergs' ethnicity stood quietly in the background. A more significant feature of the Goldberg family apartment's modest decor was the large portrait of George Washington hanging in the living room, iconic of the primacy of American values and sensibilities in the world of "The Goldbergs." The protagonists' Jewishness—or, rather, their generic immigrant ethnicity in an urban American context—was also signaled by a conventionalized English dialect, with its sing-song intonation, occasional malapropisms, and inversions of syntax. In her reminiscences, Berg explains that she strove to make her characters ordinary, their ethnicity inoffensive to the general public. Thus, though the program's title recalls Abraham Cahan's novel *The Rise of David Levinsky* (1917), which chronicles an earlier generation of immigrants' struggle to escape the confines of their ethnicity, "The Goldbergs" are presented as having risen to a certain level of cultural "at-homeness" in America. A more complex and difficult reality of being Jewish in postwar America was performed off-camera, in the tragic blacklisting and eventual suicide of actor Philip Loeb, who played the Goldberg *pater familias*. As a result, "The Goldbergs" was cancelled at the height of its popularity.

Ironically, the success of Jews in the early years of television has often been attributed specifically to their ability to derive energy from their ethnic heritage. By exploiting this inherently creative power—attributed variously to shtetl folk wisdom, Talmudic acumen, the ironic humor of oppression, the ferment of a people asserting their new-found national culture, the antidote to the immigrants' urban anomie—Jewish performers in American television (as well as radio, theater, and vaudeville) are seen as having transcended their parochial background to emerge as national celebrities. The oft-cited archetype of this success is Sid Caesar, whose "Your Show of Shows" (1949–1954) and "Caesar's Hour" (1954–1957), are hailed as the fountainhead of television comedy-variety programs. The achievement of these programs is largely attributed to the collaboration among Caesar, his co-stars, producer-director Max Liebman, and his writers—whose ranks included Woody Allen, Mel Brooks, Selma Diamond, Larry Gelbart, Carl Reiner, Aaron Rubin, Neil Simon, Joe Stein, Mel Tolkin—the majority of whom were American-born children of East European Jewish immigrants.

The "Caesar" aesthetic was derived from revues that he and some of his first collaborators had staged at Jewish resort hotels in the Catskills in the late 1940s. (Similarly, Gertrude Berg's career began with the amateur theatricals she presented at her family's Catskill hotel.) Caesar's material differed from other comedy-variety television fare of the time by offering humor in the form of narrative sketches, as opposed to the series of "stand-up" jokes and pranks performed by vaudevilleans who had crossed over to television, epitomized by Milton Berle. Exploiting their star's virtuosity in both verbal and physical comedy, the writers of "Your Show of Shows" and "Caesar's Hour" developed a range of genres of sketches—the amusing misadventures of daily life (especially among married couples); the comic world-view of such diverse creatures and objects as a fly, an infant, and an old automobile tire; parodies of various performance genres (opera, westerns, rock and roll). A common feature of many of these sketches was a mocking of the culturally serious, epitomized by Caesar's pseudo-omniscient character, the Professor. This particular kind of humor—which required both a considerable level of "high" cultural literacy as well as a sense of distance from this culture—has its antecedents in the satirical writings of American Jewish humorists S. J. Perelman and George S. Kaufman, whose works included screenplays for the Marx brothers in the 1930s.

THE COMIC IMAGE OF THE JEW ON TELEVISION. Caesar's shows, together with series featuring Milton Berle, Jack Benny, Phil Silvers, and Groucho Marx, as well as frequent guest appearances on variety shows by a host of humorists and comedians—Morey Amsterdam, Shelley Berman, Jack Carter, Myron Cohen, Buddy Hackett, Sam Levenson, Jackie Mason, Marilyn Michaels, Joan Rivers, Menashe Skulnick, Henny Youngman, among others—established an essentially comic image of Jews in the American consciousness during the first postwar decades, and they transformed an immigrant Jewish rhetoric into a national discourse of humor. Thus, in the highly encoded art of television, Jewishness was first established primarily as a signal for laughter.

Yiddish has played an essential role in the codification of Jews as inherently comic, and its presence on American television—whether explicit or implicit—has become a key element of the medium's discourse of humor. As the children of immigrants, many of the Jews working in television in its early years heard or spoke Yiddish in their childhood homes and communities. More-over, it was often the language of their earliest exposure to theater, vaudeville, radio, and film, where it implicitly established a communal intimacy between performer and audience. However, the use of the language—with its associations of Old-World provinciality and exoticism, as well as of parochial insularity and secrecy—on a modern, nationally broadcast medium created a disparity that was quickly codified as being inherently comic. Thus, the insertions of isolated Yiddish words and expressions into one's speech—Yiddish rarely appears on American television as a full language, but rather as a fragment of one—has become a signal of humor. Thus, Yiddish—and by extension, Jews—have come to be understood by the American television audience as inherently funny. The use of Yiddishisms by non-Jews (Johnny Carson being a salient but by no means sole example) generates a comic disparity of its own—that of the Gentile outsider having insider knowledge of the "secret" language. (It should be noted here that Yiddish words and expressions permeate the argot of the television industry both on camera and off, evinced by such terms as spiel, glitch, kaka, etc.)

Yiddish is also identified as having an implicit presence in television's comic discourse by serving as a structural model for humorous idioms of speech. Attributed to Yiddish, or described as "Jewish rhythms," are such devices as rhetorical questions and the answering of questions with questions, sing-song speech cadences, and inverted syntax. Variously codified as Jewish modes of discourse are guilt, arrogance, intellectual pretentiousness, intellectual irreverence, earthiness, moral conscientiousness, saccharine sentiment, vitriolic wit, and, above all, irony. This notion of "Jewish-style" rhetoric is not confined to television writing; it is also applied to plays, novels, and screenplays by American Jews.

THE "SERIOUS" IMAGE OF JEWS ON TELEVISION. Complementing the comic, ethnic image of yiddishkeit is the serious, religious image of Judaism. Though the codification of Jewry as a religious group avoids the difficulties attending an ethnic identity, analogizing Jews with Methodists or Muslims presents problems of its own. Admittedly, the only forum in which Jewishness is regularly, explicitly discussed are the commercial networks' ecumenical religious series ("Lamp Unto My Feet," "Frontiers of Faith," "Look Up and Live," "Directions," and "The Eternal Light"). However, the range of

Jewish programs presented over the course of more than four decades on "The Eternal Light"—which includes dramatizations of stories by S. Y. Agnon, Isaac Bashevis Singer, Y. L. Peretz, and Sholem Aleichem, biographies of famous Jewish figures in history, interviews with contemporary Jewish politicians, musicians, writers, and artists, stories of important events in Jewish history as well as dramatizations of Bible stories and discussions with theologians—demonstrates that mainstream American Jewry's notion of Jewishness has been, in fact, much more extensive than what is covered under the category of "religion."

Jews have also appeared occasionally as serious presences in television dramas. Here, they are largely respected religious figures (e.g., Paddy Chayevsky's "Holiday Song" (Philco Television Playhouse, 1952), Zionist heroes (e.g., "A Woman Called Golda," 1982), or the undeserving victims of persecution, usually instigated by Nazis (e.g., "Holocaust," 1978, "Skokie," 1981). Despite the generally limited presence of Jews as serious subjects on television, certain figures (Anne Frank, Marc Chagall, Simon Wiesenthal) and events (Jewish incarceration in Auschwitz or the Warsaw Ghetto uprising) have achieved extensive, repeated coverage, while the bulk of Jewish biographies, history, literature, and culture remains a largely untapped resource.

The single, most extensive attempt to present Jews as "serious" has been American public television's 9-hour series "Heritage: Civilization and the Jews" (1984), a history of Jewish national and communal experience as well as a chronicle of the contributions of Jewry to world culture. The series title recalls—and suggests that it should be seen at least in part as a response to—public television's watershed series, "Civilisation" (1970), Kenneth Clark's 13-hour history of Western culture through the visual arts, in which Jews are virtually absent.

JEWS AND TELEVISION NEWS. The Jewishness of a number of prominent television journalists, though often a well-known fact, is hardly ever commented on in the context of television news reporting. This is most likely a result of journalistic notions of a reporter's objectivity, although it is reinforced by the phenomenon of Jewish "invisibility" on American television as codified during its early years.

The coverage of Jewish individuals, issues, and events on television news programming like-

wise remains largely devoid of explicit discussion of Jewishness, except in its perceived "relevance" to larger issues. Though notions of the relevance of Jewishness have changed over the years, the Jewish identity of famous (or infamous) figures in the news is still rarely mentioned outright; an individual's Jewishness is usually codified as one's religious confession and is therefore regarded as a private matter, categorically separated from the realm of public life. The coverage of Diaspora Jewish issues and events in television news is largely shaped by the organizing principle of anti-Semitism, which is usually understood in American terms as an assault on a Jewish person's or community's civil rights. The organizing principle of anti-Semitism presents Jewish activities and responses to issues as essentially defensive rather than creative; thus American Jewish community life and cultural activity are rarely the subject of news stories, except for occasional features on local news programs, usually oriented around holiday celebrations.

The single, largest presence of Jews in television news reporting is found in the ongoing chronicle of the State of Israel. Having come into existence at the same time as the medium, the history of Israel is distinctively linked with television, especially in the American consciousness. Indeed, most Americans' sense of modern Israel comes almost exclusively from this source. The discussion of Israel's internal political, economic, and cultural life as well as its relations with neighboring states and to world politics is, like most foreign coverage, largely shaped by American sensibilities and domestic political concerns. Nonetheless, American television reporting plays a role of great importance in the American Jewish community's sense of commitment to Zionism. Television coverage of the Israeli incursion in Lebanon in the early 1980s and the more recent Intifada has thus played an instrumental role in the American Jewish community's crisis of confidence in Zionism by showing the Jewish state as aggressor, where it had previously been presented on American television as a utopian, redemptive response to the horrors of Jewish persecution during World War II.

The extensive attention given to Israel on television has, in turn, been instrumental in establishing Jews as a political presence in America. Reporters have addressed the issue of the "Jewish vote" as a strategic factor in both national and local elections, and television news has given more attention to the political implications of such issues as anti-Semitism among white supremacists and increased tensions between African and Jewish Americans. Moreover, television news programming has emerged as a forum where Jewish spokesmen can address the nation and the world on a range of political and moral issues. Salient among these figures is Elie Wiesel, whom television has canonized as something of a voice of universal moral conscience. Wiesel not only spoke out on camera against President Reagan's controversial visit to Nazi graves in Bitburg in 1985 as the renowned author of Holocaust literature was being honored at the White House, but he has also been invited to discuss on the airwaves the moral implications of subjects as diverse as the Cambodian genocide and nuclear war, the latter following the screening of "The Day After" (1983), a television movie dramatizing the aftermath of an atomic holocaust.

THE JEWISH PRESENCE ON TELEVISION IN THE 1970s. The image of Jews on television series underwent a significant change beginning in the early 1970s, along with much of the medium's programming in general, as a consequence of the transformations in American life wrought by mass movements against poverty and the Vietnam War and on behalf of civil rights, blacks, women, students, and gays. Producer Norman Lear's "All in the Family" (1971–1979) is often pointed to as marking this new era in television programming. Lear used the tried-and-true situation comedy format centering around the lives of two married couples (cf. "I Love Lucy," "The Honeymooners") as a forum for airing debate on a series of topics—the antiwar movement, the Watergate scandal, as well as racism, sexism, and other prejudices encountered in daily life—previously regarded as too controversial for discussion on television, except perhaps in the ostensibly dispassionate, serious format of news reportage or documentary. "All in the Family," the shows that it spawned ("Maude," "The Jeffersons"), and the many others that it inspired (including "Good Times," "Mary Hartman," "One Day at a Time," "Sanford and Son") were hailed as "ground-breaking" television, expanding the roster of themes, situations, and characters that could be acceptable to audiences seeking entertainment in prime-time hours. The impact of these innovations have also been felt in other kinds of television programming, ranging from daytime soap operas and talk shows to late-night entertainments, notably "Saturday Night Live."

On this comedy series, which premiered in 1975, Jews, along with virtually every other segment of American culture, have been the explicit subjects of satirical sketches.

Lear's programs are recognized not only for having brought a wider range of social and political issues into the forum of prime-time television entertainment, but also for explicitly promoting an American liberal agenda. This phenomenon recalls the "social-conscience" films made in Hollywood during the 1930s and 1940s. Here, too, Jewish producers used their medium as a forum for presenting the American public with ideologically charged narrative lessons in combatting social intolerance and intellectual orthodoxy, championing underdogs against the wielders of power, and promoting an American patriotism embracing cultural and political diversity. In both cases, the Jewishness of these promoters of liberalism is masked. Just as Hollywood often disguised the ethnic identity of characters who were Jewish in their literary or journalistic sources, "All in the Family"'s Michael Stivic is a Polish-American, the title character of "Maude" is a Westchester WASP (yet both are played by Jewish actors).

Thus, whereas Jewish producers and writers may have begun to draw on their experiences as Jews as the paradigm for the various kinds of "otherness"—being ethnic, black, female, radical, disabled, gay, old—that they were exploring and celebrating in television programs of the 1970s, the paradigm was largely an encoded one. Thus, the short-lived "Bridget Loves Bernie" (1972–1973), a situation comedy about intermarriage à la Broadway's *Abie's Irish Rose* (1922) treated the subject with dated frivolity at the same time that Lear was challenging the limits of topical discourse in prime-time television entertainments. (The formula was revived more recently, with even less success, with the short-lived series *Chicken Soup* (1989), featuring Jackie Mason and Lynn Redgrave as the interfaith lovers.)

Indeed, the producers of television entertainment series had already demonstrated their willingness to perpetuate Hollywood's tendency to "deracinate" Jewish sources. Thus the Gentile character Rob Petrie, protagonist of "The Dick Van Dyke Show" (1961–1966), was based on the life of the show's producer, Carl Reiner, inspired by his experiences writing and performing with Sid Caesar (transformed in the situation comedy into the perennially offstage character Alan Brady); likewise Felix Unger and Oscar Madison of "The Odd Couple" (1970–1975, derived from

Neil Simon's 1965 Broadway comedy of the same name) were implicitly Jewish—as manifested in the "Jewish-style" rhetoric of their banter and by the Jewishness of the actors portraying them—despite their last names. In both these series, Jews were obliquely present in the form of comic foils to the protagonists—Murray, the bumbling cop; Buddy Sorrel, the wisecracking gag writer.

The Jewish "other" appeared explicitly in the guise of Rhoda Morgenstern, the Bronx-bred neighbor of the midwestern WASP protagonist of "The Mary Tyler Moore Show" (1970–1977), though the role was still essentially a foil. Beside Moore's Mary Richards, Valerie Harper's Rhoda was more appetitive, earthy, sensual, colorful, irrational, emotionally labile. Thus Rhoda embodied another archetypal role for Jews on American television—and in the iconography of American culture—that of the carnivalesque. In the dramatic world of television series, the role of the carnivalesque "other" requires a culturally centric "straight man" (or woman) to play off. (Indeed, when Rhoda became the protagonist and title role of a spin-off series in 1974, a younger sister, Brenda, was invented to fill the role of the relatively unattractive and unhappy "other" that Rhoda had previously played to Mary Richards.) Thus Jews are rarely seen as sage raisonneurs when they appear among the ethnic salad of characters that populate situation comedies and serial dramas, such roles usually being reserved for adult WASP males. The occasional exceptions—the title role in "Barney Miller" (1975–1982), Alex Reiger in "Taxi" (1978–1983)—cast the Jew as the wise man in an inverted, carnivalesque world.

THE CONTEMPORARY IMAGE OF JEWS ON TELEVISION. The Jewish presence on American television has undergone yet another significant development in the 1980s. An increasingly sizable and diverse number of Jewish characters have populated programs such as "Hill Street Blues," "St. Elsewhere," "LA Law," "A Year in the Life," and "thirtysomething," constituting an ongoing exercise in self-conscious self-portraiture on the part of Jewish producers, writers, directors, and actors in the television industry. This differs from other forms of Jewish self-imaging in literature and drama, as it is the product of a corporate aesthetic rather than a single artist's vision. The range of characters provides the means for exploration of a number of clearly Jewish concerns—anti-Semitism, Jewish

family dynamics, morality, and stereotypes (especially sexual ones)—and life-cycle events as they are experienced by Jews—birth, circumcision, bar mitzvah, marriage, and death. Of particular importance among these is the subject of intermarriage; indeed, all of the abovementioned programs have featured an interfaith couple. Not only is this a reflection of a growing trend among American Jews, but intermarriage is exploited to "problematize" the greater issue of having a Jewish identity in largely Gentile America. In addition, interfaith marriages are a dramatic device for exploring, in an extreme case, a problem inherent in all marriages, namely, the ongoing need of the two partners to negotiate the differences in their cultural backgrounds and personalities.

Rather than being dealt with in an isolated "Jewish" episode, as was typical of television series from the sixties and seventies, the Jewishness of these characters is usually part of an ongoing exploration of their personalities and relationships. Thus, a character's Jewishness receives extended treatment over the course of several seasons, much like other identities such as being an alcoholic, single parent, cancer patient, or mentally retarded. When this is combined with a number of regular Jewish characters, as is the case on "LA Law," the resulting image of being Jewish in contemporary American society assumes an unprecedented richness and complexity. In addition to treating topics clearly marked as Jewish—anti-Jewish prejudice, feelings about the Holocaust, separation of church and state, etc.—the series explores subtler issues, notably the difference between WASP and Jewish law (and lawyers). The result evinces both a new, distinctive sense of Jewish "at-homeness" in America as well as an exceptional comfort in using the television serial as a medium for self-presentation and even self-exploration.

The Jewish presence in television remains a largely unexplored field critically. The major initiative toward providing a corpus for its analysis is the National Archive of Jewish Broadcasting, established in 1981 at the Jewish Museum in New York, where a collection of some 2800 news reports, documentaries, dramatic and comic series episodes, special programs, and commercials have been gathered and inventoried for scholarly purposes. Though the parameters of this unique collection themselves pose interesting problems—for how does one determine what constitutes a piece of "Jewish media"?—this archive provides a valuable resource both for analyses of the images of Jews presented on television to the American public as well as studies of how a Jewish presence has fashioned the sensibilities of the medium and of American popular culture.

JEFFREY SHANDLER

BIBLIOGRAPHY

Altman, Sig. *The Comic Image of the Jew: Explorations of a Pop Culture Phenomenon.* Teaneck, N.J.: Fairleigh Dickinson University Press, 1975.

Berg, Gertrude, with Cherney Berg. *Molly and Me.* New York: Amerean, 1961.

Caesar, Sid, with Bill Davidson. *Where Have I Been?: An Autobiography.* New York: Crown, 1982.

Chayevsky, Paddy. *Television Plays.* New York: Simon & Schuster, 1955.

Cohen, Sarah Blacher, ed. *From Hester Street to Hollywood: The Jewish-American Stage and Screen.* Bloomington: Indiana University Press, 1983.

Friedman, Lester. *Hollywood's Image of the Jew.* New York: Ungar, 1982.

Temple Emanu-El (New York City). Congregation Emanu-El of New York City is considered the foremost Reform congregation in the United States. The congregation grew out of a cultural society established on New York's Lower East Side in 1844. In April 1845, 33 members of the society decided to form a Reform congregation and consulted with leaders of Charleston's Reform congregation (the first such congregation in the United States) and with Reform leaders in Baltimore. The German immigrant founders at first made minimal modifications of traditional practice. In 1854, however, the second days of festivals were abolished, and the following year a "Reformed" prayer book came into use. In 1854, too, the congregation moved from the Lower East Side uptown to Twelfth Street, to a former Baptist Church that had been refurbished as a synagogue. Membership increased rapidly, in both numbers and influence. In 1868, the congregation was able to build its own building on Fifth Avenue at Forty-third Street, an imposing house of worship in the heart of New York's best residential area. This was the age of the fashionable church, and Emanu-El exemplified the Jewish community's place in this phase of religion. The ritual had been reorganized after the Protestant style, the music was impressive, and the sermon had become the central feature of worship.

The course adopted by the congregation appears to have been determined by its lay leaders. In 1906, Stephen Wise refused the pulpit when he learned that the freedom on which he insisted could not be granted; in 1910, Judah Leon Magnes withdrew from the pulpit when the board of trustees rejected his proposals for a modification of the congregation's extreme Reform stance. This was a period in which the congregation numbered among its leaders many of American Jewry's outstanding figures in business and finance as well as the leaders of Jewish institutions. The congregation, however, did not lose sight of the plight of its less fortunate coreligionists and concerned itself with their welfare through practical social work on the Lower East Side.

In 1927, Emanu-El, which had combined with Temple Beth-El, began construction of a new building and moved its headquarters, until 1929, to Beth-El at Fifth Avenue and Seventy-sixth Street. The first service to be held at the newly built temple was the funeral in September 1929 for Louis Marshall, an outstanding leader of American Jewry who as the president of Emanu-El was largely responsible for the construction of the building. Today, Temple Emanu-El at Fifth Avenue and Sixty-fifth Street continues to be an architectural landmark of New York City. Adjoining it is the Beth-El Chapel and the Community House. In 1964, the Goldsmith Religious School Building was opened to provide school facilities and additional space for the temple's expanding programs. Its congregation includes many of New York City's most prominent Jewish families. *See also* Reform Judaism.

S. D. TEMKIN

BIBLIOGRAPHY

Goren, Arthur A. *New York Jews and the Quest for Community.* New York: Columbia University Press, 1970.

Grossman, Cissy; Sobel, Ronald B.; and Kirschberg, Reva G. *A Temple Treasury: The Judaica Collection of Congregation Emanu-El of the City of New York.* New York: Hudson Hills Press, 1989.

Hyman, B. *The Rise of the Jewish Community of New York, 1654–1860.* Philadelphia: Jewish Publication Society, 1945.

Theater. The relationship between Jews and the American stage goes back to the early days of the republic. Prior to the Civil War, most plays produced in the United States included unsympathetic Jewish characters. The earliest depiction of a Jew in an American play was in *Slaves of Algiero*

(1794) by Susanna Haswell Rowson, in which the villain is a Jewish character. Foreign dramas brought to the States such as *The Jew and the Doctor* (1809) or *The Jew of Luheck* (1819) similarly treated Jewish characters negatively as did such plays as *London Assurance* (1841) and *The Ticket-of-Leave Man* (1853).

The few Jewish playwrights of the nineteenth century, such as Mordecai Manuel Noah (1785–1851), Isaac Harby (1789–1828), and Jonas B. Phillip (d. 1862), avoided using Jewish themes in their plays.

Negative images of Jews on the stage began to change after the Civil War. George H. Jessop's *Sam'l of Pasem* (1861, written for the Jewish actor M. B. V. Curtis) signals the beginning of the sympathetic portrayal of Jews on the American stage. Throughout the nineteenth century, however, Jewish actors were very popular. In fact, the earliest Jewish stars were women. Rachel (née Elisa Felid; 1820–1858), Rose Eytinge (1835–1911), and French actress Sarah Bernhardt (née Bernard), who toured the States frequently, were among the best-known stars of the American stage, and Eytinge, at one point, was hailed as the leading lady of the American stage—much as in 1970 Barbra Streisand (b. 1942) would be presented with a special Tony award as Broadway Performer of the Decade.

Although there were no paramount Jewish playwrights until the twentieth century, Jews were prominent in the business side of the theater. H. B. Philips was the manager of Ford's Theater, Washington, D.C.; David Belasco (1859–1931) —actor, playwright, producer, and director—was also the founder of the Belasco Theater (1906), New York City; the Frohman brothers (David, 1851–1940, and Charles, 1860–1915) were responsible for the American premieres of such playwrights as Oscar Wilde, Somerset Maugham, and James Barrie. Sol Hurok (1888–1974) frequently brought over major figures and major foreign theatrical companies to America, including the HaBimah Players in 1926. In recent years, David Merrick (né Margulois; b. 1911) and Hal Prince (b. 1928) are among Broadway's most successful producers.

As Jews continued to play a major role in all aspects of theatrical life in the twentieth century, they also pioneered as teachers and founders of acting schools. Among the more important of these teachers were Stella Adler (b. 1920), who founded the Stella Adler Conservatory of Acting in 1949, and Lee Strasberg (né Israel Strassberg; 1901–1982), who introduced the "method school" of acting at the Actors Studio when he came to the organization in 1948.

The nativism of the 1920s as it manifested itself in the form of anti-Semitism was confronted in two plays during this decade: Aaron Hoffman's *Welcome Stranger* (1920) and John Galsworthy's *Loyalties* (1922), a play about English anti-Semitism. Clearly the negative stereotyping of Jews by Gentiles on the American stage was a thing of the past. Yet one could not speak of a Jewish-American stage genre although there were many Jews involved in the theater. The emergence of this genre would come in the aftermath of the Great Depression.

The immediate ancestor of Jewish-American drama is the vibrant but not awesome Yiddish theater, whose valuable legacy has not overwhelmed its heirs but enabled them to use only what they most cherished and could comfortably assimilate. Among its treasures the Yiddish theater generously made available its serious literature—its weighty dramas of filial disobedience and parental anguish, of loyalties divided between Old World and New, of Jew–Gentile confrontations, of personal versus communal betterment. It also provided intentional and unintentional humorous fare—its saccharine melodramas, eclectic musicals, and broad comedies. By both stressing and diminishing the importance of being earnest, the Yiddish theater created its own brand of parables and parodies, a rich source of didacticism and levity for Jewish-American drama. The Yiddish theater had the most emotional impact on its immigrant audience—the majority of the 1.3 million Yiddish-speaking Jews who between 1882 and World War I left Eastern Europe for a better life in America. By depicting shtetl life and types—and most of all, with its language—the Yiddish theater preserved the familiar within the unknown and made the new aliens less homesick.

Thus, the Yiddish theater was the common meeting place, the common topic of conversation, the common dispeller of estrangement. Its heartrending plots permitted the immigrants to give full vent to their feelings, "to bathe in this homey theatrical bathhouse." Its makeshift spectacles and grandiloquent acting provided a glamorous respite from their grim Hester Street lives. Its self-ordained playwright-preachers—the Gordons, the Pinskis, the Asches—became their New World rabbis whose moralizations replaced Old World Torah instruction and spiritual counsel. The Yiddish theater generated such a consuming passion for works of the imagination that it became a secular temple where its audiences regularly worshiped the aesthetic. Or if the mode of dramatic expression was not to their liking and they opposed the values depicted, the Yiddish theater became an arena for cultural debate, a place to exercise their newly gained freedom of expression. As journalist Lincoln Steffens observed: "A remarkable phenomenon it was, a community of thousands of people fighting over an art question, dividing families, setting brother against brother, breaking up business firms, and finally actually forcing the organization of a rival theater with a company pledged to realism against the old theater which would play any good piece."

Despite such great differences of artistic opinion, the establishment by 1918 of some 20 Yiddish theaters in New York City alone suggested that these enterprises were catalysts for social cohesion rather than sources of communal disruption. The Jewish immigrants may have had heated arguments over the aesthetic merits of a given play, but the Yiddish theater was still their *own* theater. It offered them, as Nahma Sandrow points out, the "intimate atmosphere of an 'insider's event' for people who were still outsiders in America. The play was for them and often about them, and in their own language."

Though the Yiddish theater flourished during the twenties and early thirties, the immigrant audience rapidly became more Americanized, more affluent. Changing their names, language, and occupations, they moved from the Lower East Side to better parts of the city and suburbs. They left the clannish "theatrical bathhouse" to jump into the nonsectarian melting pot to wash away their greenhorn identity. The more talented actors and actresses—Paul Muni (1895–1967), Stella Adler, Molly Picon (b. 1898)—also abandoned the sinking Yiddish theater for smoother sailing on Yankee showboats. The few fans who remained loyal to the Yiddish theater could no longer see a variety of engaging plays by gifted playwrights, for once an impoverished company had a success, they performed it for an entire season. And the hit, more often than not, was a form of *shund* (trash), the lowbrow fare which in the earlier Yiddish theater was a mishmash of "classical Yiddish songs, topical jokes, pilfered dialogue, irrelevant new show tunes," all expressed in a "diluted, crippled, macaronic, or eviscerated Yiddish." The distinguishing feature of this newer brand of *shund* was that it was performed in "potato Yiddish—a corrupt version diluted with English words and Americanisms."

The appeal of this new Yiddish theater, itself a prime casualty of the acculturation it had instigated, was the bastardization of the language it so lovingly nurtured. Promoted as bilingual hilarity, its fractured Yiddish and English, its crude puns and malapropisms, its obscene jests struck audiences as terribly funny. Yiddish in this context was so held up to ridicule that even the sound appeared comical, especially to the young who did not speak or understand the language.

The juxtaposition of Yiddish with English for humorous purposes may have been a sign of the ebbing vitality of the Yiddish theater, but it added new comic gusto to the emerging vaudeville routines of American Jewish entertainers and Borscht Belt comedians who themselves were the irreverent descendants of the shtetl *badkhn*, the facile-tongued wedding jester and itinerant funnyman. While Weber and Fields performed a variation of Yiddish dialect humor in America as early as the 1870s and "Hebe comedians" devised trite Yiddish parodies at the turn of the century, not until the next decade did Eddie Cantor (1892–1964), Georgie Jessel (1898–1981), Sophie Tucker (1884–1966), Al Jolson (1886–1950), and Fanny Brice (1891–1951) begin infusing new life into ethnic song and jest. In crowded vaudeville and burlesque halls, primarily owned and operated by Jews, they catered to former Yiddish performers who mingled breezy Americanisms with racy Yiddishisms. These performers became comic universe changers, importing into one sphere an entire "universe of discourse with all sorts of associations from an entirely different sphere." Eddie Cantor, singing "Cohen Owes Me Ninety-Seven Dollars" and "Yiddle on Your Fiddle, Play Some Ragtime," Fanny Brice as Rosie Rosenstein performing "I'm an Indian" in a Yiddish accent, Al Jolson, the cantor's son in blackface, belting out "Mammy," and Sophie Tucker with her Yiddish and English tear-jerker, "My Yiddishe Mamma," capitalized on the rich humor of their hyphenated origins. Unashamed of being Jewish, they seasoned their acts with spicy Yiddish to amuse, not malign, their people. Fanny Brice's justification for her Jewish routines expressed their general attitude: "In anything Jewish I ever did, I wasn't standing apart, making fun of the race, and what happened to me on the stage is what could happen to them. They identified with me, and then it was all right to get a laugh, because they were laughing at me as well as at themselves." Many of these entertainers used Yiddish to establish an immediate intimacy with their Jewish audiences, to evoke the bittersweet experiences of a shared immigrant background. Later, Barbra Streisand would employ much the same techniques to endear herself to a wider, American audience as she brought Fanny Brice to the screen as *Funny Girl*. The Yiddish language's earthy expressions also brought the luminaries down to earth and briefly transformed them into commoners once again. As Irving Howe perceptively states, for "a Jolson or a Cantor, Yiddish had served as a kind of secret sign, a gleeful or desperate wave to the folks back home by a performer who liked it to be known that he was still a Jewish boy faithful to the old plebeian ways and the bracing street vulgarisms."

The female performers' use of Yiddish had a somewhat different effect, however. Fanny Brice's Yiddish accent in Irving Berlin's "Sadie Salome Go Home," the song of a clumsy Jewish girl eager to become a shimmy dancer, both differentiated her from more agile Gentile girls and underscored her ineptitude. Her enactment of Jewish ladies in distress, whose English was faulty as well, made her doubly vulnerable. She was still the oppressed greenhorn girl beneath her glamorous Ziegfeld Follies exterior. Sophie Tucker, on the other hand, used Yiddish, especially its four-letter vocabulary, to establish her sexual equality with men. In her off-color numbers she candidly expressed her sexual needs and destroyed the stereotype of the frigid Jewish woman. By being lascivious, she also violated the code of gentility observed by respectable Jewish women. But Tucker did not alienate her audience with her breaches of decency. Her Yiddish equivalents of foul language made her act more comic than shocking. It also enabled her more effectively to mask her hostility so she could mock men with impunity.

Whatever they might have been, Fanny Brice and Sophie Tucker were not Molly Picons. The use of Yiddish phrases, intonations, and character types was not a principal feature of their routines. According to June Sochen, feminist historian, "both Brice and Tucker ultimately used their femaleness rather than their Jewishness to make their enduring point, but their Jewish heritage surely added a deep and subtle layer to the meaning of vulnerability and the need to be assertive." This was also true of the Jewish male comedians of the same period. Their Jewishness was not the predominant trait of their theatrical personas, nor in their acts did they examine their Jewishness in any great depth. In blackface they facilely combined black spontaneity and Jewish sentimentality. As paleface vaudevillians, they rattled off innocuous Jewish jokes, related clever but uncomplicated dialect stories, improvised benignly comic skits of ethnic misunderstanding. Their chief distinction was the invention of themselves as stars, fired by the need to rise above their immigrant depths and sustained in the heights by their Jewish energy and talent. But theirs were not parochial Stars of David shining on one segment of the people, but the more worldly, show-biz variety illuminating the entire tribe. In the decade after World War II the Jewish comic appeared undisguisedly as a Jew. True of both a smiling Milton Berle and a seething Lenny Bruce, this later comic's "Jewishness," Anthony Lewis claims, "may embarrass, motivate or anger him, but the connection between performance and cultural background is clear to him, and, he assumes, the audience as well." Instead of hiding or subordinating his Jewish identity, he virtually advertised the fact.

Such uninhibited presentation of the Jew had been possible in the intimate quarters of a night-club stage. But such an uncamouflaged portrait of the Jew could not be the focal point in the beginnings of Jewish-American drama in, for example, the 1920s melting-pot plays of Elmer Rice. Just as the more established German Jewish community tried to suppress the early Yiddish theater for making "spectacles of themselves before all of New York," so the newly assimilated Eastern European Jews of the 1920s did not want Jewish-American dramatists to depict them as significantly different from their fellow Americans. Reinforcing their desire for a low dramatic profile were the passage in the same decade of the National Origins Act restricting immigration and an upsurge of anti-Semitism fomented by the Ku Klux Klan. Moreover, Broadway producers, knowing that drama evoking prejudice or battling it would be bad for business, backed only those plays that would not offend any sizable group. Thus, the most popular play of the times, the one that best kept the peace and the profits, was Gentile playwright Ann Nichol's *Abie's Irish Rose* (1922), the amiable comedy of Jewish and Irish star-crossed lovers and their feuding fathers. The Old World prejudices and exaggerated dialects of the stereotypical immigrant parents, Solomon Levy and Patrick Murphy, provide the engaging humor of the piece; the New World triumph of romantic love and brotherhood over religious clannishness—the blissful union of Abie and his

Irish Rose—contributes an even more winning sentimentality. To dispel any reservations about the appropriateness of intermarriage, Ann Nichols has two liberal clergymen, Father Whalen and Rabbi Jacob Samuels, give their respective blessings to the happy couple and try to gain their parents' approval. Assuming that all faiths and creeds are essentially the same, both clergymen express pleasure at the merging of customs and ceremonies in the young couple's home: "a Christmas tree in the parlor, kosher food in the cabinets, and a ham in the oven." But most important, the inflexibilities of Jewish tradition and Irish Catholicism have been eliminated and the goal of total assimilation achieved.

Had Elmer Rice (1892–1967), born Elmer Leopold Reizenstein, written plays about Jews significantly more subtle than the more obvious acculturation plays of an Ann Nichols, he would have been deemed illegitimate on the legitimate stage. Jules Chametzky tells us that Rice, rather than openly dramatizing the complexities of the Leo Frank case, the 1913 lynching in Atlanta of a northern Jew, treated the subject ten years afterward "in the more oblique and stylized expressionistic manner of *The Adding Machine* (1923)," depicting "the potential for mindless violence in the average man frustrated by forces beyond his comprehension." Even in Rice's less oblique Pulitzer Prize plays (e.g., the 1929 *Street Scene*), Jews appear as one of many minorities in a crowded urban tenement, a miniature United Nations of warring factions. Here the Kaplan family and their ethnic neighbors are powerless to prevent the domestic tragedy enacted before them— the murder of the oppressed Mrs. Maurrant and her milkman lover by her authoritarian, drunken husband.

Unlike the indifferent Irish, Italian, German, and Scandinavian witnesses of the event's prelude and aftermath, the Kaplans are more sympathetic choric figures, the more articulate armchair critics of American slum conditions that brutalize the individual. Yet despite their heartfelt condolences and perceptive social criticism, these Jews are not fully delineated. They are eclipsed by the street they inhabit—the kaleidoscopic setting for the sensational dramas of city life. Thus Rice's remark about his Jewish background, "I have never paraded my origin, but I have never tried to deny it," applies to the Jewish characters of *Street Scene* and his later plays *Counsellor-at-Law* (1931) and *Flight to the West* (1940). His protagonists are liberal intellectuals who accept the external world's designation of them as Jews, but they do not act the part with any distinctiveness.

Such ethnic blandness is not the case in Clifford Odets (1906–1963). His most celebrated play, *Awake and Sing!* (1935), is certainly America's best dramatic treatment of the Depression. Though Baird Shuman believes that "Odets will be remembered historically more as a proletarian playwright than as a Jewish playwright," nevertheless, he acknowledges that "[Odets's] background and upbringing imposed a Jewishness upon his work, a Hebrewtude," reflected in his use of theme, character, and language. Unlike other leftist dramatists, Odets did not write about the generalized proletariat but about the social class and institution he knew best: the Jewish bourgeois family. In one respect, he agrees with Jacob Berger, the Marxist grandfather in *Awake and Sing!* who wants to "abolish such families" since they breed selfishness and hypocrisy, stifle personal growth, destroy spiritual values. Yet Odets also admires the personal sacrifice the Jewish mother, Bessie Berger, makes for the economic survival of her family and the revolutionary zeal Jacob imparts to his grandson, inspiring him to improve the family of humankind.

Such a desire to better society at large is clearly Marxist, but it can also be traced to the universalist concerns of Judaism, for the title Odets chose to replace the original one of *I Got the Blues* is taken from Isaiah 26:19, which prophesies the resurrection of all peoples: "Awake and sing, ye that dwell in dust: for the dew is as the dew of herbs, and the earth shall cast out the dead." Thus, the Jewish prophetic tradition as well as Marxism were responsible for Odets's commitment to social reform in the thirties.

Such lofty biblical allusions lent depth to *Awake and Sing*'s thematic concerns, but the more earthy Yiddishized English gave the play its great vitality. Of its street-tough dialogue, Alfred Kazin appreciatively remarked: "In Odets's play there was a lyric uplifting of blunt Jewish speech, boiling over the explosive, that did more to arouse the audience than the political catch words that brought the curtain down." Odets's inimitable use of the ironic echoes of Old World Yiddish mingled with the sassy banter of New World colloquialism produced an original idiom for the theater. Unconcerned with correctness or the niceties of expression, brimming with raciness and impudence, this idiom enabled Odets to fashion a new Jewish literary style that subsequently induced Jewish-American fiction writers to take similar liberties with language.

However, the other two leading social dramatists who were Jewish, Lillian Hellman (1905–1984) and Arthur Miller (b. 1915), did not in the majority of their plays cultivate Odets's brand of "Yinglish," nor did they intentionally create recognizably Jewish characters. Their efforts to Americanize characters was due in large measure to the emergence of Hitler whose presence Henry Popkin believes had the following effect: "When Hitler forced Americans to take anti-Semitism seriously . . . the most eloquent reply that could be made was dead silence: the American answer to the banishment of Jews in public life in Germany was the banishment of Jewish figures from popular arts in the United States." Even in Lillian Hellman's two World War II plays, *Watch on the Rhine* (1941) and *The Searching Wind* (1944), there were no Jewish characters nor any direct reference to the persecution of the Jews. Her primary concern was to alert Americans to the encroaching evils of fascism, to rally impotent liberals to combat the powerful enemy in their midst.

Undoubtedly, Hellman's dramas were a response to the period's unwritten censorship of things Jewish in the arts. But they also seem to reflect her own anti-Jewish feelings. Her memoirs reveal that she wanted to banish objectionable Jews and Jewish traits from her life, and she apparently wanted to banish them from her plays as well. The notable exception to this is her adaptation, *My Mother, My Father and Me* (1963), where she focuses on the Jewish middle class but then with caustic humor indicts them for their hypocrisy and philistinism. In her original dramas, what she values most is the physical and emotional bravery of Gentiles, a kind of Hemingwayesque "grace under pressure," in contrast to the Jews in her life, whom she sees as unduly fearful and self-seeking. Thus Bonnie Lyons concludes that Hellman's "negative image of the Jew coupled with her Hemingwayesque world view suggests a flight from her own Jewishness."

Arthur Miller's attitude toward his Jewish heritage in his plays is more complex than Hellman's and more subject to change through the years. His earliest works of the 1930s, *Honors at Dawn* and *No Villain*, plays of social protest that he wrote as a student at the University of Michigan, are about a middle-class Jewish family in the Depression torn between principle and the need for profit. Miller, however, did not continue in this vein, for in his 1940s bid for Broadway, he, like Elmer Rice in the 1920s, sensed that the climate was unfavorable for homegrown ethnic

drama. Moreover, he himself did not want to be known as a producer of parochial stock; rather he aspired to be a great public playwright able to capture the essence of the generic American, the universal tragedy of the common man. The result, of course, was the rough-hewn *All My Sons* (1947) and the superbly crafted *Death of a Salesman* (1949), in which errant fathers struggling with self-righteous sons try to make "of the outside world a home." True to Miller's new ecumenicalism, the homes of Joe Keller and Willy Loman are purposely not identified as Jewish, nor do the family members reveal any specific religious or ethnic affiliation. For these omissions Miller was chastened not by a Jewish critic but by the Irish Catholic Mary McCarthy: "A disturbing aspect of the *Death of a Salesman* was that Willy Loman seemed to be Jewish, to judge by his speech cadences, but there was no mention of this on stage. He could not be Jewish because he had to be 'America,' which is not so much a setting as a big, amorphous idea: the puzzle for the audience . . . is to guess where these living rooms, roughly, are and who is living in them, which might make it possible to measure the plausibility of the action." Miller's reply to such a charge was that the themes of these particular plays did not require their characters to be Jewish. Who they were was not determined by their cultural or religious background.

He does concede, however, that two of his later plays, *Incident at Vichy* (1964), depicting the plight of Jews in Nazi-occupied France, and *The Price* (1968), with its comically sage Jewish appraiser of furniture and life, and, this writer would add, his 1980 television drama, "Playing for Time," based on Fania Fenelon's Auschwitz memoirs, and his semiautobiographical Depression play, *The American Clock* (1980), have Jewish characters in them because historical verisimilitude demands they be there. Moreover, the Jewish values they embody advance the complexities of meaning Miller intended for these works. Why he chose to write about these subjects at the particular time he did suggests another shift in his reaction to his own and the public's Jewish concerns. During the philo-Semitic 1960s, Leslie Fiedler insightfully describes the period as the "Judaization of American culture" when "Zion" became "Main Street." Miller, now the successful playwright, could afford in *The Price* to create a Gregory Solomon, the Jew as resilient survivor, and allow him to be the play's resident oracle. And America's belated confrontation with the

Holocaust gave Miller permission to tough-mindedly confront the subject in *Incident at Vichy* and later in "Playing for Time," where he intricately reveals the ambiguities of individual and collective guilt for the destruction of the Jews. But in all of these plays "ethics, not ethnicity," the Old Testament prophetic virtues of social responsibility and righteous conduct toward Jew and Gentile alike, are Miller's primary concern, for, according to Enoch Brater, Miller finds in "traditions more Judaic than Jewish the real conflicts he might still portray on stage."

The reverse is true of Paddy Chayefsky (1923–1981). In his Jewish-flavored dramas of the early sixties—*The Tenth Man* (1960) and *Gideon* (1962)—popularized ethnicity rather than probing ethics is the chief appeal for audiences yearning to recapture their vibrant immigrant pasts. In the fifties, such Broadway favorites as *The Fifth Season* (1953), *A Hole in the Heart* (1955), and *A Majority of One* (1959)—the last play an updated version of *Abie's Irish Rose*—had accustomed theatergoers to folksy comedies with sentimentalized stock characters, risibly mistaken uses of the English language, and implausibly optimistic endings. It, therefore, did not matter to audiences that *The Tenth Man*'s underlying theme was a rather hackneyed one (the healing powers of human love) as long as the play retained its amusing mixture of exotic Jewish mysticism, blatant satire of attenuated American Judaism, and the greenhorn vaudeville routines of the synagogue's elders. Similarly, theatergoers were not bothered that the thematic concerns of *Gideon*, Chayefsky's biblical drama, were more temporal than celestial. They were delighted that he transformed Jewish family members employing comic anachronism and ironic hindsight to win their arguments. However, the playful but facile reduction of profound theological issues in *Gideon* and the whimsical but simple formula for the renewal of religious faith and love in *The Tenth Man* moved Robert Brustein to dub Chayefsky "the Mahomet of Middle Seriousness." Yet he is a Mahomet with a large Jewish following, for Leslie Field maintains that Chayefsky "has produced Jewish drama as forthright, perceptive, and enjoyable as any written today in America."

Neil Simon (b. 1927) has an even larger following, perhaps because he injects urban angst, rather than Jewish "middle seriousness," into his plays. He is, for the most part, a nondenominational Pied Piper, who, with his fast-paced urban comedies, rescues people from their tedium-infested lives. When he does deal with recognizably Jewish types and topics, he unwittingly follows the same ingratiating practices that Gertrude Berg claimed made the Molly Goldberg radio and television shows so successful for 25 years. "You see, darling, I don't bring up anything that will bother people. . . . Unions, politics, fund-raising, Zionism, socialism, intergroup relations, I don't stress them. And, after all, aren't all such things secondary to daily family living? The Goldbergs are not defensive about their Jewishness, or especially aware of it. . . . I keep things average, I don't want to lose friends."

In short, Neil Simon does not "lose friends" with such Jewish-style comedies as *Come Blow Your Horn* (1961), *The Odd Couple* (1965), *The Sunshine Boys* (1973), *God's Favorite* (1974), or *Fools* (1981), although his highly acclaimed *Brighton Beach Trilogy* is every bit as much about "Jewishness" as it is about Jerome's coming of age as an artist.

Nonetheless, in the bulk of Simon's slickly written, slickly produced plays, Judaism usually takes the form of amusing eccentricities of character, language, and gastronomical preference. Be it Manhattan, Long Island, or Chelm, ethnically exaggerated modes of behavior are highlighted for humorous response, but there is no attempt to grapple with any Jewish issues that does not provide immediate comic relief. Simon's Jewish-seasoned comedies are often indistinguishable from his secular urban comedies, where conditions of residence take precedence over religious affiliation. Yet a critic such as Daniel Walden argues that though Simon is not a practicing Jew, certain of his plays are more than nominally Jewish, since his earliest, most formative "points of reference are to an upwardly mobile Jewish lower- and middle-class culture, politically and socially liberal." Or, as Lenny Bruce expressed it, "If you live in New York or any other big city, you are Jewish. It doesn't matter even if you're Catholic, if you live in New York, you're Jewish."

If we accept Bruce's equation of urban and religious origins, then the cabaret revues and full-length satires of lifelong New Yorker Jules Feiffer (b. 1929) are Jewish, though they lack explicitly Jewish themes. With their neurotic dread and defensive wit, their intellectual pretensions and schoolboy irreverence, their quick tempos and tempers, they are not much different from Neil Simon's brand of predictable urban comedies. Both are producers of what some see in the sixties and seventies as the waning of minority culture and the waxing of an American mass culture absorbing all of its distinctiveness. Yet others claim that the highly ethnic metropolitan context in which these plays are written rather than their specific content is what makes them Jewish, if only through association. In Jules Feiffer's cartoons and in their stage metamorphosis in such works as *Crawling Arnold* (1961), *Little Murders* (1967), *Grownups* (1974), and *Knock Knock* (1976), there is an unmistakably Jewish ambiance derived in part from the larger world of the popular arts, many of whose creators are Jewish. Though Feiffer has not demonstrably pledged allegiance to Judaism in his life or works, Stephen Whitfield finds that his "satiric animus, his leftist perspective, his urban irony and his psychoanalytic spirit help give his work a Jewish component in the sense that a Jew is most likely to have created it."

The Last Analysis (1965) the only full-length play of Nobel Laureate Saul Bellow (b. 1915) is also endowed with "urban irony" and the "psychoanalytic spirit," but there is no doubt a Jew created it. While his play does not possess his novels' subtle interplay of Jewish and American values or their rich humor of verbal retrieval, it does present a convincing depiction of another of his "suffering joker" heroes: Philip Bummidge, ex-television comedian. Like Tommy Wilhelm (*Seize the Day*) and Moses Herzog (*Herzog*)—the suffering jokers of Bellow's fiction—Bummidge makes a career of his problems and is compulsively funny as a way of enduring his wretched circumstances, but as he ruefully acknowledges: "When the laughter stops, there's still a big surplus of pain." A clown driven to being a theoretician, Bummidge is another of Bellow's visionary creatures who, disappointed with his fallibility, strives to become a mensch, a person of substance. But his Jewish family stands in the way of his self-improvement. In this respect the generational conflicts of *The Last Analysis* resemble those of *Awake and Sing!*, since Bummidge, like Jacob Berger, struggles to become "drenched with new meaning" despite his money-hungry family's clamoring that he be content with the old meaning. Though Berger's god is Marx and Bummidge's is Freud, they each adopt one exclusive metaphor for salvation and the interpretation of experience that ultimately isolates them from society. Jacob Berger commits suicide, and Bummidge retreats from the predatory world to his platonic academy. The fact that Bummidge severs ties with his associates and "ends up alone, like the American cowboy with a sidekick or two," makes Keith Opdahl initially think that *The Last Analysis* is a "notably Jewish play." But, on second thought, he considers that Bummidge's case of "humanities," his inability to tolerate other people, may be the "personal or emotional equivalent to the very real Jewish ambivalence about assimilation," for to affiliate with a larger group is to risk forfeiting one's identity. Therefore, Bummidge in his hermetic Institute of Nonsense may be alienated from the Jewish community, but he is all-consumed with his psychoanalysis, that Jewish talking science wherein the most profound conversations are with oneself. Unfortunately, the critics did not regard these conversations as terribly profound. *The Last Analysis* closed after 28 performances on Broadway.

The inability of one Nobel Laureate to shift gears adroitly from the fictional to the theatrical and have a long-running production did not prevent another American Nobel Laureate, the Yiddish writer Isaac Bashevis Singer (b. 1904), from creating, at age 68, his own vehicles for the stage. Foreign in appearance and antiquated in design, Singer's plays were not manufactured from their raw materials but were, with the help of collaborators, adaptations of his short stories and children's tales. Singer, however, was not the first to provide English adaptations of Yiddish literature for the American theater. In the fifties and sixties, Jewish-American dramatists, mourning the irrevocable loss of Yiddish-speaking Jews and their *shtetl* folkways, felt compelled to recapture their unique qualities and give them theatrical permanence. Since Sholom Aleichem was considered the most endearing chronicler of this quaint past, his stories became the primary source of Arnold Perl's *The World of Sholom Aleichem* (1953) and *Tevya and His Daughters* (1957) as well as the enormously successful musical version of the Tevya stories, Joseph Stein's *Fiddler on the Roof* (1964). These works ostensibly offered an intimate view of familiar Jews within their confining but accustomed quarters who, despite poverty and persecution, had a durable sense of humor and an abiding faith in God.

But a close reading of Sholom Aleichem's original stories and historical accounts of the *shtetl* reveals that these Broadway versions greatly sentimentalized Jewish life in pre-Holocaust Eastern Europe and provided what audiences wanted: heartwarming stories about close-knit, tradition-bound families who triumph over adversity. The *shtetl* of Isaac Bashevis Singer's dramas, by contrast, is not idealized. Though his fictional treatment of it departs from strict realism, his is an authentic depiction of its more sordid and anguished side. And since he is the principal adapter of his stories for the theater, his plays derived from his firsthand knowledge of the *shtetl* are certainly more authentic than those by American-born adapters produced almost a century later.

Particularly in Singer's stage verson of *Yentl* (1974), he accurately reveals the unalterable religious context of nineteenth-century Polish Jewry and captures the inner torment of a young woman forced to choose between the illicit study of sacred texts and the lawful performance of wifely duties. To lend ready-made depth to commonplace scenes, Singer also incorporates eloquent orthodox rituals, yet shocks us by employing them to commemorate unorthodox events, such as the marriage ceremony uniting two women.

What Singer has said about his participation in the theater, therefore, applies even more strongly to the cinema's appropriation of his art: "I like art to be pure. A book is written by one man. In the theater you have too many partners— the director, the producer, the actors, the writers. In a way it is already a collective." Even though the cinema's "collective" is sure to have its Jewish members, there is no guarantee the Jewish quality of Singer's work will retain its full strength.

In both the stage (1955) and film versions (1959) of *The Diary of Anne Frank* and *The Wall*, for example, Lawrence Langer states that "the American vision of the Holocaust . . . continued to insist that millions have not died in vain, trying to parlay hope, sacrifice, justice, and the future into a victory that will mitigate despair." Like Anne Frank, these versions led audiences to believe that "people are really good at heart." Yet Frank's ultimate destruction belies such affirmation. In the course of the play, however, they deleted the somber knowledge that an innocent young girl and countless like her were killed simply because they were Jewish. Such a dark truth Broadway and Hollywood were unwilling to convey.

On the other hand, recent plays such as the revival of Jerome Weidman's *I Can Get It For You Wholesale* (1962) and Jerry Sterner's *Other People's Money* (1980) suggest that negative Jewish stereotyping is no longer as threatening, as taboo, as it once had been. Moreover, plays with distinctive— and authentic—Jewish content such as Barbara Lebow's *Shaina Maidel* (1985) and Israel Horo-

vitz's trilogy (*Today, I am a Fountain Pen*, *A Rosen by any Other Name*, and *The Chopin Playoffs*, 1987) continue to be produced off-off Broadway, at the Jewish Repertory Company and at institutions such as the 92nd Street YMHA—all of which suggests that the prognosis for a vibrant Jewish-American theater is richer than many might have supposed. *See also* Comics and Comedy; Theater, Yiddish; Vaudeville.

SARAH BLACHER COHEN

BIBLIOGRAPHY

Boardman, Gerald. *The Oxford Companion to American Theatre*. New York: Oxford University Press, 1984.

Cohen, Sarah Blacher, ed. *From Hester Street to Hollywood*. Bloomington: Indiana University Press, 1983.

Kolin, Philip C., ed. *American Playwrights Since 1945*. Westport, Conn.: Greenwood Press, 1989.

Sochen, June. *Consecrate Everyday: The Public Lives of Jewish American Women, 1880–1980*. Modern Jewish History Series. New York: State University of New York Press, 1981.

———. *Enduring Values: Women in Popular Culture*. Westport, Conn.: Greenwood Press, 1987.

Theater, Yiddish. The Yiddish theater was the great cultural passion of the immigrant Jewish community in the United States. It was the theater, Harold Clurman noted in 1968, that "even more than the synagogue or the lodge, became the meeting place and the forum of the Jewish community in America between 1888 and the early 1920s."

The Yiddish theater was a new phenomenon in Jewish life. It came into being in 1876 in Jassy, Romania, and arrived in New York six years later. This novel form of entertainment quickly took hold; within less than a decade, New York turned into the undisputed world capital of the Yiddish stage. Supported by a constantly growing Yiddish-speaking immigrant population (nearly 3.5 million Jews settled in the United States between 1881 and 1925), the New York Yiddish rialto was brimming with energy. It produced celebrated stars, generated a wealth of dramatic material, and presented a rich spectrum of productions ranging from sentimental melodramas and quasi-historical operettas to sophisticated experiments inspired by the latest trends of the European, particularly the Russian, stage.

Although always in the hands of private entrepreneurs, the American Yiddish theater was a genuine people's institution insofar as its appeal was not limited to any one socioeconomic group. It was attended by rich and poor, educated and illiterate, observant and free-thinking. Statistical data attests to its popularity. In 1927, two years after mass immigration had reached a virtual halt, there were 24 Yiddish theaters across America, 11 of them in New York, 4 in Chicago, 3 in Philadelphia, and 1 each in Baltimore, Boston, Cleveland, Detroit, Los Angeles, Newark, and St. Louis. Some 10 years later, during the 1937–1938 season, when the Yiddish theater in America was well past its prime, it was estimated that 1.75 million tickets to Yiddish shows were sold in New York City alone. Such sales meant that every Yiddish-speaking adult in the city saw an average of more than three Yiddish shows per year, an impressive figure unmatched by any other ethnic group in America.

In order to understand the development of the Yiddish theater in the United States, however, it is imperative to consider its East European roots. Professional entertainment, even on a modest scale, was introduced into Jewish life only after secularization and urbanization had begun to change traditional Jewish life. Music was the only performing art for which Jews could boast of having skilled personnel. Music also provoked the least protest because of its nonrepresentational character. Hence, it was only natural that the earliest modern Jewish performers were itinerant minstrels. The first such group, the Broder Zinger, originated, as its name indicates, in the Polish town of Brody. By the mid-nineteenth century, its members began to travel across the towns and villages of Eastern Europe, presenting their comic songs and ballads to working-class audiences. As this kind of entertainment became popular, the number of such musicians increased. Some began to introduce bits of dialogue and to use some makeup and props to add continuity and dramatic flavor to their musical numbers.

These rudimentary theatrics finally evolved into a cohesive, albeit crude, performance in 1876, when Abraham Goldfaden (1840–1908), a Russian intellectual known for his popular tunes and lyrics, joined forces with Israel Gradner, a Broder singer performing in a Jassy tavern on the eve of the Russo-Turkish War. Goldfaden imposed a simple dramatic framework on Gradner's musical material and created a genre that has been compared to Italian commedia dell'arte because it combined a fixed scenario with improvised dialogue and stage business. The successful Goldfaden enlarged the troupe and began to produce full-fledged musical plays, some of which—*The Witch* (1879), *The Two Kuni Lemls* (1880) and *Shulamith* (1880)—have become classics of the Jewish stage and have been frequently revived in the original as well as in Hebrew and English translations. Known as the Father of the Yiddish Theater, Goldfaden was a man of many talents who produced, wrote, composed, directed, and designed the sets of his own productions. However, in a world of wandering troupes with little regard for copyright laws, he also suffered from his own phenomenal success: actors who were initiated into the stage by him, including Gradner, frequently opted to leave the master's majestic rule and to found their own competing traveling companies whose main repertoire consisted of Goldfaden's original plays.

In 1883, following the assassination of Czar Alexander II, the Russian government proclaimed a series of anti-Jewish laws, including the prohibition of Yiddish theatrical productions, throughout the Russian empire. Because anti-Semitism and the depressed economic conditions that afflicted Jewish communities in other East European countries were not conducive to theatrical activity, the young actors and fledgling playwrights of the new Yiddish stage joined the great migration to the West. London became the new, though temporary, center of the Yiddish stage.

Unfortunately, the poor immigrant community of the East End could not support this influx of Jewish thespians. The latter were also hampered by the fierce opposition of the Anglo-Jewish establishment and by the strict fire-safety rules of the municipal authorities. The freedom to flourish without such constraints was to be found in the Golden Land, particularly in New York, soon to become the largest Jewish urban center in the world.

It was, perhaps, the good fortune of Leon and Miron Golubok and their troupe to have left Russia and to have been stranded in London in 1882, before the influx of better-known actors began. They were also lucky to have a brother, Abe Golubok, who had already settled in New York. The American Golubok and a co-worker in the same cigar factory, an ambitious youth named Boris Tomashefsky (1868/1866?–1939) persuaded Frank Wolf, the proprietor of a downtown saloon, to become the first Yiddish impresario and to finance the importation of the Golubok troupe to New York. The company, consisting of four men and two women, arrived in the city in the summer of 1882. On August 12, assisted by local talent and featuring the young Tomashefsky, the actors premiered with Goldfaden's popular musical, *The Witch*. The performance at Turn Hall, 66 East Fourth Street, started late and ended in disaster. Tomashefsky, who some years later became a matinee idol of the Yiddish theater, offered in his memoirs (1935) a glamorized version of the event, including attempted sabotage by uptown German Jews. It seems, however, that the performance left no imprint on the life of the community, and its importance is primarily that of an historic first.

Toward the end of 1882, the group signed a lease to play weekends at the Old Bowery Garden, a narrow beer hall with a small stage usually devoted to American vaudeville. The Yiddish shows were presented regularly on Friday nights and Saturday matinees, offering mostly Goldfaden's popular operettas and the early plays written by Nokhem Meyer Shomer-Shaikevitch (1849–1905), one of the first Yiddish playwrights to utilize Goldfaden's formula, though with considerably less talent. The company also presented two plays written by one of its actors, Israel Barsky, whose business card identified him as "Tailor, actor and playwright. Author of *The Spanish Inquisition*. Pants altered and pressed." It is interesting to note that in the absence of a centralized rabbinate, there was no opposition to performances conducted on Saturday; even Orthodox spectators frequented the theater on that day. However, no stage business that could be regarded as a violation of the holy day took place on stage: sealed envelopes arrived miraculously open, cigarettes were not lit, and all lights were turned on in advance before the performance began.

In 1883, plagued by financial problems and personal feuds, the company split into two theater groups. The Goluboks and their people stayed at the Old Bowery Garden, and Tomashefsky, joined by his two sisters and his entrepreneurial father, Pesach, leased the National, a theater on the Bowery near Grand Street. Neither fared well; the arrival in 1883 of a professional group from London, one with nine experienced actors as well as its own playwright, forced the Goluboks to move to Chicago and the Tomashefskys had to retreat for the next three years to Philadelphia.

In 1886, another major company that boasted some of the most brilliant stars of the Yiddish theater arrived in New York. Among the newcomers were comedian Sigmund Mogulseco (1858–1914) and the dramatic actors David Kessler (1860–1920) and Sigmund Feinman (1862–1909). A year later Jacob P. Adler (1855–1926) and Keni Liptzin (1856–1918) left for New York, as did Abraham Goldfaden, who hoped to capitalize on his fame and to take the town by storm. Failing in their attempts, Adler and Goldfaden returned to Europe. Adler was invited back to New York in 1890; he became the greatest dramatic actor of the Yiddish stage. Goldfaden returned to New York in 1902, a somewhat pathetic figure whose livelihood depended on the regular support of Tomashefsky and Adler. In 1907, shortly before his death, the old master was vindicated when his play, *Ben Ami*, produced by Tomashefsky, proved to be one of the hits of the season.

The fierce competition between the early two companies created a heavy demand for new scripts. Two prolific dramatists who virtually monopolized the young Yiddish stage were Joseph Lateiner (1853–1937) and "professor" Moshe Hurwitz (1884–1910). Lateiner, who originally came to the United States in 1884 as the prompter of the Karp-Silberman company, wrote some 150 plays. Hurwitz was equally prolific; he had arrived with the Romanian troupe in 1887 and served as its dramatist.

Lateiner and Hurwitz specialized in quasi-historical extravaganzas, heart-wrenching melodramas, and *tsaybilder*, spectacles depicting recent events of national or sensational significance. Their plays, a hodgepodge of tragedy, comedy, music, and spectacle, were filled with plagiarized scenes and historical inaccuracies. Nonetheless, on stage they offered the immigrants an escape from their drab existence and an entry into a magical world of glamour, turbulence, passion, and fantasy.

The scripts were mostly derivative. They either Judaized classic and current dramas, like Shakespeare's or Ibsen's, or padded original plots with scenes lifted from other sources. It is significant that nearly every play included some traditional religious ritual, such as the lighting of the Sabbath candles, a wedding ceremony, or the recitation of a well-known prayer. The theatrical enactment of these traditional rituals touched the community's nostalgic nerve, its collective yearning for the Old Country and the life it had left behind. These scenes remained an integral part of the Yiddish theater well into the 1930s.

The actors who performed in these early plays delivered their lines in *daytshmerish*, a Germanized Yiddish deemed more eloquent and more suitable to the stage. Their acting style was operatic, namely, broad, intense, with an energetic display of temperament. Often working with an unfinished script and learning a new part every two weeks, the actors took the liberty of improvising, introducing lines from other plays, and interpolating song-and-dance numbers that bore no relation to the plot.

The Yiddish stars soon became the royalty of the Lower East Side. They elicited a unique sort of adoration, and the characters they played were a major topic of discussion and controversy. This popular sentiment reached fanatic proportions with the *patriyotn*, avid fans of a specific star who regularly crowded the gallery, clapping their hands enthusiastically at whatever their favorite star did or said. It has been suggested that these devotees continued the tradition of the Hasidic followers crowding at their rabbi's court.

The grandeur of the stage was not reflected in the auditorium, whose atmosphere resembled that of an outdoor marketplace: peddlers promoted their wares, and spectators chewed apples, shelled peanuts, and popped bottles of soda both during and after the intermission.

The burgeoning intellectual circles looked down at the theaters as circuses and labeled their plays *shund*, mainly trash. Influenced by the new European theater, they wanted their Yiddish Shaw and Ibsen. Jacob Gordin (1853–1909), a Russified intellectual with no previous ties to the Yiddish stage, became their torchbearer and idol. Gordin came to the United States in 1891 with the *Am Olam* movement, which had been greatly influenced by the ideas of Tolstoyan socialism. He accidentally met Jacob P. Adler, who voiced his dissatisfaction with the repertoire of the Yiddish theater. Adler was looking for plays of greater literary value; not a song-and-dance man, he sought strong dramatic roles. Gordin wrote his first play, *Siberia*, for Adler. Its 1891 premiere marked the beginning of a new phase in the history of the Yiddish theater.

Gordin rejected escapist spectacles in favor of a realistic mode, the prevailing style of the European stage. He had serious literary aspirations and fought bitterly with actors to convince them to deliver his lines as written, and to omit their customary "shticks" and improvisations.

Gordin's plays, which did away with *daytshmerish* and which employed a more natural language, were successes. Gordin was recognized as an innovator and as the leading playwright of the Yiddish theater. His 18-year career was named the Gordin Era, also known as the Golden Epoch of the Yiddish theater in America.

Gordin, a social activist and former teacher, utilized the stage as a didactic forum. In his plays, playlets, and translations, he focused on issues relevant to American Jewish life. In *The Jewish King Lear* (1892) and *Mirele Efros* (1898), he tackled the painful subject of intergenerational estrangement; in *God, Man and the Devil* (1900), he criticized the manic pursuit of the almighty dollar; in *The Kreutzer Sonata* (1902), he dealt with the subject of women's emancipation. Gordin's plays, essentially domestic melodramas, became classics of the Yiddish theater and are still periodically revived.

One of the greatest playwrights of the later Yiddish stage, David Pinski, noted that Gordin did not write plays, but parts. Indeed, the more ambitious actors of the early Yiddish stage quickly recognized Gordin's plays as effective star vehicles and were often eager to perform in them. Four actors were closely associated with Gordin's repertoire: Jacob P. Adler, the most revered dramatic actor of his generation; David Kessler, who excelled in portraying simple characters; Keni Liptzin, nicknamed the Yiddish Eleonora Duse; and Bertha Kalish, a romantic prima donna.

Gordin's success encouraged more Yiddish writers to devote their energy to the theater. Leon Kobrin (1872–1946) tried to follow in Gordin's footsteps and wrote the first plays that offered a realistic portrayal of Jewish life in America. His 20 plays were full of melodrama and vaudevillian elements, yet were instrumental as a stepping stone for the introduction of meritorious literary plays.

Following the successful reception of Gordin's and Kobrin's plays, the star managers began to produce a more gutsy repertoire. Adler and Kessler staged plays by Sholem Asch; Adler and Tomashefsky produced plays by Sholem Aleichem; and Bertha Kalish introduced I. L. Peretz's plays to the American Yiddish stage.

According to historian Moses Rischin, the four major Yiddish theaters—the Thalia, the Windsor, the People's, and the Grand—presented 1100 performances annually during the turn of the century, for an estimated audience of 2 million patrons. The theaters, all in the Bowery area, were a far cry from the modest halls of the 1880s. The

Thalia was a 3000-seat house devoted to more literary plays; it often featured David Kessler and Keni Liptzin. The Grand, managed by Jacob Adler, was the second house devoted to so-called "better theater." Specifically built for Yiddish shows, it opened in 1903 and seated 2000. The Windsor opened in 1893. With 3500 seats, it was the largest playhouse devoted to popular plays, particularly those by Hurwitz. The People's had a 2500-seat capacity and was leased by Tomashefsky in 1900. It housed the greatest Yiddish hit of its day, Tomashefsky's *Dos Pintele Yid* (The Jewish Essence, 1907), a magnificent spectacle that ran for an entire season and was seen by tens of thousands of people.

The four theaters employed a repertory system, which meant that various plays from their repertoire were presented during the week, usually to theater parties. To attract a mid-week audience, they offered "benefits," i.e., discount sale of an entire performance to volunteer organizations. The organization, in turn, sold the tickets to their members at full price, and the particular charitable and/or social cause benefitted from the proceeds.

The theaters' current hits were presented on the weekend at regular box office prices, ranging from 25 cents to $1. Hutchins Hopgood noted in 1902 that many who earned $10 per week were willing to spend half of their income on the theater, virtually the only amusement available to the immigrant Yiddish-speaking Jew.

Like its English-language counterpart, Yiddish theater enjoyed an economic boom during World War I. Money poured into the box office, and the theaters offered increasingly lavish shows, often at the expense of the more literary repertoire whose popularity was waning after Gordin's death. After the United States entered the war, the Yiddish stage was full of patriotic musicals, with such titles as *Jewish War Brides*, *Orphans of the World*, and *Jewish Martyrs of America*.

The prosperity, on the one hand, and the decline of the Bowery area, on the other, led to the formation of a new Yiddish theater district on Second Avenue. On the avenue, between Houston and Fourteenth streets, stood the Yiddish flagship theaters and related businesses, such as music, flower, and photography stores, costume houses, and several restaurants and cafes, the most famous of which was the Cafe Royal, the legendary meeting place of the theatrical crowd. The first Yiddish theaters to open on this "Yiddish Broadway" were the Second Avenue Theater

(1911), a 1986-seat house built especially for David Kessler, and the National (1912), a 2000-seat house built for Tomashefsky. Both were elegant theaters that cost nearly $1 million each. The opening ceremonies of these playhouses were important social events attended by an array of dignitaries, including the mayor of New York. The last two theaters to open on the avenue were completed in 1926—Maurice Schwartz's 1236-seat Yiddish Art Theater, and the Public, a 1752-seat house. Both were elegant structures that attested to the social mobility of their patrons.

Second Avenue was synonymous with the great stars of the popular theater of the 1920s and 1930s. The first lady of the musical stage was Molly Picon, introduced to American audiences in 1923 as "the greatest sensation from Europe." Other big names in musical comedy were Menasha Skulnik, Herman Yablokoff, Aaron Lebedeff, Ludwig Satz, and Mikhel Mikhalesco. Jennie Goldstein was the queen of Yiddish melodramatic musical spectacles.

Despite the enormous popularity of these stars, the postwar period was associated, first and foremost, with the art theater movement. The movement, in turn, was brought about by the young, relatively un-Americanized post-1905 immigrants, many of whom were radicals with a serious relation to culture, particularly to literature and drama. Many of these culturally oriented workers had become familiar in Russia with amateur dramatic groups whose goal was to improve the folksy ways of the Yiddish theater. Out of this tradition emerged the semiprofessional troupe, established in 1905 by Peretz Hirshbein. It is credited as the first art theater of the Yiddish stage.

Upon their arrival in America, many young immigrants joined amateur dramatic clubs. Soon the clubs proliferated, and in 1917, they tried unsuccessfully to form an umbrella organization. One of the major clubs in this "better theater" movement was New York's Hebrew Dramatic League, which, in 1915, became the drama section of the Workmen's Circle fraternal organization. The league changed its name to *Fraye Yidishe Folksbine* (the Free Yiddish People's Stage). Its first production was Ibsen's *Enemy of the People*. In 1918, the Folksbine produced *Green Fields* by Peretz Hirshbein. The production's success went beyond expectation, and some regard its premiere as marking the birth of the Yiddish art theater. Inadvertently, the production also served as a touchstone, and it proved to Maurice

Schwartz (1890–1960), who had recently opened his Irving Place Theater, the existence of new audiences who were looking for a new sort of theater.

Maurice Schwartz, producer, director, actor, and occasional playwright, was a powerhouse of a man who, more than anyone else, defined the shape of the artistic Yiddish theater in America during the 1920s and 1930s. In 1918, the young Schwartz took over the Irving Place Theater, hired Jacob Ben-Ami, the finest young actor of the Yiddish stage, and other known actors such as Celia Adler and Bertha Gerstein. Schwartz was persuaded by Ben-Ami, a serious actor committed to the principles of the modern European theater, to offer a modest production of Hirshbein's play *Forsaken Nook*. The 1918 production made theatrical history. The play and its mode of production were a complete reversal of the customary bravura of the Yiddish stage. Simple and modest, it was captivating in its tenderness.

The Yiddish art theater replaced traditional Yiddish acting with Stanislavsky's psychological realism. It was not, however, committed to one particular theatrical style. Schwartz was not a theatrical thinker, but he was greatly interested in new theatrical forms. In the 1920s, he was willing to risk box-office proceeds to produce lavish modernistic shows, such as the constructivist production of Goldfaden's *The Tenth Commandment* (1926), designed by Boris Aronson.

The Yiddish art theater's greatest success was *Yoshe Kalb* (1932), a dramatization of I. J. Singer's popular novel. The enormous success of this domestic melodrama had an adverse impact on the future of the theater. Playing for an entire season, it destroyed the theater's repertory system and made Schwartz eager to cash in on its reputation by touring extensively. The Yiddish art theater that returned to New York in the late 1930s did not regain its adventurous spirit, though it continued to be considered New York's primary Yiddish theater.

Among other innovative and noteworthy theaters of the period was the Unzer Teater (Our Theater), which opened in 1925 in a small Bronx playhouse. Playwrights David Pinski, Peretz Hirshbein, and H. Leivick were involved in its formation, but the group could not maintain itself economically for more than one season. The Shildkraut Theater, organized a year later, was forced to close for a similar reason. The 1930s saw more of the same phenomena—groups formed, presented one or two noteworthy pro-

ductions, and then disbanded for lack of financial resources.

The one small art theater that thrived during the 1930s was the Artef Theater. Originally a group of amateurs affiliated with the American Yiddish Communist movement, the Artef was greatly influenced by the Russian avant-garde of the 1920s. Directed by Benno Schneider, possibly the best and most innovative director working on the American Yiddish stage, the Artef developed a unique style characterized by a measure of stylization and genuine ensemble work. The Artef gradually professionalized itself and, in 1934, moved to a small Broadway house, far removed from the downtown Yiddish rialto. Despite its successful shows and community-based support, the Artef suspended operation in 1937 for lack of funds. It reopened for the 1938–1939 season, after which it closed permanently.

It was the tragic misfortune of the Yiddish theater in America that during the 1930s, when it reached its highest artistic level, it was losing its hold on the masses. The decline in attendance was an irreversible process. Jewish immigration to the United States was at an all-time low, averaging 7000 per year. The foreign-born became more acculturated, and as the number of American-born Jews increased, Yiddish gradually and consistently lost its status as the primary language of the American Jewish community.

The Yiddish theater continued to hang on. As the theater season became increasingly short and as the elegant playhouses were abandoned, the actors, aging with their audiences, began to tour the Jewish communities around the world, and became a twentieth-century variation of the itinerant players of the century before. By the 1960s the Yiddish theater was no longer a viable phenomenon, and sporadic efforts to revive it tended to be amateurish and short-lived. The curtain had come down on a major chapter in Jewish creativity.

EDNA NAHSHON

BIBLIOGRAPHY

Hapgood, Hutchins. *The Spirit of the Ghetto.* Cambridge: Belknap Press of Harvard University Press, 1967.

Howe, Irving. *World of Our Fathers.* New York: Harcourt Brace Jovanovich, 1976.

Lifson, David S. *The Yiddish Theatre in America.* Cranbury, N.J.: Yoseloff, 1965.

———. "Yiddish Theatre." In *Ethnic Theater in the United States.* Edited by Maxine S. Seller. Westport, Conn.: Greenwood Press, 1983.

Rosenfeld, Lulla. *Bright Star of Exile: Jacob Adler and the Yiddish Theatre.* New York: Crowell, 1977.

Sanders, Ronald. *The Downtown Jews.* New York: Harper & Row, 1969.

Sandrow, Nahma. *Vagabond Stars, a World History of Yiddish Theater.* New York: Harper & Row, 1977.

Touro Synagogue. Newport, Rhode Island's Touro Synagogue, originally named Yeshuath Israel, was founded in 1759 and dedicated in 1763. Although it was not the first synagogue built in the United States, it is the oldest still standing. It has always been and remains a congregational synagogue.

Early Jewish immigrants in America did not build synagogues and formally join congregations until the 1700s; the only synagogue that dated to the seventeenth century was in New York City. In 1759, members of the Newport Jewish community wrote to members of New York's Shearith Israel asking for their financial help in building a synagogue. The members of Shearith Israel held a fund raiser during Passover, and the money raised was used to begin building Yeshuath Israel.

Touro Synagogue was designed by Paul Harrison, a Newport architect. Harrison used an English Georgian style. The synagogue sits diagonally on its plot so that the worshippers face Jerusalem. Originally, the synagogue was Sephardic in both ritual and design. The building has a women's gallery, the reader's table faces the ark, and the congregation sits on either side. One of the most unusual features is the trap door under the reader's table that leads to an escape tunnel. Many of the founders came from Spain and Portugal, and they remembered the Inquisition. Writers speculate that this "escape route" was a reminder of the times when practicing Judaism was illegal and religious observances had to be kept secret.

The first hazan (reader) of the congregation was Isaac Touro. He and his sons, Abraham and Judah, were very generous to the new synagogue. Judah Touro eventually moved to New Orleans, Louisiana, where he opened a store. He donated his money generously to his country, his people, and the synagogue at Newport. As a result, Yeshuath Israel became widely known as Touro Synagogue. President Harry S Truman proclaimed the Touro Synagogue a National Historic shrine in 1947.

LINDA GLAZER

BIBLIOGRAPHY

Kenvin, Helen Schwartz. *This Land of Liberty.* New York: Behrman House, 1986.

Klaperman, Gilbert and Libby. *The Story of the Jewish People.* Vol. 4. New York: Behrman House, 1961.

Raphael, Marc Lee. *Profiles in American Judaism—The Reform, Conservative, Orthodox and Reconstructionist Traditions in Historical Perspective.* San Francisco: Harper & Row, 1984.

Trilling, Lionel (1905–1975). Literary critic, educator, and author, Lionel Trilling published his first critical study, *Matthew Arnold,* in 1939, a product of his doctoral thesis at Columbia University a year before. Arnold, the famous Victorian literary and social critic and poet, influenced Trilling to relate literary criticism to general ideas and to maintain a scholarly disinterestedness, not committing oneself uncritically to any political program. Trilling followed this work with a study of the British novelist E. M. Forster in 1943, which helped affirm Forster's reputation. But the work that brought Trilling his widest recognition was *The Liberal Imagination* (1950), his first collection of essays, a probing examination, especially as manifested in literature, of liberalism and radicalism, dominant traditions in American thought and letters in the 1930s and 1940s. A liberal himself, Trilling, like Arnold before him, pointed to the rigidities or stereotypes of the liberal tradition. He wrote in the Preface: "The job of criticism would seem to me, then, to recall liberalism to its first essential imagination of variousness and possibility, which implies the awareness of complexity and difficulty." Later, he manifested little sympathy for the neoradicalism of the 1960s. Therefore, it might be said that Trilling was an initiator of the neoconservative movement, prominent among many American Jewish writers and intellectuals, in the 1970s and 1980s.

His only novel, *The Middle of the Journey* (1947), though lacking in vitality as fiction, interests as a novel of ideas. It attempts to undermine the simplistic attitudes of Communist Party members and fellow travelers living in New York before World War II. At the same time, it deplores the conversion of Stalinists into reactionaries, exchanging one set of dogmas for another.

His later collections of essays, including *The Opposing Self* (1955) and *Beyond Culture* (1965), though diverse in subject matter, are unified around the theme of the opposing claims of self and culture. This theme—important in the conforming 1950s and the rebellious 1960s—pertains to the difficulty of maintaining a cherishable personal identity in a culture directed toward ends more and more socialized and standards more and more external. Much in American life is good and must be acknowledged, but much is destructive of selfhood. Trilling finds the solution to this dilemma in Freud's *Civilization and Its Discontents*: acquiescence to society is a tragic necessity. He writes: "We do well to accept it, although we also do well to cast a cold eye on the fate that makes it our better part to accept it."

His last work, *Sincerity and Authenticity* (1972), is a masterful sketch, ranging over four centuries, of the history of the idea of the authenticity or sincerity of self, threatened, on the one hand, by the burden of social forces and, on the other, by a rejection of society that borders on and even becomes madness.

Trilling was a native son of New York City. His parents were David W. and Fannie Cohen Trilling. He was educated in the city and earned his undergraduate and graduate degrees at Columbia University. Before getting his doctorate, he contributed, beginning in 1923, stories and reviews to the *Menorah Journal* and other periodicals, taught at the University of Wisconsin and Hunter College, and then began a long career as instructor and professor at Columbia. In 1929, he married Diana Rubin, known later for her critical writings as Diana Trilling. During this earlier period, he worried over the ambiguous role of the Jewish teacher in an academic area, English literature, which had been traditionally non-Jewish. He later wrote: "When I decided to go into academic life, my friends thought me naive to the point of absurdity, nor were they wholly wrong—my appointment to an instructorship in Columbia College was pretty openly regarded as an experiment, and for some time my career in the College was complicated by my being Jewish." Somewhat ironically, he was to be laden with academic honors toward the end of his career.

His early stories, usually with an academic background, such as "Impediments" (1925) and "Notes on a Departure" (1929), as well as, indirectly, his later and best story, "Of This Time, Of That Place" (1943), suggest that Trilling rejected the idea of assimilation, though the time was not ripe for the Jewish assertiveness of such later scholars as Harold Bloom and Geoffrey H. Hartman. In Trilling's later essays, his interest in Judaism reveals itself in his brilliant essay on Isaac

Babel (1955), pointing to the Soviet writer's clinging to the memories of his Jewish childhood yet being drawn to the more adventurous world outside, and in "Wordsworth and the Rabbis" (1955), in which Trilling draws likenesses between Wordsworth's religious acceptance of nature and the religious acceptance of Torah of the authors of the Pirke Avoth. The latter essay marks a milestone in critical literature—a blending of reflections on Jewish religious literature and on English literature.

Trilling's chief innovation as critic and scholar, at a time when historicism or formal analysis was stressed, was his concern for the moral aspects of literature, for the ways great works throw light upon and measure political and social ideas. Second, in the combating claims of self and culture, he advocated a posture of civilized moderation, of minimal acceptance instead of surrender to either of these opposing claims. *See also* Critics, Literary.

SEYMOUR LAINOFF

BIBLIOGRAPHY

Boyers, Robert. *Lionel Trilling: Negative Capability and the Wisdom of Avoidance.* Columbia: University of Missouri Press, 1977.

Chace, William M. *Lionel Trilling: Criticism and Politics.* Stanford, Calif.: Stanford University Press, 1980.

Shoben, J. Edward, Jr. *Lionel Trilling: Mind and Character.* New York: Ungar, 1982.

Tuchman, Barbara W. (1912–1989). Historian and author, Barbara W. Tuchman was born in New York City to Maurice and Alma Morganthau Wertheim. Her father was an international banker and owner of the *Nation.* Her grandfather, Henry Morganthau, Sr., was a successful businessman and ambassador to Turkey under Woodrow Wilson and her uncle, Henry Morganthau, Jr., was Franklin D. Roosevelt's secretary of the treasury. She was brought up in a family that advocated Jewish assimilation, and though her grandfather aided Jewish families in Palestine during World War I, he was never pro-Zionist.

Tuchman was educated at Radcliffe, earning a B.A. in 1933. Her first job was a nonpaying position for the American Council of the Institute of Pacific Relations (IPR). She was sent to Tokyo where she worked as assistant to William L. Holland, supervisor of IPR's *The Economic Handbook of the Pacific.* While in Tokyo she had several pieces published in IPR publications *Far Eastern Survey* and *Pacific Affairs*. Upon her return to America, she had an article published in *Foreign Affairs*, at the age of 24.

In 1936, she went to work for the *Nation* as a staff writer and foreign correspondent. During the Spanish Civil War she was sent to Valencia and Madrid (1937–1938) to cover the war. She also worked for a weekly bulletin, the *War in Spain*, that was subsidized by the Spanish government. During this time she had her first book published, *The Lost British Policy: Britain and Spain Since 1700* (1938), which was written to show that England's policy in Spain was to keep it free of Hitler's control.

On June 18, 1940, she married New York physician Dr. Lester Reginald Tuchman. During World War II, while her husband was in the medical corps, she worked for the Office of War Information (OWI) in New York, where she was assigned to the Far East desk because of her knowledge of Japan. Her task was to explain the Pacific war and the American effort in Asia to the European listeners.

Her second book, *Bible and the Sword: England and Palestine from the Bronze Age to Balfour* (1956) in which she supported the idea of a Jewish homeland, took six years to write because she was dividing her time between her book and family. By this time she was the mother of three girls.

Tuchman is best known for her narrative history. Besides *The Lost British Policy* and *Bible and the Sword*, she is also the author of the following books: *The Zimmerman Telegram* (1958); *The Guns of August* (1962), which was published in England under the title *August, 1914*; *The Proud Tower: A Portrait of the World Before the War, 1890–1914* (1966); *Stilwell and the American Experience in China, 1911–1945* (1979), which was published in England under the title *Sand Against the Wind: Stilwell and the American Experience in China, 1911–1945*; *Notes from China* (1972); *A Distant Mirror: The Calamitous 14th Century* (1978); *Practicing History: Selected Essays* (1981); *The March of Folly: From Troy to Vietnam* (1984); and *The First Salute* (1988). For these works Tuchman received many awards and honors. *The Zimmerman Telegram* was her first best-seller. She won her first Pulitzer Prize in 1962 for *The Guns of August*, which was also a Book-of-the-Month Club Selection, and a 1964 documentary film of the same title, produced by Nathan Kroll, was based on the book. *Stilwell and the American Experience, 1911–1945* won her a second Pulitzer

Prize in 1971 and was a Book-of-the-Month Club Selection, as was *The Proud Tower*.

Tuchman was also honored in other ways. Among the awards and honors she received were the Gold Medal for History, American Academy of Arts and Sciences (1978), of which she served as president; Regent Medal of Excellence, University of the State of New York (1984); the Order of Leopold from the Kingdom of Belgium; and honorary degrees from Boston University, Columbia University, Hamilton College, Harvard University, Mount Holyoke College, New York University, Smith College, University of Massachusetts, Williams College, and Yale University, plus many more.

Though Tuchman was never a trained historian, her well-researched books were often on the best-seller list for nonfiction. When she died in February 1989, her final book *The First Salute* reached number nine on the *New York Times* best-seller list.

JANET L. DOTTERER

BIBLIOGRAPHY

American Women Writers: A Critical Reference Guide from Colonial Times to the Present. New York: Ungar, 1982.

"Barbara Tuchman Dead at 77, A Pulitzer-Winning Historian." *New York Times*, February 7, 1989, A1, B7.

Contemporary Authors: Bio-Bibliographical Guide to Current Writers in Fiction, General Nonfiction, Poetry, Journalism, Drama, Motion Pictures, Television, and Other Fields. Detroit: Gale, 1988.

Tuchman, Barbara W. *Practicing History: Selected Essays.* New York: Knopf, 1981.

Who's Who of American Women, 1989–1990, 16th ed. Chicago: Marquis, 1990.

Tussman, Malka Heifetz (1893–1987). Although she declared the natural rhythms of speech and breath as her *ars poetica*, at the peak of her powers the Yiddish poet Malka Heifetz Tussman introduced into Yiddish one of the most rigid verse forms, the triolet, and mastered another, the sonnet corona. A teacher of Yiddish language and literature in the Midwest and the West, Tussman published her six books of poetry relatively late in life, in 1949, 1958, 1965, 1972, 1974, and 1977. She was awarded the Itsik Manger Prize for Yiddish poetry in Tel Aviv in 1981. Born on Shevuot, Tussman herself disputed the exact year, stating it variously as 1893, 1895, or 1896. Her parents were the third generation of the Hasidic Heifetz family to manage an estate in the village of her birth, Khaytshe or Bolshaya-Chaitcha, in the Ukrainian province of Volhynia. The second of eight children, Tussman and her siblings were educated in Hebrew, Yiddish, Russian, and English, initially by private tutors and later in the Russian schools in the nearby towns of Norinsk and Korostyen. At a young age, Tussman began to write poems in Russian about the poverty of the neighboring peasants.

She came to America in 1912 and joined family members in Chicago. "Under terrible conditions she pursued her learning," as Tussman once wrote about herself. Her first Yiddish short story appeared in 1918, and her first poem was published in 1919. She also wrote in English for the Chicago anarchist publication, *Alarm*, in 1914.

After her marriage to the cantor Shloyme Tussman and the birth of her two sons (in 1914 and 1917), the family lived in Milwaukee, Wisconsin. In 1924, Tussman began to teach in a Yiddish secular school; at the same time she studied at the University of Wisconsin. She also studied briefly at the University of California, Berkeley. Later the family moved to Los Angeles, where Tussman taught Yiddish elementary and high school students. In 1949, she became an instructor of Yiddish language and literature at the University of Judaism. After her husband's death in 1971, she lived for a year in Israel. Upon her return, she moved to Berkeley, where she resided until her death.

Although she lived far from the centers of Yiddish letters, Tussman's poems, short stories, and essays appeared in the leading Yiddish newspapers and journals from 1918 onward. These publications included the New York papers *Fraye arbeter shtime* and *Der vokh*, as well as the journals *Oyfkum*, *Inzikh*, *Yidisher kemfer*, *Sviva*, *Kinder zshurnal*, and *Di tsukunft*; the Warsaw weekly *Literarishe bleter*; the Toronto literary magazine *Tint un feder*; and the Tel Aviv quarterly, *Di goldene keyt*. Her poems were represented in collections of Yiddish poetry, such as *Antologye—mitvest-mayrev* (From Midwest to North Pacific; Chicago, 1933) and *Amerike in yidishn vort* (America in Yiddish Literature; New York, 1955).

Six volumes of her poems were published: *Lider* (Poems; Los Angeles, 1949), *Mild mayn vild* (Mild My Wild; Los Angeles, 1958), *Shotns*

fun gedenken (Shadows of Remembering; Tel Aviv, 1965), *Bleter faln nit* (Leaves Do Not Fall; Tel Aviv, 1972), *Unter dayn tseykhn* (Under Your Sign; Tel Aviv, 1974), and *Haynt iz eybik* (Now Is Ever; Tel Aviv, 1977). Until her death, Tussman continued to work on a seventh volume, *Un ikh shmeykhl* (And I Smile).

Throughout her career as a poet, Tussman sustained literary friendships and extensive correspondences with Yiddish writers in the United States, Canada, Poland, France, and Israel, including the poets Kalman Marmor, Yankev Glatshteyn, H. Leyvik, Rokhl Korn, Kadya Molodowsky, Melekh Ravitsh, and Avraham Sutzkever. She read poetry of many languages, modern and ancient, and exercised her poetic voice by translating poems by writers as various as Yeats, Rossetti, Auden, and Tagore into Yiddish. By maintaining a ferocious poetic independence from any school or movement, Tussman achieved a compressed lyrical style noted by the critic M. Littvin for its elliptical syntax and free verse rhythms that render the strophe inconspicuous but dense. Avraham Sutzkever praised her poetry for asserting an ever more flexible, youthful voice, the older the poet herself grew.

Tussman has significance as a woman poet in Yiddish. Although she did not believe that poetry should be read or written in terms of gender, her poems are fueled by an explicitly female sensuality. Denying any feminist orientation, she, nonetheless, acknowledged the difficulties that women writing poetry in Yiddish had, even in the heyday of Yiddish poetry in America, to publish their poems in periodicals or to find sponsors for the publication of their books. In an interview she once expressed her sense that women who excelled in writing poems for children, such as Kadya Molodowsky, were often categorized by the Yiddish literary establishment as "merely children's poets," so that their other work remained unacknowledged. In her later years, she taught informally and befriended a number of younger poets, many American-born and writing in English, who helped disseminate her poetry through their translations. She also served as a mentor for some younger Yiddish poets, of whom an Israeli recipient of the Manger Prize, the late Rokhl Fishman, was the best known. Malka Heifetz Tussman thus served as a bridge between the generations of Yiddish poets who emigrated from Eastern Europe and of those American-born Jewish poets who have taken up the task of making Yiddish poetry known to a readership that knows little Yiddish. *See also* Literature, Yiddish.

KATHRYN HELLERSTEIN

BIBLIOGRAPHY

Bankier, Joanna; Cosman, Carol; Earnshaw, Doris; et al., eds. *The Other Voice: Twentieth Century Women's Poetry in Translation*. New York: Norton, 1976.

Diament, Zeyhvi. "Kheyfets-Tuzman, Malke," in *Leksikon fun der Neyet Yiddisher Literatur*, Shmuel Nigera and Yankev Shatski, eds. New York: Alveltlekhn Yidishn Kultur-Kongres, 1980. Vol. 3, pp. 744–745.

Harshav, Benjamin and Barbara, eds. *American Yiddish Poetry: A Bilingual Anthology*. Los Angeles: University of California Press, 1986.

Hellerstein, Kathryn. "A Question of Tradition; Women Poets in Yiddish." In *Handbook of American-Jewish Literature*, edited by Lewis Fried. Pp. 195–237. Westport, Conn.: Greenwood Press, 1988.

Howe, Irving; Wisse, Ruth R.; and Shmeruk, Khone, eds. *The Penguin Book of Modern Yiddish Verse*. New York: Penguin, 1987.

Littvin, M. "Dos poetishe verk fun malke kheyfetstuzman." *Di goldene keyt* 89 (1976): 80–88.

Sutzkever, Avraham. "Haynt is eybik (tsum toyt fun malke kheyfets tuzman)." *Di goldene keyt* 122 (1987): 52.

U

Union of American Hebrew Congregations. The Union of American Hebrew Congregations (founded 1873) is an association of Reform synagogues, comprising some 850 congregations as of 1991.

Shortly after he settled in the United States in 1846, Rabbi Isaac Mayer Wise (1819–1900) called for a national body to serve the scattered congregations making up the growing American Jewish community. He envisaged the publication of a standard prayer book and other religious literature, the establishment of a college for training rabbis, and a religious authority that would legitimize changes in religious practice necessitated by conditions in the New World.

For many years Wise's efforts were lost in the controversies they stimulated, particularly among the rabbis. At length the congregations of Cincinnati, where Wise was serving as rabbi, agreed to call a conference of Jewish congregations in the South and West. The outcome was the establishment in 1873 of the Union of American Hebrew Congregations (UAHC), with headquarters in Cincinnati.

The constitution of the union set forth that it was not to interfere "in any manner whatsoever with the affairs and management of any congregation." The "primary object" of the body was to establish a "Hebrew Theological Institute," but it did permit a broad program of activities without limitation to any single religious tendency. The geographical limitation on UAHC's comprehensiveness disappeared in 1879 when the major congregations in the East joined the Union and the

Board of Delegates of American Israelites (est. 1859) was absorbed.

In 1875, Hebrew Union College was opened under Wise's presidency, and in 1883 it ordained its first rabbis. Wise's energy and devotion sustained the college for 25 years, but for the rest, though many projects were discussed, little by way of action ensued. UAHC lost its religious comprehensiveness and became a body of Reform congregations, with little relationship to the new and larger Jewish community brought into being by the heavy immigration from Eastern Europe. Having its headquarters in Cincinnati, at a distance from the burgeoning Jewish communities of the East Coast, did not lessen UAHC's aloofness from the problems of the day.

Some development of activities was recorded, particularly in the preparation of educational curricula and literature, but by 1940 the feeling had grown within the Reform camp that the Union had failed to meet the challenge of the times. Rabbi Maurice Eisendrath became director in 1943 (in 1946 he received the title "president"), and under his leadership UAHC was transformed. Existing programs were intensified, a regional structure built up, and the establishment of new Reform congregations encouraged. In 1951, headquarters were moved to New York. UAHC already had begun to make its presence felt in the major controversies affecting the American Jewish community, particularly with regard to the formation of the American Jewish Conference and the struggle for a Jewish state. In 1964, a Religious Action Center was opened in Washington, D.C., indicating a determination to make the voice of Reform Judaism heard in matters of public concern, such as civil rights. This trend in UAHC's activities aroused disquiet among some of its more conservative members, leading to threats of secession, but the differences were resolved. The Union has developed a strong regional organization and affiliated bodies representing women's groups, and youth and men's clubs.

The 400 affiliated congregations of 1943 grew to 733 in 1981 and by 1991 to 850. In 1973, Rabbi Eisendrath was succeeded as president by Rabbi Alex Schindler. Naturally the zest which accompanied the great expansion of activities during the immediate postwar years could not be maintained, but the extended range of activities that UAHC developed has continued, and its place as Reform Judaism's representative body is unchallenged. *See also* Reform Judaism.

S. D. Temkin

BIBLIOGRAPHY

Landsberger, Franz. *Union of American Hebrew Congregations*. Cincinnati: Union of American Hebrew Congregations, 1946.

Meyer, Michael A. *Response to Modernity: A History of the Reform Movement in Judaism*. New York: Oxford University Press, 1988.

United Jewish Appeal (UJA). From the end of the nineteenth century to the early 1930s, the Jewish community began to "come of age" in the United States. Thousands of Jewish philanthropic associations competed for funds from the Jewish community. This chaotic situation led to the formation of federations. The federations would raise and distribute funds, thus reducing competition and duplication among the various philanthropic associations. Although federations did solve many of the problems, three major agencies continued to pull and divide major fund-raising efforts. The Joint Distribution Committee served Jews all over the world; the United Palestine Appeal worked specifically in Palestine; and the United Service for New Americans helped rehabilitate refugees and settle them in the United States. These three agencies united in 1939 to form a single organization—the United Jewish Appeal.

The United Jewish Appeal (UJA) was established by the American Jewish community as a direct response to Hitler's *Kristallnacht* of No-

vember 8 and 9, 1939. This traumatizing crisis forced Jewish Americans to consolidate their fund-raising efforts under one agency.

Although UJA is primarily devoted to fund raising, it also has come to be the collective voice through which American Jewry asserts its commitments, interests, and political views. During World War II, UJA worked to rescue as many Jews as possible. Once the war ended, the agency's primary concern shifted from Europe to Israel. UJA and local federations in many cities began to combine their annual fund-raising campaigns. Together they became a collective voice for the Jewish community.

UJA establishes funds for special projects. For example, the costs of Operation Magic Carpet (the airlifting in 1948–1949 of Yemenite Jews to Israel) were defrayed by UJA. The Israel Emergency Fund (1967–1977) was in response to the Six-Day War. Operation Moses (1984–1985) was funded to provide for the absorption and integration of Ethiopian Jewry in Israel. Operation Exodus is the newest UJA special project. It is the most ambitious project ever undertaken by the UJA, with a goal of raising $420 million as part of a worldwide effort to assist Soviet Jews settling in Israel.

The major share of the funds received by UJA are transmitted to the Israeli-based United Israel Appeal. That organization allocates funds to support the programs of the Jewish Agency for Israel. The Jewish Agency accomplishes its goals through the operations of seven departments: Immigration and Absorption, Rural Settlement (establishing new settlements inside the pre-1967 boundaries and the care and development of kibbutzim), Youth Aliyah, Education (provides scholarships for students to study in Israel and financial assistance to strengthen Jewish education in the Diaspora), Social Programs (activities for disadvantaged children, the elderly, and the handicapped and housing assistance for young couples), Project Renewal (rehabilitation program to improve the quality of life in distressed immigrant neighborhoods), and Housing and Community Facilities (renovating houses and playgrounds and establishing social clubs and playgrounds).

Linda Glazer

BIBLIOGRAPHY

Karp, Abraham J. *Haven and Home*. New York: Schocken, 1985.

Klaperman, Gilbert and Libby. *The Story of the Jewish People*. Vol. I. New York: Behrman House, 1961.

Meller, Charles. "An Introduction to the Jewish Federation." New York: Council of Jewish Federations, 1985.

Rockland, Mae Schaffer. *New Jewish Yellow Pages*. New York: SBS, 1980.

"The United Jewish Appeal." New York: Council of Jewish Federations, n.d.

"UJA Plans Operation Exodus to Fund Soviet Jewish Resettlement in Israel." *Jewish Exponent* (Philadelphia) January 26, 1990, 5, 33.

Yoffe, James. *The American Jews*. New York: Random House, 1969.

United States-Israeli Relations.

Relations between the United States and Israel, while certainly damaged in recent years by such incidents as Israel's invasion of Lebanon, the Jonathan Jay Pollard spy scandal, and the Palestinian uprising on the West Bank and Gaza Strip, generally remain in rather good overall shape. Indeed, the day-to-day level of military, intelligence, economic, and diplomatic cooperation is impressive. There are differences of opinion that surface from time to time—as is the case between all friendly countries. But leaders in both Washington and Jerusalem strive to contain those differences. There are too many mutual interests at stake, especially in the aftermath of the war in the Persian Gulf in 1991.

Thus, the relationship of today has grown to the point that even when serious differences surface, neither government will allow them to overly strain the relationship. There is an almost built-in cushion, including a set of incentives, fueled by public opinion in both countries, to limit the negative fallout.

In Israel, the top leadership of the Labor and Likud parties is very well aware of the fact that Israel has become very dependent on U.S. support. They know that this situation automatically limits Israel's maneuverability. Israeli officials say they would like to reduce that dependency, but they insist that the only alternative, given Israel's enormous security problems, is a wholesale reduction in the population's standard of living. The political leadership in Jerusalem is clearly not prepared to accept that approach.

Every Israeli government, in addition, is also very sensitive to the fact that the United States is the home of the largest Jewish community in the world. Thus, no Israeli government will want to find itself in a real rift with Washington for too long. "If Israel gets into trouble with the United States," former Foreign Minister Moshe Arens told the writer in an interview, "I think, inevitably, it's going to mean that a certain part of the American Jewish community is not going to be as supportive of Israel as it was before because there might be some hesitancy about taking a position against the administration's position." Arens said that Israel would be misleading itself if it thought that American Jews were going to side with Israel on every issue no matter what.

Still, what could seriously strain the overall relationship would be a major effort to resolve the Arab-Israeli conflict. There are long-standing differences between Washington and Jerusalem (including Israeli hawks and doves) on the ultimate disposition of the West Bank and Gaza. Bringing those sensitive issues to the bargaining table would quickly expose those differences, upsetting the relationship.

Since 1948, every American president has faced a basic dilemma in conducting a proper Middle East policy. The United States has sought to maintain strong ties with Israel, but at the same time it has tried to reach out to the Arab world where the United States also has important economic, military, and political interests. Some presidents have walked that delicate tightrope better than others. Richard Nixon and Jimmy Carter, for example, managed to maintain close relations with Israel while strengthening U.S. interests in the Arab world at the same time.

Israel, over all these years, has been blessed with a strong reservoir of domestic American political backing, spearheaded by the Jewish community but including many non-Jews as well. They have been active and very effective in generating support for Israel, especially on Capitol Hill. Israel has good friends among Republicans and Democrats, liberals and conservatives. Support for Israel, generally, has been nonpartisan and nonideological. These supporters can be expected to continue to weigh in very heavily as the United States continues to grope toward a proper Middle Eastern strategy.

By all accounts, American Jews were invigorated by the 1967 Six-Day War. Since then, they have managed to play the political power game in Washington very effectively. There was much greater consciousness of and vicarious identification with Israel. American Jews sharpened their political skills. They became more sophisticated.

The American Jewish community's support for Israel, while very important indeed in shaping United States-Israeli relations, is but only one factor in the overall scheme of things. Support by the United States, which has been quite impressive over the years, has been based on other factors as well.

There are long-standing moral considerations, partially resulting from the birth of Israel out of the ashes of the Holocaust. There are shared values and democratic traditions. Israel is the only functioning democracy in the Middle East. For many Americans, there are deeply felt religious connections to the Holy Land. And in recent years, Israel also has emerged as a major strategic ally. Things have started to happen in the United States-Israeli military relationship that would have been considered unheard of only a few years earlier. Both countries have benefited.

Thus, neither the United States nor Israel permitted the Pollard affair to strain their connection overly. This was underscored by President Ronald Reagan's February 1987 announcement that Israel's official status had been elevated to that of a "major non-NATO ally." That announcement came 15 months after Pollard's arrest and just on the eve of his sentencing. The top leadership in both countries appreciate those common interests even if lower-level officials remain angry.

It is important to keep the American-Israeli relationship in its proper perspective. The relationship has dramatically matured and improved since 1948. At that time, even as Israel was fighting for its very survival in its War of Independence, the Truman administration included Israel in a regional arms embargo. The State Department, which had failed to convince Truman not to recognize Israel's independence formally, had still managed to convince the White House that any U.S. arms sales to Israel would completely poison U.S. ties with the Arab world. The Soviet Union would then exploit that opportunity to strengthen its influence there.

Prime Minister David Ben-Gurion's fledgling government was, therefore, forced to turn to all sorts of sources for badly needed weaponry. Five neighboring Arab armies, after all, had just invaded the newly born state. There had been some illegal gun-running operations to Israel involving private American citizens—some of whom were later arrested and even sent to jail. They included Jews as well as non-Jews. But, ironically, it was the Soviet Union that gave Czechoslovakia the green light to sell Israel some elementary weapons—machine guns, hand grenades, ammunition. It was that sale that helped Israel to stave off the Arab assault and to sign armistice agreements with its Arab neighbors in 1949.

The Truman arms embargo against Israel basically remained in effect throughout the balance of his administration and then throughout the Eisenhower administrations. It was not until the first year of the Kennedy presidency in 1961 that the United States actually shipped an early version of the Hawk anti-aircraft missile system to Israel—although most of the political and military ingredients leading up to that sale had been effectively concluded during Eisenhower's final year in office. Since then, the United States-Israeli military relationship has expanded rapidly, especially after the 1967 and 1973 wars. The United States is today Israel's major source of weapons.

There are many reasons for this dramatic expansion of the military relationship. Before 1967, France had been Israel's chief weapons supplier. But the Franco-Israeli link virtually ended with the war when President Charles deGaulle decided to embargo weapons to Israel. The United States quickly came to fill that vacuum.

Certainly, the American Jewish community, proud of Israel's victory and emboldened by Israel's scrappy and popular image then so widely portrayed in the news media, played a significant role in lobbying for greater U.S. military sales to Israel during those years. The American Israel Public Affairs Committee (AIPAC), the official pro-Israeli lobbying organization then headed by the late Isaiah "Si" Kenen, urged senators and representatives to support such transfers. The pro-Israeli lobby began to come of age in the aftermath of the 1967 war.

American defense companies, of course, were also anxious to conclude lucrative sales. At the Pentagon, military chiefs were very much impressed by Israel's six-day victory. They were anxious to learn the lessons drawn from Israel's battle experience. Quickly, a new level of mutual cooperation developed between U.S. and Israeli air forces, especially as American-made F-4 Phantoms became the major fighter bomber in the Israeli inventory.

The Soviet Union, moreover, severed diplomatic ties with Israel during the 1967 war. Israel was thus perceived as now firmly part of the Western—American—strategic camp. The Arabs, by and large, were purchasing Soviet weapons. There was a growing political inclination in Washington to side with Israel, a trend that has continued ever since.

Beginning in November 1983, the two countries have also formally strengthened their strategic cooperation in a whole host of areas. As far as Israel is concerned, this was the major legacy of the eight-year Reagan administration—this institutionalization of the American-Israeli military connection.

In its own modest way, Israel has come to play a role in support of the United States. There is extensive intelligence sharing, especially in the area of counterterrorism. Israel has made available a considerable amount of captured Soviet weaponry. It has presented to the United States the military lessons it has learned from its combat experiences against Soviet-supplied armies. Haifa, Israel's largest port, has today emerged as a major U.S. naval facility in the eastern Mediterranean. On any given day, there are likely to be several U.S. battleships, patrol boats, destroyers, and aircraft carriers in Haifa with a large number of American sailors on shore leave in Israel. This development is especially important for the United States at a time when other friendly countries in that part of the world, including Greece, Turkey, and Egypt, have been backing away from their own willingness to maintain a high-visibility profile with Washington. And over the past few years, Israel and the United States also have quietly been involved in joint military maneuvers, medical evacuation exercises, and strategic planning operations. The United States, quietly without a whole lot of fanfare, has prepositioned some military equipment in Israel. The Reagan administration, as part of this closer cooperation, invited Israel to participate in the Strategic Defense Initiative. The Israeli government quickly accepted since there were important economic, military, and political benefits to be gained. Israel also agreed to a U.S. request that the Voice of America build huge radio transmitters in the Negev. Finally, the two countries concluded a formal Free Trade Area agreement removing all trade barriers between them—the most far-reaching trade liberalization agreement the United States has entered into with any country, including Canada.

Today's government-to-government relationship, therefore, is not simply a one-way street, whereby the United States does all the giving and Israel does all the taking. Israel has emerged as a strategic asset for the United States in the Middle East. It can assemble, after three or four days, a 500,000-man army, battle-tested, reliable, using some of the finest conventional weaponry in the world, most of it American made. That is something that the Soviet Union and its allies certainly have to consider in their own defense calculations. It is also something that American strategic planners can automatically include in their own overall force assessments. Still, the United States asked Israel to remain on the sidelines during the 1991 war in the Persian Gulf to avoid the possible fracturing of the U.S.-Arab coalition.

Whenever the governments of the United States and Israel are at odds, there is a temptation to predict a wrenching change in the overall relationship. The supposedly inevitable "crunch" between Washington and Jerusalem is said to have arrived. But no matter how tense the relationship appears to be at any one moment, and occasionally it has become quite tense, that all-out confrontation has not materialized. The two countries somehow manage to put their relationship in order. Thus, whenever a real confrontation has appeared likely, either the United States or Israel—and usually both—has taken the necessary steps to avoid it. Positions have changed. Concessions have been made. And the basic United States-Israeli connection has survived intact.

Still, Israeli officials and their American supporters, extremely sensitive to the potential for long-term damage, are concerned. With each new incident, no matter how trivial, there is automatically some erosion, some damage. No matter how strong the overall relationship, some support for Israel in America can eventually be whittled away.

On the whole, relations between the two countries are not merely one of patron-client, even though Israel is clearly the junior partner. Yes, Israel has become extremely dependent on the United States for economic, military, and political support. Some will say that Israel has even become "hooked" on American largess. "As a Zionist and an Israeli who cares deeply about the future of my country, I think this partnership has hurt as much as it has helped us," said Chaim Shur, editor of *New Outlook*, a leftist monthly published in Israel. "The Israeli government is not a puppet on an American string, but reliance on the United States for political, economic, and military support has badly compromised our foreign policy. Israel is increasingly being pushed to see the world through the eyes of U.S. policymakers and to adopt the assumptions of the Cold War."

But at the same time, others disagree. The United States, they argue, cannot simply impose demands on Israel and expect them to be implemented. Israel has too many powerful political friends in the United States and has become too powerful in the Middle East in its own right for that scenario to unfold. Today's relationship between Washington and Jerusalem has become much more complex.

Thus, when he was foreign minister, Moshe Arens could make the case that the United States needs a strong and reliable Israel as much as Israel needs the United States. "There is a recognition of our contribution," he said. "Israel makes a significant contribution to the strategic interests of the Western world." There is, therefore, no need to feel uncomfortable about the billions of dollars in U.S. economic and military assistance to Israel. These huge sums represent an investment in America's own national security.

There are some critics of the relationship who argue that Israel actually calls most of the shots. They insist that the American-Israeli connection has become an example of the tail (Israel) wagging the dog (the United States). They have raised the Iran arms affair as a supposed example of this tendency. Israel, they insist, managed successfully to pressure the United States into getting involved in the arms-for-hostage operation in the first place. Israel had its own objectives for doing so.

The syndicated columnists Rowland Evans and Robert Novak have repeatedly made this case. And writing of the Iran affair in the *Wall Street Journal*, columnist Alexander Cockburn said: "Not only was it a long-term Israeli diplomatic objective to cultivate friendships in Teheran and sustain Iran in its war against Iraq, it also was an enormously lucrative proposition for an Israeli arms industry crucial to the country's economic fortunes and well populated with Shimon Peres's friends. One of the most conspicuous failings of the mainstream U.S. press, with the exception of the *Chicago Tribune*, has been its coverage of the bountiful examples of vigor with which this industry, sustained by U.S. aid, has pursued its own self-interest."

But this is also an overly simplistic explanation of the United States-Israeli relationship.

Since Israel's establishment in 1948, it has basically had two "patrons"—France until the 1967 Six-Day War and the United States since. Given Israel's security headaches, it probably has had little choice but to depend on one bigger power for support. Earlier visions of a "neutral" Israel maintaining good ties with both East and West were never very realistic, given Arab and Soviet hostility. Early in Israel's history, David Ben-Gurion moved the country into the Western camp, from which it has never left.

There are some similarities in the way Israel has behaved toward France and the United States but many differences. The two cases are by no means completely the same. Even when Israel supported France in Algeria, it was acting out of self-interest. Israeli officials recognized that an independent Algeria would automatically become another hostile Arab state—as it did.

And there is little likelihood that any administration in Washington in the foreseeable future—either Republican or Democratic—will be in a position to walk away from Israel the way de Gaulle did during the 1967 war. Israel's domestic political standing in France and the basic structure of the political system there were never as conducive to maintaining strong ties with Israel as is the case in the United States.

Recognizing its great dependence on the United States (and France during earlier years), every Israeli government is certainly always anxious to reciprocate whenever and wherever possible. But in almost all of the cases where Israel has met some perceived geostrategic need for its most important ally, there has been a parallel Israeli interest served. Rarely will Israel undertake delicate military or political moves in complete isolation of its own objectives. "As Golda Meir used to put it," recalled former Under Secretary of State Joseph Sisco, "Israel can only make one mistake. If it makes one mistake, it will be death." Burdened with incredible security and political problems, Israel simply does not have that kind of luxury. And this is also the case involving foreign arms sales to controversial regimes.

Thus, Israel has indeed been selling weapons and training troops in Central America, as has been widely reported. And yes, the United States has often encouraged Israel to move ahead with that policy, convinced that Israel was bolstering America's friends. On occasion, the administration has actually coordinated such Israeli activity, given congressional restrictions on direct American assistance. But Israel also has its own reasons for pursuing this policy.

For one thing, Israel has a very important financial reason for getting involved in such weapons exports. They are good for Israel's military-industrial complex, which is a source of considerable foreign currency revenue for the country. Military sales, moreover, almost always bring automatic political benefits with them. Countries armed by Israel are more likely to support Israel in the United Nations and other international arenas. The fact that this Israeli policy toward Central America was in tune with what the Reagan administration had had in mind was a mere by-product of Israel's thinking—albeit a very positive one.

The same is true in the case of the U.S. arms sales to Iran. Israel may have been asked by Washington to get involved in the affair, but Israel certainly had its own interests at heart when it did. There has long been a prevailing sense in Jerusalem, spanning both Labor and Likud leaderships, that Israel and Iran have some common long-term interests. Iran, while Islamic, is also anti-Arab. Under the Shah, Iran maintained close ties with Israel. Even today in Israel, there is a tendency to believe that ayatollahs will come and go, but the fundamental link between Jerusalem and Teheran will continue.

In this particular case, therefore, it is by no means accurate to suggest that Israel was simply doing the Reagan administration's "dirty" errands. Indeed, as the Senate Intelligence Committee's final report on the Iran affair concluded, Israel had its own agenda at the focus of its attention and that agenda may have differed from Washington's occasionally. Reagan's Secretary of State George Shultz, a great friend of Israel, even warned the administration of the peril of undertaking such an initiative with Israel, whose own reasons for selling arms to Iran, according to the Senate report, were in some respects contrary to U.S. objectives. The report noted that Israeli interests "might be served by a continuation of the Iran-Iraq war so as to keep the Iraqi Army occupied." Israeli arms dealers also had a financial stake in weapons sales—as did the overall Israeli economy. Thus, the report cited "previous Israeli attempts to circumvent Operation Staunch, the U.S. program to embargo arms shipments to Iran."

Still, despite the strains generated by the Iran affair, the Jonathan Jay Pollard spy scandal, and other lesser diplomatic spats, American-Israeli relations remain strong. The relationship between Washington and Jerusalem has dramatically matured and improved since 1948.

Newsweek magazine, for example, has reported that American fighter pilots attached to the Sixth Fleet in the Mediterranean have started to train at Israeli bombing ranges in the Negev Desert. "The Negev range is equipped with advanced technology that provides pilots almost instantaneous readings on the accuracy of their strikes," a senior administration official was quoted as having said.

Given the extraordinary degree of U.S. support for Israel, any Israeli government finds it very difficult to say "no" to a Washington request. The United States, after all, has been providing Israel with $3 billion a year in economic and military grants.

But despite this impressive state of relations, it would be a mistake to assume that Washington and Jerusalem are going to find themselves always in full agreement on every issue. There are no two countries, no matter how close their alliance, who will always agree. The United States occasionally finds itself differing over all sorts of things with even its closest friends and allies, including Britain, France, Canada, Japan, and Mexico.

But no Israeli government will want to find itself in a real rift with Washington. That does not mean that Israel is always going to do whatever the United States wants. Israel, after all, is a sovereign, independent country who in the end must make up its own mind about its best national interest. It certainly does mean, however, that every Israeli leader will always factor the U.S. position, as conveyed by the President, the secretary of state, and their advisers, into their decision-making process.

What is still apparent today is that the upward curve in United States-Israeli relations has become a constant feature—and is almost certain to remain so in the future even if there are some negative blips on the way. *See also* Politics, Zionism.

WOLF BLITZER

BIBLIOGRAPHY

Blitzer, Wolf. *Between Washington and Jerusalem: A Reporter's Notebook.* New York: Oxford University Press, 1985.

Spiegel, Steven L. *The Other Arab-Israeli Conflict.* Chicago: University of Chicago Press, 1985.

United Synagogue of America. The United Synagogue of America is the membership organization of Conservative congregations in the United States. Beginning with 22 congregations in 1913, it has grown to approximately 850. The United Synagogue, the Jewish Theological Seminary, and the Rabbinical Assembly are the three organizational branches of the Conservative Movement.

United Synagogue was founded in 1913 under the direction of Solomon Schechter. Schechter felt that "Conservative Judaism unit[es] what is desirable in modern life with the precious heritage of our faith . . . that has come down to us from ancient times." At first, Schechter and his followers hoped that the organization would unite all non-Reform congregations into a single non-denominational movement. Schechter believed that the survival of Judaism in the United States depended on its Americanization and that the United Synagogue would help congregations blend the American influence with more traditional Jewry (Orthodox) without going as far as the Reform Movement. They felt that a general loyalty to tradition could unite most congregations without requiring detailed and full conformance to the tradition.

It was not long before Schechter and others in the Conservative Movement realized that the differences between Conservative and Orthodox ideology would prevent such a union. The United Synagogue of America then became a solely Conservative organization with a denominational program that made few compromises to either Reform or Orthodox Judaism. The organization emphasized the observance of Shabbat, kashrut, home celebrations of the holidays, the founding of Jewish religious schools, the publishing of modern prayer books and textbooks, the use of Hebrew in worship, and the use of English for sermons (not Yiddish). It also supported rabbis as they trained at the Jewish Theological Seminary. Conservative Judaism was the first movement to support Zionism, believing Jewish nationality and religion were inseparable.

Conservative Judaism attracted second-generation Eastern European Jews who wanted to affiliate with a synagogue but whose Americanization had progressed to the point where they could not remain within the confines of the first generation's orthodoxy. By the end of the 1920s, United Synagogue had 229 affiliates. The 1950s was a time for the revival of religion throughout the United States. The decade also saw the growth of suburbia. Conservative Judaism ex-

panded dramatically during that time. Jewish communities in newly developing suburban areas who were organizing their first synagogue often turned to the Conservative Movement as a compromise that would best "satisfy everyone." The original criticism that Conservative Judaism was too ideologically loose turned out to be its greatest strength. By the end of the 1960s, when the suburban boom ended, over 800 synagogues were affiliated with the United Synagogue of America. Conservative Judaism was now the largest branch in the United States.

The United Synagogue of America made a commitment to work for the good of all members of society. For example, in 1954, it formed the Joint Commission on Social Action. This commission played a vigorous role in the civil rights movement. In supporting the passage of the Civil Rights Act of 1964, it was forced to review its own position on the role of women in the synagogue because the act included sections on sex discrimination. As a direct result of this, women within the Conservative Movement now play active roles in all phases of synagogue activities and leadership.

Currently, the United Synagogue of America consists of 850 affiliated synagogues and over 1.5 million members. *See also* Conservative Judaism, Jewish Theological Seminary.

LINDA GLAZER

BIBLIOGRAPHY

Karp, Abraham J. *Haven and Home*. New York: Schocken, 1985.

Klaperman, Gilbert and Libby. *The Story of the Jewish People*. Vol. 4. New York: Behrman House, 1961.

Marcus, Jacob R. *The American Jewish Woman: A Documentary History*. Hoboken, N.J.: Ktav, 1981.

"Questions and Answers About the United Synagogue of America and the Conservative Movement." New York: United Synagogue of America, 1989.

Raphael, Marc Lee. *Profiles in American Judaism: The Reform, Conservative, Orthodox and Reconstructionist Traditions in Historical Perspective*. New York: Harper & Row, 1984.

Rosenberg, Stuart. *The New Jewish Identity in America*. New York: Hippocrene Books, 1985.

V

Vaudeville. The most eclectic and yet uniquely American form of entertainment—vaudeville—has long been a gold mine of Jewish participation. Begun in the late 1840s or early 1850s, "vaudeville" derived from a French term "Val de Vire," the valley of the Vire River in Normandy, a place known for folk songs and ballads. Douglas Gilbert wrote in his book *American Vaudeville* "Vaudeville was America in motley, the national relaxation. To the Palace, the Colonial, the Alhambra, the Orpheum, the Keith circuit and a chain of variety houses, New York and Los Angeles, we flocked. Vaudeville was the theatre of the people, its simplicity as naive as a circus. Its social implications . . . are pronounced because its entertainment was largely topical fun."

Vaudeville was not only the famous comedians, singers, and stage shows; it included magicians, specialty acts, humorists, serious actors, musicians, dancers, animal acts, in fact, almost any kind of entertainment.

Erich "Ernie" Weiss, better known as Harry Houdini (1874–1926) was the world's best-known escape artist. His type of performance, trapeze artists, dancers, animal acts, jugglers, etc., were known as "dumb acts" because they could be performed without dialogue. Houdini, the most successful of all "dumb acts," earned star billing in many vaudeville shows. In fact, "to do a Houdini" became a generic term meaning doing an escape act.

Dancing and music were two important facets of vaudeville. Although difficult to imagine, two of our most famous comedians began their careers as dancers. The famous dance team of Jose and Burns started George Burns (b. 1896) in his career; later he became half of the comedy team of Burns and Allen, and he achieved even greater fame going solo in stage, television, and motion pictures after his wife Gracie's death.

Fanny Brice (1891–1951), too, danced her way to fame with her "dying swan" burlesque of classical ballet. From vaudeville she joined the Ziegfeld Follies and achieved international fame.

Classical musicians enjoyed huge popularity with vaudeville audiences, increasing the "highbrow quotient" of many shows. Cornetist Jules Levi, and fine violinists, such as Jules Saranoff, Ben Bernie (1891–1943), and Jack Benny (1894–1975), lent their names to vaudeville classical music billing. In Bernie and Benny's careers, humor and comedy provided far greater personal and financial success. A well-known pianist, Will H. Fox, did burlesque take-offs of famous composers and musicians of his day such as his parody of Polish pianist Ignace Paderweski, calling himself "the Padawhiskey of the Piano!"

Classical and religious singers were not inured to the attraction of vaudeville. Even the greatest hazan of his time, Cantor Josef Rosenblatt (1882–1933) played the vaudeville circuit, using as his encore piece, "When Irish Eyes Are Smiling!"

Vaudeville's stars were big business. Song publishers realized that to have their new tunes introduced by a great vaudeville headliner would boost a song toward success. Therefore, many publishers used various forms of encouragement for headliners to introduce their new songs. They provided "song slides"—illustrations and lyrics to songs for the audience to sing, special clothing, orchestrations and arrangements geared to the performer, and even "song pluggers," the ubiquitous member of the audience who, after hearing a song "only once," could stand up and sing it perfectly. Such stars as Sophie Tucker (1884–1966), Fanny Brice, Molly Picon (b. 1898), were among the song plugger stars whose imprimatur meant success for a new song.

Sophie Tucker, "the last of the red-hot mamas," easily made the jump from vaudeville to the nightclub and theatrical stage. Her theme song, "Some of These Days" and her famous signature tune, "My Yiddishe Mamma," imprinted a Jewish flavor on all of her performances. Fanny Brice's first Yiddish humorous song was written for her by Irving Berlin (1888–1989). Both women brought the Jewish persona into the modern musical theater, but they were not the first to parody the Jewish immigrant to America.

As early as 1897, the first great Jewish team of Burt and Leon toured the variety halls of the East coast. Both were products of the streets of Philadelphia, and in their humor they personified the racial comedy of the 1880s and 1890s as Jewish and Gentile. Much of Burt and Leon's humor came from parody, as they gave popular poetry of the day a Jewish nuance.

Another great Jewish comedian of the nineteenth century was Frank Bush (1856–1927). He appeared on a bill as a grotesque Jewish caricature, wearing a long black coat, a pointed black beard, oversized glasses and shabby pants, mimicking and deriding the new European immigrant. His act included songs and dances with lyrics of mixed English and Yiddish that he created:

Oh my name is Solomon Moses,
I'm a bully Sheeny man.
I always treat my customers
The very best what I can.
I keep a clothing store way down on
Baxter Street
where you can get your clothing now,
I sell so awful cheap.

Joe Welch, in 1896, became the first "Hebrew monologist." Where other comics had used Jewish stories or jokes, Welch did complete speeches and scenes in Yiddish or Jewish dialect.

Andy Rice (1881–1963) changed the Hebrew monologue, using only the slightest dialect and dressing beautifully. Rice related many wonderful stories about life in the Jewish world of the 1920s. One of his most famous stories was about a wedding: "There were 200 in the grand march. We invited 100, expected 80, so we ordered supper for 50 . . . we had three detectives watch the presents and my three brothers watched them!"

The Jewish caricature of the "shlemiel and shlemazel" became the trademark of several Jewish comedians. The most successful duo was Joe Weber (1867–1942), the shlemazel figure, a dumb simpleton, and Lew Fields (1867–1941), the clever sophisticate. After successfully working together for several decades, Weber and Fields split, each going his own way to great success. Fields became active in the American musical theater and "fathered" several of America's most creative theatrical producers, librettists, and lyricists. In 1902, Edward Leopold, better known as Ed Wynn (1886–1966), the son of a wealthy Philadelphia family, began his more than six-decade career in vaudeville, theater, and movies, with skits that lampooned college youth of the day. His "perfect fool," a permutation of the shlemazel character, was hugely successful. By 1913, Wynn went into the legitimate musical theater and later scored his greatest popularity on radio.

The shlemiels and the shlemazels, comedians and comediennes, singers and hazanim, producers and impresarios were all acceptable roles for Jews to undertake in vaudeville, but one of the most popular areas for those in vaudeville is the racially insensitive yet important ethnic, historic entertainment genre—the blackface acts. Several Jews achieved their fame by playing these acts in variety and minstrel shows, even in the Broadway musical. Al Jolson (1886–1950), Eddie Cantor (1892–1964), and George Jessel (1898–1981) began their careers in cork and pancake makeup. Although they did not speak in "black" dialect, they became known for the black on their faces and the white gloves on their hands.

Vaudeville was peopled not only by talented men and women on the stage, but also equally talented men and women behind the stage. Such names as William Morris (1893–1932), a German born in Schwarzenau, became the greatest producer and booker of talent in the world. His legacy is the William Morris Agency of today. Marcus Loewe (1870–1927), an immigrant furrier, became not only a millionaire, but also owner of many of the greatest theaters in the United States, founding Metro-Goldwyn-Mayer productions in the process.

William Hammerstein (1873–1958), of the great opera and musical impresario family, was the son of Oscar the first (1847–1919), great popularizer of grand opera in the United States, and was the father of Oscar the second (1895–1960), one of our most prolific and successful lyricists and librettists, author of such magnificent theatrical events as *Showboat*, *Oklahoma!* and *Carousel*. William Hammerstein was the manager and producer of the Victoria Theater in New York, the most successful vaudeville house in the world. In seventeen years (1904–1921) it made a profit of almost $5 million on grosses of $20 million. William's business success was only one aspect of the many achievements for which the Hammerstein family is known.

If vaudeville showed our American patchwork pastiche, the much vaunted melting pot, so it illustrated the simplicity and unsophistication of America in the late nineteenth and early twentieth centuries as it grew in its national self-awareness. For many Jews, vaudeville was the open door to the "Golden Land." It was a wonderful start to what has become a glorious chapter in the social and cultural history of our country. *See also* Comedians and Comedy, Theater.

KENNETH A. KANTER

BIBLIOGRAPHY

Gilbert, Douglas. *American Vaudeville, Its Life and Times*. New York: Dover, 1963.

Green, Abel, and Laurie, Jr., Joe. *Show Biz: From Vaude to Video*. New York: Holt, 1951.

Laurie, Jr., Joe. *Vaudeville: From the Honky-tonks to the Palace*. New York: Holt, 1953.

Stein, Charles W., ed. *American Vaudeville as Seen by Its Contemporaries*. New York: Knopf, 1984.

W

Wald, Lillian (1867–1940). Social worker, nurse, and sociologist Lillian Wald was a descendant of German and Polish Jews who came to America in 1848 seeking better opportunities. Wald was born in Cincinnati, but the family moved to Rochester, New York, the nation's center for the optical business, her father's profession. As a youngster, Wald was an avid reader and curious about the world around her. It was her sister's illness that aroused Wald's interest in nursing and humane care for the less fortunate. She had long conversations with the nurse who cared for her sister and was fascinated by the nurse's knowledge of anatomy, medical terminology, and therapeutic techniques. After many conversations with her, it was apparent how Wald wished to spend the rest of her life.

Following an 18-month nurse's training period, Wald worked with the New York Juvenile Asylum. This work was her first exposure to poverty, and she was unsettled by what she witnessed. As a result, Wald began a program to offer nursing training to women of the Lower East Side in New York City. At this time the East Side was largely comprised of Jewish immigrants from Eastern Europe. Poverty, ignorance, and sickness were prevalent. Through her nursing education program, Wald wished to create a setting where people would learn to care for themselves, their families, and the community at large. Ahead of her times, she emphasized preventative medicine. Working and living on the East Side, where poverty, filth, and disease pervaded the lives of those who resided in its tenements, determined Wald's

life pursuit—aiding the afflicted East Siders. To succeed in this endeavor, money was needed. Wald approached Jacob Schiff, a wealthy German Jewish philanthropist, and informed him of her activities and hopes for the future. Schiff, struck by Wald's idealism and energy, agreed to provide funds for the project. Thus, in 1893 began a visiting nurses program that was eventually to serve as the model for America's first venture in public health. In time, Wald was able to influence the city of New York to start a program of public health and nursing. Wald was indefatigable.

Not only did she expend great energy and time aiding the sick, she also struggled with how the economic and social causes of poverty could eventually be eliminated. Her efforts to help the East Side, inhabited by 190,000 people residing within a densely populated area, living in cheaply built, tiny rooms with few windows and inadequate ventilation, made her a revered and legendary figure. In 1895, Schiff bought a house at 265 Henry Street to be used as a center for the Visiting Nurses Service. Eventually, 267 Henry Street was acquired to accommodate all of the nurses working with Wald. The house became a sanctuary for the sick and needy of the East Side and known as the Henry Street Settlement.

Being a person with deep and varied interests, Wald was also active in a campaign to keep the Metropolitan Art Museum open on Sunday, helped to publicize the Women's Trade Union League and fought to create the Federal Children's Bureau. She also convinced the Board of Education to hire nurses for the public schools and worked on committees opposing child labor and for creating more recreational space in the city. It should also be noted that Wald was a pacifist during World War I.

Difficult as it is to summarize a life as eventful and productive as Wald's, Irving Howe in *World of Our Fathers* (1976) put it succinctly, Wald "grew within her lifetime into a figure of legend, known and adored on every street."

HOWARD SHAKER

BIBLIOGRAPHY

Epstein, Beryl (Williams). *Angel of Henry Street.* New York: Messner, 1951.

Howe, Irving. *World of Our Fathers.* New York: Harcourt Brace Jovanovich, 1976.

Siegel, Beatrice. *Lillian Wald of Henry Street.* New York: Macmillan, 1983.

Wald, Lillian. *The House on Henry Street.* New York: Dover, rpt. 1971.

West, The. Since the end of the eighteenth century Jews, along with their fellow citizens, have fanned out from the urban areas of concentrated Jewish settlement along the East Coast. By the middle of the nineteenth century, still in company with pioneers of other faiths and national origins, Jewish Americans began to move into the newly opening lands stretching from the Mississippi to the Pacific Coast. Jews settled on the Great Plains, took up residence in the Southwest and Northwest, and joined the gold seekers in California.

By the middle of the twentieth century Jewish migration west of the Mississippi River had resulted in a shift of the demographic balance of the American Jewish population toward the Pacific. Although New York City remained the capital of Jewish America, by 1950 a rival center of Jewish life had arisen in Los Angeles, which had emerged as the city with the second largest population of Jews in the United States. Although often ignored and frequently dismissed as insignificant, the western Jewish experience is an important component of the larger story of the history of Jews in the United States.

Reflecting the movement of Jews into the territory west of the 90th meridian was the percentage of Jews living in the area when the first, albeit imprecise, census of the Jewish population of the United States (*Statistics of the Jews of the United States*, 1880) was taken by the Board of Delegates of American Israelites in 1877. Among 26 communities with 1000 or more Jews, four were west of the Mississippi (San Francisco, New Orleans, St. Louis, and Galveston) and accounted for 16 percent of all Jews living in the larger Jewish centers. Perhaps more significantly, San Francisco, with a Jewish population of 16,000, claimed the second largest concentration of Jews in the United States, trailing behind only New York City and larger than Philadelphia, Chicago, and Baltimore. The *Statistics* also listed 134 communities with from 100 to 999 Jewish residents of which 36 (27 percent) were in states west of the Mississippi. California led with 7, followed by Texas (6), Louisiana (5), Iowa and Arkansas (3), Minnesota, Missouri, and Nevada (2), and Colorado, Kansas, Montana, New Mexico, Oregon, and Utah with one each. While dispersed among 14 states, the smaller Jewish communities west of the Mississippi accounted for only 2.6 percent of all Jews located in communities with a Jewish population between 100 and 999. On the other hand, the western Jewish population (37,082) was 16 percent of the total American Jewish population (232,257).

A little over 100 years later, as reported in the *American Jewish Year Book 1987*, the states west of the Mississippi contained 1,299,100 Jews or 22 percent of the total Jewish population of the United States. Among the western states, California was still, by far, the preeminent locus of Jewish population, claiming 868,200, or 14 percent, of all Jews in the United States. Within California, however, a shift had occurred; southern California and Los Angeles had replaced San Francisco as the center of Jewish life. Indeed, by 1950, Los Angeles had risen to the rank of the second largest Jewish city in the nation with a Jewish population in 1986 recorded at 501,000.

Although residing in every state west of the Mississippi, 61 percent of Jews living between the Mississippi and the Pacific in 1987 were concentrated in the nine urban centers of Los Angeles, San Francisco, San Diego, Phoenix, Denver, Minneapolis-St. Paul, Houston, Dallas, and Kansas City. Each of these western cities recorded a Jewish population of more than 20,000. Despite the rural character of so much of the West, Jewish westerners have followed the long-established preference of Jews for choosing the city over the village or the small town.

The growth and expansion of the western Jewish population can be charted as neither a straight line nor an uninterrupted process. In fact, the demography of western Jewry developed in three distinct phases. From the mid-nineteenth century until the Depression decade of the 1890s, Jews migrated in large numbers relative to total population as reflected in *Statistics of Jews in the United States*. From the 1890s until the boom times in the West occasioned by World War II, Jews were less attracted to the states beyond the Mississippi than they were to the burgeoning industrial cities of the Northeast and North Central regions of the country. In these years Jews from Eastern Europe arrived in ever larger numbers to settle in Boston, New York, Philadelphia, Baltimore, and Chicago and the smaller cities and towns of the industrial heartland. Because western migration slacked off precisely when the character of the American Jewish population was being transformed by the arrival of Eastern Europeans, the percentage of Eastern Europeans in the western Jewish population did not keep pace with trends elsewhere outside the South. With the outbreak of World War II and the rapid recovery from the 1930s Depression that followed, as the West Coast shipbuilding and aircraft industries expanded to meet wartime needs, the West experienced a new burst of economic prosperity and proved attractive once again to mobile Americans seeking better opportunities. Between 1940 and 1980, Jews also moved to the West in larger numbers than ever before, transforming the established areas of Jewish settlement and creating new Jewish communities where none had previously existed.

That patterns of immigration and population growth in the West did not parallel those in the Northeast and North Central regions after 1890 should caution historians that the commonly accepted periodization of American Jewish history is not applicable to the history of Jews in the West. The West did share with other regions the influx of Jews from Central Europe from 1840 to 1880, but, as noted above, the dramatic increase in Jewish population in the United States caused by the mass migration of Jews from Eastern Europe between 1881 and 1924 did not have the same impact on western Jewry it did elsewhere. Likewise, the decline in Jewish migration to the United States as the 1924 Immigration Act took effect did not have any immediate consequences for the western Jewish population. Finally, the great expansion in the Jewish population of the West between 1940 and 1980 occurred at a time when the Jewish population of the East and Middle West was stable or even in decline. The history of Jews in the West, at least when measured

by its demography, is sufficiently different from the contours of the Jewish experience in the older centers of concentrated Jewish settlement as to require its own periodization. Western Jewish history cannot be properly understood simply as a variant of the history of the Jews of New York, however central the New York experience has been for American Jewry at large.

In the middle and late decades of the nineteenth century, Jews joined other Americans in the march westward, most essentially to seek their fortunes. Unlike so many others, however, Jews did not migrate west with hopes of becoming farmers, miners, cattle ranchers, or timber barons. Rather, Jews sought the commercial opportunities as store owners, sutlers, or merchants that became available as the new territories were opened that matched their entrepreneurial skills and experience. Thus, Jews were attracted to the villages, small towns, and instant cities of the West, often arriving in the first wave of settlement. They were valued by their neighbors for establishing the economic links with markets and sources of supply upon which the future health of nascent communities ultimately depended. Whether in the mining camps of California, Nevada, or Colorado, the supply centers of Portland, Denver, and Kansas City, the smaller towns that served an agricultural hinterland, such as Tucson, Santa Fe, and Trinidad, Colorado, or in the western metropolis of San Francisco, Jews could be found who were ready to invest their time, their energy, and their small capital in dreams of mercantile success. The growth of western Jewish communities was frequently a family matter as once one member of a family achieved some limited success, he would call for brothers and brothers-in-law, nephews, or cousins to come join and share in the potential prosperity. In many smaller locales on the western frontier of the nineteenth century, the Jewish community appeared as something of a network of extended families tied together by both blood and marriage.

If a goodly number of Jews found moderate economic success in the trans-Mississippi West in the latter half of the nineteenth century, some few were inordinately fortunate. Although they do not represent the careers of the majority of pioneer western Jews, the Guggenheims of Colorado, Jesse Seligman of San Francisco, the Speigelbergs of New Mexico, Adolph Sutro of San Francisco, who connected the Comstock Lode to the Carson Valley, and Levi Strauss, famed for his work pants fixed by rivets designed for miners in the California gold fields, have entered into the mercantile mythology of the West. These nineteenth-century exemplars of the American Dream were joined in the twentieth century by the movie moguls of Hollywood, most of whom (for example, Louis B. Mayer, Adolph Zukor, William Fox, Samuel Goldwyn) were Eastern European Jewish immigrants.

Still other western Jews pursued activities associated with the myth of the American West, even if they did not accumulate the vast fortunes of those mentioned in the previous paragraph. Josephine Sarah Marcus ran away from her San Francisco home to the Arizona territory where she eventually became the common-law wife of Wyatt Earp. Emil Harris struggled against the violence and lawlessness of the West in Los Angeles first as a patrolman, then as a detective, and in 1877 as the city's first chief of police. Solomon Bibo of New Mexico married Juana Valle, granddaughter of an Acoma Indian chief, and was himself appointed pueblo governor for a time in the 1880s, thus becoming a certified Jewish Indian chief.

For some Jews the journey West was occasioned not by a search for wealth but a desperate quest for health. In the nineteenth century, tuberculosis (consumption) was the number-one killer disease, and those who lived in crowded cities with poor sanitation, labored in factories or sweat shops, and worked long hours at physically demanding jobs were particularly susceptible. A regimen of fresh air and proper diet were the standard treatments for the disease at the time, making the mountain West and the Southwest attractive to those who suffered from tuberculosis and other respiratory illnesses. As the number of Jews concentrated in the unhealthy environment of the East coast ghettos increased, due to the continued migration from Eastern Europe, the incidence of tuberculosis among Jews rose correspondingly. Thus, by the late nineteenth century some western Jewish communities, Denver in particular, confronted an influx of poor, Eastern European Jews who arrived in their midsts hoping that the salubrious climate of mountain or desert would be the medicine required to restore broken bodies.

As Eastern European Jewish health seekers relocated in the West, their presence often placed inordinate pressures upon the limited philanthropic resources available within the already established Jewish communities. Local Jewish leadership, both male and female, struggled to meet the needs of their co-religionists as best they could. In Denver, because so many of the ill selected the city as their destination, the decision was taken to build a Jewish hospital for the treatment of tuberculosis financed by Jews from around the country. After several false starts, the National Jewish Hospital opened its doors in 1899, supported by the national fraternal organization B'nai B'rith and wealthy, mostly Reform, Jews from the East. Five years later (1904) a second Jewish facility in Denver for the treatment of tuberculosis, the Jewish Consumptives' Relief Society, was launched, organized by Eastern European Jews, some socialists and others Orthodox. It relied on small contributions from a large number of poor donors contacted throughout the nation. In consequence, the history of the Jewish community of Denver was uniquely affected by the establishment of two national institutions dedicated to the treatment of Jewish tuberculars, many of whom remained in the city after release from the hospital and increased the proportion of Eastern Europeans in the Jewish population beyond what would otherwise have been the case. (That Golda Meir lived in Denver for two years, graduated from Denver's West High School, and met her husband while resident in the city was occasioned by the fact that her sister was a patient at National Jewish when the young teenager and future prime minister of the State of Israel decided to leave her parents' home in Milwaukee.)

One last group of Jewish pioneers deserve mention less for their numbers than for their idealism. Influenced by the Russian back-to-the-soil movement prior to emigration, convinced that they could regain the ancient Jewish connection to the soil, and anxious to demonstrate to anti-Semites that Jews could be productive members of society, some Eastern Europeans struggled to build agricultural settlements, based on collective ownership and co-operation, in the American West. In North and South Dakota and in Kansas, Colorado, Oregon, and Utah, from the 1880s until 1913 efforts to plant agricultural colonies of Jews were tried and in every case failed. Often the settlers were encouraged and aided by Americanized Jews who did not wish to see the further ghettoization of Eastern European Jews in the port cities of the East, who feared that the new immigrants would fuel the fires of anti-Semitism that might threaten the hard-won respectability and status the acculturated German Jews had achieved, and who were anxious to find some means of quickly Americanizing the new immigrants while simultaneously meeting the financial drain that philanthropic support of the recently arrived Jewish poor entailed. But the support offered was insufficient, and the colonists themselves were able to raise only limited capital from their own meager resources. Inadequate capitalization contributed to the demise of every effort at Jewish colonization in the West. In addition, historians have noted that the settlers' lack of farming experience, the choice of poor lands, bad weather, and ideological conflicts all contributed to the downfall of these experiments in agrarian utopianism.

The reception that Jews in the West encountered from their Gentile neighbors was generally hospitable. While incidents of anti-Semitism occurred west of the Mississippi, in the nineteenth century hostility to the Jew was less prevalent in the region than in the Northeast. One important sign of Jewish acceptance in the West was the surprisingly large number of Jews who were elected to public office at the local, state, and even national levels by an electorate in which Jews were a decided minority. Since historians no longer accept Frederick Jackson Turner's thesis that the West was more democratic and egalitarian than other sections (as the western treatment of racial minorities—American Indian, Asian, black, and Hispanic—demonstrates), an explanation for the relative absence of anti-Semitism must be sought elsewhere. Some scholars have speculated that western Jews were immune from the anti-Semitism virus because they arrived with the original white settlers and were included among the founding fathers of many western towns. Others have attributed the weakened strain of western anti-Semitism to the underrepresentation of Eastern Europeans in the western Jewish population. No consensus on this matter has yet emerged, and it is a subject that deserves further investigation.

One sign that anti-Semitism may have been less prevalent in the West was the incidence of intermarriage. Compared to other regions, the rates of intermarriage in the West have always appeared significantly higher. While it might be reasonable to conclude that this situation reflected the social democracy and equality that Frederick Jackson Turner claimed for the frontier West, it should be remembered that in the nineteenth century Jewish men were likely to outnumber Jewish women in the most sparsely settled areas of the West. The appearance of greater numbers of intermarriages in the West may, therefore, have had more to do with the shortage of suitable Jewish brides for Jewish bachelors than with an absence of western anti-Semitism.

Since 1970, demographic surveys of Jewish communities that have counted intermarrieds clearly document a dramatically higher number of intermarriages for western cities than in Jewish communities in other regions, although intermarriage has increased everywhere. This is especially true for the studies conducted in Los Angeles, Phoenix, and Denver. How to explain the increase in western rates of intermarriage remains problematic. It may be that in the West Jews yet face less hostility from Gentiles and are thus freer to intermarry. But, what all studies of intermarriage indicate is that the segment of the Jewish population most prone to intermarriage is young, college educated, and managerial or professional in occupation—precisely that slice of the Jewish population that has migrated west in ever growing numbers since 1945. Perhaps, then, the extraordinary rates of intermarriage in the West more accurately reflect the transplantation of younger, eastern Jews to the states of the Southwest, Rocky Mountains, and the Pacific coast than any increase in the propensity of Jews born in the West to intermarry.

As Jews gathered together in western towns and cities in sufficient numbers, they began to construct the communal institutions required for the maintenance of Jewish life. The development of local Jewish organizations in the West offered no regionally distinctive model and replicated a pattern that had characterized American Jewish life since its beginning. Frequently the first organizations to appear were the male and female benevolent societies that dispensed charity to the poor and also provided a forum for social interaction in a Jewish environment. If not established as the initial institution of the Jewish community, a burial society and a Jewish cemetery association were early on the list of communal agencies. Once children were present, Jewish education was quickly recognized as a communal need. As the western Jewish communities increased in size, a number of purely social clubs made their appearance, including local lodges of the B'nai B'rith. Not until the community had attracted a large enough population and resources were adequate, however, did a synagogue appear, and then differences over *minhag* or allegiance to Reform, Conservative, or Orthodox Judaism often led to the formation of additional houses of worship.

With the arrival of Eastern European Jews in

the West, institutions serving their brand of Jewish life began to appear. At first, the newer immigrants formed religious associations to satisfy their spiritual lives and associations to meet the pressing economic needs of landsmen even more recently settled in the West free from the domination of the older, Americanized, and primarily Reform-established communal Jewish leadership. Usually somewhat later, organizations reflecting attempts to establish the social and political aspects of Yiddishkeit made their appearance in the West as they had in the East. Depending on the size of the Eastern European component of the Jewish population, by the 1920s western communities could boast of free loan societies, branches of the Workmen's Circle, and chapters of various Zionist organizations, whose minutes were recorded in Yiddish.

The first and second generation of Eastern European Jews in the West, however, were never able to create the full spectrum of institutional life supporting Yiddishkeit that could be found on the Lower East Side of New York. The West could maintain neither an active Yiddish press nor a permanently established Yiddish theater. Specifically, Jewish labor unions were nonexistent, due primarily to the fact that until World War II the western economy remained dependent on agriculture, mining, and commerce rather than industry. Although Jewish socialist and other radical political organizations attractive to Eastern Europeans surfaced, Jewish radicalism in the West was less significant than in the industrial centers of the East and Middle West.

As Jewish philanthropic organizations proliferated in western towns and cities, some led by the established leadership and others by transplanted Eastern Europeans, efforts to coordinate the charities on a community-wide basis were attempted, temporarily uniting Yehudin (German Jews) and Yiddin (Eastern Europeans). Thus, the Jews of Kansas City joined together in a Bureau of Associated Charities in 1888. By the end of the nineteenth century, Jewish communities throughout the country were adopting the federation plan for charitable fund raising and allocation in order to reduce the number of solicitations now that so many different agencies existed and to bring some rational order to what appeared to some as a system that was inefficient, redundant, and chaotic. Led by Boston in 1895 and in emulation of the national movement for "scientific charity" and professionalization, by 1912 federations had

been founded in many of the major Jewish communities west of the Mississippi, including St. Louis, Kansas City, San Francisco, and Los Angeles. In the latter half of the twentieth century, federations had become a dominant force in western Jewish communities, as was so throughout the United States, and served to forge important links between the Jews of the West and the network of national Jewish organizations with headquarters located most often in New York City.

If local federations reached out from the West to the East, national Jewish organizations extended their membership from East to West in the post-World War II era as they recognized the flow of Jewish population into the region. Associated with the maturation of Jewish communities in the West and the sophistication of American Jewish life in general, local branches of most national organizations could be found in western cities by the mid-twentieth century. These agencies included the American Jewish Committee, the American Jewish Congress, the Anti-Defamation League, Hadassah, the National Council of Jewish Women, Jewish Children and Family Service, and the Jewish Community Center. Replicating national trends, Jewish social services in the West underwent professionalization as each agency hired trained personnel, usually social workers, as paid directors. By 1950, the leading western Jewish communities were large enough, wealthy enough, and self-conscious enough to have in place the full panoply of organizations, agencies, and services that could be found in Jewish communities anywhere in the United States.

By the mid-twentieth century, western Jewry differed little from Jewish communities throughout the country in organizational structure and demography. On the other hand, western Jews remained convinced that there was something different about the western Jewish experience that distinguished it from Jewish existence in other regions of the United States. Identifying and documenting the unique characteristics that describe the Jews of the West remains a matter of dispute among scholars (some would argue that no such marks of distinction any longer exist), but western Jews persist in claiming that life in the open expanses of the West has been and continues to be more free, less stratified, and more open to change. In such an atmosphere, it has been claimed, the challenges that the future holds for all of American Jewry (assimilation and intermarriage especially) have been encountered first in the West, and the responses of western Jewry may well set the pattern to be followed by American Jewry at large. *See also* Los Angeles.

JOHN LIVINGSTON

BIBLIOGRAPHY

Goldberg, Robert A. *Back to the Soil: The Jewish Farmers of Clarion, Utah*. Salt Lake City: University of Utah Press, 1986.

Herscher, Uri D. *Jewish Agricultural Utopias in America, 1880–1910*. Detroit: Wayne State University Press, 1981.

Levinson, Robert. *The Jews of the California Gold Rush*. Hoboken, N.J.: Ktav, 1978.

Libo, Kenneth, and Howe, Irving. *We Lived There Too*. New York: St. Martin's/Marek, 1984.

Narell, Irene. *Our City: The Jews of San Francisco*. San Diego: Howell-North, 1980.

Parish, William J. *The Charles Ilfeld Company: A Study of the Rise and Decline of Mercantile Capitalism in New Mexico*. Cambridge: Harvard University Press, 1961.

Plaut, W. Gunther. *The Jews in Minnesota: The First Seventy-five Years*. New York: American Jewish Historical Society, 1959.

Rischen, Moses. *The Jews of the West: The Metropolitan Years*. Berkeley, Calif.: Western Jewish History Center, Judah L. Magnes Museum, 1979.

———, and John Livingston. *The Jew of the American West*. Detroit: Wayne State University Press, 1991.

Rochlin, Harriet and Fred. *Pioneer Jews: A New Life in the Far West*. Boston: Houghton Mifflin, 1984.

Rosenbaum, Fred. *Architects of Reform: Congregational and Community Leadership, Emanu-El of San Francisco, 1849–1980*. Berkeley, Calif.: Western Jewish History Center, Judah L. Magnes Museum, 1980.

Toll, William. *The Making of an Ethnic Community: Portland Jewry Over Four Generations*. Albany: State University of New York Press, 1982.

Vorspan, Max, and Gartner, Lloyd P. *History of the Jews of Los Angeles*. San Marino, Calif.: Huntington Library, 1970.

White, Theodore H. (1915–1986). Journalist and author Theodore H. White, who was born in Boston's Jewish ghetto, was descended from a line of rabbis on his father's side, one of whom was claimed to be Baal Shem-Tov, founder of Hasidism. White's father, an atheist socialist, was the first family member to break from the chain of religious orthodoxy. Several events in White's youth left a permanent mark on him. The first was the Great Depression. White's family, like millions of others in this period, suffered economically, especially after his father's death in the early years of the Great Depression. One of White's earliest memories was of his mother's sorrow in not having the money to provide her children with new shoes. White attributed his later obsession with money as having derived from this experience. Another childhood experience to leave an imprint on White's life was his work as a newspaper boy. He gained from this undertaking an awareness of the profound importance world events have on everyone's life. As a newspaper carrier, he spent a great deal of time on the streets, often jumping from trolley car to trolley car to sell his papers. The time on the streets imbued White with worldly wisdom, a trait that one day would benefit his journalistic enterprise.

Among White's most pivotal childhood experiences was Hebrew school. Initially, White resented his parents forcing him to attend yet another school when he would have preferred being out on the streets with his friends. This resentment diminished with time. White's Hebrew school instructors were recent immigrants to America who were seeking secular education in Boston's many universities. Teaching Hebrew school in the evening enabled them to earn their living expenses while they were full-time students. If there was one common thread to these instructors' lives, it was their Zionism. Hebrew was the chief tool for imparting their Zionist vision to the students. The following quotation from White's *In Search of History* captures the intensity of his Hebrew experience: "We learned it, absorbed it, thought in it, until the ancient Hebrew became a working rhythm in the mind." Of equal value were the Bible lessons. These lessons, White wrote, were his "first intensive seminar in history." History, like religion, White believed, is an attempt to explore man's place and purpose in the world. Unlike many upwardly mobile Jews of his generation, White's passion for Judaism and Zion (ingrained as a student despite his resistance) was not eroded over time.

Despite White's undistinguished academic record at Boston's elite Latin School, his high college entrance examination scores gained him admittance at Harvard. Interestingly, like his former Hebrew instructors, White was able to earn money while a student by teaching Hebrew. White described himself as a "stern but effective teacher of tradition to the young." He also commented on how listening to his young students reading aloud the Song of Songs stirred him with a passion no other reading was ever able to equal.

After graduating summa cum laude with a degree in history from Harvard in 1938, White was the recipient of a Sheldon Traveling Fellowship, enabling him to travel extensively. As a student of Charles Fairbanks (famed Chinese scholar at Harvard), he had cultivated an interest in Chinese culture and history. This interest led him to China. It was in China that John Hersey, a foreign correspondent for *Time* magazine, recruited White as a writer for Henry R. Luce's publishing empire. Following China, White would cover events in India, Europe, and the Japanese surrender ending World War II aboard the battleship *Missouri*. He left *Time* in 1946 and in 1947 became senior editor of the *New Republic*, but left after only six months. After leaving the *New Republic* White free-lanced for the *Saturday Review of Literature*, the *New York Times Magazine*, and *Harper's Magazine*. White also wrote several books during these years, including *Thunder out of China* (1946), *Fire and Ashes* (1953) and *The Mountain Road* (1958). The latter, a novel, was based on White's experience in China.

The enterprise that more than any other would establish White's reputation and fame were his books on the presidential elections, beginning with *The Making of a President 1960*, for which he won the 1962 Pulitzer Prize. For the first time American presidential elections were reported in a narrative form. For White, presidential elections represented an American adventure story, where Americans would discover their identities and history through the democratic process.

In addition to the Pulitzer Prize, White won over twenty major journalism awards, a number of Emmys, and the Benjamin Franklin award for magazine writing.

At a memorial service at Temple Emanu-El, New York City, in May 1986 White was eulogized and honored by people of many backgrounds and diverse political leanings. His exuberance for life, love of the intellect, and passion for human history are part of a legacy that lives on through his writings. *See also* Journalism, Politics.

HOWARD SHAKER
JANET L. DOTTERER

BIBLIOGRAPHY

White, Theodore Harold. *In Search of History: A Personal Adventure*. New York: Harper & Row, 1978.

Wiesel, Elie (b. 1928). Writer, educator, Holocaust survivor and witness, Elie Wiesel has become a voice of conscience in the Jewish community as well as in the world community. In recognition of his deep commitment to human rights, he was awarded the Nobel Peace Prize (1986) and the Congressional Gold Medal of Achievement (1984). Recipient of numerous literary and humanitarian awards from organizations throughout the United States, Israel, and Europe, Wiesel served as chairman of the U.S. President's Commission on the Holocaust (1979–1980) and the U.S. Holocaust Memorial Council (1980–1986). He taught at City College, City University of New York (1972–1976), Yale University (1982–1983), and since 1976 has been the Andrew W. Mellon Professor in the Humanities at Boston University.

Born in Sighet, Romania, Wiesel grew up immersed in Orthodox Jewish teachings. In 1944, at the age of 15, he was deported to Auschwitz with his parents, Shlomo and Sarah (Feig), three sisters, and the rest of Sighet's 15,000 Jews. His mother and younger sister died in the gas chambers, while his two older sisters survived. He and his father stayed together as they were shunted from Auschwitz to Buchenwald, where the young boy watched his father slowly die of disease and starvation. This experience that was to mark him for the rest of his life is recounted in his memoir, *Night* (1960), first published in Yiddish as *Un di velt Hot Geshvign* (1956), then condensed and translated into French in 1958. After World War II, Wiesel lived in Paris, where he attended the Sorbonne (1948–1951) and worked as a journalist for French (*L'Arche*) and Israeli (*Yedioth Ahronot*) newspapers. He adopted French as his literary language as a way of distancing himself from the past. In 1956, he went to New York to live and wrote for the *Jewish Daily Forward*. He was naturalized as an American citizen in 1963, married Marion Erster (1969), and had a son, Shlomo-Elisha, born in 1972.

Wiesel is the author of 30 volumes, including novels, collections of essays, dialogues, and stories (*Legends of Our Time*, 1968; *One Generation After*, 1970; *A Jew Today*, 1978), Hasidic tales (*Souls on Fire*, 1972), biblical portraits (*Messengers of God*, 1976), plays (*Zalmen or the Madness of God*, 1974, and *The Trial of God*, 1978), and cantatas (*Ani Maamin*, 1973). He has also written an eyewitness report on Soviet Jewry based on a trip he took to Russia (*The Jews of Silence*, 1966). While only his first book, *Night*, deals directly with the concentration-camp experience, the Holocaust lies at the core of all of his writing. His works depict the personal and historical events that have structured his universe: life in the Jewish shtetl of pre-war Eastern Europe, the encounter with death, and survival in the aftermath of catastrophe. Each of his novels explores a different option open to the survivor: killing (*Dawn*, 1961), suicide (*The Accident*, 1962), madness (*The Town Beyond the Wall*, 1964, and *Twilight*, 1988), faith and friendship (*The Gates of the Forest*, 1966), return from exile (*A Beggar in Jerusalem*, 1970), silence (*The Oath*, 1973), and involvement in political movements (*The Testament*, 1981). *The Fifth Son* (1985) portrays a child of survivors who seeks to learn about a past from which he has been excluded. As in *The Accident*, the last section of *The Gates of the Forest*, and *Twilight*, the setting for this novel is the United States.

Wiesel's identity as a Jew is central to his writing and to his significant role in public service. He is actively involved in the American Jewish community, participating in countless organizations such as the National Jewish Center for Learning and Leadership, the American Jewish Heritage Center, the American Gathering of Jewish Holocaust Survivors (Honorary President, 1985), and lecturing for over 20 years on Jewish topics at the 92nd Street YM&YWHA in New York City.

Wiesel is a leading figure in American Jewry today because of his commitment to Judaism, his affirmation of Jewish identity, and his concern with the need to correct injustice inflicted upon Jews and other oppressed peoples throughout the world. His primary task as a writer and thinker is to bear witness to the Jewish experience in order to transmit Jewish memory and to assure its continuity. Wiesel brings to the American Jewish community a universal perspective and a sense of Jewish history. *See also* Holocaust, Literature of.

ELLEN S. FINE

BIBLIOGRAPHY

Abramowitz, Molly. *Elie Wiesel: A Bibliography*. Metuchen, N.J.: Scarecrow Press, 1974.

Abramson, Irving, ed. *Against Silence: The Voice and Vision of Elie Wiesel*. 3 vols. New York: Holocaust Library, 1985.

Berenbaum, Michael. *The Vision of the Void: Theological Reflections on the Works of Elie Wiesel*. Middletown, Conn.: Wesleyan University, 1979.

Brown, Robert McAfee. *Elie Wiesel: Messenger to All Humanity*, rev. ed. Notre Dame, Ind.: University of Notre Dame Press, 1989.

Cargas, Harry. *Conversations with Elie Wiesel*. Paramus, N.J.: Paulist/Newman Press, 1976.

Estess, Ted. *Elie Wiesel*. New York: Ungar, 1980.

Fine, Ellen S. *Legacy of Night: The Literary Universe of Elie Wiesel*. Albany: State University of New York Press, 1982.

Rittner, Carol. *Elie Wiesel: Between Memory and Hope*. New York: New York University Press, 1990.

Rosenfeld, Alvin, and Greenberg, Irving, eds. *Confronting the Holocaust; The Impact of Elie Wiesel*. Bloomington: Indiana University Press, 1979.

Wiesenthal Center. *See* SIMON WIESENTHAL CENTER.

Wise, Isaac Mayer (1819–1900). Rabbi and principal organizer of Reform Judaism in North America, Isaac Mayer Wise was born in Steingrub, Bohemia, and received a traditional Talmudic education at various yeshivas. He was certified as a *Religionsweiser* (religious officiant) and served the small Jewish community of Radnitz for three years before emigrating from Bohemia to the United States in 1846. The exact circumstances of his departure from Europe are unknown, although it is possible that either his liberal political views or unauthorized officiation at weddings were brought to the attention of Hapsburg officials causing him to be subjected to censure.

Less than a month after arriving in New York, Wise introduced himself to Max Lilienthal, the chief rabbi of New York's three traditional German synagogues. Lilienthal, who subsequently embraced Reform Judaism, engaged the articulate and energetic newcomer as his personal emissary. A speaking trip to Albany, New York, resulted in a rabbinic position for Wise at the local synagogue, Beth El. Empowered by his new situation and liberated by the democratic traditions of his adopted country, Wise began to fashion a uniquely "American Judaism" with the hope of organizing the United States's chaotic Jewish community under its banner.

Controversy erupted at Beth El because of Wise's introduction of select religious reforms, his increasingly heterodox beliefs, and, above all, his unwillingness to be controlled by his lay leadership. In 1850, following a widely reported melee in the synagogue on Rosh Hashanah, Wise's supporters organized a new congregation, Anshe

Emeth, and named him its rabbi. The new synagogue was the first in the United States to allow mixed seating. The congregation had bought a church and decided to use its family pews. Apparently, the idea of men and women sitting together at Anshe Emeth was not debated.

In 1854, Wise moved to Cincinnati to serve as rabbi of Congregation B'nai Jeshurun (Bene Yeshurun, recently renamed the Wise Center) and remained there for the rest of his life. Shortly after relocating in the "Queen City," he began publishing an English-language paper, the *Israelite*, subsequently renamed the *American Israelite*, and a German supplement called *Die Deborah*. Both papers enjoyed a national circulation. The following year, 1855, Wise organized his first successful rabbinic conference. Meeting in Cleveland, a small group of moderate reformers as well as Isaac Leeser, the leading spokesman for traditional Judaism in America, endorsed a number of Wise's ideas. Subsequently, Leeser distanced himself from the positions and programs adopted at the conference. The harshest criticism of the Cleveland meetings, however, came from radical reformers, especially David Einhorn, who claimed Wise had conceded too much to the Orthodox camp. Undeterred, Wise issued his own prayerbook, *Minhag America*, in 1856 and continued to call for a union of congregations as well as a college to train rabbis in the United States.

During the Civil War, Wise articulated what is widely held to have been the political position of the majority of American Jews of the period. A Copperhead Democrat, he was prepared to tolerate slavery to preserve the Union. Wise even flirted with the idea of running for public office in Ohio until his congregation forced him to drop the idea. During the war years, B'nai Jeshurun built a monumental brick sanctuary in downtown Cincinnati that combined Moorish and Gothic themes. Now a national historical landmark, the Plum St. Temple helped to popularize the "cathedral synagogue" concept in the United States.

Following the war, Wise and Einhorn resumed their fierce ideological feud. Wise attended a rabbinic conference organized by Einhorn in Philadelphia in 1869 but determined that its radical decisions were inconsistent with his vision of a united American Jewry. The German radicals, on the other hand, boycotted meetings called by Wise in Cleveland, Cincinnati, and New York. Frustrated by the sharp divisions in the American rabbinate, laymen, largely associated with Wise's congregation, took matters into their own hands and organized the Union of American Hebrew Congregations (UAHC) in 1873. One of UAHC's principal goals was to establish a rabbinic school, and in 1875 the Hebrew Union College was organized. Wise was named president, and he successfully built the Cincinnati-based institution into an important center of modern Jewish scholarship. Largely estranged from the radicals who prepared the Pittsburgh Platform in 1885, Wise, graduates from the Hebrew Union College, and his rabbinical allies organized the Central Conference of American Rabbis in 1889 as a regional organization. The conference quickly developed a national following and thus emerged as the third and final of the parent bodies that continue to shape the development of American Reform Judaism.

Although he was remarkably prolific and addressed nearly all the major issues of philosophy, religion, and science of the nineteenth century, Wise was not a systematic thinker. Scholars continue to debate the content of his personal religious beliefs. Influenced by Mendelssohnian ideas while still in Europe, he also felt challenged by the rational religion of Unitarianism in the United States. He rejected biblical criticism and, late in life, vociferously opposed political Zionism. Wise's intellectual flexibility and personal dynamism greatly contributed to his effectiveness as a religious leader in the United States during the nineteenth century. He never abandoned his vision of a singular American Judaism; in effect, however, he established the basic pattern of denominational Judaism in North America. The current institutional strength of the American Reform Movement is testimony to his foresightedness and tenacity.

Wise married Therese Bloch in 1844. They had ten children. She died in 1874. Two years later, Wise married Selma Bondi. They had four children, including Rabbi Jonah B. Wise. *See also* Reform Judaism.

LANCE J. SUSSMAN

BIBLIOGRAPHY

Heller, James G. *Isaac M. Wise: His Life, Work and Thought.* New York: Union of American Hebrew Congregations, 1965.

Kraut, Benny. "Judaism Triumphant: Isaac Mayer Wise on Unitarianism and Liberal Christianity." *AJS Review* 7–8 (1982–1983): 179–230.

Meyer, Michael A. *Response to Modernity: A History of the Reform Movement in Judaism.* New York: Oxford University Press, 1988.

Temkin, Sefton D. "Isaac Mayer Wise and the Civil War." *American Jewish Archives* 15 (November 1963): 120-142.

Wise, Stephen (1874-1949). Reform Rabbi Stephen Wise, born in Budapest, Hungary, was a descendant of a long line of rabbis, which included his father Rabbi Aaron Weisz, who in turn was the son of the chief rabbi of Hungary. His mother, Sabine, was the daughter of Moritz Fisher, who had founded the porcelain industry in Hungary and had received the rare distinction of being knighted and then raised to the rank of baron.

The Wise family, upon reaching America in 1875, settled on East Fifth Street in New York. Stephen, a product of the public school system, eventually attended City College followed by studies at Columbia University. His academic interests were in Latin and Greek; however, his first love was English. He invested time and energy gleaning the works of the great English poets and prose stylists.

After Columbia, Stephen Wise was ordained as rabbi in Vienna under the tutelage of Rabbi Jellinek. This was followed by graduate work at Oxford University. While in his mid-twenties Wise was made rabbi of the Madison Avenue Synagogue, a prestigious Conservative congregation in New York. During his tenure as rabbi, the Dreyfus affair in France and pogroms in czarist Russia were front-page news stories. Because of these events, Wise was attracted to the budding Zionist Movement in America. In a time when Zionism received little support from American Jews, he founded the Zionist Federation in New York on July 4, 1897. This was also the period when Wise married Louise Waterman, an artist.

In 1900, the Wise family moved to Portland, Oregon. Their move was motivated by a desire to live in a smaller city where Wise would have more time to read, study, and write. Also, Wise's beliefs had become increasingly liberal, and he felt that the Reform Movement (the affiliation of his congregation in Portland) would be more hospitable toward his changing convictions. In Portland, Wise became politically involved in the community and became part of a movement to institute good government in a time when state and city governments were riddled with corruption. In addition, he was a speaker in frequent demand and was often invited to speak before Christian congregations to explain Judaism.

Rabbi Wise, a person of indefatigable energy,

was also an ardent supporter of the labor movement. He served on a commission dealing with the issue of child labor and was Oregon's commissioner of child labor. A speech given after the Triangle fire of 1911 in New York City, which resulted in the needless death of garment workers, illustrates Stephen Wise's passion on this issue. "While prosperity is good, life is better, that while possessions are valuable, life is priceless. The meaning of the hour is that the life of the lowest worker in the nation is sacred and inviolable, and, if that sacred human right be violated, we shall stand adjudged and condemned before the tribunal of God and history."

Wise traveled to Europe in 1904 to attend the Greater Actions Committee of the World Zionist Organization (WZO) meeting in Vienna. As a member of the Federation of American Zionists (FAZ), he expected to be treated as an equal by members of the European counterpart of WZO. He had long admired Theodore Herzl and was hurt when ignored by the Greater Actions Committee. Herzl was able to smooth things over with Wise, but it was to be just one of many such incidents to occur between American and European Jewry leadership throughout the coming years.

In 1906, Wise returned to New York City. Among his many considerable achievements was the establishment of the Free Synagogue there in 1907. Braving criticism from Jewish establishment groups, Wise established a synagogue built upon liberal and egalitarian principles. The synagogue was managed democratically and not by a hierarchy where those who made the largest contributions dictated policy.

In 1918, Wise, as chairman of the Provisional Committee, shouldered the responsibility of preparing and effecting the reorganization of the newly created Zionist Organization of America (ZOA). In 1920, he resigned as first vice-president of ZOA but reconsidered after considerable pressure from Louis Brandeis. In 1936, Wise became president of the ZOA and chairman of the United Palestine Appeal (UPA). He remained president of the ZOA until 1943, when he was ousted by Abba Hillel Silver.

In the 1930s, Wise found himself in opposition to Jewish organizations on the issue of Nazi Germany. He advocated a more assertive response to the excesses of the Nazis and used his close relationship with President Franklin D. Roosevelt to put pressure on the German government with regard to the persecution of its Jews.

In recent years, Holocaust historiography has focused on Stephen Wise's controversial decision in August 1942 to withhold from the American Jewish community news of the "final solution" as it was relayed to him by the World Jewish Congress. Trusting the Roosevelt administration was sincere in its efforts to save European Jewry, Wise deferred to Under Secretary of State Sumner Welles's request that the story of the mass murder of the Jews be withheld until it could be confirmed. Thus, it was not until November 1942 that a reluctant Roosevelt administration confirmed the truth of the reports of the "final solution."

Stephen Wise was also co-chairman of the American Zionist Emergency Committee (1939–1945), perhaps the most influential Zionist lobbying group in its time. Wise was associated with the moderates within AZEC who were willing to compromise on the idea of a Jewish state in return for non-Zionist support of unlimited immigration into Palestine. As in the matter of the Holocaust, Wise placed great faith in President Roosevelt's ability to persuade the British to revoke the White Paper of 1939.

Wise's strategy of quiet diplomacy brought him into conflict with Rabbi Abba Hillel Silver (1893–1963), the leader of the more militant wing of AZEC. The militants argued for the immediate creation of a Jewish state in Palestine. Whereas Wise and his moderates looked to the President for support of this agenda, the militants believed their objectives could best be achieved through lobbying Congress. *See also* Reform Judaism, Zionism.

HOWARD SHAKER
JANET L. DOTTERER

BIBLIOGRAPHY

Feingold, Henry. *The Politics of Wise Rescue*. New York: Holocaust Library, 1970.

Urofsky, Melvin. *A Voice that Spoke for Justice: The Life and Times of Stephen S. Wise*. Albany: State University of New York Press, 1982.

Wise, Stephen. *As I See It*. New York: Marstin Press, 1944.

———. *Challenging Years: The Autobiography of Stephen Wise*. New York: Putnam, 1949.

Wolfson, Harry (1887–1974). Born in Ostrin, Lithuania, Harry Wolfson studied at yeshivas in Grodno, Slonim, Bialystock, Kovno, Slobodka, and Vilna before coming to the United States in 1903. His family settled in Scranton, Pennsylvania. After graduating from Harvard College, Wolfson was awarded a traveling fellowship to study in Europe, 1912–1914. On his return he joined the Harvard faculty in 1915. He became professor of Hebrew literature and philosophy in 1925, which position he held until his retirement in 1958.

Wolfson was the author of numerous scholarly works. His *Crescas' Critique of Aristotle* (completed in 1918, published in 1929) included a critical edition of a section of Crescas's *Or Adonai*. This work was described by Arthur Hyaman (in the *Encyclopaedia Judaica*) as of special importance because of the notes that fill half of the volume: "In these notes Wolfson discusses with great erudition the origin and development of the terms and arguments discussed by Crescas and . . . clarifies Crescas' often enigmatic text." Wolfson also introduced in his *Crescas' Critique* the method of hypothetical deduction ("hypotheico-deductive method of textual study") that guided his work for the future. The premise of the method is that authors write with sufficient accuracy that "every term, expression, generalization, or exception is significant not so much for what it states as for what it implies." The work of scholarship then is to resolve contradictions through harmonistic interpretation, and that demands probing the "latent processes" of the author.

Wolfson turned to the commentaries on Aristotle by the Muslim philosopher Averroes and undertook to edit and publish the manuscripts, with the Arabic originals and Hebrew and Latin translations as well as English translations. In 1934, he published *The Philosophy of Spinoza*, investigating the processes of Spinoza's reasoning. From this study he developed the conception of investigating, in "the structure and the growth of philosophic systems from Plato to Spinoza." His conception, that philosophy began with Plato and ended with Spinoza, led him next to Philo, and he published *Philo: Foundation of Religious Philosophy in Judaism, Christianity, and Islam* (1947). Wolfson here demonstrated that Philo did more than make philosophical statements; he developed a philosophical system, and, further, that system was the foundation of the religious philosophies of Judaism, Christianity, and Islam. This system stood until Spinoza demolished it. Wolfson moved on from Philo to the Church Fathers, which yielded, in 1956, *The Philosophy of the Church Fathers*. From Judaism, then Christianity, he turned to

Islam, with *The Philosophy of the Kalam* (1976) and *Repercussions in Jewish Philosophy*. He also wrote numerous essays, 116 items being listed in his bibliography as of 1963, and some of the more important essays were published in 1961 as *Religious Philosophy: A Group of Essays*. In 1973 and 1976, he published two more volumes of essays, *Studies in the History of Philosophy and Religion* (in two volumes).

As a teacher of graduate students, Wolfson taught several generations of historians of philosophy. He also taught undergraduates at Harvard and served as adviser to incoming freshmen, with whom, in many cases, he developed lifelong and warm relationships. His counsel to young students was long remembered, and his hospitality and courtesy were legendary among those fortunate enough to know him. While scholarly and profoundly devoted to his academic program, he also was a man of great warmth and deep wisdom, and his charm, as much as his erudition, form part of the legacy he left to those who knew him.

It is due to Wolfson's scholarly activity while at Harvard that Jewish studies has become entrenched in humanistic research in the United States. Wolfson's tireless work laid the foundation for the development of the Harvard College Library's Judaica Collection as the leading university research collection in Jewish studies. During his tenure at Harvard he served as curator of Hebraica and Judaica in Harvard College Library.

Wolfson's successor at Harvard and his student, Isadore Twersky, summarizes Wolfson's life's work in academe as follows: "Wolfson's life work at Harvard marks the emergence of Judaica in great universities as a respectable, self-sufficient discipline with its own integrity, autonomy, and comprehensiveness. The establishment of the Littauer chair at Harvard for Harry Wolfson gave Judaica its own station on the frontiers of knowledge and pursuit of truth. . . . Wolfson's impact was great not only because of institutional leverage, but also because of the broad range of his own creative scholarship. . . . Personal, professional, and institutional preeminence . . . carved out a central niche for Harry Wolfson in the development of Jewish scholarship in America." *See also* Academe.

JACOB NEUSNER

BIBLIOGRAPHY

Schwarz, Leo W. *Wolfson of Harvard: Portrait of a Scholar*. Philadelphia: Jewish Publication Society, 1978.

Women. Jewish-American women have lived in multiple worlds simultaneously. Since the first appearance of Jews in colonial America, the women have had to create Jewish homes for their families while adjusting to the new American realities. They had to face, and absorb, the individualistic rhetoric of this country and reconcile it with their communally structured Jewish life. In so doing, they devised new forms and values for the Jewish-American community while attaining unprecedented heights in individual accomplishments.

Jewish-American women have been responsible for the maintenance of religious Judaism within the home where ritual practices form the foundation of observance. They have also been essential to the building of, and the continuance of, religious and secular communal organizations. The sisterhoods of every congregation have raised money for their synagogues. Beginning in the nineteenth century, especially in Reform Jewish congregations, Jewish women became the teachers of the newly formed Sunday schools. Rebecca Gratz (1781–1869), born and raised in Philadelphia, founded the first Jewish Sunday School in America in 1838. She also started the Female Hebrew Benevolent Society in 1819. Gratz and scores of middle- and upper-class Jewish women in each Jewish community provided relief for the poor, the widows, and the orphans. The words of the Prophets were acted upon.

Prior to the 1880s, most Jews came from either Sephardic or Germanic-Central European backgrounds. Their particular customs and practices differed from the newly arriving Eastern European Jews. While the earlier settlers were already comfortably middle class and many were Reform Jews, the newcomers were largely working class and Orthodox. But the women in both communities shared many essential values and concerns: most wanted to provide their children with a Jewish home and education; they all worried about the temptations of the American schools, streets, and stores; and most experimented with their own personal growth and change in the egalitarian atmosphere of America.

The newer immigrant women also participated in social service organizations. For all of them, volunteer work satisfied their need for companionship while helping the needy. Further, the Orthodox created their own hospitals so as to insure the observance of the dietary laws. In Chicago, for example, while Reform Jewish women volunteered at Michael Reese Hospital in the

1890s, Orthodox Jewish women worked at Mt. Sinai Hospital.

By 1900, essential patterns in Jewish-American women's lives were emerging. Economic fortune often determined the fate of the women in the family. While voluntarism characterized some lives, working-class women, especially the young, unmarried women, worked in the garment factories of New York and Chicago. Jewish manufacturers, who dominated the clothing industry, hired young, seemingly pliant, women to work 12- to 14-hour shifts. Married women took in boarders and did piece work at home. Jewish women left the factories within one generation, and the daughters of immigrants worked in the new department stores and offices of America. With the improvement in their fathers' fortunes, they completed high school and even went off to college in greater numbers.

Jewish women dominated the ranks of the garment workers, and they played a significant role in organizing the most successful trade union in America, the International Ladies Garment Workers Union (ILGWU). In the shirtwaist industry, Jewish women led the first mass strike of women workers in this country. On November 22, 1909, Local 25 of the Ladies Waistmakers Union voted to strike for union recognition, better conditions, and the elimination of the hated charges on equipment. Twenty thousand women workers went into the streets, most being Jewish, though a small number of Italian women joined them.

Many young women distinguished themselves during the more than two months that the women struck. Pauline Newman (1894?–1986) became the first woman organizer following the strike and went on to become the executive secretary of the Joint Board of Sanitary Control, a committee created to negotiate labor disputes between the manufacturers and the workers. In 1919, she became the educational director of the ILGWU's Unity Health Center, a position she held for many years. Fania Cohn (1885?–1962) became the ILGWU's only woman vice president in 1916. Earlier, in August, 1915, she had led the first successful strike of Chicago's dress and white-goods workers. Following this accomplishment, she became the head of the ILGWU's worker education programs, programs that were renowned for their wide-ranging opportunities for workers to expand their education.

The overwhelming majority of Jewish women workers were temporary workers, 16- to 20-year-olds, who worked in the factories until they married or until their first child was born. Afterward, they helped support the family with various kinds of home work. The few women who attained leadership positions in the union were generally single women for whom the union became a surrogate family. Further, Jewish women found the male leadership of the unions unwilling to share power with them; the cultural attitudes toward women, common to both the Jewish and Christian traditions, prevailed among the Jewish unions' male leadership.

The labor experience produced two extraordinary rebels whose speaking and writing distinguished them from all others. Emma Goldman (1869–1940) and Rose Pastor Stokes (1879–1933), both daughters of immigrants, experienced the hardships of the sweatshop, Goldman in a garment factory and Stokes in a cigar factory. Both abandoned Judaism in search of a more satisfying philosophy for ambitious, able women who found traditional Judaism patriarchal and stultifying. Goldman found sympathy for her message of anarchism among the Jewish workers, and she often spoke in Yiddish. Stokes became a socialist and later, a founding member of the U.S. Communist Party. Both women were feminists also and combined their struggle for human equality with women's equality. They embraced a universalist vision, claiming that the particularism of Judaism was too restrictive. Though they abandoned the faith of their mothers and fathers, they were products of the first-generational encounter between Jewish immigrants and America.

While the new labor unions provided some members of the immigrant generation with leadership possibilities, Jewish women of the middle class whose families had been here much longer also emerged into positions of prominence. Lillian Wald (1867–1940), a nurse from Rochester, New York, founded the Henry Street Settlement House in 1893 for Jewish immigrants on the Lower East Side of New York. Her training gave her settlement house a preventive health focus; Wald established a visiting nurses program while offering classes in nutrition and prenatal care to the young mothers in the neighborhood. Wald had the financial and social support of the Jewish male leaders of the city. During the early years of World War I, before the United States entered the war, she was a leader of the American Union Against Militarism, a peace group. Though she never achieved the public recognition accorded Jane Addams, Wald's activities for Jewish immigrants established impressive patterns that became part of the newly emerging profession of social work.

Julia Richman (1855–1912), a daughter of immigrants, became a professional educator. A native New Yorker, Richman graduated from Normal College (later Hunter College), became a teacher in 1872, a principal in 1884, and in 1903, the first Jewish woman district superintendent in the New York City school system. Richman chose "Little Italy" and "Little Israel," the Lower East Side, for her district. She tried to inculcate American values into the children while believing that their religious and cultural heritage was to be taught in religious schools. Though she often encountered stiff opposition from Jewish parents who objected to her English-only policy and her vigorous efforts at acculturation, Richman displayed her commitment to her Jewish roots by actively writing curriculum for Reform Jewish Sunday schools and by lecturing on the value of religious education.

Two outstanding creators of Jewish women's organizations were Hannah Greenebaum Solomon (1858–1942) and Henrietta Szold (1860–1945). Solomon, a member of the well-established Chicago German Jewish Greenebaums, founded the National Council of Jewish Women after having brought representatives from all over the country to the Parliament of Religions at the World Columbian Exposition in Chicago in 1893. The nationwide group of women representatives became the basis for an organization that returned to its respective communities committed to perpetuating the Jewish religion, philanthropy, and education. While each chapter of the National Council devised its own particular set of projects, the yearly meetings of the national organization served to unify the group. The New York City chapter distinguished itself with its programs to visit Jewish women in prison and to greet new arrivals at the city's docks. During the Depression of 1893, the Chicago chapter established a workroom for needy women.

Henrietta Szold founded Hadassah, the Women's Zionist Organization, on Purim, 1912. Szold came from a religious Hungarian family in Baltimore, where her father, Rabbi Benjamin Szold, had been a leader in the newly emerging Conservative branch of Judaism. Being the eldest in a family of daughers, Henrietta Szold learned Torah from her father and later in life, when she settled in Palestine after 1920, took up conversational Hebrew. As early as 1896, she had spoken before a local group of the National Council of Jewish Women on the Zionist cause. At a time when that philosophy had few adherents among American Jews, Szold spoke and wrote on the importance of a return to Zion for the Jewish people.

Hadassah became the most successful Zionist organization in America, the largest women's organization in the world, and a most effective fund raiser during the 1920s and 1930s. Szold combined her fervent commitment to Zionism with her knowledge of Judaism and Jewish leaders, and her acceptance of Progressive American ideals. She was a Jewish pragmatist who shaped Hadassah in two directions: to provide medical and nursing care to Jews and Arabs in Palestine and to educate American Jews to Judaism and Zionism. Beginning with the sending of two nurses to Palestine, Hadassah's goals and accomplishments steadily increased. Hadassah hospital, begun in the 1930s, has become one of the most modern and complete medical facilities in the Middle East. Henrietta Szold moved permanently to Palestine in 1920; except for a brief return to New York (1923–1926), she lived out her life there. In the 1930s, among her many projects was Youth Aliyah, aimed at getting Jewish children out of Europe. Szold remained an inspiration to her followers long after her death.

Jewish women writers also emerged early in the century as sensitive commentators on the Jewish experience in America. Natives Fannie Hurst (1889–1968) and Edna Ferber (1887–1968) were removed, both geographically and emotionally, from the immigrant experience, while immigrant Anzia Yezierska (1880–1970) was a part of that life. Ferber, growing up in Wisconsin and Illinois, wrote an autobiographical novel called *Fanny Herself* (1917), which featured a Jewish widow, Molly Brandeis, in Winnebago, Wisconsin; the widow supported her children by operating a dry goods store. As one of the few Jewish families in the town, the Brandeises felt isolated, though the daughter Fanny never abandoned her love of Judaism. Ferber's most popular fiction, however, dealt with American pioneer types, such as the widow farmer in *So Big* and the oil entrepreneurs in *Giant*. Ferber's mother Julia may have been the prototype for her heroic characters; her commitment to Judaism was also expressed in her two autobiographical volumes, *A Peculiar Treasure* and *A Kind of Magic*.

Fannie Hurst grew up in St. Louis, the daughter of a prosperous German Jewish family, and knew little about immigrant Jews until she moved to New York City in the second decade of the twentieth century. In a short story called "The Gold in Fish"(1927), she satirized the eager assimilation of Jewish children; the author's sympathies were with the older generation. Like Ferber, her most successful fiction dealt with un-ethnic Americans. Hurst became the queen of melodrama, with stories like *Back Street* becoming the basis of successful movies. Yezierska, by con-trast, portrayed in many of her stories a tyrannical Orthodox father who denied his daughter free-dom. *Bread Givers* (1925), her best-known novel, described a young woman's efforts to separate herself from her demanding father to obtain an education and to lead a life different from her mother and sisters. She succeeded and reconciled with her father at the story's end.

Subsequent generations of Jewish women writers have dealt with the problems of their re-spective generation. Middle-generation daughters such as Tillie Olsen (b. 1913), Grace Paley (b. 1922), and Cynthia Ozick (b. 1928) de-scribed their adjustments to America. Women growing up in the 1940s and 1950s, such as Gail Parent (b. 1940) and Susan Fromberg Schaeffer (b. 1941) incorporated the new feminism of the 1960s in their literary identity quests. Ozick has emerged as the most consciously Jewish woman writer today. Her fiction and nonfiction alike grapple with the problem of idolatry in the mod-ern world, paganism versus theism, and material-ism versus morality.

Advice literature has a long and successful history in America as well as in the Jewish com-munity. From the "Bintel Brief" in the *Jewish Daily Forward* to the daily advice columns in the newspapers, women have contributed their knowledge and experience. Three of America's most popular advice columnists are Jewish: Ann Landers (b. 1918) (Esther Friedman Lederer), her twin sister Abigail Van Buren (Pauline Fried-man Phillips), and Sylvia Porter (1913-1991). While the twin sisters advise millions of Ameri-cans daily on how to deal with personal problems, Sylvia Porter offers them financial advice. In all three cases, the columns are syndicated and reach multiple millions of people each day. Collec-tively, these three Jewish women writers have secularized and universalized the immigrant Jew-ish concern for adjustment to American life.

Show business attracted many of the daugh-ters of immigrants. Sophie Tucker (1884-1966) came to this country as a child and began singing in her father's Hartford, Connecticut restaurant. The touring Yiddish actors who frequented the restaurant encouraged her to pursue a career on the Yiddish stage. Tucker chose vaudeville and became a successful nightclub singer of Yiddish and bawdy songs. Her largely Jewish clientele enjoyed her rendition of "My Yiddishe Mamma," which she sang for over 50 years. Fanny Brice (1891-1951) was the daughter of immigrants who learned Yiddish mannerisms and intonations from the composer Irving Berlin. He wrote "Sadie Salome Go Home" for Brice in 1909 and sug-gested that she sing it with a Yiddish accent. She did and incorporated this stylistic device into her act. Brice became the star of the Ziegfeld Follies from 1910 to 1923 and was regarded as one of the greatest stars in show business.

As the economic fortunes of the fathers im-proved, the daughters benefited by increased edu-cational opportunities. Though marriage re-mained the major adult occupation for Jewish daughters, college attendance increased, so that by the mid-1970s, an equal number of Jewish girls and boys were going to college. The number of Jewish women professionals increased steadily; by 1980, 23 percent of Jewish women were col-lege graduates while only 14 percent of all Ameri-can women had college degrees. Jewish women are represented in the traditional female profes-sions, teaching, social work, and librarianship, as well as the male-defined fields of law and medi-cine.

Better-educated Jewish-American women displayed both their self-confidence and their confidence in America by assuming public roles in politics and the academy. Two of the most vocal and visible women politicians of the 1970s were Bella Abzug (b. 1920), three-term member of the House of Representatives from 1970 to 1976, and Elizabeth Holtzman (b. 1941), a member of the U.S. Congress from 1972 to 1982. Holtzman left Washington to become Brooklyn's district attorney and then was elected to be New York City comptroller. Both women spoke out on behalf of Israel as well as women's issues. Two distinguished professors who consciously iden-tify as Jews are Lucy Dawidowicz (1915-1990), professor of Holocaust Studies at Yeshiva Univer-sity, and Rosalyn Yalow (b. 1921), a nuclear physicist and Nobel Prize winner. For Dawido-wicz, of course, her academic interest focused upon the Jewish fate in Europe during World War II.

Jewish-American women have also entered

the field of rabbinic studies in the last 20 years. The first woman to be ordained was Sally Priesand, a 1972 graduate of the Hebrew Union College in Cincinnati. She not only opened the door for women in the Reform Movement but also in the Reconstructionist and Conservative movements. In 1990, there were 168 Reformed women rabbis in the United States. In 1974, Sandy Sasso became the first Reconstructionist woman rabbi in the United States; by 1990, there were 46 ordained women rabbis in the Reconstructionist Movement. It would not be until 1985 that the Conservative Movement would ordain Amy Eilberg as its first woman rabbi. In 1990, there were 27 Conservative ordained women rabbis.

Jewish-American women have maintained their commitments to Jewish religious, philanthropic, social, and educational organizations. Post-1945 groups such as Women's American ORT (Organization Through Rehabilitation and Training) preserve the strong ties to Israel. Hadassah, the National Council of Jewish Women as well as the sisterhoods of synagogues and temples and the boards of Jewish federations and community centers continue to win support from them. Simultaneous with this impressive involvement in communal activities, Jewish-American women have attained impressive educational credentials; they pursue individual careers and meet family and community obligations. They have successfully merged the social and religious values of Judaism with the individualistic rhetoric of America. *See also* Feminist Movement.

JUNE SOCHEN

BIBLIOGRAPHY

Baum, Charlotte; Hyman, Paula; and Michel, Sonya. *The Jewish Woman in America.* New York: New American Library, 1977.

Dash, Joan. *Summoned to Jerusalem: The Life of Henrietta Szold.* New York: Harper & Row, 1979.

Glanz, Rudolph. *The Jewish Woman in America: Two Female Immigrant Generations, 1820–1929.* Hoboken, N.J.: Ktav, 1976.

Harris, Alice Kessler. "Organizing the Unorganizable: Three Jewish Women and Their Union." *Labor History* 17 (Winter 1976): 5–23.

Lebeson, Anita Libman. *Recall to Life: Jewish Women in American History.* New York: Yoseloff, 1970.

Levine, Louis. *The Women's Garment Workers: A History of the International Ladies Garment Workers Union.* New York: Huebsch, 1924.

Lowenthal, Marvin. *Henrietta Szold: Life and Letters.* New York: Viking Press, 1942.

Marcus, Jacob Rader. *The American Jewish Woman.* Hoboken, N.J.: Ktav, 1981.

Sochen, June. *Consecrate Every Day: The Public Lives of Jewish American Women, 1880–1980.* New York: SUNY Press, 1981.

Solomon, Hannah Greenebaum. *Fabric of My Life.* New York: Bloch, 1946.

Workmen's Circle. Although the historic founding date of the Workmen's Circle is September 4, 1900, its founding took place in spirit on April 4, 1892, in the tenement flat of one Sam Greenberg at 151 Essex Street in Manhattan. There, some six Jewish immigrant workers founded the Workingmen's Circle (Arbeter Ring). It was here, with Eastern European Jews streaming into the streets of America, especially the ghetto of the Lower East Side of New York, that the seeds of the labor movement of America itself began to take hold. The Workmen's Circle came out of the years of struggle by Yiddish-speaking-and-reading sweatshop workers to form not only Jewish unions, but also a self-help organization that would involve itself in trade union organization, health insurance, medical assistance, death benefits, hospitalization, cultural interests, and a fraternalism that encompassed all of these ingredients.

When, on September 4, 1900, the Workmen's Circle became a national order, the eight years prior to Workmen's Circle becoming a national order had been spent in intense organization and in designing what became for the decades that followed the pioneering of social legislation that led to the ingredients of the New Deal, Great Society, and New Frontier. The Workmen's Circle program ran the gamut from social security and medicare to human rights, from fighting against all forms of totalitarianism to organizing against child labor, sweatshops, slums, etc. In May 1933, the Workmen's Circle was the first to hold a public demonstration of some 50,000 in Union Square (New York) against the rise of Hitlerism—months after he came into power. It was in the forefront of the anti-Nazi boycott movement as it was in 1934 helping, together with the labor movement, to create the Jewish Labor Committee to rescue and aid the Jewish and non-Jewish labor victims of Hitlerism. During the earlier years of labor organization in the United States, the Workmen's Circle's Labor Lyceums, located in major industrial areas throughout the United States and Canada, were used by a then fledgling labor movement as headquarters for organization and strikes. Soup kitchens and clothing depots for strikers were established on the premises of the Circle, and the Circle was dubbed "The Red Cross of the Labor Movement" by the late AFL President William Green.

Impresario Sol Hurok began his artistic career as educational director of the Lyceums and brought such new (then) talent to the Jewish immigrants as Yascha Heifetz and Mischa Elman and the voices of Lauritz Melchior and Feodor Chaliapin.

Stressing a common bond through Yiddish, the Workmen's Circle was the conduit for, and by, the *Jewish Daily Forward*. To this day, both share officers, on occasion, and occupy the same headquarters building in Manhattan. Wherever and whenever Yiddish cultural pursuits are in need of financial and moral nourishment, the Workmen's Circle is a leading sponsor. From YIVO to its own secular schools, from Third Seders to the "Yiddish Vinkels" in the Soviet Union, France, Israel, or Australia, the cultural department of the organization since its inception has pursued a vigorous course of involvement. In the early years of the twentieth century, the organization created The Folksbiene, the world-renowned "amateur" drama troupe that has displayed theatrical works of noted Jewish writers, from Isaac Bashevis Singer, Sholem Aleichem, Sholem Asch, Peretz Hirschbein to Clifford Odets (in Yiddish translation, of course).

Prominent Yiddish writers including Sholem Aleichem, labor leaders, and socialists are buried in the organization's Old Carmel Cemetery in New York, which is known as the Pantheon of the Jewish labor movement. Interred there also are B. Charey Vladeck, Meyer London, and the distinguished author and editor of the *Jewish Daily Forward*, Abraham Cahan, among others.

In the 1940s, the Workmen's Circle reached a peak membership of close to 75,000; in 1990, the organization still had some 50,000 members and a multimillion dollar reserve in assets. Despite the decline in membership experienced by all Jewish fraternal groups (many of whom have since faded), the Workmen's Circle has redesigned itself for the "New Decade" and "New Century." It still maintains a modern summer resort in upper New York State for both adults and children—with an emphasis on the latter. When in the 1920s and 1930s tuberculosis was the scourge of the sweatshops, the Workmen's Circle maintained the first sanitarium for the afflicted in Liberty, New

York. Subsequently it sold that property to the famous Borscht Belt resort Grossinger's and invested in building community centers in Los Angeles, Boston, Philadelphia, Cleveland, Detroit, New York, Montreal, and Toronto and throughout Florida.

To keep pace with modern technology, the Workmen's Circle has installed an extensive computer system to service members. Medical facilities have also been updated. The VCR has become a tool for worldwide dissemination of Yiddish films and entertainment. From book fairs in New York to Moscow, the Workmen's Circle's image of literary Yiddishkeit is displayed to the public. The organization and its officers have never forgotten their roots—just refined them, never forgotten their objectives—just updated them. While maintaining geriatric centers in New Jersey and the Bronx, New York, Workmen's Circle has been busy setting up new "young" branches in Boston, New York, Detroit, Cleveland, and other Jewish centers. The balance of "old" and "young" is attempted through public affairs forums and statements to retain old values in a changing society.

While other Jewish organizations may be older, the Workmen's Circle is one of the oldest fraternal bodies in continuous existence. Whether in the President's Conference of Major American Jewish Organizations, or local community councils, or in Israel, it maintains contacts not only with Jewish leaders throughout the world, but also labor leaders and leaders of free democratic causes. Thus the organization continues its concern for human freedom and dignity in the spirit of its motto: "All for One, One for All."

W. KIRSCHENBAUM

BIBLIOGRAPHY

Levin, Nora. *While Messiah Tarried: Jewish Socialist Movements, 1871–1917.* New York: Schocken, 1977.

Shapiro, Judah J. *The Friendly Society: A History of the Workmen's Circle.* New York: Schocken, 1977.

Shepard, Richard. *Live and Be Well.* New York: Simon & Schuster, 1987.

Wouk, Herman (b. 1915). A best-selling American fictionist and playwright, Herman Wouk grew up in New York City. In many respects, his early childhood followed the typical pattern of Jewish immigrant children: his parents were Russian Jewish immigrants; his father worked as a laundry laborer for $3 per hour; and the Wouk family made do as best they could amid the clutter and poverty of the Bronx.

By 1931, however, their situation had changed dramatically. Wouk's father became a success in the power laundry business, and the family moved to the more fashionable surroundings of Manhattan's West Side—the affluent world Wouk would later chronicle in *Marjorie Morningstar*.

Wouk graduated from Columbia University in 1934 and began his literary career as a gag man for radio comedians. His apprentice labor (1934–1935) landed him a more prestigious job as a scriptwriter for Fred Allen, a post he held from 1936 to 1941.

By 1950, Wouk had written a handful of reasonably successful books, including *The City Boy: The Adventures of Herbie Bookbinder and His Cousin, Cliff* (a 1948 Book-of-the-Month Club selection and Reader's Digest Condensed Book Club selection), but widespread fame, and "name recognition," came with *The Caine Mutiny* (1951), which won that year's Pulitzer Prize. Wouk has basked in the popular limelight ever since, with one best-selling novel after another: *Marjorie Morningstar* (1955), *Youngblood Hawke* (1962), *The Winds of War* (1971), and *War and Remembrance* (1978). In each case, motion picture version or elaborate television miniseries have followed publication.

Not surprisingly, some critics have taken Wouk to task as a literary middleweight, partly because he cares little about symbolism or the niceties of a sophisticated "style," and partly because he delivers the large, sprawling canvases that mass audiences love. Malcolm Cowley, for example, dismissed him contemptuously as an "all-right-nik," one singled out for praise by *Life* magazine as a writer of "positivist" fiction. Others objected to the unjustified swings in Wouk's plot lines, especially Lieutenant Greewald's final speech (in *The Caine Mutiny*) defending both Captain Queeg and the United States Navy. Wouk fared no better—indeed, probably much worse—where drama critics were concerned. As one reviewer put it, "All Wouk, no play."

Nonetheless, Wouk is not only a popular success, but also a significant Jewish phenomenon. As Pearl K. Bell points out, he is an "unembarrassed believer in such 'discredited' forms of commitment as valor, gallantry, leadership, patriotism." He is also a Jewish-American writer "unembarrassed" by his Jewishness. His undergraduate years at Columbia may have taken a toll on the Orthodoxy of his youth, but in 1940, he began a slow return to the faith of his fathers, and more particularly to the Lubavitcher Hasidism of his grandfather, Mendel Leib Levine, a rabbi from Minsk. *This Is My God* (1959) is Wouk's nonfictional, highly personal account of the Jewish faith. It, too, was a Book-of-the-Month Club selection and later reissued as a Reader's Digest condensed book. *See also* Fiction.

SANFORD PINSKER
MICHAEL HARMATZ

BIBLIOGRAPHY

Guttman, Allen. *The Jewish Writer in America*. New York: Oxford University Press, 1971.

Y

Yeshiva University. A multifaceted institution of higher education, Yeshiva University, New York City, is the outgrowth of one of the many schools established on the Lower East Side to serve the needs of the immigrant Jewish community.

In the community's early days Hebrew and religious education did not receive high priority, but as early as 1886 the Yeshivah Etz Chayim was established in New York. Despite its name, it was primarily an elementary school. Nearer in its curriculum to the East European yeshivas was the Rabbi Isaac Elhanan Theological Seminary, established in 1897 in memory of Rabbi Isaac Elhanan Spektor, of Kovno. Many of its students expected to enter the rabbinate, and in 1908, there was unrest over student demands that the curriculum should not be limited to Talmud and codes but should be broadened to include subjects needed to enable a rabbi to function in an American congregation.

In 1915, the two schools amalgamated. Using the name Rabbi Isaac Elhanan Theological Seminary (RIETS), the combined institution came under the presidency of Bernard Revel (1885–1940), whose concept of combining talmudic and secular studies in one college set the course for future development. First Revel established a high school in connection with the yeshivah; in 1922, the teachers' institute set up by the Mizrachi in 1917 was taken over; and in 1928, the State of New York chartered Yeshiva College, with the power to grant bachelor's degrees in the liberal arts and sciences.

This expansion in the educational field was sealed by the construction of a spacious college building in Washington Heights. Progress was not unimpeded. Scarcely had the college moved to Washington Heights than the Great Depression brought financial disaster. Further, the institution always had to face the hostility of those sections of Orthodox opinion to whom the combination of talmudic and secular studies was anathema.

Under Samuel Belkin, who was president from 1943 to 1975, and his successor, Norman Lamm, progress was considerable. In 1945, the college became Yeshiva University, empowered to grant higher degrees. Several programs for advanced study were instituted, and new branches opened, including the Stern College for Women (1954), the Wurzweiler School of Jewish Social Work (1957), and the Benjamin N. Cardozo School of Law (1976). The most notable event for the university in the 1950s was the establishment of the Albert Einstein College of Medicine and its associated hospital (1955) in the Bronx.

Yeshiva University has expanded geographically as well as educationally, opening centers in Los Angeles and Jerusalem. The diverse schools and programs that are now part of the university can hardly be considered subsidiary to the original RIETS, which still exists as an autonomous division and is considered the country's leading institution for training Orthodox rabbis.

Often it is RIETS that is thought of when Yeshiva University is mentioned. The most eminent figure among its scholars is Rabbi Joseph Dov Soloveitchik, who became professor of Talmud in 1941. His erudition in both Talmud and philosophy and his gifts as a teacher exemplified the standpoint of the institution and enhanced its reputation among the various strands of Orthodox opinion. *See also* ORTHODOXY.

S. D. TEMKIN

BIBLIOGRAPHY

Gurock, Jeffrey S. *The Men and Women of Yeshiva University: Higher Education, Orthodoxy and American Judaism.* New York: Columbia University Press, 1988.
Stein, Barbara. "The Yeshiva Decision." *Today's Education* 69 (November–December 1980): 10.
Wiesel, Elie. "Echoes of Yesterday." *New York Times Magazine,* September 28, 1986, 37.
Wouk, Herman. "Centennial of a Citadel." *New York Times Magazine,* September 28, 1986, 36.
"Yeshiva University." *New York Times,* May 29, 1987, 11.

Yiddish Literature. *See* LITERATURE, YIDDISH.

Yiddish Music. *See* MUSIC, YIDDISH.

Yiddish Poetry. *See* POETRY, YIDDISH.

Yiddish Theater. *See* THEATER, YIDDISH.

YIVO Institute for Jewish Research. The YIVO Institute for Jewish Research was founded in 1925 in Wilno (Vilna), Poland—now Vilnius, Lithuania. In 1940, its headquarters were transferred to New York City. Originally known in Yiddish as Yidisher visnshaftlekher institut, or simply by its acronym YIVO, the institute is dedicated to preserving and transmitting the heritage of Eastern European Ashkenazic Jewry, with particular emphasis in the following areas: Yiddish language, literature, theater, and folklore; Jewish history and culture in Eastern Europe; Eastern European Jewish immigration to North America; anti-Semitism; and the Nazi Holocaust.

The principal subdivisions of YIVO are its library and archives, which function as two separate departments, and the Max Weinreich Center for Advanced Jewish Studies, which is accredited by the New York State Regents to serve as a non-degree-granting graduate center in YIVO's fields of interest. In 1990, the library had book and periodical holdings of more than 320,000 volumes and the archives had approximately 22 million items.

As of 1938, the Vilna YIVO had library holdings of approximately 40,000 books and 10,000 periodical volumes plus extensive archival holdings. These collections were plundered by the Nazis who intended to include them in a museum dedicated to the extinct Jews of Europe. After World War II, about 50 percent of the archival materials and a substantial portion of the press and library holdings of the collections were recovered in West Germany and sent to the New York YIVO, where they are now housed as the Vilna Collection. Today the New York Vilna Collection includes over 40,000 volumes (many of them originally in the Strashun Library of Vilna) in the following categories: rabbinica, Yiddish secular books, Hebrew secular books, books in other languages, and periodicals in various languages. There are also 30,000 archival folders in the Vilna collection. Of the remaining original Vilna archival material, about 40 percent has been located in three repositories in Vilnius, and attempts are being made to identify and microfilm these items as well as other YIVO materials that still remain in Vilnius.

The YIVO Library's massive holdings on the Holocaust served as the basis of the multivolume Yad Vashem—YIVO Joint Documentary Projects Bibliographical Series, published in the 1960s and early 1970s. Among the library's frequently consulted Holocaust materials are memorial volumes for over 500 Eastern European Jewish communities that were annihilated during World War II.

Much of the European and American Yiddish press is available on microfilm at YIVO. *The Yiddish Card Catalog and Authority File of the YIVO Library* was published in 1990 (G. K. Hall).

The YIVO Archives are particularly strong in the following areas: original literary papers of Yiddish writers, scripts of Yiddish plays, sheet music for Yiddish songs and operettas, immigration-related collections, records of national and local American Jewish organizations, landsmanshaftn records (a published catalogue is available), European Jewish community records, Holocaust documentation, and photographs of Jewish life in Europe and the Americas, including over 100,000 total images.

Also attached to the archives are the following divisions: (1) the Slide Bank, a circulating collection of over 3000 slides on topics of Jewish interest; (2) the Sound Archives, with large collections of 78-rpm records and other audio material, which are being preserved on tape; (3) the Videodisk, which includes some 18,000 photographic images of European Jewish life, with subjects searchable by computer.

A soon to be published *Guide to the YIVO Archives* contains descriptions of YIVO's archival collections on a record group level.

In addition to its important library and archival collections, through its Max Weinreich Center YIVO offers courses in Yiddish language and literature, modern Jewish history, and the Holocaust. Each year, YIVO and Columbia University jointly offer the Uriel Weinreich Summer Yiddish Program.

YIVO has also been active both as publisher and editor of important scholarly and educational publications. Among the most important books published by YIVO are *The History of the Yiddish Language*, by Max Weinreich (Chicago: University of Chicago Press, 1980; first published in Yiddish by YIVO, in 1973); *College Yiddish*, by Uriel Weinreich (New York: YIVO, 1949 and subsequent editions), and the *Modern English-Yiddish Yiddish-English Dictionary*, by Uriel Weinreich (New York: YIVO and McGraw-Hill, 1968). YIVO also publishes the scholarly journals *YIVO-bleter*, *Yidishe shprakh* (both in Yiddish), and *YIVO Annual* (in English).

ZACHARY M. BAKER

BIBLIOGRAPHY

Abramowicz, Dina. "The YIVO Library." *Jewish Book Annual* 25 (1967/1968): 87–102.

Dawidowicz, Lucy S. *From that Place and Time: A Memoir, 1938–1947*. New York: Norton, 1989.

Gilson, Estelle. "YIVO—Where Yiddish Scholarship Lives: History and Mission on Fifth Avenue." *Present Tense* (Autumn 1976): 57–65.

Z

Zionism.

PRE-HERZLIAN ZIONISM. During the long centuries of persecution in Europe, Jews continually prayed for redemption to Zion, for it seemed that only in their historic homeland could they be free. But in the early nineteenth century, European Jews learned of an alternative, another place where they could practice their religion without fear of state-sponsored persecution. Although small Jewish communities in the New World dated to the early seventeenth century, the first great migration of Jews to the United States occurred in the 1840s when 200,000 German Jews emigrated across the Atlantic, to be followed after 1881 by 2.5 million Jews from Eastern Europe and Russia.

The German Jews came from a community already assimilating into modernity, and the Reform Judaism they practiced no longer called for a return to Zion. The Jews from Eastern Europe, however, still clung to Orthodoxy, continued to pray for a return to Eretz Yisroel, and established societies similar to those in Europe that had begun building Jewish colonies in Palestine. On July 4, 1882, Dr. Joseph Bluestone proposed the creation of a Hoveve Zion (Lovers of Zion) society. It would be another two years before one actually came into existence in New York, but within a few years similar societies could be found in all the cities with significant Jewish populations. In addition, two publications, a regular supplement to the New York *Yiddisher Zeitung* and *Shulamith*, a Yiddish journal, advocated Palestinian colonization.

Troubles beset the Hoveve Zion groups from the start. Orthodox Jews believed that redemption could only come through divine intervention, while German Jews saw Zionism as raising the spectre of "dual loyalty," which would undermine Jewish status in America. In some of the larger communities, rival groups competed for the relatively small number of potential Hoveve Zion members. The Hoveve Zion in America raised some money to support the early settlements in Palestine, but the movement never gained the strength it enjoyed in Eastern Europe. Most of its members eventually found their way into later Zionist organizations.

FEDERATION OF AMERICAN ZIONISTS. Modern Zionism begins with the publication of Theodor Herzl's *The Jewish State* in 1896 and the First Zionist Congress the following year held in Basel, Switzerland. All of American Jewry, including those opposed to the whole notion, followed news of the congress closely, and within a few years Zionist societies, inspired by the world movement but American in outlook, took root in the United States. After the initial enthusiasm, however, the Zionist societies ran into the same problems that had plagued the Hoveve Zion—opposition from the Orthodox on the one side and from Reform Germans on the other, as well as internal bickering.

In an effort to eliminate factionalism, Gustav Gottheil, one of the few Reform rabbis sympathetic to Zionism, and Joseph Bluestone organized an umbrella organization of 13 local clubs in November 1897, the Federation of Zionist Societies of Greater New York and Vicinity. Similar groups soon sprouted in other major cities, and in July 1898 they agreed to the formation of a national body, the Federation of American Zionists (FAZ). The FAZ endorsed the Basel program and affiliated itself with the World Zionist Organization (WZO). It elected as its first officers Professor Richard Gottheil of Columbia University as president, Bluestone and Herman Rosenthal as vice presidents, and Stephen S. Wise as secretary.

Within a year the federation grew from 25 to 125 societies, and 10,000 men and women purchased the 50-cent shekel of membership. The FAZ sent 11 delegates to the Third Zionist Congress in 1899, and Gottheil, elected as a second vice president of the WZO, reported that Zionism was now receiving serious attention in America.

Underneath the surface vitality, however, serious problems plagued the FAZ from the start. An umbrella organization, it had no real power over its constituent societies, many of whom had their own Zionist agendas. The Hoveve Zion, with its emphasis on colonies, feared the political aspects of Herzlian Zionism; the Orthodox attacked the alleged godlessness of the socialists; the socialists complained that the FAZ leadership ignored social problems. Despite the strenuous efforts of Gottheil, Wise, and a few others, the FAZ lacked an effective administrative structure and relied on one or two paid clerks and various volunteers to handle daily activities.

The most serious problem confronting the FAZ, however, involved the strenuous opposition of the established German Jewish community, which saw support for a Jewish homeland in Palestine as incompatible with complete loyalty to the United States. Non-Jews would say that Jews were not patriotic but owed their allegiance to a foreign country, and, as a result, the current status of Jews as equal citizens of the United States would be undermined.

The charge struck a responsive chord with many American Jews. The Reform contingent had already eliminated the notion of a return to Zion as part of their religious ideology. The Orthodox newcomers, despite their religious attachment to Zion, had emigrated not to the new colonies in Palestine but to the United States, where they desperately wanted to become "Amerikaners." The warnings of the established German-American Jews that Zionism could undermine their acceptance kept many from joining the movement.

Like the Hoveve Zion, the FAZ could point to some accomplishments. It established the groundwork for the new leadership that took over in 1914 and brought into the movement young men and women who would be the nucleus of American Zionist leadership for the next generation. It publicized many of the WZO's activities, such as the purchase of land in Palestine and the regeneration of Hebrew as a living language. Under the editorship of Louis Lipsky, the FAZ began publishing the *Maccabean* in 1901, which quickly became one of the outstanding Jewish journals in America. *Dos Yiddishe Folk* faced stiffer competition from an established Yiddish press, but it too raised a potent Zionist voice in the immigrant community.

To reach different interest groups, the FAZ sponsored fraternal orders such as the Sons of Zion and at its 1909 convention established Young Judea to reach boys and girls aged 10 to 18. Within five years Young Judea had 175 clubs with more than 5000 members.

The FAZ also raised money for a number of Zionist projects in Palestine, such as Bezalel Arts School, the Herzliya Academy, Aaron Aaronsohn's agricultural experiment station, and the Technion in Haifa. For many of these projects the Zionists secured funds from men like Jacob Schiff who, although opposed to the idea of a Jewish political state, nonetheless believed in developing Jewish life in its ancestral homeland.

In 1912, several chapters of the Daughters of Zion united to form Hadassah, the women's Zionist organization, which ultimately became the single largest Zionist membership agency in the world. Under the leadership of Henrietta Szold, and with the financial support of Mr. and Mrs. Nathan Straus, Hadassah adopted medical work in Palestine as the major focus of its energies. It sent two nurses to the Holy Land in early 1914, forerunners of what would ultimately be a great comprehensive medical and health program.

Nonetheless, at the 1914 FAZ convention, the secretary reported that only 12,000 persons had paid the membership shekel (out of an American Jewish population of well over 2 million) and that the proposed budget of $12,150 exceeded estimated income by $2600.

THE BRANDEIS ERA. When war erupted in August 1914, the American Jewish Committee, representing the established German-American leadership, immediately began raising relief funds for European Jewish communities in the war zones. But the committee had little interest in aiding the Zionist settlements in Palestine, which faced economic ruin because the war had cut off their European markets for citrus. The Zionists convened an emergency meeting at the Hotel Marseilles in New York on August 30, 1914, for the express purpose of raising funds for the Palestinian colonies. They prevailed upon a relative newcomer to the cause, the famed "people's attorney" Louis Dembitz Brandeis, to take the chairmanship of what they called the Provisional Executive Committee for General Zionist Affairs (PEC). Much to the surprise—and joy—of American Zionist leaders, Brandeis took hold of the PEC and not only raised money for the *yishuv*, but turned Zionism into a major force in American Jewish life and in American political affairs as well.

Brandeis brought a new group of American-born or Americanized Jews into the PEC, men like Judge William Mack, Professor Felix Frankfurter, and Rabbi Stephen S. Wise (who had resigned in despair from the FAZ), and the success of this new leadership derived from several factors.

All had been leaders in American progressive reforms, and they brought their publicity and organizational skills with them. Their motto— "Men! Money! Discipline!"—had been the implicit slogan of dozens of progressive crusades; one needed people and funds, which, used effectively, could then achieve the desired results. Under the Brandeis leadership membership in American Zionism grew from 12,000 in the FAZ in 1914 to over 176,000 in the Zionist Organization of America (ZOA) in 1919, with thousands of others affiliated with Orthodox and socialist groups. Brandeis introduced modern accounting, so that money could be managed effectively, and for the first time developed extensive membership lists.

Perhaps most important, the so-called "Brandeisian synthesis" resolved the problem of alleged dual loyalty. The German-American community clung to an essentially European notion of patriotism, based on a relatively homogeneous society in which one could only be loyal to single entity. Horace Meyer Kallen, whom Brandeis knew well, had already begun writing about pluralism in America, claiming that in contradistinction to Europe, American strength derived from the heterogeneous nature of society. Instead of trying to turn all immigrants into copies of native-born Yankees, America should revel in the variety and resulting vitality that immigrants brought to community life.

Brandeis expanded upon Kallen's theme by arguing that one could indeed have multiple loyalties provided they did not contradict one another. For example, every American could be loyal to his community and his state as well as his national government, to his church and social club and college, since all of these operated in harmony. Zionism, he claimed, embodied the traditional Jewish *and* American ideals of democracy and justice. The Zionists were attempting to build in Palestine the type of free and democratic society that Jefferson and the Founding Fathers had envisioned for the United States. To be Zionists, therefore, did not mean being disloyal to America; to the contrary, it expressed loyalty to America's noblest ideals. "To be good Americans," he repeated in speech after speech, "we must be better Jews, and to be better Jews, we must become Zionists!"

Perhaps the greatest achievement of American Zionism in these years was securing the American government's approval of the idea of a Jewish homeland in Palestine. Because the United States was not at war with Turkey, which controlled Palestine, the State Department opposed a policy that would have stripped land from a country with which we were trying to maintain at least neutral relations. Nonetheless, pleas from Wise and Brandeis led President Woodrow Wilson to endorse the concept, and that cleared away the last hurdle for the British government to issue the Balfour Declaration in November 1917, calling for the establishment of a Jewish homeland after the war.

The Brandeis leadership also successfully reorganized American Zionism. Individual Zionists still belonged to local clubs or fraternal groups, although during the war all these bodies followed the Brandeis leadership. Aside from moral suasion, though, the PEC could do little to enforce discipline. In 1918, the leadership finally secured approval for a radical reorganization of the movement. The new Zionist Organization of America (ZOA) included all groups except the socialist Po'ale Zion and the religious Mizrachi and was based on the idea of individual membership organized along geographic lines.

The ZOA also adopted a statement of *American* Zionist policy. The FAZ had, like all other Zionist groups, endorsed the Basel program's call for a Jewish homeland, but it had never developed an independent articulation of what American

Zionists hoped for in that homeland. The 1918 Pittsburgh Platform, more than any other document, exemplified the analogous nature of the Brandeis leadership to American progressive reform. The platform called for political and civil equality of all inhabitants of Palestine, regardless of race, sex, or faith; equality of opportunity, with public ownership of land, natural resources, and utilities; free public education; the cooperative principle in economic development; and Hebrew as the national language.

With the exception of the last plank, there was little in the Pittsburgh Platform that was Zionist as Europeans understood the matter, that is, as a question of religious identification and the mystic identification of a people with its ancient homeland. Because Brandeis and his colleagues interpreted Zionism in these American terms, they made it possible for assimilated Jews as well as non-Jews to endorse Zionism as compatible with American ideals. At the same time, they sowed the seeds of future conflict between American and European Zionists, and even later with the Israelis.

THE SCHISM AT CLEVELAND. The Zionist movement in general, and American Zionists in particular, emerged from the war period with increased membership and political influence. What had only been Herzl's dream, the establishment of a Jewish homeland in Palestine, was now the official policy of the League of Nations. What had been the weakest of all Zionist territorial federations, the FAZ, had now become the strongest, with a leadership respected not only within the Jewish community, but in the highest levels of national government as well.

Following the signing of the San Remo Treaty on April 24, 1920, which affirmed the Balfour Declaration and assigned the mandate for Palestine to Great Britain, Zionist leaders agreed they should meet to map out the next steps in turning the dream into reality. At the London Zionist Conference in July, however, significant differences developed between the American Zionists, under Brandeis's leadership, and the Europeans, led by Chaim Weizmann and Nahum Sokolow.

The split has often been characterized as "merely" a difference in financial outlooks and the nature of a new Zionist fund, the Keren Hayesod. The WZO had earlier established specialized funds for specific purposes, such as the Jewish National Fund to purchase land in Palestine. Both

the Americans and the Europeans recognized that massive amounts of money would be needed, both in the form of outright donations as well as investment money. To Brandeis, donations and investments aimed at two different purposes and had to be used accordingly. Donation funds had no restrictions and could be used for public works, education, and health and welfare projects that were not intended as profitable enterprises. Investment funds, however, could only be used in potentially profitable undertakings. People who invested in Palestine did not, of course, expect to receive large returns; rather, such funds would foster that element of private initiative necessary to achieve a balanced and dynamic economy. Brandeis no more wanted Palestine to be developed as a model of private enterprise than Weizmann wanted for it to be socialist. To Brandeis, however, so-called "commingling" of funds not only violated accounting rules but moral principles as well.

This the Europeans could never understand, nor could they comprehend Brandeis's insistence on more efficient organization and emphasis on practical as opposed to political work. He believed—wrongly as it turned out—that the Zionist political program had been achieved in the San Remo Treaty and that the Zionists now had to concentrate on the practical work of turning Palestine into the Jewish homeland. To do this, he wanted the WZO to streamline its organization, eliminate unnecessary tasks and positions, and employ trained experts to oversee its projects in Palestine. For the Europeans, for whom Zionism was a way of life as well as a means toward an end, the American proposals threatened not only their jobs, but also the nature of Zionism; it might become more efficient, but at a cost of losing its Jewishness, and they strenuously opposed the Brandeis program.

As a gesture of unity, Weizmann agreed to the creation of a special commission to look into alleged charges of inefficiency and promised to abide by its findings and recommendations. When the commission confirmed all of the American charges, however, Weizmann repudiated it, and encouraged by his supporters, he set out to depose the Brandeis group and claim full control of the world movement.

The task proved easier than expected. Despite their high prestige in the community, Brandeis and his group with their emphasis on American principles had alienated many of the Yiddish-speaking Eastern Europeans, who still clung to the more religious and mystical aspects of Jewish redemption. They neither understood nor cared very much about the American leadership's emphasis on proper accounting and efficient organization. They did care for Yiddishkeit, a pervasive sense of Jewishness, and for that they looked to Chaim Weizmann—and not to Louis Brandeis.

Weizmann arrived in the United States in the spring of 1921 to attend the Zionist conference in Cleveland and almost immediately proclaimed the Keren Hayesod, despite his earlier promise not to do so until the ZOA convention could meet and discuss the question. He then made the issue one of personality, his Jewishness versus the austere nature of Justice Brandeis. He also found a number of willing allies among American Zionists, people like Louis Lipsky who had been shunted aside by the Brandeis group. Aside from personal pique, they too found the Americanized Zionism of the Pittsburgh Platform too anemic and lacking in traditional Jewish values. When the vote over the Keren Hayesod came at 1:30 in the morning of June 6, the Weizmann-Lipsky forces triumphed, 153 to 71.

A weary Julian Mack then thanked the delegates for the opportunity they had given him to serve the movement, and then he and all of the Brandeisists resigned their positions in the ZOA. As Brandeis later explained, the Keren Hayesod affronted their principles, and for Palestine to be won, it had to be won with clean hands. They would continue to work for Zionism, but through other agencies, such as the newly created Palestine Economic Committee (PEC). Control of American Zionism would now be in the hands of Weizmann, Lipsky, and their associates.

ZIONISM IN THE 1920s AND 1930s. For the next decade, American Zionism remained split among several factions. The Weizmann-Lipsky group controlled the ZOA; the Hadassah leadership, however, with its close ties to Brandeis and Mack, asserted its independence and refused to follow ZOA policy. The Brandeisians worked for Palestine through the PEC, but it never controlled enough money to underwrite more than a few modest projects. Po'ale Zion and the Mizrachi also kept their distance from the ZOA. At the same time, Weizmann launched his grand plan to bring all Jews into the Zionist fold and mostly ignored the ineffectual Lipsky leadership.

The extent of this disarray was not immediately apparent. In fact, the Zionists appeared to have won a major political and propaganda vic-

tory in 1922 when they secured congressional approval of the Lodge-Fish Resolution. Signed by President Harding, this became the first formal American endorsement of the idea of a Jewish homeland in Palestine.

Aside from this one victory, American Zionism as a movement had few accomplishments in the 1920s. The enormous membership built up during the war dwindled away, partly because of the Brandeis-Weizmann split, partly because of the ineffectiveness of the Lipsky regime, and partly because the wartime emergency had passed. Jews in Europe had been helped, the new European nations recognized—at least on paper— Jewish rights, and the League of Nations had endorsed the Balfour program. For many American Jews, the battles had been won, and it was now time to get on with their own business of becoming successful Americans.

The growth of the *yishuv* in Palestine did, however, affect not only Zionists but non-Zionist Jews as well. Even those opposed to political Zionism could still support the rebuilding of the ancient homeland on religious or cultural grounds. Louis Marshall, Jacob Schiff, and other non-Zionists had begun to cooperate with Brandeis during the war when they realized that his interpretation of Zionism did not endanger their self-perceptions as Americans. Now Chaim Weizmann, in order to make the Keren Hayesod the vehicle he hoped would underwrite Palestinian development, began a campaign to involve non-Zionist Jews more closely in Zionist projects through the Jewish Agency. The agency would be a cooperative venture, with both Zionist and non-Zionist members, and its efforts would be strictly economic, social, and cultural; all political work would be undertaken by the WZO alone. Weizmann and Marshall finally brought the Jewish Agency into existence at the Sixteenth Zionist Congress in August 1929.

The agency never developed into the great enterprise its two architects had envisioned. Within weeks after its founding, Marshall died. At the same time, the Arab population in Palestine, restless over the rapid growth of the *yishuv*, began a series of riots and protests that led to a British reevaluation of what it meant in the Balfour Declaration by a "Jewish homeland." In October, the stock market crash ushered in a decade of economic depression in America and Europe. Then, in 1933, Adolf Hitler came to power in Germany.

Whether it wanted to or not, the Jewish Agency became involved in politics. As the designated representative of world Jewry called for in the League of Nations mandate, the agency presented the case for continued Jewish development in Palestine and fought against British efforts to restrict immigration. It was Cyrus Adler, the chairman of the American Jewish Committee and a non-Zionist member of the agency, who prepared the presentation to the League of Nations after Arabs attempted to cut off Jewish access to the Western Wall. It was Felix Warburg, who assumed the chairmanship of the agency after Marshall's death, who led the protest against the British White Paper of 1930.

By 1930, in fact, American Jews could well wonder if there was in fact an organized Zionist movement aside from Hadassah, with its medical programs. The Lipsky leadership presided over a hollow shell, and many of those who had worked to oust the Brandeisians in 1921, such as Emanuel Neumann, now opposed Lipsky. The ZOA had no money, practically no members, and no independent programs or policies. It was totally unable to respond to the crises that arose one after another in 1929 and 1930. In 1931, Robert Szold assumed the leadership of the ZOA as the designated lieutenant of Louis Brandeis and Julian Mack.

Given the economic, social, and political conditions, no group of leaders could have revivified American Zionism. The primary issues in American Jewish life in the early 1930s were not Zionism or Palestine, but the same concerns that dominated non-Jewish interests, namely, economic survival. The Szold committee did the best it could, getting ZOA internal affairs in order so that when conditions improved, the movement would be ready to act.

The rise of Adolf Hitler, the Nazi threat to Jewish survival in Germany, increased Arab resistance to the *yishuv*, and British abandonment of the Balfour policy all forced the Zionists to act sooner than had been anticipated. One crisis after another in the 1930s required action, but the ZOA lacked the political power it had exercised during World War I and did not yet have the influence it would enjoy in the 1960s and 1970s. There has been much criticism of American Jewry in general, and especially of the Zionists, in their response to Hitler. While one can always say that more should have been attempted, given the circumstances, the community reacted as best it could.

The Zionists, like all American Jews, were concerned over the Nazi menace, but they had a specific solution—establishment of a Jewish homeland in Palestine. They kept up a constant barrage of criticism against the British for not living up to the Balfour promise, and although Great Britain tried to cut off Jewish immigration beginning with the 1930 White Paper, the Zionists managed to stave off this act until the 1939 White Paper. As a result, tens of thousands of Jews fled Germany and settled in Palestine before World War II. The Zionists criticized American immigration restrictions, but for several reasons they put the bulk of their efforts into Palestine. They recognized that in the face of the Depression, the American people and Congress would not lower immigration barriers, even if they disapproved of Nazi persecutions. They also had limited resources and, although they joined in such anti-Hitler protests as the boycott, believed that the only viable solution to anti-Semitism was a Jewish homeland.

The Nazi menace, however, did lead to a renewed sense of crisis in American Jewry. The American Jewish Committee continued to urge a cautious, behind-the-scenes diplomatic approach, a policy that failed to satisfy people who wanted a more vigorous and open protest. The Zionists organized public protests, and the fact that they had an answer—one that did not require Congress to change the immigration laws—gradually brought American Jews to join the movement. By 1941, the ZOA counted 46,000 members, Hadassah 80,000, and the various smaller groups had another 55,000. The old Brandeisian slogan of "Men! Money! Discipline!" took on a new urgency, and American Zionism finally emerged from two decades of debilitating factional strife.

REVIVAL DURING WORLD WAR II. Membership continued to climb during the war years, and by the establishment of the State of Israel in 1948, 1 million American Jews had formally joined the movement; another million belonged to groups like the fraternal order B'nai B'rith which had endorsed Zionist goals. The revelation of Hitler's "Final Solution" and the price Jews had to pay for British perfidy led to a new militancy in Zionist circles. The destruction of European Jewry left effective control of Zionism outside the United States in the hands of Palestinian Jewry, led by David Ben-Gurion. In the United States, Abba Hillel Silver gradually took over control of the movement from the more moderate forces led by Stephen S. Wise.

The outstanding event of the war years was the Biltmore Conference of May 9–11, 1942. Not only were the American leaders there, but also Weizmann, Ben-Gurion, and those WZO executives not captured by Nazi forces. The militants called for and received a new mandate for the movement to replace the Basel statement. The Biltmore Program demanded that after the war an autonomous Jewish state should be established in Palestine, with full control over immigration. From then until 1948, the Biltmore Program served as the official policy of American and world Zionism.

To lobby for that goal, American Zionists formed the American Zionist Emergency Council (AZEC) to coordinate political activities. The agency had several troubled years due to the friction between its co-leaders, Abba Hillel Silver and Stephen S. Wise. The latter, a friend and admirer of President Franklin Roosevelt, did not want to do anything that might embarrass the administration during the war. He believed Roosevelt a friend to Zionist aspirations and urged the ZOA to trust in the President, a trust that Wise later conceded was misplaced. Silver, on the other hand, wanted to pressure the administration as much as possible, to threaten political activity if it did not do more for the victims of the Holocaust and for Zionism.

During the actual war years Wise's caution usually won out, as the community, still unsure of its full acceptance into American society, hesitated to call undue attention to itself. But the continued destruction of European Jewry, as well as the refusal of Great Britain to let in refugees, led to a shift in community values. The extent of this shift could be seen at the American Jewish Conference in 1943, organized to unite Zionists and non-Zionists into one umbrella agency to seek help for Hitler's victims.

Wise originally agreed, in order to win the cooperation of the non-Zionist American Jewish Committee, that Zionism should not be on the conference agenda. Silver originally acceded to the plan, but midway through the conference his friends urged him to speak out. When he did so, the conference endorsed the Biltmore Program almost unanimously. The American Jewish Committee left but soon discovered that its anti-Zionist stance now led to rejection of any claims it might have to leadership in the community. By the end of the war, no major Jewish organization opposed the Biltmore Program.

AMERICAN ZIONISTS AND THE ESTABLISHMENT OF ISRAEL. The ultimate success

of the Zionist enterprise resided with the *yishuv*; independence was won on the battlefields of Palestine and paid for in the blood of the *chalutzim*. But American Zionism played an important supporting role. It raised funds for the *yishuv* and secretly helped to arm the Haganah; it helped develop public support, especially among non-Jews, for the establishment of a Jewish state; and it brought political pressure to bear on the Truman administration, first to force the British into opening Palestine to the survivors and to recognizing the new Jewish state moments after its independence had been proclaimed on May 14, 1948.

The Zionists accurately assessed that despite the Holocaust, the American public would prove no more receptive to immigrants in 1945 than it had in 1935, and Zionist propaganda focused on Palestine as a haven for the survivors. Under the brilliant guidance of Emanuel Neuman, the American Christian Palestine Committee worked relentlessly to build non-Jewish support for the Zionist program. Following the 22nd Zionist Congress in Basel in December 1946, leadership of the movement passed completely into the hands of the militants—Abba Hillel Silver in the United States and David Ben-Gurion in Palestine—and Zionism stood pledged to ending British rule in the Holy Land as soon as possible in order to establish a Jewish state there.

An immediate decision stepped up underground military opposition to the British. Efforts would be made to bring thousands of immigrants into Palestine, legally if possible, illegally if not. This work, done by the *yishuv*, was politically supported by the newly created American Section of the Jewish Agency, headed by Silver, which also secretly sent funds to help arm the *yishuv*. Americans also played an important part in securing ships and acquiring large amounts of surplus war goods sold by the War Department.

A word is necessary about the so-called Bergson group, the American branch of the Irgun Tzvi Leumi. Led by Peter Bergson, this group called for an active role in opposing Hitler during the war and in arming Jews to fight the British afterward. There is much scholarly debate over whether or not the Bergson group actually accomplished anything; certainly its claims for smuggling thousands of Jews into Palestine have been proven highly inflated. Nonetheless, at a time when many American Jewish groups, including the Zionists, hesitated over what actions to take, Bergson called for political action both legal and illegal. Those who claim American Zionists did not do enough to save Jewish lives during the Holocaust often point to the highly visible protests of the Bergson group as evidence of what should have been done. Within the Zionist movement, however, both Wise and Silver saw the Bergsonites as irresponsibles, whose failure to work with AZEC and other Zionist groups undermined the effort to develop a politically potent united front.

Zionist pressure began to achieve results in 1946 when President Harry S Truman called for the immediate admission of 100,000 survivors into Palestine. The American Section had played a significant role in presenting evidence to the Anglo-American commission on the need to open the gates of Palestine, and following Truman's acceptance of the 100,000 proposal, it launched a massive campaign to win public endorsement of it. When Great Britain finally agreed to give up the mandate and threw the Palestine issue into the lap of the United Nations, Silver led the American delegation at Lake Success. The Americans worked unceasingly for the UN resolution calling for partition of Palestine into Jewish and Arab states, a resolution adopted on November 29, 1947. Six months later the British mandate over Palestine ended, and the provisional government in Tel-Aviv declared Israeli independence on May 14, 1948. Eleven minutes after British rule formally came to an end, the United States recognized the new State of Israel.

During the Israeli War for Independence, American Zionism continued the role it had played since 1945, raising millions of dollars to support the war and to aid the survivors of the Holocaust while keeping public pressure on the Congress and the administration to help the new state.

AMERICAN ZIONISM IN THE POST-STATE ERA. The establishment of the State of Israel marked the fulfillment of the Zionist enterprise, and American Zionists understood that basic modifications in the movement would have to be made. Its leaders never anticipated, however, that within a few years the American movement would again be reduced to a shell of its former self.

Prior to 1948, American Zionism had three major tasks: raising funds for Jewish settlements in Palestine, managing political relations between the Zionist movement and the American government, and educating both the Jewish and non-Jewish communities about Zionism. The call for aliyah that had been so integral a part of European Zionism never played an important role in the United States, and there is some truth to charges that American Zionism had more of a philanthropic rather than a spiritual base.

With the establishment of Israel, the new state properly assumed control of its own diplomatic relations. The financial needs of Israel, both military and humanitarian, could no longer be met by Zionist funds, which had always been inadequate. The Zionization of the community led the United Jewish Appeal, which had access to the richer elements of the community, to take over the chief responsibility for humanitarian fund raising, while the American government provided millions and later billions in military and economic assistance. Even the educational program fell into disarray, since the Zionists had no clear-cut *American* program they could foster in the community. All American Jews now supported Israel, and they did not care to learn about the niceties of Zionist ideology or what divided one Zionist faction from another.

With the exception of Hadassah, Zionist membership fell drastically, and the ZOA lost much of its influence in American Jewish affairs. The women's organization not only kept its membership, but grew, primarily because it had a nonpolitical program that appealed to many people—the providing of quality medical care through the Hadassah Hospital in Jerusalem and its related programs.

Israeli leaders did not lament the decline of the ZOA. Ben-Gurion, in fact, helped speed the process along by indicating that the Israeli government preferred to work with the United Jewish Appeal and its leaders, most of whom were non-Zionists, rather than with the ZOA. In February 1949, Silver and Neumann resigned from the Zionist Executive in protest. Two years later when Ben-Gurion visited the United States to launch the first Israel bond drive, he avoided all mention of Zionism. Jews who chose not to make aliyah could still be considered friends of Israel, while those who did settle in Israel fulfilled the Zionist dream. Given such a situation, he implied, there was no longer any need for a Zionist organization. In the 1950s, continued dissension within the American movement led to its near collapse.

Although the 1967 and 1973 wars aroused great sympathy for Israel and support from within the American Jewish community, American Zionism continued a desultory existence.

Some of the constituent bodies, such as Hadassah, maintained active programs that drew sustained support. American Zionists tried to work out a new relationship with the Jewish state, but the Israelis continued to insist that true Zionism meant aliyah, an idea embodied in the Jerusalem Program of 1968. A slight modification of this view was adopted by the Twenty-ninth Zionist Congress in 1979, but Israeli leaders refused to implement any programs that would have recognized parity between Jewish groups in the Diaspora and in Israel.

In the United States today, a variety of Zionist organizations claim approximately 800,000 to 1 million members, although most of these are inactive. The agencies all cooperate, to some extent, under the umbrella of the American Zionist Federation (AZF), established in accordance with the territorial reorganization adopted by the 27th Zionist Congress in 1968. The AZF does operate a number of public programs, such as the annual celebration of Israel Independence Day, and serves as a central address for numerous Zionist-related activities. But it is often torn between the demands of its constituent bodies and the American Section of the Jewish Agency, consisting of the American members of the Zionist Executive.

On the one hand, one might say that American Zionism is a victim of its own success. From a small, marginal group at the turn of the century, it grew and managed to impress its idea upon the entire Jewish community. It convinced the larger non-Jewish community to support the Zionist dream of a Jewish homeland in Palestine and organized enormous political pressure to help make that dream a reality. Today, most American Jews believe in Israel and believe that Zionism is no more than support for the Jewish state.

Zionism, however, was always more than that. The movement in the end had to concentrate on the political goal because of the ravages of the Holocaust, but it had always spoken to wider ideals of cultural and spiritual regeneration. By ignoring these aspects, a decision that could not be avoided in the light of genocide, American Zionism had little to say following the establishment of the State of Israel.

MELVIN I. UROFSKY

BIBLIOGRAPHY

Cohen, Naomi W. *American Jews and the Zionist Idea.* Hoboken, N.J.: Ktav, 1975.

Feinstein, Marnin. *American Zionism, 1884–1904.* New York: Herzl Press, 1965.

Ganin, Zvi. *Truman, American Jewry, and Israel, 1945–1948.* New York: Holmes & Meier, 1979.

Halperin, Samuel. *The Political World of American Zionism.* Detroit: Wayne State University Press, 1961.

Meyer, Isadore, ed. *Early History of Zionism in America.* New York: American Jewish History Society, 1958.

Shapiro, Yonathan. *Leadership of the American Zionist Organization, 1897–1930.* Urbana: University of Illinois Press, 1971.

Urofsky, Melvin. *American Zionism from Herzl to the Holocaust.* New York: Doubleday, 1975.

——— . *We Are One! American Jewry and Israel.* New York: Doubleday, 1978.

Index